Handbook of Digital
Signal Processing
Engineering Applications

Handbook of Digital Signal Processing
Engineering Applications

Edited by

Douglas F. Elliott

Rockwell International Corporation
Anaheim, California

ACADEMIC PRESS, INC.
Harcourt Brace Jovanovich, Publishers

San Diego   New York   Berkeley   Boston
London   Sydney   Tokyo   Toronto

ACADEMIC PRESS, INC.
1250 Sixth Avenue, San Diego, California 92101

United Kingdom Edition published by
ACADEMIC PRESS INC. (LONDON) LTD.
24–28 Oval Road, London NW1 7DX

Library of Congress Cataloging in Publication Data

Handbook of digital signal processing.

Includes index.
1. Signal processing—Digital techniques—Handbooks,
manuals, etc.   I. Elliott, Douglas F.
TK5102.5.H32   1986   621.38'043   86-26490
ISBN 0–12–237075–9 (alk. paper)

PRINTED IN THE UNITED STATES OF AMERICA

87 88 89 90   9 8 7 6 5 4 3 2 1

Contents

Preface		xi
Acronyms and Abbreviations		xiii
Notation		xvii

Chapter 1   Transforms and Transform Properties
DOUGLAS F. ELLIOTT

I.	Introduction	1
II.	Review of Fourier Series	2
III.	Discrete-Time Fourier Transform	6
IV.	z-Transform	16
V.	Laplace Transform	24
VI.	Table of z-Transforms and Laplace Transforms	27
VII.	Discrete Fourier Transform	27
VIII.	Discrete-Time Random Sequences	41
IX.	Correlation and Covariance Sequences	45
X.	Power Spectral Density	50
XI.	Summary	51
	References	53

Chapter 2   Design and Implementation of Digital FIR Filters
P. P. VAIDYANATHAN

I.	Introduction	55
II.	FIR Digital Filter Preliminaries	56
III.	FIR Filter Design Based on Windowing	61
IV.	Equiripple Approximations for FIR Filters	71
V.	Maximally Flat Approximations for FIR Filters	90
VI.	Linear Programming Approach for FIR Filter Designs	95
VII.	Frequency Transformations in FIR Filters	100
VIII.	Two-Dimensional Linear-Phase FIR Filter Design and Implementation	112
IX.	Recent Techniques for Efficient FIR Filter Design	118
X.	Other Useful Types of FIR Filters	136
XI.	Summary	146
Appendix A.	Design Charts for Digital FIR Differentiators and Hilbert Transformers	147
Appendix B.	Program Listings for Linear-Phase FIR Filter Design	150
	References	170

Chapter 3   Multirate FIR Filters for Interpolating and Desampling
FREDERIC J. HARRIS

I.	Introduction	173
II.	Characteristics of Bandwidth-Reducing FIR Filters	180

III. Data Rate Reduction (Desampling) by $1/M$ Filters   208
IV. Heterodyne Processing   223
V. Interpolating Filters   234
VI. Architectural Models for FIR Filters   245
VII. Summary   252
Appendix. Windows as Narrowband Filters   253
References   286

Chapter 4 IIR Digital Filters
NAZIR A. PASHTOON

I. Introduction   289
II. Preliminaries   290
III. Stability   291
IV. Digital Filter Realizations   295
V. Frequency Domain Design   300
VI. Analog Filter Design and Filter Types   306
VII. Frequency Transformations   331
VIII. Digital Filter Design Based on Analog Transfer Functions   332
IX. Spectral Transformations   343
X. Digital Filters Based on Continuous-Time Ladder Filters   344
XI. Summary   353
Appendix. IIR Digital Filter CAD Programs   355
References   355

Chapter 5 Low-Noise and Low-Sensitivity Digital Filters
P. P. VAIDYANATHAN

I. Introduction   359
II. Binary Numbers—Representation and Quantization   361
III. Generation and Propagation of Roundoff Noise in Digital Filters 369
IV. Dynamic Range Constraints and Scaling   373
V. Signal-to-Roundoff-Noise Ratio in Simple IIR Filter Structures   378
VI. Low-Noise IIR Filter Sections Based on Error-Spectrum Shaping   387
VII. Signal-to-Noise Ratio in General Digital Filter Structures   395
VIII. Low-Noise Cascade-Form Digital Filter Implementation   396
IX. Noise Reduction in the Cascade Form by ESS   399
X. Low-Noise Designs via State-Space Optimization   402
XI. Parameter Quantization and Low-Sensitivity Digital Filters   412
XII. Low-Sensitivity Second-Order Sections   416
XIII. Wave Digital Filters   419
XIV. The Lossless Bounded Real Approach for the Design of Low-
Sensitivity Filter Structures   434
XV. Structural Losslessness and Passivity   443
XVI. Low-Sensitivity All-Pass-Based Digital Filter Structures   444
XVII. Digital All-Pass Functions   453
XVIII. Orthogonal Digital Filters   458
XIX. Quantization Effects in FIR Digital Filters   460
XX. Low-Sensitive FIR Filters Based on Structural Passivity   465
XXI. Limit Cycles in IIR Digital Filters   469
References   475

Chapter 6 Fast Discrete Transforms
PAT YIP AND K. RAMAMOHAN RAO

I.	Introduction	481
II.	Unitary Discrete Transforms	482
III.	The Optimum Karhunen Loève Transform	483
IV.	Sinusoidal Discrete Transforms	485
V.	Nonsinusoidal Discrete Transforms	499
VI.	Performance Criteria	510
VII.	Computational Complexity and Summary	516
Appendix A.	Fast Implementation of DCT via FFT	517
Appendix B.	DCT Calculation Using an FFT	521
Appendix C.	Walsh–Hadamard Computer Program	523
	References	523

Chapter 7 Fast Fourier Transforms
DOUGLAS F. ELLIOTT

I.	Introduction	527
II.	DFTs and DFT Representations	528
III.	FFTs Derived from the MIR	532
IV.	Radix-2 FFTs	553
V.	Radix-3 and Radix-6 FFTs	558
VI.	Radix-4 FFTs	564
VII.	Small-N DFTs	565
VIII.	FFTs Derived from the Ruritanian Correspondence (RC)	567
IX.	FFTs Derived from the Chinese Remainder Theorem	571
X.	Good's FFT	573
XI.	Kronecker Product Representation of Good's FFT	574
XII.	Polynomial Transforms	579
XIII.	Comparison of Algorithms	580
XIV.	FFT Word Lengths	587
XV.	Summary	595
Appendix A.	Small-N DFT Algorithms	596
Appendix B.	FFT Computer Programs	600
Appendix C.	Radix-2 FFT Program	602
Appendix D.	Prime Factor Algorithm (PFA)	605
Appendix E.	Highly Efficient PFA Assembly Language Computer Program	621
	References	630

Chapter 8 Time Domain Signal Processing with the DFT
FREDERIC J. HARRIS

I.	Introduction	633
II.	The DFT as a Bank of Narrowband Filters	639
III.	Fast Convolution and Correlation	666
IV.	The DFT as an Interpolator and Signal Generator	683
V.	Summary	698
	References	698

Chapter 9 Spectral Analysis
JAMES A. CADZOW

I.	Introduction	701
II.	Rational Spectral Models	702
III.	Rational Modeling: Exact Autocorrelation Knowledge	707
IV.	Overdetermined Equation Modeling Approach	714
V.	Detection of Multiple Sinusoids in White Noise	716
VI.	MA Modeling: Time Series Observations	721
VII.	AR Modeling: Time Series Observations	723
VIII.	ARMA Modeling: Time Series Observations	724
IX.	ARMA Modeling: A Singular Value Decomposition Approach	726
X.	Numerical Examples	731
XI.	Conclusions	739
	References	739

Chapter 10 Deconvolution
MANUEL T. SILVIA

I.	Introduction	741
II.	Deconvolution and LTI Systems with No Measurement Noise	746
III.	Deconvolution and the Identification of DTLTI Systems with	
	Measurement Noise	760
IV.	Fast Algorithms for Deconvolution Problems	766
V.	Some Practical Applications of Deconvolution	777
VI.	Summary	784
Appendix A.	References for Obtaining Computational Algorithms	785
Appendix B.	Implementing the Levinson or Toeplitz Recursion	786
Appendix C.	Implementing the Lattice Form of the Levinson Recursion	787
	References	787

Chapter 11 Time Delay Estimation
MANUEL T. SILVIA

I.	Introduction	789
II.	Time Delay Estimation for Active Sensors	793
III.	Time Delay Estimation for Passive Sensors	818
IV.	Cross-Correlation and Its Relationship to the Time Delay	
	Estimation Problem	833
V.	The Implementation of Some Time Delay Estimation Algorithms	
	Using the Fast Fourier Transform (FFT)	837
VI.	Algorithm Performance	844
VII.	Summary	853
	References	853

Chapter 12 Adaptive Filtering
NASIR AHMED

I.	Introduction	857
II.	Some Matrix Operations	858
III.	A Class of Optimal Filters	860
IV.	Least-Mean-Squares (LMS) Algorithm	866

V.	LMS Lattice Algorithms	882
VI.	Concluding Remarks	888
Appendix.	Four FORTRAN-77 Programs	889
	References	896

Chapter 13 Recursive Estimation
GENE H. HOSTETTER

I.	Introduction	899
II.	Least Squares Estimation	900
III.	Linear Minimum Mean Square Estimation	908
IV.	Discrete Kalman Filtering Examples	915
V.	Extensions	922
VI.	Some Computational Considerations	929
VII.	Summary	938
	References	938

Chapter 14 Mechanization of Digital Signal Processors
LESTER MINTZER

I.	Introduction	941
II.	Digital Machine Fundamentals	942
III.	The Essence of Digital Signal Processing	947
IV.	Number Representations	947
V.	Hardware Components	950
VI.	Microprogramming	959
VII.	Keeping Things in Perspective	963
VIII.	Distributed Arithmetic	964
IX.	Summary	972
	References	972

Addendum to
Chapter 3 Window Generation Computer Program   975
FREDERIC J. HARRIS

Index   987

Preface

When Academic Press approached me with the proposal that I serve as editor of a handbook for digital signal processing, I was aware of the need for such a book in my work in the aerospace industry. Specifically, I wanted basic digital signal processing principles and approaches described in a book that a person with a standard engineering background could understand. Also, I wanted the book to cover the more advanced approaches, to outline the advantages and disadvantages of each approach, and to list references in which I could find detailed derivations and descriptions of the approaches that might be most applicable to given implementation problems.

The various authors in this volume have done an outstanding job of accomplishing these goals. Coverage of the fundamentals alone makes the book self-sufficient, yet many advanced techniques are described in readable, descriptive prose without formal proofs. Detailing fundamental approaches and describing other available techniques provide an easily understandable book containing information on a wide range of approaches. For example, the chapter on adaptive filters derives basic adaptive filter structures and provides the reader with a background to "see the forest" of adaptive filtering. The chapter then describes various alternatives, including adaptive lattice structures that might be applicable to particular engineering problems. This description is provided without the detailed derivations that get one "lost in the trees."

Many new useful ideas are presented in this handbook, including new finite impulse response (FIR) filter design techniques, half-band and multiplierless FIR filters, interpolated FIR (IFIR) structures, and error spectrum shaping. The advanced digital filter design techniques provide for low-noise, low-sensitivity, state-space, and limit-cycle free filters. Filters for decimation and interpolation are described from an intuitive and easily understandable viewpoint. New fast Fourier transform (FFT) ideas include in-place and in-order mixed-radix FFTs, FFTs computed in nonorthogonal coordinates, and prime factor and Winograd Fourier transform algorithms. Transmultiplexing discussions carefully describe how to control crosstalk, how to satisfy dynamic range requirements, and how to avoid aliasing when resampling. Using an over-determined set of Yule–Walker equations is a key concept described for reducing data-induced hypersensitivities of parameters in model-based spectral estimation. Tools are provided for understanding the basic theory, physics, and computational algorithms associated with deconvolution and time delay estimation. Recursive least squares adaptive filter algorithms for both lattice and transversal structures are compared to other approaches, and their advantage in terms of rapid convergence at the expense of a modest computational increase is discussed. Extensions of Kalman filtering include square-root filtering. The simplicity and regularity of distributed arithmetic are lucidly described and are shown to be attractive for VLSI implementation.

There is some overlap in the material covered in various chapters, but readers will find the overlap helpful. For example, in Chapter 2 there is an excellent derivation of FIR digital filters that provides the necessary mathematical framework, and in the first part of Chapter 3 there is an intuitive explanation of how various FIR filter parameters, such as impulse response length, affect the filter performance. Similarly, in Chapter 9 the Yule–Walker equations are discussed in the context of spectral analysis, whereas in Chapter 10 these equations appear from a different viewpoint in the context of deconvolution.

Many applications in digital signal processing involve the use of computer programs. After many discussions the chapter authors decided to include useful programs and to give references to publications in which related program listings can be found. For example, Chapter 7 points out that a large percentage of FFT applications are probably best accomplished with a radix-2 FFT, and such an FFT is found in Appendix 7-C. However, Appendixes 7-D and 7-E present prime factor algorithms designed for IBM ATs and XTs. The listing in Appendix 7-E is a highly efficient 1008-point assembly language program. Other sources for FFTs are also listed in Appendix 7-B.

The encouragement of Academic Press was crucial to the development of this book, and I would like to thank the editors for their support and advice. I would also like to express my appreciation to Stanley A. White for his behind-the-scenes contribution as an advisor, and to thank all of the chapter authors for their diligent efforts in developing the book. Finally, I would like to thank my wife, Carol, for her patience regarding time I spent compiling, editing, and writing several chapters for the book.

Acronyms and Abbreviations

lsb	Least significant bit
msb	Most significant bit
ADC	Analog-to-digital converter
AGC	Automatic gain control
ALE	Adaptive line enhancer
AR	Autoregressive
ARMA	Autoregressive moving average
BP	Bandpass
BPF	Bandpass filter
BR	Bounded real
BRO	Bit-reversed order
CAD	Computer-aided design
CCW	Counterclockwise
CG	Coherent gain
CMOS	Complementary metal-on-silicon
CMT	C-matrix transform
CRT	Chinese remainder theorem
CSD	Canonic sign digit
DA	Distributed arithmetic
DAC	Digital-to-analog converter
DCT	Discrete cosine transform
DFT	Discrete Fourier transform
DF2	Direct-form 2
DIF	Decimation-in-frequency
DIT	Decimation-in-time
DPCM	Differential pulse code modulation
DRO	Digit-reversed order
DSP	Digital signal processing
DST	Discrete sine transform
DTFT	Discrete-time Fourier transform
DTLTI	Discrete-time linear time-invariant
DTRS	Discrete-time random sequence
DWT	Discrete Walsh transform
EFB	Error feedback
ENBW	Equivalent noise bandwidth
EPE	Energy packing efficiency
ESS	Error-spectrum shaping
FDM	Frequency-division (domain) multiplexing
FDST	Fast discrete sine transform
FFT	Fast Fourier transform
FIR	Finite impulse response
GT	General orthogonal transform
HHT	Hadamard–Haar transform

HPF	Highpass filter
HT	Haar transform
IDFT	Inverse discrete Fourier transform
IDTFT	Inverse discrete-time Fourier transform
IFFT	Inverse fast Fourier transform
IFIR	Interpolated finite impulse response
IIR	Infinite-duration impulse response
IQ	In-phase and quadrature
IT	Inverse transform; identity transform
KLT	Karhunen–Loève transform
KT	Kumaresan–Tufts
LBR	Lossless bounded real
LC	Inductance–capacitance
LDI	Lossless discrete integrator
LHP	Left half-plane
LMS	Least-mean-square
LP	Lowpass
LPC	Linear predictive coding
LPF	Lowpass filter
LS	Least squares
LSA	Least squares analysis
LSI	Large-scale integration
LTI	Linear time-invariant
MA	Moving average
MAC	Multiplier-accumulator
MFIR	Multiplicative finite impulse response
MIR	Mixed-radix integer representation
MLMS	Modified least-mean-square
MMS	Minimum mean-square
MP	McClellan–Parks
MSE	Mean-squared error
MSP	Most significant product
NO	Natural order
NTSC	National Television Systems Committee
NTT	Number-theoretic transform
PFA	Prime factor algorithm
PROM	Programmable read-only memory
PSD	Power spectrum density
PSR	Parallel-to-serial register
QMF	Quadrature mirror filter
RAM	Random-access memory
RC	Ruritanian correspondence
RCFA	Recursive cyclotomic factorization algorithm
RHT	Rationalized Haar transform
RLS	Recursive least squares
ROM	Read-only memory
RRS	Recursive running sum
RT	Rapid transform
SD	Sign digit
SDSLSI	Silicon-on-sapphire large-scale integration
SER	Sequential regression
SFG	Signal-flow graph
SNR	Signal-to-noise ratio

SPR	Serial-to-parallel register
SR	Shift register
SRFFT	Split-register fast Fourier transform
SSBFDM	Single-sideband frequency-division multiplexing
ST	Slant transform
SVD	Singular value decomposition
TDM	Time division (domain) multiplexed
VLSI	Very large-scale integration
WDF	Wave digital filter
WFTA	Winograd Fourier transform algorithm
WHT	Walsh-Hadamard transform
WSS	Wide-sense stationary

Notation

Symbol	Meaning
$a \leftarrow b$	Give variable a the value of expression b (or replace a by b)
$a, x, \ldots$	Lowercase denotes scalars
$\underline{a}, \underline{x}, \ldots$	Underbar denotes a random variable
$a^*, x^*, \ldots$	The complex conjugate of a. x, ...
$a_k, b_k, c_k,$ $\ldots$	Filter coefficients
a_k	Coefficients for the numerator polynomial of a transfer function, coefficients of corresponding difference equation
b_i, c_i, d_i, y_i	Elements of Jury's array for stability testing
b	Number of bits used to represent the value of a number (does not include the sign bit)
b_k	Coefficients of the denominator for polynomial of a transfer function, coefficients in the corresponding difference equation
c	Recursive least squares scalar divisor, initial state mean
c_j	Scale factor given by $$c_j = \begin{cases} 1 & \text{if } i \neq 0 \text{ or } N \\ 1/\sqrt{2} & \text{if } i = 0 \text{ or } N \end{cases}$$
$c_{xx}(m)$	Autocovariance sequence for the discrete-time random sequence $\underline{x}(n)$ where $c_{xx}(m) = E\{[\underline{x}(n) - \mu_x][\underline{x}(n-m) - \mu_x]^*\}$
$c_{xy}(m)$	Cross-covariance sequence for the discrete-time random sequences $\underline{x}(n)$ and $\underline{y}(n)$ where $c_{xy}(m) = E\{[\underline{x}(n) - \mu_x][\underline{y}(n-m) - \mu_y]^*\}$
d	Discrimination factor
$d(n), g(n)$	Input output sequences
$\hat{d}(n)$	Hilbert transform of $\hat{d}(n)$
$[d(n), j\hat{d}(n)]$	Analytic signal
$d(s,n)$	Data sequence where s is slow time index (identifies groups) and n is fast time index (identifies position in a group)
$e^{j\omega T}$	Steady-state frequency domain contour in the z-plane
$e(n)$	Error sequence
f	Frequency in hertz (Hz)
f_0	Filter center frequency
f_p	Passband upper edge frequency in hertz
f_q	Stopband lower edge frequency in hertz
f_r	Stopband (rejection band) edge frequency in hertz
f_s	Sampling frequency in hertz; $f_s = 1/T$
f_s'	Resampling frequency
$f(z)$	A linear factor $(z - re^{j\theta})$
$f'(z)$	A linear factor $(rz - e^{j\theta})$
$g(n), h(n), \ldots$	Time domain scalars
$h(n)$	Filter impulse response, filter coefficient, data sequence window
$h_a(t)$	Impulse response of an analog prototype filter

Symbol	Meaning
i, j, k, l, m, n	Integer indices
$i \equiv m$ (modulo n)	i is congruent to m (modulo n), i.e., $i = ln + m$ where i, l, m, and n are integers
j	$\sqrt{-1}$
k	Transform sequence number, integer step index, selectivity parameter
ln	Logarithm to the base e
log	Logarithm to the base 10
$\log_2$	Logarithm to the base 2
m_i	ith multiplier coefficient
n	Data sequence number (time index), system dynamic order
$q(k,s)$	Data sequence from filter bank where k is the filter index and s is the time index
r	Magnitude of a complex number (pole, zero)
$r_{xx}(m)$	Autocorrelation sequence for the discrete-time random sequence $\underline{x}(n)$ where $r_{xx}(m) = E[\underline{x}(n)\underline{x}^*(n-m)]$
$r_{xy}(m)$	Cross-correlation sequence for the discrete-time random sequences $\underline{x}(n)$ and $\underline{y}(n)$ where $r_{xy}(m) = E[\underline{x}(n)\underline{y}^*(n-m)]$
s	Laplace transform variable, $s = \sigma + j\omega$
s_m	Zeros of the inverse Chebyshev filters
$u(n)$	Unit step sequence defined by $u(n) = \begin{cases} 1, & n \geq 0 \\ 0 & \text{otherwise} \end{cases}$
x_i	Value of inductance or capacitance
$x(n)$	Input sequence; nth data sample
$\underline{x}(n), \underline{y}(n), \ldots$	Discrete-time random sequences
$x(t)$	Time domain scalar-valued function at time t
$x_s(t)$	Sampled function
$\hat{\underline{x}}$	Estimate of the random variable $\underline{x}$
$x(n) * y(n)$	The convolution of the sequences $x(n)$ and $y(n)$ where $$x(n) * y(n) = \sum_{m=-\infty}^{\infty} x(m)y(n-m)$$
$y(n)$	Output sequence
z	z-transform independent variable, $z = e^{sT}$, but used in this book for a normalized sampling period of $T = 1$ unless otherwise indicated
A	Minimum stopband attenuation
A_p	Filter passband attenuation in decibels, $A_p = -20 \log_{10} \delta_1$
A_r	Minimum acceptable filter stopband attenuation in decibels, $A_r = 20 \log_{10} \delta_2$
$A \oplus B$	Bit by bit addition of the binary numbers A and B
$\text{Arg}[H(e^{j\omega T})]$	Steady-state frequency domain phase response
A_p	Maximum allowable specified passband ripple in decibels
B	BPF bandwidth (rad s^{-1})
C_k^i	$\cos(i\pi/k)$
$C_n(\omega)$	Chebyshev polynomial of degree n (Chapter 4)
D	Distortion function
$\hat{D}(e^{j\omega})$	The desired frequency response of a digital filter
$D(z)$	Denominator polynomial of a transfer function
$\text{DFT}[x(n)]$	The discrete Fourier transform of the sequence $x(n)$
$\text{DTFT}[X(n)]$	The discrete-time Fourier transform of the sequence $x(n)$
$E\{\ \}$	Expected value, expectation
$E(\omega)$	Approximation error spectrum

Symbol	Meaning
$E_2 \ddagger E_1$	Shorthand notation for the matrices of exponents defined by $W_{N^2}^{E_2} W_{N^1}^{E_1}$
F	Analog frequency in hertz
$F_m(z^{-1})$	A causal approximant to predictor z
$G(e^{j\omega})$, $H(e^{j\omega})$, ..., $G(z)$, $H(z)$, ...	Transform domain scalars
$G(z)$	An intermediate complex variable
$G_i(z)$	Intermediate complex variable in cascade description
$H_a(j\omega)$	Steady-state frequency response function for an analog prototype filter
$H(e^{j\omega T})$	Steady-state frequency response function of a digital filter
$|H(e^{j\omega T})|$	Steady-state frequency domain magnitude response
$H(f)$	Spectral response (Chapter 3)
$H_i(z)$	Transfer function of individual quadratic blocks in a parallel realization of a digital filter
$H(z)$	Transfer function of a digital filter
$H_0(z)$	Zero-phase part of linear-phase filter with $(N + 1)$-point impulse response, $H(z) = z^{-N/2}H_0(z)$
H_w	Wiener filter transfer function
$H*$	Complex conjugate of the point spread transfer function
$H(\omega)$	Window (filter) spectrum (Chapter 3)
I, J, K, L, M, N	Integer indices
$I(z)$	Discrete integration operator
$I_B(z)$	$(1 + z^{-1})/(1 - z^{-1})$
$\text{Im}[\ ]$	The imaginary part of the quantity in brackets
I_N	The $N \times N$ identity matrix
$I_0(x)$	Modified zeroth-order Bessel function of the first kind
J	Performance measure
$K(A)$	Attenuation-related scale factor
M	The highest power of z in the numerator polynomial of a transfer function $H(z)$, number of filter weights (coefficients)
N	Transform dimension order of a digital filter (the highest power of z in the characteristic polynomial)
$N(z)$	Numerator polynomial of a transfer function
Q	Filter quality factor defined by ratio of center frequency to bandwidth
$Q[x(n)]$	Quantized value of $x(n)$ where $Q[x(n)] = x(n) + \underline{e}(n)$
$\text{Re}[\ ]$	The real part of the quantity in brackets
$R_n(\omega)$	Chebyshev rational function
$S_{xx}(e^{j\omega})$	Spectrum of the autocorrelation sequence $r_{xx}(m)$ where $S_{xx}(e^{j\omega}) = \text{DTFT}[r_{xx}(m)]$
T	Sampling interval in seconds
W_N	$\exp(-j2\pi/N)$
W_N^E	The matrix defined by $(W_N^{E(k,n)})$ where $(E(k,n)$ is a matrix with rows $k = 0, 1, ..., K-1$ and columns $n = 0, 1, ..., N-1$
$\hat{W}(e^{j\omega})$	Weighted error function that allocates relative errors between a filter passband and stopband
$X(e^{j\omega})$	The spectrum of the sequence $x(n)$ where $X(e^{j\omega}) = \text{DTFT}[x(n)] = X(z)|_{z=e^{j\omega}}$
$X(k)$	Coefficient number k in a series expansion of a periodic sequence
$X(z)$	The z-transform domain representation of the sequence $x(n)$
$X'(z)$	$dX(z)/dz$
$X'(e^{j\omega})$	$dX(e^{j\omega})/d\omega$ (compare with above)

Symbol	*Meaning*
a, b, x, ...	Vectors are designated by lowercase boldfaced letters
a	Measurement noise mean vector
b	State noise mean, constant measurement bias
u	Arbitrary vector
v	Measurement noise vector, arbitrary vector
w	State noise vector
x	State vector
y	Arbitrary vector
z	Measurement vector
A, B, X, ...	Matrices are designated by capital boldfaced letters
A	Arbitrary matrix, noise-shaping filter state coupling matrix
A^{-1}	The inverse of matrix **A**
A***	Complex conjugate of matrix **A**
A^T	The transpose of matrix **A**
A†	$(\mathbf{A}^T)^*$
A(z)	$\mathbf{A}^T(z^{-1})$
A ∘ **B**	The $M \times N$ matrix formed from element by element multiplication of the elements in the $M \times N$ matrices A and B; i.e., $A \circ B = (A(k,n)B(k,n))$
A ⊗ **B**	The Kronecker product of A and B
B	Arbitrary matrix, noise-shaping filter input coupling matrix
C	Noise-shaping filter output coupling matrix
D	Composite system input coupling matrix
F	State coupling matrix
G	Deterministic input coupling matrix
H	Equation coefficient matrix, output coupling matrix
Ha(k)	Haar transform of size 2^k
I$_M$	Opposite diagonal matrix
I$_R$	Identity matrix of size $R \times R$
K	Gain matrix, Kalman gain
L	Input noise coupling matrix
M	Measurement noise coupling matrix, state error covariance square root
N	Square root of inverse state error covariance matrix
O	Null matrix
P	Covariance matrix, state covariance matrix
P$_1$	Steady state prediction error covariance matrix
P$_N$	Permutation matrix
P$_O$	Initial state covariance matrix
Q	State noise covariance matrix
R	Measurement noise covariance matrix
RH(k)	Rationalized Haar transform of size 2^k
S(ℓ)	Slant transform of size 2^{ℓ}
W	Symmetric weighting matrix
X	A transform domain vector resulting from the data vector **x**
X$_c$	DCT of $x(n)$
X$_F$	DFT of $x(n)$
X$_k$	Coefficients of kth basis function
$w(n)$	Data sequence window function; also called a weighting function (Chapters 1 and 2)
$\mathscr{L}[x(t)]$	The Laplace transform of the function $x(t)$
$\mathscr{R}(i/m)$	The remainder when i is divided by m
$\mathscr{W}(e^{j\omega})$	Window function spectrum (Chapters 1 and 2)

Symbol	Meaning
$\mathscr{Z}[x(n)]$	The z-transform of the sequence $x(n)$ where $X(z) = \mathscr{Z}[x(n)]$
A, B, C, D	Chain parameters of digital two-pair
$\mathscr{T}$	Transfer matrix of digital two-pair
$\mathscr{T}_M$	Chebyshev polynomial of degree M (Chapter 5)
α	Ratio of 6-dB bandwidth to sample rate
αf_s	6-dB bandwidth referred to sample rate
α_i	Digital filter coefficients
δ_k	Peak error in kth filter band, where $2\delta_k$ is the peak-to-peak error
$\delta(n)$	Unit impulse (also called discrete-time impulse, impulse, or unit sample), defined by

$$\delta(n) = \begin{cases} 1, & n = 0 \\ 0, & n \neq 0 \end{cases}$$

Symbol	Meaning
ϵ	Mean-squared error ripple factor
$E(n)$	Quantization error at sample number n
η or η_x or μ	The mean value of the random variable $\underline{x}$ given by $\eta = E[\underline{x}]$
Θ	Argument (phase) of a complex number (pole, zero)
λ	Eigenvalue
ν	Covergence parameter
ξ	Noise-shaping filter state coupling
ρ	Adjacent correlation coefficient
σ	Real part of s (the Laplace transform variable)
σ^2	$E[(\underline{x} - \mu)^2]$
$\tau(\omega)$	Group delay
ϕ_f	Signal power spectra
ϕ_n	Noise power spectra
ω	Frequency in radians per second, $\omega = 2\pi f$, where f is usually normalized to $f_s = 1$ Hz in discrete-time systems
ω_c	Cutoff frequency of a filter, the -3dB cutoff frequency
ω_ℓ	The lower cutoff frequency of a bandpass or bandstop filter
ω_m	Geometric mean frequencey for bandpass transformation
ω_0	Center frequency (elliptic filters)
ω_p	Passband edge frequency
ω_p'	Specified passband edge frequency
ω_r	Stopband (rejection band) edge frequency
ω_s	Sampling radian frequency given by $\omega_s = 2\pi/T$
ω_u	The upper cutoff frequency of a bandpass or bandstop filter
Δf	Transition bandwidth of a filter, $\Delta f = (\omega_s - \omega_r)/2\pi$
Δx	State error
Δz	Measurement error
Ω	Continuous-time frequency in radians per second, $\Omega = 2\pi f$
λ_j	jth eigenvalue
ϕ	$N \times N$ basis vector
$\phi_k(t)$	kth basis function
ϕ_{ik}	ith element of kth basis vector
Γ	Arbitrary square matrix, noise-shaping filter initial covariance matrix
Ψ	Covariance matrix, composite system state coupling matrix
Ω	Inverse of state error covariance matrix

Symbol	*Meaning*
∇	The gradient operator
$[C^m]$	DCT of type m
$[A]$	Factored matrices
$[A(L)]$	DCT of size $(2^L \times 2^L)$
$[H(L)]$	Walsh–Hadamard matrix of size $(2^L \times 2^L)$
$[R(L)]$	Product of sparse matrices
$[S^N]$	DST of type N
$\lvert(\cdot)\rvert$	Magnitude of $(\cdot)$
$\lVert(\cdot)\rVert$	The L_2-norm (Euclidean norm) of $(\cdot)$
$\lVert X(e^{j\omega}) \rVert$	Without subscript means $\lVert X(e^{j\omega}) \rVert_2$
$\lVert X(e^{j\omega}) \rVert_2$	$\int_0^{2\pi} \lvert X(e^{j\omega}) \rvert^2 \, d\omega/2\pi$
$\lVert X(e^{j\omega}) \rVert_p$	The L_p-norm of $X(e^{j\omega})$
$\lfloor(\cdot)\rfloor$	Largest integer $\leqslant(\cdot)$; e.g., $\lfloor 3.5 \rfloor = 3$, $\lfloor -2.5 \rfloor = -3$
$\lceil(\cdot)\rceil$	Smallest integer $\geqslant(\cdot)$; e.g., $\lceil 3.5 \rceil = 4$, $\lceil -2.5 \rceil = -2$

Chapter 1

Transforms and
Transform Properties

DOUGLAS F. ELLIOTT
Rockwell International Corporation
Anaheim, California 92803

INTRODUCTION I

Transforms and transform properties occupy an important compartment of an engineer's "tool kit" for solving new problems and gaining insight into old ones. By resolving a time-varying waveform into sinusoidal components, engineers transform a problem from that of studying time domain phenomena to that of evaluating frequency domain properties. These properties often lead to simple explanations of otherwise complicated occurrences.

Continuous waveforms are not alone in being amenable to analysis by transforms and transform properties. Data sequences that result from sampling waveforms likewise may be studied in terms of their frequency content. Sampling, however, introduces a new problem: analog waveforms that do not look anything alike before sampling yield exactly the same sampled data; one sampled waveform "aliases" as the other.

This chapter briefly reviews the nature of sampled data and develops transforms and transform properties for the analysis of data sequences. We start by reviewing Fourier series that represent periodic waveforms. We note that the aliasing phenomenon leads to a periodic spectrum for data sequences so that the spectrum has a Fourier representation in terms of the data. We can find this representation from the data by using the discrete-time Fourier transform (DTFT).

The (DTFT) is generalized to the z-transform, which is a powerful tool for data sequence analysis. We also review the discrete Fourier transform (DFT) and recall the Laplace transform. We review discrete-time random sequences before discussing correlation and covariance sequences and their power spectral densities. Tables of properties are presented for each transform.

HANDBOOK OF DIGITAL SIGNAL PROCESSING

II REVIEW OF FOURIER SERIES

Fourier series have been a fundamental engineering tool since J. Fourier announced in 1807 that an arbitrary periodic function could be represented as the summation of scaled cosine and sine waveforms. We shall use Fourier series as a basis for developing the DTFT in the next section. We show that the integrals defining the series coefficients correspond to the inverse discrete-time Fourier transform (IDTFT).

This section simply recalls for the reader's convenience the definition of Fourier series. We consider one- and two-dimensional series.

A One-Dimensional Fourier Series

Let $X(\alpha)$ have period P and be the function to be represented by a one-dimensional (1-D) series. Let $X(\alpha)$ be such that

$$\int_{-P/2}^{P/2} |X(\alpha)|\, d\alpha = K_0 < \infty \tag{1.1}$$

Then $X(\alpha)$ has the 1-D Fourier series representation

$$X(\alpha) = \sum_{n=-\infty}^{\infty} x(n) e^{-j2\pi\alpha n/P} \tag{1.2}$$

At a point of discontinuity, α_0, the series converges to $[X(\alpha_0^+) + X(\alpha_0^-)]/2$, where $X(\alpha_0^+)$ and $X(\alpha_0^-)$ are the function's values at the left and right sides of the discontinuity, respectively. The $x(n)$, $n = 0,\ \pm 1,\ \pm 2,\ldots$, are Fourier series coefficients given by

$$x(n) = \frac{1}{P} \int_{-P/2}^{P/2} X(\alpha) e^{j2\pi\alpha n/P}\, d\alpha \tag{1.3}$$

We can easily derive Eq. (1.3) from Eq. (1.2) by using the orthogonality property for exponential functions:

$$\frac{1}{P} \int_{-P/2}^{P/2} e^{-j2\pi\alpha n/P} e^{j2\pi\alpha k/P}\, d\alpha = \delta_{kn} \tag{1.4}$$

where

$$\delta_{kn} = \begin{cases} 1, & k = n \\ 0, & \text{otherwise} \end{cases} \tag{1.5}$$

is the Kronecker delta function. Multiplying both sides of Eq. (1.2) by $\exp(j2\pi\alpha k/P)$, integrating from $-P/2$ to $P/2$, and using Eq. (1.5) yield Eq. (1.3).

For most engineering applications the function $X(\alpha)$ is bounded and continuous, except, possibly, at a finite number of points. In this case the Fourier series holds for very general integrability conditions. The orthogonality condition, Eq. (1.4), makes the Fourier series useful by allowing a function to be converted from one domain (frequency, etc.) to another (time, etc.). Other

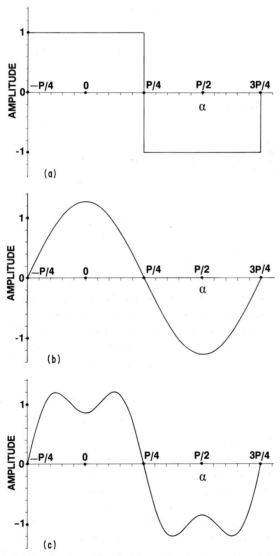

Fig. 1.1. A periodic waveform and its Fourier series representation. (a) One period of the waveform; (b) One-term approximation. (c) Two term-approximation. (d) Three-term approximation. (e) Ten-term approximation.

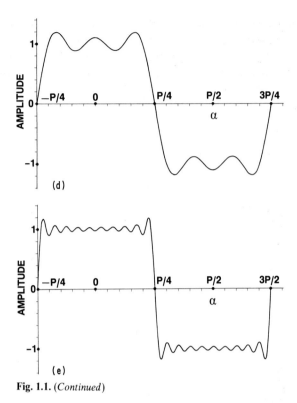

Fig. 1.1. (*Continued*)

ransforms (Walsh, etc.; see Chapter 6) also have orthogonality conditions and may be considered for the analysis of periodic functions.

Figure 1.1(a) shows one period of a square wave of period P. Figure 1.1(b)–(e) shows Fourier series representations using 1, 2, 3, or 10 terms of the series. The reader may verify that the N-term approximation, $X_N(\alpha)$, to the square wave reduces to

$$X_N(\alpha) = \sum_{m=1}^{N} (-1)^{m-1} \frac{4}{(2m-1)\pi} \cos\left[\frac{2\pi(2m-1)\alpha}{P}\right] \tag{1.6}$$

If we let $x(n) = 2a_n/\pi$, we note that $a_0 = 0$, $a_n = (-1)^{(n-1)/2}/n$ when the index n is an odd integer, and $a_n = 0$ when n is even. The series coefficients a_n are plotted versus both n and n/P in Fig. 1.2.

Figure 1.1(e) illustrates an advantage and a disadvantage of the Fourier series representation of the square wave. An advantage is that only 10 terms of the series give a fairly accurate approximation to the waveform. A disadvantage is the overshoot, or Gibbs phenomenon, at the points of discontinuity of the waveform. Further discussion of this phenomenon and Fourier series in general is in [1].

We have illustrated the representation of a periodic continuous function $X(\alpha)$ by a sequence of coefficients $x(n)$. Given the sequence $x(n)$, we can find the

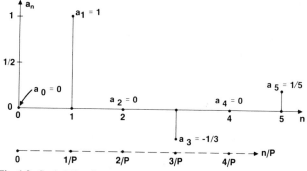

Fig. 1.2. Scaled Fourier series coefficients for the waveform in Fig. 1.1.

function $X(\alpha)$, and, indeed, the procedure of taking a data sequence and finding the corresponding $X(\alpha)$ is that of the DTFT, discussed in Section III.

Two-Dimensional Fourier Series   B

Let $X(\alpha, \beta)$ be an image with period P_1 along the α axis and period P_2 along the β axis (see Fig. 1.3). Note that the periodic image is generated by simply repeating a single image in both the horizontal and vertical directions. Let

$$\int_{-P_1/2}^{P_1/2} \int_{-P_2/2}^{P_2/2} |X(\alpha, \beta)| \, d\alpha \, d\beta = K_1 < \infty \tag{1.7}$$

Then $X(\alpha, \beta)$ has the 2-D Fourier series representation

$$X(\alpha, \beta) = \sum_{m=-\infty}^{\infty} \sum_{n=-\infty}^{\infty} x(n, m) e^{-j2\pi\alpha n/P_1} e^{-j2\pi\beta m/P_2} \tag{1.8}$$

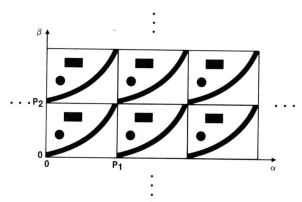

Fig. 1.3. Two-dimensional function with periods P_1 along the horizontal axis and P_2 along the vertical axis.

Paralleling the derivation of the Fourier coefficients for the 1-D series, we obtain the Fourier coefficients for the 2-D series:

$$x(m, n) = \frac{1}{P_1 P_2} \int_{-P_1/2}^{P_1/2} \int_{-P_2/2}^{P_2/2} X(\alpha, \beta) e^{j 2\pi\alpha m/P_1} e^{j 2\pi\beta n/P_2} \, d\alpha \, d\beta \qquad (1.9)$$

The coefficient $x(m, n)$ scales the product of complex sinusoids $\exp(-j2\pi\alpha m/P_1)\exp(-j2\pi\beta n/P_2)$ that have m cycles per P_1 units in the horizontal direction and n cycles per P_2 units in the vertical direction. Remarks concerning integrability conditions, advantages, and disadvantages for the 1-D series apply equally to the 2-D series.

The reader will doubtless see a pattern emerging from the 1-D and 2-D series development. This pattern leads to series representations for N-D functions, $N = 3, 4, \ldots$. We will not present these representations but will exploit a similar pattern in a later section to develop N-D discrete Fourier transforms.

III DISCRETE-TIME FOURIER TRANSFORM

The periodic waveforms discussed in the previous section have Fourier series representations determined, in general, by an infinite number of coefficients. Given the waveform, we can determine the sequence of coefficients. Conversely, given a sequence, we can find the continuous waveform. It is this latter procedure that yields the DTFT.

The DTFT provides a frequency domain representation of a data sequence that might result, for example, from sampling an analog waveform every T seconds (s). The distinct difference between the frequency spectrum of the analog signal and the discrete-time sequence derived from it is that the sampling process causes the analog spectrum to repeat periodically at intervals of f_s, where $f_s = 1/T$ is the sampling frequency. This section reviews the reason for the periodicity of the discrete-time spectrum, derives the DTFT and IDTFT, and presents a table of DTFT properties.

A Reason for Periodicity in Discrete-Time Spectra

Figure 1.4 shows cosine waveforms with frequencies of 1 and 9 Hz. There is no chance of mistaking one of these analog waveforms for the other. However, when they are sampled every $\frac{1}{8}$ s, the situation changes dramatically because the cosine functions intersect at $\frac{1}{8}$ s, $\frac{2}{8}$ s, ...

$$\cos[2\pi(\tfrac{1}{8})] = \cos[2\pi 9(\tfrac{1}{8})], \quad \cos[2\pi(\tfrac{2}{8})] = \cos[2\pi 9(\tfrac{2}{8})], \ldots$$

respectively; the sampled data from one is exactly the same as the sampled data from the other, and we say that sampled data from one "aliases" as sampled data

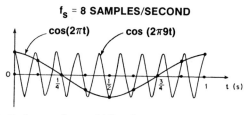

Fig. 1.4. Cosine waveforms yielding the same data at sampling instants.

from the other. It is easy to verify cosines of frequencies $1 + kf_s$, $f_s = 1/T$, $k = \pm 1, \pm 2,...$, go through the same points of intersection. Although Fig. 1.4 depicts cosine waveforms, aliasing will occur for any sinusoid.

We have shown that sampled sinusoids of frequency 1 Hz are indistinguishable from those of $1 + kf_s$ Hz, where k is any integer. Likewise, sampled sinusoids of frequencies f and $f + kf_s$ are indistinguishable:

$$\cos[2\pi f nT + \phi] = \cos[2\pi(f + kf_s)nT + \phi]$$

where ϕ is an arbitrary phase angle. Consequently, a spectrum analyzer would get the same value at f as at $f + kf_s$. We conclude that if by some means we determine the frequency spectrum of a discrete-time data sequence, the aliasing feature causes the spectrum to repeat at intervals of f_s, as shown in Fig. 1.5. In general, the frequency spectrum $X(f)$ is complex, so only the magnitude is plotted in the figure. The nonsymmetry of the spectrum about 0 Hz is due to a complex-valued data sequence that might result, for example, from frequency shifting (i.e., complex demodulation), which is described later.

Fourier Series Representation of Periodic Spectra B

We have found that the spectrum of a data sequence is periodic. If the data results from sampling a continuous-time signal every T s, then the period of the spectrum is $f_s = 1/T$ Hz. Since periodic functions can be represented by Fourier

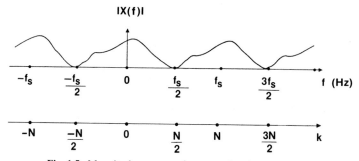

Fig. 1.5. Magnitude spectrum for a complex data sequence.

series under relatively mild conditions, we can use Eq. (1.2) to represent the spectrum by the series

$$X_1(f) = \sum_{n=-\infty}^{\infty} x(n)e^{-j2\pi fn/f_s} \tag{1.10}$$

where the series coefficient $x(n)$ is given by

$$x(n) = \frac{1}{f_s} \int_{-f_s/2}^{f_s/2} X_1(f)e^{j2\pi fn/f_s} \, df \tag{1.11}$$

The series coefficient $x(n)$ is the data sequence giving rise to the spectrum. We use $x(n)$ for samples of the continuous-time function $x(t)$ sampled at $t = nT$ and for data sequences in general. We know that $x(n)$ has a periodic spectrum. Substituting $f + kf_s$, where k is an integer, for f_s in (1.10) shows that $X_1(f)$ is the same for f as for $f + kf_s$. Thus, $X_1(f)$ has period f Hz, as required.

Note that in the Fourier series development we assumed a periodic function was given, and we found the sequence of coefficients for the Fourier series representation, using Eq. (1.11). If we are given a sequence of coefficients instead of the spectrum, we can use the coefficients to find the spectrum by using Eq. (1.10). When dealing with sequences, we are more likely to be given data that corresponds to the coefficients. If the data is the sequence $x(n)$, we find its spectrum using Eq. (1.10). We recover the data sequence from its spectrum by using Eq. (1.11). In any case Eqs. (1.2) and (1.3) or Eqs. (1.10) and (1.11) are a *transform pair*.

Another transform pair is the continuous-time Fourier transform and its inverse defined, respectively, by

$$X_1(f) = \int_{-\infty}^{\infty} x(t)e^{-j2\pi ft} \, dt \tag{1.12}$$

$$x(t) = \int_{-\infty}^{\infty} X_1(f)e^{j2\pi ft} \, df \tag{1.13}$$

We can gain additional intuition for Eq. (1.10) by noting that it is the Fourier transform of

$$x(t)\left[\sum_{n=-\infty}^{\infty} \delta(t - nT) \right] \tag{1.14}$$

where for any continuous function $y(t)$,

$$\int_{-\infty}^{\infty} y(t)\,\delta(t - nT)\, dt = y(nT) \tag{1.15}$$

The function $\delta(t - nT)$ is a Dirac delta function that acts as a sampling function in the sense that it derives $y(nT)$ from $y(t)$ through Eq. (1.15). If we let Eq. (1.14) be the integrand of Eq. (1.12), then Eq. (1.15) yields

$$y(nT) = x(nT)\exp(-j2\pi fnT) = x(n)\exp(-j2\pi fn/f_s)$$

which is a term in Eq. (1.10). Thus, Eq. (1.10) is the Fourier transform of Eq. (1.14). Whereas Eq. (1.12) yields the same answer as Eq. (1.10) if $x(t)$ is sampled with delta functions, Eqs. (1.11) and (1.13) do not correspond directly because Eq. (1.11) applies to a sequence and Eq. (1.13) applies to a continuous-time function. Since the spectrum given by Eq. (1.10) is periodic, only one period is required to obtain the sample $x(n)$, as Eq. (1.11) shows. This is in contrast to Eq. (1.13), where the entire spectrum is used to obtain $x(t)$.

One-Dimensional DTFT and IDTFT   C

We will now simplify the notation by using a normalized sampling interval of $T = 1$ s and radian frequency $\omega = 2\pi f$. Let $X_1(f) = X(e^{j\omega T})$. Then rewriting Eqs. (1.10) and (1.11) for $T = 1$ s gives

$$X(e^{j\omega}) = \sum_{n=-\infty}^{\infty} x(n)e^{-j\omega n} \tag{1.16}$$

$$x(n) = \frac{1}{2\pi} \int_{-\pi}^{\pi} X(e^{j\omega})e^{j\omega n}\,d\omega \tag{1.17}$$

Equations (1.16) and (1.17) are defined as the 1-D DTFT and 1-D IDTFT, respectively. The DTFT yields a periodic spectrum $X(e^{j\omega})$ for a given data sequence $x(n)$. The IDTFT recovers the data sequence from the spectrum. We will also use the notation

$$X(e^{j\omega}) = \mathrm{DTFT}[x(n)] \tag{1.18}$$

$$x(n) = \mathrm{IDTFT}[X(e^{j\omega})] \tag{1.19}$$

for Eqs. (1.16) and (1.17), respectively. Let Ω be the analog radian frequency. Then conversion from the radian frequency ω normalized for a sampling interval of 1 s to analog radian frequency Ω for an arbitrary sampling interval T requires only the substitution $\omega = \Omega T$. Figure 1.6 indicates corresponding points on the

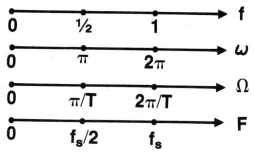

Fig. 1.6. Corresponding points on frequency axes for normalized variables f and ω and for analog variables Ω and F.

frequency axes for the variables $f, \omega = 2\pi f, \Omega = 2\pi F$, and F, where F is the analog frequency in hertz.

D   DTFT Properties

Table I summarizes properties of the 1-D DTFT. A property is described by a transform pair consisting of a data sequence representation and a transform sequence representation. For example, $x(n)$ and $X(e^{j\omega})$ constitute a transform pair. We will illustrate derivation of the pairs with several examples. For further details see [2, 3].

1   Frequency Shifting

Let the sequence $x(n)$ have the DTFT $X(e^{j\omega})$. Then the frequency-shifted sequence is $e^{j\omega_0 n}x(n)$, and its DTFT is

$$\text{DTFT}[e^{j\omega_0 n}x(n)] = \sum_{n=-\infty}^{\infty} e^{j\omega_0 n}x(n)e^{-j\omega n}$$

$$= \sum_{n=-\infty}^{\infty} x(n)e^{-j(\omega - \omega_0)n} = X(e^{j(\omega - \omega_0)}) \qquad (1.20)$$

The transform of $e^{j\omega_0 n}x(n)$ is right-shifted by ω_0 rad s^{-1}, and the DTFT of $e^{-j\omega_0 n}x(n)$ is left-shifted in frequency so that $e^{\pm j\omega_0 n}x(n)$ and $X(e^{j(\omega \mp \omega_0)})$ constitute a pair.

2   Data Sequence Convolution

Convolution of the sequence $x(n)$ with $y(n)$ is represented by $x(n) * y(n)$ and is defined by

$$x(n) * y(n) = \sum_{m=-\infty}^{\infty} x(m)y(n - m) = \sum_{m=-\infty}^{\infty} y(m)x(n - m) \qquad (1.21)$$

The transform of Eq. (1.21) is

$$\sum_{n=-\infty}^{\infty} x(n) * y(n)e^{-j\omega n} = \sum_{n=-\infty}^{\infty} \sum_{m=-\infty}^{\infty} x(m)y(n - m)e^{-j\omega n} \qquad (1.22)$$

Interchanging summations on the right of Eq. (1.22) and letting $i = n - m$ yield

$$\text{DTFT}[x(n) * y(n)] = \sum_{m=-\infty}^{\infty} x(m)e^{-j\omega m} \sum_{i=-\infty}^{\infty} y(i)e^{-j\omega i}$$

$$= X(e^{j\omega})Y(e^{j\omega}) \qquad (1.23)$$

as stated in Table I.

TABLE I
Summary of Discrete-Time Fourier Transform Properties

Property	Data sequence representation	DTFT representation
Discrete-time Fourier transform	$x(n)$	$X(e^{j\omega})$
Linearity	$ax(n) + by(n)$	$aX(e^{j\omega}) + bY(e^{j\omega})$
Horizontal data axis sign change	$x(-n)$	$X(e^{-j\omega})$
Complex conjugation	$x^*(n)$	$X^*(e^{-j\omega})$
Both of the above	$x^*(-n)$	$X^*(e^{j\omega})$
Sample shift	$x(n \pm m)$	$e^{\pm j\omega m} X(e^{j\omega})$
Frequency shift	$e^{\pm j\omega_0 n} x(n)$	$X(e^{j(\omega \mp \omega_0)})$
Double-sideband modulation	$\cos(\omega_0 n)x(n)$ $\sin(\omega_0 n)x(n)$	$\frac{1}{2}[X(e^{j(\omega + \omega_0)}) + X(e^{j(\omega - \omega_0)})]$ $\frac{1}{2j}[X(e^{j(\omega + \omega_0)}) - X(e^{j(\omega - \omega_0)})]$
Data sequence convolution (transform product)	$x(n) * y(n)$	$X(e^{j\omega})Y(e^{j\omega})$
Frequency domain convolution (data sequence product)	$x(n)y(n)$	$X(e^{j\omega}) * Y(e^{j\omega})$
Discrete-time impulse $\delta(n - n_0)$	$\delta(n - n_0) = \begin{cases} 1, & n = n_0 \\ 0 & \text{otherwise} \end{cases}$	$e^{-j\omega n_0}$
Frequency domain delta function	$e^{j2\pi f_0 n}$	$\delta(f - f_0)$
Discrete-time cosine waveform	$\cos(2\pi f_0 n)$	$\frac{1}{2}\delta(f + f_0) + \frac{1}{2}\delta(f - f_0)$

(continued)

TABLE I (*Continued*)

Property	Data sequence representation	DTFT representation
Discrete-time sine waveform	$\sin(2\pi f_0 n)$	$\frac{1}{2}j\delta(f + f_0) - \frac{1}{2}j\delta(f - f_0)$
N sample step sequence	$u_N(n) = \begin{cases} 1, & n = 0, 1, 2, \ldots, N-1 \\ 0 & \text{otherwise} \end{cases}$	$e^{-j\omega(N-1)/2}\dfrac{\sin(\omega N/2)}{\sin(\omega/2)}$
Two-sided step truncated for $\|n\| > N$	$s_N(n) = \begin{cases} 1, & \|n\| \le N \\ 0, & \|n\| > N \end{cases}$	$\dfrac{\sin[\omega(N + 1/2)]}{\sin(\omega/2)}$
Triangular sequence	$\text{tri}(n) = \begin{cases} N - \|n\|, & \|n\| \le N \\ 0, & \|n\| > N \end{cases}$	$\dfrac{\sin^2(\omega N/2)}{\sin^2(\omega/2)}$
Sequence truncated for $\|n\| > N$	$x(n)s_N(n)$	$X(e^{j\omega}) * \left\{ \dfrac{\sin[\omega(N + 1/2)]}{\sin(\omega/2)} \right\}$
Sequence truncated for $n < 0$ and $n \ge N$	$x(n)u_N(n)$	$X(e^{j\omega}) * \left[e^{-j\omega(N-1)/2}\dfrac{\sin(\omega N/2)}{\sin(\omega/2)} \right]$
Two-sided decaying exponential	$e^{-\alpha\|n\|}$	$\dfrac{1 - e^{-2\alpha}}{1 - 2e^{-\alpha}\cos\omega + e^{-2\alpha}}$
Damped sinusoid	$e^{-\alpha\|n\|}\cos(2\pi n\omega_0)$	$\dfrac{1}{2}\left[\dfrac{1 - e^{-2\alpha}}{1 - 2e^{-\alpha}\cos(\omega + \omega_0) + e^{-2\alpha}} + \dfrac{1 - e^{-2\alpha}}{1 - 2e^{-\alpha}\cos(\omega - \omega_0) + e^{-2\alpha}} \right]$
Conjugate symmetry of the transform of a real sequence	$x(n)$	$X(e^{j\omega}) = X^*(e^{-j\omega})$

Decomposition of a real sequence $x(n)$ into an even part $x_e(n)$ plus an odd $x_o(n)$	$x(n) = x_e(n) + x_o(n)$ $x_e(n) = \frac{1}{2}[x(n) + x(-n)]$ $x_o(n) = \frac{1}{2}[x(n) - x(-n)]$	$X(e^{j\omega})$ $\text{Re}[X(e^{j\omega})]$ $j\text{Im}[X(e^{j\omega})]$
Decomposition of a complex data sequence $x(n)$ into a conjugate symmetric part $x_e(n)$ and a conjugate antisymmetric part $x_o(n)$	$x(n) = x_e(n) + x_o(n)$ $x_e(n) = \frac{1}{2}[x(n) + x^*(-n)]$ $x_o(n) = \frac{1}{2}[x(n) - x^*(-n)]$	$X(e^{j\omega})$ $\text{Re}[X(e^{j\omega})]$ $j\text{Im}[X(e^{j\omega})]$
Decomposition of a complex transform $X(e^{j\omega})$	$x(n)$ $\text{Re}[x(n)]$ $j\text{Im}[x(n)]$	$X(e^{j\omega}) = X_e(e^{j\omega}) + X_o(e^{j\omega})$ $X_e(e^{j\omega}) = \frac{1}{2}[X(e^{j\omega}) + X^*(e^{-j\omega})]$ $X_o(e^{j\omega}) = \frac{1}{2}[X(e^{j\omega}) - X^*(e^{-j\omega})]$
Energy spectral density	$x(n)$	$|X(e^{j\omega})|^2$
Increasing sampling frequency by M—i.e., transforming a data sequence $x_1(n)$ padded with zeros by a factor of M	$x(n) = \begin{cases} x_1(n) & \text{if } n/M = m \\ 0 & \text{otherwise} \end{cases}$	$X_1(e^{jM\omega})$
Reducing sampling frequency by M—i.e., decimating a sequence $x_1(n)$ by a factor of M	$x(n) = x_1(Mn),$ $n = 0, \pm 1, \pm 2, \ldots$	$\dfrac{1}{M}\displaystyle\sum_{l=0}^{M-1} X_1(e^{j(\omega - 2\pi l)/M})$
Parseval's theorem	$\displaystyle\sum_{n=-\infty}^{\infty} x(n)y^*(n)$ $=$	$\dfrac{1}{2\pi}\displaystyle\int_{-\pi}^{\pi} X(e^{j\omega})Y^*(e^{j\omega})\,d\omega$

3 *Frequency Domain Convolution*

Frequency domain convolution is defined by

$$X(e^{j\omega}) * Y(e^{j\omega}) = \frac{1}{2\pi} \int_{-\pi}^{\pi} X(e^{j\theta}) Y(e^{j(\omega - \theta)}) \, d\theta \qquad (1.24)$$

Using the IDTFT definition, Eq. (1.17), interchanging integrations, and making a change of variables yield

$$\text{IDTFT}[X(e^{j\omega}) * Y(e^{j\omega})] = x(n)y(n) \qquad (1.25)$$

as stated in Table I.

4 *Symmetry Properties*

Several properties in Table I deal with conjugate symmetric sequences satisfying $x(n) = x^*(-n)$ and conjugate antisymmetric sequences satisfying $x(n) = -x^*(-n)$. If a sequence is real, then conjugate symmetric or antisymmetric correspond to even or odd, respectively.

5 *Sampling Frequency Change*

As an example of the utility of transform properties, consider the sampling frequency change properties (the two entries before Parseval's theorem at the end of Table I). Let the periodic repetitions of a spectrum of a sequence $x_1(n)$ be widely spaced so that the signal bandwidth (BW) satisfies BW $\leq f_s/M$. Then the sequence may be desampled by $M : 1$; that is, only 1 of every M samples is retained [see Fig. 1.7(a), (b)]. This reduces the spectral amplitude by $1/M$ and causes the spectrum to repeat at the new sampling frequency f_s/M [Fig. 1.7(c); the curve for $X_3(e^{j2\pi f})$ applies to $X_2(e^{j2\pi f})$ after frequency units are changed to Hz/3]. Desampling is used, for example, to more efficiently analyze a signal with a DFT. Before going to the DFT, the signal is desampled as much as possible without introducing aliasing, and, as a consequence of the desampling, the DFT can be run at a lower rate.

A signal can be interpolated by a $1 : M$ upsampling that adds $M - 1$ zeros to every sample (padding with zeros by $1 : M$). Although the upsampling increases the sampling frequency, it does not effect the spectrum, which still repeats at f_s/M (Fig. 1.7(c)). When we remove the spectral replicas at integer multiples of f_s/M by filtering, the zero values introduced by padding disappear and we obtain the original sequence $x_1(n)$. If we start with the signal $x_2(n)$ and wish to interpolate to find intermediate sample values, we simply pad with zeros by $1 : M$ and use a lowpass filter with a zero frequency gain of M to get a sequence $x_1(n)$ such that every Mth value matches $x_2(n)$. Another interesting application of upsampling is to effect a sampling frequency change (see Chapter 3).

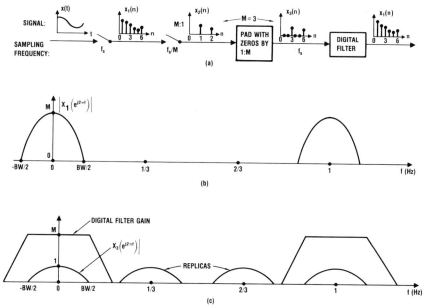

Fig. 1.7. For $f_s \geq M \cdot BW$ desampling by $M{:}1$ reduces computation rate while upsampling by $1{:}M$ interpolates the signal. (a) Block diagram showing desampling, upsampling, and filter to remove replicas. (b) Spectral magnitude for $x_1(n)$. (c) Spectral magnitude of $x_3(n)$ for $M = 3$.

Two-Dimensional DTFT   E

Let an image $x(r, s)$ be sampled at intervals of T_1 and T_2 along the r and s axes, respectively, yielding the 2-D sequence $x(m, n)$. The spectrum will be 2-D with periods $1/T_1$ and $1/T_2$ along the f_1 and f_2 axes, respectively, for the same reason that a 1-D spectrum is periodic. Since the 2-D spectrum is periodic, we can represent it by a 2-D Fourier series. Paralleling the steps for the 1-D DTF and IDTFT leads to

$$X(e^{j\omega_1}, e^{j\omega_2}) = \sum_{m=-\infty}^{\infty} \sum_{n=-\infty}^{\infty} x(m, n) e^{-j\omega_1 m} e^{-j\omega_2 n} \tag{1.26}$$

$$x(m, n) = \left(\frac{1}{2\pi}\right)^2 \int_{-\pi}^{\pi} \int_{-\pi}^{\pi} X(e^{j\omega_1}, e^{j\omega_2}) e^{j\omega_1 m} e^{j\omega_2 n} \, d\omega_1 \, d\omega_2 \tag{1.27}$$

We define Eqs. (1.26) and (1.27) as the 2-D DTFT and 2-D IDTFT, respectively. Extension of Table I to the 2-D case using Eqs. (1.26) and (1.27) is straightforward.

IV   z-TRANSFORM

The z-transform generalizes the DTFT and gives additional information on system stability. This section discusses the z-transform, the inverse z-transform, and a table of properties.

A   One-Dimensional z-Transform

Equation (1.16) defines the 1-D DTFT:

$$X(e^{j\omega}) = \sum_{n=-\infty}^{\infty} x(n)e^{-j\omega n} \tag{1.16}$$

We can generalize this equation by replacing $e^{-j\omega n}$ by $e^{-\sigma n - j\omega n}$, letting $z = e^{\sigma + j\omega}$, and defining the resulting summation as the two-sided, 1-D z-transform of $x(n)$ or, simply, the *z-transform* of $x(n)$, denoted by

$$X(z) = \mathscr{Z}[x(n)] = \sum_{n=-\infty}^{\infty} x(n)z^{-n} \tag{1.28}$$

For $\sigma = 0$, $z = e^{j\omega}$, and Eq. (1.28) is the same as Eq. (1.16). In this case $|z| = |e^{j\omega}| = |\cos \omega + j \sin \omega|$, which defines the *unit circle* (a circle with unity radius centered at the origin). Evaluating the z-transform on the unit circle in the z-plane corresponds to the DTFT.

B   Region of Convergence

The infinite series in Eq. (1.28) is meaningful only if it converges. One test of convergence is the ratio test: a series converges if the magnitude of the ratio of term $n + 1$ to term n (term $-n - 1$ to term $-n$ on the negative axis) is less than 1 as $n \to \infty$. For $n > 0$ we require that

$$\lim_{n \to \infty} \left| \frac{x(n + 1)z^{-n-1}}{x(n)z^{-n}} \right| < 1 \quad \text{or} \quad |z| > \lim_{n \to \infty} \left| \frac{x(n + 1)}{x(n)} \right| = R_1 \tag{1.29}$$

whereas for $n < 0$ we require that

$$\lim_{n \to \infty} \left| \frac{x(-n - 1)z^{n+1}}{x(-n)z^{n}} \right| < 1 \quad \text{or} \quad |z| < \lim_{n \to \infty} \left| \frac{x(-n)}{x(-n - 1)} \right| = R_2 \tag{1.30}$$

The region where Eqs. (1.29) and (1.30) are satisfied is called *the region of convergence*; R_1 and R_2 are called the *radii of convergence*. As an example, let

$$x(n) = \begin{cases} a^n, & n \geq 0 \\ -b^n, & n < 0 \end{cases} \tag{1.31}$$

Applying the geometric series summation formula

$$1 + c + c^2 + \cdots + c^{N-1} = \frac{1 - c^N}{1 - c}$$ (1.32)

to the z-transform of Eq. (1.31) gives

$$
\begin{aligned}
X(z) &= \sum_{n=0}^{\infty} a^n z^{-n} - \sum_{n=-1}^{-\infty} b^n z^{-n} \\
&= \frac{1}{1 - az^{-1}} + 1 - \sum_{n=0}^{\infty} b^{-n} z^n \\
&= \frac{z}{z - a} + \frac{z}{z - b} = \frac{2z[z - (a + b)/2]}{(z - a)(z - b)}
\end{aligned}
$$ (1.33)

where

$$\sum_{n=0}^{\infty} a^n z^{-n} \text{ converges for } |z| > a \quad \text{and}$$

$$\sum_{n=0}^{\infty} b^{-n} z^n \text{ converges for } |z| < b$$ (1.34)

From Eq. (1.34) we conclude that the region of convergence for Eq. (1.33) is the annulus defined by $|z| > a$ and $|z| < b$, as shown in Fig. 1.8. As is evident from Eq. (1.33), the function $X(z)$ diverges at $z = a$ and $z = b$. Such points are called *poles* of the function. Similarly, $X(z) = 0$ at $z = (a + b)/2$ and $z = 0$. Such points are called *zeros* of the function. If $b < a$, there is no region of convergence for (1.33) because the z-transform diverges everywhere.

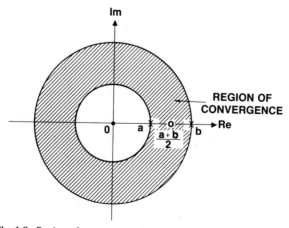

Fig. 1.8. Region of convergence for $x(n) = (a^n, n \geq 0; -b^{-n}, n < 0)$.

C One-Sided z-Transform

Many sequences considered in this book are zero for $n < 0$. Such a sequence is *right-sided*, and the 1-D z-transform, given by Eq. (1.28), becomes

$$X(z) = \sum_{n=0}^{\infty} x(n)z^{-n} \tag{1.35}$$

Similarly, if $x(n) = 0$ for $n > 0$, the sequence is *left-sided* and its 1-D z-transform is

$$X(z) = \sum_{n=-\infty}^{0} x(n)z^{-n} \tag{1.36}$$

Equations (1.35) and (1.36) define one-sided z-transforms. Section VI gives the z-transform of a number of right-sided sequences along with the corresponding continuous-time function $x(t)$ from which the sampled version, the sequence $x(n)$, is derived and the Laplace transform of $x(t)$.

D Inverse One-Dimensional z-transform

Given the function $X(z)$, we derive the data sequence $x(n)$ by taking the inverse z-transform of $X(z)$. Equation (1.28) defines the z-transform:

$$X(z) = \sum_{n=-\infty}^{\infty} x(n)z^{-n} \tag{1.28}$$

Multiplying both sides of Eq. (1.28) by $z^{m-1}/2\pi j$ and integrating over a counterclockwise (CCW) contour C, which is in the region of convergence of $X(z)$ and encircles the origin, yields

$$\frac{1}{2\pi j} \oint_C X(z)z^{m-1}\, dz = \sum_{n=-\infty}^{\infty} x(n)\left[\frac{1}{2\pi j} \oint_C z^{-n}z^{m-1}\, dz\right] \tag{1.37}$$

where we have substituted the right side Eq. (1.28) for $X(z)$ and have then interchanged summation and integration. We evaluate the integral in the brackets by the Cauchy integral theorem:

$$\frac{1}{2\pi j} \oint_C z^{m-n-1}\, dz = \delta(n - m) \tag{1.38}$$

where

$$\delta(n - m) = \begin{cases} 1, & n = m \\ 0 & \text{otherwise} \end{cases} \tag{1.39}$$

is the discrete time impulse. Since $\sum_{n=-\infty}^{\infty} x(n)\delta(n - m) = x(n)$, Eq. (1.37) reduces to the inverse z-transform:

$$x(n) = \mathscr{Z}^{-1}[X(z)] = \frac{1}{2\pi j} \oint_C X(z)z^{n-1}\, dz \tag{1.40}$$

When C is the unit circle $z = e^{j\omega}$, the preceding integral reduces to

$$x(n) = \frac{1}{2\pi} \int_{-\pi}^{\pi} X(e^{j\omega})e^{j\omega n}\, d\omega \tag{1.17}$$

which is the IDTFT defined previously.

We can evaluate the integral on the right of Eq. (1.40) by Cauchy's residue theorem:

$$x(n) = \sum [\text{Residues of } X(z)z^{n-1} \text{ at poles inside } C] \tag{1.41}$$

However, in practice it is often easier to use either long division or a partial-fraction expansion rather than Eq. (1.40) or Eq. (1.41). As an example of long division, consider the right-sided z-transform $X(z) = 1/(1 - az^{-1})$. Dividing numerator by denominator yields

$$X(z) = 1 + az^{-1} + a^2z^{-2} + \cdots + a^nz^{-n} + \cdots = \sum_{n=0}^{\infty} x(n)z^{-n} \tag{1.42}$$

Comparing coefficients of z^{-n} gives $x(n) = a^n$.

As an example of using a partial-fraction expansion, consider the right-sided transform

$$X(z) = \frac{1}{(1 - az^{-1})(1 - bz^{-1})} = \frac{a/(a-b)}{1 - az^{-1}} + \frac{b/(b-a)}{1 - bz^{-1}} \tag{1.43}$$

We may evaluate each term in the summation on the right of Eq. (1.43) by using Eq. (1.42) to get $x(n) = (a^{n+1} - b^{n+1})/(a - b)$, or we can use z-transform pairs. Some z-transform pairs are stated for right- and left-sided sequences in Table II. In the table ω and a are real numbers; right- and left-sided sequences converge for $|z| > p$ and $|z| < q$, respectively, where p is a right-sided sequence pole and q is a left-sided sequence pole. More extensive right-sided z-transforms are in Section VI.

z-Transform Properties   E

Table III summarizes a number of 1-D z-transform properties, most of which apply to either one- or two-sided data sequences. When the property applies only to a one-sided sequence, this is stated. For example, the initial value theorem in the table applies to right-sided sequences. Derivation of the properties is treated in [3–13, 19]. Most of the properties are a straightforward application of the z-transform definition, as the following examples illustrate.

TABLE II

z-Transform Pairs

Data sequence, $x(n)$	z-Transform, $X(z)$	
	Right-sided	Left-sided
$\delta(n)$	1	1
$a^{\lvert n\rvert}$	$\dfrac{1}{1 - az^{-1}}$	$\dfrac{1}{1 - az}$
$\lvert n\rvert a^{\lvert n\rvert}$	$\dfrac{az^{-1}}{(1 - az^{-1})^2}$	$\dfrac{az}{(1 - az)^2}$
$\lvert n\rvert^2 a^{\lvert n\rvert}$	$\dfrac{az^{-1}(1 + az^{-1})}{(1 - az^{-1})^3}$	$\dfrac{az(1 + az)}{(1 - az)^3}$
$a^{\lvert n\rvert}\sin\lvert n\rvert\omega T$	$\dfrac{a\sin(\omega T)z^{-1}}{1 - 2a\cos(\omega T)z^{-1} + a^2 z^{-2}}$	$\dfrac{a\sin(\omega T)z}{1 - 2a\cos(\omega T)z + a^2 z^2}$
$a^{\lvert n\rvert}\cos\lvert n\rvert\omega T$	$\dfrac{1 - a\cos(\omega T)z^{-1}}{1 - 2a\cos(\omega T)z^{-1} + a^2 z^{-2}}$	$\dfrac{1 - a\cos(\omega T)z}{1 - 2a\cos(\omega T)z + a^2 z^2}$

TABLE III

Summary of z-Transform Properties

Property	Data sequence representation	z-Transform representation
z-Transform	$x(n)$	$X(z)$
Equivalence of the DTFT and the z-transform evaluated on the unit circle	$x(n)$	$\text{DTFT}[x(n)] = X(z)\big|_{z = e^{j\omega}}$
Linearity	$ax(n) + by(n)$	$aX(z) + bY(z)$
Data sequence horizontal axis sign change	$x(-n)$	$X(1/z)$
Complex conjugation	$x^*(n)$	$X^*(z^*)$
Both of the above	$x^*(-n)$	$X^*(1/z^*)$
Transform of real part of data sequence	$\text{Re}[x(n)]$	$\frac{1}{2j}[X(z) + X^*(z^*)]$
Transform of imaginary part of data sequence	$\text{Im}[x(n)]$	$\frac{1}{2}[X(z) - X^*(z^*)]$
Sample shift	$x(n \pm m)$	$z^{\pm m}X(z)$
Left shift of right-sided sequence	$x(n + m)$	$z^m\left[X(z) - \displaystyle\sum_{n=0}^{m-1} x(n)z^{-n}\right]$
z-plane complex scale change	$w^{-n}x(n)$	$X(wz)$

(continued)

TABLE III (*Continued*)

Property	Data sequence representation	z-Transform representation
Convolution of data sequences (transform product)	$x(n) * y(n)$	$X(z)Y(z)$
Periodic convolution of transforms (data sequence product)[a]	$x(n)y(n)$	$\dfrac{1}{2\pi j}\displaystyle\oint_C X(v)\,Y\!\left(\dfrac{z}{v}\right)v^{-1}\,dv$
Data sequence multiplication by n	$nx(n)$	$-z\dfrac{dX(z)}{dz}$
Right-sided data sequence[b] division by n [12]	$\dfrac{x(n+1)}{n}$ where $x(n)=0$ for $n<2$	$\displaystyle\int_z^{\infty} X(w)\,dw \quad \text{for } |z| > R$
Initial value theorem for right-sided sequence	$x(0)$	$\displaystyle\lim_{z\to\infty} X(z)$
Final value theorem for right-sided sequence[c]	$\displaystyle\lim_{n\to\infty} x(n)$	$\displaystyle\lim_{z\to 1}(1-z^{-1})X(z)$
Right-sided data sequence $x(n)$ with period N	$x_1(n)=\begin{cases} x(n), & 0\le n<N \\ 0 & \text{otherwise}\end{cases}$	$\dfrac{X_1(z)}{1-z^{-N}}$
Increasing sampling frequency by M—i.e., transforming a data sequence $x_1(n)$ padded with zeros by a factor of M	$x(n)=\begin{cases} x_1(m) & \text{if } n/M=m \\ 0 & \text{otherwise}\end{cases}$	$X_1(z^M)$
Reducing sampling frequency by M—i.e., decimating a sequence $x_1(n)$ by a factor of M	$x(n)=x_1(Mn),$ $n=0,\pm 1,\pm 2,\dots$	$\dfrac{1}{M}\displaystyle\sum_{l=0}^{M-1} X_1(z^{1/M}e^{-j2\pi l/M})$
Parseval's theorem[d]	$\displaystyle\sum_{n=-\infty}^{\infty} x(n)y^*(n) \quad =$	$\dfrac{1}{2\pi}\displaystyle\int_{-\pi}^{\pi} X(e^{j\omega})Y^*(e^{j\omega})\,d\omega$

[a] C is in the region of convergence of $X(v)$ and $Y(z/v)$.
[b] R is the radius of convergence of $X(z)$.
[c] The poles of $X(z)$ must lie within the unit circle except for possibly a first-order pole at $z=1$.
[d] The poles of $X(z)$ and $Y(z)$ must lie within the unit circle.

Data Sequence Horizontal Axis Sign Change   1

Let $x(n)$ be replaced by $x(-n)$—for example, by a time reversal in taking data. The z-transform of the sequence $x(-n)$ is, by definition,

$$\sum_{n=-\infty}^{\infty} x(-n)z^{-n} = \sum_{m=-\infty}^{\infty} x(m)z^m = \sum_{m=-\infty}^{\infty} x(m)\left(\frac{1}{z}\right)^{-m} = X\left(\frac{1}{z}\right) \quad (1.44)$$

The data sequence horizontal axis sign change yields $x(-n)$, which has the z-transform $X(1/z)$, whereas $x(n)$ has the z-transform $X(z)$.

2   Convolution of Data Sequences

This property states that the z-transform of the convolution of data sequences yields the product of the z-transforms of each sequence. Let $x(n)$ and $y(n)$ be the sequences convolved, and let $w(n)$ be the resulting sequence:

$$w(n) = x(n) * y(n) = \sum_{m=-\infty}^{\infty} x(m)y(n-m) \tag{1.45}$$

By definition the z-transform of $w(n)$ is

$$W(z) = \sum_{n=-\infty}^{\infty} w(n)z^{-n} = \sum_{n=-\infty}^{\infty}\sum_{m=-\infty}^{\infty} x(m)y(n-m)z^{-n} \tag{1.46}$$

Interchanging the summations and letting $k = n - m$ yield

$$W(z) = \sum_{m=-\infty}^{\infty} x(m)\sum_{n=-\infty}^{\infty} y(n-m)z^{-n} = \sum_{m=-\infty}^{\infty} x(m)\sum_{k=-\infty}^{\infty} y(k)z^{-k-m} = X(z)Y(z) \tag{1.47}$$

so the z-transform of $x(n) * y(n)$ is $X(z)Y(z)$.

3   Periodic Convolution of Transforms

This property states that the z-transform of the sequence formed from the term-by-term product of two data sequences is given by a contour integral. If the region of convergence of the z-transform of each sequence includes the unit circle in the z-plane, then the contour integral is a periodic convolution. Let $w(n) = x(n)y(n)$. Then the z-transform of $w(n)$ is

$$W(z) = \sum_{n=-\infty}^{\infty} x(n)y(n)z^{-n} = \sum_{n=-\infty}^{\infty} x(n)\frac{1}{2\pi j}\oint_{C_1} Y(v)v^{n-1}\,dv\,z^{-n} \tag{1.48}$$

where Eq. (1.40) was used to express $y(n)$ and C_1 is a CCW contour around the origin in the region of convergence of $Y(v)$. Interchanging the integration and summation in Eq. (1.48) yields

$$W(z) = \frac{1}{2\pi j}\oint_{C_1}\sum_{n=-\infty}^{\infty} x(n)\left(\frac{z}{v}\right)^{-n} Y(v)v^{-1}\,dv$$

$$= \frac{1}{2\pi j}\oint_{C_1} X\left(\frac{z}{v}\right) Y(v)v^{-1}\,dv \tag{1.49}$$

where now C_1 must lie in the region of convergence of $X(z/v)$ as well as that of $Y(v)$. Interchanging the roles of $x(n)$ and $y(n)$ yields another form of the integral:

$$W(z) = \frac{1}{2\pi j}\oint_{C} X(v)Y\left(\frac{z}{v}\right)v^{-1}\,dv \tag{1.50}$$

where C is a CCW contour that encircles the origin and lies in the regions of convergence of $X(v)$ and $Y(z/v)$. Combining Eqs. (1.48) and (1.50) gives the result that the z-transform of the sequence $x(n)y(n)$ is a contour integration. Let C include the circles with radii ρ and r/ρ. Let $z = re^{j\phi}$ and $v = \rho e^{j\omega}$. Then Eq. (1.50) gives

$$W(re^{j\phi}) = \frac{1}{2\pi} \int_{-\pi}^{\pi} X(\rho e^{j\omega}) Y\left[\frac{r}{\rho} e^{j(\phi - \omega)}\right] d\omega \tag{1.51a}$$

which is called a periodic convolution because $W(re^{j\phi})$ has period 2π. When the circles of convergence include $r = \rho = 1$, we interchange the roles of ϕ and ω and denote the periodic convolution by

$$W(e^{j\omega}) = X(e^{j\omega}) * Y(e^{j\omega}) \tag{1.51b}$$

which is the same as frequency domain convolution for the DTFT [see Eq. (1.24)].

Two-Dimensional z-Transform   **F**

Just as we generalized the 1-D DTFT to obtain the 1-D z-transform, we shall generalize the 2-D DTFT to obtain the 2-D z-transform. Let $x(m, n)$ be a 2-D sequence representing, for example, a sampled image. We obtain the 2-D z-transform of $x(m, n)$, $\mathcal{Z}_{2\text{-D}}[x(m, n)]$, by generalizing Eq. (1.26), letting $z_i = e^{\sigma_i + j\omega_i}$, $i = 1, 2$, which gives

$$X(z_1, z_2) = \mathcal{Z}_{2\text{-D}}[x(m, n)] = \sum_{m=-\infty}^{\infty} \sum_{n=-\infty}^{\infty} x(m, n) z_1^{-m} z_2^{-n} \tag{1.52}$$

The region of convergence of $X(z_1, z_2)$ is that region in z_1, z_2 space for which Eq. (1.52) is absolutely summable:

$$\sum_{m=-\infty}^{\infty} \sum_{n=-\infty}^{\infty} |x(m, n) z_1^{-m} z_2^{-n}| < \infty \tag{1.53}$$

Likewise, the 2-D inverse z-transform results from generalizing Eq. (1.27):

$$x(m, n) = \mathcal{Z}_{2\text{-D}}^{-1}(X(z_1, z_2)) = \left(\frac{1}{2\pi j}\right)^2 \oint_{C_1} \oint_{C_2} X(z_1, z_2) z_1^{m-1} z_2^{n-1} \, dz_1 \, dz_2 \tag{1.54}$$

where C_i is a closed contour encircling the origin of the z_i-plane, $i = 1, 2$. The contours C_i are generally difficult to specify unless the 2-D z-transform is separable: $X(z_1, z_2) = X_1(z_1) X_2(z_2)$, which is true if and only if the data sequence is separable.

The table of 1-D z-transform properties extends in a straightforward manner to 2-D properties. For example, the z-transform of a 2-D convolution gives the product of transforms:

$$\mathscr{Z}_{2-D}[x(m, n) * y(m, n)] = X(z_1, z_2)Y(z_1, z_2) \tag{1.55}$$

The 2-D z-transform is important in the development of 2-D digital filters used in image processing. Thus, stability of the 2-D filter is an important consideration, and the stability assessment requires us to determine the location of the zeros of the denominator polynomial of the filter transfer function. The filter is stable if the denominator polynomial is never zero for any values of z_1 and z_2 such that $|z_1| > 1$ and $|z_2| > 1$.

V LAPLACE TRANSFORM

Whereas the z-transform is the primary tool for analysis of discrete-time systems, the Laplace transform is often the primary tool for analysis of continuous-time systems. Laplace transforms were originally developed by Oliver Heaviside to solve ordinary differential equations by algebraic means without finding a general solution and evaluating arbitrary constants.

Laplace transforms have several applications in this book. We use them principally to describe an analog filter *transfer function*. We can convert this transfer function to a digital filter by the techniques described in Chapter 4.

A Definition of the One-Sided Laplace Transform

Let $x(t)$ be a function such that

$$\int_0^\infty |x(t)|e^{-\sigma t}\,dt = K < \infty \tag{1.56}$$

for some finite, real-valued constant σ. Then the one-sided *Laplace transform* of $x(t)$, $\mathscr{L}[x(t)]$, is defined as $X(s)$ and given by

$$X(s) = \mathscr{L}[x(t)] = \int_0^\infty x(t)e^{-st}\,dt, \qquad s = \sigma + j\Omega \tag{1.57}$$

To insure essential uniqueness of the function $x(t)$, if we are given $X(s)$, we require that

$$x(t) = 0, \qquad t < 0 \tag{1.58}$$

Then the inverse Laplace transform of $X(s)$ is

$$x(t) = \frac{1}{2\pi j}\int_{\sigma_1 - j\infty}^{\sigma_1 + j\infty} F(s)e^{st}\,ds \tag{1.59}$$

where $\sigma_1 > \sigma$ and the latter is the σ in Eq. (1.56).

Table IV summarizes some Laplace transform properties. In the table all functions are zero for negative time; that is, if $t < 0$, then $x(t) = x_1(t) = x_2(t) = 0$. Other notational definitions include

$$x'(0) = \frac{dx(t)}{dt}\bigg|_{t=0}, \qquad x''(0) = \frac{d^n x(t)}{dt}\bigg|_{t=0} \tag{1.60}$$

$$u(t) = \begin{cases} 1, & t \geq 0 \\ 0, & t < 0 \end{cases} \tag{1.61}$$

We illustrate derivation of the pairs with several examples.

Laplace Transform of e^{-at} 1

For $\mathrm{Re}[s] > a$ the transform of e^{-at} is

$$\int_0^\infty e^{-at} e^{-st}\, dt = -\frac{e^{-(s+a)t}}{s+a}\bigg|_0^\infty = \frac{1}{s+a} \tag{1.62}$$

Laplace Transform of $\int_0^t x(\tau)\, d\tau$ 2

The Laplace transform of $\int_0^t x(\tau)\, d\tau$ is

$$\int_0^\infty \left[\int_0^t x(\tau)\, d\tau\right] e^{-st}\, dt = \left[\frac{e^{-st}}{-s}\int_0^t x(\tau)\, d\tau\right]\bigg|_0^\infty - \frac{1}{-s}\int_0^\infty e^{-st} x(t)\, dt \tag{1.63}$$

$$= \frac{X(s)}{s}$$

where we used $\int u\, dv = uv - \int v\, du$, $u = \int_0^t x(\tau)\, d\tau$, and $dv = e^{-st}\, dt$, and where the expression in brackets when evaluated at zero and infinity equals zero [14].

Laplace Transform of $dx(t)/dt$ 3

Let $\lim_{t \to \infty} [e^{-st} x(t)] = 0$. Then

$$\int_0^\infty e^{-st} \frac{dx(t)}{dt}\, dt = e^{-st} x(t)\bigg|_0^\infty + s \int_0^\infty x(t) e^{-st}\, dt \tag{1.64}$$

$$= -x(0) + sX(s)$$

where again we integrated by parts, using $u = e^{-st}$ and $dv = dx(t)$.

TABLE IV
Summary of Laplace Transform Properties[c]

Property	Time domain representation	Laplace transform representation
Laplace transform	$x(t)$	$X(s)$
Time domain first-order derivative	$dx(t)/dt$	$sX(s) - x(0)$
Time domain second-order derivative	$d^2x(t)/dt^2$	$s^2X(s) - sx(0) - x'(0)$
Time domain nth-order derivative	$d^nx(t)/dt^n$	$s^nX(s) - s^{n-1}x(0) - \cdots x^{n-1}(0)$
Time domain integration	$\displaystyle\int_0^t x(t)\,dt$	$\dfrac{X(s)}{s}$
Right-shifted time function	$x(t-a),\quad a \geq 0$	$e^{-as}X(s)$
Left-shifted time function	$x(t+a)u(t),\quad a \geq 0$	$e^{as}\mathscr{L}[x(t)u(t-a)]$
Function $x(t)$ with period P	$x_1(t) = \begin{cases} x(t), & 0 \leq t < P \\ 0 & \text{otherwise} \end{cases}$	$\dfrac{X_1(s)}{1 - e^{-Ps}}$
Attenuated time function	$e^{-at}x(t),\quad a \geq 0$	$X(s+a)$
Horizontal time axis scaling	$x(at),\quad a \geq 0$	$\dfrac{1}{a}X\left(\dfrac{s}{a}\right)$
Time domain convolution (frequency domain product)	$x_1(t) * x_2(t)$ $= \displaystyle\int_0^t x_1(\tau)x_2(t-\tau)\,d\tau$	$X_1(s)X_2(s)$
Frequency domain convolution (time domain product)[a]	$x_1(t)x_2(t)$	$X_1(s) * X_2(s)$ $= \dfrac{1}{2\pi j}\displaystyle\int_{c-j\infty}^{c+j\infty} X_1(w)X_2(s-w)\,dw$
Time function partial derivative with respect to a parameter	$\dfrac{\partial x(t,a)}{\partial a}$	$\dfrac{\partial X(s,a)}{\partial a}$
Time function integration with respect to a parameter	$\displaystyle\int_{a_1}^{a_2} x(t,a)\,da$	$\displaystyle\int_{a_1}^{a_2} X(s,a)\,da$
Product of time function and t^n	$t^nx(t)$	$(-1)^n\dfrac{d^nX(s)}{ds^n}$
Division of time function by t	$\dfrac{x(t)}{t}$	$\displaystyle\int_s^\infty X(s)\,ds$
Decomposition of a complex time function	$x(t) = \text{Re}[x(t)] + j\text{Im}[x(t)]$	$X(s) = \text{Re}[X(s)] + j\text{Im}[X(s)]$
Initial value theorem	$x(0)$	$\displaystyle\lim_{s\to\infty} sX(s)$
Final value theorem[b]	$x(\infty)$	$\displaystyle\lim_{s\to 0} sX(s)$

[a] $\text{Re}[w] = c$ lies to the right of the poles of $X_1(w)$ and to the left of the poles of $X_2(s-w)$.
[b] The poles of $sX(s)$ must be in the left half of the s-plane.
[c] Adapted from [14].

TABLE OF z-TRANSFORMS AND LAPLACE TRANSFORMS VI

Table V states the Laplace transform for each listed function $x(t)$, as well as the z-transform of the right-sided sequence $x(n)$, $x(n) = x(t)$ evaluated at $t = nT$, where T is the sampling interval. Note that the z-transforms have not been stated for a normalized sampling frequency of 1 Hz, but the sampling interval is contained explicitly in the transforms.

DISCRETE FOURIER TRANSFORM VII

The DTFT discussed in Section III yields a periodic, continuous spectrum for a nonperiodic data sequence of infinite length. The DFT of this section also yields a periodic spectrum characteristic of sampled data. In contrast to the DTFT, the DFT has a line spectrum that represents a sequence of period N. The term "discrete Fourier transform" is somewhat of a misnomer since the DFT provides a Fourier series representation for a finite sequence, whereas the DTFT yields a true Fourier transform of an infinite sequence incorporating Dirac delta functions [see Eq. (1.14)].

Series Representation of an N-Point Sequence A

Let an N-point sequence, $x(n)$, be given for $n = 0, 1, 2, \ldots, N - 1$. Then we form the periodic sequence, $x_p(n)$, from $x(n)$ by simply repeating $x(n)$ with period N:

$$x_p(n) = x(i), \qquad i = 0, 1, 2, \ldots, N - 1, i = n \bmod N \qquad (1.65)$$

where for some integer $mn = i + Nm$. Thus, i is the remainder of n/N, or, stated another way, i is *congruent* to n (modulo N). These equivalent statements are written as

$$i = n \bmod N \qquad \text{or} \qquad i \equiv n \quad (\text{modulo } N) \qquad (1.66)$$

As discussed in Section II, periodic functions can be represented by a Fourier series. There is a periodic function $x_p(t)$ that yields the sequence $x(n)$ when sampled at $t = nT$, $n = 0, 1, 2, \ldots, N - 1$, where $P = NT$ is the period of the function. The Fourier coefficients $X_p(k)$ for the series represent a line spectrum where the lines are at intervals of $1/P = f_s/N$ as illustrated in Fig. 1.2. Thus, the lines in the spectrum are at the frequencies

$$f = \frac{kf_s}{N}, \qquad k = 0, 1, 2, \ldots, N - 1 \qquad (1.67)$$

where just N values are required for k because $X_p(k)$ has the period N.

TABLE V
Table of Laplace and z-Transforms[a]

Laplace transform $X(s)$	Time function $x(t)$	z-transform $X(z)$
1	$\delta(t)$	1
e^{-nTs}	$\delta(t-nT)$	z^{-n}
$\dfrac{1}{s}$	$u(t)$	$\dfrac{z}{z-1}$
$\dfrac{1}{s^2}$	t	$\dfrac{Tz}{(z-1)^2}$
$\dfrac{2!}{s^3}$	t^2	$\dfrac{T^2 z(z+1)}{(z-1)^3}$
$\dfrac{(n-1)!}{s^n}$	t^{n-1}	$\displaystyle\lim_{a\to 0}(-1)^{n-1}\dfrac{\partial^{n-1}}{\partial a^{n-1}}\left(\dfrac{z}{z-e^{-aT}}\right)$
$\dfrac{1}{s+a}$	e^{-at}	$\dfrac{z}{z-e^{-aT}}$
$\dfrac{1}{(s+a)(s+b)}$	$\dfrac{1}{b-a}(e^{-at}-e^{-bt})$	$\dfrac{1}{b-a}\left(\dfrac{z}{z-e^{-aT}}-\dfrac{z}{z-e^{-bT}}\right)$
$\dfrac{1}{s(s+a)}$	$\dfrac{1}{a}(u(t)-e^{-at})$	$\dfrac{1}{a}\dfrac{(1-e^{-aT})z}{(z-1)(z-e^{-aT})}$
$\dfrac{1}{s^2(s+a)}$	$\dfrac{1}{a}\left(t-\dfrac{1-e^{-at}}{a}\right)$	$\dfrac{1}{a}\left[\dfrac{Tz}{(z-1)^2}-\dfrac{(1-e^{-aT})z}{a(z-1)(z-e^{-aT})}\right]$
$\dfrac{(s+b)}{s^2(s+a)}$	$\dfrac{a-b}{a^2}u(t)+\dfrac{b}{a}t+\dfrac{1}{a}\left(\dfrac{b}{a}-1\right)e^{-at}$	$\dfrac{1}{a}\left[\dfrac{bTz}{(z-1)^2}+\dfrac{(a-b)(1-e^{-aT})z}{a(z-1)(z-e^{-aT})}\right]$
$\dfrac{1}{s(s+a)(s+b)}$	$\dfrac{1}{ab}\left(u(t)+\dfrac{b}{a-b}e^{-at}-\dfrac{a}{a-b}e^{-bt}\right)$	$\dfrac{1}{ab}\left[\dfrac{z}{z-1}+\dfrac{bz}{(a-b)(z-e^{-aT})}-\dfrac{az}{(a-b)(z-e^{-aT})}\right]$
$\dfrac{1}{(s+a)^2}$	te^{-at}	$\dfrac{Tze^{-aT}}{(z-e^{-aT})^2}$

$\dfrac{1}{s^3(s+a)}$	$\dfrac{1}{2a}\left(t^2 - \dfrac{2}{a}t + \dfrac{2}{a^2}u(t) - \dfrac{2}{a^2}e^{-at}\right)$	$\dfrac{1}{a}\left[\dfrac{T^2 z}{(z-1)^3} + \dfrac{(aT-2)Tz}{2a(z-1)^2} + \dfrac{z}{a^2(z-1)} - \dfrac{z}{a^2(z-e^{-aT})}\right]$
$\dfrac{a}{s^2+a^2}$	$\sin at$	$\dfrac{z\sin aT}{z^2 - 2z\cos aT + 1}$
$\dfrac{s}{s^2+a^2}$	$\cos at$	$\dfrac{z(z-\cos aT)}{z^2 - 2z\cos aT + 1}$
$\dfrac{a}{s^2-a^2}$	$\sinh aT$	$\dfrac{z\sinh aT}{z^2 - 2z\cosh aT + 1}$
$\dfrac{s}{s^2-a^2}$	$\cosh aT$	$\dfrac{z(z-\cosh aT)}{z^2 - 2z\cosh aT + 1}$
$\dfrac{a}{s(s^2+a^2)}$	$\dfrac{1}{a}(u(t) - \cos at)$	$\dfrac{1}{a}\left[\dfrac{z}{z-1} - \dfrac{z(z-\cos aT)}{z^2 - 2z\cos aT + 1}\right]$
$\dfrac{a^2}{s^2(s^2+a^2)}$	$t - \dfrac{1}{a}\sin at$	$\dfrac{Tz}{(z-1)^2} - \dfrac{1}{a}\dfrac{z\sin aT}{z^2 - 2z\cos aT + 1}$
$\dfrac{1}{s(s+a)^2}$	$\dfrac{1}{a^2}[u(t) - (1+at)e^{-at}]$	$\dfrac{1}{a^2}\left[\dfrac{z}{z-1} - \dfrac{z}{z-e^{-aT}} - \dfrac{aTe^{-aT}z}{(z-e^{-aT})^2}\right]$
$\dfrac{1}{s^2(s+a)^2}$	$\dfrac{t}{a^2} - \dfrac{2}{a^3}u(t) + \left(\dfrac{t}{a^2} + \dfrac{2}{a^3}\right)e^{-at}$	$\dfrac{1}{a^3}\left[\dfrac{(aT+2)z - 2z^2}{(z-1)^2} + \dfrac{2z}{z-e^{-aT}} + \dfrac{aTe^{-aT}z}{(z-e^{-aT})^2}\right]$
$\dfrac{1}{(s+a)^2+b^2}$	$\dfrac{1}{b}e^{-at}\sin bt$	$\dfrac{1}{b}\left(\dfrac{ze^{-aT}\sin bT}{z^2 - 2ze^{-aT}\cos bT + e^{-2aT}}\right)$
$\dfrac{s+a}{(s+a)^2+b^2}$	$e^{-at}\cos bt$	$\dfrac{z^2 - ze^{-aT}\cos bT}{z^2 - 2ze^{-aT}\cos bT + e^{-2aT}}$
$\dfrac{1}{s[(s+a)^2+b^2]}$	$\dfrac{1}{a^2+b^2}[1 - e^{-at}\sec\phi\cos(bt+\phi)]$	$\dfrac{1}{a^2+b^2}\left[\dfrac{z}{z-1} - \dfrac{z^2 - ze^{-aT}\sec\phi\cos(bT-\phi)}{z^2 - 2ze^{-aT}\cos bT + e^{-2aT}}\right]$
	$\phi = \tan^{-1}\left(\dfrac{-a}{b}\right)$	

[a] From [8].

B   Inverse Discrete Fourier Transform

We just showed that the spectrum for $x_p(n)$ is a line spectrum with period N. In Section III.B we showed that a sequence, $x_p(n)$ in this case, defines the Fourier series for the periodic spectrum. Since the spectrum is now a line spectrum, we find $x_p(n)$ from a summation over a period rather than an integration over a period as in Eq. (1.11), which is repeated here for convenience:

$$x(n) = \frac{1}{f_s} \int_0^{f_s} X_1(f) e^{j2\pi fn/f_s} \, df \tag{1.68}$$

where the limits have been shifted from $-f_s/2$ and $f_s/2$ to 0 and f_s. This shift has no effect on the value of the integral because we are integrating the product of a periodic function and a complex sinusoid that completes an integer number of cycles per period. Integration of the product gives the same answer if the limits are shifted, provided the limits span the period. Let $a \leftarrow b$ mean that b replaces a. Then the integral yielding $x(n)$ is approximated by an N-point summation as follows:

$$df = \frac{f_s}{N}, \qquad f = k\,df = \frac{kf_s}{N},$$

$$\frac{1}{f_s} \int_0^{f_s} (\cdot)\,df \leftarrow \frac{1}{f_s} \sum_{k=0}^{N-1} (\cdot) \frac{f_s}{N}, \qquad X_1(f) = X_p\left(\frac{kf_s}{N}\right) \overset{d}{=} X_p(k) \tag{1.69}$$

These substitutions yield

$$x_p(n) = \frac{1}{N} \sum_{k=0}^{N-1} X_p(k) (e^{-j2\pi/N})^{-kn} \tag{1.70}$$

Defining

$$W_N = e^{-j2\pi/N} \tag{1.71}$$

and dropping the subscript p in Eq. (1.70) yield the inverse discrete Fourier transform (IDFT):

$$x(n) = \frac{1}{N} \sum_{k=0}^{N-1} X(k) W_N^{-kn}, \qquad n = 0, 1, 2, \ldots, N-1 \tag{1.72}$$

Note that the sampling frequency does not appear in Eq. (1.70), and we can assume a normalized value of $f_s = 1$ Hz in accordance with Fig. 1.6.

The IDFT in Eq. (1.72) determines the data sequence $x(n)$ given the transform sequence $X(k)$, $k = 0, 1, 2, \ldots, N-1$. The DFT obtains the transform sequence $X(k)$ from the data sequence $x(n)$, which is described next.

Suppose we want the coefficient $X(l)$ in the summation in Eq. (1.72). We get it by multiplying $x(n)$ by W_N^{ln} and summing over n:

$$\sum_{n=0}^{N-1} x(n) W_N^{ln} = \sum_{n=0}^{N-1} \left[\frac{1}{N} \sum_{k=0}^{N-1} X(k) W_N^{-kn} \right] W_N^{ln} \qquad (1.73)$$

$$= \frac{1}{N} \sum_{k=0}^{N-1} X(k) \sum_{n=0}^{N-1} W_N^{(l-k)n}$$

where we interchanged the summations over n and k on the right side of the last equals sign. We evaluate the summation over n on the right side of (1.73) with the geometric summation formula Eq. (1.32) and get

$$\frac{1 - W_N^{N(l-k)}}{1 - W_N^{(l-k)}} = \frac{W_N^{N(l-k)/2}}{W_N^{(l-k)/2}} \frac{\sin[\pi(l-k)]}{\sin[\pi(l-k)/N]}$$

$$= \begin{cases} N, & l = k \\ 0, & l \neq k \text{ and } l, k = 0, 1, 2, \dots, N-1 \end{cases} \qquad (1.74)$$

Thus,

$$\sum_{n=0}^{N-1} x(n) W_N^{ln} = \frac{1}{N} \sum_{k=0}^{N-1} X(k) N \delta_{kl} \qquad (1.75)$$

which is the DFT

$$X(k) = \sum_{n=0}^{N-1} x(n) W_N^{kn} \qquad (1.76)$$

We could have started our development with the Fourier series for $x(n)$, using

$$x_p(n) = \sum_{k=0}^{N-1} X_p(k) W_N^{-kn} \qquad (1.77)$$

in which case we get

$$X_p(k) = \frac{1}{N} \sum_{n=0}^{N-1} x_p(n) W_N^{kn} \qquad (1.78)$$

Since this switches the factor $1/N$ from the IDFT to the DFT, we conclude that the role of N in the DFT and IDFT is arbitrary. We will use Eq. (1.76) and (1.72) for the DFT and IDFT, respectively, in this book because these definitions are the most common.

The DFT is usually implemented by a fast Fourier transform (FFT) algorithm, as discussed in Chapter 7. If the mechanization involves fixed-point hardware, then Eq. (1.78) is often more convenient than Eq. (1.76), because the $1/N$ can be used for scaling the outputs of FFT stages to prevent overflow. The $1/N$ also has the advantage of normalizing the peak DFT frequency response to unity (see [2, Chapter 6]).

E DFT Properties

The notation

$$X(k) = \text{DFT}[x(n)] \qquad \text{and} \qquad x(n) = \text{IDFT}[X(k)] \qquad (1.79)$$

means that the DFT and its inverse are defined by the N-point sequences $x(n)$ and $X(k)$, respectively. When both $X(k)$ and $x(n)$ exist, we say that they constitute a *DFT pair*. Let $x(n)$ and $y(n)$ be two sequences with a period of N points. Then Table VI lists some DFT pairs that are labeled by an identifying property. A brief discussion of some of the DFT properties follows. More detailed discussions are in the references at the end of this chapter.

1 Convolution

Circular convolution is defined for periodic sequences, whereas convolution is defined for aperiodic sequences. The circular convolution of two N-point periodic sequences $x(n)$ and $y(n)$ is the N-point sequence $a(m) = x(n) * y(n)$, defined by

$$a(m) = x(m) * y(m) = \sum_{n=0}^{N-1} x(n)y(m-n), \qquad m = 0, 1, 2, \ldots, N-1 \quad (1.80)$$

Since $a(m + N) = a(m)$, the sequence $a(m)$ is periodic with period N. Therefore $A(k) = \text{DFT}[a(m)]$ has period N and is determined by $A(k) = X(k)Y(k)$.

The noncircular (i.e., aperiodic) convolution of two sequences $x(n)$ and $y(n)$ of lengths P and Q, respectively, yields another sequence $a(n)$ of length $N = P + Q - 1$:

$$a(m) = \sum_{n=0}^{N-1} x(n)y(m-n), \qquad m = 0, 1, \ldots, P + Q - 2 \qquad (1.81)$$

Note that the convolution property of the DFT [see Eq. (1.80)] implies circular convolution. Noncircular convolution, as implied in Eq. (1.81), requires that the sequences $x(n)$ and $y(n)$ be extended to length $N \geq P + Q - 1$ by appending

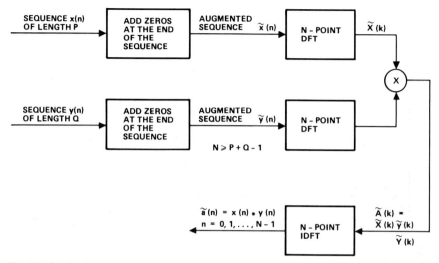

Fig. 1.9. Application of DFT to obtain the noncircular convolution of two sequences $x(n)$ and $y(n)$.

zeros to yield the augmented N-point sequences

$$\{\tilde{x}(n)\} = \{x(0), x(1), \ldots, x(P-1), 0, 0, \ldots, 0\} \tag{1.82}$$

$$\{\tilde{y}(n)\} = \{y(0), y(1), \ldots, y(Q-1), 0, 0, \ldots, 0\} \tag{1.83}$$

Then the circular convolution of $\tilde{x}(n)$ and $\tilde{y}(n)$ yields a periodic sequence $a(n)$ with period N. However, $\tilde{a}(m) = a(m)$ for $m = 0, 1, \ldots, P + Q - 2$. Hence

$$\text{DFT}[\tilde{a}(n)] = \text{DFT}[\tilde{x}(n) * \tilde{y}(n)] = \tilde{X}(k)\tilde{Y}(k) \tag{1.84}$$

where $\tilde{X}(k)$ and $\tilde{Y}(k)$ are the N-point DFTs of $\tilde{x}(n)$ and $\tilde{y}(n)$, respectively, and

$$\tilde{a}(n) = \text{IDFT}[\tilde{X}(k)\tilde{Y}(k)] \tag{1.85}$$

These operations are illustrated in block diagram form in Fig. 1.9. Of course, an FFT is applied to implement the DFT.

Overflow can be a problem when implementing convolution in a digital computer. Therefore, a factor of $1/N$ is often included before the summations in Eqs. (1.80) and (1.81), and this scaling precludes overflow with floating-point as well as properly scaled fixed-point sequences. Convolution is discussed in more detail in Chapter 8, starting on page 666.

Periodicity of the Data Sequence   2

Data sequence periodicity follows from the IDFT:

$$x(n) = \frac{1}{N}\sum_{k=0}^{N-1} X(k)W_N^{-kn} \tag{1.86}$$

TABLE VI
Summary of Discrete Fourier Transform Properties

Property	Data sequence representation	Transform sequence representation
DFT	$x(n)$	$X(k)$
Linearity	$ax(n) + by(n)$	$aX(k) + bY(k)$
Periodicity of data and transform sequences	$x(n + iN)$ $i, m = \ldots, -1, 0, 1, \ldots$	$X(k + mN)$
Horizontal axis sign change	$x(-n)$	$X(-k)$
Complex conjugation	$x^*(n)$	$X^*(-k)$
Both of the above	$x^*(-n)$	$X^*(k)$
Sample shift	$x(n \pm m)$	$W_N^{\mp km} X(k)$
Frequency shift	$W_N^{\pm k_0 n} x(n)$	$X(k \pm k_0)$
Double-sideband modulation	$\cos(2\pi k_0 n/N)x(n)$ $\sin(2\pi k_0 n/N)x(n)$	$\frac{1}{2}[X(k + k_0) + X(k - k_0)]$ $\frac{1}{2j}[X(k + k_0) - X(k - k_0)]$
Data sequence circular convolution (transform sequence product)	$x(n) * y(n)$	$X(k)Y(k)$
Transform sequence circular convolution (data sequence product)	$x(n)y(n)$	$X(k) * Y(k)$
Data sequence convolution (transform product)	$\tilde{x}(n) * \tilde{y}(n)$ (augmented N-point sequences)	$\tilde{X}(k)\tilde{Y}(k)$
Transform sequence convolution (data sequence product)	$\tilde{x}(n)\tilde{y}(n)$	$\tilde{X}(k) * \tilde{Y}(k)$ (augmented N-point sequences)
Data sequence cross-correlation	$\frac{1}{N}\tilde{x}(-n) * \tilde{y}^*(n)$ (augmented N-point sequences)	$\frac{1}{N}\tilde{X}(-k)\tilde{Y}^*(-k)$

Data sequence autocorrelation	$\frac{1}{N}\tilde{x}(-n) * \bar{x}^*(n)$	$\frac{1}{N}|\tilde{X}(-k)|^2$
Conjugate symmetry of the transform of a real-valued sequence	$x(n)$	$X(k) = X^*(N-k)$
Decomposition of a real sequence $x(n)$ into an even part $x_e(n)$ plus an odd part $x_o(n)$	$x(n) = x_e(n) + x_o(n)$ $x_e(n) = \frac{1}{2}[x(n) + x(-n)]$ $x_o(n) = \frac{1}{2}[x(n) - x(-n)]$	$X(k)$ $\mathrm{Re}[X(k)]$ $j\mathrm{Im}[X(k)]$
Decomposition of a complex data sequence $x(n)$ into a conjugate symmetric part $x_e(n)$ and a conjugate antisymmetric part $x_o(n)$	$x(n) = x_e(n) + x_o(n)$ $x_e(n) = \frac{1}{2}[x(n) + x^*(-n)]$ $x_o(n) = \frac{1}{2}[x(n) - x^*(-n)]$	$X(k)$ $\mathrm{Re}[X(k)]$ $j\mathrm{Im}[X(k)]$
Decomposition of a complex transform $X(k)$ into a conjugate symmetric part $X_e(k)$ and a conjugate antisymmetric part $X_o(k)$	$x(n) = \mathrm{Re}[x(n)] + j\mathrm{Im}[x(n)]$ $\mathrm{Re}[x(n)]$ $j\mathrm{Im}[x(n)]$	$X(k) = X_e(k) + X_o(k)$ $X_e(k) = \frac{1}{2}[X(k) + X^*(-k)]$ $X_e(k) = \frac{1}{2}[X(k) - X^*(-k)]$
Symmetry	$X(-n)/N$ $X(n)$	$x(k)$ $Nx(-k)$
IDFT by means of DFT	$\frac{1}{N}X^*(n)$	$x^*(k)$
DFT by means of IDFT	$X^*(n)$	$Nx^*(k)$
DFT of two real N-point sequences $x(n)$ and $y(n)$ by means of one N-point DFT	$a(n) = x(n) + jy(n)$	$A(k) = X_e(k) + j\tilde{X}_o(k) + jY_e(k)$ $\qquad + \tilde{Y}_o(k), \quad k = 0, 1, \ldots, N/2$ $X_e(k) = \frac{1}{2}\mathrm{Re}[A(k) + A(N-k)]$ $\tilde{Y}_o(k) = \frac{1}{2}\mathrm{Re}[A(k) - A(N-k)]$ $\tilde{X}_o(k) = \frac{1}{2}\mathrm{Im}[A(k) - A(N-k)]$ $Y_e(k) = \frac{1}{2}\mathrm{Im}[A(k) + A(N-k)]$
DFT of a $2N$-point real data sequence using an N-point DFT	$a(n) = x(2n) + jx(2n+1),$ $n = 0, 1, \ldots, N-1$	$X(k) = \frac{1}{2}\mathrm{Re}[A(k) + A(N-k)]$ $\qquad + \frac{j}{2}\mathrm{Im}[A(k) - A(N-k)]$ $\qquad - W_{2N}^k\{\frac{j}{2}\mathrm{Re}[A(k) - A(N-k)]$ $\qquad - \frac{1}{2}\mathrm{Im}[A(k) + A(N-k)]\},$ $\qquad k = 0, 1, \ldots, N$

(continued)

TABLE VI (*Continued*)

Property	Data sequence representation	Transform sequence representation
IDFT of a 2N-point complex transform sequence, which resulted from a 2N-point real sequence using an N-point DFT and IDFT by means of a DFT	$Y(n) = \frac{1}{2}\{\mathrm{Re}[X(n)] + \mathrm{Im}[X(n)]\}$ $Y(2N - n) = \frac{1}{2}\{\mathrm{Re}[X(n)] - \mathrm{Im}[X(n)]\}$ $A(n) = Y(2n) + jY(2n + 1)$, etc.	$x(k) = \frac{1}{2N}\{Re[y(k)] + \mathrm{Im}[y(k)]\}$, $x(2N - k) = \frac{1}{2N}\{Re[y(k)] - \mathrm{Im}[y(k)]\}$ $k = 0, 1, \ldots, N$
Complex exponential data sequence (DFT frequency response)	$e^{j2\pi f n/N}$	$e^{-j\pi(k - f)(1 - 1/N)}\,\dfrac{\sin[\pi(k - f)]}{\sin[\pi(k - f)/N]}$
Unity data sequence	$u_N(n) = \begin{cases} 1, & n = 0, 1, \ldots, N - 1 \\ 0 & \text{otherwise} \end{cases}$	$U_N(e^{j\omega})\Big|_{\omega = 2\pi k/N} = e^{-j\pi f(N - 1)}\dfrac{\sin(\pi f N)}{\sin(\pi f)}\Big|_{f = k/N}$ $= \begin{cases} N, & k = 0 \\ 0, & k = 1, 2, \ldots, N - 1 \end{cases}$
DFT output in response to an arbitrary input[a]	$x(n)$	$U_N(e^{j\omega}) * X_a(e^{j\omega})$ evaluated at $\omega = 2\pi k/N$
DFT output with an input weighing[b] that is nonzero only for $0 \leq n < N$	$x(n)w(n)$ $w(n) = 0$ for $n < 0$ and $n \geq N$	$W(e^{j\omega}) * X_a(e^{j\omega})$ evaluated at $\omega = 2\pi k/N$
DFT output with an input weighing that is nonzero for $n < 0$ and $n \geq N$	$x(n)w(n)$ $w(n) \neq 0$ for $n < 0$ and $n \geq N$	$\mathcal{W}(e^{j\omega}) * U_N(e^{j\omega}) * X_a(e^{j\omega})$ evaluated at $\omega = 2\pi k/N$

N-point DFT response to $u_M(n)$	$u_M(n) = \begin{cases} 1, & n = 0, 1, \ldots, M-1 \\ 0, & \text{otherwise} \end{cases}$	$U_M(e^{j2\pi k/N}) = e^{-j\pi k(M-1)/N} \dfrac{\sin(\pi k M/N)}{\sin(\pi k/N)}$
M-points into an N-point DFT (zero extending a data sequence)	$x(n) = \begin{cases} x_1(n), & n = 0, 1, \ldots, M-1 \\ 0, & \text{otherwise} \end{cases}$	$X(k) = U_M(e^{j2\pi f}) \ast X_a(e^{j2\pi f})\big|_{f=k/N}$
MN-point DFT[c] of a data sequence padded with zeros by a factor of M	$x(n) = \begin{cases} x_1(m), & \text{if } n/M = m \\ 0, & \text{otherwise} \end{cases}$	$X_{MN}(k) = X_N(k \bmod N) = \text{DFT}_N[x_1(n)]$
Interpolation of an N-point data sequence to an MN-point sequence[d]	$U_N^*(e^{j2\pi n/MN}) \ast x(n)$ where $x(n)$ is padded with zeros by a factor of M	$X_{MN}(k) = \begin{cases} X_N(k), & k = 0, 1, \ldots, N-1 \\ 0 & k = N, \ldots, MN-1 \end{cases}$
Interpolation of an N-point data sequence to an MN-point sequence using a frequency domain window that is nonzero only for $0 \le k < MN - 1$[d]	$\mathcal{W}^*(e^{j2\pi n/MN}) \ast x(n)$ where $x(n)$ is padded with zeros by a factor of M	$X_{MN}(k) = \omega(k) X_N(k \bmod N)$
L-dimensional DFT	$x(n_1, n_2, \ldots, n_L)$	$X(k_1, k_2, \ldots, k_L)$
Parseval's theorem	$\displaystyle\sum_{n=0}^{N-1} |x(n)|^2 =$	$\dfrac{1}{N} \displaystyle\sum_{k=0}^{N-1} |X(k)|^2$

[a] $X_a(e^{j\omega}) = \text{DTFT}[x(n)]$
[b] $\mathcal{W}(e^{j\omega}) = \text{DTFT}[w(n)]$
[c] $X_M(k) = \text{DFT}_M[x(n)] = \sum_{n=0}^{M-1} x(n) W_M^{kn}$
[d] See Fig. 8.36.

If we replace n by $n + iN$, where i is an integer, we have

$$W_N^{-k(n+iN)} = (e^{-j2\pi/N})^{-k(n+iN)} = W_N^{-kn} \tag{1.87}$$

since $\exp[(j2\pi/N)(iNk)] = 1$. Thus,

$$x(n + iN) = \frac{1}{N} \sum_{k=0}^{N-1} X(k) W_N^{-k(n+iN)} = \frac{1}{N} \sum_{k=0}^{N-1} X(k) W_N^{-kn} = x(n) \tag{1.88}$$

Since $x(n) = x(n + iN)$, $i = \ldots, -1, 0, 1, \ldots$, the data sequence has period N, at least when we use the IDFT to derive the data. Unfortunately, when we take N samples of a time waveform at a sampling interval of T s, it is unusual that the period $P = NT$ of the time waveform is known, and indeed the waveform may not be periodic. The implication of this is discussed next.

3   DFT Output in Response to an Arbitrary Input

The use of the DFT presumes a periodic input whose known period is spanned by the N samples used in the DFT. Such an input has a line spectrum, and if it is properly bandlimited the DFT measures it exactly. In general, either the period is unknown or the signal may be nonperiodic or even a continuum of frequencies. The result is that the DFT transform coefficient $X(k)$ measures a windowed spectrum from 0 to f_s Hz. To determine the characteristics of the windowed spectrum, note that the DFT is evaluating the DTFT at specific frequencies

$$f = \frac{k}{N}, \quad k = 0, 1, \ldots, N-1 \tag{1.89}$$

for an input, $x(n)$, that is truncated for $n < 0$ and $n \geq N$. This can be achieved by multiplying $x(n)$ by $u_N(n)$, where

$$u_N(n) = \begin{cases} 1, & n = 0, 1, 2, \ldots, N-1 \\ 0 & \text{otherwise} \end{cases} \tag{1.90}$$

The sequence $u_N(n)x(n)$ is that required by the DFT and

$$\text{DFT}[u_N(n)x(n)] = \text{DTFT}[u_N(n)x(n)]\Big|_{f=k/N} \tag{1.91}$$

Let frequency domain convolution be defined by (1.24), let $X_a(e^{j\omega}) = \text{DTFT}[x(n)]$, and let $\text{DTFT}[u_N(n)] = U_N(e^{j\omega})$. Then using the entries in Table I for frequency domain convolution (data sequence product) and for the transform of the N sample step sequence, we get

$$X(k) = \text{DFT}[u_N(n)x(n)] = U_N(e^{j\omega}) * X_a(e^{j\omega})\Big|_{\omega = 2\pi k/N}$$

$$= \int_{-1/2}^{1/2} e^{-j\pi(k-fN)(1-1/N)} \frac{\sin[\pi(k-fN)]}{\sin[\pi(k-fN)/N]} X_a(e^{j2\pi f}) \, df \tag{1.92}$$

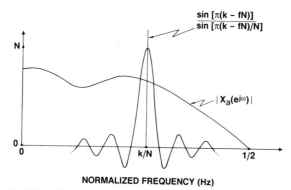

$$\frac{\sin[\pi(k - fN)]}{\sin[\pi(k - fN)/N]}$$

NORMALIZED FREQUENCY (Hz)

Fig. 1.10. The DFT frequency response admits spectral leakage.

The DFT has a $|\sin(\pi fN)/\sin(\pi f)|$ frequency response magnitude that has nulls every $1/N$ Hz. If the input has a spectrum of only N delta functions that are spaced $1/N$ Hz apart starting at $f = 0$ and that have strength $X(k)/N$, then the DFT determines these lines exactly because only the line at $f = k/N$ is not at a null of $\sin[\pi(k - fN)]/\sin[\pi(k - fN)/N]$. Otherwise, Eq. (1.92) shows that the DFT output is an integral of the product of the responses of $U_N(e^{j\omega})$ shifted to $\omega = 2\pi k/N$ and $X_a(e^{j\omega})$. Figure 1.10 shows the magnitude of $X_a(e^{j\omega})$ and $U_N(e^{j2\pi(k - fN)/N})$ (the complex exponential factor is not shown), and illustrates how the sidelobes of $U_N(e^{j\omega})$ pick up energy (called *spectral leakage*) included in $X(k)$ by the integration in Eq. (1.92). Furthermore, Fig. 1.10 shows that the mainlobe of the DFT frequency response includes a band of frequencies in the input, $X_a(e^{j\omega})$. This band, plus the spectral leakage, determines the output coefficient $X(k)$ and leads to the term DFT filter response with a rectangular weighting on the input. Thus the DFT can be regarded as a bank of filters where the magnitude response of adjacent DFT filters is given in Fig. 8.32.

DFT Output in Response to a Weighted Input 4

The $\sin(\pi fN)/\sin(\pi f)$ frequency response of the DFT can be changed by data sequence *weighting* (also called a *data sequence window* [2]). Let the weighting, $w(n)$, be nonzero only for $0 \leq n < N$. Then $w(n)$ truncates the data sequence in the same manner as $u_N(n)$. Let $\text{DTFT}[w(n)] = \mathscr{W}(e^{j\omega})$. Then

$$\text{DFT}[w(n)x(n)] = \text{DTFT}[w(n)x(n)]\Big|_{\omega = 2\pi k/N} = \mathscr{W}(e^{j\omega}) * X_a(e^{j\omega})\Big|_{\omega = 2\pi k/N}$$

$$(1.93)$$

On the other hand, if $w(n)$ is nonzero for $n < 0$ and $n \geq N$, the sequence $x(n)$ must again be truncated by $u_N(n)$ with the result that

$$\text{DFT}[w(n)u_N(n)x(n)] = \mathcal{W}(e^{j\omega}) * U_N(e^{j\omega}) * X_a(e^{j\omega})\Big|_{\omega = 2\pi k/N} \quad (1.94)$$

As in Eq. (1.92), the convolutions in Eqs. (1.93) and (1.94) are defined by Eq. (1.24). Displaying Eqs. (1.93) and (1.94) as convolutions evaluated at $f = 2\pi k/N$ shows that the DFT output is the integral of the product of the data spectrum and a *frequency domain window* determined by $\mathcal{W}(e^{j\omega}) * U_N(e^{j\omega})$ in Eq. (1.94). These windows are selected to achieve desirable modifications to the basic DFT window, $U_N(e^{j\omega})$. The modifications include the following: (1) reduce the peak amplitude of the sidelobes; (2) change the width of the mainlobe of the frequency (filter) response; (3) increase the rate at which successive sidelobes decay; (4) vary the locations of the sidelobe nulls; and (5) simultaneously do (1)–(4). Similar to Fig. 1.10, the frequency domain windows have the appearance of filter responses and are referred to as *DFT filters*. Weighted, overlapping blocks of data plus a frequency bin phase shift accomplish filtering operations such as multiplexing and demultiplexing (see Chapter 8). The Appendix in Chapter 3 includes windows, and its Table AI lists some of their properties.

5   Horizontal Axis Sign Change

Taking the DFT of the sequence $x(-n)$ gives the horizontal axis sign change:

$$\text{DFT}[x(-n)] = \sum_{n=0}^{N-1} x(-n)W_N^{kn} = \sum_{l=0}^{-N+1} x(l)W_N^{-kl} \quad (1.95)$$

where we let $l = -n$. The periodicity of W_N^{-kl} and the sequence $x(l)$ allow us to shift the indices to between 0 and $N - 1$, giving

$$\sum_{l=0}^{N-1} x(l)W_N^{-kl} = X(-k) \quad (1.96)$$

so $\text{DFT}[x(-n)] = X(-k)$.

6   DFT of Two Real N-Point Sequences

Let $x(n)$ and $y(n)$ be two real N-point sequences and let $a(n) = x(n) + jy(n)$. Let $\text{DFT}_N[x(n)] = X_e(k) + jX_o(k)$, where $X_e(k)$ and $X_o(k)$ are the DFTs of the even and odd parts, respectively, of $x(n)$, and DFT_N means an N-point DFT. Similarly, let $\text{DFT}_N[y(n)] = Y_e(k) + jY_o(k)$ and $\text{DFT}_N[a(n)] = A(k)$. Then we can determine $X(k)$ and $Y(k)$ from $A(k)$, using the formulas in Table VI: $X_e(k) = \frac{1}{2}\text{Re}[A(k) + A(N - k)]$, etc. This algorithm is for determining the DFTs of two real N-point sequences by just one N-point DFT; see Fig. 8.30(a). Other algorithms are available to take the DFT of a $2N$-point real sequence by using an N-point DFT and the DFT of a $4N$-point even or odd sequence by using an N-point DFT [15, 16].

The multidimensional DFT is a direct extension of the 1-D DFT and is defined by

$$X(k_L, k_{L-1}, \ldots, k_1) = \sum_{n_L=0}^{N_L-1} \sum_{n_{L-1}=0}^{N_{L-1}-1} \cdots \sum_{n_1=0}^{N_1-1} x(n_L, n_{L-1}, \ldots, n_1) \qquad (1.97)$$
$$\times \; W_{N_L}^{k_L n_L} W_{N_{L-1}}^{k_{L-1} n_{L-1}} \cdots W_{N_1}^{k_1 n_1}$$

where

$$W_{N_i} = e^{-j2\pi/N_i} \qquad (1.98)$$

The multidimensional DFT is the basis for developing several FFT algorithms in Chapter 7.

DISCRETE-TIME RANDOM SEQUENCES VIII

So far we have discussed signals that are periodic in the frequency domain (for the DFT, the data sequence is assumed to be periodic as well). If a signal is deterministic, it has a definite value as a function of sample number and, unless we admit Dirac delta functions, has finite energy over its duration or, in the case of the DFT, over a period. If a signal is a discrete-time random sequence (DTRS), it also has a periodic spectrum, like all data sequences. In contrast to the deterministic signals the value of a DTRS at a given sample number can only be specified by a probability distribution function, and, furthermore, a DTRS may have infinite energy.

A DTRS is also referred to as a stochastic signal, stochastic process, random function, random time series, or random process. At any sample number the data is a random variable. Many of the properties of the DTRS are summarized in terms of its correlation sequence and power spectrum. We shall briefly review random variables and then discuss correlation sequences and power spectra.

Random Variables A

A DTRS is a sequence of random variables, $\underline{x}(n)$, where for a given n, $\underline{x}(n)$ is a random variable described by a probability distribution function, $F_{\underline{x}(n)}(x, n)$; that is, in general it is a function of the data sequence number and is given by

$$F_{\underline{x}(n)}(x, n) = \mathrm{Pr}\{\underline{x}(n) \leq x\} \qquad (1.99)$$

where Pr means the probability that the event in braces occurs, and x is a real number. The random variables can assume either a continuous range of values or a discrete set of values. If the partial derivative of $F_{\underline{x}(n)}(x, n)$ with respect to x exists for all x, then $\underline{x}(n)$ is described by the probability density function

$$f_{\underline{x}(n)}(x, n) = \frac{\partial}{\partial x} F_{\underline{x}(n)}(x, n) \tag{1.100}$$

On the other hand, if $\underline{x}(n)$ assumes only a countable set of values, it is described by the discrete probability density function (also called a *probability mass* function)

$$f_{\underline{x}(n)}(x, n) = \sum_{k=-\infty}^{\infty} p_{\underline{x}(n)}(x_k, n)\delta(x - x_k) \tag{1.101}$$

where $p_{\underline{x}(n)}(x_k, n)$ is the probability mass function, and the Dirac delta function $\delta(x - x_k)$ is described in Eqs. (1.14) and (1.15). For the continuous and discrete-valued random variables the distribution function is given by

$$F_{\underline{x}(n)}(x, n) = \int_{-\infty}^{x} f_{\underline{x}(n)}(\alpha, n)\, d\alpha \tag{1.102a}$$

$$= \sum_{k=-\infty}^{m} p_{\underline{x}(n)}(x_k, n) \qquad \text{(discrete type only)},$$

$$m = \{m : x_m \le x < x_{m+1}\} \tag{1.102b}$$

where Eq. (1.102a) holds for both and Eq. (1.102b) holds only for the discrete type. The following examples illustrate the two types of random variables.

1   Gaussian Distributed

The continuous random variable $\underline{x}$ is Gaussian distributed if the density function is given by

$$f_{\underline{x}}(x) = \frac{1}{\sqrt{2\pi\sigma^2}} \exp\left[-\frac{1}{2}\left(\frac{x - \eta}{\sigma}\right)^2 \right] \tag{1.103}$$

where we have suppressed the data sequence index n, and η and σ^2 are the mean and variance, respectively, of $\underline{x}$. Figure 1.11 shows the normalized density and distribution functions $\sigma f_{\underline{x}}(x/\sigma)$ and $F_{\underline{x}}(x/\sigma)$, respectively.

2   Binomial Distributed

The discrete random variable $\underline{x}$ is binomial distributed if, for example, it describes the probability of getting k heads in N tosses of a coin, $0 \le k \le N$. Let p be the probability of getting a head and $q = 1 - p$ be the probability of getting a tail. Then $\underline{x}$ takes discrete values according to the density

$$f_{\underline{x}}(x) = \sum_{k=0}^{N} \frac{N!}{(N - k)!k!} p^k q^{N-k}\delta(x - k) \tag{1.104}$$

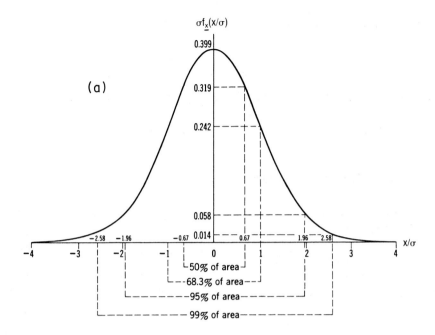

(a)

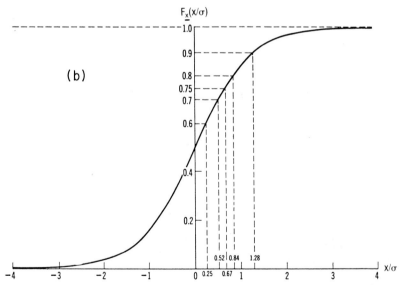

(b)

Fig. 1.11. Gaussian (a) density and (b) distribution functions. [From E. Parzen, *Modern Probability Theory and Its Applications*, Wiley, New York. Copyright © 1960, John Wiley and Sons, Inc. Reprinted with permission.]

where again we have suppressed the index n. For $N = 3$ the probability mass function

$$p_{\underline{x}}(k) = \frac{N!}{(N - k)!k!} p^k q^{N-k}$$

takes values only at $k = 0, 1, 2,$ and 3, yielding $p_{\underline{x}}(0) = \frac{1}{8}$, $p_{\underline{x}}(1) = p_{\underline{x}}(2) = \frac{3}{8}$, and $p_{\underline{x}}(3) = \frac{1}{8}$. The distribution function is stair-step-like, steps up only at $k = 0, 1, 2,$ and 3, yielding $F_{\underline{x}}(0) = \frac{1}{8}$, $F_{\underline{x}}(1) = \frac{1}{2}$, $F_{\underline{x}}(2) = \frac{7}{8}$, and $F_{\underline{x}}(3) = 1$.

B Jointly Distributed Random Sequences

Two discrete-time sequences $\underline{x}(n)$ and $\underline{y}(m)$ are described by a joint probability distribution function $F_{\underline{x}(n),\underline{y}(m)}(x, n, y, m)$:

$$F_{\underline{x}(n),\underline{y}(n)}(x, n, y, m) = \Pr\{\underline{x}(n) \leq x \text{ and } \underline{y}(m) \leq y\} \tag{1.105}$$

When $\underline{x}(n)$ and $\underline{y}(m)$ assume a continuous range of values and $F_{\underline{x}(n),\underline{y}(m)}(x, n, y, m)$ is differentiable with respect to x and y, the joint probability density function of $\underline{x}(n)$ and $\underline{y}(m)$ is

$$f_{\underline{x}(n),\underline{y}(m)}(x, n, y, m) = \frac{\partial^2}{\partial x \, \partial y} F_{\underline{x}(n),\underline{y}(m)}(x, n, y, m) \tag{1.106}$$

Equations (1.105) and (1.106) extend to three, four, or more random variables straightforwardly. Likewise, Eq. (1.101) extends to two, three, or more random variables.

C Stationary Discrete-Time Random Sequences

A DTRS is stationary if its statistical characterization is not affected by a shift in the data sequence origin. For example, the probability distribution function of the stationary sequence $\underline{x}(n)$ satisfies

$$F_{\underline{x}(n)}(x, n) = F_{\underline{x}(n+k)}(x, n + k) = F_{\underline{x}}(x) \tag{1.107}$$

for all integers k and n. In addition, the joint distribution function satisfies

$$F_{\underline{x}(n),\underline{y}(m)}(x, n, y, m) = F_{\underline{x}(n+k),\underline{y}(m+k)}(x, n + k, y, m + k) \tag{1.108}$$

for all integers k, m, and n.

D Expectations

Let $g(\underline{x})$ be a function of the random variable $\underline{x}$. (We are suppressing the index n in $\underline{x}(n)$ for notational convenience.) Then we define the *expected value* of $g(\underline{x})$,

$E[g(\underline{x})]$, as

$$E[g(\underline{x})] = \int_{-\infty}^{\infty} g(x) f_x(x)\, dx \qquad (1.109)$$

$E[g(\underline{x})]$ is also called the *average value* or the *mean value* of $g(\underline{x})$. For example, let $g(\underline{x}) = \underline{x}$. Then the mean value, η_x, of the random variable x is

$$\eta_x = E[\underline{x}] = \int_{-\infty}^{\infty} x f_x(x)\, dx \qquad (1.110)$$

If $\underline{x}$ is Gaussian distributed, we obtain $\eta_x = \eta$ by using Eq. (1.103). The mean-squared value of $\underline{x}$ is $E[\underline{x}^2]$, while the variance of $\underline{x}$, σ_x^2, is defined by

$$\sigma_x^2 = E[(\underline{x} - \eta_x)^2] \qquad (1.111)$$

Statistically Independent and Uncorrelated Random Variables E

The random variables $\underline{x}$ and $\underline{y}$ are statistically independent (or simply independent) if their joint probability density and distribution functions factor into the product of two functions:

$$f_{\underline{x},\underline{y}}(x, y) = f_{\underline{x}}(x) f_{\underline{y}}(y) \qquad (1.112)$$

They are uncorrelated if

$$E[\underline{x}\underline{y}] = E[\underline{x}]E[\underline{y}] \qquad (1.113)$$

It follows from Eq. (1.112) that independent random variables are uncorrelated; the converse is not necessarily true.

CORRELATION AND COVARIANCE SEQUENCES IX

Much useful information about DTRSs is available from their correlation and covariance sequences. In this book we shall discuss wide-sense stationary (WSS) sequences. These sequences have a mean value that is independent of the data sequence index, and a correlation and covariance that are functions only of the difference in the time indices of two random variables. To state this mathematically, let $\underline{x}(n)$ be a wide-sense stationary DTRS. Then

$$E[\underline{x}(n)] = \eta_x \qquad \text{for all } n \qquad (1.114)$$

where η_x is a constant. The *autocorrelation sequence* for $\underline{x}(n)$, $r_{xx}(m)$, is defined for all integers m and n by

$$r_{xx}(m) = E[\underline{x}(n)\underline{x}^*(n - m)] = E[\underline{x}(n + m)\underline{x}^*(n)] \qquad (1.115)$$

and is a function only of the difference in the indices. Conversely, sequences satisfying Eqs. (1.114) and (1.115) for all n are WSS.

Similarly, if $\underline{x}(n)$ and $\underline{y}(n)$ are two WSS DTRSs, their *cross-correlation sequence* is defined for all integers m and n by

$$r_{xy}(m) = E[\underline{x}(n)\underline{y}^*(n-m)] = E[\underline{x}(n+m)\underline{y}^*(n)] \tag{1.116}$$

Covariance sequences differ from correlation sequences only in that the mean value of a DTRS is removed before taking an expected value. Thus, the *autocovariance* and *cross-covariance sequences* of WSS DTRSs are defined, respectively, by

$$c_{xx}(m) = E\{[\underline{x}(n) - \eta_x][\underline{x}(n-m) - \eta_x]^*\} = r_{xx}(m) - |\eta_x|^2 \tag{1.117}$$

$$c_{xy}(m) = E\{[\underline{x}(n) - \eta_x][\underline{y}(n-m) - \eta_y]^*\} = r_{xy}(m) - \eta_x\eta_y^* \tag{1.118}$$

The variance of $\underline{x}(n)$ in Eq. (1.111) is also given by

$$\sigma_x^2 = c_{xx}(0) \tag{1.119}$$

A   Time Averages and Ergodicity

Time averages are often used to infer statistical properties for DTRSs. Let $\underline{x}(n)$ be a WSS DTRS. Then the $(2N + 1)$-point time average for the $\underline{x}(n)$ defined by

$$\langle \underline{x}(n) \rangle_N = \frac{1}{2N + 1} \sum_{n=-N}^{N} \underline{x}(n) \tag{1.120}$$

provides an estimate of the mean. If this estimate converges as N approaches infinity, we define

$$\langle \underline{x}(n) \rangle = \lim_{N \to \infty} \langle \underline{x}(n) \rangle_N \tag{1.121}$$

as the average of the entire sequence. By comparison, $E[\underline{x}(n)]$ is an ensemble average; that is, it is the mean of all possible values of $\underline{x}(n)$ at a specific value of n.

Similar to Eq. (1.120), an estimate of the autocorrelation sequence is

$$\langle \underline{x}(n)\underline{x}^*(n-m) \rangle_N = \frac{1}{2N + 1} \sum_{n=-N}^{N} \underline{x}(n)\underline{x}^*(n-m) \tag{1.122}$$

While similar to Eq. (1.121), if the estimate in Eq. (1.122) converges, we have

$$\langle \underline{x}(n)\underline{x}^*(n-m) \rangle = \lim_{N \to \infty} \langle \underline{x}(n)\underline{x}^*(n-m) \rangle_N \tag{1.123}$$

If $x(n)$ is not only WSS but also satisfies the *ergodic* theorems for the mean and autocorrelation [17, 18], then

$$\langle \underline{x}(n) \rangle = E[\underline{x}(n)] \tag{1.124}$$

$$\langle \underline{x}(n)\underline{x}^*(n-m) \rangle = r_{xx}(m) \tag{1.125}$$

Equation (1.124) says that an average of $\underline{x}(n)$ over all possible values of the index n is equal to the expected value (average) of $\underline{x}(n)$ for a specific integer n. Thus, engineers are apt to say that, if a sequence is ergodic, time averages are equivalent to ensemble averages, where the ensemble is all possible values of the random variable $\underline{x}(n)$, with n fixed. A similar interpretation applies to Eq. (1.125). Likewise, if $\underline{x}(n)$ is WSS and satisfies the ergodic theorems for the mean and autocorrelation, then

$$c_{xx}(m) = \langle [\underline{x}(n) - \eta_x][\underline{x}(n - m) - \eta_x]^* \rangle \qquad (1.126)$$

If $\underline{x}(n)$ and $\underline{y}(n)$ are both ergodic sequences, then

$$r_{xy}(m) = \langle \underline{x}(n)\underline{y}^*(n - m) \rangle \qquad (1.127)$$

$$c_{xy}(m) = \langle [\underline{x}(n) - \eta_x][\underline{y}(n - m) - \eta_y]^* \rangle \qquad (1.128)$$

Ergodic sequences are important in engineering applications of digital signal processing because we can determine their mean values and correlations by using many samples from one sequence rather than specific samples from many sequences.

Correlation and Covariance Properties   B

Table VII gives some properties of the correlation and covariance sequences for WSS sequences $\underline{x}(n)$ and $\underline{v}(n)$. The properties result mainly from applying definitions already stated. Some examples and clarification follow.

Conjugate Symmetry   1

Conjugate symmetry results from taking the complex conjugate of a correlation or covariance sequence. For example, since $\underline{x}(n)\underline{x}^*(n - m) = \underline{x}^*(n - m)\underline{x}(n)$, we have

$$r_{xx}(m) = E[\underline{x}^*(n - m)\underline{x}(n)] = E[\underline{x}^*(n)\underline{x}(n + m)] \qquad (1.129)$$

where the indices can be shifted because the sequences are stationary. Taking the complex conjugate in Eq. (1.129) outside the expection yields

$$r_{xx}(m) = \{E[\underline{x}(n)\underline{x}^*(n + m)]\}^* = r_{xx}^*(-m) \qquad (1.130)$$

as stated in Table VII.

Autocorrelation is Maximum at the Origin   2

Let $\underline{x}(n)$ and $\underline{y}(n)$ be two real sequences. Then solving

$$E\{[\underline{x}(n + m) + \alpha\underline{y}(n)]^2\} \qquad (1.131)$$

TABLE VII

Properties of the Correlation and Covariance Sequences for Wide-Sense Stationary Sequences

Property	Sequence	Equivalent representation
Autocorrelation	$r_{xx}(m)$	$E[x(n)x^*(n-m)]$
Autocovariance	$c_{xx}(m)$	$E\{[x(n)-\eta_x][x(n-m)-\eta_x]^*\}$
Cross-correlation	$r_{xy}(m)$	$E[x(n)y^*(n-m)]$
Cross-covariance	$c_{xy}(m)$	$E\{[x(n)-\eta_x][y(n-m)-\eta_y]^*\}$
Conjugate symmetry	$r_{xx}(m)$ $c_{xx}(m)$ $r_{xy}(m)$ $c_{xy}(m)$	$r_{xx}^*(-m)$ $c_{xx}^*(-m)$ $r_{yx}^*(-m)$ $c_{yx}^*(-m)$
Relation of autocovariance and autocorrelation	$c_{xx}(m)$ $c_{xy}(m)$	$r_{xx}(m)-|\eta_x|^2$ $r_{xy}(m)-\eta_x\eta_y^*$
Uncorrelated sequences	$r_{xy}(m)$	$\eta_x\eta_y^*$
Orthogonal sequences	$r_{xy}(m)$	0
Sum of orthogonal sequences $x(n)$ and $y(n)$ $w(n)=x(n)+y(n)$	$r_{ww}(m)$	$r_{xx}(m)+r_{yy}(m)$
Product of independent sequences $w(n)=x(n)y(n)$	$r_{ww}(m)$	$r_{xx}(m)r_{yy}(m)$
Ergodicity	$r_{xx}(m)$	$\lim_{N\to\infty}\left[\dfrac{1}{2N+1}x(m)*_N x^*(-m)\right]$
	$c_{xx}(m)$	$\lim_{N\to\infty}\left\{\dfrac{1}{2N+1}[x(m)-\eta_x]*_N[x(-m)-\eta_x]^*\right\}$
	$r_{xy}(m)$	$\lim_{N\to\infty}\left[\dfrac{1}{2N+1}x(m)*_N y^*(-m)\right]$
	$c_{xy}(m)$	$\lim_{N\to\infty}\left\{\dfrac{1}{2N+1}[x(m)-\eta_x]*_N[y(-m)-\eta_y]^*\right\}$
Output of a linear, stable, shift-invariant system with impulse response $h(n)$, $y(n)=h(n)*x(n)$	$r_{xy}(m)$ $r_{yx}(m)$ $r_{yy}(m)$	$r_{xx}(m)*h^*(-m)$ $r_{xx}(m)*h(m)$ $r_{xx}(m)*h(m)*h^*(-m)$

The following properties apply only to sequences that become uncorrelated for large index shifts of one sequence

Decorrelation of sequences for large shifts of one sequence	$\lim\limits_{m\to\infty} r_{xx}(m)$	$\eta_x\eta_x^*$
	$\lim\limits_{m\to\infty} c_{xx}(m)$	0
	$\lim\limits_{m\to\infty} r_{xy}(m)$	$\eta_x\eta_y^*$
	$\lim\limits_{m\to\infty} c_{xy}(m)$	0

TABLE VII (*Continued*)

Property	Sequence	Equivalent representation
The following properties apply only to real sequences		
Autocorrelation is real	$r_{xx}(m)$	$r_{xx}^*(n)$
Autocorrelation is even	$r_{xx}(m)$	$r_{xx}(-m)$
Autocorrelation is maximum at the origin	$r_{xx}(0)$ $r_{xx}(0) + r_{yy}(0)$ $r_{xx}(0)r_{yy}(0)$	$\geq \|r_{xx}(m)\|$ $\geq 2\|r_{xy}(m)\|$ $\geq r_{xy}^2(m)$
Equivalence of autocovariance and variance at the origin	$c_{xx}(0)$	σ_x^2
Autocorrelation at the origin	$r_{xx}(0)$	$\sigma_x^2 + \eta_x^2$

for α and concluding that the discriminate is nonpositive give $r_{xy}^2(m) \leq r_{xx}(0)r_{yy}(0)$. Noting that Eq. (1.131) is greater than or equal to zero for $\alpha = -1$ yields $2r_{xy}(m) \leq r_{xx}(0) + r_{yy}(0)$. In like manner we get the useful identity $|r_{xx}(m)| \leq r_{xx}(0)$.

Ergodicity 3

Define the $(2N + 1)$-point convolution of $\underline{x}(m)$ and $\underline{y}(m)$ as

$$\underline{x}(n) *_N \underline{y}(m) = \sum_{i=-N}^{N} \underline{x}(i)\underline{y}(m - i) \tag{1.132}$$

Comparing Eqs. (1.132) and (1.122) shows that the cross-correlation for ergodic sequences $\underline{x}(n)$ and $\underline{y}(n)$ can be expressed in terms of the convolution

$$r_{xy}(n) = \lim_{N \to \infty} \left[\frac{1}{2N + 1} \underline{x}(m) *_N \underline{y}^*(-m) \right] \tag{1.133}$$

with similar expressions holding for $r_{xx}(m)$, $c_{xx}(m)$, and $c_{xy}(m)$, as shown in Table VII.

Output of a Linear System 4

Let $h(n)$ be the impulse response of a linear, stable, shift-invariant discrete-time system. In general, $h(n)$ can be complex. Let the system have input $\underline{x}(n)$ and output $\underline{y}(n)$, as illustrated in Fig. 1.12, where the output is determined by

$$\underline{y}(n) = \underline{x}(n) * h(n) \tag{1.134}$$

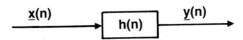

Fig. 1.12. Linear system relationships.

The cross-correlation sequence $r_{yx}(m)$ relating a WSS input and system output is

$$r_{yx}(m) = E[\underline{y}(n)\underline{x}^*(n-m)] = E\left[\sum_{i=-\infty}^{\infty} \underline{x}(n-i)h(i)\underline{x}^*(n-m)\right]$$

$$= \sum_{i=-\infty}^{\infty} r_{xx}(m-i)h(i) = r_{xx}(m) * h(m) \qquad (1.135)$$

as stated in Table VII. Similar computations yield the entries shown in the table for $r_{xy}(m)$ and $r_{yy}(m)$.

X POWER SPECTRAL DENSITY

The DTFT of the covariance sequence yields a function of frequency variously called the power spectral density (PSD), power density spectrum, power spectrum, or spectrum. Let $S_{xx}(\omega)$ denote the PSD for the sequence $\underline{x}(n)$. Then

$$S_{xx}(\omega) = \text{DTFT}[c_{xx}(n)] = \mathscr{Z}[c_{xx}(n)]\Big|_{z=e^{j\omega}} \qquad (1.136)$$

The cross-power spectral densities, $S_{xy}(\omega)$ and $S_{yx}(\omega)$, are similarly defined:

$$S_{xy}(\omega) = \text{DTFT}[c_{xy}(n)] = \mathscr{Z}[c_{xy}(n)]\Big|_{z=e^{j\omega}} \qquad (1.137)$$

$$S_{yx}(\omega) = \text{DTFT}[c_{yx}(n)] = \mathscr{Z}[c_{yx}(n)]\Big|_{z=e^{j\omega}} \qquad (1.138)$$

A Convergence Conditions

The sequences $c_{xx}(n)$, $c_{xy}(n)$, and $c_{yx}(n)$ are defined for $n = 0, \pm 1, \pm 2, \ldots$, so the z-transforms in Eq. (1.136)–(1.138) are two-sided and the usual convergence conditions apply. From Table VII we get

$$r_{xx}(n) = c_{xx}(n) + |\eta_x|^2 \qquad (1.139)$$

$$\mathscr{Z}[r_{xx}(n)] = \mathscr{Z}[c_{xx}(n)] + \mathscr{Z}[|\eta_x|^2] \qquad (1.140)$$

Comparing Eqs. (1.140) and (1.34), we see that the region of convergence for $\mathscr{Z}[|\eta_x|^2]$ is $1 < |z| < 1$, which cannot be satisfied, so we require that $\eta_x = 0$. Thus, if we do not admit delta functions, the PSD of the autocorrelation sequence $r_{xx}(n)$ exists only if the DTRS $\underline{x}(n)$ has a mean value of zero. Likewise, the PSD of $r_{xy}(n)$ exists only if $\eta_x = 0$ and/or $\eta_y = 0$. We conclude that the PSD of an autocorrelation (or cross-correlation) function exists only if the mean value(s) of the DTRS(s) is (are) zero, in which case the PSD of the correlation is the same as the PSD of the covariance. Nevertheless, the PSD provides a very general approach to the study of DTRS(s), since if a DTRS has a nonzero mean value the mean can be subtracted, yielding a DTRS that has a zero mean and therefore has a PSD if its z-transform converges on the unit circle in the complex plane.

Table of Properties B

Table VIII states some properties of the PSD of a WSS sequence. Most of the properties follow directly from PSD definitions. An example and some discussion follow.

PSD Relating System Input and Output 1

Table VIII shows that the cross-covariance relating the output of a linear, stable, shift-invariant system is $r_{yy}(m) = r_{xx}(m) * h(m) * h^*(-m)$. Using the data sequence convolution, horizontal axis sign change, and complex conjugation properties in Table I, we get a relation between the PSD of the system output and its input:

$$S_{yy}(\omega) = \text{DTFT}[r_{yy}(n)] = S_{xx}(\omega)|H(\omega)|^2 \qquad (1.141)$$

PSD for Ergodic Sequences 2

Table VIII gives representations for these sequences in terms of the average of a convolution. We apply the DTFT to the right entry in the table and define the PSD in terms of averages of $X(e^{j\omega})$ and $Y(e^{j\omega})$. When we do this, we must consider convergence conditions that are a lengthy digression. We refer the reader to several references [3, 18].

SUMMARY XI

In this chapter we presented a brief summary of transforms and transform properties. We started our development by recalling the Fourier series representation of a periodic function. We showed that sampled data from cosine

TABLE VIII

Power Spectral Density Properties for Wide-Sense-Stationary Sequences

Property	Power spectral density	Equivalent representation
Power spectral density (PSD)	$S_{xx}(\omega)$	$\text{DTFT}[c_{xx}(n)]$
PSD of a zero mean sequence	$S_{xx}(\omega)$	$\text{DTFT}[r_{xx}(n)]$
Cross PSD	$S_{xy}(\omega)$	$\text{DTFT}[c_{xy}(n)]$
Cross PSD of zero mean sequences	$S_{xy}(\omega)$	$\text{DTFT}[r_{xy}(n)]$
The covariance function is analytically defined (see, e.g., below)	$S_{xx}(\omega)$ or $S_{xy}(\omega)$	See Table I or Table V with $z = e^{j\omega}$
$r_{xx}(n) = s_N(n)$ (see Table I)	$\dfrac{\sin[\omega(N + 1/2)]}{\sin(\omega/2)}$	$\text{DTFT}[s_N(n)]; \; s_N(n) = \begin{cases} 1, & \|n\| \le N \\ 0, & \|n\| > N \end{cases}$
The PSD of a sequence is real	$S_{xx}(\omega)$	$S_{xx}^*(\omega)$
Conjugate symmetry of cross PSD of WSS sequences	$S_{xy}(\omega)$	$S_{yx}^*(\omega)$
Orthogonal sequences, $x(n)$ and $y(n)$	$S_{xy}(\omega)$	0
PSD for $w(n) = x(n) + y(n)$ where $x(n)$ and $y(n)$ are orthogonal sequences	$S_{ww}(\omega)$	$S_{xx}(\omega) + S_{yy}(\omega)$
The PSD of a real sequence, $x(n)$, is real, even, and nonnegative	$S_{xx}(\omega)$ $S_{xx}(\omega)$ $S_{xx}(\omega)$	$S_{xx}^*(\omega)$ $S_{xx}(-\omega)$ ≥ 0
Output of a linear, a stable, shift-invariant system: $y(n) = x(n) * h(n)$	$S_{yx}(\omega)$ $S_{xy}(\omega)$ $S_{yy}(\omega)$	$S_{xx}(\omega)H(\omega)$ $S_{xx}(\omega)H^*(\omega)$ $S_{xx}(\omega)\|H(\omega)\|^2$
Ergodic sequence cross-correlation[a]	$S_{xy}(\omega)$	$\lim\limits_{N \to \infty} \left[\dfrac{1}{2N + 1} X_N(e^{j\omega}) Y_N^*(e^{j\omega}) \right]$
Erodic sequence autocorrelation[a]	$S_{xx}(\omega)$	$\lim\limits_{N \to \infty} \dfrac{1}{2N + 1} \|X_N(e^{j\omega})\|^2$

[a] $X_N(e^{j\omega}) = \sum\limits_{n=-N}^{N} x(n)e^{-j\omega n}$

waveforms separated in frequency by the sampling frequency, f_s, went through exactly the same points, so the spectrum of sampled data is periodic and can be represented by a Fourier series called the discrete-time Fourier transform. We generalized the DTFT to derive the z-transform, and we then stated the Laplace transform. The discrete Fourier transform was derived from a Fourier series representation of an N-point sequence that was assumed to repeat with period N.

To introduce correlation and covariance sequences, we reviewed discrete-time random sequences. We concluded the chapter by stating some properties of the power spectral density of the covariance sequence.

REFERENCES

1. R. W. Hamming, *Digital Filters*, Prentice-Hall, Englewood Cliffs, N.J., 1977.
2. D. F. Elliott and K. R. Rao, *Fast Transforms—Algorithms, Analyses and Applications*, Academic Press, New York, 1982.
3. A. V. Oppenheim and R. W. Schafer, *Digital Signal Processing*, Prentice-Hall, Englewood Cliffs, N.J., 1975.
4. N. Ahmed and T. Natarajan, *Discrete-Time Signals and Systems*, Reston, Reston, Va., 1983.
5. A. Antoniou, *Digital Filters: Analysis and Design*, McGraw-Hill, New York, 1979.
6. C. Chen, *One-Dimensional Digital Signal Processing*. Dekker, New York, 1979.
7. B. Gold and C. M. Rader, *Digital Processing of Signals*, McGraw-Hill, New York, 1969.
8. B. C. Kuo, *Analysis and Synthesis of Sampled-Data Control Systems*, Prentice-Hall, Englewood Cliffs, N.J., 1963.
9. L. R. Rabiner and B. Gold, *Theory and Application of Digital Signal Processing*, Prentice-Hall, Englewood Cliffs, N.J., 1975.
10. S. D. Stearns, *Digital Signal Analysis*, Hayden Book, Rochelle Park, N.J., 1975.
11. J. T. Tou, *Digital and Sampled-Data Control Systems*, McGraw-Hill, New York, 1959.
12. S. A. Tretter, *Introduction to Discrete-Time Signal Processing*, Wiley, New York, 1976.
13. J. Cadzow, *Signal Processing and Time Series Analysis*, MacMillan, New York, 1986.
14. J. A. Aseltine, *Transform Method in Linear System Analysis*, McGraw-Hill, New York, 1958.
15. J. W. Cooley, P. A. Lewis, and P. D. Welch, The fast Fourier transform algorithm. Programming considerations in the calculation of sine, cosine and Laplace transforms, *J. Sound Vib.* **12,** 315–337 (1970).
16. L. R. Rabiner, On the use of symmetry in FFT computation, *IEEE Trans. Acoust. Speech Signal Process.* **ASSP-27,** 233–239 (1979).
17. A. Papoulis, *Probability, Random Variables, and Stochastic Processes*, McGraw-Hill, New York, 1965.
18. M. Schwartz and L. Shaw, *Signal Processing—Discrete Spectral Analysis, Detection, and Estimation*, McGraw-Hill, New York, 1975.
19. J. Cadzow and H. Van Landingham, *Signals, Systems, and Transforms*, Prentice-Hall, Englewood Cliffs, N.J., 1985.

Chapter **2**

Design and Implementation
of Digital FIR Filters

P. P. VAIDYANATHAN
Department of Electrical Engineering
California Institute of Technology
Pasadena, California 91125

INTRODUCTION **I**

Digital filters [1, 2] can be classified into two main types: finite impulse response (FIR) filters, and infinite impulse response (IIR) filters. Finite impulse response digital filters possess several desirable properties that make them attractive for a wide range of applications. An exactly linear phase-response can be achieved with FIR filters, with the result that they can be used in the faithful reconstruction of signals without phase distortion. In addition, FIR filters are inherently stable, and hence the question of stability does not arise either in the design or in the implementation of these filters (unless they are implemented with recursive building blocks [1]). This is very attractive in such applications as echo cancelers, where an adaptive transversal filter is used, whose coefficients are time varying. Moreover, even though FIR filter typically requires a large order, it can usually be realized by implementing the convolution sum efficiently with fast Fourier transform (FFT) algorithms [3]. Furthermore, recent publications show that under most practical situations FIR filters of high orders can be implemented efficiently by indirect design approaches. Another major advantage of FIR filters is that near-optimal multidimensional FIR filters (in image processing applications, for example) can be designed easily starting from one-dimensional (1-D) prototypes and using spectral transformations. The resulting multidimensional filters are guaranteed to be stable and can be implemented without impairing this stability in spite of coefficient quantization. Finally, FIR filters naturally lend themselves to efficient implementation of multirate signal processing algorithms and can be used to achieve extremely efficient sampling

55

HANDBOOK OF DIGITAL SIGNAL PROCESSING

rate conversions, as discussed in Chapter 3. The only possible disadvantage of linear-phase FIR filters in certain applications is that the overall group delay is equal to $(N - 1)/2$. This quantity is large for high filter orders, and in communications applications where echos of transmitted signals cannot be tolerated, this tends to be objectionable (unless echo cancelers are employed). Moreover, in digital feedback control applications, a large delay in the feedback loop is generally not acceptable.

In the past 20 years many techniques have been advanced for the design and implementation of FIR filters. This chapter outlines the most important techniques so that you can choose the appropriate design methodology for the applications involved.

Section II reviews FIR filter preliminaries. Section III discusses the windowing technique for FIR design, with particular emphasis on Kaiser's window. This method is one of the earliest but is surprisingly efficient for numerous applications. Section IV discusses optimal FIR designs with equiripple weighted error, emphasizing Remez exchange techniques developed for FIR filters by McClellan and Parks. This class of filters is the most well known and widely used, primarily because its flexibility enables the designer to realize a very wide range of requirements. Section V deals with maximally flat FIR filters. An attractive feature of this type of filter is that for low orders it can be implemented without multipliers, and high-order multiplierless filters can be designed by combining such low-order building blocks. Section VI discusses linear programming techniques for FIR designs, originally introduced by Rabiner *et al.* Even though these designs have their own limitations (such as numerical difficulties, large convergence time etc.), they are useful in certain applications where Remez exchange techniques are not suitable. Examples include designs that require a certain degree of flatness (or tangency) in the passband. Section VII deals with frequency transformations in FIR filters, and Section VIII extends these concepts so that a 1-D linear-phase FIR filter can be converted into a 2-D FIR filter. Section IX describes recent unconventional design approaches that meet all conventional design requirements but are more efficient from an implementation point of view. The techniques of Sections IX are based primarily on suitable modifications of those in Sections IV and V. Section X discusses designs of useful types of FIR filters, such as minimum-phase, half-band, and power-complementary filters.

II FIR DIGITAL FILTER PRELIMINARIES

A causal FIR filter [2] of length N has transfer function

$$H(z) = h(0) + h(1)z^{-1} + \cdots + h(N - 1)z^{-(N - 1)} \tag{2.1}$$

where $N - 1$ is the filter order and $h(n)$ are the impulse response coefficients. In this chapter we assume that these coefficients are real numbers. Such a filter has a linear phase-response if the impulse response is either symmetric [i.e., $h(n) = h(N-1-n)$] or antisymmetric [i.e., $h(n) = -h(N-1-n)$]. Depending upon whether the filter order is even or odd and whether $h(n)$ is symmetric or antisymmetric, four classes of linear-phase FIR filters can be distinguished. We discuss these classes in greater detail in Section IV. For now we consider a filter with a symmetric impulse response. The corresponding frequency response, which is the discrete-time Fourier transform (DTFT) of the sequence $h(n)$, can be written as (see Chapter 1)

$$H(e^{j\omega}) = e^{-j\omega(N-1)/2} H_0(e^{j\omega}) \tag{2.2}$$

$$H_0(e^{j\omega}) = \begin{cases} \displaystyle\sum_{n=0}^{(N-1)/2} b_n \cos(\omega n) & \text{if } (N-1) \text{ is even} \\[2mm] \displaystyle\sum_{n=1}^{N/2} b_n \cos\omega\left(n-\frac{1}{2}\right) & \text{if } (N-1) \text{ is odd} \end{cases} \tag{2.3}$$

where $H_0(e^{j\omega})$ is a real function of ω. The coefficients b_n [see Table IV] for $N-1$ even are given by

$$b_n = \begin{cases} h\left(\dfrac{N-1}{2}\right), & n = 0 \\[3mm] 2h\left(\dfrac{N-1}{2} - n\right), & n \neq 0 \end{cases} \tag{2.4}$$

Thus the phase response of the filter is

$$\phi(\omega) = -\left(\frac{N-1}{2}\right)\omega \tag{2.5}$$

which shows that it is a linear-phase filter with a group delay equal to $(N-1)/2$. For $N-1$ even, this delay is an integral number of samples, whereas for $N-1$ odd, the delay is nonintegral. If the order $N-1$ is even, then a zero-phase filter with the same magnitude response as that of $H(z)$ can be obtained by constructing the noncausal transfer function

$$H_0(z) = z^{(N-1)/2} H(z) \tag{2.6}$$

where $H_0(z)$ has the frequency response in Eq. (2.3).

Filter Characteristics   A

A FIR transfer function of the form in Eq. (2.1) can be implemented with N multipliers and $N-1$ adders, as shown in Fig. 2.1(a). This structure is called the *direct form*. For linear-phase filters, the symmetry of the coefficients $h(n)$ permits a more efficient implementation. Figure 2.1(b) demonstrates this for a sixth-order

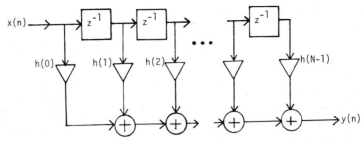

Fig. 2.1(a). The direct-form implementation of a FIR filter of order $N - 1$.

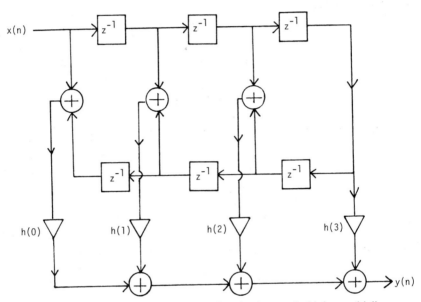

Fig. 2.1(b). Sixth-order linear-phase FIR filter implemented with four multipliers.

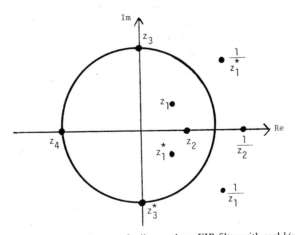

Fig. 2.1(c). Symmetry of zeros of a linear-phase FIR filter with real $h(n)$.

filter (i.e., $N - 1 = 6$). In general, a linear-phase FIR filter of order $N - 1$ can be implemented with $(N - 1)/2 + 1$ multipliers if $N - 1$ is even, and with $N/2$ multipliers if $N - 1$ is odd.

Note that the frequency response $H(e^{j\omega})$ is always periodic in ω with period 2π. If $N - 1$ is even, then $e^{-j\omega(N-1)/2} = e^{-j(\omega + 2\pi)(N-1)/2}$; if $N - 1$ is odd, then $e^{-j\omega(N-1)/2} = -e^{-j(\omega + 2\pi)(N-1)/2}$. Accordingly, $H_0(e^{j\omega})$ has a period of 2π for $N - 1$ even and 4π for $N - 1$ odd. If the impulse response coefficients $h(n)$ are real, then $H(e^{j\omega})$ is such that $|H(e^{j\omega})|$ is symmetric and $\arg(H(e^{j\omega}))$ is antisymmetric:

$$|H(e^{j\omega})| = |H(e^{-j\omega})|, \qquad \arg(H(e^{j\omega})) = -\arg(H(e^{-j\omega}))$$

Accordingly, it is sufficient to plot $|H(e^{j\omega})|$ and $\arg H(e^{j\omega})$ in the range $0 \le \omega \le \pi$.

If z_0 is a zero of $H(z)$ for any linear-phase FIR filter, then $1/z_0$ is also a zero [1]. Thus, zeros are restricted to be either on the unit circle or in reciprocal pairs with respect to the unit circle in the z-plane. Figure 2.1(c) shows the possible types of zeros for such linear-phase filters.

It is sometimes of interest to design FIR filters that have a *minimum-phase* (rather than a linear-phase) response. For such filters none of the zeros are outside the unit circle, and the phase lag at any frequency is the smallest possible among all FIR filters having the same magnitude response. These filters are discussed in Section X.

Design Specifications B

The simplest type of design specification is the lowpass frequency response. Other types will be taken up in later sections. Figure 2.2 shows an ideal lowpass response, and Fig. 2.3 shows a typical tolerance requirement. Here δ_1 and δ_2 represent the peak permissible errors in the passband and stopband, respectively. The transition bandwidth Δf is

$$\Delta f = \frac{\omega_r - \omega_p}{2\pi} \tag{2.7a}$$

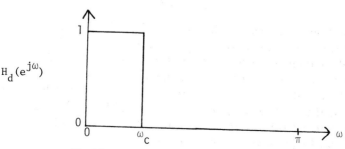

Fig. 2.2. An ideal lowpass filter specification.

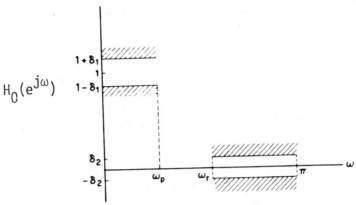

Fig. 2.3. Tolerance scheme for a practical lowpass filter specification.

where ω_p and ω_r are the passband and stopband (rejection band) edges, respectively. The *cutoff* frequency ω_c of a lowpass filter is defined to be the arithmetic mean of the bandedges:

$$\omega_c = \frac{\omega_p + \omega_r}{2} \tag{2.7b}$$

The variable f, defined as $f = \omega/2\pi$, is called the *normalized frequency* (see Fig. 1.6). Thus, for real $h(n)$ we plot $|H(e^{j\omega})|$ in the range $0 \le f \le 0.5$. A typical design problem is to find FIR filter transfer function $H(z)$ such that the frequency response magnitude lies within the tolerance region of Fig. 2.3.

The *minimum* stopband attenuation in dB is defined as

$$A_r = -20\log_{10}\delta_2 \tag{2.8}$$

and the *peak* passband attenuation in dB is defined as

$$A_p = -20\log_{10}(1 - \delta_1) \tag{2.9}$$

For small δ_1,

$$A_p \approx 8.686\delta_1 \quad \text{dB} \tag{2.10}$$

The notation A_{max} denotes the quantity $2A_p$. If the frequency response is normalized so that its maximum magnitude (in the passband) is unity, A_{max} essentially represents the *maximum* passband attenuation in dB for small δ_1.

In most of the numerical design examples we show the frequency response plots, along with passband details (see, for example, Fig. 2.9). The response is plotted in dB; that is, $20\log_{10}|H(e^{j\omega})|$ is plotted. The passband details, however, are not plotted in dB, but $|H(e^{j\omega})|$ is displayed. The passband edges (for example, normalized frequencies 0.0 and 0.08) are always explicitly indicated in the passband blowups.

FIR FILTER DESIGN BASED ON WINDOWING   III

Windowing is one of the earliest design techniques for FIR filter design, is one of the simplest [4, 5], and is further discussed in the Appendix to Chapter 3. The technique is simple because the filter coefficients can be obtained in closed form without elaborate optimization procedures. Thus, the design time is very small, and most designs can be done on a calculator. This simplicity continues to make the technique attractive today, in spite of more sophisticated FIR design algorithms developed during the last 15 years. Moreover, FIR designs based on Kaiser's windows [5] are quite flexible, and experience shows that they are close to optimal.

To explain the windowing technique, first consider Fig. 2.2, which shows an ideal (or *desired*) lowpass response $H_d(e^{j\omega})$ with cutoff frequency ω_c radians. The corresponding impulse response coefficients given by the inverse DTFT (IDTFT) of $H_d(e^{j\omega})$ are

$$h_d(n) = \frac{\omega_c}{\pi}\left(\frac{\sin \omega_c n}{\omega_c n}\right), \qquad -\infty \le n \le \infty \qquad (2.11)$$

Clearly, Eq. (2.11) represents a noncausal IIR filter that, in addition, is unstable (i.e., the impulse response $h_d(n)$ is not absolutely summable [1]). It is therefore unrealizable. To obtain a FIR filter that approximates the response of Fig. 2.2, we can truncate the above impulse response to a finite-length sequence as

$$h(n) = \begin{cases} h_d(n), & -(N-1)/2 \le n \le (N-1)/2 \\ 0 & \text{otherwise} \end{cases} \qquad (2.12)$$

The impulse response $h(n)$ represents a FIR filter of order $N-1$ (which turns out to be even). A causal filter can be obtained simply by delaying the impulse response by $(N-1)/2$ units of time. For the rest of this section we will assume for notational convenience that the impulse response is noncausal [i.e., of the form of Eq. (2.12)] so that $H(z)$ is a zero-phase filter and $H(e^{j\omega})$ is real valued for all ω.

Now, the above process of obtaining $h(n)$ from $h_d(n)$ can be viewed as multiplying the sequence $h(n)$ with the *rectangular window function*

$$w(n) = \begin{cases} 1, & -(N-1)/2 \le n \le (N-1)/2 \\ 0 & \text{otherwise} \end{cases} \qquad (2.13)$$

Equivalently, $H(e^{j\omega})$ is the convolution of $H_d(e^{j\omega})$ with the transform of the rectangular window (see Table I in Chapter 1)

$$\mathcal{W}(e^{j\omega}) = \frac{\sin(\omega N/2)}{\sin(\omega/2)} \qquad (2.14)$$

where N is the window length or span ($=$ filter length). Figure 2.4 is a plot of $\mathcal{W}(e^{j\omega})$ for $N-1=16$. The peak sidelobe of the window transform is only a *weak* function of N and corresponds to about -13 dB, regardless of how large N is.

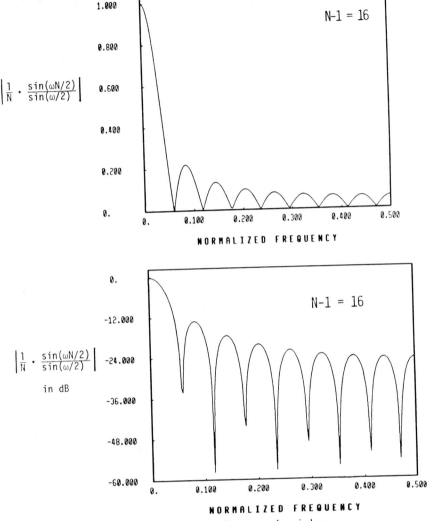

Fig. 2.4. The transform of a rectangular window.

The resulting response $H(e^{j\omega}) = H_0(e^{j\omega})$ has ripples, as shown in Fig. 2.5, with ripple size increasing toward the bandedge. Increasing the filter order has the effect of confining the ripples closer to the bandedge but does not decrease the ripple magnitude. The first sidelobe of the stopband in the lowpass response has a height of about -21 dB, regardless of how large N is, assuming a passband response of about 0 dB. (For example, Fig. 2.5(b) shows the frequency response of a lowpass filter of order $N - 1 = 64$ designed with a rectangular window.) The explanation for this behavior is that $h_d(n)$, given by Eq. (2.11), is the Fourier series expansion of the periodic frequency domain response of Fig. 2.2, and this series gives rise to the well-known Gibbs phenomenon [6].

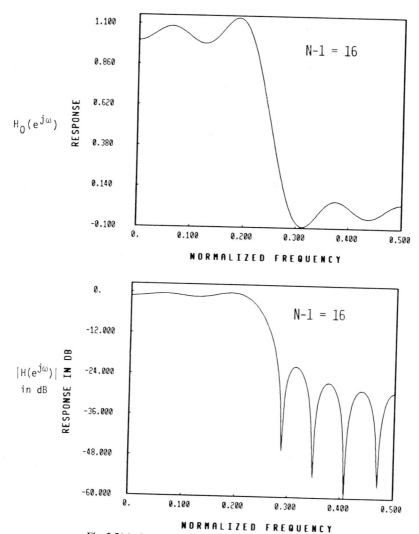

Fig. 2.5(a). Lowpass filter with rectangular window.

Decreasing the Ripple Size   A

We can decrease the ripple size by using windows $w(n)$ that are *less abrupt* than the rectangular window—the *triangle* window, for example. The $(2M + 1)$-point triangular window (also called the Bartlett window) is defined as

$$w(n) = 1 - \frac{|n|}{M} \qquad \text{for } -M \leq n \leq M$$

$$= 0 \qquad\qquad \text{otherwise}$$

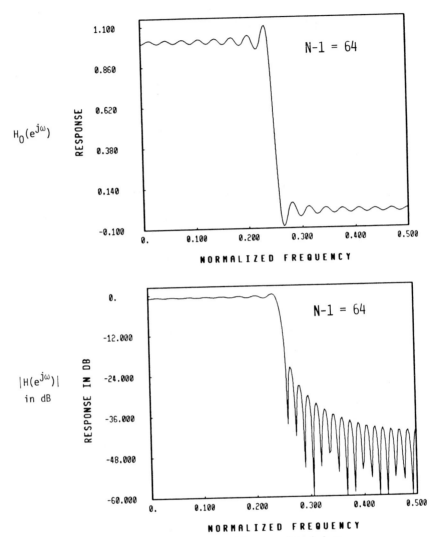

$H_0(e^{j\omega})$

$|H(e^{j\omega})|$
in dB

Fig. 2.5(b). Lowpass filter with rectangular window.

For a given window length the mainlobe width (defined to be twice the first zero crossing) of $\mathscr{W}(e^{j\omega})$ for a triangular window is double that of the corresponding rectangular window. Consequently, Δf of the resulting lowpass response increases. We can compensate for this increase of Δf simply by increasing the window span N, because Δf varies as $1/N$.

Figure 2.6 shows the transform of a 33-point triangular window ($M = 16$). The mainlobe width is the same as that of the 17-point rectangular window (Fig. 2.4), but the sidelobe level of the window transform is now about -26 dB. Thus a lowpass filter design based on this triangular window has the same transition

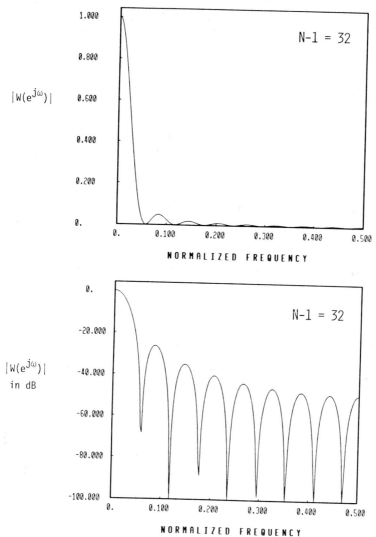

Fig. 2.6. The transform of a triangular window.

bandwidth as in Fig. 2.5(a), but has a minimum stopband attenuation of about −25 dB. In general, depending on the required stopband attenuation, the designer chooses an appropriate window and then, depending on the specification for Δf, chooses the filter length N.

For a given filter length N the attainable stopband attenuation A_r is higher for a window with smaller sidelobe level, and the transition bandwidth Δf of the filter response is smaller for a window with narrower mainlobe. This gives an overall guideline for choosing of the window. Historically, many window

TABLE I
Commonly Used Windows for FIR Design

Window	$w(n)$	
Rectangular	1	$-\dfrac{N-1}{2} \le n \le \dfrac{N-1}{2}$
Triangular or Bartlett ($N = 2M + 1$ point)	$1 - \dfrac{|n|}{M}$	$-M \le n \le M$
Hann	$\dfrac{1}{2}\left(1 + \cos\dfrac{2\pi n}{N}\right)$	$-\dfrac{N-1}{2} \le n \le \dfrac{N-1}{2}$
Hamming	$0\cdot54 + 0\cdot46\cos\dfrac{2\pi n}{N}$	$-\dfrac{N-1}{2} \le n \le \dfrac{N-1}{2}$
Blackman	$0\cdot42 + 0\cdot5\cos\dfrac{2\pi n}{N} + 0\cdot08\cos\dfrac{4\pi n}{N}$	$-\dfrac{N-1}{2} \le n \le \dfrac{N-1}{2}$

(a) Time Domain Representation

Window	Transform $\mathcal{W}(e^{j\omega})$
Rectangular	$S(\omega) \triangleq \dfrac{\sin(\omega N/2)}{\sin(\omega/2)}$
Triangular	$S^2(\omega)$
Hann	$0\cdot5\,S(\omega) + 0\cdot25\,S\left(\omega - \dfrac{2\pi}{N}\right) + 0\cdot25\,S\left(\omega + \dfrac{2\pi}{N}\right)$
Hamming	$0\cdot54\,S(\omega) + 0\cdot23\,S\left(\omega - \dfrac{2\pi}{N}\right) + 0\cdot23\,S\left(\omega + \dfrac{2\pi}{N}\right)$
Blackman	$0\cdot42\,S(\omega) + 0\cdot25\,S\left(\omega - \dfrac{2\pi}{N}\right) + 0\cdot25\,S\left(\omega + \dfrac{2\pi}{N}\right)$ $+ 0\cdot04\,S\left(\omega - \dfrac{4\pi}{N}\right) + 0\cdot04\,S\left(\omega + \dfrac{4\pi}{N}\right)$

(b) Transform Domain Representation

Window	Width of mainlobe of $|\mathcal{W}(e^{j\omega})|$	Peak sidelobe level of $|\mathcal{W}(e^{j\omega})|$ in dB	Minimum stopband attenuation A_r of the resulting lowpass filter
Rectangular	$4\pi/N$	-13	-21
Triangular	$8\pi/N$	-26	-25
Hann	$8\pi/N$	-31	-44
Hamming	$8\pi/N$	-41	-53
Blackman	$12\pi/N$	-57	-74

(c) Relevant Details

functions are known, such as the Bartlett, Hann, Hamming, and Blackman windows and many more [7, 8]. Some of these windows are optimal in certain respects. For example, consider windows of length N with the following form for $w(n)$:

$$w(n) = \alpha + (1 - \alpha)\cos\left(\frac{2\pi n}{N}\right), \qquad -\frac{N-1}{2} \le n \le \frac{N-1}{2} \qquad (2.15)$$

Among all windows of this form, the Hamming window has the smallest first-sidelobe level. Even the rectangular window is optimal in a certain sense—, it leads to a frequency response that is the best *least squares fit* to the desired frequency response. However, none of these windows leads to *optimal filters*—filters with minimum length for a given set of specifications.

An extensive tabulation of windows functions is in the appendix to Chapter 3. Table I shows some window functions along with their transforms. In Table II(c), we list the mainlobe width and the peak sidelobe amplitude of $\mathscr{W}(e^{j\omega})$ for each N-point window, where $\mathscr{W}(e^{j0})$ is normalized to unity. The mainlobe width is defined as twice the first zero-crossing frequency of $\mathscr{W}(e^{j\omega})$. Table I(c) also shows the attainable minimum stopband attenuation A_r for the lowpass filter. The transition bandwidths Δf of the lowpass filters, designed using some of these windows, are as follows: $0.9375/N$ for rectangular-window-based designs; $3.3125/N$ for Hamming-window-based designs; and $5.06/N$ for Kaiser-window-based designs (with $\beta = 7.865$).

TABLE II

**Minimum Stopband Attenuation
Versus Beta for Kaiser Window**

Minimum stopband attenuation	β
25.0	1.333
30.0	2.117
35.0	2.783
40.0	3.395
45.0	3.975
50.0	4.551
55.0	5.102
60.0	5.653
65.0	6.204
70.0	6.755
75.0	7.306
80.0	7.857
85.0	8.408
90.0	8.959
95.0	9.510
100.0	10.061

B   The Kaiser Window

In 1974, Kaiser [5] advanced a new window, now known as the Kaiser window, based on discrete-time approximations of the prolate spheroidal wave functions. This window has a flexible parameter β that can be chosen to meet a given stopband attenuation, and then the window length N can be chosen to meet the requirements on Δf. Due to the parameter β, the Kaiser window essentially subsumes several other windows for FIR design.

Recall that a window is essentially a time-limited function with a lowpass type of transform. One would like the transform $\mathcal{W}(e^{j\omega})$ to resemble an impulse function so that the result of convolution of $\mathcal{W}(e^{j\omega})$ with $H_d(e^{j\omega})$ resembles $H_d(e^{j\omega})$ as closely as possible. One possible approach for obtaining an optimal *window* is therefore to minimize the *energy* in the sidelobes of $\mathcal{W}(e^{j\omega})$. The Kaiser window is a discrete-time approximation of such an optimal continuous-time family of functions [9], and is

$$
w(n) = \begin{cases} I_0\left[\beta\sqrt{1 - \left(\frac{n}{(N-1)/2}\right)^2}\right] \bigg/ I_0(\beta), & -\frac{N-1}{2} \leq n \leq \frac{N-1}{2} \\ 0 & \text{otherwise} \end{cases} \tag{2.16}
$$

where $I_0(x)$ is the modified zeroth-order Bessel function, which can be computed easily as

$$
I_0(x) = 1 + \sum_{k=1}^{\infty} \left[\frac{(x/2)^k}{k!}\right]^2 \tag{2.17}
$$

Analytical expressions for $\mathcal{W}(e^{j\omega})$ are not available for the Kaiser window, but they are not required for designing FIR filters based on this window. The argument x in Eq. (2.17) is clearly in the range $(0, \beta)$. The parameter β, to be discussed next, is typically in the range 2 to 10, and for this range of arguments about 20 terms in the summation of Eq. (2.17) are sufficient to yield accurate values of $w(n)$.

As the value of β increases, the stopband attenuation of the lowpass filter increases and the transition band widens. Proper choice of N then leads to the final design. Accurate design formulas are available for choosing β and N. Thus, we can design a lowpass filter with equal passband and stopband peak ripples $(\delta_1 = \delta_2)$ by choosing

$$
\beta = \begin{cases} 0.1102(A_r - 8.7) & \text{if } A_r > 50 \\ 0.5842(A_r - 21)^{0.4} + 0.07886(A_r - 21) & \text{if } 21 < A_r < 50 \\ 0 & \text{if } A_r < 21 \end{cases} \tag{2.18}
$$

Moreover Kaiser has found the following closed-form expression for estimating the window length N (i.e., the filter length) in terms of the desired specifications Δf and A_r [see Eq. (2.7(a)) and (2.8)]:

$$
N - 1 = \frac{A_r - 7.95}{14.36\,\Delta f} \tag{2.19}
$$

which is an elegant and quick design aid. Thus, given the specifications in terms of A_r, ω_p, and ω_r, we compute Δf from Eq. (2.7a) and then estimate β and $N - 1$ from Eqs. (2.18) and (2.19). We compute the window coefficients $w(n)$ from Eq. (2.16) and take the filter coefficients to be $h(n) = h_d(n)w(n)$, where $h_d(n)$ is as in Eq. (2.11). If the resulting filter response is not satisfactory, we can increase β and $N - 1$ as required. Usually, a couple of trials of this kind bring about very satisfactory results. Experience with lowpass designs shows that the required order is close to the order of an optimal equiripple design (the topic of the next section).

Table II shows a list of values of β for various possible attenuation requirements. Table III shows the required order $N - 1$ for various typical combinations of A_r and Δf.

Design Example 1. Consider a lowpass design with specifications

$$\omega_p = 0.16\pi, \quad \omega_r = 0.24\pi, \quad A_r = 39 \text{ dB} \tag{2.20}$$

$$\delta_1 = \delta_2 \tag{2.21}$$

Recall that A_r is defined to be $-20\log_{10}\delta_2$. The frequency ω_c in Eq. (2.11) is the arithmetic mean of ω_p and ω_r. For a Kaiser-window-based design, we estimate β and the filter order from Eqs. (2.18) and (2.19), respectively. Thus the parameters for the window-based design are

$$N - 1 = \text{order} = 54, \quad \beta = 3.276, \quad \omega_c = 0.2\pi \tag{2.22}$$

Figure 2.7 shows the relevant frequency response plots. Note that all the desired specifications are satisfied, thus demonstrating the accuracy of the estimates of β and N.

TABLE III
Estimated Order of Kaiser-Window-Based Lowpass Filter

Δf	A_r							
	30.0	40.0	50.0	60.0	70.0	80.0	90.0	100.0
0.010	153	223	292	362	432	501	571	641
0.015	102	148	195	241	288	334	380	427
0.020	76	111	146	181	216	250	285	320
0.025	61	89	117	144	172	200	228	256
0.030	51	74	97	120	144	167	190	213
0.035	43	63	83	103	123	143	163	183
0.040	38	55	73	90	108	125	142	160
0.050	30	44	58	72	86	100	114	128
0.060	25	37	48	60	72	83	95	106
0.070	21	31	41	51	61	71	81	91
0.085	18	26	34	42	50	59	67	75
0.100	15	22	29	36	43	50	57	64
0.110	13	20	26	32	39	45	51	58
0.120	12	18	24	30	36	41	47	53

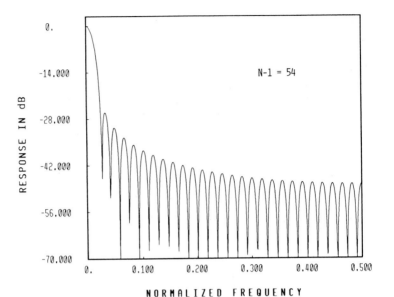

Fig. 2.7(a). Example 1: $|W(e^{j\omega})|$ for Kaiser window.

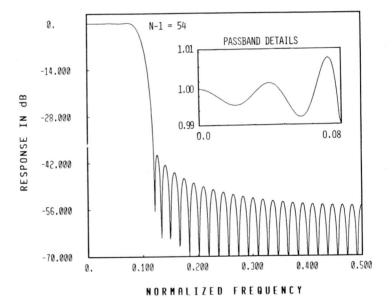

Fig. 2.7(b). Example 1: Lowpass filter designed with Kaiser window.

One limitation of the windowing approach is that the designer has no simultaneous control over the passband and stopband errors. The peak errors δ_1 and δ_2 are always equal. Secondly, filters with unconventional responses, such as multiband filters with different attenuations in different bands, cannot be designed. Also, the design of such filtering functions as optimal digital differentiators and Hilbert transformers requires a completely different approach, which is described in Section IV.

EQUIRIPPLE APPROXIMATIONS FOR FIR FILTERS   IV

Perhaps the most well-known and widely used linear-phase FIR filters are those that have an equiripple *weighted approximation error* [10]. The main reason for this is that such *equiripple filters* (also called minimax designs, Chebyshev designs, and sometimes simply *optimal designs*) are optimal in the sense that, for a given set of specifications (such as for instance, ω_p, ω_r, δ_1, and δ_2), these filters have the lowest order $N - 1$. Thus a direct-form implementation (Fig. 2.1) of the filter requires the smallest number of multiplications (equal to $(N - 1)/2 + 1$ for odd N and $N/2$ for even N). Moreover, McClellan and Parks [11] have developed a general design algorithm (called the MP algorithm in this chapter) that can be used to design optimal FIR filters, in the above sense, for a wide variety of requirements. For example, filters with several passbands and stopbands, with each band having its own error tolerance δ_k can be designed. In addition, a nonuniform tolerance over a given passband also can be achieved. Digital differentiators and Hilbert transformers [2] with exact linear phase can be designed with this algorithm. Even IIR filters can be designed by carefully adapting the principles involved here [12].

In view of its numerous merits, this entire section is dedicated to the principles and applications of the MP algorithm. Section IX presents novel applications of this algorithm that lead to surprisingly efficient FIR designs.

Four Basic Types of Linear-Phase FIR Filters   A

Recall that an FIR transfer function has the form of Eq. (2.1) and that for a linear phase-response, the coefficients must be symmetric $[h(n) = h(N - 1 - n)]$ or antisymmetric $[h(n) = -h(N - 1 - n)]$. The order $N - 1$ can be even or odd. Thus four types of linear-phase FIR filters can be distinguished [10], and their properties are summarized in Table IV. For each type, the frequency response can

TABLE IV(a)
The Four Types of Linear-Phase FIR Filters

Type	$N-1$ ($=$ order)	$h(n)$	$H_0(e^{j\omega})$	b_n
1	Even	Symm.	$\sum_{n=0}^{(N-1)/2} b_n \cos(n\omega)$	$b_0 = h\left(\dfrac{N-1}{2}\right)$
				$b_n = 2h\left(\dfrac{N-1}{2} - n\right),\, n \neq 0$
2	Odd	Symm.	$\sum_{n=1}^{N/2} b_n \cos \omega\left(n - \dfrac{1}{2}\right)$	$b_n = 2h\left(\dfrac{N}{2} - n\right)$
3	Even	Antisymm.	$\sum_{n=1}^{(N-1)/2} b_n \sin(n\omega)$	$b_n = 2h\left(\dfrac{N-1}{2} - n\right)$
4	Odd	Antisymm.	$\sum_{n=1}^{N/2} b_n \sin \omega\left(n - \dfrac{1}{2}\right)$	$b_n = 2h\left(\dfrac{N}{2} - n\right)$

$H(e^{j\omega}) = $ frequency response $= (j)^l e^{-j\omega(N-1)/2} H_0(e^{j\omega})$, where $l = 0$ for types 1 and 2 and $l = 1$ for types 3 and 4.

TABLE IV(b)
Equivalent Expressions for $H_0(e^{j\omega})$ for the Four Types

Type	Equivalent expression for $H_0(e^{j\omega})$	Relation between b_n and $\tilde{b}_n$
1	$\sum_{n=0}^{(N-1)/2} \tilde{b}_n \cos(n\omega)$	$\tilde{b}_n = b_n$
2	$\cos\dfrac{\omega}{2} \sum_{n=0}^{(N-2)/2} \tilde{b}_n \cos(n\omega)$	$b_1 = \tilde{b}_0 + \tilde{b}_1/2$ $\begin{cases} b_k = \frac{1}{2}(\tilde{b}_{k-1} + \tilde{b}_k) \\ k = 2, 3, \ldots, (N-2)/2 \end{cases}$ $b_{N/2} = \frac{1}{2}\tilde{b}_{(N-2)/2}$
3	$\sin \omega \sum_{n=0}^{(N-3)/2} \tilde{b}_n \cos(n\omega)$	$b_1 = \tilde{b}_0 - \frac{1}{2}\tilde{b}_2$ $\begin{cases} b_k = \frac{1}{2}(\tilde{b}_{k-1} - \tilde{b}_{k+1}), \\ k = 2, \ldots, (N-1)/2 - 2 \end{cases}$ $b_{(N-1)/2-1} = \frac{1}{2}\tilde{b}_{(N-1)/2-2}$ $b_{(N-1)/2} = \frac{1}{2}\tilde{b}_{(N-1)/2-1}$
4	$\sin\dfrac{\omega}{2} \sum_{n=0}^{(N-2)/2} \tilde{b}_n \cos(n\omega)$	$b_1 = \tilde{b}_0 - \frac{1}{2}\tilde{b}_1$ $\begin{cases} b_k = \frac{1}{2}(\tilde{b}_{k-1} - \tilde{b}_k), \\ k = 2, \ldots, N/2 - 1 \end{cases}$ $b_{N/2} = \frac{1}{2}\tilde{b}_{(N-2)/2}$

TABLE IV(c)
Further Properties of the Four Types of Linear-Phase FIR Filters

Type	Value of $H_0(e^{j\omega})$ at $\omega = 0$	Value of $H_0(e^{j\omega})$ at $\omega = \pi$	Typical application
1	Unconstrained	Unconstrained	Bandpass filter design
2	Unconstrained	Zero	Bandpass filter design (except highpass)
3	Zero	Zero	Differentiators and Hilbert transformers
4	Zero	Unconstrained	Differentiator and Hilbert transformers

Note: "Bandpass" in general stands for lowpass, highpass, bandpass, and multiband designs, with a constant attenuation requirement in a given band.

be written in the form

$$H(e^{j\omega}) = (j)^k e^{-j\omega(N-1)/2} H_0(e^{j\omega}) \qquad (2.23)$$

where $j = \sqrt{-1}$, and $H_0(e^{j\omega})$ is the zero-phase part (i.e., $H_0(e^{j\omega})$ is real valued for all values of ω). The exponent k in Eq. (2.23) is equal to 0 for types 1 and 2 and is equal to 1 for types 3 and 4. Tables IV(a) and IV(b) show two equivalent ways of writing $H_0(e^{j\omega})$, where the meaning of b_n is explained in Table IV(b). Table IV(c) lists the behaviors of the four types at $\omega = 0$ and $\omega = \pi$; these constraints are useful when making judgments as to which type should be used.

We identify four different types because each type has a different application. For example, bandpass filters with constant attenuation in each band can be designed with types 1 and 2. Types 3 and 4 must not be used for designs that require a nonzero response at $\omega = 0$. To design differentiators and Hilbert transformers, we must use only type 3 or type 4 because the constant factor j is required in these designs. It is also clear from Table IV that if a filter with nonzero response at $\omega = \pi$ is required, then it cannot be designed with a type 2 or type 3 transfer function. Type 4 transfer functions are more general than type 3 in this sense. Similarly, type 1 transfer functions are more general than type 2. However, there are some applications in multirate signal processing (the "QMF filter banks") where *only* type 2 filters can be used for signal splitting and reconstruction [13] (unless special structures with additional forward delays are incorporated). Further implications of the properties of the various types will be clarified in later subsections.

The Alternation Theorem **B**

Most of the results on equiripple FIR filters are based on the alternation theorem, suitably adapted for FIR transfer functions [11]. In Fig. 2.3, which shows a typical lowpass specification, it is intuitively clear that if the approximation error is uniformly distributed throughout the band of interest, then the resulting transfer function will be optimal in the sense that the filter order is minimized. The alternation theorem makes this intuition more precise.

A result from the Alternation Theorem. Let $\mathscr{F}$ be any closed subset of the closed interval $0 \leq \omega \leq \pi$. Let $P(e^{j\omega})$ be a linear combination of cosines:

$$P(e^{j\omega}) = \sum_{n=0}^{M} \alpha(n)\cos(\omega n) \tag{2.24}$$

Let $\hat{D}(e^{j\omega})$ be any (desired) continuous function on $\mathscr{F}$. Define a weighted error function $E(e^{j\omega})$ by

$$E(e^{j\omega}) = \hat{W}(e^{j\omega})[\hat{D}(e^{j\omega}) - P(e^{j\omega})] \tag{2.25}$$

Then $P(e^{j\omega})$ is said to be the best weighted Chebyshev approximation to $\hat{D}(e^{j\omega})$ [with weight $\hat{W}(e^{j\omega})$] if the quantity

$$\max_{\omega \in \mathscr{F}} |E(e^{j\omega})| \tag{2.26}$$

is the smallest over all possible sets of $\alpha(n)$ in Eq. (2.24). The alternation theorem says that $P(e^{j\omega})$ is the unique best weighted Chebyshev approximation to $\hat{D}(e^{j\omega})$ if and only if there exist at least $M + 2$ points ω_i in $\mathscr{F}$ such that $\omega_1 < \omega_2 < \cdots < \omega_{M+2}$ and such that

$$E(e^{j\omega_i}) = -E(e^{j\omega_{i+1}}), \qquad i = 1, 2, \ldots, M + 1 \tag{2.27}$$

and

$$|E(e^{j\omega_i})| = \max_{\omega \in \mathscr{F}} |E(e^{j\omega})|, \qquad i = 1, 2, \ldots, M + 2 \tag{2.28}$$

Most of the optimal design techniques are essentially iterative schemes for satisfying the above alternation conditions on the weighted approximation error $E(e^{j\omega})$.

C Method Due to Hermann

Hermann [14] showed in 1970 how a set of nonlinear constraints on the function $H_0(e^{j\omega})$ can lead to an equiripple solution. To explain the method, we consider type 1 filters, where, as in Table IV,

$$H_0(e^{j\omega}) = \sum_{n=0}^{M} b_n \cos(\omega n), \qquad M = \frac{N-1}{2} \tag{2.29}$$

The function $H_0(e^{j\omega})$ is required to be equiripple as shown in Figure 2.8, where δ_1, δ_2, and N (and hence M) are assumed to be given. The quantities b_n are then computed so as to make $H_0(e^{j\omega})$ an equiripple function with peak errors δ_1 and

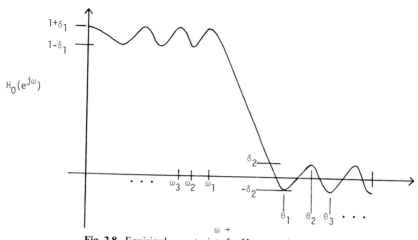

Fig. 2.8. Equiripple constraints for Herrmann's method.

δ_2. There is no direct control over the bandedges ω_p and ω_r, but an indirect control can be exercised by constraining the number of extrema N_p in the passband and the number of extrema N_r in the stopband. [In this section, the term "extrema" stands for the zeros of the derivative $H_0'(e^{j\omega})$.][†] For a filter of a given order $N - 1$, we therefore have only a *finite* number of choices for the bandedges of the equiripple filter.

Let us now look into the actual details of Herrmann's method. The function $H_0(e^{j\omega})$ can have at most $M - 1$ extrema in the open interval $0 < \omega < \pi$. Moreover, it always has one extremum at $\omega = 0$ and one at $\omega = \pi$, regardless of the unknown coefficients b_n. Let N_p and N_r represent the total number of extrema in the ranges $0 \leq \omega \leq \omega_p$ and $\omega_r \leq \omega \leq \pi$, respectively. Clearly $N_p + N_r \leq M + 1$. Hermann showed how to obtain the coefficients such that there are precisely $M + 1$ extrema of $H_0(e^{j\omega})$ in the region $0 \leq \omega \leq \pi$. For this, the following constraints are imposed:

$$
\begin{aligned}
H_0(e^{j\omega_k}) &= 1 - (-1)^k \delta_1, & k &= 1, 2, \ldots, N_p \\
H_0'(e^{j\omega_k}) &= 0, & k &= 1, 2, \ldots, N_p - 1 \\
H_0(e^{j\theta_k}) &= (-1)^k \delta_2, & k &= 1, 2, \ldots, N_r \\
H_0'(e^{j\theta_k}) &= 0, & k &= 1, 2, \ldots, N_r - 1
\end{aligned}
\tag{2.30}
$$

Note that $\omega_{N_p} = 0$ and $\theta_{N_r} = \pi$ and the derivatives are automatically zero at these frequencies, and, moreover, $M + 1 = N_p + N_r$. We solve the above set of $2M$ equations to obtain the $2M$ unknowns $(\omega_1, \omega_2, \ldots, \omega_{N_p - 1})$, $(\theta_1, \theta_2, \ldots, \theta_{N_r - 1})$, and $(b_0, b_1, \ldots, b_M)$. The filter coefficients $h(n)$ can then be calculated from b_n. The bandedges ω_p and ω_r are those frequencies in the range $\omega_1 < \omega < \theta_1$, where

[†] Here the superscript prime denotes derivative with respect to ω.

$H_0(e^{j\omega})$ is equal to $1 - \delta_1$ and δ_2, respectively. These points are automatically determined in the process.

As a comment on Herrmann's method, first note that there are precisely $M + 1$ extrema; hence, if we count the bandedges, there are $M + 3$ distinct frequencies where the approximation error $E(e^{j\omega})$ attains its maximum value. Moreover, the error clearly alternates between positive and negative extrema. Thus, all the conditions of the alternation theorem are satisfied, and the resulting design is therefore optimal in the Chebyshev sense. However, according to the alternation theorem it is *sufficient* to have $M + 2$ frequencies where the error attains its peak magnitude. We thus have one more ripple than the minimum number required to satisfy the theorem. For this reason, Herrmann's solutions are called *extraripple* solutions.

The above equations that must be solved to obtain the filter coefficients are highly nonlinear in terms of the unknowns ω_k and θ_k. The method is therefore limited to the solution of low-order extraripple filters only. Moreover, the modification of the method for designing other filter shapes is generally complicated.

Using an elegant technique of Hofstetter *et al.* [15]; we can overcome the disadvantage of solving a set of highly nonlinear equations. Hofstetter's method has exactly the same formulation as Herrmann's method, and most of the preceding discussion is valid. However, the solution for the $2M$ unknowns is now based on a *multiple-exchange* procedure. Since this procedure is also basic to the widely used McClellan–Parks algorithm, we now describe the latter.

D   The McClellan–Parks (MP) Algorithm

Let us again begin with a lowpass specification, as in Fig. 2.3. Recall that in the algorithms of Herrmann and Hofstetter *et al.* N, δ_1, and δ_2 were specified and ω_p and ω_r were automatically constrained by the resulting design. In the MP algorithm, however, the quantities specified are N, ω_p, ω_r, and the ratio of passband to stopband error, $K = \delta_1/\delta_2$. The peak errors δ_1 and δ_2 are determined by the resulting optimal solution. If these errors are not small enough, we can increase N and redesign the transfer function. Given the more common specifications δ_1, δ_2, ω_p, and ω_r, we can estimate the desired order and use this estimate as the input to the MP algorithm. The resulting design is usually very close to being satisfactory and can always be improved by slightly increasing the order $N - 1$. Kaiser has reported a simple and useful estimate for $N - 1$, based on experience with window-based designs that $N - 1$ is inversely proportional to Δf and proportional to the arithmetic mean of the errors $\log_{10}\delta_1$ and $\log_{10}\delta_2$. Based on this intuition and the design data for *equiripple* filters due to Herrmann [14], the following estimate has been reported [5]:

$$N - 1 = \frac{-20\log_{10}\sqrt{\delta_1\delta_2} - 13}{14.6\,\Delta f} \qquad (2.31)$$

This estimate of filter order for optimal filters is reasonably close to the estimate in Eq. (2.19) for window-based designs for the special case $\delta_1 = \delta_2$. Table V shows the computed order estimates based on Eq. (2.31) for various combinations of Δf and A_r (where $A_r = -20 \log_{10} \sqrt{\delta_1 \delta_2}$). Herrmann obtained a somewhat more accurate formula by measuring an extensive set of optimal linear-phase lowpass filters; the formula is given by [16]

$$N - 1 = \frac{D_\infty(\delta_1, \delta_2) - F(\delta_1, \delta_2)(\Delta f)^2}{\Delta f} \tag{2.32}$$

where

$$D_\infty(\delta_1, \delta_2) = [a_1(\log_{10} \delta_1)^2 + a_2 \log_{10} \delta_1 + a_3] \log_{10} \delta_2$$
$$+ [a_4(\log_{10} \delta_1)^2 + a_5 \log_{10} \delta_1 + a_6] \tag{2.33}$$

and

$$F(\delta_1, \delta_2) = b_1 + b_2[\log_{10} \delta_1 - \log_{10} \delta_2] \tag{2.34}$$

The constants a_k and b_k are given by

$$a_1 = 0.005309, \qquad a_2 = 0.07114, \qquad a_3 = -0.4761,$$
$$a_4 = -0.00266, \qquad a_5 = -0.5941, \qquad a_6 = -0.4278 \tag{2.35}$$

and

$$b_1 = 11.01217, \qquad b_2 = 0.51244 \tag{2.36}$$

TABLE V
Estimated Equiripple Filter Order, Kaiser's Formula

Δf	A_r							
	30.0	40.0	50.0	60.0	70.0	80.0	90.0	100.0
0.010	116	184	253	321	390	458	527	595
0.015	77	123	168	214	260	305	351	397
0.020	58	92	126	160	195	229	263	297
0.025	46	73	101	128	156	183	210	238
0.030	38	61	84	107	130	152	175	198
0.035	33	52	72	91	111	131	150	170
0.040	29	46	63	80	97	114	131	148
0.050	23	36	50	64	78	91	105	119
0.060	19	30	42	53	65	76	87	99
0.070	16	26	36	45	55	65	75	85
0.085	13	21	29	37	45	53	62	70
0.100	11	18	25	32	39	45	52	59
0.110	10	16	23	29	35	41	47	54
0.120	9	15	21	26	32	38	43	49

Table VI shows the value of the estimate $N - 1$, computed from (2.32), for various typical combinations of Δf and $A_r = -20\log_{10}\sqrt{\delta_1\delta_2}$. Based on (2.32), we can estimate the value of any of the five parameters $\omega_p, \omega_r, \delta_1, \delta_2$, and N, given the remaining four. Rabiner [17] has presented useful algorithms, based on simple iterative schemes, for obtaining such accurate estimates.

Note: Extensive design experience has shown that the order $N - 1$ does not necessarily increase as Δf decreases! For example, Rabiner demonstrates in [16] that, with $\delta_1 = \delta_2 = 0.1$, Δf is smaller for a filter with $N - 1 = 8$ than for a filter with $N - 1 = 9$, for *certain* values of ω_p. However, if we compare $N - 1$ within the subclass of filters with even $N - 1$ (or odd $N - 1$), then it is found that $N - 1$ is monotone increasing with decreasing Δf.

To explain the MP algorithm, let us get back to the lowpass specifications in Fig. 2.3. For lowpass designs, only type 1 or type 2 transfer functions are relevant. Assume, for simplicity, that a type 1 function is used so that the order $N - 1$ is even. Given $N - 1$, ω_p, ω_r, and the ratio of passband to stopband errors $K = \delta_1/\delta_2$, we should minimize the weighted error function of Eq. (2.25), where $P(e^{j\omega})$ is as in Eq. (2.24), and

$$\hat{W}(e^{j\omega}) = \begin{cases} 1, & 0 \leq \omega \leq \omega_p \\ K = \delta_1/\delta_2, & \omega_r \leq \omega \leq \pi \end{cases} \qquad (2.37)$$

and

$$\hat{D}(e^{j\omega}) = \begin{cases} 1, & 0 \leq \omega \leq \omega_p \\ 0, & \omega_r \leq \omega \leq \pi \end{cases} \qquad (2.38)$$

TABLE VI

Estimated Equiripple Filter Order, Herrmann's Formula

Δf	\multicolumn{8}{c}{A_r}							
	30.0	40.0	50.0	60.0	70.0	80.0	90.0	100.0
0.010	131	194	259	325	392	460	528	597
0.015	87	129	172	216	261	307	352	397
0.020	65	96	129	162	196	230	264	298
0.025	52	77	103	129	156	184	211	238
0.030	43	64	86	108	130	153	176	198
0.035	37	55	73	92	111	131	150	170
0.040	32	48	64	80	97	114	131	148
0.050	25	38	51	64	78	91	105	118
0.060	21	31	42	53	64	76	87	98
0.070	17	27	36	45	55	65	74	84
0.085	14	21	29	37	45	53	61	69
0.100	12	18	24	31	38	44	51	58
0.110	10	16	22	28	34	40	46	53
0.120	9	14	20	25	31	37	42	48

To find $b_n = \alpha(n)$ in Eq. (2.24) such that the maximum error of Eq. (2.26) is minimized, we suitably adapt the *Remez exchange procedure* [10, 11], which is described next.

Assume that we are given a set S of $M + 2$ trial extremal frequencies

$$\omega_1, \omega_2, \ldots, \omega_{M+2} \tag{2.39}$$

and that we want to force the weighted error function to satisfy the alternation condition at these frequencies:

$$\rho = E(e^{j\omega_k}) = -E(e^{j\omega_{k+1}}), \qquad k = 1, 2, \ldots, M + 1 \tag{2.40}$$

where ρ is yet unknown. We can always solve for the $M + 2$ unknowns

$$\alpha(0), \alpha(1), \ldots, \alpha(M), \rho \tag{2.41}$$

in Eq. (2.24) from the $M + 2$ equations

$$-(-1)^k \rho = \hat{W}(e^{j\omega})[\hat{D}(e^{j\omega}) - P(e^{j\omega})] \tag{2.42}$$

where ω takes on the $M + 2$ values given in Eq. (2.39). After we obtain the $\alpha(i)$, $i = 0, 1, \ldots, M$, in this manner, we calculate the actual error function $E(e^{j\omega})$ at any frequency by using Eq. (2.25), because the right side of Eq. (2.25) is now known. However, the set of frequencies in Eq. (2.39) may not turn out to be *extremal* (i.e., points with zero derivatives). Thus, the quantity in Eq. (2.26) may not be equal to ρ in Eq. (2.40). However, since $E(e^{j\omega})$ is now completely known, we can compute a new set of frequencies where $E(e^{j\omega})$ is *actually* extremal [but not necessarily satisfying Eq. (2.40)], and then again solve for a new set of $\alpha(i)$ and ρ such that Eq. (2.40) is again satisfied at these new frequencies. We repeat this process until it converges. At convergence, the frequencies in Eq. (2.39) at which Eq. (2.40) holds are *also* extremal frequencies—that is, Eq. (2.28) is *also* satisfied.

Thus we repeat two steps in the exchange procedure, until convergence occurs:

1. Given a set S of extremal frequencies as in Eq. (2.39), compute ρ and $P(e^{j\omega})$ from Eq. (2.42).

2. From this $P(e^{j\omega})$, compute a new set $\hat{S}$ of extremal frequencies, where the error $E(e^{j\omega})$ actually has maximum magnitude. If S and $\hat{S}$ are the same within a certain tolerance, stop the iteration. Otherwise set $S = \hat{S}$ and go to step 1.

In practice, we need not explicitly solve the $M + 2$ simultaneous equations Eq. (2.42). We can compute ρ by using a closed-form expression [10, 11] and then obtain the values of $P(e^{j\omega})$ at frequencies ω_k from Eq. (2.42); we then obtain the entire function $P(e^{j\omega})$ by interpolation. We use this interpolation to evaluate $P(e^{j\omega})$ at a dense set of frequencies, and we thereby obtain a new set $\hat{S}$ of trial extremal frequencies ω_k. Details of computations involved can be found in [10].

In step 2, the computation of the new set of extremal frequencies that maximize $E(e^{j\omega})$ is generally time consuming. The usual procedure here is to compute $E(e^{j\omega})$ at a dense grid of equispaced frequencies in the range $0 \leq \omega \leq \pi$ such that about $10M$ to $20M$ values are computed during each iteration. After computing these values, we find the set of extremal frequencies merely by locating $M + 2$ maxima among the computed values. Clearly M is large for large filter orders; hence the number of evaluations is large, and the time required for *each* evaluation goes up as M increases. Antoniou [18] has developed a procedure for significantly reducing this computational overload; the procedure is based on the fact that, as the iteration proceeds, the extremal frequencies take favored locations closer and closer to the optimal locations, and hence an equispaced search for extremal frequencies is not necessary. Antoniou shows how, based on derivative information, the search can be dramatically speeded up (more than 80% saving in computational load has been reported in [18]!). The details of this improved technique are, however, beyond the scope of this chapter.

If we want the filter order $N - 1$ to be odd, then $H_0(e^{j\omega})$ is no longer a sum of cosines as required by the alternation theorem (see Table IV); instead, we can modify the above formulation simply by suitably redefining $\hat{W}(e^{j\omega})$ and $\hat{D}(e^{j\omega})$ so that $P(e^{j\omega})$ in Eq. (2.25) is still a sum of cosines. A wide range of filter requirements can be met by a simple redefinition of the quantities on the right side of Eq. (2.25) to suit the problem at hand. The next few subsections demonstrate this flexibility. The software due to McClellan *et al.* (available in [19] incorporates this flexibility and has many applications. We conclude this subsection with a few design examples.

Design Example 2. Consider again the lowpass specifications of Design Example 1 [Eqs. (2.20) and (2.21)]. We estimate the required filter order from

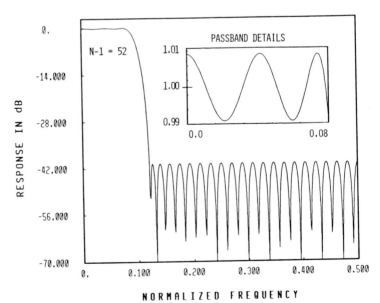

Fig. 2.9. Example 2: Lowpass filter, equiripple design.

Eq. (2.32) to be 48. Then we complete the design, based on the program in [19], and find that the resulting stopband attenuation A_r is about 38.7 dB. By increasing the order to 50, we achieve an attenuation of 39.4 dB, which is just about sufficient. It is, however, safest to slightly increase the order because the inevitable coefficient quantization in an actual implementation usually leads to a loss of stopband attenuation. An order of 52 offers an attenuation of 40.7 dB, which is quite satisfactory. Figure 2.9 shows the frequency response plots, which should be compared with the plots of Fig. 2.7.

As a comparison with the optimal IIR designs discussed in Chapter 4, the above specifications can also be met with an IIR elliptic filter of order as low as 5. The relevant frequency response plots in Fig. 2.10(a) show that (approximately) the same specifications are met. The transfer function is

$$H_5(z) = k\left(\frac{1 - 0.9066z^{-1} + z^{-2}}{1 - 1.5544z^{-1} + 0.6969z^{-2}}\right)\left(\frac{1 - 1.4304z^{-1} + z^{-2}}{1 - 1.6522z^{-1} + 0.9053z^{-2}}\right)$$
$$\times \left(\frac{1 + z^{-1}}{1 - 0.7541z^{-1}}\right) \tag{2.43}$$

where $k = 0.0071171$, so $|H_5(e^{j\omega})|$ has a maximum value of unity in the passband. This IIR transfer function can be implemented with only seven multiplications and a scaling multiplier k. In contrast, the optimal (minimum-order) FIR design requires 27 multipliers! The price paid for the high efficiency of the IIR implementation is that the group delay is not constant but has a large peak near the bandedge. This is demonstrated in Fig. 2.10(b).

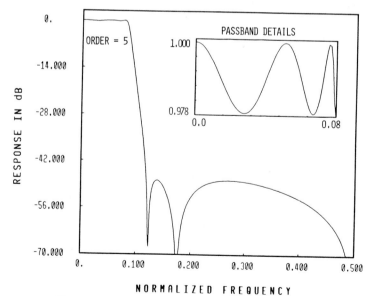

Fig. 2.10(a). Example 2: Lowpass filter, elliptic IIR design.

P. P. Vaidyanathan

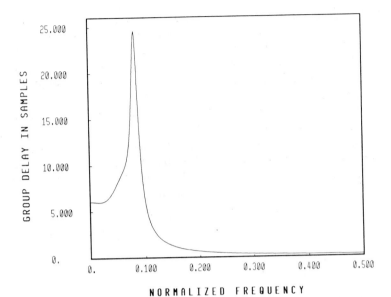

Fig. 2.10(b). Example 2: Lowpass filter, elliptic IIR design, group-delay response.

Design Example 3.   Assume that we want to design a filter that is essentially lowpass, except that zero frequency should be suppressed. Let the bandedges be $\omega_p = 0.64\pi$, $\omega_r = 0.7\pi$, and suppose we want a stopband attenuation exceeding 39 dB. Also assume that the stopband error should be twice as small as the passband error. Let the required attenuation at zero frequency be greater than 20 dB. These requirements can be met by designing a bandpass filter with specifications as indicated in Fig. 2.11, where

$$\delta_1 = 0.112, \quad \delta_2 = 0.0224, \quad \delta_3 = 0.0112 \tag{2.44}$$

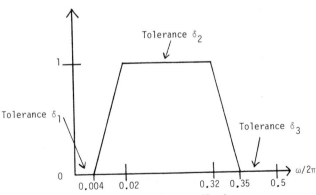

Fig. 2.11. The bandpass specifications.

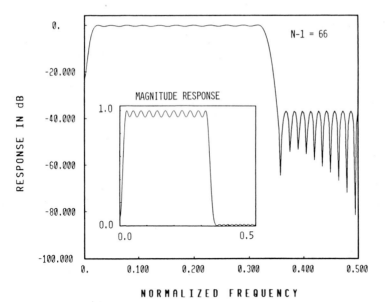

Fig. 2.12. Example 3: Bandpass filter, equiripple design.

In other words, the weighting function $W(e^{j\omega})$ should be chosen as

$$W(e^{j\omega}) = \begin{cases} 1, & 0 \le \omega \le 0.008\pi \\ \delta_1/\delta_2 = 5, & 0.04\pi \le \omega \le 0.64\pi \\ \delta_1/\delta_3 = 10, & 0.7\pi \le \omega \le \pi \end{cases} \qquad (2.45)$$

A filter of order $N - 1 = 66$ is found to meet the desired specifications satisfactorily. Figure 2.12 shows the frequency response of such a filter designed with the program in [19].

Design of Digital Differentiators **E**

Digital differentiators are characterized by a frequency response of the form

$$H(e^{j\omega}) = \begin{cases} \dfrac{j\omega}{\pi} e^{-j\omega(N-1)/2}, & 0 \le \omega \le \omega_p \\ (-1)^N j \dfrac{2\pi - \omega}{\pi} e^{-j\omega(N-1)/2}, & 2\pi - \omega_p \le \omega \le 2\pi \end{cases} \qquad (2.46)$$

Notice that the phase response is still linear in ω, except for the additional constant phase shift of $\pi/2$ rad at all frequencies due to the j factor. We can obtain this j factor simply by using type 3 or type 4 linear-phase FIR filters. Thus, we should always use an *antisymmetric* impulse response for designing differentiators.

The fact that types 3 and 4 have $H(e^{j0}) = 0$ is not a limitation, because this is precisely what Eq. (2.46) requires. Note that the approximation is required only in the range $0 < \omega \le \pi$. The symmetry properties of $H(e^{j\omega})$ automatically insure the rest.

To be specific, let us assume that type 3 filters are used. Then, referring to Table IV, we can define a weighted error function[†]

$$E(e^{j\omega}) = W(e^{j\omega})\left[\frac{\omega}{\pi} - \sin\omega \sum_{n=0}^{(N-1)/2-1} \tilde{b}_n \cos(n\omega)\right] \quad (2.47)$$

Now, in the region near $\omega = 0$, the magnitude response is very small, whereas it is largest near $\omega = \pi$. Thus, we wish to have a smaller approximation error near zero frequency. We can obtain that by defining the weight function $W(e^{j\omega})$ as

$$W(e^{j\omega}) = \frac{1}{\omega}, \quad 0 < \omega \le \omega_p \quad (2.48)$$

This enables us to rewrite Eq. (2.47) as

$$E(e^{j\omega}) = \frac{\sin\omega}{\omega}\left[\frac{\omega}{\pi\sin\omega} - \sum_{n=0}^{(N-1)/2-1} \tilde{b}_n \cos(n\omega)\right]. \quad (2.49)$$

This error function is of the form in Eq. (2.25) with $\hat{D}(e^{j\omega})$, $\hat{W}(e^{j\omega})$, and $P(e^{j\omega})$ identified as

$$\hat{D}(e^{j\omega}) = \frac{\omega}{\pi\sin\omega}, \quad \hat{W}(e^{j\omega}) = \frac{\sin\omega}{\omega}, \quad P(e^{j\omega}) = \sum_{n=0}^{(N-1)/2-1} \tilde{b}_n \cos(n\omega)$$

Simply by defining the function $P(e^{j\omega})$ as the sum of cosines appearing in Eq. (2.49), we can use the iteration described earlier to solve this approximation problem. The result of approximation produces an equiripple behavior of the *weighted* error $E(e^{j\omega})$, and the actual error therefore grows as ω increases.

1 *Remarks on the Choice of N and ω_p for Differentiators*

Table IV shows that filters with an antisymmetric impulse response have zero response at $\omega = \pi$ if the order $N - 1$ is even. Thus, odd orders (type 4) should be used for differentiators with $\omega_p = \pi$. Even if ω_p is less than π, but very close to π, it is preferable to use odd orders so that the approximation error near the bandedge ω_p is not too large. The design charts included in [2] indeed show that, for a given permissible peak relative error δ and a given value of ω_p, the filter length is much smaller for odd $N - 1$, compared to even $N - 1$. (Figure 2.A.1 includes "design charts" that aid in the choice of filter order $N - 1$ for differentiators.)

[†] This is also termed as the relative error.

Next, for a given N, the designer, if he or she has some flexibility about the choice of ω_p, should make ω_p as small as possible to minimize the approximation error.

Further Remarks on the Choice of ω_p　2

Let $x(t)$ be a continuous-time waveform, bandlimited to the range $(0, \Omega_{max})$. Let us assume that we wish to pass this signal through a differentiator $H_a(s)$. Clearly we require an approximation to the response

$$H_a(j\Omega) = \begin{cases} j\Omega, & 0 \le \Omega \le \Omega_{max} \\ -j\Omega, & -\Omega_{max} \le \Omega \le 0 \end{cases} \qquad (2.50)$$

To perform this filtering digitally, we would sample the waveform $x(t)$ at a frequency $\Omega_r > 2\Omega_{max}$ and then design a digital differentiator with

$$\omega_p = \frac{\Omega_{max}}{\Omega_r} 2\pi \qquad (2.51)$$

Thus, it is a simple matter to choose Ω_r to be large enough so that ω_p is sufficiently smaller than π. This enables us to design very accurate linear-phase FIR differentiators with reasonably low orders.

Design Example 4. Consider a differentiator whose cutoff frequency is required to be $\omega_p = \pi$. Assume that the relative error of Eq. (2.47), which is equiripple, is required to have a peak value δ not exceeding 0.0065. Since ω_p is equal to π, a type 4 filter should be used. From the design charts in Fig. 2.A.1 we can estimate the required order to be about 35. An order $N - 1 = 31$ is actually found to be sufficient, and the relevant responses are plotted in Fig. 2.13.

Design of Digital Hilbert Transformers　F

In the continuous-time domain an ideal Hilbert transformer is characterized by a frequency response of the form

$$H(j\Omega) = \begin{cases} -j & \text{for } \Omega > 0 \\ j & \text{for } \Omega < 0 \end{cases}$$

Accordingly, we would expect a digital Hilbert transformer to have the response

$$H(e^{j\omega}) = \begin{cases} -j, & 0 \le \omega \le \pi \\ j, & \pi \le \omega \le 2\pi \end{cases} \qquad (2.52)$$

Clearly, there is an inconsistency (or discontinuity) at $\omega = \pi$ and moreover, as $H(e^{j0}) = H(e^{j2\pi})$, there is an inconsistency at $\omega = 0$. Moreover, from Table IV(a), it is clear that an antisymmetric impulse response is required. For such an

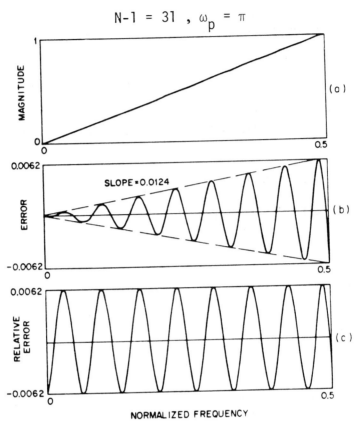

Fig. 2.13. Example 4: Optimal differentiator with equiripple (relative) error [58](© 1973 IEEE).

impulse response the frequency response at $\omega = 0$ is always zero, as we see from Table IV(c). Theoretically therefore, there does not exist a linear-phase FIR Hilbert transformer. In practice, therefore, a FIR digital Hilbert transformer is specified to have a response

$$H(e^{j\omega}) = \begin{cases} je^{-j\omega(N-1)/2}, & \omega_L \leq \omega \leq \omega_H \\ (-1)^N je^{-j\omega(N-1)/2}, & 2\pi - \omega_H \leq \omega \leq 2\pi - \omega_L \end{cases} \qquad (2.53)$$

where $\omega_L > 0$ and $\omega_H \leq \pi$. For antisymmetric impulse responses of even order $N - 1$, ω_H is restricted to be strictly less than π, because of the constraint $H(e^{j\pi}) = 0$.

We can now formulate the approximation problem by simply defining the weighted error function

$$E(e^{j\omega}) = W(e^{j\omega})[1 - H_0(e^{j\omega})] \qquad (2.54)$$

where $H_0(e^{j\omega})$ is as in Table IV (type 3 or type 4). Equation (2.54) can be rewritten in the form of Eq. (2.25) by suitably defining $\hat{W}(e^{j\omega})$ and $\hat{D}(e^{j\omega})$ so that $P(e^{j\omega})$ is a sum of cosines.

Commenting on the choice of the order $N - 1$, once again, if we are interested in $\omega_H = \pi$, only type 4 filters (odd order) should be employed. If, however, $\omega_H < \pi$, then either a type 3 or a type 4 filter can be used. Detailed guidelines pertaining to the choice of ω_L, ω_H, and $N - 1$ are in [2].

If the Hilbert transformer specifications are symmetric with respect to $\pi/2$ (i.e., if $\omega_L + \omega_H = \pi$) and if the order $N - 1$ is even (type 3), then it can be shown that the resulting FIR filter has $b_n = 0$ for even values of n. Only about half of the impulse response coefficients are therefore nonzero. We thus require only about $(N - 1)/4 + 1$ multiplications in the implementation of the filter. If the designer has the freedom to choose symmetric specifications, it can be exploited in this manner. Figure 2.A.2 aids in the choice of $N - 1$ for Hilbert transformers with $\omega_L + \omega_H = \pi$. (In the figure $\Delta f = \omega_L/2\pi$.) The quantity δ represents the peak value of the weighted equiripple error.

Design Example 5. We wish to design a Hilbert transformer with $\omega_L = 0.1\pi$ and $\omega_H = 0.9\pi$. Let the peak equiripple error be required to be less than 0.006. From the design charts in Fig. 2.A.2, we estimate that an order of about 30 is sufficient. An order $N - 1 = 28$ is actually found to be sufficient, and the relevant responses are shown in Fig. 2.14. Only 14 of the 29 coefficients $h(n)$ are nonzero, so only seven multipliers are required.

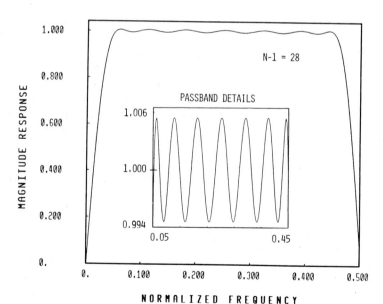

Fig. 2.14. Example 5: Hilbert transformer design.

G   Flexibility of the McClellan–Parks Algorithm

The most remarkable feature of the MP algorithm is the flexibility it offers for the design of a wide range of filter responses, as seen from the examples earlier in this section. This flexibility results from a suitable definition of the functions $\hat{D}(e^{j\omega})$ and $\hat{W}(e^{j\omega})$ in Eq. (2.25) so that the *weighted* error function $E(e^{j\omega})$ of the resulting design has the equiripple property. In the design program (Program 5.1), which is available in the IEEE software package [19]–, two user-definable functions (EFF and WATE) are included, which enable the designer to choose $\hat{D}(e^{j\omega})$ and $\hat{W}(e^{j\omega})$ according to specific requirements. The design of bandpass filters (i.e., filters with a piecewise constant attenuation requirement), differentiators, and Hilbert transformers can be done without modifying the functions EFF and WATE. However, if the designer has other unconventional specifications, these functions should be appropriately redefined.

Design Example 6.   As an example of the usefulness of these functions, consider a lowpass design specification with

$$\omega_p = 0.28\pi, \quad \omega_r = 0.36\pi, \quad \delta_1 = \delta_2 \tag{2.55}$$

and

$$A_r = -20\log_{10}\delta_2 \geq 35 \quad \text{dB} \tag{2.56}$$

The estimated filter order from Eq. (2.31) is equal to 38. Let us now assume that, in addition to the above requirements, a transmission zero is required at $\omega_0 = 0.78\pi$. (This is a typical requirement when there are unwanted sinusoids of known frequency in the input signal.) However, since we do not have direct control over the location of transmission zeros, one possible way to deal with this problem is to uniformly increase the stopband attenuation everywhere to a very large value, say 60 dB. A conventional FIR filter with the same specifications as in Eqs. (2.55) and (2.56) can now be designed, except that δ_2 is now much smaller than δ_1. Specifically, δ_2 is taken to be such that A_r in Eq. (2.56) is about 60 dB. The resulting filter order, as estimated from Eq. (2.31) is 59. The order $N - 1 = 60$ is actually found to be sufficient, and Fig. 2.15 shows the response.

The preceding solution is highly inefficient because we require only about 35 dB in most of the stopband (which can be achieved with a filter of order 38), and a filter with order 60 is therefore injudicious. One possible way to obtain a more efficient solution is to design a multiband filter with one passband and three stopbands, where the first and third stopbands provide an attenuation exceeding 35 dB, whereas the second stopband has an attenuation exceeding 60 dB. An even more elegant solution is as outlined next. Let us first define a transfer function

$$H_2(z) = (1 - 2z^{-1}\cos\omega_0 + z^{-2}) \tag{2.57}$$

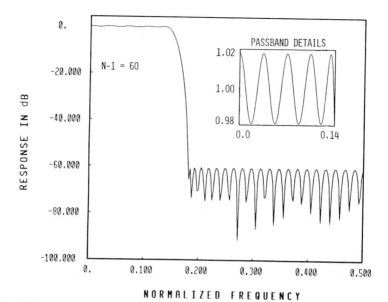

Fig. 2.15. Example 6: Conventional method for increased attenuation around $\omega_0 = 0.78\pi$.

that has a transmission zero at $\omega_0 = 0.78\pi$. The overall transfer function $H(z)$ is obtained in the form of a cascade

$$H(z) = H_1(z)H_2(z) \tag{2.58}$$

where $H_1(z)$ is designed so that $H(z)$ satisfies the tolerance requirements δ_1 and δ_2 and has equiripple passband behavior. This is accomplished by defining $\hat{D}(e^{j\omega})$ and $\hat{W}(e^{j\omega})$ in Eq. (2.25) as

$$\hat{D}(e^{j\omega}) = \begin{cases} \dfrac{1}{|H_2(e^{j\omega})|}, & 0 \le \omega \le \omega_p \\ 0, & \omega_r \le \omega \le \pi \end{cases} \tag{2.59}$$

$$\hat{W}(e^{j\omega}) = \begin{cases} |H_2(e^{j\omega})|, & 0 \le \omega \le \omega_p \\ \dfrac{\delta_1}{\delta_2}|H_2(e^{j\omega})|, & \omega_r \le \omega \le \pi \end{cases} \tag{2.60}$$

We get an approximate estimate of the order $N_1 - 1$ of $H_1(z)$ by using Eq. (2.31), which gives $N_1 - 1 = 38$, as mentioned earlier. The value $N_1 - 1 = 40$ is actually found to be sufficient. Figure 2.16 shows the relevant frequency responses. Notice the effect of the transmission zero at $\omega = 0.78\pi = 0.39(2\pi)$. The total number of multipliers in the final implementation is 22. This number is about the same as that required for the conventional transfer function that meets the specifications of Eqs. (2.55) and (2.56) without the additional transmission zero requirement!

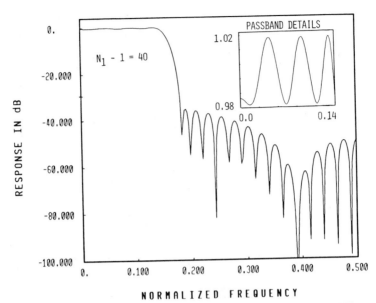

Fig. 2.16. Example 6: Efficient way to obtain transmission zero at $\omega = 0.78\pi$.

Section IX discusses research contributions that make further use of the flexibility offered by the generalized error function of Eq. (2.25) in order to obtain new efficient filter designs for conventional and unconventional design requirements.

V MAXIMALLY FLAT APPROXIMATIONS FOR FIR FILTERS

In Section III we described design techniques for FIR filters based on windowing. The design procedures in that section do not involve computer-aided optimizations but are based on closed-form expressions for the window coefficients. The advantages of this simplicity were also discussed in Section III. In this section we introduce another class of linear-phase FIR filters with closed-form expressions for the transfer function. This class of filters has a *maximally flat* frequency response around $\omega = 0$ and $\omega = \pi$ and was introduced by Herrmann [20] in 1971.

These filters are useful in applications where a signal should be filtered with considerable accuracy near zero frequency. Because the transfer function of this class of filters has a closed-form expression, the design is extremely simple. The frequency response of these filters is monotone in each frequency band, which is required in certain applications. However, for a given set of tolerances, such as δ_1

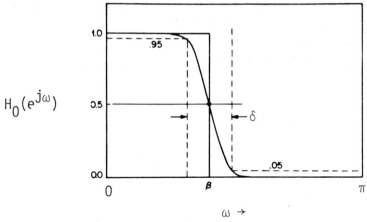

Fig. 2.17. Specifications for a maximally flat lowpass response.

and δ_2, these filters do not have the smallest order, unlike the equiripple designs of Section IV.

The frequency response of a maximally flat, linear-phase FIR filter $H(z)$ is $H(e^{j\omega}) = e^{-j\omega(N-1)/2} H_0(e^{j\omega})$, where $H_0(e^{j\omega})$ is given by [21]

$$H_0(e^{j\omega}) = \cos^{2K}\left(\frac{\omega}{2}\right) \sum_{n=0}^{L-1} d(n)\sin^{2n}\left(\frac{\omega}{2}\right) \qquad (2.61)$$

$$d(n) = \frac{(K-1+n)!}{(K-1)!n!} \qquad (2.62)$$

The filter order is

$$N - 1 = 2(K + L - 1) \qquad (2.63)$$

Note that $d(n)$ are positive integers. The integers K and L, which *completely characterize* the transfer function, are determined from the specifications β and δ indicated in Fig. 2.17. The significances of K and L are clear from Eq. (2.61). Thus, the first $2K - 1$ derivatives of the magnitude response are equal to zero at $\omega = \pi$, and the first $2L - 1$ derivatives are zero at $\omega = 0$. For the rest of this chapter the abbreviation $I_{K,L}(z)$ is used to denote a transfer function $H(z)$ of the above form.

Design Procedure   A

Given the specifications β and δ, the design procedure is simply to compute K and L such that these specifications are satisfied. Kaiser has developed a method for this computation. Once K and L are computed, the response of Eq. (2.61) is then known, and an N-point IDFT is performed to obtain the filter coefficients. A

FORTRAN code for the design of these filters, due to Kaiser, is included in the IEEE software package [19, Program 5.3].

For given β and δ, the algorithm for finding K and L is as follows [21]: first obtain an estimate of the filter order as

$$N - 1 = 2\left(\frac{\pi}{\delta}\right)^2 \tag{2.64}$$

Note that the estimated order grows as $1/\delta^2$. Next, define

$$\alpha = \cos^2\left(\frac{\beta}{2}\right) \tag{2.65}$$

and obtain the best rational approximation to α to be

$$\alpha \simeq \frac{K}{N_{\mathrm{p}}} \tag{2.66}$$

$$\frac{N-1}{2} \leq N_{\mathrm{p}} \leq N - 1 \tag{2.67}$$

After determining the above rational approximation, we identify its numerator with the quantity K. With K thus determined, we next find that $L = N_{\mathrm{p}} - K$. We then get the impulse response $h(n)$ from Eq. (2.61) by performing an N-point IDFT. That $h(n)$ is real and symmetric considerably simplifies the IDFT com-

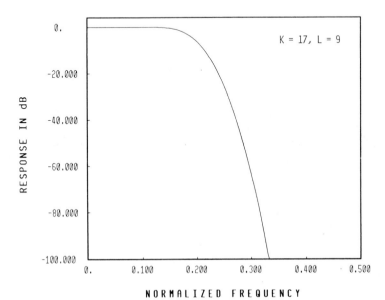

Fig. 2.18. Example 7: Maximally flat lowpass filter.

putation. After $h(n)$ is computed, we can obtain a direct-form implementation with $K + L$ multipliers.

Design Example 7.   Let $\beta = 0.4\pi$ and $\delta = 0.2\pi$ be the required specifications. The values of K and L computed as described above are $K = 17$ and $L = 9$. This corresponds to FIR filter of order $N - 1 = 50$. The computed impulse response coefficients are as shown in Table VII, whereas the frequency response is shown in Fig. 2.18. Note that the frequency response is monotone, and the stopband attenuation is large (exceeding 100 dB) almost everywhere.

We see from Table VII that many of the filter coefficients are very small. Depending upon the required stopband accuracy around $\omega = \pi$, some of these coefficients can be set to zero, leading to more efficient implementations.

TABLE VII

**Example 7: Impulse Response
Coefficients for Maximally Flat
FIR Filter with $K = 17$, $L = 9$
(order = 50) [21]**

$B(1) =$	.39847448
$B(2) =$	.29650429
$B(3) =$	.08785310
$B(4) =$	$-.05124769$
$B(5) =$	$-.05604429$
$B(6) =$	$-.00136329$
$B(7) =$	.02472394
$B(8) =$	.01120456
$B(9) =$	$-.00592278$
$B(10) =$	$-.00709112$
$B(11) =$	$-.00061605$
$B(12) =$	.00232969
$B(13) =$	.00113164
$B(14) =$	$-.00028640$
$B(15) =$	$-.00043241$
$B(16) =$	$-.00008700$
$B(17) =$	.00006961
$B(18) =$	.00004320
$B(19) =$	.00000222
$B(20) =$	$-.00000624$
$B(21) =$	$-.00000241$
$B(22) =$	$-.00000007$
$B(23) =$	.00000016
$B(24) =$	.00000002
$B(25) =$	$-.00000002$
$B(26) =$	$-.00000001$

Note: $B(26)$ stands for $h(0) = h(50)$.
In general, $B(n + 1)$ stands for
$h(25 - n) = h(25 + n)$.   [21] (©
1979 IEEE).

B Minimum-Multiplier Implementations

Sometimes we can obtain an implementation that is more convenient than the direct form by noting that the actual causal transfer function corresponding to Eq. (2.61) can be written as

$$I_{K,L}(z) = H(z) = \left(\frac{1+z^{-1}}{2}\right)^{2K} \sum_{n=0}^{L-1} d(n)(-1)^n \left(\frac{1-z^{-1}}{2}\right)^{2n} z^{-(L-n-1)} \quad (2.68)$$

which can be implemented as shown in Fig. 2.19(a). The advantages of this implementation are that it requires only $L-1$ multipliers and, during the *design* phase, there is no need to compute the actual impulse response coefficients. An equivalent implementation can be obtained with only $K-1$ multipliers. This is useful when K is smaller than L. At the end of Section VII.C we shall explain how this can be accomplished.

For large values of K and L the structure of Fig. 2.19(a) is inconvenient because the coefficients $d(n)$ grow very fast. Thus, with $K = 17$, the coefficients derived from Eq. (2.62) are given by

$$d(0) = 1, d(1) = 17, d(2) = 153, d(3) = 969, d(4) = 4845, \ldots, d(7) = 24, 5157, \ldots$$
$$(2.69)$$

As a result, either a direct-form implementation or the modified implementation of Fig. 2.19(b) as outlined in [22] is preferable. However, for small values of K

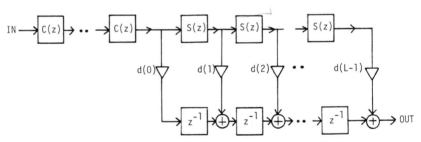

Fig. 2.19(a). $(L-1)$-Multiplier implementation of the maximally flat filter.

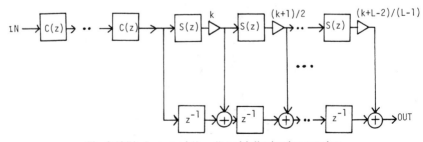

Fig. 2.19(b). Improved $(L-1)$ multiplier implementation.

TABLE VIII

The (K, L) Pair for Maximally Flat FIR Filters (beta and delta are in multiples of π)

β	δ					
	0.1	0.2	0.3	0.4	0.5	0.6
0.1	159, 4	40, 1				
0.2	161, 17	38, 4	19, 2	9, 1		
0.3	104, 27	27, 7	15, 4	8, 2	4, 1	3, 1
0.4	72, 38	17, 9	13, 7	4, 2	4, 2	2, 1
0.5	50, 50	12, 12	6, 6	3, 3	2, 2	1, 1
0.6	38, 72	9, 17	7, 13	2, 4	2, 4	1, 2

and L, the structures of Fig. 2.19(a) are very efficient and are essentially multiplierless because the $d(n)$ are very simple combinations of powers of 2. In view of this we find it convenient to tabulate (Table VIII), for quick design purposes, the values of K and L for various combinations of β and δ. Note that if $\delta/2$ exceeds β or $\pi - \beta$, then the response of Fig. 2.17 is not meaningful. The feasibility of the structures of Fig. 2.19 also depends the roundoff noise level (see Chapter 5).

Further discussions concerning the usefulness of this class of filters are included in Section IX, where several unconventional design methods and implementation strategies are presented. Also, a new class of multiplierless digital FIR filters with very sharp cutoff, based on maximally flat building blocks, is reported in [23].

LINEAR PROGRAMMING APPROACH FOR FIR FILTER DESIGNS   VI

In several situations a linear-phase FIR filter is required to be optimal, subject to certain other constraints. For example, in certain applications the transient part of the step response is required to have as small a ripple size δ_3 as possible. Thus, one has to optimize the frequency response under the constraint that this transient be bounded in magnitude by a desired amount. Another application is in the design of a frequency response with a given fixed passband error δ_1; the filter coefficients are to be chosen so that the stopband error is as small as possible, for fixed filter order $N - 1$, and fixed ω_p and ω_r. Furthermore, some applications require a *flatness* constraint in the passband of the response. Linear programming offers a considerable amount of flexibility for handling these situations and always converges to a solution. In addition, many of the optimal (equiripple) designs described in Section IV can also be handled by linear programming. However, the design time in linear programming is rather large, compared to the techniques of Section IV. It is therefore preferred only in situations that cannot be handled by conventional, faster techniques.

Rabiner [24] has studied the use of linear programming techniques for FIR filter design. Steiglitz and Kaiser [25, 26] have also considered the application of linear programming techiques for designing FIR filters with constraints on the derivatives at certain frequencies. Rabiner, Graham, and Helms have also shown how IIR filters with arbitrary magnitude response specifications can be designed with linear programming techniques [27].

A   The Basic Idea

Let us reconsider the lowpass specification as depicted in Fig. 2.3. Assume for simplicity that the FIR filter order $N - 1$ is even. The response is then given by Eq. (2.2), where

$$H_0(e^{j\omega}) = \sum_{n=0}^{M} b_n \cos(\omega n), \qquad M = \frac{N - 1}{2} \qquad (2.70)$$

from Eq. (2.3). The frequency response requirement can be written in the form of a set of inequalities:

$$H_0(e^{j\omega}) \leq 1 + \delta_1, \qquad 0 \leq \omega \leq \omega_p \qquad (2.71)$$

$$H_0(e^{j\omega}) \geq 1 - \delta_1, \qquad 0 \leq \omega \leq \omega_p \qquad (2.72)$$

$$H_0(e^{j\omega}) \leq \delta_2, \qquad \omega_r \leq \omega \leq \pi \qquad (2.73)$$

$$H_0(e^{j\omega}) \geq -\delta_2, \qquad \omega_r \leq \omega \leq \pi \qquad (2.74)$$

where ω_p, ω_r, and $N - 1$ are assumed to be given. The above constraints are written at a dense grid of frequencies,

$$\omega_1, \omega_2, \ldots, \omega_{rM} \qquad (2.75)$$

where rM is a properly chosen integral multiple of M. Since $H_0(e^{j\omega})$ is in the form of Eq. (2.70), Eqs. (2.71)–(2.74) represent a set of *linear* inequalities. The objective function Φ to be minimized is typically a linear combination of δ_1 and δ_2, but there are other possible choices. For example, δ_1 can be fixed at a predetermined value, and $\Phi = \delta_2$ then minimized. In any case, since the inequalities and Φ are linear in the unknown variables b_n we can minimize Φ by linear programming.

B   Examples of Constraints

Let us consider the case where δ_1 is fixed and $\Phi = \delta_2$ should be minimized. There are a total of $M + 2$ variables, $b_0, b_1, \ldots, b_M$, *and* δ_2, in the problem. If a linear programming problem of the above form has N_1 variables and N_2

inequalities, where $N_2 \geq N_1$, then the optimal solution is such that at least N_1 of the N_2 inequalities are satisfied with equality [24]. Thus, in the above design problem there are at least $M + 2$ frequencies in the region of interest where the approximation error attains the peak value. In other words, the conditions of the alternation theorem of Section IV are satisfied by the solution, which is therefore optimal.

Constraints on the step response can be imposed simply by incorporating additional inequalities of the form

$$-\delta_3 \leq g(n) \leq \delta_3, \qquad 0 \leq n \leq n_1 \tag{2.76}$$

where $g(n)$ is the step response given by

$$g(n) = \sum_{m=0}^{n} h(m) \tag{2.77}$$

In Eq. (2.76), n_1 is the sample number up to which the step response is expected to oscillate around zero. Note that the constraints are still linear in terms of the coefficients $h(n)$, which are linearly related to b_n, as shown in Table IV. The objective function now can be a linear combination of δ_1, δ_2, and δ_3. Or one could fix δ_3 to be a desired value and then optimize a linear combination of δ_1 and δ_2. Clearly there are now several possible choices of the objective function.

Similarly, if one is interested in constraining the flatness of the response at a given frequency, say at ω_k, then the following constraints can be added:

$$\left. \frac{d^m H_0(e^{j\omega})}{d\omega^m} \right|_{\omega = \omega_k} \leq 0, \qquad m = 1, 2, \ldots, N_1 \tag{2.78}$$

$$\left. \frac{d^m H_0(e^{j\omega})}{d\omega^m} \right|_{\omega = \omega_k} \geq 0, \qquad m = 1, 2, \ldots, N_1 \tag{2.79}$$

This is to insure that the first N_1 derivatives of the response are zero at ω_k. The constraints of Eqs. (2.78) and (2.79) are still linear in the coefficients b_n. We can design FIR filters with monotone passbands and equiripple stopbands by incorporating flatness as described above; Steiglitz [25] has presented a FORTRAN source code for this purpose. In applications where passband ripples are objectionable [6], these monotone filters serve as the next best alternative. For example, in a communication link with several repeater stations, the filters in the stations form a long cascade, and, as a result, the passband error δ_1 accumulates. If, however, each of these filters has an extremely flat passband, then the overall passband error of the entire link is within acceptable bounds.

The linear programming approach can be used for designing arbitrary shapes of the frequency response, including multiband filters with arbitrary specifications and differentiators. In general, if $D(e^{j\omega})$ is the response to be approximated by the quantity $H_0(e^{j\omega})$, then the set of linear inequalities

$$-W(e^{j\omega})\delta \leq |H_0(e^{j\omega}) - D(e^{j\omega})| \leq W(e^{j\omega})\delta \tag{2.80}$$

is used at a dense grid of frequencies. Here $W(e^{j\omega})$ is the weighting function, which serves a purpose analogous to the weighting function in Eq. (2.25). In particular, if $W(e^{j\omega})$ is chosen to be equal to $1/D(e^{j\omega})$ (assuming that $D(e^{j\omega})$ is nonzero) then the *relative* error of approximation has equiripple behavior.

A number of FIR filter design examples based on linear programming can be found in [24]–[26]. We conclude this section with an example from [24].

Design Example 8. Consider an optimal FIR design with a constraint on the step response as in Eq. (2.76). Assume that δ_3 is required to be 0.03, and that the filter order is $N - 1 = 24$. Assume further that the constraint $\delta_1 = 25\delta_2$ is

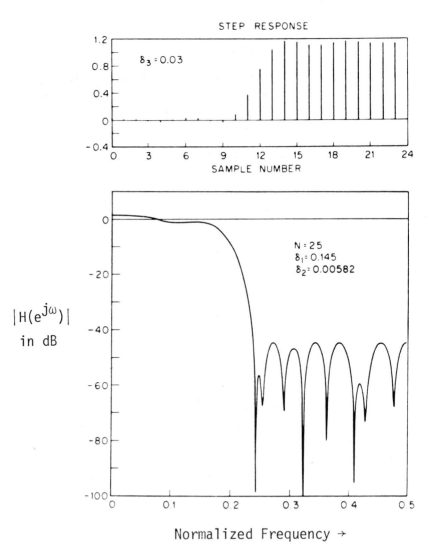

Fig. 2.20. Example 8: Lowpass FIR design based on linear programming (after Rabiner [24]) (© 1972 IEEE).

included along with Eqs. (2.71)–(2.74). Then the solution to the linear program-ming formulation yields the values $\delta_1 = 0.145$ and $\delta_2 = 0.00582$ for the passband and stopband errors. The resulting filter is not equiripple any more, as seen from the frequency response plot of Fig. 2.20.

In the above example, if δ_3 is left unconstrained and the optimization performed with linear programming, the result is an equiripple design, with the response as shown in Fig. 2.21. The resulting values of the errors are $\delta_1 = 0.06$, $\delta_2 = 0.00237$, $\delta_3 = 0.12$. Figures 2.20 and 2.21 also show the step responses.

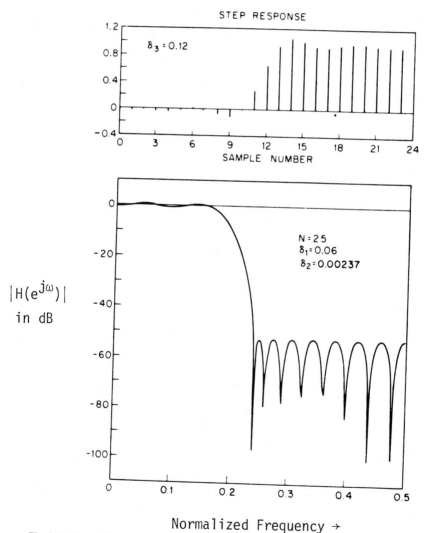

Fig. 2.21. Repetition of Example 8 with the step-response ripple δ_3 unconstrained [24] (© 1972 IEEE).

VII FREQUENCY TRANSFORMATIONS IN FIR FILTERS

Let us assume that a digital filter, say lowpass, has been designed and implemented as an interconnection of multipliers, delays, and adders. There are
applications in which it is desirable to change the cutoff frequency ω_p by
changing the multiplier values in the *implementation*, typically in real time. An
obvious way to change the cutoff frequency is to redesign the entire filter, but this
may be impractical for several reasons. With optimal FIR filters of a given length,
for example, redesigning involves rerunning the entire Remez exchange algorithm. This may not be feasible within the time frame available for readjusting
the cutoff frequency. It is therefore of interest to design the filter circuit such that
the change of one or a few parameters results in the desired tuning over the
desired frequency range. In this section we discuss methods for achieving this.

A All-Pass-Based Transformations

Consider a linear-phase lowpass FIR filter with bandedges Ω_p and Ω_r. Assume
that we wish to have a single parameter that controls the exact value of Ω_p. This
can be accomplished by first designing a prototype filter with passband edge ω_p
(where ω_p is the nominal value of Ω_p) and then replacing each delay unit z^{-1} with
a stable all-pass function. For example,

$$z^{-1} = \frac{\alpha + Z^{-1}}{1 + \alpha Z^{-1}} \tag{2.81}$$

Letting $Z = e^{j\Omega}$ and $z = e^{j\omega}$, the prototype frequency ω is related to the actual
frequency Ω by

$$\Omega = \omega + 2\tan^{-1}\left[\frac{\alpha \sin \omega}{1 - \alpha \cos \omega}\right] \tag{2.82}$$

For each real-valued Ω there exists a unique real-valued ω, and the converse is
also true. The above is therefore a valid *frequency transformation* (or spectral
transformation). The tuning parameter α controls the actual passband edge.
Further details can be found in [28]. Since the substitution of Eq. (2.81) can
actually be incorporated into the structure, we therefore have a means of
adjusting the cutoff frequency by varying the physical multiplier-parameter α.

The obvious disadvantage of this all-pass-based spectral transformation is
that the resulting filter is not FIR and therefore does not have linear-phase
characteristics, even though the prototype filter may have linear phase. For FIR
filters, therefore, a different frequency transformation is required.

Transformations Based on Trigonometric Building Blocks   B

An elegant approach to this problem was outlined by Oppenheim *et al.* in 1976 for type 1 FIR filters [29]. This method, however, is not based on replacement of delay units but on replacement of another type of building block, to be described shortly. The direct-form structure of Fig. 2.1, which has delays as the building blocks, is not suitable for application of the proposed transformation technique; we should first derive a new filter structure that contains the building blocks on which the transformation operates. We now proceed to do this.

Recall that for type 1 filter the zero-phase part can be written as a sum of cosines, as shown in Table IV. From this we get

$$H_0(z) = \frac{1}{2} \sum_{n=1}^{(N-1)/2} b_n(z^n + z^{-n}) + b_0 \tag{2.83}$$

Now $z^n + z^{-n}$ represents $2\cos n\omega$ on the unit circle. But $\cos n\omega$ can be written as

$$\cos n\omega = \mathscr{T}_n[\cos \omega] \tag{2.84}$$

where $\mathscr{T}_n(X)$ represents the nth-order Chebyshev polynomial in the variable X. Thus we can write $H_0(z)$ as

$$H_0(z) = \sum_{n=1}^{(N-1)/2} b_n \mathscr{T}_n\left(\frac{z + z^{-1}}{2}\right) + b_0 \tag{2.85}$$

This can be rearranged as a polynomial in $(z + z^{-1})/2$:

$$H_0(z) = \sum_{k=0}^{(N-1)/2} a_k \left(\frac{z + z^{-1}}{2}\right)^k \tag{2.86}$$

The frequency response corresponding to Eq. (2.86) is

$$H_0(e^{j\omega}) = \sum_{k=0}^{(N-1)/2} a_k \cos^k \omega \tag{2.87}$$

Thus, the response can be written entirely in terms of the variable $\cos \omega$. Let us now assume that a circuit with building blocks of the form $(z + z^{-1})/2$ has been built in order to realize Eq. (2.86), as shown in Fig. 2.22(a). (We show later how to overcome the noncausality of the building blocks, caused by the positive powers of z.) If we now replace $(z + z^{-1})/2$ with functions $F(Z)$, real valued on the unit circle and satisfying

$$-1 \le F(e^{j\Omega}) \le 1 \tag{2.88}$$

then for each frequency Ω we can find a unique prototype frequency ω from the relation

$$\omega = \cos^{-1}(F(e^{j\Omega})) \tag{2.89}$$

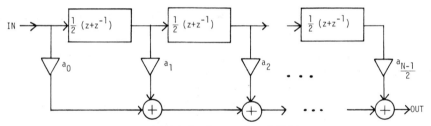

Fig. 2.22(a). Implementation of $H_0(z)$.

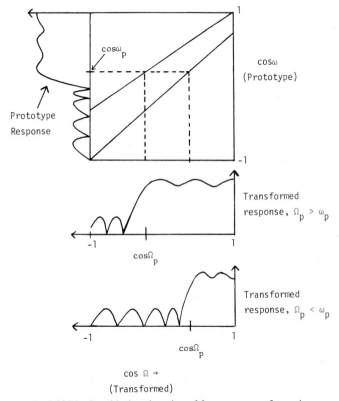

Fig. 2.22(b). Graphical explanation of frequency transformation.

Thus we have a valid frequency transformation. For example, we can obtain the transformation

$$\cos \omega = \sum_{k=0}^{P} A_k \cos^k \Omega \tag{2.90}$$

$$F(Z) = \sum_{k=0}^{P} A_k \left(\frac{Z + Z^{-1}}{2} \right)^k \tag{2.91}$$

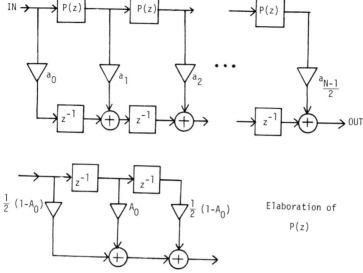

Fig. 2.22(c). Implementation of transformed filter.

where A_k are such that Eq. (2.88) is satisfied. Note that, even though Eq. (2.88) holds by construction of the right side of Eq. (2.90), $\cos \Omega$ in Eq. (2.90) may not turn out to be of magnitude less than unity for an arbitrary prototype frequency ω. In other words, there may exist certain portions of the prototype frequency response that do not map onto the unit circle of the transformed plane. This is not generally harmful for frequency responses that are piecewise constant.

As a specific special case consider the transformation

$$\cos \omega = A_0 + A_1 \cos \Omega \qquad (2.92)$$

In terms of the z variables,

$$\frac{z + z^{-1}}{2} = A_0 + A_1 \left(\frac{Z + Z^{-1}}{2} \right)$$

Essentially, given a prototype filter with attenuation α_p at some frequency ω_p, the transformed filter has the same attenuation at frequency Ω_p, where ω_p and Ω_p are related by Eq. (2.92).

Figure 2.22(b) graphically explains how the transformation works. A major requirement on a *legal* transformation is that, for every *actual* frequency Ω in the range $0 \le \Omega \le 2\pi$, there should exist a unique frequency ω in the range $0 \le \omega \le 2\pi$ satisfying Eq. (2.92). In other words, a straight line representing Eq. (2.92) in Fig. 2.22(b) should satisfy

$$-1 \le A_0 + A_1 \cos \Omega \le 1 \qquad (2.93)$$

Let us assume that we wish to convert a lowpass prototype filter with cutoff frequency ω_p into a lowpass filter with cutoff frequency Ω_p. Figure 2.22(b) shows the cases $\Omega_p < \omega_p$ and $\Omega_p > \omega_p$. In either case, once the passband edge has been mapped as desired, we wish the stopband edge ω_r to map into a frequency Ω_r such that Ω_r is as close to the mapped Ω_p as possible. This is desirable because the transformed filter then has the narrowest possible transition bandwidth (for a given order and for a given set of tolerances δ_1 and δ_2). From Fig. 2.22(b) it is clear how this can be accomplished: the straight line representing the mapping of Eq. (2.92), which passes through the point $(\cos \Omega_p, \cos \omega_p)$, must have the largest possible slope, subject to the constraint of Eq. (2.93). Thus, when we want $\Omega_p > \omega_p$ (i.e., when we want to expand the passband width), the point $\omega = 0$ must map onto $\Omega = 0$. Similarly, if we wish to *shrink* the passband width, the best possible transformation is the one that maps $\omega = \pi$ to $\Omega = \pi$.

When we attempt to expand the bandwidth ($\Omega_p > \omega_p$), the requirement that $\omega = 0$ maps onto to $\Omega = 0$ gives the constraint $A_0 + A_1 = 1$. Thus, the mapping

$$\cos \omega = A_0 + (1 - A_0)\cos \Omega \qquad (2.94)$$

leads to such a variable-cutoff filter provided $0 \le A_0 < 1$. Similarly, to shrink the passband with ($\Omega_p < \omega_p$), we should use

$$\cos \omega = A_0 + (1 + A_0)\cos \Omega \qquad (2.95)$$

with $-1 < A_0 \le 0$.

By choosing A_0 and A_1 properly, we can use the same transformation of Eq. (2.92) for highpass filters as well.

If the transformation of Eq. (2.94) is applied to the transfer function Eq. (2.86), the resulting transfer function is

$$G_0(Z) = \sum_{k=0}^{(N-1)/2} a_k Z^k \left(\frac{1 - A_0 + 2A_0 Z^{-1} + (1 - A_0)Z^{-2}}{2} \right)^k \qquad (2.96)$$

which represents a noncausal transfer function. The causal version is

$$Z^{-(N-1)/2} G_0(Z) = \sum_{k=0}^{(N-1)/2} a_k Z^{-((N-1)/2 - k)} \left(\frac{1 - A_0 + 2A_0 Z^{-1} + (1 - A_0)Z^{-2}}{2} \right)^k \qquad (2.97)$$

which can be implemented as in Fig. 2.22(c). Thus, simply by changing the parameter A_0 in Fig. 2.22(c), we can obtain a wide range of transfer functions.

Design Example 9. For a numerical example of the first-order transformation of Eq. (2.92), consider again the FIR filter of Example 2, which is an equiripple filter of order $N - 1 = 52$, with passband cutoff frequency $\omega_p = 0.16\pi$. We wish to design a new lowpass filter with the same passband and stopband errors δ_1 and δ_2 but with passband edge at $\Omega_p = 0.3\pi$. Since $\Omega_p > \omega_p$, we use Eq. (2.94), from which we can compute $A_0 = 0.7$. The response of the transformed filter is shown in Fig. 2.23. Note that the entire passband region $(0, \omega_p)$ gets mapped into $(0, \Omega_p)$, whereas only a portion of the stopband response (ω_r, ω_{max}) gets mapped onto (Ω_r, π), where

$$\Omega_r = \cos^{-1}\left(\frac{\cos \omega_r - A_0}{1 - A_0}\right) \tag{2.98}$$

In other words, only a portion of the unit circle of the prototype gets mapped onto the unit circle of the resulting filter. Clearly, this is not harmful, because the transformed response is a well-defined lowpass response with desired tolerances δ_1 and δ_2.

The first-order transformation of Eq. (2.92) leaves the filter order unchanged. Moreover, δ_1 and δ_2 remain unchanged for obvious reasons. Thus, if the prototype is optimal, the resulting filter is usually not optimal, because the transition bandwidth can only *increase* as a result of transformation.

Using Eq. (2.91), we can define higher-order transformations in order to get lowpass to bandpass conversions, and so on. The concept of frequency transformations in FIR filters is important not only for the design of variable-cutoff filters but also for certain other applications: for example, [23] develops a "hierarchical" procedure for designing multiplierless FIR filters based on the frequency transformation concept. Details of these filters are beyond the scope of this chapter.

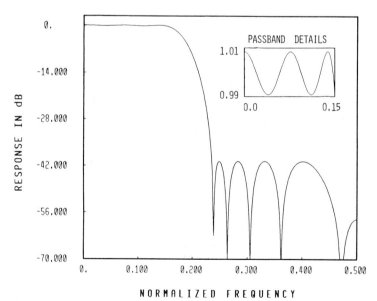

Fig. 2.23. Example 9. The response of Example 2 (Fig. 2.9) frequency transformed.

C   Other Types of Transformations

We next proceed to describe certain related transformation techniques that are extremely useful in FIR design practice. Let $H(z)$ represent the transfer function of a linear-phase FIR filter, as given by Eq. (2.1). The frequency response $H(e^{j\omega})$ can be written in terms of the zero-phase response $H_0(e^{j\omega})$, as in Eq. (2.2). Assuming that $H(z)$ is lowpass with $N - 1$ even, we can write

$$H_0(e^{j\omega}) = \sum_{n=0}^{(N-1)/2} b_n \cos \omega n \qquad (2.99)$$

Note that $H_0(e^{j\omega})$ is an even function of ω. A typical plot of $H_0(e^{j\omega})$ in Eq. (2.99) is shown in Fig. 2.24(a). Let us now define a new transfer function

$$H_1(z) = z^{-(N-1)/2} - H(z) = z^{-(N-1)/2}(1 - H_0(z)) \qquad (2.100)$$

Clearly, the zero-phase response $H_{10}(z)$ of $H_1(z)$ is

$$H_{10}(e^{j\omega}) = 1 - H_0(e^{j\omega}) \qquad (2.101)$$

Figure 2.24(b) shows the function $H_{10}(e^{j\omega})$, which is clearly highpass, with passband edge equal to ω_r and stopband edge equal to ω_p. Next define a transfer function

$$G(z) = H_1(-z) = (-z)^{-(N-1)/2}(1 - H_0(-z)) \qquad (2.102)$$

Note that on the unit circle $H_0(-z)$ becomes

$$H_0(-z) = H_0(-e^{j\omega}) = H_0(e^{j(\omega - \pi)}) = H_0(e^{j(\pi - \omega)}) \qquad (2.103)$$

where we used the fact that $H_0(e^{j\omega})$ is an even function of ω. Thus, letting $G(e^{j\omega}) = e^{-j\omega(N-1)/2} G_0(e^{j\omega})$, we obtain the zero-phase response $G_0(e^{j\omega})$ of $G(z)$:

$$(-1)^{(N-1)/2} G_0(e^{j\omega}) = 1 - H_0(e^{j(\pi - \omega)}) = H_{10}(e^{j(\pi - \omega)}) \qquad (2.104)$$

Thus, based on the plot of H_{10} in Fig. 2.24(b), we can plot the response $G_0(e^{j\omega})$ given by Eq. (2.104). This is shown in Fig. 2.24(c).

It is thus clear that $G(z)$ again represents a linear-phase lowpass FIR filter of order $N - 1$, but its passband edge is $\theta_p = \pi - \omega_r$, whereas the stopband edge is $\theta_r = \pi - \omega_p$. Moreover, the passband tolerance for $G(z)$ is δ_2, whereas the stopband tolerance is δ_1. The above sequence of operations is therefore a simple procedure to convert a linear-phase lowpass filter $H(z)$ into a linear-phase lowpass filter $G(z)$ such that the passband parameters and stopband parameters are merely interchanged. These ideas are summarized in Table IX. Figure 2.24(d) shows a physical circuit for obtaining $G(z)$ from $H(z)$. Note that there are two crucial requirements to be satisfied for this "trick" to work. The first is that the transfer function $H(z)$ must have linear phase so we can subtract the zero-phase response from unity, as in Eq. (2.100). The second requirement is that the order $N - 1$ should be even so that the delay $z^{-(N-1)/2}$ in Fig. 2.24(d) is realizable.

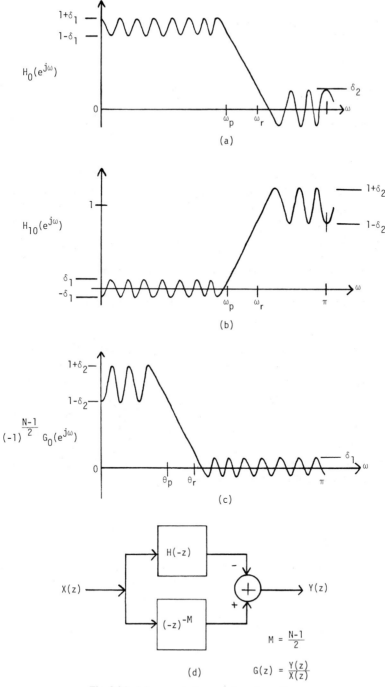

Fig. 2.24. A lowpass to lowpass transformation.

TABLE IX

Interchanging the Passband and Stopband Characteristics

Transfer function	Passband edge	Stopband edge	Passband tolerance	Stopband tolerance
$H(z)$ (lowpass)	ω_p	ω_r	δ_1	δ_2
$H_1(z)$ (highpass)	ω_r	ω_p	δ_2	δ_1
$G(z)$ (lowpass)	$\pi - \omega_r$	$\pi - \omega_p$	δ_2	δ_1

The above idea of interchanging passband characteristics with stopband characteristics has other important applications. For example, assume that we wish to design a linear-phase FIR filter with a maximally flat passband and an equiripple stopband. A direct design procedure for such specifications is complicated [25–26] and time consuming. However, as will be shown in Section IX, it is much easier to first design a lowpass transfer function $H(z)$ having an equiripple passband and maximally flat stopband. We can then obtain the desired transfer function $G(z)$ from $H(z)$ prescisely as in Fig. 2.24(d). Section IX outlines the detailed procedure for dealing with this problem; related ideas and methods are in [30].

As another application of the above idea, recall that in Section V.B we mentioned that maximally flat FIR filters can be built with only $L - 1$ multipliers by implementing (2.68) directly. We also commented that it is possible to obtain an implementation with $K - 1$ rather than $L - 1$ multipliers, which is suitable when $K < L$. For example, let $K = 3$ and $L = 5$. Let us first design a maximally flat lowpass filter $H(z)$ with K and L interchanged (i.e., $K = 5$ and $L = 3$). Thus $H(z)$ can be built with only two multipliers. From the structure for $H(z)$ if we now obtain the structure of Fig. 2.24(d), the resulting transfer function $G(z)$ is maximally flat lowpass, with K and L restored (i.e., $K = 3$ and $L = 5$). Thus, we have obtained an implementation of $G(z)$ with only $K - 1 = 2$ multipliers.

D Multiple Use of a Given Filter For Response-Sharpening

Consider a lowpass linear-phase FIR transfer function $H(z)$ of order $N - 1$ with response as shown in Fig. 2.24(a). Let us assume that this filter is available in the form of a module (a software module, for example) and that we wish to use this filter to obtain filters with smaller passband and/or stopband errors. If the output sequence generated by $H(z)$ is again passed through $H(z)$, this produces an overall transfer function

$$G_1(z) = H^2(z) = z^{-(N-1)}H_0^2(z) = z^{-(N-1)}G_{10}(z) \qquad (2.105)$$

The response $G_{10}(e^{j\omega})$ is shown in Fig. 2.25(a). The bandedges ω_p and ω_r

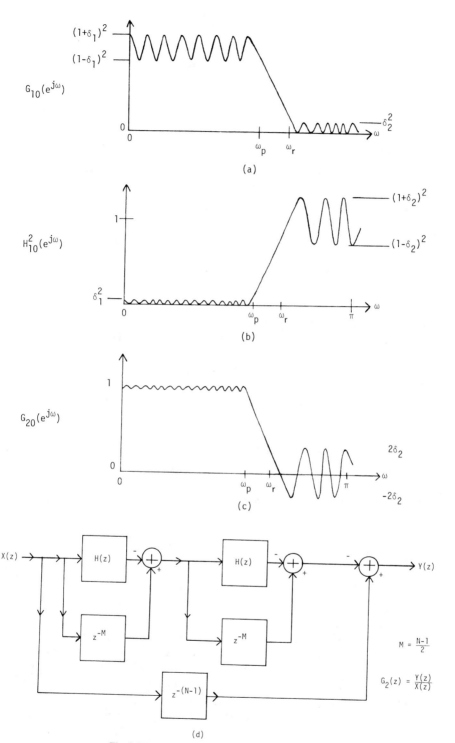

Fig. 2.25. Multiple use of a given filter module.

are unchanged by the squaring operation. Clearly, the peak passband error for $G_1(z)$ is

$$\hat{\delta}_1 = \frac{(1 + \delta_1)^2 - (1 - \delta_1)^2}{2} = 2\delta_1 \tag{2.106}$$

whereas the peak stopband error for $G_1(z)$ is

$$\hat{\delta}_2 = \frac{\delta_2^2}{2} \tag{2.107}$$

Thus, multiple use of the same filter decreases the stopband error, but, unfortunately, the passband error *increases*.

Note that the order of $G_1(z)$ is $2(N - 1)$. Now assume that we want to obtain a transfer function $G_2(z)$ of order $2(N - 1)$ by twice employing $H(z)$ as above, but we want to have a smaller *passband* error. We can do this by the following sequence of operations: first define a transfer function $H_1(z)$ as in Eq. (2.100). The response of $H_1(z)$ is as in Fig. 2.24(b). (This requires that $N - 1$ be even.) Next form the transfer function $H_2(z) = H_1^2(z) = z^{-(N-1)}H_{10}^2(z)$. Figure 2.25(b) shows the response $H_{10}^2(e^{j\omega})$, which is highpass with peak passband error

$$\epsilon_1 = \frac{(1 + \delta_2)^2 - (1 - \delta_2)^2}{2} = 2\delta_2 \tag{2.108}$$

and peak stopband error

$$\epsilon_2 = \delta_1^2/2 \tag{2.109}$$

Finally, define the transfer function

$$G_2(z) = z^{-(N-1)} - H_2(z) \tag{2.110}$$

Figure 2.25(c) shows the response of $G_2(z)$. The peak passband error for $G_2(z)$ is

$$\hat{\delta}_1 = \epsilon_2 = \frac{\delta_1^2}{2} \tag{2.111}$$

whereas the peak stopband error is

$$\hat{\delta}_2 = \epsilon_1 = 2\delta_2 \tag{2.112}$$

Thus the passband error is reduced, but the stopband error increases. Figure 2.25(d) shows the physical structure for the implementation of $G_2(z)$.

Next suppose we want to devise a scheme so that using the filter $H(z)$ several times improves the passband and stopband errors. We can do this if we make judicious use of $H(z)$ three times rather than twice, which gives an overall filter order of $3(N - 1)$. A general theory for accomplishing this kind of improvement, based on the concept of *amplitude change function*, was introduced by Kaiser and Hamming [31]. The details of this ingenious concept are beyond the scope of this chapter, so we present the simplest result that is of immediate relevance to our discussion.

Basically, given a linear-phase FIR transfer function $H(z) = z^{-(N-1)/2}H_0(z)$ of order $N - 1$, we wish to construct the linear-phase FIR function $G(z) = z^{-3(N-1)/2}G_0(z)$ such that the real-valued function $G_0(e^{j\omega})$ has smaller passband and stopband errors than the function $H_0(e^{j\omega})$. Let $G_0 = f(H_0)$ denote the functional dependency of G_0 on H_0. The quantity H_0 is close to unity in the passband and close to zero in the stopband. Accordingly, $f(H_0)$ should satisfy $f(0) = 0$, $f(1) = 1$. Furthermore, we would like small deviations of H_0 around *zero* and around *unity* to be reflected as even smaller deviations in G_0. We do this by forcing the derivative of $f(H_0)$ to be equal to zero for $H_0 = 0$ and $H_0 = 1$. The simplest function satisfying all these conditions is $G_0 = f(H_0) = H_0^2(3 - 2H_0)$. Figure 2.26(a) is a sketch of $f(H_0)$.

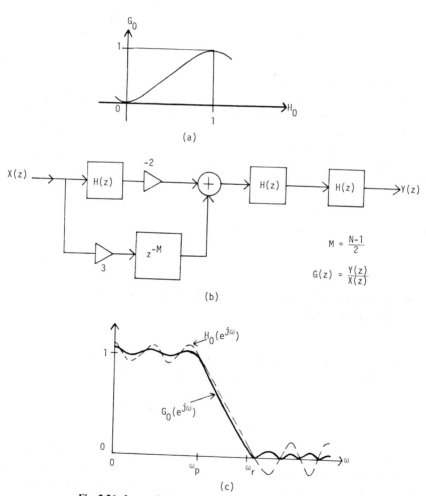

Fig. 2.26. Improving both the passband and the stopband.

TABLE X

**Improving the Passband and Stopband Characteristics by Multiple
Use of the Same Filter**

	Peak passband error	Peak stopband error
$H(z)$	δ_1	δ_2
$G(z)$	$6\delta_1^2$	$\frac{3}{2}\delta_2^2$

The relation in Fig. 2.26(a) can be realized in practice by implementing the scheme in Fig. 2.26(b). Clearly,

$$G(z) = H^2(z)(3z^{-(N-1)/2} - 2H(z)) \tag{2.113}$$

Thus, letting $G(z) = z^{-3(N-1)/2}G_0(z)$ and $H(z) = z^{-(N-1)/2}H_0(z)$, we have

$$G_0(z) = H_0^2(z)(3 - 2H_0(z)) \tag{2.114}$$

as required. The effect of zero slope at $(0, 0)$ and $(1, 1)$ is that the error is reduced in the passband and in the stopband. A Typical plot of $H_0(e^{j\omega})$, shown in Fig. 2.26(c), leads to a corresponding plot of $G_0(e^{j\omega})$, shown in the same figure. Notice that $G_0(e^{j\omega})$ has equiripple behavior in the passband but not in the stopband. However, for small δ_2 the stopband of $G_0(e^{j\omega})$ is almost equiripple. It is easily shown that $G(z)$ has peak passband error of about $6\delta_1^2$ and peak stopband error of about $1.5\delta_2^2$. Table X summarizes these results. For small δ_1 and δ_2 there is a remarkable improvement in passband and stopband errors. However, if he original filter $H(z)$ has large δ_1 and δ_2, then the resulting filter $G(z)$ may be even worse than $H(z)$. To summarize in a qualitative way, the structure of Fig. 2.26(b) makes *good filters better* and *bad filters worse*.

VIII TWO-DIMENSIONAL LINEAR-PHASE FIR FILTER DESIGN AND IMPLEMENTATION

A two-dimensional (2-D) FIR filter with impulse response coefficients $h(n_1, n_2)$, $0 \le n_1 \le N_1 - 1, 0 \le n_2 \le N_2 - 1$, has transfer function

$$H(z_1, z_2) = \sum_{n_1=0}^{N_1-1} \sum_{n_2=0}^{N_2-1} h(n_1, n_2)z_1^{-n_1}z_2^{-n_2} \tag{2.115}$$

The impulse response $h(n_1, n_2)$ is *causal*—that is, it vanishes for $n_1 \le 0$ and for $n_2 \le 0$. The above filter is said to be an $(N_1 \times N_2)$-point FIR filter. We obtain the frequency response from Eq. (2.115) by setting $z_1 = e^{j\omega_1}$ and $z_2 = e^{j\omega_2}$. Such filters are used in image processing problems, such as image enhancement and compensation for linear optical degradations, and so on [32]. The input signal

$x(n_1, n_2)$ and the output signal $y(n_1, n_2)$ are related through the convolution sum

$$y(n_1, n_2) = \sum_{m_1=0}^{n_1} \sum_{m_2=0}^{n_2} x(m_1, m_2) h(n_1 - m_1, n_2 - m_2) \qquad (2.116)$$

where $h(n_1, n_2)$ and $x(n_1, n_2)$ are assumed to be causal.

Two-Dimensional Filter Implementation A

The implementation of such filters can be accomplished by directly computing the 2-D convolution sum of Eq. (2.116). For an $N \times N$ filter the number of multiplications involved per computed output sample is proportional to N^2. For large N the implementation is therefore expensive, and fast convolution methods (based on 2-D FFT techniques) must be adopted. For filters with impulse response arrays larger than 10×10, FFT methods are more efficient than direct convolution.

Many of the linear-phase FIR design methods for one-dimensional (1-D) filters can be extended to the 2-D case. Windowing techniques can be directly extended; optimization methods based on the linear programming approach or the Remez exchange techniques can all be extended as described in [2]. A major disadvantage of such a direct optimization is that the optimization time tends to be very large for a filter of moderate size because the number of constraint equations and problem variables tends to be large. As a result, direct optimization techniques are limited to moderate-sized 2-D filters, such as 10×10 impulse response filters. For filters of higher orders an elegant indirect approach proposed by McClellan [33] is the most suitable technique; it is the topic of the next subsection.

McClellan's Transformation Technique B

In 1973, McClellan [33] showed how 1-D linear-phase FIR filters can be transformed to 2-D linear-phase FIR filters. The method is based on the idea of frequency transformation discussed in Section VII. Mecklenbrauker, Mersereau, and Quatieri have studied the design and implementation of such filters in considerable detail [32, 34].

The advantage of such an indirect mapping-based method is clear: the design time is much less because 1-D filters can be designed very efficiently by algorithms described earlier in this chapter. As a result, higher-order filters (such as 40×40 or more) can be designed with very little computational effort (compared to a direct 2-D method). The 2-D filters designed by mapping are often optimal. Finally, the actual implementation of these filters is much more efficient (in terms of number of multiplications) than a direct implementation of a directly designed

2-D filter. The implementation of a mapping-based filter is more efficient than an FFT-based implementation of a directly designed optimal filter [2], up to an impulse response size of about 45×45. (Recall that an FFT-based method is better than a direct convolution approach for orders exceeding only 10×10.)

To understand the basic idea, recall that a linear-phase FIR filter of even order can be written as in Eq. (2.2), where $H_0(e^\omega)$ is as in Eq. (2.87). Instead of replacing $\cos \omega$ in Eq. (2.87) by $F(e^{j\Omega})$, suppose that we replace it as follows:

$$\cos \omega = A \cos \omega_1 + B \cos \omega_2 + C \cos \omega_1 \cos \omega_2 + D \qquad (2.117)$$

where ω_1 and ω_2 are the frequencies of the 2-D filter. The constants A, B, C, D are such that the right side of Eq. (2.117) is in the range $[-1, 1]$ for $0 \le \omega_1, \omega_2 \le \pi$. Thus, for each frequency pair (ω_1, ω_2), we get a unique *prototype* frequency ω, so Eq. (2.117) represents a meaningful transformation. The response of Eq. (2.87) gets mapped into

$$H_0(e^{j\omega_1}, e^{j\omega_2}) = \sum_{m=0}^{M_1} \sum_{n=0}^{M_2} b(m, n)\cos(m\omega_1)\cos(n\omega_2) \qquad (2.118)$$

so the filter design involves designing the parameters A, B, C, D and the prototype. Since the former has been described in earlier sections, we deal only with the design of the mapping parameters A, B, C, D.

From Eq. (2.117) we can write

$$\omega_2 = \cos^{-1}\left(\frac{\cos \omega - D - A \cos \omega_1}{B + C \cos \omega_1}\right) \qquad (2.119)$$

Thus a given value of ω is represented by a contour in the (ω_1, ω_2)-plane, whose exact shape is governed by the contour parameters A, B, C, D. From Eq. (2.119) it can be shown that the conditions $|C| \le |A|$ and $|C| \le |B|$ insure, respectively, that there are no horizontal or vertical contours (except at the boundaries of the square $[0, \pi] \times [0, \pi]$ in the (ω_1, ω_2)-plane. Moreover, the contours are always monotone [33], with the mapping as in Eq. (2.117). McClellan [33] considers two examples: one with a monotone decreasing set of contours, and one with a monotone increasing set. These contours can be used, respectively, to design 2-D lowpass and 2-D fan filters, starting from a 1-D prototype. For lowpass designs, we can choose the contour parameters such that

$$C = -D \qquad A = 1 - B \qquad (2.120)$$

so that the contours are monotone decreasing, as shown in Fig. 2.27. (In Fig. 2.27, the labels on the contour represent the normalized 1-D frequency $f = \omega/2\pi$.) Note that, for each 2-D frequency ω_1, ω_2, there corresponds a unique frequency ω of the 1-D prototype, and hence the ripple sizes δ_1 and δ_2 are preserved during the transformation. For fan filters, a typical choice would be $C = D$ and $A = B + 1$.

As a specific example, let $A = 0.5$ and $C = 0.5$ and assume that a lowpass 1-D prototype should be transformed into a lowpass 2-D filter. Then $B = 1 - A =$

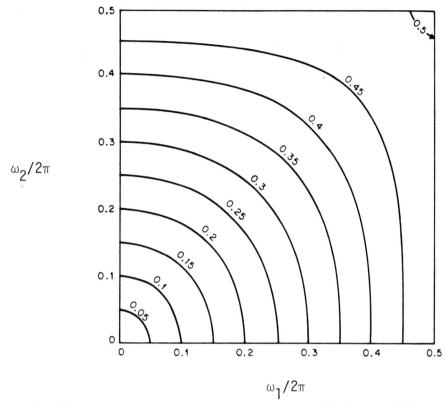

$\omega_2/2\pi$

$\omega_1/2\pi$

Fig. 2.27. Contours of constant ω, when $A = B = C = -D = 0.5$. [16] (© 1975 IEEE).

0.5 and $D = -C = -0.5$. This leads to

$$\cos \omega = 0.5(\cos \omega_1 + \cos \omega_2) + 0.5 \cos \omega_1 \cos \omega_2 - 0.5 \qquad (2.121)$$

which shows that the point $\omega = 0$ maps into ($\omega_1 = \omega_2 = \pi$). Moreover, for small values of ω, ω_1, and ω_2 we get the approximate relation $\omega^2 = \omega_1^2 + \omega_2^2$, which shows that the contours of constant ω are circular for small frequencies (Fig. 2.27). Note that for large ω the contours flatten out and resemble rectangles.

Design Example 10. Assume that we wish to design a lowpass 2-D equiripple filter with the passband edge and stopband edge represented by approximately circular contours with radii $2\pi/6$ and $2\pi/3$, respectively. [See Fig. 2.28(a)]. Assume that the peak passband and stopband errors of the 2-D filters are required to be $\delta_1 \leq 0.08$ and $\delta_2 \leq 0.008$. The transformation of Eq. (2.121) gives contours that are only approximately circular, so we adopt the following intuitive guideline to compute the bandedges of the prototype 1-D filter: the 2-D frequency $(0, 2\pi/6)$ is a point on the contour representing the passband edge. Substituting these values of ω_1 and ω_2 in Eq. (2.121), we get $\omega = 2\pi/6$. Thus, the

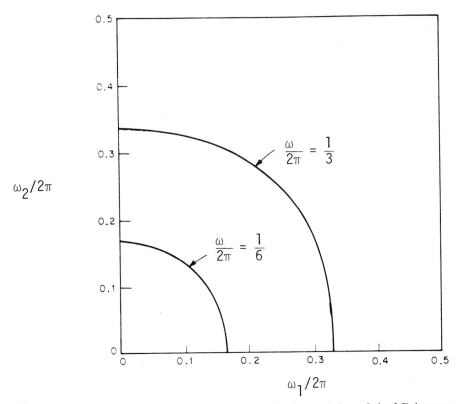

$\omega_2/2\pi$

$\omega_1/2\pi$

Fig. 2.28(a). Example 10: Circular contours representing the bandedges of the 2-D lowpass specification.

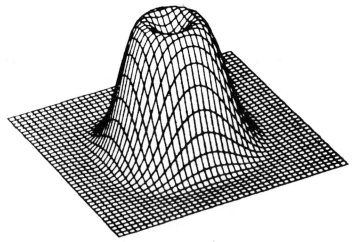

Fig. 2.28(b). Example 10: The frequency response of the resulting 9×9 2-D FIR filter [59].

1-D prototype can be designed to have $\omega_p = 2\pi/6$. In an analogous manner we can find $\omega_r = 2\pi/3$.

Now δ_1 and δ_2 of the 2-D filter are the same as those of the 1-D prototype. We therefore have the complete specifications for the 1-D equiripple design:

$$\omega_p = \frac{2\pi}{6}, \quad \omega_r = \frac{2\pi}{3}, \quad \delta_1 = 0.08, \quad \delta_2 = 0.008 \tag{2.122}$$

These requirements are satisfied by a filter of order $N - 1 = 8$. The transformation of Eq. (2.121) now gives rise to a 2-D filter of length 9×9. Figure 2.28(b) shows the frequency response.

Generalization of McClellan's Transformation   C

McClellan's transformation has been generalized by Mersereau *et al.* [32] to a considerable extent, making it possible for the designer to have a wide variety of choices for contour shaping and contour optimization. This generalization is based on the observations that the mapping of Eq. (2.117) is a special case of the transformation

$$\cos \omega = F(\omega_1, \omega_2) \tag{2.123}$$

where

$$F(\omega_1, \omega_2) = \sum_{p=0}^{P} \sum_{q=0}^{Q} t(p, q) \cos(p\omega_1)\cos(q\omega_2) \tag{2.124}$$

If the prototype 1-D filter has an impulse response of length $N = 2M + 1$, then the 2-D filter has a $(2MP + 1) \times (2MQ + 1)$ impulse response. However, the design process is made considerably simpler by designing the contour parameters $t(p, q)$ first and then the prototype impulse response. This then involves only $(P + 1) \times (Q + 1) + M + 1$ parameters.

Mersereau *et al.* [32] actually show how $t(p, q)$ can be chosen optimally. In general, there are two known methods for designing the contour parameters $t(p, q)$. In the first method, called the *contour matching approach*, we formulate an optimization problem that enables us to approximate certain contour shapes. For instance, we can force the passband edge of the 2-D response to be as close as possible to an ellipse. Or we can design a circularly symmetric lowpass filter where the contour representing the passband edge is as close as possible to a circle. At the other extreme, the method can also be used to design the types of responses required in applications such as reconstruction of objects from their projections [32]. Contour mapping problems can be solved by linear optimization techniques, as elaborated in [32].

The second method, which works well only for frequency responses that are piecewise constant, is based on the viewpoint that the design of $t(p, q)$ is itself a filter design problem. The basic idea is to design the contour parameters such that the transition bandwidth $\omega_r - \omega_p$ of the prototype 1-D filter is maximized. Clearly, this minimizes the peak errors in the passband and stopband for a given prototype filter length. This problem can also be formulated as a linear programming design problem to solve for the coefficients $t(p, q)$. Techniques more efficient than linear programming are also known from works of Kamp and Thiran [35]. All details are omitted here in the interests of brevity.

D Implementation Considerations

The most efficient way to implement 2-D FIR filters using McClellan's transformation is to recognize that a zero-phase 1-D FIR filter can be implemented exactly as in (2.86), and hence the 2-D design is obtainable simply by replacing the building blocks $(z + z^{-1})/2$ with the z-domain equivalent of $F(\omega_1, \omega_2)$ in Eq. (2.124). Such an implementation is computationally much more efficient than a direct implementation of the convolution sum, because the number of multiplication operations in Eq. (2.86) per computed output sample is proportional to N rather than N^2. The above implementation is known to be even more efficient than FFT-based 2-D convolution techniques for filters of orders up to about 45×45. The only disadvantage of the implementations based on Eq. (2.86) is that the coefficients a_k span a large dynamic range because of the Chebyshev transformation involved in Eq. (2.85). For a detailed treatment refer to [34], where the effects of finite word length in these implementations are also studied.

IX RECENT TECHNIQUES FOR EFFICIENT FIR FILTER DESIGN

Newer techniques have been reported for the design and implementation of FIR filters. Compared to equiripple designs, these techniques require less design time and are computationally more efficient from an implementation viewpoint. This section outlines some of these techniques.

An *implementation* of a filter is simply a scheme that computes the output sequence $y(n)$ in response to an arbitrary input sequence $x(n)$. Let N_m and N_a represent, respectively, the number of multiplications and additions required to compute each sample of the output sequence. Also, let N_z represent the number of delay units (i.e., amount of memory required) in the implementation. The relative importance of the three quantities N_m, N_a, and N_z depends upon the exact architecture of implementation (i.e., whether it is special-purpose hardware, or programmable-chip based, or simply a mainframe computer program). However, in many cases of practical interest, the multipliers are the most time consuming (or equivalently space consuming), and much more significance usually needs to be attached to N_m than to N_a and N_z. The methods discussed here are particularly suited to such situations. In situations where high-speed parallel multipliers are *already* available, so that multiplication time is not significantly higher than addition time, there is little motivation to reduce N_m at the expense of increased N_a and N_z.

To see the basic philosophy behind some of the new methods, recall that equiripple designs are optimal in the sense that the filter order $N - 1$ is the smallest among all filters that have the same specifications (for example, the same specified values of ω_p, ω_r, δ_1, and δ_2). As a result, a *direct-form* implementation requires the fewest multiplications (approximately half the order). However, there may be *other* implementations that require a higher overall order than the equiripple designs (to meet the same set of specifications) but require *fewer* multipliers. Such implementations can be very attractive when N_z is not as crucial as N_m. Most designs discussed in this section are based on this viewpoint.

The Interpolated FIR (or IFIR) Approach   A

The IFIR technique is valuable in situations where a FIR filter with a "narrow passband" is desired. For notational simplicity let us confine our attention to the lowpass design. Referring to the specification shown in Fig. 2.3, recall that a direct optimal design requires an order as estimated by Eq. (2.31). Consequently, a narrow transition bandwidth Δf implies a high order. The number of multipliers in a direct implementation is therefore very large (about half the order $N - 1$). However, it is sometimes possible to design this filter indirectly so that the actual number of multipliers is much less, *even though* the order is higher than for optimal designs.

The approach can be described by referring to a lowpass design. Corresponding to the lowpass specifications as in Fig. 2.29(a), consider a new set of *stretched* specifications as in Fig. 2.29(b), where the bandedges have been stretched by a factor of 2 but the tolerances δ_1 and δ_2 are unchanged. The new specifications are meaningful, provided $2\omega_r < \pi$. The modified specifications can be met by a *model filter* $H_M(z)$ of order given by

$$N_M - 1 = \frac{-20\log_{10}\sqrt{\delta_1\delta_2} - 13}{14.6(2\,\Delta f)} \tag{2.125}$$

which is half the value given by Eq. (2.31). Now consider the frequency response corresponding to $H_M(z^2)$, which is shown in Fig. 2.30(a). This is precisely as in Fig. 2.29(a), except for the unwanted passband around $\omega = \pi$. The unwanted passband can be suppressed by cascading $H_M(z^2)$ with a filter having a transfer

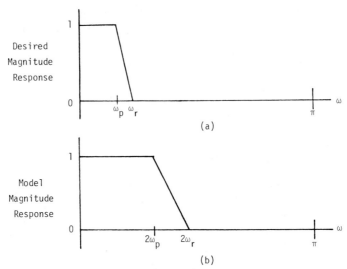

Fig. 2.29. Pertaining to the IFIR method.

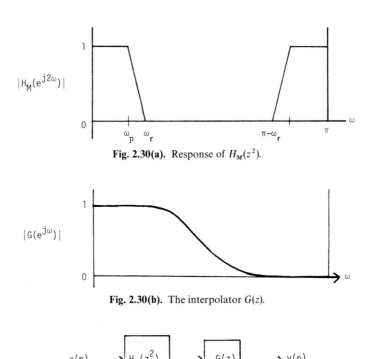

Fig. 2.30(a). Response of $H_M(z^2)$.

Fig. 2.30(b). The interpolator $G(z)$.

Fig. 2.30(c). The overall IFIR implementation.

function $G(z)$ and frequency response as in Fig. 2.30(b). Thus the overall transfer function is

$$H(z) = H_M(z^2)G(z) \tag{2.126}$$

Figure 2.30(c) shows the overall implementation. The main point is that as long as ω_r is not very close to $\pi/2$ the response of $G(z)$ *need not* have a sharp transition, although it needs to have a large attenuation in the region $\pi - \omega_r \leq \omega \leq \pi$. Thus $G(z)$ is, in general, inexpensive, as we shall demonstrate by design examples. The overall implementation requires only $(N_M - 1)/2 + 1$ multiplications (for even $N_M - 1$). This is half as many as that required by a direct design.

The choice of $G(z)$ is governed by the fact that it should have large attenuation in the range $\pi - \omega_r \leq \omega \leq \pi$. This itself is easily accomplished, for example, by taking

$$G(z) = \left(\frac{1 + z^{-1}}{2}\right)^R \tag{2.127}$$

where the integer R is large enough to attenuate the unwanted passband around $\omega = \pi$. However, the obvious disadvantage of this is that, for large R, the filter $G(z)$ causes unacceptable deterioration of the passband of $H(z)$. One way to avoid this is to *predistort* the model filter $H_M(z)$ such that its passband compensates for the deterioration. For example, if we are designing $H_M(z)$ by using the MP algorithm, then we need only choose the desired response to be

$$D(e^{j\omega}) = \begin{cases} 1/|G(e^{j\omega/2})|, & 0 \leq \omega \leq 2\omega_p \\ 0, & \omega \geq 2\omega_r \end{cases} \tag{2.128}$$

and the weighting function to be

$$W(e^{j\omega}) = \begin{cases} |G(e^{j\omega/2})|, & 0 \leq \omega \leq 2\omega_p \\ \text{constant}, & \omega \geq 2\omega_r \end{cases} \tag{2.129}$$

Thus, the overall filter $H(z)$ has equiripple passband response. Note, however, that if the interpolator causes a large droop in the passband, then $D(e^{j\omega})$ in Eq. (2.128) has a large dynamic range in the passband region. As a result, the impulse response coefficients of $H_M(z)$ tend to have large magnitudes, even though they add up to approximately unity around $\omega = 0$. This implies that the *passband sensitivity* of the resulting design can be large with respect to the coefficients of $H_M(z)$. Thus, interpolators that cause a large droop should be avoided.

A simple way to overcome the above sensitivity problem is to choose $G(z)$ such that it not only attenuates the signals around $\omega = \pi$ but is also very flat in the passband region $0 \leq \omega \leq \omega_p$. This can generally be done with inexpensive $G(z)$ because the transition bandwidth Δf of $G(z)$ can still be quite large. An excellent choice of $G(z)$ based on this observation is the class of maximally flat FIR filters discussed in Section V. Recall that these lowpass filters have a high degree of flatness around $\omega = 0$ and $\omega = \pi$. Design experience [23, 36] shows that, because of the flatness of this type of interpolator, the *predistortion* described by Eq. (2.128) is not necessary in most situations. It is also found in practice that small values of K and L are quite sufficient in most designs. Recall from Section V that (for small K and L) $G(z)$ can be implemented very efficiently in a multiplierless manner.

We now make some comments. First, the impulse response corresponding to $H_M(z^2)$ has every odd-numbered coefficient equal to zero. The cascading of $G(z)$ with $H_M(z^2)$ as in Eq. (2.126) is equivalent to filling in these zero-valued coefficients with a weighted average of surrounding coefficients. For this reason $G(z)$ is termed the *interpolator*. If the interpolator happens to be a maximally flat transfer function of the form of Eq. (2.68), then we call it a *maximally flat interpolator*. Note, however, that no explicit *signal interpolation* is involved in the structure of Fig. 2.30(c). In other words, the structure represents a single-rate, rather than a multirate, implementation.

Second, if ω_r is sufficiently small, we can extend the above idea and stretch the frequency axis by more than a factor of 2. Thus, we can define a model lowpass filter $H_M(z)$ with bandedges $l\omega_p$ and $l\omega_r$, where l is an integer such that $l\omega_r < \pi$. The final design $H(z)$ is then

$$H(z) = H_M(z^l)G(z) \qquad\qquad (2.130)$$

where $G(z)$ is a suitably chosen interpolator that suppresses the $l - 1$ unwanted passbands. The overall design now has about l times fewer multipliers than a conventional equiripple design, provided that $G(z)$ continues to be a simple circuit. Note, however, that if $l\omega_r$, which is less than π, is very close to π, then the interpolator $G(z)$ is expensive to design because it now must have *sharp* transition bands. Accordingly, it is a good design strategy not to make l too large. In any case, a theoretical upper bound on l is the integer part of π/ω_r.

Design Example 11. Reconsider the specifications of Example 2. Since ω_r is sufficiently small, we can employ the IFIR approach for the design. Note that $\pi/\omega_r = 1/0.24$, and, theoretically speaking, we can use $l = 4$. However, to keep the design of the interpolator simple, let us pick $l = 2$. The model lowpass filter $H_M(z)$ has bandedges

$$\hat{\omega}_p = 0.32\pi, \qquad \hat{\omega}_r = 0.48\pi \qquad\qquad (2.131)$$

and requires an order $N_M - 1$ of 26. A maximally flat interpolator with $K = L = 3$ is found suitable for removing the unwanted passband of $H_M(z^2)$ around $\omega = \pi$. Figure 2.31 shows the frequency response of the resulting design, which meets all design specifications, even though it requires only 14 multipliers. Note that no prewarping of the passband has been necessary.

Designing highpass and bandpass filters based on the IFIR technique can be done in a similar manner. See [37] for further details. For lowpass filters with $\omega_r > \pi/2$, we can still use fewer multipliers by first designing the complementary

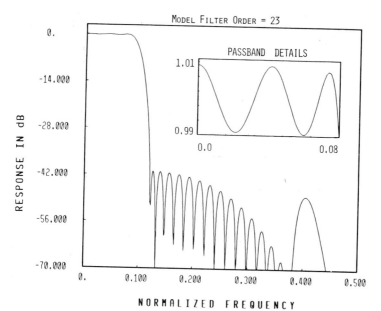

Fig. 2.31. Example 11: Lowpass filter, IFIR design.

lowpass filter $H_c(z)$ with passband edge $\pi - \omega_r$, stopband edge $\pi - \omega_p$, passband peak error δ_2, and stopband peak error δ_1. After efficiently designing it using the IFIR approach, we obtain the desired transfer function

$$H(z) = (-z)^{-(N-1)/2} - H_c(-z) \tag{2.132}$$

Other choices of $G(z)$ are possible. The choice

$$G(z) = 1 + z^{-1} + \cdots + z^{-(S-1)} = \frac{1 - z^{-S}}{1 - z^{-1}} \tag{2.133}$$

called the *recursive running sum* (RRS), is particularly useful. (The use of the RRS for efficient FIR filter design was recognized earlier in a different context by Adams and Willson [38].) This building block can be implemented with only two addition operations, and provides a minimum stopband attenuation of about 13 dB (see Fig. 2.32). The parameter S essentially determines the width of the mainlobe of the RRS interpolator. A typical design rule is to choose S so that $\Delta = 2\pi/S > \omega_r$. If the difference $\Delta - \omega_r$ is too small, then designing $H_M(z)$ is difficult because its passband needs to have a large variation to compensate for the droop in the passband caused by $G(z)$. Such a large variation leads to noise and sensitivity problems.

In Section V we mentioned that the design of maximally flat FIR filters with small transition widths is extremely expensive because the order $N - 1$ grows as the inverse square of this width. From the discussions of this section, it is clear

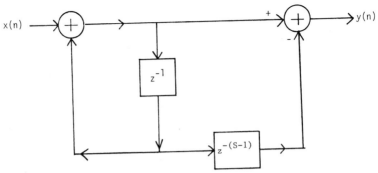

Fig. 2.32(a). Implementation of the recursive running sum.

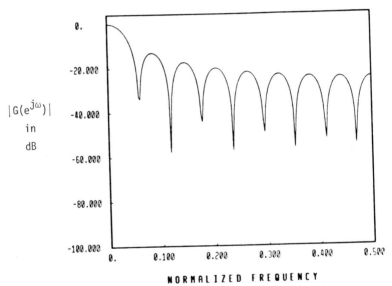

NORMALIZED FREQUENCY

Fig. 2.32(b). The magnitude response of the recursive running sum.

that the IFIR approach can be applied for the design of these filters as well. This is demonstrated in the next example.

Design Example 12.   Assume we want a monotone response as in Section V with $\beta = 0.2\pi$ and $\delta = 0.1\pi$. A direct design requires $K = 161$ and $L = 17$, which means that a direct-form implementation requires about 178 multipliers! However, we can design indirectly a monotone filter with the same bandedges by using the IFIR approach as follows: first design $H_M(z)$ with $\beta = 0.4\pi$ and $\delta = 0.2\pi$, requiring $K = 17$ and $L = 9$. This involves only 26 multipliers. We obtain the

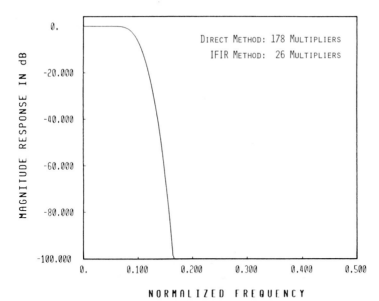

Fig. 2.33. Example 12: IFIR-based design of monotone response.

overall transfer function $H(z)$ as in Eq. (2.126), where $G(z)$ is itself a maximally flat interpolator (or a cascade of such interpolators) characterized by small values of K and L. In the example under consideration, the choice $G(z) = I^3_{3,3}(z)$ is found to suppress the unwanted passband satisfactorily. [Recall that, $I_{K,L}(z)$ is the abbreviation for a maximally flat FIR transfer function as in Eq. (2.68).] Thus, the overall implementation is dramatically simplified since it involves only 26 multipliers (compared to 178 in a direct design) and three multiplierless building blocks. Figure 2.33 shows the frequency response plot. For further details and examples of this nature, see [23, 36]. Note that the resulting indirect designs have responses that are not maximally flat, even though they are *very* flat, and are usually monotone.

The Prefilter–Equalizer Approach to FIR Design[†]   **B**

Reconsider a typical lowpass response as shown in Fig. 2.3. The desired transfer function has two important roles: it should provide a good stopband attenuation, and it should keep the passband signals as undistorted as possible. Instead of directly designing a transfer function $H(z)$ satisfying these requirements, we can take an indirect approach as follows. First design a transfer

[†] See reference [38].

function $H_2(z)$ that provides considerable stopband attenuation but not necessarily a good passband response. Then design a transfer function $H_1(z)$ such that in the passband $H_1(z)$ compensates for the response of $H_2(z)$ so that the cascaded transfer function $H_1(z)H_2(z)$ has its passband response within the required tolerance.

The advantage of such an approach is that $H_2(z)$ can usually be designed in an efficient manner without multipliers. An example is the RRS of Eq. (2.133), which has all transmission zeros on the unit circle of the z-plane. As mentioned earlier, this can be implemented with only two digital adders and no multipliers. The RRS provides a minimum attenuation of about 13 dB. The filter $H_1(z)$, which provides the additional attenuation in the stopband and also shapes the passband, has an order that is considerably lower than the order of a directly designed optimum filter. Since $H_2(z)$ is multiplierless, the overall implementation of $H_1(z)H_2(z)$ is therefore computationally less expensive even though the resulting filter order is higher than that of an optimal filter.

Adams and Willson [38, 39] have introduced several building blocks for the transfer function $H_2(z)$, which is called the prefilter. The prefilter $H_2(z)$ should be chosen to have all zeros on the unit circle to provide a good stopband attenuation. The prefilters proposed in [38] and [39] are based on the RRS of Eq. (2.133). By suitably combining RRS building blocks, we can easily construct prefilters with attenuation exceeding 13 dB. The function $H_1(z)$ is designed such that $H_1(z)H_2(z)$ has an equiripple passband. We can do this by designing $H_1(z)$ with the help of the MP algorithm. We choose the desired response $D(e^{j\omega})$ and weighting function $W(e^{j\omega})$ to be input to the MP algorithm in an obvious manner:

$$D(e^{j\omega}) = \begin{cases} |1/H_2(e^{j\omega})|, & 0 \le \omega \le \omega_p \\ 0, & \omega \ge \omega_r \end{cases} \qquad (2.134)$$

and

$$W(e^{j\omega}) = \begin{cases} |H_2(e^{j\omega})|, & 0 \le \omega \le \omega_p \\ \delta_1/\delta_2|H_2(e^{j\omega})|, & \omega \ge \omega_r \end{cases} \qquad (2.135)$$

Design Example 13. As a simple illustration of the prefilter–equalizer approach, consider a lowpass specification with bandedges $\omega_p = 0.042\pi$, $\omega_r = 0.146\pi$, A_{max} = maximum passband attenuation = 0.28 dB, and A_r = minimum stopband attenuation = 36 dB. A direct design based on the MP algorithm leads to an equiripple design $H_e(z)$ of order 33, requiring 17 multipliers. An RRS of the form of Eq. (2.133) with $S = 13$ has mainlobe extending from $\omega = 0$ to $\omega = 2\pi/13 = 0.1538\pi$, and is a suitable prefilter for this problem. The optimal equalizer designed using the MP algorithm has order 27, and the overall design therefore requires 14 multipliers. Figure 2.34 shows the relevant frequency responses.

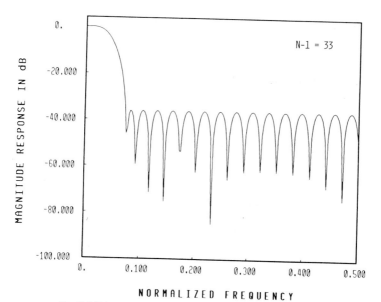

Fig. 2.34(a). Example 13: Lowpass filter equiripple design.

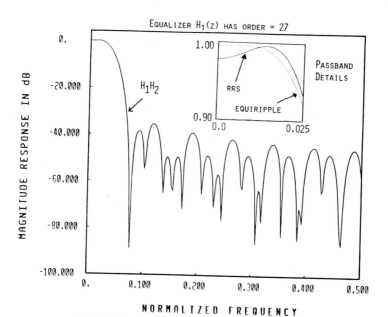

Fig. 2.34(b). Example 13: Lowpass filter, RRS-based.

C   Prefilters Based on Dolph–Chebyshev Polynomials

A new class of prefilters, introduced in [40], is based on Dolph–Chebyshev polynomials. A Dolph–Chebyshev function of order M and cutoff frequency ω_c is defined by

$$D_{M,\omega_c}(\omega) = \frac{\mathcal{T}_M(X)}{\mathcal{T}_M(X_c)} \qquad (2.136)$$

where

$$X = \frac{\cos(\omega/2)}{\cos(\omega_c/2)}, \qquad X_c = \frac{1}{\cos(\omega_c/2)} \qquad (2.137)$$

and $\mathcal{T}_M(X)$ is the Mth-order Chebyshev polynomial in X. Figure 2.35 is a typical plot of this lowpass function. The minimum stopband attenuation is

$$A_r = 20\log_{10}\mathcal{T}_M(X_c) \qquad (2.138)$$

We can design a linear-phase FIR filter with frequency response as in Eq. (2.2), where $H_0(e^{j\omega})$ is of the form of Eq. (2.136), simply by recognizing that the response $\cos(\omega/2)$ is realizable (in causal form) as $(1 + z^{-1})/2$. As a result, FIR filters with responses as in Eq. (2.136) can be built as in Fig. 2.36(a), where the tap weights are the coefficients of the Chebyshev polynomial. Each box labeled X in Fig. 2.36(a) corresponds to the X defined in Eq. (2.137). We can write

$$X = \frac{z^{1/2} + z^{-1/2}}{2\cos(\omega_c/2)} = z^{1/2}\left(\frac{1 + z^{-1}}{2\cos(\omega_c/2)}\right) \qquad (2.139)$$

Thus

$$\mathcal{T}_M(X) = \sum_{k=0}^{M} c_k z^{k/2}\left(\frac{1 + z^{-1}}{2\cos(\omega_c/2)}\right)^k \qquad (2.140)$$

Two difficulties are associated with a direct implementation of Eq. (2.140). The first is the noncausality of the building blocks caused by positive powers of z; the second is the presence of fractional powers of z, which do not correspond to

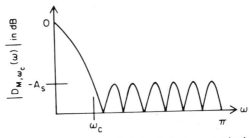

Fig. 2.35. A typical plot of the Dolph–Chebyshev magnitude [40]
(© 1985 IEEE).

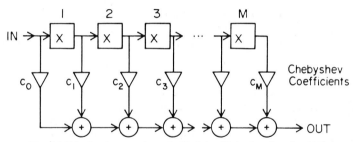

Fig. 2.36(a). Implementation of a Dolph–Chebyshev function [40] (© 1985 IEEE).

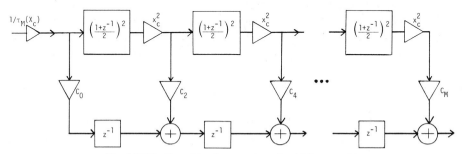

Fig. 2.36(b). Causal implementation of $\tau_M(x)$ for even M.

physical operators. Both of these difficulties are trivially overcome in practice, as we outline next.

From the property of Chebyshev polynomials [1, 41], it is known that if M is odd then $\mathcal{T}_M(X)$ has only odd powers of X, whereas if M is even it has only even powers of X. Thus for even M,

$$\mathcal{T}_M(X) = \sum_{k=0}^{M/2} c_{2k} z^k \left(\frac{1 + z^{-1}}{2 \cos(\omega_c/2)} \right)^{2k} \tag{2.141}$$

The noncausality in Eq. (2.141) is avoided by introducing $M/2$ units of delay:

$$z^{-M/2} \mathcal{T}_M(X) = \sum_{k=0}^{M/2} c_{2k} z^{-(M/2-k)} \left(\frac{1 + z^{-1}}{2 \cos(\omega_c/2)} \right)^{2k} \tag{2.142}$$

Figure 2.36(b) shows the overall causal implementation of (2.136), which is free from fractional powers of z. For odd M an analogous derivation leads to a causal structure.

Note the X_c^2 in Fig. 2.36(b). These multipliers imply additional computational overhead, but they can often be judiciously avoided, as we demonstrate in a latter example.

Prefilters with response of the form of Eq. (2.136) are attractive for several reasons. First, even for small M the stopband attenuation is quite large for typical values of ω_c. Second, the tap coefficients c_k in Fig. 2.36 are very simple combinations of powers of 2 for small M, leading to an inexpensive implementation of $H_2(z)$. By proper choice of ω_c, we can make the values of the multipliers X_c in Fig. 2.36 equal to a simple power of 2.

From Fig. 2.35 it is clear that ω_c should be chosen such that $\omega_c > \omega_r$. Moreover, ω_c should be as close to ω_r as possible so that the attenuating effect of the prefilter is available throughout the stopband. However, the smaller the value of ω_c, the smaller is the equiripple attenuation A_r shown in Fig. 2.35. Clearly, a compromise is necessary. For filters with a narrow passband, ω_r is typically small, and it may not be desirable to reduce ω_c to a comparably small value. A simple solution to this problem is to first construct an intermediate function $\hat{H}_2(z)$ based on the Dolph–Chebyshev function with $\omega_c > 2\omega_r$, and then define the prefilter $H_2(z)$ to be $H_2(z) = \hat{H}_2(z^2)\hat{H}_2(z)$. A number of other prefilters can be generated based on the Dolph–Chebyshev prefilter. A three-parameter family of functions for this purpose is reported in [40] and has magnitude response

$$|\hat{H}_2(e^{j\omega})| = \left| \frac{\mathscr{T}_M(X^k)}{\mathscr{T}_M(X_c^k)} \right| \tag{2.143}$$

The prefilter $H_2(z)$ is then generated as

$$H_2(z) = \hat{H}_2(z^2)\hat{H}_2(z) \tag{2.144}$$

Guidelines for choice of the parameters k, M, and ω_c are discussed in [40].

Design Example 14. Let us now reconsider Design Example 13. A prefilter of the form Eq. (2.144), where $\hat{H}_2(z)$ is given by Eq. (2.143) with $M = 5$ and $\omega_c = 0.2951672\pi$, is most suited to obtain an efficient design.[†] An equalizer $H_1(z)$ corresponding to this prefilter requires an order of 13. Thus, the overall implementation $H_1(z)H_2(z)$ requires only 7 multipliers compared to 17 required by the direct approach. Figure 2.37 shows all the relevant responses. Clearly the new design meets all specifications met by the conventional equiripple design.

The above design can be further improved by combining the IFIR approach with the *Dolph–Chebyshev prefilter–equalizer* approach. Thus, with the prefilter as in Design Example 14, we can first design an equalizer $H_1(z)$ with bandedges $\hat{\omega}_p = 0.084\pi$ and $\hat{\omega}_r = 0.292\pi$ and then obtain the overall transfer function $H(z)$ as $H(z) = H_1(z^2)H_2(z)$. The required order of $H_1(z)$ is now only 8. Figure 2.38 shows the frequency response of the resulting design, which clearly meets all specifications and requires only five multipliers.

Table XI shows a comparison of computational complexity for the design example. The quantities N_m and N_a are shown for the direct equiripple approach, the RRS prefilter approach, and the Chebyshev-function-based prefilter approach (with and without incorporating the IFIR technique).

[†] This choice of ω_c corresponds to $X_c^2 = 1.25 = 1 + 2^{-2}$: hence the multipliers in Fig. 2.36b are simple.

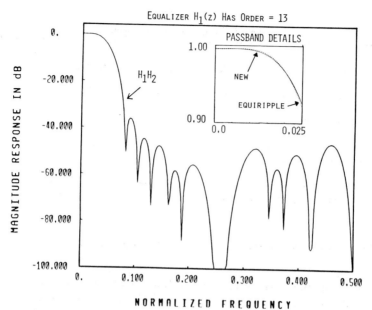

Fig. 2.37. Example 14: Lowpass filter, Chebyshev prefilter based.

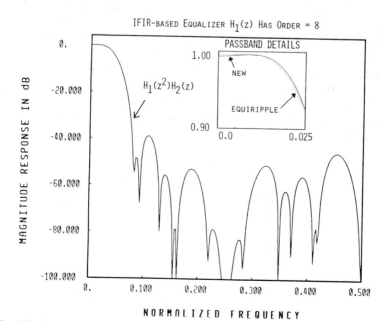

Fig. 2.38. Example 14: Lowpass filter, with Chebyshev prefilter and IFIR-based equalizer.

TABLE XI

Complexity Comparison for the Examples

Example	Prefilter (adders)	Equalizer[a]	Total for $H_1(z)H_2(z)$[a]	Direct equiripple design[a]
Example 14 Dolph–Chebyshev prefilter	38	13	51	33
		7	7	17
Example 13 RRS prefilter	2 (RRS)	27	29	33
		14	14	17
Example 14 Dolph–Chebyshev prefilter with IFIR-based equalizer	38	8	46	33
		5	5	17

[a] The first number is the number of adders; the second, the number of multipliers.

D FIR Filters with Very Flat Passbands and Equiripple Stopbands

In certain applications it is required to design a lowpass transfer function $G(z)$ with cutoff frequency ω_p such that the response is very flat around $\omega = 0$ and the peak passband error is less than a prescribed value, say δ_1, in the rest of the passband. As mentioned in Section VI, such specifications can be handled by a linear programming formulation, as shown by Steiglitz [25]. However, as pointed out by Kaiser and Steiglitz [26], this might lead to numerical problems during the design phase, in addition to requiring long convergence time. Such specifications can also be met by using the MP algorithm, with the weighting function properly chosen. However, a more efficient way to use the MP algorithm to achieve the same purpose is outlined next [30].

Assume that we require a flatness of degree $M - 1$ at $\omega = 0$ (i.e., $M - 1$ derivatives of the response $G(e^{j\omega})$ are zero at $\omega = 0$); also assume that the peak passband and stopband errors permitted are δ_1 and δ_2. The stopband is required to be equiripple so that δ_2 is minimized for a given filter order. Figure 2.39 represents these specifications.

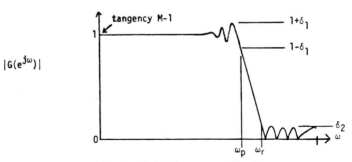

Fig. 2.39. The desired lowpass specifications.

We can obtain such a response by first designing a transfer function $H(z)$ to meet the complementary specifications defined in Fig. 2.40(a). The complementary transfer function has a tangency of $M - 1$ at $\omega = \pi$ and can therefore be decomposed as

$$H(z) = H_1(z)H_2(z) \tag{2.145}$$

where

$$H_2(z) = \left(\frac{1 + z^{-1}}{2}\right)^M \tag{2.146}$$

Next we can design $H_1(z)$ by using the MP algorithm with the following specifications for $D(e^{j\omega})$ and $W(e^{j\omega})$:

$$D(e^{j\omega}) = \begin{cases} 1/|H_2(e^{j\omega})|, & 0 \leq \omega \leq \pi - \omega_r \\ 0, & \pi - \omega_p \leq \omega \leq \pi \end{cases} \tag{2.147}$$

and

$$W(e^{j\omega}) = \begin{cases} |H_2(e^{j\omega})|, & 0 \leq \omega \leq \pi - \omega_r \\ \delta_2/\delta_1|H_2(e^{j(\pi - \omega_p)})|, & \pi - \omega_p \leq \omega \leq \pi \end{cases} \tag{2.148}$$

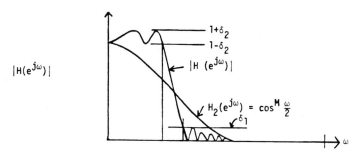

Fig. 2.40(a). The complementary specifications.

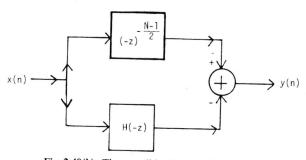

Fig. 2.40(b). The overall implementation of $G(z)$.

This insures an overall equiripple passband for the cascade $H(z)$ in Eq. (2.145). The desired transfer function $G(z)$ is then[†]

$$G(z) = (-z)^{-(N-1)/2} - H(-z) \qquad (2.149)$$

so that it has an equiripple stopband and a passband with degree of flatness of $M - 1$ at zero frequency. The choice of $W(e^{j\omega})$ as in Eq. (2.148) also insures that the peak passband to equiripple stopband error of $G(z)$ is δ_1/δ_2 as desired. The choice of the order $N_1 - 1$ of $H_1(z)$ should be done to meet the actual requirement on δ_2 for a given δ_1/δ_2. An approximate estimate can once again be obtained from the right side of Eq. (2.31).

The overall implementation of $G(z)$ is shown in Fig. 2.40(b). Note that the overall order $N - 1 = N_1 - 1 + M$ is required to be even so that the complementation indicated in Eq. (2.149) can be performed. Even though the filter order is $N - 1$, the number of multipliers is only about $(N_1 - 1)/2$. Thus, the passband flatness of $G(z)$ is achieved in a multiplierless manner by $H_2(-z)$, and the stopband of $G(z)$ is taken care of by $H_1(-z)$. Finally note that only the MP algorithm is required in the entire design process, and no other optimization routines are involved.

The key point to be noticed in the above method is that the flatness requirement at $\omega = 0$ has been *exploited* to extract the building block $H_2(z)$, which can be implemented without multipliers. If a linear programming approach [or a direct Remez exchange approach with a suitably chosen $W(e^{j\omega})$] were employed for this design problem, then such a *building block extraction* would not be possible.

Design Example 15. Referring to Fig. 2.39, consider the following specifications: $\delta_1 = 0.016$, $\delta_2 = 0.2\delta_1$, $\omega_p = 0.6\pi$, $\omega_r = 0.7\pi$, $M = 16$. Note that δ_2 corresponds to about 50-dB attenuation in the stopband. The order $N_1 - 1$ of $H_1(z)$ can be estimated from the right side of Eq. (2.31) as

$$N_1 - 1 = \frac{-20\log_{10}\sqrt{\delta_1\delta_2} - 13}{(14.6)(0.05)} = 44 \qquad (2.150)$$

With $H_2(z)$ as in Eq. (2.146) where $M = 16$, and with $H_1(z)$ designed as described above, the overall transfer function $G(z)$ has the frequency response as in Fig. 2.41(a). Figure 2.41(b) shows an equiripple FIR filter of order 44 with the same stopband attenuation. Note that the equiripple design requires the same number of multipliers (23) as the new design. Figure 2.41(b) also shows a comparison of passband details of the new design and the equiripple design. Note that for the new design the stopband is equiripple, the passband is extremely flat around $\omega = 0$, and the remaining specifications are also met satisfactorily.

[†] See also Section VII.C and Table IX.

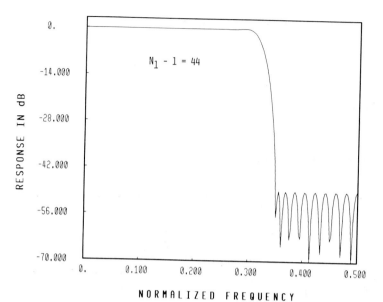

Fig. 2.41(a). Example 15: The new design for flat passband filters.

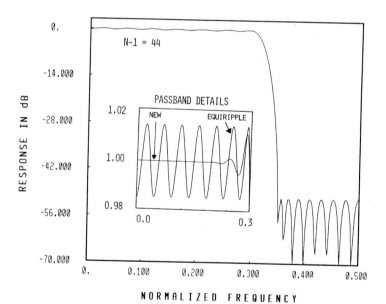

Fig. 2.41(b). An equiripple design of order 44, for comparison.

X OTHER USEFUL TYPES OF FIR FILTERS

This section discusses certain useful additional topics on FIR filter design. These include minimum-phase filters, half-band filters, and power-complementary filters.

A Minimum-Phase FIR Filters

As outlined in Section I, FIR filters have several advantages in addition to the (optional) linear-phase property. Thus, if an application does not particularly require the linear-phase property, we still have motivations for using FIR rather than IIR filters. These motivations include guaranteed stability in spite of parameter quantization and absence of limit cycles. In addition, in multirate signal processing applications FIR filters are extremely efficient and, in general, outperform their IIR counterparts even in terms of computational complexity [42, 43].

A major price paid for the linear-phase nature of a FIR filter is that the overall group delay, which is equal to $(N - 1)/2$, is large. The reason is that for a given set of frequency response specifications (such as δ_1, δ_2, ω_p, and ω_r), the required order $N - 1$ of a FIR design is much higher than that of an IIR design. (Design Example 2 in Section IV demonstrates this.) If linear phase is not a requirement, then FIR filters can be designed to have acceptably small group delays in the passband, even though $N - 1$ may continue to be large. In addition, a linear-phase filter has a 50% redundancy in the coefficients, due to impulse response symmetry. Thus, a nonlinear-phase FIR filter meeting a set of magnitude response specifications is expected to have lower order (though not necessarily by a factor of 2 [16]), compared to a linear-phase design.

Some authors have addressed the problem of optimal FIR design with minimum phase [44–48]. A minimum-phase FIR transfer function $G(z)$ has the property that all the zeros z_k of $G(z)$ satisfy $|z_k| \le 1$. Consequently, among all transfer functions that have the same magnitude response $|G(e^{j\omega})|$, the minimum-phase function has the smallest phase lag. Thus, if $\phi_{min}(\omega)$ denotes the phase response $\arg(G(e^{j\omega}))$ of a minimum-phase transfer function $G(z)$, then

$$-\phi_{min}(\omega) \le -\phi(\omega) \qquad \text{for all } \omega \tag{2.151}$$

where $\phi(\omega)$ is the phase response of any other transfer function having the same magnitude response.

The simplest technique [44] for designing a minimum-phase lowpass FIR filter with equiripple magnitude response is to first design a linear-phase transfer function $H(z)$ with a response as in Fig. 2.42 and then obtain a new transfer

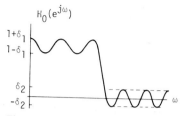

Fig. 2.42. Linear-phase function $H(z)$.

function $H_1(z)$ as

$$H_1(z) = H(z) + \delta_2 z^{-(N-1)/2} \tag{2.152}$$

assuming that $N - 1$ is even. The frequency response of $H_1(z)$ now has *double* zeros at the frequencies ω_k, as indicated in Fig. 2.43. Thus $H_1(e^{j\omega})$ can be written as

$$H_1(e^{j\omega}) = e^{-j\omega(N-1)/2}H_{10}(e^{j\omega}) \tag{2.153}$$

where $H_{10}(e^{j\omega})$ is real and positive. We can therefore factorize $H_1(z)$ to yield

$$H_1(z) = z^{-(N-1)/2}G(z)G(z^{-1}) \tag{2.154}$$

where $G(z)$ has real coefficients and has its zeros in the region $|z| \leq 1$. Thus, $G(z)$ is a minimum-phase function and has an equiripple magnitude response as shown in Fig. 2.44, where the peak errors are given approximately by

$$\hat{\delta}_1 = \frac{\delta_1}{2}, \qquad \hat{\delta}_2 = \sqrt{2\delta_2} \tag{2.155}$$

for small δ_1 and δ_2.

The design procedure is therefore as follows: given the lowpass specifications $\omega_p, \omega_r, \hat{\delta}_1, \hat{\delta}_2$, compute δ_1 and δ_2 using Eq. (2.155), and then design a linear-phase transfer function $H(z)$ with lowpass specifications $\omega_p, \omega_r, \delta_1,$ and δ_2. Next compute $H_1(z)$ as in Eq. (2.152). The spectral factor $G(z)$, which is the desired minimum-phase filter, is then computed.

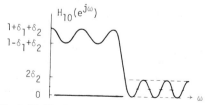

Fig. 2.43. The function $H_1(z)$ with double zeros.

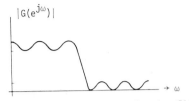

Fig. 2.44. The minimum-phase function $G(z)$.

One disadvantage of this approach is that the computation of the spectral factor $G(z)$ involves computation of the zeros of the polynomial $H_1(z)$, which is time consuming and leads to severe numerical inaccuracies for large values of N. A simple way to partially overcome this difficulty is as follows. When the equiripple filter $H(z)$ is designed using the MP algorithm, the values of the extremal frequencies ω_k in Fig. 2.42 are automatically available. A subset of these values is precisely the double zeros of $H_1(e^{j\omega})$ and their accuracy can be refined if necessary by means of standard root-refining techniques [49]. Thus, the spectral factorization is rendered easier because many of the roots have already been located. Great care should still be exercised because deflation of a high-degree polynomial $H_1(z)$ with known roots on the unit circle is known to be a highly inaccurate process [50].

If we are interested in designing optimal minimum-phase filters with arbitrary magnitude response, such as nonequiripple stopbands or several stopbands with different peak errors, a more general design procedure is called for. For example, we could first obtain a weighted equiripple linear-phase FIR filter with the constraint that the response $H_0(e^{j\omega})$ be positive for all ω. The next step is to perform the spectral factorization as described above. Detailed results on these and related techniques are in [45, 46].

Mian and Nainer [47] have proposed a new technique to circumvent the problem of having to locate the roots of $H_1(z)$. The method is based on a useful property of the complex cepstrum [1] and converts the factorization problem to a computation of two FFTs. The basic idea is that the impulse response $g(n)$ corresponding to $G(z)$ can be obtained from the cepstral sequence $G_G(n)$ corresponding to $G(z)$, which in turn can be obtained easily from the cepstral sequence corresponding to $H_1(z)$. For further related discussions, see [47, 48].

Design Example 16. As an example of minimum-phase FIR design, let us assume that we wish to design a lowpass FIR filter $G(z)$, having minimum phase, to meet the following requirements: $\omega_p = 0.08(2\pi)$, $\omega_r = 0.12(2\pi)$, $\hat{\delta}_1 \le 0.012$, $-20\log_{10}\hat{\delta}_2 \ge 25$ dB. We find δ_1 and δ_2 of the corresponding linear-phase FIR filter $H(z)$ from Eq. (2.155). Note that $H(z)$ is required to have the same ω_p and ω_r as the minimum-phase filter $G(z)$. We obtain the estimate for the order of $H(z)$ as usual from Eq. (2.31) or Eq. (2.32). An order of $N - 1 = 60$ is found to be sufficient. Figure 2.45(a) shows the response of $H(z)$ and also the response of

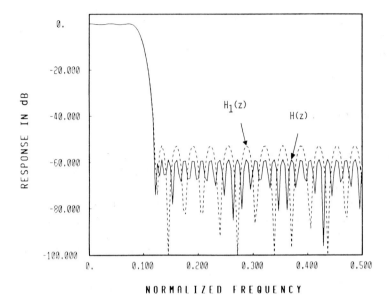

Fig. 2.45(a). Example 16: The response of the linear-phase filter $H(z)$.

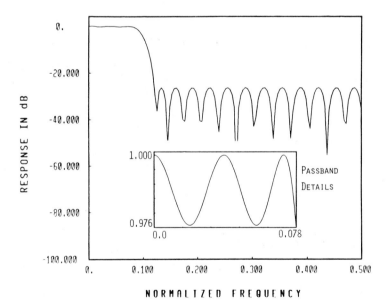

Fig. 2.45(b). Example 16: Magnitude response of the resulting minimum-phase $G(z)$.

$H_1(z)$ defined in Eq. (2.152). We arrive at the minimum-phase spectral factor $G(z)$ defined in Eq. (2.154) by using the method described in [47]. Figure 2.45(b) shows the magnitude response of $G(z)$. Note that all specifications requirements are satisfied.

B   Half-Band FIR Filters

Certain applications [51–54] need a lowpass filter with cutoff frequency $\pi/2$. Thus "half" of the frequency band is "passed," and the other half is attenuated. Such half-band filters have interesting properties under certain additional *symmetry constraints*, which make them attractive from an implementation viewpoint. In this subsection we indicate some of these properties.

Let $H(z)$ be a linear-phase FIR transfer function of even order $N - 1$ and with symmetric impulse response (i.e., type 1 filter, Table IV). Then the real-valued quantity $H_0(e^{j\omega})$ is

$$H_0(e^{j\omega}) = \sum_{n=0}^{M} b_n \cos n\omega, \qquad M = \frac{N-1}{2} \tag{2.156}$$

Since $\omega_c = \pi/2$, we have, by Eq. (2.7b)

$$\omega_p + \omega_r = \pi \tag{2.157}$$

Moreover, assume that the passband ripple and the stopband ripple are the same (i.e., $\delta_1 = \delta_2 = \delta$). Thus, the response exhibits symmetry around $\pi/2$. Figure 2.46 (solid curve) shows a representative plot of such a symmetric half-band response. In view of the symmetry, we easily verify that

$$H_0(e^{j\omega}) = 1 - H_0(e^{j(\pi - \omega)}) \tag{2.158}$$

Equivalently, in terms of $H(z)$,

$$H_0(z) + H_0(-z) = 1 \tag{2.159}$$

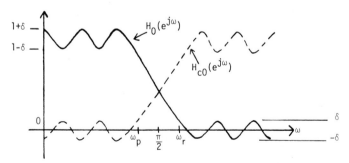

Fig. 2.46. Symmetric half-band response.

that is,

$$H(z) + (-1)^{(N-1)/2} H(-z) = z^{-(N-1)/2} \qquad (2.160)$$

Substituting Eq. (2.156) in Eq. (2.158), we can verify that the coefficients b_n are constrained as follows:

$$b_{2n} = 0, \qquad n \neq 0 \qquad (2.161)$$

and $b_0 = h(M) = 0.5$. As a result, the impulse response sequence (Table IV) has every odd-numbered sample equal to zero for M odd and every even-numbered sample equal to zero for M even (except the coefficient $h(M) = b(0) = 0.5$). Thus, for M even, $h(0) = h(N-1) = 0$; hence the filter order is actually *not* $N-1$. Since $h(0)$ is zero, we can shift the impulse response by one sample and redefine $h(1)$ to be the zeroth sample; this makes the filter order equal to $N-3$. In summary, for half-band symmetric frequency responses, $N-1$ can *always* be taken to be of the form

$$N - 1 = 4n_0 + 2, \qquad n_0 = \text{integer} \qquad (2.162)$$

In other words, M can be assumed to be odd without loss of generality. Correspondingly, half-band symmetric linear-phase FIR filters can be assumed to satisfy

$$h(n) = \begin{cases} 0, & n = \text{odd} \neq M \\ 0.5, & n = M \end{cases} \qquad (2.163)$$

without loss of generality.

A direct-form implementation of half-band symmetric FIR filters as in Fig. 2.1(b) requires only about $(M+1)/2$ rather than M multipliers. In addition, once we implement $H(z)$ with about $(M+1)/2$ multipliers, we can get the *complementary* half-band highpass function $H_c(z)$, defined as

$$H_c(z) = z^{-(N-1)/2} - H(z) = z^{-(N-1)/2} H_{co}(z) \qquad (2.164)$$

without using additional multipliers. Figure 2.46 (dashed curve) also shows the response of the highpass linear-phase filter obtained in this manner. In summary, at the expense of a total of only about $(N-1)/4$ multipliers, we have obtained *two* half-band filters, operating on the same input signal.

Efficient Use of the MP Algorithm for Half-Band Filter Design   1

We can design the half-band transfer function $H(z)$, which has $\delta_1 = \delta_2$ and which satisfies Eq. (2.157), using the MP algorithm by requesting a filter order as in Eq. (2.162). However, because of computational inaccuracies, the odd-numbered impulse response coefficients do not *exactly* satisfy Eq. (2.163) even though in practice, at the end of the MP design, these coefficients come out to be very close to that in (2.163). Since we *know* $h(M) = 0.5$ and the other odd values of

$h(n)$ are zero, as indicated in Eq. (2.163), it is judicious to eliminate these coefficients from the approximation problem, and solve only for the unknown coefficients (i.e., even-numbered coefficients of the impulse response), thus saving considerable design time. We now show how this can be accomplished by designing a linear-phase FIR filter $V(z)$ of odd order $(N - 1)/2 = M$, and then manipulating the result.

Let $V(z)$ be a linear-phase FIR filter of odd order M with *symmetric* impulse response (i.e., type 2, Table IV). We know that $V(e^{j\pi})$ is equal to zero. Let $V(z)$ be designed to be a lowpass filter such that its passband edge is θ_p and its stopband edge is $\theta_r = \pi$. Letting

$$V(e^{j\omega}) = e^{-j\omega M/2} V_0(e^{j\omega}) \qquad (2.165)$$

we see that $V_0(e^{j\omega})$ has the typical form shown in Fig. 2.47(a) for $0 \le \omega \le 2\pi$. (The plot is antisymmetric with respect to π because of the factor $\cos(\omega/2)$ in $V_0(e^{j\omega})$, as indicated in Table IV.) Now consider a filter with transfer function $V(z^2)$. The corresponding response $V(e^{2j\omega})$ is shown in Fig. 2.47(b). If this curve is now shifted up by adding a constant equal to unity, the result is *precisely* the half-band

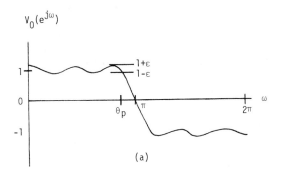

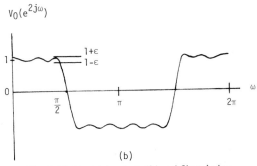

Fig. 2.47. Pertaining to half-band filter design.

symmetric response[†] $H_0(e^{j\omega})$, as shown in Fig. 2.46! Thus $H(z)$ can be designed as

$$H(z) = \frac{V(z^2) + z^{-(N-1)/2}}{2} \tag{2.166}$$

After we find the coefficients $v(n)$ of the filter $V(z)$ of order $(N-1)/2$, we determine the coefficients of $H(z)$ to be

$$h(n) = \begin{cases} 0.5v(n/2), & n = \text{even} \\ 0, & n = \text{odd} \neq M \\ 0.5, & n = M \end{cases} \tag{2.167}$$

In summary, given the specifications for the half-band filter $H(z)$ in the form of ω_p and ω_r satisfying Eq. (2.157) and δ, we find $\epsilon = 2\delta$ and $\theta_p = 2\omega_p$ in Fig. 2.47(a), and design $V(z)$ using the MP algorithm. We obtain $H(z)$ by using Eq. (2.167).

Applications 2

An interesting application of such half-band filter banks is in signal splitting and reconstruction in the frequency domain (such as in subband coding [53, 54]). An accurate discussion of this involves introducing multirate concepts to take into account sampling-rate alterations, which is the subject of Chapter 3. We therefore outline the concept of frequency-band splitting and reconstruction, under the assumption that there is no sampling-rate change involved.

Referring to Fig. 2.46, which represents the symmetric half-band response, we can see clearly that the function $G_0(e^{j\omega}) = H_0(e^{j\omega}) + \delta$ is positive for all ω, and hence if we define

$$G(z) = H(z) + \delta z^{-(N-1)/2} = z^{-(N-1)/2}G_0(z) \tag{2.168}$$

then $G(z)$ can be factorized as

$$G(z) = z^{-(N-1)/2}G_1(z^{-1})G_1(z) \tag{2.169}$$

where $G_1(z)$ has real-valued coefficients. Moreover, because of Eq. (2.160) $G(z)$ satisfies

$$G(z) + (-1)^{(N-1)/2}G(-z) = (1 + 2\delta)z^{-(N-1)/2} \tag{2.170}$$

Substituting Eq. (2.169) into Eq. (2.170), we arrive at

$$G_1(z^{-1})G_1(z) + G_1(-z^{-1})G_1(-z) = (1 + 2\delta) \tag{2.171}$$

Note that the transfer function $G_1(z)$ in Eq. (2.169) has order $M = (N-1)/2$. We can simplify notation in Eq. (2.171) by defining

$$G_2(z) = z^{-(N-1)/2}G_1(-z^{-1}) \tag{2.172}$$

[†] Except for a scale factor of 2.

Writing $G_1(z)$ in terms of its impulse response

$$G_1(z) = \sum_{n=0}^{(N-1)/2} g_1(n)z^{-n} \qquad (2.173)$$

we then have

$$G_2(z) = (-1)^{(N-1)/2} \sum_{n=0}^{(N-1)/2} g_1\left(\frac{N-1}{2} - n\right)(-z)^{-n} \qquad (2.174)$$

Notice that $G_2(z)$ is causal. The zeros of $G_2(z)$ are obtained by replacing each zero z_r of $G_1(z)$ with $-1/z_r$. It is easily verified that if $G_1(z)$ is lowpass, then $G_2(z)$ is highpass, and vice versa. Moreover, if $G_1(z)$ has minimum phase, then $G_2(z)$ has maximum phase, and vice versa. On the unit circle, Eq. (2.171) can be equivalently rewritten now as

$$|G_1(e^{j\omega})|^2 + |G_2(e^{j\omega})|^2 = 1 \qquad (2.175)$$

which shows that $G_1(z)$ and $G_2(z)$ form a power-complementary pair.[†] For example, if $G_1(z)$ is lowpass, then $G_2(z)$ has a highpass response such that the sum of magnitude squares adds up *exactly* to unity for all frequencies. This property is extremely useful in reconstruction of a signal that has been split into lowpass and highpass bands. Thus, see Fig. 2.48 in which the signal $x(n)$ has been split into a lowpass signal $x_1(n)$ and a highpass signal $x_2(n)$. Figure 2.48 also shows how the components $x_1(n)$ and $x_2(n)$ can be recombined by using the reconstruction filters (or synthesis filters)

$$F_1(z) = z^{-(N-1)/2}G_1(z^{-1}), \qquad F_2(z) = z^{-(N-1)/2}G_2(z^{-1}) \qquad (2.176)$$

By making use of Eq. (2.171), we can verify that the *reconstructed* signal $\hat{x}(n)$ is

$$\hat{x}(n) = x\left(n - \frac{N-1}{2}\right) \qquad (2.177)$$

Thus, the power-complementary property represented by Eq. (2.171) or, equivalently, by Eq. (2.175) enables us to reconstruct $x(n)$ with no error except for an overall delay of $(N-1)/2$ samples!

Note that even though we started with a linear-phase transfer function $H(z)$ [see Eq. (2.156)], the factorized transfer function $G_1(z)$ does not necessarily have linear phase. As a result, $G_2(z)$, which is obtained from $G_1(z)$ by using Eq. (2.172), does not have linear phase in general.[‡]

[†] Equation (2.175) may itself be taken as the definition of a power-complementary pair of transfer functions $G_1(z)$, $G_2(z)$.

[‡] It can be shown [55] that if $P(z)$ and $Q(z)$ are two linear-phase FIR filters satisfying the power-complementary property (i.e., $|P(e^{j\omega})|^2 + |Q(e^{j\omega})|^2 = 1$), then the magnitude responses $|P(e^{j\omega})|$ and $|Q(e^{j\omega})|$ are trivial; specifically, they are either constants or functions of the form $|\cos(K\omega)|$ and $|\sin(K\omega)|$.

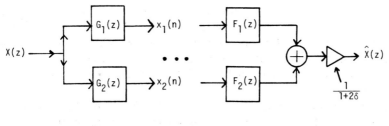

analysis stage   synthesis stage

Fig. 2.48. Signal splitting and reconstruction.

Design Example 17. We wish to design a lowpass filter $G_1(z)$ and a corresponding highpass filter $G_2(z)$, defined as in Eq. (2.172), such that Eq. (2.175) is satisfied. To do this, we first design the linear-phase symmetric, half-band transfer function $H(z)$. The specifications ω_p and ω_r for $H(z)$ are the same as those of $G_1(z)$, which in turn should satisfy the symmetry condition of Eq. (2.157). Moreover, $H(z)$ should have $\delta_1 = \delta_2$, which we can find from the attenuation requirements of $G_1(z)$ by using Eq. (2.155). (Note that since $\delta_1 = \delta_2$, then $\hat{\delta}_1$, $\hat{\delta}_2$ in Eq. (2.155) cannot be independently specified.) Let the resulting specifications of $H(z)$ for certain given specifications of $G_1(z)$ be

$$\omega_p = 0.2(2\pi), \quad \omega_r = 0.3(2\pi), \quad \delta_1 = \delta_2 \le 0.00035 \qquad (2.178)$$

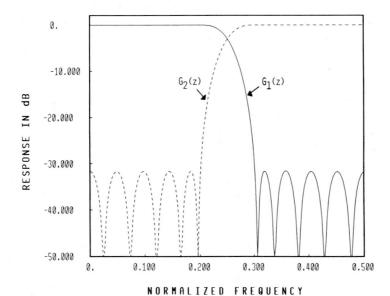

NORMALIZED FREQUENCY

Fig. 2.49. Example 17: The power-complementary pair of FIR filters.

An order $N - 1 = 38$ is found sufficient for $H(z)$. The linear-phase, symmetric, half-band FIR filter $H(z)$ can be designed by the MP algorithm efficiently, as described earlier. Since $H(z)$ is thus known, $G_1(z)$ in Eq. (2.169) can be computed. The algorithm due to Mian and Nainer [47] can again be used, if $G_1(z)$ is required to be a minimum-phase function. Figure 2.49 shows the response of the resulting power-complementary pair.

We conclude this section by noting that filter banks of the form described above can also be used with slight modification to reconstruct $x(n)$ after undersampling the filtered versions $x_1(n)$ and $x_2(n)$ in Fig. 2.48. Smith and Barnwell [54] have shown how *exact* reconstruction can be done in this manner with no distortion (except for an overall delay).

XI SUMMARY

In this chapter we presented several techniques for the design of FIR digital filters, including recent procedures that lead to efficient implementations. The window-based methods of Section III are the simplest to use, whereas the Remez exchange methods of Section IV give rise to a much wider class of filter functions. Almost any kind of design requirements (except *tangency* requirements in the frequency domain and *time domain* constraints) encountered in practice can be met with the methods of Section IV. Certain specific tangency requirements can be met with the maximally flat filters of Section V, whereas more general tangency requirements *and* time domain requirements can be met by the linear programming approach of Section VI. The methods of Section V, however, have the advantage of design simplicity, because no optimization programs are required. In addition, the methods of Section V can be used to design multiplierless filters.

Once a linear-phase FIR filter has been designed, its cutoff frequency (and the entire response) can be changed and manipulated in other ways by invoking the *transformation* tools and sharpening techniques described in Section VII. A linear-phase FIR filter can easily be converted to a two-dimensional FIR filter through the mapping procedures of Section VIII.

Even though many of the methods in Sections III to VIII are optimal or suboptimal in certain theoretical ways, they do not necessarily lead to optimal *implementations* in the sense of network complexity. Section IX describes filter design techniques that lead to implementations that are better than direct implementations of the methods of earlier sections. The methods of Section IX are essentially variations and combinations of the methods of earlier sections, so the importance of the methods of Sections III to VIII should not be underestimated. Finally, Section X introduces the designer to useful types of FIR filters that are of interest for specific applications.

A question of prime importance that a digital filter designer encounters is whether to design a FIR filter or an IIR filter for a given application. There is no definite answer to this question because the decision depends on the design specifications, requirements on the group delay, internal word length available, choice of architecture, and so on. However, some guidelines are available to partially help the designer in this regard; the excellent study by Rabiner *et al.* [56] gives such guidelines for the specific case of equiripple direct-form FIR and cascade-form IIR filters. Basically, for most combinations of specifications IIR filters are more economical (in terms of multiplications per output sample), but they introduce a phase distortion. FIR filters, on the other hand, can be designed with exact linear phase. IIR filters with group-delay equalizers in cascade, which have approximately linear phase in the overall passband, are generally *more* expensive that direct-form FIR filters meeting the same specifications [56]. Thus in applications requiring linear phase, FIR filters have a very important place; in addition, nonrecursive FIR implementations are always stable in spite of coefficient quantization. Moreover, instead of comparing IIR filters with equiripple FIR designs, if a comparison is made with recent FIR designs (Section IX), then FIR filters are *even* more efficient than IIR designs with no group-delay equalization.

APPENDIX A.   DESIGN CHARTS FOR DIGITAL FIR DIFFERENTIATORS AND HILBERT TRANSFORMERS

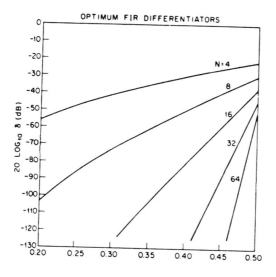

Fig. A2.1. Design chart for optimal FIR differentiators [60].

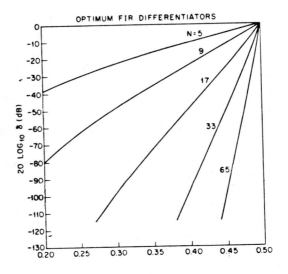

Passband Cutoff Frequency $\dfrac{\omega_p}{2\pi}$

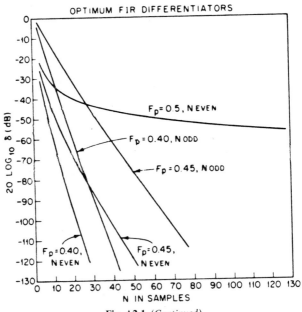

Fig. A2.1. (*Continued*)

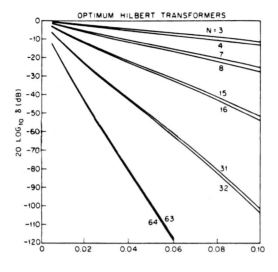

Transition Width Δf ⟶

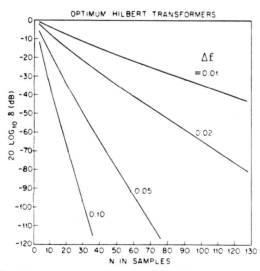

Fig. A2.2. Design charts for optimal FIR Hilbert transformers [61] .

APPENDIX B. PROGRAM LISTINGS FOR LINEAR-PHASE FIR FILTER DESIGN

As mentioned in the text, references [19, 21, 25] contain useful design programs for linear-phase FIR filters. The accompanying listing is based on the program due to McClellan, Parks, and Rabiner, published in [19]. This program is appropriately modified here in order to be able to obtain new and more efficient designs. As an illustration, Design Examples 6 and 13 can be obtained by selecting an appropriate set of input data.

The program in [19] is used here as a *subroutine*, invoked by the main program MAIN.f. The following distinct program files should be compiled and linked together before execution:

1. Main program: MAIN.f.
2. Subprograms: maclel.f, magres.f, effw1.f, extfun.f, rrs.f, zero.f and compe.f.

The program efffw1.f which invokes extfun.f, zero.f, and rrs.f is crucial when we attempt to exploit the flexibility of the Remez exchange technique. Comments are included in the listings which clarify some of these facts. The user should study these comments carefully before attempting to use the programs for applications.

The listings are obtained from a FORTRAN 77 version running on the VAX machine under the Berkeley Unix V4.2 operating system. The input and output files are conveniently designated as FORT.n files. The program can be adapted to other environments simply by changing the READ, WRITE, and FORMAT statements.

To run the compiled executable code, one must prepare the following input file (and keep it in the name FORT.9):

> IMETH, NFILT, JTYPE, NBANDS, LGRID.
> BAND EDGES.
> DESIRED VALUES IN THE BANDS.
> DESIRED WEIGHTS IN THE BANDS.

The meanings of each of the above lines are elaborated in the accompanying listing of MACLEL.f. By choosing the parameter IMETH appropriately, one can use the programs for many applications. Note that the parameters specified in the input file FORT.9 describe the filter designed by the MP algorithm, which is not necessarily the final transfer function. Similarly, the file FORT.3, which contains some of the *results* of the design, pertain to the filter designed by the MP algorithm. As an illustration, in Design Example 6, the filter $H_1(z)$ is the one specified in FORT.9. Thus, $H_1(z)$ in Eq. (2.58) is designed by creating FORT.9 as follows:

$$3, 41, 1, 2, 0$$
$$0, .14, .18, .5$$
$$1, 0$$
$$1, 1$$

The impulse response of $H_1(z)$ and other details pertaining to $H_1(z)$ are written in FORT.3 by the program MACLEL.f.

The frequency response of the overall filter [for example, $H_1(z)H_2(z)$ in (2.58)] is computed by the program COMPE.f automatically before the execution terminates. This response is written in the output file FORT.18. The file FORT.7 is used for an intermediate purpose, and the user is requested not to interfere with the contents of FORT.7.

```fortran
c MAIN.f
c
c ***********************************************************************
c
c This main program demonstrates the use of the McClellan-Parks
c program in [19], as a subroutine.
c The input and output statements and files are
c compatible with a Fortran 77 version running under the Berkeley
c Version 4.2 of the Unix operating system.
c With simple changes in the input-output details, this program
c can be run in other operating environments..
c
c ***********************************************************************
c
          dimension h(1025),hresp(514)
          call ieee21
          in=7
          rewind(9)
          read(9,*)imeth
          iout=18
          m=9
          nfft=2**m
          nout=nfft/2+1
          rewind(in)
          rewind(iout)
          read(in,*)norder
          nag=1 +norder/2
          do 1 i=1,nag
          read(in,*)h(i)
          h(norder+2-i)=h(i)
1         continue
          do 5 i=norder+1,fft
5         h(i)=0.0
          call magres(h,hresp,m)
          nout1=nout-1
          call compe(hresp,nout1)
c
c Normalize the maximum magnitude to unity:
c
          do 3 i=1,nout
          if(hmax.lt.abs(hresp(i)))hmax=abs(hresp(i))
3         continue
          do 4 i=1,nout
4         hresp(i)=hresp(i)/hmax
          rewind(iout)
          write(iout,*)nout1
          do 2 i=1,nout
          x=(i-1.0)/(nout-1.0)
          write(iout,*)x/2,hresp(i),hresp(i)
2         continue
          stop
          end
```

```
c MACLEL.f
c
c
c-----------------------------------------------------------------------
c This program is being used here as a subroutine.
c Calling sequence: call ieee21
c There are no arguments to be passed; all input is read by ieee21
c from the file FORT.9
c
c
c
c Original authors: james h. mcclellan
c                   department of electrical engineering and computer science
c                   massachusetts institute of technology
c                   cambridge, mass. 02139
c
c                   thomas w. parks
c                   department of electrical engineering
c                   rice university
c                   houston, texas 77001
c
c                   lawrence r. rabiner
c                   bell laboratories
c                   murray hill, new jersey 07974
c
c input:
c   imeth-- Method of design
c           1=Conventional equiripple design
c           2=Prefilter-equalizer based design, using the recursive
c             running sum.
c           3=Design as in Eqn. (2.58), where (2.57) represents
c             a transmission zero.
c   nfilt-- filter length
c   jtype-- type of filter
c           1 = multiple passband/stopband filter
c           2 = differentiator
c           3 = hilbert transform filter
c   nbands-- number of bands
c   lgrid-- grid density, will be set to 16 unless
c           specified otherwise by a positive constant.
c
c   edge(2*nbands)-- bandedge array, lower and upper edges for each band
c                    with a maximum of 10 bands.
c
c   fx(nbands)-- desired function array (or desired slope if a
c                differentiator) for each band.
c
c   wtx(nbands)-- weight function array in each band.  for a
c                 differentiator, the weight function is inversely
c                 proportional to f.
c
c   sample input data setup:
c       3,41,1,2,0
c       0,.14,.18,.5
c       1,0
c       1,1
c       this data specifies a length 41 lowpass filter with
c       passband 0 to 0.14 and stopband  0.18 to 0.5.
```

```
c       The passband weight is equal to the stopband weight.
c       Since imeth=3, the desired passband shape, and
c       the detailed shape of the weighting function are
c       governed by EXTFUN.f, in a manner detailed in the
c       listing of this function.
c       The grid density defaults to 16.
c
c       the following input data specifies a length 32 fullband
c       differentiator with slope 1 and weighting of 1/f.
c       the grid density will be set to 20.
c          1,32,2,1,20
c          0,0.5
c          1.0
c          1.0
c       Since imeth=1 here, the design is a conventional
c       weighted equiripple design.
c
c-----------------------------------------------------------------------
c
        subroutine ieee21
        common pi2,ad,dev,x,y,grid,des,wt,alpha,iext,nfcns,ngrid
        common /oops/niter,iout
        dimension iext(252),ad(252),alpha(252),x(252),y(252)
        dimension h(252)
        dimension des(4032),grid(4032),wt(4032)
        dimension edge(20),fx(10),wtx(10),deviat(10)
        double precision pi2,pi
        double precision ad,dev,x,y
        double precision gee,d
        integer bd1,bd2,bd3,bd4
        data bd1,bd2,bd3,bd4/1hb,1ha,1hn,1hd/
          input=9
        rewind(3)
        iout=3
          rewind(iout)
        pi=4.0*datan(1.0d0)
        pi2=2.0d00*pi
          iout2=7
          rewind(iout2)
c
c  the program is set up for a maximum length of 128, but
c  this upper limit can be changed by redimensioning the
c  arrays iext, ad, alpha, x, y, h to be nfmax/2 + 2.
c  the arrays des, grid, and wt must dimensioned
c  16(nfmax/2 + 2).
c
        nfmax=500
    100 continue
        jtype=0
c
c  program input section
c
        read(input,*)imeth, nfilt,jtype,nbands,lgrid
c replace stop by return
        if(nfilt.eq.0)return
    110 format(4i5)
        if(nfilt.le.nfmax.or.nfilt.ge.3) go to 115
        call error
c replace stop by return
        return
    115 if(nbands.le.0) nbands=1
```

```
c
c   grid density is assumed to be 16 unless specified
c   otherwise
c
      if(lgrid.le.0) lgrid=16
      jb=2*nbands
      read(input,*) (edge(j),j=1,jb)
         freqs=edge(3)
  120 format(4f15.9)
      read(input,*) (fx(j),j=1,nbands)
      read(input,*) (wtx(j),j=1,nbands)
         rewind(input)
      if(jtype.gt.0.and.jtype.le.3) go to 125
      call error
c replace stop by return
      return
  125 neg=1
      if(jtype.eq.1) neg=0
      nodd=nfilt/2
      nodd=nfilt-2*nodd
      nfcns=nfilt/2
      if(nodd.eq.1.and.neg.eq.0) nfcns=nfcns+1
c
c   set up the dense grid.  the number of points in the grid
c   is (filter length + 1)*grid density/2
c
      grid(1)=edge(1)
      delf=lgrid*nfcns
      delf=0.5/delf
      if(neg.eq.0) go to 135
      if(edge(1).lt.delf) grid(1)=delf
  135 continue
      j=1
      l=1
      lband=1
  140 fup=edge(l+1)
  145 temp=grid(j)
c
c   calculate the desired magnitude response and the weight
c   function on the grid
c
      des(j)=eff(temp,fx,wtx,lband,jtype)
      wt(j)=wate(temp,fx,wtx,lband,jtype,freqs)
      j=j+1
      grid(j)=temp+delf
      if(grid(j).gt.fup) go to 150
      go to 145
  150 grid(j-1)=fup
      des(j-1)=eff(fup,fx,wtx,lband,jtype)
      wt(j-1)=wate(fup,fx,wtx,lband,jtype,freqs)
      lband=lband+1
      l=l+2
      if(lband.gt.nbands) go to 160
      grid(j)=edge(l)
      go to 140
  160 ngrid=j-1
      if(neg.ne.nodd) go to 165
      if(grid(ngrid).gt.(0.5-delf)) ngrid=ngrid-1
  165 continue
```

```
c
c  set up a new approximation problem which is equivalent
c  to the original problem
c
      if(neg) 170,170,180
  170 if(nodd.eq.1) go to 200
      do 175 j=1,ngrid
      change=dcos(pi*grid(j))
      des(j)=des(j)/change
  175 wt(j)=wt(j)*change
      go to 200
  180 if(nodd.eq.1) go to 190
      do 185 j=1,ngrid
      change=dsin(pi*grid(j))
      des(j)=des(j)/change
  185 wt(j)=wt(j)*change
      go to 200
  190 do 195 j=1,ngrid
      change=dsin(pi2*grid(j))
      des(j)=des(j)/change
  195 wt(j)=wt(j)*change
c
c  initial guess for the extremal frequencies--equally
c  spaced along the grid
c
  200 temp=float(ngrid-1)/float(nfcns)
      do 210 j=1,nfcns
      xt=j-1
  210 iext(j)=xt*temp+1.0
      iext(nfcns+1)=ngrid
      nm1=nfcns-1
      nz=nfcns+1
c
c  call the remez exchange algorithm to do the approximation
c  problem
c
      call remez
c
c  calculate the impulse response.
c
      if(neg) 300,300,320
  300 if(nodd.eq.0) go to 310
      do 305 j=1,nm1
      nzmj=nz-j
  305 h(j)=0.5*alpha(nzmj)
      h(nfcns)=alpha(1)
      go to 350
  310 h(1)=0.25*alpha(nfcns)
      do 315 j=2,nm1
      nzmj=nz-j
      nf2j=nfcns+2-j
  315 h(j)=0.25*(alpha(nzmj)+alpha(nf2j))
      h(nfcns)=0.5*alpha(1)+0.25*alpha(2)
      go to 350
  320 if(nodd.eq.0) go to 330
      h(1)=0.25*alpha(nfcns)
      h(2)=0.25*alpha(nm1)
      do 325 j=3,nm1
      nzmj=nz-j
      nf3j=nfcns+3-j
```

```
    325 h(j)=0.25*(alpha(nzmj)-alpha(nf3j))
        h(nfcns)=0.5*alpha(1)-0.25*alpha(3)
        h(nz)=0.0
        go to 350
    330 h(1)=0.25*alpha(nfcns)
        do 335 j=2,nm1
        nzmj=nz-j
        nf2j=nfcns+2-j
    335 h(j)=0.25*(alpha(nzmj)-alpha(nf2j))
        h(nfcns)=0.5*alpha(1)-0.25*alpha(2)
c
c  program output section.
c
    350 write(iout,360)
    360 format(1h1, 70(1h*)//15x,29hfinite impulse response (fir)/
       113x,34hlinear phase digital filter design/
       217x,24hremez exchange algorithm/)
        if(jtype.eq.1) write(iout,365)
    365 format(22x,15hbandpass filter/)
        if(jtype.eq.2) write(iout,370)
    370 format(22x,14hdifferentiator/)
        if(jtype.eq.3) write(iout,375)
    375 format(20x,19hhilbert transformer/)
        write(iout,378) nfilt
    378 format(20x,16hfilter length = ,i3/)
        write(iout,380)
    380 format(15x,28h***** impulse response *****)
        norder=nfilt-1
        write(iout2,*)norder
        do 381 j=1,nfcns
        write(iout2,*)h(j)
        k=nfilt+1-j
        if(neg.eq.0) write(iout,382) j,h(j),k
        if(neg.eq.1) write(iout,383) j,h(j),k
    381 continue
    382 format(13x,2hh(,i2,4h)  = ,e15.8,5h = h(,i3,1h))
    383 format(13x,2hh(,i2,4h)  = ,e15.8,6h = -h(,i3,1h))
        if(neg.eq.1.and.nodd.eq.1) write(iout,384) nz
    384 format(13x,2hh(,i2,8h)  =  0.0)
        do 450 k=1,nbands,4
        kup=k+3
        if(kup.gt.nbands) kup=nbands
        write(iout,385) (bd1,bd2,bd3,bd4,j,j=k,kup)
    385 format(/24x,4(4a1,i3,7x))
        write(iout,390) (edge(2*j-1),j=k,kup)
    390 format(2x,15hlower band edge,5f14.7)
        write(iout,395) (edge(2*j),j=k,kup)
    395 format(2x,15hupper band edge,5f14.7)
        if(jtype.ne.2) write(iout,400) (fx(j),j=k,kup)
    400 format(2x,13hdesired value,2x,5f14.7)
        if(jtype.eq.2) write(iout,405) (fx(j),j=k,kup)
    405 format(2x,13hdesired slope,2x,5f14.7)
        write(iout,410) (wtx(j),j=k,kup)
    410 format(2x,9hweighting,6x,5f14.7)
        do 420 j=k,kup
    420 deviat(j)=dev/wtx(j)
        write(iout,425) (deviat(j),j=k,kup)
    425 format(2x,9hdeviation,6x,5f14.7)
        if(jtype.ne.1) go to 450
        do 430 i=k.kup
```

```
      430 deviat(j)=20.0*alog10(deviat(j)+fx(j))
          write(iout,435) (deviat(j),j=k,kup)
      435 format(2x,15hdeviation in db,5f14.7)
      450 continue
          do 452 j=1,nz
          ix=iext(j)
      452 grid(j)=grid(ix)
c the following writes the extremal frequencies
c in the output. please also copy them into fort.4
          write(iout,455) (grid(j),j=1,nz)
c         iout1=4
c         write(iout1,456) (grid(j),j=1,nz)
456       format(1x,f14.9)
      455 format(/2x,47hextremal frequencies--maxima of the error curve/
         1 (2x,5f12.7))
          write(iout,460)
      460 format(/1x,70(1h*)/1h1)
          go to 100
          end
c
c----------------------------------------------------------------------
c subroutine: error
c    this routine writes an error message if an
c    error has been detected in the input data.
c----------------------------------------------------------------------
c
          subroutine error
          common /oops/niter,iout
          write(iout,1)
        1 format(44h *********** error in input data **********)
          return
          end
c
c----------------------------------------------------------------------
c subroutine: remez
c    this subroutine implements the remez exchange algorithm
c    for the weighted chebyshev approximation of a continuous
c    function with a sum of cosines.  inputs to the subroutine
c    are a dense grid which replaces the frequency axis, the
c    desired function on this grid, the weight function on the
c    grid, the number of cosines, and an initial guess of the
c    extremal frequencies.  the program minimizes the chebyshev
c    error by determining the best location of the extremal
c    frequencies (points of maximum error) and then calculates
c    the coefficients of the best approximation.
c----------------------------------------------------------------------
c
          subroutine remez
          common pi2,ad,dev,x,y,grid,des,wt,alpha,iext,nfcns,ngrid
          common /oops/niter,iout
          dimension iext(252),ad(252),alpha(252),x(252),y(252)
          dimension des(4032),grid(4032),wt(4032)
          dimension a(66),p(65),q(65)
          double precision pi2,dnum,dden,dtemp,a,p,q
          double precision dk,dak
          double precision ad,dev,x,y
          double precision gee,d
```

```
c
c   the program allows a maximum number of iterations of 25
c
      itrmax=25
      dev1=-1.0
      nz=nfcns+1
      nzz=nfcns+2
      niter=0
  100 continue
      iext(nzz)=ngrid+1
      niter=niter+1
      if(niter.gt.itrmax) go to 400
      do 110 j=1,nz
      jxt=iext(j)
      dtemp=grid(jxt)
      dtemp=dcos(dtemp*pi2)
  110 x(j)=dtemp
      jet=(nfcns-1)/15+1
      do 120 j=1,nz
  120 ad(j)=d(j,nz,jet)
      dnum=0.0
      dden=0.0
      k=1
      do 130 j=1,nz
      l=iext(j)
      dtemp=ad(j)*des(l)
      dnum=dnum+dtemp
      dtemp=float(k)*ad(j)/wt(l)
      dden=dden+dtemp
  130 k=-k
      dev=dnum/dden
      write(iout,131) dev
  131 format(1x,12hdeviation = ,f12.9)
      nu=1
      if(dev.gt.0.0) nu=-1
      dev=-float(nu)*dev
      k=nu
      do 140 j=1,nz
      l=iext(j)
      dtemp=float(k)*dev/wt(l)
      y(j)=des(l)+dtemp
  140 k=-k
      if(dev.gt.dev1) go to 150
      call ouch
      go to 400
  150 dev1=dev
      jchnge=0
      k1=iext(1)
      knz=iext(nz)
      klow=0
      nut=-nu
      j=1
c
c   search for the extremal frequencies of the best
c   approximation
c
```

```
200 if(j.eq.nzz) ynz=comp
    if(j.ge.nzz) go to 300
    kup=iext(j+1)
    l=iext(j)+1
    nut=-nut
    if(j.eq.2) yl=comp
    comp=dev
    if(l.ge.kup) go to 220
    err=gee(l,nz)
    err=(err-des(l))*wt(l)
    dtemp=float(nut)*err-comp
    if(dtemp.le.0.0) go to 220
    comp=float(nut)*err
210 l=l+1
    if(l.ge.kup) go to 215
    err=gee(l,nz)
    err=(err-des(l))*wt(l)
    dtemp=float(nut)*err-comp
    if(dtemp.le.0.0) go to 215
    comp=float(nut)*err
    go to 210
215 iext(j)=l-1
    j=j+1
    klow=l-1
    jchnge=jchnge+1
    go to 200
220 l=l-1
225 l=l-1
    if(l.le.klow) go to 250
    err=gee(l,nz)
    err=(err-des(l))*wt(l)
    dtemp=float(nut)*err-comp
    if(dtemp.gt.0.0) go to 230
    if(jchnge.le.0) go to 225
    go to 260
230 comp=float(nut)*err
235 l=l-1
    if(l.le.klow) go to 240
    err=gee(l,nz)
    err=(err-des(l))*wt(l)
    dtemp=float(nut)*err-comp
    if(dtemp.le.0.0) go to 240
    comp=float(nut)*err
    go to 235
240 klow=iext(j)
    iext(j)=l+1
    j=j+1
    jchnge=jchnge+1
    go to 200
250 l=iext(j)+1
    if(jchnge.gt.0) go to 215
255 l=l+1
    if(l.ge.kup) go to 260
    err=gee(l,nz)
    err=(err-des(l))*wt(l)
    dtemp=float(nut)*err-comp
    if(dtemp.le.0.0) go to 255
    comp=float(nut)*err
    go to 210
```

```
260 klow=iext(j)
    j=j+1
    go to 200
300 if(j.gt.nzz) go to 320
    if(k1.gt.iext(1)) k1=iext(1)
    if(knz.lt.iext(nz)) knz=iext(nz)
    nut1=nut
    nut=-nu
    l=0
    kup=k1
    comp=ynz*(1.00001)
    luck=1
310 l=l+1
    if(l.ge.kup) go to 315
    err=gee(l,nz)
    err=(err-des(l))*wt(l)
    dtemp=float(nut)*err-comp
    if(dtemp.le.0.0) go to 310
    comp=float(nut)*err
    j=nzz
    go to 210
315 luck=6
    go to 325
320 if(luck.gt.9) go to 350
    if(comp.gt.y1) y1=comp
    k1=iext(nzz)
325 l=ngrid+1
    klow=knz
    nut=-nut1
    comp=y1*(1.00001)
330 l=l-1
    if(l.le.klow) go to 340
    err=gee(l,nz)
    err=(err-des(l))*wt(l)
    dtemp=float(nut)*err-comp
    if(dtemp.le.0.0) go to 330
    j=nzz
    comp=float(nut)*err
    luck=luck+10
    go to 235
340 if(luck.eq.6) go to 370
    do 345 j=1,nfcns
    nzzmj=nzz-j
    nzmj=nz-j
345 iext(nzzmj)=iext(nzmj)
    iext(1)=k1
    go to 100
350 kn=iext(nzz)
    do 360 j=1,nfcns
360 iext(j)=iext(j+1)
    iext(nz)=kn
    go to 100
370 if(jchnge.gt.0) go to 100
c
c   calculation of the coefficients of the best approximation
c   using the inverse discrete fourier transform
c
```

```
400 continue
    nm1=nfcns-1
    fsh=1.0e-06
    gtemp=grid(1)
    x(nzz)=-2.0
    cn=2*nfcns-1
    delf=1.0/cn
    l=1
    kkk=0
    if(grid(1).lt.0.01.and.grid(ngrid).gt.0.49) kkk=1
    if(nfcns.le.3) kkk=1
    if(kkk.eq.1) go to 405
    dtemp=dcos(pi2*grid(1))
    dnum=dcos(pi2*grid(ngrid))
    aa=2.0/(dtemp-dnum)
    bb=-(dtemp+dnum)/(dtemp-dnum)
405 continue
    do 430 j=1,nfcns
    ft=j-1
    ft=ft*delf
    xt=dcos(pi2*ft)
    if(kkk.eq.1) go to 410
    xt=(xt-bb)/aa
    xt1=sqrt(1.0-xt*xt)
    ft=atan2(xt1,xt)/pi2
410 xe=x(1)
    if(xt.gt.xe) go to 420
    if((xe-xt).lt.fsh) go to 415
    l=l+1
    go to 410
415 a(j)=y(l)
    go to 425
420 if((xt-xe).lt.fsh) go to 415
    grid(l)=ft
    a(j)=gee(l,nz)
425 continue
    if(l.gt.1) l=l-1
430 continue
    grid(1)=gtemp
    dden=pi2/cn
    do 510 j=1,nfcns
    dtemp=0.0
    dnum=j-1
    dnum=dnum*dden
    if(nm1.lt.1) go to 505
    do 500 k=1,nm1
    dak=a(k+1)
    dk=k
500 dtemp=dtemp+dak*dcos(dnum*dk)
505 dtemp=2.0*dtemp+a(1)
510 alpha(j)=dtemp
    do 550 j=2,nfcns
550 alpha(j)=2.0*alpha(j)/cn
    alpha(1)=alpha(1)/cn
    if(kkk.eq.1) go to 545
    p(1)=2.0*alpha(nfcns)*bb+alpha(nm1)
    p(2)=2.0*aa*alpha(nfcns)
    q(1)=alpha(nfcns-2)-alpha(nfcns)
    do 540 j=2,nm1
    if(j.lt.nm1) go to 515
    aa=0.5*aa
    bb=0.5*bb
```

```
  515 continue
      p(j+1)=0.0
      do 520 k=1,j
      a(k)=p(k)
  520 p(k)=2.0*bb*a(k)
      p(2)=p(2)+a(1)*2.0*aa
      jm1=j-1
      do 525 k=1,jm1
  525 p(k)=p(k)+q(k)+aa*a(k+1)
      jp1=j+1
      do 530 k=3,jp1
  530 p(k)=p(k)+aa*a(k-1)
      if(j.eq.nm1) go to 540
      do 535 k=1,j
  535 q(k)=-a(k)
      nf1j=nfcns-1-j
      q(1)=q(1)+alpha(nf1j)
  540 continue
      do 543 j=1,nfcns
  543 alpha(j)=p(j)
  545 continue
      if(nfcns.gt.3) return
      alpha(nfcns+1)=0.0
      alpha(nfcns+2)=0.0
      return
      end
c
c------------------------------------------------------------------
c function: d
c   function to calculate the lagrange interpolation
c   coefficients for use in the function gee.
c------------------------------------------------------------------
c
      double precision function d(k,n,m)
      common pi2,ad,dev,x,y,grid,des,wt,alpha,iext,nfcns,ngrid
      dimension iext(252),ad(252),alpha(252),x(252),y(252)
      dimension des(4032),grid(4032),wt(4032)
      double precision ad,dev,x,y
      double precision q
      double precision pi2
      d=1.0
      q=x(k)
      do 3 l=1,m
      do 2 j=l,n,m
      if(j-k)1,2,1
    1 d=2.0*d*(q-x(j))
    2 continue
    3 continue
      d=1.0/d
      return
      end
c
c------------------------------------------------------------------
c function: gee
c   function to evaluate the frequency response using the
c   lagrange interpolation formula in the barycentric form
c------------------------------------------------------------------
c
      double precision function gee(k,n)
      common pi2,ad,dev,x,y,grid,des,wt,alpha,iext,nfcns,ngrid
      dimension iext(252),ad(252),alpha(252),x(252),y(252)
```

```
      dimension des(4032),grid(4032),wt(4032)
      double precision p,c,d,xf
      double precision pi2
      double precision ad,dev,x,y
      p=0.0
      xf=grid(k)
      xf=dcos(pi2*xf)
      d=0.0
      do 1 j=1,n
      c=xf-x(j)
      c=ad(j)/c
      d=d+c
    1 p=p+c*y(j)
      gee=p/d
      return
      end
c
c-----------------------------------------------------------------------
c subroutine: ouch
c    writes an error message when the algorithm fails to
c    converge. there seem to be two conditions under which
c    the algorithm fails to converge: (1) the initial
c    guess for the extremal frequencies is so poor that
c    the exchange iteration cannot get started, or
c    (2) near the termination of a correct design,
c    the deviation decreases due to rounding errors
c    and the program stops. in this latter case the
c    filter design is probably acceptable, but should
c    be checked by computing a frequency response.
c-----------------------------------------------------------------------
c
      subroutine ouch
      common /oops/niter,iout
      write(iout,1)niter
    1 format(44h *********** failure to converge *********/
     141hOprobable cause is machine rounding error/
     223hOnumber of iterations =,i4/
     339hOif the number of iterations exceeds 3,/
     462hOthe design may be correct, but should be verified with an fft)
      return
      end
```

```
c MAGRES.f
c
c
c
c  ********************************************************************
c
c INPUTS: fr(1) .... fr(2^m): real valued data
c         m: where 2^m is the number of points
c
c OUTPTS: fmag(1) .. fmag(2^m): The magnitude of DFT
c
c  ********************************************************************
c
      subroutine magres(fr,fmag,m)
      dimension fr(1),frnw(1025),finw(1025),fmag(1)
      pi=4*atan(1.d00)
      n=2**m
      do 222 i=1,n
            frnw(i)=fr(i)
            finw(i)=0.0
222   continue
      mm=1
      ll=n/2
      do 1 k=1,m
      tta=pi/ll
      ti=sin(tta/2)
      cs=-2*ti*ti
      sd=sin(tta)
      c=1
      s=0
      do 2 l=1,mm
      i=1+(l-1)*ll*2
      ii=i+ll
      a=frnw(i)-frnw(ii)
      b=finw(i)-finw(ii)
      frnw(i)= frnw(i)+frnw(ii)
      finw(i)=finw(i)+finw(ii)
      frnw(ii)=a
2     finw(ii)=b
      if (ll-2)6,5,5
5     do 4 j=2,ll
3     cold=c
      c=cs*c-sd*s+c
      s=cs*s+sd*cold+s
      do 4 l=1,mm
      i=j+(l-1)*ll*2
      ii=i+ll
      a=frnw(i)-frnw(ii)
      b=finw(i)-finw(ii)
      frnw(i)=frnw(i)+frnw(ii)
      finw(i)=finw(i)+finw(ii)
      frnw(ii)=a*c+b*s
4     finw(ii)=b*c-a*s
      ll=ll/2
1     mm=mm*2
6     call fftbi(frnw,finw,m)
      do 111 i=1,n
```

```
111     fmag(i)=cabs(cmplx(frnw(i),finw(i)))
        return
        end
        subroutine fftbi(fr,fi,m)
        dimension fr(1),fi(1)
        n=2**m
        ib=0
        nil=n-1
        do 1 i=2,nil
        do 2 j=1,m
        nt=n/(2**j)
        if (ib-nt)3,2,2
2       ib=ib-nt
        go to 7
3       ib=ib+nt
        if (ib+1-i)1,1,5
5       t=fr(i)
        fr(i)=fr(ib+1)
        fr(ib+1)=t
        t=fi(i)
        fi(i)=fi(ib+1)
        fi(ib+1)=t
1       continue
7       return
        end
```

```
c
c **********************************************************************
c EFFW1.f
c
c This program now works in conjunction with the Fortran functions
c "EXTFUN.f", "RRS.f", and "ZERO.f".
c Modified by P. P.Vaidyanathan, Dept. EE, Caltech, Pasadena, CA 91125.
c
c------------------------------------------------------------------------
c
c    EFF: Function to calculate the desired magnitude response
c    as a function of frequency.
c    An arbitrary function of frequency can be
c    approximated if the user replaces this function
c    with the appropriate code to evaluate the ideal
c    magnitude.  note that the parameter freq is the
c    value of normalized frequency needed for evaluation.
c
c
c    _____
c
      function eff(freq,fx,wtx,lband,jtype)
      dimension fx(5),wtx(5)
      if(jtype.eq.2) go to 1
      if(fx(lband).lt.0.0001) go to 2
        eff=fx(lband)/extfun(freq*2)
      return
    2 eff=fx(lband)
      return
    1 eff=fx(lband)*freq
      return
      end
c-------------------------------------------------------------------------
c function: wate
c    function to calculate the weight function as a function
c    of frequency.  Similar to the function eff, this function can
c    be replaced by a user-written routine to calculate any
c    desired weighting function.
c-------------------------------------------------------------------------
c
      function wate(freq,fx,wtx,lband,jtype,freqs)
      dimension fx(5),wtx(5)
      if(jtype.eq.2) go to 1
      if(fx(lband).lt.0.0001) go to 2
      wate=wtx(lband)*extfun(freq*2)
      return
c
      return
    1 if(fx(lband).lt.0.0001) go to 2
      wate=wtx(lband)/freq
      return
      end
c
c **********************************************************************
c
c   EXTFUN.f
c
c By appropriate choice of this function, a wide variety of
c linear-phase filters can be designed. This function essentially
c affects the function-subprograms EFF and WATE.
c Please look at the listings of EFF and WATE above, to see
c how "extfun" comes in.
```

```
c EFF corresponds to the "desired response" to be approximated
c by the Remez algorithm, whereas the function WATE corresponds
c to the weighting function.
c
c As an illustration, consider design example 6, where we designed
c H(z) as in Eqn. (2.58). Here, H2(z) is fixed as in (2.57),
c whereas H1(z) is designed using the Remez-exchange algorithm
c in such a manner that H(z) has equiripple passband. The choice
c of "extfun" in this problem corresponds to "IMETH=3" below.
c As another illustration, consider Design Example 13. Here again
c the overall transfer function is H(z)=H1(z)H2(z), where H2(z)
c is the RRS of Eqn. (2.133) with S=13. The linear-phase FIR
c transfer function H1(z) is obtained such that H(z) has equiripple
c passband behavior as shown in Fig. 2.34(b).
c The choice of "extfun" in this problem corresponds
c to "imeth=2" below.
c
c The sixth item on line 1 of FORT.9 is the variable imeth;
c
c        IMETH=        1 For usual equiripple design
c                      2 Prefilter-equalizer method based on Running sum
c                      3 To obtain transmission zero at freq0(mul of PI)
c                        where freq0 should somehow be made known
c                        to the program; we have chosen to include
c                        the statement  "freq0=0.78"  in here, but
c                        this is only an example.
c
c        Freq, freq0 are in mul of PI
c
         function extfun(freq)
         rewind(9)
         read(9,*)imeth
         goto(1,2,3)imeth
1        extfun=1.0
         return
2        extfun=rrs(freq,N)
         return
3        freq0=0.78
         extfun=zero(freq,freq0)
         return
         end
c
c ****************************************************************
c
c RRS.f
c
c Freq is in multiple of PI
c
c "N" here corresponds to "S" in Eqn. (2.133)
c The value of N (which is the length of the recursive running sum)
c must somehow be fed into the program. As an example,
c we have punched in "N=13" in here.
c
         function rrs(freq,N)
         N=13
         if(freq.eq.0)rrs=1.0
         if(freq.eq.0)return
         pi=4*atan(1.00)
         omega=pi*freq
         rrs=sin(omega*N*0.5)/sin(omega*0.5)
```

```
              rrs=rrs/N
              return
              end
c
c  **************************************************************
c
c  ZERO.f
c
              function zero(freq,freq0)
              pi=4*atan(1.00)
              omega0=pi*freq0
              omega=pi*freq
              zero=cos(omega)-cos(omega0)
              return
              end
c
c  **************************************************************
c
c  COMPE.f
c
c  The purpose of this program is to evaluate the magnitude
c  response of H(z)=H1(z)H2(z), where H1(z) has magnitude
c  response stored in the array hresp(i), and where the magnitude
c  response of H2(z) is obtained by invoking "extfun". The
c  applications of this program are in design examples such as
c  6 and 13.
c
c          INPUTS:   hresp(1)  ......  hresp(nout+1)
c          OUTPUT:   hresp(1)  ......  hresp(nout+1)
c                    modified by multiplying with extfun(i).
c
              subroutine compe(hresp,nout)
              dimension hresp(1)
2             do 3 i=1 , nout+1
                    freq=(i-1.00)/nout
                    htemp=extfun(freq)
              old=hresp(i)
                    hresp(i)=hresp(i)*abs(htemp)
              htemp1=abs(htemp)
3             continue
              return
              end
```

REFERENCES

1. A. V. Oppenheim and R. W. Schafer, *Digital Signal Processing*, Prentice-Hall, Englewood Cliffs, N.J., 1975.
2. L. R. Rabiner and B. Gold, *Theory and Application of Digital Signal Processing*, Prentice-Hall, Englewood Cliffs, N.J., 1975.
3. T. G. Stockham, Jr., High speed convolution and correlation, AFIPS Conf. Proceedings, Spring Joint Computer Conference, 1966.
4. L. R. Rabiner, Techniques for designing finite duration impulse response digital filters, *IEEE Trans. Comm. Technol.* **COM-19**, 188–195 (April 1971).
5. J. F. Kaiser, Nonrecursive digital filter design using the I_0–sinh window function, *Proc. 1974 IEEE Int. Symp. Circuits Systems* April 1974, 20–23.
6. R. W. Hamming, *Digital Filters*, Prentice-Hall, Englewood Cliffs, N.J., 1977.
7. F. J. Harris, On the use of windows for harmonic analysis with the discrete fourier transform, *Proc. IEEE* **66**, 51–83 (January 1978).
8. D. F. Elliott and K. R. Rao, *Fast Transforms—Algorithms, Analyses, and Applications*, Academic Press, New York, 1982.
9. D. Slepian, H. O. Pollak, and H. J. Landau, Prolate spheroidal wave functions, Fourier analysis and uncertainity, parts I, II, *Bell System Technical J.* **40**, 43–84 (January 1961).
10. T. W. Parks and J. H. McClellan, Chebyshev approximation for nonrecursive digital filters with linear phase, *IEEE Trans. Circuit Theory* **19**, 189–194 (March 1972).
11. J. H. McClellan and T. W. Parks, A unified approach to the design of optimum FIR linear-phase digital filters, *IEEE Trans. Circuit Theory* **20**, 697–701 (November 1973).
12. H. G. Martinez and T. W. Parks, Design of recursive digital filters with optimum magnitude and attenuation poles on the unit circle, *IEEE Trans Acoust. Speech Signal Proc.* **26**, 150–156 (April 1978).
13. C. R. Galand and H. J. Nussbaumer, New quadrature mirror filter structures, *IEEE Trans. Acoust. Speech Signal Proc.* **32**, 522–531 (June 1984).
14. O. Herrmann, Design of nonrecursive digital filters with linear phase, *Electron. Letters* **6**, (May 1970).
15. E. Hofstetter, A. V. Oppenheim, and J. Siegel, A new technique for the design of nonrecursive digital filters, *Proc. Fifth Annual Princeton Conf. Inform. Sci. Systems*, 1971, pp. 64–72.
16. L. R. Rabiner, J. H. McClellan, and T. W. Parks, FIR digital filter design techniques using weighted Chebyshev approximation, *Proc. IEEE* **63**, 595–610 (April 1975).
17. L. R. Rabiner, Approximate design relationships for lowpass FIR digital filters, *IEEE. Trans. Audio Electroacoustics* **21**, 456–460 (October 1973).
18. A. Antoniou, New improved method for the design of weighted-Chebyshev, nonrecursive, digital filters, *IEEE Trans. Circuits Systems* **CAS-30**, 740–750 (October 1983).
19. IEEE Digital Signal Processing Committee, Editor, *Programs for Digital Signal Processing*, IEEE Press, New York, 1979.
20. O. Herrmann, On the approximation problem in nonrecursive digital filter design, *IEEE Trans. Circuit Theory* **18**, 411–413 (May 1971).
21. J. F. Kaiser, Design subroutine (MXFLAT) for symmetric FIR low pass digital filters with maximally flat pass and stop bands, in *Programs for Digital Signal Processing*, edited by IEEE Digital Signal Processing Committee, IEEE Press, New York, 1979.
22. P. P. Vaidyanathan, On maximally flat linear phase FIR filters, *IEEE Trans. Circuits Systems* **31**, 830–832 (September 1984).
23. P. P. Vaidyanathan, Efficient and multiplierless design of FIR filters with very sharp cutoff via maximally flat building blocks, *IEEE Trans. Circuits Systems* **32**, 236–244 (March 1985).
24. L. R. Rabiner, Linear program design of FIR digital filters, *IEEE Trans. Audio Electroacoustics* **20**, 280–288 (October 1972).
25. K. Steiglitz, Optimal design of FIR digital filters with monotone passband response, *IEEE Trans. Acoust., Speech Signal Proc.* **27**, 643–649 (December 1979).

26. J. F. Kaiser and K. Steiglitz, Design of FIR filters with flatness constraints, *IEEE Int. Conf. on Acoust., Speech and Signal Proc.*, April 1983, pp. 197–199.

27. L. R. Rabiner, N, Y. Graham, and H. D. Helms, Linear programming design of IIR digital filters with arbitrary magnitude function, *IEEE Trans. Acoust., Speech Signal Proc.* **22**, 117–123 (April 1974).

28. A. G. Constantinides, Spectral transformations for digital filters, *Proc. IEEE* **117**, 1585–1590 (August 1970).

29. A. V. Oppenheim, W. F. G. Mecklenbrauker, and R. M. Mersereau, Variable cutoff linear phase digital filters, *IEEE Trans. Circuits Systems* **23**, 199–203 (April 1976).

30. P. P. Vaidyanathan, Optimal design of linear-phase FIR digital filters with very flat passbands and equiripple stopbands, *IEEE Trans. Circuits Systems* **CAS-32** (September 1985).

31. J. F. Kaiser and R. W. Hamming, Sharpening the response of a symmetric nonrecursive filter by multiple use of the same filter, *IEEE Trans. Acoust., Speech Signal Proc.* **ASSP-25**, 415–422 (October 1977).

32. R. M. Mersereau, W. F. G. Mecklenbrauker, and T. F. Quatieri, McClellan transformations for two dimensional digital filtering. I Design, *IEEE Trans. Circuits Systems* **23**, 405–413 (July 1976).

33. J. H. McClellan, The design of two-dimensional digital filters by transformations, *Proc. Seventh Annual Princeton Conf. Information Sciences and Systems*, 1973, pp. 247–251.

34. W. F. G. Mecklenbrauker and R. M. Mersereau, McClellan transformations for two-dimensional digital filtering. II: Implementation, *IEEE Trans.* **23**, 414–422 (July 1976).

35. Y. Kamp and J. P. Thiran, Chebyshev approximation for two-dimensional nonrecursive digital filters, *IEEE Trans. Circuits Systems* **22**, 208–218 (March 1975).

36. P. P. Vaidyanathan, Fast design of efficient FIR digital filters, based on maximally flat building blocks, *Proc. Annual Princeton Conf. Information Sciences and Systems*, March 1984, pp. 387–391.

37. Y. Neuvo, C.-Y. Dong, and S. K. Mitra, Interpolated finite impulse response filters, *IEEE Trans. Acoust., Speech Signal Proc.* **32**, 563–570 (June 1984).

38. J. W. Adams and A. N. Willson, Jr., A new approach to FIR digital filters with fewer multipliers and reduced sensitivity, *IEEE Trans. Circuits Systems* **30**, 277–283 (May 1983).

39. J. W. Adams and A. N. Willson, Jr., Some efficient digital prefilter structures, *IEEE Trans. Circuits Systems* **31**, 260–266 (March 1984).

40. P. P. Vaidyanathan and G. Beitman, On prefilters for digital FIR filter design, *IEEE Trans. Circuits Systems* **32**, 494–499 (May 1985).

41. M. E. Van Valkenburg, *Modern Network Synthesis*, Wiley, New York 1964.

42. T. Saramaki, A class of linear-phase FIR filters for decimation, interpolation and narrow-band filtering, *IEEE Trans. Acoust., Speech Signal Proc.* **32**, 1023–1036 (October 1984).

43. S. Chu and C. S. Burrus, Multirate filter design using comb filters, *IEEE Trans. Circuits Systems* **31**, 913–924 (November 1984).

44. O. Herrmann and W. Schussler, Design of nonrecursive digital filters with minimum phase, *Electron. Letters* (May 1970).

45. E. Goldberg, R. Kurshan, and D. Malah, Design of FIR digital filters with nonlinear phase response, *IEEE Trans. Acoust., Speech Signal Proc.* **29**, 1003–1010 (October 1981).

46. Y. Kamp and C. J. Wellekens, Optimal design of minimum phase FIR filters, *IEEE Trans. Acoust., Speech Signal Proc.* **31**, 922–926 (August 1983).

47. G. A. Mian and A. P. Nainer, A fast procedure to design equiripple minimum-phase FIR filters, *IEEE Trans. Circuits Systems* **29**, 327–331 (May 1982).

48. R. Boite and H. Leich, Comments on "A fast procedure to design equiripple minimum-phase FIR filters," *IEEE Trans Circuits System* **31**, 503–504 (May 1984).

49. S. Acton, *Numerical Methods That Work*, Harper & Row, New York, 1970.

50. C. E. Schmidt and L. R. Rabiner, A study of techniques for finding the zeros of linear phase FIR digital filters, *IEEE Trans. Acoust., Speech Signal Proc.* **25**, 96–98 (February 1977).

51. M. G. Bellanger, J. L. Daguet, and G. P. Lepagnol, Interpolation, extrapolation, and reduction of

computation speed in digital filters, *IEEE Trans. Acoust., Speech Signal Proc.* **ASSP-22,** 231–235 (August 1974).

52. F. Mintzer, On half-band, third-band and Nth-band FIR filters and their design, *IEEE Trans. Acoust., Speech Signal Proc.* **ASSP-30,** 734–738 (October 1982).
53. R. E. Crochiere and L. R. Rabiner, *Multirate Digital Signal Processing,* Prentice-Hall, Englewoods Cliffs, N.J., 1983.
54. M. J. T. Smith and T. P. Barnwell, A procedure for designing exact reconstruction filter banks for tree-structured subband coders, *IEEE Int. Conf. on Acoustics, Speech and Signal Processing,* Vol. 2 March 1984, pp. 27.1.1–27.1.4.
55. P. P. Vaidyanathan, On power complementary FIR filters, *IEEE Trans. Circuits Systems* **32,** 1308–1310 (December 1985).
56. L. R. Rabiner, J. F. Kaiser, O. Herrmann, and M. T. Dolan, Some comparisons between FIR and IIR digital filters, *Bell System Technical J.* **53,** 305–331 (February 1974).
57. H. D. Helms, Nonrecursive digital filters: design methods for achieving specifications on frequency response, *IEEE Trans. Audio Electroacoust.* **16,** 336–342 (September 1968).
58. J. H. McClellan, T. W. Parks, and L. R. Rabiner, A computer program for designing optimum FIR linear phase digital filters. *IEEE Trans. Audio Electroacoust.* **AU-21,** 506–526 (December 1973).
59. L. R. Rabiner and B. Gold, *Theory and Application of Digital Signal Processing,* Prentice-Hall, Englewood Cliffs, N.J., 1975.
60. L. R. Rabiner and R. Shafer, On the behavior of minimax relative error FIR digital differentiators, *Bell Syst. Tech. J.* **53,** 333–361 (February 1974).
61. L. R. Rabiner and R. Schafer, On the behavior of minimax FIR digital Hilbert transformers, *Bell Syst. Tech. J.* **53,** 363–390 (February 1974).

Chapter **3**

Multirate FIR Filters for Interpolating and Desampling

FREDERIC J. HARRIS
Department of Electrical and Computer Engineering
San Diego State University
San Diego, California 92182

INTRODUCTION I

In many signal processing applications it is desirable to have the output sample rate be different from the input sample rate. The process of altering the data rates within a digital filter is known as resampling, and the algorithms that perform this resampling are called multirate filters. By extension, a multirate filter may achieve a desired change in sample rate by using a cascade of simple multirate subfilters. Each subfilter performs a segment of the resampling process. The partition is often selected to minimize the total computational burden.

If the output rate of a filter is less than the input rate, we say we have downsampled (or decimated or desampled) the output. On the other hand, if the output rate is greater than the input rate, we say we have upsampled (or interpolated) the output. The ratio of output to input sample rates can be any ratio of integers, P/M. Here either integer (P or M) can be unity. It is also possible to make this ratio slowly time varying. Figure 3.1 presents examples of sample-rate change filter configurations. To help us understand the constraints of the resampling process, we will examine desamplings of $1/M$ and unsamplings of $P/1$.

173

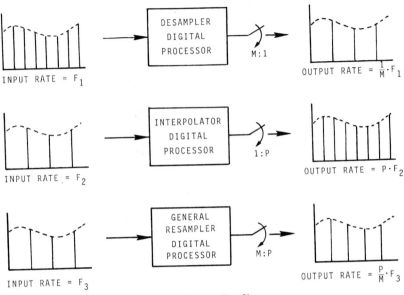

Fig. 3.1. Resampling filters.

A   Examples of Systems with Multirate Filters

We will now identify a number of examples of systems that use multirate processing [1]. The list will certainly not be exhaustive. The value of this section is to help the novice understand how system considerations lead to a multirate design. It also gives us specific systems to which we can refer when we later develop the design techniques for multirate filters.

1   Zoom Transform

For this example, we describe an application for desampling. In particular, let us consider the spectral analysis scheme known as a zoom transform. A conventional discrete Fourier transform (DFT) algorithm processes N points of input data. The output of the algorithm is N points of the input data's spectrum. These spectral points are analogous to those obtained from a bank of equally spaced contiguous narrowband filters. The spectral resolution (i.e., filter spacing) of this bank is the input sample rate divided by the transform size, f_s/N.

To obtain a finer spectral resolution, we must either increase the transform size N or decrease the sample rate f_s. The zoom transform uses the multirate filter to accomplish the latter. We preprocess the input data with a complex heterodyne and a lowpass filter. The complex heterodyne first shifts a desired (but arbitrary) center frequency to zero frequency. The lowpass filter then reduces the bandwidth of this shifted signal by convolving (a weighted average) the filter impulse

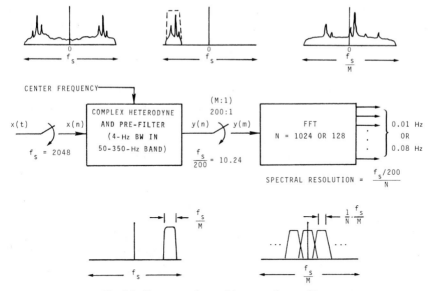

Fig. 3.2. Zoom transform with resampling prefilter.

response with the shifted input series. The output bandwidth of the lowpass is approximately the inverse of the averaging time interval. The output of this heterodyne and average process is a time series representing the complex envelope of the narrowband signal centered at the heterodyne frequency and with the bandwidth of the lowpass filter. Note we have independent control of the center frequency and of the bandwidth for this series.

Since the bandwidth of this series has been reduced by, say, a factor of $M:1$, we can still satisfy the Nyquist criterion if we reduce the output sample rate by the same factor. Thus we select the output sample rate f'_s to be f_s/M. Now if the time series at this rate is presented to the DFT, the DFT output spectral resolution is f'_s/N (or f_s/MN). An example of this process is shown in Fig. 3.2. Here the input data, sampled at 2048 samples per second, is prefiltered to a 4-Hz bandwidth prior to a 200:1 sample-rate reduction to 10.24 samples/s.

Fractional Octave Spectrum Analyzer **2**

In this example we examine another application for desampling filters. The DFT can be visualized as an algorithm to synthesize a bank of constant-bandwidth, equally spaced contiguous filters. A variation of this filter bank is a contiguous filter set characterized by constant bandwidth and equal spacing on a logarithmic scale [1]. Filters defined by these specifications are called constant-Q filters because the ratio of center frequency to bandwidth (classical definition of filter quality factor) is a constant.

Spectra of vibrating mechanical systems are normally described or analyzed by equal increments on a logarithmic scale. Examples include the Western world's tempered music scale, (in which the frequency ratio of adjacent notes is $2^{1/12}$), and fractional octave (third-octave and tenth-octave) filter banks used in sound-level measurements.

Figure 3.3 is a block diagram of a third-octave spectrum analyzer. Here, the sampled data is presented to two subprocessors. The upper processor is a bank of three filters designed to perform the constant-Q decomposition at the top analysis octave, say 10.0–20.0 kHz. The input sample rate (assume for our example this is 50.0 kHz) is chosen at least twice the highest analysis frequency. Thus the top octave is located between 20% and 40% of the input sample rate. The next lower analysis octave would be between 10% and 20% of the input sample rate. We access this next octave by processing the series obtained from the lower subprocessor.

The lower segment of the process is a baseband filter designed to reduce the input bandwidth by a factor of 2. The output of this filter is then desampled by the same factor. We note that the second octave band, which is located between

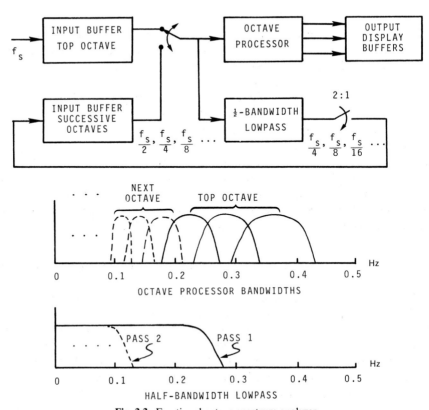

Fig. 3.3. Fractional octave spectrum analyzer.

10% and 20% of the input rate, is also located between 20% and 40% of the output rate. The upper processor can now filter this data (at its lower rate) to access the next lower octave. The lower subprocessor also prepares this data by again filtering and desampling for the next lower octave. This combination of decomposing the data into its top octave (by the upper processor) while preparing the data for decomposing the next lower octave (by the lower processor) is performed by nested passes through the two subprocessors for as many octaves of analysis as desired. (Figure 3.24, presented later, shows the equivalent sequence of filter desample, filter desample, etc., as a cascade of identical filters.)

We note that with 2:1 resampling between processing successive octaves, a particular octave is decomposed with the same computational burden as the next higher octave, but at half the data rate. Thus each lower octave requires half the previous computation rate. Since the total computation rate is proportional to the sum $1 + \frac{1}{2} + \frac{1}{4} + \frac{1}{8} + \frac{1}{16} + \cdots$. The total workload to compute the outputs for all the lower octaves is never greater than that required to decompose the top octave. The overhead of the filtering performed in the lower subprocessor is less than that of the upper processor but, as a first estimate, can be considered comparable. The lower processor also operates on successive desampled series with the total work for all lower bands not exceeding that of the top octave.

Interpolation for Complex-to-Real Data Conversion **3**

In this example we examine the postprocessing task of converting a complex time series at one sampling rate to a real series at a higher rate [3]. Many signal processing algorithms process time series as the in-phase and quadrature-phase (I-Q) components of a complex series. The advantage of this form of processing is that the signal magnitude and phase are preserved at its minimum bandwidth; hence the signal can be processed at the minimum sample rate. One example of this form of processing is the demultiplexing of a single-sideband frequency-division-multiplexed (SSB-FDM) signal, which we will examine closely in Chapter 8. The result of the demultiplexing is a collection of separated channels of complex data. In telephone traffic each channel is nominally 3.6 kHz wide, and the demultiplexed complex data rate is typically 4.0–6.0 kHz. This complex data must then be converted to real data at rates between 8.0 and 10.0 kHz.

The example in Fig. 3.4 demonstrates the process of converting a complex data set at 6-kHz rate to a real data set of 8 kHz. A simplified description of the process is that the real and imaginary series are separately interpolated up to a new sample frequency of 24 kHz. The data at this new data rate is then desampled by a factor of 3 to obtain the desired data rate of 8 kHz. A complex heterodyne is then applied to the complex data, which is now at the proper sample rate, to move the center frequency from 0 to 2 kHz. The real part of this spectrally shifted series is the desired output. In actual fact the processing is altered slightly so that the data discarded by the two desampling operations (after the interpolation and after the complex heterodyne) is not computed. We will examine this example in detail at the end of this chapter.

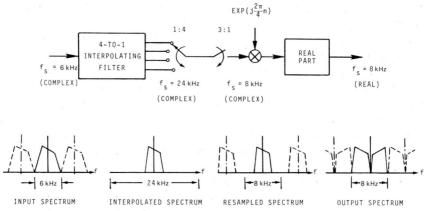

Fig. 3.4. Complex-to-real resampling filter.

4   Interpolating For Time Domain Beamforming

In this example we describe a system that uses the resampling interpolator filter, not to raise the sample rate, but to generate data samples shifted a small increment in time from the original input data sample positions. This system is a time domain beamformer. Beamforming, a spatial filtering operation, is used to separate signals arriving from many simultaneous directions into distinct subsignals that are ordered by direction of arrival. Beamforming entails delay and addition of signals collected over a spatial aperture. In a time delay beamformer, coarse delay is realized as transport delay in a tapped delay line. Fine delay, a fraction of the interval between the available coarse delays, is realized with a broadband time delay filter. Narrowband beamformers often approximate the desired time delays by additive phase shift in the frequency domain; in this case they are known as phased-array beamformers [4].

In an array beamformer the signals intercepted by the aperture are collected at distinct (often equally spaced) element locations across that aperture. The beam is steered by inserting time delays in the separate signal paths to compensate for the delays associated with a specified wavefront crossing the array. Beam steering by digital signal processing techniques is facilitated by uniformly sampling in time the signals observed at each spatial location. Thus the raw data collected for an array beamformer can be thought of as a two-dimensional data array, the dimensions being distance and time.

A mapping of a memory containing the data collected from a uniformly spaced array of hydrophones is suggested in Fig. 3.5. Indicated in Fig. 3.5 are three time-space contours over which data points must be summed to form beams facing the indicated directions. (The spatial direction is scaled by the propagation velocity so that both directions are proportional to time). Note that along contour 2 some of the time series do not have a time data point along the contour of summation

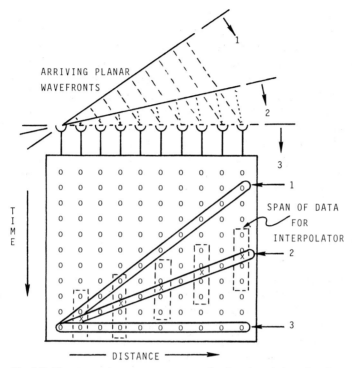

Fig. 3.5. Time-space data memory contours for time domain beamforming.

(the missing points are denoted by an X). If the ratio of sample rate to bandwidth is sufficiently high (to insure high intersample correlation), we could select the nearest-neighbor data point as an acceptable approximation to the desired data point. Alternatively, we can interpolate to the desired position from the data points in the neighborhood, such as over the data spans in Fig. 3.5.

As in amplitude quantization, the time quantization (i.e., the deviation from the line of summation) has an effect similar to additive noise and must be made acceptably small. We could reduce the time quantization by simply increasing the sample rate for each spatial element. For instance, rather than sample near the Nyquist rate, say 2.5 times the highest frequency, we might choose to sample 30.0 times the highest frequency. This solution is not generally desirable for the following reasons. Most of the extra data points would not be used in any of the beam summations, but a higher speed and larger memory space would have to be used to store them. (Partial-sum beamformers manage to get around this objection by storing the desired sums rather than the raw data.) In addition, the higher-speed analog-to-digital converter (ADC) is a hardware item with a significantly higher cost that we may wish to avoid.

An alternative to the higher sample rate is the use of interpolating filters. The filters can be used to upsample the data from each spatial element to synthesize the desired higher sample rate. But we do not really want a higher sample rate, but one new data point at some location in the time interval between two collected data points. We realize the two requirements by first upsampling, via the interpolating filter, to the acceptable time quantization and then desampling back to the original data rate with the selected time delay. Hence the interpolating filter operates at an output rate that matches the input data rate and outputs data only at the time position required for the given beam summation. We will see later that by imbedding the desampling operation in the upsampling filter, we obtain a filter architecture with a particularly simple structure. The filter can be viewed as partitioned into a collection of subinterpolators known as polyphase filters, and the resampling to the desired output time position is performed by selecting the proper polyphase subfilter.

B   Overview of Chapter

In this chapter we shall identify the parameters that describe FIR filter characteristics, and we shall review how these parameters interact. The emphasis will be on how the coupling between these parameters affects the design of multirate filters. We start with classical frequency and time domain specifications of lowpass FIR filters and present a number of quick, first-order approximations to the ways they interact. We then show how data rate reduction is achieved with lowpass FIR filters. Here we demonstrate, via the McClellan-Parks (MP) design algorithm (see Section IV.D in Chapter 2), how the choice of filter parameters controls filter characteristics and how these parameters can be traded for desirable performance gains. We then examine data rate reduction techniques that use carrier-centered FIR filters, and we also examine center frequencies with interesting signal processing characteristics. We next investigate interpolating filters used to obtain increases in the data rate by integer multiples and then increases by multiples that are a ratio of integers. Finally we look at simple architectural models of FIR filters. One strength of this chapter is the liberal use of graphical presentations to demonstrate the important FIR filter relationships.

II   CHARACTERISTICS OF BANDWIDTH-REDUCING FIR FILTERS

Finite duration impulse response (FIR) filters were introduced in the previous chapter. They perform their filtering operation as a collection of finite inner products. These inner products are implemented by a sequence of multiplications and additions. For each output point computed during the filtering operation, there is one addition per filter coefficient and (if symmetric) one multiplication per pair of coefficients. Thus the computational burden to implement a FIR filter is proportional to the number of its coefficients (or, equivalently, to its length).

Since the number of multiplications and additions per output point is an important consideration in implementing a filter, a major descriptor of a FIR filter is its length N. We saw in the last chapter that the filter length is controlled by a combination of frequency domain specifications, primarily transition bandwidth and passband and stopband ripple [see (2.19) and (2.31)]. A secondary descriptor is the filter impulse response or, equivalently, the particular set of coefficients.

A major attraction of the FIR filter is the (usually exercised) option to have the frequency response exhibit linear phase. Linear phase is so desirable that we sometimes forget that it is only an option. Filters exhibiting linear-phase characteristics are constrained to have either even or odd symmetry about their midpoint. This constraint permits us to reduce the number of multiplications per output point by precombining data points that will be multiplied by identical coefficients.

Filters used in multirate processing are usually bandwidth-reducing filters, which we will show are related to a simple lowpass filter. Most of these filters are designed to be even frequency domain functions and will have an envelope reminiscent of the $\sin(wt)/(wt)$ function.

Frequency Domain Characteristics   A

We now examine the frequency domain characteristics of realizable lowpass filters [5–7]. Since we are discussing sampled data filters, it will be convenient to describe all frequencies as a fraction of the sample rate. This is equivalent to dividing (normalizing) all frequencies by the sampling frequency. Thus the sampling frequency becomes 1.0, the half-sampling frequency becomes 0.5, etc. (See Fig. 1.4.)

The ideal lowpass filter has unity gain between the frequencies $\pm f_p$, and zero gain elsewhere. The realizable filter can only approximate the ideal. The approximation includes an acceptable deviation envelope about unity gain in the passband region, an acceptable deviation envelope about zero gain in the stopband region, and an interval over which the filter gain must make the transition from unity gain to zero gain. The transition interval, Δf, is normally implied by (the difference between) the upper edge of the passband f_p and the lower edge of the stopband (rejection band) f_r. These parameters are indicated in Fig. 3.6. In the next section we will see how to convert a set of resampling specifications into these filter parameters.

Typical Specifications for a Lowpass Filter   1

Chapter 2 introduced techniques for designing FIR filters. Here we will concentrate on lowpass filters and will demonstrate a design philosophy. A design proceeds iteratively from coarse boundaries to fine detail. Part of the

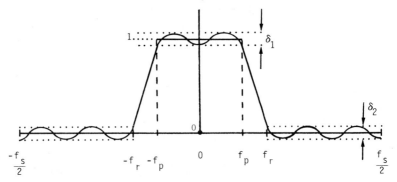

Fig. 3.6. Typical frequency domain characteristics of sampled data lowpass filter.

procedure requires the designer to review a number of options for performance or workload comparisons. The designer should have access to quick estimation procedures early in the process. We will now develop some useful relationships between filter parameters which are compact approximations to the relationships presented in Chapter 2.

The transition bandwidth of a lowpass filter is the spectral interval for the magnitude response to make the transition between the passband and the stopband tolerance bands. For a minimum bandwidth narrowband filter, the transition bandwidth is identically the filter bandwidth. We know the narrowest bandwidth a filter can realize is f_s/N, where N is the filter length. This filter has uniform (or equal) weights, with the spectral width of the Dirichlet kernel. The length-N uniform weight set can be used as a window to truncate the impulse response duration of any arbitrary filter. (This approach to FIR filter design was discussed in Section III of Chapter 2, and is being discussed here to develop a simple estimate of transition bandwidth.) The multiplication of the two sequences in time is equivalent to a convolution of their spectra in frequency. Abrupt spectral transitions of the filter are smoothed by the convolution with the window spectrum, which results in a transition width equal to the spectral width of the window's mainlobe. Hence we have the remarkable property that all filters of the same length N exhibit a transition bandwidth that is essentially the same (the truncating function's mainlobe width) and is independent of the original (untruncated) filter bandwidth.

A filter designed with a rectangular window has sidelobes related to the -13-dB sidelobes of the $\sin(\pi f N)/\sin(\pi f)$ function resulting from the periodic extension of the $\sin(\pi f T)/(\pi f)$ kernel (see Section VII.E of Chapter 1). The sidelobe levels are slightly lower for wider bandwidths due to averaging of the sidelobes during the spectral convolution of the ideal filter and the window. To design filters with lower prescribed sidelobe levels, we have to allow for an increase in transition bandwidth. From classical window design considerations we know the transition bandwidth of a filter is of the form

$$\Delta f = K(A)\frac{f_s}{N} \qquad (3.1)$$

where A is the minimum stopband attenuation (e.g., $A = 0.001$) and $K(A)$ is an attenuation-related scale factor. From filter design experience we find the parameter $K(A)$ in Eq. (3.1) is bounded by

$$\frac{-20\log(A)}{25} < K(A) < \frac{-20\log(A)}{20} \qquad (3.2)$$

In comparing Eq. (3.2) to the approximations of Eqs. (2.19) and (2.31), we see that we now have access to a quick first-order estimate of filter length for a given sidelobe level and transition bandwidth as follows:

$$N = K(A)\frac{f_s}{\Delta f} < \frac{-20\log(A)}{20}\frac{f_s}{\Delta f} = \frac{A\,(\text{dB})}{20}\frac{f_s}{\Delta f} \qquad (3.3)$$

This relationship is demonstrated in Fig. 3.7, which is a collection of 21-point FIR filters. These filters were designed to have a transition bandwidth of 0.1 with the -50-dB stopband edges located at 0.1, 0.2, 0.3, and 0.4 Hz, respectively. The parameters of attenuation value (-50 dB) and transition bandwidth used in Eq. (3.3) result in an upper bound to the filter length of 25 points. This estimate for N is 16% too high because a 21-point filter meets the specifications for this example. The narrowband filter response of Fig. 3.7(a) is superimposed at the right side of the other filter's transition regions for ease of comparing the transition bandwidths.

How the Filter Specification Parameters Interact **2**

Since FIR filter design is iterative, the designer should have an idea of how the parameters interact so that reasonable trades in the parameters can be made during the design. We will now demonstrate how a change in a single parameter alters the frequency and time description of a selected prototype filter. The filters presented here were designed by the (MP) algorithm, which was altered to obtain a sidelobe peak decay of -15 dB/decade (-4.5 dB/octave).

We start with a 16-point impulse response filter with a passband ending at 0.1 Hz and a stopband starting at 0.2 Hz. Since the filter length N and the transition bandwidth Δf are already fixed, the only parameters we can adjust are the approximation tolerance bands in the passband and stopband. Since only three of these four parameters are independent, the MP algorithm operates with a fixed (but user-selected) ratio of the two tolerances and then minimizes the amplitude of both tolerance bands. Using a ratio of passband ripple to stopband ripple of 1, 10, and 100, respectively, we obtain the time and frequency responses shown in Fig. 3.8. Since the transition bandwidth is specified and the filter length is known, we can use Eq. (3.3) to predict that the minimum stopband attenuation level will be between -32 and -40 dB. We obtain minimum attenuation levels of -29, -41, and -51 dB respectively, We note that the additional stopband attenuation is achieved at the expense of greater passband ripple; peak ripples are

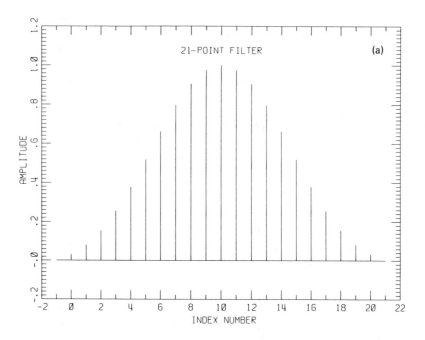

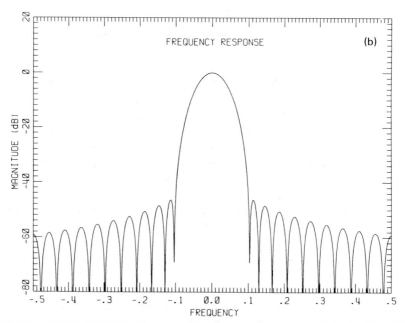

Fig. 3.7(a). 21-Point FIR filter impulse and frequency responses, respectively, for (a) and (b) a transition band of 0.0–0.1 Hz.

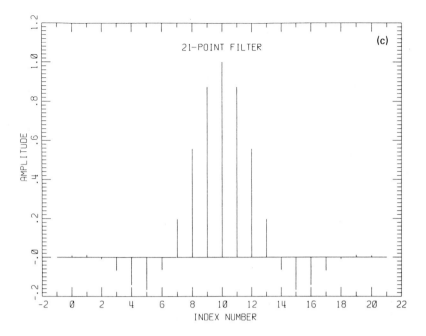

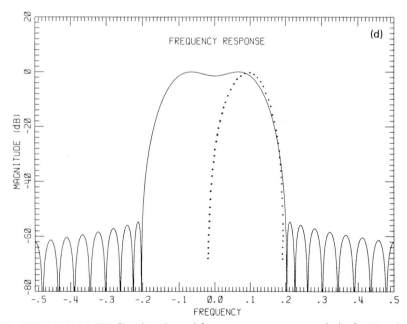

Fig. 3.7(b). 21-Point FIR filter impulse and frequency responses, respectively, for (c) and (d) a transition band of 0.1–0.2 Hz.

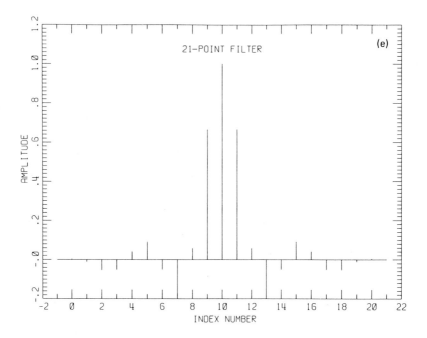

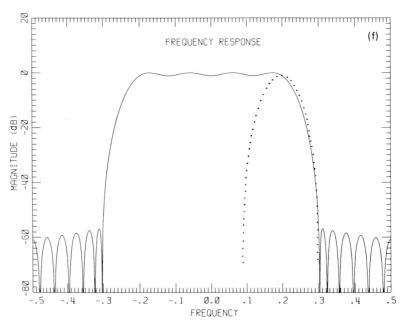

Fig. 3.7(c). 21-Point FIR filter impulse and frequency responses, respectively, for (e) and (f) a transition band of 0.2–0.3 Hz.

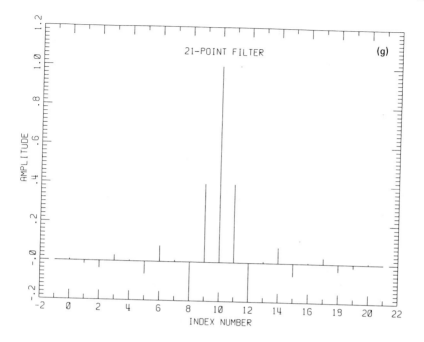

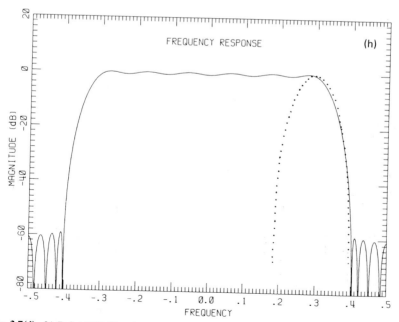

Fig. 3.7(d). 21-Point FIR filter impulse and frequency responses, respectively, for (g) and (h) a transition band of 0.3–0.4 Hz.

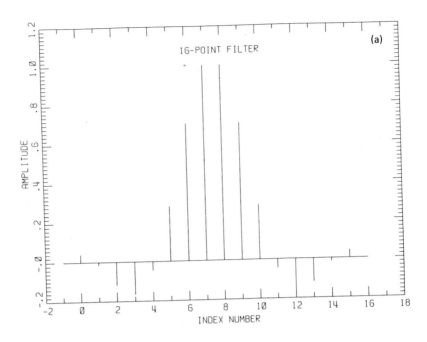

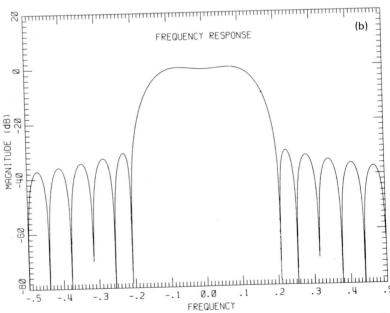

Fig. 3.8(a). 16-Point FIR filter impulse and frequency responses, respectively, for (a) and (b) the ratio $\delta_1/\delta_2 = 1.0$.

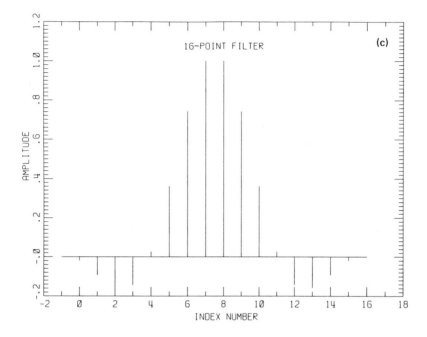

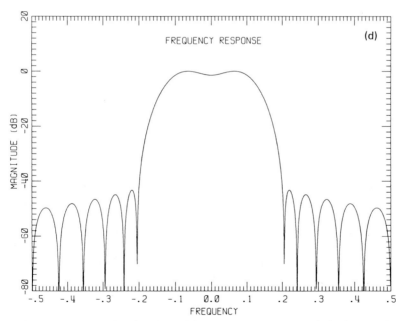

Fig. 3.8(b). 16-Point FIR filter impulse and frequency responses, respectively, for (c) and (d) the ratio $\delta_1/\delta_2 = 10.0$.

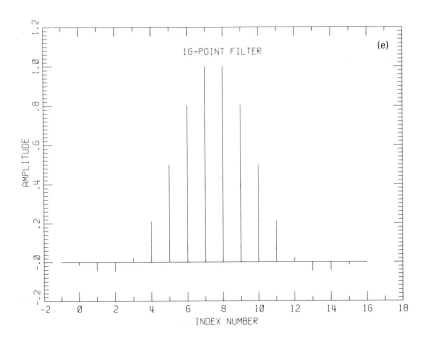

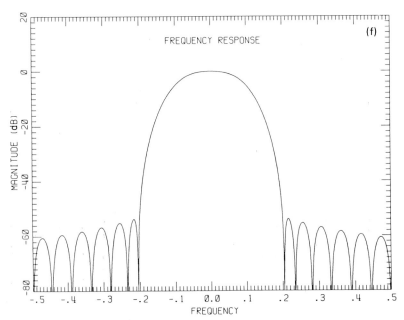

Fig. 3.8(c). 16-Point FIR filter impulse and frequency responses, respectively, for (e) and (f) the ratio $\delta_1/\delta_2 = 100.0$.

0.30, 0.74, and 2.88 dB, respectively. Equation (3.3) works well when the ratio of stopband ripple to passband ripple is between 10 and 100; I regularly use 40.

In Figs. 3.9 and 3.10 we see the impulse and frequency responses for filters of length 16, 32, and 64 points, respectively. Here, as in the previous example, the passband ends at 0.1 Hz and the stopband starts at 0.2 Hz. In Fig. 3.9 the ratio of passband ripple to stopband ripple is 1.0, and in Fig. 3.10 this ratio is 40.0. As expected from Eq. (3.3), for fixed transition bandwidth, the sidelobe levels decrease with increased filter length.

We continue with a 16-point filter but with an increase in transition bandwidth obtained by modifying the location of the passband, stopband, or both. Figure 3.11 presents the time and frequency responses obtained by modifying the transition bandwidth. We first present, for comparison, the nominal 16-point impulse response filter with passband set to 0.1 Hz and stopband set to 0.2 Hz. The expected sidelobe level is between -32 and -48 dB, the actual level is seen to be -49 dB. In each of the cases that follow, the transition bandwidth is increased 50% to 0.15 Hz. For the first modification we move the stopband edge to 0.25 Hz and keep the same passband at 0.1 Hz. Note that the spectral sidelobes are further down, and the impulse response mainlobe width is narrower. We expect sidelobes between -48 dB and -60 dB and realize -59 dB. For the second modification we move the passband edge to 0.05 Hz and keep the stopband edge at 0.2 Hz. Here too the wider transition bandwidth has led to increased peak stopband attenuation, but it is now -54 dB, and, as expected, the mainlobe time response has widened. For the final modification we split the direction of the transition bandwidth increase by moving the passband edge to 0.075 Hz and the stopband edge to 0.225 Hz. This yields sidelobe levels of -64 dB.

Time Domain Characteristics and Scaling Consideration   B

We note by scanning Figs. 3.7 through 3.11 that the impulse responses of these filters are essentially smoothly truncated versions of the $\sin(wt)/(wt)$ function (see Section III in Chapter 2). The minimal filter response appears to include the mainlobe and first sidelobes of the $\sin(wt)/(wt)$ envelope. The mainlobe width (in time) varies inversely with passband width (in frequency). If the (single-sided) -6-dB passband width (slightly greater than f_p) is αf_s, the impulse response mainlobe width, measured between the first nulls, is $1/\alpha f_s$ or $1/\alpha$ samples. Thus $1/\alpha$, the ratio of sample rate to -6-dB bandwidth, is an estimate of the number of coefficients in the mainlobe time response. For the examples presented in Fig. 3.7 the one-sided -6-dB bandwidths are 0.045, 0.135, 0.240, and 0.340, respectively. The expected mainlobe widths are 22, 7, 4, and 3; the actual mainlobe widths are 21, 7, 5, and 3, respectively. For Figs. 3.8 through 3.11, the -6-dB one-sided bandwidth is 0.15, so we expect the number of mainlobe samples to be 7. The actual number of samples is either 6 or 8, depending

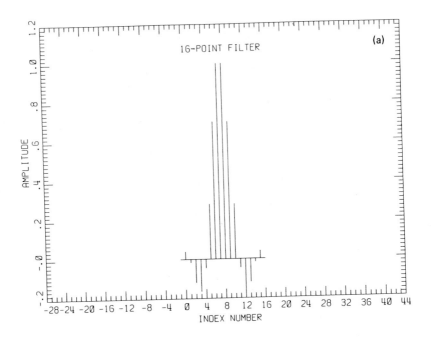

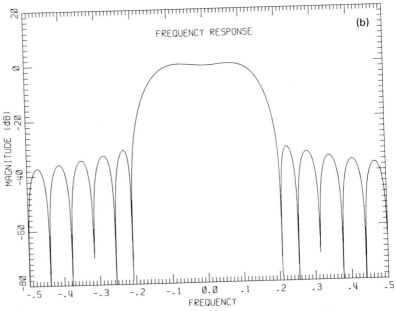

Fig. 3.9(a). FIR filter for the ratio $\delta_1/\delta_2 = 1.0$. Impulse response and frequency response magnitudes, respectively, are shown for a filter of length (a) and (b) 16 points.

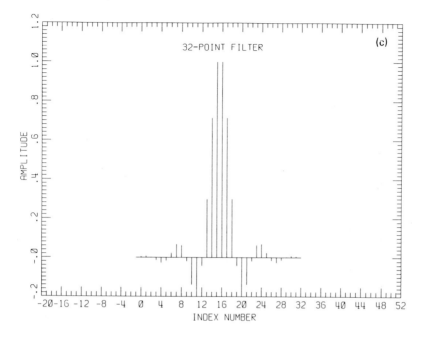

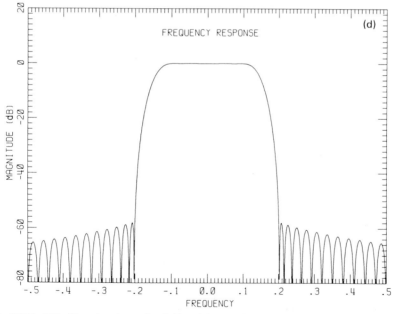

Fig. 3.9(b). FIR filter for the ratio $\delta_1/\delta_2 = 1.0$. Impulse response and frequency response magnitudes, respectively, are shown for a filter of length (c) and (d) 32 points.

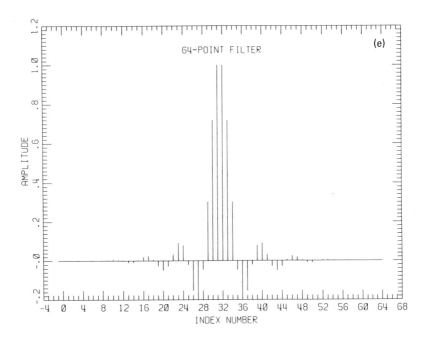

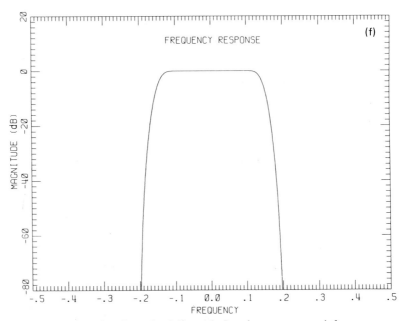

Fig. 3.9(c). FIR filter for the ratio $\delta_1/\delta_2 = 1.0$. Impulse response and frequency response magnitudes, respectively, are shown for a filter of length (e) and (f) 64 points.

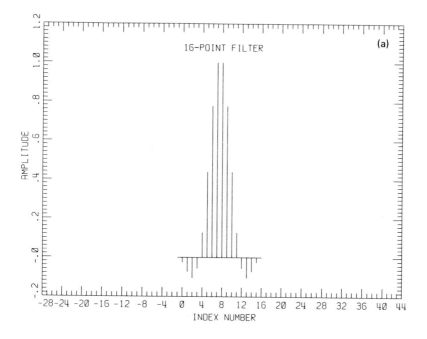

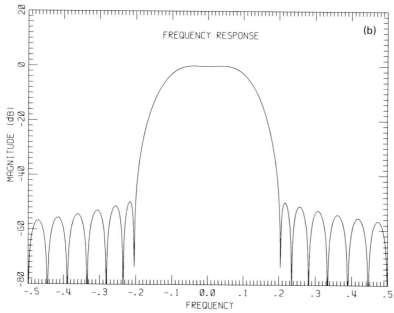

Fig. 3.10(a). FIR filter for the ratio $\delta_1/\delta_2 = 40.0$. Impulse and frequency responses, respectively, are shown for a filter of length (a) and (b) 16 points.

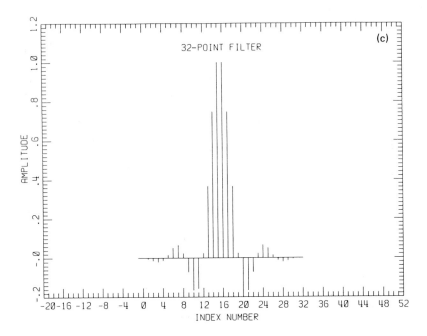

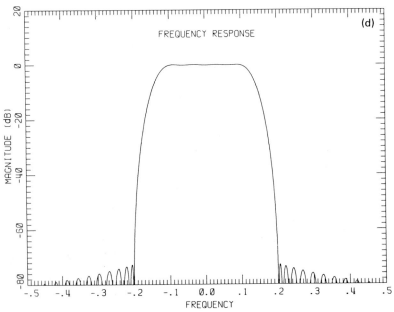

Fig. 3.10(b). FIR filter for the ratio $\delta_1/\delta_2 = 40.0$. Impulse and frequency responses, respectively, are shown for a filter of length (c) and (d) 32 points.

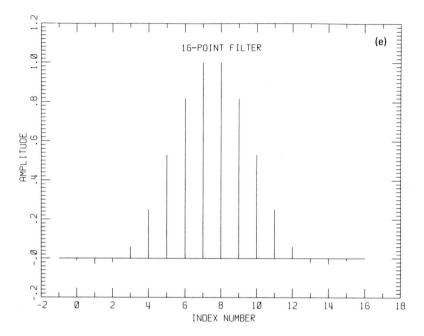

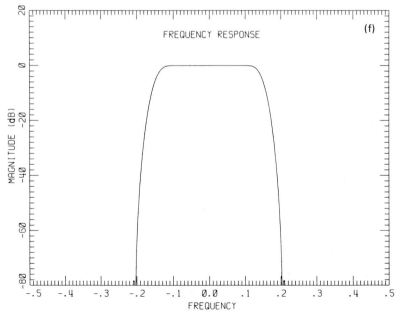

Fig. 3.10(c). FIR filter for the ratio $\delta_1/\delta_2 = 40.0$. Impulse and frequency responses, are shown for a filter of length (e) and (f) 64 points.

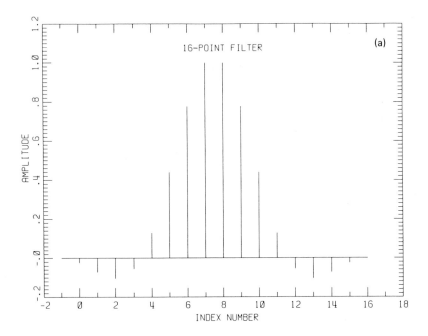

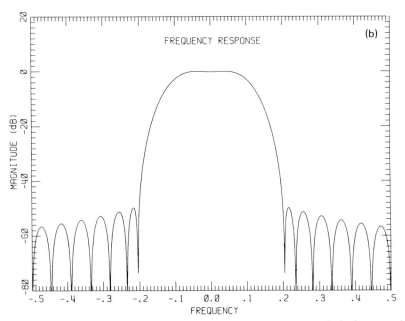

Fig. 3.11(a). 16-Point FIR filter impulse and frequency responses, respectively, for a transition band of (a) and (b) 0.1–0.2 Hz.

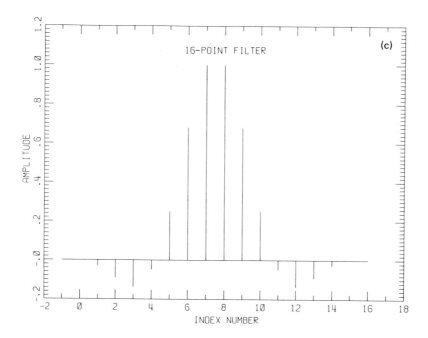

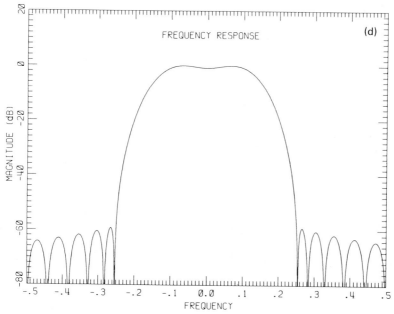

Fig. 3.11(b). 16-Point FIR filter impulse and frequency responses, respectively, for a transition band of (c) and (d) 0.1–0.25 Hz.

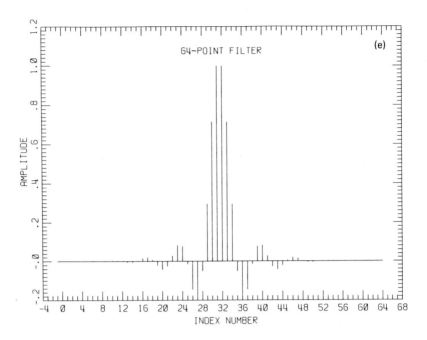

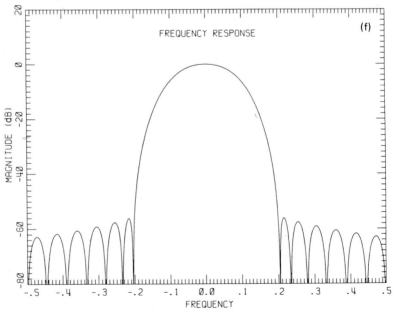

Fig. 3.11(c). 16-Point FIR filter impulse and frequency responses, respectively, for a transition band of (e) and (f) 0.05–0.20 Hz.

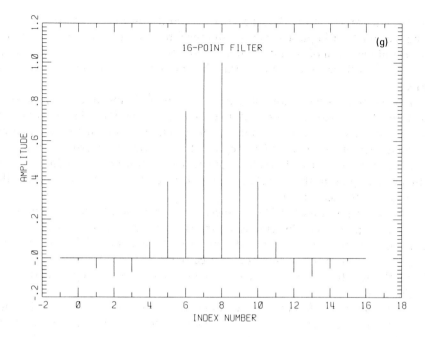

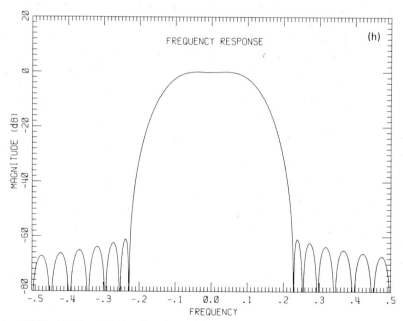

Fig. 3.11(d). 16-Point FIR filter impulse and frequency responses, respectively, for a transition band of (g) and (h) 0.075–0.225 Hz.

on the filter length. Note that the filter's spectral transition width controls the length of the filter impulse response, and the filter's spectral bandwidth controls the mainlobe width of the filter impulse response. We need to estimate the filter mainlobe width because of a concern related to finite arithmetic realizations of FIR filters.

The weighted summation of data to accomplish the filtering process is performed by a sequence of multiplications and additions. The partial sum formed by the sequence of additions resides in a finite word-length accumulator. The number of bits required to represent the partial sum grows during the accumulation. This growth is called numerical gain. A scaling procedure must be employed to prevent the maximum width of the partial sum from exceeding the bit width of the accumulator.

One option is to scale the filter coefficients for a peak steady-state gain of unity. For the lowpass filters this entails scaling so that the sum of the coefficients is unity. If there are a large number of samples in the mainlobe of the filter impulse response, this form of scaling could force the samples with small magnitudes below the quantization resolution of the finite registers used to represent the filter coefficients.

To minimize the effect of finite word-length representation of the coefficients, we normally scale them so that the maximum coefficient is between one and one half of the largest number that can be held by the coefficient registers. Often this scaling corresponds to setting the maximum filter coefficient to match the register's largest number. For ease of discussion, let us consider the binary point to be left justified so that this largest coefficient is unity. We now can see why an estimate of the mainlobe impulse response width is important. Since the large coefficients of the filter are located in the mainlobe of the impulse response, most of the numerical gain in the filtering process occurs in the summation of the mainlobe coefficients. We conclude that smaller bandwidth filters (with wider mainlobe impulse responses) exhibit a greater numerical gain, which must be managed in the finite-width accumulators. For example, if there are 10 coefficients in the mainlobe of the impulse response (with the maximum coefficient scaled to unity) and we use a triangle approximation to the mainlobe shape, we can expect a numerical gain of 5; if there are 100 coefficients, we can expect a numerical gain of 50. We note that if the filter coefficients are scaled for unity maximum value, the numerical gain is approximately $1/2\alpha$, the ratio of sample frequency to two-sided passband bandwidth. Thus filters with a very narrow bandwidth relative to sample rate will exhibit large numerical gain. Unless scaling is imbedded in the accumulation process, the finite accumulator width will limit the range of possible desampling ratios.

We observed from Figs. 3.7 through 3.11 that the impulse response mainlobe width is controlled by the spectral bandwidth of the filter. We now note that the total filter length, in turn, controls the spectral sidelobes of the filter. Figures 3.9 and 3.10 show that an increased filter length permits additional sidelobes in the impulse response and results in decreased spectral sidelobes. The time domain sidelobes introduced by lengthening the filter are successively smaller and smaller valued. The low-level coefficients in these sidelobes can (and do) drop below the quantizing noise of the finite-length coefficient words. As mentioned, careful scaling is required during the sum of products process to prevent the finite coefficient lengths from limiting the effective filter length and hence the achievable low-amplitude spectral sidelobe levels. As an example of this limiting effect, Fig. 3.12 compares the response of a 32-point lowpass filter obtainable with floating-point coefficients to one obtainable with fixed-point coefficients with word lengths of 16, 14, 12, 10, and 8 bits respectively. We see that the 16-bit coefficient quantizing effects are down 75 dB relative to the peak response and that shorter coefficient lengths result in poorer sidelobe behavior in the stopband. Additional filter length realized with 16-bit accuracy will not result in lower spectral sidelobes. Figure 3.13 compares the achievable sidelobe levels using floating-point and 16-bit fixed-point coefficients for a 128-point narrowband filter. We will address block floating-point coefficients sets when we examine FIR filter architectures.

In the previous section we observed that the FIR filter time domain impulse response closely resembles the envelope of a smoothly truncated $\sin(wt)/(wt)$ function. The response included the central mainlobe and (usually, at least) a pair of sidelobes. The step responses of these filters exhibit ringing precursors and postcursors due to the sidelobes of the impulse response. These are most clearly seen as the ringing we call the Gibbs phenomenon, which occurs in the neighborhood of a discontinuity. In some applications this ringing is undesirable, for example video pulse processing. Here the ringing represents spatial interpixel coupling, which results in reduced image quality.

We will now examine lowpass FIR filters with monotonic step response. The impulse response of such a filter has no sidelobes. We still require the filter to have a specified transition bandwidth and sidelobe level. The only filter parameter yet to be specified is the passband bandwidth. We noted in Fig. 3.7 that for a selected transition bandwidth and sidelobe levels, narrower bandwidth results in the mainlobe portion of the impulse response occupying a larger fraction of the impulse response width. A filter with a sufficiently narrow bandwidth has an impulse response that consists entirely of mainlobe response. Thus filters with monotonic impulse responses are narrowband filters, so narrow that their entire spectral characteristic is described by the transition bandwidth and sidelobe levels. Are such filters of any value? Yes! They are usually called time domain windows or weightings and are used in spectral analysis to shape the spectral characteristics of a DFT. We have used the classic filter design routines to design windows with specified characteristics, such as sidelobe levels and sidelobe slopes. Figure 3.13 presents the spectrum of a window designed by the Remez multiple-exchange filter design routine to have peak sidelobe levels of -70 dB with -15 dB/decade sidelobe falloff rate.

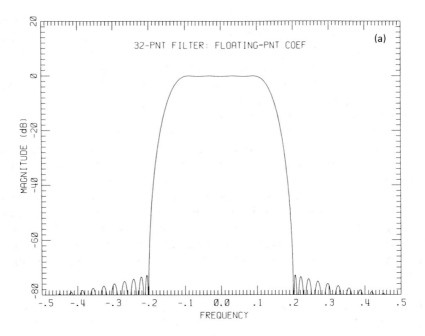

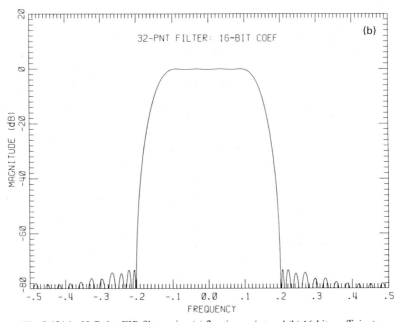

Fig. 3.12(a). 32-Point FIR filter using (a) floating-point and (b) 16-bit coefficients.

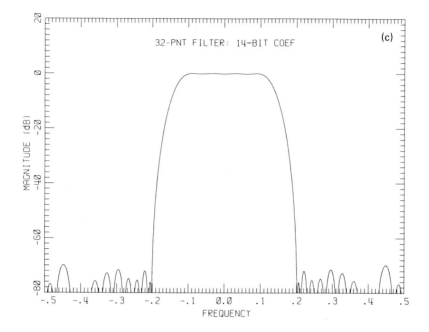

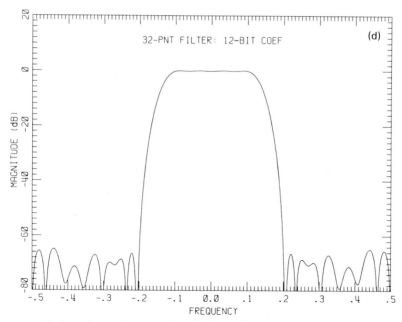

Fig. 3.12(b). 32-Point FIR filter using (c) 14-bit and (d) 12-bit coefficients.

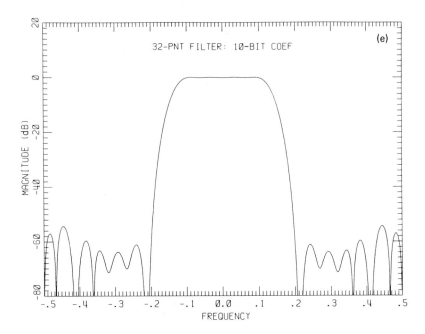

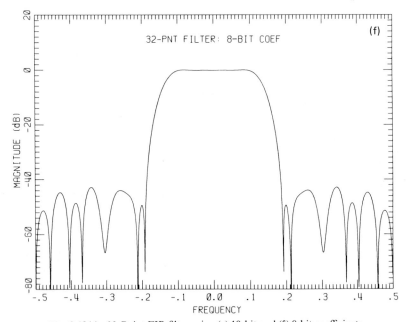

Fig. 3.12(c). 32-Point FIR filter using (e) 10-bit and (f) 8-bit coefficients.

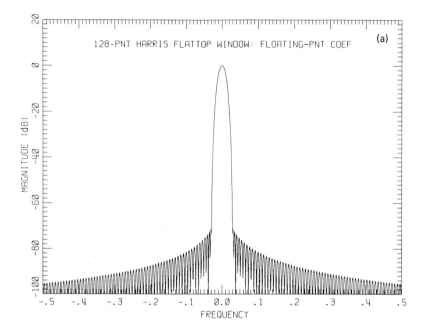

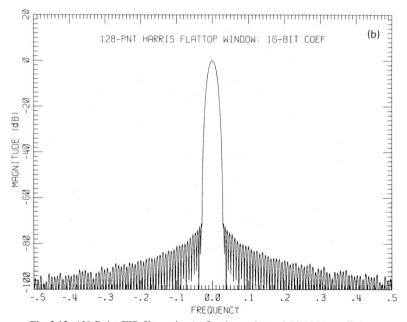

Fig. 3.13. 128-Point FIR filter using (a) floating-point and (b) 16-bit coefficients.

Any of the classic time domain windows designed for spectral analysis can be used as the impuse response of a minimum bandwidth filter with monotonic step response. The windows are easy to generate and satisfy standard filter constraints such as minimum stopband attenuation [23]. The Appendix presents time and spectral descriptions of some of the better windows filters as well as the standard rectangular and triangular weightings for comparison. The Hamming, the Blackman, and the Blackman–Harris windows are regularly used as prototype lowpass filters because they are simply formed as the weighted sum of two, three, or four cosines. Table AI lists these windows along with standard figures of merit that are useful for comparing their performance as lowpass filters. A computer program to generate samples of classic window functions is included in this handbook as an addendum to Chapter 3.

The filters that we have designed and described can be used in any application. Examples include windows for spectral analysis and shadings for phased-array beamformers. In Chapter 8 we will use these filters in conjunction with the DFT to synthesize banks of narrowband filters with arbitrary spectral shapes.

III   DATA RATE REDUCTION (DESAMPLING) BY 1/M FILTERS

We now examine techniques that permit us to reduce the sampling rate of a time series [9–18]. The rate reduction will occur in conjunction with a filtering operation that reduces the bandwidth of the data set. Thus the filter will be characterized by two sampling rates: the input rate and the output rate. Until now, we have found it convenient to describe filter bands in terms of frequencies normalized by the filter sampling rate. Now that we have two sampling rates, what do we do? We can interpret the resampling process as two distinct operations: (1) a bandwidth-reducing filtering operation followed by (2) an editing operation. This perspective is reflected by the presence of the two sampling switches at the input and at the output of the filter indicated in Fig. 3.14. Here we see quite clearly that the filtering operation occurs at the input sampling rate, and it is the input rate to which we must normalize the filter characteristics. We will see shortly that the filter specifications are often presented in terms of the output sampling rate. As part of the design process, we will be required to recast those specifications to the input rate. If there is any possibility of confusion, we will explicitly state that the input and output frequencies are f_s and $f_s P/M$,

Fig. 3.14. Input and output rates of resampling digital filter.

respectively; that is, for every M samples into the filter only P output samples are used.

Baseband Filters   A

The resampling process is most easily visualized as an extension of the lowpass antialiasing filter applied to a signal before periodic sampling. We first select the desired bandwidth required to adequately describe the input signal. We will refer to the one-sided filter bandwidth as the analysis bandwidth and denote it by f_p. The analysis bandwidth defines the passband width of the antialiasing lowpass filter. We must also select the required dynamic range (the ratio of the minimum to maximum spectral levels) to be recognized in the analysis band. The dynamic range, denoted by $1/A$, identifies the highest level (or minimum attenuation) of sampling-related artifacts permitted in the analysis band. The dynamic range, in turn, helps define the transition bandwidth of the antialiasing filter. The transition bandwidth, denoted Δf, is the interval between the passband edge and the frequency for which the filter achieves the minimum attenuation $1/A$. Filter parameters are shown in Fig. 3.15. We see that the sampling rate, f_s, required to obtain an alias-free passband down to the level $1/A$ satisfies

$$f_s = 2f_p + \Delta f \tag{3.4}$$

Equation (3.4) is the engineer's version of the Nyquist sampling theorem. We note that the sampling rate exceeds the Nyquist rate by the transition bandwidth of the antialiasing filter. For a given analysis bandwidth and dynamic range, we can obtain a reduced sampling rate only by using a filter with a narrower transition bandwidth.

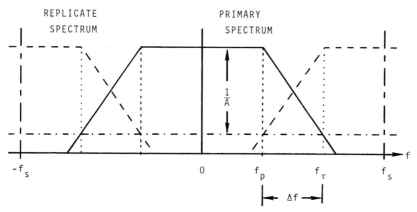

Fig. 3.15. Spectral description of resampling lowpass filter.

1 Filter Length Versus Fractional Bandwidth and Desampling Rate

The discussion of the previous section described the relationship between analysis bandwidth, transition bandwidth, and sampling rate for an antialiasing filter. A desampling filter is also an antialiasing filter! A change in sampling rate does not affect the relationship between desired analysis bandwidth, transition bandwidth of the filter and the final sampling rate. The change in sampling rate from f_s to f_s/M affects the filter length through the selected transition bandwidth and dynamic range.

The new sampling rate after $M:1$ desampling is f_s/M. The new sampling rate defines the total postdesampling bandwidth of the output signal. The integer M is sometimes called the decimation rate. Within this bandwidth the (two-sided) fraction α will be alias free [19]. The width of this alias-free band is determined by the transition width of the antialiasing FIR filter. We now demonstrate the relationship between filter length N and the new analysis bandwidth (the alias-free desampled bandwidth). The new (two-sided) analysis bandwidth is

$$2f_p = \alpha \frac{f_s}{M} \tag{3.5}$$

The transition bandwidth of the FIR antialiasing filter, from Eq. (3.3), is

$$\Delta f = K(A)\frac{f_s}{N} \quad \text{where } K(A) = \frac{-20\log(A)}{20} = \frac{A\,(\text{dB})}{20}. \tag{3.6}$$

Substituting Eqs. (3.5) and (3.6) into Eq. (3.4) gives

$$\frac{f_s}{M} = \alpha\frac{f_s}{M} + K(A)\frac{f_s}{N} \tag{3.7}$$

Rearranging Eq. (3.7), we obtain

$$N = K(A)\frac{M}{1-\alpha} = K(A)\frac{M}{\Delta f/f_s} = K(A)\frac{f_s}{\Delta f}M \tag{3.8}$$

Equation (3.8) is a good estimate of the required filter length for a given set of specifications. Note that in Eq. (3.8) the term $1-\alpha$ is the transition bandwidth of the filter relative to the filter final output rate f_s/M. Comparing Eq. (3.8) to Eq. (3.1), we see that the filter length for $M:1$ desampling is M times that of the filter satisfying the same spectral description without including the desampling. This reflects our awareness that the alias-free bandwidth is specified relative to the output rate, but that the filtering is performed at the input rate, which is M times greater.

For example, suppose we need an $8:1$ desampling filter with a dynamic range of 60 dB, and we require that 50% of the bandwidth be alias free after desampling. Equation (3.8) tells us to use a filter length between 38 and 48. For this example we selected an impulse response of length 40. These filter specifications were cast into parameters required for the MP version of the Remez multiple-exchange

TABLE I
Parameter List for McClellan-Parks Algorithm

FL, FT, NB, SD = 40, 1, 2, 16	
F0, F1, F2, F3 = 0.0, 0.03125, 0.09375, 0.50	
G1, G2 = 1.0, 0.0	
P1, P2 = 1.0, 100.0	

TABLE II
Definition of Parameter List for Table I

FL: Filter length
FT: Filter type (1 = lowpass)
NB: Number of bands (one passband and one stopband)
SD: Sampling density (default is 16)
F0, F1: Frequencies of beginning and end of band 1
F2, F3: Frequencies of beginning and end of band 2
G1, G2: Gain desired in bands 1 and 2
P1, P2: (Penalty) weighs in bands 1 and 2

algorithm. This parameter list is shown in Table I for a lowpass filter. Table II identifies the parameters of Table I. Figure 3.16 shows the relationship between these parameters relative to the input and output sampling rates. When these parameters were used with the algorithm, the filter design lead to a passband ripple of 0.96 dB and a peak stopband ripple of -64.0 dB. The impulse and frequency response of this design are shown in Fig. 3.17. Figure 3.18 emphasizes the aliasing regions associated with the resampling process by presenting the frequency response of this filter after resampling at both the input and output sample rates. This figure shows the individual aliased spectral levels that fold back into the passband due to the resampling process. Note the advantage of the sloping sidelobes in the filter design. Had the sidelobes been of equal amplitude, the folded sidelobe power would add at 3 dB per doubling. On the other hand, the

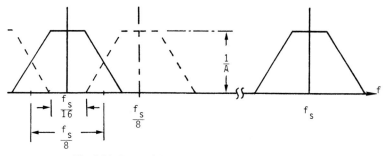

Fig. 3.16. Spectral description of 8:1 resampling filter.

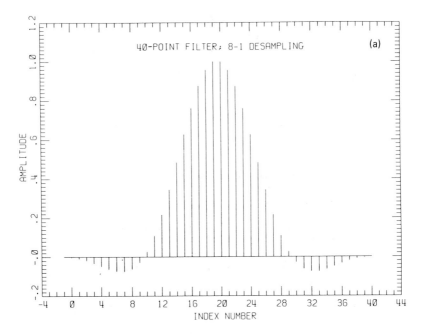

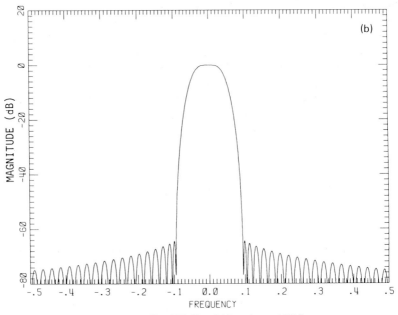

Fig. 3.17. 40-Point 8:1 desampling FIR filter (a) impulse and (b) frequency responses.

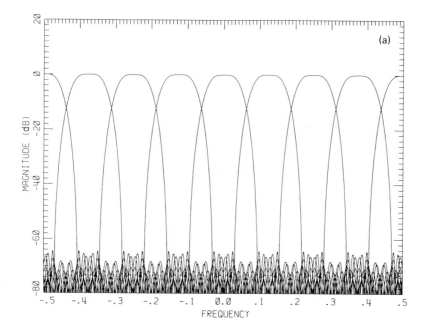

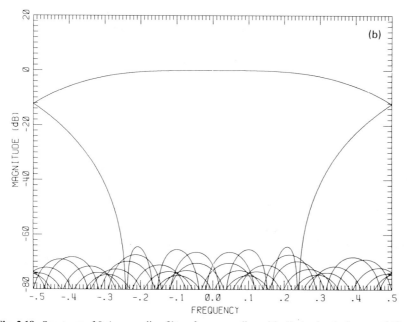

Fig. 3.18. Spectrum of 8 : 1 resampling filter after resampling with aliasing levels shown at (a) input and (b) output rates.

power sum of unequal level sidelobes is dominated by the largest, so there is no significant increase in the summed sidelobes.

Continuing with the example of the last paragraph, we note that the 40-point filter more than satisfied the -60-dB sidelobe requirement and exhibited about a 1.0-dB passband ripple. The designer has several choices. If the design as realized is acceptable, the extra stopband attenuation can be used to absorb unwanted power due to spectral folding and the design is complete. Alternatively, the filter length can be held fixed and a decreased penalty weight in the stopband, which results in a slight increase in the stopband ripple, can be tried. This will result in a slight decrease of passband ripple. A second choice is to decrease the filter length by a small integer and retry the algorithm. An iterative combination of these options converges rapidly to the specified design. One other option is to review the design specifications. Often a slight relaxation of a parameter will simplify the design. This was demonstrated in Fig. 3.11 where a reduction of bandwidth or an increase of passband tolerance resulted in additional sidelobe attenuation. Yet another option, which will be presented in Section III.A.3, is to realize the desampling filter as a set of shorter multistage filters.

2 Processing Overlap

In the last section we showed how to determine the filter length N required to realize an $M:1$ desampling filter with specified fractional bandwidth and specified sidelobe levels. The filter must perform an N-point inner product for each output data point. If we assume an even symmetric response, the N-point filter will require $N/2$ multiplications and N additions per output point. The output data rate is $1/M$ of the input data rate, so the computational workload per input point is

$$\frac{\text{Mult}}{\text{Input}} = \frac{1}{M}\frac{N}{2} = \frac{K(A)}{2(1-\alpha)} \tag{3.9a}$$

$$\frac{\text{Adds}}{\text{Input}} = \frac{1}{M}N = \frac{K(A)}{(1-\alpha)} \tag{3.9b}$$

Notice that on the right sides of Eq. (3.9) the workload per input point is independent of the filter length and desampling ratio, but is directly proportional to the sidelobe level attenuation and inversely proportional to the fractional transition bandwidth. For example, a filtering operation that specifies a -60-dB peak sidelobe level and 50% fractional bandwidth will require four multiplications and eight additions per input point. This workload per input point is the same if the desampling ratio is $8:1$ or $80:1$. Thus, knowing the input data rate, we can easily estimate the computational speed required to perform real-time signal processing. Conversely, knowing multiplier speeds, we can infer a maximum input sample rate for real-time processing.

The N/M ratio in Eq. (3.9) has an important interpretation. It tells us the overlap (or shift) factor of the filter. The desampling filter is a sliding block operation. The N-point inner product is applied to successive blocks of data separated by intervals of M data points. Each data block of length M will experience N/M shifts (and hence contribute to N/M outputs) as it passes through the filter. For some architectures the number of output points to which a data block contributes is an indicator of the network complexity. For instance, in the partial-sum architecture (which we will examine in a later section) the N/M ratio is the number of partial accumulators in the process. Alternatively, the reciprocal ratio, M/N, is the fractional shift of the filter length between successive application of the inner product.

Cascade Filters **3**

In previous sections we determined the filter length required to obtain a desired resampling ratio for a specified fractional bandwidth and sidelobe level. We then determined the computational burden per input point for that filter. We found that the multiplication and addition rates were defined only by the fractional transition bandwidth and sidelobe levels. We now consider the option of reducing the sampling rate in a succession of cascade filters [20, 21]. Each filter in the cascade must not exceed some sidelobe level to protect the final passband from aliasing artifacts, and the analysis bandwidth of each section must also have the same value. Then where is the advantage?—in the fact that fractional (not actual) transition bandwidth of the spectral description affects the filter length and computation rate.

To see how cascading affects the processing workload, we consider the two-stage partition. The first-stage filter performs a coarse bandwidth reduction, which accommodates most of the sample-rate reduction but leaves an overly wide transition bandwidth. The second-stage filter finishes the resampling process and forms the desired transition bandwidth. The workload performed by the second filter proceeds at the reduced data rate established by the first filter. In addition, the second filter length is considerably reduced due to the smaller ratio of (new) sample rate to transition bandwidth.

As an example of the available gain due to cascading, let us consider a 20:1 resampling filter of the type described in the previous section. The useful partition is a 10:1 filter followed by a 2:1 filter. Figure 3.19 presents the bandwidth reduction and resampling that occurs in each stage. The corresponding filter parameters are listed in Table III. The cycles-per-output parameter indicates how often the filter is exercised per output point. For instance, in this example the output filter operates with a 2:1 resampling rate, which means the previous filter must operate twice to allow the next filter to operate once.

As seen from the last entry in Table III, for this example there is a 23% saving in the number of multiplications due to the cascading. The saving becomes more significant when the original resampling ratio is larger. Another factor in favor of the cascade filter set is the reduced amount of data storage along with the reduced number of filter coefficients that must be stored. In this example, a filter of length 120 is replaced with two filters of combined length 52. For small integer

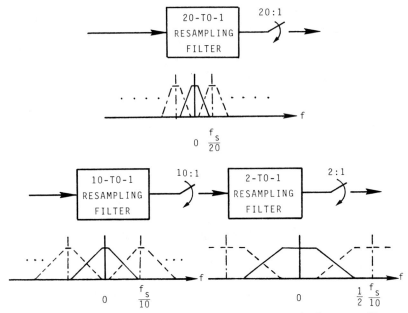

Fig. 3.19. 20:1 resampling as a single-stage filter and as a cascade of two-stage filters.

TABLE III

Parameters of Single-Stage and Two-Stage Filter for 20:1 Desampling

| | | Two-stage filter | |
Parameter	Single filter	Filter 1	Filter 2
Input sample rate	f_s	f_s	$f_s/10$
Output sample rate	$f_s/20$	$f_s/10$	$f_s/20$
Resampling ratio [M]	20	10	2
Analysis bandwidth [f_p]	$f_s/40$	$f_s/40$	$f_s/40$
Fractional bandwidth [α] (rel. output rate)	0.5	0.25	0.5
Filter length [$KM/(1-\alpha)$]	120	40	12
Cycles per output	1	2	1
Multiplication per output	60	40	6
Composite mult/output	60		46

resampling the benefits of cascaded filters are small and the overhead of operating separate subfilters may overcome the small gains.

Figures 3.20 present the impulse and frequency responses of the 20:1 resampling filters described in this example. Also shown is the aliasing, which folds back into the (final) passband for the one-stage and two-stage realizations.

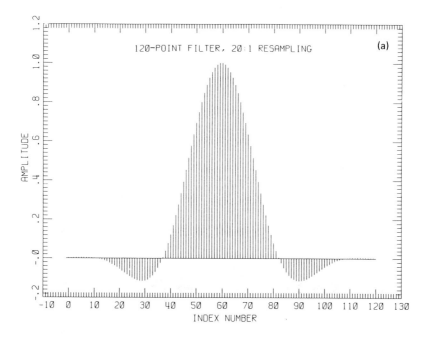

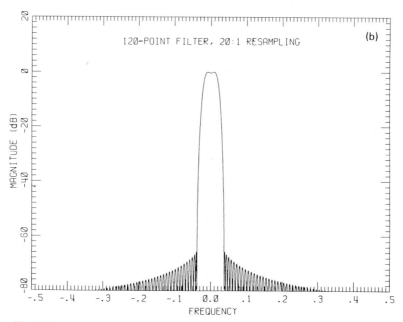

Fig. 3.20(a). 120-Point 20:1 resampling filter (a) impulse and (b) frequency responses.

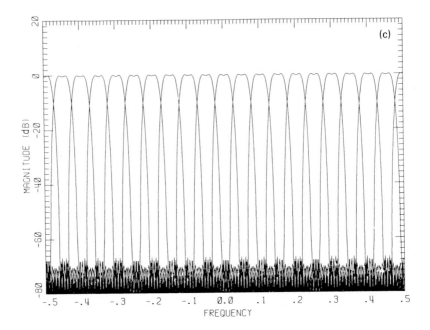

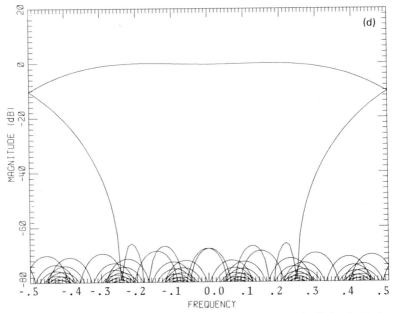

Fig. 3.20(b). Spectrum of 20:1 resampling filter after resampling with aliasing levels shown at (c) input and (d) output rates.

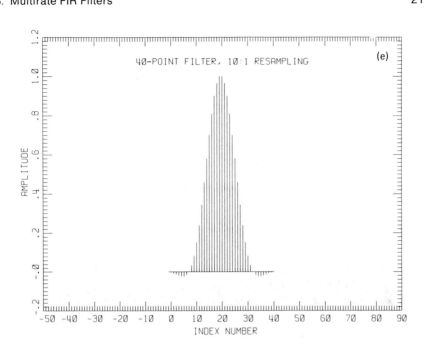

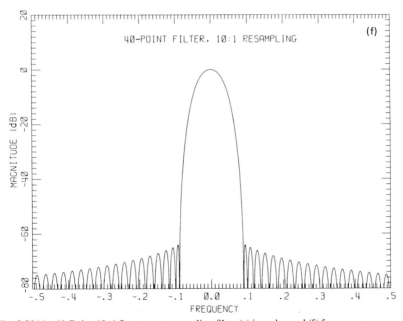

Fig. 3.20(c). 40-Point 10:1 first-stage resampling filter (e) impulse and (f) frequency responses.

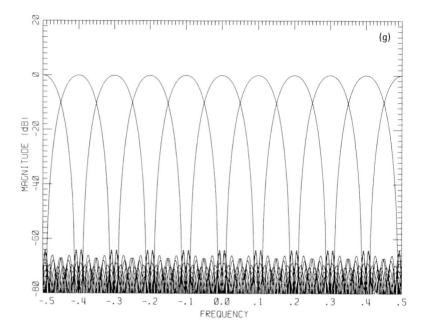

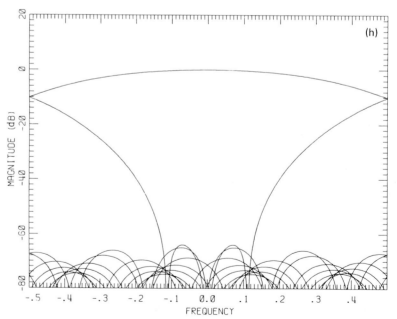

Fig. 3.20(d). Spectrum of 10:1 resampling filter after resampling with aliasing levels shown at (g) input and (h) output rates.

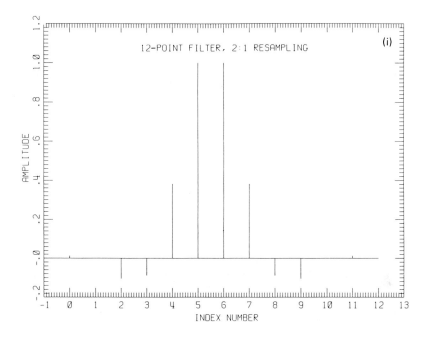

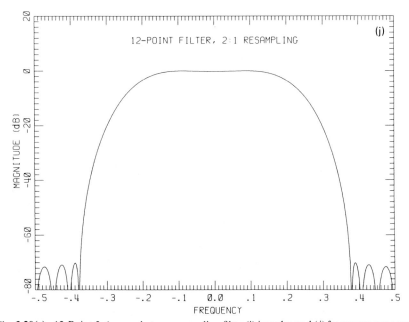

Fig. 3.20(e). 12-Point 2:1 second-stage resampling filter (i) impulse and (j) frequency responses.

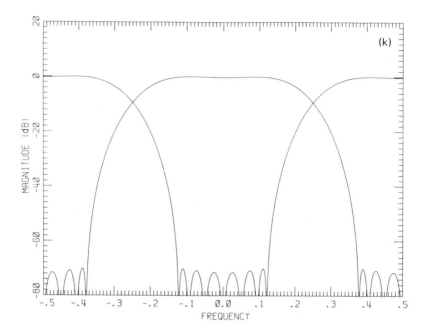

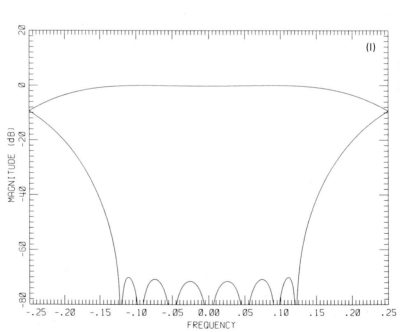

Fig. 3.20(f). Spectrum of 2:1 resampling filter after resampling with aliasing levels shown at (k) input and (l) output rates.

HETERODYNE PROCESSING   IV

In the previous section we addressed the task of resampling a baseband signal. We have been assuming that the signal was real, so a single filter accomplished the task. Had the signal been complex (i.e., an ordered pair), the filtering operation would proceed separately on each of the ordered pairs using identical versions of the designed baseband filter. We now consider the task of resampling carrier-centered signals.

We may have an interest in the structure of a signal occupying a reduced bandwidth at some center frequency other than zero [22, 23]. An inital approach would be to design a baseband filter to eliminate signal components that lie above the desired bandwidth. The cutoff frequency of this filter output would then be the sum of the center frequency and the one-sided bandwidth of the signal. The bandwidth of the signal may be considerably smaller than the center frequency of the signal, and it may not be necessary to select the sample rate based on the highest frequency. It is possible to sample at a rate based only upon the signal bandwidth by accounting for the known center frequency in some auxiliary processing. We have a number of options that allow us to sample at the bandwidth-related rate rather than at the highest frequency-related rate.

The first option is to move the center frequency of the spectral region of interest to zero and proceed to filter and desample as we have in earlier sections. The shifting of a spectrum is called frequency shifting or heterodyning from the Greek hetero, which means "different," and dyne, which means "move." The shift to zero frequency is called basebanding. If the spectrum does not exhibit conjugate symmetry about the center frequency, the shift requires two heterodynes: a complex heterodyne on an I-Q (in phase–quadrature) heterodyne (also called complex demodulation). Signals that exhibit conjugate symmetry about a carrier can be shown to result from either amplitude or phase modulation of the carrier. On the other hand, signals that do not exhibit conjugate symmetry about the carrier must be described by both amplitude and phase modulation of the carrier (or equivalently by independent amplitude modulation of the quadrature carrier components, cos and sin). The modulation of the color subcarrier in the National Television System Committee NTSC: American TV standard and quadraphase modulation of modems are examples of this type of modulation. In the absence of a priori information about signal structure, a basebanding operation must be performed by a complex heterodyne.

The second option is to form the narrowband filter at the carrier-centered frequency of f_0 Hz. If we resample this output by a factor of $M:1$, the carrier-centered frequency will alias to the new frequency of $[f_0] \bmod(f_s/M)$ Hz where $x \bmod y$ means the remainder of x divided by y. The aliasing may or not result in spectral folding with the negative frequency components, depending on the center frequency and the bandwidth of the signal. To prevent the possibility of spectral aliasing, we can perform complex narrowband filtering to eliminate the negative frequency components. If desired, the new center frequency can then be shifted to zero frequency by a heterodyne at the output rate (as opposed to one at the input rate). We will examine both options in the next section. Note that there is no inherent coupling between the desired bandwidth, the selected center frequency, and the resampling ratio (except for aliasing considerations). Later we will also examine systems that realize computational efficiencies by requiring coupling between these parameters.

A Complex Bandshifting of Input Data

Complex bandshifting, also referred to as frequency shifting or I-Q demodulation, is a direct application of the modulation theorem, which is stated below for both continuous and sampled data.

Modulation Theorem.   Given a transform pair

$$h(t) \text{ and } H(f) \qquad h(nT) \text{ and } H(2\pi fT)$$

a second transform pair is

$$h(t)\exp(-j2\pi f_0 t) \text{ and } H(f - f_0)$$

$$h(nT)\exp(-j2\pi f_0 Tn) \text{ and } H(2\pi fT - 2\pi f_0 T)$$

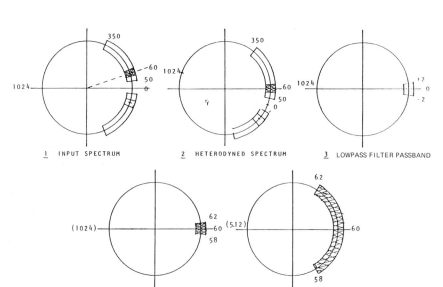

Fig. 3.21. Heterodyning a desired spectrum to baseband.

Hence to shift the spectral band of interest from the center frequency f_0 to zero frequency, we multiply the input data by the ordered pair $\exp(-j2\pi f_0 nT)$. Since the sampled data spectrum is periodic, this represents a rotation of the spectrum about the unit circle by the amount f_0/f_s Hz. The lowpass filtering operation is then performed on the two separate data sets presented by the ordered pair at the output of the heterodyne operation. This operation and the spectral description corresponding to points in that process are presented in Fig. 3.21. In the figure the crosshatched region is the frequency band of interest.

We have already examined the computational workload of the separate lowpass filters in the basebanding operation. For the complex heterodyne processing we have to account for the presence of two lowpass filters and for the complex heterodyne. In the heterodyning each real input data point is multiplied by a cos and sin value, which represents an increase of two real multiplications per input point. Therefore, if the input data is complex, there is an increase of four real multiplications and two real additions per input point. Merging this additional workload with that of the two N-point FIR filters yields

$$\text{Re mult/input} = \frac{N}{M} + 2 = \frac{K(A)}{1 - \alpha} + 2 \qquad \text{[real input data]}$$

$$= \frac{N}{M} + 4 = \frac{K(A)}{1 - \alpha} + 4 \qquad \text{[cmplx input data]} \quad (3.10a)$$

$$\text{Re adds/input} = \frac{2N}{M} = \frac{2K(A)}{1 - \alpha} \qquad \text{[real input data]}$$

$$= \frac{2N}{M} + 2 = \frac{2K(A)}{1 - \alpha} + 2 \qquad \text{[cmplx input data]} \quad (3.10b)$$

Complex Bandshifting of Filter **B**

In Section IV.A we alluded to the possibility of frequency shifting the LPF (lowpass filter) response rather than demodulating the data spectrum. Let $d(n)$ and $g(n)$ denote the system's input and output, respectively. Then the convolution performed by the N-point impulse response filter in the previous section is of the form

$$g(n) = [d(n)\exp(-j2\pi f_0 Tn)] * h(n) \qquad (3.11a)$$

$$= \sum_{k=0}^{N-1} d(n-k)\exp[-j2\pi f_0 T(n-k)]h(k) \qquad (3.11b)$$

$$= \exp(-j2\pi f_0 Tn) \sum_{k=0}^{N-1} d(n-k)h(k)\exp(j2\pi f_0 Tk) \qquad (3.11c)$$

$$= \exp(-j2\pi f_0 Tn)[d(n) * h(n)\exp(j2\pi f_0 Tn)] \qquad (3.11d)$$

Equation (3.11d) shows that the heterodyne, which we had originally applied to the data, can also be applied to the lowpass filter (forming a different set of weights) off line. In this scheme the narrowband carrier-centered filtering is performed first, and the heterodyne is applied at the output. If the filter input and output rate were identical, there would be a slight disadvantage of the second technique over the first. If the heterodyning is performed at the filter input (on real data), we have a single real-complex multiplication (2 Re mult) per input point. If it is performed at the filter output, we have a complex-complex multiplication (4 Re mult and 2 Re adds) per output point. If the output sample rate is sufficiently lower than the input rate, we may realize a saving in the heterodyne by not having to heterodyne the data points we discard by the resampling process. In sliding the complex exponential through the resampler, we find that the frequency (in hertz) has aliased to $[f_0] \bmod (f_s/M)$. The workload to apply this new heterodyne at the output rate is given by

$$\text{Re mult/input} = \frac{2N}{M} + \frac{4}{M} = \frac{K(A)}{1-\alpha} + \frac{4}{M} \tag{3.12a}$$

$$\text{Re adds/input} = \frac{2N}{M} + \frac{2}{M} = \frac{2K(A)}{1-\alpha} + \frac{2}{M} \tag{3.12b}$$

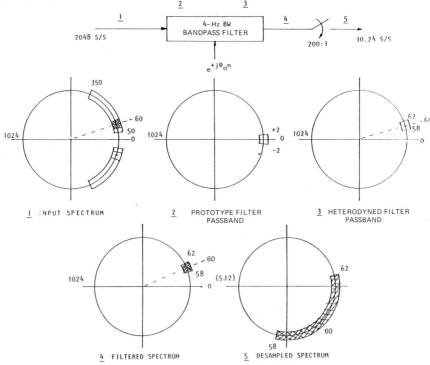

Fig. 3.22. Heterodyning a filter to desired spectrum.

Comparing with Eq. (3.10), we see a saving accrues to heterodyning the filter output if the resampling ratio is greater than $2:1$.

Figure 3.22 presents the form of the filter in which the coefficient set has been heterodyned and the heterodyne occurs at the output data rate. A second benefit in heterodyning the narrowband desampled filter output results if the sin-cos values used in the heterodyne are taken from a table. Since the table is finite, only those frequencies commensurate with the table length can be heterodyned. This is true at both the input rate and the output rate. To achieve a selected frequency resolution at the output of the system would require a resolution at the input that is M times as great. Hence for a fixed-length sin-cos table, the frequency resolution of an output heterodyne is M times better than that of an input heterodyne.

If the data from the filter is to be presented to a DFT routine for spectral decomposition, we have access to one additional option—don't do the heterodyning! The heterodyne only accomplishes a shifting of a specified frequency to the zero frequency of the spectrum. As long as we know where in the spectrum that frequency resides, we need only reassign the DFT bin to frequency correspondence. The only concern here is that the desired center frequency might not reside in the center of a DFT bin, but this residual offset can be avoided by clever selection of the input sample frequency. If the residual frequency offset is important, it can be removed by the output heterodyne.

Center Frequencies with Special Properties C

Earlier we mentioned that there is no coupling between the parameters of bandwidth, center frequency, and resampling rate of the resampling filters. We can, however, require that these parameters be constrained in particular ways to obtain a desired simplification or improvement of the filtering process. One simple example we have already seen is that symmetric filters can be implemented with half of the multiplications of an arbitrary filter. We had easy access to an implementation simplification through a simple constraint.

Four frequencies on the unit circle can be moved to zero frequency with no special processing. They are zero (an easy one to miss), plus or minus a quarter of the sampling frequency, and half the sampling frequency. A heterodyne can rotate the spectrum from any arbitrary center frequency to zero frequency by a set of complex multiplications. For the frequencies just identified, the complex multiplications are free; they are achieved by sign changes or by interchanging the real and imaginary parts of a number (data steering) and appropriate sign changes.

The half sampling frequency is easily interchanged with zero frequency by sign reversals on alternate data points. Alternatively, a lowpass filter can be rotated to half the sampling frequency (thus becoming a highpass filter) by the same procedure of alternating the sign of adjacent coefficients. If the lowpass filter is a half-bandwidth filter[†], that is, has 3-dB points at a quarter of the sampling frequency, then the reflected highpass filter will also be. Let the outputs of the two filters be resampled by $2:1$. Then at a quarter of the sampling input frequency, the power gain sum of the two filters is precisely unity. In the regions where one of the filters exhibits large attenuation, the other exhibits unity gain, so the power gain sum is again very nearly unity. By using an optimization scheme, we can fine-tune the filter so that the power gain sum in the transition bandwidth of the pair is essentially unity (within fractions of a dB). The important property here is that the sum of the two filter gains is unity even in their transition bands. Figure 3.23 shows the frequency response of a half-bandwidth lowpass and half-bandwidth highpass filter as well as the power sum of the pair. The benefit of this property is seen in the next paragraph.

If the filter is used with $2:1$ resampling, the aliasing of the highpass filter will yield a bandwidth coinciding precisely with the bandwidth of the mirror filter. It does because the mirror is the same filter simply heterodyned to half the sampling frequency by the coefficient sign changes. These filter pairs are called quadrature mirror filters (QMF) [24–27]. They are used in speech analysis and synthesis of half-bandwidth spectral regions by a chain of successive $2:1$ desampling operations. This form of processing is akin to the constant-Q spectral decomposition discussed in this chapter's introduction. Figure 3.24 presents the structure of a spectral decomposition by a cascade of resampling QMFs. Here the upper path reduces the data rate by a sequence of filter and resampling stages while the lower path(s) extracts the upper half-bandwidth from each successive stage. Figure 3.25 presents the spectral response of a QMF and the spectral resolution of the first six stages of a QMF decomposition.

The quarter sampling frequency is another spectral location that exhibits particularly attractive properties. The complex heterodyne required to shift a quarter of the sampling frequency to zero frequency is

$$\exp(-j2\pi f_0 Tn) = \exp\left(-j2\pi \frac{1}{4T} Tn\right) = \exp\left(-j\frac{\pi}{2}n\right) \qquad (3.13)$$

$$= (-j)^n$$

This is also a trivial sequence to apply either to data or to any baseband filter to shift its spectral properties to the quarter sampling frequency. The heterodyned coefficient sets are zero valued at alternate positions in the real set and are zero valued at (single offset) alternate positions in the imaginary set. Thus there are half as many multiplications and additions, all of which are trivial, as we would expect for an arbitrary complex filter. The proportional bandwidth filter bank described in the introduction to this chapter takes advantage of this reduced workload filter heterodyned by a quarter of the sampling frequency.

[†] These filters are also called half-band filters.

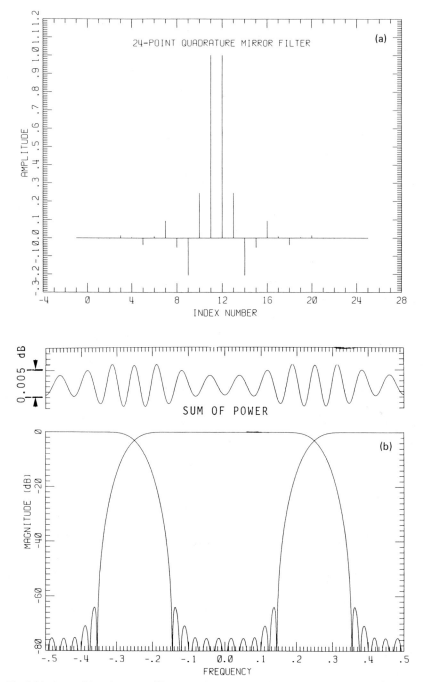

Fig. 3.23. (a) Half-band lowpass filter impulse response. (b) Frequency response of half-band lowpass and highpass filters, i.e., quadrature mirror filters.

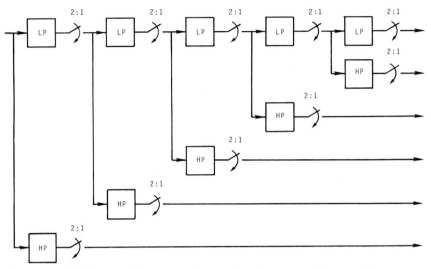

Fig. 3.24. Structural form of quadrature mirror filter spectral decomposition.

We now examine a filter with an interesting coupling of bandwidth, center frequency, and resampling rate. The filter is a half-bandwidth filter of the type described in the discussion on QMFs. In particular, we can select the impulse response to be samples of a Nyquist pulse. Figure 3.26 presents the time and spectral domain descriptions of this impulse response. Note that the coefficients of the half-bandwidth filter are samples of a smoothly truncated version of the $\sin(wt)/(wt)$ envelope. After the samples of the mainlobe, alternate samples coincide with the zeros of the envelope.

When we align the coefficients of this baseband filter with those of the quarter sampling frequency sin heterodyne, we see that they have the same zero set (except at the origin). Also we note that the nonzero sin coefficients have the same sign as the filter impulse response coefficients in the negative time interval and opposing signs in the positive time interval. Thus the nonzero product terms are all negative valued in positive time and all positive valued in negative time.

When we align the coefficients of the baseband filter with those of the quarter sampling frequency cos heterodyne, we have a surprise. The zeros of the cos samples coincide with the nonzero values of the baseband filter (except at the origin), and the zeros of the filter coincide with the nonzero values of the cos samples. Thus the product of the two series is zero everywhere but at the origin. The real part of our filter has almost disappeared; all that remains is a single path of unity gain. What we have just designed is a filter that passes only the spectral content of the positive frequency axis and, when desampled 2:1, exhibits the constant power gain (as in the QMFs) even in the transition bands.

This filter forms a complex signal that has the property that its DFT is (essentially) zero over the negative frequencies. For the continuous case such a

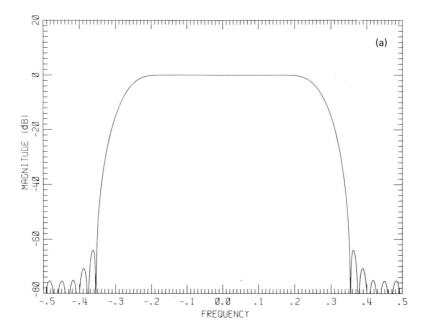

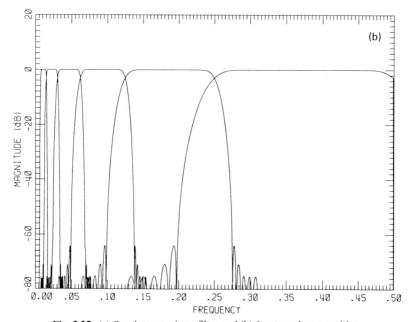

Fig. 3.25. (a) Quadrature mirror filter and (b) 6-octave decomposition.

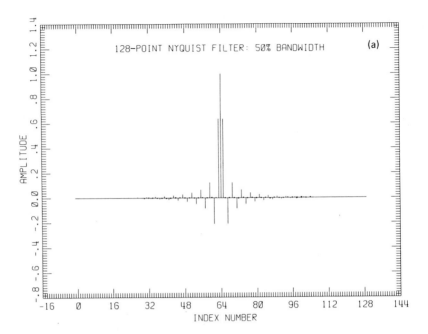

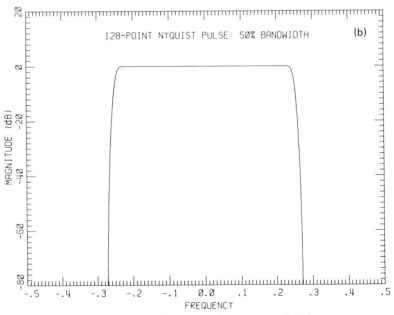

Fig. 3.26. Half-bandwidth nyquist filter (a) impulse response and (b) frequency response.

signal is called analytic. By extension, we denote these sequences as analytic sequences. This signal is the minimum bandwidth representation of real signals and is particularly useful in describing the properties of narrowband signals. The filter supplying the imaginary output is a wideband 90° phase shifter. Hence the filter performs a Hilbert transform on the input data $d(n)$ and generates the signal $\hat{d}(n)$ [28]. The ordered pair

$$a(n) = [d(n) + j\hat{d}(n)] \tag{3.14}$$

from this process is the analytic signal, the signal with a single-sided spectrum. We can easily see this in Fig. 3.27, which presents the complex impulse response and the frequency response (prior to resampling) of the QMF set designed as a Hilbert transform filter.

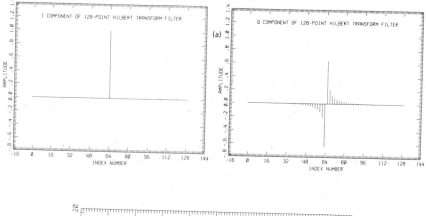

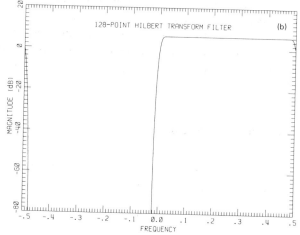

Fig. 3.27. (a) I-Q Components of Hilbert transform filter derived from Nyquist half-bandwidth pulse and (b) filter frequency response before 2:1 resampling.

V   INTERPOLATING FILTERS

Interpolation is the process of computing sample values of a sequence in an interval between existing data points. We note that before the advent of the pocket calculator it was common practice to interpolate between entries in tables of transcendental functions to improve the accuracy of computations. Interpolation is performed by first computing the parameters of a function selected to pass through (or fit) a chosen set of sample points and then sampling the resultant curve at the desired locations. Classically the curve selected for the data fit is a low-order polynomial. The most familiar of these are the zero-order, the first-order, and the second-order polynomials. These are often called, respectively, the boxcar or zero-order hold, the linear interpolator, and the quadratic interpolator. The primary attraction of a polynomial interpolator is computational simplicity. The primary disadvantages is that the user has no guideline for selecting the order of the polynomial fit. Intuition leads us to select a polynomial of sufficient order to match the order of the significant local derivatives of the underlying function (from which the samples came). If we do not know the local derivatives, we can estimate them (by successive differences), or we can try a different approach. This section deals with the alternative approach.

In general, our data points correspond to samples of a bandlimited but otherwise unknown function. Knowing this, we put aside the burden of estimating local derivatives and choose instead to pass a simple bandlimited interpolator through our data points. We will show shortly that the structure of this bandlimited interpolator is intimately related to our ubiquitous $\sin(\pi f N)/(\pi f N)$ lowpass filter function. The $\sin(\pi f N)/(\pi f N)$ function is often called the cardinal (bandlimited) interpolator. The very practical problem associated with this interpolator is its unbounded length. To have a useful interpolator, we have to select finite-length approximations to this function. We will demonstrate that the selection of such a finite-length approximation is akin to the design of the impulse response of a lowpass FIR filter. The performance measures of the approximation will be in terms of the spectral characteristics of the equivalent filter.

A   Increasing the Data Rate by a Factor of P

Given a set of equally spaced data points $x(nT)$, we can perform bandlimited interpolation to the arbitrary position T_0 by

$$x(T_0) = \sum_n x(nT)D(T_0 - nT) \tag{3.15}$$

One interpretation of (3.15) is the replacement of each sample value $x(nT)$ by a weighted copy of the interpolating function $D(t)$ centered at the sample locations

nT followed by the summation of each contributor at the desired sample position. This interpretation, the classic cardinal reconstruction, is shown in Fig. 3.28. An alternative interpretation places the cardinal interpolator at the desired sample position T_0 and then forms the weighted summation of the data values of each sample position that intersects that cardinal function. The data is weighted by the value of the cardinal function at each intersection position. Shown in Fig. 3.29 is a set of data points and the cardinal function located at the desired interpolation position.

We now examine the task of interpolating an arbitrarily long sequence of data at P equally spaced subintervals between the existing data [29, 30]. These subintervals are indicated in Fig. 3.30. We can slide the weighting function to each of the desired positions and then form the appropriate weighted summation. This sequence of operations looks amazingly like a convolution. With the inclusion of one final detail, this weighted summation will be seen to be a FIR filtering operation. We start with a naive, but still useful, initial approach to increase the data rate by the factor P. We first identify positions for the $P - 1$ new data points between each pair of existing data points by placing zero values at those desired equally spaced positions. This is called zero-packing (as opposed to zero-extending) the data, and we will soon develop design insight by examining this operation in more detail. The interpolation task is now that of a simple moving weighted average through this zero-packed data, which can be performed with a FIR filter. The filtering process replaces the zero-packed data with the

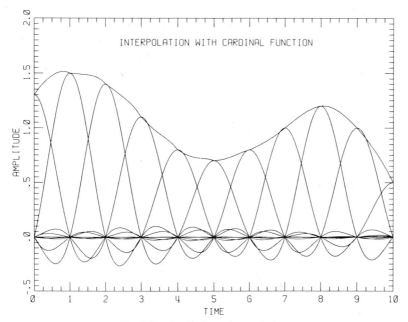

Fig. 3.28. Cardinal sum interpolation.

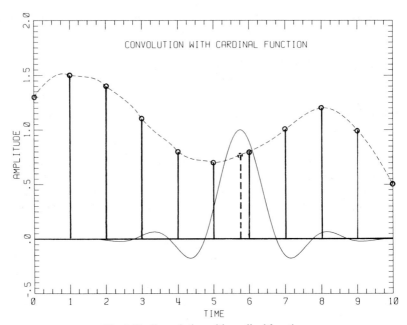

Fig. 3.29. Convolution with cardinal function.

bandlimited interpolation values. If the lowpass filter coefficients were originally scaled for unity gain at zero frequency, a final scale factor of value P must be applied to the output data to maintain the unity again at 0 Hz.

We still have to address the problem of selecting the proper length filter and examine processing schemes that take advantage of the zero-valued data points of the input series. Speaking of zeros, we note that the cardinal weighting sequence has its own set of equally spaced zeros and that by choosing the bandwidth to be an integer fraction of the sample rate these zeros can be made to coincide with sample positions. These approximations, called Nyquist pulses, are obtained by windowing the cardinal function. Because the distance between these zeros is the same as the distance between the input data points, we see that filter weights based on the Nyquist pulse require no computation to form output values at the output positions that match the input data positions. Thus only data

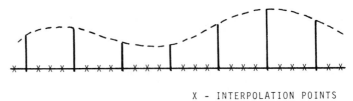

X - INTERPOLATION POINTS

Fig. 3.30. 4:1 Interpolation: desired subintervals indicated.

at the interpolated positions have to be computed. For a non-Nyquist pulse, data has to be computed at all positions, even those that correspond to input data positions.

Spectral Effects of Zero-Packing Input Data   B

In the previous section we cast the interpolation process in terms of lowpass filtering of zero-packed data. The zero-packing can be visualized as multiplexing the input data with $P - 1$ additional zero-valued data points, as indicated in Fig. 3.31. We note that the data rate out of the multiplexer is P times the input data rate. Also, in spite of the new rate, the only nonzero data present is the input data. Then what have we accomplished by multiplexing with the zeros? We have changed the quantity we identify as the sample rate from $1/T$ samples/s to P/T samples/s. Since the spectra associated with sampled data is periodic in the sampling frequency, we have redefined a spectral period as P cycles of spectra rather than one such cycle. The spectra is still periodic in $1/T$ since it satisfies

$$H(f) = H\left(f + \frac{K}{T}\right) \tag{3.16}$$

for all frequencies f; but Eq. (3.16) must also be satisfied for all integers K and particularly for the desired integer P. The task of the interpolating filter is to reject the spectral copies that occur at the integer multiples (less than P) of the input sampling frequency. This is the same task the lowpass filter had to perform as part of the desampling process described in Section III. We call attention to the similarity of the filtering functions of upsampling and downsampling so that we have access to the design techniques presented earlier. The spectral description of the data at the indicated points in Fig. 3.31 is shown in Fig. 3.32.

If we compare the spectral relationships for the upsampling filter (Fig. 3.32) with those of the desampling filter (Fig. 3.16), we realize that the relationships are

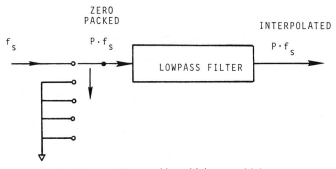

Fig. 3.31. $P:1$ Zero-packing with input multiplexer.

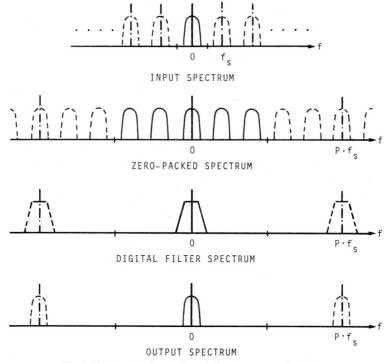

Fig. 3.32. Spectral description of filtering zero-packed data.

identical. In both of the filters the parameters M and P denote the ratio of the higher sample rate to that of the lower sample rate. The difference in the two filter cases is that for the desampling filter the higher sampler rate is the input rate, and for the upsampling filter it is the output rate. Thus we find that Eq. (3.8) establishes the length of the lowpass filter for both desampling and upsampling operations (with the parameter P substituted for the parameter M if required). For the upsampling filters the parameter $K(A)$ no longer reflects control of aliased spectral terms but control of replicated spectral terms.

C   Partitioning Filters For Polyphase Structures

In the previous two sections we presented the technique of interpolation by zero-packing and lowpass filtering. We further showed that the length of the lowpass filter is chosen to satisfy the same spectral constraints required for a desampling filter. This relationship, originally Eq. (3.8), is repeated here as

$$N = P\frac{K(A)}{1 - \alpha} \qquad (3.17)$$

We now note that of every P samples of zero-packed data presented to the filter only one point is nonzero. The contribution of the remaining $P - 1$ zero-valued data points to the output weighted summation is identically zero. We may reduce the computational burden of the N-point filter by suppressing those multiplications (and additions) of the filter coefficients that operate on these known zero-valued data points. Figure 3.33 indicates, by a set of indicator flags, the position of the nonzero data values for a sequence of zero-packed data in a filter performing a 4:1 upsampling interpolation. Since only one out of P samples is nonzero, if we count the nonsuppressed arithmetic operations performed by the length-N filter, we find only N/P multiplications and additions per output point. Comparing this to Eq. (3.9), we see that the number of operations per output point is the same for the process of desampling and upsampling and that this number depends only on sidelobe levels and fractional bandwidth of the filtered data. The total workload may be greater for upsampling simply because more output points are being computed.

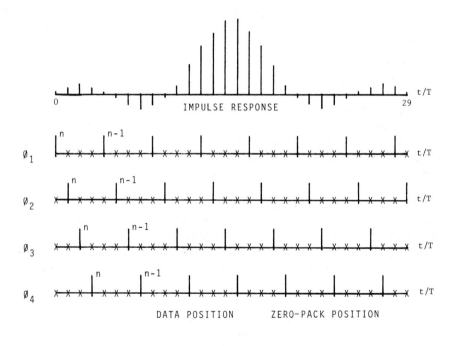

Fig. 3.33. Partition of impulse response by indicator set from 4:1 zero-packed data set.

We now partition the lowpass filter into a collection of subfilters known as *polyphase filters* [31]. The subset of filter coefficients needed to compute a given output point are those that intersect the nonzero data points in the span of the filter's total impulse response. On successive shifts, the nonzero input data samples intersect different subsets of the filter's impulse response needed to compute a particular output sample. We use the indicator set of Fig. 3.33 to identify the coefficient subset required for each particular output shift. These subsets define the polyphase subfilters, of which there must be precisely P, the upsampling ratio.

Shown in Fig. 3.33 is a partition of a 30-point filter into the four subfilters required for a 4:1 upsampling operation. The four successive indicator time lines correspond to successive time shifts of data through the filter. Note that only four distinct subsets are defined by this partition because the next time shift time line cycles back to the first such line. We also note that there may not be an equal number of coefficients in each subset. The average length of the subsets is N/P, and if this is not an integer, the actual lengths are either the next integer higher or lower. If we count the indicator set in Fig. 3.33, we find two subfilters of length 8 and two of length 7. A consideration for identical architectural structure in the subsets may lead us to require that N/P be an integer and this can be trivially arranged by choosing a larger N in the filter specification or by zero-extending the existing coefficient set.

The filter structure can now be modified to take advantage of this partition of coefficients. Examining Fig. 3.33, we note a curious relationship between the nonzero data locations and the filter coefficients. The data indicated on the first time line is processed by the eight coefficients of the phase 1 filter. On the next three time lines we note that the same data is successively processed by the next successive phases of the filter. The important observation here is that it is the same data! We might reason that the data could stay still while a succession of four filter sets is applied between successive (nonzero) input samples. Rather than visualize zero-packed data sliding through a single N-point filter and intersecting P distinct subsets, we can imagine the non-zero-packed data sliding simultaneously through P distinct filters of length N/P. Each filter receives a new data point at the input sample rate, and we increase the output rate by multiplexing

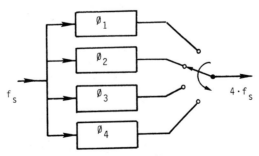

Fig. 3.34. 4:1 Polyphase filter structure.

through the outputs of the P polyphase filters. Figure 3.34 shows this structure. Note that the input commutator, which originally was used to zero-pack the input data, is now used to sequentially address the outputs of the polyphase filter.

Arbitrary Change in Sample Rate by P/M D

In Section III we presented techniques to decrease the filter output rate by an integer factor M, and in Section V we described techniques to increase the filter output rate by the integer factor P. We now combine the two methods to realize ratios of output to input sampling frequency equal to the ratio of arbitrary integers P/M. The rational fraction P/M can be greater or less than unity. Often the fraction is a ratio of small integers such as 5/2 or 3/4, but a ratio such as 18/6145 can also be managed. There are cases, such as in time delay interpolators, for which the ratio is precisely unity but realized as P/P (such as 20/20). We alluded to such an option in the introduction as the interpolators used in time domain beamformers. We can even accommodate a ratio that is slowly time varying about a nominal value by imbedding occasional input zero sample padding and/or output sample skipping in the filtering process.

The philosophy of this technique is to upsample the data by the numerator integer (P) but with a transition bandwidth on the interpolating filter to allow a desampling by the denominator integer (M). Figure 3.35 shows the shifting indicator set for a 3:1 desampling imbedded in a 1:4 upsampling filter. Figure 3.36 shows the polyphase structure of the filter; note that it operates on the shift schedule listed in Fig. 3.35.

This method is best described with the aid of a specific example. For an example of a resampling of arbitrary ratio, let us consider the task of interpolating complex data at an input rate of 6 kHz to a real output rate of 8 kHz. For example, data could be a voice-grade telephone channel that has been zero centered by a complex heterodyne and has a normal one-sided alias-free bandwidth of 1.8 kHz. The first task is to upsample the data to the lowest common factor of the input and output frequencies; this is 24 kHz, so we require an initial 4:1 interpolating filter. If our only need was to upsample by a factor of 4, the required transition bandwidth of the filter, as shown in Fig. 3.37, would be 2.4 kHz (4.2 kHz − 1.8 kHz). The desampling and conversion to a real signal, which follows the upsampling operation, reduces the bandwidth spacing between the spectral replicates, thus necessitating a narrower transition bandwidth. Hence we see that the upsampling and desampling operations are coupled through the transition bandwidth specifications of the interpolating filter. For our example the required transition bandwidth is seen to be 0.4 kHz (2.2 kHz − 1.8 kHz), and since the LPF must operate at the equivalent input data rate of 24.0 kHz, we find that the required filter length for 40-dB sidelobes is

$$N = K(A)\frac{f_s}{\Delta f} = 2\frac{24.0}{0.4} = 120 \qquad (3.18)$$

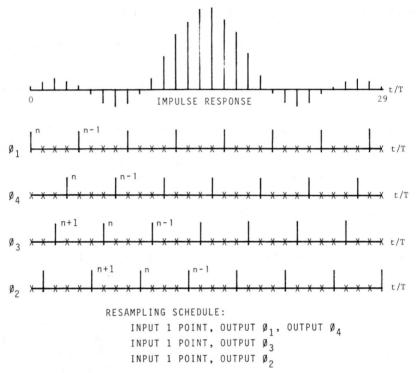

Fig. 3.35. Partition of impulse response by indicator set from 4:1 zero-packed data with imbedded 3:1 desampling for a total 4:3 resampling.

With this interpolator implemented in a polyphase structure, we can imbed the desampling operation in the phasing of the input clock and output commutator clock. Figure 3.35 presented a sequence of time lines showing the zero-packed data sliding past the filter coefficients and pausing at each third input to compute the desampled output. Comparing the input sequence to the polyphase filter taps, we see the input-output phase relationships are indicated in Fig. 3.36. The final

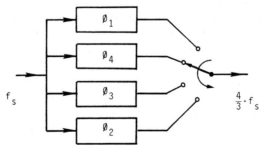

Fig. 3.36. 3:4 Resampling filter with a 4:1 polyphase filter and imbedded 1:3 resampling.

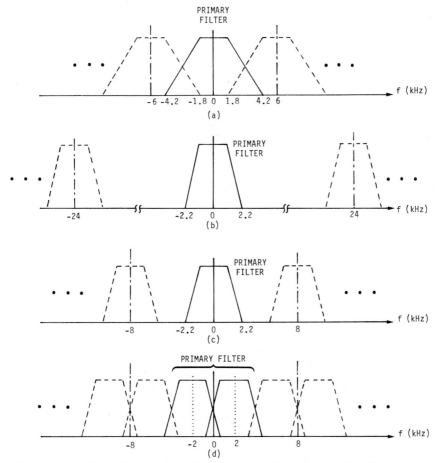

Fig. 3.37. Spectral descriptions of 6-kHz-complex-to-8-kHz-real resampling filter. (a) Input spectrum; output spectrum after (b) 4:1 and (c) 3:4 resampling; and (d) output spectrum of real part of heterodyned signal after 3:4 resampling.

operation applied to the output is the complex heterodyne to shift the data by one quarter of the sampling frequency. Since we are only interested in the real part of that heterodyne product, we will only form that part of the complex multiplication that contributes to the real part. This operation is

$$d(n) = \text{Re}\{[x(n) + jy(n)] * [\cos(\theta n) + j\sin(\theta n)]\} \qquad (3.19)$$

$$= x(n) * \cos(\theta n) - y(n) * \sin(\theta n)$$

$$= x(n) * \cos\left(\frac{\pi}{2}n\right) - y(n) * \sin\left(\frac{\pi}{2}n\right)$$

We note that the sequence of cos and sin values needed for the complex multiplication are cyclically the values

$$\left\{\cos\left(\frac{\pi}{2}n\right)\right\} = +1.0,\ 0.0,\ -1.0,\ 0.0 \tag{3.20}$$

$$\left\{\sin\left(\frac{\pi}{2}n\right)\right\} = 0.0,\ +1.0,\ 0.0,\ -1.0$$

Since these products are trivial, the sequence $d(n)$ of Eq. (3.18) can be formed as cyclically multiplexed and sign-reversed filter outputs such as

$$\{d(n)\} = x(n),\ y(n+1),\ -x(n+2),\ -y(n+3),\dots \tag{3.21}$$

Figure 3.37 shows the spectral descriptions of the signal in the conversion of the 6-kHz complex signal to an 8-kHz real signal. Figure 3.38 shows the final

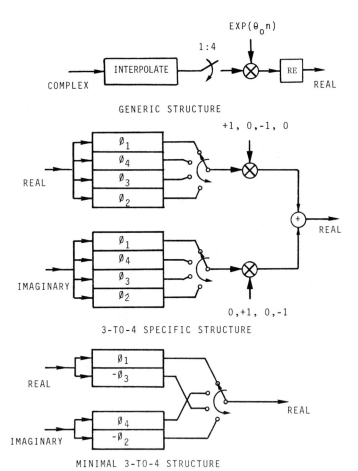

Fig. 3.38. Complex-to-real polyphase filter structure.

structure of the complex-to-real interpolator, in which the desampling is performed with the polyphase output commutator, and the output heterodyne is imbedded in the multiplexer along with appropriate sign changes. Note that the workload for this filter is 30 multiplications and additions per real output point. Also note that for this example the coefficients for phases 1 and 2 are the same set but in reversed order; this is also true for phases 3 and 4.

ARCHITECTURAL MODELS FOR FIR FILTERS   VI

The FIR filter directly implements the convolution process as a weighted summation of data points. The various names by which the filter is known include "tapped delay line," "moving average," "transversal," "all zero," "nonrecursive," and "linear phase" (As explained in Chapter 2, a FIR filter is not necessarily linear phase.) These names reflect properties or structure of the filter. The first three names are architectural descriptors and represent the signal flow model that first comes to mind for most of us. Figure 3.39 presents a block diagram of the classical tapped-delay-line model. The model describes the way we would manipulate data stored in a sequence of memory cells. The first observation is that the adder junction of the model is an $(N - 1)$-input adder that does not exist. Occasionally the model is redrawn to reflect the use of two-input adders for the actual implementation. One such version is shown in Fig. 3.40.

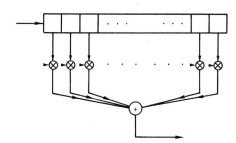

Fig. 3.39. Classical tapped-delay-line FIR filter model.

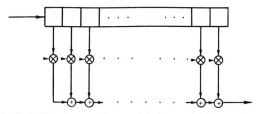

Fig. 3.40. Two-input adders model of tapped-delay-line filter.

Note that we are free to rearrange the order in which we perform the additions of the product terms to obtain reduced computational noise. We will discuss this option soon. This form also suggests various levels of parallelism in terms of adder trees, as indicated in Fig. 3.41.

The simplest adder chains are implemented by successive additions in an accumulator. This form of the adder chain is the digital version of an integrate and dump recursive filter and model is shown in Fig. 3.42.

The N multiplication operations distributed through the models in Figs. 3.39 through 3.41 could be performed by parallel multipliers. Most implementations of the FIR filter use only one multiplier, which sequentially accesses the coefficient and data pairs as suggested in the block diagrams. Signal processors designed with four multipliers (an architecture optimized for complex computations such as in an FFT) have options for some parallelism in the multiplier chain or in the successive inner products of sequential (shifted) filter outputs.

The combination of a single multiplier and accumulator along with data and coefficient memories leads to the minimal FIR filter processing architecture shown in Fig. 3.43. We now leave this level of architectural detail and return to the block diagram level. If the filter response exhibits symmetry about its midpoint, the block diagram model is modified to reflect a sum-product-sum

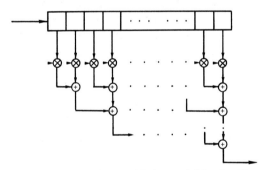

Fig. 3.41. Parallel adder model of tapped-delay-line filter.

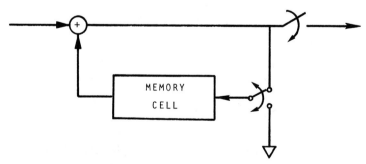

Fig. 3.42. Integrate and dump accumulator.

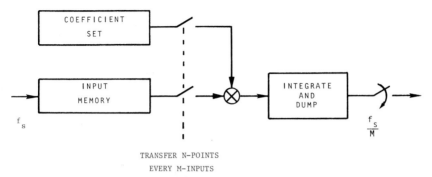

TRANSFER N-POINTS
EVERY M-INPUTS

Fig. 3.43. Minimal FIR filter architecture.

sequence of operations [32]. This is shown in Fig. 3.44 and again in Fig. 3.45. In this form the coefficient memory is half of the filter.

While we are fine tuning the filter architecture to reflect our knowledge about the coefficient set, we can modify that set to minimize computational noise. We can do this by storing the coefficients as short blocks of successive weights that share common binary exponents. This is called a block floating-point set. We recall that the overall response of the lowpass filter is a smoothly truncated version of the $\sin(wt)/(wt)$ function. The envelope of the time response mono-tonically decreases as we leave the central peak. Moving away from the co-efficient peak, we mark the coefficient boundary beyond which the magnitude of the coefficients is alway less than half of the peak. We store the boundary marker (as a count away from the peak) and simply double the coefficient values that reside across that boundary on either side of the peak. We do this bound-ary marking and coefficient doubling recursively till we reach the end of the set. This process reduces the effects of coefficient quantization errors, which we have observed limit the achievable stopband sidelobe attenuation.

The filtering process of multiplication and addition proceeds from the tail of the filter toward the center point. On each call to the coefficient memory we examine the exponent flag (to identify a crossing of an exponent boundary). If the flag is set, while performing the multiplication we simultaneously align the

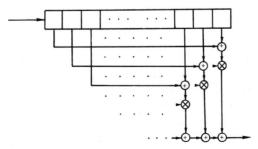

Fig. 3.44. Sum-product-sum FIR filter model.

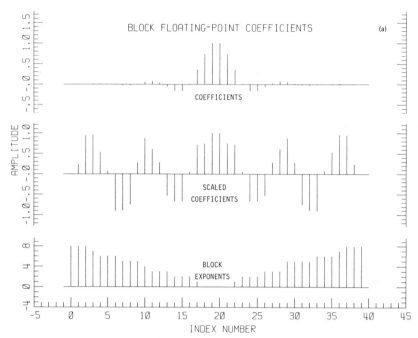

Fig. 3.45(a). Block floating-point FIR filter coefficients.

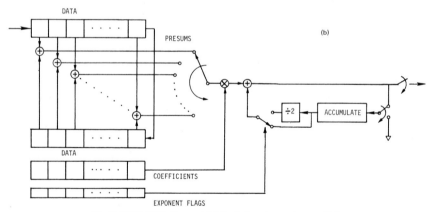

Fig. 3.45(b). FIR filter with Block floating-point coefficients.

exponent of the partial sum with that of the coefficient (by a binary shift and sign extension) prior to the recursive addition. This recursive exponent alignment continues through the entire coefficient set and, when finished, results in the properly aligned summation. Here we have the advantage that the partial summations are performed with more accurate coefficients before the scaling.

The original filter coefficient set indicated in Fig. 3.45 has been modified by the block floating-point operation to become the second set shown in the same figure.

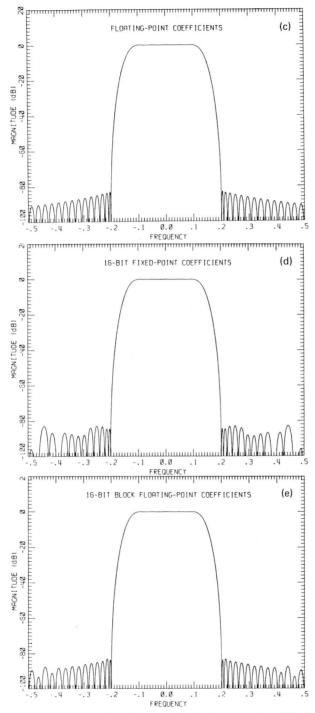

Fig. 3.45(c). Spectra of 40-point FIR filter with (c) floating-point, (d) 16-bit fixed-point, and (e) 16-bit block floating-point coefficients.

Also shown in Fig. 3.45(c), (d), and (e) is the frequency response of the filter realized, respectively, with floating-point, with 16-bit fixed-point, and with 16-bit block floating-point coefficients, respectively. This technique requires the data to be buffered in random access memory so that the partial sums can be performed in the selected order. We cannot apply this scaling technique if the memory is sequential access, such as in a shift register memory, nor can we apply it if the architecture is not of the tapped delay form, such as in the partial-sum models.

A   Partial-Sum FIR Filter Structure

The partial-sum model is a minimum data memory realization of the resampling FIR filter [33]. In this architecture partial summations instead of raw input data are stored. In the tapped-delay-line model each data point shifts through the delay line with periodic pauses to compute the product and summation required for its contribution to a given output point. In the partial-sum model the set of products and summations, normally formed sequentially as a data point moves in the tapped-delay-line model, are all formed simultaneously

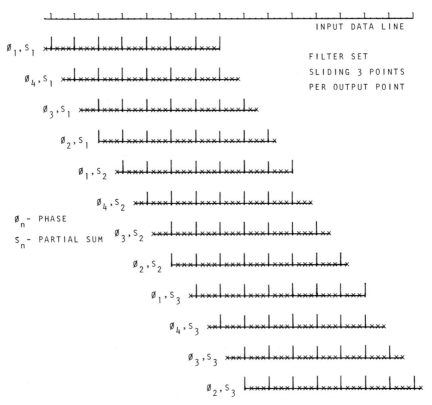

Fig. 3.46. Partial-sum partition of polyphase filter set.

upon the data point's arrival. The additions are made to partial-sum accumulators, which are cleared only upon completion of each summation. Since
the data's contribution to each filter output point is stored as a collection of
partial summations, there is no need to store the raw data. Storage consists
entirely of the partial summations. This consideration is important in very high-
speed applications where memory access times would limit processing speeds.

We now address the number of partial summations required for a given filter.
The number of partial summations required to form a resampling FIR filter
depends on filter length, number of polyphase segments (upsampling parameter),
and the imbedded desampling parameter (if any). The required number is most
easily seen by keeping track of the clearing rate for the accumulators. The
contents of a partial-sum accumulator are cleared upon the completion of the
polyphase inner product. Upon clearing, the accumulator becomes available to
form the next partial sum.

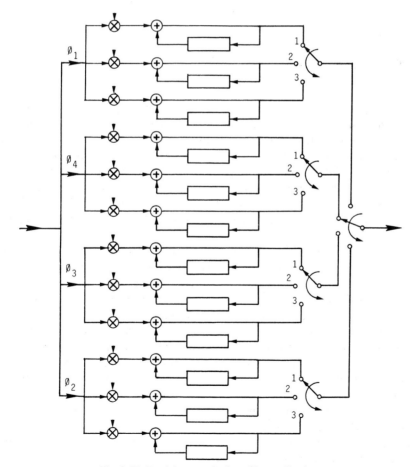

Fig. 3.47. Partial-sum polyphase filter realization.

Let us follow a specific example, in particular the 30-point 4:1 upsampling filter with the imbedded 1:3 desampling of Fig. 3.35. Assume the first three data points have just contributed to a freshly cleared phase 1 segment. Since the segment has not finished its run (of eight), it cannot clear. The next three input points arrive and contribute to this first partial sum and to the start of a second partial sum. The first sum has now accumulated six of its required eight points; hence it has not completed its run and still cannot clear. The second accumulator, holding a fresher sum, obviously has not finished its run of eight, and it too cannot be cleared. The next three input points arrive; two of them contribute to the first sum and finish its run of eight points, thus allowing an output and a clearing. These same input points contribute to the second partial sum and to a fresh third partial sum. When the next three input points arrive, they start a fresh partial sum run in the original first accumulator. Thus we find that three partial sums had to be in operation for the phase 1 segment. This accounting technique is shown in Fig. 3.46 for all four phases. Shown in Fig. 3.47 is the partial sum polyphase structure of this same filter.

VII SUMMARY

This chapter has examined the structure of resampling filters. We found that the resampling filter is essentially a lowpass filter and a system of input and output switches operating at two or more frequencies. These frequencies are related by integer ratios $M:1$, $1:P$, and $M:P$. In our review of lowpass filters we found that the filter length is proportional to the ratio of sampling rate to transition bandwidth. The proportionality coefficient was shown to be inversely related to stopband attenuation. We formed a simple estimate of this attenuation-related coefficient and demonstrated some designs using our estimates.

An interesting result of our review of resampling filters is that the filter design is the same for desampling and upsampling ratios of $M:1$ and $1:P$, respectively. We showed that, as with nonresampling lowpass filters, the filter length is proportional to the ratio of the sample rate to transition bandwidth, where the sample rate is the larger of the pair of input and output sampling rates.

We introduced upsampling filters through the technique of lowpass filtering a zero-packed input data stream. We then used the nonzero positions in the zero-packed data to identify filter subsets that formed distinct subfilters. These subfilters were used as the polyphase components of computationally efficient interpolating filters.

We also introduced other architectural variations of the FIR filter that permit enhanced performance options related to speed, finite accuracy coefficients, and memory requirements. These included the add-multiply-add structure, block floating-point coefficient structrue, and the partial-sim structures.

APPENDIX WINDOWS AS NARROWBAND FILTERS

Introduction   A

Windows were discussed in Section III in conjunction with FIR filter design. Windows are also used in conjunction with the DFT to perform spectral analysis on data sets observed over finite intervals. In support of that task, the window serves various functions. the most important of which is to shape the spectral response of the equivalent filter set. For this reason, windows designed for spectral analysis applications can also be used as the impulse response of narrowband FIR filters. In this appendix we shall review the important properties of windows from the classical viewpoint of spectral decomposition. As part of this review, we shall cite how those properties that make windows useful for spectral decomposition can be interpreted as desirable properties for narrowband FIR filters.

The first function a data sequence window (also called a data sequence weighting) serves in spectral analysis is to define the duration of the observation. For sampled data systems the duration is the number of samples N, which along with the known time interval between samples T defines the total time duration of the observation NT. This in turn defines the analysis' minimum spectral resolution, which is the inverse of the observation length $1/NT$, where the units are inverse seconds or hertz. This minimum resolution can be factored to emphasis that the minimum resolution is equal to the sample rate divided by the number of data points: $(1/N)(1/T)$. This minimum achievable bandwidth is obtained with the rectangular weighted window, sometimes called the default window. By analogy, a FIR lowpass filter defined by the rectangular weights will exhibit this minimum bandwidth response for the given number of points. From the inverse viewpoint a FIR filter designed to pass a band of frequencies that represents $1/N$ of the sample rate must span an input interval of at least N data points. Data sequence shaping and additional filter length are required to obtain filter sidelobe control for a given spectral bandwidth.

Figures of Merit   B

We must share the same concern about the maximum levels of the out-of-band spectral response of FIR filters and data sequence windows. Table AI lists common figures of merit for windows that can aid in comparing the important performance considerations. The first parameter listed in Table AI is the highest sidelobe level — that is, the minimum stopband attenuation. Filters are normally specified by a minimum required attenuation level, and windows are identified as exhibiting particular sidelobe levels or are designed to realize a given sidelobe

TABLE AI

Figures of Merit for Shaped DFT Filters

	Highest sidelobe level (dB)	Sidelobe falloff (dB/octave)	Coherent gain	Figure of merit					Overlap correlation (%)	
				Equivalent noise BW (bins)	3.0-dB BW (bins)	Scallop loss (dB)	Worst-case process loss (dB)	6.0-dB BW (bins)	75% OL	50% OL
Weighting										
Rectangle	−13	−6	1.00	1.00	0.89	3.92	3.92	1.21	75.0	50.0
Triangle	−27	−12	0.50	1.33	1.28	1.82	3.07	1.78	71.9	25.0
cos²(x) α = 1.0	−23	−12	0.64	1.23	1.20	2.10	3.01	1.65	75.5	31.8
α = 2.0	−32	−18	0.50	1.50	1.44	1.42	3.18	2.00	65.9	16.7
Hann α = 3.0	−39	−24	0.42	1.73	1.66	1.08	3.47	2.32	56.7	8.5
α = 4.0	−47	−30	0.38	1.94	1.86	0.86	3.75	2.59	48.6	4.3
Hamming	−43	−6	0.54	1.36	1.30	1.78	3.10	1.81	70.7	23.5
Parabolic	−21	−12	0.67	1.20	1.16	2.22	3.01	1.59	76.5	34.4
Riemann	−26	−12	0.59	1.30	1.26	1.89	3.03	1.74	73.4	27.4
Cubic	−53	−24	0.38	1.92	1.82	0.90	3.72	2.55	49.3	5.0
Tukey α = 0.25	−14	−18	0.88	1.10	1.01	2.96	3.39	1.38	74.1	44.4
α = 0.50	−15	−18	0.75	1.22	1.15	2.24	3.11	1.57	72.7	36.4
α = 0.75	−19	−18	0.63	1.36	1.31	1.73	3.07	1.80	70.5	25.1
Bohman	−46	−24	0.41	1.79	1.71	1.02	3.54	2.38	54.5	7.4
Poisson α = 2.0	−19	−6	0.44	1.30	1.21	2.09	3.23	1.69	69.9	27.8
α = 3.0	−24	−6	0.32	1.65	1.45	1.46	3.64	2.08	54.8	15.1
α = 4.0	−31	−6	0.25	2.08	1.75	1.03	4.21	2.58	40.4	7.4
Hamming– α = 0.5	−35	−18	0.43	1.61	1.54	1.26	3.33	2.14	61.3	12.6
Poisson α = 1.0	−39	−18	0.38	1.73	1.64	1.11	3.50	2.30	56.0	9.2
α = 2.0	none	−18	0.29	2.02	1.87	0.87	3.94	2.65	44.6	4.7
Cauchy α = 3.0	−31	−6	0.42	1.48	1.34	1.71	3.40	1.90	61.6	20.2
α = 4.0	−35	−6	0.33	1.76	1.50	1.36	3.83	2.20	48.8	13.2
α = 5.0	−30	−6	0.28	2.06	1.68	1.13	4.28	2.53	38.3	9.0

Window		Highest Side-Lobe Level (dB)	Side-Lobe Fall-Off (dB/oct)	Coherent Gain	Equiv. Noise BW (bins)	3.0-dB BW (bins)	Scallop Loss (dB)	Worst Case Process Loss (dB)	6.0-dB BW (bins)	Overlap Correlation 75% (%)	Overlap Correlation 50% (%)
Taylor	α = 2.0	−40	−6	0.57	1.30	1.25	1.91	3.06	1.74	75.7	28.3
	α = 2.5	−50	−6	0.51	1.43	1.36	1.60	3.15	1.90	71.3	21.4
	α = 3.0	−60	−6	0.47	1.55	1.47	1.37	3.26	2.06	67.0	16.1
	α = 3.5	−70	−6	0.44	1.66	1.58	1.20	3.40	2.21	62.9	12.1
	α = 4.0	−80	−6	0.41	1.76	1.67	1.06	3.52	2.35	59.1	9.1
Gaussian	α = 2.5	−42	−6	0.51	1.39	1.33	1.69	3.14	1.86	67.7	20.0
	α = 3.0	−55	−6	0.43	1.64	1.55	1.25	3.40	2.18	57.5	10.6
	α = 3.5	−69	−6	0.37	1.90	1.79	0.94	3.73	2.52	47.2	4.9
Dolph–Chebyshev	α = 2.5	−50	0	0.53	1.39	1.33	1.70	3.12	1.85	69.6	22.3
	α = 3.0	−60	0	0.48	1.51	1.44	1.44	3.23	2.01	64.7	16.3
	α = 3.5	−70	0	0.45	1.62	1.55	1.25	3.35	2.17	60.2	11.9
	α = 4.0	−80	0	0.42	1.73	1.65	1.10	3.48	2.31	55.9	8.7
Kaiser–Bessel	α = 2.0	−46	−6	0.49	1.50	1.43	1.46	3.20	1.99	65.7	16.9
	α = 2.5	−57	−6	0.44	1.65	1.57	1.20	3.38	2.20	59.5	11.2
	α = 3.0	−69	−6	0.40	1.80	1.71	1.02	3.56	2.39	53.9	7.4
	α = 3.5	−82	−6	0.37	1.93	1.83	0.89	3.74	2.57	48.8	4.8
Barcilon–Temes	α = 3.0	−53	−6	0.47	1.56	1.49	1.34	3.27	2.07	63.0	14.2
	α = 3.5	−58	−6	0.43	1.67	1.59	1.18	3.40	2.23	58.6	10.4
	α = 4.0	−68	−6	0.41	1.77	1.69	1.05	3.52	2.36	54.4	7.6
Exact Blackman		−68	−6	0.46	1.57	1.52	1.33	3.29	2.13	62.7	14.0
Blackman		−58	−18	0.42	1.73	1.68	1.10	3.47	2.35	56.7	9.0
Minimum 3-sample Blackman–Harris		−71	−6	0.42	1.71	1.66	1.13	3.45	1.81	57.2	9.6
Minimum 4-sample Blackman–Harris		−92	−6	0.36	2.00	1.90	0.83	3.85	2.72	46.0	3.8
62-dB 3-sample Blackman–Harris		−62	−6	0.45	1.61	1.56	1.27	3.34	2.19	61.0	12.6
74-dB 4-sample Blackman–Harris		−74	−6	0.40	1.79	1.74	1.03	3.56	2.44	53.9	7.4
4-sample Kaiser–Bessel	α = 3.0	−69	−6	0.40	1.80	1.74	1.02	3.56	2.44	53.9	7.4

level. The sidelobe levels are specified to reflect dynamic range considerations, such as the noise floor of an input ADC (at -6.0 dB/bit). Windows are also characterized by asymptotic rates of decay for the out-of-band sidelobe levels. This traditionally is not a specification for FIR filters. As explained in Chapter 3, however, a FIR filter with rates of decay between -4.5 and -6.0 dB/octave (or -15 to -20 dB/decade) exhibits reduced levels of sidelobe aliasing under the resampling operation. This asymptotic sidelobe decay rate is the second parameter listed for each window in Table AI.

The coherent gain (CG) of the window (or prototype lowpass FIR filter) is the zero frequency gain (also referred to as the dc gain) of the window, which is found as the summation of the window weights. The weights are normalized to a peak value of unity, and the summation over the N points is bounded by N. The CG parameter listed in Table AI is the summation scaled by the number of terms N:

$$CG = \frac{1}{N} \sum_{n=0}^{N-1} w(n) \tag{A3.1}$$

This term is the numerical gain referred to in Chapter 3 and is required to estimate the width of the accumulators needed when forming the weighted summation of the FIR filter.

It is difficult to assess and compare the bandwidth-reducing abilities of filters with different spectral shapes. One useful measure of this ability is the equivalent noise bandwidth (ENBW). We can conduct test to measure the ENBW of a filter by passing white noise with a known spectral density through the filter and then measuring the output variance. The variance of the output noise is a measure of the filter bandwidth. In particular, the ENBW of a window or filter is the width of an equivalent ideal rectangular spectral response that will pass the same noise power as the filter under test. The filter under test is first normalized for unity zero frequency gain. If we assume unity sample rate and unity noise power spectral density, the ENBW of a filter is given by

$$ENBW = \frac{\sum_n w^2(n)}{\left| \sum_n w(n) \right|^2} \tag{A3.2}$$

For a rectangular weighted summation of N terms, the ENBW is $1/N$, which is also the filter's spectral resolution. For other weightings the ENBW is larger. In many cases we are willing to accept a larger ENBW in order to control the out-of-band sidelobe levels. The ENBW parameter listed in Table AI has been normalized relative to the ENBW of the rectangular weights of the same filter length.

Another important set of parameters is related to the shape of the filter's mainlobe spectral response. In particular, the spectral interval between the peak gain and the -3.0-dB and -6.0-dB response levels is a convenient measure of the filter mainlobe width. Normalized versions of these parameters are listed in

Table AI for N-point weighting sequences. The normalization is in terms of bins, where a bin is the frequency resolution using rectangular weightings ($1/N$ of the input sample rate).

The scallop loss is the attenuation of the window at one-half a bin separation from the mainlobe peak spectral position. It is an important consideration when the window is used to form a bank of adjacent filters that are spaced at one-bin intervals such as in a DFT. The scallop loss represents the apparent reduction in signal level due to a sinusoid whose frequency is midway between two adjacent filter center frequencies. An allied figure of merit is the worst-case processing loss. This term is the sum of the scallop loss and the ENBW (converted to dB) of the filter. This represents the apparent reduction in SNR for a sinusoid in additive white noise and can be attributed to use of the window. It is due to the position of the input sinusoid in the filter bandwidth and to increased noise variance resulting from the increased mainlobe widths. This figure is useful for detection considerations but is often replaced with an average loss over the bandwidth (as opposed to the maximum loss).

The last figure of merit listed in Table AI is the percent overlap correlation for filters used to reduce the bandwidth of the input series. In many applications the sample rate is reduced commensurately with the bandwidth reduction. For a white noise input, filter output samples separated by more than the filter length are independent. Those taken from the filter that are closer than the filter length are correlated, because some of the same input data has contributed to each output. The correlation coefficients represent the degree of correlation of filter output points that are separated by 25% and 50% of the filter length. These terms are useful in quantifying the estimation uncertainty (or variance reduction) related to incoherent averaging of filter data.

Window (Filter) Descriptions   **C**

Rectangular Window   *1*

The rectangular window is unity over its entire interval. When this data sequence window is represented by an even symmetric FIR filter impulse response, it is defined as

$$h(n) = 1.0, \qquad n = -\frac{N}{2}, \ldots, -1, 0, 1, \ldots, \frac{N}{2} \qquad (A3.3)$$

The sequence is shifted $N/2$ locations to the right to make it realizable. The spectral response of the realizable weights is given by

$$H(\omega) = \exp\left[-j\frac{N}{2}\omega\right] \frac{\sin[((N+1)/2)\omega]}{\sin[(1/2)\omega]} \qquad (A3.4)$$

The time response of this filter for $N/2 = 25$ is shown in Fig. A3.1(a); the spectral response is shown in Fig. A3.1(b). The filter has the narrowest mainlobe width for an N-point filter but exhibits high sidelobes. The first sidelobe is attenuated approximately 13.0 dB relative to the mainlobe, and the remaining sidelobes fall off at 6 dB/octave.

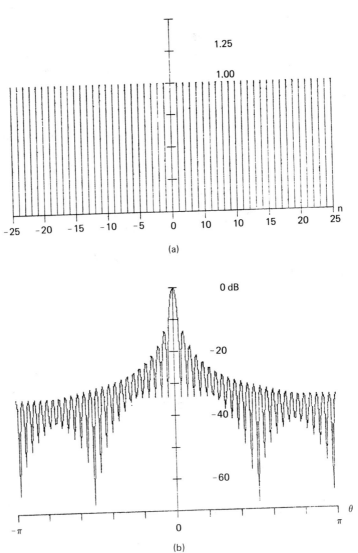

(a)

(b)

Fig. A3.1. (a) Rectangle window and (b) log-magnitude of window's frequency response.

Triangular (Fejer, Bartlett) Window **2**

The triangular window, when represented by an even symmetric FIR filter impulse response, is defined by

$$h(n) = 1.0 - \frac{|n|}{N/2} \qquad n = -\frac{N}{2}, \ldots, -1, 0, 1, \ldots, \frac{N}{2} \qquad (A3.5)$$

This sequence is shifted $N/2 - 1$ positions to the right to make it realizable. The spectral response of the realizable weighting is

$$H(\omega) = \exp\left[-j\left(\frac{N}{2} - 1\right)\omega\right]\left[\frac{\sin[(N/4)\omega]}{\sin[(1/2)\omega]}\right]^2 \qquad (A3.6)$$

The time and spectral responses of this filter are shown in Fig A3.2. This filter's frequency response is seen to be the magnitude squared of the response of a rectangular window of length $N/2 + 1$. The reason is that the triangle can be obtained as the convolution of two (half-width) rectangles, so the resultant transform is the product of the rectangle's spectrum with itself. Note that the mainlobe width has been doubled and that the sidelobes start at -26 dB and decay at 12 dB/octave. The spectrum is everywhere positive, which is a property of a filter response obtained by self-correlation of an arbitrary sequence.

Cos*(x) Windows **3**

The $\cos(x)$ windows are a family of windows defined on the parameter α. The window used as a symmetric FIR filter is defined by

$$h(n) = \text{Cos}^{\alpha}\left[\left(\frac{n}{N}\right)\pi\right] \qquad n = -\frac{N}{2}, \ldots, -1, 0, 1, \ldots, \frac{N}{2} \qquad (A3.7)$$

The window is formed by raising to the power α the samples of half a cycle of a cosine, which extends over the $N + 1$ points of the impulse response. The zeros at the end of the interval become repeated zeros as the power α increases. The repeated zeros of the resultant function suggest that not only is the function zero at the boundaries, but also a number of the function's derivatives are zero. This has the effect of forcing the spectral sidelobe structure to decay more rapidly. This also causes the time function (i.e., the impulse response) to the narrower so that its spectral response widens. The time response and spectral responses for the filter are presented in Fig. A3.3 for $\alpha = 2.0$. This is the Hann window, which is sometimes referred to as a raised cosine window. The window is defined by

$$h(n) = \text{Cos}^2\left[\left(\frac{\pi}{N}\right)n\right] = 0.5[1.0 + \cos\left[\left(\frac{2\pi}{N}\right)n\right], \qquad (A3.8)$$

$$n = -\frac{N}{2}, \ldots, -1, 0, \ldots, \frac{N}{2}$$

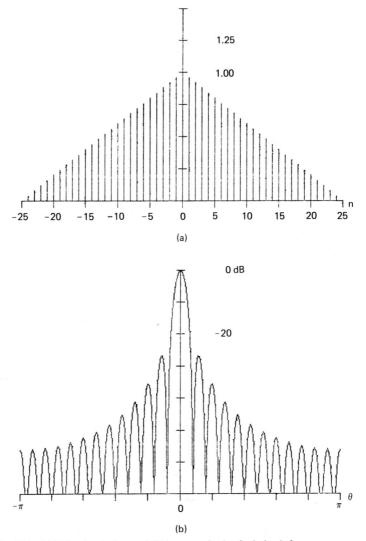

Fig. A3.2. (a) Triangle window and (b) log-magnitude of window's frequency response.

Since the time domain description of the Hann window is that of a two-term cosine series, the spectral description is particularly simple, being a summation of Dirichlet kernels of the form

$$H(\omega) = 0.5D(\omega) + 0.25\left[D\left(\omega - \frac{2\pi}{N}\right) + D\left(\omega + \frac{2\pi}{N}\right)\right] \qquad (A3.9)$$

where

$$D(\omega) = \frac{\sin[(N/2)\omega]}{\sin[(1/2)\omega]}$$

The spectrum of the Hann window has a mainlobe width twice that of the rectangular window (as does the triangular window), a highest sidelobe attenuated relative to the mainlobe by 32 dB, and an asymptotic rate of sidelobe

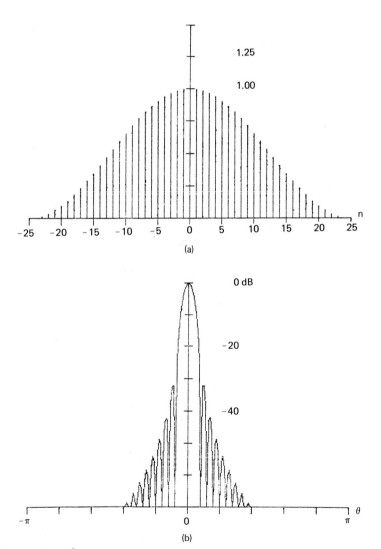

Fig. A3.3. (a) $\text{Cos}^2(n\pi/N)$ window and (b) log-magnitude of window's frequency response.

decay of 18 dB/octave. The reduced sidelobe levels can be visualized as resulting from the destructive cancellation of sidelobes from the offset Dirichlet kernels of Eq. (A3.9).

4 Hamming Window

The Hamming window is an extension of the Hann window in the sense that it is a raised cosine window of the form

$$h(n) = \alpha + (1.0 - \alpha)\cos\left[\left(\frac{2\pi}{N}\right)n\right] \tag{A3.10}$$

with a corresponding spectrum of the form

$$H(\theta) = \alpha D(\omega) + \frac{(1.0 - \alpha)}{2}\left[D\left(\omega - \frac{2\pi}{N}\right) + D\left(\omega + \frac{2\pi}{N}\right)\right] \tag{A3.11}$$

The parameter α permits the optimization of the destructive sidelobe cancellation mentioned in the description of the Hann window. In particular, when α is adjusted to 25/46 (0.543478261...), the first sidelobe (see the Hann window) is canceled. The common approximation to this value of α is 0.54, for which the window is called the Hamming window and is of the form

$$H(\theta) = 0.54 + 0.46\cos\left[\left(\frac{2\pi}{N}\right)n\right] \tag{A3.12}$$

The time and spectral responses of this filter are shown in Fig. A3.4. Note that the mainlobe width matches that of the Hann, that the highest sidelobe is attenuated with respect to the mainlobe by 43 dB, and that the asymptotic rate of attenuation is 6 dB/octave.

5 Short Cosine Series Windows

The Hamming and the Hann windows are examples of windows constructed by the summation of shifted Dirichlet kernels. The general time domain description of such a window is of the form

$$h(n) = \sum_{k=0}^{K/2} a(k)\cos\left[\left(\frac{2\pi}{N}\right)kn\right] \qquad n = -\frac{N}{2}, \ldots, -1, 0, 1, \ldots, \frac{N}{2} \tag{A3.13}$$

which has a spectral description of the form

$$H(\omega) = a(0)D(\omega) + \sum_{k=1}^{K/2} \frac{a(k)}{2}\left[D\left(\omega - k\frac{2\pi}{N}\right) + D\left(\omega + k\frac{2\pi}{N}\right)\right] \tag{A3.14}$$

subject to the constraint

$$\sum_{k=0}^{K/2} a(k) = 1.0 \tag{A3.15}$$

We see that the Hamming and the Hann windows are of this form with only two nonzero coefficients. Constructing a window with a small number of nonzero coefficients is one way to control the mainlobe width of the spectral response.

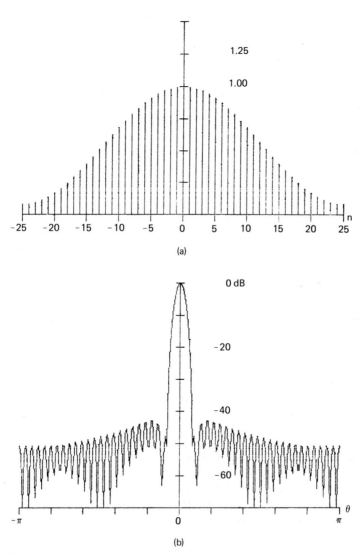

(a)

(b)

Fig. A3.4. (a) Hamming window and (b) log-magnitude of window's frequency response.

a. Blackman Window. Blackman examined windows with three terms and found the values that placed zeros at the nominal position of the first two sidelobes outside the mainlobe interval. These exact values and their two-place approximations are

$$a(0) = \frac{793}{18,608} = 0.426\ 590\ 71 \approx 0.42$$

$$a(1) = \frac{9240}{18,608} = 0.496\ 560\ 62 \approx 0.50$$

$$a(3) = \frac{1403}{18,608} = 0.076\ 848\ 67 \approx 0.08$$

The window defined by the two-place approximations is known as the Blackman window and is of the form

$$h(n) = 0.42 + 0.50 \cos\left[\frac{2\pi}{N} n\right] + 0.08 \cos\left[\frac{2\pi}{N} 2n\right]. \qquad \text{(A3.16)}$$

$$n = -\frac{N}{2}, \ldots, -1, 0, 1, \ldots, \frac{N}{2}$$

The time and spectral responses of this filter are presented in Fig. A3.5. Note that the first sidelobe is attenuated 59 dB relative to the mainlobe and that the sidelobes fall off at 18 dB/octave. The time and spectral responses for the exact Blackman weights are presented in Fig. A3.6. Note that the highest sidelobe is attenuated by 69 dB relative to the mainlobe response and that the sidelobes decay at 6 dB/octave.

b. Blackman–Harris Window. Using a gradient search technique, Harris found three-term and four-term windows that achieve minimum sidelobe level responses. Nutall subsequently published corrected coefficients for the same windows. These three- and four-term windows are called Blackman–Harris or Harris–Nutall windows. These windows achieve sidelobe levels of −74 and −94 dB, respectively. The coefficients for these windows are listed in Table AII. The three-term (−74-dB) window formed by this short cosine series and its spectrum are given in Fig. A3.7.

c. Sampled Kaiser–Bessel Window. Any good window with acceptable sidelobe levels can be the prototype of a small number of term cosine series. We simply sample the mainlobe spectral response of the prototype filter and use scaled versions of those samples as the coefficients of the cosine series terms in (A3.13). For instance, the spectral description of the Kaiser–Bessel window is of the form

$$H(\omega) = \frac{\sinh \sqrt{\pi^2 \alpha^2 - (\omega N/2)^2}}{\sqrt{\pi^2 \alpha^2 - (\omega N/2)^2}}, \qquad 0 \le \alpha \le 4 \qquad \text{(A3.17)}$$

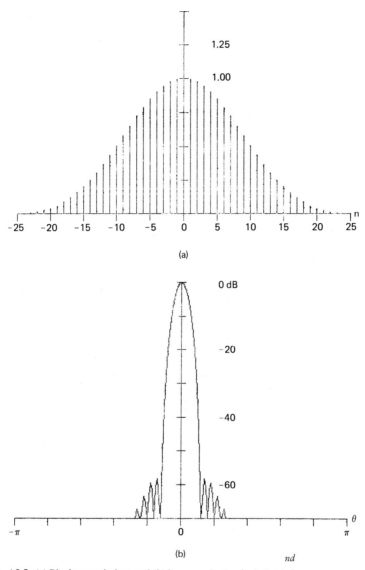

(a)

(b)   *nd*

Fig. A3.5. (a) Blackman window and (b) log-magnitude of window's frequency response.

TABLE AII

Coefficients of Three- and Four-Term Blackman–Harris (Harris–Nutall) Windows

	3 Term (−61 dB)	3 Term (−67 dB)	4 Term (−74 dB)	4 Term (−94 dB)
$a(0)$	0.449 59	0.423 23	0.402 17	0.358 75
$a(1)$	0.493 64	0.497 55	0.497 03	0.488 29
$a(2)$	0.056 77	0.079 22	0.098 92	0.141 28
$a(4)$	—	—	0.001 83	0.011 68

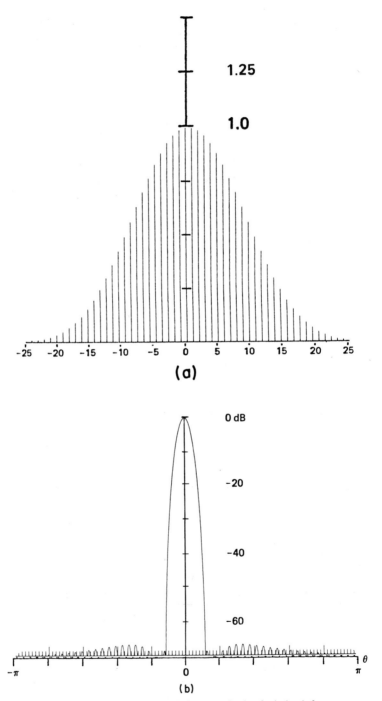

Fig. A3.6. (a) Exact Blackman window and (b) log-magnitude of window's frequency response.

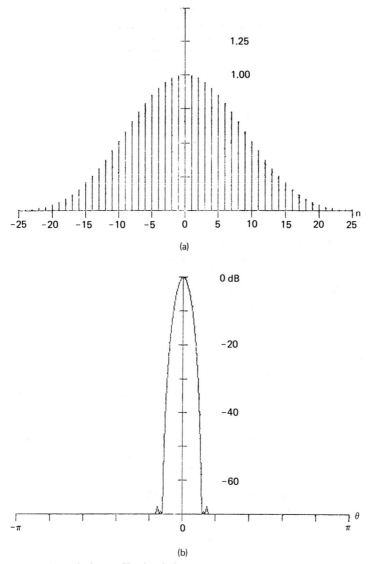

(a)

(b)

Fig. A3.7. (a) Three-Blackman–Harris window and (b) log-magnitude of window's frequency response.

In Eq. (A3.17) let $\omega = m(2\pi/N)$, the equally spaced spectral points of a DFT; then we have

$$H_1(m) = \frac{\sinh(\pi\sqrt{\alpha^2 - m^2})}{\pi\sqrt{\alpha^2 - m^2}} \tag{A3.18}$$

TABLE AIII

**Coefficients of Four-Term Sampled
Kaiser–Bessel Window**

$a(0) = 0.402\ 43$
$a(1) = 0.498\ 04$
$a(2) = 0.098\ 31$
$a(3) = 0.001\ 22$

Now scaling the sampled results of Eq. (A3.17) gives

$$c = H_1(0) + 2H_1(1) + 2H_1(2) + [2H_1(3)] \tag{A3.19}$$

$$a(0) = \frac{H_1(0)}{c}, \qquad a(m) = \frac{2H_1(m)}{c}, \quad m = 1, 2, (3)$$

The four coefficients for the sampled Kaiser–Bessel window corresponding to the parameter $\alpha = 3$ (for -70-dB sidelobes) are listed in Table AIII. The window formed by this four-term cosine series and its spectrum are presented in Fig. A3.8. Note that the four-term approximating window maintains essentially the same sidelobe performance of the original prototype.

6   Constructed Windows

Numerous windows have been constructed as the product, as the sum, as sections, and as convolutions of simple functions and of other simple windows. In general, these constructed windows do not exhibit the good spectral properties of narrow mainlobe width and low sidelobe levels. We include them here to help the user avoid taking well-trod pathways that have not led to useful results. For these windows we simply describe the function and give their time and frequency responses with no other comments.

a. Parabolic (Riesz, Bochner, Parzen) window.   The parabolic window is a simple polynomial function (quadratic) of the form

$$h(n) = 1.0 - \left[\frac{n}{N/2}\right]^2, \qquad 0 \le |n| \le \frac{N}{2} \tag{A3.20}$$

The time and frequency responses of this window are given in Fig. A3.9.

b. Riemann Window.   The Riemann window is a set of samples of the central (main) lobe of the $\sin(x)/(x)$ function and is of the form

$$h(n) = \frac{\sin\dfrac{2\pi n}{N}}{\dfrac{2\pi n}{N}}, \qquad 0 \le |n| \le \frac{N}{2} \tag{A3.21}$$

The time and frequency responses of this window are given in Fig. A3.10.

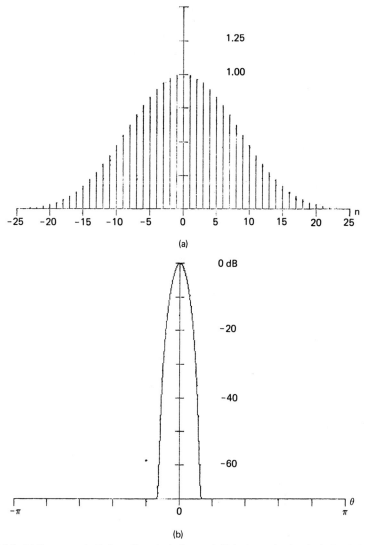

Fig. A3.8. (a) Four sample Kaiser–Bessel window and (b) log-magnitude of window's frequency response.

c. De La Vallé–Poussin (Jackson, Parzen) window. This window is a piecewise cubic curve obtained by self-convolving two triangles of half extent or four rectangles of one-fourth extent. It is defined by

$$h(n) = \begin{cases} 1.0 - 6\left[\dfrac{n}{N/2}\right]^2\left[1.0 - \dfrac{|n|}{N/2}\right], & 0 \le |n| \le \dfrac{N}{4} \\[3mm] 2\left[1.0 - \dfrac{|n|}{N/2}\right]^3 & \dfrac{N}{4} \le |n| \le \dfrac{N}{2} \end{cases} \tag{A3.22}$$

The time and frequency responses are given in Fig. A3.11.

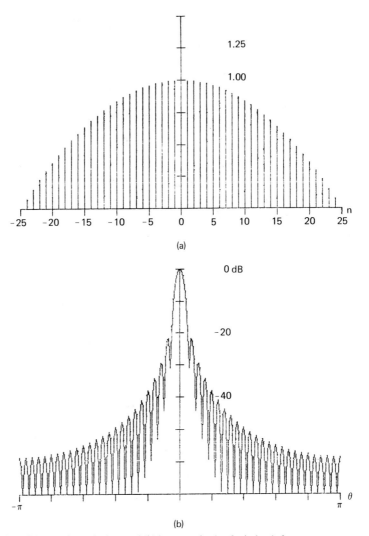

Fig. A3.9. (a) Riesz window and (b) log-magnitude of window's frequency response.

d. Cosine Taper (Tukey) Window. The Tukey window is unity amplitude over $(1 - \alpha/2)N$ points, with the remaining $(\alpha/2)N$ points forming a cosine taper from unity to zero at its boundaries. The window is equivalent to convolving a rectangle of width $(1 - \alpha/2)N$ with a raised cosine (the Hann window) of width $(\alpha/2)N$. The resultant window is of the form

$$
h(n) = \begin{cases}
1.0, & 0 \le |n| \le \alpha\dfrac{N}{2} \\[2ex]
0.5\left(1.0 + \cos\left[\pi\dfrac{n - \alpha(N/2)}{2(1 - \alpha)(N/2)}\right]\right), & \alpha\dfrac{N}{2} \le |n| < \dfrac{N}{2}
\end{cases} \tag{A3.23}
$$

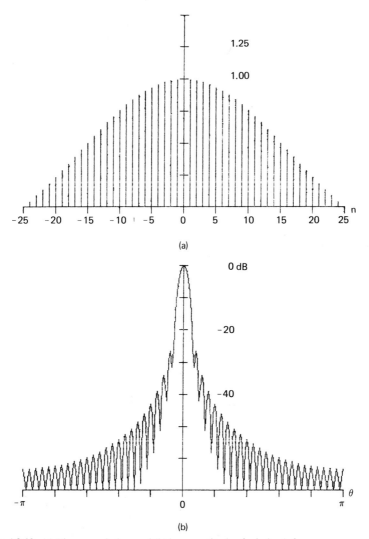

Fig. A3.10. (a) Riemann window and (b) log-magnitude of window's frequency response.

The time and frequency responses of this window are given for $\alpha = 0.75$ in Fig. A3.12.

e. Bohman Window. The Bohman window is obtained by the convolution of two half-duration cosine functions (Eq. (A3.7) with $\alpha = 1.0$); thus its transform is the square of the corresponding cosine function's transform. The window is of the form

$$h(n) = \left[1.0 - \frac{|n|}{N/2} \right] \cos\left[\pi \frac{|n|}{N/2} \right] + \frac{1}{\pi} \sin\left[\pi \frac{|n|}{N/2} \right], \qquad 0 \leq |n| \leq \frac{N}{2} \quad (A3.24)$$

The time and frequency responses of this window are given in Fig. A3.13.

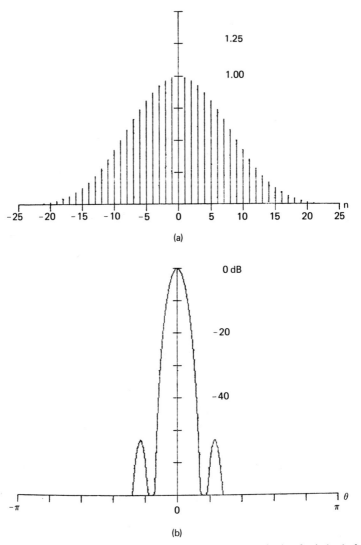

Fig. A3.11. (a) De La Vallée-Poussin window and (b) log-magnitude of window's frequency response.

f. Poisson Window.   The Poisson is a family of truncated two-sided exponentials defined by

$$h(n) = \exp\left[-\alpha \frac{|n|}{N/2}\right], \qquad 0 \le |n| \le \frac{N}{2} \qquad (A3.25)$$

The parameter α in this family corresponds to the reciprocal time constant of an exponential sequence. The time and frequency responses of this window for $\alpha = 3.0$ are given in Fig. A3.14.

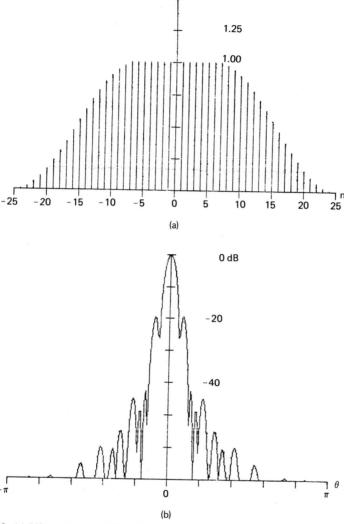

(b)

Fig. A3.12. (a) 75% cosine taper (Tukey) window and (b) log-magnitude of window's frequency response.

g. Hann–Poisson Window. The Hann–Poisson family of windows is obtained as the product of the Hann and the Poisson windows and is of the form

$$h(n) = 0.5\left[1.0 + \cos\left(\pi\frac{n}{N/2}\right)\right]\exp\left(-\alpha\frac{|n|}{N/2}\right), \qquad 0 \le |n| \le \frac{N}{2} \quad (A3.26)$$

The time and frequency responses of this window are given for $\alpha = 0.5$ in Fig. A3.15.

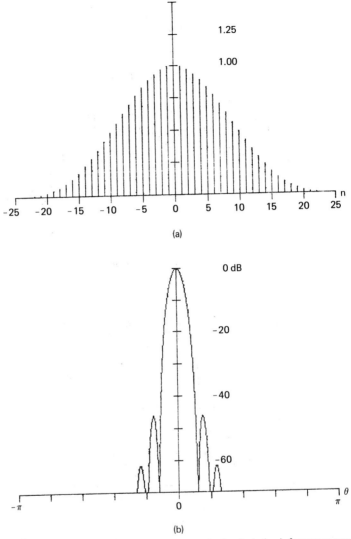

Fig. A3.13. (a) Bohman window and (b) log-magnitude of window's frequency response.

h. Cauchy (Abel, Poisson) Window. The Cauchy is a family of windows obtained from samples of a truncated Cauchy function. This function is the power spectrum of a first-order analog filter and is the form

$$h(n) = \frac{1.0}{1.0 + [\alpha n/(N/2)]^2}, \qquad 0 \le |n| \le \frac{N}{2} \qquad (A3.27)$$

The time and frequency responses of this window are given for 4.0 in Fig. A3.16.

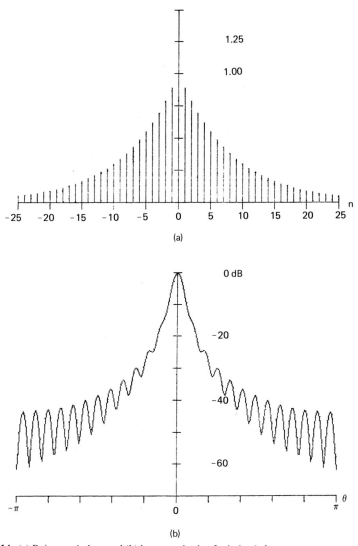

Fig. A3.14. (a) Poisson window and (b) log-magnitude of window's frequency response ($\alpha = 3.0$).

Gaussian (Weierstrass) Window   7

Windows are smooth (usually positive) functions with tall, thin (i.e., concentrated) frequency responses. From the uncertainty principle we know that the mean-square time duration T and the mean-square bandwidth W (in hertz)

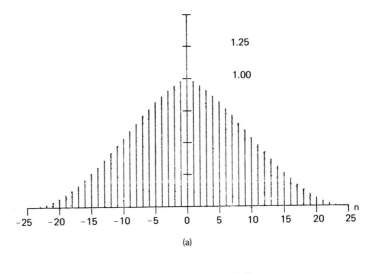

(a)

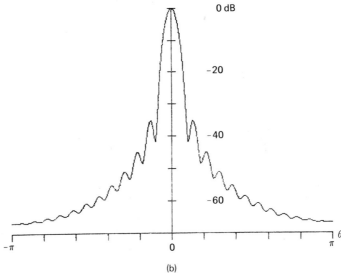

(b)

Fig. A3.15. (a) Hanning–Poisson window and (b) log-magnitude of window's frequency response $(\alpha = 0.5)$.

satisfies

$$TW \geq \frac{1}{2} \tag{A3.28}$$

The Gaussian function is the minimum time-bandwidth function because it alone satisfies Eq. (A3.28) with equality. The Gaussian window obtained as samples of a

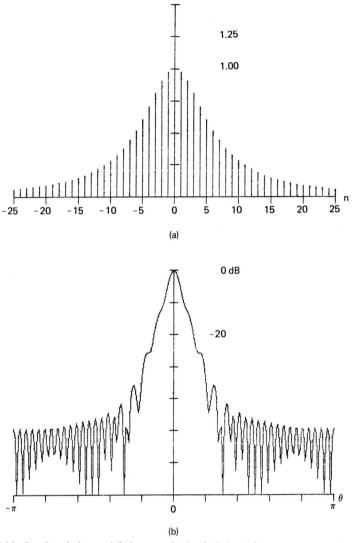

Fig. A3.16. Cauchy window and (b) log-magnitude of window's frequency response ($\alpha = 4.0$).

truncated Gaussian function is no longer minimum time-bandwidth and is of the form

$$h(n) = \exp\left[-\frac{1}{2}\left(\alpha\frac{n}{N/2} \right)^2 \right], \qquad 0 \le |n| \le \frac{N}{2} \qquad (A3.29)$$

The time and frequency responses of the window for $\alpha = 3.0$ are given in Fig. A3.17.

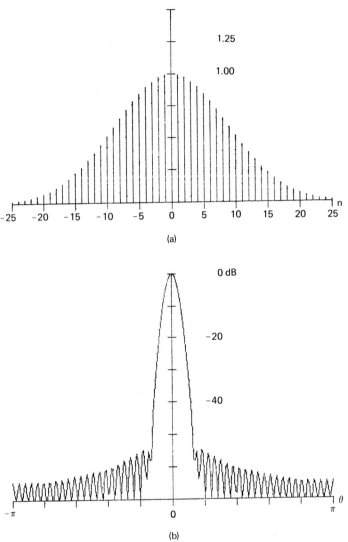

Fig. A3.17. (a) Gaussian window and (b) log-magnitude of window's frequency response ($\alpha = 3.0$).

8   Dolph–Chebyshev Window

The Dolph–Chebyshev window is an optimum window in the sense that it exhibits the narrowest mainlobe width for a given maximum sidelobe level. The peak sidelobe levels are all of the same size and are selectable. The window is most easily described by its DFT in the frequency domain and then the inverse DFT determines the time domain samples. The DFT description is of the form

$$H(k) = \frac{\cosh(N \cosh^{-1}(\beta \cosh(\pi k/N)))}{\cosh(N \cosh^{-1}[\beta])} \tag{A3.30a}$$

where

$$\cosh^{-1}(X) = \ln[X + \sqrt{X^2 - 1.0}], \qquad |X| > 1.0$$

$$H(k) = \frac{\cos(N \cos^{-1}(\beta \cos(\pi k/N)))}{\cosh(N \cosh^{-1}[\beta])} \tag{A3.30b}$$

where

$$\cos^{-1}(X) = \frac{\pi}{2} - \tan^{-1}\left(\frac{X}{\sqrt{X^2 - 1.0}}\right), \qquad |X| \le 1.0$$

where β satisfies

$$\beta = \cosh\left(\frac{1}{N} \cosh^{-1} 10^{\alpha}\right) \tag{A3.30c}$$

and

$$h(n) = \sum_{k=0}^{N-1} H(k) \exp\left(j\frac{2\pi}{N} nk\right) \tag{A3.31}$$

The parameter α has the interpretation of sidelobe level in decades of attenuation. The time and frequency responses of this window are presented for $\alpha = 3.0$ in Fig. A3.18. Note that the constant-level sidelobes in the spectrum imply that the filter impulse response exhibits an impulse that resides at the boundary of the time response. (In Fig. A3.18(a) the impulse amplitude is so small that the impulse is not noticeable.)

Taylor Window 9

The Taylor window is an approximation to the Chebyshev window, which holds a subset of the sidelobes at a constant level and permits the remaining sidelobes to fall off at 6 dB/octave. This avoids the impulse in the time response description of the window. The number of sidelobes held at the designated fixed level depends on the chosen attenuation level. The spectral description of the window is a short cosine transform exhibiting nonzero coefficients only over the bandwidth of the constant-level sidelobes.

The Taylor weightings can also be described by the coefficients of the short cosine series. Table AIV lists the nonzero coefficients of the short cosine series for Taylor weights with sidelobe levels of -40, -50, -60, and -70 dB. The time and frequency responses of a 51-point Taylor window for a maximum sidelobe level of -60 dB are shown in Fig. A3.19.

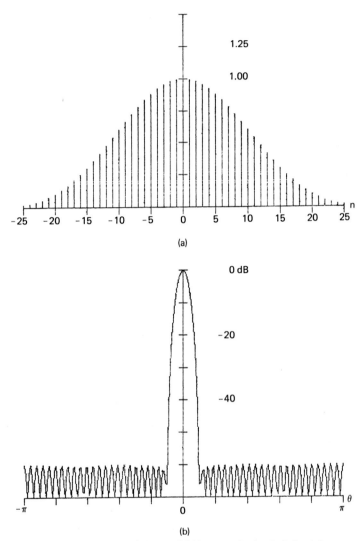

Fig. A3.18. (a) Dolph–Chebyshev window and (b) log-magnitude of window's frequency response ($\alpha = 3.0$).

10   Kaiser–Bessel Window

The Kaiser–Bessel window (see also Section III.B in Chapter 2) is an optimum window in the sense that it achieves the smallest time-bandwidth product for functions of finite duration. In a manner similar to the Gaussian function, which is its own transform (in the absence of truncation), this window is its own

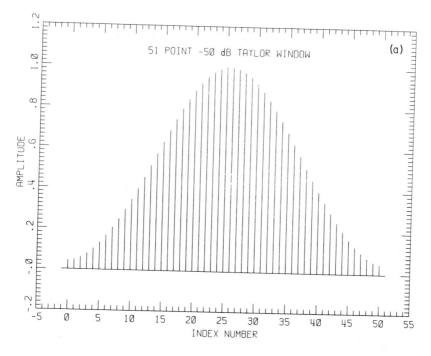

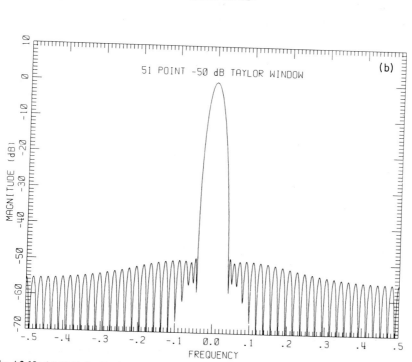

Fig. A3.19. (a) 51-Point Taylor window and (b) log-magnitude of window's frequency response.

TABLE AIV

Coefficients for Short Cos Expansion of Taylor Window

	-40 dB	-50 dB	-60 dB	-70 dB
$a(0)$	0.566 071	0.511 488	0.469 792	0.464 840
$a(1)$	0.440 535	0.473 578	0.489 709	0.528 340
$a(2)$	$-0.010\ 702$	0.013 046	0.040 543	0.007 174
$a(3)$	0.005 527	0.003 098	0.000 465	$-0.000\ 292$
$a(4)$	$-0.001\ 824$	$-0.001\ 837$	$-0.000\ 893$	$-0.000\ 225$
$a(5)$	0.000 393	0.000 919	0.000 631	0.000 285
$a(6)$	—	$-0.000\ 410$	$-0.000\ 397$	$-0.000\ 228$
$a(7)$	—	0.000 146	0.000 237	0.000 166
$a(8)$	—	$-0.000\ 028$	$-0.000\ 132$	$-0.000\ 116$
$a(9)$	—	—	0.000 066	0.000 078
$a(10)$	—	—	$-0.000\ 027$	$-0.000\ 051$
$a(11)$	—	—	0.000 007	0.000 032
$a(12)$	—	—	—	$-0.000\ 018$
$a(13)$	—	—	—	0.000 009
$a(14)$	—	—	—	$-0.000\ 004$
$a(15)$	—	—	—	0.000 001

transform when we include the truncation operation. As such, we can define the window either by samples of its spectrum or by samples of its time description. In the sample domain description the window is defined in terms of the zero-order Bessel function (of the first kind) by

$$h(n) = \frac{I_0(\pi\alpha\sqrt{1.0 - (n/(N/2)^2)})}{I_0(\pi\alpha)}, \qquad 0 \le |n| \le \frac{N}{2} \qquad (A3.32)$$

where

$$I_0(X) = \sum_{k=0}^{\infty} \left| \frac{(X/2)^k}{k!} \right|^2 \qquad (A3.33)$$

An alternative description in terms of its spectra is

$$h(n) = \frac{\sinh((\pi/\alpha\sqrt{1.0 - (n/N/2)^2})}{\sinh(\pi/\alpha)} \qquad (A3.34)$$

The time and frequency responses for the Kaiser–Bessel window for $\alpha = 2.5$ are given in Fig. A3.20.

11   Barcilon–Temes Window

Whereas the Kaiser–Bessel window achieved its performance by maximizing the energy contained in the mainlobe, the Barcilon–Temes window achieves its performance by minimizing the weighted energy outside the mainlobe. This

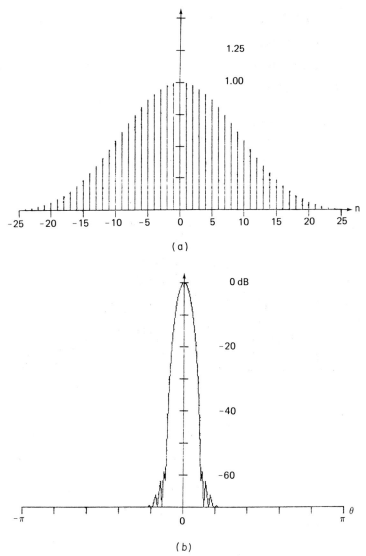

Fig. A3.20. (a) Kaiser–Bessel window and (b) log-magnitude of window's frequency response ($\alpha = 2.5$).

window, like the Dolph–Chebyshev, is described by equally spaced samples in the frequency domain, and then an inverse DFT transforms the window to the time domain. The frequency domain samples are defined by

$$W(k) = \frac{A\cos\{[y(k)] + B[y(k)/C]\sin[y(k)]\}}{(C + AB)\{[y(k)/C]^2 + 1.0\}} \qquad (A3.35)$$

where $A = \sinh C = \sqrt{10^{2\alpha} - 1.0}$

$B = \cosh C = 10^{\alpha}$

$C = \cosh^{-1} 10^{\alpha}$

$\beta = \cosh(C/N)$

$y(k) = N \cos^{-1}\left[\beta \cos\left(\frac{\pi k}{N}\right) \right]$

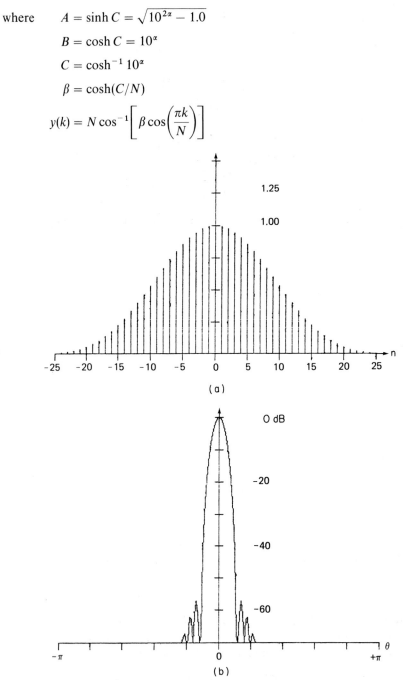

(a)

(b)

Fig. A3.21. (a) Barcilon–Temes window and (b) log-magnitude of window's frequency response ($\alpha = 3.5$).

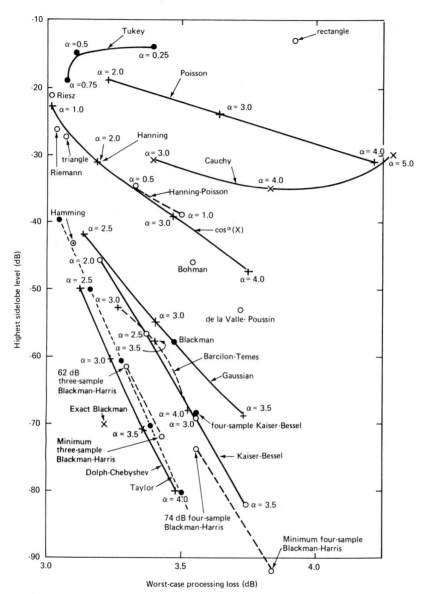

Fig. A3.22. Highest sidelobe level versus worst-case processing loss. Shaped DFT filters in the lower left tend to perform well.

The time and frequency descriptions of the window are presented for $\alpha = 3.5$ in Fig. A3.21.

D Closing Comments

We have described some classic windows that may be used as the impulse response of narrowband FIR filters. We have also presented a table of important figures of merit with which different windows/filters can be compared. A quick comparison of important figures of merit is possible with Fig. A3.22. Here the highest sidelobe level is plotted against worst-case processing loss for the different windows described in this appendix. These parameters are important for detecting sinusoids of unknown frequency in additive white noise. Robust filters should exhibit low sidelobes and low processing loss—should be located in this figure toward the lower left corner. By this criterion we see that the better filters are the Dolph–Chebyshev, the Taylor, the Blackman–Harris, and the Kaiser–Bessel weightings. If we include the consideration that the out-of-band sidelobes should not be of constant amplitude, the Blackman–Harris and the Kaiser–Bessel weightings are the most desirable.

Some of the windows identified here are particularly useful because of their simplicity of form. For example, the short cosine series expansions for the Blackman–Harris windows make it possible to compute the filter coefficients for very large filters when standard filter design algorithms (e.g., the Remez algorithm described in Appendix 2A) fail to converge.

REFERENCES

1. S. L. Freeney, J. F. Kaiser, and H. S. McDonald, Some applications of digital signal processing in telecommunications, in *Applications of Digital Signal Processing*, edited by A. V. Oppenheim, Prentice-Hall, Englewood Cliffs, N.J., 1978.
2. G. A. Nelson, L. L. Pfeifer, and R. C. Wood, High-speed octave band digital filtering, *IEEE Trans. Audio Electroacoust.* **AU-20,** 58–65 (March 1972).
3. T. A. Ramstad, Methods for conversion between arbitrary sampling frequencies, *IEEE Trans. Acoust. Speech Signal Process.* **ASSP-32,** 577–591 (June 1985).
4. R. E. Crochiere, L. R. Rabiner, and R. R. Shively, A novel implementation of digital phase shifters, Bell Systems Technical J. **54,** 1497–1502 (October 1975).
5. O. Herrman, L. R. Rabiner, and D. S. Chan, Practical design rules for optimum finite impulse response lowpass digital filters, Bell Systems Technical J. **52,** 769–799 (July–August 1973).
6. A. V. Oppenheim and R. W. Shafer, *Digital Signal Processing*, Prentice-Hall, Englewood Cliffs, N.J., 1975.
7. L. R. Rabiner and B. Gold, *Theory and Applications of Digital Signal Processing*, Prentice-Hall, Englewood Cliffs, N.J., 1975.
8. F. J. Harris, On the use of windows for harmonic analysis with the discrete Fourier transform, *Proc. IEEE* **66,** 51–83 (January 1978).
9. A. W. Crooke and J. W. Craig, Digital filters for sample-rate reduction, *IEEE Trans. Audio Electroacoust.* **AU-20,** 308–315 (October 1972).

10. R. E. Crochiere and L. R. Rabiner, Optimum FIR digital filter implementations for decimation, interpolation, and narrow-band filtering, *IEEE Trans. Acoust. Speech Signal Process.* **ASSP-23,** 444–456 (October 1975).

11. L. R. Rabiner and R. E. Crochiere, A novel implementation for narrow-band FIR digital filters, *IEEE Trans. Acoust. Speech Signal Process.* **ASSP-23,** 457–463 (October 1975).

12. R. A. Meyer and C. S. Burrus, Design and implementation of multirate digital filters, *IEEE Trans. Acoust. Speech Signal Process.* **ASSP-24,** 53–57 (February 1976).

13. R. E. Crochiere and L. R. Rabiner, Further considerations in the design of decimators and interpolators, *IEEE Trans. Acoust. Speech Signal Process.* **ASSP-24,** 296–311 (August 1976).

14. D. J. Goodman and M. J. Carey, Nine digital filters for decimation and interpolation, *IEEE Trans. Acoust. Speech Signal Process.* **ASSP-25,** 121–126 (April 1977).

15. R. E. Crochiere and L. R. Rabiner, Interpolation and decimation of digital signals — A tutorial review, *Proc. IEEE* **69,** 300–331 (March 1981).

16. E. B. Hogenauer, An economical class of digital filters for decimation and interpolation, *IEEE Trans. Acoust. Speech Signal Process.* **ASSP-29,** 155–162 (April 1981).

17. I. Paul and J. W. Woods, Intersection filters for general decimation/interpolation, *IEEE Trans. Acoust. Speech Signal Process.* **ASSP-29,** 934–936 (August 1981).

18. T. Saramaki, A class of linear-phase FIR filters for decimation, interpolating, and narrow-band filtering, *IEEE Trans. Acoust. Speech Signal Process.* **ASSP-32,** 1023–1036 (October 1984).

19. F. Mintzer and B. Liu, Aliasing error in the design of multirate filters, *IEEE Trans. Acoust. Speech Signal Process.* **ASSP-26,** 76–87 (February 1978).

20. R. R. Shively, On multistage finite impulse response (FIR) filters with decimation, *IEEE Trans. Acoust. Speech Signal Process.* **ASSP-23,** 353–356 (August 1975).

21. Z. Jing and A. Fam, A new structure for narrow transition band, lowpass digital filter design, *IEEE Trans. Acoust. Speech Signal Process.* **ASSP-32,** 362–370 (April 1984).

22. F. Mintzer and B. Liu, The design of optimal multirate bandpass and bandstop filters. *IEEE Trans. Acoust. Speech Signal Process.* **ASSP-26,** 534–543 (December 1978).

23. F. Mintzer and B. Liu, Practical design rules for optimum FIR bandpass digital filters, *IEEE Trans. Acoust. Speech Signal Process.* **ASSP-27,** 204–206 (April 1979).

24. V. K. Jain and R. E. Crochiere, Quadrature mirror design in the time domain, *IEEE Trans. Acoust. Speech Signal Process.* **ASSP-32,** 353–361 (April 1984).

25. C. R. Garland and H. J. Nussbaumer, New quadrature mirror filter structures, *IEEE Trans. Acoust. Speech Signal Process.* **ASSP-32,** 522–531 (June 1984).

26. F. Mintzer, Filters for distortion-free two band multirate filter banks, *IEEE Trans. Acoust. Speech Signal Process.* **ASSP-33,** 626–630 (June 1985).

27. G. Pirani and V. Zingarelli, An analytical formula for the design of quadrature mirror-filters, *IEEE Trans. Acoust. Speech Signal Process.* **ASSP-32,** 645–648 (June 1985).

28. L. B. Jackson, On the relationship between digital Hilbert transformers and certain lowpass filters, *IEEE Trans. Acoust. Speech Signal Process.* **ASSP-23,** 381–383 (August 1975).

29. R. W. Schafer and L. R. Rabiner, A digital signal processing approach to interpolation, *Proc. IEEE* **61,** 692–702 (June 1973).

30. G. Oetken, T. W. Parks, and H. W. Schussler, New results in the design of digital interpolators, *IEEE Trans. Acoust. Speech Signal Process.* **ASSP-23,** (June 1975). 301–308.

31. M. G. Bellanger, G. Bonnerot, and M. Caudreuse, Digital filtering by polyphase network: Application to sample-rate alteration and filter banks," *IEEE Trans. Acoust. Speech Signal Process.* **ASSP-24,** 109–114 (April 1976).

32. N. Narasimha and A. Peterson, On using the symmetry of FIR filters for digital interpolation, *IEEE Trans. Acoust. Speech Signal Process.* **ASSP-26,** 267–268 (June 1978).

33. M. G. Bellanger and G. Bonnerot, Premultiplication schemes for digital FIR filters with application to multirate filtering, *IEEE Trans. Acoust. Speech Signal Process.* **ASSP-26,** 50–55 (February 1978).

Chapter **4**

IIR Digital Filters

NAZIR A. PASHTOON
Electrical Engineering Department
State University of New York
Stony Brook, New York 11794

INTRODUCTION **I**

The unit sample response (impulse response) of discrete-time linear time-invariant digital filters is either of infinite duration or of finite duration. Thus, from the point of view of the impulse response duration, filters can be classified as infinite-duration impulse response (IIR), or finite-duration impulse response (FIR) digital filters. IIR digital filters are commonly realized recursively by feeding back a weighted sum of past output values and adding these values to a weighted sum of present and past input values. In principle, IIR digital filters have infinite memory. In contrast, the nonrecursive realization of FIR digital filters has finite memory, where an output sample is generated as a weighted sum of present and past input values.

The major advantage of IIR digital filters, compared to FIR digital filters, is that, for a given order N, highly selective recursive digital filters can be designed. In other words, the recursive realizations of IIR digital filters are computationally efficient. The disadvantage of the recursive realization is that the designer must pay attention to stability, parasitic phenomena, and (when a design consideration) phase nonlinearity [1–4].

The title of this chapter covers numerous classes of digital filters. Indeed, the topic of IIR digital filters will, deservedly, require a whole book. Some important and interesting low-noise and low-coefficient-sensitivity IIR digital filters [5–8] appear in Chapter 5. Special design requirements may dictate an investigation of these structures and others.

Our purpose is to present standard techniques for designing IIR digital filters. We emphasize indirect approach of designing digital filters from analog filter prototypes [1–4] meeting given magnitude response specifications.

289

Sections I and II contain an introduction and some definitions. Section III discusses the stability of IIR digital filters. Standard digital filter realizations are discussed in Section IV. Section V describes filter specifications in the frequency domain, as well as the use of analog filters as prototypes. Various analog filter types and their design are discussed in Section VI. Section VII discusses analog transformations for converting the lowpass prototypes of Section VI to lowpass, highpass bandpass, and bandstop filters. Section VIII discusses various transformations necessary for the "digitalization" of analog prototype filters. Section IX examines spectral transformations, which are used for transforming a prototype lowpass digital filter to bandpass, highpass, etc.

These techniques require precise knowledge of the transfer functions of analog and digital filters at some stage of the design process. Section X presents two types of IIR digital filters [9, 10] that start with a doubly terminated analog lossless ladder network as a prototype, thus obviating the need for exact knowledge of transfer functions. These filters have low sensitivity to coefficient quantization errors and are well suited for narrowband designs.

II   PRELIMINARIES

The output sequence $y(n)$ of a causal, linear, and time-invariant digital filter in response to an input sequence $x(n)$ is given by the convolution sum

$$y(n) = \sum_{m=0}^{\infty} h(n-m)x(m) = \sum_{m=0}^{\infty} h(m)x(n-m) \tag{4.1}$$

where $h(m)$ is the unit-sample (impulse) response of the digital filter. The digital filter is called a FIR digital filter if $h(m)$ is identically zero outside a range $m_2 < m < m_1$. Otherwise, it is called an IIR digital filter. Assuming a causal input sequence, we can write the convolution sum representation of digital filters as

$$y(n) = \sum_{m=0}^{n} h(n-m)x(m) = \sum_{m=0}^{n} h(m)x(n-m) \tag{4.2}$$

We obtain the frequency domain characterization of the digital filter by taking the z-transform of Eq. (4.2), assuming the initial conditions are zero, which yields the filter transfer function

$$H(z) = \frac{Y(z)}{X(z)} \tag{4.3}$$

We obtain the steady-state frequency domain response of the digital filter by evaluating $H(z)$ on the unit circle of the z-plane:

$$H(z)\bigg|_{z=e^{j\omega T}} = H(e^{j\omega T}) = |H(e^{j\omega T})| \operatorname{Arg} H(e^{j\omega T}) \tag{4.4}$$

where T is the sampling period.

The transfer function $H(z)$ can be expressed as a ratio of two polynomials

$$H(z) = \frac{\displaystyle\sum_{k=0}^{M} a_k z^{-k}}{1 + \displaystyle\sum_{k=1}^{N} b_k z^{-k}} = \frac{N(z)}{D(z)} \tag{4.5}$$

For causal filters, considered in this chapter, $N \geq M$. If the denominator and numerator do not have common factors, there will be N poles and zeros, with $N - M$ zeros at $z = 0$.

A time domain characterization of Eq. (4.5) as a recursive difference equation, provided not all b_k are zero, is given by

$$y(n) = -\sum_{k=1}^{N} b_k y(n-k) + \sum_{k=0}^{M} a_k x(n-k) \tag{4.6}$$

In Eq. (4.6) the output of the filter is a weighted sum of past outputs and inputs and the present input. If all b_k are zero, then the output is a weighted sum of present and past inputs. The resulting difference equation is nonrecursive.

STABILITY   III

In the design of IIR digital filters stability is an important consideration. A paper design might indicate a perfectly stable filter, whereas the actual filter implemented may be unstable. An illustrative example will be the design of highly selective filters, with poles inside but close to the unit circle of the z-plane (high-Q poles). In the actual implementation of the digital filter, the finite precision representation of coefficients could cause the poles in the proximity of the unit circle to wander out and produce an unstable digital filter.

A discrete-time linear time-invariant causal digital filter is considered stable if a bounded input creates a bounded output. In a *stable* system the impulse response $h(n)$ vanishes after a sufficiently long time. In an *unstable* system $h(n)$ grows without bound after a sufficiently long time. The impulse response $h(n)$ approaches a constant (nonzero) or a bounded oscillation for a *marginally stable* system.

Mathematically, a necessary and sufficient condition for the stability of the digital filters under consideration is that the impulse response be absolutely summable:

$$\sum_{n=0}^{\infty} |h(n)| < \infty \qquad (4.7)$$

The implication of Eq. (4.7) is that the stability of digital filters can be ascertained by restricting the location of the poles of the transfer function $H(z)$ of the digital filter. In general, the stability requirements for the pole–zero location of $H(z)$ can be summarized as follows:

a. For a stable system the poles of $H(z)$ can lie anywhere inside the unit circle of the z-plane, regardless of their order (multiplicity).

b. If $H(z)$ has poles outside the unit circle of the z-plane, regardless of the order, the system is unstable.

c. If $H(z)$ has first-order poles on the unit circle, the system is marginally stable. Multiple-order poles on the unit circle make the system unstable.

d. In general, zeros of $H(z)$ are allowed to lie anywhere in the z-plane.

A   Testing for Stability

In the previous section we summarized the stability requirements for digital filters. Given a transfer function

$$H(z) = \frac{N(z)}{D(z)} = \frac{N(z)}{\sum_{k=0}^{N} b_k z^{N-k}} \qquad (4.8)$$

the stability testing of $H(z)$ requires that the location of the roots in the z-plane of $D(z)$ (characteristic polynomial) be investigated.

1   Direct Approach

A direct approach for ascertaining that the poles of $H(z)$ lie inside the unit circle is through root-finding routines, which are part of the standard repertoire of computer libraries. However, for narrowband filters the roots of $D(z)$ clump together very close to the unit circle in a small region of the z-plane. Some root-finding routines might require proper initial guesses, or might even provide inaccurate results. Therefore, it is a good idea to verify that the roots found do satisfy the characteristic equation.

Jury's stability test is similar to the Routh–Hurwitz test for stability testing of continuous-time systems. The coefficients of the characteristic polynomial $D(z)$ are used to construct an array of numbers, known as Jury's array, as illustrated in Table I. The procedure for constructing the array is as follows:

a. Form the first two rows of the array by writing the coefficients of $D(z)$ as shown.

b. Form the third and fourth rows of the array by evaluating the determinants

$$c_j = \begin{vmatrix} b_0 & b_{N-j} \\ b_N & b_j \end{vmatrix}, \qquad j = 0, 1, 2, \ldots, N-1 \tag{4.9}$$

c. Form the fifth and sixth rows of the array from the third and fourth rows by calculating its elements from

$$d_j = \begin{vmatrix} c_0 & c_{N-1-J} \\ c_{N-1} & c_j \end{vmatrix}, \qquad j = 0, 1, 2, \ldots, N-2 \tag{4.10}$$

d. Continue this procedure until you obtain $2N - 3$ rows, with the last row having three elements y_0, y_1, y_2.

Jury's stability criterion states that a digital filter with a transfer function $H(z)$ and a characteristic polynomial $D(z)$ is stable if it passes the following tests:

a. $D(z)|_{z=1} > 0$
b. $(-1)^N D(z)|_{z=-1} > 0$
c. $|b_0| > |b_N|, |c_0| > |c_{N-1}|, |d_0| > |d_{N-2}|, \ldots, |y_0| > |y_2|$.

TABLE I

Jury's Array for Stability Testing

Row	Coefficients		
1	b_0 b_1	$\cdots$	b_N
2	b_N b_{N-1}	$\cdots$	b_0
3	c_0 c_1	$\cdots$	c_{N-1}
4	c_{N-1} c_{N-2}	$\cdots$	c_0
5	d_0 d_1	$\cdots$	d_{N-2}
6	d_{N-2} d_{N-3}	$\cdots$	d_0
$\vdots$	$\vdots$	$\cdots$	$\vdots$
$2N - 3$	y_0	y_1	y_2

† See references [4, 11].

TABLE II
Jury's Array for Example 4.1

Row	Coefficient				
1	8	4	2	−1	−1
2	−1	−1	2	4	8
3	63	31	18	−4	
4	−4	18	31	63	
5	3953	2025	1258		

Example 4.1. To check the transfer function

$$H(z) = \frac{z^4 + 2z^3 + z^2}{8z^4 + 4z^3 + 2z^2 - z - 1}$$

for stability, we form Jury's array as shown in Table II. Performing the various tests gives the following results:

a. $D(z)|_{z=1} = 12 > 0$
b. $(-1)^N D(z)|_{z=-1} = (-1)^4 D(-1) = 6 > 0$
c. $|8| > |-1|, |63| > |-4|, |3953| > |1258|$

Therefore the roots of $D(z)$ are all within the unit circle of the z-plane, so the given digital filter is stable.

B Stabilization

During computer-aided design (CAD) of digital filters, we may, while optimizing, meet the magnitude response specification, but the transfer function may be unstable. Also, using spectral transformations to derive from a given lowpass prototype a digital filter with different passband specifications may produce an unstable transfer function. In situations like the above, it is possible to stabilize the digital filters [12] and still meet the magnitude response specifications. To illustrate, let us assume that a pole of $H(z)$ is outside the unit circle of the z-plane. Thus $D(z)$ has a factor

$$f(z) = (z - re^{j\theta}) \qquad r > 1 \tag{4.11}$$

For stabilization purposes let us replace $f(z)$ by the factor

$$f'(z) = r(z - r^{-1}e^{j\theta}) = (rz - e^{j\theta}) \tag{4.12}$$

Clearly, replacing the pole $re^{j\theta}$ by $r^{-1}e^{j\theta}$ stabilizes the filter. The substitution leaves the overall magnitude response unaffected because both factors have similar magnitude responses. To see this, consider

$$|f(e^{j\omega T})| = \left| z - re^{j\theta} \right|_{z=e^{j\omega T}} = [(\cos\omega T - r\cos\theta)^2 + (\sin\omega T - r\sin\theta)^2]^{1/2}$$

$$(4.13)$$

Now

$$|f'(e^{j\omega T})| = r(z - r^{-1}e^{j\theta})\Big|_{z=e^{j\omega T}} = |e^{j\omega T}e^{j\theta}(re^{-j\theta} - e^{-j\omega T})| = |e^{-j\omega T} - re^{-j\theta}|$$

$$= |(\cos\omega T - r\cos\theta)^2 + (\sin\omega T - r\sin\theta)^2]^{1/2} \qquad (4.14)$$

$$|f(e^{j\omega T})| = |f'(e^{j\omega T})| \qquad (4.15)$$

DIGITAL FILTER REALIZATIONS   IV

For a given transfer function $H(z)$ or the difference equations of a digital filter meeting given specifications, we can implement the digital filter using special-purpose hardware or as a software algorithm. A realization will consist of converting the input-output relation of the digital filter into an algorithm of basic operations, which are described next.

Realization Building Blocks   A

The basic operations involved in realizing digital filters require the following building blocks:

a. Summer (adder). We assume that the summer can perform subtraction as well.

b. Multiplier or scaler.

c. Delay units, which can be registers or memory references for storage and recall of past values of signals.

Figure 4.1 shows the basic building blocks used in realizing digital filters.

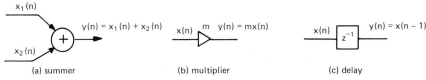

(a) summer   (b) multiplier   (c) delay

Fig. 4.1. Basic building blocks.

Using the basic building blocks, we can realize a digital filter in many different forms. From a practical standpoint, different realizations will exhibit different noise characteristics, and the responses will show different sensitivities to coefficient quantization, as discussed in the next chapter. In the following subsections some standard realizations are shown.

B Direct-Form Realizations

The transfer function of a digital filter expressed as a ratio of two polynomials is

$$H(z) = \frac{Y(z)}{X(z)} = \frac{\sum\limits_{i=0}^{N} a_i z^{-i}}{\sum\limits_{i=0}^{N} b_i z^{-i}} \qquad (4.16)$$

We will let $b_0 = 1$, without loss of generality. The difference equation corresponding to Eq. (4.16) is

$$y(n) = \sum_{i=0}^{N} a_i x(n-i) - \sum_{i=1}^{N} b_i y(n-i) \qquad (4.17)$$

A realization of Eq. (4.17) known as direct-form 1 is shown in Fig. 4.2.

We will derive an alternative realization known as direct-form 2 by introducing an intermediate variable $G(z)$:

$$H(z) = \frac{Y(z)}{G(z)} \cdot \frac{G(z)}{X(z)} \qquad (4.18)$$

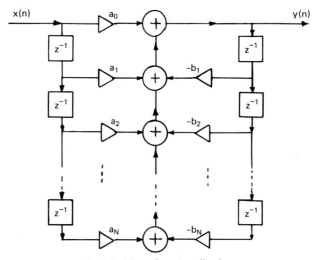

Fig. 4.2. Direct-form 1 realization.

Let $Y(z)/G(z)$ be the numerator polynomial

$$\frac{Y(z)}{G(z)} = \sum_{i=0}^{N} a_i z^{-i} \tag{4.19}$$

and let $G(z)/X(z)$ be the denominator polynomial

$$\frac{G(z)}{X(z)} = \frac{1}{1 + \displaystyle\sum_{i=0}^{N} b_i z^{-i}} \tag{4.20}$$

The difference equations corresponding to Eq. (4.19) and Eq. (4.20), respectively, are

$$y(n) = \sum_{i=0}^{N} a_i g(n-i) \tag{4.21}$$

and

$$g(n) = x(n) - \sum_{i=1}^{N} b_i g(n-i) \tag{4.22}$$

Equation (4.21) can be viewed as the nonrecursive part of the algorithm of the digital filter, shown at the right of the realization diagram in Fig. 4.3. Equation (4.22) is the recursive part, as illustrated on the left of Fig. 4.3.

Figure 4.3 shows two sets of delays. Since a single set of delays is sufficient, the delays are combined in Fig. 4.4, which results in what is called a direct-form 2

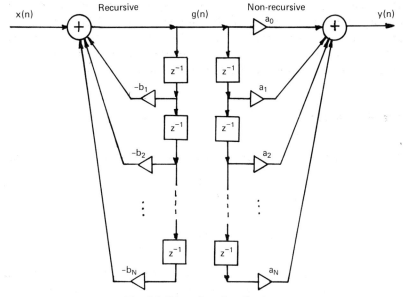

Fig. 4.3. Direct-form 2 realization.

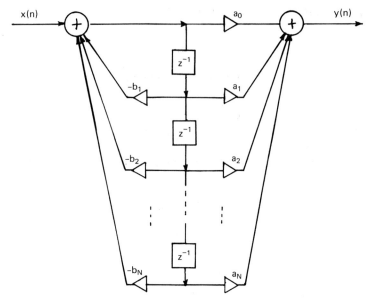

Fig. 4.4. Direct-form 2 canonic realization.

canonic realization. This realization is canonic in the sense that, for the given transfer function, the structure has the fewest adders, multipliers, and delays. The maximum number of adders, multipliers, and delays is $2N$, $2N + 1$, and N, respectively.

The direct realizations, though simple in appearance, have severe response sensitivity problems because of coefficient quantization effects, especially as the order of the filter increases. To reduce these effects, we can decompose the transfer function into quadratic blocks, realized either as parallel or cascade sections. These realizations, called nondirect realizations, are described next.

C Parallel Realization

A given transfer function $H(z)$ can be expressed as a sum of quadratic sections:

$$H(z) = \frac{Y(z)}{X(z)} = \sum_{i=1}^{K} H_i(z) \qquad (4.23)$$

where

$$H_i(z) = \frac{a_{0i} + a_{1i}z^{-1}}{1 + b_{1i}z^{-1} + b_{2i}z^{-2}} \qquad (4.24)$$

To obtain the $H_i(z)$, we use a partial-fraction expansion (see Section IV.D in Chapter 1) to get the various sections. Figure 4.5 shows the parallel realization, and Fig. 4.6 illustrates a typical section.

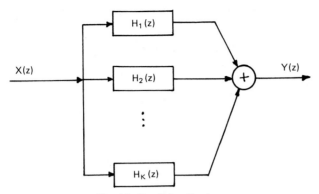

Fig. 4.5. Parallel realization.

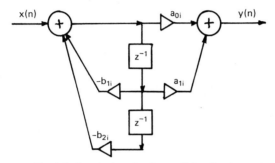

Fig. 4.6. A typical section in parallel realization.

Cascade Realization **D**

A transfer function $H(z)$ can also be decomposed as a cascade of quadratic sections:

$$H(z) = \frac{Y(z)}{X(z)} = \frac{G_1(z)}{X(z)} \cdot \frac{G_2(z)}{G_1(z)} \cdots \frac{Y(z)}{G_K(z)}$$

$$= H_1(z) \cdot H_2(z) \cdots H_K(z) = \prod_{i=1}^{K} H_i(z) \tag{4.25}$$

where the $G_i(z)$, $i = 1, 2, \ldots, K$, are intermediate variables and

$$H_i(z) = \frac{a_{0i} + a_{1i} z^{-1} + a_{2i} z^{-2}}{1 + b_{1i} z^{-1} + b_{2i} z^{-2}} \tag{4.26}$$

A typical cascade realization is shown in Fig. 4.7, and the realization of Eq. (4.26) is shown in Fig. 4.8.

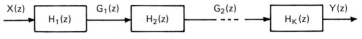

Fig. 4.7. Typical cascade realization.

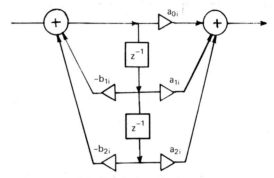

Fig. 4.8. A typical quadratic section.

Using the *transposition theorem* from signal flow graph (SFG) theory, we can derive alternative realizations, which may have different noise performance characteristics. The theorem states that if the direction of each and every branch in an SFG is reversed, the transfer function is unchanged [4, 13].

V   FREQUENCY DOMAIN DESIGN

As stated in the introduction, this chapter deals with the design of frequency selective IIR digital filters. More specifically, these filters meet prescribed magnitude response specifications for the band of frequencies the filters will pass or reject. We can approximate the given magnitude response specifications by direct methods, such as computer-aided design, or indirect methods, such as digitalizing an analog filter. The characterization of magnitude response of filters and the notation used is explained next.

A   Magnitude Response Characterization

The magnitude response of filters can be characterized in terms of the frequency bands the filter will pass or reject. In Fig. 4.9 the ideal magnitude responses of the four most frequently used filter types are illustrated as a function of ω in radians per second. Note that the periodicity of frequency response with respect to the sampling frequency is not shown.

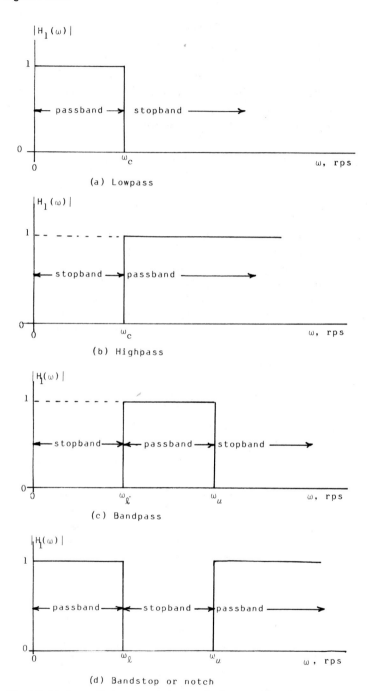

Fig. 4.9. Ideal magnitude response characterization or brick-wall characteristics.

In Fig. 4.9(a) the ideal magnitude response of a lowpass filter is illustrated. The range of frequencies from 0 to ω_c is the passband of the filter, and ω_c is known as the cutoff frequency. The stopband of the filter starts from ω_c. Figure 4.9(b) shows the response of an ideal highpass filter. The stopband of the filter is from 0 to ω_c. The passband of the filter starts from ω_c. The magnitude response of an ideal bandpass filter is shown in Fig. 4.9(c). Frequencies in the passband between ω_l and ω_u are passed. Frequencies above and below ω_u and ω_l are in the stopband of the filter and are rejected. Figure 4.9(d) is the response of an ideal bandstop filter that behaves in a complementary fashion to the bandpass filter.

The response characteristics in Fig. 4.9 are also known as "brick wall" filter specifications because of their shape. Although we cannot realize a brick-wall characteristic by using a finite number of building blocks or elements, their use does allow us to approximate the ideal responses closely.

To facilitate the approximation, we illustrate more realistic magnitude response specifications in Fig. 4.10. In addition to passbands and stopbands, the figures show a transition band for each type of filter. Furthermore, the passband and stopband specifications also provide for response tolerances, indicated by the crosshatched horizontal zones. The magnitude function is designated with the nondescript notation $|H_1(\omega)|$. The reason is that the steady-state frequency domain magnitude specifications for analog and digital filters are basically similar, except for the periodicity of the digital filter response with respect to ω_s, the sampling radian frequency:

$$\omega_s = 2\pi f_s = \frac{2\pi}{T} \quad \text{rad s}^{-1} \tag{4.27}$$

Later when we need to distinguish between the transfer functions of analog and digital filters, we use $H_a(j\omega)$ and $H(e^{j\omega T})$, respectively. The maximum value of $|H_1(\omega)|$ is assumed to be 1. The passband tolerance makes allowance for $|H_1(\omega)|$ to fluctuate from 1 to $1/\sqrt{1 + \epsilon^2}$, where ϵ, the ripple factor, is related to passband ripple. Frequency ω_p designates the passband edge frequency. Frequency ω_r designates the rejection frequency or stopband edge frequency, where $|H_1(\omega)|$ should deviate from 0 by no more than $1/\alpha$. The symbol ω_c will be used to designate the cutoff frequency (half-power point) of the filter magnitude response. Furthermore we let

$$H_1(\omega) = |H_1(\omega)|e^{j\theta(\omega)} \tag{4.28}$$

where

$$\theta(\omega) = \text{Arg} \, H_1(\omega) \tag{4.29}$$

is the phase angle. The *group delay* of the filter is defined as

$$\tau(\omega) = -\frac{d\theta(\omega)}{d\omega} \tag{4.30}$$

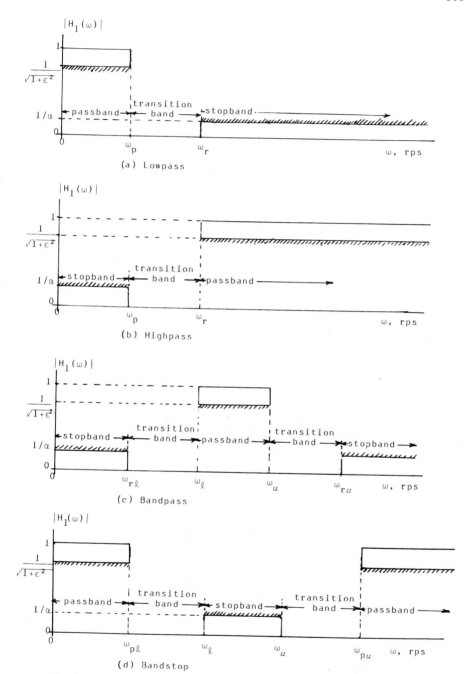

Fig. 4.10. Practical magnitude response specifications with allowance for tolerances.

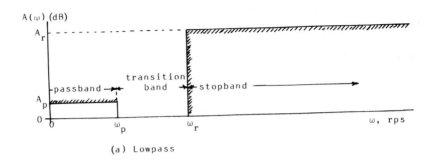

(a) Lowpass

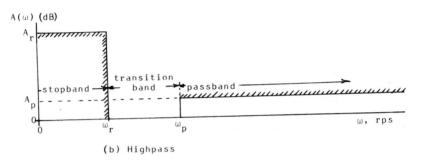

(b) Highpass

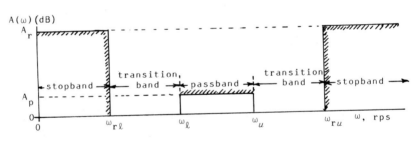

(c) Bandpass

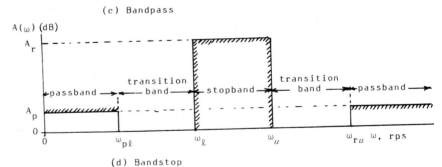

(d) Bandstop

Fig. 4.11. Filter specifications in terms of attenuation in dB.

The steady-state frequency domain response of filters is frequently specified in terms of the attenuation or loss characteristics in the bands of interest. The attenuation in dB is defined as

$$A(\omega) = -10 \log|H_1(\omega)|^2 \quad \text{dB} \qquad (4.31)$$

Figure 4.11 shows filter characterizations based on attenuation specifications. The passband tolerance (maximum allowed ripple in dB) is designated by A_p, and the minimum acceptable stopband attenuation is designated by A_r.

Specifications to Realization   B

Filter design, in general, deals with the problem of finding an approximation to given response specifications. The magnitude response specifications allow for tolerances on in-band ripple as well as out-of-band rejection. For a given realization the designer's task is to find the unknown coefficients in the digital filter transfer function in order to approximate the desired magnitude response meeting or exceeding the specifications. Direct methods such as pole–zero placement in the z-plane, error minimization, and optimization techniques [14–17, 3] can be used. Indirect methods, such as the transformation of prototype analog filters to digital filters, a standard design technique [1–4], will be presented later.

CAD Technique[†]   C

The direct approach of computer-aided design (CAD) of IIR digital filters deals with approximating an arbitrary set of magnitude response specifications. It is useful in finding digital filter coefficients for filters with multiple passbands and stopbands. In this approach the arbitrary magnitude response specifications are represented by a set of values α_n at frequencies ω_n. For a given realization the transfer function $H(z)$, whose coefficients are unknown, is also evaluated at ω_n. An error criterion, which can be minimized, is defined. Optimization techniques [15–17, 3] can be used to good effect. The application of the techniques may give unstable poles, which can be stabilized by the method outlined in Section III.B.

Use of Analog Filters as Prototypes   D

The design of digital filters, namely, finding the coefficients of the transfer function $H(z)$ in order to meet a given response specification can be achieved

---

[†] See references [3, 15–17].

without reference to analog (continuous-time) filters. However, the use of analog filters as prototypes has been popular [1] because of the preponderance of design aids and information available about these filters.

VI   ANALOG FILTER DESIGN AND FILTER TYPES†

The design task at hand constitutes designing first an analog filter that meets the desired specifications and then utilizing simple transformations to map the analog filter to the desired digital filter. The next section discusses the design of some widely used analog lowpass filters, are the basis for many IIR filters, because, by using frequency transformations, we can convert them to highpass, bandpass, or bandstop filters.

A   Butterworth Filters

Butterworth filters have a monotonically decreasing response with respect to frequency. The magnitude-squared Butterworth function of order n is

$$|H_a(j\omega)|^2 = \frac{1}{1 + (\omega/\omega_c)^{2n}} \tag{4.32}$$

where ω_c is the frequency for which $|H_a(j\omega_c)|^2 = 1/2$. Alternatively, since

$$20\log|H_a(j\omega)|\bigg|_{\omega=\omega_c} = -3 \quad \text{dB} \tag{4.33}$$

ω_c is also known as the -3dB cutoff frequency. Plots of Butterworth filters are shown in Fig. 4.12. The Butterworth type of response is also known as a maximally flat response because it is the response that is the flattest at $\omega = 0$ in the sense that

$$\frac{d^i|H_a(j\omega)|}{d\omega^i}\bigg|_{\omega=0} = 0, \quad i = 0, 1, 2, \ldots, m \tag{4.34}$$

where Eq. (4.34) holds for the largest m among all transfer functions with constant numerators (all-pole transfer functions) and denominators of the same order.

To obtain a transfer function in the s-domain, we use analytic continuation:

$$|H_a(j\omega)|^2 = H_a(s)H_a(-s)\bigg|_{s=j\omega} = \frac{1}{1 + (\omega/\omega_c)^{2n}} \tag{4.35}$$

† See references [4, 18–22].

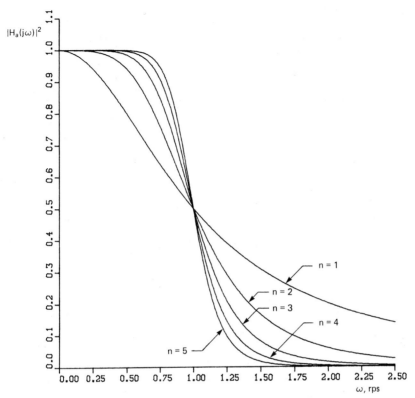

Fig. 4.12. Magnitude-squared characteristic of the normalized Butterworth lowpass filter.

or

$$H_a(s)H_a(-s) = \frac{1}{1 + (-1)^n (s/\omega_c)^{2n}} \tag{4.36}$$

The $2n$ poles of $H_a(s)H_a(-s)$ are the roots of

$$1 + (-1)^n \left(\frac{s}{\omega_c}\right)^{2n} = 0 \tag{4.37}$$

which are given by

$$s_K = \omega_c e^{j\pi(1-n+2K)/2n}, \qquad K = 0, 1, 2, \ldots, 2n - 1 \tag{4.38}$$

Thus the poles are all on a circle of radius ω_c and are π/n rad apart. Figure 4.13(a) and (b) shows the distribution of the poles for $n = 5$ and $n = 6$, respectively, for $\omega_c = 1$.

To obtain a stable transfer function, all the left-half-plane poles in Eq. (4.38) are assigned to $H_a(s)$. The left-half s-plane poles are

$$s_K = \omega_c \left[-\sin\frac{(2K+1)\pi}{2n} + j\cos\frac{(2K+1)\pi}{2n} \right], \qquad K = 0, 1, \ldots, n - 1 \tag{4.39}$$

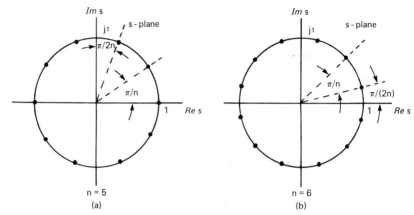

Fig. 4.13. Pole locations of $H(s)H(-s)$ for Butterworth filters for (a) $n = 5$ and (b) $n = 6$.

The transfer function of Butterworth filters is given by

$$H_a(s) = (-1)^n \prod_{K=0}^{n-1} \frac{s_K}{s - s_K} \tag{4.40}$$

In Table III the denominator polynomials in Eq. (4.40), known as Butterworth polynomials, are tabulated in factored form for normalized ($\omega_c = 1$) filters.

Practical filter specifications are usually provided in the form of Fig. 4.11. In other words, given the maximum passband attenuation A_p, the passband edge frequency f_p, the minimum allowable attenuation in the stopband, and the stopband edge frequency f_r, we are required to find the order and transfer function of the Butterworth filter. Applying the definition of attenuation, Eq. (4.31), to Eq. (4.35) yields

$$10\log\left[1 + \left(\frac{\omega_p}{\omega_c}\right)^{2n}\right] = A_p \tag{4.41}$$

TABLE III
Factored Butterworth Polynomials for Normalized Lowpass Filters

n	Butterworth polynomial
1	$s + 1$
2	$s^2 + 1.41421s + 1$
3	$(s + 1)(s^2 + s + 1)$
4	$(s^2 + 0.76537s + 1)(s^2 + 1.84776s + 1)$
5	$(s + 1)(s^2 + 0.61803s + 1)(s^2 + 1.61803s + 1)$
6	$(s^2 + 0.51764s + 1)(s^2 + 1.41421s + 1)(s^2 + 1.93185s + 1)$
7	$(s + 1)(s^2 + 0.44504s + 1)(s^2 + 1.24798s + 1)(s^2 + 1.80194s + 1)$
8	$(s^2 + 0.39018s + 1)(s^2 + 1.11114s + 1)(s^2 + 1.66294s + 1)(s^2 + 1.96157s + 1)$
9	$(s + 1)(s^2 + 0.34730s + 1)(s^2 + s + 1)(s^2 + 1.53209s + 1)(s^2 + 1.87939s + 1)$
10	$(s^2 + 0.31287s + 1)(s^2 + 0.90798s + 1)(s^2 + 1.41421s + 1)(s^2 + 1.78201s + 1)(s^2 + 1.97538s + 1)$

and

$$10\log\left[1 + \left(\frac{\omega_r}{\omega_c}\right)^{2n}\right] = A_r \qquad (4.42)$$

where

$$\omega_p = 2\pi f_p \qquad (4.43)$$

and

$$\omega_r = 2\pi f_r \qquad (4.44)$$

Dividing Eq. (4.41) by Eq. (4.42) and solving for n gives

$$n = \frac{|\log[(10^{0.1A_p} - 1)/(10^{0.1A_r} - 1)]|}{|\log(\omega_p/\omega_r)|} \qquad (4.45)$$

Equation (4.45) can be written in more compact form by defining a *selectivity parameter*

$$k = \triangleq \frac{\omega_p}{\omega_r} = \frac{f_p}{f_r} < 1 \qquad (4.46)$$

and a *discrimination factor*

$$d \triangleq \left(\frac{10^{0.1A_p} - 1}{10^{0.1A_r} - 1}\right)^{1/2} < 1 \qquad (4.47)$$

for the filter. Larger k values imply narrower transition width Δf—that is, steeper rolloff. Smaller d values of the discrimination factor imply a greater difference between A_p and A_r. Substituting Eqs. (4.46) and (4.47) in Eq. (4.45) gives a design equation

$$n \geq \frac{|\log d|}{|\log k|} = \frac{\log(1/d)}{\log(1/k)} \qquad (4.48)$$

From Eq. (4.48), n will almost always be a noninteger value. To meet or exceed specifications, select the next higher integer value for n. The cutoff frequency ω_c can be calculated from Eq. (4.41) or Eq. (4.42). Thus to meet the passband attenuation requirement exactly and exceed the stopband specification, we need

$$\omega_c = \frac{\omega_p}{(10^{0.1A_p} - 1)^{1/2n}} \qquad (4.49)$$

To meet the stopband attenuation requirement exactly and exceed the requirement of passband specification, we need

$$\omega_c = \frac{\omega_r}{(10^{0.1A_r} - 1)^{1/2n}} \qquad (4.50)$$

Example 4.2.   Find the transfer function of a lowpass filter with Butterworth magnitude response. The filter is to have no more than 1-dB deviation from ideal magnitude response up to a frequency of 1000 Hz. The filter must reject frequencies above 5000 Hz by at least 30 dB.

From the information supplied the specifications of the filter are

$$A_p = 1 \quad \text{dB}, \qquad \omega_p = 2\pi \times 1000 \quad \text{rad s}^{-1}$$

$$A_r = 30 \quad \text{dB}, \qquad \omega_r = 2\pi \times 5000 \quad \text{rad s}^{-1}$$

The selectivity parameter of the filter is

$$k = \frac{f_p}{f_r} = \frac{1000}{5000} = 0.2$$

The discrimination factor of the filter is

$$d = \frac{\sqrt{10^{0.1A_p} - 1}}{\sqrt{10^{0.1A_r} - 1}} = \frac{\sqrt{10^{0.1} - 1}}{\sqrt{10^3 - 1}} = 1.6099 \times 10^{-2}$$

The order of the filter is

$$n \geq \frac{|\log d|}{|\log k|} = \frac{|\log 1.6099 \times 10^{-2}|}{|\log 0.2|} = 2.565$$

Selecting the next higher integer, we use $n = 3$. The poles for the normalized filter can be obtained from a table (Table III) or calculated as

$$s_K = -\sin\frac{(2K + 1)\pi}{2n} + j\cos\frac{(2K + 1)\pi}{2n}, \qquad K = 0, 1, \ldots, n - 1$$

Therefore

$$s_0 = -\sin\frac{\pi}{6} + j\cos\frac{\pi}{6} = -1/2 + j\sqrt{3/2}$$

$$s_1 = -\sin\frac{3\pi}{6} + j\cos\frac{3\pi}{6} = -1$$

$$s_2 = -\sin\frac{5\pi}{6} + j\cos\frac{5\pi}{6} = -1/2 - j\sqrt{3/2} = \bar{s}_0.$$

The normalized transfer function is given as

$$H_a(s) = (-1)^n \prod_{K=0}^{n-1} \frac{s_K}{s - s_K} = \frac{1}{(s + 1)(s^2 + s + 1)}$$

To find the denormalized transfer function, we need to calculate the actual cutoff frequency ω_c:

$$\omega_c = \omega_p(10^{0.1A_p} - 1)^{-1/2n} = 2\pi \times 1000(10^{0.1} - 1)^{-1/6}$$

$$= 1253 \times 2\pi = 7870 \quad \text{rad s}^{-1}$$

Denormalization is achieved by replacing every s in the transfer function by s/ω_c:

$$H_a\left(\frac{s}{\omega_c}\right) = \frac{1}{(s/7870 + 1)((s/7870)^2 + s/7870 + 1)}$$

Chebyshev Filters   B

A filter's magnitude response specification can be approximated in a band of frequencies (the passband) by minimizing the peak error of the approximating function in the band. Using this strategy, we get the Chebyshev magnitude response filters. The magnitude response is characterized by an equiripple passband and a much sharper transition band rolloff than in Butterworth filters.

The squared magnitude transfer function of the normalized ($\omega_p = 1$) lowpass Chebyshev prototype filter is

$$|H_a(j\omega)|^2 = \frac{1}{1 + \epsilon^2 C_n^2(\omega)} \tag{4.51}$$

where $C_n(\omega)$ is the nth-order Chebyshev polynomial:

$$C_n(\omega) = \cos(n\cos^{-1}\omega), \qquad 0 \le \omega \le 1$$
$$= \cosh(n\cosh^{-1}\omega), \qquad \omega > 1 \tag{4.52}$$

and ϵ (called the ripple factor) is a free variable that determines the amplitude of the ripple. To establish that $C_n(\omega)$ are polynomials in ω, let

$$u = \cos^{-1}\omega \tag{4.53}$$

Then

$$C_n(\omega) = \cos nu \tag{4.54}$$

Using trigonometric identities, we get

$$C_0(\omega) = \cos 0 = 1$$
$$C_1(\omega) = \cos u = \cos(\cos^{-1}\omega) = \omega \tag{4.55}$$
$$C_2(\omega) = \cos 2u = 2\cos^2 u - 1 = 2\omega^2 - 1 \tag{4.56}$$
$$C_3(\omega) = \cos 3u = 4\cos^3 u - 3\cos u = 4\omega^3 - 3\omega \tag{4.57}$$

The preceding relations are called Chebyshev polynomials. Table IV lists them for $n = 1,\dots, 10$. Utilizing the trigonometric identity

$$\cos[(n + 1)u] = 2\cos(nu)\cos(u) - \cos[(n - 1)u] \tag{4.58}$$

we get a recursive formula for Chebyshev polynomials:

$$C_{n+1}(\omega) = 2\omega C_n(\omega) - C_{n-1}(\omega); \quad n = 0, 1, 2,\dots \tag{4.59}$$

TABLE IV

Chebyshev Polynomials $C_n(\omega)$

n	Chebyshev polynomial $C_n(\omega)$
0	1
1	ω
2	$2\omega^2 - 1$
3	$4\omega^3 - 3\omega$
4	$8\omega^4 - 8\omega^2 + 1$
5	$16\omega^5 - 20\omega^3 + 5\omega$
6	$32\omega^6 - 48\omega^4 + 18\omega^2 - 1$
7	$64\omega^7 - 112\omega^5 + 56\omega^3 - 7\omega$
8	$128\omega^8 - 256\omega^6 + 160\omega^4 - 32\omega^2 + 1$
9	$256\omega^9 - 576\omega^7 + 432\omega^5 - 120\omega^3 + 9\omega$
10	$512\omega^{10} - 1280\omega^8 + 1120\omega^6 - 400\omega^4 + 50\omega^2 - 1$

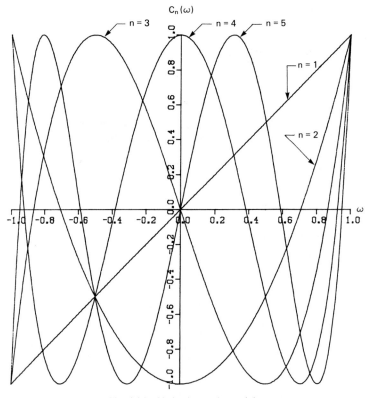

Fig. 4.14. Chebyshev polynomials.

with $C_0(\omega) = 1$ and $C_1(\omega) = \omega$. We can obtain the higher-order Chebyshev polynomials by using Eq. (4.59).

Figure 4.14 contains plots of the Chebyshev functions. Using Fig. 4.14 and Eqs. (4.52) and (4.59) we can deduce the following properties of $C_n(\omega)$:

1. For any order n

$$0 \le |C_n(\omega)| \le 1 \qquad \text{for } 0 \le |\omega| \le 1$$

$$|C_n(\omega)| > 1 \qquad \text{for } |\omega| > 1$$

Also, $C_n(1) = 1$ for any n.
   2. $|C_n(\omega)|$ increases monotonically for $\omega > 1$.
   3. $C_n(\omega)$ is an even (odd) polynomial if n is even (odd).
   4. $|C_n(0)| = 0$ for odd n. $|C_n(0)| = 1$ for even n.

In light of the above, the Chebyshev magnitude response is characterized by the following properties.

1.

$$|H_a(j\omega)|_{\omega=0} = \begin{cases} 1 & \text{when } n \text{ is odd} \\ 1/\sqrt{1 + \epsilon^2} & \text{when is even} \end{cases}$$

2. Since $C_n(1) = 1$ for any n, then $|H_a(j1)| = 1/\sqrt{1 + \epsilon^2}$ for any n.
   3. $|H_a(j\omega)|$ decreases monotonically for $|\omega| > 1$.

In Fig. 4.15 typical response for odd and even n are shown.

Pole Location of Chebyshev Filters   1

Consider

$$|H_a(j\omega)|^2 = \frac{1}{1 + \epsilon^2 C_n^2(\omega)} = \frac{1}{1 + \epsilon^2 C_n^2(-js)}\bigg|_{s=j\omega} \qquad (4.60)$$

The poles are obtained by finding the roots of the denominator

$$1 + \epsilon^2 C_n^2(-js) = 0 \rightarrow C_n(-js) = \pm \frac{j}{\epsilon} \qquad (4.61)$$

Letting

$$s = \sigma + j\omega \rightarrow -js = -j\sigma + \omega \qquad (4.62)$$

yields

$$\cos[n\cos^{-1}(\omega - j\sigma)] = \pm \frac{j}{\epsilon} \qquad (4.63)$$

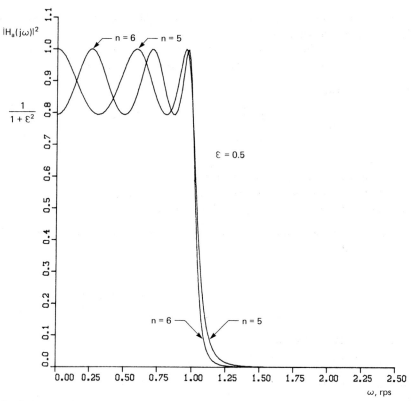

Fig. 4.15. Magnitude-squared response of an even-order and an odd-order normalized lowpass Chebyshev filter.

Let

$$\cos^{-1}(\omega - j\sigma) = x + jy \tag{4.64}$$

Substituting Eq. (4.64) in Eq. (4.63) gives

$$\cos(nx + jny) = \pm \frac{j}{\epsilon} \tag{4.65}$$

$$\cos(nx) \cdot \cos(jny) - \sin(nx) \cdot \sin(jny) = \pm \frac{j}{\epsilon} \tag{4.66}$$

Since $\cos(jx) = \cosh(x)$ and $\sin(jy) = j\sinh(y)$, we get

$$\cos(nx)\cosh(ny) - j\sin(nx)\sinh(ny) = \pm \frac{j}{\epsilon} \tag{4.67}$$

Equation (4.67) is satisfied if

$$\cos(nx) \cdot \cosh(ny) = 0 \tag{4.68}$$

and

$$\sin(nx) \cdot \sinh(ny) = \mp \frac{1}{\epsilon} \tag{4.69}$$

Since $\cosh(ny) \neq 0$, in Eq. (4.68), $\cos(nx) = 0$ so

$$x = (2K + 1)\frac{\pi}{2n}, \qquad K = 0, 1, 2, \dots, 2n - 1 \tag{4.70}$$

$$y = \pm \frac{1}{n}\sinh^{-1}\frac{1}{\epsilon} \tag{4.71}$$

From Eqs. (4.70) and (4.71) we obtain the real and imaginary parts of the roots, which specify the pole locations:

$$\sigma_K = \pm\sin\left[(2K + 1)\frac{\pi}{2n}\right] \cdot \sinh\left[\frac{1}{n}\sinh^{-1}\frac{1}{\epsilon}\right] \tag{4.72}$$

$$\omega_K = \cos\left[(2K + 1)\frac{\pi}{2n}\right] \cdot \cosh\left[\frac{1}{n}\sinh^{-1}\frac{1}{\epsilon}\right] \tag{4.73}$$

where $K = 0, 1, 2, \dots, 2n - 1$. From this we have

$$\frac{\sigma_K}{\sinh^2 y} + \frac{\omega_K}{\cosh^2 y} = 1, \qquad y = \frac{1}{n}\sinh^{-1}\frac{1}{\epsilon} \tag{4.74}$$

This is the equation of an ellipse with foci at $\omega = \pm 1$, and with minor and major axes on the σ- and $j\omega$-axes of the s-plane, respectively. A typical pole distribution of Chebyshev filters is shown in Fig. 4.16.

We now give design relations when maximum passband attenuation (A_p), minimum stopband attenuation (A_r), passband edge frequency $(\omega_p = 2\pi f_p)$, and stopband edge frequency $(\omega_r = 2\pi f_r)$ are given. The denormalized magnitude-squared function is

$$|H_a(j\omega)|^2 = \frac{1}{1 + \epsilon^2 C_n^2(\omega/\omega_p)} \tag{4.75}$$

so that

$$|H_a(j\omega_p)|^2 = \frac{1}{1 + \epsilon^2 C_n^2(\omega/\omega_p)}\bigg|_{\omega = \omega_p} = \frac{1}{1 + \epsilon^2} \tag{4.76}$$

$$A_p = 10\log(1 + \epsilon^2) \tag{4.77}$$

From Eq. (4.77) we obtain

$$\epsilon = \sqrt{10^{0.1A_p} - 1} \tag{4.78}$$

Now

$$A_r = 10\log\left(1 + \epsilon^2 C_n^2\left(\frac{\omega_r}{\omega_p}\right)\right) \tag{4.79}$$

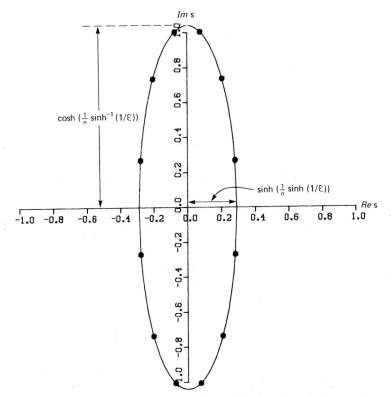

Fig. 4.16. Pole locations of $H(s)H(-s)$ for a Chebyshev filter of order $n = 6$.

Using Eq. (4.52) gives us

$$A_r = 10\log\left(1 + \epsilon^2\cosh^2\left(n\cosh^{-1}\left(\frac{\omega_r}{\omega_p}\right)\right)\right) \qquad (4.80)$$

from which

$$n \geq \cosh^{-1}\left(\frac{10^{0.1A_r} - 1}{\epsilon^2}\right)^{1/2}\bigg/\cosh^{-1}\left(\frac{\omega_r}{\omega_p}\right) \qquad (4.81)$$

Using the discrimination factor (d), Eq. (4.47) and the selectivity factor k, Eq. (4.46), we can write the order n of a Chebyshev filter very compactly:

$$n \geq \frac{\cosh^{-1}(1/d)}{\cosh^{-1}(1/k)} \qquad (4.82)$$

Note that

$$\cosh^{-1}(x) = \ln(x + \sqrt{x^2 - 1}) \qquad (4.83)$$

Knowing ϵ and n from the design equations, Eq. (4.78) and Eq. (4.82), we can calculate the LHP poles of the transfer function from (4.72) and (4.73):

$$s_K = \sin\left[(2K + 1)\frac{\pi}{2n}\right] \cdot \sinh\left[\frac{1}{n}\sinh^{-1}\frac{1}{\epsilon}\right]$$

$$+ j\cos\left[(2K + 1)\frac{\pi}{2n}\right]\cosh\left[\frac{1}{n}\sinh^{-1}\frac{1}{\epsilon}\right] \quad (4.84)$$

Note that

$$\sinh^{-1}(x) = \ln(x + \sqrt{x^2 + 1}) \quad (4.85)$$

The transfer function is

$$H_a(s) = -\prod_{K=0}^{n-1}\frac{s_K}{s - s_K}, \quad n \text{ odd} \quad (4.86)$$

and

$$H_a(s) = \frac{1}{\sqrt{1 + \epsilon^2}}\prod_{K=0}^{n-1}\frac{s_K}{s - s_K}, \quad n \text{ even} \quad (4.87)$$

The poles obtained by using Eq. (4.84) are the poles of the normalized filter (i.e., $\omega_p = 1$). To denormalize to an edge frequency $\omega_p = 2\pi f_p$, replace every s in the transfer function with s/ω_p.

Finally, we can obtain the 3-dB cutoff frequency ω_c by observing that

$$|H_a(j\omega_c)|^2 = \frac{1}{2} = \frac{1}{1 + \epsilon^2 C_n^2(\omega_c)} \quad (4.88)$$

Using Eq. (4.52), we get

$$1 + \epsilon^2\cosh^2(n\cosh^{-1}\omega_c) = 2 \quad (4.89)$$

Solving Eq. (4.89) for ω_c, we obtain

$$\omega_c = \cosh\left(\frac{1}{n}\cosh^{-1}\frac{1}{\epsilon}\right) \quad (4.90)$$

Example 4.3. A lowpass filter is to be designed with the passband ripple not exceeding 2 dB up to a frequency of ω_p. The filter is to reject out-of-band signals by at least 50 dB in the frequency range above $5\omega_p$.

The filter specifications based on the description are

$$A_p \leq 2 \text{ dB} \quad \text{at } \omega = \omega_p$$

$$A_r \geq 50 \text{ dB} \quad \text{at } \omega = \omega_r = 5\omega_p$$

The ripple factor is

$$\epsilon = \sqrt{10^{0.1A_p} - 1} = \sqrt{10^{0.2} - 1} = 0.76478$$

The selectivity parameter is

$$k = \frac{\omega_p}{\omega_r} = \frac{\omega_p}{5\omega_p} = 0.2$$

The discrimination factor is

$$d = \frac{\epsilon}{\sqrt{10^{0.1A_r} - 1}} = \frac{0.764783}{\sqrt{10^5 - 1}} = 2.4185 \times 10^{-3}$$

Using d and k, we may now solve for the filter order:

$$n \geq \frac{\cosh^{-1}(1/d)}{\cosh^{-1}(1/k)}$$

$$= \frac{\ln(1/d + \sqrt{1/d^2 + 1})}{\ln(1/k + \sqrt{1/k^2 + 1})}$$

$$= \frac{6.7177}{2.3124} = 2.9051$$

Selecting the next higher integer yields $n = 3$. The poles can be obtained from (Table V). To calculate s_K for a normalized filter, we have

$$y = \frac{1}{n}\sinh^{-1}\frac{1}{\epsilon} = \frac{1}{n}\ln\left(\frac{1}{\epsilon} + \sqrt{\frac{1}{\epsilon^2} + 1}\right)$$

$$= \frac{1}{3}\ln(1.3076 + \sqrt{2.7097}) = 0.3610$$

Now

$$\sinh y = \frac{e^y - e^{-y}}{2} = 0.3689, \qquad \cosh y = \frac{e^y + e^{-y}}{2} = 1.0659$$

$$s_K = \sin\left[(2K + 1)\frac{\pi}{2n}\right] \cdot \sinh y + j\cos\left[(2K + 1)\frac{\pi}{2n}\right] \cdot \cosh y$$

Thus

$$s_0 = -\sin\left(\frac{\pi}{6}\right)(0.3689) + j\cos\left(\frac{\pi}{6}\right)1.0659 = -0.1844 + j0.9231$$

$$s_1 = \sin\left(\frac{\pi}{2}\right)(0.3689) + j\cos\left(\frac{\pi}{2}\right)1.0659 = -0.3689$$

$$s_2 = -\sin\left(\frac{5\pi}{6}\right)(0.3689) + j\cos\left(\frac{5\pi}{6}\right)1.0659 = -0.1844 - j0.9231 = \bar{s}_0$$

The normalized transfer function is

$$H_a(s) = \frac{0.3269}{(s + 0.3689)(s^2 + 0.3688s + 0.8861)}$$

To denormalize to any other frequency $\omega_p = 2\pi f_p$, replace every s in the transfer function by s/ω_p.

TABLE V

Factors of the Denominator Polynomials of Normalized Chebyshev Lowpass Filters

n	0.1-dB Ripple ($\epsilon = 0.15262$)
1	$s + 6.55220$
2	$s^2 + 2.37236s + 3.31403$
3	$(s + 0.96941)(s^2 + 0.96941s + 1.68975)$
4	$(s^2 + 0.52831s + 1.33003)(s^2 + 1.27546s + 0.62292)$
5	$(s + 0.53891)(s^2 + 0.33307s + 1.19494)(s^2 + 0.87198s + 0.63592)$
6	$(s^2 + 0.22939s + 1.12939)(s^2 + 0.62670s + 0.69637)(s^2 + 0.85608s + 0.26336)$
7	$(s + 0.37678)(s^2 + 0.16768s + 1.09245)(s^2 + 0.46983s + 0.75322)(s^2 + 0.67893s + 0.33022)$
8	$(s^2 + 0.12796s + 1.06949)(s^2 + 0.36440s + 0.79889)(s^2 + 0.54536s + 0.41621)(s^2 + 0.64330s + 0.14561)$
9	$(s + 0.29046)(s^2 + 0.10088s + 1.05421)(s^2 + 0.29046s + 0.83437)$
	$\cdot (s^2 + 0.44501s + 0.49754)(s^2 + 0.54589s + 0.20134)$
10	$(s^2 + 0.08158s + 1.04351)(s^2 + 0.23675s + 0.86188)(s^2 + 0.36874s + 0.56799)$
	$\cdot (s^2 + 0.46464s + 0.27409)(s^2 + 0.51506s + 0.09246)$

n	0.2-dB Ripple ($\epsilon = 0.21709$)
1	$(s + 4.60636)$
2	$(s^2 + 1.92709s + 2.35683)$
3	$(s + 0.81463)(s^2 + 0.81463s + 1.41363)$
4	$(s^2 + 0.44962s + 1.19866)(s^2 + 1.08548s + 0.49155)$
5	$(s + 0.46141)(s^2 + 0.28517s + 1.11741)(s^2 + 0.74658s + 0.55839)$
6	$(s^2 + 0.19705s + 1.07792)(s^2 + 0.53835s + 0.64491)(s^2 + 0.73540s + 0.21190)$
7	$(s + 0.32431)(s^2 + 0.14433s + 1.05566)(s^2 + 0.40441s + 0.71644)(s^2 + 0.58439s + 0.29343)$
8	$(s^2 + 0.11028s + 1.04183)(s^2 + 0.31407s + 0.77124)(s^2 + 0.47004s + 0.38855)$
	$\cdot (s^2 + 0.55445s + 0.11795)$
9	$(s + 0.25057)(s^2 + 0.08702s + 1.03263)(s^2 + 0.25057s + 0.81278)$
	$\cdot (s^2 + 0.38389s + 0.47596)(s^2 + 0.47092s + 0.17976)$
10	$(s^2 + 0.44461s + 0.07513)(s^2 + 0.40109s + 0.25677)(s^2 + 0.31830s + 0.55066)$
	$\cdot (s^2 + 0.20436s + 0.84455)(s^2 + 0.07042s + 1.02619)$

(continued)

TABLE V (*Continued*)

n	0.5-dB Ripple ($\epsilon = 0.34931$)
1	$s + 2.86278$
2	$s^2 + 1.42562s + 1.51620$
3	$(s + 0.62646)(s^2 + 0.62646s + 1.14245)$
4	$(s^2 + 0.35071s + 1.06352)(s^2 + 0.84668s + 0.35641)$
5	$(s^2 + 0.36232)(s^2 + 0.22393s + 1.03578)(s^2 + 0.58625s + 0.47677)$
6	$(s^2 + 0.15530s + 1.02302)(s^2 + 0.42429s + 0.59001)(s^2 + 0.57959s + 0.15610)$
7	$(s^2 + 0.25617)(s^2 + 0.11401s + 1.01611)(s^2 + 0.31944s + 0.67688)(s^2 + 0.46160s + 0.25388)$
8	$(s^2 + 0.08724s + 1.01193)(s^2 + 0.24844s + 0.74133)(s^2 + 0.37182s + 0.35865)$
	$\cdot (s^2 + 0.43859s + 0.08805)$
9	$(s + 0.19841)(s^2 + 0.06891s + 1.00921)(s^2 + 0.19841s + 0.78937)$
	$\cdot (s^2 + 0.30398s + 0.45254)(s^2 + 0.37288s + 0.15634)$
10	$(s^2 + 0.05580s + 1.00734)(s^2 + 0.161934s + 0.82570)(s^2 + 0.25222s + 0.53181)$
	$\cdot (s^2 + 0.31781s + 0.23791)(s^2 + 0.35230s + 0.05628)$

n	1-dB Ripple ($\epsilon = 0.50885$)
1	$s + 1.96523$
2	$s^2 + 1.09773s + 1.10251$
3	$(s + 0.49417)(s^2 + 0.49417s + 0.99421)$
4	$(s^2 + 0.27907s + 0.98651)(s^2 + 0.67374s + 0.27940)$
5	$(s^2 + 0.28949s + 0.17892s + 0.98832)(s^2 + 0.46841s + 0.42930)$
6	$(s^2 + 0.12436s + 0.99073)(s^2 + 0.33976s + 0.55772)(s^2 + 0.46413s + 0.12471)$
7	$(s^2 + 0.20541)(s^2 + 0.09142s + 0.99268)(s^2 + 0.25615s + 0.65346)(s^2 + 0.37014s + 0.23045)$
8	$(s^2 + 0.07002s + 0.99414)(s^2 + 0.19939s + 0.72354)(s^2 + 0.29841s + 0.34086)$
	$\cdot (s^2 + 0.35110s + 0.07026)$
9	$(s + 0.15933)(s^2 + 0.05533s + 0.99523)(s^2 + 0.15933s + 0.77539)$
	$\cdot (s^2 + 0.24411s + 0.43856)(s^2 + 0.29944s + 0.14236)$
10	$(s^2 + 0.04483s + 0.99606)(s^2 + 0.13010s + 0.81442)(s^2 + 0.20263s + 0.52053)$
	$\cdot (s^2 + 0.25533s + 0.22664)(s^2 + 0.28304s + 0.04500)$

n	
	1.5-dB Ripple ($\epsilon = 0.64229$)
1	$s + 1.55693$
2	$s^2 + 0.92218s + 0.92521$
3	$(s + 0.42011)(s^2 + 0.42011s + 0.92649)$
4	$(s^2 + 0.23826s + 0.95046)(s^2 + 0.57521s + 0.24336)$
5	$(s^2 + 0.24765)(s^2 + 0.15306s + 0.96584)(s^2 + 0.40071s + 0.40682)$
6	$(s^2 + 0.10650s + 0.97534)(s^2 + 0.29097s + 0.54233)(s^2 + 0.39747s + 0.10932)$
7	$(s + 0.17603)(s^2 + 0.07834s + 0.98147)(s^2 + 0.21951s + 0.64225)(s^2 + 0.31720s + 0.21924)$
8	$(s^2 + 0.06003s + 0.98561)(s^2 + 0.17094s + 0.71501)(s^2 + 0.25583s + 0.33233)$
	$\cdot (s^2 + 0.30177s + 0.06173)$
9	$(s + 0.13667)(s^2 + 0.04745s + 0.98852)(s^2 + 0.13664s + 0.76867)$
	$\cdot (s^2 + 0.20934s + 0.43185)(s^2 + 0.25679s + 0.13565)$
10	$(s^2 + 0.03845s + 0.99063)(s^2 + 0.11159s + 0.80900)(s^2 + 0.17381s + 0.51510)$
	$\cdot (s^2 + 0.21901s + 0.22121)(s^2 + 0.24277s + 0.03958)$

n	
	2-dB Ripple ($\epsilon = 0.76478$)
1	$s + 1.30756$
2	$s^2 + 0.80382s + 0.82306$
3	$(s + 0.36891)(s^2 + 0.36891s + 0.88610)$
4	$(s^2 + 0.20978s + 0.92868)(s^2 + 0.50644s + 0.22157)$
5	$(s^2 + 0.21831)(s^2 + 0.13492s + 0.95217)(s^2 + 0.35323s + 0.39315)$
6	$(s^2 + 0.09395s + 0.96595)(s^2 + 0.25667s + 0.53294)(s^2 + 0.35061s + 0.09993)$
7	$(s + 0.15533)(s^2 + 0.06913s + 0.97462)(s^2 + 0.19371s + 0.63539)(s^2 + 0.27991s + 0.21239)$
8	$(s^2 + 0.05298s + 0.98038)(s^2 + 0.15089s + 0.70978)$
	$\cdot (s^2 + 0.22582s + 0.32710)(s^2 + 0.26637s + 0.05650)$
9	$(s + 0.12063)(s^2 + 0.04189s + 0.98440)(s^2 + 0.12063s + 0.76455)$
	$\cdot (s^2 + 0.18482s + 0.42773)(s^2 + 0.22671s + 0.13153)$
10	$(s^2 + 0.03395s + 0.98730)(s^2 + 0.09853s + 0.80567)(s^2 + 0.15347s + 0.51178)$
	$\cdot (s^2 + 0.19338s + 0.21788)(s^2 + 0.21436s + 0.03625)$

(continued)

TABLE V (*Continued*)

2.5-dB Ripple ($\epsilon = 0.88220$)

n	
1	$(s + 1.13353)$
2	$(s^2 + 0.71525s + 0.75579)$
3	$(s + 0.32995)(s^2 + 0.32995s + 0.85887)$
4	$(s^2 + 0.18796s + 0.91386)(s^2 + 0.45378s + 0.20676)$
5	$(s + 0.19577)(s^2 + 0.12099s + 0.94284)(s^2 + 0.31677s + 0.38382)$
6	$(s^2 + 0.08429s + 0.95953)(s^2 + 0.23028s + 0.52651)(s^2 + 0.31456s + 0.09350)$
7	$(s + 0.13941)(s^2 + 0.06204s + 0.96992)(s^2 + 0.17384s + 0.63070)(s^2 + 0.25120s + 0.20769)$
8	$(s^2 + 0.04756s + 0.97680)(s^2 + 0.1354s + 0.70620)(s^2 + 0.20269s + 0.32352)$
	$\cdot (s^2 + 0.23909s + 0.05292)$
9	$(s + 0.10829)(s^2 + 0.03761s + 0.98157)(s^2 + 0.10829s + 0.76173)$
	$\cdot (s^2 + 0.16591s + 0.42490)(s^2 + 0.20352s + 0.12870)$
10	$(s^2 + 0.19245s + 0.03396)(s^2 + 0.17361s + 0.21560)(s^2 + 0.13778s + 0.50949)$
	$\cdot (s^2 + 0.08846s + 0.80338)(s^2 + 0.03048s + 0.98502)$

3-dB Ripple ($\epsilon = 0.99763$)

n	
1	$s + 1.00238$
2	$s^2 + 0.64490s + 0.70795$
3	$(s + 0.29862)(s^2 + 0.29862s + 0.83917)$
4	$(s^2 + 0.17034s + 0.90309)(s^2 + 0.41124s + 0.19598)$
5	$(s + 0.17753)(s^2 + 0.10970s + 0.93603)(s^2 + 0.28725s + 0.37701)$
6	$(s^2 + 0.07646s + 0.95483)(s^2 + 0.20889s + 0.52182)(s^2 + 0.28535s + 0.08880)$
7	$(s + 0.12649)(s^2 + 0.05629s + 0.96648)(s^2 + 0.15773s + 0.62726)(s^2 + 0.22792s + 0.20425)$
8	$(s^2 + 0.04316s + 0.97417)(s^2 + 0.12290s + 0.70358)(s^2 + 0.18393s + 0.32089)$
	$\cdot (s^2 + 0.21696s + 0.05029)$
9	$(s + 0.09827)(s^2 + 0.03413s + 0.97950)(s^2 + 0.09827s + 0.75966)$
	$\cdot (s^2 + 0.15057s + 0.42283)(s^2 + 0.18470s + 0.12664)$
10	$(s^2 + 0.02766s + 0.98335)(s^2 + 0.08028s + 0.80171)(s^2 + 0.12504s + 0.50782)$
	$\cdot (s^2 + 0.15757s + 0.21393)(s^2 + 0.17466s + 0.03229)$

Inverse, or type 2, Chebyshev filters have a flat magnitude in the passband and equiripple in the stopband. Standard Chebyshev filters of type 1, discussed in Section VI.B, were all-pole filters. In contrast, inverse Chebyshev filters have transmission zeros in the stopband. For a given filter order n, the magnitude response is flatter in the passband for an inverse Chebyshev filter than for a comparable Butterworth filter. The magnitude-squared transfer function is

$$|H_a(j\omega)|^2 = \frac{\epsilon^2 C_n^2(\omega_r/\omega)}{1 + \epsilon^2 C_n^2(\omega_r/\omega)} \tag{4.91}$$

where $C_n(\omega)$ is the Chebyshev polynomial and ω_r is the stopband edge frequency where the ripple starts. The attenuation in dB is

$$A(\omega) = 10 \log\left(1 + \frac{1}{\epsilon^2 C_n^2(\omega_r/\omega)}\right) \quad \text{dB.} \tag{4.92}$$

The ripple factor ϵ can be calculated by noting that at the stopband edge, where $\omega = \omega_r$, the specified attenuation requirement must be satisfied as follows:

$$A_r = 10 \log\left(1 + \frac{1}{\epsilon^2 C_n^2(1)}\right) \tag{4.93}$$

Since $C_n(1) = 1$,

$$\epsilon = \frac{1}{\sqrt{10^{0.1 A_r} - 1}} \tag{4.94}$$

To meet the attenuation requirements in the passband, the maximum allowable attenuation A_p cannot be exceeded at $\omega = \omega_p$:

$$A_p = 10 \log\left(1 + \frac{1}{\epsilon^2 C_n^2(\omega_r/\omega_p)}\right) \tag{4.95}$$

Using Eqs. (4.94) and (4.95), we obtain the order of the filter as

$$n \geq \frac{\cosh^{-1}(1/d)}{\cosh^{-1}(1/k)} \tag{4.96}$$

which is the same as for Chebyshev filters [see Eq. (4.82)].
   Analytic continuation is used in Eq. (4.91) to find the poles and zeros

$$H_a(s)H_a(-s) = \frac{\epsilon^2 C_n^2(j\omega_r/s)}{1 + \epsilon^2 C_n^2(j\omega_r/s)} \tag{4.97}$$

We obtain the zeros by setting.

$$C_n\left(\frac{j\omega_r}{s}\right) = 0 \tag{4.98}$$

Using Eq. (4.52), we write (4.98) as

$$\cos\left(n\cos^{-1}\left(\frac{j\omega_r}{s}\right)\right) = 0 \qquad (4.99)$$

which is satisfied if

$$\cos^{-1}\left(\frac{j\omega_r}{s}\right) = \frac{m\pi}{2n}, \qquad m \text{ odd} \qquad (4.100)$$

The zeros, designated as s_m, are

$$s_m = j\omega_r \sec\left(\frac{m\pi}{2n}\right), \qquad m = 1, 3, \ldots, 2n - 1 \qquad (4.101)$$

The poles of the inverse Chebyshev filters are the roots of

$$1 + \epsilon^2 C_n^2\left(\frac{j\omega_r}{s}\right) = 0 \qquad (4.102)$$

which is the same as Eq. (4.60) except that $-s$ is replaced by $1/s$. Note that for standard Chebyshev filters the denormalization of the transfer function is with respect to ω_p [see Eq. (4.75)], whereas for inverse Chebyshev filters the denormalization is with respect to the stopband edge frequency ω_r. Therefore, we determine the poles of a standard Chebyshev filter and then perform a pole reciprocation to obtain the poles for the inverse Chebyshev filter. Pole reciprocation consists of replacing each and every pole s_p of the standard Chebyshev filter by $1/s_p$. Note that the poles of the inverse Chebyshev filter lie on an almost elliptical contour in the s-plane.

D Elliptic Filters[†]

The requirements of a given magnitude response specification can be met by spreading the approximation error in the passband and the stopband. A strategy of minimizing the peak error of the approximating function results in a filter magnitude response characteristic that is equiripple in the passband and the stopband. Filters having such a response are known as elliptic or Cauer filters. Elliptic filters have transmission zeros (loss poles) in the stopband. The magnitude response of elliptic filters is optimum in the sense that for a given order n the rolloff in the transition band is the steepest, and for this reason elliptic filters are used very widely.

The square magnitude response function for elliptic filters is

$$|H_a(j\omega)|^2 = \frac{1}{1 + \epsilon^2 R_n^2(\omega)} \qquad (4.103)$$

[†] See references [4, 18, 21–26].

where $R_n(\omega)$ is known as the Chebyshev rational function and ϵ is the ripple factor. The roots of $R_n(\omega)$ are related to the Jacobi elliptic sine function. The calculation of the pole–zero locations of the transfer function requires elaboration of elliptic function theory and its properties [23, 27, 22, 4, 3]. An extensive tabulation of lowpass elliptic filter pole–zero locations is available [28]. For design purposes the pole–zero locations can also be calculated by using series approximation for the elliptic functions. The design procedure presented herein was proposed in [23], with full discussion of elliptic functions and a computer program of the design equations in [4]. Also see [24] for a FORTRAN program of these equations.

The following is a summary of the properties of Chebyshev rational functions. Note the similarities with the properties of Chebyshev polynomials.

1. $R_n(\omega)$ is an even function of ω when n is even. It is an odd function of ω when n is odd.
2. The zeros of $R_n(\omega)$ are in the range $|\omega| < 1$, and the poles of $R_n(\omega)$ are in the range $|\omega| > 1$.
3. The function $R_n(\omega)$ oscillates between the values ± 1 in the passband.
4. $R_n(\omega) = 1$ at $\omega = 1$.
5. $R_n(\omega)$ oscillates between $\pm 1/d$ and infinity in the stopband, where d is the discrimination factor defined (Eq. 4.47).

The Chebyshev rational function, normalized to a "center frequency" $\omega_0 = 1$, has the form

$$R_n(\omega) = \omega \prod_{i=1}^{(n-1)/2} \frac{\omega_i^2 - \omega^2}{1 - \omega_i^2 \omega^2} \qquad \text{for } n \text{ odd} \qquad (4.104)$$

and

$$R_n(\omega) = \prod_{i=1}^{n/2} \frac{\omega_i^2 - \omega^2}{1 - \omega_i^2 \omega^2} \qquad \text{for } n \text{ even} \qquad (4.105)$$

The poles and zeros of $R_n(\omega)$ are reciprocals of each other and exhibit geometric symmetry with respect to the center frequency ω_0. Furthermore,

$$R_n\left(\frac{1}{\omega}\right) = \frac{1}{R_n(\omega)} \qquad (4.106)$$

that is, the Chebyshev rational function $R_n(\omega)$ exhibits a symmetry with respect to the center frequency $\omega_0 = 1$ such that its value at a frequency ω_j in the range $0 \le \omega < \omega_0$ is the reciprocal of a value at the geometrically symmetric frequency $1/\omega_j$ (or generally ω_0/ω_j).

A typical magnitude-squared response is shown in Fig. 4.17. The transition region is exaggerated to show clearly some frequencies of interest. The figure shows the equiripple passband and stopband characteristic. In the passband $|H_a(j\omega)|^2$ oscillates between 1 and $1/(1 + \epsilon^2)$ up to the passband edge frequency

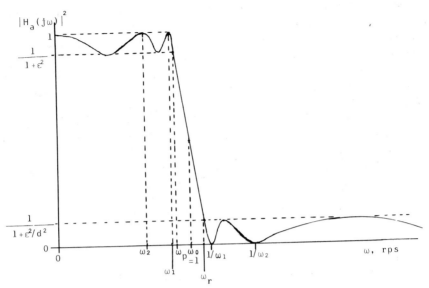

Fig. 4.17. Magnitude-squared response of a normalized lowpass elliptic filter.

at $\omega = \omega_p$. The passband specification requirement is that the attenuation (ripple) be at most A_p dB.

$$A_p = 10\log(1 + \epsilon^2) \tag{4.107}$$

$$\epsilon = \sqrt{10^{0.1A_p} - 1} \tag{4.108}$$

The figure also shows the stopband response oscillating between zero and $1/(1 + \epsilon^2/d^2)$. The specification requires that the filter reject (attenuate) unwanted frequencies in the stopband by at least A_r dB. Thus at the stopband edge, $\omega = \omega_r$, we can write

$$A_r = 10\log\left(1 + \frac{\epsilon^2}{d^2}\right) \tag{4.109}$$

$$d = \frac{\epsilon}{\sqrt{10^{0.1A_r} - 1}} \tag{4.110}$$

or

$$d = \left(\frac{10^{0.1A_p} - 1}{10^{0.1A_r} - 1}\right)^{1/2} \tag{4.111}$$

which is the same as Eq. (4.47); that is, d is the discrimination factor. The normalization frequency ω_0, which for simplicity, has a value of 1 in the figure is easily calculated from the passband and stopband edge frequencies:

$$\omega_0 = \sqrt{\omega_p \omega_r} \tag{4.112}$$

The selectivity factor k can be calculated from its definition:

$$k = \frac{\omega_p}{\omega_r} \qquad (4.113)$$

The transfer function of an nth-order lowpass, normalized ($\omega_0 = 1$), elliptic filter is

$$H_a(s) = H_0 \prod_{i=1}^{n/2} \frac{s^2 + a_i}{s^2 + b_i s + c_i}, \qquad n \text{ even} \qquad (4.114)$$

$$H_a(s) = \frac{H_0}{s + a} \prod_{i=1}^{(n-1)/2} \frac{s^2 + a_i}{s^2 + b_i s + c_i}, \qquad n \text{ odd} \qquad (4.115)$$

To calculate the pole–zero locations of the filter and the quadratic factors in the transfer function from the given specifications, A_p, ω_p, A_r, ω_r, use the following formulas [23, 4, 24]. The computation sequence shown can be readily programmed on a programmable calculator or computer.

1. Calculate k from Eq. (4.113).
2. Let

$$q_0 = \frac{1}{2}\left(\frac{1 - (1 - k^2)^{1/4}}{1 + (1 - k^2)^{1/4}}\right) \qquad (4.116)$$

3. Calculate

$$q = q_0 + 2q_0^5 + 15q_0^9 + 150q_0^{13} \qquad (4.117)$$

4. Calculate d from Eq. (4.111).
5. The order of the filter is

$$n \geq \frac{\log(16/d^2)}{\log(1/q)} \qquad (4.118)$$

6. Calculate ϵ from Eq. (4.108).
7. Let

$$\beta = \frac{1}{2n} \ln \frac{(1 + \epsilon^2)^{1/2} + 1}{(1 + \epsilon^2)^{1/2} - 1} \qquad (4.119)$$

8. Calculate

$$a = \frac{2q^{1/4} \sum\limits_{m=0}^{\infty} (-1)^m q^{m(m+1)} \sinh[(2m + 1)\beta]}{1 + 2 \sum\limits_{m=1}^{\infty} (-1)^m q^{m^2} \cosh(2m\beta)} \qquad (4.120)$$

9. Let

$$U = \sqrt{(1 + ka^2)\left(1 + \frac{a^2}{k}\right)} \qquad (4.121)$$

10. Then

$$\omega_1 = \frac{2q^{1/4} \sum\limits_{m=0}^{\infty} (-1)^m q^{m(m+1)} \sin[(2m+1)\pi l/n]}{1 + 2 \sum\limits_{m=1}^{\infty} (-1)^m q^{m^2} \cos(2\pi m l/n)} \tag{4.122}$$

where $l = i - 1/2, i = 1, 2, \ldots, n/2, n$ even, and $l = i, i = 1, 2, \ldots, (n-1)/2, n$ odd.

11.

$$V_i = \sqrt{(1 - k\omega_i^2)\left(1 - \frac{\omega_i^2}{k}\right)} \tag{4.123}$$

12. Then

$$a_i = \frac{1}{\omega_i^2} \tag{4.124}$$

13.

$$b_i = \frac{2aV_i}{1 + a^2\omega_i^2} \tag{4.125}$$

14.

$$c_i = \frac{(aV_i)^2 + (\omega_i U)^2}{(1 + a^2\omega_i^2)^2} \tag{4.126}$$

15. Finally

$$H_0 = a \prod_{i=1}^{(n-1)/2} \frac{c_i}{a_i} \qquad \text{for } n \text{ odd} \tag{4.127}$$

$$H_0 = \frac{1}{\sqrt{1 + \epsilon^2}} \prod_{i=1}^{n/2} \frac{c_i}{a_i} \qquad \text{for } n \text{ even} \tag{4.128}$$

Replacing each s by s/ω_0 in the transfer function, where ω_0 is the center frequency given by Eq. (4.112), denormalizes the transfer function to the desired frequency range.

Example 4.4. The transfer function of a lowpass analog filter is to be found. The filter is to have no more than 2-dB ripple in the passband up to an edge frequency of 3000 Hz. The filter is to attenuate the out-of-band signals beyond 4000 Hz by at least 60 dB.

The filter specifications are summarized as

$$A_p \leq 2 \text{ dB}, \qquad \omega_p = 2\pi f_p = 2\pi \times 3000 \text{ rad s}^{-1}$$

$$A_r \geq 60 \text{ dB}, \qquad \omega_r = 2\pi f_r = 2\pi \times 4000 \text{ rad s}^{-1}$$

The selectivity factor is $k = 0.75$. The discrimination factor is $d = 7.6478 \times 10^{-4}$. The filter order, from Eqs. (4.116) and (4.117), is $n \geq 5.7$. Selecting the next higher integer in order to meet or exceed the given specifications, we get $n = 6$. Carrying out the computation sequence according to Eqs. (4.119)–(4.128) and using Eq. (4.114), we obtain the normalized transfer function

$$H_a(s) = 7.1374 \times 10^{-4} \frac{(s^2 + 13.8451)(s^2 + 2.2153)(s^2 + 1.3955)}{(s^2 + 0.35518s + 0.10903)(s^2 + 0.194425s + 0.48045)} \times (s^2 + 0.053863s + 0.73417)$$

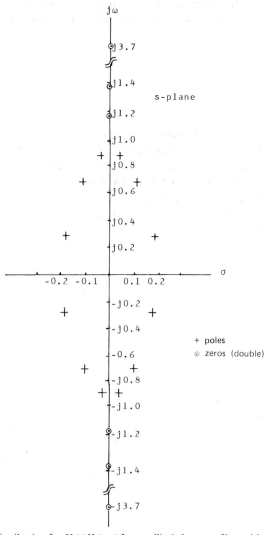

Fig. 4.18. Pole–zero distribution for $H_a(s)H_a(-s)$ for an elliptic lowpass filter with $n = 6$.

Note that transmission zeros are all on the $j\omega$-axis above the normalized stopband edge frequency, $\omega_r = 1/\sqrt{k} = 1.155$ rad s^{-1}. The pole–zero distribution for the normalized transfer function is shown in Fig. 4.18, which is typical of elliptic filters. The specified filter's center frequency, which is the geometric mean of the passband and stopband edge frequencies, is $\omega_0 = 2\pi \times 3464$ rad s^{-1}. The transfer function of the specified filter is obtained by replacing each s in the normalized transfer function by s/ω_0.

The series in Eqs. (4.120) and (4.122) are fast converging. In many filter design calculations, up to four or five terms in the series will provide sufficient accuracy. In Example 4.4 the computation was stopped when the difference between the mth and $(m - 1)$st term was less than 10^{-6}. The required value of m was at most $m = 3$.

E   Bessel Filters[†]

The group delay of the filters in the previous sections is a nonlinear function of frequency. The group delay becomes progressively more nonlinear as filters with steeper skirt rolloff characteristics are developed. The nonlinearity is more pronounced as one goes from Butterworth to elliptic filters, especially in the vicinity of the passband edge frequency [19]. Bessel filters, on the other hand, are characterized by maximally flat group delay. The transfer function of Bessel filters has the form

$$H_a(s) = \frac{B_0^n}{\displaystyle\sum_{i=0}^{n} B_i s^i} \tag{4.129}$$

where

$$B_i = \frac{(2n - 1)!}{2^{n-i} i!(n - 1)!} \tag{4.130}$$

As can be seen, Bessel filters are of the all-pole type. The roots of the characteristic polynomial can be found by computer methods. A table of the quadratic factors for up to $n = 10$ and a filter design procedure are available in references [29, 30]. To meet given magnitude response specifications, Bessel filters require substantially higher orders than some of the filters in the previous sections, which makes them undesirable. Also, a digital filter designer has the choice of designing perfectly linear-phase (constant group-delay) filters, using the techniques of Chapter 2.

[†] See references [8, 21, 29, 30].

Section VI discussed design methods for some popular normalized analog filters. The magnitude responses of all-pole filters such as Bessel, Butterworth, and Chebyshev (type 1) are monotonically decreasing functions of frequency in the stopband. Bessel filters are characterized by a maximally flat group-delay characteristic. Butterworth filters have a maximally flat magnitude response characteristic. Chebyshev filters, on the other hand, have an equiripple magnitude response characteristic in the passband. For a given order n a Butterworth filter has a higher attenuation in the stopband and steeper rolloff in the transition band than does a Bessel filter. We can make similar observation between Chebyshev and Butterworth filters. The design tradeoff is between achieving magnitude response specifications with the lowest filter order n and the increased group-delay nonlinearity for the sharper rolloff filter types.

The inverse Chebyshev (Chebyshev type 2) filters have a maximally flat magnitude response in the passband and an equiripple characteristic in the stopband. Inverse Chebyshev filters exhibit a flatter passband magnitude response than does a Butterworth filter of the same order. Flatness is achieved by including the stopband zeros (loss poles) in the transfer function. Inverse Chebyshev filters have sharper rolloffs than standard Chebyshev filters [21] and have group-delay characteristics more nonlinear than Butterworth filters but less so than standard Chebyshev filters.

The magnitude response of elliptic filters is equiripple in the passband and the stopband and is characterized by the steepest rolloff for a given order n. For example, for $k = 0.75$, $A_p = 2$ dB, and $A_r = 60$ dB, a sixth-order elliptic filter is required. In contrast, a Chebyshev filter of order 10 and a 25th-order Butterworth filter would have to be specified to meet or exceed the given specifications. The group delay of elliptic filters is the most nonlinear, especially near the passband edge. When such sharp rolloffs are desirable and group-delay linearity is a concern, the designer can alleviate the problem by cascading the filter with delay equalizers.

The filters mentioned here are the most frequently used. A broad overview of other filters along with a good selection of nomographs and design curves is available in [31].

FREQUENCY TRANSFORMATIONS   **VII**

The normalized lowpass analog filters described in Section VI can be easily transformed to a lowpass filter with different edge frequency or to a highpass, bandpass, or bandstop filter. The transformations are as follows:

1. *Lowpass to lowpass:* This is the frequency scaling transformation illustrated in the examples of Section VI and is given by

$$s \to \frac{s}{\omega_p} \tag{4.131}$$

In words, every s in the normalized filter is replaced by s/ω_p, where ω_p is the new edge frequency in radians per second.

2. *Lowpass to highpass:* The transformation is

$$s \to \frac{\omega_p}{s} \tag{4.132}$$

where ω_p is the new edge frequency for the highpass filter.

3. *Lowpass to bandpass:* The transformation is

$$s \to \frac{s^2 + \omega_m^2}{Bs} \tag{4.133}$$

where ω_m is the geometric mean of the upper bandedge frequency ω_u and the lower bandedge frequency ω_l:

$$\omega_m = \sqrt{\omega_u \omega_l} \tag{4.134}$$

and B is the bandwidth of the filter:

$$B = \omega_u - \omega_l \tag{4.135}$$

4. *Lowpass to bandstop:* The transformation is

$$s \to \frac{Bs}{s^2 + \omega_m^2} \tag{4.136}$$

where ω_m and B are defined as above.

VIII DIGITAL FILTER DESIGN BASED ON ANALOG TRANSFER FUNCTIONS

A widely used technique for the design of digital filters is the transformation or mapping of an analog filter that meets given specifications. In other words, we first calculate the transfer function $H_a(s)$ of an analog filter that meets the design requirements. Then, using a suitable transformation from the s-plane to the z-plane, we obtain the transfer function $H(z)$ of the desired digital filter. From z-transform theory the transformation relating the Laplace transform variable

s to the z-transform variable z is

$$z = e^{sT} \tag{4.137}$$

or

$$s = \frac{1}{T} \ln z \tag{4.138}$$

The mapping of points from the s-plane to the z-plane indicated by (4.137) is such that all points in the right-half s-plane are mapped outside of the unit circle in the z-plane; the left-half s-plane is mapped inside the unit circle of the z-plane. The steady-state frequency domain in the s-plane (i.e., the $j\omega$-axis) is mapped onto the unit circle in a periodic manner such that every circuit on the unit circle corresponds to a period of $\omega_s = 2\pi/T$. The transformation maps stable analog filters to stable digital filters.

Using Eq. (4.138) to map an analog filter with transfer function $H_a(s)$ to a digital filter $H(z)$ causes a realization problem because the substitution called for in Eq. (4.138) gives an irrational $H(z)$, which is not realizable. To obtain a rational digital filter transfer function $H(z)$, we need a rational function of z for the transformation from the s-plane to the z-plane. To preserve the steady-state frequency domain characteristic of the analog filter and map it to a stable digital filter, the transformation should have the following properties:

1. The transformation maps the steady-state frequency domain of the s-plane onto the unit circle of the z-plane.
2. The transformation maps the left-half s-plane (Re $s < 0$) inside the unit circle of the z-plane.

For example, consider the digitalization of an analog filter using numerical integration techniques [3, 20]. In this method the derivative of a continuous-time function is approximated by finite differences:

$$\left.\frac{dy}{dt}\right|_{t=nT} = \frac{1}{T} \sum_{i=0}^{M} a_i y(nT - iT) \tag{4.139}$$

Euler's approximation is a special case of Eq. (4.139):

$$\left.\frac{dy}{dt}\right|_{t=nT} = \frac{y(nT) - y(nT - T)}{T} \tag{4.140}$$

The transformation between the s-plane and the z-plane corresponding to Euler's approximation is

$$s = \frac{1 - z^{-1}}{T} \tag{4.141}$$

A study of the mapping properties of Eq. (4.141) reveals [20] that property 1 of the mapping requirements is not satisfied, the consequence of which is that the transformation in Eq. (4.141) can be adequately used only for the design of very narrowband lowpass filters.

In the following subsections we describe digital filter design techniques based on other transformations.

A   The Impulse-Invariant Transformation[†]

The concept underlying the impulse-invariant transformation technique is to match the impulse response of the prototype analog filter to the impulse response of the digital filter at the sampling instants:

$$h_a(t)\Big|_{t=nT} = h(nT) \tag{4.142}$$

The impulse response of the analog prototype can be obtained from its transfer function:

$$H_a(s) = \sum_{i=1}^{N} \frac{A_i}{s - s_i} \tag{4.143}$$

The inverse Laplace transform of Eq. (4.143) gives

$$h_a(t) = \sum_{i=1}^{N} A_i e^{s_i t} \tag{4.144}$$

Using Eq. (4.142) in Eq. (4.144) and taking the z-transform give the transfer function of the digital filter as

$$H(z) = \sum_{i=1}^{N} \frac{A_i z}{z - p_i} \tag{4.145}$$

where the relation between the poles of the digital and analog filters is

$$p_i = e^{s_i T} \tag{4.146}$$

The frequency responses of the digital filter and the analog prototype filter are related by

$$H(e^{j\omega T}) = \frac{1}{T} \sum_{n=-\infty}^{\infty} H_a(j\omega + jn\omega_s) \tag{4.147}$$

Equation (4.147) shows that the digital filter frequency response is a periodic version of the analog filter frequency response, where the period is ω_s, the sampling radian frequency. Thus if the analog filter frequency response is not bandlimited to the folding frequency ($\omega_s/2$), aliasing errors, which could be severe, will occur. Thus the design technique is useful in digitalizing bandlimiting

[†] See references [1, 3].

filters, such as lowpass and bandpass, and should not be used for highpass and bandstop filter designs. In lowpass and bandpass designs select a sampling rate that is high enough to maintain tolerable aliasing errors. Equation (4.147) indicates that as T is decreased the digital filter exhibits higher gains. To achieve comparable gains for the digital and analog prototype filters, multiply $H(z)$ by T in Eq. (4.145)

Example 4.5. Use the impulse-invariant design procedure to transform a lowpass analog filter whose specifications are

$$A_p = 1 \text{ dB}, \qquad \omega_p = 2\pi \times 1000 \text{ rad s}^{-1}$$
$$A_r = 25 \text{ dB}, \qquad \omega_r = 2\pi \times 4000 \text{ rad s}^{-1}$$

The sampling rate for the digital filter is $f_s = 10{,}000$ Hz. The analog prototype Butterworth filter is the same filter as in Example 4.2, except for the stopband specifications. From Example 4.2 the transfer function of the analog filter is

$$H_a\left(\frac{s}{\omega_c}\right) = \left[\left(\frac{s}{7870} + 1\right)\left(\left(\frac{s}{7870}\right)^2 + \frac{s}{7870} + 1\right)\right]^{-1}$$

with $\omega_c = 7870$ rad s^{-1}. Expanding the transfer funcction using partial fractions and making the substitution as called for in Eqs. (4.145) and (4.146), with a gain adjustment such that the analog and digital filter magnitudes match at zero frequency, we obtain the transfer function of the digital filter, $f_s = 10{,}000$

$$H(z) = 0.7878\left[\frac{z}{z - 0.4552} - \frac{z(z - 0.7694)}{z^2 - 1.0479z + 0.4552}\right] \qquad (4.148)$$

In order to see the effect of the aliasing error due to a reduced sampling rate, we redesigned the filter a sampling rate $f_s = 6000$ Hz. The transfer function is then

$$H(z) = 1.3223\left[\frac{z}{z - 0.2694} - \frac{z(z - 0.4904)}{z^2 - 0.4373z + 0.2694}\right] \qquad (4.149)$$

The steady-state frequency domain magnitude response of the digital filters in Eqs. (4.148) and (4.149) is plotted in Fig. 4.19(a), (b). When $f_s = 10{,}000$ Hz, the digital filter meets the design requirements. When $f_s = 6000$ Hz, the aliasing error is severe enough that the design requirements are not met.

Matched z-Transform   B

In the impulse-invariant transformation the poles of the continuous-time domain transfer function $H_a(s)$ are mapped into poles of $H(z)$ via Eq. (4.146). In the matched z-transform the poles and zeros of $H_a(s)$ are mapped by using

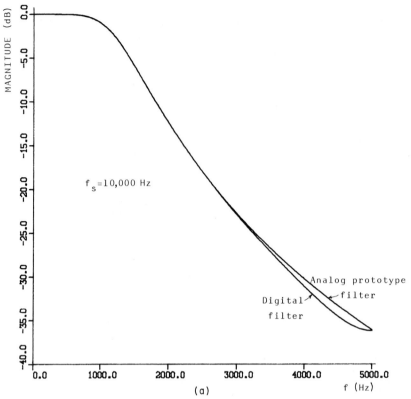

Fig. 4.19. Magnitude response of a third-order digital filter using the impulse-invariant transformation with (a) $f_s = 10{,}000$ Hz and (b) $f_s = 6000$ Hz.

Eq. (4.146) to create the digital filter transfer function $H(z)$. Thus given

$$H_a(s) = \frac{\prod\limits_{i=1}^{M}(s - s_{0l})}{\prod\limits_{i=1}^{N}(s - s_{pl})} \qquad (4.150)$$

the corresponding digital filter transfer function is

$$H(z) = \frac{\prod\limits_{i=1}^{M}(1 - e^{s_{0i}T}z^{-1})}{\prod\limits_{i=1}^{N}(1 - e^{s_{pl}T}z^{-1})} \qquad (4.151)$$

The method can be used for designing highpass and bandstop filters, but it will not preserve the equiripple magnitude response characteristic of Chebyshev and elliptic filters. Because the transformation does not preserve any time or frequency domain properties of the prototype analog filter, it is not widely used.

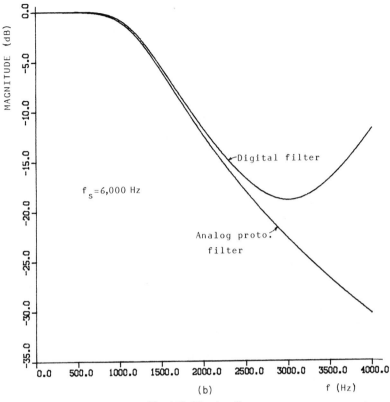

Fig. 4.19. (*Continued*)

Bilinear z-Transformation   C

The aliasing phenomenon inherent in the impulse-invariant and matched z-transformations are caused by the one-to-many mapping from the s-plane to the z-plane. The bilinear transformation, on the other hand, is a one-to-one mapping from the s-plane to the z-plane defined by

$$s = \frac{2}{T}\frac{z-1}{z+1} \qquad (4.152)$$

where

$$z = \frac{2/T + s}{2/T - s} \qquad (4.153)$$

The bilinear z-transformation is bandlimiting in its action, eliminating the aliasing effect observed with previous designs. It is widely used for transforming analog filter designs, which approximate piecewise constant-magnitude specifications, to digital filters with similar characteristics. The mapping preserves the equiripple magnitude characteristic of the prototype filter.

Using Eqs. (4.152) and (4.153), we can study the mapping properties of the bilinear z-transformation. Consider the mapping of a point $z = re^{j\theta}$ in the z-plane to a point $s = \sigma + j\omega$ in the s-plane. Using Eq. (4.153) we can write

$$re^{j\theta} = \frac{2/T + \sigma + j\omega}{2/T - \sigma - j\omega} \tag{4.154}$$

which yields

$$r = \left(\frac{(2/T + \sigma)^2 + \omega^2}{(2/T - \sigma)^2 + \omega^2} \right)^{1/2} \tag{4.155}$$

and

$$\theta = \tan^{-1}\left(\frac{\omega}{2/T + \sigma}\right) + \tan^{-1}\left(\frac{\omega}{2/T - \sigma}\right) \tag{4.156}$$

From Eq. (4.155), if we let $\sigma > 0$ (right-half s-plane), then $r > 1$; that is, the right-half s-plane is mapped to the exterior of the unit circle of the z-plane. When $\sigma < 0$, then $r < 1$; that is, the left-half s-plane is mapped to the interior of the unit circle of the z-plane. If $\sigma = 0$, then $r = 1$; that is, the steady-state frequency domain in the s-plane ($j\omega$-axis) is mapped onto the unit circle of the z-plane. Thus the bilinear z-transformation meets the mapping requirements mentioned in the beginning of Section VIII.

The bilinear z-transform maps the entire $j\omega$-axis of the s-plane onto the unit circle of the z-plane; that is, the $j\omega$-axis is compressed (or warped) into the unit circle. The implication of the warping phenomenon is that the scales of the analog filter frequencies and the digital filter frequencies are different. For example, consider the relationship between the frequencies of the analog filter and the derived digital filter. To reduce confusion in notaion, let the analog filter frequency variable be Ω, and let the corresponding digital filter frequency variable be ω. To study the effect of warping, substitute $s = j\Omega$ and $z = e^{j\omega T}$ in Eq. (4.152):

$$j\Omega = \frac{2}{T}\left[\frac{e^{j\omega T} - 1}{e^{j\omega T} + 1}\right] = \frac{2}{T}\left[\frac{(e^{j\omega T/2} - e^{-j\omega T/2})/j2}{(e^{j\omega T/2} + e^{-j\omega T/2})/j2}\right]$$

$$= j\frac{2}{T}\tan\frac{\omega T}{2} \tag{4.157}$$

Thus the relationship between the frequency scales of the analog and digital filters is

$$\Omega = \frac{2}{T}\tan\frac{\omega T}{2} \tag{4.158}$$

which is nonlinear. Figure 4.20 is a plot of Eq. (4.158). It illustrates the nonlinear warping of the frequency scale as well as the effect of the warping on mapping the analog filter magnitude response to that of a digital filter. When $\omega T/2 \ll 1$, the relationship between the two scales is approximately linear because

$$\Omega \cong \frac{2}{T}\omega\frac{T}{2} = \omega \qquad (4.159)$$

We can correct the warping error by using Eq. (4.158). Given the critical frequencies of the digital filter per specifications, we can calculate a set of critical frequencies of the analog filter by using Eq. (4.158). For example, if the specified passband edge frequency for the digital filter is ω_p, then the passband edge frequency for the analog prototype filter is

$$\Omega_p = \frac{2}{T}\tan\frac{\omega_p T}{2} \qquad (4.160)$$

Similarly for the stopband edge frequency

$$\Omega_r = \frac{2}{T}\tan\frac{\omega_r T}{2} \qquad (4.161)$$

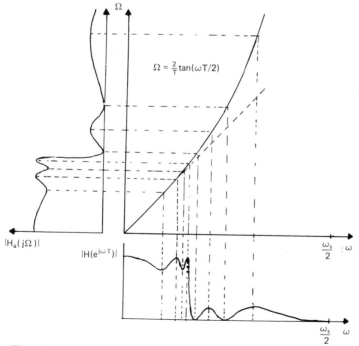

Fig. 4.20. The effect of a bilinear z-transformation on $|H_a(j\Omega)|$ to $|H(e^{j\omega T})|$.

The design steps are outlined below:

1. Given a set of critical frequencies as part of the digital filter specification, calculate the critical frequencies for the analog filter. The analog prototype filter obtained in this way is said to be prewarped.

2. Find the transfer function of the prewarped filter $H_a(s)$ meeting the magnitude response specifications.

3. Substitute the bilinear z-transformation for every s in $H_a(s)$ of step 2 and obtain the desired digital filter transfer function $H(z)$.

The calculation of $H(z)$ from $H_a(s)$ is easier if we apply the bilinear z-transformation to the poles and zeros. Thus if

$$H_a(s) = H_{a0} \frac{\displaystyle\sum_{i=1}^{M} (s - s_{0i})}{\displaystyle\prod_{l=1}^{N} (s - s_{pl})} \tag{4.162}$$

When the bilinear z-transform is used, then by [2],

$$H(z) = H_0(1 + z^{-1})^{N-M} \frac{\displaystyle\sum_{i=1}^{M} (1 - z_i z^{-1})}{\displaystyle\sum_{l=1}^{N} (1 - p_l z^{-1})} \tag{4.163}$$

The poles p_l are given by

$$p_l = \frac{1 + Ts_{pl}/2}{1 - Ts_{pl}/2} \tag{4.164}$$

and the zeros z_i are given by

$$z_i = \frac{1 + Ts_{0i}/2}{1 - Ts_{0i}/2} \tag{4.165}$$

The gain factor H_0 is adjusted so that $H(1) = H_a(0)$.

We can also use the following relationships to simplify the calculation of the linear and quadratic factors in the transfer function:

$$s + \lambda \xrightarrow{s = 2T^{-1}(z-1)(z+1)^{-1}} \frac{(2/T + \lambda)z - (2/T - \lambda)}{z + 1} \tag{4.166}$$

$$(s + a + jb)(s + a - jb) = s^2 + 2as + (a^2 + b^2)$$

$$\xrightarrow{s = 2T^{-1}(z-1)(z+1)^{-1}} \frac{[(2/T+a)^2+b^2]z^2 - 2[(2/T)^2-a^2-b^2]z + [(2/T-a)^2+b^2]}{(z + 1)^2} \tag{4.167}$$

Example 4.6. Design a digital lowpass filter so that the passband ripple does not exceed 2 dB for up to $\omega_p = 7870$ rad s^{-1} and the stopband attenuation is greater than 50 dB for frequencies above $5\omega_p$. The sampling rate is $f_s = 8000$ Hz.

If we choose a Chebyshev filter for the design, the normalized analog filter is exactly the same third-order Chebyshev lowpass filter obtained in Example 4.3. The normalized analog lowpass filter has a transfer function

$$H_a(s) = \frac{0.3269}{(s + 0.3689)(s^2 + 0.3688s + 0.8861)}$$

To illustrate the effect of warping, we find the denormalized transfer function with an edge frequency $\Omega_p = 7870$ rad s^{-1}:

$$H_a\left(\frac{s}{7870}\right) = \frac{0.3269}{(s/7870 + 0.3689)((s/7870)^2 + 0.3688(s/7870) + 0.8861)}$$

Substituting the bilinear z-transformation for every s, we get the transfer function

$$H(z) = \frac{0.0236(z + 1)^3}{(z - 0.6929)(z^2 - 1.1257z + 0.7401)} \tag{4.168}$$

We calculate the magnitude spectrum of the digital filter by evaluating $|H(e^{j\omega T})|$ from Eq. (4.168). A plot of the magnitude spectrum is shown in Fig. 4.21(a). Note

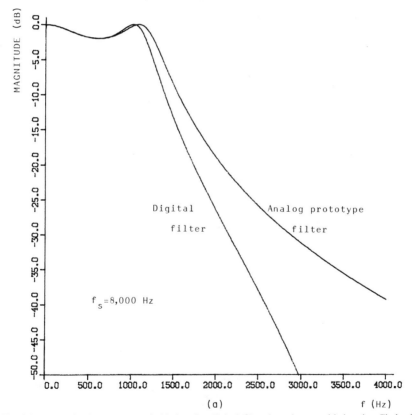

Fig. 4.21. Magnitude response of third-order digital filter based on a third-order Chebyshev analog prototype. (a) Bilinear z-transform with warping; (b) with prewarping correction.

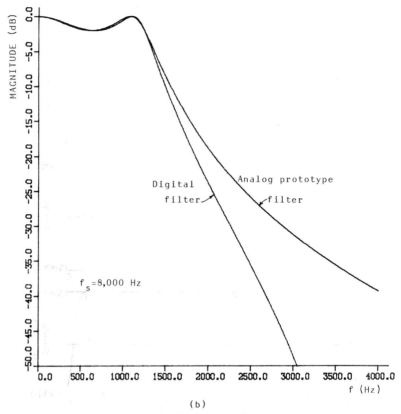

Fig. 4.21. (*Continued*)

that the passband edge frequency of the digital filter is incorrect. Further note the bandlimiting action of the bilinear z-transform, which causes the digital filter to have "better" magnitude response in the stopband than does the analog prototype.

To incorporate the prewarping correction, let us calculate the passband edge frequency for the prewarped analog filter:

$$\Omega_p = \frac{2}{T}\tan \omega_p T = 16{,}000 \tan\frac{7870}{16{,}000} = 8572.8 \quad \text{rad s}^{-1}$$

The transfer function of the prewarped denormalized analog filter is

$$H_a\!\left(\frac{s}{\Omega_p}\right) = \frac{0.3269}{(s/\Omega_p + 0.3689)((s/\Omega_p)^2 + 0.3688(s/\Omega_p) + 0.8861)}$$

The transfer function of the desired digital filter is

$$H(z) = \frac{0.02892(z + 1)^3}{(z - 0.6699)(z^2 - 1.0270z + 0.7278)} \tag{4.169}$$

A plot of the magnitude response corresponding to Eq. (4.169) is shown in Fig. 4.21(b). The passband edge frequency meets the specifications. Note also that at times it is possible to meet the given specifications, especially in the stopband, by a lower-order digital filter than the analog prototype filter indicates.

SPECTRAL TRANSFORMATIONS[†]   IX

In the design of digital filters a prototype lowpass digital filter can be transformed to a lowpass, highpass, bandpass, or bandstop digital filter. The spectral transformations are as follows:

1. *Lowpass to lowpass:*   The transformation is

$$z \rightarrow \frac{z - \beta}{1 - \beta z} \tag{4.170}$$

$$\beta = \frac{\sin[(\omega_p T - \omega_p' T)/2]}{\sin[(\omega_p T + \omega_p' T)/2]} \tag{4.171}$$

where ω_p is the passband edge frequency of the existing prototype lowpass filter, and ω_p' is the specified passband edge frequency.

2. *Lowpass to highpass:*   The transformation is

$$z \rightarrow -\left(\frac{z - \beta}{1 - \beta z}\right) \tag{4.172}$$

$$\beta = -\frac{\cos[(\omega_p T - \omega_p' T)/2]}{\cos[(\omega_p T + \omega_p' T)/2]} \tag{4.173}$$

ω_p' is the passband edge frequency for the specified highpass filter.

3. *Lowpass to bandpass:*   The transformation is

$$z \rightarrow -\left(\frac{z^2 + \beta_1 z + \beta_2}{1 + \beta_1 z + \beta_2}\right) \tag{4.174}$$

$$\beta_2 = \frac{h - 1}{h + 1}, \qquad \beta_1 = \frac{-2\beta h}{h + 1} \tag{4.175}$$

$$\beta = \frac{\cos[(\omega_u T + \omega_l T)/2]}{\cos[(\omega_u T - \omega_l T)/2]} \tag{4.176}$$

$$h = \tan\left(\frac{\omega_p T}{2}\right) \cot\left[\frac{\omega_u T - \omega_l T}{2}\right] \tag{4.177}$$

[†] See references [32–34].

where ω_u and ω_l are the upper and lower bandedge frequencies and ω_p is the passband edge frequency of the prototype lowpass digital filter.

4. *Lowpass to bandstop:* The transformation is

$$z \rightarrow \frac{z^2 + \beta_1 z + \beta_2}{1 + \beta_1 z + \beta_2 z^2} \tag{4.178}$$

$$\beta_2 = \frac{h - 1}{h + 1}, \qquad \beta_1 = \frac{-2\beta}{h + 1} \tag{4.179}$$

$$\beta = \frac{\cos[(\omega_u T + \omega_l T)/2]}{\cos[(\omega_u T - \omega_l T)/2]} \tag{4.180}$$

$$h = \tan\left(\frac{\omega_p T}{2}\right)\tan\left[\frac{\omega_u T - \omega_l T}{2}\right] \tag{4.181}$$

where ω_u and ω_l are the upper and lower edge frequencies and ω_p is the prototype filter's edge frequency.

DIGITAL FILTERS BASED ON CONTINUOUS-TIME LADDER FILTERS

The digital filter design procedures discussed in the previous sections require the computation of pole–zero locations in the s-domain, z-domain, or both. Digital filters can also be designed that capitalize on the wealth of design tables and charts developed for analog lossless ladder networks composed of inductors and capacitors (LC ladder networks). The doubly terminated lossless LC ladder is especially interesting as a model because of the low sensitivity of the frequency response to perturbations in the element values [35, 36]. The basic idea behind the synthesis procedures is to design a doubly terminated analog ladder network that meets the specifications and then digitalize the network by a suitable transformation from the s-domain to the z-domain.

Consider the doubly terminated nth-order lowpass LC ladder prototype in Fig. 4.22(a). An SFG description of the network in the voltage-current (V-I) domain, known as the *leapfrog* [37] SFG structure, is shown in Fig. 4.22(b). Note that the LC elements of the original ladder are represented as integrators with gain constants that bear a one-to-one correspondence to the element values of the original ladder network. Also, the identity of each and every state variable of the original ladder is preserved in the SFG. Indeed, the original motivation for the development of this structure was the simulation of passive LC filters with active networks using operational amplifiers. In Section VIII the bilinear z-transformation, because of its excellent mapping properties, was judged to be the best transformation for digitalizing analog transfer functions, which approximate

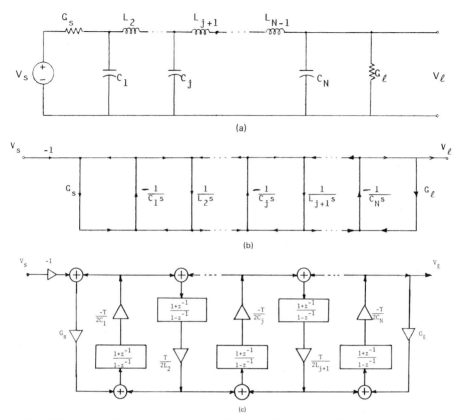

Fig. 4.22. (a) A doubly terminated analog LC ladder, (b) its leapfrog SFG representation, and (c) the substitution of the bilinear z-transformation for integrators.

brick-wall magnitude response specifications. If we attempt to digitalize the leapfrog SFG by substituting the bilinear z-transformation for each integrator [Fig. 4.22(c)], that is,

$$\frac{1}{s} \to \frac{T}{2} I_B(z) \tag{4.182}$$

where

$$I_B(z) = \frac{1 + z^{-1}}{1 - z^{-1}} \tag{4.183}$$

then we encounter the problem that each transmittance in Fig. 4.22(c) that represents an impedance or admittance (immittance) of the capacitors and inductors has no delay in its forward path. Therefore delay-free loops occur in the digital network of Fig. 4.22(c), which makes the digital network variables incomputable. In other words, the digital filter obtained is nonrealizable because of the incomputability problem.

We can circumvent the problem of nonrealizability associated with the leapfrog SFG [8] by using an incident-reflected wave description of transmission line filters modeled after LC filters. Interconnecting elements through the use of "adaptors" so that proper boundary conditions for incident and reflected waves are met and incorporating delays for breaking delay-free loops are described in Chapter 5. The digital filters obtained are known as *wave digital filters* (WDF). These filters faithfully "imitate" the response of classical ladders. They perform especially well in narrowband designs, where the magnitude response deterioration of a cascade design with coefficients quantized to 12-bit accuracy is no better than a WDF with coefficients quantized to 5-bit accuracy [38].

To digitalize the *V-I* domain leap-frog structure, we have to use a transformation with delays in the forward path of its transmittance. In [39, 40] it is proven that meeting the mapping requirements of Section VIII and the requirement in the leapfrog simulation of maintaining a one-to-one correspondence between element values and the coefficients in the digital filter makes delay-free loops inevitable. We will describe two methods of digitalizing the leapfrog SFG that are especially useful for narrowband filter designs. In both methods we use transformations from the *s*-domain to the *z*-domain that relax the mapping requirements.

1 Method 1[†]

The transformation known as the *lossless discrete integrator* (LDI) was originally proposed for digitalizing the leapfrog SFG of doubly terminated LC ladders [9]. The original approach that we describe has an intuitive appeal, even though [39–41] the synthesis procedure was later extended so that LDI digital filters could be designed directly in the *z*-domain without reference to analog filters. Note that LDI digital filters have become the basis of synthesizing switched capacitor filters with large-scale integration (LSI) implementations.

Consider the leapfrog SFG of the prototype low pass LC prototype of Fig. 4.22(b). The substitution of the LDI transformation

$$\frac{1}{s} \to T \frac{z^{-1/2}}{1 - z^{-1}} \tag{4.184}$$

for every continuous-time integrator is shown in Fig. 4.23(a). Since the transmittances in the forward paths have half-delays, the delay-free loop problem is resolved, but we face a nonrealizability problem in a full synchronic system of another sort; namely, the existence of half-delays. Using SFG manipulation or, equivalently, transform immittance scaling of the original network immittances by $z^{-1/2}$, we can move the-half delays so that they appear only at the network terminations, as shown in Fig. 4.23(b). For the network to be realizable,

---

[†] See references [39–41].

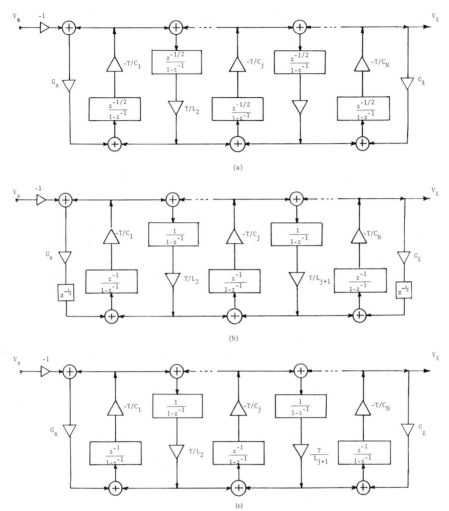

Fig. 4.23. (a) The application of the LDI transformation to the leapfrog SFG, and (b), (c) the various steps in removing half-delays.

the half-delays appearing at the terminations can be eliminated or replaced by full delays of z^{-1}. Eliminating the half-delays, as shown in Fig. 4.23(c), is equivalent to having parasitic elements across the source and load conductances and has little effect on the specified magnitude response, especially for narrowband operation. The digital network of Fig. 4.23(c) is the required digital filter. Note that the LDI transformation in Eq. (4.184) gives absolutely unstable digital filters [42]. Eliminating the half-delays [Fig. 4.23(c)] stabilizes the filter.

The passband response of LDI digital filters is excellent. But since the transformation lacks transmission zeros at the folding frequency (i.e., the $z + 1$

factors) in its transfer function, the stopband and transition band response may suffer at lower sampling rates [39, 43]. Improved response is possible by incorporating these factors in the design.

2   Method 2[†]

Consider the bilinear z-transformation [see Eq. (4.182)]

$$\frac{1}{s} \to \frac{T}{2} z \cdot z^{-1} I_B(z) \tag{4.185}$$

Our objective in digital filter design is to achieve desirable filter characteristics in the steady-state frequency domain. The transformation in Eq. (4.185) has the predictor z. We propose to approximate z on the unit circle of the z-plane by a causal approximant designated by $F_m(z^{-1})$. The simultaneous maximally flat approximation of the predictor z in the steady-state frequency domain is [10]

$$z\Big|_{z=e^{j\omega T}} = \sum_{l=0}^{m} (-1)^l \binom{m+1}{l+1} z^{-l}\Big|_{z=e^{j\omega T}} \triangleq F_m(z^{-1})\Big|_{z=e^{j\omega T}}. \tag{4.186}$$

where $\binom{k}{n}$ is the number of combinations of k objects taken n at a time. Note that m is the order of the approximant. Substituting Eq. (4.186), the causal approximant to predictor z in Eq. (4.185) gives

$$\frac{1}{s} \to \frac{T}{2} z^{-1} F_m(z^{-1}) I_B(z) \triangleq I(z) \tag{4.187}$$

and the above substitution results in a realizable digital filter network. The existence of the delay z^{-1} in the forward path of the transmittances breaks the delay-free loops in Fig. 4.24(a). Higher values of m in the transformation in Eq. (4.187) provide more accurate responses with more complex networks. From an implementation point of view the case $m = 1$ is of special interest. When $m = 1$,

$$F_1(z^{-1}) = 2 - z^{-1} \tag{4.188}$$

and

$$I(z) = \frac{T}{2} z^{-1}(2 - z^{-1})\left(\frac{1 + z^{-1}}{1 - z^{-1}}\right) = T\left(0.5z^{-1} + \frac{1}{1 - z^{-1}}\right)z^{-1} \tag{4.189}$$

The building block corresponding to Eq. (4.189) is shown in Fig. 4.24(b).

In general, the coefficients in methods 1 and 2 are related to the LC element values of the denormalized analog ladder. Using the element numbering scheme

---

[†] See reference [10].

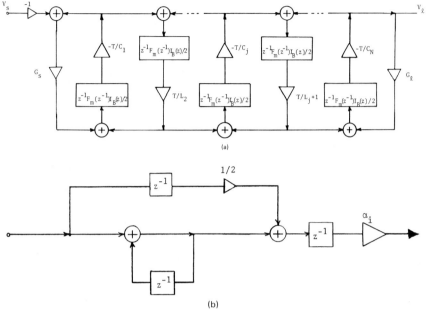

Fig. 4.24. (a) The generalized form of the digital filter of method 2 and (b) the building block representing $z^{-1}F_m(z^{-1})I_B(z)/2$ when $m = 1$.

for the LC elements as shown in Fig. 4.23(a), we get the coefficients of the digital filters

$$\alpha_i = (-1)^i \frac{T}{x_i} \tag{4.190}$$

where $x_i = C_i$ or L_i, depending on the branch of the original network.

Note: If the transformations in Section IX are used, the resulting networks will have delay-free loops. The following transformations are useful for replacing delays in situ without creating delay-free loops:

1. *Lowpass to highpass*

$$z^{-1} \to z^{-1} \tag{4.191}$$

2. *Lowpass to bandpass*

$$z^{-1} \to z^{-1} \frac{z^{-1} - \beta}{1 - \beta z^{-1}} \tag{4.192}$$

where

$$\beta = \frac{\cos(\omega_0 T)}{\cos(\omega_p T/2)} \tag{4.193}$$

and where ω_0 is the desired center frequency and ω_p is the edge frequency of the lowpass digital filter obtained by methods 1 or 2. The transformation in

Eq. (4.192) preserves the bandwidth of the lowpass digital filter. The factor β thus controls the center frequency of the bandpass filter.

Example 4.7. In this example we apply the digitalization technique of the previous two methods to the leapfrog representation of a fifth-order lowpass analog LC filter. The element values of the normalized (-3-dB gain at $\omega_c = 1$) analog filter, with a 0.5-dB equiripple (Chebyshev) characteristic in the passband, are [19]

$$G_s = G_l = 1.0, \quad C_1 = 1.8068 = C_5, \quad L_2 = 1.3025 = L_4, \quad C_3 = 2.6914$$

The sampling rate is $f_s = 9759$ Hz. Narrowband lowpass digital filters are to be designed such that the ratio of the cutoff frequency to the sampling rate is $1:25$.

From the preceding description, the cutoff frequency specification is $f_c = f_s/25 = 390.4$ Hz. The LC element values have to be denormalized by ω_c, where

$$\omega_c = 2\pi f_c = 2425.8 \quad \text{rad s}^{-1}$$

Dividing the element values by ω_c and using Eq. (4.190), we obtain the coefficients for the digital filters:

$$G_s = G_L = 1.0, \quad \alpha_1 = -0.1391 = \alpha_5, \quad \alpha_2 = 0.1930 = \alpha_4, \quad \alpha_3 = -0.09338$$

In Fig. 4.25 the schematic diagrams of the digital filters corresponding to

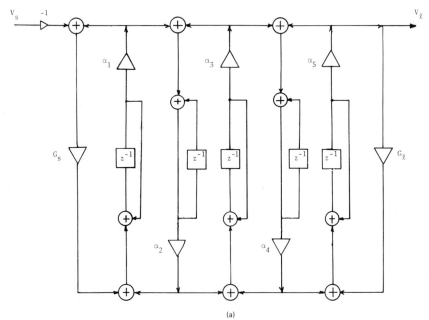

(a)

Fig. 4.25. (a) LDI digital filter and (b) the digital filter of method 2 based on a fifth-order all-pole analog ladder.

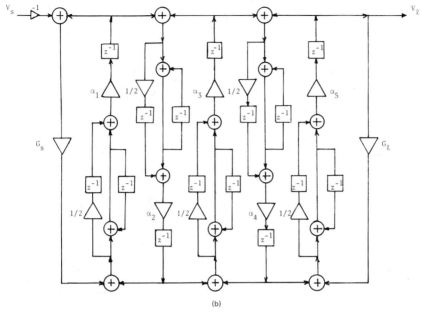

(b)

Fig. 4.25. (*Continued*)

methods 1 and 2, respectively, are shown. The magnitude spectra of the filters are shown in Figs. 4.26 and 4.27. In Fig. 4.28 the magnitude spectrum for the wave digital filter is also shown.

The digital filters were implemented on a Texas Instruments TMS 32010 system. The data word length for the TMS 32010 is 16 bits. Multiplier coefficient accuracy was 13 bits, with the result of each multiplication truncated to 16 bits. The analog-to-digital and digital-to-analog conversions on the system have 12-bit accuracy. The sinusoidal sweep input to the filters was supplied from a tracking sinusoidal sweep generator from the spectrum analyzer. The input level was adjusted just below the threshold of overflow occurrence. The analog prefilter and the smoothing postfilter were removed. Removing the postfilter produces a higher noise floor than would normally be observed.

The magnitude spectra in the figures show good passband responses for the LDI and WDF. The filter of method 2 has a peaky response in the passband, which is due to the approximation error (1.5-dB ripple in the passband). The transition band and stopband responses of all three filters are good, with the filter of method 2 having slightly better response. With the noise floor as an indicator of signal-to-noise performance, the three filters have a noise floor that is down by at least 40 dB, with the filter of method 2 showing the lowest noise floor. For the filters of this example the WDF, when once driven into overflow, exhibited a high-level (7 dB below passband level) limit-cycle oscillation at $f = f_s/4$, and this oscillation could not be eliminated even when the input was set to

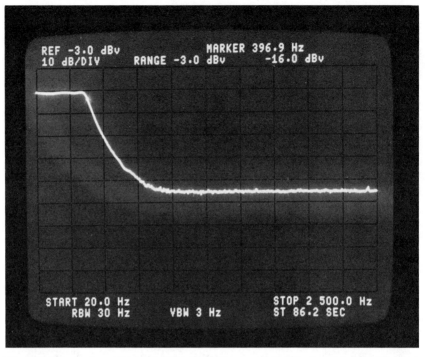

Fig. 4.26. Magnitude spectrum of LDI (method 1) lowpass digital filter based on fifth-order analog lowpass prototype with 0.5-dB ripple in the passband, $f_s/f_c = 25$. Vertical: 10 dB/div. Horizontal: 250 Hz/div.

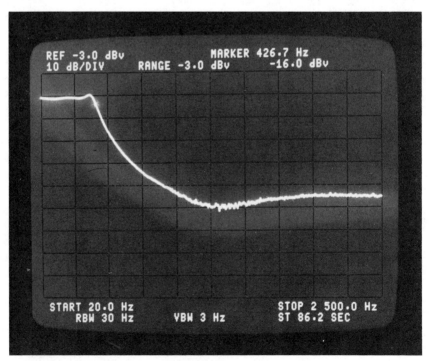

Fig. 4.27. Magnitude spectrum of a lowpass digital filter using a predictor z (method 2), $f_s/f_c = 25$. The same analog prototype as in Fig. 4.26 was used. Vertical: 10 dB/div. Horizontal: 250 Hz/div.

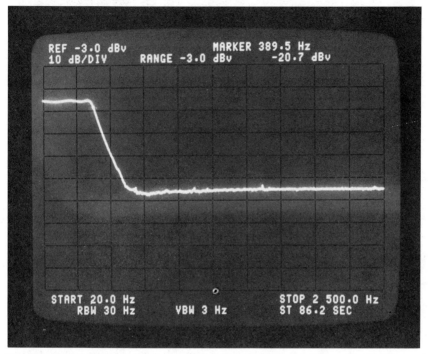

Fig. 4.28. Magnitude spectrum of wave digital filter modeled after the same analog filter as in Fig. 4.26, $f_s/f_c = 25$. Vertical: 10 dB/div. Horizontal: 250 Hz/div.

zero. The oscillation was suppressed by using "front chopping" [45, 46]. The LDI (method 1) and predictor z (method 2) filters recovered rapidly from overflow without degradation of response or limit-cycle oscillations.

In Fig. 4.29 the magnitude spectrum of a very narrowband ($f_s/f_c = 50$) implementation of the digital filter of the predictor z synthesis method is shown. As expected, a rise in the noise floor is observed. The filter meets the passband specifications of 0.5 dB. The magnitude spectra in Figs. 4.26–4.29 show small deviations from the specified cutoff frequency. The small error can be corrected by prewarping correction of the coefficients.

SUMMARY XI

This chapter dealt with IIR digital filter designs based on the transfer functions of continuous time domain (analog) filters as well as digital filters modeled after classical doubly terminated lossless ladders. The design procedures for calculating the transfer functions of some popular normalized analog lowpass filters were presented. The type of filters discussed were the maximally flat magnitude

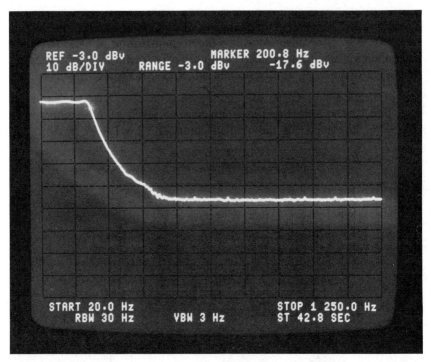

Fig. 4.29. Magnitude spectrum of the digital filter modeled after the same analog filter as in Fig. 4.26 using method 2, $f_s/f_c = 50$. Vertical: 10 dB/div. Horizontal: 125 Hz/div.

response (Butterworth), equiripple magnitude in the passband (Chebyshev), equiripple magnitude in the stopband (inverse Chebyshev), and equiripple magnitude in the passband and the stopband (elliptic). The choice of filter type from Butterworth to elliptic filters is dictated by the design tradeoff between lower complexity of the filter (lower order) and the increasing nonlinearity of the group-delay function. The normalized analog lowpass filter can be denormalized and frequency transformed to generate lowpass, highpass, bandpass, and bandstop prototype filters meeting the design requirements. The prototype analog filters were transformed to digital filters by the impulse-invariant, modified z-transform, and bilinear z-transform approaches. The bilinear z-transform approach was judged the best, as far as its mapping properties are concerned, for the design of digital filters meeting piecewise constant specification requirements. The group-delay nonlinearity can be tackled by cascading the digital filter meeting given magnitude specifications with delay equalizer networks [12, 4]. Lastly, two methods of designing narrowband digital filters, modeled after classical doubly terminated lossless ladders, were presented. These digital filters, capitalize on the low magnitude response sensitivity of the prototype analog ladder to perturbation of its element values, exhibit low sensitivity to coefficient quantization and low noise.

APPENDIX: IIR DIGITAL FILTER CAD PROGRAMS

This appendix summarizes some readily available computer programs for designing IIR digital filters.

IIR Filter Design Programs Described in the Open Literature   A

1. Listings of five IIR digital filter design programs are given in [40]. A tape is available from IEEE.

2. Listings of IIR digital filter design programs are available in [4, 24, 14].

IIR Filter Design Programs Available in Commercial Packages   B

1. FILSYN is a filter design package that has evolved through many years. The package, besides IIR and FIR digital filter design and optimization features, also has design and optimization routines for passive, active, switched capacitor, and microwave filters. Available from DGS Associates, 1353 Sarita Way, Santa Clara, California 95051.

2. DIG-FIL- is a program package used for designing digital filters in cascade form. The Peled–Liu (See Chapter 5) heuristic optimization technique is used for scaling a signal between filter sections to achieve the best signal to round off noise ratio. The program was written by the author, utilizing the techniques presented in this chapter. Versions of the program for Commodore's Amiga and IBM PC are available.

3. The ILS package from STI is an extensive digital signal processing package that, in addition to digital filter design capabilities, has routines for parameter estimation, cepstral analysis, speech processing (analysis, synthesis, pitch extracting, and format tracking), and pattern analysis/recognition. The package is written in ANSI FORTRAN, and versions are available for different computers. The package is available from STI, 5951 Encina Road, Goleta, California 93117.

4. DFDP is a digital filter design package for the TI and IBM PCs and is available from ASPI. The package is used for designing standard IIR digital filters using the bilinear z-transform, as well as for FIR digital filters optimized by the McClellan-Parks procedure. The package is interactive and makes extensive use of TI/IBM PC color graphics capabilities. The package can produce assembly language code for the TMS 32010 processor and is available from ASPI, 770 Spring St., N.W., Atlanta, Georgia 30308.

REFERENCES

1. J. F. Kaiser, Digital filters, in *System Analysis by Digital Computer*, edited by F. F. Kuo and J. F. Kaiser, Wiley, New York, 1966.
2. L. B. Jackson, *Digital Filters and Signal Processing*, Kluwer Academic, Boston, 1986.
3. L. R. Rabiner and B. Gold, *Theory and Applications of Digital Signal Processing*, Prentice-Hall, Englewoods Cliffs, N.J., 1976.

4. A. Antoniou, *Digital Filters: Analysis and Design*, McGraw-Hill, New York, 1979.
5. C. T. Mullis and R. A. Roberts, Synthesis of minimum roundoff noise fixed point digital filters, *IEEE Trans. Circuits Systems* **CAS-23**, 551–562 (September 1976).
6. C. W. Barnes and S. Leung, The normal lattice—a casade digital filter structure, *IEEE Trans. Circuits Systems* **CAS-29**, 393–400 (June 1982).
7. A. H. Gray and J. D. Markel, Digital lattice and ladder filter synthesis, *IEEE Trans. Audio Electroacoust.* **AU-21**, 491–500 (December 1973).
8. A. Fettweis, Digital filter structures related to classical filter networks, *Arch. Elek Ubertrangung* **25**, 78–89 (1971).
9. L. T. Bruton, Low sensitivity digital ladder filters, *IEEE Trans. Circuits Systems* **CAS-22**, 168–176 (March 1975).
10. N. A. Pashtoon and P. M. Chirlian, *New Transformational Digital Filters* (publication pending).
11. E. I. Jury, *Theory and Application of the z-Transform Method*, Wiley, New York, 1964.
12. C. T. Chen, *One Dimensional Digital Signal Processing*, Dekker, New York, 1979.
13. A. V. Oppenheim and R. W. Schafer, *Digital Signal Processing*, Prentice-Hall, Englewood Cliffs, N.J., 1975.
14. A. Durling and D. Childers, *Digital Filtering and Signal Processing*, West, St. Paul, Minn., 1975.
15. K. Steiglitz, Computer-aided design of recursive digital filters, *IEEE Trans. Audio Electrocoust.* **AU-18**, 123–129 (June 1970).
16. A. Peled and B. Liu, *Digital Signal Processing*, Wiley, New York, 1976.
17. A. G. Deczky, Equiripple and minimax (Chebyshev) approximations for recursive digital filters, *IEEE Trans. Acoust., Speech Signal Process.* **ASSP-22**, 98–111 (1974).
18. L. Weinberg, *Network Analysis and Synthesis*, McGraw-Hill, New Work, 1962.
19. A. I. Zverev, *Handbook of Filter Synthesis*, Wiley, New York, 1967.
20. H. Y.-F. Lam, *Analog and Digital Filters: Design and Realization*, Prentice-Hall, Englewood Cliffs, N.J., 1979.
21. M. E. Valkenberg, *Analog Filter Design*, Holt, Rinehart and Winston, New York, 1982.
22. R. W. Daniels, *Approximation Methods for Electronic Filter Design*, McGraw-Hill, New York, 1974.
23. A. J. Grossman, Synthesis of Tchebycheff parameter symmetrical filters, *Proc. IRE* **45**, 454–473 (April 1957).
24. M. T. Jung, *Methods of Discrete Signal and System Analysis*, McGraw-Hill, New York, 1982.
25. B. Gold and C. M. Rader, *Digital Processing of Signals*, McGraw-Hill, New York, 1969.
26. M. Bellanger, *Digital Processing of Signals, Theory, and Practice*, Wiley, New York, 1984.
27. F. Bowman, *Introduction to Elliptic Functions with Application*, Dover, New York, 1961.
28. E. Christian and E. Eisenman, *Filter Design Tables and Graph*, Transmission Networks Int'l., Raleigh, N.C., 1977.
29. N. Balabanian, *Network Synthesis*, Prentice-Hall Englewood Cliffs, N.J., 1958.
30. G. C. Temes and J. W. LaPatra, *Introduction to Circuit Synthesis and Design*, McGraw-Hill, New York, 1977.
31. C. S. Lindquist, *Active Network Design with Signal Filtering Applications*, Steward, Long Beach, Calif., 1977.
32. A. G. Constantanides, Spectral Transformations for Digital Filters, *Proc. IEE* **117**, (August 1970).
33. R. E. Bogner and A. G. Constantanides, *Introduction to Digital Filtering*, Wiley, New York, 1975.
34. V. Cappellini, A. G. Constantanides, and P. Emiliani, *Digital Filters and Their Applications*, Academic Press, London, 1978.
35. H. J. Orchard, Inductorless filters, *Electron. Letters* **2**, 224–245 (June 1966).
36. G. C. Temes and H. J. Orchard, First order sensitivity and worst case analysis of doubly terminated reactance two-ports, *IEEE Trans. Circuits Systems* **CT-20**, 567–571 (September 1973).
37. F. E. J. Girling and E. F. Good, Active filters-12. The leap-frog or active-ladder synthesis, *Wireless World* **76**, 341–345 (July 1970).

38. R. E. Crochiere, Digital filter structures and coefficient sensitivity, *IEEE Trans. Audio Electroacoust.* **AU-20,** 240–246 (October 1972).
39. D. A. Vaughn-Pope, Low sensitivity digital ladder filters, Ph.D. Thesis, Univ. of Calgary, May 1976.
40. D. A. Vaughn-Pope and L. T. Bruton, Transfer function synthesis using generalized doubly terminated two-port networks, *IEEE Trans. Circuits Systems* **CAS-24,** 79–88 (February 1977).
41. E. S. K. Liu, L. E. Turner, and L. T. Bruton, Exact design of LDI and LDD ladder filters, *IEEE Circuits Systems* **CAS-31,** 369–381 (April 1984).
42. L. T. Bruton and D. A. Vaughn-Pope, Synthesis of digital ladder filters from LC filters, *IEEE Trans. Circuits Systems* **CAS-23,** 395–402 (June 1976).
43. J. L. Levy and T. N. Trick, Roundoff noise properties of some low sensitivity recursive digital filters, *Proc. IEEE ISCBP,* 1978, pp. 121.
44. A. Fettweis and K. Meekrotter, Suppression of parasitic oscillations in wave digital filters, *IEEE Trans. Circuits Systems* **CAS-22,** 239–246 (March 1975).
45. A. Fettweis, Wave digital filters: Theory and practice, *Proc. IEEE* 270–327 (February 1986).

Chapter **5**

Low-Noise and
Low-Sensitivity Digital Filters

P. P. VAIDYANATHAN
Department of Electrical Engineering
California Institute of Technology
Pasadena, California 91125

INTRODUCTION   **I**

When one implements a digital filter transfer function using a digital machine, it invariably involves quantization of signals and coefficients in the system. As a result, the overall input-output behavior is not ideal. Two basic types of quantization effects should be distinguished in any implementation [1, 2]. The first is due to *parameter* quantization, where the term "parameter" refers to the fixed digital-filter coefficients (or multipliers). The result of parameter quantization is that the actual implemented transfer function $H_q(z)$ is different from $H(z)$. Once the quantization has been done, this error is a fixed, well-determined quantity.

The second type of quantization is due to signal rounding; the internal signals in a digital filter, which take part in the filtering process, are invariably subject to quantization, causing an error in the computed output. Such quantization is a nonlinear phenomenon and can be further subdivided into two types of effects, called limit-cycle oscillations [3] and roundoff noise. Limit-cycle oscillations, which contribute to undesirable periodic components at the filter output, are due to the fact that quantization is a nonlinear operation (when such nonlinearities exist in feedback paths, they can lead to oscillations). Roundoff noise, on the other hand, affects the filter output in the form of a random disturbance, and can be analyzed by suitable noise modeling and by the use of linear system theory.

Given a digital filter transfer function $H(z)$, there exist an infinite number of structures[†] to implement it. Of these, some structures are less sensitive to

---

[†] A *structure* is any interconnection of digital multipliers, delays, and adders.

HANDBOOK OF DIGITAL SIGNAL PROCESSING

coefficient quantization than others, and some structures generate less roundoff noise than others. Moreover, certain structures can be designed to be independent of limit cycles. A "low-sensitivity" structure is one for which the transfer function $H_q(z)$ after coefficient quantization does not differ substantially from the ideal $H(z)$. A *low-noise* structure is one for which the variance of the noise *at the filter output* is "low" in comparison to the signal level.

The simplest form of digital filter structures is the direct form structure [4, 5] shown in Fig. 5.1. The transfer function implemented by Fig. 5.1 is

$$H(z) = \frac{q_0 + q_1 z^{-1} + \cdots + q_N z^{-N}}{1 + p_1 z^{-1} + \cdots + p_N z^{-N}} = \frac{Q(z)}{P(z)}$$

For large N, the locations of the poles and zeros of $H(z)$ [which are roots of the polynomials $P(z)$ and $Q(z)$] are very sensitive [4–6] with respect to the coefficients p_n and q_n. In addition, the direct form structure generates large roundoff noise for transfer functions having sharp frequency response behaviors and often supports limit cycles. In view of these considerations, the direct-form structure is not employed for $N > 2$. Several other structures have much better behavior in a quantized environment, and the purpose of this chapter is to present the most important of these structures.

Section II is a brief introduction to binary arithmetic and quantization of binary sequences, along with statistical properties. Section III is an introduction to noise propagation in digital filters. Scaling and dynamic range considerations are introduced in Section IV, and Section V deals with signal-to-noise ratio (SNR) performance in simple structures. A class of low-noise second-order structures based on error-spectrum shaping (ESS) is described in Section VI. Section VII generalizes the concept of SNR to arbitrary structures. Sections VIII and IX deal with cascade-form implementations and noise-reduction strategies in

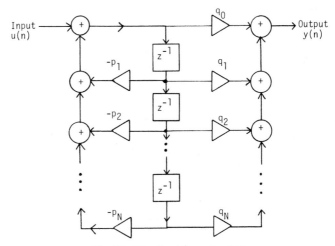

Fig. 5.1. The direct-form structure.

such implementations. State-space structures for low-noise design are considered in Section X; closed-form expressions for certain minimum-noise state-space structures are included. Sections XI and XII deal with low-sensitivity digital filter realizations, with emphasis on second-order sections, whereas Section XIII introduces wave digital filters (WDFs), which are well known for low sensitivity (and often low noise). Sections XIV–XVI deal with various low-sensitivity digital filter z-domain design procedures based on passivity concepts. Section XVII briefly summarizes digital all-pass structures, which form a crucial building block in many low-sensitivity realizations. Section XVIII deals with orthogonal digital filters. Sections XIX and XX present results concerning low-sensitivity finite impulse response (FIR) design. The design of limit-cycle free digital filters is described in Section XXI.

A Word on Notation. To distinguish input sequences from unit-step sequences, we use $u(n)$ for the input and $1(n)$ for the unit step. The notation $\delta(n)$ stands for the unit-pulse (or "impulse") function. Boldface letters denote matrices and vectors. Superscript T stands for matrix transpose; tilde is defined to be such that $\tilde{\mathbf{A}}(z) = \mathbf{A}^T(z^{-1})$. A dagger ($\dagger$) indicates transposition followed by complex conjugation. Thus, on the unit circle of the z-plane, $\tilde{}$ and $\dagger$ imply the same operation. The symbols $\mathbf{I}$ and $\mathbf{0}$ stand for the identity matrix and the null matrix (or null vector), respectively. A real symmetric matrix $\mathbf{P}$ is said to be positive definite if the scalar $\mathbf{y}^\dagger \mathbf{P} \mathbf{y}$ is positive for all $\mathbf{y} \neq \mathbf{0}$. We call $\mathbf{P}$ positive semidefinite (nonnegative definite) if $\mathbf{y}^\dagger \mathbf{P} \mathbf{y}$ is nonnegative for all $\mathbf{y} \neq \mathbf{0}$. We abbreviate the positive definite property as $\mathbf{P} > \mathbf{0}$, and the positive semidefinite property as $\mathbf{P} \geq \mathbf{0}$.

BINARY NUMBERS—REPRESENTATION AND QUANTIZATION II

We briefly summarize various binary number systems used in digital filtering and outline the statistical characterization of quantization properties of different number systems. We then establish the noise propagation properties in a digital filter implementation.

Binary Number Systems A

A binary representation of a number [4, 5, 7, 8] is a means of writing the number in terms of powers of 2. For example, the decimal number 6.375 can be represented as 110.011, an abbreviation for $2^2 + 2^1 + 0 \cdot 2^0 + 0 \cdot 2^{-1} + 2^{-2} + 2^{-3}$. Thus, a binary number in this form comes with a "binary point." The portion to the left represents an integer (e.g., $110 = 6$), and the part to the right (0.011) represents fractions less than unity.

In fixed-point binary arithmetic, the binary point is held fixed. The addition of two fixed-point numbers does not depend on the location of the binary point. When we multiply two fixed-point numbers, it is convenient to assume both to be integers or both to be fractions, because the product is also accordingly an integer or fraction. When two fixed-point integers with b bit representations are multiplied, the result is a $2b$-bit integer; hence, if we use integer arithmetic in feedback loops, the required number of bits accumulates with every cycle of operation and produces overflow. Accordingly, for digital filtering applications, it is most convenient to consider all arithmetic to be fixed-point fraction arithmetic. In such arithmetic, if two b-bit numbers are multiplied, we still have a $2b$-bit result, but we can reduce it to a b-bit number simply by rounding or truncating the least significant b bits. For example, $(0.101) \times (0.110) = (0.011110) \simeq (0.100)$, which in decimal language translates to $\frac{5}{8} \times \frac{6}{8} = \frac{15}{32} \simeq \frac{1}{2}$. This kind of rounding operation after a multiplication is the root cause of "roundoff error" in digital filter implementation. A substantial part of this chapter is dedicated to methods that minimize the *effect* of such error on the filtered output signal. Notice, in this context, that if two fixed-point b-bit binary fractions are *added*, then the result usually has b bits in the fractional part and a possible nonzero bit to the left of the binary point. This extra nonzero bit is called the overflow bit. Under certain conditions, this extra bit can be discarded (i.e., simply thrown away) without affecting the ultimate filter output. This point will be elaborated on in Section IV. In any case, unlike multiplication,[†] adding two fixed-point numbers does not produce roundoff error.

In contrast to fixed-point arithmetic, a digital filter can also be implemented in floating-point arithmetic. Here, each number x is represented as $x = 2^c \cdot M$, where M is the binary b-bit mantissa and is always in the range $\frac{1}{2} \le M < 1$. The exponent or characteristic c is an integer (of either sign). Two floating-point numbers $x_1 = 2^{c_1} \cdot M_1$ and $x_2 = 2^{c_2} \cdot M_2$ are multiplied as follows: $x = x_1 x_2 = 2^{c_1 + c_2} M_1 M_2$. The new mantissa $M_1 M_2$ is then renormalized to be in the range $\frac{1}{2} \le M_1 M_2 < 1$, and the exponent $c_1 + c_2$ is adjusted accordingly. Adding two floating-point numbers is more involved, because the mantissa of the smaller number must be right-shifted until its characteristic matches that of the larger number. From this discussion it is clear that in floating-point arithmetic roundoff error is generated during addition and multiplication. Moreover, unlike fixed-point arithmetic, which is inherently simple to implement, floating-point operations are more involved and usually require longer execution times [7]. However, a major advantage of floating-point arithmetic is that it covers a much wider signal dynamic range. For example, if we permit 8 bits for the characteristic c, then the dynamic range (i.e., the range of representable numbers) is approximately $2^{-128} < x < 2^{127}$ (the exact range actually depends on the convention for representing negative numbers, see Section II.B). In view of

---

† Remember that roundoff errors are small, noiselike errors, whereas overflow errors are huge and cause severe distortion of the output signal.

TABLE I
Features of Various Arithmetic Schemes

Features	Fixed-point fractions	Fixed-point integers	Floating-point
Overflow under multiplication	Not possible	Possible	Possible but unlikely
Overflow under addition	Possible[a] but not harmful in most occasions	Possible	Possible but unlikely
Roundoff noise due to addition	Does not occur	Does not occur	Occurs
Roundoff noise due to multiplication	Occurs	Does not occur	Occurs
Dynamic range available	Moderate	Moderate	Enormous
Ease of implementation	Simple	Simple	Involved; more hardware and/or execution time required

[a] To be elaborated in Section IV, which deals with scaling and dynamic range.

this, signal overflow during floating-point implementation of a digital filter is far less likely, compared to a fixed-point implementation.

Table I summarizes the main features of the three types of number representations. Each type has its own advantages and disadvantages. Note that integer arithmetic is entirely free from roundoff noise, but is very likely to generate overflow errors; it also offers very limited dynamic range. In view of its simplicity and freedom from overflow (during multiplication), the fixed-point fraction representation has been the most frequently used scheme. Therefore, in this chapter, we primarily deal with this representation.

Oppenheim [9] has advanced an arithmetic system called the block floating-point system, which sometimes forms an excellent compromise between fixed-point and floating-point systems. We do not deal with this system here, even though it offers certain attractions for certain implementations.

Handling Negative Numbers   B

In Section II.A we gave an overall view of the three kinds of number representations, but we did not carefully distinguish between negative and positive numbers. Now that we have decided to narrow down most of our discussions to the fixed-point fraction representations, we make use of this representation to state and clarify our conventions for negative numbers.

When we say "b-bit fixed-point fraction" we mean a binary number as shown in Fig. 5.2. There are b bits after the decimal point, and there is a separate bit s, called the sign bit. The quantities a_k and s can take on only the values 0 and 1. If $s = 0$, then $x = \sum_{k=1}^{b} a_k 2^{-k}$ (a nonnegative quantity); if $s = 1$, $x < 0$ and its precise value depends on the "convention." Three conventions are common: the sign magnitude, 2's complement, and 1's complement. In the sign-magnitude representation, $\sum_{k=1}^{b} a_k 2^{-k}$ always represents the magnitude. Thus, addition and multiplication are performed on the magnitudes and the signs are kept track of separately.

The 2's complement representation of a positive number is the same as that of the sign-magnitude representation (e.g., $\frac{1}{4} = 0.01$). The representation of a negative number results from computing it mod 2 (e.g., $-\frac{1}{4} = 10.00 - 0.01 = 1.11$). In 2's complement representation the *value* of a number x is always given by

$$x = -s \cdot 2^0 + \sum_{k=1}^{b} a_k 2^{-k} = -s \cdot 2^1 + s \cdot 2^0 + \sum_{k=1}^{b} a_k 2^{-k} \tag{5.1}$$

In other words, s is looked upon as a *weight* for -1. Thus the *magnitude* of a negative number is

$$|x| = 1 - \sum_{k=1}^{b} a_k 2^{-k} = 2 - \left[s + \sum_{k=1}^{b} a_k 2^{-k} \right] \tag{5.2}$$

The name "2's complement" comes from Eq. (5.2). For example, the magnitude of 1.101 is $2 - [1 + \frac{5}{8}] = \frac{3}{8}$, so 1.101 represents $-\frac{3}{8}$. Given a 2's complement number x as in Eq. (5.1), we have

$$-x = s \cdot 2^0 - \sum_{k=1}^{b} a_k 2^{-k} \tag{5.3}$$

Since $1 = \sum_{k=1}^{b} 2^{-k} + 2^{-b}$, (5.3) is equivalent to

$$-x = -(1 - s)2^0 + \sum_{k=1}^{b} (1 - a_k)2^{-k} + 2^{-b} \tag{5.4}$$

By comparing Eq. (5.1) and Eq. (5.4), we see that we can negate (i.e., complement) a 2's complement number simply by replacing each 1 with a 0 (and each 0 with a 1), including the sign bit s, and then adding the least significant bit 2^{-b}. For example, if $x = 1.101$, then $-x = 0.011$ (here $b = 3$) whereas if $y = 0.0101$ then $-y = 1.1011$ (here $b = 4$). Rules for addition and multiplication are simple and can be found in [7, 8]. Clearly multiplication cannot cause overflow, and the

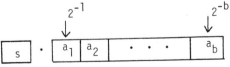

Fig. 5.2. Fixed-point b-bit fraction representation.

result is always correct.[†] On the other hand, if x_1 and x_2 have the same sign, it is possible to have an overflow error due to addition. We emphasize that the rules for basic arithmetic operations of negation (complementation), addition, and multiplication of 2's complement fractions are independent of the signs of the operands, and this is a significant advantage over other representations. (Subtraction is not a "basic" operation because it can be performed by preceding addition with a 2's complement negation.)

The 1's complement representation of a positive number is the same as that of the sign-magnitude representation (e.g., $\frac{1}{4} = 0.01$). The representation of a negative number results from computing it mod $(2 - 2^{-b})$ (e.g., for $b = 2$, $-\frac{1}{4} = 1.11 - 0.01 = 1.10$. In 1's complement representation, the value of a number x is given by

$$x = -s(1 - 2^{-b}) + \sum_{k=1}^{b} a_k 2^{-k} \qquad (5.5)$$

In other words,

$$x = s + \sum_{k=1}^{b} a_k 2^{-k} - 2s + 2^{-b} \cdot s \qquad (5.6)$$

Thus 1.010 stands for $(\frac{10}{8} - 2 + 2^{-3}) = (10 - 15)/8 = -\frac{5}{8}$, whereas the representation of $-\frac{13}{16}$ is obtained by noting that $-\frac{13}{16} = (\frac{18}{16} - \frac{32}{16} + \frac{1}{16}) = (\frac{18}{16} - 2 + 2^{-4})$; hence the representation is 1.0010. It is easy to verify that a 1's complement number can be "complemented" (i.e., negated) simply by complementing each bit. Thus -1.0110 is 0.1001, and so on. Detailed rules for addition and multiplication can be found in several standard texts [7, 8] and are omitted here, because they are not needed to understand the rest of the chapter. Note, however, that 2's complement arithmetic is easy to implement (for adding and multiplying numbers) and elegantly handles negative numbers. Thus it is unnecessary to keep track of signs of operands and results. (For this reason, 2's complement arithmetic has been found most suitable for serial arithmetic also [10].)

Accordingly, our primary emphasis is on 2's complement fixed-point fraction arithmetic. Note that the range of numbers represented is $-1 \le x \le 1 - 2^{-b}$ for 2's complement representation, and $-(1 - 2^{-b}) \le x \le 1 - 2^{-b}$ for 1's complement and sign-magnitude representations. Table II gives a quick review of the three representations, and Table III summarizes the main features. We abbreviate the dynamic range spanned by the 1's complement and sign-magnitude representations by $(-1, 1)$, and the corresponding range for 2's complement by $[-1, 1)$, to emphasize that -1 is represented in the 2's complement case. When the number representation is not explicitly specified, we denote the dynamic range by $(-1, 1)$ for simplicity.

[†] Multiplication of two numbers x_1 and x_2 could produce a nonzero bit to the left of s (i.e., corresponding to the 2^1 location), but this "physical overflow" does not mean that the product is incorrect. The product is always correct, once the overflow is ignored. Thus 2^1 can be treated as "zero;" hence, 2's complement arithmetic is essentially modulo 2 arithmetic [4, 5].

TABLE II

The Three Numbering Systems, Demonstrated for 3-Bit Binary Fractions (i.e., $b = 3$)

Binary number	Interpretation		
	Sign and magnitude	2's complement	1's complement
$0_\Delta 111$	7/8	7/8	7/8
$0_\Delta 110$	6/8	6/8	6/8
$0_\Delta 101$	5/8	5/8	5/8
$0_\Delta 100$	4/8	4/8	4/8
$0_\Delta 011$	3/8	3/8	3/8
$0_\Delta 010$	2/8	2/8	2/8
$0_\Delta 001$	1/8	1/8	1/8
$0_\Delta 000$	0	0	0
$1_\Delta 000$	-0	-1	$-7/8$
$1_\Delta 001$	$-1/8$	$-7/8$	$-6/8$
$1_\Delta 010$	$-2/8$	$-6/8$	$-5/8$
$1_\Delta 011$	$-3/8$	$-5/8$	$-4/8$
$1_\Delta 100$	$-4/8$	$-4/8$	$-3/8$
$1_\Delta 101$	$-5/8$	$-3/8$	$-2/8$
$1_\Delta 110$	$-6/8$	$-2/8$	$-1/8$
$1_\Delta 111$	$-7/8$	$-1/8$	-1

TABLE III

Main Features of the Three Representation

Features	Sign and magnitude	2's complement	1's complement
Range	$-(1 - 2^{-b}) \le x$ $\le (1 - 2^{-b})$	$-1 \le x$ $\le (1 - 2^{-b})$	$-(1 - 2^{-b}) \le x$ $\le (1 - 2^{-b})$
Representation of zero	0.000 and 1.000	0.000	0.000 and 1.111
Arithmetic rules	Signs must be kept track of, separately	Simple; negative numbers elegantly handled	Simple, but "end around carry" should be carefully handled [8]
Suitability for serial arithmetic [10]	Not so good	Excellent	Good

C Quantization of Binary Numbers

In digital implementations it is often necessary to quantize a binary fixed-point b_1-bit number to a b-bit number, as shown in Fig. 5.3. The quantization error is denoted by

$$e = Q[x] - x \tag{5.7}$$

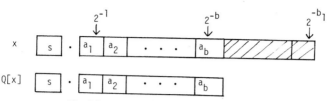

Fig. 5.3. Quantizing a fixed-point fraction.

The properties of e and its statistical behavior (when x is a random variable belonging to a sequence) depend, in general, on the choice of representation we use for negative numbers. Regardless of the representation of negative numbers, the quantization itself could be one of several types, such as truncation, magnitude truncation, rounding, and so on. This section carefully distinguishes these cases and outlines the quantization properties for each case.

Truncation Arithmetic   1

Truncation is a process in which the least significant $b_1 - b$ bits (shown shaded in Fig. 5.3) are simply dropped, regardless of the sign of the number and the convention for representing negative numbers. If $x > 0$, then clearly $-(2^{-b} - 2^{-b_1}) \le e \le 0$, where e is defined in Eq. (5.7). If $x < 0$, we can then verify that e depends upon the representation as follows:

a. sign-magnitude: $0 \le e \le 2^{-b} - 2^{-b_1}$ and $|Q[x]| \le |x|$;
b. 1's complement: $0 \le e \le 2^{-b} - 2^{-b_1}$ and $|Q[x]| \le |x|$;
c. 2's complement: $-(2^{-b} - 2^{-b_1}) \le e \le 0$ and $|Q[x]| \ge |x|$.

Certain important features now emerge. First, for both sign-magnitude and 1's complement representations, the sign of e is the opposite of the sign of x. Thus, e is *correlated* with x. In contrast, the error e is always nonpositive for the 2's complement case, regardless of the sign of x. Second, for both sign-magnitude and 1's complement representations, truncation decreases the magnitude, whereas for 2's complement numbers, $|Q(x)| \ge |x|$ for negative x. Thus, truncation does not imply "magnitude truncation" for 2's complement negative numbers. This fact has far-reaching consequences when we attempt to suppress limit-cycle oscillations in digital filters, based on passivity concepts. We elaborate on this fact in Section XXI.

If we think of x as a uniformly distributed random variable, and if b and $b_1 - b$ are sufficiently "large," then the quantization error e can be modeled as a random variable with uniform probability density. Based on the above discussion of the behavior of e, we can draw the probability density function $p(e)$ as shown in Fig. 5.4(a),(b) for the three subcases of *truncation* arithmetic. Strictly speaking, e is a discrete variable, and the continuous plots of Fig. 5.4 hold only when

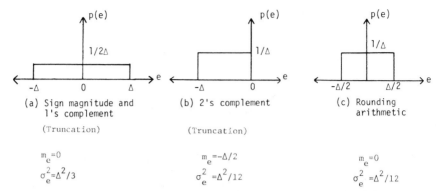

Fig. 5.4. Probability density functions for quantization errors; $\Delta = 2^{-b}$.

$b_1 - b$ is large. In practice, this is generally true, and we rely on Fig. 5.4 for additional guidelines on noise analysis. Note that Δ in Fig. 5.4 represents $2^{-b} - 2^{-b_1}$, but with $b_1 - b$ large we can take

$$\Delta = 2^{-b} \tag{5.8}$$

for all practical purposes. Figure 5.4 also shows the statistical mean m_e and variance σ_e^2 of the roundoff error e. Note that 2's complement truncation leads to lower noise variance (by a factor of 4) compared to the other two representations. As a tradeoff, 2's complement truncation gives rise to a nonzero mean value, which causes a mean value in the output roundoff noise of the digital filter.

2 Magnitude-Truncation Arithmetic

Magnitude-truncation arithmetic is defined to be any type of arithmetic for which $|Q(x)| \leq |x|$. Thus, conventional truncation arithmetic is also magnitude-truncation arithmetic for sign-magnitude and 1's complement representations. For 2's complement representations, we can convert truncation arithmetic to magnitude truncation simply by adding 2^{-b} to $Q[x]$ whenever $x < 0$ (i.e., $s = 1$) and $e \neq 0$. The price we pay is that the resultant error $e = Q[x] + s \cdot 2^{-b}$ has a sign correlated with x.

3 Rounding Arithmetic

Let x be as in Fig. 5.3. In rounding arithmetic we take $Q[x]$ to be the nearest b-bit number; that is,

$$-\frac{\Delta}{2} \leq e \leq \frac{\Delta}{2} \tag{5.9}$$

where Δ is as in Eq. (5.8) and e is as in Eq. (5.7). Thus, regardless of the

TABLE IV
Number Systems and Quantization Effects

Features	Truncation arithmetic		Rounding arithmetic (features are independent of number representation)
	1's complement and sign magnitude	2's complement	
Sign of error	Opposite the sign of x	Uncorrelated with x; always nonpositive	Uncorrelated with x
Mean of error, m_e	0	$-\Delta/2$	0
Variance of error, σ_e^2	$\Delta^2/3$	$\Delta^2/12$	$\Delta^2/12$
$\lvert Q(x)\rvert$	$\leq \lvert x\rvert$	$\leq \lvert x\rvert, x > 0$ $\geq \lvert x\rvert, x < 0$	Could be $\leq$ or $\geq \lvert x\rvert$, uncorrelated with the sign of x
Same as magnitude truncation?	Yes	No	No
Ease of implementation	Easy	Easy	Not particularly easy

$e \triangleq Q[x] - x$ where $Q[x] = $ quantized number; $\Delta \simeq 2^{-b}$.

representation of negative numbers (i.e., sign magnitude or 1's or 2's complement), the sign of e is uncorrelated with that of x, and Fig. 5.4(c) can be used to represent the probability density $p(e)$. Therefore, rounding arithmetic has several desirable features: the variance is only $\Delta^2/12$, and m_e is 0 regardless of how negative numbers are represented; in addition, the sign of e is independent of the sign of x. However, the magnitude $\lvert Q(x)\rvert$ is not restricted to be less than $\lvert(x)\rvert$, and it might create problems when we attempt to suppress limit cycles in digital filters.

A summary of quantization effects in fixed-point fraction representations appears in Table IV. Be aware that even though there exist several quantization schemes (rounding, truncation, and so on), the quantization noise is generally referred to as *roundoff* noise. This does not necessarily mean that roundoff quantization is being employed. For simplicity we adopt this loose language.

GENERATION AND PROPAGATION OF ROUNDOFF NOISE IN DIGITAL FILTERS   III

Consider the first-order infinite impulse response (IIR) digital filter structure[†] of Fig. 5.5, which corresponds to the all-pole transfer function

$$H(z) = (1 - \alpha z^{-1})^{-1} \tag{5.10}$$

[†] In this chapter $u(n)$ and $U(e^{j\omega})$ denote the input sequence and its transform. The symbol $x_k(n)$ will be reserved for state variables.

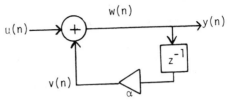

Fig. 5.5. A first-order digital filter.

where $-1 < \alpha < 1$ for stability. This structure involves one multiplier, α, one two-input adder, and a delay (storage register). Assume that $u(n)$ and $y(n)$ are b-bit fixed-point fractions as in Fig. 5.2 ($w(n)$ and $y(n)$ denote the same signal). The quantity

$$v(n) = \alpha y(n-1) \tag{5.11}$$

is the output of the multiplier α. If we use b' bits to represent α, then $v(n)$ actually has $b + b'$ bits. Thus, $y(n)$, which is given by $u(n) + v(n)$, has $b + b'$ bits during the succeeding cycle. In this manner, the number of bits required to represent $v(n)$ and $y(n)$ accumulates indefinitely because of the feedback loop. To avoid such accumulation, we must insert a quantizer Q that converts a $(b + b')$-bit number to a b-bit number. Figure 5.6 shows two ways of doing this.

In Fig. 5.6(a) the signal $v(n)$ is added to $u(n)$ and the result $w(n)$ is quantized; in Fig. 5.6(b) the signal $v(n)$ is quantized to b bits and added to $u(n)$. The scheme of

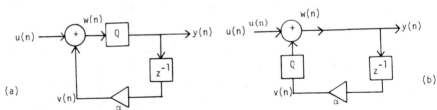

Fig. 5.6. Signal quantization in the first-order structure.

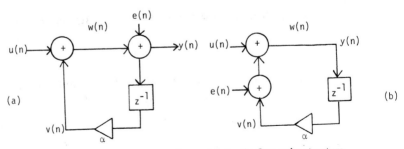

Fig. 5.7. Quantization noise models for the first-order structure.

Fig. 5.6(a) requires a $(b + b')$-bit adder, whereas that of Fig. 5.6(b) requires a b-bit adder. The tradeoff is that Fig. 5.6(b) represents a noisier circuit than Fig. 5.6(a).

The result of such quantization is to introduce the quantization error $e(n)$, defined according to Eq. (5.7). Thus, equivalent models [1, 4, 5] for the schemes in Fig. 5.6 can be drawn as shown in Fig. 5.7. The noise source $e(n)$ can thus be considered as a second input to the filter. Its effect can then be analyzed using linear-system theory (even though quantization itself is a nonlinear effect). Such analysis is generally done with the following assumptions about $e(n)$:

Assumptions about the Noise Source e(n)   1

a. $e(n)$ is a wide-sense stationary (WSS) random process [11]; that is, the statistical quantities

$$E[e(n)] = \text{statistical expected value} = m_e$$

$$E[e(n) - m_e][e(n + m) - m_e] = \text{covariance sequence} = c_{ee}(m)$$

are independent of the time index n.

b. $e(n)$ is "white"; i.e.,[†] $c_{ee}(m) = \sigma_e^2 \cdot \delta(m)$. Thus the autocorrelation sequence is

$$r_{ee}(m) = E[e(n)e(n + m)] = \sigma_e^2 \delta(m) + m_e^2$$

c. $e(n)$ is uncorrelated to all other signals such as $x(n)$, $w(n)$, and $v(n)$.

d. $e(n)$ is uniformly distributed, as shown in the typical plots of Fig. 5.4.

These assumptions are generally valid when b and b_1 (Fig. 5.3) are sufficiently large and when $x(n)$ is "sufficiently random." A quantitative analysis concerning validity of these assumptions can be found in [12] and references thereof.

In Fig. 5.7, the signals $e(n)$ "pass through" the filter just like the signals $u(n)$. The transfer functions from the noise sources to the outputs $w(n)$ and $y(n)$ are

$$\left. \frac{W(z)}{E(z)} \right|_{U(z)=0} = \begin{cases} \dfrac{\alpha z^{-1}}{1 - \alpha z^{-1}} & \text{for Fig. 5.7(a)} \\[3mm] \dfrac{1}{1 - \alpha z^{-1}} & \text{for Fig. 5.7(b)} \end{cases} \qquad (5.12)$$

and

$$\left. \frac{Y(z)}{E(z)} \right|_{U(z)=0} = \frac{1}{1 - \alpha z^{-1}} \qquad \text{for both Fig. 5.7(a),(b)} \qquad (5.13)$$

The quantization noise gets "amplified" through the "noise transfer functions" of

---

[†] Recall that $\delta(m)$ is the unit pulse defined as $\delta(m) = 0$ for $m \neq 0$ and $\delta(0) = 1$.

Eqs. (5.12) and (5.13). Thus, even though $e(n)$ may be "small," its effect on $w(n)$ and $y(n)$ can be large. Note that since $|\alpha| < 1$ for stability, the scheme of Fig. 5.7(a) is less noisy than that of Fig. 5.7(b) as far as $w(n)$ is concerned. In practice, however, it is more natural to take $y(n)$ as the output, because it is typically cascaded to a succeeding stage.

For the rest of the section, only the schemes of Figs. 5.6(a) and 5.7(a) with $y(n)$ defined to be the filter output will be considered. Thus the noise transfer function is

$$G(z) = (1 - \alpha z^{-1})^{-1} \tag{5.14a}$$

which results in an impulse response given by

$$g(n) = \alpha^n 1(n) \tag{5.14b}$$

where $1(n)$ stands for the unit step. The noise contribution at the filter output due to $e(n)$ is

$$y_e(n) = \sum_{m=0}^{\infty} g(m)e(n - m) \tag{5.15}$$

From the aforementioned assumptions concerning the noise source $e(n)$, we easily verify [4,5] that $y_e(n)$ is a WSS random process with the following mean and variance:

$$m_f \triangleq E[y_e(n)] = m_e \sum_{n=0}^{\infty} g(n) \tag{5.16}$$

$$\sigma_f^2 \triangleq E[y_e(n) - m_f]^2 = \sigma_e^2 \sum_{n=0}^{\infty} g^2(n) \tag{5.17}$$

where m_e and σ_e^2 are the mean and variance of $e(n)$ as tabulated in Table IV for various kinds of quantization and number representations. Notice that for 2's complement truncation arithmetic, there is a nonzero mean value for the output error $y_e(n)$.

In view of the expression for $g(n)$ in Eq. (5.14), it is clear that Eqs. (5.16) and (5.17) imply

$$m_f = m_e(1 - \alpha)^{-1} \tag{5.18}$$

$$\sigma_f^2 = \sigma_e^2(1 - \alpha^2)^{-1} \tag{5.19}$$

For narrowband filters, $|\alpha|$ is typically very close to 1. For such filters the noise variance σ_e^2 gets amplified enormously. For example, with $\alpha = 0.997$ (which is not uncommon), $\sigma_f^2 = 167\sigma_e^2$, which corresponds to a noise gain of $10 \log_{10} 167 = 22$ dB.

Before proceeding further, note that the noise level σ_f^2 itself is not as meaningful as the SNR at the filter output. As a simple example, if the input signal $u(n)$ is itself a white WSS random process with variance σ_u^2, then the output signal $y(n)$ has variance

$$\sigma_y^2 = (1 - \alpha^2)^{-1} \sigma_u^2 \qquad (5.20)$$

and hence the noise-to-signal ratio is

$$\frac{N}{S} = \frac{\sigma_f^2}{\sigma_y^2} = \frac{\sigma_e^2}{\sigma_u^2} \qquad (5.21)$$

Thus, the noise gain $(1 - \alpha^2)^{-1}$ cancels with the signal gain. In other words, α does not enter Eq. (5.21) at all, and the S/N ratio is apparently independent of pole location. This, however, is a false conclusion for the following fundamental reason: in fixed-point arithmetic, since we wish to confine $y(n)$ to the dynamic range $(-1, 1)$, it is necessary to scale down $u(n)$ accordingly. Otherwise the computed signal $y(n)$ suffers from possible overflow. The scaling of $u(n)$ required depends on the signal gain (hence on α). Thus for $\alpha \to 1$, the gain $(1 - \alpha^2)^{-1}$ is large and σ_u^2 in (5.21) is small, thus deteriorating the SNR.

In view of these considerations, we now proceed to the topic of scaling and dynamic range in digital filters. After this, we shall return to Fig. 5.7 and obtain a more useful and practical expression for the SNR.

DYNAMIC RANGE CONSTRAINTS AND SCALING   IV

In general, a digital filter structure is more complicated than that of Fig. 5.5 and is an elaborate interconnection of multipliers, adders, and delays (Fig. 5.8). Let us assume that all the signals involved (including $u(n)$, $y(n)$, and the internal signals) are represented by b-bit fixed-point fractions (Fig. 5.2). It is thus desirable that, during the computation process, none of the signals exceeds the dynamic range $(-1, 1)$. Let us now assume that the transfer function $H(z)$ and input $u(n)$ are

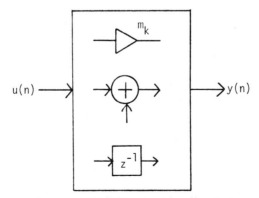

Fig. 5.8. Components of a general digital filter structure are multipliers, adders, and delays.

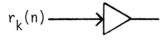

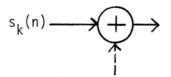

Fig. 5.9. Internal signals in a filter structure.

such that the output $y(n)$ stays in the range $(-1, 1)$ for all n. Thus, if there is no overflow of internal signals [i.e., if all internal signals are in the range $(-1, 1)$], then the computed $y(n)$ is the correct result. "Scaling" is a process of readjusting certain internal gain parameters in order to accomplish this goal.

An "internal signal" is a signal that is neither $u(n)$ nor $y(n)$. The set of all internal signals that participate in computations can be divided into two classes (Fig. 5.9):

1. Signals $r_k(n)$ that are inputs to (nonintegral)[†] multipliers. (These signals could simultaneously be inputs to adders as well.)

2. Signals $s_k(n)$ that are not inputs to multipliers. Such signals are inputs to adders.

For a number of standard arithmetic systems (such as 1's and 2's complement systems), it is necessary only to scale the $r_k(n)$. In other words, given an infinite precision, infinite dynamic range theoretical circuit, if $r_k(n)$ remains in the range $(-1, 1)$ for all k and n, then in a practical circuit with dynamic range $(-1, 1)$ the signals $r_k(n)$ will continue to be the correct values (and $y(n)$ will continue to be correct) even if the signals $s_k(n)$ undergo several overflows. The reasoning for this is outlined in [4, 10, 13] and a mathematically rigorous proof can be given, but we omit details here.

If a digital filter structure is such that $|r_k(n)| < 1$ for a certain class of inputs under ideal conditions, then it is said to be scaled *for this particular class of inputs*. In his original work [13] Jackson shows how scaling should be performed, depending on the class of inputs. Let $f_k(n)$ denote the impulse response from the input $u(n)$ to the node of $r_k(n)$. The transform $F_k(z) = \sum_{n=0}^{\infty} f_k(n)z^{-n}$ is called the *scaling transfer function*. It can be shown that $|r_k(n)|$ is bounded for all indices n as follows:

$$|r_k(n)| \le \|F_k\|_p \|U\|_q \tag{5.22}$$

[†] Note that the integer portion of any multiplier can be looked upon as a set of adders. Thus, without loss of generality, for analysis purposes, a "multiplier" can be assumed to be a fraction in the range $(-1, 1)$.

where p and q are constrained by

$$\frac{1}{p} + \frac{1}{q} = 1 \tag{5.23}$$

and where the symbol $\|\cdot\|_p$ denotes the L_p norm:

$$\|S\|_p \triangleq \left[\frac{1}{2\pi} \int_0^{2\pi} |S(e^{j\omega})|^p \, d\omega \right]^{1/p} \tag{5.24}$$

Note that $p = \infty$ corresponds to taking the maximum value; that is,

$$\|S\|_\infty = \max_\omega |S(e^{j\omega})| \tag{5.25}$$

Based on the inequality Eq. (5.22) it is easy to derive conditions on $F_k(z)$ to satisfy $|r_k(n)| < 1$. For example, let the input be such that $|U(e^{j\omega})|_{\max} < 1$; that is, $\|U\|_\infty < 1$; then from Eqs. (5.22) and (5.23) it is clear that if we scale the filter such that $\|F_k\|_1 \leq 1$, then overflow of $r_k(n)$ can be avoided. This corresponds to $p = 1, q = \infty$ in (5.23).

On the other hand, let the input be a pure cosine wave, $\cos \omega_0 n$, of arbitrary (unknown) frequency ω_0. In this case

$$U(e^{j\omega}) = \pi \sum_{k=-\infty}^{\infty} [\delta(\omega - \omega_0 - 2\pi k) + \delta(\omega + \omega_0 - 2\pi k)]$$

where in this context $\delta(\cdot)$ is the impulse function with a *continuous* argument. Note that $\|U\|_q$ is well defined only when $q = 1$. In fact, $\|U\|_1 = 1$, and thus the scaling policy is obtained by setting $q = 1, p = \infty$ in (5.22). In other words, if the structure is scaled such that $\|F_k\|_\infty < 1$, then overflow of $r_k(n)$ can be avoided. This represents the most "stringent" of all L_p scaling policies because it can be shown that the norm in Eq. (5.24) satisfies

$$\|S\|_p \leq \|S\|_\infty \qquad \text{for all } p \tag{5.26}$$

Thus, if $\|F_k\|_\infty < 1$ for all k, then it implies that the filter is scaled for all possible input signals (not only sinusoids) satisfying $\|U\|_1 \leq 1$. Next, the case $p = 2, q = 2$ is useful when $U(e^{j\omega})$ is known to have bounded *energy*; that is,

$$\|U\|_2^2 = \int_0^{2\pi} |U(e^{j\omega})|^2 \frac{d\omega}{2\pi} \leq 1 \tag{5.27}$$

Under this condition, it is sufficient to scale $\|F_k\|_2$ such that $\|F_k\|_2 < 1$.

Finally, suppose that we do not have any a priori knowledge on the input, except, of course, that $|u(n)| \leq 1$ because of the natural input register dynamic range. Under this condition,

$$|r_k(n)| = \left| \sum_{m=0}^{\infty} f_k(m)u(n-m) \right| \leq \sum_{m=0}^{\infty} |f_k(m)| \tag{5.28}$$

TABLE V
Various Useful Types of Scaling
(In each row, at least one of the two inequalities must be strict)

Condition on input, i.e., available knowledge about input	Requirement on $f_k(n)$ to avoid overflow of $r_k(n)$ for all n	Terminology used for the scaling policy	Comments
None, except $\|u(n)\| \leq 1$	$L = \sum\limits_{n=0}^{\infty} \|f_k(n)\| \leq 1$	Sum-scaling	Most stringent scaling policy; entirely overflow-proof
$\|U(e^{j\omega})\|_1 \leq 1$ (example: sinusoids)	$L_\infty = \max\limits_{\omega} \|F_k(e^{j\omega})\| \leq 1$	Peak-scaling or L_∞-scaling	Most stringent among all L_p-scaling policies
$\|U(e^{j\omega})\|_2 \leq 1$ (finite-energy inputs)	$L_2 = \|F_k(e^{j\omega})\|_2 \leq 1$	L_2-scaling	Commonly used; mathematically tractable
$\max\limits_{\omega} \|U(e^{j\omega})\| \leq 1$	$L_1 = \|F_k(e^{j\omega})\|_1 \leq 1$	L_1-scaling	Most stringent knowledge requirement on $U(e^{j\omega})$

$\|S\|_p$ stands for $\left[\dfrac{1}{2\pi}\displaystyle\int_0^{2\pi} \|S(e^{j\omega})\|^p\, d\omega\right]^{1/p}$

Note that $\max\limits_{\omega} \|S(e^{j\omega})\| = \|S\|_\infty$.

Thus, the only way to ensure freedom from overflow is to make $\sum_{m=0}^{\infty} \|f_k(m)\| < 1$. This then represents the most stringent scaling requirement. Table V summarizes some of the main points concerning scaling and includes standard names for scaling policies. In view of the well-known inequality Eq. (5.26), L_∞-scaling is more stringent than L_p-scaling, $p < \infty$. Sum-scaling on the other hand is the most stringent and hence provides complete freedom from overflow. Finally, L_1-scaling is the least stringent, but in view of Eq. (5.26) puts the maximum constraint on the nature of input.

1   Stochastic Input Sequences

When the input sequence $u(n)$ is a sample of a random process, $U(e^{j\omega})$ does not, in general, exist, and we should formulate more meaningful guidelines for scaling. Assuming that $u(n)$ represents a WSS random process, let $S_{uu}(e^{j\omega})$ be the power spectral density of $u(n)$; that is,

$$S_{uu}(e^{j\omega}) = \sum_{m=-\infty}^{\infty} r_{uu}(m)e^{-j\omega m} \tag{5.29}$$

where $r_{uu}(m)$ is the autocorrelation sequence; that is, $r_{uu}(m) = E[u(n)u(n + m)]$. Assuming for notational simplicity that $u(n)$ has zero mean, we obtain the variance of $r_k(n)$:

$$\sigma_{r_k}^2 = \frac{1}{2\pi} \int_0^{2\pi} |F_k(e^{j\omega})|^2 S_{uu}(e^{j\omega})\, d\omega \qquad (5.30)$$

It can be shown [13] that Eq. (5.30) implies

$$\sigma_{r_k}^2 \le \|F_k^2\|_p \|S_{uu}\|_q \qquad (5.31)$$

where p and q are related as in Eq. (5.23).

We have thus found an upper bound on the variance of the random variable $r_k(n)$. The usefulness of this can be seen as follows: $r_k(n)$ is the output of a causal linear system $F_k(z)$ in response to $u(n)$. Hence $r_k(n)$ is a linear combination of $u(n)$, $u(n-1)$, $u(n-2),\ldots$, and so on. So, by the central limit theorem [11] $r_k(n)$ is expected to be Gaussian (particularly if $F_k(z)$ is IIR). Thus, any bound on the standard deviation σ_{r_k} reveals an upper bound on the overflow probability of $r_k(n)$. For example, if $\sigma_{r_k} < \frac{1}{3}$, then the probability of overflow is not greater than about 0.003 (i.e., 0.3%). For quick reference, Table VI lists the probability of overflow for various bounds on σ_{r_k}. We constructed the table from standard data [14] on Gaussian distributions.

It is clear from Table VI that we can achieve arbitrarily small probability of overflow by decreasing $\|S_{uu}\|_q$ [see (5.31)], which in turn can be accomplished by scaling down $u(n)$. The obvious tradeoff is that the signal level $\sigma_{r_k}^2$ accordingly decreases, eventually deteriorating the output SNR. (We will soon elaborate on the SNR behavior under scaled conditions.)

Summarizing this section, given a digital filter structure as in Fig. 5.8 to be implemented in fixed-point fractional arithmetic, the circuit is said to be "scaled" if none of the signals $r_k(n)$ (inputs to nonintegral multipliers) overflow. This can be accomplished if each of the impulse response sequences $f_k(n)$ satisfies $\sum |f_k(n)| \le 1$. If, however, we have some a priori knowledge on the input $u(n)$, then

TABLE VI

Bounds on Overflow Probability

Upper bound on σ_{r_k}	Upper bound on probability of overflow
1	0.318
0.80	0.212
0.60	0.096
0.40	0.012
0.333	0.0028
0.30	0.00092
0.25	6.4×10^{-5}
0.22	6.0×10^{-6}
0.20	6.0×10^{-7}

it is sufficient to scale $f_k(n)$ such that a suitable norm $\|F_k\|_p$ is bounded above by 1. Guidelines for this are given in Table V. Finally, if $u(n)$ is a stochastic input, useful bounds can be obtained for the variance of internal signals, thus giving us the necessary scaling information.

An unscaled digital filter structure (i.e., one for which $f_k(n)$ do not satisfy the necessary bounds) can be scaled by restructuring the internal details. These are best explained with practical examples, and so we defer the details to later sections.

A *normalized* digital filter is a scaled digital filter for which the quantities $f_k(n)$ are scaled such that the upper bound is actually attained. For example, based on available knowledge on $u(n)$, assume that we know $\|U\|_2 \le 1$. Then a scaled structure has $\|f_k\|_2 \le 1$ for all k, whereas a normalized structure has $\|f_k\|_2 = 1$ for all k. Clearly, for a normalized structure, the internal signals span the maximum permissible dynamic range without, at the same time, undergoing overflow. The SNR accordingly, is expected to be maximized.

V   SIGNAL-TO-ROUNDOFF NOISE RATIO IN SIMPLE IIR FILTER STRUCTURES

In this section, first- and second-order IIR sections are considered and expressions for noise-to-signal ratios are obtained.

A   First-Order IIR Sections

In Section III we derived an expression [see Eq. (5.19)] for the quantization noise variance σ_f^2 at the output of the filter shown in Fig. 5.5:

$$\sigma_f^2 = \text{quantization noise variance} = \sigma_e^2(1 - \alpha^2)^{-1} \qquad (5.32)$$

where σ_e^2 is as in Table IV and where $|\alpha| < 1$. It is clear from Fig. 5.5 that the only type of signal $r_k(n)$ that "enters a multiplier" is $y(n)$ itself. Thus, in order to scale the circuit we should force a bound on the transfer function $H(z) = (1 - \alpha z^{-1})^{-1}$, which is analogous to the quantity $F_k(z)$ in Section IV. Thus

$$F_k(z) = H(z) = (1 - \alpha z^{-1})^{-1} \qquad (5.33)$$

$$f_k(n) = h(n) = \alpha^n 1(n) \qquad (5.34)$$

The parameter L (Table V) depends on the scaling policy. Thus

$$\sum_{n=0}^{\infty} |f_k(n)| = \frac{1}{1 - |\alpha|} \qquad (5.35)$$

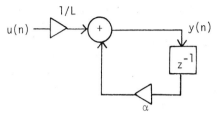

Fig. 5.10. The scaled structure.

$$\|F_k\|_2 = \frac{1}{\sqrt{1 - \alpha^2}} \qquad (5.36)$$

$$\max_{\omega} |F_k(e^{j\omega})| = \|F_k\|_\infty = \frac{1}{1 - |\alpha|} \qquad (5.37)$$

and so on.[†] Let us assume that the quantity L has been computed from Table V. In order to scale the circuit, we introduce the scaling multiplier $1/L$ as shown in Fig. 5.10. Note that this is equivalent to simply scaling down the input signal. (Such equivalence does not generally hold, as we shall see in Section X on state-space structures.) In practice, to avoid the use of an expensive multiplier $1/L$, we can replace it with the nearest power of 2 or merge it with a multiplier of the preceding filter stage. We now examine typical cases.

Let us assume that complete freedom from overflow is desired. Then we should take

$$L = \sum |h(n)| = \frac{1}{1 - |\alpha|} \qquad (5.38)$$

If $u(n)$ is a WSS random process with a uniform probability density function, then, since $-1 \le u(n) \le 1$, we have

$$\sigma_u^2 = \text{variance of } u(n) = \tfrac{1}{3} \qquad (5.39)$$

Thus in Fig. 5.10 the output signal variance is

$$\sigma_y^2 = \tfrac{1}{3} L^{-2} (1 - \alpha^2)^{-1} \qquad (5.40)$$

With quantization noise given by (5.19), the output noise-to-signal ratio is

$$\frac{N}{S} = \frac{\sigma_f^2}{\sigma_y^2} = 3L^2 \sigma_e^2 = \frac{3\sigma_e^2}{(1 - |\alpha|)^2} \qquad (5.41)$$

For poles close to the unit circle ($|\alpha| \to 1$), the noise-to-signal ratio is large. For a given α, the only way to decrease this ratio is to decrease σ_e^2 by increasing the number of bits b (see Table IV).

[†] In this chapter, filter coefficients are always assumed to be real. Equivalently, all impulse response sequences are real valued.

Next assume that $u(n)$ is again a WSS random process that is Gaussian (this is typically so if $u(n)$ itself is the output of a digital filter, which occurs in cascade-form implementations). We would then like to "fit in" the values of $u(n)$ into the register dynamic range $(-1, 1)$ for most of the time. Referring to Fig. 5.11, this is facilitated by using a small σ_u. Thus $\sigma_u = \frac{1}{3}$ ensures that for about 99.72% of the time, $u(n)$ is faithfully represented by the input register. With this choice, we have for the output signal variance,

$$\sigma_y^2 = \tfrac{1}{9}L^{-2}(1 - \alpha^2)^{-1} \tag{5.42}$$

whence

$$\frac{N}{S} = \frac{\sigma_f^2}{\sigma_y^2} = 3\frac{3\sigma_e^2}{(1 - |\alpha|)^2} \tag{5.43}$$

Comparing Eq. (5.43) with Eq. (5.41) reveals that with a Gaussian input the structure is three times as noisy.

Next assume that $u(n)$ is a sinusoid with *known* frequency ω_0. (This assumption is useful when studying narrowband bandpass filters.) Then L should be chosen such that the output sinusoid has amplitude close to unity. Thus

$$S = \text{output signal power} = \tfrac{1}{2} \tag{5.44}$$

whence the noise-to-signal ratio is

$$\frac{N}{S} = \frac{\sigma_f^2}{S} = \frac{2\sigma_e^2}{1 - \alpha^2} \tag{5.45}$$

Note in this example that the scale factor L does not explicitly enter Eq. (5.45). Consequently in Eq. (5.45), $1 - \alpha^2$ appears in the denominator, whereas in Eqs. (5.41) and (5.43) $(1 - |\alpha|)^2$ appears in the denominator. Thus, for poles close to the unit circle, the noise-to-signal level is much higher in Eqs. (5.41) and (5.43) than in Eq. (5.45). Note that, even though L does not appear in Eq. (5.45), an appropriate scale factor $1/L$ *does* need to be inserted in Fig. 5.10 in order to perform the scaling.

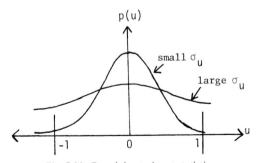

Fig. 5.11. Pertaining to input statistics.

As a final example, assume again that we have a white WSS input $u(n)$, but let us change our scaling policy. Instead of making the circuit entirely free of overflow, let us assume we wish to reduce the overflow probability of $y(n)$ to less than 0.003. From Table VI it is clear that σ_y should be $\frac{1}{3}$ or less. Assuming $\sigma_y = \frac{1}{3}$, we have the signal power $S = \frac{1}{9}$. The noise variance is given by Eq. (5.19) and hence the noise-to-signal ratio is

$$\frac{N}{S} = \frac{9}{1 - \alpha^2} \sigma_e^2 \tag{5.46}$$

Once again, as for sinusoidal inputs of known frequency, the noise-to-signal ratio does not contain L explicitly. Thus, N/S has only $1 - \alpha^2$ in the denominator, rather than $1 - |\alpha|$.

In practice, it is often convenient to compute and tabulate noise-to-signal ratios in dB. For example, Eq. (5.46) can be expressed as

$$\left. \frac{N}{S} \right|_{\text{dB}} = 10 \log_{10} \frac{N}{S} = -10 \log_{10}(1 - \alpha^2) + 20 \log_{10} \sigma_e + 9.542 \tag{5.47}$$

To be specific, let us assume roundoff arithmetic. Then from Table IV

$$\sigma_e^2 = \frac{\Delta^2}{12} = \frac{2^{-2b}}{12} \tag{5.48}$$

whence

$$\left. \frac{N}{S} \right|_{\text{dB}} = -10 \log_{10}(1 - \alpha^2) - 6.02b - 1.25 \tag{5.49}$$

Equation (5.49) reveals that the SNR can be improved (i.e., N/S decreased) by 6.02 dB by increasing b by 1. Thus, every additional bit of internal word length improves the SNR by about 6 dB. Even though we derived this condition for a specific example, it is true in general.

Table VII summarizes some of the instructive results derived above. It is clearly seen that as $|\alpha|$ moves closer to 1, the SNR deteriorates in all cases. The deterioration is severe for entries 1 and 2 compared to entries 3 and 4, because of the $(1 - |\alpha|)^2$ rather than $1 - \alpha^2$ dependence. Figure 5.12 is a plot of N/S that clearly places this in evidence. For a given α and a given desired N/S, the required number of bits b can be readily computed from Table VII. Figure 5.13 shows such a plot for typical α.

Let $\delta = 1 - |\alpha|$. Thus δ represents the shortest distance of the pole from the unit circle. For small δ we have $1 - \alpha^2 \simeq 2\delta$, and Table VII also includes the N/S expressions in terms of δ. Clearly, as $\delta \to 0$, entries 1 and 2 show more severe noise amplification than do entries 3 and 4.

For the case of 16-bit fixed-point implementation with roundoff arithmetic, Table VII includes the N/S ratios for $|\alpha| = 0.99$. Notice that the difference between entry 4 and entries 1 and 2 is significant. Thus, it is a better strategy to

TABLE VII

Noise-to-Signal Ratio in First-Order IIR Sections

Entry No.	Type of input	Scaling policy	N/S ratio	N/S in dB for rounding arithmeti $\sigma_e^2 = 2^{-2b}/12$
1	WSS, uniform density, white	Completely avoid overflow	$\dfrac{3\sigma_e^2}{(1-|\alpha|)^2}$ $\left(=\dfrac{3\sigma_e^2}{\delta^2}\right)$	$-10\log_{10}(1-|\alpha|)^2 - 6{\cdot}02b - 6{\cdot}0$ $(= -62.34 \text{ dB for } b = 16, |\alpha| = 0{\cdot}9$
2	WSS, Gaussian density, white	Completely avoid overflow	$\dfrac{9\sigma_e^2}{(1-|\alpha|)^2}$ $\left(=\dfrac{9\sigma_e^2}{\delta^2}\right)$	$-10\log_{10}(1-|\alpha|)^2 - 6{\cdot}02b - 1{\cdot}2$ $(= -57{\cdot}6 \text{ dB for } b = 16, |\alpha| = 0.99$
3	Sinusoid, known frequency	Completely avoid overflow	$\dfrac{2\sigma_e^2}{1-\alpha^2}$ $\left(\simeq\dfrac{\sigma_e^2}{\delta}\right)$	$-10\log_{10}(1-\alpha^2) - 6{\cdot}02b - 7{\cdot}78$ $(= -87{\cdot}1 \text{ dB for } b = 16, |\alpha| = 0{\cdot}9$
4	WSS unknown density, white	Reduce overflow probability to <0.003	$\dfrac{9\sigma_e^2}{1-\alpha^2}$ $\left(\simeq\dfrac{4.5\sigma_e^2}{\delta}\right)$	$-10\log_{10}(1-\alpha^2) - 6{\cdot}02b - 1.2$ $(= -80{\cdot}6 \text{ dB for } b = 16, |\alpha| = 0.99$

Here α represents pole location. In column 3, δ represents $(1-|\alpha|)$, and the expressions in parentheses h when $\delta \ll 1$.

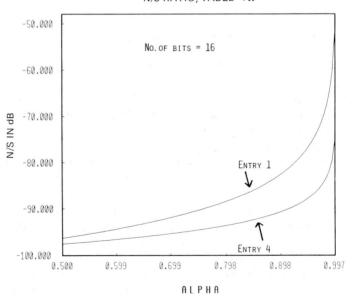

Fig. 5.12. Plot of N/S vs. α for first-order filter.

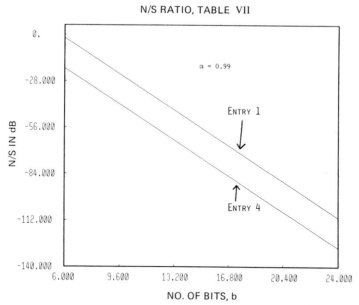

Fig. 5.13. Plot of N/S vs. b for first-order section (only integer values of abscissa have physical meaning).

scale the filter to reduce the probability of overflow than to scale the filter to *completely suppress* overflow. For entries 1 and 2 the quantity $[-10\log(1 - |\alpha|)^2]/6.02$ can be considered to be the "number of bits of noise deterioration" due to noise gain from the quantizer output to the filter output. We can similarly interpret $[-10\log(1 - \alpha^2)]/6.02$ in entries 3 and 4 of Table VII.

From our discussion in this section, it is clear that there is an inherent tradeoff involved between roundoff noise and dynamic range. Thus, if we try to decrease the probability of overflow, it increases the N/S ratio. Such an interaction between noise and dynamic range [13] exists in all implementations of digital filters, particularly with those that employ a fixed-point arithmetic scheme.

Another point that should be reemphasized is that, for a fixed-point implementation, the quantization noise σ_f^2 at the filter output alone does not form a meaningful measure. The SNR *under scaled conditions* is the only meaningful parameter of interest.

Second-Order IIR Sections   B

Let us now turn our attention to second-order IIR transfer functions. These play a centrol role in the implementation of several practical digital filter circuits, such as the parallel form and cascade form. Accordingly, careful attention must be paid to the behavior of such sections under signal quantization.

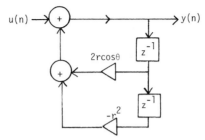

Fig. 5.14. Direct-form implementation for complex pole pair.

Consider the structure of Fig. 5.14, which shows a direct-form implementation of the transfer function

$$H(z) = \frac{1}{1 - 2r(\cos\theta)z^{-1} + r^2z^{-2}} \tag{5.50}$$

This is an all-pole function with a pair of complex conjugate poles at $z_p = re^{\pm j\theta}$. (If the poles were real, we could have implemented $H(z)$ as a cascade of two sections as in Fig. 5.5.) Assume once again that fixed-point fractions are used to represent all numbers, and that the dynamic range is $(-1, 1)$. The only signal that enters "multipliers" is $y(n)$, and the structure can be scaled by ensuring that $|y(n)| \le 1$ for all inputs $u(n)$ of interest.

The impulse response corresponding to Eq. (5.50) is [4]

$$h(n) = \frac{r^n \sin(n + 1)\theta}{\sin\theta} \cdot 1(n) \tag{5.51}$$

where $1(n)$ represents the unit step. To keep $y(n)$ from overflowing for inputs in $(-1, 1)$, we must insert a scale factor $1/L$ as in Fig. 5.15, where

$$L = \sum_{n=0}^{\infty} |h(n)| \tag{5.52}$$

Once again, in practice, the scale factor $1/L$ is either merged with the preceding section (if it exists) or replaced with a power of 2 to avoid expensive

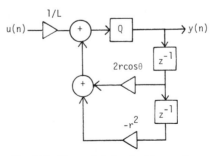

Fig. 5.15. The scaled circuit with quantizer.

multiplication overhead. Because the computation of Eq. (5.52) is difficult, particularly for r close to 1, it is avoided in practice. Instead certain bounds on L have been established [4, 5] that enable us to obtain an estimate of the extent of scaling necessary. Thus, it can be shown that

$$\frac{1}{(1 - r)^2(1 - 2r\cos 2\theta + r^2)} \le L^2 \le \frac{1}{(1 - r)^2 \sin^2 \theta} \qquad (5.53a)$$

An improved (i.e., smaller) upper bound has been proposed in [15]. We omit the details here, but the bound is

$$L^2 \le \frac{16}{\pi^2} \frac{1}{(1 - r^2)^2 \sin^2 \theta} \qquad (5.53b)$$

The bound in Eq. (5.53b) is smaller than that in Eq. (5.53a) for $r > 0.273$. These bounds are easily computed, giving us the desired estimate on L. Now consider the circuit of Fig. 5.15, which shows the scale factor $1/L$ and the quantizer Q. Note that even though there are two multipliers, it is sufficient to insert only one quantizer in a branch that is common to both feedback loops. The quantization noise model is shown in Fig. 5.16. The noise transfer function (i.e., $Y(z)/E(z)$ with $U(z) = 0$) is clearly $H(z)$ itself, and hence the noise variance at the filter output is

$$\sigma_f^2 = \sigma_e^2 \sum_{n=0}^{\infty} h^2(n) \qquad (5.54)$$

With $h(n)$ given as in Eq. (5.51) Eq. (5.54) simplifies to

$$\sigma_f^2 = \frac{1 + r^2}{1 - r^2} \frac{1}{r^4 - 2r^2 \cos 2\theta + 1} \cdot \sigma_e^2 \qquad (5.55)$$

Now assume that $u(n)$ is a WSS white process with a uniform density function. Since the dynamic range of $u(n)$ is $(-1, 1)$, we have $\sigma_u^2 = \frac{1}{3}$. Hence the signal power at the output is

$$S = \sigma_y^2 = \frac{1}{3} \frac{1}{L^2} \sum_{n=0}^{\infty} h^2(n) \qquad (5.56)$$

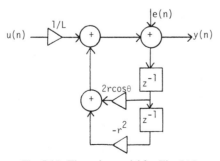

Fig. 5.16. The noise model for Fig. 5.15.

whence the noise-to-signal ratio is

$$\frac{N}{S} = \frac{\sigma_f^2}{\sigma_y^2} = 3L^2\sigma_e^2 \tag{5.57}$$

where L is bounded as in Eq. (5.53). Thus, with rounding arithmetic where $\sigma_e^2 = 2^{-2b}/12$, we have

$$\frac{2^{-2b}}{4(1-r)^2(1-2r\cos 2\theta + r^2)} \le \frac{N}{S} \le \frac{4}{\pi^2} \frac{2^{-2b}}{(1-r^2)^2 \sin^2\theta} \tag{5.58}$$

If $u(n)$ is Gaussian rather than uniform, then we can take $\sigma_u = \frac{1}{3}$, using the same reasoning as in the case of the first-order structure. Then the output signal power is

$$S = \sigma_y^2 = \frac{1}{9}\frac{1}{L^2}\sum_{n=0}^{\infty} h^2(n) \tag{5.59}$$

whence the N/S ratio is as in (5.58) except for an increase by a factor of 3.

If we assume that $u(n)$ is a sine wave of *known* frequency ω_0, it can be verified that the noise-to-signal ratio becomes

$$\frac{N}{S} = \frac{\sigma_f^2}{\sigma_y^2} = \frac{1+r^2}{1-r^2}\frac{2^{-2b}}{6(r^4 - 2r^2\cos 2\theta + 1)} \tag{5.60}$$

for rounding arithmetic. The scale factor $1/L$ does not enter Eq. (5.60) even though an appropriate value of $1/L$ appears in Fig. 5.15 in order to obtain an output sine wave that has a peak amplitude equal to unity.

Finally, consider the case of white WSS input with unknown probability density function for $u(n)$. Let us assume that we wish to reduce the probability of overflow of $y(n)$ to about 0.0030. Thus σ_y should be chosen as $\frac{1}{3}$, as explained for the corresponding situation in the case of first-order sections. Thus $S = \sigma_y^2 = \frac{1}{9}$, N is still given by Eq. (5.55), and

$$\frac{N}{S} = \frac{\sigma_f^2}{\sigma_y^2} = \frac{1+r^2}{1-r^2}\frac{3\cdot 2^{-2b}}{4(r^4 - 2r^2\cos 2\theta + 1)} \tag{5.61}$$

for rounding arithmetic.

Much better insight into the above relations can be gained by using the notation $\delta = 1 - r$ (which is the radical distance of the pole from the unit circle) and simplifying the above expressions for $\delta \to 0$. Table VIII shows the N/S ratio for the preceding four cases, with roundoff arithmetic and δ very small. A commonly encountered situation is to have small θ and δ such that $\theta \gg \delta$. Table VIII also shows the corresponding simplification. The quantity δ appears in the denominators of N/S in entries 3 and 4, where as δ^2 appears in entries 1 and 2. Thus, for small δ the effect of noise is much more severe in entries 1 and 2 of the table, as seen from the example in the fifth column of Table VIII. The reason for this is that in entry 3 of the table, we once again have considerable

TABLE VIII

Summary of N/S for Second-Order All-Pole Direct-Form Structures, for Various Types of Inputs

Entry No.	Type of input	Scaling policy	N/S ratio	Example: N/S in dB for $r = 0.995$, $\theta = 0.07\pi$ and $b = 16$
1	WSS, uniform density, white	Completely avoid overflow	$\dfrac{2^{-2b}}{4\delta^2(\delta^2 + 4\theta^2)}$ $\leq \dfrac{N}{S} \leq \dfrac{1}{\pi^2}\dfrac{2^{-2b}}{\delta^2\theta^2}$	$-49 \leq N/S \leq -47.1$
2	WSS, Gaussian density, white	Completely avoid overflow	$2^{-2b} \cdot \dfrac{3}{4\delta^2(\delta^2 + 4\theta^2)}$ $\leq \dfrac{N}{S} \leq \dfrac{3}{\pi^2}\dfrac{2^{-2b}}{\delta^2\theta^2}$	$-44.23 \leq N/S \leq -42.33$
3	Sinusoid, known frequency	Completely avoid overflow	$\dfrac{2^{-2b}}{24\delta(\delta^2 + \theta^2)}$ $\simeq \dfrac{2^{-2b}}{24\delta\theta^2}$	-74
4	WSS, unknown density, white	Reduce overflow probability to < 0.003	$\dfrac{2^{-2b} \cdot 3}{16\delta(\delta^2 + \theta^2)}$ $\simeq \dfrac{2^{-2b} \cdot 3}{16\delta\theta^2}$	-67.42

The quantization rule is b-bit rounding. Here $\delta \triangleq 1 - r$, and we assume δ is "very small."

knowledge of the input. In entry 4 we perform the scaling to attain a certain degree of freedom from overflow, rather than complete freedom; thus a judicious choice of the scaling policy has considerable effect on the SNR attainable.

LOW-NOISE IIR FILTER SECTIONS BASED ON VI
ERROR-SPECTRUM SHAPING

From our discussions in Section V it is clear that for first- and second-order IIR filters, the SNR deteriorates as the poles move close to the unit circle. Thus, for the second-order section when $r \to 1$, $\delta \to 0$, from Table VIII we see that the noise-to-signal ratio increases. The same is true as $\theta \to 0$—that is, as the pole moves close to the real axis. For digital filters having a narrowband lowpass response, the conditions $\theta \to 0$ and $\delta \to 0$ tend to be true. Accordingly, an implementation based on interconnection of (first- and) second-order sections tends to be noisy.

An obvious way to obtain a satisfactorily low N/S is to increase b to the required extent. This, however, increases the cost of the implementation and is impractical when δ and θ are very small.

An elegant and *powerful* alternative is to use the concept of error-spectrum shaping (ESS) in the digital filter structure [16–19]. Analogous ideas have been known in the areas of communications and coding [20], but the adaptation and application of such techniques for digital filters is novel and rewarding; a dramatic amount of noise reduction can be achieved with little additional cost. In this section we present some design guidelines and results on this. We consider only first- and second-order sections since any higher-order section can always be built based on a cascade or parallel connection of these sections.

A ESS in First-Order Sections

Let us again consider Fig. 5.10, which represents the scaled first-order structure. For b-bit fixed-point fractional arithmetic (Fig. 5.2), the appearance of the signals in binary format is shown in Fig. 5.17, where the quantizer is also included. The multiplier α is assumed to be a b-bit fraction. Notice that when we say b-bit arithmetic, we mean that the *output* of the quantizer is a b-bit fraction as in Fig. 5.2. Thus, z^{-1} represents a b-bit (or single-precision) storage, α represents a single-precision multiplier with two b-bit inputs and a $2b$-bit output, and the adder is a double-precision device. (We can convert the adder to a single-precision device by moving the quantizer to the adder inputs, if necessary). The unshaded areas in Fig. 5.17 represent 0's (or 1's for negative numbers). The crosshatched area in Fig. 5.17 is what gives rise to the quantization error; it is not necessarily *equal* to the quantization error $e(n)$ because $e(n)$ [defined to be

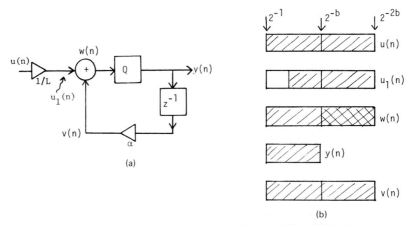

Fig. 5.17. (a) Appearance of internal signals in a first-order digital filter. (b) Word lengths of signals in (a).

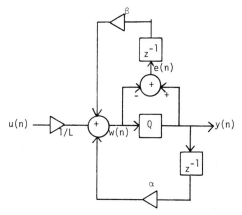

Fig. 5.18. The error feedback technique.

$y(n) - w(n)$ according to (5.7)] depends on the exact quantization rule. However, it is easy to find $e(n)$ from the crosshatched portion shown.

Now, instead of discarding the error $e(n)$, let us consider feeding it back, as shown in Fig. 5.18. Such error feedback (EFB) often leads to noise reduction, as shown next. The quantity β is called the EFB coefficient.

Analysis of the EFB Circuit 1

Since $e(n)$ is represented by b bits in the range $2^{-(b+1)}$ to 2^{-2b}, the product $\beta e(n)$ produces additional secondary quantization error at the 2^{-2b} level unless β is an integer. Moreover, an integral value of β such as $\pm 1, \pm 2$ is much simpler to implement without multipliers. Under the assumption that multiplication by β does not generate quantization error, we can show

$$w(n) = \alpha w(n-1) + \frac{u(n)}{L} + (\alpha + \beta)e(n-1) \tag{5.62}$$

$$y(n) = \alpha y(n-1) + \frac{u(n)}{L} + e(n) + \beta e(n-1) \tag{5.63}$$

Note that the difference between $y(n)$ and $w(n)$ is $e(n)$, which is the negligible unamplified quantization error. The noise transfer function with EFB is

$$G_1(z) = \begin{cases} \dfrac{(\alpha + \beta)z^{-1}}{1 - \alpha z^{-1}} & \text{if } W(z) \text{ is the output signal} \tag{5.64a} \\[3mm] \dfrac{1 + \beta z^{-1}}{1 - \alpha z^{-1}} & \text{if } Y(z) \text{ is the output signal} \tag{5.64b} \end{cases}$$

Because of EFB, the noise transfer function has changed (compare with the results of Section III). However, as from Eqs. (5.62) and (5.63), the input-output transfer function is unaffected:

$$\frac{Y(z)}{U(z)}\bigg|_{E(z)=0} = \frac{1}{L(1 - \alpha z^{-1})}$$

Thus, EFB has the effect of changing the noise transfer function without changing either the input-output transfer function or the scaling properties.

2   Choice of the EFB Parameter β

Careful choice of β leads to reduced noise variance at the filter output. From Eq. (5.64) it is clear that if α is close to unity, then the choice $\beta = -1$ has the effect of reducing the noise. It is easily verified that the noise variance at the filter output is (with $W(z)$ considered as output)

$$\sigma_f^2 = \frac{(\alpha + \beta)^2}{1 - \alpha^2} \sigma_e^2 \tag{5.65}$$

where σ_e^2 is the basic quantizer noise variance (Table IV). Thus, if we restrict β to be an integer, the following choice is the "best" from the viewpoint of minimizing the noise variance:

$$\beta = \begin{cases} 0, & |\alpha| \le \frac{1}{2} \\ -1, & \frac{1}{2} < \alpha < 1 \\ 1, & -1 < \alpha < -\frac{1}{2} \end{cases} \tag{5.66}$$

With $|\alpha| \le \frac{1}{2}$, the noise level σ_f^2 is not high and does not represent an interesting case (the pole is not sufficiently close to the unit circle to be of concern). With $|\alpha| > \frac{1}{2}$ and with the choice of Eq. (5.66), Eq. (5.65) becomes

$$\sigma_f^2 = \frac{(1 - |\alpha|)^2}{1 - \alpha^2} \sigma_e^2 = \frac{1 - |\alpha|}{1 + |\alpha|} \sigma_e^2, \qquad |\alpha| > \frac{1}{2} \tag{5.67}$$

Thus the N/S ratio is decreased by $-10 \log(1 - |\alpha|)^2$ dB. For example, with $|\alpha| = 0.995$, we obtain $-10 \log(25 \times 10^{-6}) = 46$ dB of improvement (equivalent to $46/6.02 \simeq 7$ bits of increased accuracy!).

Comparing Eq. (5.67) with Eq. (5.32), which is the noise variance in absence of EFB, it is clear that for $|\alpha| \to 1$, Eq. (5.32) is very large, whereas Eq. (5.67) is not. The denominator of Eq. (5.32) can get arbitrarily small for $|\alpha| \to 1$, but this is not the case in Eq. (5.67). The noise gain in Eq. (5.67) does not exceed $\frac{1}{3}$ for any α in the range $\frac{1}{2} \le |\alpha| < 1$!

The price paid for the dramatic noise reduction is the additional b-bit register that holds $e(n)$, and the extra double-precision adder in the EFB path. If we assume that b is 8 (i.e., single precision $\equiv$ 8 bits), then the above EFB scheme is almost equivalent to replacing single-precision multipliers with double-precision multipliers [21].

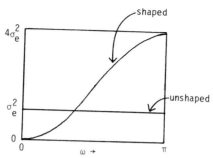

Fig. 5.19. The error power spectrum.

The name "error-spectrum shaping" derives from the fact that the quantization error $E(z)$ has effectively been shaped to become $E_S(z) = (1 + \beta z^{-1})E(z)$, which then passes through the *usual* noise transfer function $1/(1 - \alpha z^{-1})$, as seen from Eq. (5.64b). Thus, with narrowband lowpass filters (where $\alpha \to 1$), the choice $\beta = -1$ [see Eq. (5.66)] leads to the "shaped" spectrum $E_S(z) = (1 - z^{-1}) E(z)$. In other words, there is a *zero* in the spectrum of $E_S(z)$ at $z = 1$ (i.e., $\omega = 0$). The power spectral density of the shaped error $e_S(n)$ is thus redistributed to lie mostly in the stopband (Fig. 5.19) and is given by $4\sin^2(\omega/2)\sigma_e^2$, where σ_e^2 is the flat power spectral density of the unshaped quantization error $e(n)$. Since $1/(1 - \alpha z^{-1})$ has a lowpass nature for $\alpha > 0$, the effective output noise variance is reduced by the ESS technique.

Note that the choice $\beta = -\alpha$ corresponds to a double-precision implementation of Fig. 5.17 (i.e., $2b$-bit multiplier, $4b$-bit adder, etc.) See [21] for detailed discussions on this. Under this condition, Eqs. (5.64) and (5.65) are not meaningful because the secondary noise generated by β in the EFB path cannot be ignored any more (since this is the *only* noise source and corresponds to the usual error in a double-precision implementation). Essentially, ESS offers a compromise between single-precision and double-precision implementations.

ESS in Second-Order Sections   B

The noise-reduction strategy outlined above can readily be extended to second-order IIR sections. Figure 5.20 shows a typical second-order filter with EFB incorporated. The overall transfer function under ideal (unquantized) conditions is

$$H(z) = \frac{1/L}{1 + b_1 z^{-1} + b_2 z^{-2}} \tag{5.68}$$

The scaling multiplier $1/L$ is chosen as indicated in Section V.B. If the poles are

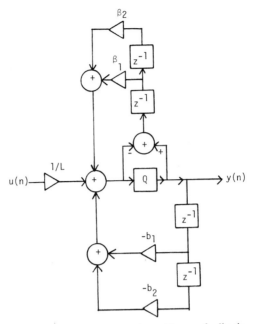

Fig. 5.20. Second-order section with error feedback.

complex conjugates, then

$$b_1 = -2r\cos\theta, \qquad b_2 = r^2 \tag{5.69}$$

In practice, the EFB coefficients β_1 and β_2 should be chosen such that they are simple to implement and do not generate additional quantization error, if possible. Some practical choices have been studied in [22, 23], and several examples of this scheme can be found in the literature. From the viewpoint of simplicity, we restrict, in this chapter, the choice of β_1 and β_2 to the set $\{\pm 2, \pm 1, 0\}$. For the structure of Fig. 5.20 we have the relation

$$y(n) = -b_1 y(n-1) - b_2 y(n-2) + \frac{u(n)}{L} + e(n) + \beta_1 e(n-1) + \beta_2 e(n-2) \tag{5.70}$$

where $e(n) = y(n) - w(n)$ is the basic quantizer error. The noise transfer function with EFB is thus

$$G(z) = \frac{1 + \beta_1 z^{-1} + \beta_2 z^{-2}}{1 + b_1 z^{-1} + b_2 z^{-2}} \tag{5.71}$$

whence the noise variance at the filter output is

$$\sigma_f^2 = \sigma_e^2 \|G\|_2^2 \tag{5.72}$$

where σ_e^2 is as in Table IV and $\|G\|_2^2$ is the L_2 norm of $G(z)$. The choice $\beta_1 =$

$b_1, \beta_2 = b_2$ in Eq. (5.71) implies $G(z) = 1$, and hence $\sigma_f^2 = \sigma_e^2$. This seems to be (and can be shown to be [23]) the optimal choice, since the basic quantizer noise is thus not amplified. However, under this condition, the EFB network itself generates quantization noise at the 2^{-2b} level (which we have ignored in our analysis) and the circuit with EFB becomes equivalent to a double-precision implementation [21].

A more practical and useful strategy is to choose β_1 and β_2 to be integers nearest to b_1 and b_2, respectively. Thus, for poles $z_p = re^{\pm j\theta}$ close to the unit circle and close to the real axis, we have $b_1 \to -2$ and $b_2 \to 1$ so that the choice

$$\beta_1 = -2, \qquad \beta_2 = 1 \tag{5.73}$$

is most appropriate. This situation is common in narrowband lowpass filters. With this choice the noise transfer function is

$$G(z) = \frac{1 - 2z^{-1} + z^{-2}}{1 - 2r(\cos\theta)z^{-1} + r^2 z^{-2}} \tag{5.74}$$

It can be shown [24] that for $r \to 1$ and $\theta \to 0$, $\|G\|_2^2$ is approximately given by

$$\|G\|_2^2 = 1 + \frac{\theta^4}{4\delta(\theta^2 + \delta^2)} \tag{5.75}$$

where $\delta = 1 - r$. We can now proceed to calculate the noise-to-signal ratio for the structure of Fig. 5.20 under scaled conditions (i.e., with $1/L$ present). Note that the presence of EFB does not affect the overall input-output transfer function $H(z)$ or the required value of L in Fig. 5.20 for a given class of inputs (see Table VIII).

Table VIII can now be revised, with the above type of EFB. Assuming that β_1 and β_2 are as in Eq. (5.73), and with $\delta = 1 - r \to 0$ and $\theta \to 0$, Table IX shows a complete summary. In case of bounds on N/S as in entry 1 of Table VIII, the lower bound is taken as N/S for simplicity in Table IX. The low-noise performance of the circuit with EFB is clearly placed in evidence by this table. Thus, for entry #1, N/S varies as $1/\delta^2\theta^2$ with no EFB and as θ^2/δ^2 with EFB; for small θ, this clearly implies a significant improvement. Table 5.9 also shows a numerical example, which demonstrates about 26 dB improvement in N/S. This is equivalent to increasing the word length of conventional direct form (i.e., without EFB) by $26/6.02 \simeq 4$ bits.

Note that the only additional complexity introduced by the above EFB scheme is the inclusion of two adders and two b-bit storage registers. Once again, ESS is a compromise between single- and double-precision implementations.

The justification for the name "error-spectrum shaping" is once again evident from Eq. (5.74). The conventional noise transfer function [as in Eq. (5.50)] is replaced by Eq. (5.74), which is equivalent to adding *two zeros* at $z = 1$ in the noise spectrum. Thus, the "shaped" noise source has power spectral density $16\sin^4(\omega/2)\sigma_e^2$, whereas the unshaped noise source has a (white) spectral density equal to σ_e^2 for all ω.

TABLE IX

Noise Reduction in Second-Order Filter Sections with ESS

Entry No.	N/S ratio; $\delta \to 0, \theta \to 0, \theta \gg \delta$		Numerical example; $r = 0.995, \theta = 0.07\pi, b = 16,$ $\beta_1 = -2, \beta_2 = 1$ (N/S in dB)	
	No EFB	With EFB	No EFB	With EFB
1	$\dfrac{2^{-2b}}{16\delta^2\theta^2}$	$\dfrac{2^{-2b}\theta^2}{16\delta^2}$	-49.0	-75.17
2	$2^{-2b}\dfrac{3}{16\delta^2\theta^2}$	$2^{-2b}\dfrac{3\theta^2}{16\delta^2}$	-44.23	-70.4
3	$\dfrac{2^{-2b}}{24\delta\theta^2}$	$\dfrac{2^{-2b}}{24\delta}$	-74.0	-99.94
4	$2^{-2b}\dfrac{3}{16\delta\theta^2}$	$2^{-2b}\dfrac{3\theta^2}{16\delta}$	-67.42	-93.4

See Table VIII for meaning of "Entry No." In this table, b-bit rounding arithmetic is assumed; δ stands for $1 - r$.

1 Relation to the Agarwal and Burrus Structures

In 1975 Agarwal and Burrus [25] proposed a family of second-order IIR structures having low sensitivity and quantization noise for certain pole locations. Later on, Chang [26] used a different approach to show that some of the structures proposed by Agarwal and Burrus are equivalent to EFB structures. Chang's approach gives a natural explanation of the low-noise behavior of some of the structures in [25].

Consider once again the structure of Fig. 5.20. We know that if the pole locations are such that $r \to 1$ and $\theta \to 0$, then the choice $\beta_1 = -2, \beta_2 = 1$ leads to a low-noise implementation. Figure 5.20 can then be redrawn as in Fig. 5.21a, which in turn can be redrawn as in Fig. 5.21b. In this structure the multipliers involved are $\hat{b}_1 = -2 - b_1$ and $\hat{b}_2 = 1 - b_2$. Since b_1 is close to -2 and b_2 is close to 1, the quantities $\hat{b}_1$ and $\hat{b}_2$ are "small numbers." Let $\hat{b}_1 = m_1 \cdot 2^{c_1}, \hat{b}_2 = m_2 \cdot 2^{c_2}$, where $\frac{1}{2} \leq |m_1|, |m_2| < 1$ and c_1 and c_2 are appropriate integers. If m_1 and m_2 are implemented as b-bit fractions, then the equivalent accuracies of b_1 and b_2 are much higher. The representations of c_1 and c_2 do not require storage because they represent equivalent hardwired shifts of the signals being multiplied. Note that we are not digressing into a floating-point system because c_1 and c_2 are fixed for a given second-order filter. Because of the increased equivalent accuracy of b_1 and b_2, coefficient quantization effects are dramatically reduced [26]. This structure is precisely one of the structures proposed in [25], where certain judicious internal scaling schemes are incorporated to obtain a good SNR.

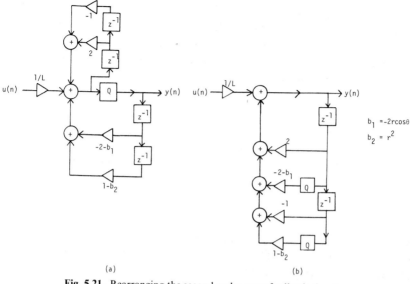

Fig. 5.21. Rearranging the second-order error feedback circuit.

Other related structures [24, 27–29] have been proposed by other authors for reducing noise and coefficient sensitivity. For want of space we refrain from elaborating further on these.

SIGNAL-TO-NOISE RATIO IN GENERAL DIGITAL   VII FILTER STRUCTURES

Digital filter structures are in practice more complicated than the simple structures of Figs. 5.5 and 5.14. For example, structures can be built by parallel or cascade interconnection of these sections. There exist even more sophisticated structures such as state-space structures [30–32], wave digital filters [33], and orthogonal digital filters [34], for which the scaling and quantization noise analysis cannot be performed as readily. A more general procedure is required in such cases.

Consider again Fig. 5.8, which shows a general digital filter structure. Recall from Section IV that there exists a subset of signals $r_k(n)$, $k = 1, 2, \ldots, P$, which alone need to be scaled, according to an appropriate scaling policy (see Table V). Now, let $e_1(n), e_2(n), \ldots, e_M(n)$ represent the errors due to quantizers in the structure. (It is *sufficient* to have a quantizer at the output of each multiplier, even though this is not *necessary*, for avoiding infinite bit accumulation. For example, in Fig. 5.15 it is necessary to use only one quantizer because the two loops containing the multipliers have a common branch.) Each $e_k(n)$ is assumed to satisfy the assumptions listed in Section III concerning noise sources. In addition, we assume that any pair of noise sources is uncorrelated. Let $G_k(z)$ denote the noise transfer functions from these noise sources to the filter output for the unscaled structure. Then the total quantization noise variance at the filter output for the unscaled structure is

$$\sigma_f^2 = \sigma_e^2 \sum_{k=1}^{M} \|G_k\|_2^2 \tag{5.76}$$

where σ_e^2 is as in Table IV.

We thus have two sets of transfer functions $F_k(z)$, $k = 1,\ldots, P$, and $G_k(z)$, $k = 1,\ldots, M$. *Scaling* is a process by which the transfer functions $F_k(z)$ are converted to F_k' such that $F_k'(z)$ satisfy one of the conditions in Table V; for example,

$$L_k \triangleq \|F_k'\|_2 \leq 1, \qquad 1 \leq k \leq P \tag{5.77}$$

In the process the functions $G_k(z)$ change to a new set $G_k'(z)$. But the overall transfer function $H(z) = Y(z)/X(z)$ should not change due to the scaling process. The scaled structure has output noise variance

$$\sigma_f^2 = \sigma_e^2 \sum_{k=1}^{M} \|G_k'\|_2^2 \tag{5.78}$$

Assuming for simplicity that the input $u(n)$ is white and WSS with uniform density, we obtain the output signal power

$$\sigma_y^2 = \tfrac{1}{3}\|H\|_2^2 \tag{5.79}$$

whence

$$\frac{N}{S} = 3\sigma_e^2 \frac{\displaystyle\sum_{k=1}^{M} \|G_k'\|_2^2}{\|H\|_2^2} \tag{5.80}$$

For a given scaling policy, Eq. (5.80) gives a meaningful performance measure. Note that the noise variance Eq. (5.76) for the unscaled structure is itself not meaningful, because there might be some internal signals that frequently overflow and other internal signals that occupy only a fraction of the dynamic range available to them.

VIII   LOW-NOISE CASCADE-FORM DIGITAL FILTER IMPLEMENTATION

Given a higher order IIR transfer function $H(z)$, a direct-form implementation as in Fig. 5.1 has several undesirable properties, as discussed earlier, such as high roundoff error, high coefficient sensitivity, and possibility of limit cycles. Accordingly, there exist several methods of implementing such a transfer func-

tion based of first- and second-order building blocks. Prominent among these
are the cascade-form and parallel-form structures [35].

Figure 5.22 shows a cascade-form structure for $H(z)$ where

$$H(z) = a_0 \prod_{k=1}^{M} H_k(z) \tag{5.81}$$

The building blocks $H_k(z)$ are second-order sections with

$$H_k(z) = \frac{1 + a_{1k}z^{-1} + a_{2k}z^{-2}}{1 + b_{1k}z^{-1} + b_{2k}z^{-2}} = \frac{A_k(z)}{B_k(z)} \tag{5.82}$$

These can, in general, be in direct form, coupled form, direct form with EFB, and
so on. Each second-order section can thus be implemented in any of several
possible ways. The order of $H(z)$ is clearly $2M$. If $H(z)$ has odd order, an
additional first-order section should be added. There are several types of direct-
form structures [4]. The structures in Fig. 5.22 are called direct-form 2 (DF2)
structures. For b-bit fixed-point fractional arithmetic, each internal signal has a
binary representation as in Fig. 5.2, so it is necessary to scale the structure to
avoid overflow. Recall from Section IV that only the inputs to (nonintegral)
multipliers need be scaled. Thus it is sufficient to ensure that the nodes indicated 1
through M are scaled.

Let $F_k(z)$ represent the transfer functions

$$F_k(z) \triangleq \frac{1}{1 + b_{1k}z^{-1} + b_{2k}z^{-2}} \prod_{l=1}^{k-1} H_l(z), \qquad k = 1, 2, \ldots, M \tag{5.83}$$

(For $k = 1$ the product $\prod_{l=1}^{k-1} H_l(z)$ is taken as unity.) Depending on the scaling
policy (Table V), an appropriate measure of $F_k(z)$ should be bounded by unity in
order to get a scaled structure. For L_p scaling let us define the numbers

$$S_k = \|F_k\|_p \tag{5.84}$$

Then the scaled structure is as shown in Fig. 5.23, which also shows the
quantizers. The noise transfer functions for the quantizer noise sources $e_k(n)$ in
the scaled structure are clearly

$$G'_k(z) = a_0 S_k \prod_{l=k}^{M} H_l(z) = S_k G_k(z) \tag{5.85}$$

With the usual assumptions on $e_k(n)$ (Sections III and VII), the noise variance at

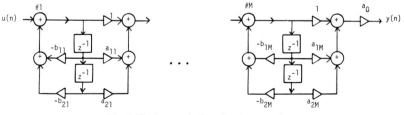

Fig. 5.22. A cascade-form implementation.

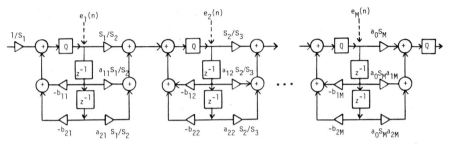

Fig. 5.23. The scaled cascade form; noise sources are also indicated.

the output of the scaled structure is

$$\sigma_f^2 = \sigma_e^2 \left[1 + \sum_{k=1}^{M} \| G_k' \|_2^2 \right] \tag{5.86}$$

where the unity term in brackets is due to the rightmost quantization in Fig. 5.23. Notice that scaling has not affected the overall transfer function Eq. (5.81); hence the output signal level for a given input signal is unaffected. The effect of scaling is to reduce the internal overflow probability, and this in turn affects the quantization noise variance at the filter output, as seen from the factors S_k in Eq. (5.85).

It has been observed [35] that the noise variance in Eq. (5.86) depends on the ordering of the sections and the pairing of second-order numerators (zeros) with the second-order denominators (poles). Jackson [35] has given intuitive guidelines for choosing the ordering scheme and pairing scheme. For L_2-scaling the section ordering does not seem to have a significant effect on Eq. (5.86). For L_∞-scaling, however, a judicious ordering scheme can reduce the output noise. We can see this by writing Eq. (5.86) as

$$\sigma_f^2 = \sigma_e^2 [1 + \| F_1 \|_p^2 \| G_1 \|_2^2 + \| F_2 \|_p^2 \| G_2 \|_2^2 + \cdots] \tag{5.87}$$

In Eq. (5.87), $p = \infty$ corresponds to L_∞-scaling. Recall from Table V that $\| F_k \|_\infty$ corresponds to $\max_\omega |F_k(e^{j\omega})|$; hence for L_∞-scaling,

$$\sigma_f^2 = \sigma_e^2 [1 + |F_1|_{\max}^2 \| G_1 \|_2^2 + |F_2|_{\max}^2 \| G_2 \|_2^2 + \cdots] \tag{5.88}$$

To minimize the effect of the "peak values" in the scaling transfer functions, it is judicious to order the sections according to increasing "peakedness." (Thus, the first section should have the least peakedness.) A quantitative measure of peakedness of the kth section $H_k(z)$ has been defined by Jackson [35] as

$$\rho_k = \frac{\| H_k \|_\infty}{\| H_k \|_2} \tag{5.89}$$

Thus, for L_∞-scaling, the section with smallest ρ_k should be the first section, and so on.

An intuitive guideline for the pairing of sections is to realize that if a pole is paired with the "nearest" zero, then the peakedness of the section is smallest, and therefore the overall noise variance is low. Several examples and further elaborate discussions on the above topic can be found in [35].

The Optimization Due to Liu and Peled 1

In general, a cascade-form structure having M sections gives rise to $M!$ different implementations because of $M!$ possible section orderings. Moreover, since each numerator can be paired with any one of the M denominators, there is a total of $(M!)^2$ possible cascade-form realizations. For example, with $M = 5$ (tenth-order filter), $(M!)^2 = 14,400$ different structures exist. The noise variance Eq. (5.86) under scaled conditions is, in general, different for these different structures. The natural question is, how can we find the best ordering (i.e., one that minimizes σ_f^2)? For digital filters having all transmission zeros at one point (such as lowpass Butterworth and Chebyshev filters, which have all zeros at $z = -1$), the number of distinct cascade-form structures is only $M!$, and an exhaustive search might be possible. However, for more general transfer functions (such as elliptic filters), in view of the large value of $(M!)^2$, an exhaustive search is not feasible. Hwang [36] has suggested a dynamic programming approach to reduce the search time for such cases. Liu and Peled [37] have proposed a heuristic procedure for arriving at a suboptimal cascade-form realization. The Liu–Peled procedure is much faster and generally leads to a solution that is very close to optimal. This algorithm can be described as follows:

1. Generate a random ordering of the numerators $\{A_k(z)\}$ and denominators $\{B_k(z)\}$ [see Eq. (5.82)].

2. By keeping the ordering of $\{A_k(z)\}$ fixed, interchange all possible pairs of $B_k(z)$. For each resulting cascade form, evaluate the noise variance σ_f^2 under scaled conditions [i.e., (5.86)]. This requires $[\binom{M}{2} + 1]$ evaluations of σ_f^2. Then the smallest σ_f^2 corresponds to a local optimum.

3. Repeat steps 1 and 2 a prescribed number of times L. Thus there are L local optima to choose from.

4. Pick the ordering and pairing that corresponds to the best local optimum.

Note that the above algorithm takes care of section ordering as well as pole–zero pairing. Even though it is heuristic and does not result in the global optimum, it generally leads to near-optimal results. Several examples demonstrating the usefulness of this technique can be found in [37].

NOISE REDUCTION IN THE CASCADE FORM BY ESS IX

In Section VI we found that ESS is a powerful approach to noise reduction in first- and second-order IIR filter sections. Since these sections are the basic building blocks in cascade-form implementations, we can design very low-noise cascade-form filters by ESS. In Section VI.B we saw that the most suitable choice of the EFB coefficients β_1, β_2 is obtained by rounding b_1 and b_2 to the nearest integers. Thus for narrowband lowpass designs, the choice of Eq. (5.73) is best. This choice is also compatible with the viewpoint that the ESS technique is a compromise between single- and double-precision implementations.

Let us now reconsider the scaled cascade-form structure of Fig. 5.23. If we incorporate EFB into each section, the resulting structure is as shown in Fig. 5.24. Notice that a scaled structure continues to remain scaled, even after EFB is incorporated. Thus EFB has the effect of changing the noise transfer functions without affecting either the scaling properties or the input-output behavior. The total noise variance at the output of the scaled filter is now given by an expression similar to Eq. (5.86), except that the spectral shaping factors

$$1 + \beta_{1k}z^{-1} + \beta_{2k}z^{-2} \tag{5.90a}$$

are now to be taken into account. (See Eq. (5.71) and discussions thereof.) Thus the output noise variance for the scaled filter is

$$\sigma_f^2 = \sigma_e^2 \left[1 + \sum_{k=1}^{M} \|(1 + \beta_{1k}z^{-1} + \beta_{2k}z^{-2})G_k'\|_2^2 \right] \tag{5.90b}$$

where G_k' is as in Eq. (5.85). The EFB coefficients β_{1k}, β_{2k} for the kth section affect only the kth term in the summation of Eq. (5.90b), so the best choices of β_{1k}, β_{2k} are obtained by minimizing the kth term in Eq. (5.90b) independent of other terms. Thus β_{1k}, β_{2k} are found by solving the following problem:

$$\underset{\beta_{1k},\beta_{2k}}{\text{minimize}} \, \|(1 + \beta_{1k}z^{-1} + \beta_{2k}z^{-2}) \prod_{l=k}^{M} H_l(z)\|_2^2 \tag{5.91}$$

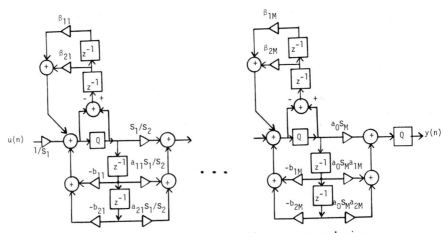

Fig. 5.24. The scaled cascade-form with error-spectrum shaping.

The solution to this problem is derived in [22], and the results are as follows:

$$\beta_{1k} = \frac{J_1 J_2 - J_1 J_3}{J_3^2 - J_1^2}, \qquad \beta_{2k} = \frac{J_1^2 - J_2 J_3}{J_3^2 - J_1^2} \tag{5.92}$$

where

$$J_1 = \frac{1}{\pi} \int_0^{2\pi} Q(\omega)\cos \omega \, d\omega \tag{5.93a}$$

$$J_2 = \frac{1}{\pi} \int_0^{2\pi} Q(\omega)\cos(2\omega) \, d\omega \tag{5.93b}$$

$$J_3 = \frac{1}{\pi} \int_0^{2\pi} Q(\omega) \, d\omega \tag{5.93c}$$

The quantities J_1, J_2, J_3, and $Q(\omega)$ depend on the section number k, though this dependence is not indicated in Eq. (5.93) for simplicity of notation. Here $Q(\omega)$ is defined by

$$Q(\omega) = \prod_{l=k}^{M} |H_l(e^{j\omega})|^2 \tag{5.94}$$

where $H_l(z)$ are the second-order transfer functions in Eq. (5.82). Thus, in practice, one would compute β_{1k} and β_{2k} for all k using Eq. (5.92) and then round the results to the nearest integers (or powers of 2) for simplicity of EFB network. Note that, unlike in single, isolated second-order sections, the optimal choice of Eq. (5.92) does not necessarily represent a simple "double-precision" implementation. The reason is that the optimal choice in Eq. (5.92) depends on all the transfer functions $H_k(z)$, $H_{k+1}(z), \ldots, H_M(z)$.

If we are interested only in applying a first-order EFB to the second-order sections, then the optimal choice [22] is given by $\beta_{1k} = -J_1/J_3$ and β_{2k} is, of course, zero.

As a design example [22], consider a tenth-order elliptic lowpass filter with passband edge equal to $\pi/4$. The scaled cascade-form structure of Fig. 5.23 has noise gain σ_f^2/σ_e^2 equal to 20.77 dB, whereas the EFB-based cascade form of Fig. 5.24 has noise gain equal to 5.91 dB. The EFB coefficients, which are taken as power-of-2 approximations to (5.90) are given by $\beta_{1k} = -2$, $\beta_{2k} = 1$ for all k, in this example.[†]

It is thus clear that ESS techniques can reduce the effect of quantization errors in cascade-form implementations. Once again, section ordering and pole pairing should be carefully considered for further improvement in SNR. Further discussions and guidelines can be found in [22].

[†] The comparison is made for a fixed ordering and pole–zero pairing. See [22] for details.

X LOW-NOISE DESIGNS VIA STATE-SPACE OPTIMIZATION

Any IIR digital filter transfer function $H(z)$ given by

$$H(z) = \frac{Y(z)}{U(z)} = \frac{q_0 + q_1 z^{-1} + \cdots + q_N z^{-N}}{1 + p_1 z^{-1} + \cdots + p_N z^{-N}} \tag{5.95}$$

can be implemented as [30–32] follows:

$$\mathbf{x}(n + 1) = \mathbf{A}\mathbf{x}(n) + \mathbf{B}u(n) \tag{5.96a}$$

$$y(n) = \mathbf{C}\mathbf{x}(n) + Du(n) \tag{5.96b}$$

where $\mathbf{x}(n)$ is an N-vector called the state vector, $\mathbf{A}$ is an $N \times N$ matrix, $\mathbf{B}$ is an $N \times 1$ matrix (column vector), $\mathbf{C}$ is a $1 \times N$ matrix (row vector), and D is a scalar.[†] Thus the output sequence $\{y(n)\}$ is related to the input sequence $\{u(n)\}$ by N coupled first-order difference equations (5.96). Recall, in contrast, that the direct-form structure implements $H(z)$ as a single Nth-order difference equation:

$$\sum_{k=0}^{N} p_k y(n - k) = \sum_{k=0}^{N} q_k u(n - k) \tag{5.97}$$

Given a direct-form implementation as in Fig. 5.25, the state variables $x_k(n)$ can be identified as shown. Essentially, these are the outputs of the delay elements.

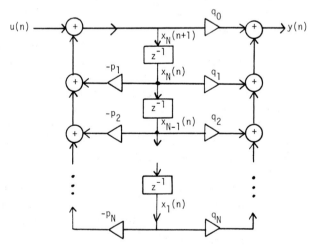

Fig. 5.25. State variables in the direct-form structure.

[†] The reader may want to review Section I on matrix notation.

With $\mathbf{x}(n)$ defined as

$$\mathbf{x}(n) = [x_1(n), x_2(n), \ldots, x_N(n)]^{\mathrm{T}} \qquad (5.98)$$

it is easily verified that for the direct form are given by

$$\mathbf{A} = \begin{bmatrix} 0 & 1 & 0 & \cdots & & 0 \\ 0 & 0 & 1 & \cdots & & 0 \\ \vdots & & & & & \\ 0 & \cdots & & & 0 & 1 \\ -p_N & -p_{N-1} & \cdots & & -p_2 & -p_1 \end{bmatrix}$$

$$\mathbf{B} = [0 \quad 0 \quad \cdots \quad 0 \quad 1]^{\mathrm{T}}$$

$$\mathbf{C} = [q_N - q_0 p_N \quad q_{N-1} - q_0 p_{N-1} \quad \cdots \quad q_1 - q_0 p_1]$$

$$D = q_0 \qquad (5.99)$$

A *state-space implementation* $(\mathbf{A}, \mathbf{B}, \mathbf{C}, D)$ is an implementation in which the elements of $\mathbf{A}, \mathbf{B}, \mathbf{C}, D$ are the multiplier coefficients. Thus the state-space implementation corresponding to Eq. (5.99) is as shown in Fig. 5.26. Note that Fig. 5.25, strictly speaking, is not a state-space implementation.

For emphasis, we wish to observe that, given any digital filter structure, we can always *write* a set of state equations as in Eq. (5.96), thus obtaining a state-space representation. However, the digital filter structure is said to be an implementation of the state equations so obtained only if the elements of $\mathbf{A}, \mathbf{B}, \mathbf{C}, D$ physically appear as multipliers in the structure.

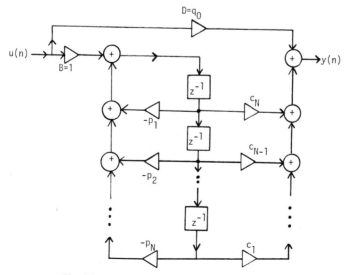

Fig. 5.26. The state-space structure of Eq. (5.99).

A Analysis of the State Equations

It is easily verified that the impulse response $h(n)$ from $u(n)$ to $y(n)$ (i.e., the filter impulse response) is given in terms of A, B, C, D by

$$h(n) = CA^{(n-1)}B1(n-1) + D\,\delta(n) \tag{5.100}$$

where $1(\cdot)$ represents the unit-step function. The transfer function $H(z)$ is related to the state-space parameters by

$$H(z) = C(zI - A)^{-1}B + D \tag{5.101}$$

It can be shown that the eigenvalues of A are precisely the poles of $H(z)$. Throughout this chapter we assume that there is no pole–zero cancellation in Eq. (5.95) and that $p_N \neq 0$. Thus Eq. (5.95) represents a minimal rational function, and Eq. (5.96) represents a minimal realization. Moreover, we assume for obvious practical reasons that $H(z)$ is stable and, hence, that the magnitudes of all eigenvalues of A are strictly less than unity.

Assuming zero initial conditions (i.e., $x(0) = 0$), if we apply an impulse for the input $u(n)$, then the state vector is

$$x(n) = A^{n-1}B1(n-1) \tag{5.102}$$

Thus, Eq. (5.102) represents the impulse response vector from $u(n)$ to $x(n)$. Similarly, under zero input conditions, if x_0 represents the state vector at $n = 0$ (i.e., $x(0) = x_0$), then

$$y(n) = CA^n x_0 1(n) \tag{5.103}$$

Thus, the impulse response from $u(n)$ to $x_k(n)$ is

$$f_k(n) = \begin{cases} [A^{n-1} \quad B]_k, & n > 0 \\ 0, & n \le 0 \end{cases} \tag{5.104}$$

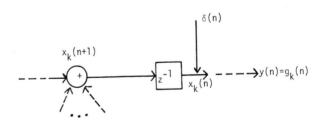

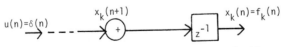

Fig. 5.27. The responses $f_k(n)$ and $g_k(n)$.

whereas the impulse response from the kth state terminal to the output terminal is

$$g_k(n) = \begin{cases} [\mathbf{C} \ \mathbf{A}^n]_k, & n \geq 0 \\ 0, & n < 0 \end{cases} \tag{5.105}$$

Figure 5.27 demonstrates this. The quantities $f_k(n)$ and $g_k(n)$ play an important role in the noise-minimization procedure [31], as elaborated later.

Similarity Transformations   B

Given a state-space structure $(\mathbf{A}, \mathbf{B}, \mathbf{C}, D)$ for a digital filter, the transfer function is given by Eq. (5.101). The following set of manipulations leave $H(z)$ unchanged:

$$\begin{aligned} H(z) &= \mathbf{C}(z\mathbf{I} - \mathbf{A})^{-1}\mathbf{B} + D \\ &= \mathbf{C}\mathbf{T}\mathbf{T}^{-1}(z\mathbf{I} - \mathbf{A})^{-1}\mathbf{T}\mathbf{T}^{-1}\mathbf{B} + D \\ &= \mathbf{C}\mathbf{T}(z\mathbf{I} - \mathbf{T}^{-1}\mathbf{A}\mathbf{T})^{-1}\mathbf{T}^{-1}\mathbf{B} + D \\ &= H(z) \end{aligned} \tag{5.106}$$

where $\mathbf{T}$ is *any* $N \times N$ nonsingular matrix. Thus, given a state-space structure $(\mathbf{A}, \mathbf{B}, \mathbf{C}, D)$, we can trivially obtain an equivalent representation

$$\mathbf{A}_1 = \mathbf{T}^{-1}\mathbf{A}\mathbf{T}, \quad \mathbf{B}_1 = \mathbf{T}^{-1}\mathbf{B}, \quad \mathbf{C}_1 = \mathbf{C}\mathbf{T}, \quad D_1 = D \tag{5.107}$$

having the same transfer function $H(z)$. Transformations of the form in Eq. (5.107) are called *similarity transformations*. Since $\mathbf{T}$ is an entirely arbitrary (nonsingular) matrix, we have an infinite number of state-variable structures for implementing the same transfer function.

The natural question now is whether these structures all yield the same output SNR. It turns out that the SNR under scaled conditions is strongly dependent upon the actual state-space realization. In other words, given an arbitrary realization $(\mathbf{A}, \mathbf{B}, \mathbf{C}, D)$ for a particular transfer function $H(z)$, there exists an optimal equivalent structure $(\mathbf{A}_1, \mathbf{B}_1, \mathbf{C}_1, D_1)$ derivable as in Eq. (5.107), which has the lowest noise-to-signal ratio under scaled conditions. The purpose of this section is to present design rules and algorithms for obtaining such structures.

Complexity of State-Space Structures   1

We can easily verify that an explicit implementation of Eq. (5.96) requires $(N + 1)^2$ multipliers and $(N + 1)N$ two-input adders. (The example of Eq. (5.99) is a special case where many of the multiplier coefficients are zero.) In comparison, a direct-form implementation (Fig. 5.25) of Eq. (5.95) requires only $(2N + 1)$ multipliers, whereas a cascade form (Fig. 5.23) requires $5N/2 + 1$ multipliers (for

N even). Thus, for $N = 10$ the general multiplier count is

$$\begin{array}{ll}
\text{Direct form} & 21 \\
\text{Cascade form} & 26 \\
\text{State-space} & 121
\end{array} \qquad (5.108)$$

In other words, the cost of implementation of a general Nth-order state-space structure is exorbitantly high. Thus, even though the roundoff noise can be minimized for a given N, enabling us to use a smaller value for b, the overall implementation cost might be much higher because of the increased multiplier requirement. Moreover, in examples of the form in (5.99), many of the multipliers are 0's and 1's and therefore do not generate roundoff noise. Since this fact is not easily taken into account in the noise-minimization process for general state-space structures, the minimum-noise state-space implementation might even have *higher* noise than an implementation with fewer nontrivial multipliers.

In view of these problems the fundamental results reported in [31] have been adapted for the generation of minimum-noise, second-order, state-space filters by several authors [38–41]. For $N = 2$ the number of multipliers is not large, and the minimum-noise state-space structure often represents a global minimum-noise structure, particularly for narrowband filters. In this section simple and useful guidelines for such designs are presented.

C Roundoff Noise and Dynamic Range in State-Space Structures

Assume that $u(n)$, $y(n)$ and all internal signals, $\mathbf{x}(n)$, are represented by b-bit fixed-point fractions as in Fig. 5.2. Figure 5.28 shows a schematic of the state-space structure. To avoid internal overflow, it is necessary and sufficient for us to scale the signals $x_k(n)$ (which are inputs to multipliers). Recall that the impulse response from the filter input to the kth state variable is given as in Eq. (5.104).

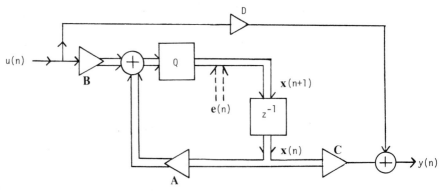

Fig. 5.28. The state-space structure with quantizer.

Thus, for L_2-scaling policy we would like to have

$$\|F_k(z)\|_2^2 \triangleq \sum_{n=0}^{\infty} f_k^2(n) = 1, \qquad 1 \le k \le N \tag{5.109}$$

Next consider the quantization noise vector $e(n) = [e_1(n), \ldots, e_N(n)]^{\mathrm{T}}$, where

$$e_k(n) = Q[(\mathbf{Ax}(n) + \mathbf{B}u(n))_k] - (\mathbf{Ax}(n) + \mathbf{B}u(n))_k \tag{5.110}$$

We assume that each $e_k(n)$ satisfies the assumptions made in Section III, and that $e_k(n)$ and $e_l(n)$ are uncorrelated for $k \ne l$. We easily verify that the impulse response from the location of the noise sources $e(n)$ to the output terminal $y(n)$ is $\mathbf{CA}^{n-1}\mathbf{1}(n-1)$. In other words, $g_k(n)$ in Eq. (5.105) precisely represent the impulse responses of the noise transfer functions $G_k(z)$ (except for a delay). Thus the noise variance at the output is

$$\sigma_f^2 = \sigma_e^2 \sum_{k=1}^{N} \|G_k\|_2^2 \tag{5.111}$$

where

$$\|G_k\|_2^2 = \int_0^{2\pi} |G_k(e^{j\omega})|^2 \frac{d\omega}{2\pi} = \sum_{n=0}^{\infty} g_k^2(n) \tag{5.112}$$

and σ_e^2 is as in Table 5.4. When we apply a similarity transformation, the quantities $f_k(n)$ and $g_k(n)$ change. Thus, both the scaling (i.e., dynamic range) and noise properties are altered by $\mathbf{T}$ in Eq. (5.107). An efficient way to keep track of these changes of $f_k(n)$ and $g_k(n)$ is through the so-called $\mathbf{K}$ and $\mathbf{W}$ matrices [31].

The Matrices K and W   1

Since $g_k(n)$ is the kth component of the row vector $\mathbf{CA}^n$, the diagonal elements of the $N \times N$ matrix $(\mathbf{CA}^n)^{\mathrm{T}}(\mathbf{CA}^n)$ are precisely the quantities $g_k^2(n)$. Now define the $N \times N$ matrix

$$\mathbf{W} = \sum_{n=0}^{\infty} (\mathbf{CA}^n)^{\mathrm{T}}(\mathbf{CA}^n) \tag{5.113}$$

Clearly

$$W_{kk} = \sum_{n=0}^{\infty} g_k^2(n) = \|G_k\|_2^2 \tag{5.114}$$

In a similar manner, defining the $N \times N$ matrix

$$\mathbf{K} = \sum_{n=0}^{\infty} \mathbf{A}^n \mathbf{B} (\mathbf{A}^n \mathbf{B})^{\mathrm{T}} \tag{5.115}$$

we clearly see that the diagonal elements of $\mathbf{K}$ are

$$K_{kk} = \sum_{n=0}^{\infty} f_k^2(n) = \|F_k\|_2^2 \tag{5.116}$$

Thus, a state-space structure has total output noise variance Eq. (5.111) given by

$$\sigma_f^2 = \sigma_e^2 \sum_{k=1}^{N} W_{kk} \tag{5.117}$$

and a state-space structure is said to be scaled in the L_2-sense if

$$K_{kk} = 1, \qquad 0 \le k \le N \tag{5.118}$$

Equation (5.118) is called the *scaling constraint*.

By definition, $\mathbf{K}$ and $\mathbf{W}$ are real, symmetric, positive semidefinite matrices satisfying the matrix equalities

$$\mathbf{K} = \mathbf{AKA}^T + \mathbf{BB}^T \tag{5.119}$$

$$\mathbf{W} = \mathbf{A}^T\mathbf{WA} + \mathbf{C}^T\mathbf{C} \tag{5.120}$$

Moreover, since Eq. (5.96) is assumed to represent a minimal stable system, it can be verified that $\mathbf{K}$ and $\mathbf{W}$ are strictly positive definite. Thus

$$\mathbf{K} = \mathbf{K}^T > 0, \qquad \mathbf{W} = \mathbf{W}^T > 0 \tag{5.121}$$

It can also be shown that, under a similarity transformation Eq. (5.107), $\mathbf{K}$ and $\mathbf{W}$ transform as follows:

$$\mathbf{K}_1 = \mathbf{T}^{-1}\mathbf{KT}^{-T}, \qquad \mathbf{W}_1 = \mathbf{T}^T\mathbf{WT} \tag{5.122}$$

Thus, in particular,

$$\mathbf{K}_1\mathbf{W}_1 = \mathbf{T}^{-1}(\mathbf{KW})\mathbf{T} \tag{5.123}$$

whence the eigenvalues $\mathbf{KW}$ are invariant under a similarity transformation. These eigenvalues, which are always positive, are denoted μ_k^2, and μ_k are called the "second-order modes" [31] of the system $H(z)$.

2 Scaling the State-Space Structure

Given a state-space realization as in Eq. (5.96) with matrices $\mathbf{W}$, $\mathbf{K}$ as in Eqs. (5.113) and (5.115), we can easily obtain a scaled realization $(\mathbf{A}_1, \mathbf{B}_1, \mathbf{C}_1, D_1)$ by applying the diagonal transformation

$$\mathbf{T} = \begin{bmatrix} \sqrt{K_{11}} & & & \\ & \sqrt{K_{22}} & & 0 \\ & & \ddots & \\ 0 & & & \sqrt{K_{NN}} \end{bmatrix} \tag{5.124}$$

because, by Eq. (5.122), we get

$$\mathbf{K}_1 = \mathbf{T}^{-1}\mathbf{KT}^{-T} = \begin{bmatrix} 1 & & & \\ & 1 & & \times \\ & & \ddots & \\ & \times & & 1 \end{bmatrix} \tag{5.125}$$

that is, $(\mathbf{K}_1)_{ii} = 1$ for all i, satisfying the scaling constraint. The **W**-matrix of the scaled realization is[†]

$$
\mathbf{W}_1 = \mathbf{T}^{\mathsf{T}}\mathbf{W}\mathbf{T} =
\begin{bmatrix}
K_{11}W_{11} & & & \times \\
& K_{22}W_{22} & & \\
& & \ddots & \\
\times & & & K_{NN}W_{NN}
\end{bmatrix}
\tag{5.126}
$$

Thus the noise variance at the output of the scaled realization is

$$
\sigma_f^2 = \sigma_e^2 \sum_{k=1}^{N} (\mathbf{W}_1)_{kk} = \sigma_e^2 \sum_{k=1}^{N} K_{kk} W_{kk}
\tag{5.127}
$$

Equation (5.127) expresses the noise variance for the scaled structure in terms of the parameters **K**, **W** of the unscaled structure.

Thus, the noise-minimization problem can be stated as follows: given an initial state-space realization $\mathbf{A}_0, \mathbf{B}_0, \mathbf{C}_0, \mathbf{D}_0$ for $H(z)$, find a new equivalent description **A, B, C, D**,

$$
\mathbf{A} = \mathbf{T}^{-1}\mathbf{A}_0\mathbf{T}, \quad \mathbf{B} = \mathbf{T}^{-1}\mathbf{B}_0, \quad \mathbf{C} = \mathbf{C}_0\mathbf{T}, \quad D = D_0
\tag{5.128}
$$

such that $\sum_{k=1}^{N} K_{kk} W_{kk}$ is minimized—that is, smallest among all equivalent state-space realizations of $H(z)$. Once we find such a realization, it is trivial to obtain a scaled realization $\mathbf{A}_1, \mathbf{B}_1, \mathbf{C}_1, D_1$ as described above.

Mullis and Roberts [31] have laid down the necessary and sufficient conditions for $(\mathbf{A}, \mathbf{B}, \mathbf{C}, D)$ to represent such an optimal realization. We next state these conditions. The detailed proofs, based on intricate linear algebraic inequalities, are omitted.

Necessary and Sufficient Conditions for (A, B, C, D) to Represent a Minimum-Noise Realization

Consider the state-space realization Eq. (5.96), implemented as in Fig. 5.28. The quantization noise source $e(n)$ has components $e_k(n)$ as in Eq. (5.110). Assuming equal word length for each $x_k(n)$, and under the usual assumptions about noise sources, we have

$$
\sigma_e^2 = \text{variance of each noise source } e_k(n)
$$

as in Table IV. The output noise variance is as in Eq. (5.117), whereas the output noise variance of the scaled realization in terms of the unscaled parameters is as in Eq. (5.127).

Theorem 5.1. Under the above conditions and noise modeling, $(\mathbf{A}, \mathbf{B}, \mathbf{C}, D)$

[†] The cross in Eqs. (5.125) and (5.126) indicates that the nondiagonal entries are unconstrained.

represents a minimum-noise realization if and only if **K** and **W** satisfy

(i) $\mathbf{K} = \mathbf{D}_0\mathbf{W}\mathbf{D}_0$,
(ii) $K_{kk}W_{kk} = $ constant independent of k

for some diagonal matrix $\mathbf{D}_0$ of positive elements.

The above condition implies that for L_2-scaled structures (i.e., when $K_{kk} = 1$ for all k), the roundoff noise is minimum if and only if $\mathbf{W} = \rho^2\mathbf{K}$, where ρ is some scalar constant. Note that for such systems $W_{kk} = $ constant; that is, the noise contribution to the output is the same from all N noise sources. In view of the practical significance, we state these results as a lemma:

Lemma 5.1. A scaled realization—a realization with $K_{kk} = 1$ for all k—has the smallest possible roundoff noise if and only if

$$\mathbf{W} = \rho^2\mathbf{K} \qquad (5.129)$$

for some real scalar ρ. Under this condition, $W_{kk} = $ constant, thus equalizing the noise contribution at the output due to all internal quantizers.

Based on these results, several authors have obtained closed-form expressions and design equations for second-order state-space structures having minimum noise. If such structures are used in cascade-form or parallel-form realizations, the resulting structures have impressively low noise performance.

4   Minimum-Noise Second-Order IIR Filters

Jackson et al. [38] showed that the conditions for minimum roundoff noise in second-order sections can be expressed in a particularly simple form. Based on this, they obtained closed-form expressions for the matrices **A**, **B**, **C** of a minimum-noise realization. Jackson et al. showed that the conditions of Lemma 5.1 are satisfied by any second-order state-space structure such that

$$a_{11} = a_{22} \qquad (5.130a)$$

$$b_1c_1 = b_2c_2 \qquad (5.130b)$$

Thus Eqs. (5.130a) and (5.130b) form a set of sufficient conditions[†] for a scaled structure to have minimum noise. The synthesis of low-noise second-order sections thus reduces to the problem of satisfying Eq. (5.130) while preserving the property $k_{11} = k_{22} = 1$.

With Jackson's conditions as a starting point, a number of authors have approached this problem from different viewpoints [39–41] and obtained alternative and simpler expressions for **A**, **B**, **C** and the noise gain σ_f^2/σ_e^2 of the optimal realization.

[†] It has not been proved, however, that these conditions are necessary. Perhaps they are not.

For want of space we include only one of these approaches to second-order minimum-noise design. The method we describe is due to Barnes [40]. Let

$$H(z) = \frac{q_0 + q_1 z^{-1} + q_2 z^{-2}}{1 + p_1 z^{-1} + p_2 z^{-2}} \tag{5.131}$$

represent a second-order section. We assume that the poles are complex conjugates given by[†]

$$\lambda = \sigma + j\omega, \quad \lambda* \tag{5.132}$$

Since q_0 in Eq. (5.131) is equal to D in Eq. (5.96), which is invariant under similarity transformations, it is sufficient to obtain the optimal (minimum-noise) state-space structure for $G(z) = H(z) - q_0$:

$$G(z) = \frac{q_1' z^{-1} + q_2' z^{-2}}{1 + p_1 z^{-1} + p_2 z^{-2}} = \frac{q_1' z + q_2'}{z^2 + p_1 z + p_2} \tag{5.133a}$$

which can be expressed in partial-fraction form as

$$G(z) = \frac{\alpha}{z - \lambda} + \frac{\alpha*}{z - \lambda*} \tag{5.133b}$$

where the residue α is in general complex:

$$\alpha = \alpha_r + j\alpha_i \tag{5.133c}$$

Let us define the intermediate real-valued parameters P, Q, R by

$$P = \frac{|\alpha|}{1 - |\lambda|^2}, \quad R + jQ = \frac{\alpha}{1 - \lambda^2} \tag{5.134}$$

Then a scaled minimum-noise state-space structure for $G(z)$ is

$$A = \begin{bmatrix} \sigma & k\omega \\ -\omega/k & \sigma \end{bmatrix}, \quad B = \begin{bmatrix} b_1 \\ b_2 \end{bmatrix}, \quad C = [c_1 \quad c_2] \tag{5.135}$$

where

$$k = \sqrt{\frac{P + Q}{P - Q}} \tag{5.136a}$$

$$b_1 = \sqrt{\frac{|\alpha| - \alpha_i}{P - Q}}, \quad b_2 = -\sqrt{\frac{|\alpha| + \alpha_i}{P + Q}} \, \text{sgn}(\alpha_r) \tag{5.136b}$$

and

$$c_1 = \frac{\alpha_r}{b_1}, \quad c_2 = \frac{\alpha_r}{b_2} \tag{5.137a}$$

[†] Recall that asterisk denotes complex conjugation.

This structure is scaled in the L_2-sense; that is, $\mathbf{K}_{11} = \mathbf{K}_{22} = 1$. The noise gain of the structure σ_f^2/σ_e^2 is

$$\frac{\sigma_f^2}{\sigma_e^2} = 2[P^2 - Q^2] \qquad (5.137b)$$

Thus, given the transfer function $H(z)$, we have a simple and elegant way of designing the L_2-scaled minimum-noise structure and computing the noise gain of the resulting structure. Closed-form expressions for structures scaled in a L_p-sense, with $p \neq 2$, have not been reported in the literature to the best of our knowledge.

XI PARAMETER QUANTIZATION AND LOW-SENSITIVITY DIGITAL FILTERS

Given a digital filter structure as in Fig. 5.8, the multiplier coefficients m_k in practice can be represented only with a limited number of bits. This multiplier-quantization produces a deviation of $|H(e^{j\omega})|$ from its ideal value, and this is termed the "sensitivity problem." The sensitivity of the phase response $\arg(H(e^{j\omega}))$ has not received as much attention as the magnitude response sensitivity. This is partially because the latter is generally more important in applications. In situations where the phase distortion cannot be tolerated, one can generally employ linear-phase FIR filters, which have an exact linear phase in spite of multiplier quantization. For the rest of this chapter, "sensitivity" refers only to sensitivity of $|H(e^{j\omega})|$.

For a low-sensitivity structure the variation of $|H(e^{j\omega})|$ with respect to multiplier values is small; hence we can obtain an implementation with very few bits per multiplier that reduces the implementation expense.

For large filter order N the IIR direct-form structure of Fig. 5.25 has very high sensitivity; that is, in order to obtain a response that is satisfactorily close to the infinite-precision response, one has to use an exorbitantly large number of bits per multiplier. The reason for this is that the roots of a polynomial are very sensitive to the coefficients, so the poles and zeros of $H(z)$ are very sensitive to the multipliers p_k and q_k in Fig. 5.25. If z_i represents a pole of $H(z)$ in Eq. (5.95), then it can be shown [4] that

$$\frac{\partial z_i}{\partial p_k} = \frac{-z_i^{N-k}}{\displaystyle\prod_{l=1; l \neq i}^{N} (z_i - z_l)} \qquad (5.138)$$

For standard filters such as lowpass and bandpass, the poles are generally crowded at angles close to the bandedge, as shown in Fig. 5.29. Hence, the quantities $z_i - z_l$ are very small in Eq. (5.138), and their product is exceedingly

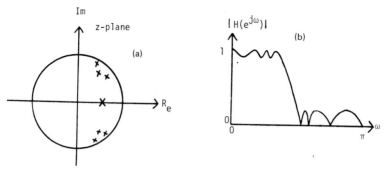

Fig. 5.29. Pole crowding in IIR transfer functions (a) Example of pole locations. (b) Typical magnitude response.

small. Thus, a small change in p_k leads to a large change in z_i. This effect is called *pole crowding*.

The simplest way to avoid this sensitivity problem is to implement $H(z)$ as a sum or a product of first- and second-order sections leading, respectively, to parallel-form and cascade-form implementations [4, 5]. This clearly eliminates the pole-crowding effect to a large extent. However, for complex-conjugate poles with small pole angles, we still have high-sensitivity problems even with second-order sections. Accordingly, researchers have developed new second-order sections with low sensitivity. If these sections are used in cascade or parallel structures, the resulting sensitivity is generally acceptable.

An entirely different approach to the synthesis of low-sensitivity digital filters is to simulate continuous-time LC (i.e., inductance-capacitance) filters digitally. Certain continuous-time LC filters (the doubly terminated lossless networks) are well known for low *passband* sensitivity [42, 43]. Fettweis has shown how a realizable digital filter structure can be developed by simulating certain "wave variables" pertaining to the LC structure. Such wave filters [33, 44] have been studied extensively. In particular, the potentiality and usefulness of lattice wave filters has been well established [45, 46].

Another family of structures having low passband sensitivity is the class of orthogonal digital filters [34]. Certain digital lattice filters introduced by Gray and Markel [47–49] are known to be "partially orthogonal" in the sense that the recursive part [i.e., the denominator of $H(z)$] is realized in an orthogonal manner. Truly orthogonal filters can be implemented entirely in terms of planar rotation building blocks and are suitable for very large-scale integration (VLSI) architectures [50].

Wave filters and orthogonal filters have several other desirable properties in addition to low passband sensitivity. Thus, they can be designed so as to be free of "limit cycles" [51, 52]. In addition, the multiplier parameters in these structures can always be quantized in such a way that the quantized implementation is guaranteed to be stable. Many of these structures also have low roundoff noise.

Finally, certain wave filters (the lattice wave filters) and certain orthogonal filters [46, 50] lend themselves to implementations with a high amount of computational parallelism.

In the next few sections we present results and design-oriented aspects concerning some of these of low-sensitivity digital filters. It can be shown that, as a general rule, low-sensitivity digital filters also have low quantization noise under scaled conditions [53]. Even though this is not a direct proportionality relation, it gives us a fairly dependable guideline for relating sensitivity to roundoff noise. Some of these aspects are also explored in the succeeding sections.

1 "Measuring" Sensitivity

There have been a variety of "measures" of sensitivity that authors have used for comparing the sensitivity of different structures. In general, it is difficult to define a single measure that is applicable in all contexts.

Some authors use as a measure of sensitivity the fractional change in $|H(e^{j\omega})|$ defined as

$$S_{m_k}^{|H|} = \frac{m_k}{|H(e^{j\omega})|} \frac{\partial |H(e^{j\omega})|}{\partial m_k} \tag{5.139}$$

where this quantity is clearly a function of ω and should be specified for every multiplier m_k. The fractional change in $|H(e^{j\omega})|$ due to the perturbation of m_k is

$$\frac{\Delta |H(e^{j\omega})|}{|H(e^{j\omega})|} = S_{m_k}^{|H|} \frac{\Delta m_k}{m_k} \tag{5.140}$$

Thus, the fractional changes $\Delta |H|/|H|$ and $\Delta m_k/m_k$ are related by $S_{m_k}^{|H|}$.

The sensitivity of the poles with respect to multipliers is often a useful measure. For second-order sections with poles at $re^{\pm j\theta}$, the measures

$$\frac{\partial r}{\partial m_k}, \quad \frac{\partial \theta}{\partial m_k} \tag{5.141}$$

are commonly used, where m_k is the kth distinct multiplier. For state-space structures (of any order) the sensitivity of the poles (which are eigenvalues λ_k of $\mathbf{A}$) with respect to the elements a_{nm} of $\mathbf{A}$ is often employed [40]:

$$\frac{\partial \lambda_k}{\partial a_{nm}}, \quad 1 \leq k, n, m \leq N \tag{5.142}$$

The only disadvantage of Eq. (5.142) is that there are N^3 numbers characterizing the sensitivity. Some authors [40] prefer to use a global measure of sensitivity for state-space structures, defined by

$$S(\lambda_k, \mathbf{A}) = \left[\sum_{n,m} \left| \frac{\partial \lambda_k}{\partial a_{nm}} \right|^2 \right]^{1/2} \tag{5.143}$$

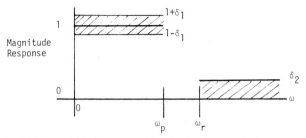

Fig. 5.30. A typical tolerance specification for the magnitude response.

It can be shown that $S(\lambda_k, \mathbf{A})$ has a lower bound of unity for any realization. This lower bound is achieved by certain structures, such as the normal form [54].

Crochiere [55] has used some useful and intuitive measures for comparing the sensitivity of digital filter structures. Consider a typical lowpass filter specification as in Fig. 5.30. The passband response of an equiripple design under unquantized conditions is shown in Fig. 5.31, which also shows a typical response with multipliers quantized to b bits. The peak-to-peak error $H_{max} - H_{min}$ is greater than the ideal tolerance A_M. The fractional deterioration defined as

$$\frac{H_{max} - H_{min} - A_M}{A_M} \tag{5.144}$$

is a meaningful single number representing the passband sensitivity. A different, but useful measure, can be defined by taking the total shaded area shown in Fig. 5.32. The advantage of this measure is that if the tolerance is exceeded by a large amount only in a small region of frequencies, then its contribution to sensitivity is correspondingly small. Thus under situations where the input signal has a more or less flat spectrum, this measure is quite meaningful.

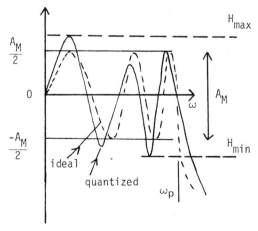

Fig. 5.31. A typical passband magnitude response (dB) under quantization.

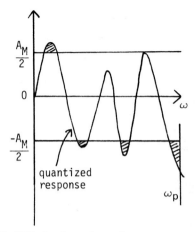

Fig. 5.32. An alternative performance measure.

XII LOW-SENSITIVITY SECOND-ORDER SECTIONS

A second-order all-pole section with complex conjugate poles has transfer function

$$H(z) = \frac{1}{1 - 2r(\cos\theta)z^{-1} + r^2 z^{-2}} \tag{5.145}$$

and can be implemented in direct form as in Fig. 5.33, where the multipliers are $m_1 = 2r\cos\theta$ and $m_2 = -r^2$. It can be shown that the poles $re^{\pm j\theta}$ have the following sensitivities:

$$\frac{\partial r}{\partial m_1} = 0, \quad \frac{\partial r}{\partial m_2} = -\frac{1}{2r}, \quad \frac{\partial\theta}{\partial m_1} = -\frac{1}{2r\sin\theta}, \quad \frac{\partial\theta}{\partial m_2} = -\frac{1}{2r^2\tan\theta} \tag{5.146}$$

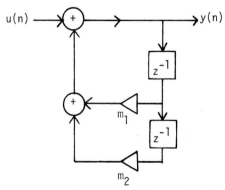

Fig. 5.33. The conventional two-multiplier second-order section.

For narrowband filters where $\theta \to 0$, the sensitivities $\partial\theta/\partial m_1$ and $\partial\theta/\partial m_2$ are very large. This makes second-order direct-form sections unsuitable for narrowband lowpass designs. This can also be seen from the pole–grid diagram in Fig. 5.34, which shows the set of possible pole locations when m_1 and m_2 are quantized to three bits. Since the poles are crowded near the imaginary axis and close to the unit circle, it is clear that for small θ and small r, large errors in pole location are created by quantizing m_1 and m_2. The pole–grid pattern can be made uniform all over the z-plane in $|z| < 1$ simply by implementing $r\cos\theta$ and $r\sin\theta$ as multipliers rather than $2r\cos\theta$ and $-r^2$. Such a structure, called the *coupled-form structure*, is shown in Fig. 5.35, which also shows the pole–grid pattern [4]. It can be shown that

$$\frac{\partial r}{\partial m_1} = \cos\theta, \quad \frac{\partial r}{\partial m_2} = \sin\theta, \quad \frac{\partial\theta}{\partial m_1} = -\frac{\sin\theta}{r}, \quad \frac{\partial\theta}{\partial m_2} = \frac{\cos\theta}{r} \quad (5.147)$$

so the sensitivities are well behaved for all θ. For $r \to 1$ all the functions in Eq. (5.147) have magnitudes bounded above by 1 for all θ.

Some authors [28] have derived modified coupled-form structures that are particularly well suited for certain pole locations. Figure 5.36 shows two such circuits. The sensitivities are

$$\frac{\partial r}{\partial m_1} = \frac{1}{\cos\theta}, \quad \frac{\partial r}{\partial m_2} = r\sin\theta\cos\theta, \quad \frac{\partial\theta}{\partial m_1} = 0, \quad \frac{\partial\theta}{\partial m_2} = \cos^2\theta \quad (5.148)$$

for Fig. 5.36(a) and

$$\frac{\partial r}{\partial m_1} = \frac{1}{\sin\theta}, \quad \frac{\partial r}{\partial m_2} = r\sin\theta\cos\theta, \quad \frac{\partial\theta}{\partial m_1} = 0, \quad \frac{\partial\theta}{\partial m_2} = -\sin^2\theta \quad (5.149)$$

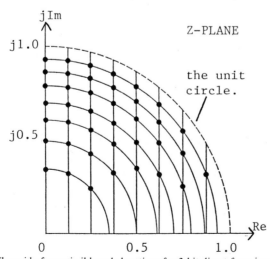

Fig. 5.34. The grid of permissible pole locations for 3-bit direct-form implementation.

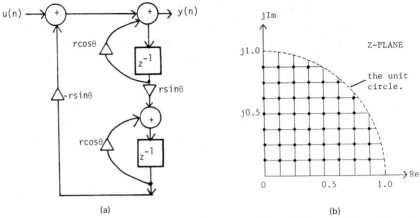

(a)   (b)

Fig. 5.35. The coupled-form structure and the corresponding grid of permissible pole locations (3 bits).

for Fig. 5.36(b). Thus for $\theta \to 0$ Fig. 5.36(a) represents a particularly useful structure, whereas for $\theta \to \pi/2$ Fig. 5.36(b) represents a good structure. Finally, consider the Agarwal–Burrus structure in Fig. 5.21(b). Define

$$m_1 = -2 - b_1 = -2 + 2r\cos\theta \qquad (5.150)$$

$$m_2 = 1 - b_2 = 1 - r^2 \qquad (5.151)$$

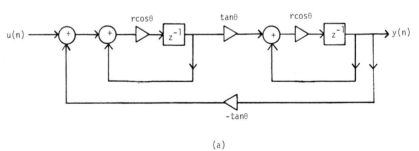

(a)

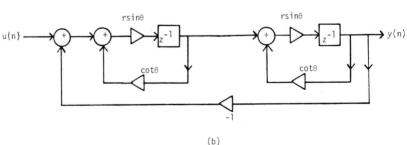

(b)

Fig. 5.36. Modified coupled forms.

TABLE X
Sensitivities for Various Second-Order Sections

	Direct form	Agarwal and Burrus	Coupled form	Modified coupled forms	
				1	2
$\dfrac{\partial r}{\partial m_1}$	0	0	$\cos\theta$	$\dfrac{1}{\cos\theta}$	$\dfrac{1}{\sin\theta}$
$\dfrac{\partial r}{\partial m_2}$	$-\dfrac{1}{2r}$	$-\dfrac{1}{2r}$	$\sin\theta$	$r\sin\theta\cos\theta$	$r\sin\theta\cos\theta$
$\dfrac{\partial\theta}{\partial m_1}$	$-\dfrac{1}{2r\sin\theta}$	$-\dfrac{1}{2r\sin\theta}$	$-\dfrac{\sin\theta}{r}$	0	0
$\dfrac{\partial\theta}{\partial m_2}$	$-\dfrac{1}{2r^2\tan\theta}$	$-\dfrac{1}{2r^2\tan\theta}$	$\dfrac{\cos\theta}{r}$	$\cos^2\theta$	$-\sin^2\theta$
When to use?	$\theta\to\dfrac{\pi}{2}$ $r\to 1$	$\theta\to 0,\dfrac{\pi}{2}$ $r\to 1$ (see text)	$r\to 1$	$\theta\to 0$	$\theta\to\dfrac{\pi}{2}$

Thus, m_1 and m_2 are the physical multipliers. The sensitivities are now again given by Eq. (5.146). However, with b bits the quantization errors Δm_1 and Δm_2 of the multipliers in the Agarwal–Burrus structure are much smaller than the corresponding error in the direct form (see Section VI.B for explanation). Consequently, the Agarwal–Burrus structure represents a low-sensitivity structure for $r\to 1$ and $\theta\to 0$, even though the sensitivity expressions are the same as in Eq. (5.146). Table X summarizes these results pertaining to second-order sections.

The Agarwal–Burrus structure, introduced in Section VI.B in the context of low-noise designs, also has low sensitivity, as we observed above (assuming that $r\to 1$ and $\theta\to 0$). This gives evidence that sensitivity and roundoff noise are closely related.

WAVE DIGITAL FILTERS   XIII

In Section XII we presented a number of all-pole second-order sections that have low sensitivity for *certain* pole locations. Thus, depending on the pole location, we can choose a second-order structure with the help of Table X so that the sensitivity is low. A higher-order filter can be designed by a cascade or parallel combination of such sections with appropriate numerators.

In 1971 an entirely new approach [33] to the design of low-sensitivity digital filters was introduced by Fettweis. This approach is based on digital simulation of continuous-time LC filters. There exists a class of continuous-time LC filters, called doubly terminated LC structures [42]. When "properly" designed [43], these structures exhibit very low passband sensitivity with respect to electrical element variations. The explanation for this is based on the concepts of maximum available power and perfect impedence matching [43]. When a digital filter structure is built to simulate such a "prototype" LC network, it inherits the low passband sensitivity property. In addition, due to the inherent passivity of the LC prototype, the digital filter is also passive in a certain sense [51], and this can be exploited to suppress limit cycle oscillations.

The purpose of this section is to briefly outline the procedure for designing WDF structures. Several excellent papers have been published in the last 15 years, but for want of space we will not attempt to discuss in detail all these contributions.

A   The Overall Design Procedure

Consider, for example, the design of a digital lowpass filter with specifications as in Fig. 5.37(a). The first step in the WDF design procedure is to translate these specifications to the continuous-time domain by application of the bilinear transformation, that is,[†]

$$sT = \frac{1 - z^{-1}}{1 + z^{-1}} \tag{5.152}$$

With

$$s = j\Omega \quad \text{and} \quad z = e^{j\omega} \tag{5.153}$$

we get from Eq. (5.152)

$$\Omega T = \tan(\omega/2) \tag{5.154}$$

Thus, the bandedges of the continuous-time filter are

$$\Omega_{\mathrm{p}} = \frac{1}{T}\tan\frac{\omega_{\mathrm{p}}}{2}, \qquad \Omega_{\mathrm{r}} = \frac{1}{T}\tan\frac{\omega_{\mathrm{r}}}{2} \tag{5.155}$$

The second step is then to design a doubly terminated lossless (LC) network whose transfer function has magnitude response as in Fig. 5.37(b). This can be done by standard software, such as FILSYN [56], FILTOR [57], etc., or by

---

[†] For our discussion we can think of T as an arbitrary constant with the dimension of time.

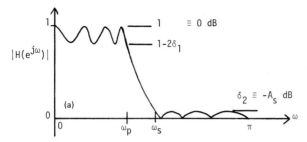

Fig. 5.37(a). Typical lowpass specifications.

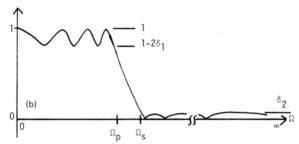

Fig. 5.37(b). The mapped continuous-time specification.

design charts and tables [58]. Figure 5.38 shows a typical example of such a filter network.

The third step is to translate this LC network into the digital domain in such a way that the resulting network has no delay-free loops [33]. This is by far the most involved step because digital simulation of voltages and currents in a network such as Fig. 5.38 always produces delay-free loops. To overcome such loops, Fettweis introduced wave variables that are linear combinations of voltages and currents. By careful manipulation and simulation of wave variables in the digital domain, we can avoid delay-free loops. This leads to the ingenious concept of WDF. The rest of this section is dedicated to an elaboration of step 3. Several standard references [42, 56–58] are available for obtaining details on step 2.

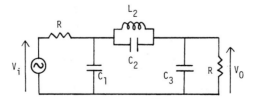

Fig. 5.38. A doubly terminated LC filter.

B   Wave Digital Simulation of Electrical Elements

We begin with a simple example. Consider the inductor L in Fig. 5.39. The voltage and current are related by

$$V(s) = sLI(s) \qquad (5.156)$$

Let us define two new variables $A_1(s)$ and $B_1(s)$ as follows:

$$A_1(s) = V(s) + RI(s), \qquad B_1(s) = V(s) - RI(s) \qquad (5.157)$$

where R is a positive constant with dimensions of resistance. The inductor, which is completely described by Eq. (5.156), can equally well be described by the "corresponding" relation between $A_1(s)$ and $B_1(s)$, obtained by substituting Eq. (5.156) in Eq. (5.157). Thus

$$B_1(s) = \frac{sL/R - 1}{sL/R + 1} A_1(s) \qquad (5.158)$$

Now apply the bilinear transformation Eq. (5.152) to Eq. (5.158). Let

$$B(z) = B_1(s) \Big|_{s = T^{-1}(1 - z^{-1})(1 + z^{-1})^{-1}} \qquad (5.159)$$

and similarly define $A(z)$. Then $B(z)$ and $A(z)$ are related by

$$B(z) = \frac{(1 - z^{-1})(1 + z^{-1})^{-1}(L/RT) - 1}{(1 - z^{-1})(1 + z^{-1})^{-1}(L/RT) + 1} A(z) \qquad (5.160)$$

The quantity T in these equations is used only to match the physical dimensions. Hereafter, we shall set $T = 1$ without loss of generality. Next, if we choose

$$R = L \qquad (5.161)$$

the variables $B(z)$ and $A(z)$ in the digital world are related by

$$B(z) = -z^{-1}A(z) \qquad (5.162)$$

Thus, Fig. 5.40(b) is a "discrete-time" simulation of the inductor of Fig. 5.39. In

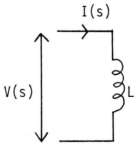

Fig. 5.39. An inductor.

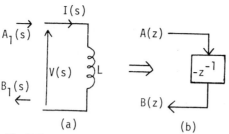

Fig. 5.40. The wave equivalent for the inductor.

essence, an inductor translates into a simple delay with a negative sign. The variables being simulated are $A(z)$ and $B(z)$ rather than discrete versions of $V(s)$ and $I(s)$. By conventions of drawing figures, the variables $A_1(s)$ and $B_1(s)$ are indicated in the inductor diagram. The classical name for $A_1(s)$ is the *incident wave*, and $B_1(s)$ is called the *reflected wave*. As far as the LC network is concerned, such wave variables are fictitious, but in the digital world these variables are the physical signals that are manipulated inside a WDF.

The value L does not explicitly appear in Fig. 5.40(b). The definitions of A and B, however, implicitly have L because of Eq. (5.161) and the relations

$$A = V + RI, \qquad B = V - RI \tag{5.163}$$

The simulation in Fig. 5.40 is referred to as a *one-port* simulation. The port, which is characterized by the unique relation Eq. (5.156), has thus been "digitally" simulated. The exact result of the simulation itself depends on the choice of the arbitrary constant R. If R is chosen as in Eq. (5.161), then the network of Fig. 5.40(b) occurs. R is called the *port resistance* of the one-port being simulated. Similarly other circuit elements can be simulated. Table XI shows a few such simulations, some of which we plan to use in this chapter. A more complete list is in [33].

Certain comments are in order. First consider the simulated resistor R_1. The resulting digital network has $B = V - RI = 0$, if we choose $R = R_1$; hence $A = V + RI$ is arbitrary. Thus, regardless of what the value of the incident "wave" is, no wave gets reflected. In other words, we have a "wave sink" in the digital domain. The new notation in Table XI implies this fact. Next, the voltage source e with internal resistance R_1 ($= R$) is simulated simply by setting $A = V + RI = e$ and ignoring B, which is arbitrary.

Interconnection of Simulated One-Port Elements   C

For the LCR circuit of Fig. 5.38 it is easy to draw, based on the previous subsection, the wave digital equivalent for each circuit element in isolation. However, when we try to interconnect these simulated equivalents, we

TABLE XI
Wave-Simulation of Electrical Elements

Electrical element	Discrete-time wave-variable simulation	Choice of R where $A = V+RI$, $B = V-RI$
		$R = L$
		$R = \dfrac{1}{C}$
	Wave sink $B = 0$	$R = R_1$
(open circuit)		R = arbitrary
(short circuit)		R = arbitrary
		$R = R_1$

encounter a major problem: the $A(z)$ and $B(z)$ variables attached to various circuit elements are not compatible because their definitions involve R, which in turn varies from one-port to one-port. We can overcome this difficulty by using the ingenious concept of wave adaptors [33, 44, 59], which serve to interconnect several one-ports. For our purposes it is sufficient to deal with series and parallel interconnections of three one-ports at a time; we now do this.

Parallel Three-Port Wave Adaptors 1

Figure 5.41 shows the parallel connection of three one-ports. The port resistances are defined as R_1, R_2, and R_3. The port voltages and currents are constrained by

$$V_1 = V_2 = V_3 \tag{5.164}$$

$$I_1 + I_2 + I_3 = 0 \tag{5.165}$$

The wave variables are also accordingly constrained. Using the definitions

$$A_k = V_k + R_k I_k \tag{5.166}$$

$$B_k = V_k - R_k I_k \tag{5.167}$$

we easily verify that Eqs. (5.164) and (5.165) translate, in terms of wave

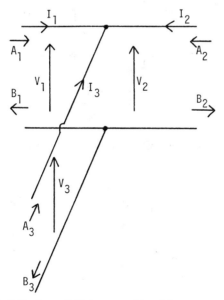

Fig. 5.41. A parallel interconnection of three one-ports.

variables, to

$$B_k = 2A_3 - A_k + \sum_{l=1}^{2} \alpha_l(A_l - A_3) \qquad (5.168)$$

for $k = 1, 2, 3$, where

$$\alpha_l = \frac{2G_l}{G_1 + G_2 + G_3}, \qquad G_k = \frac{1}{R_k} \qquad (5.169)$$

Thus, to obtain the wave digital equivalent of Fig. 5.41, we first replace each of the three one-ports with its equivalent from Table XI and then interconnect them with the "parallel wave adaptor," which is a three-input three-output memoryless device satisfying Eq. (5.168). Figure 5.42 is a notation for this device. Figure 5.43 shows the use of a parallel adaptor.

An implementation of Eq. (5.168) is shown in Fig. 5.44, which therefore depicts the internal details of the parallel adaptor of Fig. 5.42. Notice that the implementation requires seven two-input adders and two multipliers. When adaptors are interconnected to other adaptors, it results in a delay-free loop unless special precautions are taken. Under specific conditions, certain degrees of freedom are available in the choice of port resistances R_k (this will be demonstrated with a design example in the next subsection). These degrees of freedom enable us to avoid such delay-free loops.

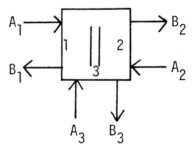

Fig. 5.42. The parallel adaptor schematic.

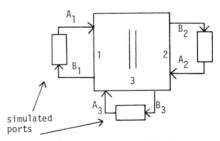

Fig. 5.43. The use of a parallel adaptor.

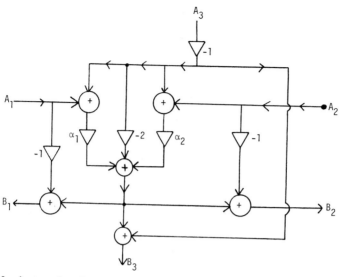

Fig. 5.44. Implementation of a parallel adaptor with two multipliers and seven two-input adders.

For example, let us assume that we are free to choose the port resistance R_2 in Fig. 5.41. If we choose R_2 such that

$$\frac{1}{R_2} = \frac{1}{R_1} + \frac{1}{R_3} \tag{5.170}$$

then we can show that B_2 in Eq. (5.168) does not depend on A_2. Thus, there is no direct connection between B_2 and A_2, and if port 2 of such an adaptor is connected to another device it does not lead to delay-free loops. Since B_2 is zero regardless of A_2 whenever $A_1 = A_3 = 0$, port 2 is called a *reflection-free* port.

We can use Eq. (5.170) to simplify Eq. (5.168) as follows:

$$\begin{bmatrix} B_1 \\ B_2 \\ B_3 \end{bmatrix} = \begin{bmatrix} -1+\alpha & 1 & 1-\alpha \\ \alpha & 0 & 1-\alpha \\ \alpha & 1 & -\alpha \end{bmatrix} \begin{bmatrix} A_1 \\ A_2 \\ A_3 \end{bmatrix} \tag{5.171}$$

where $\alpha = \alpha_1$ is as in Eq. (5.169). Figure 5.45 shows an implementation of the three-port parallel adaptor, with port 2 being reflection free. Note that only one multiplier and four adders are required for its implementation. The reflection-free nature of port 2 is indicated in Fig. 5.45.

Series Three-Port Wave Adaptors 2

Consider next a series interconnection of three ports as in Fig. 5.46. There are three ports connected in series, with port resistances R_1, R_2, and R_3. Once again,

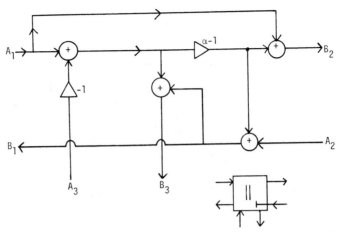

Fig. 5.45. Parallel adaptor with one multiplier and four two-input adders (port 2 is reflection free).

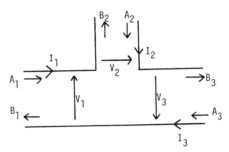

Fig. 5.46. Series interconnection of three one-ports.

each one-port can be simulated by a corresponding wave digital one-port. To interconnect the ports, we need "series wave adaptors."

The port voltages and currents in Fig. 5.46 are constrained by

$$V_1 + V_2 + V_3 = 0 \tag{5.172}$$

$$I_1 = I_2 = I_3 \tag{5.173}$$

It can be shown that the corresponding constraint on the wave variables A_k, B_k defined in Eqs. (5.166) and (5.167) is

$$B_k = A_k - \beta_k \sum_{l=1}^{3} A_l \tag{5.174}$$

where

$$\beta_k = \frac{2R_k}{R_1 + R_2 + R_3} \tag{5.175}$$

The three-port series wave adaptor is a device that implements Eq. (5.174). Fig-

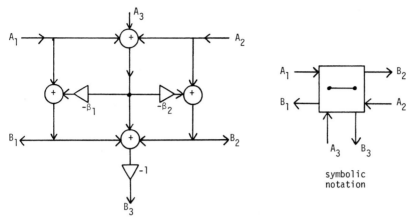

Fig. 5.47. The series adaptor with two multipliers and six two-input adders.

ure 5.47 shows this adaptor along with the block diagram notation. Notice that two multipliers and six two-input adders are required for this implementation.

To avoid delay-free loops, we once again need reflection-free ports. We can make port 2 in Fig. 5.47 reflection free simply by choosing

$$R_2 = R_1 + R_3 \qquad (5.176)$$

This is possible only if R_2 is not constrained for other reasons. In practical wave filter design, such freedom to choose R_2 is always available; hence reflection-free adaptors are quite commonly employed.

Figure 5.48 shows such a reflection-free three-port series adaptor along with building-block notation. Only one multiplier and four adders are required for its implementation.

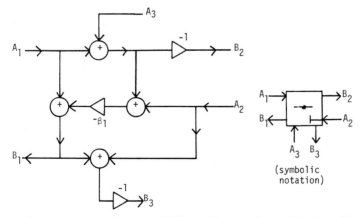

Fig. 5.48. The series adaptor with one multiplier and four two-input adders (port 2 is reflection free).

D   Design Summary And A Design Example

Given an LCR network as in Fig. 5.38, for instance, the first step in converting it to a wave digital network is to identify the "interconnections" (i.e., series and parallel interconnection of one-ports). The second step is to assign "port resistances" to the wire interconnection ports. During this step the guidelines in column 3 of Table XI along with the rules for obtaining reflection-free ports [Eqs. (5.170) and (5.176)] should be judiciously used (as demonstrated in the examples to follow). The third step is to use Table XI to replace the electrical elements with wave one-ports, and then interconnect these with appropriate wave adaptors. The wave filter design is then complete.

As a design example, consider the circuit of Fig. 5.38 again. The various interconnections are identified as in Fig. 5.49. Interconnections "1," "3," and "4" represent parallel interconnections, whereas "2" represents a series interconnection. These interconnections must be simulated with adaptors. For each interconnection the "ports" have been numbered. Let R_{1k}, R_{2k}, R_{3k} represent the three port resistances for the kth interconnection. We now assign these resistances as follows:

1. $R_{11} = R =$ internal resistance of voltage source
2. $R_{31} = 1/C_1$ (according to Table XI)
3. $1/R_{21} = 1/R_{11} + 1/R_{31}$ [according to Eq. (5.170)]
4. $R_{14} = L_2$ (according to Table XI)
5. $R_{34} = 1/C_2$ (according to Table XI)
6. $1/R_{24} = 1/R_{14} + 1/R_{34}$ [according to Eq. (5.170)]
7. $R_{12} = R_{21}$
8. $R_{32} = R_{24}$

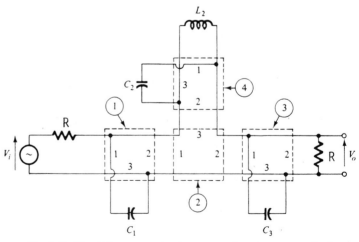

Fig. 5.49. Identifying appropriate interconnections for Fig. 5.38 [30].

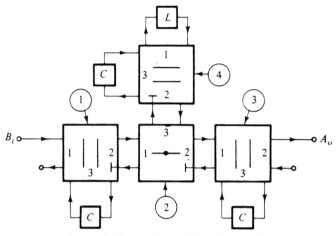

Fig. 5.50. The resulting WDF structure [30] .

9. $R_{22} = R_{12} + R_{32}$ [according to Eq. (5.176)]
10. $R_{13} = R_{22}$
11. $R_{33} = 1/C_3$ (according to Table XI)
12. $R_{23} = R$

Assignments 1, 2, 4, 5, and 11 have been made according to Table XI. Assignments 7, 8, and 10 have been made in order to make the port resistances of connected ports compatible. Assignments 3, 6, and 9 have been made to force ports 2 of adaptors corresponding to the interconnections 1, 2, and 4 to be reflection-free ports. The freedom to choose R_{21}, R_{24}, and R_{22} according to Eq. (5.170) or Eq. (5.176) was available and exploited accordingly.

Figure 5.50 shows the resulting WDF. Note that port 2 of adaptor 3 is not reflection free. This, however, is not harmful because there is no possibility of a delay-free loop being caused by this port.

Other Types Of WDFs 1

Several authors have taken other viewpoints in order to obtain different types of WDFs. An important family of WDFs results from considering each electrical element as a two-port rather than a one-port [60, 61]. The advantage of such a viewpoint is that "adaptors" are not necessary for interconnection purposes. However, these adaptors are implicitly taken care of in the simulated digital two-ports. The main advantage of this class of wave filters is the simplicity of the design procedure.

Although we do not give details of this class of filters, we do indicate the nature of the resulting structures. Thus, consider Fig. 5.38 again. Here each series and parallel branch is regarded as a two-port. Each two-port is assigned port resistances as shown in Fig. 5.51. (Thus the capacitor C_1 is a two-port with port resistances R_1 and R_2.) Each such two-port has a standard wave digital equivalent two-port, as demonstrated in Fig. 5.52, where the "wave variables" are

$$A_1 = V_1 + R_1 I_1, \qquad A_2 = V_2 + R_2 I_2 \tag{5.177}$$

$$B_1 = V_1 - R_1 I_1, \qquad B_2 = V_2 - R_2 I_2 \tag{5.178}$$

The port resistances R_1, R_2,... are chosen such that there is no delay-free connection between A_1 and B_1 (or between A_2 and B_2). If such equivalent digital networks are cascaded as in Fig. 5.53, there are then no delay-free loops, and the resulting cascade represents a realizable digital equivalent of the LC network. The design rules for such a class of filters are in [61] and are quite simple to apply.

As a typical example, Fig. 5.54 shows the two-port wave equivalent [61] of a series inductor L. For a given L, R_1 and R_2 are chosen such that there is no delay-free path from A_2 to B_2. This occurs when $R_2 = R_1 + L$. In practice, we can choose either R_1 or R_2 as convenient, and we exploit this to force $R_2 = R_1 + L$. The multiplier σ in Fig. 5.54(b) is

$$\sigma = \frac{R_1}{R_2} = \frac{R_2 - L}{R_2}, \qquad 0 < \sigma < 1 \tag{5.179}$$

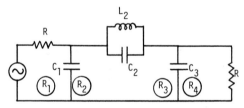

Fig. 5.51. Viewing each circuit element as a two-port.

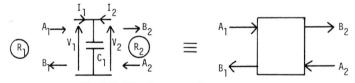

Fig. 5.52. The shunt capacitor as a two-port.

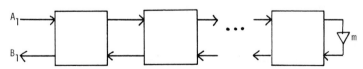

Fig. 5.53. Cascading the wave two-ports.

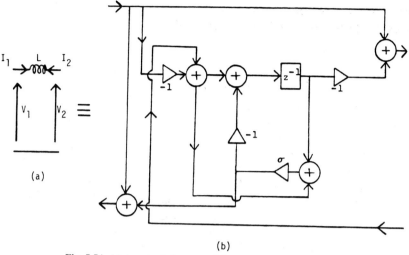

Fig. 5.54. (a) A series inductor and (b) its two port equivalent.

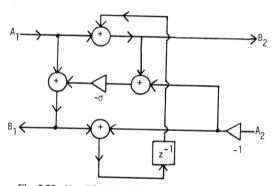

Fig. 5.55. Simplification of the circuit of Fig. 5.54(b).

There are five adders and one multiplier in Fig. 5.54(b). It can, however, be shown that the input-output relation of the circuit in Fig. 5.54(b) is the same as the structure in Fig. 5.55, which requires only four adders and one multiplier. The striking point here is that Fig. 5.55 is precisely the same as the series adaptor in a conventional wave filter, with the wave equivalent of an inductor (i.e., $-z^{-1}$) connected between B_3 and A_3 (see Fig. 5.48). Thus, the complexity of implementation of these structures is really the same as the wave filters presented earlier. However, the design rules seem to be simpler. For complete details see [61].

XIV   THE LOSSLESS BOUNDED REAL APPROACH FOR THE DESIGN OF LOW-SENSITIVITY FILTER STRUCTURES

As outlined in Section XIII, WDFs have several desirable properties under finite word-length constraints. To design structures with these properties, we must map the filter specifications into the continuous-time domain and then synthesize the LC network. It is only after this that we can translate the LC filter back to the wave digital world.

The intermediate step of going into the continuous-time domain and designing the LC prototype and then translating back into the digital domain is actually unnecessary and can be eliminated by direct cascade synthesis (not to be confused with conventional cascade-form synthesis of Fig. 5.22) in the digital domain itself. To do this, we require a general theory for low-sensitivity digital filters, and a formal procedure for synthesizing such filters in the z-domain. Such developments have been reported recently [62, 63].

An important advantage, among others, of such a procedure is that familiarity with LC networks and classical filter synthesis is not a prerequisite either for designing the filters or for comprehending the procedure. This situation is particularly attractive in view of the fact that digital filtering is an important and popular tool in other branches of engineering.

This section outlines these independent z-domain methods. For all theoretical details see [62–64].

A   The Basic Principle

Wave digital filters have low passband sensitivity because they are derived from passive continuous-time circuits are designed to satisfy certain maximum-power bounds [51]. If we can somehow accomplish such "bounds" by designing structures independently in the z-domain, then we have a means for direct low-sensitivity digital filter design. To be more specific, consider a typical lowpass transfer function magnitude as shown in Fig. 5.56. The magnitude $|H(e^{j\omega})|$ attains the maximum of unity at certain frequencies ω_k in the passband. Let us now assume that we have invented a structural interconnection such that, regardless of the multiplier values m_k (i.e., as long as the multiplier values stay within a well-defined range, such as, for example $0 < |m_k| < 1$), the quantity $|H(e^{j\omega})|$ is bounded above by unity. In other words, the structure forces the bound

$$|H(e^{j\omega})| \leq 1 \qquad \text{for all } \omega \qquad (5.180)$$

Now consider $|H(e^{j\omega_k})|$, which is unity when the multiplier values are "ideal" (i.e., have infinite precision). Now if a multiplier m_k is perturbed (quantized), then $|H(e^{j\omega_k})|$ can only decrease because of the bound (5.180). Hence a plot of $|H(e^{j\omega_k})|$

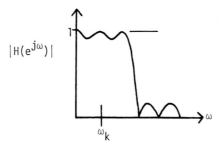

Fig. 5.56. A typical lowpass response.

looks like Fig. 5.57, exhibiting a zero derivative; that is,

$$\frac{\partial |H(e^{j\omega_k})|}{\partial m_i}\Bigg|_{m_i = m_{i_0}} = 0 \tag{5.181}$$

In other words, the first-order sensitivity of $|H(e^{j\omega})|$ with respect to each multiplier m_i is zero at each ω_k where $|H(e^{j\omega})|$ attains its maximum. Clearly, if there exist several frequencies ω_k in the passband where this happens, we can expect very low passband sensitivity.

Since the structure forces the bound in Eq. (5.180) rather than the incidental values of the multipliers, we call it *structural boundedness* or *structural passivity*. Basically, if we can find an implementation that is structurally bounded or structurally passive, then we can design low passband sensitivity digital filters.

If the structure is such that Eq. (5.180) holds with equality for all ω (i.e., $H(z)$ is all-pass), then we have structural *losslessness*, and this leads to a structurally lossless implementation of the all-pass function; thus in spite of coefficient quantization, the transfer function continues to remain all-pass.

We now introduce some useful terminology. Any *stable* transfer function $H(z)$ with *real* coefficients satisfying Eq. (5.180) is called a *bounded real* (BR) function [62], whereas if Eq. (5.180) holds with equality for all ω, then $H(z)$ is said to be *lossless bounded real* (LBR). An LBR function is any stable all-pass function with real coefficients. A stable transfer matrix $\mathcal{T}(z) = [T_{ij}(z)]$ is said to be LBR if $\mathcal{T}(z)$

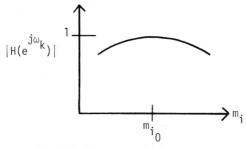

Fig. 5.57. The zero-sensitivity property.

is real for real z, and satisfies[†]

$$\mathcal{T}^\dagger(e^{j\omega})\mathcal{T}(e^{j\omega}) = \mathbf{I} \qquad \text{for all } \omega \qquad (5.182)$$

It can be shown that if $\mathcal{T}(z)$ is LBR, then each component $T_{ij}(z)$ is BR.

B The Design of Structurally Bounded Implementations

It is a simple matter to find elementary examples of structurally bounded implementations. Consider a first-order transfer function

$$H_1(z) = \frac{1 - a}{1 - az^{-1}} \qquad (5.183)$$

where a is assumed to be positive. Clearly, $|H_1(e^{j\omega})|$ has maximum value (equal to 1) at $\omega = 0$. A structure that implements this is shown in Fig. 5.58. It is clear that, regardless of the value of a in Fig. 5.58, as long as a satisfies $0 < a < 1$, $|H(e^{j\omega})|$ continues to be bounded by unity. Thus, Fig. 5.58 represents a structurally bounded (or passive) implementation of (5.183).

The numerator and denominator of Eq. (5.183) have the same coefficient a, which is what enabled us to obtain the implementation of Fig. 5.58. In general, if we have a higher-order transfer function with essentially unrelated numerator and denominator, it is nontrivial to obtain structurally bounded implementations. To explain the procedure we adopt in such cases, consider Fig. 5.59. Here, a transfer function $G_m(z)$ is obtained by starting with a two-input, two-output system and forcing the second input $X_2(z)$ to be $G_{m-1}(z)$ times $Y_2(z)$.

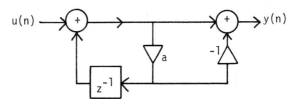

Fig. 5.58. A structurally passive implementation.

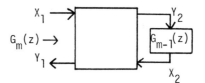

Fig. 5.59. A constrained two-pair.

[†] Matrices and vectors satisfying Eq. (5.182) are also termed all-pass matrices and all-pass vectors.

The two-input, two-output system is called a (digital) two-pair [62] and is described by a 2×2 transfer matrix $\mathscr{T}_m(z) = [T_{ij}(z)]$.

$$\begin{bmatrix} Y_1(z) \\ Y_2(z) \end{bmatrix} = \begin{bmatrix} T_{11}(z) & T_{12}(z) \\ T_{21}(z) & T_{22}(z) \end{bmatrix} \begin{bmatrix} X_1(z) \\ X_2(z) \end{bmatrix}$$ (5.184a)

Another equivalent way of describing the two-pair is via the chain parameters A, B, C, D:

$$\begin{bmatrix} X_1(z) \\ Y_1(z) \end{bmatrix} = \begin{bmatrix} A(z) & B(z) \\ C(z) & D(z) \end{bmatrix} \begin{bmatrix} Y_2(z) \\ X_2(z) \end{bmatrix}$$ (5.184b)

Thus, $G_m(z)$ in Fig. 5.59 is obtained by constraining the two-pair at the right side by the transfer function $G_{m-1}(z)$. A typical situation is where the two-pair is of first-order (has one delay), whereas $G_m(z)$ and $G_{m-1}(z)$ have orders m and $m-1$, respectively.

Referring to Fig. 5.59, the basic idea pertaining to structural boundedness is as follows: Let the two-pair $\mathscr{T}_m(z)$ have the following property:

Property 1. If $|G_{m-1}(e^{j\omega})| \leq 1$ for some frequency ω, then $|G_m(e^{j\omega})| \leq 1$ for the same ω.

This in turn means that if $G_{m-1}(z)$ has a structurally bounded implementation, then $G_m(z)$ in Fig. 5.59 is certainly structurally bounded. Thus, Fig. 5.59 helps to convert the problem of structural boundedness of $G_m(z)$ into a problem of structurally bounding the lower-order function $G_{m-1}(z)$. If we now repeat this idea, we obtain the cascade of two-pairs in Fig. 5.60. Each two-pair $\mathscr{T}_m(z)$, $m = 1, 2, \ldots, N$, in this figure is such that if $G_{m-1}(z)$ is structurally bounded, then so is $G_m(z)$. G_0 is a constant and is automatically structurally bounded as long as $|G_0| < 1$. Thus, by inductive reasoning, $G_1(z)$ is structurally bounded and so are $G_2(z)$, $G_3(z), \ldots$. In essence, the higher-order transfer function $G_N(z)$ is structurally bounded as long as $|G_0| < 1$ and each two-pair satisfies Property 1.

We now encounter two design-related questions. (i) What kind of two-pair matrices $\mathscr{T}_m(z)$ satisfy Property 1? (ii) Given an arbitrary $G_N(z)$, under what conditions can we construct the cascaded structure in Fig. 5.60, where each $\mathscr{T}_m(z)$ satisfies Property 1? What, in essence, is the procedure for synthesizing such a cascade?

Both of these issues have been recently handled in the literature [62–64]. We now proceed to present some of the related basic results without proofs.

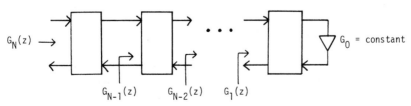

Fig. 5.60. The cascaded two-pair.

1 The Concept of Digital Two-Pair Extraction

Given a transfer function $G_m(z)$, let us assume that we have identified a transfer matrix $\mathcal{T}_m(z)$ (typically, first order or second order) such that $G_m(z)$ can be realized as in Fig. 5.59, where $G_{m-1}(z)$ is a reduced-order "remainder function." This process is called (digital) *two-pair extraction*. It can be shown that $G_m(z)$ and the remainder $G_{m-1}(z)$ are related through the parameters of the extracted two-pair in the following manner:

$$G_{m-1} = \frac{C - AG_m}{BG_m - D} \tag{5.185a}$$

$$G_m = \frac{C + DG_{m-1}}{A + BG_{m-1}} \tag{5.185b}$$

If the extracted two-pair is LBR, then the above process is simply termed *LBR extraction*.

Given a stable tranfer function $G_N(z)$, assume that it is scaled such that it satisfies $|G_N(e^{j\omega})| \leq 1$ for all ω. If $|G_N(e^{j\omega})|$ is not equal to unity for any ω, it can be scaled up so that it is equal to unity for some ω. Therefore assume, without loss of generality, that $G_N(z)$ is BR and such that its magnitude attains the maximum of unity at some frequency ω_k. Clearly, if $\omega_k = 0$ or π, then $G_N(e^{j\omega_k})$ is either 1 or -1. If, on the other hand, $0 < \omega_k < \pi$, then $G_N(e^{j\omega_k})$ might be complex. Thus we have three distinct cases to handle:

Case 1. $\omega_k = 0$ or π; that is, $z_k = 1$ or -1.

Case 2. $0 < \omega_k < \pi$ and $G_N(e^{j\omega_k}) = \pm 1$.

Case 3. $0 < \omega_k < \pi$ and $G_N(e^{j\omega_k}) = e^{j\phi}$.

It is shown in [62] that in Cases 1–3 there exists an LBR two-pair such that when it is "extracted" from $G_N(z)$ the remainder $G_{N-1}(z)$ is lower-order BR. It is also indicated in [62, 63] how such a two-pair can be determined from the known transfer function $G_N(z)$. If Case 1 is true, then the LBR two-pair is first order and $G_{N-1}(z)$ has order one less than that of $G_N(z)$. For Cases 2 and 3 the extracted LBR two-pair is second order, and the order of $G_{N-1}(z)$ is two less than that of $G_N(z)$. Since the reduced-order remainder $G_{N-1}(z)$ continues to be BR, the above procedure can be repeated until the cascade of Fig. 5.60 is obtained, with $|G_0| \leq 1$. $G_N(z)$ has thus been synthesized as a cascade of LBR two-pairs terminated in a BR constant G_0.

We will have a complete set of rules for synthesis once we specify the transfer matrices of the LBR two-pairs to be extracted in each of the three cases. The first three entries of Table XII give us this information for Cases 1 and 2. The LBR two-pairs in the first two entries are characterized by a single parameter σ that can readily be computed from the transfer function $G_m(z)$. Similarly, the LBR two-pair in the third entry is characterized by two parameters σ and β, both of which can be computed from $G_m(z)$. Also note that the LBR two-pairs in entries 1 and 2 can be implemented with one delay element, whereas those in the third entry require two delays.

To handle Case 3, we first extract a type 1A two-pair from $G_m(z)$ with $\sigma = \sigma_1$, as shown in the fourth entry of Table XII. The result is a remainder $G_{m-1}(z)$ such that $G_{m-1}(e^{j\omega_k}) = -1$. Now a type 2B LBR two-pair (with $\sigma = \sigma_2$, $\beta = \beta_2$) is extracted so that the remainder $G_{m-2}(z)$ has order two less than that of $G_{m-1}(z)$. This is then followed by a further two-pair extraction of type 1A with $\sigma = \sigma_3$ for reasons established in [62]. The required value of σ_3 is

$$(1 - \sigma_1)(1 - \beta_2)\sigma_3 + (1 - \sigma_3)(1 - \beta_2)\sigma_2 + 2(1 - \sigma_1)(1 - \sigma_2)(1 - \sigma_3) = 0$$

$$(5.186)$$

The final remainder $G_{m-3}(z)$ has order two less than that of $G_m(z)$. Figure 5.61 summarizes the situation. Moreover, $G_{m-3}(z)$ is BR (assuming $G_m(z)$ is BR), and the cascade of the three two-pairs is LBR. However, only one of the two first-order two-pairs in Fig. 5.61 is LBR. The three two-pairs in Fig. 5.58 can be

TABLE XII

Rules for Two-Pair Extraction

Type	Condition when used	$T_{ij}(z)$	σ
1A	$G_m(-1) = 1$	$T_{11} = 1 - \sigma$ $T_{12} = T_{21} = \sqrt{\sigma}(1 + z^{-1})$ $T_{22} = (\sigma - 1)z^{-1}$ common denominator $= 1 + \sigma z^{-1}$	$\dfrac{G'_m}{G'_m - 1}\bigg\|_{z^{-1} = -1}$
1C	$G_m(1) = 1$	$T_{11} = 1 - \sigma$ $T_{12} = T_{21} = \sqrt{\sigma}(1 - z^{-1})$ $T_{22} = -(\sigma - 1)z^{-1}$ common denominator $= 1 - \sigma z^{-1}$	$\dfrac{G'_m}{G'_m + 1}\bigg\|_{z^{-1} = 1}$
2A	$G_m(e^{j\omega_k}) = 1$	$T_{11} = -(\sigma - 1)(1 + \beta z^{-1})$ $T_{12} = \sqrt{\sigma}(1 + 2\beta z^{-1} + z^{-2}) = T_{21}$ $T_{22} = (\sigma - 1)z^{-1}(\beta + z^{-1})$ common denominator $= 1 + \beta(1 + \sigma)z^{-1} + \sigma z^{-2}$	$\dfrac{1}{1 + 2z/G'_m}\bigg\|_{z = z_k}$
1A	When $G_{m-1}(e^{j\omega_k})$ should be forced to -1	$T_{11} = 1 - \sigma$ $T_{12} = T_{21} = \sqrt{\sigma}(1 + z^{-1})$ $T_{22} = (\sigma - 1)z^{-1}$ common denominator $= 1 + \sigma z^{-1}$	$\dfrac{1}{2} - \dfrac{\operatorname{Re} z + \operatorname{Re} G_m}{\|1 + z^{-1}G_m\|^2}\bigg\|_{z = z_k}$
2B	After 1A extraction in Case 3	$T_{11} = (\sigma - 1)(1 + \beta z^{-1})$ $T_{12} = \sqrt{\sigma}(1 + 2\beta z^{-1} + z^{-2}) = T_{21}$ $T_{22} = -(\sigma - 1)z^{-1}(\beta + z^{-1})$ common denominator $= 1 + \beta(1 + \sigma)z^{-1} + \sigma z^{-2}$	$\dfrac{1}{1 - 2z/G'_m}\bigg\|_{z = z_k}$

Prime denotes derivative with respect to z^{-1}; $z_k = e^{j\omega_k}$ and $\beta = -\cos \omega_k$.

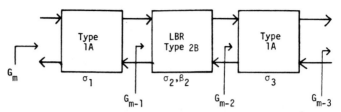

Fig. 5.61. The cascade of three two-pairs.

combined into a single *second-order* two-pair (called type 3 LBR two-pair) and implemented with two delay units. Thus the structure is canonic in delays.

It can be shown that a type 1A LBR two-pair can be implemented as in Fig. 5.62 in terms of planar rotation operators [63]. Type 1C can be implemented simply by replacing z^{-1} with $-z^{-1}$ in Fig. 5.62. Also, type 2A can be obtained from type 1A by replacing z^{-1} as shown in Fig. 5.63; the overall structure involves a total of three planar rotation operators. Finally, type 3 LBR two-

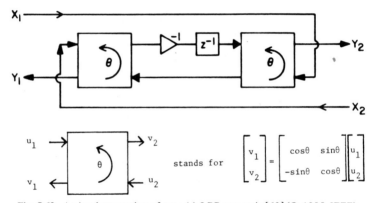

Fig. 5.62. An implementation of type 1A LBR two-pair [63] (© 1985 IEEE).

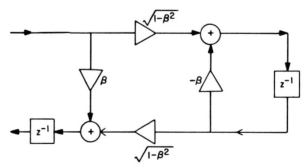

Fig. 5.63. The building block that should replace z^{-1} in a type 1A two-pair to get a type 2A two-pair [63] (© 1985 IEEE).

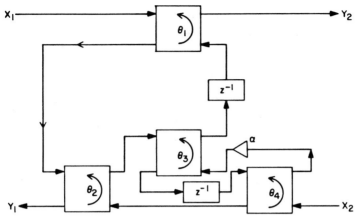

Fig. 5.64. Implementation of type 3 two-pair in terms of planar rotation operators [63] (© 1985 IEEE).

pairs (Fig. 5.61) can be implemented with two delays and four planar rotation operators as shown in Fig. 5.64. Detailed justifications for these are quite involved and can be found in [63].

More Economic Implementations   2

Consider the implementation of the first-order LBR two-pair in Fig. 5.62. This implementation involves two "planar rotators" and a delay unit and is called an *orthogonal implementation*, since planar rotators are orthogonal operators; in other words, if

$$R = \begin{bmatrix} \cos\theta & \sin\theta \\ -\sin\theta & \cos\theta \end{bmatrix}$$

then $R^T R = I$. Such implementations have the desirable feature that internal signals that normally require scaling (i.e., multiplier inputs) are automatically scaled in an L_2-sense.

We can obtain unscaled and less expensive implementations of the two-pair building blocks by noting that if we replace $T_{12}(z)$ and $T_{21}(z)$ with $\alpha T_{12}(z)$ and $\alpha^{-1} T_{21}(z)$ in the two-pair structure of Fig. 5.59, where α is a scalar, then $G_m(z)$ is unchanged for a given $G_{m-1}(z)$. Thus, in the two-pairs of Table 5.12 the quantities $\sqrt{\sigma}$ can be avoided by taking $\alpha = 1/\sqrt{\sigma}$ or $\sqrt{\sigma}$. Such resulting structures are more economical in the sense that the first-order two-pairs can be implemented with one multiplier, four adders, and a delay, and second-order two-pairs (type 2) can be implemented with two multipliers, six adders, and two delays. Notice that Property 1, which was crucial for accomplishing structural boundedness, is still preserved. Figure 5.65 shows the type 1A two-pair implemented in this manner, whereas Fig. 5.66 shows the corresponding type 2A two-pair.

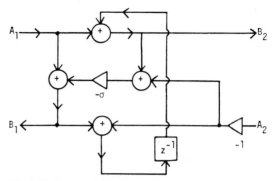

Fig. 5.65. Economic implementation of type 1A two-pair.

Notice that the structure of Fig. 5.65 is precisely the same as that of Fig. 5.55, which in turn represents the wave filters due to Swamy and Thyagarajan [61]. In addition, these structures are also equivalent to the series-adaptor-based realization of an inductor as shown in Section XIII.D.

In summary, the LBR approach has placed in evidence a new synthesis procedure for digital transfer functions. The procedure is such that the resulting implementation is structurally passive and hence has low passband sensitivity. The procedure is based entirely in the z-domain and does not require the use of

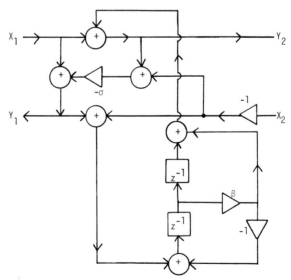

Fig. 5.66. Implementing a type 2A LBR two-pair with six additions and two multiplications.

an *LCR* prototype. However, the implementation of LBR-based filters with building blocks as in Figures 5.65 and 5.66 shows that WDFs are special cases of this approach; thus the low-sensitivity property of the WDFs is essentially a consequence of structural passivity or structural boundedness. On the other hand, planar-rotation-based implementations as in Figs. 5.62 and 5.64 show that orthogonal digital filters can be derived based on this approach, too. Because of the generality of the LBR approach, it can be used with proper modification even for the design of low-sensitivity FIR filters [65, 65a]. This issue will be taken up later.

STRUCTURAL LOSSLESSNESS AND PASSIVITY   XV

In the previous section we saw that a structurally passive implementation leads to low-sensitivity digital filters. Wave digital filters, the LBR-based filters, and orthogonal digital filters are all specific instances of such structural passivity [66, 67]. Recall that structure passivity (or structural boundedness) implies a situation where the structure forces the bound of Eq. (5.180) automatically. Accordingly, the magnitude response is robust with respect to quantization effects. In the LBR-based approach this boundedness was forced by employing lossless 2×2 matrix building blocks (the LBR two-pairs) and scaled versions thereof (Figs. 5.65 and 5.66). So is the case with wave filters and orthogonal filters.

Several authors have noticed in the past that a low-sensitivity structure also has low roundoff noise, and vice versa [53, 68]. (Recall that we made a similar observation in Section XI with respect to the Agarwal–Burrus structure.) Accordingly, any structurally passive implementation is also expected to have low roundoff noise.

Because of the passivity (actually losslessness) of the building blocks, several other interesting properties [66] can be established. For example, we can suppress unwanted granular oscillations (limit cycles) by proper quantization rules. In addition to the above-mentioned structures, there exist several other structures ("normal" digital filters [69], minimum-noise second-order filters [70], etc.), which are based on different viewpoints and possess excellent properties such as low sensitivity, low noise, and freedom from limit cycles. It turns out that the properties in these structures are also attributable to internal passivity and/or losslessness of building blocks.

Therefore the major conclusion emphasized here is that structural passivity plays a key role in minimizing the effects of several kinds of quantization effects—sensitivity, limit cycles, and roundoff noise in digital filters. From an engineering viewpoint it is therefore of considerable interest to explore newer and simpler ways to accomplish structural passivity. The next section outlines one such new method.

XVI LOW-SENSITIVITY ALL-PASS-BASED DIGITAL FILTER STRUCTURES

In this section we outline an exceptionally simple and attractive procedure for attaining structural boundedness for certain transfer functions. The method is once again entirely z-domain based and leads to low sensitivity in the passband. In addition, the resulting structures have very few multipliers per transfer function. The basic building blocks are again structurally lossless, and limit cycles can therefore be suppressed. Moreover, the resulting structures have more inherent parallelism and lend themselves to pipelinable implementations using VLSI technology. An additional advantage of these structures is that they are ideally suited for multirate filtering (see quadrature mirror filters in Chapter 8) even though the details of this particular aspect are outside the scope of this chapter.

The basic idea is as follows: consider once again the magnitude response $|H(e^{j\omega})|$ in Fig. 5.56. Let us assume that $H(z)$ has the property that it can be written as a sum of two stable all-pass functions $A_0(z)$ and $A_1(z)$:

$$H(z) = \tfrac{1}{2}[A_0(z) + A_1(z)] \tag{5.187}$$

$$|A_0(e^{j\omega})| = |A_1(e^{j\omega})| = 1 \qquad \text{for all } \omega \tag{5.188}$$

Since $A_0(z)$ and $A_1(z)$ are all-pass, they can be written as

$$A_0(e^{j\omega}) = e^{j\phi_0(\omega)} \tag{5.189}$$

$$A_1(e^{j\omega}) = e^{j\phi_1(\omega)} \tag{5.190}$$

where $\phi_0(\omega)$ and $\phi_1(\omega)$ are real-valued functions of ω. At frequency ω_k, where $|H(e^{j\omega_k})| = 1$ (see Fig. 5.56), it is clear that the complex numbers A_0 and A_1 are in phase [i.e., $\phi_0(\omega) = \phi_1(\omega)$] so that they add up to 2. It is also clear that if A_0 and A_1 remain all-pass in spite of coefficient quantization, then $|H(e^{j\omega})|$ can never exceed unity in spite of coefficient quantization. Thus we have a structurally passive implementation of $H(z)$ (Fig. 5.67) provided A_0 and A_1 are implemented in a structurally lossless manner.

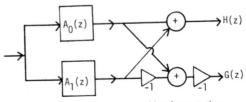

Fig. 5.67. The all-pass-based implementation.

There exist several methods of implementing digital all-pass functions such that they remain all-pass in spite of multiplier quantization [47, 71]. Hence the preceding method can be applied successfully as long as $H(z)$ satisfies Eq. (5.187). Fortunately, it turns out that several transfer functions of practical interest do satisfy the requirement of Eq. (5.187)—that is, can be written as the sum of all-pass functions. For example, this is possible for Butterworth, Chebyshev, and elliptic-digital filters of odd order [72]. More generally, a much wider class of transfer functions satisfies Eq. (5.187), as revealed by the following theorem.

Theorem 5.2. Let $H(z) = P(z)/D(z)$ be BR and such that the numerator $P(z) = \sum_{n=0}^{N} p_n z^{-n}$ is a symmetric polynomial; that is,

$$p_n = p_{N-n} \tag{5.191}$$

where N represents the orders of $P(z)$ and $D(z)$. Consider $|D(e^{j\omega})|^2 - |P(e^{j\omega})|^2$. If there exists a spectral factor $Q(z) = \sum_{n=0}^{N} q_n z^{-n}$ of this quantity such that $Q(z)$ is an antisymmetric polynomial—that is, if

$$|Q(e^{j\omega})|^2 = |D(e^{j\omega})|^2 - |P(e^{j\omega})|^2 \tag{5.192}$$

with

$$q_n = -q_{N-n} \tag{5.193}$$

—then $H(z)$ can be written as a sum of two all-pass functions. More specifically, defining $G(z) = Q(z)/D(z)$, we have the all-pass decomposition property

$$H(z) = \tfrac{1}{2}[A_0(z) + A_1(z)] \tag{5.194}$$

$$G(z) = \tfrac{1}{2}[A_1(z) - A_0(z)] \tag{5.195}$$

where $A_0(z)$ and $A_1(z)$ are all-pass functions.

Comments. Note first that since $H(z)$ is BR, we have $|H(e^{j\omega})| \leq 1$; hence the right side of Eq. (5.192) is nonnegative, as required for spectral factorization. Second, the symmetry condition Eq. (5.191) is not very restrictive. Most digital filter transfer functions have zeros on the unit circle; hence $P(z)$ is symmetric (or possibly antisymmetric if highpass). Third, in view of Eq. (5.192), we have, by construction of $G(z)$,

$$|H(e^{j\omega})|^2 + |G(e^{j\omega})|^2 = 1 \tag{5.196}$$

In other words, $H(z)$ and $G(z)$ form a power-complementary pair (Section X, Chapter 2). Thus, if $H(z)$ is lowpass, then $G(z)$ is highpass, and vice versa.

If $H(z)$ satisfies the conditions of the Theorem 5.2, it only remains to show how A_0 and A_1 in (5.194) should be identified so that we can build the structure of Fig. 5.67. The details of this can be found in [72], and we give only the results. The procedure is as follows:

Step 1. Given $H(z) = P(z)/D(z)$, find $Q(z)$ such that (5.192) is satisfied.

Step 2. Compute the roots of the polynomial $P(z) + Q(z)$. Let these be $z_1, z_2, \ldots, z_r, z_{r+1}, \ldots, z_N$, where $z_1, \ldots, z_r$ are strictly inside the unit circle, and $z_{r+1}, \ldots, z_N$ are strictly outside.

Step 3. Construct $A_0(z)$ and $A_1(z)$ as

$$A_1(z) = \prod_{k=r+1}^{N} \frac{z^{-1} - z_k^{-1}}{1 - z^{-1} z_k^{-1}} \tag{5.197}$$

$$A_0(z) = \prod_{k=1}^{r} \frac{z^{-1} - z_k}{1 - z_k z^{-1}} \tag{5.198}$$

Note that $A_0(z)$ and $A_1(z)$ identified in the above manner are *stable* all-pass functions. It can be shown that $P(z) + Q(z)$ *cannot* have any zero on the unit circle (as long as $H(z)$ is stable); hence step 2 always succeeds.

While performing step 1 we need not go through an elaborate and general spectral factorization algorithm. Since $Q(z)$ is antisymmetric, we can find its coefficients q_k simply by using the closed-form formula

$$q_0 = \sqrt{r_0}, \qquad q_1 = \frac{r_1}{2q_0} \tag{5.199}$$

$$q_n = -q_{N-n} = \frac{r_n - \sum_{k=1}^{n-1} q_k q_{n-k}}{2q_0}, \qquad n = 2, 3, \ldots \tag{5.200}$$

where $R(z) = \sum_{n=0}^{2N} r_n z^{-n}$ is the polynomial

$$R(z) \triangleq z^{-N}(P(z^{-1})P(z) - D(z^{-1})D(z)) \tag{5.201}$$

1 Complexity of the Implementation

Any all-pass function of order m has only m distinct coefficients, because the numerator polynomial is the flipped version (i.e., mirror image) of the denominator. It is therefore always possible to implement it with only m multipliers (rather than the $2m + 1$ multiplers required for a general mth-order transfer function). Thus $A_0(z)$ requires r multipliers, whereas $A_1(z)$ requires $N - r$ multipliers, making a total of N multipliers in Fig. 5.67. Thus we obtain two transfer functions $H(z)$ and $G(z)$ with only N multipliers that is. $\lceil N/2 \rceil$ multipliers per transfer function where $\lceil x \rceil$ is the smallest integer greater than or equal to x. In contrast, a direct implementation of $H(z)$ alone would normally require $N + \lceil N/2 \rceil \simeq 3(N/2)$ multipliers! Thus, there is a reduction by a factor of 3 in the complexity of the implementation as a result of the all-pass based structure in Fig. 5.67. In addition, each multiplier coefficient requires fewer bits in Fig. 5.67 because of the low passband sensitivity property, as explained earlier. We now proceed to demonstrate these ideas with a design example.

As mentioned above, odd-order digital Butterworth, Chebyshev, and elliptic filters (classical optimal filters) can always be implemented in the computationally efficient form of Fig. 5.67. However, the class of transfer functions satisfying Theorem 5.2 is much wider. To demonstrate this, we take a transfer function $H(z)$ that is not a classical optimal filter and obtain the design of Fig. 5.67. Thus consider the BR transfer function

$$H(z) = \frac{P(z)}{D(z)}$$

$$= k \frac{1 + 1.73306z^{-1} + 2.83075z^{-2} + 2.83075z^{-3} + 1.73306z^{-4} + z^{-5}}{1 - 0.7004z^{-1} + 1.42787z^{-2} - 0.57995z^{-3} + 0.40866z^{-4} - 0.05463z^{-5}}$$

$$(5.202)$$

where $k = 0.13494$, so $|H(e^{j\omega})|_{max} = 1$. Clearly,

$$P(z) = 0.13494(1 + 1.73306z^{-1} + 2.83075z^{-2} + 2.83075z^{-3} + 1.73306z^{-4} + z^{-5})$$

whereas

$$D(z) = 1 - 0.7004z^{-1} + 1.42787z^{-2} - 0.57995z^{-3} + 0.40866z^{-4} - 0.05463z^{-5}$$

Computing $\tilde{D}(z)D(z) - \tilde{P}(z)P(z)$ (see Section I for the meaning of $\sim$) and employing Eqs. (5.199) and (5.200), we obtain its anti-symmetric spectral factor $Q(z)$:

$$Q(z) = 0.26989(1 - 2.63479z^{-1} + 4.09366z^{-2} - 4.09366z^{-3} + 2.63479z^{-4} - z^{-5})$$

Next, we determine the zeros of $P(z) + Q(z)$:

$$z_1 = 0.155661, \qquad z_2 = 0.109659 + j0.924586$$

$$z_3 = z_2^*, \qquad z_4 = 0.401930 + j1.51943$$

$$z_5 = z_4^*$$

Of these, z_1, z_2, and z_3 are inside the unit circle, and z_4 and z_5 are outside. We therefore construct the two all-pass functions

$$A_1(z) = \frac{(1 - z_4 z^{-1})(1 - z_5 z^{-1})}{(-z_4 + z^{-1})(-z_5 + z^{-1})}$$

$$A_0(z) = \frac{(-z_1 + z^{-1})(-z_2 + z^{-1})(-z_3 + z^{-1})}{(1 - z_1 z^{-1})(1 - z_2 z^{-1})(1 - z_3 z^{-1})}$$

Thus $A_1(z)$ is a second-order section, whereas $A_0(z)$ is a cascade of a first-order section $A_{01}(z)$ and a second-order section $A_{02}(z)$, where

$$A_{01}(z) = \frac{-z_1 + z^{-1}}{1 - z_1 z^{-1}}, \qquad A_{02}(z) = \frac{(-z_2 + z^{-1})(-z_3 + z^{-1})}{(1 - z_2 z^{-1})(1 - z_3 z^{-1})}$$

The appropriate all-pass functions are therefore

$$A_1(z) = \frac{0.40482 - 0.32542z^{-1} + z^{-2}}{1 - 0.32542z^{-1} + 0.40482z^{-2}} \tag{5.203}$$

and

$$A_0(z) = \frac{-0.13494 + 0.90102z^{-1} - 0.37498z^{-2} + z^{-3}}{1 - 0.37498z^{-1} + 0.90102z^{-2} - 0.13494z^{-3}} \tag{5.204}$$

To study the sensitivity properties, we quantized the coefficients of the all-pass filters $A_1(z)$ and $A_0(z)$ to 3 bits of mantissa in canonic sign digit code (SD code), and the structure of Fig. 5.67 simulated. Note that each multiplier has a complexity equivalent to two additions. Figure 5.68 shows the relevant frequency responses. In all the plots the dashed curve indicates the ideal (infinite-precision) response. The excellent sensitivity properties of the structurally passive implementation are evident from the response plots, particularly in the passband. In the present example, $H(z)$ has been chosen to be a filter transfer function that is not optimal in any classical sense, as seen from the ideal response plots in Fig. 5.68. We purposely chose $H(z)$ this way to emphasize the point we made earlier that to obtain an implementation as in Fig. 5.68, $H(z)$ need not necessarily be optimal.

As a comparison, the transfer function of (5.202) was also implemented in direct form with the same amount of parameter quantization (3 bits of SD code per mantissa). Figure 5.69 shows the relevant frequency response plots. Not surprisingly, the performance is unacceptable.

In the new structures, since $A_1(z)$ and $A_0(z)$ are all-pass functions, they require only two and three multipliers, respectively. Thus a total of five multiplications are involved per computed output sample, and we get two filters, $H(z)$ and $G(z)$. Thus the average multiplier count is 2.5. In contrast, the direct form requires seven multipliers [even after taking into account the symmetry of the numerator $P(z)$] and more precision for each multiplier.

As a further demonstration, the all-pass functions of Eqs. (5.203) and (5.204) were implemented with only 2 bits of SD code per multiplier mantissa. (Note that each multiplier is then as complex as one addition operation.) The resulting quantized all-pass functions are

$$A_1(z) = \frac{0.375 - 0.3125z^{-1} + z^{-2}}{1 - 0.3125z^{-1} + 0.375z^{-2}} \tag{5.205}$$

and

$$A_0(z) = \frac{-0.1328125 + 0.875z^{-1} - 0.375z^{-2} + z^{-3}}{1 - 0.375z^{-1} + 0.875z^{-2} - 0.1328125z^{-3}} \tag{5.206}$$

Figure 5.70 shows the resulting frequency responses obtained with the implementation of Fig. 5.67. Notice that the passband behavior continues to be

OVERALL RESPONSE

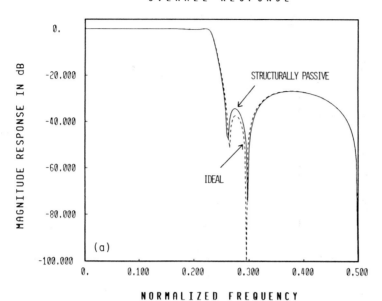

Fig. 5.68(a). The new implementation with 3 bits per multiplier.

PASSBAND DETAILS

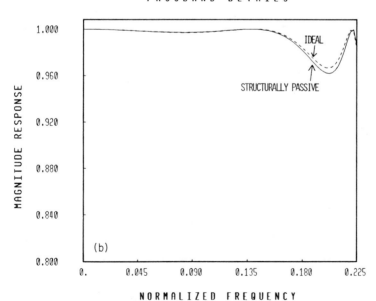

Fig. 5.68(b). The new implementation with 3 bits per multiplier.

OVERALL RESPONSE

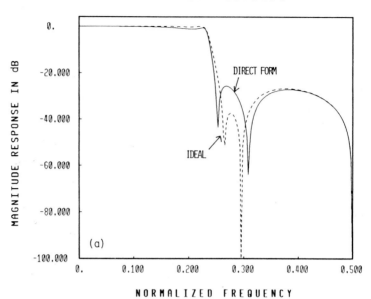

Fig. 5.69(a). The direct form with 3 bits per multiplier.

PASSBAND DETAILS

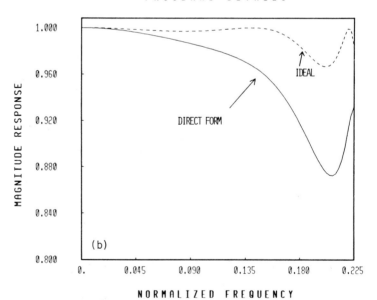

Fig. 5.69(b). The direct form with 3 bits per multiplier.

OVERALL   RESPONSE

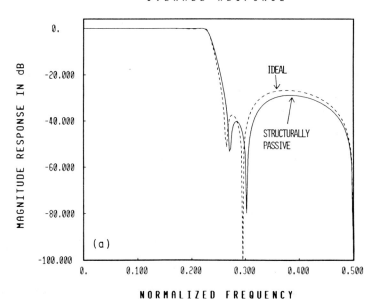

Fig. 5.70(a). The new implementation with 2 bits per multiplier.

PASSBAND   DETAILS

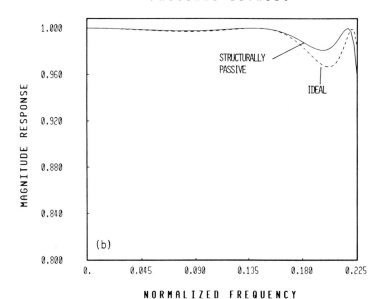

Fig. 5.70(b). The new implementation with 2 bits per multiplier.

excellent. The quantized response has *less* error in the passband and stopband than does the ideal response! The reason is that the quantized response has a wider transition band. The improved behavior is not surprising since the ideal response is not optimal in any way. Since each multiplier is equivalent to one addition in complexity, the total complexity of the quantized circuit of Fig. 5.67 is now only 16 addition operations (equivalent to a single 17-bit multiplier coefficient!). With this low complexity the structure still achieves about 30-dB stopband attenuation and 0.1 dB peak passband ripple. This example therefore demonstrates the excellent potentiality of the circuit of Fig. 5.67 from a sensitivity viewpoint. (For completeness we note that with a quantization level of 2 bits of SD code per multiplier mantissa the direct-form structure became unstable in this example.)

3 Comment on Stopband Sensitivity

The passband sensitivity of the complementary filter $G(z)$ is expected to be excellent for the same reason that the passband sensitivity of $H(z)$ is excellent. In spite of parameter quantization, Eqs. (5.194) and (5.195) hold; hence Eq. (5.196) holds for each frequency. Thus, the stopband sensitivity of $H(z)$ is expected to be good. However, in terms of decibels, a small passband error in $G(z)$ corresponds to a large stopband error in $H(z)$, particularly in the region of low passband and stopband error. Figure 5.71 shows a plot of α versus β, where

$$\alpha = -20\log_{10} a, \qquad \beta = -20\log_{10} b, \qquad a^2 + b^2 = 1 \qquad (5.207)$$

Notice that the quantity α decreases very sharply for small changes in β in the region of large α. This figure demonstrates that if $H(z)$ has large stopband attenuation, then low *passband* sensitivity of $G(z)$ does not necessarily imply low *stopband* sensitivity of $H(z)$.

4 Comments on the All-Pass Filters

As we mentioned earlier, the implementation in Fig. 5.67, based on all-pass decomposition, always exhibits low passband sensitivity regardless of how the all-pass filters are implemented as long as they are implemented in a structurally lossless manner.

A structurally lossless implementation of an all-pass function $A(z)$ of order m can be obtained by implementing $A(z)$ with m multipliers (rather than $2m$). The use of the smallest number of multipliers ensures that the numerator of $A(z)$ is a mirror image of the denominator in spite of parameter quantization. Accordingly, $A(z)$ remains all-pass even after multiplier quantization.

There are several well-known all-pass structures [47–49, 72] requiring the smallest number of multipliers, and hence possessing structure losslessness. Among them, some have the additional property that crucial internal nodes

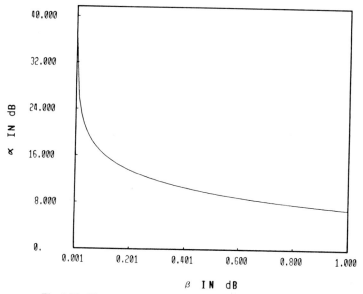

Fig. 5.71. The tradeoff between passband and stopband errors.

(multiplier inputs) are automatically scaled [48]; and some have the property that limit-cycle oscillations can be suppressed [49]. In addition, a particular choice of the all-pass implementation gives rise to certain well-known WDFs called the lattice wave filters [45, 46].

Because of the crucial role of all-pass filters in several applications (including the applications of this section), we dedicate the next section to a summary of results in the literature in this connection.

DIGITAL ALL-PASS FUNCTIONS   XVII

A digital all-pass function is of the form

$$A(z) = \frac{b_N + b_{N-1}z^{-1} + \cdots + b_1 z^{-(N-1)} + z^{-N}}{1 + b_1 z^{-1} + b_2 z^{-2} + \cdots + b_{N-1}z^{-(N-1)} + b_N z^{-N}} \qquad (5.208)$$

Thus the numerator is the flipped version (or mirror image) of the denominator. Therefore it is possible to implement it with only N multipliers. Figure 5.72 shows how a first-order all-pass function

$$A(z) = \frac{b_1 + z^{-1}}{1 + b_1 z^{-1}} \qquad (5.209)$$

can be built using one multiplier. This structure has two delays even though the

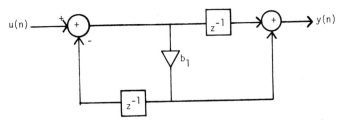

Fig. 5.72. A one-multiplier, two-delay implementation of the first-order all-pass function.

order is only unity. A structure with one multiplier and one delay can be obtained as shown in Fig. 5.73.

For second-order all-pass functions it is once again possible to obtain structures having only two multipliers and two delays. Figure 5.74 is a typical example where

$$A(z) = \frac{b_2 + b_1 z^{-1} + z^{-2}}{1 + b_1 z^{-1} + b_2 z^{-2}} \tag{5.210}$$

A systematic way to generate first- and second-order all-pass structures with a minimum number of multipliers is advanced in [71] based on the "multiplier extraction approach." Four first-order structures and 24 second-order structures are catalogued in [71]. More and newer structures can be found in [73]. Based on these structures, one can readily obtain a cascade-form implementation of an all-pass function having arbitrary order. In addition, for each such all-pass structure, closed-form expressions for roundoff noise variance are included in [71]. Sufficient information for scaling these structures in the L_2-sense can be found in [72].

An entirely different family of all-pass structures is the Gray and Markel (untapped) recursive structures. The overall appearance is shown in Fig. 5.75, where each building block is a digital two-pair characterized by a single parameter k_m, making a total of N parameters altogether. The building block has a

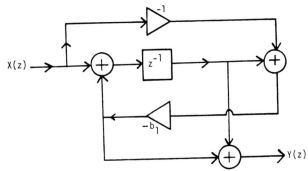

Fig. 5.73. A one-multiplier, one-delay implementation of the first-order all-pass function.

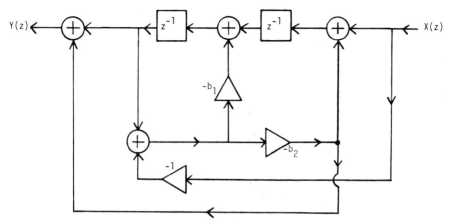

Fig. 5.74. A two-multiplier, two-delay implementation for a second-order all-pass function.

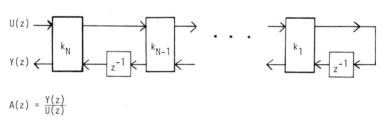

$$A(z) = \frac{Y(z)}{U(z)}$$

Fig. 5.75. The cascaded Gray and Markel lattice structures.

transfer matrix

$$\mathcal{T}_m = \begin{bmatrix} k_m & 1 + k_m \\ 1 - k_m & -k_m \end{bmatrix} \tag{5.211}$$

and is drawn in Fig. 5.76. Note that only one multiplier and one delay are required per stage in Fig. 5.75.

It can be shown that if $\mathcal{T}_m(z)$ in Eq. (5.211) is replaced by

$$\mathcal{T}_m = \begin{bmatrix} k_m & (1 + k_m)\alpha_m \\ (1 - k_m)/\alpha_m & -k_m \end{bmatrix} \tag{5.212}$$

for arbitrary α_m, the transfer function $A(z)$ in Fig. 5.75 remains unchanged. With $\alpha_m = 1 - k_m$ we get the two-multiplier implementation of Fig. 5.77, whereas with $\alpha_m = \sqrt{(1 - k_m)/(1 + k_m)}$ we get the structure of Fig. 5.78. Note that Fig. 5.78 requires four multipliers and is called the *normalized structure*. When each section in Fig. 5.75 has the form of Fig. 5.78, the cascade of Fig. 5.75 are automatically internally scaled in the L_2-sense. The price paid for this is sections in the increased number of multipliers.

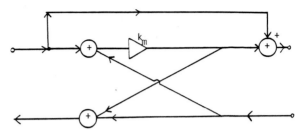

Fig. 5.76. The one-multiplier Gray–Markel lattice.

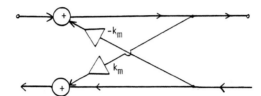

Fig. 5.77. The two-multiplier Gray–Markel lattice.

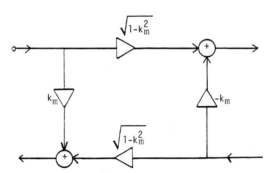

Fig. 5.78. The four-multiplier Gray–Markel lattice.

It has been shown by Gray [49] that building blocks of the form in Figs. 5.76–5.78 are passive; hence Fig. 5.75 represents a passive implementation. Therefore interesting properties can be established, including freedom from limit cycles [49].

For a given all-pass function the coefficients k_m do not depend on whether we use building blocks of Figs. 5.76, 5.77, or 5.78. Indeed, we can even use an arbitrary combination of them. Given $A(z)$ as in Eq. (5.208), the most important question is, how does one compute $\{k_m, m = 1, 2, \ldots, N\}$ so that the structure of Fig. 5.75 can be built? Here is an algorithm for computing all k_m: let

$$A_N(z) = 1 + b_1 z^{-1} + \cdots + b_{N-1} z^{-(N-1)} + b_N z^{-N} \tag{5.213}$$

$$B_N(z) = z^{-N} A_N(z^{-1}) \tag{5.214}$$

be the denominator and numerator polynomials of $A(z)$. Recursively define the polynomials

$$A_{m-1}(z) = A_m(z) - k_m B_m(z) \tag{5.215}$$

$$B_{m-1}(z) = z^{-(m-1)} A_{m-1}(z^{-1}) \tag{5.216}$$

where

$$k_m = B_m(\infty)/A_m(\infty) \tag{5.217}$$

Repeated use of Eqs. (5.215)–(5.217) reveals the values of all k_m. For a proof of this procedure see [74, 74a].

It can be shown that newer all-pass structures can be obtained by using the building blocks of Fig. 5.55 as the two-pairs in Fig. 5.75. The resulting structures are, however, not as simple and may not offer specific attractions.

Design of Arbitrary Transfer Functions Based on the All-Pass Structure of Figure 5.75

Gray and Markel have developed structures that are extensions of Fig. 5.75 in order to realize arbitrary (i.e., not necessarily all-pass) transfer functions. These structures are called *tapped cascaded lattice structures* [47] (Fig. 5.79), where the tap coefficients α_m are computed depending on the desired transfer function numerator. These structures are known to exhibit low sensitivity and roundoff noise and can be made free of limit cycles.

We conclude this section with an important remark. If the all-pass sections in the low-sensitivity structure of Section XVI (Fig. 5.67) are implemented as in Fig. 5.75 with building blocks (two-pairs) as in Fig. 5.76, the resulting structures are precisely the wave digital lattice filters studied in [75]. This observation once again shows the relation between structural passivity methods, wave digital methods, and the Gray–Markel lattice structures.

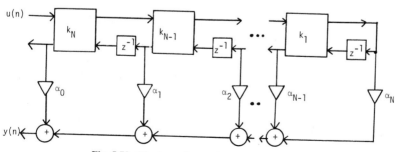

Fig. 5.79. The tapped cascaded lattice structure.

XVIII   ORTHOGONAL DIGITAL FILTERS

We saw earlier that filters based on passive and lossless building blocks tend to have several excellent properties when word lengths are quantized . We also saw that the LBR approach gave rise to wave filters as special cases. In addition, the LBR approach also leads to certain structures having orthogonal building blocks (Figs. 5.62 and 5.64); these structures are actually a class of orthogonal digital filters [34, 63].

Several other classes of orthogonal digital filter structures exist. Some of them are truly orthogonal, and some have an orthogonal implementation of the recursive part. The tapped cascaded Gray and Markel lattice of Fig. 5.79 has an orthogonal recursive part if each building block is as in Fig. 5.78. The transfer matrix of such a building block is an orthogonal matrix

$$\mathscr{T}_m = \begin{bmatrix} k_m & \sqrt{1 - k_m^2} \\ \sqrt{1 - k_m^2} & -k_m \end{bmatrix} \tag{5.218}$$

and hence corresponds to a planar rotation.

A particular class of orthogonal filters that can be implemented with N delays (N being the transfer function order) and that are highly pipelinable is described in [76] and [50]. These structures have the advantages of a conventional orthogonal filter [34], but at the same time permit a high degree of concurrency in implementation. In this section we describe only these structures, and we base our discussion on the LBR framework [63].

Given any Nth-order IIR BR transfer function $H(z) = P(z)/D(z)$, assume that we have constructed the complementary function $G(z) = Q(z)/D(z)$ satisfying Eq. (5.196). Define the vector

$$\mathbf{G}_N(z) = \begin{bmatrix} H(z) \\ G(z) \end{bmatrix} = \frac{\begin{bmatrix} P(z) \\ Q(z) \end{bmatrix}}{D(z)} \tag{5.219}$$

Clearly $\mathbf{G}_N(z)$ is an LBR vector (i.e., an all-pass vector) because

$$\mathbf{G}_N^\dagger(e^{j\omega})\mathbf{G}_N(e^{j\omega}) = 1 \tag{5.220}$$

for all ω. Note that the components of an all-pass vector satisfy Eq. (5.196); each component can be any function bounded by unity for $z = e^{j\omega}$. It therefore leads us

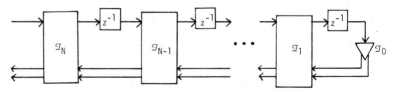

Fig. 5.80. Cascaded lattice realization of a vector all-pass function.

to believe that this vector all-pass function can be realized by a vector version of the Gray–Markel cascaded lattice of Fig. 5.75, illustrated in Fig. 5.80. This indeed turns out to be the case. Each 3×3 building block in Fig. 5.80 has a transfer matrix[†]

$$\mathscr{T}_m = \begin{bmatrix} \mathbf{k}_m & (\mathbf{I} - \mathbf{k}_m \mathbf{k}_m^t)^{1/2} \\ \sqrt{1 - \mathbf{k}_m^t \mathbf{k}_m} & -\mathbf{k}_m^t \left(\dfrac{\mathbf{I} - \mathbf{k}_m \mathbf{k}_m^t}{1 - \mathbf{k}_m^t \mathbf{k}_m} \right)^{-t/2} \end{bmatrix} \tag{5.221}$$

which is orthogonal and is analogous to Eq. (5.218) in the scalar-all-pass case. Since Eq. (5.221) represents an orthogonal matrix, it can be written as a succession of planar rotations. It can be shown that

$$\mathscr{T}_m = \begin{bmatrix} 1 & 0 & 0 \\ 0 & \cos \alpha_2 & \sin \alpha_2 \\ 0 & \sin \alpha_2 & -\cos \alpha_2 \end{bmatrix} \begin{bmatrix} -\cos \alpha_1 & \sin \alpha_1 & 0 \\ \sin \alpha_1 & \cos \alpha_1 & 0 \\ 0 & 0 & 1 \end{bmatrix}$$

where $k_1 = -\cos \alpha_1$ and $k_2 = \sin \alpha_1 \cos \alpha_2$. Figure 5.81 shows an implementation of this building block. See Fig. 5.62 for the definition of the "θ-block." In Eq. (5.221) $\mathbf{k}_m$ is a column vector with two components. Given $\mathbf{G}_N(z)$, the structure of Fig. 5.80 can be obtained once we compute $\mathbf{k}_m$ for all m. We do it by a vector extension of the earlier recursive procedure described in Eqs. (5.215)–(5.217). The details are as follows:

Given $\mathbf{G}_m(z) = \mathbf{N}_m(z)/\mathbf{D}_m(z)$, compute

$$\mathbf{k}_m = \mathbf{G}_m(\infty) \tag{5.222}$$

$$z^{-1}\mathbf{N}_{m-1}(z) = (\mathbf{I} - \mathbf{k}_m \mathbf{k}_m^t)^{-1/2}(\mathbf{N}_m(z) - \mathbf{k}_m \mathbf{D}_m(z)) \tag{5.223}$$

$$\mathbf{D}_{m-1}(z) = (1 - \mathbf{k}_m^t \mathbf{k}_m)^{-1/2}(\mathbf{D}_m(z) - \mathbf{k}_m^t \mathbf{N}_m(z)) \tag{5.224}$$

If this process is repeated starting from $m = N$ downward, we obtain all $\mathbf{k}_m$ coefficients. The above recursion is initialized by

$$\mathbf{N}_N(z) = \begin{bmatrix} P(z) \\ Q(z) \end{bmatrix} \tag{5.225}$$

$$\mathbf{D}_N(z) = D(z) \tag{5.226}$$

because of Eq. (5.219).

In Fig. 5.80 the column vector $\mathscr{T}_0$ is

$$\mathscr{T}_0 = \frac{\mathbf{N}_0}{\mathbf{D}_0} \tag{5.227}$$

Futher details concerning these and related structures can be found in [50] and [63].

[†] Matrix notation is reviewed in Section I.

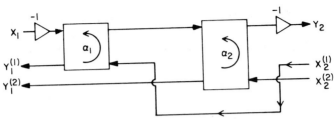

Fig. 5.81. A typical 3×3 building block in Fig. 5.80.

XIX QUANTIZATION EFFECTS IN FIR DIGITAL FILTERS

Consider the FIR transfer function

$$H(z) = h_0 + h_1 z^{-1} + \cdots + h_{N-1} z^{-(N-1)} \tag{5.228}$$

A direct-form implementation is shown in Fig. 2.1(a), requiring N multipliers, $N - 1$ delays, and $N - 1$ adders. If $H(z)$ has linear phase, then it can be any of four types (Table IV in Chapter 2) and, because of the impulse response symmetry, requires only $\lceil N/2 \rceil$ multipliers. Figure 2.1(b) shows a type 1, sixth-order linear-phase FIR filter implemented in direct form.

If we introduce a quantizer after each multiplier m_k, then the quantization error $e_k(n)$ introduced at the output of each multiplier contributes to the output noise variance. It is readily seen that the output quantization noise variance is

$$\sigma_f^2 = \begin{cases} N\sigma_e^2 & [\text{Fig. 2.1(a)}] \qquad (5.229) \\ \lceil N/2 \rceil \sigma_e^2 & [\text{Fig. 2.1(b)}] \qquad (5.230) \end{cases}$$

where σ_e^2 is defined in Table 5.4 and the usual assumptions concerning noise sources are made (Section III). If, however, we quantize not after each multiplier but only *after* all additions have been performed, then

$$\sigma_f^2 = \sigma_e^2 \tag{5.231}$$

and is the smallest possible output roundoff noise we can hope to get. This scheme requires double-precision adders to preserve the unquantized internal precision before quantizing at the output. For large N, Eqs. (5.229) and (5.230) imply large noise gain. We recall (Chapter 2) that for FIR filters the order $N - 1$ is generally large. Thus, $N - 1 = 10$ is considered low, whereas $N - 1 = 50$ is quite common.

Scaling the Direct-Form FIR Structure. From Fig. 2.1 it is clear that the signals that are inputs to multipliers are nothing but delayed versions of the input signal. Thus as long as the input is scaled to be in the range $(-1, 1)$, there is no possibility of internal overflow. To avoid overflow at the output node, we must insert a scale factor $1/L$ (as we did for IIR filters, Sections IV, V), where

$$L = \sum_{n=0}^{N-1} |h(n)| \tag{5.232}$$

Even though the choice of L as in Eq. (5.232) guarantees complete freedom from overflow, it is too conservative. Less stringent scaling rules (and improved SNR) can be obtained if further knowledge concerning the input is available, as summarized in Table V.

Direct-Form Versus Cascade-Form FIR Filters   A

It is clear from the above discussions that the direct form is an exceptionally simple structure and offers very low roundoff noise. In addition, the scaling rules are simple and well understood. Thus unlike IIR filters, direct-form FIR filters are quite widely used, even if the order $N-1$ is large.

However, there is the problem of coefficient sensitivity in FIR filters. For direct-form filters Herrmann and Schuessler [77] have demonstrated that for high filter orders and stopband sensitivity under quantization is rather large while the passband sensitivity is generally acceptably low. The basic explanation is that, as the filter coefficients are rounded, the transmission zeros on the unit circle generally move off, causing a loss of stopband attenuation. (Notice however that structures such as in Fig. 2.1(b) continue to offer exact linear phase in spite of quantization of multipliers.)

An obvious attempt to remedy this situation is to use the cascade-form structure. Any FIR transfer function with real-valued $h(n)$ can be written in the form of a product of sections of the form $1 + a_k z^{-1} + b_k z^{-2}$, where a_k and b_k are real. (If $H(z)$ has odd order, one of the b_k can be taken as zero.) The zeros on the unit circle contribute to factors of the form $1 - 2\cos(\theta_k)z^{-1} + z^{-2}$. Thus, upon quantization of the multipliers the zeros on the unit circle can move only *along* the unit circle, causing reduced stopband sensitivity. In view of the linear phase of $H(z)$, each factor of the form $1 + a_k z^{-1} + b_k z^{-2}$ (representing a zero not on the unit circle) has associated with it the factor $b_k + a_k z^{-1} + z^{-2}$. As long as the a_k's (and b_k's) in these factors are the same even after quantization, the linear-phase property continues to be preserved. The major disadvantage here, however, is that such a cascade of (first-and) second-order sections requires more multipliers than $\lceil N/2 \rceil$. We can remedy this by implementing the factors $1 + a_k z^{-1} + b_k z^{-2}$ and $b_k + a_k z^{-1} + z^{-2}$ after combining (and rescaling) as

$$1 + c_k z^{-1} + d_k z^{-2} + c_k z^{-3} + z^{-4} \tag{5.233}$$

which is a fourth-order linear-phase section requiring only two multipliers (c_k and d_k). Thus the total number of multipliers is minimum, as in linear-phase direct forms. Obviously, phase linearity is still preserved in spite of quantization. Such a structure, based on fourth-order sections, unfortunately has an unforeseen disadvantage: the section of Eq. (5.233) has very high zero sensitivity with respect to the multiplier coefficients [77]. Accordingly, this kind of cascade form has high passband sensitivity, even though the stopband sensitivity is low.

1 Section-Ordering Problems

A further disadvantage of cascade-form FIR filters is that the output roundoff noise depends very strongly on the ordering of sections. Thus the SNR at the filter output under scaled condition depends crucially on this ordering [78]. (Schuessler has demonstrated the example of a thirty-second-order FIR filter in cascade form for which the noise gain is 2.4 for one ordering and 1.5×10^8 for another ordering!) Thus it is important to search efficiently for an optimal ordering; because there are so many sections, the number of possible orderings is enormous and a direct search is impractical. Chan and Rabiner [78] have come up with efficient procedures for finding a good ordering scheme.

In addition to the direct and cascade forms, several authors have proposed novel FIR filter structures, some of which are known to exhibit low roundoff noise, and sensitivity properties. Schuessler [79] has introduced structures based on polynomial interpolation formulae; Jing and Fam [80] have advanced a class of structures called the multiplicative FIR (MFIR) structures. In addition, the novel concept of "space-time duality" has been introduced in [81] to obtain efficient FIR implementations. Mahanta et al. [82] have studied FIR filter structures with permuted coefficients in order to accomplish remarkable reductions in quantization effects. In addition, the concept of structural passivity introduced in Section XIV has recently been employed [65] to design certain very low-sensitivity FIR structures (called the FIRBR structures).

B Estimation of Coefficient Accuracy Requirements

Unlike IIR filters, the problem of coefficient sensitivity in FIR filters is much more tractable in the sense that it is possible to get estimates for the number of bits per multiplier required to obtain a certain degree of accuracy in the frequency response. A number of contributions pertaining to this problem have appeared in the literature [83, 84].

Chan and Rabiner [83] proposed a technique in 1973 for estimating the frequency response error due to parameter quantization. Let $H(e^{j\omega})$ be the frequency response of a type 1 linear-phase FIR filter given by

$$H(e^{j\omega}) = e^{-j\omega(N-1)/2}H_0(e^{j\omega}) \tag{5.234}$$

where

$$H_0(e^{j\omega}) = \sum_{n=0}^{M} b_n \cos \omega n$$

and, as in Chapter 2,

$$b_n = \begin{cases} 2h\left(\dfrac{N-1}{2} - n\right), & n \neq 0 \\[2mm] h\left(\dfrac{N-1}{2}\right), & n = 0 \end{cases} \tag{5.235}$$

After quantizing the coefficients $h(n)$ in a direct-form implementation, the error in $H_0(e^{j\omega})$ is

$$E(e^{j\omega}) = \bar{H}_0(e^{j\omega}) - H_0(e^{j\omega}) \tag{5.236}$$

where $\bar{H}_0(e^{j\omega})$ corresponds to the response of the quantized direct form. Clearly, $E(e^{j\omega})$ can be written as

$$E(e^{j\omega}) = \sum_{n=1}^{M} 2e(n)\cos \omega n + e(0) \tag{5.237}$$

where $e(n)$ are the quantization errors in the impulse response coefficients $h((N-1)/2 - n)$. If each $h(n)$ is represented by b bits as in Fig. 5.2, then $e(n)$ behaves as in Table IV. Assuming rounding arithmetic, we have an upper bound for $E(e^{j\omega})$ as follows:

$$|E(e^{j\omega})| \leq (2M + 1)\Delta/2, \qquad \Delta = 2^{-b} \tag{5.238}$$

where $2M + 1 = N$ is the filter length. The above upper bound is pessimistic in the sense that the error $E(e^{j\omega})$ will hardly ever attain this magnitude. Chan and Rabiner have taken a more practical viewpoint to derive useful bounds. Even though a filter structure, once quantized, remains fixed, a statistical viewpoint gives us a preliminary guideline for choice of the required number of bits b per coefficient $h(n)$. Thus, assume $e(n)$ to be an uncorrelated random sequence satisfying all the assumptions of Section III concerning error sources. $E(e^{j\omega})$ is then a real-valued random variable and can be assumed to be Gaussian [12] for large N. Its standard deviation is

$$\sigma_E(e^{j\omega}) = \Delta \sqrt{\frac{2N-1}{12}} \, W_N(\omega) \tag{5.239}$$

where

$$W_N(\omega) = \left[\frac{1}{2N-1}\left(-\frac{1}{2} + \frac{\sin N\omega}{\sin \omega}\right) + \frac{1}{2}\right]^{1/2} \tag{5.240}$$

Notice that $W_N(\omega)$ is in the range $(0, 1)$, as shown in the plot of Fig. 5.82. Thus, the

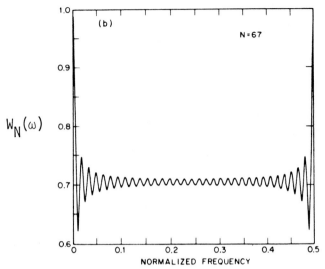

Fig. 5.82. A typical plot of $W_N(\omega)$ [83] (© 1973 IEEE).

standard deviation is bounded for all ω by

$$\sigma_E(e^{j\omega}) \le \Delta \sqrt{\frac{2N-1}{12}} \qquad (5.241)$$

Since $E(e^{j\omega})$ is assumed to be Gaussian, we can say that $E(e^{j\omega})$ lies in the range $(-3\sigma_E, 3\sigma_E)$ with very high probability. Based on this, Chan and Rabiner [83] could actually derive estimates for the required number of bits b per filter coefficient $h(n)$ for a specified tolerance requirement in the passband and stopband.

Heute [85] has pointed out that the bound in Eq. (5.241) underestimates peak errors in the frequency response. Gersho et al. [86] have shown that the new bound due to Heute [85] overestimates the peak errors; in [86] are presented new bounds based on some fundamental mathematical results concerning trigonomentric polynomials.

A major point is that most of the literature available for estimating the number of bits b assumes that the coefficients are represented as in Fig. 5.2. However, it is often much more efficient to represent coefficients in canonic sign digit code (CSD) [87], which permits the digits 1, -1, and 0 in the representation. As an example, 111101 in binary corresponds to 1000 -101 in CSD code, requiring only three rather than five active bits (i.e., nonzero bits). If the digital filter architecture is such that multiplications are to be performed by shift-and-add operations, then CSD is an efficient way to represent coefficients. The true meaning of "number of bits" in CSD should be taken as the number of nonzero bits. With this definition, it is nontrivial to obtain simple formulas for the error such as Eq. (5.239).

LOW-SENSITIVE FIR FILTERS BASED ON STRUCTURAL PASSIVITY   XX

In Sections XIII–XVI we saw that structural boundedness (or passivity) enables us to obtain low-sensitivity digital filters with additional favorable properties. We also saw that the LBR approach is sufficiently general and z-domain based. Hence it is possible to design structurally passive FIR filters without referring to any continuous-time LC filters.

An Approach for Designing FIRBR Structures[†]   A

Most of the FIR filters that are of interest in practice have linear phase. There are four types of linear-phase FIR filters (Chapter 2). Types 3 and 4 are used for the design of Hilbert transformers and differentiators, and we will not consider them here. Type 2 filters have the restriction that $H(e^{j\pi}) = 0$, and therefore are less general than type 1 filters. Therefore, in this section we shall consider only type 1 linear-phase FIR filters. The frequency response of such a filter is

$$H(e^{j\omega}) = e^{-j\omega(N-1)/2}H_0(e^{j\omega}) \tag{5.242}$$

where $H_0(e^{j\omega})$ is a real function of ω. Let us now consider a "complementary transfer function" $G(z)$, defined as

$$G(z) = z^{-(N-1)/2} - H(z) \tag{5.243}$$

Clearly,

$$G(e^{j\omega}) = e^{-j\omega(N-1)/2}[1 - H_0(e^{j\omega})] = e^{-j\omega(N-1)/2}G_0(e^{j\omega}) \tag{5.244}$$

and $G(z)$ is again a linear-phase transfer function of type 1. Figure 5.83 shows typical plots of $H_0(e^{j\omega})$ and $G_0(e^{j\omega})$. Note that $G_0(e^{j\omega})$ has double zeros at the frequencies $\omega_1, \omega_2, \ldots, \omega_M$ where $|H(e^{j\omega})|$ is equal to unity. In other words, $G(z)$ has factors of the form

$$G_{1,k}(z) = (1 - 2\cos(\omega_k)z^{-1} + z^{-2})^2 \tag{5.245}$$

and can therefore be written as

$$G(z) = G_2(z)\prod_{k=1}^{M}(1 - 2\cos(\omega_k)z^{-1} + z^{-2})^2 = G_2(z)G_1(z) \tag{5.246}$$

Let us now implement $H(z)$ in the form

$$H(z) = z^{-(N-1)/2} - G(z) \tag{5.247}$$

where $G(z)$ is implemented as in Eq. (5.246). Let us consider the effect of

---

[†] See reference [65].

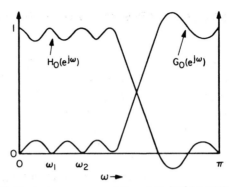

Fig. 5.83. Typical appearances of G_0 and H_0 [65] (© 1985 IEEE).

quantizing the multiplier coefficients $2\cos\omega_k$ in Eq. (5.246). Clearly, the sign of $G_0(e^{j\omega})$ is not affected by the quantization, because the zeros of G_0 represented by Eq. (5.245) are all double. In other words, $G_0(e^{j\omega})$ cannot become negative in the passband of $H(z)$. Consequently, $H_0(e^{j\omega})$, defined to be

$$H_0(e^{j\omega}) = 1 - G_0(e^{j\omega}) \qquad (5.248)$$

cannot exceed unity in the passband. Thus $H(z)$ is "structurally bounded" with respect to all the multiplier coefficients involved in the implementation of $G_1(z)$. Next, $G_2(z)$ has no zeros on the unit circle, so quantization of multipliers in $G_2(z)$ cannot affect the sign of $G_0(e^{j\omega})$. In conclusion, therefore, the implementation in Fig. 5.84 is structurally bounded with respect to all the digital multipliers involved. We call these structures FIRBR structures.

For completeness of the theoretical argument, we note that in Eq. (5.246) that the zeros of $G_2(z)$, even though not on the unit circle of the z-plane, occur in reciprocal pairs, thus if z_0 is a zero, so is $1/z_0$. Under extreme conditions of multiplier quantization, a zero of $G_2(z)$, say, $z_0 = re^{j\theta}$, may move onto the unit circle. This is possible if r is very close to unity. Such zero pairs can then be implemented by combining the factors $1 - 2r\cos(\theta)z^{-1} + r^2z^{-2}$ and $r^2 - 2r\cos(\theta)z^{-1} + z^{-2}$ in such a manner that if z_0 moves onto the unit circle because of quantization, then so does $1/z_0$. Thus the zeros (of the quantized

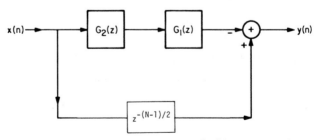

Fig. 5.84. The FIRBR implementation [65] (© 1985 IEEE).

implementation) on the unit circle are still double zeros; hence $H(z)$ is still structurally bounded.

The FIRBR implementation requires the same number of multipliers as the direct form and one adder more than the direct form, which is a negligible overhead. According to our arguments in Section XIV, the FIRBR structure in Fig. 5.84 is expected to have low sensitivity. We give an example to show this.

An Example B

A thirty-fourth-order wideband lowpass FIR filter with equiripple passband extending from 0 to 0.8π and equiripple stopband extending from 0.9π to π was designed with the McClellan–Parks (MP) algorithm [88]. The resulting transfer

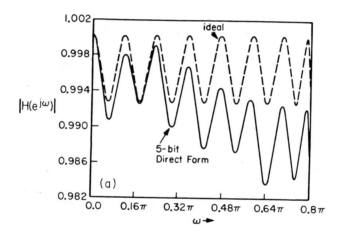

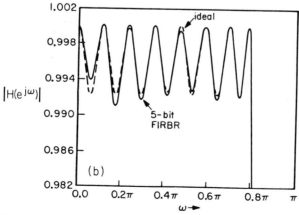

Fig. 5.85. Passband response of the quantized implementations (5-bits per multiplier) [65] (© 1985 IEEE).

function $H(z)$ has maximum magnitude of unity at the following frequencies:

$$\omega_0 = 0.0, \qquad \omega_1 = 0.1182\pi, \quad \omega_2 = 0.236\pi, \quad \omega_3 = 0.354\pi$$
$$\omega_4 = 0.472\pi, \quad \omega_5 = 0.588\pi, \qquad \omega_6 = 0.698\pi, \quad \omega_7 = 0.784\pi \qquad (5.249)$$

Thus,

$$G_1(z) = (1 - z^{-1})^2 \prod_{k=1}^{7} (1 - 2\cos(\omega_k)z^{-1} + z^{-2})^2 \qquad (5.250)$$

with degree 30. $G_2(z)$, therefore, is a fourth-order linear-phase filter.

At this point we have several choices for implementing $G(z)$. Instead of implementing $G(z)$ with all factors of the form of Eq. (5.245) grouped together, we may pick a subset of these and group them together. For example, instead of

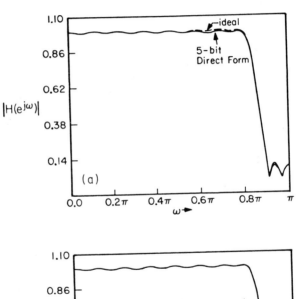

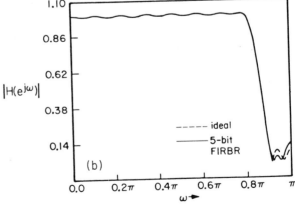

Fig. 5.86. Overall response of the quantized implementations [65] (© 1985 IEEE).

using Eq. (5.250) we could define

$$G_1(z) = (1 - 2\cos(\omega_1)z^{-1} + z^{-2})^2(1 - 2\cos(\omega_3)z^{-1} + z^{-2})^2$$
$$\times (1 - 2\cos(\omega_5)z^{-1} + z^{-2})^2(1 - 2\cos(\omega_7)z^{-1} + z^{-2})^2 \quad (5.251)$$

and we would redefine $G_2(z)$ accordingly. This flexibility allows us to have a tradeoff between the passband and stopband sensitivities. In the example under consideration, we define $G_1(z)$ to be as in Eq. (5.251) and we implement $H(z)$ as in Fig. 5.84.

Figure 5.85 shows the passband frequency response of the direct form and FIRBR implementations with 5 bits per multiplier, compared to the ideal frequency response. Figure 5.86 shows the entire frequency response with 5 bits per multiplier. It is clear from these implementations that the FIRBR structure has excellent passband sensitivity properties. Results on roundoff noise in FIRBR structures can be found in [65].

LIMIT CYCLES IN IIR DIGITAL FILTERS   XXI

In any IIR filter implementation we always have feedback loops, and in order to use practical word lengths, we always have quantizers in the loops, as explained in Section III. A typical situation is shown in Fig. 5.87 where Q is a quantizer in a feedback loop and $T(z)$ is the transfer function as seen by the quantizer. Since $Q(\cdot)$ is a nonlinear operation, stability of the system is not guaranteed, even though the ideal system (with no quantizer) may be stable.

Such instability due to (nonlinear) quantization effects can produce undesirable oscillations called *limit cycles*. Instructive examples of this are in [4]. Even if the quantizer is a magnitude-truncation type so that $|Q(x)| \le |x|$, it is still possible to have limit cycles because of the gain that $T(z)$ might offer. Excellent and comprehensive results are in [89, 90].

Two types of limit cycles can be distinguished: (1) *granular or roundoff* and (2) *overflow*. Granular limit cycles occur because of the quantization error $e(n) = Q[x(n)] - x(n)$, which behaves as in Table IV. These oscillations are

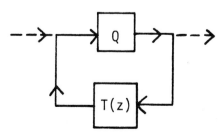

Fig. 5.87. A closed loop with quantizer nonlinearity.

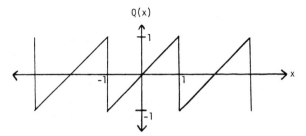

Fig. 5.88. Overflow characteristics in 2's complement arithmetic.

usually "small" (but large enough to be objectionable), and one can often place bounds on their amplitudes [91]. Overflow oscillations are the result of internal signal overflow. Thus, if $|x(n)| > 1$ in a fixed-point fraction implementation, then, because of overflow, $Q[x(n)]$ is drastically different from $x(n)$, as depicted in Fig. 5.88 for 2's complement arithmetic. Since an overflow is a nonlinear operation, it can lead to oscillations. These oscillations are large amplitude and must be avoided.

The most straightforward approach to avoiding overflow oscillations is to avoid overflow. This in turn can be accomplished by ensuring that all crucial internal signals (multiplier inputs) are most conservatively scaled ("sumscaling," Table V). However, such an approach leads to an enormous decrease of SNR for b bits. If we instead take a statistical approach to scaling and reduce overflow probability (as in Section V), then we still have some chance of overflow. Such overflow should not cause overflow oscillations (it has been shown to be possible to avoid these oscillations). Wave digital filters [52], lattice and orthogonal filters [49, 34], minimum-norm and normal digital filters [69], and "minimum-noise second-order filters" [70] are structures that can be designed to avoid overflow oscillations. Turning our attention now to granular oscillations, we can show that some of these same structures can be made free of such oscillations simply by restricting the quantizers to be the magnitude-truncation type.

All the above-mentioned structures that have the potentiality to suppress limit cycles are more complicated than the simple cascade-form structure. For a second-order direct-form section, Classen et al. [92] have shown that with truncation arithmetic the probability of limit cycles is very small. Mitra and Lawrence [93] have advanced a set of arithmetic rules (which are neither simple truncation nor rounding) for the inherently simple second-order direct-form. These rules suppress all zero-input limit cycle oscillations but are somewhat involved.

When discussing limit cycles, one should clearly distinguish between oscillations in absence of an input (zero-input limit cycles) and oscillations in presence of some input signal. Most of the results available thus far and mentioned in the above paragraphs are related only to zero-input limit cycles.

A second-order IIR transfer function of the form

$$H(z) = (1 + a_1 z^{-1} + a_2 z^{-2})^{-1} \qquad (2.252)$$

is known to be stable (i.e., all poles inside the unit circle) when a_1 and a_2 lie within the triangular region shown in Fig. 5.89(a). However, in an actual 2's complement fixed-point fraction implementation as in Fig. 5.90, the effects of possible overflow at the adder output $w(n)$ can cause oscillations. We can show [94] that if a_1 and a_2 belong to the shaded diamond region of Fig. 5.89(b), there cannot be any overflow under zero input with arbitrary initial state. If, however, a_1 and a_2 do not belong to this region, then there always exists an overflow limit cycle for some suitable internal starting state, even with zero input. The shaded area in

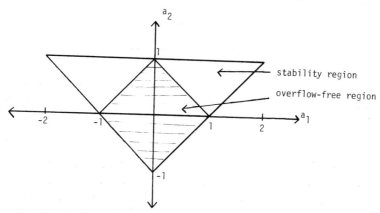

Fig. 5.89. Stability region and overflow-free region for second-order IIR filters.

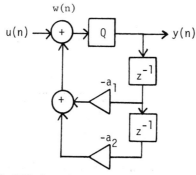

Fig. 5.90. Second-order section with quantizer.

Fig. 5.89(b) is characterized by

$$|a_1| + |a_2| < 1 \tag{5.253}$$

which represents a necessary and sufficient condition for avoiding overflow oscillations in second-order direct-form filters using 2's complement arithmetic in absence of an input.

Thus to guarantee freedom from limit cycles, we must find a different structure, even if it involves additional multipliers.

1 A Fundamental Result Concerning Overflow Oscillations

Mills, Mullis, and Roberts [70] showed that certain state-space realizations can be made entirely free from zero-input overflow oscillations due to 2's complement arithmetic. Referring to Fig. 5.91, where $\mathbf{A}$ represents the state-transition matrix [Eq. 5.96(a)], we have the physical set of equations

$$\mathbf{w}(n + 1) = \mathbf{A}\mathbf{x}(n) \tag{5.254}$$

$$\mathbf{x}(n + 1) = Q[\mathbf{w}(n + 1)] \tag{5.255}$$

instead of the ideal equation $\mathbf{x}(n + 1) = \mathbf{A}\mathbf{x}(n)$. Assume that Eq. (5.254) is an exact equation (not involving any rounding or overflow) and that the possibility of overflow is accounted for by Eq. (5.255). The actual interpretation of Eq. (5.255) is

$$x_k(n + 1) = Q[w_k(n + 1)] \tag{5.256}$$

where the subscript k refers to the kth component of the vector and $Q(\cdot)$ is as in Fig. 5.88. Since $|Q(x)| \leq |x|$ for any x, $Q(\cdot)$ can be regarded as a "passive" operation. If the matrix $\mathbf{A}$ is also "passive" in a certain sense, then the closed loop of Fig. 5.91 cannot sustain overflow oscillations.[†] The following result is derived in [70].

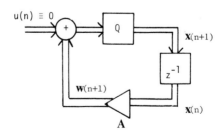

Fig. 5.91. The state-space feedback loop with quantizer.

[†] The term "passive" has not been used in [70], but we believe that the conditions in [70] are closely related to the role of passivity in limit-cycle suppression [66, 67].

Theorem 5.3. Let $\mathbf{A}$ be such that $\mathbf{D} - \mathbf{A}^T\mathbf{D}\mathbf{A}$ is positive definite for some diagonal matrix $\mathbf{D}$ with postive elements. Then there can be no overflow oscillations with 2's complement arithmetic under zero-input conditions.

For the case of second-order stable systems with

$$\mathbf{A} = \begin{bmatrix} a_{11} & a_{12} \\ a_{21} & a_{22} \end{bmatrix}$$

the above condition for absence of overflow oscillations reduces to the following simple conditions:

i. either $a_{12}\,a_{21} \geq 0$,
ii. or, if $a_{12}\,a_{21} < 0$, then $|a_{11} - a_{22}| + \det(A) < 1$.

Because of its simplicity, this condition is extremely useful and attractive.

Some very interesting structures have been proposed by various authors before Theorem 5.3 was available. However, the theorem serves to unify all of these earlier results. We now consider some specific examples of practical structures satisfying the conditions of the theorem. Notice that if $\mathbf{A}$ satisfies these conditions, it continues to satisfy it even if a diagonal similarity transformation is applied. Thus, *scaling* does not affect the above result.

Minimum-Norm Digital Filters **2**

Consider a state-space structure with state transition matrix $\mathbf{A}$. The *norm* of $\mathbf{A}$ (also called the *induced L_2-norm*) denoted $\|\mathbf{A}\|_2$ is defined by

$$\|\mathbf{A}\|_2^2 = \max_{\mathbf{x} \neq \mathbf{0}}\left(\frac{\mathbf{x}^\dagger \mathbf{A}^\dagger \mathbf{A}\mathbf{x}}{\mathbf{x}^\dagger\mathbf{x}}\right) \qquad (5.257)$$

The quantity in Eq. (5.257) is nothing but the maximum eigenvalue of $\mathbf{A}^\dagger\mathbf{A}$. The smallest possible value that $\|\mathbf{A}\|_2$ can ever attain is equal to the maximum-magnitude eigenvalue of $\mathbf{A}$. For a stable system all eigenvalues of $\mathbf{A}$ have magnitudes strictly less than unity. Barnes and Fam [69] have defined a minimum-norm structure to be a state-space structure with the property that $\|\mathbf{A}\|_2$ is precisely equal to the smallest possible value; that is,

$$\|\mathbf{A}\|_2 = |\lambda(\mathbf{A})|_{\max} \qquad (5.258)$$

where $\lambda(\mathbf{A})$ denotes an eigenvalue of $\mathbf{A}$. For such structures it can be shown [69] that no overflow limit cycles are sustained under 2's complement arithmetic. The reason is that such structures satisfy the conditions of Theorem 5.3.

Normal-Form Digital Filters **3**

Normal-form digital filters are structures with the matrix $\mathbf{A}$ satisfying the condition $\mathbf{A}^T\mathbf{A} = \mathbf{A}\mathbf{A}^T$. This condition implies that the norm of $\mathbf{A}$ is a minimum [as in Eq. (5.258)] and hence overflow oscillations are suppressed. A second-order normal form has state transition matrix

$$\mathbf{A} = \begin{bmatrix} \sigma & \beta \\ -\beta & \sigma \end{bmatrix} \tag{5.259}$$

where the poles of the transfer function are given by $\lambda_{1,2} = \sigma \pm j\beta$. If the poles are real, then the matrix

$$\mathbf{A} = \begin{bmatrix} \lambda_1 & 0 \\ 0 & \lambda_2 \end{bmatrix} \tag{5.260}$$

serves as a normal realization. Higher-order implementations free of limit cycles can be obtained simply by cascading such second-order sections (and possibly a first-order section). Reference [69] contains a direct state-space approach for higher-order normal forms.

4 Minimum-Noise Second-Order Sections

We saw in Section X that minimum-noise, second-order, state-space realizations satisfy $a_{11} = a_{22}$ [Eq. (5.130(a))]. Thus, the conditions of Theorem 5.3 are satisfied, and these structures are free from overflow oscillations under 2's complement arithmetic.

5 Wave and Lattice Digital Filters

Based on the notions of pseudopassivity, wave filters can be made entirely free from limit cycles of both types [52] (granular as well as overflow) as long as 2's complement magnitude-truncation rules are used. These claims hold true regardless of the filter order N and are therefore strong results. Similar results have also been established for cascaded lattice digital filters [49] and more generally are known to hold for orthogonal digital filters [34]. Mills, Mullis, and Roberts [70] have shown the connection between these results and Theorem 5.3, which therefore leads to a unified outlook.

6 The Role of Passivity in Limit-Cycle-Free Filters

It has recently been shown [66, 67] that several digital filters can be classified under the framework of structural passivity and that properties relating to freedom from limit cycles can be established based only on this. The major conclusion is that structural passivity leads to low-noise, low-sensitivity structures that are free from limit cycles, as evidenced by several well-known special cases.

Closed-Form Expressions For Normal-Form Digital Filters   B

In view of the advantages that have been outlined above, normal forms play an important role in digital filter design. For the second-order transfer function $H(z)$ it is possible to obtain the quantities **A**, **B**, **C**, **D** of a normal structure based on closed-form expressions advanced in [39]. Let

$$H(z) = \frac{Q(z)}{P(z)} = \frac{q_0 + q_1 z^{-1} + q_2 z^{-2}}{1 + p_1 z^{-1} + p_2 z^{-2}} \tag{5.261}$$

have poles $\lambda = a + j\beta$ and $\lambda^* = \alpha - j\beta$. Define

$$r = \frac{|Q(\lambda^*)|}{\beta} \tag{5.262}$$

$$\phi = \arg[Q(\lambda^*)] + \pi \tag{5.263}$$

$$\theta = -\tfrac{1}{2}\arg(1 - \lambda^2) \tag{5.264}$$

Then the state-space realization

$$\mathbf{A} = \begin{bmatrix} \alpha & -\beta \\ \beta & \alpha \end{bmatrix}, \tag{5.265}$$

$$\mathbf{B} = \sqrt{2(1 - |\lambda|^2)} \begin{bmatrix} -\sin\left(\theta - \dfrac{\pi}{4}\right) \\ \cos\left(\theta - \dfrac{\pi}{4}\right) \end{bmatrix} \tag{5.266}$$

$$\mathbf{C} = \frac{1}{\sqrt{2(1 - |\lambda|^2)}} \left[r\cos\left(\phi - \theta + \dfrac{\pi}{4}\right) \quad r\sin\left(\phi - \theta + \dfrac{\pi}{4}\right) \right] \tag{5.267}$$

$$D = H(\infty) = q_0 \tag{5.268}$$

is a normal-form realization. Furthermore, it is scaled in the L_2-sense—that is, the **K**-matrix of Section X satisfies $K_{11} = K_{22} = 1$.

Even though normal structures are not the same as minimum-noise structures, they do have very low roundoff noise in most cases. Further results and alternative closed-form expressions for normal-form filters, minimum-noise filters, and suboptimal filters are in [39–41].

REFERENCES

1. A. V. Oppenheim and C. J. Weinstein, Effects of finite register length in digital filtering and the fast fourier transform, *Proc. IEEE* **60**, 957–976 (August 1972).
2. B. Liu, Effects of finite wordlength on the accuracy of digital filters—A review, *IEEE Trans. Circuit Theory* **CT-18**, 670–677 (November 1971).
3. S. R. Parker and S. F. Hess, Limit-cycle oscillations in digital filters, *IEEE Trans. Circuit Theory* **CT-8**, 687–697 (November 1971).

4. A. V. Oppenheim and R. W. Schafer, *Digital Signal Processing*, Prentice-Hall, Englewood Cliffs, N.J., 1975.
5. L. R. Rabiner and B. Gold, *Theory and Applications of Digital Signal Processing*, Prentice-Hall, Englewood Cliffs, N.J., 1975.
6. J. F. Kaiser, *System Analysis by Digital Computer*, edited by F. F. Kuo and J. F. Kaiser, Wiley, New York, 1966.
7. K. Hwang, *Computer Arithmetic*, Wiley, New York, 1979.
8. I. Flores, *The Logic of Computer Arithmetic*, Prentice-Hall, Englewood Cliffs, N.J., 1963.
9. A. V. Oppenheim, Realization of digital filters using block-floating-point-arithmetic, *IEEE Trans. Audio Electroacoust.* **AU-18,** 130–136 (January 1970).
10. L. B. Jackson, J. F. Kaiser, and H. S. McDonald, An approach to the implementation of digital filters, *IEEE Trans. Audio Electroacoust.* **AU-16,** 413–421 (September 1968).
11. A. Papoulis, *Probability, Random Variables and Stochastic Processes*, McGraw-Hill, New York, 1965.
12. C. W. Barnes, A parametric approach to the realization of second-order digital filter sections, *IEEE Trans. Circuits Systems* **CAS-32,** 530–539 (June 1985).
13. L. B. Jackson, On the interaction of roundoff noise and dynamic range in digital filters, *Bell Systems Technical J.* **49,** 159–184 (1970).
14. M. Abramowitz and I. A. Stegun, Editors, *Handbook of Mathematical Functions*, National Bureau of Standards, Applied Mathematics Series (1964).
15. Z. Unver and K. Abdullah, A tighter practical bound on quantization errors in second-order digital filters with complex conjugate poles, *IEEE Trans. Circuits Systems* **CAS-22,** 632–633 (July 1975).
16. T. Thong and B. Liu, Error spectrum shaping in narrowband recursive digital filters, *IEEE Trans. Acoust. Speech, Signal Process.* **ASSP-25,** 200–203 (April 1977).
17. T. L. Chang and S. A. White, An error cancellation digital filter structure and its distributed-arithmetic implementation, *IEEE Trans. Circuits Systems* **CAS-28,** 339–342 (April 1981).
18. D. C. Munson, Jr., and B. Liu, Narrowband recursive filters with error spectrum shaping, *IEEE Trans. Circuits Systems* **CAS-28,** 160–163 (February 1981).
19. P. P. Vaidyanathan, On error-spectrum shaping in state-space digital filters, *IEEE Trans. Circuits Systems* **CAS-32,** 88–92 (January 1985).
20. N. S. Jayant, *Waveform Quantization and Coding*, IEEE Press, New York, 1976.
21. C. T. Mullis and R. A. Roberts. An interpretation of error spectrum shaping in digital filter structures, *IEEE Trans. Acoust., Speech Signal Process.* **ASSP-30,** 1013–1015 (December 1982).
22. W. E. Higgins and D. C. Munson, Jr., Optimal and suboptimal error spectrum shaping for cascade-form digital filters, *IEEE Trans. Circuits Systems* **CAS-31,** 429–437 (May 1984).
23. W. E. Higgins and D. C. Munson, Jr., Noise reduction strategies for digital filters: Error spectrum shaping versus the optimal linear state-space formulation, *IEEE Trans. Acoust. Speech, Signal Process.* **ASSP-30,** 963–972 (December 1982).
24. D. C. Munson, Jr. and B. Liu, Low-noise realizations for narrowband recursive digital filters, *IEEE Trans. Acoust. Speech Signal Process.* **ASSP-28,** 41–54 (February 1980).
25. R. C. Agarwal and C. S. Burrus, New recursive digital filter structures having very low sensitivity and roundoff noise, *IEEE Trans. Circuits Systems* **22,** 921–926 (December 1975).
26. T. L. Chang, On low-roundoff noise and low-sensitivity digital filter structures, *IEEE Trans. Acoust. Speech, Signal Process.* **ASSP-29,** 1077–1080 (October 1981).
27. J. Szczupak and S. K. Mitra. On digital filter structures with low coefficient sensitivities, *Proc. IEEE* **66,** 1082–1083 (September 1978).
28. G. T. Yan and S. K. Mitra, Modified coupled-form digital-filter structures, *Proc. IEEE* **70,** 762–763 (July 1982).
29. S. Nishimura, K. Hirano, and R. N. Pal, A new class of very low sensitivity and low roundoff noise recursive digital filter structures, *IEEE Trans. Circuits Systems* **CAS-28,** 1151–1157 (December 1981).
30. A. Antoniou, *Digital Filters: Analysis and Design*, McGraw-Hill, 1979.

31. C. T. Mullis and R. A. Roberts, Synthesis of minimum roundoff noise fixed point digital filters, *IEEE Trans. Circuits Systems* **CAS-23**, 551–562 (September 1976).

32. S. Y. Hwang, Minimum uncorrelated unit-noise in state-space digital filtering, *IEEE Trans. Acoust. Speech, Signal Process.* **ASSP-25**, 273–281 (August 1977).

33. A. Fettweis, Digital filter structures related to classical filter networks, *Arch Elek, Ubertrangung.* **25**, 79–81 (February 1971).

34. P. DeWilde and E. Deprettere, Orthogonal cascade realization of real multiport digital filters, *Int. J. Circuit Theory Appl.* **8**, 245–277 (1980).

35. L. B. Jackson, Roundoff-noise analysis for fixed-point digital filters realized in cascade or parallel form, *IEEE Trans. Audio Electroacoust.* **AU-18**, 107–122 (June 1970).

36. S. Y. Hwang, On optimization of cascade fixed-point digital filters, *IEEE Trans. Circuits Systems* **21**, 163–166 (January 1974).

37. B. Liu and A. Peled, Heuristic optimization of the cascade realization of fixed-point digital filters, *IEEE Trans. Acoust. Speech, Signal Process.* **23**, 464–473 (October 1975).

38. L. B. Jackson, A. G. Lindgren, and Y. Kim, Optimal synthesis of second-order state-space structures for digital filters, *IEEE Trans. Circuits Systems* **26**, 149–153 (March 1979).

39. W. L. Mills, C. T. Mullis, and R. A. Roberts, Low roundoff noise and normal realizations of fixed-point IIR digital filters, *IEEE Trans. Acoust. Speech, Signal Process.* **29**, 893–903 (August 1981).

40. C. W. Barnes, On the design of optimal state-space realizations of second-order digital filters, *IEEE Trans. Circuits Systems* **CAS-31**, 602–608 (July 1984).

41. B. W. Bomar, New second-order state-space structures for realizing low roundoff noise digital filters, *IEEE Trans. Acoust. Speech, Signal Process.* **33**, 106–110 (February 1985).

42. G. C. Temes and J. W. La Patra, *Circuit Synthesis and Design*, McGraw-Hill, New York, 1977.

43. H. J. Orchard, Inductorless filters, *Electron. Letters* 224–225 (September 1966).

44. A Sedlmeyer and A. Fettweis, Digital filters with true ladder configuration, *Int. J. Circuit Theory Appl.* **1**, 5–10 (March 1973).

45. A. Fettweis, Wave digital lattice filters, *Int. J. Circuit Theory Appl.* **2**, 203–211 (June 1974).

46. L. Gazsi, Explicit formulas for lattice wave digital filters, *IEEE Trans. Circuits Systems* **32**, 68–88 (January 1985).

47. A. H. Gray, Jr., and J. D. Markel, Digital lattice and ladder filter synthesis, *IEEE Trans. Audio Electroacoust.* **AU-21**, 491–500 (December 1973).

48. A. H. Gray, Jr., and J. D. Markel, A normalized digital filter structure, *IEEE Trans. Acoust. Speech, Signal Process.* **ASSP-23**, 268–277 (June 1975).

49. A. H. Gray, Jr., Passive cascaded lattice digital filters, *IEEE Trans. Circuits Systems* **CAS-27**, 337–344 (May 1980).

50. S. K. Rao and T. Kailath, Orthogonal digital filters for VLSI implementation, *IEEE Trans. Circuits Systems* **31**, 933–945 (November 1984).

51. A. Fettweis, "Pseudopassivity, sensitivity, and stability of wave digital filter, *IEEE Trans. Circuit Theory* **19**, 668–673 (November 1973).

52. A. Fettweis and K. Meerkotter, Suppression of parasitic oscillations in wave filters, *IEEE Trans. Circuit Systems* **22**, 239–246 (March 1975).

53. A. Fettweis, Roundoff noise and attenuation sensitivity in digital filters with fixed-point arithmetic, *IEEE Trans. Circuit Theory* **CT-20**, 174–175 (March 1973).

54. C. W. Barnes, A parametric approach to the realization of second-order digital filter sections, *IEEE Trans. Circuits Systems* **CAS-32**, 530–539 (June 1985).

55. R. E. Crochiere, Digital ladder structures and coefficient sensitivity, *IEEE Trans. Audio Electroacoust.* **20**, 240–246 (October 1972).

56. G. Szentirmai, S/FILSTN—Filter Synthesis Package, 1983.

57. A. S. Sedra and P. O. Brackett, *Filter Theory and Design: Active and Passive*, Matrix Publishers Beaverton, Ore., 1978.

58. R. Saal and E. Ulbrick, On the design of filters by synthesis, *IRE Trans. Circuit Theory*, 284–327 (December 1958).

59. A. Fettweis and K. Meerkotter, *On adaptors for wave digital filters, IEEE Trans Acoust. Speech, Signal Process.* **ASSP-23,** 516–525 (December 1975).

60. A. G. Constantinides, Alternative approach to design of wave digital filters, *Electron. Letters* **10,** 59–60 (1974).

61. M. N. S. Swamy and K. Thyagarajan, A new type of wave digital filters, *J. Franklin Inst.* **300,** 41–58 (July 1975).

62. P. P. Vaidyanathan and S. K. Mitra, Low passband sensitivity digital filters: A generalized viewpoint and synthesis procedures, *Proc. IEEE* **72,** 404–423 (April 1984).

63. P. P. Vaidyanathan, A unified approach to orthogonal digital filters and wave digital filters based on LBR two-pair extraction, *IEEE Trans. Circuits Systems* **CAS-32,** 673–686 (July 1985).

64. P. P. Vaidyanathan, A general theorem for degree-reduction of a digital BR function, *IEEE Trans. Circuits Systems* **CAS-32,** 414–415 (April 1985).

65. P. P. Vaidyanathan and S. K. Mitra, Very low-sensitivity FIR filter implementation using "structural passivity" concept, *IEEE Trans. Circuits Systems,* 360–364 (April 1985).

65a. P. P. Vaidyanathan, Passive cascaded lattice structures for low-sensitivity FIR filter design, with applications to filter banks, *IEEE Trans. Circuits Systems* **33,** 1045–1064 (November 1986).

66. P. P. Vaidyanathan and S. K. Mitra, Passivity properties of low sensitivity digital filter structures, *IEEE Trans. Circuits Systems,* 217–224 (March 1985).

67. P. P. Vaidyanathan, The discrete-time bounded real lemma in digital filtering, *IEEE Trans. Circuits Systems* **CAS-32,** 918–924 (September 1985).

68. L. B. Jackson, Roundoff noise bounds derived from coefficient sensitivities for digital filters, *IEEE Trans. Circuits Systems* **CAS-23,** 481–485 (August 1976).

69. C. W. Barnes and A. T. Fam, Minimum norm recursive digital filters that are free of overflow limit cycles, *IEEE Trans. Circuits Systems* **CAS-24,** 569–574 (October 1977).

70. W. L. Mills, C. T. Mullis, and R. A. Roberts, Digital filter realizations without overflow oscillations, *IEEE Trans. Acoust. Speech, Signal Process.* **ASSP-26,** 334–338 (August 1978).

71. S. K. Mitra and K. Hirano, Digital all-pass networks, *IEEE Trans. Circuits Systems* **CAS-21,** 688–700 (September 1974).

72. P. P. Vaidyanathan, S. K. Mitra, and Y. Neuvo, A new approach to the realization of low sensitivity IIR digital filters, *IEEE Trans. Acoust. Speech, Signal Process.* **ASSP-34** (1986).

73. R. Ansari and B. Liu, A class of low-noise computationally efficient recursive digital filters with applications to sampling rate alterations, *IEEE Trans. Acoust. Speech, Signal Process.* **33,** 90–97 (February 1985).

74. J. D. Markel and A. H. Gray, Jr., *Linear Prediction of Speech,* Springer-Verlag, New York, 1976.

74a. P. P. Vaidyanathan and S. K. Mitra, A unified structural interpretation of some well-known stability-test procedures for linear systems, *Proc. IEEE* **75,** 478–497 (April 1987).

75. J. K. L. Van Ginderdeuren, H. J. DeMan, N. F. Gonclaves, and W. A. M. Van Noije, Compact NMOS building blocks and a methodology for dedicated digital filter applications, *IEEE Trans. Solid State Circuits* **SC-18,** 306–316 (June 1983).

76. D. Henrot and C. T. Mullis, A modular and orthogonal digital filter structure for parallel processing, *IEEE Int. Conf. on Acoustics, Speech, and Signal Processing,* pp. 623–626, April 1983.

77. O. Herrmann and W. Schuessler, On the accuracy problem in the design of nonrecursive digital filters, *Arch. Electronik. Ubertragungstechnik* **24,** 525–526 (1970).

78. D. S. K. Chan and L. R. Rabiner, An algorithm for minimizing roundoff noise in cascade realizations of finite impulse response digital filters, *Bell System Tech. J.* **52,** 347–385 (1973).

79. W. Schuessler, "On structures for nonrecursive digital filters," Arch. Elek. Uberstrangung. **26,** 255–258 (1972).

80. Z. Jing and A. T. Fam, A new structure for narrow transition band, lowpass digital filter design, *IEEE Trans. Acoust. Speech, Signal Process.* **32,** 362–370 (April 1984).

81. A. T. Fam, Space-time duality in digital filter structures, *IEEE Trans. Acoust. Speech, Signal Process.* **31,** 550–556 (June 1983).

82. A. Mahanta, R. C. Agarwal, and S. C. Dutta Ray, FIR filter structures having low sensitivity and roundoff noise, *IEEE Trans. Acoust. Speech, Signal Process.* **ASSP-30,** 913–920 (December 1982).

83. D. S. K. Chan and L. R. Rabiner, Analysis of quantization errors in the direct form for finite impulse response digital filters, *IEEE Trans. Audio Electroacoust.* **AU-21,** 354–366 (August 1973).

84. W. P. Niedringhaus, K. Steiglitz, and D. Kodek, An easily computed performance bound for finite wordlength direct-form FIR digital filters, *IEEE Trans. Circuits Systems* **CAS-29,** 191–193 (March 1983).

85. U. Heute, Necessary and efficient expenditure for nonrecursive digital filters in direct-structure, *European Conf. on Circuit Theory and Design,* IEEE Conf. Pub. No. 116, pp. 13–19, July 1974.

86. A. Gersho, B. Gopinath, and A. M. Odlyzko, Coefficient inaccuracy in transversal filtering, *Bell Systems Technical J.* **58,** 2301–2316 (December 1979).

87. A. Avizienis, Signed-digit number representations for fast parallel arithmetic, *IRE Trans. Elec. Computers* **EC-10,** 389–400 (September 1961).

88. J. H. McClellan and T. W. Parks, A unified approach to the design of optimum FIR linear-phase digital filters, *IEEE Trans. Circuit Theory* **CT-20,** 697–701 (November 1973).

89. S. R. Parker, Limit cycles and correlated noise in digital filters, in *Digital Signal Processing,* edited by J. K. Aggarwal, Western Periodicals, North Hollywood, Calif., 1979, pp. 117–179.

90. T. A. C. M. Classen, W. F. G. Mecklenbrauker, and J. B. H. Peek, Frequency domain criteria for the absence of zero-input limit cycles in nonlinear discrete-time systems, with applications to digital filters, *IEEE Trans. Circuits Systems* **CAS-22,** 232–239 (March 1975).

91. J. L. Long and T. N. Trick, An absolute bound on limit cycles due to roundoff errors in digital filters, *IEEE Trans. Audio Electroacoust.* **AU-21,** 27–30 (February 1973).

92. T. A. C. M. Classen, W. F. G. Mecklenbrauker, and J. B. H. Peek, Second-order digital filter with only one magnitude-truncation quantizer and having practically no limit cycles, *Electron. Letters* **9,** 531–532 (November 1973).

93. D. Mitra and V. B. Lawrence, Controlled rounding arithmetics, for second-order direct-form digital filters, that eliminate all self-sustained oscillations, *IEEE Trans. Circuits Systems* **CAS-28,** 894–905 (September 1981).

94. P. M. Ebert, J. E. Mazo, and M. G. Taylor, Overflow oscillations in digital filters, *Bell Systems Technical J.* **48,** 2999–3020 (November 1969).

Chapter **6**
Fast Discrete Transforms

PAT YIP
Department of Mathematics and Statistics
McMaster University
Hamilton, Ontario L8 S4K1

K. RAMAMOHAN RAO
Department of Electrical Engineering
The University of Texas at Arlington
Arlington, Texas 76019

INTRODUCTION   I

The solution of a mathematical problem is often made more tractable when the problem is first transformed into a different domain. The Fourier, Laplace, and z-transforms are well-known transforms (see Chapter 1). So when a signal in the time domain is to be processed, the task may often be more easily or quickly accomplished by first transforming the signal into the frequency domain. Although this is theoretically true, such an approach was very often avoided in the past because of the added labor of transforming between the two conjugate domains. The added computation had often made this approach less than attractive. Even with high-speed digital computers, the transform domain processing was time consuming and real-time implementation was deemed almost impossible. All this was changed when Cooley and Tukey [1] introduced an efficient computational algorithm for the Fourier transform, which was aptly named the fast Fourier transform (FFT). Since then, many discrete transforms based on different sets of basis functions have been examined. The basis functions for some of these transforms date back to the early 1900s: for example, Walsh functions [2] and Haar functions [3]. Others, such as the discrete cosine transform (DCT) [4], rapid transform (RT) [5], and discrete sine transform (DST) [6] are more recent developments.

As for a mathematical problem, where the choice of a transform depends on the nature of the problem, engineers also have to choose a transform that is

HANDBOOK OF DIGITAL SIGNAL PROCESSING

appropriate for the signal processing task at hand. Very often, however, this choice is determined not by any objective criterion, but by the user's own familiarity with the transform. This chapter briefly discusses the theoretical bases of the various transforms, their basic properties, performance criteria, and various fast algorithmic implementations so that sufficient objective information is available for the user to make an informed choice.

The next section is devoted to the theoretical aspects of unitary transforms. Section III discusses the optimal Karhunen–Loève transform. The suboptimal transforms are grouped into sinusoidal ones in Section IV and nonsinusoidal ones in Section V. Section VI discusses various performance criteria that form a basis for selecting a particular transform. Section VII summarizes the chapter as well as the computational complexities of the various algorithms.

II UNITARY DISCRETE TRANSFORMS

Consider a real signal $x(t)$ in the time domain. If $\{\phi_k\}$, $k = 1,\ldots, \infty$, is a complete set of basis functions in the signal space, then

$$x(t) = \sum_{k=1}^{\infty} X_k \phi_k(t) \tag{6.1}$$

If the signal is sampled at a regular time interval Δt, then the ith sample can be similarly expressed:

$$x(i\Delta t) = \sum_{k=1}^{\infty} X_k \phi_k(i\Delta t) \tag{6.2}$$

When the signal is of finite duration, such that only N samples are of interest, Eq. (6.2) reduces to the finite case:

$$x_i = \sum_{k=1}^{N} \phi_{ik} X_k, \qquad i = 1,\ldots, N \tag{6.3}$$

where $x_i = x(i\Delta t)$, $\phi_{ik} = \phi_k(i\Delta t)$, and the X_k are the coefficients of expansion. (See, for example, [7].) In matrix notation Eq. (6.3) is reduced to

$$\mathbf{x} = \phi \mathbf{X} \tag{6.4}$$

where $\mathbf{x} = \{x_1,\ldots, x_N\}^T$, $\mathbf{X} = \{X_1,\ldots, X_N\}^T$, and ϕ is the $N \times N$ matrix

$$\phi = \begin{bmatrix} \phi_{11} & \phi_{12} & \cdots & \phi_{1N} \\ \vdots & \vdots & & \vdots \\ \phi_{N1} & \phi_{N2} & \cdots & \phi_{NN} \end{bmatrix} \tag{6.5}$$

Equation (6.4) states that $\mathbf{x}$, the "time" signal, is represented as a linear combination of "frequency" functions ϕ_{ik}, with coefficients given by the vector $\mathbf{X}$.

X is said to be the transform of x. All the properties of the transform are contained in the matrix ϕ. If ϕ is nonsingular so that

$$\phi^{-1}\phi = \phi^{\dagger}\phi = I \tag{6.6}$$

where the superscript † denotes complex conjugate transpose, the transform is said to be unitary. If, in addition, ϕ is real, and the superscript T denotes transpose, then

$$\phi^{T}\phi = I \tag{6.7}$$

Unitary transforms have a preeminent position in the realm of discrete transforms because they are easy to invert and because they preserve energy. The vector

$$X = \phi^{-1}x \tag{6.8}$$

is said to be the transform of x. Many properties of integral transforms are directly transferable to the discrete case. These properties form part of the discussion on specific discrete transforms.

A discrete transform is not necessarily a unitary transform, since the matrix ϕ need only contain linearly independent row vectors. We concentrate only on unitary transforms and begin by looking at what is considered the optimal transform, the Karhunen–Loève transform.

THE OPTIMUM KARHUNEN–LOÈVE TRANSFORM   III

If ϕ_i is used to denote the ith column of ϕ and X_i the ith component of X, Eq. (6.4) reduces to

$$x = \sum_{i=1}^{N} X_i \phi_i \tag{6.9}$$

There are many ways of choosing the complete set ϕ_i; one is to effect a maximum amount of decorrelation in the coefficients X_i. This is the basic premise of the Karhunen–Loève transform (KLT). If Eq. (6.9) is truncated so that $\hat{x}$ represents an approximation to x in the equation

$$\hat{x}(t) = \sum_{k=1}^{D} X_i \phi_i \tag{6.10}$$

a measure of the approximation is given by the mean-square error (MSE)

$$\epsilon = E\left[\sum_{j=D+1}^{N} \phi_j^{\dagger} [xx^{T}] \phi_j \right] = \sum_{j=D+1}^{N} \phi_j^{\dagger} E[xx^{T}] \phi_j \tag{6.11}$$

where E is the expectation operator, and the covariance matrix is

$$\psi = E[xx^{T}] \tag{6.12}$$

assuming the mean of $\mathbf{x}$ is zero. The minimization of ϵ in Eq. (6.11) subject to the normality condition for the ϕ_i leads to the eigenvalue problem

$$(\psi - \lambda_i \mathbf{I})\phi_i = 0 \tag{6.13}$$

Thus the basis vectors ϕ_i are the eigenvectors of the covariance matrix $\mathbf{\Psi}$. This set of vectors forms the bases for the KL expansion. We note also that the MSE due to truncation is

$$\epsilon = \sum_{i=D+1}^{N} \lambda_i \tag{6.14}$$

Thus the error of truncation is minimized by ranking the eigenvalues λ_i and the corresponding eigenvectors ϕ_i in decreasing order. (For more detail, see [8].)

Since Eq. (6.13) indicates that ϕ_i are the eigenvectors, the corresponding matrix ϕ, representing the transform, diagonalizes the covariance matrix ψ for the signal $\mathbf{x}$. This property is both a blessing and a curse for the KLT, as can be seen by the following lists of advantages and disadvantages.

1 Advantages

    1. It completely decorrelates the signal in the transform domain.

    2. It minimizes the MSE in bandwidth reduction or data compression.

    3. It packs the most energy (variance) in the fewest number of transform coefficients.

    4. It minimizes the total representation entropy of the sequence, which is linked to the rate-distortion criterion of transform performance (see Section VI.D).

2 Disadvantages

    1. Each data sequence requires its own KLT basis set.

    2. The covariance matrix diagonalized by the KLT has to be estimated, or else a large amount of sampling has to be done.

    3. There is considerable computational effort in generating the KLT basis set.

    4. Even after the basis set is obtained, there is no readily available fast algorithm for implementation.

On balance, the KLT is often used not in the practical sense but as a measure of performance for other so-called suboptimal transforms. If we assume that the signal sequence has a certain statistical distribution (e.g., Marköv-1), it is possible to generate deterministic basis sets that will approximate the KLT performance in the limit [9].

In Fig. 6.1 the basis functions for the KL expansion are shown for $N = 16$. The sampled signal is assumed to have a Markov-1 statistic with adjacent correlation

Basis function
Number

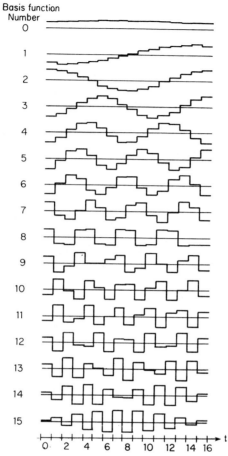

Fig. 6.1. KL basis functions for $N = 16$ and $\rho = 0.95$ for a Markov-1 signal.

coefficient $\rho = 0.95$. The corresponding covariance matrix is

$$\boldsymbol{\psi} = (\psi_{ij}) = (\rho^{|i-j|}) \tag{6.15}$$

Note the similarity between these functions and sampled sinusoids.

SINUSOIDAL DISCRETE TRANSFORMS   IV

As pointed out in the last section, the KLT, which is optimal in the sense of decorrelation, is difficult to implement, mainly because the basis functions are essentially signal dependent. In most signal processing situations deterministic basis functions are more practical. Since these deterministic functions are not, in general, the eigenvectors of the covariance matrix of the signal in question, the corresponding transforms are necessarily suboptimal. In this section we shall discuss in more detail those suboptimal transforms based on sinusoidal functions. The discrete Fourier transform (DFT), which belongs to this category, has already been developed in Chapter 1. Fast algorithms for efficient implementation of the DFT are developed in Chapter 7.

A   Discrete Cosine Transforms

When the basis functions in Eq. (6.3) are cosine functions, the signal is said to undergo a DCT. The first such transform was developed in 1974 by Ahmed *et al.* based on a class of discrete Chebyshev polynomials. A symmetric version of the DCT was later developed by Kitajima (1980). By reversing the roles of the indices k and i in the basis functions and by phase shifting the basis functions, Wang (1984) was able to develop and systematically study the fast implementations of these DCTs.

There are four types of DCTs, defined as follows:

DCT type I $\quad \phi_{ik} \equiv [\mathbf{C}^{\mathrm{I}}]_{ik} = \sqrt{\dfrac{2}{N}} \left[c_i c_k \cos\left(\dfrac{ik\pi}{N}\right) \right], \qquad\qquad i, k = 0, \ldots, N$

DCT type II $\quad \phi_{ik} \equiv [\mathbf{C}^{\mathrm{II}}]_{ik} = \sqrt{\dfrac{2}{N}} \left[c_i \cos\left(\dfrac{i(k + \frac{1}{2})\pi}{N}\right) \right], \qquad i, k = 0, \ldots, N-1$

DCT type III $\quad \phi_{ik} \equiv [\mathbf{C}^{\mathrm{III}}]_{ik} = \sqrt{\dfrac{2}{N}} \left[c_k \cos\left(\dfrac{k(i + \frac{1}{2})\pi}{N}\right) \right], \qquad i, k = 0, \ldots, N-1$

DCT type IV $\quad \phi_{ik} \equiv [\mathbf{C}^{\mathrm{IV}}]_{ik} = \sqrt{\dfrac{2}{N}} \left[\cos\left(\left(i + \dfrac{1}{2}\right)\dfrac{(k + \frac{1}{2})\pi}{N}\right) \right], \quad i, k = 0, \ldots, N-1$

$$\text{(6.16)}$$

where

$$c_i = \begin{cases} 1 & \text{if } i \neq 0 \text{ or } N \\ 1/\sqrt{2} & \text{if } i = 0 \text{ or } N \end{cases}$$

We note that the normalization factor $\sqrt{2/N}$ and the scale factors c_i are included in the input and transform sequences in all of the flow diagrams shown.

Since the basis functions are real, only real arithmetic is involved in the computation of DCTs. A storage-efficient way of implementing $[\mathbf{C}^{\mathrm{II}}]$ and $[\mathbf{C}^{\mathrm{III}}]$ was first examined by Haralick (1976). Several ways of implementing $[\mathbf{C}^{\mathrm{II}}]$ via the FFT are described in Appendix A. Chen *et al.* (1977) provided the first significant sparse-matrix factorization with a recursive algorithm. Wang (1984) evaluated the various DCTs through what are called W-transforms, and Lee (1984) studied the decimation-in-time (DIT) version of $[\mathbf{C}^{\mathrm{II}}]$. Yip and Rao (1984) extended the analysis to all DCTs.

Figure 6.2 shows an $N = 16$ flow diagram based on sparse-matrix factorization of $[\mathbf{C}^{\mathrm{II}}]$ developed by Chen *et al.* (1977). Note the modular and recursive nature of the algorithm. The number of arithmetic operations in this algorithm makes it almost three times as fast as the corresponding FFT of the same size and six times as fast as the conventional way of evaluating the DCT with a $2N$-point FFT. The transform sequence is obtained in the bit-reversed order (BRO). A real-time 32-point DCT processor using CMOS/SOS-LSI circuitry has been built based on this algorithm (see [16]). For $N = 2^L$ the recursive sparse-matrix factorization is

$$\mathbf{X} = [\mathbf{A}(L)]\mathbf{x} \qquad (6.17)$$

where $\mathbf{X}$ and $\mathbf{x}$ are the properly scaled and normalized transform and input sequences, respectively. If $\mathbf{x}$ is in natural order (i.e., 0, 1, 2,...), then $\mathbf{X}$ will be in BRO. The transform matrix $\mathbf{A}(L)$ is recursively generated as

$$[\mathbf{A}(L)] = \left[\begin{array}{c|c} [\mathbf{A}(L-1)] & \mathbf{0} \\ \hline \mathbf{0} & [\mathbf{R}(L-1)] \end{array}\right][\mathbf{B}_N], \qquad L \geq 2 \qquad (6.18)$$

where $[(\cdot)]$ means $(\cdot)$ is a recursively generated or index-dependent matrix, $\mathbf{0}$

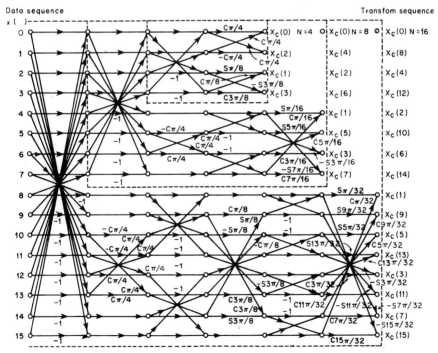

Fig. 6.2. Signal-flow graph for efficient computation of the DCT for $N = 4, 8, 16$ [13]. For notational simplicity, the multipliers $c\theta$ and $s\theta$ stand for $\cos\theta$ and $\sin\theta$, respectively.

means a zero matrix, and $[\mathbf{R}(L-1)]$ is factored into $2L-3$ sparse matrices. Thus

$$[\mathbf{R}(L-1)] = [\mathbf{M}_1][\mathbf{M}_2]\cdots[\mathbf{M}_{2L-3}] \qquad (6.19)$$

and

$$[\mathbf{B}_N] = \begin{bmatrix} \mathbf{I}_{N/2} & \bar{\mathbf{I}}_{N/2} \\ \bar{\mathbf{I}}_{N/2} & -\mathbf{I}_{N/2} \end{bmatrix} \qquad (6.20)$$

where $\mathbf{I}_M$ is an $M \times M$ diagonal unit matrix and $\bar{\mathbf{I}}_M$ is an $M \times M$ opposite diagonal unit matrix:

$$\bar{\mathbf{I}}_M = \begin{bmatrix} 0 & & \cdots & & 1 \\ \vdots & & & \cdot\cdot & \\ & & 1 & & \vdots \\ 1 & & \cdots & & 0 \end{bmatrix}$$

The starting matrix for $\mathbf{A}$ is

$$[\mathbf{A}(1)] = \frac{1}{\sqrt{2}}\begin{bmatrix} 1 & 1 \\ 1 & -1 \end{bmatrix}$$

In Eq. (6.19) the factor matrices are of four distinct types[†]

   i. $[\mathbf{M}_1]$ the first
  ii. $[\mathbf{M}_{2L-3}]$ the last
 iii. $[\mathbf{M}_q]$ the odd-numbered ones ($[\mathbf{M}_3]$, $[\mathbf{M}_5]$, etc.)
 iv. $[\mathbf{M}_p]$ the even-numbered ones ($[\mathbf{M}_2]$, $[\mathbf{M}_4]$, etc.)

For example,

$$[\mathbf{R}(3)] = \begin{bmatrix} \sin\dfrac{\pi}{32} & & & & & & & & \cos\dfrac{\pi}{3} \\ & \sin\dfrac{9\pi}{32} & & & & & & \cos\dfrac{9\pi}{32} \\ & & \sin\dfrac{5\pi}{32} & & & & \cos\dfrac{5\pi}{32} \\ & & & \sin\dfrac{13\pi}{32} & \cos\dfrac{13\pi}{32} \\ & & & -\sin\dfrac{3\pi}{32} & \cos\dfrac{3\pi}{32} \\ & & -\sin\dfrac{11\pi}{32} & & & & \cos\dfrac{11\pi}{32} \\ & -\sin\dfrac{7\pi}{32} & & & & & & \cos\dfrac{7\pi}{32} \\ -\sin\dfrac{15\pi}{32} & & & & & & & & \cos\dfrac{15}{3} \end{bmatrix}$$

[†] For details, see [13] or [7].

$$\times \begin{bmatrix} 1 & 1 & & & & & & \\ 1 & -1 & & & & & & \\ & & -1 & 1 & & & & \\ & & 1 & 1 & & & & \\ & & & & 1 & 1 & & \\ & & & & 1 & -1 & & \\ & & & & & & -1 & 1 \\ & & & & & & 1 & 1 \end{bmatrix} \begin{bmatrix} 1 & & & & & & & 0 \\ & -\cos\dfrac{\pi}{8} & & & & & \sin\dfrac{\pi}{8} & \\ & -\sin\dfrac{\pi}{8} & & & & & -\cos\dfrac{\pi}{8} & \\ & & & 1 & 0 & & & \\ & & & 0 & 1 & & & \\ & -\sin\dfrac{3\pi}{8} & & & & & \cos\dfrac{3\pi}{8} & \\ & \cos\dfrac{3\pi}{8} & & & & & \sin\dfrac{3\pi}{8} & \\ 0 & & & & & & & 1 \end{bmatrix}$$

$$\times \begin{bmatrix} 1 & & & 1 & & & & \\ & 1 & 1 & & & & & \\ & 1 & -1 & & & & & \\ 1 & & & -1 & & & & \\ & & & & -1 & & & 1 \\ & & & & & -1 & 1 & \\ & & & & & 1 & 1 & \\ & & & & 1 & & & 1 \end{bmatrix}$$

$$\times \begin{bmatrix} 1 & & & & & & & 0 \\ & 1 & & & & & & \\ & & -\cos\dfrac{\pi}{4} & & & \cos\dfrac{\pi}{4} & & \\ & & & -\cos\dfrac{\pi}{4} & \cos\dfrac{\pi}{4} & & & \\ & & & \cos\dfrac{\pi}{4} & \cos\dfrac{\pi}{4} & & & \\ & & \cos\dfrac{3\pi}{4} & & & \cos\dfrac{\pi}{4} & & \\ 0 & & & & & & 1 & \\ 0 & & & & & & & 1 \end{bmatrix} \qquad (6.21)$$

where all entries not shown are zeros.

Fast algorithms can also be generated for all four types of DCTs by DIT (i.e., rearranging and combining nonsequential input points for processing). For $N = 2^L$ Yip and Rao (1984) have provided systematic factorization, which reduces the computational complexities of Chen's and Wang's algorithms. The relevant equations are summarized as follows:

(i) $[C^I]$, type I DCT

$$\left.\begin{array}{l} X(k) = G_1(k) + H_1(k) \\ X(N - k) = G_1(k) - H_1(k) \end{array}\right\} \quad k = 0, 1, \ldots, \frac{N}{2} - 1 \qquad (6.22)$$

$$X\left(\frac{N}{2}\right) = G_1\left(\frac{N}{2}\right)$$

where
$$G_1(k) = \sum_{i=0}^{N/2} x(2i) C_{N/2}^{ik}$$

$$H_1(k) = \frac{1}{2C_N^k} \sum_{i=0}^{N/2} C_{N/2}^{ik} [x(2i + 1) + x(2i - 1)]$$

and $x(-1) \equiv 0$.

Here C_k^i is defined as $\cos(i\pi/k)$. Note that $G_1(k)$ and $H_1(k)$ are both $[C^I]$ of half the original size. This successive reduction in size is the key to the fast algorithm. Similar features persist for the remaining DCTs.

(ii) $[C^{II}]$, type II DCT

$$\left.\begin{array}{l} X(k) = G_{II}(k) + H_{II}(k) \\ X(N - k - 1) = G_{II}(k) - H_{II}(k) \end{array}\right\} \quad k = 0, 1, \ldots, \frac{N}{2} - 1 \qquad (6.23)$$

where
$$G_{II}(k) = \sum_{i=0}^{N/2-1} x(2i) C_N^{(2k+1)i}$$

$$H_{II}(k) = \frac{1}{2C_{2N}^{2k+1}} \left\{ \sum_{i=0}^{N/2} [x(2i + 1) + x(2i - 1)] C_N^{(2k+1)i} \right\}$$

and $x(-1) \equiv 0$

(iii) $[C^{III}]$, type III DCT

$$\left.\begin{array}{l} X(k) = \dfrac{1}{2C_{2N}^k} [G_{III}(k) + H_{III}(k)] \\[2mm] X(N - k - 1) = \dfrac{1}{2C_{2N}^{N-k-1}} [G_{III}(k + 1) - H_{III}(k + 1)] \end{array}\right\} \quad k = 0, \ldots, \frac{N}{2} - 1$$

where
$$G_{III}(k) = \sum_{i=0}^{N/2} [x(2i) + x(2i - 1)] C_{N/2}^{ik}$$

$$H_{III}(k) = \sum_{i=0}^{N/2} [x(2i) + x(2i + 1)] C_N^{(2i+1)k} \qquad (6.24)$$

and $x(-1) \equiv x(N) \equiv 0$. Note that $H_{III}(k)$ is $[C^{III}]$ of size $N/2$ and $G_{III}(k)$ is $[C^I]$ of size $N/2$.

(iv) $[\mathbf{C}^{IV}]$ type IV DCT

$$
\left.\begin{array}{l}
X(k) = \dfrac{1}{2C_{4N}^{2k+1}}\,[G_{IV}(k) + H_{IV}(k)] \\[3mm]
X(N - k - 1) = \dfrac{1}{2S_{4N}^{2k+1}}\,[G_{IV}(k) - H_{IV}(k)]
\end{array}\right\}
\quad k = 0, \dots, \dfrac{N}{2} - 1 \quad (6.25)
$$

where

$$
G_{IV}(k) = \sum_{i=0}^{N/2-1} [x(2i) + x(2i + 1)]C_{2N}^{(2i+1)(2k+1)}
$$

$$
H_{IV}(k) = \sum_{i=0}^{N/2-1} [x(2i) + x(2i - 1)]C_{N}^{i(2k+1)}
$$

and $x(-1) \equiv 0$.

The flow diagrams for $N = 16$ are shown in Figs. 6.3–6.6. Note that for $[\mathbf{C}^{III}]$ and $[\mathbf{C}^{IV}]$, decimation occurs after one stage of preprocessing.

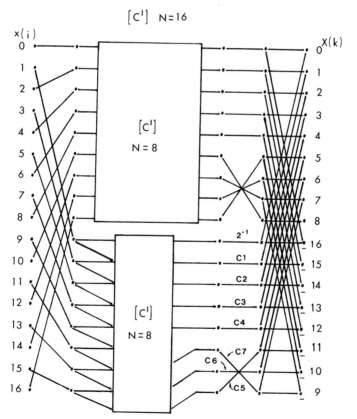

Fig. 6.3. DCT type I, $N = 16$. Here $C_j = (2\cos j\pi/16)^{-1}$.

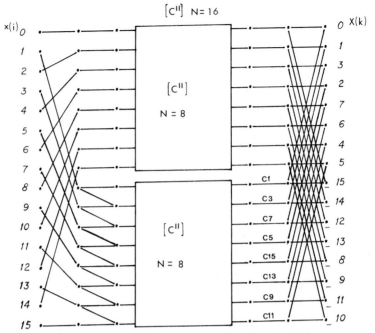

Fig. 6.4. DCT type II, $N = 16$. Here $C_j = (2 \cos j\pi/32)^{-1}$.

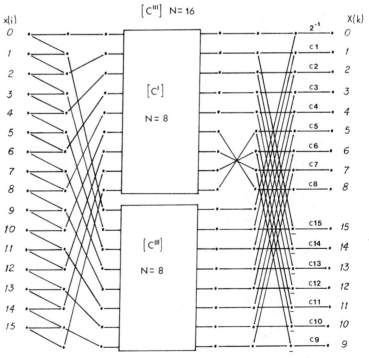

Fig. 6.5. DCT type III, $N = 16$. Here $C_j = (2 \cos j\pi/32)^{-1}$.

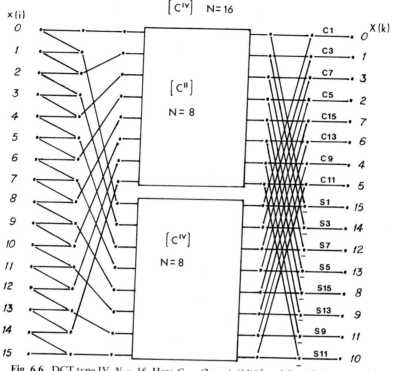

Fig. 6.6. DCT type IV, $N = 16$. Here $C_j = (2 \cos j\pi/64)^{-1}$ and $S_j = (2 \sin j\pi/64)^{-1}$.

Discrete Sine Transforms   B

When the basis functions in Eq. (6.3) are sine functions, the signal is said to undergo a DST. Jain [6] first proposed such a transform when he diagonalized a matrix asymptotically equivalent to the covariance matrix of a Markov-1 signal and found that the eigenvectors were the DST basis functions. Kekre and Solanki [17] developed another version of DST in their study of unitary trigonometric transforms. Wang [11] has also investigated the fast implementation of these DSTs.

The four types of DSTs are defined as follows:

$$\text{DST type I} \quad \phi_{ik} \equiv [\mathbf{S}^I]_{ik} = \sqrt{\frac{2}{N}} \left[\sin\left(\frac{ik\pi}{N}\right) \right],$$

$$i, k = 1, 2, \ldots, N - 1$$

$$\text{DST type II} \quad \phi_{ik} \equiv [\mathbf{S}^{II}]_{ik} = \sqrt{\frac{2}{N}} \left[c_i \sin\left(\frac{i(k - \frac{1}{2})\pi}{N}\right) \right],$$

$$i, k = 1, 2, \ldots, N$$

$$\text{DST type III}\quad \phi_{ik} \equiv [\mathbf{S}^{\text{III}}]_{ik} = \sqrt{\frac{2}{N}}\left[c_k \sin\left(\frac{k(i - \frac{1}{2})\pi}{N}\right)\right],$$

$$i, k = 1, 2, \ldots, N$$

$$\text{DST type IV}\quad \phi_{ik} \equiv [\mathbf{S}^{\text{IV}}]_{ik} = \sqrt{\frac{2}{N}}\left[\sin\left(\left(i - \frac{1}{2}\right)\left(\frac{(k - \frac{1}{2})\pi}{N}\right)\right)\right],$$

$$i, k = 1, 2, \ldots, N$$

$$(6.26)$$

where

$$c_i = \begin{cases} 1 & \text{if } i \neq 0 \text{ or } N \\ 1/\sqrt{2} & \text{if } i = 0 \text{ or } N \end{cases}$$

A comparison between Eq. (6.16) and Eq. (6.26) reveals the similarity between the two sets of transforms. As would be expected, a fast implementation similar to the algorithm of [13] exists. Yip and Rao [18] developed such an algorithm. DIT algorithms were developed later (see [15]). The speeds of computation of the DSTs were comparable to, and in some cases faster than, those for DCTs. Figure 6.7 shows the flow diagram of the DST developed by Yip and Rao for $N = 16$. (Note the actual size of the transform is $N - 1$ or 15 in this case.)

For $N = 2^L$, with notation consistent with Eq. (6.18), a DST of size $N - 1$ has the following recursive sparse-matrix factorization for $L \geq 2$:

$$[\mathbf{A}_{N-1}] = \left[\begin{array}{c|c} [\mathbf{A}_{N/2}] & 0 \\ \hline 0 & [\mathbf{D}_{N/2-1}][\mathbf{A}_{N/2-1}] \end{array}\right][\mathbf{B}_{N-1}]$$

where[‡]

$$[\mathbf{D}_{N/2-1}] = \text{diag}[\mathbf{I}_{N/4}, -\mathbf{I}_{N/4-1}] \qquad (6.27)$$

and

$$[\mathbf{B}_{N-1}] = \begin{bmatrix} 1 & & & & & & & 1 \\ & 1 & & & & & 1 & \\ & & 1 & & & 1 & & \\ & & & \ddots & 1 & \ddots & & \\ & & 1 & & & -1 & & \\ & 1 & & & & & -1 & \\ 1 & & & & & & & -1 \end{bmatrix}$$

[‡] The matrix factor $[\mathbf{D}_{N/2-1}]$ was left out in the original paper [18].

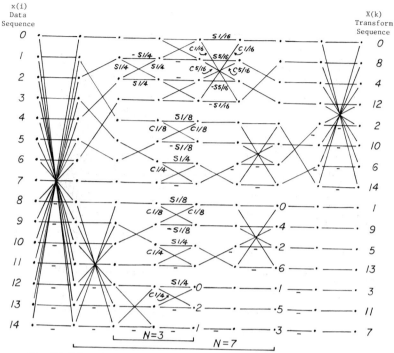

Fig. 6.7. FDST flow graph: $N = 3, 7, 15$, $cj/k = \cos(j\pi/k)$, $sj/k = \sin(j\pi/k)$.

Matrices $[\mathbf{A}_{N-1}]$ of odd size are recursively generated by Eq. (6.27) with $[\mathbf{A}_1] = 1$, and matrices $[\mathbf{A}_N]$ of even size are generated by the equation

$$[\mathbf{A}_N] = [\mathbf{P}_N]\left[\sin\frac{(2i+1)(k+1)\pi}{2N}\right], \qquad i, k = 0, 1, \ldots, N-1 \quad (6.28)$$

where $[\mathbf{P}_N]$ is a permutation matrix. The matrix can be further factored into sparse matrices (see [18]). The transform sequence is, as before, in BRO.

The following equations provide the basis for the DST DIT flow diagrams in Figs. 6.8–6.11:

(i) $[\mathbf{S}^1]$, type I DST

$$\left.\begin{array}{l} X(k) = \tilde{G}_1(k) + \tilde{H}_1(k) \\ X(N-k) = \tilde{G}_1(k) - \tilde{H}_1(k) \end{array}\right\} \qquad k = 1, 2, \ldots, \frac{N}{2} - 1 \quad (6.29)$$

and

$$X\left(\frac{N}{2}\right) = \sum_{i=0}^{N/2-1} (-1)^i x(2i+1)$$

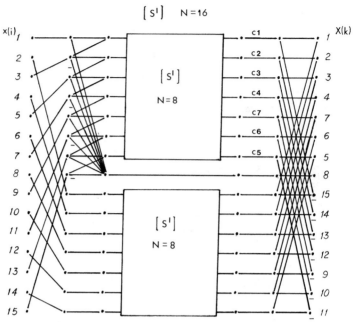

Fig. 6.8. DST type I, $N = 16$. Here $C_j = (2 \cos j\pi/16)^{-1}$.

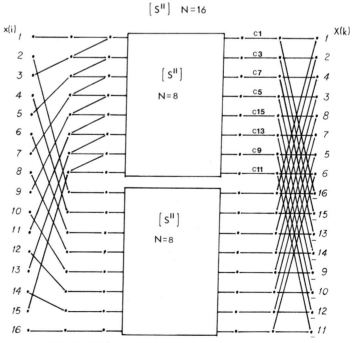

Fig. 6.9. DST type II, $N = 16$. Here $C_j = (2 \cos j\pi/32)^{-1}$.

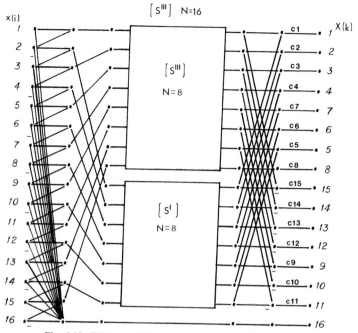

Fig. 6.10. DST type III, $N = 16$. Here $C_j = (2\cos j\pi/32)^{-1}$.

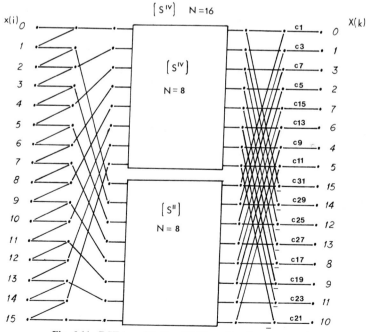

Fig. 6.11. DST type IV, $N = 16$. Here $C_j = (2\cos j\pi/64)^{-1}$.

where

$$\tilde{G}_1(k) = \frac{1}{2C_N^k} \sum_{i=1}^{N/2-1} [x(2i+1) + x(2i-1)]S_{N/2}^{ik}$$

$$\tilde{H}_1(k) = \sum_{i=1}^{N/2-1} x(2i)S_{N/2}^{ik}$$

where S_k^i is defined as $\sin(i\pi/k)$. Note that both $\tilde{G}_1(k)$ and $\tilde{H}_1(k)$ are DST type I of size $N/2$.

(ii) $[S^{II}]$, type II DST

$$\left.\begin{array}{r} X(k) = \tilde{G}_{II}(k) + \tilde{H}_{II}(k) \\ X(N-k-1) = \tilde{G}_{II}(k) - \tilde{H}_{II}(k) \end{array}\right\} \quad k = 1, 2, \ldots, \frac{N}{2} \qquad (6.30)$$

where

$$\tilde{G}_{II}(k) = \frac{1}{2C_N^{2i-1}} \sum_{i=1}^{N/2} [x(2i-1) + x(2i+1)]S_N^{i(2k-1)}$$

$$\tilde{H}_{II}(k) = \sum_{i=1}^{N/2} x(2i)S_N^{i(2k-1)}$$

(iii) $[S^{III}]$, type III DST

$$\left.\begin{array}{r} X(k) = \frac{1}{2C_{2N}^k}[\tilde{G}_{III}(k) + \tilde{H}_{III}(k)] \\ X(N-k) = \frac{1}{2C_{2N}^{N-k}}[\tilde{G}_{III}(k) - \tilde{H}_{III}(k)] \end{array}\right\} \quad k = 1, 2, \ldots, \frac{N}{2} - 1 \qquad (6.31)$$

where

$$\tilde{G}_{III}(k) = \sum_{i=1}^{N/2} [x(2i) + x(2i-1)]S_N^{(2i-1)k}$$

$$\tilde{H}_{III}(k) = \sum_{i=1}^{N/2-1} [x(2i) + x(2i+1)]S_{N/2}^{ik}$$

Note that while $\tilde{G}_{III}(k)$ is a type III DST, $\tilde{H}_{III}(k)$ is a type I DST.

(iv) $[S^{IV}]$, type IV DST

$$\left.\begin{array}{r} X(k) = \frac{1}{2C_{4N}^{2k+1}}[\tilde{G}_{IV}(k) + \tilde{H}_{IV}(k)] \\ X(N-k-1) = \frac{1}{2C_{4N}^{2N-2k-1}}[\tilde{G}_{IV}(k) - \tilde{H}_{IV}(k)] \end{array}\right\} \quad k = 0, 1, \ldots, \frac{N}{2} - 1 \qquad (6.32)$$

where

$$\tilde{G}_{IV}(k) = \sum_{i=0}^{N/2-1} [x(2i) + x(2i + 1)] S_{2N}^{(2i+1)(2k+1)}$$

$$\tilde{H}_{IV}(k) = \sum_{i=1}^{N/2-1} [x(2i) + x(2i - 1)] S_{N}^{i(2k+1)}$$

and $x(N) \equiv 0$. Although $\tilde{G}_{IV}(k)$ is a type IV DST, $\tilde{H}_{IV}(k)$ is a type II DST.

In both $[\mathbf{S}^{III}]$ and $[\mathbf{S}^{IV}]$ the decimation process is performed after one stage of preprocessing on the input data.

Inverse DCT and DST   C

In both DST and DCT, because of the orthogonality and symmetry properties, the inverse transforms are directly related to the forward transforms and therefore have similar sparse-matrix factorizations. We summarize these as follows:

$$[\mathbf{C}^{I}]^{-1} = [\mathbf{C}^{I}]; \quad [\mathbf{C}^{II}]^{-1} = [\mathbf{C}^{III}]; \quad [\mathbf{C}^{IV}]^{-1} = [\mathbf{C}^{IV}]$$
$$[\mathbf{S}^{I}]^{-1} = [\mathbf{S}^{I}]; \quad [\mathbf{S}^{II}]^{-1} = [\mathbf{S}^{III}]; \quad [\mathbf{S}^{IV}]^{-1} = [\mathbf{S}^{IV}]$$

(6.33)

NONSINUSOIDAL DISCRETE TRANSFORMS   V

The sinusoidal discrete transforms discussed in Section IV are suboptimal in terms of decorrelating the signal. They are, however, asymptotically equivalent to the KLT under some constraints of signal statistics. There are, nevertheless, other transforms that simplify computation when decorrelation is not the prime objective. For example, the discrete Walsh transform (DWT) and Walsh–Hadamard transform (WHT) require no multiplications since the values of the basis functions are equal to ± 1 [19]. This feature makes WHT capable of extremely fast implementations. The Haar transform (HT) (see [20]) basis functions are particularly suitable for coding edges for the transmission of images. Irrational numbers such as $\sqrt{2}$ are used in the HT. When these irrational numbers are replaced by rational numbers under a special rationalization scheme, the resulting transform is said to be the rationalized Haar transform (RHT) (see, e.g., [21]). The uniform changes in the basis functions of the slant transform (ST) [22] make it a good candidate to represent the gradual brightness changes in TV images. Attempts to simplify the DCT by replacing some of its elements by integers led to the development of the C-matrix transform (CMT) [23], which can also be applied to image processing. Finally, RT, a singular transform with no theoretical inverse, has been found useful in character recognition because of its invariance properties with respect to small shifts and rotations [24].

Before discussing each of these nonsinusoidal transforms in some detail, we point out that the concept of frequency associated with the sinusoids has to be generalized. The term "sequency" is used to denote one half of the number of zero crossings per second (zps) in the basis functions (see, e.g., [24, 25]).

A   The Walsh–Hadamard Transform

A complete set of orthonormal rectangular functions developed by Walsh (1923) for the normalized interval of $[0, 1]$ can be used as basis functions in Eq. (6.9). The resulting transform is the WHT. The basis functions for $N = 16$ are shown in Fig. 6.12. The functions can be ordered according to the sequency (i.e., zero crossings per unit interval), according to the dyadic representation, (Paley or dyadic order), or according to the recursive generation of these functions from Rademacher functions [26]. The basis functions shown in Fig. 6.12 are given in Walsh or sequency order. Half of these functions are even, and half of them are odd about the midpoint of the range $[0, 1]$. The even ones are called *cal*, and the odd ones are called *sal* in analogy to the cosine and sine functions for sinusoids. The corresponding discrete Walsh functions constitute the Walsh–Hadamard matrices. Different orderings of these matrices provide different ways of implementing the fast transforms. Figure 6.13 shows the flow diagram of WHT in sequency order for $N = 16$, and Appendix C contains a complete program implementing Fig. 6.13. The similarity between this and the decimation-in-frequency FFTs in Chapter 7 is obvious. There are, however, no twiddle factors or multipliers in the WHT. Note also that the order of the output points is in BRO.

Just as sinusoids are solutions to differential equations in the continuous domain, Walsh functions are solutions to so-called dyadic differential equations. If wal(m, t) is used to denote a Walsh function defined for $0 \leq t < 1$, where m represents the sequency, then

$$\text{wal}(m, t)\text{wal}(h, t) = \text{wal}(m \oplus h, t) \tag{6.34}$$

where $m \oplus h$ denotes bit-by-bit addition of m and h modulo 2. This closure property of Walsh functions under multiplication implies the possibility of bandwidth reduction by a factor of 2, compared to sinusoids for signal transmission. Other properties are associated with the use of Walsh functions in the transmission of information. The relevant theory and practical applications

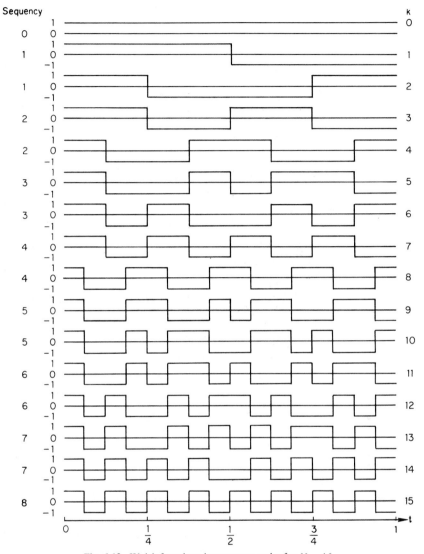

Fig. 6.12. Walsh functions in sequency order for $N = 16$.

are dealt with in great detail in [26]. (See also [27].) The discrete Walsh–
Hadamard functions for a size $N = 2^L$ transform are given nonrecursively
by [28].

$$\text{wal}(m, n) = \frac{1}{\sqrt{N}} (-1)^{q(m,n)} \tag{6.35}$$

WHT   N=16

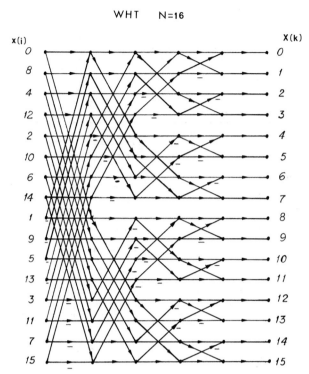

Fig. 6.13. WHT for $N = 16$, sequency ordering.

where

$$q(m, n) = \left[\sum_{i=0}^{L-1} g_i(m) n_i \right]_{\text{mod } 2} \qquad \text{for sequency or Walsh ordering}$$

$$q(m, n) = \left[\sum_{i=0}^{L-1} m_i n_i \right]_{\text{mod } 2} \qquad \text{for natural or Hadamard ordering}$$

In Eq. (6.35) m_i and n_i are the ith bits of the L-bit binary representations of m and n, respectively. $g_i(m)$ is the ith bit of the L-bit binary reversed Gray code of m, given by

$$g_0(m) = m_{L-1}, g_1(m) = m_{L-1} + m_{L-2}, \dots, g_{L-1}(m) = m_1 + m_0 \qquad (6.36)$$

It has been shown by Jones et al. [29] that all orthogonal transforms consisting of one-half even and one-half odd basis functions can be implemented in terms of the WHT. Thus frequency contents of each sequency component in the Walsh–Hadamard expansion can also be computed (see [30]).

When the WHT is computed using the natural or Hadamard orderings for the basis functions, the resulting transform is also called the binary Fourier transform or BIFORE transform [31]. The flow diagram is an exact duplicate of the FFT, with the removal of all twiddle factors and the substitution for all W^{ik} factors in the FFT by $+1$ if $(ik)_{\text{mod } N} < N/2$ and by -1 if $(ik)_{\text{mod } N} \geq N/2$. This diagram is shown in Fig. 6.14 for $N = 16$. Since the matrix is real, symmetric, and orthogonal, the inverse matrix is identical to the forward transform matrix.

We conclude this subsection by stating the recursive generation of the WHT in Hadamard or natural order. Using $H(L)$ to denote the $(\text{WHT})_h$ matrix of size $(N \times N)$, where $N = 2^L$, we obtain the recursive factorization

$$\mathbf{H}(L + 1) = \mathbf{H}(1) \otimes \mathbf{H}(L)$$

$$= \mathbf{H}(1) \otimes \mathbf{H}(1) \otimes \cdots \otimes \mathbf{H}(1)$$

with $\mathbf{H}(1) = \begin{bmatrix} 1 & 1 \\ 1 & -1 \end{bmatrix}$ and $\otimes$ denoting the Kronecker (direct) product between two matrices; that is,

$$\mathbf{H}(1) \otimes \mathbf{H}(m) = \begin{bmatrix} \mathbf{H}(m) & \mathbf{H}(m) \\ \mathbf{H}(m) & -\mathbf{H}(m) \end{bmatrix} \tag{6.37}$$

For other ordering schemes, such as Paley or cal-sal, we refer the reader to [7, 25, 27].

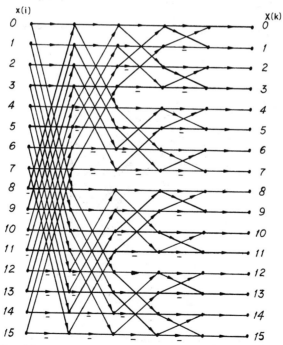

Fig. 6.14. Signal-flow graph for WHT in natural or Hadamard ordering for $N = 16$.

B The Haar Transform

When the basis functions in Eq. (6.3) are Haar functions, the input sequence **x**
undergoes a HT. The basis functions were originally developed by Haar [3], and
are shown in Fig. 6.15. The localized nature of most of the basis functions makes
HT an ideal transform for edge detection and contour extraction. Each basis
function is normalized to retain the unitary property of the transform. The
recursion relation for the matrix generation, using $[\mathbf{H}a(k+1)]$ to denote the

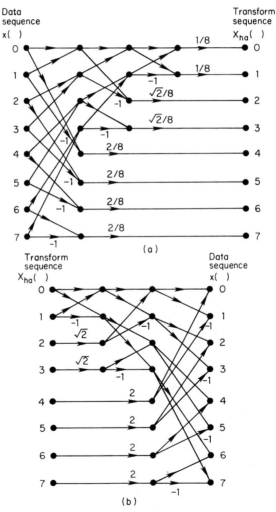

Fig. 6.15. Flow diagrams for forward (a) and inverse (b) Haar transform for $N = 8$; (c) Haar basis
functions for $N = 16$.

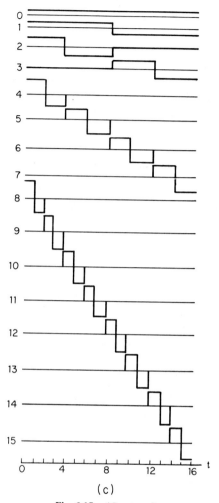

Fig. 6.15. (*Continued*)

$N = 2^{k+1}$ HT matrix, is

$$[\mathbf{H}a(k + 1)] = \begin{bmatrix} \mathbf{H}a(k) \otimes (1, 1) \\ 2^{k/2}\mathbf{I}_{2^k} \otimes (1, -1) \end{bmatrix} \qquad \text{for } k \geq 1 \qquad (6.38)$$

where

$$[\mathbf{H}a(1)] = \begin{bmatrix} 1 & 1 \\ 1 & -1 \end{bmatrix}$$

Sparse-matrix factorization of Eq. (6.38) leads to the flow diagrams in Fig. 6.15 for $N = 8$. Since the matrix is not symmetric but orthogonal, the inverse is the transpose of the forward transform as shown. This fast algorithm also lacks the in-place structure of all the previously discussed algorithms. However, Ahmed et al. [32] have developed an in-place version of the fast algorithm.

If $2^{k/2}$ is dropped in Eq. (6.38), the resulting matrix is orthogonal but not unitary. The removal of $2^{k/2}$ is referred to as rationalizing, and the resulting transform is the RHT. The modification takes into account the hardware realization of the algorithm, in which irrational numbers are difficult to implement. Denoting the matrix for the RHT as $[\mathbf{RH}(k)]$, we have the transform pair (for $N = 2^k$)

$$\mathbf{X} = [\mathbf{RH}(k)]\mathbf{x} \quad \text{and} \quad \mathbf{x} = [\mathbf{RH}(k)]^T[\mathbf{P}(k)]\mathbf{X} \tag{6.39}$$

where $[\mathbf{RH}(k)]$ is identical to $\mathbf{H}a(k)$ with the $2^{k/2}$ removed and $[\mathbf{P}(k)]$ is a 2^k diagonal matrix containing negative powers of 2, and is used to restore the normality of the transformation.

C   Slant Transform

In designing image representation for TV signals, Enomoto and Shibata [22] modified some of the Walsh functions and developed the first eight basis functions, eventually named the slant vectors. These are designed to retain the orthonormality and completeness properties, with one constant vector (for the dc component) and a combination of sampled sawtoothed functions. Using $\mathbf{S}(L)$ to denote the $N = 2^L$ transformation matrix, we have the recursive formula for $L \geq 2$

$$[\mathbf{S}(L)] = \frac{1}{\sqrt{2}}
\begin{bmatrix}
\begin{array}{cc|c} 1 & 0 & \\ a_N & b_N & 0 \\ \hline 0 & & \mathbf{I}_{N/2-2} \end{array} &
\begin{array}{cc|c} 1 & 0 & \\ -a_N & b_N & 0 \\ \hline 0 & & \mathbf{I}_{N/2-2} \end{array} \\
\begin{array}{cc|c} 0 & 1 & \\ -b_N & a_N & 0 \\ \hline 0 & & \mathbf{I}_{N/2-2} \end{array} &
\begin{array}{cc|c} 0 & -1 & \\ b_N & a_N & 0 \\ \hline 0 & & -\mathbf{I}_{N/2-2} \end{array}
\end{bmatrix}$$

$$\times \, \text{diag}\{[\mathbf{S}(L-1)], [\mathbf{S}(L-1)]\} \tag{6.40}$$

where

$$[\mathbf{S}(1)] = \frac{1}{\sqrt{2}}\begin{bmatrix} 1 & 1 \\ 1 & -1 \end{bmatrix}$$

and the parameters a_N and b_N are recursively generated by

$$a_2 = 1, \quad b_N = \frac{1}{(1 + 4a_{N/2}^2)^{1/2}}, \quad a_N = 2b_N a_{N/2}, \quad N = 4, 8, 16, \dots \tag{6.41}$$

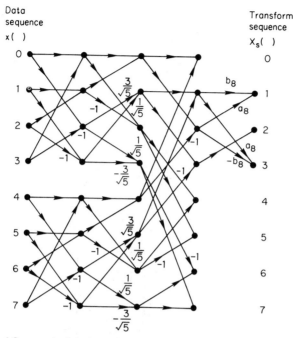

Data
sequence
x( )

Transform
sequence
$X_s(\ )$

Fig. 6.16. Signal-flow graph of the ST for $N = 8$. (For simplicity, the multiplier $1/\sqrt{8}$ is not shown.) $a_8 = 4/\sqrt{21}$, $b_8 = \sqrt{5/21}$.

Equation (6.40) implies an intrinsic fast algorithm, since $[S(L)]$ is expressed in terms of $[S(L - 1)]$. Figure 6.16 shows the flow diagram of a fast algorithm for ST for $N = 8$. Again, we note that the inverse is the transpose of the forward transform, and the flow graph is not in place. An in-place algorithm for the ST has been developed by Ahmed and Chen [33]. Figure 6.17 shows the slant basis functions for $N = 16$.

Rapid Transform D

The HT and ST in Sections V.B and V.C can be obtained by variations to the Walsh basis functions. For RT the modification is made to the flow diagram. The Hadamard ordered WHT flow diagram (e.g., Fig. 6.14) is modified by applying an absolute value operation at the output of every node subsequent to the input (see Fig. 6.18). The immediate consequence of this modification is that RT has no inverse. Thus all processing, classification, feature extraction, or identification must be performed in the transform domain. However, the modification also makes the transform invariant to circular shifts and to reflection of the input sequence. These properties lacking in the previous transforms described

Waveform number

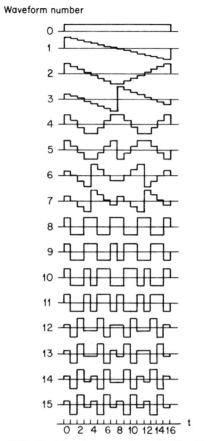

Fig. 6.17. Slant transform waveforms for $N = 16$.

in Sections V.A,B,C make the RT a good candidate for use in character recognition, feature extraction, and identification. Recovery of input data from the transform sequence is possible, given additional information (see [34].)

E Hybrid Transforms

The discrete transforms described so far can be combined in different ways to generate many hybrid transforms. The direct, or Kronecker, product of matrices as a means of combination preserves both the unitarity and the sparseness of the transform matrices. Such combinations as slant–Haar [35] and Hadamard–Haar transforms [36] result from the direct product of the corresponding

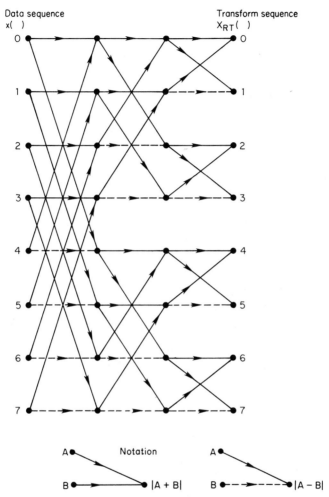

Fig. 6.18. Signal-flow graph for the rapid transform for $N = 8$. [Reprinted with permission from H. Reitbeock and T. P. Brady, A transformation with invariance under cyclic permutation for applications in pattern recognition, *Information and Control* **15**, 130–154 (1979).]

matrices. In addition, Jones *et al.* [29] have shown that all even–odd transforms are related through conversion matrices. A specific case for $N = 8$ was established for the DCT (specifically $[C^{II}]$). The cosine multipliers in the conversion matrix can be approximated closely by rational numbers (ratios of integers). This reduces the complexity of the conversion matrices and makes hardware realization much easier. Such a transform is called a CMT. However, the CMT has been developed only up to $N = 32$ (see [23]).

VI PERFORMANCE CRITERIA

How well a particular transform performs depends on the signal processing problem. Feature selection, bandwidth reduction, and pattern recognition all make demands on transform performance. We shall discuss four common criteria used in assessing particular transform performance. To obtain some idea about these criteria, we make the assumption that, in general, the data to be transformed have a sample-to-sample correlation governed by the Markov-1 model, where the covariance matrix has the form, as in Eq. (6.15),

$$
\psi = \begin{bmatrix}
1 & \rho & \rho^2 & \cdots & \rho^{N-1} \\
\rho & 1 & \rho & \cdots & \rho^{N-2} \\
\rho^2 & \rho & 1 & \rho & \cdots & \rho^{N-3} \\
\vdots & & & & \vdots \\
\rho^{N-1} & \rho^{N-2} & & \cdots & 1
\end{bmatrix} \tag{6.42}
$$

where $\rho < 1$ is the adjacent correlation coefficient of the Markov-1 model. (Note that ψ is a symmetric Toeplitz matrix of order N.) The values of ρ are usually considered to vary from 0.7 (for high-detail images) to 0.99 (for low-detail images) (see, e.g., [37]). In investigating the criteria for performance, ρ is usually allowed to vary between 0.5 and 0.99. Comparisons between different transforms very often use a typical value of $\rho = 0.9$.

A Variance Distribution and Energy Packing Efficiency

In feature selection problems of signal processing, the choice of coefficients in the transform domain determines how well a pattern may be recognized. The choice is guided by the variance of the transform coefficient, which is a measure of how much energy (proportionately speaking) is contained in the corresponding basis vector (see, e.g., [38]). The higher the variance, the more information is carried by that basis vector. If ψ denotes the covariance matrix and T denotes the transform matrix, the diagonal matrix elements in the transform domain represent the variances of the corresponding coefficients:

$$
\sigma_{jj}^2 = (T\psi T^{-1})_{jj}, \qquad j = 1, \ldots, N \tag{6.43}
$$

In particular, if T represents the KLT, then $\sigma_{jj}^2 = \lambda_j$, the eigenvalues of the KLT, since KLT diagonalizer the covariance matrix ψ. We note here that variance distribution is not defined for the RT since its inverse does not exist. Table I displays comparisons between the variances of various transforms for $N = 16$ at a correlation coefficient of $\rho = 0.9$ for a Markov-1 signal. Note that since σ_{jj}^2 is a theoretical result obtained by Eq. (6.43), it is quite independent of the algorithms

TABLE I

Variance Distribution for First-Order Markov Process Defined by $\rho = 0.9$ and $N = 16$
Where i is the Transform Coefficient Number

	Transform					
i	HT	WHT	DCT	DFT	ST	DST[a]
1	9.8346	9.8346	9.8346	9.8346	9.8346	8.8567
2	2.5364	2.5360	2.9328	1.8342	2.8536	2.4102
3	0.8638	1.0200	1.2108	1.8342	1.1963	1.3608
4	0.8638	0.7060	0.5814	0.5189	0.4610	0.6395
5	0.2755	0.3070	0.3482	0.5189	0.3468	0.4875
6	0.2755	0.3030	0.2314	0.2502	0.3424	0.2814
7	0.2755	0.2830	0.1684	0.2502	0.1461	0.2387
8	0.2755	0.1060	0.1294	0.1553	0.1460	0.1553
9	0.1000	0.1050	0.1046	0.1553	0.1047	0.1373
10	0.1000	0.1050	0.0876	0.1126	0.1044	0.0986
11	0.1000	0.1040	0.0760	0.1126	0.1044	0.0886
12	0.1000	0.1040	0.0676	0.0913	0.0631	0.0703
13	0.1000	0.1030	0.0616	0.0913	0.0631	0.0642
14	0.1000	0.1020	0.0574	0.0811	0.0631	0.0567
15	0.1000	0.0980	0.0548	0.0811	0.0631	0.0538
16	0.1000	0.0780	0.0532	0.0780	0.0631	

[a] DST is $[S^I]$ for a 15-point transform.

Note that the DST does not have a constant valued basis function as do all the others. Thus a signal with dc component removed would be a good candidate for transform analysis using DST.

used to implement the transforms. The DCT seems best in terms of the variance distribution, since it has the highest variances in the fewest coefficients. It is therefore a good candidate for feature selection and bandwidth compression.

Another very similar criterion is the energy packing efficiency (EPE) first proposed by Kitajima [39]. This is defined as the proportion of energy contained in the first K of N coefficients. When $K = 2^m$ and $N = 2^n$, the EPE η is

$$\eta(2^m) = \sum_{p=0}^{2^m-1} E(X_p^2) \bigg/ \sum_{p=0}^{2^n-1} E(X_p^2) \tag{6.44}$$

where E denotes expectation and X_p is the pth coefficient in the transform domain. Yip and Rao [28] examined η for some unitary transforms and concluded that η is invariant with respect to transforms that display block spectral structure. To see how η is related to the variance distribution, we consider

$$\sum_{p=0}^{K} E(X_p^2) = \sum_{p=1}^{K} E\left\{ \left(\sum_{i=1}^{N} \phi_{pi} x_i \right)^* \left(\sum_{j=1}^{N} \phi_{pj} x_j \right) \right\} \tag{6.45}$$

$$= \sum_{p=1}^{K} \sum_{i,j=1}^{N} \phi_{pj} E(x_j x_i^*) \phi_{pi}^* \tag{6.46}$$

If $(\phi_{pi}) = \mathbf{T}$ is the transform matrix, then $\phi_{pi}^* = (T^\dagger)_{ip}$, and if $\mathbf{T}$ is unitary, $\mathbf{T}^\dagger = \mathbf{T}^{-1}$ so that Eq. (6.46) is reduced to

$$\sum_{p=1}^{K} E(X_p^2) = \sum_{p=1}^{K} (T\psi T^{-1})_{pp} \tag{6.47}$$

where $\psi = E(x_j x_i^*)$ is the covariance matrix of the sampled data. Thus, under comparison with Eq. (6.43), the EPE η is directly equivalent to the ratio between the sum of the first K variances and the total sum of the variances. Although variance distribution is considered for transform coefficients (output sequence) in sequency order, the EPE efficiency may, quite possibly, be considered when the output sequence is in some other type of ordering.

B Residual Correlation

A measure, which indicates the amount of correlation left in the transform domain, is the residual correlation first defined by Hamidi and Pearl [40]. Let ψ'

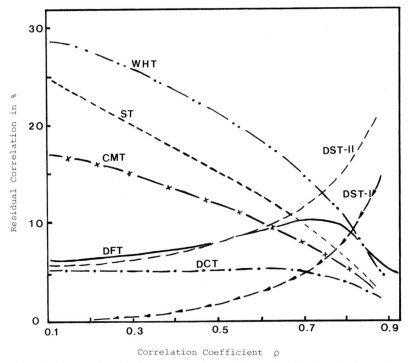

Fig. 6.19. Residual correlation vs. correlation coefficient ρ for $N = 16$. DCT is type II.

be the diagonal matrix of the variances, as defined in Eq. (6.43):

$$\psi' = (\sigma_{jj}^2) \tag{6.48}$$

The covariance ψ is then approximated in the original data domain through the inverse transformation given by

$$\psi'' = \mathbf{T}^{-1}\psi'\mathbf{T} \tag{6.49}$$

The residual correlation is then defined by

$$\text{Residual correlation} = \frac{|\psi - \psi''|^2}{|\psi - \mathbf{I}|^2} \tag{6.50}$$

where $|\ \ |^2$ is the Schmidt weak norm defined by

$$|\mathbf{M}|^2 = \frac{1}{N} \sum_{i,j=1}^{N} |(M)_{ij}|^2 \tag{6.51}$$

and $|\psi - \mathbf{I}|^2$ is a measure of the cross-correlation in the input sequence. According to Eq. (6.49), when the transform matrix $\mathbf{T}$ is the KLT, ψ'' is identical to ψ since $\mathbf{T}$ then diagonalizes ψ, and the residual correlation in Eq. (6.50) is zero for the KLT. Figure 6.19 shows the residual correlation for some of the discrete transforms as a function of ρ for $N = 16$.

Wiener Filtering   C

The Wiener filter, first derived to minimize the MSE of the linear estimate, can be formulated in the spatial and frequency domains (see [41, 42]). The Wiener filter transfer function is

$$H_{\text{w}} = \frac{H^*}{|H|^2 + \phi_n/\phi_f} \tag{6.52}$$

where H^* is the complex conjugate of the point-spread transfer function of the signal path, and ϕ_n, ϕ_f are the power spectra of the noise and signal, respectively. Thus, the estimated signal in the transform domain is

$$\hat{F} = H_{\text{w}}G \tag{6.53}$$

where $G = HF + N$ is the transform domain representation of the received signal plus noise.

Here F and N are the "frequency" transforms of the signal and noise, respectively. The Wiener filter minimizes the expected squared error:

$$\text{MSE} = E[|F - \hat{F}|^2] \tag{6.54}$$

Thus, the appropriate transform to use to effect the Wiener filter would be the one that also minimizes the MSE for a given noise statistic or for a given signal-to-noise ratio (SNR). The result for the scalar Wiener filter, that is, a diagonal matrix for H_w in Eq. (6.53), for the MSE is

$$\mathrm{MSE} = 1 - \frac{1}{N} \sum_{i=1}^{N} \frac{\psi_{ii}}{\psi_{ii} + \eta_{ii}} \qquad (6.55)$$

where ψ_{ii} and η_{ii} are the diagonal elements of the $N \times N$ covariance matrices for the signal and noise, respectively, in the transform domain. Since this performance criterion also depends on the noise statistics (or SNR), no systematic comparison of any significance has been carried out. However, Wang and Hunt [43] did compare the Wienner filter criterion for two versions of DCTs.

D Rate Distortion and Maximum Reducible Bits

A rate-distortion function can be defined to measure the information rates in bits per transform coefficient needed for coding when a certain maximum average

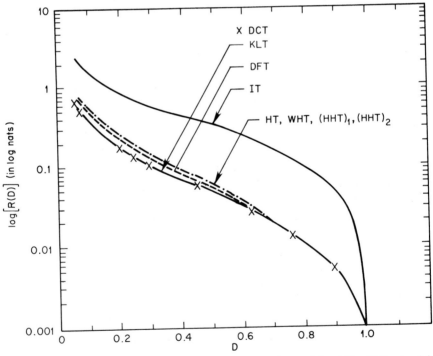

Fig. 6.20. Rate vs. distortion of a first-order Markov process for $\rho = 0.9$ and $N = 16$ (1 nat $= 1.44$ bits; i.e., $\log_2 e = 1.44$). DCT is type II.

distortion is allowed. This function is defined as

$$R(T, D) = \frac{1}{2N} \sum_{i=1}^{N} \max\left\{0, \log_2 \frac{\psi'_{ii}}{\theta}\right\} \tag{6.56}$$

where T denotes the transform used, D is the distortion function, and θ is chosen to give a predetermined value to D:

$$D(\theta) = \frac{1}{N} \sum_{i=1}^{N} \min(\theta, \psi'_{ii}) \tag{6.57}$$

ψ' are the diagonal elements of the covariance matrix in the transform domain:

$$\psi' = T\psi T^{-1} \tag{6.58}$$

Figure 6.20 compares some discrete transforms using the rate-distortion function. IT in the figure shows the rate-distortion function for the identity transform. The DST (not shown) has a curve practically identical to the DFT. If θ is chosen in Eq. (6.57) to be smaller than all ψ_{ii}, then $D = \theta$ and the rate-distortion function is reduced to

$$R(T, D) = \frac{1}{2N} \sum_{i=1}^{N} \log_2 \psi'_{ii} - \frac{1}{2} \log_2 D \tag{6.59}$$

The first term in (6.59) depends only on the transform T and is defined by Wang and Hunt [43] as the negative maximum reducible bits (mrb) from each transform component:

$$\text{mrb} = -\frac{1}{2N} \sum_{i=1}^{N} \log_2 \psi'_{ii} \tag{6.60}$$

The larger this value is, the better is the performance of the corresponding transform in the sense of bit reduction. Table II shows some mrbs for $\rho = 0.9$ and $N = 16$.

TABLE II

**Maximum Reducible Bits
for $N = 16$ and $\rho = 0.9$**

Transform	mrb
HT	0.9311
WHT	0.9374
DCT(II)	1.1172
DFT	0.9485
ST	1.0744
DST(I)	0.9752

VII COMPUTATIONAL COMPLEXITY AND SUMMARY

We have presented a collection of discrete transforms that may be used for signal processing works of various kinds. Each transform has been defined, and its main properties discussed. Fast algorithms based on radix-2 factorizations into sparse matrices were given, and many similarities and differences have been noted. Since we left out the general orthogonal transforms (GT), of Ahmed and Rao [44] and the number-theoretic transforms (NTT) of Nussbaumer [45], we have not been exhaustive. Instead, we have concentrated on the common types of sinusoidal and nonsinusoidal discrete transforms. Fast algorithms are all based on radix-2 factorizations to provide a common ground for comparing the structure and efficacy of the implementations.

The reduction of computational complexity, in particular the reduction of the number of multiplications in an algorithm, is no longer as critical as it once was. By using look-up tables, we can perform a multiplication almost as fast as an addition. However, the implication of structural simplicity based on a few multiplications is just as valid as before. The total number of arithmetic operations required in an algorithm is still a valid criterion for computational complexity. We summarize this aspect of the discrete transforms in Table III, where the number of real arithmetic operations (complex operations for the FFT) in terms of multiplications and additions is listed as a function of N, the transform size, for some of the transforms we have discussed.

Aside from this consideration of computational complexity, a recursive structure is always a desired property, since it will enable modular structures, both in software and in hardware realizations.

We have also considered different performance criteria for the various transforms. These criteria in conjunction with the computational complexity considerations will guide the engineer to choose the appropriate transform.

TABLE III

**Computational Complexity for Fast Implementations of
Various Discrete Transforms**

Transform	Number of Multiplications	Number of additions
HT	$N - 2$	$2(N - 1)$
WHT	—	$N \log_2 N$
DCT(II)[a]	$(3N/2)\log_2 N - N + 1$	$(N/2)\log_2 N$
DFT[b]	$(N/2)\log_2 N/2$	$N \log_2 N$
ST	$2(3N - 4)$	$2(3N - 2)$
DST(I)[a]	$(2N)\log_2 N - 4(N - 1)$	$(N/2)\log_2 N - N + 1$

[a] Based on DIT algorithms of Yip and Rao [15].
[b] Complex operations.

APPENDIX A. FAST IMPLEMENTATION OF DCT VIA FFT

Section IV.A discusses DCTs. This appendix discusses several methods of implementing the DCT by the FFT, since FFT computer programs are more likely to be available. By manipulating the original N-point data sequence, we can obtain its DCT by a $2N$-point or an N-point FFT using the techniques described next.

Method 1   **1**

The type II DCT (see Section IV.A) of a data sequence $x(m)$, $m = 0, 1,\ldots,$ $N - 1$, and its inverse are respectively defined as

$$X_c(k) = \sqrt{\frac{2}{N}}\,c(k)\sum_{m=0}^{N-1} x(m)\cos\left[\frac{(2m+1)k\pi}{2N}\right], \qquad k = 0, 1,\ldots, N-1 \quad (A6.1)$$

$$x(m) = \sqrt{\frac{2}{N}}\sum_{k=0}^{N-1} c(k)X_c(k)\cos\left[\frac{(2m+1)k\pi}{2N}\right], \qquad m = 0, 1,\ldots, N-1$$

where

$$c(k) = \begin{cases} 1/\sqrt{2}, & k = 0 \\ 1, & k = 1, 2,\ldots, N-1 \end{cases}$$

and $X_c(k)$, $k = 0, 1,\ldots,$ $N - 1$, is the DCT sequence. A computer program implementing Eq. (A6.1) is in Appendix B.

The DCT in Eq. (A6.1) can be also expressed as

$$X_c(k) = \sqrt{\frac{2}{N}}\,c(k)\mathrm{Re}\left[e^{-jk\pi/2N}\sum_{m=0}^{2N-1} x(m)W_{2N}^{mk}\right], \qquad k = 0, 1,\ldots, N-1$$

$$(A6.2)$$

where $W_{2N} = \exp(-j2\pi/2N)$ and $x(m) = 0$, $m = N, N+1,\ldots, 2N-1$. This implies that the DCT of an N-point sequence can be implemented by adding N

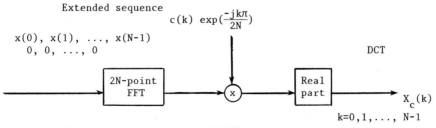

Fig. A6.1. Computation of even DCT by even length extension of **x**.

zeros to this sequence and by using a $2N$-point FFT. Other operations such as the multiplier $\exp(-jk\pi/2N)$ and real part also are needed. This is shown in block diagram form in Fig. A6.1. By using the FFT on two $2N$-point sequences, Haralick [12] has developed a DCT algorithm that is more efficient computationally and storagewise compared to that implied by Eq. (A6.2).

2 Method 2

Extending the N-point data sequence to a $2N$-point sequence in another manner eliminates the real part operation in Fig. A6.1. Let $x(n)$, $n = 0, 1, \ldots, N - 1$, be extended as follows:

$$\hat{x}(n) = \begin{cases} x(n), & n = 0, 1, \ldots, N - 1 \\ x(2N - 1 - n), & n = N, N + 1, \ldots, 2N - 1 \end{cases} \tag{A6.3}$$

Then the DFT of $\hat{x}(n)$ given by $\hat{X}_F(k)$, $k = 0, 1, \ldots, 2N - 1$, is defined as

$$\hat{X}_F(k) = \frac{1}{\sqrt{2N}} \sum_{n=0}^{2N-1} \hat{x}(n) W_{2N}^{nk} \tag{A6.4}$$

where $W_{2N} = \exp(-j2\pi/2N)$. By writing Eq. (A6.4) as

$$\hat{X}_F(k) = \frac{1}{\sqrt{2N}} \left(\sum_{n=0}^{N-1} x(n) W_{2N}^{nk} + \sum_{n=N}^{2N-1} x(n) W_{2N}^{nk} \right)$$

and using Eq. (A6.3), we can easily show that

$$\hat{X}_F(k) = \frac{1}{\sqrt{N}} e^{-j\pi k/2N} \sum_{n=0}^{N-1} x(n) \cos \frac{(2n + 1)k\pi}{2N} \tag{A6.5}$$

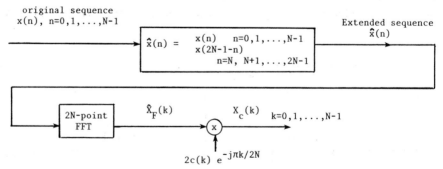

Fig. A6.2. Computation of an N-point DCT by a $2N$-point FFT without a real part operation.

Inspection of Eqs. (A6.1) and (A6.5) shows that

$$X_c(k) = 2c(k)e^{-j\pi k/2N}\hat{X}_F(k) \tag{A6.6}$$

This technique is shown schematically in Fig. A6.2.

Method 3   3

A much simpler algorithm, which requires only an N-point DFT, has been developed by Narasimha and Peterson [46]. The details are as follows: Assuming N is even, delete the constant multiplier in Eq. (A6.1). Let

$$\tilde{X}_c(k) = \sum_{m=0}^{N-1} x(m)\cos\left[\frac{(2m+1)k\pi}{2N}\right], \quad k = 0, 1, \ldots, N-1 \tag{A6.7}$$

Define a new N-point sequence $y(m)$ by

$$y(m) = x(2m), \quad y(N-1-m) = x(2m+1), \quad m = 0, 1, \ldots, N/2 - 1 \tag{A6.8}$$

Using Eq. (A6.8), we can write Eq. (A6.7) as

$$\tilde{X}_c(k) = \sum_{m=0}^{N/2-1} y(m)\cos\frac{(4m+1)k\pi}{2N}$$
$$+ \sum_{m=0}^{N/2-1} y(N-1-m)\cos\left[\frac{(4m+3)k\pi}{2N}\right], \quad k = 0, 1, \ldots, N-1 \tag{A6.9}$$

Letting $m = N - 1 - m$ in the second summation, simplifying, and recombining the two terms yield

$$\tilde{X}_c(k) = \sum_{m=0}^{N-1} y(m)\cos\left[\frac{(4m+1)k\pi}{2N}\right] = \text{Re}[H(k)]$$

where

$$H(k) = e^{j\pi k/2N}\sum_{m=0}^{N-1} y(m)e^{j2\pi mk/N}$$
$$= e^{j\pi k/2N}Y_f(k), \quad k = 0, 1, \ldots, N-1 \tag{A6.10}$$

In Eq. (A6.10), $Y_f(k)$ is the inverse DFT ((IDFT) of $y(k)$. Hence

$$H(k) = e^{j\pi k/2N}Y_f(k) \tag{A6.11}$$

It is easy to see that

$$H(N-k) = j[H(k)]^* \tag{A6.12}$$

where * implies complex conjugation. In view of Eq. (A6.12), we can evaluate

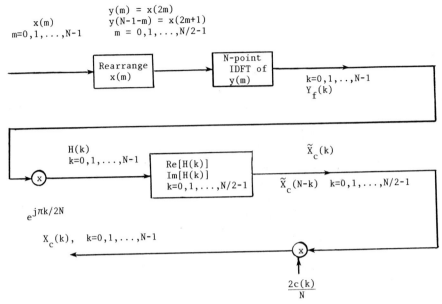

Fig. A6.3. Computation of an N-point DCT using an N-point IDFT.

$\tilde{X}_c(k)$ in Eq. (A6.9) by computing $H(k)$ for $k = 0, 1, \ldots, N/2$ as follows:

$$\tilde{X}_c(k) = \text{Re}[H(k)]$$

$$\tilde{X}_c(N - k) = \text{Im}[H(k)], \qquad k = 0, 1, \ldots, \frac{N}{2}$$

(A6.13)

The operations described by Eqs. (A6.7)–(A6.13) imply that an N-point DCT of $x(m)$ can be implemented by an N-point IDFT of a sequence $y(m)$ rearranged from $x(m)$, followed by a complex multiplication and extraction of the real and imaginary parts. If N is an integer power of 2 (i.e., $N = 2^L$), then the IDFT can be implemented by a radix-2 FFT [1]. Otherwise other fast algorithms such as the Winogard Fourier transform algorithm (WFTA) [47], prime factor algorithm (PFA) [48, 49], recursive cyclotomic factorization algorithm (RCFA) [50], radix-3 [51], radix-6 [52], and mixed radix algorithms can be used. The fast DCT algorithm described by Eqs. (A6.7)–(A6.13) is illustrated in Fig. A6.3.

APPENDIX B. DCT CALCULATION USING AN FFT

The following computer program implements Eq. (A6.1) in Appendix A by means of a FFT.

```
C     ***************************************************************
C     THIS PROGRAM IS TO FIND THE DCT MATRIX DCT(32,32) AND ITS TRANSPOSE
C     TDCT(32,32).THEN THE TEST DATA IORG(32,32) IS MULTIPLIED IN THE FORM
C     [DCT]*[IORG]*[TDCT] TO GET THE TRANSFORMED DATA TRORG(32,32) OR IF THE
C     TRANSFORMED DATA TRORG(32,32) IS THERE THE PROGRAM WILL INVERSE
C     TRANSFORM IT BY [TDCT]*[TRORG]*[DCT] TO GET THE ORIGINAL TEST DATA.
C     IN THE PROGRAM M IS THE ORDER OF THE MATRICES AND INV WHICH IS A
C     LOGICAL VARIABLE DECIDES WETHER TO PERFORM FORWARD OR INVERSE TRANSFORM
C     IF INV=.TRUE. THEN FORWARD TRANSFORM IS CARRIED OUT AND IF INV=.FALSE.
C     THEN INVERSE TRANSFORM IS CARRIED OUT.
C     THIS PROGRAM CAN TRANSFORM DATA OF 8X8,16X16,32X32 MATRICES.
C     ***************************************************************
C
C     ------------------------------------------------------------------
C     THIS PART OF THE PROGRAM GENERATES THE DCT MATRIX DCT(32,32) AND THE
C     TRANSPOSE OF THE DCT MATRIX TDCT(32,32)
C     ------------------------------------------------------------------
      LOGICAL INV
      DIMENSION IORG(33,32),DCT(32,32),TDCT(32,32),TRORG(32,32),TRORG1(32,32)
      DIMENSION TRC(32,32),TRO1(32,32),DCTI(32,32),TDCTI(32,32)
      M=4
      INV=.FALSE.
      PI=3.1415927
      RM=FLOAT(M)
      DO 15 J=1,M
      DCT(1,J)=SQRT(1.0/RM)
15    TDCT(J,1)=DCT(1,J)
      DO 20 I=2,M
      DO 20 J=1,M
      RI=FLOAT(I)
      RJ=FLOAT(J)
      DCT(I,J)=(SQRT(2.0/RM))*COS(2.0*PI*(2.0*RJ-1)*(RI-1)/(4.0*RM))
      TDCT(J,I)=DCT(I,J)
20    CONTINUE
      OPEN(UNIT=7,FILE='ORT.DAT',STATUS='NEW')
      DO 21 I=1,M
      WRITE(7,41)(DCT(I,J),J=1,M)
41    FORMAT(<M>(F11.6))
21    CONTINUE
      DO 25 I=1,M
      DO 25 J=1,M
      DCTI(I,J)=DCT(I,J)/(SQRT(2.0/RM))
      TDCTI(I,J)=TDCT(I,J)/(SQRT(2.0/RM))
      DCT(I,J)=DCT(I,J)*SQRT(2.0/RM)
      TDCT(I,J)=TDCT(I,J)*SQRT(2.0/RM)
25    CONTINUE
C     ------------------------------------------------------------------
C     IF INV IS TRUE THE FORWARD TRANSFORM IS CARRIED OUT
C     ------------------------------------------------------------------
      IF(INV.EQ.FALSE) GO TO 100
C     ------------------------------------------------------------------
C     THIS PART OF THE PROGRAM CARRIES OUT THE FORWARD TRANSFORM IN THE FORM
C     [DCT]*[IORG]*[TDCT]=[TRORG]
C     ------------------------------------------------------------------
      OPEN(UNIT=1,FILE='TEST.DAT',STATUS='OLD')
      DO 30 I=1,M
      READ(1,31) (IORG(I,J),J=1,M)
31    FORMAT(<M>(I2,2X))
30    CONTINUE
      IF(INV.EQ.FALSE) GO TO 100
```

```
           DO 50 K=1,M
           DO 50 N=1,M
           TRORG1(K,N)=0.0
           DO 50 J=1,M
           TRORG1(K,N)=TRORG1(K,N)+DCT(K,J)*IORG(J,N)
50         CONTINUE
           DO 51 K=1,M
           DO 51 N=1,M
           TRORG(K,N)=0.0
           DO 51 J=1,M
           TRORG(K,N)=TRORG(K,N)+TRORG1(K,J)*TDCT(J,N)
51         CONTINUE
           OPEN(UNIT=2,FILE='INV.DAT',STATUS='NEW')
           DO 52 I=1,M
           WRITE(2,53)(TRORG(I,J),J=1,M)
53         FORMAT(<M>(F11.6,2X))
52         CONTINUE
           GO TO 500
C          ------------------------------------------------------------------
C          THIS PART OF THE PROGRAM DOES THE INVERSE TRANSFORM IN THE FORM
C          [TDCT]*[TRORG]*[DCT] IF INV=FALSE
C          ------------------------------------------------------------------
100        OPEN(UNIT=3,FILE='INV.DAT',STATUS='OLD')
           DO 60 I=1,M
           READ(3,61)(TRORG(I,J),J=1,M)
61         FORMAT(<M>(F11.6,2X))
60         CONTINUE
           DO 70 K=1,M
           DO 70 N=1,M
           TRO1(K,N)=0.0
           DO 70 J=1,M
           TRO1(K,N)=TRO1(K,N)+TDCTI(K,J)*TRORG(J,N)
70         CONTINUE
           DO 71 K=1,M
           DO 71 N=1,M
           TRO(K,N)=0.0
           DO 71 J=1,M
           TRO(K,N)=TRO(K,N)+TRO1(K,J)*DCTI(J,N)
71         CONTINUE
           OPEN(UNIT=5,FILE='COMP.DAT',STATUS='NEW')
           DO 120 I=1,M
           WRITE(5,130)(TRO(I,J),J=1,M)
130        FORMAT(<M>(F11.6,2X))
120        CONTINUE
500        CONTINUE
           STOP
           END
```

APPENDIX C. WALSH–HADAMARD COMPUTER PROGRAM

```
C        THIS SUBROUTINE COMPUTES THE FORWARD HADAMARD TRANSFORM      C
C        OF ORDER 16.                                                 C
C        X = DATA VECTOR OF LENGTH 16.   ON RETURN X WILL BE THE      C
C        TRANSFORMED VECTOR.                                          C
C        Y = AN AUXILIARY VECTOR OF LENGTH 16.                        C
C                                                                     C

         DIMENSION X(16), Y(16)
         DO 1 I = 1, 15, 2
         Y(I) = X(I) + X(I + 1)
   1     Y(I+1) = X(I) - X(I+1)
         DO 2 I = 1, 2
         X(I) = Y(I) + Y(I+2)
         X(I+2) = Y(I) - Y(I+2)
         X(I+4) = Y(I+4) + Y(I+6)
         X(I+6) = Y(I+4) - Y(I+6)
         X(I+8) = Y(I+8) + Y(I+10)
         X(I+10) = Y(I+8) - Y(I+10)
         X(I+12) = Y(I+12)+Y(I+14)
   2     X(I+14) = Y(I+12) - Y(I+14)
         DO 3 I=1, 4
         Y(I) = X(I) + X(I+4)
         Y(I+4) = X(I) - X(I+4)
         Y(I+8) = X(I+8) + X(I+12)
   3     Y(I+12) = X(I+8) - X(I+12)
         DO 4 I=1, 8
         X(I) = (Y(I) + Y(I+8))/16.0
   4     X(I+8) = (Y(I) - Y(I+8))/16.0
         RETURN
         END
```

REFERENCES

1. J. W. Cooley and J. W. Tukey, An algorithm for the machine calculation of complex Fourier series, *Math. Comput.* **19**, 297–301 (1965).
2. J. L. Walsh, A closed set of normal orthogonal functions, *Am. J. Math.* **55**, 5–24 (1923).
3. H. Haar, Zur theori der orthogonalen funktionen-systeme, *Math. Ann.* **69**, 331–371 (1910).
4. N. Ahmed, T. Natarajan, and K. R. Rao, Discrete cosine transform, *IEEE Trans. Comput.* **C-23**, 90–93 (1974).
5. H. Reitboeck and T. P. Brody, A transformation with invariance under cyclic permutation for applications in pattern recognition, *Informat. and Cont.* **15**, 130–154 (1969).
6. A. K. Jain, A fast Karhunen–Loeve transform for a class of random processes, *IEEE Trans. Commun.* **COM-24**, 1023–1029 (1976).
7. D. F. Elliott and K. R. Rao, *Fast Transforms: Algorithms, Analyses, and Applications*, Academic Press, New York, 1982.
8. P. A. Devijer and J. Kittler, *Pattern Recognition: A Statistical Approach*, Prentice-Hall, London 1982.
9. A. K. Jain, A fast KLT for digital restoration of images degraded by white and colored noise, *IEEE Trans. Comput.* **C-26**, 560–571 (1977).
10. H. Kitajima, A symmetric cosine transform, *IEEE Trans. Comput.* **C-29**, 317–323 (1980).
11. Z. Wang, Fast algorithms for the discrete W transforms and for the discrete Fourier transforms, *IEEE Trans. Acoust. Speech, Signal Process.* **ASSP-32**, 803–816 (1984).

12. R. M. Haralick, A storage efficient way to implement the discrete cosine transform, *IEEE Trans. Comput.* **C-25,** 764–765 (1976).

13. W. H. Chen, C. H. Smith and S. C. Fralick, A fast computational algorithm for the discrete cosine transform, *IEEE Trans. Commun.* **COM-25,** 1004–1009 (1977).

14. B. G. Lee, FCT—A fast cosine transform, Proc. ICASSP-84, 28.A.3.2–28.A.3.3, San Diego, Calif. Also published in *IEEE Trans. Acoust. Speech Signal Process.* **ASSP-32,** 1243–1245 (1984).

15. P. Yip and K. R. Rao, Fast DIT algorithms for a family of discrete cosine and sine transforms, *Circuits, Systems Signal Process Circuits, Systems, and Signal Processing* **3,** 387–408 (1984).

16. H. Whitehouse *et al.*, A digital real-time intraframe video bandwidth compression system, Twenty-first SPIE Int. Tech. Symp., San Diego, Calif., pp. 64–78.

17. H. B. Kekre and J. K. Solanki, Comparative performance of various unitary trigonometric transforms for transform image coding, *Int. J. Electron.* **44,** 305–315 (1978).

18. P. Yip and K. R. Rao, Sparse-matrix factorization of discrete sine transform, *IEEE Trans. Commun.* **COM-28,** 304–307 (1980).

19. N. Ahmed, K. R. Rao, and A. L. Abdussattar, BIFORE or Hadamard transform, *IEEE Trans. Audio Electroacoust.* **AU-19,** 225–234 (1971).

20. J. E. Shore, On the application of Haar functions, *IEEE Trans. Commun.* **COM-21,** 109–216 (1973).

21. R. T. Lynch and J. J. Reis, Haar transform image coding, *Proc. Natl. Telecommun. Conf.*, Dallas, 1976, 44.3-1–44.3-5.

22. H. Enomoto and K. Shibata, Orthogonal transform coding system for television signals, *Proc. Symp. Appl. Walsh Functions*, 1971, pp. 11–17.

23. H. S. Kwak, R. Srinivasan and K. R. Rao, C-matrix transform, *IEEE Trans. Acoust. Speech Signal Process.* **ASSP-31,** 1304–1307 (1983).

24. H. F. Harmuth, *Transmission of Information by Orthogonal Functions*, 2nd ed., Springer-Verlag, New York, 1972.

25. H. F. Harmuth, *Sequency Theory: Foundations and Applications*, Academic Press, New York, 1977.

26. H. Rademacher, Einige sätze von allgemeinen orthogonalfunktionen, *Math. Ann.* **87,** 122–138 (1922).

27. M. Magus, *Applied Walsh analysis*, Heydon, Philadelphia, 1981.

28. P. Yip and K. R. Rao, Energy packing efficiency for generalized discrete transforms, *IEEE Trans. Commun.* **COM-26,** 1257–1262 (1978).

29. H. W. Jones, Jr., D. N. Hein, and S. L. Knauer, The Karhunen–Loève, discrete cosine, and related transforms obtained via the Hadamard transform, *Int. Telemeter. Conf.*, Los Angeles, Calif., 1978, pp. 87–98.

30. H. Kitai and K. Siemens, Discrete transform via Walsh transform, *IEEE Trans. Acoust. Speech Signal Process.* **ASSP-27,** 288 (1979).

31. N. Ahmed and K. R. Rao, Convolution and correlation using binary Fourier representation, *First Ann. Proc. Houston Conf. Circuits Systems and Comput.*, Houston, 1969, pp. 182–191.

32. N. Ahmed, T. Natarajan, and K. R. Rao, Cooley–Tukey type algorithm for the Haar transform, *Electron.* Letters **9,** 276–278 (1973).

33. N. Ahmed and M. C. Chen, A Cooley–Tukey algorithm for the slant transform, *Int. J. Comput. Math. Sect. B* **5,** 331–338 (1976).

34. V. Vlasenko, K. R. Rao, and V. Devarajan, Unified matrix treatment of discrete transforms, *IEEE Trans. Comput.* **C-28,** 934–938 (1979).

35. K. R. Rao, J. G. K. Kuo, and M. A. Narasimhan, Slant–Haar transform, *Int. J. Comput. Math. Sect. B* **7,** 73–83 (1979).

36. K. R. Rao *et. al.*, Hadamard–Haar transform, *Sixth Ann. Southeastern Symp. on Syst. Theory*, Session 5-A, Baton Rouge, La., 1974.

37. D. J. Conor and J. O. Limb, Properties of frame-difference signals generated by moving images, *IEEE Trans. Commun.* **COM-24,** 1023–1029 (1976).

38. H. C. Andrews, *An Introduction to Mathematical Techniques in Pattern Recognition*, Wiley, New York, 1972.

39. H. Kitajima, Energy packing efficiency of Hadamard transforms, *IEEE Trans. Commun.* **COM-24,** 1256–1258 (1976).

40. Hamidi and T. Pearl, Comparison of the cosine and Fourier transforms of Markov-1 signals, *IEEE Trans. Acoust. Speech Signal Process.* **ASSP-24,** 428–429 (1976).

41. C. W. Hellstrom, Image restoration by method of least squares, *J. Opt. Soc. Amer.* **57,** 297–303 (1967).

42. W. K. Pratt, Generalized Wienner filtering computation techniques, *IEEE Trans. Comput.* **C-21,** 636–641 (1972).

43. Z. Wang and B. R. Hunt, Comparative performance of two different versions of discrete cosine transforms, *IEEE Trans. Acoust. Speech, Signal Process.* **ASSP-32,** 450–453 (1984).

44. N. Ahmed and K. R. Rao, *Orthogonal Transforms for Digital Signal Processing*, Springer-Verlag, New York, 1975.

45. H. J. Nussbaumer, Relative evaluation of various number theoretic transforms for digital filtering applications, *IEEE Trans. Acoust. Speech Signal Process.* **ASSP-26,** 88–93 (1978).

46. M. J. Narasimha and A. M. Peterson, On the computation of discrete cosine transform, *IEEE Trans. Commun.* **COM-26,** 934–936 (1978).

47. S. Winogard, On computing the discrete Fourier transform, *Math. Comput.* **32,** 175–199 (1978).

48. D. P. Kolba and T. W. Parks, A prime factor FFT algorithm using high speed convolution, *IEEE Trans. Acoust. Speech, Signal Process.* **ASSP-25,** 281–994 (August 1977).

49. C. S. Burrus and P. W. Eschenbacher, An in-place, in-order prime factor FFT algorithm, *IEEE Trans. Accoust. Speech, Signal Process.* **ASSP-29,** 806–816 (August 1981).

50. J. B. Martens, Recursive cyclotomic factorization—A new algorithm for calculating the discrete Fourier transform, *IEEE Trans. Acoust. Speech, Signal Process.* **ASSP-32,** 750–761 (August 1984).

51. E. Dubois and A. N. Venetsanopoulos, A new algorithm for the radix-3 FFT, *IEEE Trans. Acoust. Speech, Signal Process.* **ASSP-26,** 222–225 (1979).

52. S. P. Prakash and V. V. Rao, A new radix-6 FFT algorithm, *IEEE Trans. Acoust. Speech, Signal Process.* **ASSP-29,** 939–941 (August 1981).

Chapter 7

Fast Fourier Transforms

DOUGLAS F. ELLIOTT
Rockwell International Corporation
Anaheim, California 92803

INTRODUCTION   I

The fast Fourier transform (FFT) computes the discrete Fourier transform (DFT) using a greatly reduced number of arithmetic operations as compared to brute-force evaluation of the DFT [1–5]. The method is efficient because it eliminates redundancies that result from adding certain data sequence values after they have been multiplied by the same factors of fixed complex constants during the evaluation of different DFT transform coefficients. The efficiency is achieved at the expense of reordering the data sequence and/or transform sequence, but the additional expense is generally small compared to the reduction in multiplications and additions. For example, the reduction in arithmetic using a radix-2 FFT is about $N/\log_2 N$, which for $N = 1024 = 2^{10}$ is 100, so hardware could be reduced by approximately a factor of 100 by using an FFT to compute a 1024-point DFT that continuously processes acoustic, sonar, or other data in real time.

As mentioned in Chapter 1, Fourier announced in 1807 that he had developed a method of representing an arbitrary function as a series. Consequently, the Fourier transform, DFT, and FFT bear his name. However, as Heideman *et al.* [6]† point out,

> In a recently published history of numerical analysis H. H. Goldstine attributes to Carl Friedrich Gauss, the eminent mathematician, an algorithm similar to the FFT for the computation of the coefficients of finite Fourier series. Gauss' treatise describing the algorithm was not published in his lifetime; it appeared only in his collected works as an unpublished manuscript. The presumed year of the composition of this treatise is 1805,

† © 1985 IEEE.

HANDBOOK OF DIGITAL SIGNAL PROCESSING

thereby suggesting that efficient algorithms for evaluating coefficients of Fourier series were developed at least a century earlier than had been thought previously. If this year is accurate, it predates Fourier's 1807 work on harmonic analysis.

Gauss used normal and digit-reversed number representations to obtain his FFT. In this chapter we shall use the same technique as well as several other techniques for representing integers. We shall also exploit a two-dimensional (2-D) aspect of the number representation to visualize 1-D DFTs as 2-D structures. The 2-D aspect can be extended to an L-D representation, but it is usually simpler to concatenate flow diagrams derived from 2-D developments. Matrix representations often aid in the understanding of FFTs, and we use them freely.

The next section reviews 1-D and 2-D DFTs and explains our matrix notation. The following sections derive FFTs. The first FFTs result from a mixed-radix integer representation (MIR) that includes binary, decimal, octal, etc., integers and is more familiar to engineers than the name might indicate. One FFT that follows from the MIR is the radix-2 FFT discovered by Cooley and Tukey [7] which was the first to gain wide usage. Radix-3, -4, and -6 FFTs also result from the MIR.

Integer representations with the exotic names of Chinese remainder theorem (CRT) and Ruritanian correspondence (RC) are used to derive N-point FFTs, where N is the product of relatively prime integers (e.g., $N = 3 \cdot 5 \cdot 7$, $5 \cdot 16 \cdot 3$, etc). The FFTs are therefore "prime factor" algorithms (PFAs) that include Good's FFT [8,9] and the Winograd Fourier transform algorithm (WFTA) [10].

The number of arithmetic operations required to compute various FFT algorithms is compared later in the chapter. This comparison is not the final word in efficiency, since data transfers for some of the FFTs may be significantly higher and may negate gains due to reduction of arithmetic.

Many real-time FFTs are mechanized with dedicated, fixed-point hardware. Determining the number of bits to fully utilize these FFT processors is discussed at the end of this chapter. A simple, easy to visualize graphical technique is presented to specify digital word lengths in a typical spectral analysis system.

Several appendixes are included. Appendix A gives small-N DFTs to implement the PFAs. Appendix B lists sources of other relevant FFT programs. Appendix C gives some radix-2 FFTs that satisfy many requirements for an FFT. Appendixes D and E present two program listings for efficient implementation of the PFA.

II DFTS AND DFT REPRESENTATIONS

Discrete Fourier transforms and their properties are discussed in Chapter 1, Section VII. In this section we repeat the definition of 1-D and 2-D DFTs, present 2-D flow diagrams and the equivalent operations in matrix format, and discuss DFT and FFT matrix representation.

We shall represent the 1-D DFT in vector–matrix notation and, by rearranging the matrix, shall end up with a matrix factorization leading to the FFT. Let $x(n)$ be a 1-D data sequence defined for $n = 0, 1, 2, \ldots, N - 1$. Then the N-point 1-D DFT is defined by [see Eq. (1.76)]

$$X(k) = \sum_{n=0}^{N-1} x(n) W_N^{kn}, \qquad W_N = e^{-j2\pi/N}, \, k = 0, 1, 2, \ldots, N - 1 \qquad (7.1)$$

where $X(k)$ is the transform sequence. For example, if $N = 8$, $W_8 = e^{-j2\pi/8}$ and $\mathbf{x} = (x(0), x(1), x(2), \ldots, x(7))^T$. Then Eq. (7.1) gives

$$
\begin{aligned}
X(0) &= (W^0 \quad W^0 \quad W^0 \quad W^0 \quad W^0 \quad W^0 \quad W^0 \quad W^0)\mathbf{x} \\
X(1) &= (W^0 \quad W^1 \quad W^2 \quad W^3 \quad W^4 \quad W^5 \quad W^6 \quad W^7)\mathbf{x} \\
X(2) &= (W^0 \quad W^2 \quad W^4 \quad W^6 \quad W^0 \quad W^2 \quad W^4 \quad W^6)\mathbf{x} \\
&\vdots \\
X(7) &= (W^0 \quad W^7 \quad W^6 \quad W^5 \quad W^4 \quad W^3 \quad W^2 \quad W^1)\mathbf{x}
\end{aligned}
\qquad (7.2)
$$

All of the operations in Eq. (7.2) can be combined into the matrix form

$$\mathbf{X} = W^{\mathbf{E}}\mathbf{x} = \mathbf{Dx} \qquad (7.3)$$

where $\mathbf{X} = (X(0), X(1), X(2), \ldots, X(7))^T$, $\mathbf{D} = W^{\mathbf{E}}$ is the $N \times N$ DFT matrix with row numbers $k = 0, 1, 2, \ldots, N - 1$ and column numbers $n = 0, 1, 2, \ldots, N - 1$, and the entry $W^{E(k,n)}$ is in row k and column n. For example, if $N = 8$, then $\mathbf{E}$ and $W^{\mathbf{E}}$ are given by

$$
\mathbf{E} =
\begin{array}{c}
k \diagdown n \\
0 \\ 1 \\ 2 \\ 3 \\ 4 \\ 5 \\ 6 \\ 7
\end{array}
\begin{array}{c}
0 \; 1 \; 2 \; 3 \; 4 \; 5 \; 6 \; 7 \\
\begin{bmatrix}
0 & 0 & 0 & 0 & 0 & 0 & 0 & 0 \\
0 & 1 & 2 & 3 & 4 & 5 & 6 & 7 \\
0 & 2 & 4 & 6 & 0 & 2 & 4 & 6 \\
0 & 3 & 6 & 1 & 4 & 7 & 2 & 5 \\
0 & 4 & 0 & 4 & 0 & 4 & 0 & 4 \\
0 & 5 & 2 & 7 & 4 & 1 & 6 & 3 \\
0 & 6 & 4 & 2 & 0 & 6 & 4 & 2 \\
0 & 7 & 6 & 5 & 4 & 3 & 2 & 1
\end{bmatrix}
\end{array}
= ((kn) \bmod N) \qquad (7.4)
$$

$$
W^{\mathbf{E}} =
\begin{bmatrix}
W^0 & W^0 & W^0 & W^0 & W^0 & W^0 & W^0 & W^0 \\
W^0 & W^1 & W^2 & W^3 & W^4 & W^5 & W^6 & W^7 \\
W^0 & W^2 & W^4 & W^6 & W^0 & W^2 & W^4 & W^6 \\
W^0 & W^3 & W^6 & W^1 & W^4 & W^7 & W^2 & W^5 \\
W^0 & W^4 & W^0 & W^4 & W^0 & W^4 & W^0 & W^4 \\
W^0 & W^5 & W^2 & W^7 & W^4 & W^1 & W^6 & W^3 \\
W^0 & W^6 & W^4 & W^2 & W^0 & W^6 & W^4 & W^2 \\
W^0 & W^7 & W^6 & W^5 & W^4 & W^3 & W^2 & W^1
\end{bmatrix}
\qquad (7.5)
$$

where $\mathbf{A} = (a(k, n))$ means a matrix with elements $a(k, n)$.

In the future, we shall often tag rows and columns of an E matrix with k and n values, as shown in Eq. (7.4), to clarify rearrangements of the matrix that lead to FFT algorithms. We shall find that FFTs are represented by factored matrices. As an example of an FFT in matrix form, let

$$W^{\mathbf{E}} = W^{\mathbf{E}_2} W^{\mathbf{E}_1} \tag{7.6}$$

and let $N = 4$, $W = \exp(-j2\pi/4) = -j$,

$$\mathbf{E}_2 = \begin{bmatrix} 0 & 0 & -j\infty & -j\infty \\ 0 & 2 & -j\infty & -j\infty \\ -j\infty & -j\infty & 0 & 0 \\ -j\infty & -j\infty & 0 & 2 \end{bmatrix}$$

and

$$\mathbf{E}_1 = \begin{bmatrix} 0 & -j\infty & 0 & -j\infty \\ -j\infty & 0 & -j\infty & 0 \\ 0 & -j\infty & 2 & -j\infty \\ -j\infty & 1 & -j\infty & 3 \end{bmatrix}$$

$$\tag{7.7}$$

Then

$$W^{\mathbf{E}_2} = \begin{bmatrix} 1 & 1 & 0 & 0 \\ 1 & -1 & 0 & 0 \\ 0 & 0 & 1 & 1 \\ 0 & 0 & 1 & -1 \end{bmatrix} \quad \text{and} \quad W^{\mathbf{E}_1} = \begin{bmatrix} 1 & 0 & 1 & 0 \\ 0 & 1 & 0 & 1 \\ 1 & 0 & -1 & 0 \\ 0 & -j & 0 & j \end{bmatrix} \tag{7.8}$$

since $W^{-j\infty} = e^{-j2\pi/4(-j\infty)} = e^{-\infty} = 0$. Matrices like Eq. (7.8) are called *sparse matrices* because of the zero entries that become more numerous as N increases. Substituting Eq. (7.8) in Eq. (7.6) yields

$$W^{\mathbf{E}} = W^{\mathbf{E}_2} W^{\mathbf{E}_1} = \begin{bmatrix} 1 & 1 & 1 & 1 \\ 1 & -1 & 1 & -1 \\ 1 & -j & -1 & j \\ 1 & j & -1 & -j \end{bmatrix} \tag{7.9}$$

where

$$\mathbf{E} = \begin{array}{c} \\ k \end{array} \!\! \begin{array}{c} n \\ \begin{array}{cccc} 0 & 1 & 2 & 3 \end{array} \\ \begin{array}{c} 0 \\ 2 \\ 1 \\ 3 \end{array} \!\! \begin{bmatrix} 0 & 0 & 0 & 0 \\ 0 & 2 & 0 & 2 \\ 0 & 1 & 2 & 3 \\ 0 & 3 & 2 & 1 \end{bmatrix} \end{array} \tag{7.10}$$

which is the $\mathbf{E}$ matrix of a 4-point DFT with a different ordering (called bit reversed order) of the rows.

The matrices in Eq. (7.7) have many $-j\infty$ entries. In the future, instead of making these entries we shall use the shorthand notation that a dot (no entry) in row k and column n of E means $-j\infty$. In the matrix $W^{\mathbf{E}}$ the corresponding entry in row k and column n is $W^{-j\infty} = (e^{-j2\pi/N})^{-j\infty} = e^{-\infty} = 0$. For example, in shorthand notation Eq. (7.7) is written

$$
\mathbf{E}_2 = \begin{bmatrix} 0 & 0 & \cdot & \cdot \\ 0 & 2 & \cdot & \cdot \\ \cdot & \cdot & 0 & 0 \\ \cdot & \cdot & 0 & 2 \end{bmatrix} \quad \text{and} \quad \mathbf{E}_1 = \begin{bmatrix} 0 & \cdot & 0 & \cdot \\ \cdot & 0 & \cdot & 0 \\ 0 & \cdot & 2 & \cdot \\ \cdot & 1 & \cdot & 3 \end{bmatrix} \tag{7.11}
$$

Taking the matrix product $W^{\mathbf{E}} = W^{\mathbf{E}_2} W^{\mathbf{E}_1}$ gives

$$
W^{\mathbf{E}} = \begin{bmatrix} W^0 & W^0 & 0 & 0 \\ W^0 & W^2 & 0 & 0 \\ 0 & 0 & W^0 & W^0 \\ 0 & 0 & W^0 & W^2 \end{bmatrix} \begin{bmatrix} W^0 & 0 & W^0 & 0 \\ 0 & W^0 & 0 & W^0 \\ W^0 & 0 & W^2 & 0 \\ 0 & W^1 & 0 & W^3 \end{bmatrix}
$$

$$
= \begin{bmatrix} W^{0+0} & W^{0+0} & W^{0+0} & W^{0+0} \\ W^{0+0} & W^{0+2} & W^{0+0} & W^{0+2} \\ W^{0+0} & W^{0+1} & W^{0+2} & W^{0+3} \\ W^{0+0} & W^{1+2} & W^{0+2} & W^{2+3} \end{bmatrix} \tag{7.12}
$$

The factorization of $W^{\mathbf{E}_2}$ is such that only the nonzero entry per row of $W^{\mathbf{E}_2}$ is multiplied by a nonzero entry of any column of $W^{\mathbf{E}_1}$ using the row-times-column rule of matrix multiplication. The matrix multiplication becomes addition when applied to the exponents; since $e^a e^b = e^{a+b}$, each entry in E is the sum of two exponents, so

$$
\mathbf{E} = \begin{bmatrix} 0+0 & 0+0 & 0+0 & 0+0 \\ 0+0 & 0+2 & 0+0 & 0+2 \\ 0+0 & 0+1 & 0+2 & 0+3 \\ 0+0 & 1+2 & 0+2 & 2+3 \end{bmatrix} \tag{7.13}
$$

We shall let the shorthand notation

$$
\mathbf{E} = \mathbf{E}_2 \ddagger \mathbf{E}_1 \tag{7.14}
$$

mean the matrix derived using $\mathbf{E}_1$ and $\mathbf{E}_2$. For example, $W^{\mathbf{E}} = W^{\mathbf{E}_2} W^{\mathbf{E}_1}$ in Eq. (7.12) is equivalent to

$$
\mathbf{E} = \begin{bmatrix} 0 & 0 & \cdot & \cdot \\ 0 & 2 & \cdot & \cdot \\ \cdot & \cdot & 0 & 0 \\ \cdot & \cdot & 0 & 2 \end{bmatrix} \ddagger \begin{bmatrix} 0 & \cdot & 0 & \cdot \\ \cdot & 0 & \cdot & 0 \\ 0 & \cdot & 2 & \cdot \\ \cdot & 1 & \cdot & 3 \end{bmatrix} \tag{7.15}
$$

In general, when dealing with $N \times N$ FFT matrices that factor into the product of L $N \times N$ sparse matrices, we shall use the notation [2]

$$
W^{\mathbf{E}} = W^{\mathbf{E}_L} W^{\mathbf{E}_{L-1}} \cdots W^{\mathbf{E}_1} \tag{7.16}
$$

$$
\mathbf{E} = \mathbf{E}_L \ddagger \mathbf{E}_{L-1} \ddagger \cdots \ddagger \mathbf{E}_1 \tag{7.17}
$$

B 2-D DFT Matrix Representation and 2-D Processing

Similar to the 1-D DFT let $(x(n_2, n_1))$ be an $N_2 \times N_1$ 2-D data array defined for $n_1 = 0, 1, 2, \ldots, N_1 - 1$ and $n_2 = 0, 1, 2, \ldots, N_2 - 1$. Then the 2-D DFT is defined by [see Eq. (1.97)]

$$(X(k_2, k_1)) = \sum_{n_2=0}^{N_2-1} \sum_{n_1=0}^{N_1-1} (x(n_2, n_1)) W_{N_1}^{k_1 n_1} W_{N_2}^{k_2 n_2}$$

$$W_{N_i} = e^{-j2\pi/N_i}; k_i = 0, 1, 2, \ldots, N_i - 1; i = 1, 2 \qquad (7.18)$$

where $(X(k_2, k_1))$ is an $N_2 \times N_1$ transform array. The summations over n_1 and n_2 transform the rows and columns, respectively, of the matrix $(x(n_2, n_1))$. They may be done in either order, and are referred to as the row–column rule of transformation. To express this rule using matrix notation, let

$$\mathbf{D}_1 = W_1^{\mathbf{E}_1} \qquad \text{and} \qquad \mathbf{D}_2 = W_2^{\mathbf{E}_2} \qquad (7.19)$$

where $\mathbf{D}_i$ is an $N_i \times N_i$ 1-D DFT matrix and $W_i = e^{-j2\pi/N_i}$ [see (7.3)]. Then the row–column rule is equivalent to

$$(X(k_2, k_1)) = \mathbf{D}_2(x(n_2, n_1))\mathbf{D}_1^{\mathsf{T}} = \mathbf{D}_2[\mathbf{D}_1(x(n_2, n_1))^{\mathsf{T}}]^{\mathsf{T}} \qquad (7.20)$$

According to the row–column rule of matrix multiplication, the rows of D_1 transform the columns of $(x(n_2, n_1))^{\mathsf{T}} = (x(n_1, n_2))$, yielding the array $(X(k_1, n_2))$, and the rows of $\mathbf{D}_2$ transform the columns of $(X(n_2, k_1))$, yielding the array $(X(k_2, k_1))$. Since matrix multiplication is associative, it is again apparent that the rows and columns of the 2-D data array may be transformed in either order. Figure 7.1 graphically displays the 2-D processing equivalent to Eq. (7.20) for $N_1 = 3$ and $N_2 = 2$. The 3- and 2-point DFTs, $\mathbf{D}_1$ and $\mathbf{D}_2$, respectively, can be applied to the data in either order. Figure 7.1(a) shows the 2-point DFTs applied first, and 7.1(b) shows the 3-point DFTs applied first. The coordinate axes n_1 and n_2 are below the input. After the 2-point DFTs are applied along the n_2-axis, the axes are n_1 and k_2, as shown between the 2- and 3-point in DFTs Fig. 7.1(a). After the 3-point DFTs the axes are k_1 and k_2, as shown below the output in Fig. 7.1(a). Similarly, the n_1 and n_2 coordinates in Fig. 7.1(b) get transformed to k_1 and k_2, respectively.

III FFTS DERIVED FROM THE MIR

The MIR leads to N-point FFTs, where N may be integers such as $2^L, 3^L, 4^L, 6^L$, $2^L 3^M, \ldots$, etc., where $L, M, N, \ldots$, are integers [11]. This section presents a development that applies to all these cases, and some general examples. In subsequent sections we shall develop the radix-2, -3, -4, and -6 FFTs in more detail.

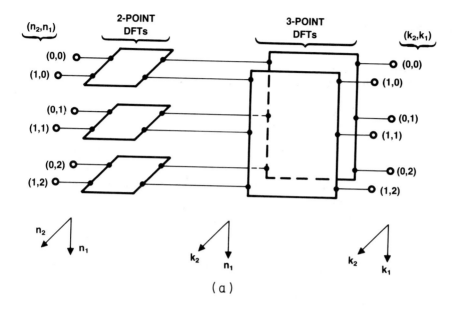

(a)

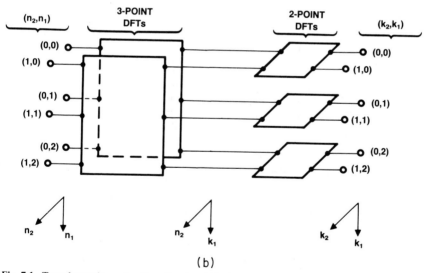

(b)

Fig. 7.1. Transformation of a (3×2)-point 2-D data array with (a) 2-point DFTs first and (b) 3-point DFTs first.

A Mixed-Radix Integer Representation

Let N_i and k_i be integers, where $0 \le k_i < N_i$, $i = 1, 2, \ldots, L$. Let $N = N_L \cdots N_2 N_1$. Then any integer k, $0 \le k < N$, has a MIR given by

$$k = k_L N_{L-1} \cdots N_2 N_1 + k_{L-1} N_{L-2} \cdots N_2 N_1$$
$$+ \cdots + k_3 N_2 N_1 + k_2 N_1 + k_1 \tag{7.21}$$

For example, if $N_i = 10$ for $i = 1, 2, \ldots$, we obtain the decimal number system. If $N_i = 2$ for all i, we obtain the binary number system, as illustrated in Table I(a) for $L = 3$. If $N_1 = 3$ and $N_2 = 4$, we get the integers in Table I(b). Rather than writing Eq. (7.21), we will let

$$k = (k_L, \ldots, k_2, k_1) \tag{7.22}$$

TABLE I

Mixed-Radix Integer Representations

		A. $N_1 = N_2 = N_3 = 2$		
k_3	k_2	k_1	k (binary)	k (decimal)
0	0	0	000	0
0	0	1	001	1
0	1	0	010	2
0	1	1	011	3
1	0	0	100	4
1	0	1	101	5
1	1	0	110	6
1	1	1	111	7

	B. $N_1 = 3$ and $N_2 = 4$		
k_2	k_1	k (MIR)	k (decimal)
0	0	00	0
0	1	01	1
0	2	02	2
1	0	10	3
1	1	11	4
1	2	12	5
2	0	20	6
2	1	21	7
2	2	22	8
3	0	30	9
3	1	31	10
3	2	32	11

mean the integer given by Eq. (7.21). To determine k_1 if we are given k, note that N_1 divides every term in the summation on the right of Eq. (7.21) except k_1. Thus, k_1 is the remainder of k divided by N_1. Likewise, k_2 is the remainder of $(k - k_1)/N_1$ divided by N_2, etc., as follows:

$$k_1 = \mathcal{R}[k/N_1], \quad k_2 = \mathcal{R}\left[\frac{k - k_1}{N_1} \middle/ N_2\right], \quad k_3 = \mathcal{R}\left[\frac{k - k_1 - k_2 N_1}{N_1 N_2} \middle/ N_3\right], \dots$$

(7.23)

where $\mathcal{R}[a/b]$ means the remainder of a divided by b.

Computing a 1-D DFT Using 2-D Processing B

We shall apply the MIR for $N = N_1 N_2$ and show that the 1-D N-point DFT can be computed using processing equivalent to 2-D processing. We demonstrate that the method leads to an FFT flow diagram for computing the N-point DFT and illustrate the processing with some simple examples. We point out that very simple matrices contain all of the required information for FFT computation.

Digit-Reversed-Order Data Sequence Index 1

Let $N = N_1 N_2$. Then Eq. (7.21) yields the integer k in *natural order* (NO):

$$k = k_2 N_1 + k_1 \triangleq (k_2, k_1)_{\text{NO}}$$

(7.24)

Furthermore, we can reverse the roles of N_1 and N_2 and express the data sequence index n in *digit-reversed order* (DRO) as

$$n = n_1 N_2 + n_2 \triangleq (n_2, n_1)_{\text{DRO}}$$

(7.25)

where $k_1, n_1 = 0, 1, \dots, N_1 - 1$ and $k_2, n_2 = 0, 1, \dots, N_2 - 1$. When using the above notations we will always let the right digit in the parentheses vary most rapidly. Note that if the subscripts 1 and 2 are switched, NO in effect becomes DRO. Table II shows the values that k and n can assume for $N_1 = 2$ and $N_2 = 3$ as well as for $N_1 = 3$ and $N_2 = 2$. The phenomena of digit reversal (bit reversal if all factors of N are 2) is evident in Table II. For example, for $n_2 = 0$ and $n_1 = 0, 1, 2$, we see that $n = 0, 2, 4$ in Table II(b), whereas for $k_2 = 0$ and $k_1 = 0, 1, 2$, Table II(b) shows that k is in normal counting order ($k = 0, 1, 2$).

Using Eqs. (7.24) and (7.25) to represent the exponent kn in Eq. (7.1) yields

$$kn \equiv k_2 n_2 N_1 + k_1 n_1 N_2 + k_1 n_2 \quad (\text{modulo } N)$$

(7.26)

The computation of kn is modulo N because exponents containing N can be set to zero, since

$$W_N^{k_2 n_1 N_1 N_2} = (e^{-j2\pi/N})^{N k_2 n_1} = 1 = W^0$$

(7.27)

TABLE II
Mixed-Radix Integer Representations of k and n

A. $N_1 = 2$ and $N_2 = 3$

k_2	k_1	k in NO (decimal)	n_2	n_1	n in DRO (decimal)
0	0	0	0	0	0
0	1	1	0	1	3
1	0	2	1	0	1
1	1	3	1	1	4
2	0	4	2	0	2
2	1	5	2	1	5

B. $N_1 = 3$ and $N_2 = 2$

k_2	k_1	k in NO (decimal)	n_2	n_1	n in DRO (decimal)
0	0	0	0	0	0
0	1	1	0	1	2
0	2	2	0	2	4
1	0	3	1	0	1
1	1	4	1	1	3
1	2	5	1	2	5

We see from Eq. (7.25) and Table II that we can obtain a summation over n by summing over n_1 for n_2 fixed, incrementing n_2, and summing again over n_1, incrementing n_2 again, etc. The summation over n is therefore equivalent to a double summation over n_1 and n_2. Using the double summation idea in Eq. (7.1) yields

$$X(k_2, k_1)_{\text{NO}} = \sum_{n_2=0}^{N_2-1} \sum_{n_1=0}^{N_1-1} x(n_2, n_1)_{\text{DRO}} W_N^{N_2 k_1 n_1} W_N^{k_1 n_2} W_N^{N_1 k_2 n_2} \qquad (7.28)$$

Noting that $W_N^{N_2} = W_{N_1 N_2}^{N_2} = W_{N_1}$, we can rewrite Eq. (7.28) as follows:

$$X(k_2, k_1)_{\text{NO}} = \sum_{n_2=0}^{N_2-1} \underbrace{\underbrace{\sum_{n_1=0}^{N_1-1} x(n_2, n_1)_{\text{DRO}} W_{N_1}^{k_1 n_1}}_{N_1\text{-point DFT}} \underbrace{W_N^{k_1 n_2}}_{\substack{\text{twiddle} \\ \text{factor}}}}_{X(n_2, k_1)} W_{N_2}^{k_2 n_2}$$

$$= \sum_{n_2=0}^{N_2-1} \underbrace{X(n_2, k_1) W_{N_2}^{k_2 n_2}}_{N_2\text{-point DFT}} \qquad (7.29)$$

where

$$X(n_2, k_1) = \left[\sum_{n_1=0}^{N_1-1} x(n_2, n_1)_{\text{DRO}} W_{N_1}^{k_1 n_1} \right] W_N^{k_1 n_2} \qquad (7.30)$$

Except for the factor $W_N^{k_1 n_2}$, known as the twiddle factor, Eq. (7.29) has the same form as a 2-D DFT [see Eq. (7.18)]. There is an input for each n_2 and n_1, and these inputs can be formatted in an $N_2 \times N_1$ 2-D array. The twiddle factor is combined with the N_1-point DFT output, giving the $N_2 \times N_1$ 2-D array $(X(n_2, k_1))$. For each value of k_1 an N_2-point DFT over the index n_2 converts the array to $(X(k_2, k_1)_{NO})$. From the $N_2 \times N_1$ array $(X(k_2, k_1)_{NO})$ we define the DFT output $X(k)$, $k = k_2 N_1 + k_1$.

Similar to Eq. (7.20), let $(x(n_2, n_1)_{DRO})$ represent the data, where the notation $(x(n_2, n_1))$ means a matrix with row numbers $n_2 = 0, 1, \ldots, N_1 - 1$. The notation $x(n_2, n_1)_{DRO}$ means that for row n_2 and column n_1 the datum in the matrix $(x(n_2, n_1)_{DRO})$ is $x(n)$, $n = n_1 N_2 + n_2$. $\mathbf{D}_1$ transforms the columns of $(x(n_2, n_1)_{DRO})$, yielding a matrix each of whose entries is multiplied by $W_N^{k_1 n_2}$. $\mathbf{D}_2$ then transforms the rows. Except for the twiddle factor these matrix operations are the same as Eq. (7.20) and may be written

$$(X(k_2, k_1)_{NO}) = \mathbf{D}_2 \{ W_N^{\text{ETF}} \circ [(x(n_2, n_1)_{DRO}) \mathbf{D}_1^T] \} \tag{7.31}$$

where W_N^{ETF} is the $N_2 \times N_1$ matrix of twiddle factors

$$W_N^{\text{ETF}} = (W_N^{k_1 n_2}) \tag{7.32}$$

and $\mathbf{A} \circ \mathbf{B} = (a_{lm} b_{lm})$; that is, $\mathbf{A} \circ \mathbf{B}$ means point-by-point multiplication of each entry in the $L \times M$ matrices $\mathbf{A} = (a_{lm})$ and $\mathbf{B} = (b_{lm})$. The operation in brackets must be performed before the point-by-point multiplication, and the matrix multiplication by $\mathbf{D}_2$ must be performed last.

We have computed a 1-D DFT, but we have used 2-D processing to do it. The result of this restructuring of the DFT is a reduction of arithmetic because smaller DFTs are computed first over one index (i.e., along one axis) and then over the other, thus eliminating redundancies in the brute-force computation over just one index (axis).

DRO Transform Sequence Index 2

Again let $N = N_1 N_2$, but let k be expressed in DRO and n in NO:

$$k = k_1 N_2 + k_2 \triangleq (k_2, k_1)_{DRO}$$
$$n = n_2 N_1 + n_1 \triangleq (n_2, n_1)_{NO} \tag{7.33}$$

In this case we obtain a DRO output given by

$$X(k_2, k_1)_{DRO} = \sum_{n_1 = 0}^{N_1 - 1} \sum_{n_2 = 0}^{N_2 - 1} x(n_2, n_1)_{NO} W_{N_2}^{k_2 n_2} W_N^{k_2 n_1} W_{N_1}^{k_1 n_1} \tag{7.34}$$

Comparing Eq. (7.34) with Eq. (7.28), we see that the order of summation is reversed. Thus, in terms of 2-D computation it is a moot point whether k or n is in DRO. However, in terms of the 2-D input and output data ordering, it is important to consider whether k or n will be in NO, since that determines whether the data or transform sequence, respectively, is in NO; the other is in DRO, unless internal formatting, discussed in Section III.E, occurs.

Similar to Eq. (7.31) we can write the 2-D processing implied by Eq. (7.34) in terms of matrices:

$$(X(k_2, k_1)_{\text{DRO}}) = \{W_N^{\text{ETF}} \circ [\mathbf{D}_2(x(n_2, n_1)_{\text{NO}})]\} \mathbf{D}_1^{\text{T}} \tag{7.35}$$

where now the input $x(n_2, n_1)_{\text{NO}}$ and the output $X(k_2, k_1)_{\text{DRO}}$ are in NO and DRO, respectively, the matrix multiplication in brackets is first, the point-by-point multiplication of the $N_2 \times N_1$ twiddle factor matrix $W_N^{\text{ETF}} = (W_N^{k_2 n_1})$ and the matrix in the brackets must be next, and the matrix multiplication by $\mathbf{D}_1^{\text{T}}$ is last.

3 DFT for $N_1 = 2$, $N_2 = 3$, and DRO Input

In this case the top line in Eq. (7.29) gives

$$X(k_2, k_1)_{\text{NO}} = \sum_{n_2=0}^{2} \sum_{n_1=0}^{1} x(n_2, n_1)_{\text{DRO}} \underbrace{\underbrace{W_2^{k_1 n_1}}_{\text{2-point DFT}} \underbrace{W_6^{k_1 n_2}}_{\substack{\text{twiddle} \\ \text{factor}}} W_3^{k_2 n_2}}_{X(n_2, k_1)}$$

$$= \sum_{n_2=0}^{2} \underbrace{X(n_2, k_1) W_3^{k_2 n_2}}_{\text{3-point DFT}} \tag{7.36}$$

Figure 7.2(a) shows the 2-D nature of the 6-point DFT [12]. The dual interpretation of k_i and n_i, $i = 1, 2$, as both indices and coordinate axes is evident in Fig. 7.2(a). The indices $k = (k_2, k_1)_{\text{NO}}$ and $n = (n_2, n_1)_{\text{DRO}}$ are in Table II(a), are in NO and DRO, respectively, and are shown in Fig. 7.2(a) along with the intermediate indices (n_2, k_1). Since

$$W_3 = e^{-j2\pi/3} = W_6^2 \tag{7.37}$$

we see that the 3-point DFT can use the same complex exponential, W_6, as the twiddle factors.

An arrow in any flow diagram indicates a multiplier whose value is shown next to the arrow. If a multiplier has unity value, the unity is not shown to simplify the diagram. Arrow heads point to summing junctions; arrows extending from a junction take the value of the sum of the inputs to the junction:

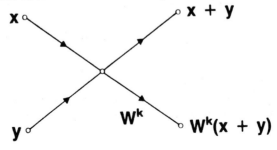

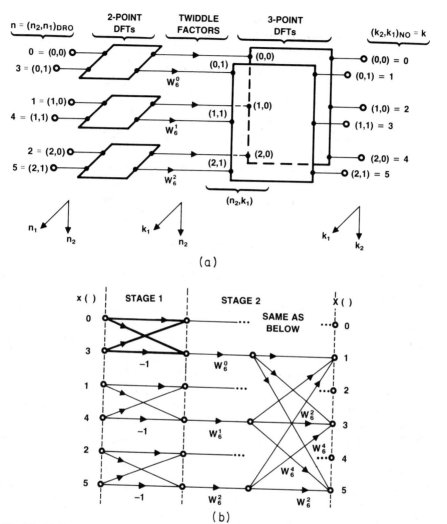

Fig. 7.2. (a) Six-point DFT reduced to 2-D processing using 2- and 3-point DFTs and twiddle factors. (b) Planar DIT FFT flow diagram for (a) with 3-point DFTs overlapping. (c) Planar DIF FFT flow diagram for (a) with 3-point DFTs separated and 2-point DFTs overlapping.

In Fig. 7.2(b) the 2-D diagram has been reduced to a planar flow diagram. The diagram shows the signal flow to compute the 2- and 3-point DFTs. For example, for a 2-point DFT with inputs $x(0)$ and $x(1)$ the outputs are

$$X(k) = \sum_{n=0}^{1} x(n) W_2^{kn} \qquad (7.38)$$

where $W_2 = -1$ and $k = 0$ or 1. Thus, $X(0) = x(0) + x(1)$ and $X(1) = x(0) - x(1)$, and the signal flow to compute the 2-point DFT simply takes the sum and difference of the inputs. The signal flow to compute the 3-point DFT is similarly

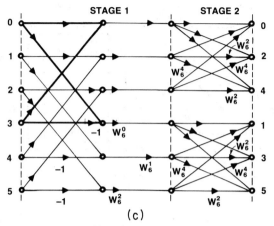

(c)

Fig. 7.2. (*Continued*)

derived. Since one 3-point DFT overlaps the other in Fig. 7.2(b), only one is shown for clarity.

Figure 7.2(c) shows Fig. 7.2(a) reduced to another planar flow diagram. This time the 3-point DFTs in Fig. 7.2(a) have been separated vertically, so the 2-point DFTs overlay. The *butterfly* shown in dark lines is the same 2-point DFT in Fig. 7.2(c) as the one shown in dark lines in Fig. 7.2(b).

Figure 7.2(b) is called a *decimation-in-time* (DIT) FFT because, going left in the 6-point DFT flow diagram, we start with an NO output and finally encounter 2-point DFTs with inputs whose indices are separated by $\frac{6}{2} = 3$. This corresponds to decimating a time sequence so as to use every third point in the 2-point DFTs. The data sequence ordering at the DIT input is $(n_2, n_1)_{\text{DRO}} = n_1 N_2 + n_2$, i.e., n_1 varies more rapidly than n_2.

Figure 7.2(c) is called a *decimation-in-frequency* (DIF) FFT because, going right in the 6-point DFT flow diagram, we start with an NO input but finally encounter 3-point DFTs with outputs whose indices are separated by $\frac{6}{3} = 2$. This corresponds to decimating a frequency sequence so as to use only every other point of the output. The transform ordering at the DIF FFT output is $(k_1, k_2)_{\text{DRO}} = k_2 N_1 + k_1$; k_2 varies more rapidly than k_1.

The FFT computation can be separated into two *stages*, as shown in Figs. 7.2(b) and (c). It is customary to show the twiddle factor at the input of a DIT stage and the output of a DIF stage [5]. From the 2-D processing viewpoint it is again a moot point as to the stage in which the twiddle factor is included.

The 6-point FFTs were derived from 2-D processing that used a DRO input and an NO output. However, when the 2-D structure in Fig. 7.2(a) is converted to 1-D structures, one structure with an NO input and another with a DRO input may be obtained. Thus, the output and input of Fig. 7.2(b) are in NO and DRO, respectively, while the reverse is true in Fig. 7.2(c). This generalizes to the interesting point that a DRO input to a 2-D structure of the type in Fig. 7.2(a) results in either a DRO or an NO FFT input, depending on how the 2-D structure is reduced to a planar diagram [see Figs. 7.2(b) and (c)].

a. 1-D Matrix Representation of the 6-Point FFT. The flow diagram in Fig. 7.2(b) is equivalent to the matrix operations

$$W^E = W^{E_2}W^{E_{TF}}W^{E_1} = W^{E_2 \ddagger E_{TF} \ddagger E_1} \tag{7.39}$$

where W^E, W^{E_2}, $W^{E_{TF}}$, and W^{E_1} are 6×6 matrices, $W = e^{-j2\pi/6}$, E_{TF} is the matrix of twiddle factors, and the matrices of exponents $E_2 \ddagger E_{TF} \ddagger E_1$ are given by

3-point DFTs

$$
\begin{array}{c}
n_2 \\
2k_2
\end{array}
\begin{array}{cccccc}
0 & 0 & 1 & 1 & 2 & 2
\end{array}
$$

$$
\begin{array}{c}
0 \\
0 \\
2 \\
2 \\
4 \\
4
\end{array}
\begin{bmatrix}
0 & \cdot & 0 & \cdot & 0 & \cdot \\
\cdot & 0 & \cdot & 0 & \cdot & 0 \\
0 & \cdot & 2 & \cdot & 4 & \cdot \\
\cdot & 0 & \cdot & 2 & \cdot & 4 \\
0 & \cdot & 4 & \cdot & 2 & \cdot \\
\cdot & 0 & \cdot & 4 & \cdot & 2
\end{bmatrix}
\ddagger
$$

twiddle factors

$$
\begin{array}{c}
k_1 \\
n_2
\end{array}
\begin{array}{cccccc}
0 & 1 & 0 & 1 & 0 & 1
\end{array}
$$

$$
\begin{array}{c}
0 \\
0 \\
1 \\
1 \\
2 \\
2
\end{array}
\begin{bmatrix}
0 & & & & & \\
& 0 & & & -j\infty & \\
& & 0 & & & \\
& & & 1 & & \\
-j\infty & & & & 0 & \\
& & & & & 2
\end{bmatrix}
$$

2-point DFTs

$$
\begin{array}{c}
n_1 \\
3k_1
\end{array}
\begin{array}{cccccc}
0 & 1 & 0 & 1 & 0 & 1
\end{array}
$$

$$
\ddagger
\begin{array}{c}
0 \\
3 \\
0 \\
3 \\
0 \\
3
\end{array}
\begin{bmatrix}
0 & 0 & & & & \\
0 & 3 & & & -j\infty & \\
& & 0 & 0 & & \\
& & 0 & 3 & & \\
-j\infty & & & & 0 & 0 \\
& & & & 0 & 3
\end{bmatrix}
\tag{7.40}
$$

where the 2-point DFTs use the complex exponentials

$$W_2^{k_1 n_1} = W_6^{3k_1 n_1} = W^{3k_1 n_1} \tag{7.41}$$

so that the transform index tag for the right matrix in Eq. (7.40) is $3k_1$ and for the left matrix $2k_2$. All entries not shown and the dots are $-j\infty$. Note that each entry other than $-j\infty$ in the matrices of exponents is the product of the data index tag above the entry's column and the transform index tag to the left of the entry's row. The matrix W^{E_1} corresponds to processing along one axis and W^{E_2} to processing along the other in the 2-D diagram in Fig. 7.2(a). The twiddle-factor matrix can be combined with either the left or the right matrix in Eq. (7.40) in the same manner that the twiddle factors can be combined with either stage 1 or stage 2 in Fig. 7.2(b). Including it with the first matrix results in some well-defined rules for generating a matrix of exponents [2].

Combining the operations in Eq. (7.40) and recalling that $k = 2k_2 + k_1$ and $n = 3n_1 + n_2$ yield

$$
\mathbf{E} =
\begin{array}{c}
\quad\overset{\displaystyle n}{\underset{k}{\diagdown}}\; 0\ \ 3\ \ 1\ \ 4\ \ 2\ \ 5 \\
\begin{array}{c}0\\1\\2\\3\\4\\5\end{array}
\left[
\begin{array}{cccccc}
0 & 0 & 0 & 0 & 0 & 0 \\
0 & 3 & 1 & 4 & 2 & 5 \\
0 & 0 & 2 & 2 & 4 & 4 \\
0 & 3 & 3 & 0 & 0 & 3 \\
0 & 0 & 4 & 4 & 2 & 2 \\
0 & 3 & 5 & 2 & 4 & 1
\end{array}
\right]
\end{array}
\tag{7.42}
$$

We see that the DIT FFT data sequence indices in Eq. (7.42) are scrambled, whereas the transform sequence indices are naturally ordered and correspond to the input and output indices in Fig. 7.2(b).

Similarly, for the DIF FFT in Fig. 7.2(c) we get

$$
\mathbf{E} =
\begin{array}{c}
\quad\overset{\displaystyle n}{\underset{k}{\diagdown}}\; 0\ \ 1\ \ 2\ \ 3\ \ 4\ \ 5 \\
\begin{array}{c}0\\2\\4\\1\\3\\5\end{array}
\left[
\begin{array}{cccccc}
0 & 0 & 0 & 0 & 0 & 0 \\
0 & 2 & 4 & 0 & 2 & 4 \\
0 & 4 & 2 & 0 & 4 & 2 \\
0 & 1 & 2 & 3 & 4 & 5 \\
0 & 3 & 0 & 3 & 0 & 3 \\
0 & 5 & 4 & 3 & 2 & 1
\end{array}
\right]
\end{array}
$$

$$
=
\begin{array}{c}
\overset{\displaystyle n_2}{\underset{2k_2}{\diagdown}}\; 0\ \ \ 1\ \ 2\ \ 0\ \ \ 1\ \ 2 \\
\begin{array}{c}0\\2\\4\\0\\2\\4\end{array}
\left[
\begin{array}{cccccc}
0 & 0 & 0 & & & \\
0 & 2 & 4 & & -j\infty & \\
0 & 4 & 2 & & & \\
& & & 0 & 0 & 0 \\
-j\infty & & & 0 & 2 & 4 \\
& & & 0 & 4 & 2
\end{array}
\right]
\end{array}
\;\overset{\ddagger}{}\;
\begin{array}{c}
\overset{\displaystyle k_1}{\underset{n_2}{\diagdown}}\; 0\ \ \ 0\ \ 0\ \ 1\ \ \ 1\ \ 1 \\
\begin{array}{c}0\\1\\2\\0\\1\\2\end{array}
\left[
\begin{array}{cccccc}
0 & & & & & \\
& 0 & & & -j\infty & \\
& & 2 & & & \\
& & & 0 & & \\
-j\infty & & & & 1 & \\
& & & & & 2
\end{array}
\right]
\end{array}
$$

$$
\overset{\ddagger}{}\;
\begin{array}{c}
\overset{\displaystyle n_1}{\underset{3k_1}{\diagdown}}\; 0\ \ 0\ \ 0\ \ 1\ \ 1\ \ 1 \\
\begin{array}{c}0\\0\\0\\3\\3\\3\end{array}
\left[
\begin{array}{cccccc}
0 & \cdot & \cdot & 0 & \cdot & \cdot \\
\cdot & 0 & \cdot & \cdot & 0 & \cdot \\
\cdot & \cdot & 0 & \cdot & \cdot & 0 \\
0 & \cdot & \cdot & 3 & \cdot & \cdot \\
\cdot & 0 & \cdot & \cdot & 3 & \cdot \\
\cdot & \cdot & 0 & \cdot & \cdot & 3
\end{array}
\right]
\end{array}
\tag{7.43}
$$

Equation (7.43) is for the DIF FFT, and we see that in this case the n index is in natural order and the k index is in scrambled order.

b. Arithmetic Operations for the 6-Point FFT. Let the input to the FFT consist of complex numbers. Then the 6-point DFT matrix in unfactored form, see for example Eq. (7.42), requires 16 complex multiplications. ($W_6^3 = -1$ and $W_6^0 = 1$ are not counted as multiplications.) The complex additions total 30. We shall next determine the number of arithmetic operations to compute the same 6-point DFT using an FFT implementation. On many computers multiplications are more time consuming than additions, so we will minimize multiplications at the expense of a few extra additions. Note that

$$W_6^4 = W_3^2 = -1 - W_3 \tag{7.44}$$

where

$$W_3 = e^{-j2\pi/3} = -\frac{1}{2} - \frac{j\sqrt{3}}{2} \tag{7.45}$$

and Eq. (7.44) is evident from Fig. 7.3(a).

The 3-point DFT in Fig. 7.2(b), (c) is redrawn in Fig. 7.3(b). Implementing each 3-point DFT as in Fig. 7.3(b) shows that the 6-point FFT is implemented with four complex multiplications, compared to 16 using a DFT. Using Eq. (7.44), we see that the multiplications by W_3^2 in Fig. 7.3(b) can be replaced by $-1 - W_3$. This substitution yields

$$X(1) = x(0) - x(2) - [x(2) - x(1)]W_3$$
$$X(2) = x(0) - x(1) + [x(2) - x(1)]W_3$$

which has the implementation in Fig. 7(c). Although Fig. 7.3(b) requires four complex multiplications, Fig. 7.3(c) requires just one.

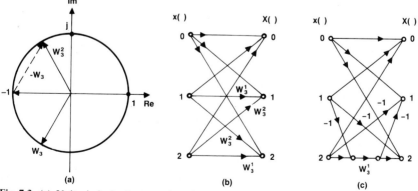

Fig. 7.3. (a) Unit circle in the complex plane showing $W_3^2 = -1 - W_3$. Three-point DFTs mechanized (b) directly and (c) using (a).

Seven complex additions are required for the 3-point DFT in Fig. 7.3(c), so the FFTs in Fig. 7.2(b), (c) require $7 + 7 + 6 = 20$ complex additions, compared to 30 using a DFT. The economy of arithmetic operations of the N-point FFT versus DFT increases rapidly as N increases.

4   DFT for $N_1 = 3$, $N_2 = 2$, and DRO Output

In this case Eq. (7.34) gives

$$X(k_2, k_1)_{\text{DRO}} = \sum_{n_1 = 0}^{2} \underbrace{\sum_{n_2 = 0}^{1} x(n_2, n_1)_{\text{NO}} \underbrace{W_2^{k_2 n_2}}_{\text{2-point DFT}} \underbrace{W_6^{k_2 n_1}}_{\substack{\text{twiddle} \\ \text{factor}}} W_3^{k_1 n_1}}$$

$$\underbrace{}_{X(k_2, n_1)}$$

$$= \underbrace{\sum_{n_1 = 0}^{2} X(k_2, n_1) W_3^{k_1 n_1}}_{\text{3-point DFT}} \qquad (7.46)$$

which is the same as Eq. (7.36) with the subscripts 1 and 2 interchanged. Figure 7.2 also applies when the subscripts 1 and 2 are interchanged and the data tags are appropriately changed. In terms of the array processing in Fig. 7.2(a), the input data is in NO and the output data is in DRO.

5   DFT for $N_1 = 3$, $N_2 = 2$, and DRO Input

Going through the same development for this case as for the previous DRO input case, in which $N_1 = 2$ and $N_2 = 3$, leads to Fig. 7.4. Figure 7.4(b), (c) show the 6-point DIF and DIT FFTs, respectively. Again $W_6 = \exp(-j2\pi/6)$, so $W_3^2 = W_6^4$, etc. Figure 7.3(c) is used to implement the 3-point DFTs in Fig. 7.4(b), (c).

The matrix of exponents for Fig. 7.4(b), $\mathbf{E} = \mathbf{E}_2 \ddagger \mathbf{E}_{\text{TF}} \ddagger \mathbf{E}_1$, is

$$\mathbf{E} = \begin{array}{c} {}^{\textstyle n} \\ k \end{array} \begin{array}{c} \begin{array}{cccccc} 0 & 1 & 2 & 3 & 4 & 5 \end{array} \\ \begin{array}{c} 0 \\ 3 \\ 1 \\ 4 \\ 2 \\ 5 \end{array} \left[\begin{array}{cccccc} 0 & 0 & 0 & 0 & 0 & 0 \\ 0 & 3 & 0 & 3 & 0 & 3 \\ 0 & 1 & 2 & 3 & 4 & 5 \\ 0 & 4 & 2 & 0 & 4 & 2 \\ 0 & 2 & 4 & 0 & 2 & 4 \\ 0 & 5 & 4 & 3 & 2 & 1 \end{array} \right] \end{array}$$

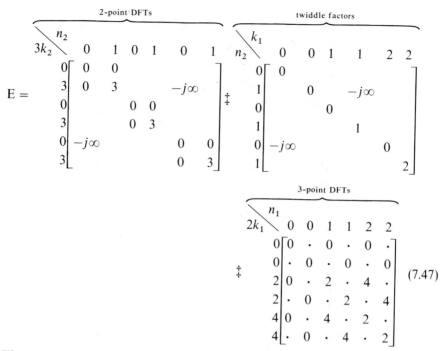

$$(7.47)$$

The transpose of the **E** matrix is equal to the **E** matrix in Eq. (7.42). Consequently, Figs. 7.2(b) and 7.4(b) are obtained from each other by *flow graph reversal* or

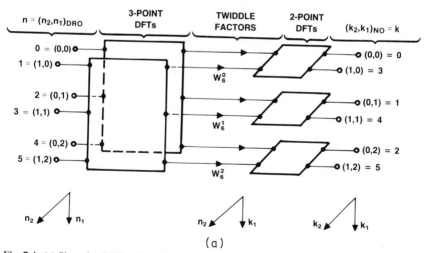

Fig. 7.4. (a) Six-point DFT reduced to 2-D processing using 3- and 2-point DFTs and twiddle factors. (b) Planar DIF FFT flow diagram for (a) with 3-point DFTs overlapping. (c) Planar DIT FFT flow diagram for (a) with 2-point DFTs overlapping.

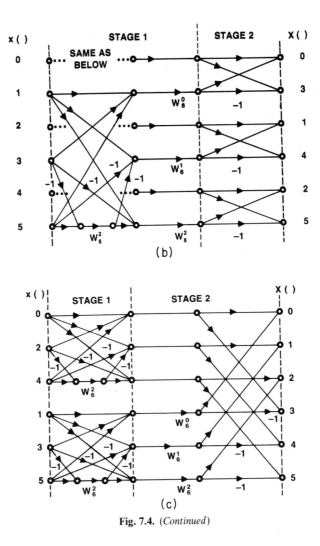

Fig. 7.4. (*Continued*)

transposition; that is, one is obtained by reversing the input, output, and direction of signal flow in the other [5].

   Figures 7.2(c) and 7.4(c) are similarly obtained from each other.

6   DFT for $N_1 = N_2 = 2$

   Figure 7.5(a) is the 2-D implementation of a 4-point DFT. Figure 7.5(b), (c) show the DIT and DIF FFTs, respectively, that result when Fig. 7.5(a) is reduced

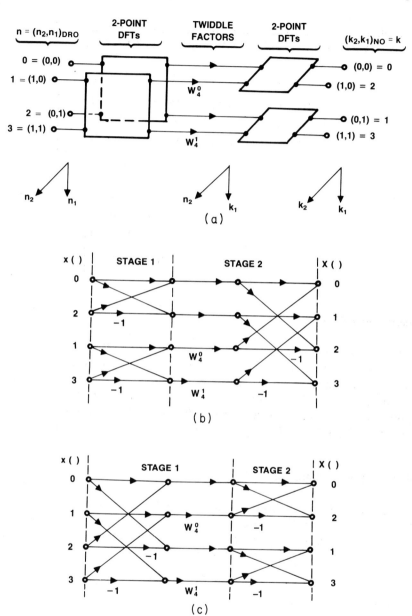

Fig. 7.5. (a) Four-point DFT reduced to 2-D processing using two 2-point DFTs and twiddle factors. (b) Planar DIT FFT flow diagram for (a) with output DFTs overlapping. (c) Planar DIF FFT flow diagram for (a) with input DFTs overlapping.

to a planar diagram. The matrix of exponents for Fig. 7.5(c) is $W^{\mathbf{E}} = W^{\mathbf{E}_2}W^{\mathbf{E}_{\mathrm{TF}}}W^{\mathbf{E}_1}$, where now $W = e^{-j2\pi/4}$ and $\mathbf{E} = \mathbf{E}_2 \ddagger \mathbf{E}_{\mathrm{TF}} \ddagger \mathbf{E}_1$ is

$$
\begin{array}{c}
\overset{\displaystyle n_2}{}\\
2k_2
\end{array}
\begin{array}{cccc}
0 & 1 & 0 & 1
\end{array}
\begin{array}{c}
0\\2\\0\\2
\end{array}
\left[
\begin{array}{cccc}
0 & 0 & & -j\infty\\
0 & 2 & & \\
-j\infty & & 0 & 0\\
& & 0 & 2
\end{array}
\right]
\ddagger
\begin{array}{c}
\overset{\displaystyle k_1}{}\\
n_2
\end{array}
\begin{array}{cccc}
0 & 0 & 1 & 1
\end{array}
\begin{array}{c}
0\\1\\0\\1
\end{array}
\left[
\begin{array}{cccc}
0 & & -j\infty & \\
& 0 & & \\
-j\infty & & 0 & \\
& & & 1
\end{array}
\right]
$$

$$
\ddagger
\begin{array}{c}
\overset{\displaystyle n_1}{}\\
2k_1
\end{array}
\begin{array}{cccc}
0 & 0 & 1 & 1
\end{array}
\begin{array}{c}
0\\0\\2\\2
\end{array}
\left[
\begin{array}{cccc}
0 & \cdot & 0 & \cdot\\
\cdot & 0 & \cdot & 0\\
0 & \cdot & 2 & \cdot\\
\cdot & 0 & \cdot & 2
\end{array}
\right]
\qquad (7.48)
$$

C Mixed-Radix FFTs

Mixed-radix FFTs result when N has factors such as $2^L 3^M$, $2 \cdot 3 \cdot 5$, etc. Figure 7.2 is an example when $N = 2 \cdot 3$. The mixed-radix FFTs can be developed by successively combining 2-D DFTs. For example, for a 15-point FFT we can use five 3-point DFTs along the n_2-axis followed by twiddle factors and three 5-point DFTs along the n_1-axis. For a 30-point FFT we can use two of the 15-point FFTs followed by twiddle factors and fifteen 2-point FFTs.

D FFTs by Matrix Transpose

We showed that implementing 6- and 4-point DFTs using 2-D processing leads to flow diagrams that correspond to the product of sparse matrices. The transpose of a matrix product leads to a new FFT. This result is very general [2, 5]. Let $W = e^{-j2\pi/N}$ and let an N-point FFT in factored form be given by

$$W^{\mathbf{E}} = W^{\mathbf{E}_L}\cdots W^{\mathbf{E}_2}W^{\mathbf{E}_1} \qquad (7.49)$$

Then another N-point FFT is

$$W^{\mathbf{E}^{\mathrm{T}}} = W^{\mathbf{E}_1^{\mathrm{T}}} W^{\mathbf{E}_2^{\mathrm{T}}}\cdots W^{\mathbf{E}_L^{\mathrm{T}}} \qquad (7.50)$$

where we have used the relation for $N \times N$ matrices $\mathbf{A}$ and $\mathbf{B}$ that $(\mathbf{AB})^{\mathrm{T}} = \mathbf{B}^{\mathrm{T}}\mathbf{A}^{\mathrm{T}}$ and the fact that

$$(W^{\mathbf{E}})^{\mathrm{T}} = W^{\mathbf{E}^{\mathrm{T}}} \qquad (7.51)$$

which can be seen, for example, from Eqs. (7.4) and (7.5).

Transposing a DIT FFT leads to a DIF FFT; both require the same arithmetic operations, and one is as good as the other in terms of internal computations. However, the input-output ordering is scrambled-natural and natural-scrambled for the DIT FFT and DIF FFT, respectively, so input-output data flow might make one FFT preferable in a given application.

Computing a 1-D DFT Using Multidimensional Processing   E

The results presented for computing a 1-D DFT using 2-D processing are readily generalized to compute the DFT using multidimensional processing. We express k and n in normal and digit-reversed MIR format, respectively, or vice versa. The DFT becomes a summation over $n_1, n_2, \ldots, n_L$, where N has L factors. A twiddle factor is applied to the output of each of the first L- DFTs. At the output of the ith stage the twiddle factor is $W_N^{t_i}$, where for a DRO input t_i is determined by k_i and $n_{i+1}, n_{i+2}, \ldots, n_L$; for an NO input t_i is determined by k_i and $n_{i-1}, n_{i-2}, \ldots, n_1$.

In-Place Computation   1

If $x(n)$ is an NO input, then an N_L-point DFT, $\mathbf{D}_L$, is computed along the n_L-axis for each combination of $n_1, n_2, \ldots, n_{L-1}$. This transforms the n_L index to k_L. Twiddle factors determined by k_L and $n_1, n_2, \ldots, n_{L-1}$ are then applied. Let T_L denote the tandem operations of $\mathbf{D}_L$ and the point-by-point application of twiddle factors. Then similar to the transform of n_L to k_L the $n_{L-1}, \ldots, n_2, n_1$ indices are converted to $k_{L-1}, \ldots, k_2, k_1$ by $T_{L-1}, \ldots, T_2, T_1$. Symbolically we indicate the transforms as follows:

$$x(n_L, \ldots, n_2, n_1) \xrightarrow{T_L} X(k_L, n_{L-1}, \ldots, n_2, n_1) \xrightarrow{T_{L-1}} X(k_L, k_{L-1}, n_{L-2}, \ldots, n_1)$$
$$\xrightarrow{T_{L-2}} \cdots \xrightarrow{T_1} X(k_L, \ldots, k_2, k_1)_{\text{DRO}} \qquad (7.52)$$

The computations are *in-place* in the sense that only N_i data points are required by the N_i-point DFT to produce N_i transform points using a maximum number of memory locations given by $N + \epsilon$, where $\epsilon \ll N$.

In-Order Computation   2

Since the n_i indices are replaced by k_i indices, the output data array ends up with the same memory map as the input, as Eq. (7.52) shows. We have found that an NO input results in a DRO output, and vice versa. However, in certain cases we can use an NO input and map the transform outputs as the computation progresses to achieve an *in-order*, that is, NO, output [13, 14]. This allows the computation to be both in-place and in-order.

In-order computation results from interchanging data between two indices. We will show why this is possible for $L = 3$. Note that for a DRO transform sequence $X(k') = X(k_3, k_2, k_1)_{\text{DRO}}$ the 1-D DFT coefficient number is

$$k' = k_1 N_2 N_3 + k_2 N_3 + k_3 \qquad (7.53)$$

whereas for an NO sequence, $X(k)$, k is

$$k = k_3 N_2 N_1 + k_2 N_1 + k_1 \qquad (7.54)$$

If $N_1 = N_3$, transform coefficients may be swapped between the k_3 and k_1 axes to convert the DFT output to the input data ordering. Alternatively, number swapping may occur during the DFT computation to achieve an in-place and in-order FFT. In the latter case, the array $x(n_3, n_2, n_1)$ is transformed by N_3-point DFTs along the n_3-axis. This is followed by twiddle factors determined by k_3, n_2, and n_1 and yields an array $X(k_3, n_2, n_1)$. Next, a mapping M_3 interchanges the k_3- and n_1-axes and the corresponding data. Then follow N_2-point DFTs and twiddle factors determined by k_2, and finally N_1-point DFTs and twiddle factors determined by k_1. Let T_i denote the application of the DFT $\mathbf{D}_i$ and twiddle factors determined by k_i, $i = 1, 2, 3$. Then symbolically we indicate the foregoing steps as follows:

$$x(n_3, n_2, n_1)_{\text{NO}} \xrightarrow{T_3} X(k_3, n_2, n_1) \xrightarrow{M_3} X(n_1, n_2, k_3)$$
$$\xrightarrow{T_2} X(n_1, k_2, k_3) \xrightarrow{T_1} X(k_1, k_2, k_3)_{\text{NO}} \qquad (7.55)$$

where $(k_1, k_2, k_3)_{\text{NO}} = k_1 N_2 N_3 + k_2 N_3 + k_3$.

Figure 7.6 is a pictorial representation of the sequence of operations in Eq. (7.55) for $N_1 = N_3 = 2$ and $N_2 = 3$. Numbers that are complex, in general, are representated by dots in Fig. 7.6. The data is in normal order, as shown by the numbers alongside the dots. The 2×2 DFT matrix $\mathbf{D}_3$ converts the n_3, n_2, n_1 space to k_3, n_2, n_1 space. Twiddle factors determined by k_3, n_2, and n_1 are then applied. These computations are in-place in the sense that, for each combination of n_1 and n_2, data are taken from the array along the n_3-axis and processed. Next, M_3 swaps points between the k_3- and n_1-axes, in effect changing the coordinate system from right-handed to left-handed. The data defined by n_2 and n_1 is still

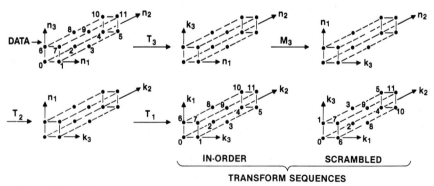

Fig. 7.6. Pictorial representation of a sequence of operations to compute a 12-point DFT.

properly ordered for transform, respectively, by the 3×3 matrix $\mathbf{D}_2$ plus twiddle factors and the 2×2 matrix $\mathbf{D}_3$ plus twiddle factors. When the transform sequence indices are computed in DRO we see that the transform sequence is in-order; that is, $X(i)$ is in the same location as $x(i)$. If the computations are done entirely in a right-handed coordinate system, the transform sequence is scrambled and must be recovered using digit reversal, as shown in the scrambled transform sequence array in Fig. 7.6.

We will say that the mixed-radix FFT is in-order if data swapping along certain axes as the computation progresses leads to an NO output. For $L = 3$ we showed the swapping requires that $N_1 = N_3$. For $L = 4$ we require $N_1 = N_4$ and $N_2 = N_3$, etc. In general, let $N_{L-i+1} = N_i$, $i = 1, 2, \ldots, \lfloor L/2 \rfloor$, where $\lfloor (\cdot) \rfloor$ is the largest integer less than or equal to $(\cdot)$, and let the data be naturally ordered. Let M_{L-i} be a mapping following the twiddle factors determined by k_{L-i}, and let M_{L-i} interchange data point by point along axes k_{L-i+1} and n_i for each combination of $k_L, k_{L-1}, \ldots, k_{L-i+2}, k_{L-i}, \ldots, k_2, k_1$ and $n_1, n_2, \ldots, n_{i-1}, n_{i+1}, \ldots, n_{L-i-1}$. Then an NO output results. Table III illustrates the DFTs the mappings for $L = 6$ [13]. $N - N/N_i$ data transfers are required per nontrivial mapping, so a total of about $\lfloor L/2 \rfloor N$ data transfers is required.

If $L = 2$ and $N_1 = N_2$, swapping data along the axes n_1 and k_2 corresponds to matrix transpose. In this case the transpose of the right side of Eq. (7.35) yields

$$(X(k_1, k_2)_{\text{NO}}) = \mathbf{D}_1 \{ W_N^{\text{ETF}} \circ [\mathbf{D}_2 (x(n_2, n_1)_{\text{NO}})] \}^{\text{T}} \tag{7.56}$$

where now both input and output data are in NO. As a simple example, let $N_1 = N_2 = 2$. Then

$$(x(n_2, n_1)_{\text{NO}}) = \begin{array}{c} n_2 \diagdown \end{array} \begin{array}{cc} 0 & 1 \\ 0 \\ 1 \end{array} \begin{bmatrix} x(0) & x(1) \\ x(2) & x(3) \end{bmatrix}, \qquad \mathbf{D}_1 = \mathbf{D}_2 = \begin{bmatrix} 1 & 1 \\ 1 & -1 \end{bmatrix}$$

$$W_4^{\text{ETF}} = \begin{bmatrix} 1 & 1 \\ 1 & W_4 \end{bmatrix}, \qquad W_4^{\text{ETF}} \circ [\mathbf{D}_2 (x(n_2, n_1))]$$

$$= \begin{array}{c} k_2 \diagdown \end{array} \begin{array}{cc} 0 & 1 \\ 0 \\ 1 \end{array} \begin{bmatrix} x(0) + x(2) & x(1) + x(3) \\ x(0) - x(2) & W_4[x(1) - x(3)] \end{bmatrix}$$

$$(X(k_1, k_2)_{\text{NO}}) = \begin{bmatrix} x(0) + x(1) + x(2) + x(3) & x(0) - x(2) + W_4[x(1) - x(3)] \\ x(0) + x(2) - x(1) - x(3) & x(0) - x(2) - W_4[x(1) - x(3)] \end{bmatrix}$$

$$= \begin{array}{c} k_1 \diagdown \end{array} \begin{array}{cc} 0 & 1 \\ 0 \\ 1 \end{array} \begin{bmatrix} X(0) & X(1) \\ X(2) & X(3) \end{bmatrix} \tag{7.57}$$

TABLE III

Memory Maps and DFTs to Yield an In-Order, In-Place Computation for $L = 6$

Mapping function	Memory map	DFT	Memory map
	$n_6, n_5, n_4, n_3, n_2, n_1$	D_6	$k_6, n_5, n_4, n_3, n_2, n_1$
M_6	$n_1, n_5, n_4, n_3, n_2, k_6$	D_5	$n_1, k_5, n_4, n_3, n_2, k_6$
M_5	$n_1, n_2, n_4, n_3, k_5, k_6$	D_4	$n_1, n_2, k_4, n_3, k_5, k_6$
M_4	$n_1, n_2, n_3, k_4, k_5, k_6$	D_3	$n_1, n_2, k_3, n_4, k_5, k_6$
I	$n_1, n_2, k_3, k_4, k_5, k_6$	D_2	$n_1, k_2, k_3, k_4, k_5, k_6$
I	$n_1, k_2, k_3, k_4, k_5, k_6$	D_1	$k_1, k_2, k_3, k_4, k_5, k_6$

where the indices n_1, n_2, k_1, and k_2 are shown explicitly several times to indicate the transposing of data. Comparing the matrices $(x(n_2, n_1)_{NO})$ and $(X(k_1, k_2)_{NO})$ shows that the input and output data sequences are in the same order. We have obtained an in-order output by physically moving (transposing) the matrix in the braces in Eq. (7.56). This represents about N data transfers, which generalizes to about $\lfloor L/2 \rfloor N$ data transfers to achieve an in-place, in-order FFT.

Figure 7.7 presents the operations in Eq. (7.56) diagrammatically. Figure 7.7(a) is a 2-D representation reduced to planar form in Fig. 7.7(b).

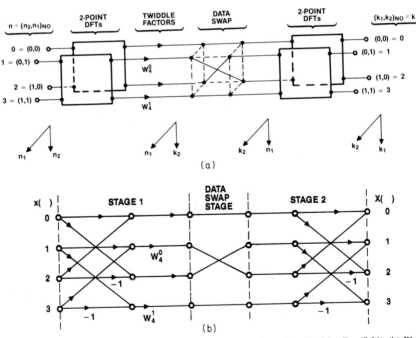

Fig. 7.7. In-place and in-order 4-point FFT. (a) 2-D operations described by Eq. (7.56). (b) Planar flow diagram for (a).

RADIX-2 FFTs

A large percentage of engineering work requiring an FFT is probably best accomplished with a radix-2 FFT. This FFT takes 2^L-data points, $L = 1, 2, \ldots,$ and produces 2^L transform coefficients. The radix-2 FFT is easy to understand and use. The only complication is that either the input or output is in bit-reversed order (BRO), but many existing general-purpose computer programs automatically take care of the bit reversal so as to accept NO inputs and provide NO outputs.

The butterfly structure of the radix-2 FFT results in a simple subroutine to do the computations. Computation is in-place: two numbers into any stage yield two output numbers that replace the input, which is not needed again.

Eight-Point DIT FFT

Applying Eq. (7.29) and Eq. (7.30) for $N_1 = 4$ and $N_2 = 2$ shows that 2-D processing computes the 8-point DFT using two 4-point DFTs followed by twiddle factors and four 2-point DFTs, as shown in Fig. 7.8(a). Figure 7.8(b) shows the planar flow diagram resulting from separating the 4-point FFTs and letting the 2-point FFTs overlap. Combining Figs. 7.5(b) and 7.8(b) yields the 8-point DIT FFT shown in Fig. 7.9.

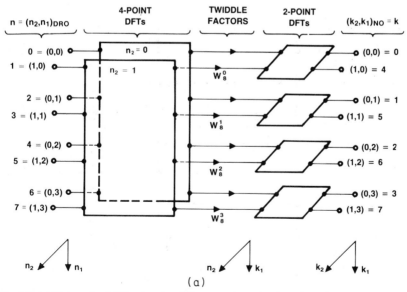

Fig. 7.8. (a) Eight-point DFT reduced to 2-D processing using 4- and 2-point DFTs and twiddle factors. (b) Planar DIT FFT flow diagram for (a) with 2-point DFTs overlapping.

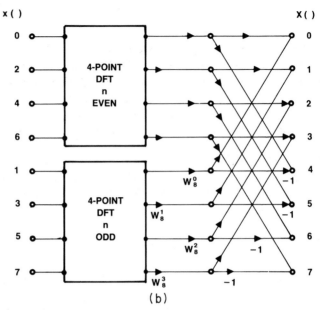

Fig. 7.8. (*Continued*)

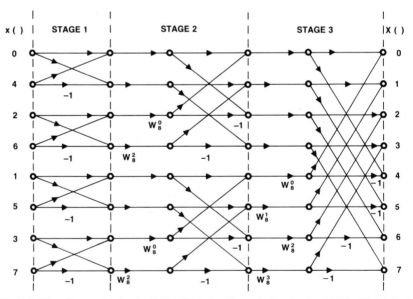

Fig. 7.9. Flow diagram for 8-point DIT FFT derived by replacing 4-point DFT in Fig. 7.8(b) with 4-point DIT FFT from Fig. 7.5(b).

a. Matrix Representation. The arithmetic operations in the three stages of Fig. 7.9 are succinctly displayed in matrix format. Moving the twiddle factors into the butterflies immediately to the right yields the matrix of exponents $E_3 \updownarrow E_2 \updownarrow E_1$ given by

$$
\begin{array}{c}
\begin{array}{c}
\diagdown n \\
k
\end{array}
\begin{array}{ccccccccc}
0 & 0 & 0 & 0 & 1 & 1 & 1 & 1
\end{array}
\\
\begin{array}{c}
0 \\ 1 \\ 2 \\ 3 \\ 4 \\ 5 \\ 6 \\ 7
\end{array}
\left[
\begin{array}{cccccccc}
0 & \cdot & \cdot & \cdot & 0 & \cdot & \cdot & \cdot \\
\cdot & 0 & \cdot & \cdot & \cdot & 1 & \cdot & \cdot \\
\cdot & \cdot & 0 & \cdot & \cdot & \cdot & 2 & \cdot \\
\cdot & \cdot & \cdot & 0 & \cdot & \cdot & \cdot & 3 \\
0 & \cdot & \cdot & \cdot & 4 & \cdot & \cdot & \cdot \\
\cdot & 0 & \cdot & \cdot & \cdot & 5 & \cdot & \cdot \\
\cdot & \cdot & 0 & \cdot & \cdot & \cdot & 6 & \cdot \\
\cdot & \cdot & \cdot & 0 & \cdot & \cdot & \cdot & 7
\end{array}
\right]
\end{array}
\updownarrow
\begin{array}{c}
\begin{array}{c}
\diagdown n \\
k
\end{array}
\begin{array}{ccccccccc}
0 & 0 & 2 & 2 & 0 & 0 & 2 & 2
\end{array}
\\
\begin{array}{c}
0 \\ 1 \\ 2 \\ 3 \\ 4 \\ 5 \\ 6 \\ 7
\end{array}
\left[
\begin{array}{cccccccc}
0 & \cdot & 0 & \cdot & & & & \\
\cdot & 0 & \cdot & 2 & & -j\infty & & \\
0 & \cdot & 4 & \cdot & & & & \\
\cdot & 0 & \cdot & 6 & & & & \\
& & & & 0 & \cdot & 0 & \cdot \\
-j\infty & & & & \cdot & 0 & \cdot & 2 \\
& & & & 0 & \cdot & 4 & \cdot \\
& & & & \cdot & 0 & \cdot & 6
\end{array}
\right]
\end{array}
$$

$$
\updownarrow
\begin{array}{c}
\begin{array}{c}
\diagdown n \\
k
\end{array}
\begin{array}{ccccccccc}
0 & 4 & 0 & 4 & 0 & 4 & 0 & 4
\end{array}
\\
\begin{array}{c}
0 \\ 1 \\ 2 \\ 3 \\ 4 \\ 5 \\ 6 \\ 7
\end{array}
\left[
\begin{array}{cccccccc}
0 & 0 & & & & & & \\
0 & 4 & & & & & & \\
& & 0 & 0 & & -j\infty & & \\
& & 0 & 4 & & & & \\
& & & & 0 & 0 & & \\
-j\infty & & & & 0 & 4 & & \\
& & & & & & 0 & 0 \\
& & & & & & 0 & 4
\end{array}
\right]
\end{array}
\quad (7.58)
$$

The matrices W^{E_1}, W^{E_2}, and W^{E_3} correspond to processing along the first, second, and third axes, respectively, of three-dimensional space.

b. Computational Considerations. When an FFT digital computer program is written, the procedure to minimize multiplications is that of Fig. 7.9. For example, on the bottom line in Fig. 7.9 the output of stage 2 should be multiplied by W_8^3 instead of moving W_8^3 into the butterfly on its right. The multiplier W_8^3 is included in the butterfly in Eq. (7.58) due to combining twiddle factor and butterfly matrices for convenience in displaying the matrices of exponents.

c. Multiplier-Free Butterflies. Note in Fig. 7.9 that the butterflies are implemented with additions and subtractions. The only multiplications are those associated with the twiddle factors. The only other known FFTs that can be implemented with multiplier-free, butterflylike structures plus twiddle factors are radix-3, -4, and -6 FFTs, as will be discussed later.

TABLE IV

Data Sequence Index Derivation for DIT Eight-Point FFT

Bits of binary index			Decimal index	
n_3	n_2	n_1	n (bit-reversed order)	n (natural order)
0	0	0	0	0
0	0	1	4	1
0	1	0	2	2
0	1	1	6	3
1	0	0	1	4
1	0	1	5	5
1	1	0	3	6
1	1	1	7	7

d. Bit-Reversed Order. The input to the 8-point DIF FFT is in a scrambled order that can be explained using Figs. 7.5 and 7.9. In the 4-point DFT (Fig. 7.5) the data sequence index is $n = 2n_1 + n_2 = 0, 1, 2, 3$, since $n_1, n_2 = 0, 1$. Let prime denote indices in the 8-point DFT (Fig. 7.5). Then $n' = 2n'_1 + n'_2$, where $n'_1 = 0, 1, 2, 3$ and $n'_2 = 0, 1$. We can replace n'_1 by n and n'_2 by n_3 to get

$$n' = 4n_1 + 2n_2 + n_3 \tag{7.59}$$

Table IV shows Eq. (7.59) with the prime discarded. It is evident from the table that n is in BRO; that is, n is the decimal number resulting from reversing the order of the bits.

B 2^L-Point DIT FFT

We have derived 2-, 4-, and 8-point FFTs that correspond to $L = 1, 2$, and 3, respectively. For $L > 3$, the 4-point DFTs in Fig. 7.8(a) are replaced by 2^{L-1}-point DFTs followed by 2^{L-1} 2-point DFTs. A 16-point FFT results from using the 8-point FFT of Fig. 7.9 for each of two 8-point DFTs, and 8 butterflies follow, similar to those in Fig. 7.8. A 32-point FFT uses two 16-point FFTs followed by 16 butterflies, etc.

a. BRO Input. Table IV shows that the data sequence into the 8-point DIT FFT is in BRO. The BRO follows from Eq. (7.59), which extends to larger FFTs with the usual result that DIT radix-2 FFTs have BRO inputs and NO outputs.

b. Arithmetic Operations for 2^L-Point FFT. We will make the pessimistic assumption that all additions and all multiplications by a power of W_N are complex operations. For example, in Fig. 7.6, $W_8^2 = -j$ will be counted as a complex multiplier, although only an exchange of real and imaginary parts of the multiplicand is required.

From Fig. 7.9 we note that there are N complex additions per stage and $\log_2 N$ stages, $N = 2^L$. In general,

$$\text{number of complex additions} = NL = N \log_2 N \qquad (7.60a)$$

The first stage is implemented with additions only, but the remaining $L - 1$ stages have $N/2$ multiplications per stage. Since $L - 1 = \log_2(N/2)$

$$\text{number of complex multiplications} = \frac{N}{2}(L - 1) = \frac{N}{2}\log_2\left(\frac{N}{2}\right) \qquad (7.60b)$$

Expressing the DFT as a matrix shows that approximately N^2 complex additions and N^2 complex multiplications are required for a brute-force approach. Thus the FFT cuts the computation of arithmetic operations by $N/\log_2 N$ complex additions and $2N/\log_2(N/2)$ complex multiplications.

2^L-Point DIF FFT C

The DIF FFT has an NO input and an output in BRO. This FFT results from starting with 2^{L-1} 2-point DFTs followed by two 2^{L-1}-point DFTs. For example, an 8-point DIF FFT is derived from representing the FFT two-dimensionally as four 2-point DFTs followed by two 4-point DFTs. The 4-point DFTs are similarly expanded. Figure 7.10 shows the resultant 8-point FFT reduced to a planar diagram. The matrix representation of Fig. 7.10 is the transpose of Eq. (7.58), so the input is in NO, whereas the output is in BRO.

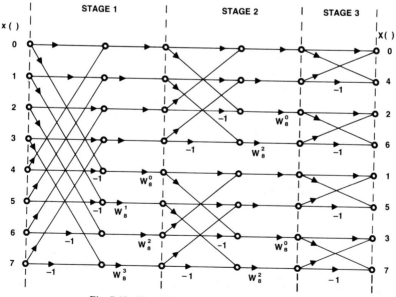

Fig. 7.10. Flow diagram for 8-point DIF FFT.

In general, a DIF FFT is characterized by a BRO output and NO input. The numbers of arithmetic operations to compute DIF and DIT FTTs are the same and are given by Eqs. (7.60a) and (7.60b).

D   Split-Radix FFT

The split-radix FFT (SRFFT) [16, 17] has the optimum number of multiplications and the minimum known number of additions for radix-2 FFTs for lengths up to and including 16 [18, 19]. The SRFFT has a good compromise arithmetic operation count for all longer radix-2 lengths. The algorithm is performed in-place using a repetitive butterfly structure and is numerically as well conditioned as radix-4 algorithms [19].

The SRFFT results from applying the DFT definition to get [18]

$$C(2k) = \sum_{n=0}^{N/2-1} \left[x(n) + x\left(n + \frac{N}{2}\right) \right] W_N^{2nk} \tag{7.61}$$

for even index terms and

$$C(4k+1) = \sum_{n=0}^{N/4-1} \left\{ x(n) - x\left(n + \frac{N}{2}\right) - j\left[x\left(n + \frac{N}{4}\right) - x\left(n + \frac{3N}{4}\right) \right] \right\} W_N^n W_N^{4nk} \tag{7.62a}$$

and

$$C(4k+3) = \sum_{n=0}^{N/4-1} \left\{ x(n) - x\left(n + \frac{N}{2}\right) + j\left[x\left(n + \frac{N}{4}\right) - x\left(n + \frac{3N}{4}\right) \right] \right\} W_N^{3n} W_N^{4nk} \tag{7.62b}$$

for odd index terms. This reduces an N-point DFT to one $N/2$-point DFT and two $N/4$-point DFTs. When applied recursively, the preceding formulas result in L-shaped butterflies that advance the top half of the butterfly by one stage and the bottom half by two stages. Figure 7.11 shows the 32-point SRFFT using the simplified notation of a small circle to represent a 2-point DFT. DIF and DIF computer programs are available for the SRFFT (see Appendix C).

V   RADIX-3 AND RADIX-6 FFTs

Radix-3 and radix-6 FFTs can be implemented with multiplier-free, butterfly-like structures plus twiddle factors similarly to radix-2 and radix-4 FFTs. Depending on the cost (i.e., time to compute a multiplication on a particular machine), the radix-3 and radix-6 FFTs can be very efficient. This efficiency is

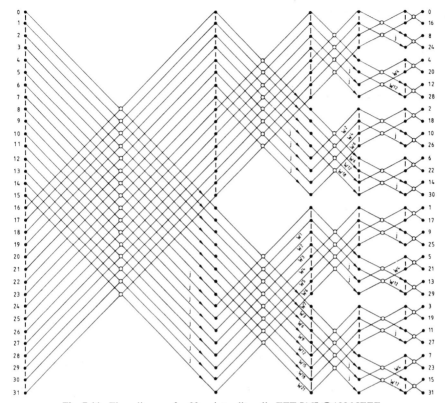

Fig. 7.11. Flow diagram for 32-point split radix FFT [16] © 1986 IEEE.

achieved by doing the FFT arithmetic in a nonorthogonal coordinate system. If the input data is complex, it must be converted to the nonorthogonal coordinates, and the conversion incurs an additional expense. The output data may or may not need conversion from the nonorthogonal coordinates, depending on the application.

The output data does not need to be converted from the nonorthogonal coordinates if convolution is being computed. The product of transforms is taken in the nonorthogonal coordinates and is inverse transformed. If the input data is real, the convolution data is also real and no transformations are required. If the input data is complex, transformations of the two data sequences and of the inverse transform are required.

Another application not requiring coordinate conversion of the output data is spectral analysis in which the squared magnitude of the DFT output is displayed. Transform coefficient magnitudes are computed in nonorthogonal coordinates.

We shall discuss nonorthogonal coordinates and then the radix-3 and radix-6 FFTs. The following radix-3 and radix-6 developments came from [20] and [21], respectively.

A   Nonorthogonal Coordinates

We can think of a complex number $a + jb$ as a vector sum of the vector $1a$ along the real axis and the vector jb along the imaginary axis, where 1 and j are unit vectors with (x, y) coordinates $(1, 0)$ and $(0, 1)$, respectively. We will say that complex numbers use the basis $(1, j)$. In most cases arithmetic is simplest using the basis $(1, j)$. However, the basis $(1, \mu)$ is equally suitable and occasionally can be the simplest, where μ is a vector of unit length and is not parallel to the real or imaginary axes.

To develop the radix-3 FFT, we let $\mu = W_3 = -\frac{1}{2} - j\sqrt{3}/2$. Then $j = -1/\sqrt{3} - W_3 2/\sqrt{3}$, and transformations between numbers using the bases $(1, j)$ and $(1, W_3)$ are accomplished by

$$a + jb \rightarrow \left(a - \frac{b}{\sqrt{3}} \right) - \frac{W_3 2b}{\sqrt{3}} \tag{7.63a}$$

$$a + W_3 b \rightarrow \left(a - \frac{b}{2} \right) - \frac{j\sqrt{3}b}{2} \tag{7.63b}$$

Addition using the basis $(1, W_3)$ is given by

$$(a + W_3 b) + (c + W_3 d) = (a + c) + W_3(b + d) \tag{7.64}$$

Using $W_3^2 = -1 - W_3$ (see Fig. 7.3), we find that multiplication is given by

$$(a + W_3 b)(c + W_3 d) = (ac - bd) + W_3[ad + b(c - d)] \tag{7.65a}$$

$$= (ac - bd) + W_3[(a + b)(c + d) - ac - 2bd] \tag{7.65b}$$

Note that Eq. (7.65a) requires four real multiplications, whereas (7.65b) requires just three plus a shift and extra additions and may be more economical, depending on the relative cost of additions and multiplications. Twiddle factors are powers of W_N expressed in nonorthogonal coordinates:

$$W_N = \cos\left(\frac{2\pi}{N} \right) + \frac{\sin(2\pi/N)}{\sqrt{3}} + \frac{W_3 2 \sin(2\pi/N)}{\sqrt{3}} \tag{7.66}$$

Finally, complex conjugation using the basis $(1, W_3)$ is

$$(a + W_3 b)^* = a + W_3^2 b = (a - b) - W_3 b \tag{7.67}$$

B   Three-Point DFT

The 3-point DFT has been discussed previously and is shown in Fig. 7.3(c). If the input to the DFT uses the basis $(1, j)$, complex multiplications are required. If the input uses the basis $(1, W_3)$, no multiplications are required, as Eq. (7.65) shows. Let the input coordinate transform yield the data sequence

$$x(n) = \text{Re}[x(n)] - \frac{1}{\sqrt{3}}\text{Im}[x(n)] - W_3\frac{2}{\sqrt{3}}\text{Im}[x(n)]$$

$$\triangleq x_1(n) + W_3 x_2(n), \qquad n = 0, 1, 2 \tag{7.68}$$

Then the 3-point DFT in Fig. 7.3(c) is implemented with additions only as shown explicitly by the equations

$$X(0) = [x_1(0) + x_1(1) + x_1(2)] + W_3[x_2(0) + x_2(1) + x_2(2)]$$
$$X(1) = [x_1(0) - x_2(1) - x_1(2) + x_2(2)]$$
$$\qquad + W_3[x_2(0) + x_1(1) - x_2(1) - x_1(2)]$$
$$X(2) = [x_1(0) - x_1(1) + x_2(1) - x_2(2)]$$
$$\qquad + W_3[x_2(0) - x_1(1) + x_1(2) - x_2(2)] \tag{7.69}$$

3^L-Point FFT   C

This FFT is mechanized as a cascade of L stages with twiddle factors in between. Each stage consists of 3^{L-1} 3-point DFTs. The 3-point DFTs are multiplier free in the basis $(1, W_3)$, so the only multiplications are due to the twiddle factors that are powers of W_N expressed with respect to the basis $(1, W_3)$ [see Eq. (7.66)]. These multiplications are implemented using Eq. (7.65a) or Eq. (7.65b).

Figure 7.12 shows the 9-point FFT in 2-D form with the input and output transformations shown explicitly. Figure 7.13 shows the 27-point DIT FFT reduced to planar form without the input and output transformations. The small circles are used to simplify the flow diagram and indicate 3-point DFTs; that is, three inputs are used to produce three outputs with additions only using Eq. (7.69). A total of $((\frac{2}{3})L - 1)N + 1$ nontrivial complex multiplications are required to implement the twiddle factors that are powers of $W = \exp(-j2\pi/27)$. The $4LN/3$ complex multiplications required by the 3-point DFTs [see Fig. 7.3(b)] are eliminated by this method.

Six-Point FFT   D

The 6-point FFT in Fig. 7.4 can be implemented without multiplications with respect to the basis $(1, W_3)$ by using the identities (see Fig. 7.14).

$$W_6 = -W_6^4 = -W_3^2 = 1 + W_3, \quad W_6^2 = -W_6^5 = W_3, \quad W_6^3 = -1$$

Thus, if $a + W_3 b$ is the input to the twiddle factors W_6 or W_6^2 in Fig. 7.4, then the

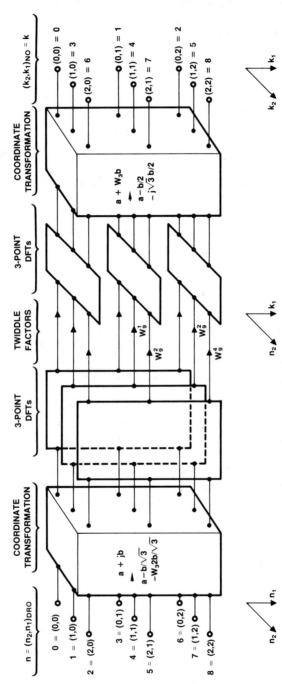

Fig. 7.12. Nine-point FFT with arithmetic using the basis $(1, W_3)$.

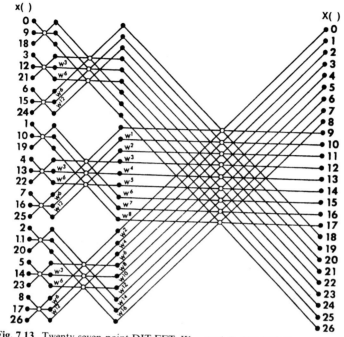

Fig. 7.13. Twenty-seven-point DIT FFT; $W = \exp(-j2\pi/27)$ [20] © 1978 IEEE.

outputs are

$$(a + W_3 b)W_6 = a - b + W_3 a, \qquad (a + W_3 b)W_6^2 = -b + W_3(a - b) \quad (7.71)$$

The twiddle factors require no multiplications, so, after the input data is converted to the basis $(1, W_3)$, the 6-point FFT requires no multiplications.

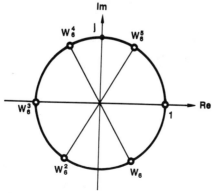

Fig. 7.14. Unit circle showing multipliers used for 6-point DFT computation.

E 6^L-Point FFT

A 6^2-pont FFT is implemented with a coordinate conversion, six 6-point FFTs along the n_1-axis (similar to Fig. 7.12), twiddle factors involving $W_{36}^{k_1 n_2}$, $k_1\, n_2 = 0, 1, \ldots, 5$, and six 6-point FFTs along the n_2-axis. A 6^3-point FFT is implemented with a coordinate conversion, thirty-six 6-point FFTs, and six 36-point FFTs. A 6^L-point FFT uses 6^{L-1} 6-point FFTs followed by six 6^{L-1}-point FFTs, etc. The twiddle factor computations are the only ones requiring multiplications. The twiddle factors are implemented using Eq. (7.66).

F $(2^L 3^M)$-Point FFT

Martens has developed a so-called recursive cyclotomic factorization algorithm (RCFA) that is efficient for transforming $2^L 3^M$-point sequences [22]. When the RCFA is for a sequence whose length is a power of 2, it can be shown to be the same as the SRFFT (Section IV.D) [17]. The RCFA requires only a few different computational cells (a cell is a few operations to accomplish a specific computation, such as a generalized butterfly). The main advantage of the RCFA is that it reduces the size of the program to compute the FFT compared to the PFA and the WFTA (Sections X and XI.B). The RCFA also offers a slight advantage over these algorithms in execution time based on run times from a VAX-11/750 computer. Martens recommends the basis $(1, W_6)$ because it is slightly more efficient. He also demonstrates how two different basis representations can be used in the same algorithm.

VI   RADIX-4 FFTs

As mentioned, the only known butterfly or butterflylike structures that can be implemented without multiplications are for radix-2, -3, -4, and -6 FFTs. For radix-3 and radix-6 FFTs it is done at the expense of computation in nonorthogonal coordinates (see Section V). Radix-4-FFTs are computed with standard complex arithmetic and are attractive for distributed arithmetic mechanizations.

A   Four-Point FFT

Figure 7.5 shows that 4-point FFT flow diagrams contain only butterflies and the multipliers $W_4^0 = 1$ and $W_4^1 = \exp(-j2\pi/4) = -j$. Multiplying $a + jb$ by $-j$ simply changes the sign of a and then interchanges $-a$ and b between their real and imaginary locations in memory. The 4-point FFT is multiplier free.

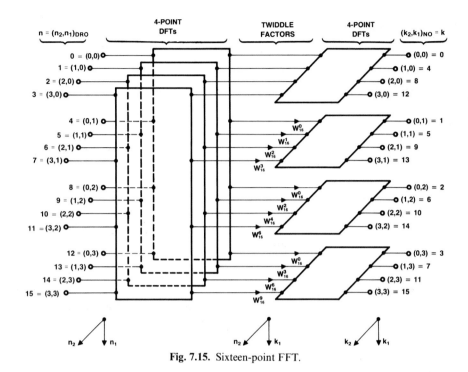

Fig. 7.15. Sixteen-point FFT.

4^L-Point FFT   **B**

The 4^L-point FFT is mechanized as a cascade of L stages where each stage consists of 4^{L-1} 4-point FFTs. Figure 7.15 shows the 2-D version of the 16-point FFT. The 64-point FFT can be mechanized as 16 parallel 4-point DFTs along the n_1-axis followed by four 16-point DFTs (implemented as FFTs) along the n_2-axis. The 4^L-point FFT can be viewed as 4^{L-1} 4-point FFTs followed by four 4^{L-1}-point FFTs.

SMALL-N DFTs   **VII**

Small-N DFTs are used in the FFTs discussed in the following sections. They are the most economical algorithms for computing the DFT in terms of minimizing multiplications, although at the expense of computations that are not in-place. Appendix A gives small-N DFTs for $N = 2-5, 7-9, 11, 13, 16,$ and 17. The theory for developing the algorithms was derived by S. Winograd using mathematical concepts that are probably less familiar to most engineers than those we have presented. Although they are not unique, only the most efficient small-N DFTs are used. You need not know how to derive them in order to use them. Therefore, we only shall state the small-N DFTs and refer the interested reader to the literature for the theoretical background [2–4, 10, 15, 23–25].

The algorithms in Appendix A are implemented with a definite sequence of operations that may be grouped as input additions, multiplications, and output additions. For example, one 3-point DFT is in Appendix A and another is

$$t_1 = x(1) + x(2), \qquad t_2 = x(1) - x(2)$$

$$m_1 = -\frac{1}{2}t_i, \qquad m_2 = -j\frac{\sqrt{3}}{2}t_2$$

$$s_1 = x(0), \qquad s_2 = m_1 + s_1$$

$$X(0) = s_1 + t_1, \qquad X(1) = s_2 + m_2, \qquad X(2) = s_2 - m_2$$

(7.72)

Evaluation of Eq. (7.72) requires six additions, one multiplication, and one shift.

For analysis purposes, it is useful to put the small-N DFTs into a factored matrix representation. The matrix representation can then be handled with matrix analysis tools to arrive at the WFTA described in a subsequent section. The factored matrices representing small-N DFTs have many zero entries and are not used to implement FFTs. Instead the equations that minimize arithmetic operations are stored in memory. These equations do not generally have the symmetrical form of radix-2 FFTs and therefore require more program storage.

Let $\mathbf{D}$ be a small-N DFT. Expression of a small-N DFT makes it possible to combine input data using only additions. All multiplications can then be performed. Finally, more additions determine the transform coefficients. These operations are represented by

$$\mathbf{D} = \mathbf{SCT} \tag{7.73}$$

where $\mathbf{T}$ accomplishes input additions, $\mathbf{C}$ accomplishes all multiplications, and $\mathbf{S}$ accomplishes output additions. For example, if $N = 3$, then Eq. (7.72) is an optimum algorithm and has the matrix representation

$$\mathbf{D} = \underbrace{\begin{bmatrix} 1 & 1 & 0 & 0 \\ 0 & 0 & 1 & 1 \\ 0 & 0 & 1 & -1 \end{bmatrix}}_{\mathbf{S}} \begin{bmatrix} 1 & 0 & 0 & 0 \\ 0 & 1 & 0 & 0 \\ 1 & 0 & 1 & 0 \\ 0 & 0 & 0 & 1 \end{bmatrix} \underbrace{\left[\begin{array}{ccc|c} 1 & 0 & 0 & 0 \\ 0 & 1 & 0 & 0 \\ 0 & 0 & -\frac{1}{2} & 0 \\ \hline 0 & 0 & 0 & -j\sqrt{3}/2 \end{array}\right]}_{\mathbf{C}}$$

$$\times \underbrace{\begin{bmatrix} 1 & 0 & 0 \\ 0 & 1 & 0 \\ 0 & 1 & 0 \\ 0 & 0 & 1 \end{bmatrix} \begin{bmatrix} 1 & 0 & 0 \\ 0 & 1 & 1 \\ 0 & 1 & -1 \end{bmatrix}}_{\mathbf{T}}$$

(7.74)

Note that some components of the factored $\mathbf{S}$ and $\mathbf{T}$ matrices in Eq. (7.74) are nonsquare; in general they are not necessarily square. Note also the following characteristics of the C matrix:

1. It is diagonal matrix implementing all the small-N algorithm's multiplications.

2. The numbers along the diagonal are either real or imaginary but not complex.

3. The real numbers along the diagonal may be grouped on one side of the C matrix; the imaginary numbers may be grouped on the other side.

FFTs DERIVED FROM THE RURITANIAN CORRESPONDENCE (RC)   VIII

The RC is another method of representing integers. It leads to N-point PFA FFTs when $N = N_1 N_2 \cdots N_L$ and the factors of N are mutually relatively prime; that is, the greatest common divisor (gcd) of N_i and N_j is 1, $i \neq j$ and $i, j = 1, 2, \ldots, L$. Thus, these FFTs are available for such values of N as $2 \cdot 3$, $3 \cdot 4$, $3 \cdot 4 \cdot 5$, $2 \cdot 5 \cdot 7 \cdot 9$, etc. We shall refer to them as RC FFTs. Their advantage is that one can implement them without twiddle factors, using the efficient small-N DFTs of the preceding chapter. Their disadvantage is that a scrambling of the transform coefficient numbers occurs and must be accounted for.

Ruritanian Correspondence   A

This is an integer representation that we will use to represent the indices k and/or n in an N-point DFT in this and later sections [2, 26]. Let $N = N_1 N_2 \cdots N_L$, where $\gcd(N_i, N_j) = 1$, $i \neq j$, and $i, j = 1, 2, \ldots, L$. Then given n_i, $0 \leq n_i < N_i$, there exists a unique n, $0 \leq n < N$, such that

$$n_i = \left[n \left\langle \left(\frac{N}{N_i} \right)^{-1} \right\rangle_{N_i} \right] \bmod N_i \tag{7.75}$$

and

$$n = \left[\sum_{i=1}^{L} n_i \frac{N}{N_i} \right] \bmod N \tag{7.76}$$

where $\langle (N/N_i)^{-1} \rangle_{N_i}$ is the multiplicative inverse of (N/N_i) (modulo N_i) and n mod N is the remainder of n/N. For example, let $L = 2$, $N_1 = 2$, and $N_2 = 3$. Then $\langle (N/N_1)^{-1} \rangle_{N_1} = \langle 3^{-1} \rangle_2 = 1$, since $3 \cdot \langle 3^{-1} \rangle_2 \bmod 2 = 3 \cdot 1 \bmod 2 = 1$; that is, the product of 3 and its multiplicative inverse is 1 when computed mod 2. Likewise, $\langle (N/N_2)^{-1} \rangle_{N_2} = \langle 2^{-1} \rangle_3 = 2$, since $2 \cdot \langle 2^{-1} \rangle_3 \bmod 3 = 2 \cdot 2 \bmod 3 = 1$. Also, $n = (n_1 N/N_1 + n_2 N/N_2) \bmod N = (3n_1 + 2n_2) \bmod 6$, as displayed in Table V.

TABLE V

Ruritanian Correspondence Integer
Representation for $N_1 = 2$ and $N_2 = 3$

RC digits		Decimal number
		$n = (3n_1 + 2n_2)$
n_2	n_1	mod 6
0	0	0
0	1	3
1	0	2
1	1	5
2	0	4
2	1	1

B   RC FFT When *N* Has Two Factors

The two-factor RC FFT occurs for $N = N_1 N_2$, where N_1 and N_2 are relatively prime, and the RC is used to represent both k and n [27, 28]:

$$k = (k_2 N_1 + k_1 N_2) \mod N \triangleq (k_2, k_1)_{\text{RC}} \tag{7.77}$$

$$n = (n_2 N_1 + n_1 N_2) \mod N \triangleq (n_2, n_1)_{\text{RC}} \tag{7.78}$$

The exponents of W_N^{kn} can be simplified by noting that

$$kn = k_1 n_1 N_2^2 + k_2 n_2 N_1^2 + N(k_1 n_2 + k_2 n_1)$$

$$kn \mod N = k_1 n_1 N_2^2 + k_2 n_2 N_1^2 \tag{7.79}$$

so that

$$W_N^{kn} = W_{N_1}^{k_1 n_1 N_2} W_{N_2}^{k_2 n_2 N_1} \tag{7.80}$$

Since the DFT input data is determined by (n_2, n_1) and the output coefficients by (k_2, k_1), we can write the DFT

$$X(k) = X(k_2, k_1)_{\text{RC}} = \sum_{n=0}^{N-1} x(n) W^{kn}$$

$$= \sum_{n_2=0}^{N_2-1} \sum_{n_1=0}^{N_1-1} x(n_2, n_1)_{\text{RC}} W_{N_1}^{k_1 n_1 N_2} W_{N_2}^{k_2 n_2 N_1} \tag{7.81}$$

Equation (7.81) is the same as a 2-D DFT except for the N_2 in the exponent of W_{N_1}, and similarly for the N_1 in the exponent of W_{N_2}.

We can nevertheless compute Eq. (7.81) as a 2-D DFT, as we explain next. Note that if N_1 and N_2 are relatively prime, then the sequence $\{0, N_2, 2N_2, \ldots, (N_1 - 1)N_2\} \mod N_1$ (i.e., each integer in the sequence is computed mod N_1

generates the sequence $\{0, 1, 2, \ldots, N_1 - 1\}$ after reordering. For example, if $N_1 = 5$ and $N_2 = 3$, then $\{0, 3, 6, 9, 12\} \bmod 5 = \{0, 3, 1, 4, 2\}$, which reorders to $\{0, 1, 2, 3, 4\}$. The sequence $k_1 N_2$ is exactly such a sequence. As k_1 takes the values in the sequence $\{0, 1, 2, \ldots, N_1 - 1\}$ we get a sequence

$$k_1' = \{0, N_2\ 2N_2, \ldots, (N_1 - 1)N_2\} \quad \bmod N_1 \tag{7.82}$$

In like manner we get a sequence

$$k_2' = \{0, N_1, 2N_1, \ldots, (N_2 - 1)N_1\} \quad \bmod N_2 \tag{7.83}$$

Using these sequences, we compute the 2-D DFT

$$X(k_2', k_1') = \sum_{n_2=0}^{N_2-1} \sum_{n_1=0}^{N_1-1} x(n_2, n_1)_{RC}\ W_{N_1}^{k_1'n}\ W_{N_2}^{k_2'n_2} \tag{7.84}$$

The 1-D DFT output is determined from Eq. (7.84) by selecting $X(k_2, k_1)$ from the array $X(k_2', k_1')$, where Eq. (7.77) is used to determine (k_2, k_1). Note that we obtain k_1 and k_2 from Eqs. (7.82) and (7.83) using the inversion formula

$$k_i = \left[k_1' \left\langle \left(\frac{N}{N_i} \right)^{-1} \right\rangle_{N_i} \right] \bmod N_i, \quad i = 1, 2 \tag{7.85}$$

For example, for $N_1 = 5$ and $N_2 = 3$, $\langle (N/N_1)^{-1} \rangle_{N_1} = \langle 3^{-1} \rangle_5 = 2$, since $3 \cdot 2 \bmod 5 = 1$. Thus, $k_1' = \{0, 3, 1, 4, 2\}$ yields $k_1 = \{0, 6, 2, 8, 4\} \bmod 5 = \{0, 1, 2, 3, 4\}$. Equation (7.84) is evaluated as follows:

$$X(k_2', k_1') = \underbrace{\sum_{n_2=0}^{N_2-1} \underbrace{\sum_{n_1=0}^{N_1-1} x(n_2, n_1)_{RC} W_{N_1}^{k_1'n_1}}_{N_1\text{-point DFT}} W_{N_2}^{k_2'n_2}}_{X(n_2, k_1')}$$

$$= \underbrace{\sum_{n_2=0}^{N_2-1} X(n_2, k_1') W_{N_2}^{k_2'n_2}}_{N_2\text{-point DFT}} \tag{7.86}$$

Note that Eq. (7.86) is similar to Eq. (7.29) except that Eq. (7.86) has no twiddle factors. We have eliminated them at the expense of mapping n into (n_2, n_1) space, using the RC and retrieving k using Eq. (7.82), Eq. (7.83), and the RC.

As an example, let $N_1 = 2$ and $N_2 = 3$. Figure 7.16 is the 6-point RC FFT. Input and output indices are in Table V and VI, respectively. Note that Figs. 7.2(a) and 7.16 are both implemented with 2- and 3-point FFTs, that the latter has no twiddle factors, and that the indexing for the two is different. Figure 7.2(a) used the MIR to represent k and n, and there are no constraints on N_1 and N_2, whereas Fig. 7.16 used the RC, so N_1 and N_2 must be relatively prime.

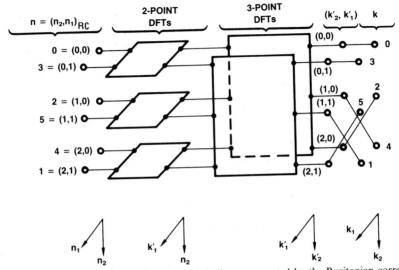

Fig. 7.16. Six-point FFT in 2-D format with indices represented by the Ruritanian correspondence.

TABLE VI

Six-Point RC FFT Output Indices

k	k_2	k_1	k_2'	$k_2' \bmod N_2$	k_1'	$k_1' \bmod N_1$
0	0	0	0	0	0	0
3	0	1	0	0	3	1
2	1	0	2	2	0	0
5	1	1	2	2	3	1
4	2	0	4	1	0	0
1	2	1	4	1	3	1

C   RC FFT When *N* Has *L* Factors

Let $N = N_1 N_2 \cdots N_L$, where the N_i are mutually relatively prime. Then using the RC to represent both k and n gives us an L-D representation of a 1-D DFT that is a direct extension of Eq. (7.81). For example, for $L = 3$ we get

$$X(k_3, k_2, k_1)_{RC} = \sum_{n_3=0}^{N_3-1} \sum_{n_2=0}^{N_2-1} \sum_{n_1=0}^{N_1-1} x(n_3, n_2, n_1)_{RC} W_{N_1}^{k_1 n_1 N_2 N_3} W_{N_2}^{k_2 n_2 N_1 N_3} W_{N_3}^{k_3 n_3 N_1 N_2}$$

$$(7.87)$$

Conversion of the 1-D DFT to an L-D DFT yields an FFT without twiddle factors. The N_1-, N_2-,..., N_L-point DFTs are evaluated in the most efficient manner, usually with the small-N DFTs in Appendix A. These FFTs can be programmed to be in-order as well as in-place, as described next.

In-Order and In-Place RC FFT D

The mapping of data into the RC FFT is determined by $(n_L, \ldots, n_2, n_1)$, where the n_i, $i = 1, 2, \ldots, L$, are determined using the RC. After the index n_i is transformed to $k_i' = k_i N/N_i$ by the N_i-point DFT, let the corresponding DFT outputs be reordered according to the index $k_i = 0, 1, 2, \ldots, N_i - 1$, where k_i is determined from k using the RC. Then the RC FFT is in-order in the sense that the RC determines the mapping for the input and the output of the DFT.

Equation (7.85) shows how scrambled output indices k_1' and k_2' are converted to NO indices k_1 and k_2, respectively, when $L = 2$. In general the mapping

$$k_i = \left[k_i' \left\langle \left(\frac{N}{N_i} \right)^{-1} \right\rangle_{N_i} \right] \bmod N_i, \qquad i = 1, 2, \ldots, L \qquad (7.88)$$

converts a scrambled-order N_i-point DFT output to an NO output; and if this is done as FFT computation progresses, the algorithm is in-order [28].

In-place computation is described for mixed-radix FFTs in Section III.E and is similar to the RC FFT.

FFTs DERIVED FROM THE CHINESE REMAINDER THEOREM IX

The CRT is still another method of representing integers that leads to N-point PFA FFTs when $N = N_1 N_2 \cdots N_L$ and factors of N are mutually relatively prime. We shall refer to these as CRT FFTs. The same remarks apply to these FFTs as to the RC FFTs.

Chinese Remainder Theorem A

Let $N = N_1 N_2 \cdots N_L$, where $\gcd(N_i, N_j) = 1$, $i \neq j$, and $i, j = 1, 2, \ldots, L$. Then given n_i, $0 \leq n_i < N_i$, there exists a unique n such that [2, 26]

$$n_i = n \bmod N_i \qquad \text{for all } i \qquad (7.89)$$

$$n = \left[\sum_{i=1}^{L} n_i \frac{N}{N_i} \left\langle \left(\frac{N}{N_i} \right)^{-1} \right\rangle_{N_i} \right] \bmod N \qquad (7.90)$$

For example, let $L = 2$, $N_1 = 2$, and $N_2 = 3$, so $n = n_1 N_2 \langle N_2^{-1} \rangle_{N_1} +$

TABLE VII

Chinese Remainder Theorem Integer
Representation for $N_1 = 2$ and $N_2 = 3$

CRT digits		Decimal number
		$n = (3n_1 + 4n_2)$
n_2	n_1	mod 6
0	0	0
0	1	3
1	0	4
1	1	1
2	0	2
2	1	5

$n_2 N_1 \langle N_1^{-1} \rangle_{N_2} = 3n_1 + 4n_2$, as displayed in Table VII. We shall also use the fact that

$$\gcd\left(N_i, \left\langle \left(\frac{N}{N_i}\right)^{-1}\right\rangle_{N_i}\right) = 1 \tag{7.91}$$

For example, for $N_1 = 8$ and $N_2 = 9$ we find that $\langle N_1^{-1}\rangle_{N_2} = 8$, since $8 \cdot \langle 8^{-1}\rangle_9 = 8 \cdot 8 \equiv 1$ (modulo 9). Also, $\langle N_2^{-1}\rangle_{N_1} = 1$, since $9 \cdot 1 \equiv 1$ (modulo 8). Thus, Eq. (7.91) reduces to $\gcd(8, 1) = \gcd(9, 8) = 1$.

B   CRT FFT When N Has Two Factors

The two-factor CRT FFT occurs when $L = 2$ and the CRT is used to represent both k and n [27, 28]:

$$k = (k_2 N_1 a_1 + k_1 N_2 a_2) \mod N \triangleq (k_2, k_1)_{\text{CRT}} \tag{7.92}$$

$$n = (n_2 N_1 a_1 + n_1 N_2 a_2) \mod N \triangleq (n_2, n_1)_{\text{CRT}} \tag{7.93}$$

where $a_i = \langle (N/N_i)^{-1}\rangle_{N_i}$, $i = 1, 2$, and, from Eq. (7.91),

$$\gcd(N_1, a_1) = \gcd(N_2, a_2) = 1 \tag{7.94}$$

The exponents of W^{kn} can be simplified by noting that

$$kn \mod N = k_1 n_1 (N_2 a_2)^2 + k_2 n_2 (N_1 a_1)^2 \tag{7.95}$$

so that

$$W_N^{kn} = W_{N_1}^{k_1 n_1 a_2} W_{N_2}^{k_2 n_2 a_1} \tag{7.96}$$

since $N_2 a_2 \bmod N_1 = N_1 a_1 \bmod N_2 = 1$. The DFT in this case can be written

$$X(k_2, k_1)_{\text{CRT}} = \sum_{n_2=0}^{N_2-1} \sum_{n_1=0}^{N_1-1} x(n_2, n_1)_{\text{CRT}} W_{N_1}^{k_1 n_1 a_2} W_{N_2}^{k_2 n_2 a_1} \qquad (7.97)$$

Equation (7.97) is the same as Eq. (7.81) when N_1 and N_2 are replaced by a_1 and a_2. Since a_1 and a_2 play the same roles in the CRT FFT development as N_1 and N_2 in the RC development, everything in Section VIII following Eq. (7.81) applies to this section after replacing N_1 and N_2 by a_1 and a_2. Also, the input and output ordering must be changed to correspond to the CRT.

As an example, let $N_1 = 2$ and $N_2 = 3$. Then Fig. 7.16 applies to the CRT FFT after the 2-point DFT input and 3-point DFT output indices are changed to those of Table VII and the unscrambling is modified appropriately.

GOOD's FFT   **X**

Good's algorithm was described in his 1958 paper [8] but went largely unnoticed until after Cooley and Tukey published their 1965 paper describing a radix-2 FFT [7]. However, Good's FFT was not competitive with the radix-2 FFT before the efficient small-N DFTs became available. Good's FFT is also called the Good–Thomas PFA or simply the PFA. Since there are a number of algorithms requiring that the factors of N be relatively prime, we shall use the terminology Good's algorithm.

The difference between Good's FFT and the RC or CRT FFT has to do with the indexing of data and transform sequences. Whereas the latter two use the RC or the CRT for indexing both sequences, Good's FFT uses the RC for one sequence and the CRT for the other.

Good's FFT When *N* Has Two Factors   **A**

Let k be represented by the CRT and n by the RC:

$$k = (k_2 N_1 a_1 + k_1 N_2 a_2) \bmod N \triangleq (k_2, k_1)_{\text{CRT}} \qquad (7.98)$$

$$n = (n_2 N_1 + n_1 N_2) \bmod N \triangleq (n_2, n_1)_{\text{RC}} \qquad (7.99)$$

where a_1 and a_2 are the multiplicative inverses of N/N_1 (modulo N_1) and N/N_2 (modulo N_2), respectively. Since $N_1 a_1 \bmod N_2 = N_2 a_2 \bmod N_1 = 1$,

$$W_N^{kn} = W_{N_1}^{k_1 n_1} W_{N_2}^{k_2 n_2} \qquad (7.100)$$

Using Eq. (7.100) in the 1-D DFT definition yields Eq. (7.18), which defines a 2-D

DFT. The indexing scheme has converted a 1-D DFT to a true 2-D DFT in which the data and transform sequences are scrambled according to Eqs. (7.99) and (7.98), respectively. If the indices k and n are represented by the RC and CRT instead of the CRT and RC, respectively, the development still applies. The only change is that the input and output indexing are reversed.

As an example, let $N_1 = 2$ and $N_2 = 3$. Let k and n be determined by the CRT and RC, respectively. Then Fig. 7.13 applies to Good's FFT after the 2-point DFT input indices are changed to those of Table VII. As another example, let $N_1 = 2$ and $N_2 = 3$, but let k and n be determined by the RC and CRT, respectively. Then Fig. 7.16 still applies to Good's FFT after the 3-point DFT output indices are changed to those of Table VII and the unscrambling is modified appropriately.

B Good's FFT When *N* Has *L* Factors

Let k and n be represented by the CRT, Eq. (7.90), and the RC, Eq. (7.76), respectively (or vice versa). Then the 2-D DFT generalizes to

$$X(k_L, \ldots, k_2, k_1)_{\mathrm{CRT}}$$

$$= \sum_{n_L=0}^{N_L-1} \cdots \left\{ \sum_{n_2=0}^{N_2-1} \left[\sum_{n_1=0}^{N_1-1} x(n_L, \ldots, n_2, n_1)_{\mathrm{RC}}\, W_{N_1}^{k_1 n_1} \right] W_{N_2}^{k_2 n_2} \right\} \cdots W_{N_L}^{k_L n_L} \quad (7.101)$$

which is an L-D DFT. The 1-D DFT data is assigned to an L-D array according to the RC. The L-D DFT is computed by the most efficient method possible to compute the N_1-, N_2-, $\ldots$, N_L-point DFTs. These efficient DFTs are generally the small-N DFTs of Appendix A. The L-D output data is reassigned to the 1-D DFT output by converting the locations in the L-D array to those in a 1-D array by the RC. Consequently, Good's FFT is in-order: the output data is in the same location as the input data, at least if we allow for determining k from $(k_L, \ldots, k_2, k_1)_{\mathrm{CRT}}$ and n from $(n_L, \ldots, n_2, n_1)_{\mathrm{RC}}$ using Eqs. (7.90) and (7.76), respectively (or vice versa).

XI KRONECKER PRODUCT REPRESENTATION OF GOOD'S FFT

Development of the WFTA is accomplished by first representing Good's FFT as a Kronecker product. Let

$$\mathbf{A} = (a_{kl}) \qquad\qquad (7.102)$$

be a $K \times L$ matrix, where $k = 0, 1, 2, \ldots, K-1$ and $l = 0, 1, 2, \ldots, L-1$. Let $\mathbf{B} = (b_{mn})$ be an $M \times N$ matrix. Then their Kronecker product is $\mathbf{A} \otimes \mathbf{B}$, where

$$\mathbf{A} \otimes \mathbf{B} = \begin{bmatrix} a_{0,0}\mathbf{B} & a_{0,1}\mathbf{B} & \cdots & a_{0,L-1}\mathbf{B} \\ a_{1,0}\mathbf{B} & a_{1,1}\mathbf{B} & \cdots & a_{1,L-1}\mathbf{B} \\ \vdots & & & \\ a_{K-1,0}\mathbf{B} & a_{K-1,1}\mathbf{B} & \cdots & a_{K-1,L-1}\mathbf{B} \end{bmatrix} \tag{7.103}$$

The Kronecker product causes $\mathbf{B}$ to be repeated KL times, each time scaled by an entry from $\mathbf{A}$. Since $\mathbf{B}$ is $M \times N$, $\mathbf{A} \otimes \mathbf{B}$ is $KM \times LN$.

DFTs can be combined into a larger DFT by taking their Kronecker product. Let $\mathbf{D}_L, \ldots, \mathbf{D}_i, \ldots, \mathbf{D}_2, \mathbf{D}_1$ be N_L-, ..., N_i-,..., N_2-, N_1-point DFTs where the N_i are relatively prime. Let $\mathbf{D}_i$ have naturally ordered indices; that is, $\mathbf{D}_i = (W_{N_i}^{k_i n_i})$, k_i, $n_i = 0, 1, 2, \ldots, N_i - 1$. Then another DFT is given by [2, 8, 10]

$$\mathbf{D} = \mathbf{D}_L \otimes \cdots \otimes D_i \otimes \cdots \otimes \mathbf{D}_2 \otimes \mathbf{D}_1 \tag{7.104}$$

where the data and transform sequence indices are determined by the RC and CRT, respectively, or vice versa. For example, let $L = 2$, $N_1 = 2$, and $N_2 = 3$. Then

$$\mathbf{D} = W_6^\mathbf{E} = W_3^{\mathbf{E}_2} \otimes W_2^{\mathbf{E}_1} \tag{7.105}$$

where

$$\mathbf{E}_2 = \begin{array}{c} \\ k_2 \end{array}\!\!\overset{\displaystyle n_2}{\begin{array}{c} 0 \;\; 1 \;\; 2 \\ \begin{array}{c} 0 \\ 1 \\ 2 \end{array}\!\!\begin{bmatrix} 0 & 0 & 0 \\ 0 & 1 & 2 \\ 0 & 2 & 1 \end{bmatrix} \end{array}, \qquad \mathbf{E}_1 = \begin{array}{c} \\ k_1 \end{array}\!\!\overset{\displaystyle n_1}{\begin{array}{c} 0 \;\; 1 \\ \begin{array}{c} 0 \\ 1 \end{array}\!\!\begin{bmatrix} 0 & 0 \\ 0 & 1 \end{bmatrix} \end{array} \tag{7.106}$$

and the matrix $\mathbf{E}$ with the n and k indices determined by the RC and CRT (see Tables V and VII), respectively, is

$$\mathbf{E} = \begin{array}{c} \\ k \end{array}\!\!\overset{\displaystyle n}{\begin{array}{c} 0 \;\; 3 \;\; 2 \;\; 5 \;\; 4 \;\; 1 \\ \begin{array}{c} 0 \\ 3 \\ 4 \\ 1 \\ 2 \\ 5 \end{array}\!\!\begin{bmatrix} 0 & 0 & 0 & 0 & 0 & 0 \\ 0 & 3 & 0 & 3 & 0 & 3 \\ 0 & 0 & 2 & 2 & 4 & 4 \\ 0 & 3 & 2 & 5 & 4 & 1 \\ 0 & 0 & 4 & 4 & 2 & 2 \\ 0 & 3 & 4 & 1 & 2 & 5 \end{bmatrix} \end{array} \tag{7.107}$$

Note that the k and n indices may be interchanged without affecting the E matrix, but the data and transform sequences are now ordered according to the CRT and RC, respectively. Note also the equivalence of the 2-D processing (Fig. 7.16 with the transform sequence indices changed to the CRT ordering) and the Kronecker product in Eq. (7.105). We conclude that L-D processing using Good's FFT, Eq. (7.101), is equivalent to the Kronecker product of L DFTs, Eq. (7.104).

A   The Winograd Fourier Transform Algorithm

The WFTA results from a Kronecker product manipulation to group input additions so that all transform multiplications follow. The multiplications are then followed by output additions that give the transform coefficients. The Kronecker product manipulation that nests the multiplications inside of the additions results from the relationship

$$(\mathbf{AB}) \otimes (\mathbf{CD}) = (\mathbf{A} \otimes \mathbf{C})(\mathbf{B} \otimes \mathbf{D}) \qquad (7.108)$$

where $\mathbf{A}, \mathbf{B}, \mathbf{C},$ and $\mathbf{D}$ are matrices with dimensions $M_1 \times N_1, N_1 \times N_2, M_3 \times N_3,$ and $N_3 \times N_4$, respectively. According to Eq. (7.73) a small-N DFT of dimension N_i can be put into the form

$$\mathbf{D}_i = \mathbf{S}_i \mathbf{C}_i \mathbf{T}_i \qquad (7.109)$$

We can construct a DFT of dimension $N = N_L \cdots N_2 N_1$ by using Eq. (7.109) in Eq. (7.104). We get

$$\mathbf{D} = (\mathbf{S}_L \mathbf{C}_L \mathbf{T}_L) \otimes \cdots \otimes (\mathbf{S}_2 \mathbf{C}_2 \mathbf{T}_2) \otimes (\mathbf{S}_1 \mathbf{C}_1 \mathbf{T}_1) \qquad (7.110)$$

Using Eq. (7.108) repeatedly in Eq. (7.110) gives [29]

$$\mathbf{D} = \underbrace{(\mathbf{S}_L \otimes \cdots \otimes \mathbf{S}_2 \otimes \mathbf{S}_1)}_{\text{output additions}} \underbrace{(\mathbf{C}_L \otimes \cdots \otimes \mathbf{C}_2 \otimes \mathbf{C}_1)}_{\text{multiplications}} \underbrace{(\mathbf{T}_L \otimes \cdots \otimes \mathbf{T}_2 \otimes \mathbf{T}_1)}_{\text{input additions}} \qquad (7.111)$$

Equation (7.111) is the WFTA. The $\mathbf{T}_i$ matrices are sparse, usually with nonzero entries of ± 1; therefore, $\mathbf{T}_L \otimes \cdots \otimes \mathbf{T}_i \otimes \cdots \otimes \mathbf{T}_2 \otimes \mathbf{T}_1$ specifies addition operations on input data. In like manner each of the $\mathbf{S}_i$ matrices accomplishes output additions. DFT multiplications are specified by the Kronecker product of the $\mathbf{C}_i$ matrices, $i = 1, 2, \ldots, L$, where each of the $\mathbf{C}_i$ matrices is diagonal and is made up of entries that are either purely real or purely imaginary.

If we write Eq. (7.111) as $\mathbf{D} = \mathbf{SCT}$, then the DFT output is

$$\mathbf{X} = \mathbf{Dx} = \mathbf{SCTx} \qquad (7.112)$$

where $\mathbf{X}$ and $\mathbf{x}$ are transform and data vectors ordered as the CRT and RC, or vice versa. The matrix operations are carried out with much fewer arithmetic operations by doing equivalent L-D processing. The data in the vector is reformatted into an L-D array that is processed in L-D space by $\mathbf{T} = \mathbf{T}_L \otimes \cdots \otimes \mathbf{T}_2 \otimes \mathbf{T}_1$. This yields an M-point output, $\mathbf{y} = \mathbf{Tx}$ in vector form, where $\mathbf{T}$ is an $M \times N$ matrix. Again $\mathbf{y}$ has L components that are processed in

L-D space by $\mathbf{C} = \mathbf{C}_L \otimes \cdots \otimes \mathbf{C}_2 \otimes \mathbf{C}_1$. Finally, L-D processing by $\mathbf{S} = \mathbf{S}_L \otimes \cdots \otimes \mathbf{S}_2 \otimes \mathbf{S}_1$ yields $X(k)$, with k determined by the CRT if n is determined by the RC. Since the $\mathbf{C}_i$ are diagonal matrices, the multiplications specified by the $\mathbf{C}_i$ are simplified, as the 2-D processing shows.

2-D WFTA   B

In the 2-D WFTA the DFT defined by $\mathbf{X} = \mathbf{D}_2 \otimes \mathbf{D}_1 \mathbf{x}$ may be processed in 2-D space, which is equivalent to

$$(X(k_2, k_1)) = \mathbf{D}_2(x(n_2, n_1))\mathbf{D}_1^{\mathrm{T}} = \mathbf{D}_2[\mathbf{D}_1(x(n_2, n_1))^{\mathrm{T}}]^{\mathrm{T}} \qquad (7.113)$$

where $(x(n_2, n_1))$ and $(X(k_2, k_1))$ are $N_2 \times N_1$ matrices, $\mathbf{D}_1$ and $\mathbf{D}_2$ are N_1- and N_2-point DFTs, and $\mathbf{D}_1$ and $\mathbf{D}_2$ transform the rows and columns of $(x(n_2, n_1))$, respectively. At this point the WFTA uses the small-N DFTs that were shown (Section VII) to have the format $\mathbf{D}_i = \mathbf{S}_i \mathbf{C}_i \mathbf{T}_i$, where $\mathbf{S}_i$, $\mathbf{C}_i$, and $\mathbf{T}_i$ are $N_i \times M_i$, $M_i \times M_i$, and $M_i \times N_i$ matrices, respectively. Using these DFTs in Eq. (7.113) yields

$$(X(k_2, k_1)) = \mathbf{S}_2 \mathbf{C}_2 \mathbf{T}_2(x(n_2, n_1))\mathbf{T}_1^{\mathrm{T}} \mathbf{C}_1^{\mathrm{T}} \mathbf{S}_1^{\mathrm{T}} \qquad (7.114)$$

$\mathbf{T}_1$ and $\mathbf{T}_2$ transform the rows and columns, respectively, of the 2-D array $(x(n_2, n_1))$. The operations equivalent to $\mathbf{T}_1$ and $\mathbf{T}_2$ are accomplished by "preweave" modules (see Fig. 7.17). Next the multiplications specified by $\mathbf{C}_1$ and

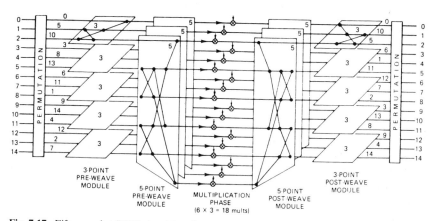

Fig. 7.17. Fifteen-point DFT algorithm decomposed using Good's mapping to obtain a two-dimensional (3×5)-point DFT and Winograd's algorithms for 3-point and 5-point DFTs. The algorithm requires $18 = 6 \times 3$ multiplications which are "nested" between the preweave and postweave modules. Reprinted with permission from J. H. McClellan and C. M. Rader, *Number Theory in Digital Signal Processing*, Prentice-Hall, Englewood Cliffs, N. J., 1979. Copyright ©1979 by Prentice-Hall, Inc.

$\mathbf{C}_2$ are carried out; they can be expedited because $\mathbf{C}_1$ and $\mathbf{C}_2$ are diagonal matrices. To illustrate, we shall compute the transpose of the center five matrices in Eq. (7.114) when they are all 2×2 matrices:

$$\mathbf{C}_1 = \begin{bmatrix} C_1(0) & 0 \\ 0 & C_1(1) \end{bmatrix}, \qquad \mathbf{C}_2 = \begin{bmatrix} C_2(0) & 0 \\ 0 & C_2(1) \end{bmatrix}$$

$$\mathbf{T}_1(x(n_2, n_1))^{\mathrm{T}} \mathbf{T}_2^{\mathrm{T}} = \begin{pmatrix} a & b \\ c & d \end{pmatrix} \tag{7.115}$$

so that

$$\mathbf{C}_1 \mathbf{T}_1(x(n_2, n_1))^{\mathrm{T}} \mathbf{T}_2^{\mathrm{T}} \mathbf{C}_2^{\mathrm{T}} = \begin{vmatrix} C_2(0)C_1(0)a & C_2(1)C_1(0)b \\ C_2(0)C_1(1)c & C_2(1)C_1(1)d \end{vmatrix}$$

$$= \mathbf{C} \circ \mathbf{T}_1(x(n_2, n_1))^{\mathrm{T}} \mathbf{T}_2^{\mathrm{T}} \tag{7.116}$$

where $\mathbf{A} \circ \mathbf{B}$ means point-by-point multiplication of corresponding points in the $M_1 \times M_2$ matrices $\mathbf{A}$ and $\mathbf{B}$, and, in general, $\mathbf{C} = (c(l_1, l_2))$ is an $M_1 \times M_2$ matrix defined by

$$c(l_1, l_2) = c_1(l_1)c_2(l_2), \qquad l_i = 0, 1, 2, \ldots, M_i - 1, i = 1, 2 \tag{7.117}$$

The significance of Eq. (7.116) is that the multiplications are combined into one phase, as illustrated in Fig. 7.17. Finally, the operations equivalent to $\mathbf{S}_1$ and $\mathbf{S}_2$ are carried out by postweave modules. Thus, alternative representations for Eq. (7.114) are

$$(X(k_2, k_1)) = \mathbf{S}_2[\mathbf{C}^{\mathrm{T}} \circ [\mathbf{T}_2(x(n_2, n_1))\mathbf{T}_1^{\mathrm{T}}]]\mathbf{S}_1^{\mathrm{T}}$$

$$= \mathbf{S}_2[\mathbf{S}_1[\mathbf{C} \circ [\mathbf{T}_1[\mathbf{T}_2(x(n_2, n_1))]^{\mathrm{T}}]]]^{\mathrm{T}} \tag{7.118a}$$

$$X(k_2, k_1) = \sum_{l_2=0}^{M_2-1} \sum_{l_1=0}^{M_1-1} S_2(k_2, l_2)S_1(k_1, l_1)C(l_2, l_1)$$

$$\times \sum_{n_2=0}^{N_2-1} \sum_{n_1=0}^{N_1-1} T_2(l_2, n_2)T_1(l_1, n_1)x(n_2, n_1) \tag{7.118b}$$

where in Eq. (7.118a) the operations must proceed from the inner brackets to the outer ones. Equations (7.118) and Fig. 7.17 illustrate the WFTA structure. The input and output data are ordered according to the RC and CRT in Fig. 7.17 (this ordering can be reversed). All input additions are done so that the number of points can be expanded along the n_2-axis and the n_1-axis, or both. Point-by-point multiplications are followed by the output additions. Combining the multipliers $c_i(l_i)$ into one [see Eq. (7.117)] gives the WFTA. It requires fewer multiplications than any FFT discussed previously, but at the expense of extra data transfers, compared to the FFTs using the in-place computations of butterfly and butterflylike structures.

In this case the DFT is defined by $\mathbf{X} = \mathbf{D}_L \otimes \cdots \otimes \mathbf{D}_2 \otimes \mathbf{D}_1 \mathbf{x}$, where $\mathbf{X}$ and $\mathbf{x}$ are N-point transform and data vectors whose entries are ordered by the CRT and RC, or vice versa. The equivalent L-D processing can be expressed by extending Eq. (7.118a) with a definition of L-D transpose [2, 29]. It is more straightforward to extend Eq. (7.118b), which gives

$$X(k_L, \ldots, k_2, k_1)_{\text{CRT}} = \sum_{l_L=0}^{M_L-1} \cdots \sum_{l_2=0}^{M_2-1} \sum_{l_1=0}^{M_1-1} S_L(k_L, l_L) \cdots S_2(k_2, l_2) S_1(k_1, l_1)$$

$$\cdot C(l_L, \ldots, l_2, l_1) \sum_{n_L=0}^{N_L-1} \cdots \sum_{n_2=0}^{N_2-1} \sum_{n_1=0}^{N_1-1} T_L(l_L, n_L) \cdots T_2(l_2, n_2)$$

$$\cdot T_1(l_1, n_1) x(n_L, \ldots, n_2, n_1)_{\text{RC}} \tag{7.119}$$

where $C(l_L, \ldots, l_2, l_1) = c_L(l_L) \cdots c_2(l_2) c_1(l_1)$ is an L-D array defining point-by-point multiplications that are nested inside the N_1-point DFT input and output additions, which in turn are nested inside the N_2-point DFT input and output additions, etc., until finally the N_L-point input and output additions determine the transform output.

In the computation of a 2-D DFT or a 1-D DFT using Good's FFT, there are many redundancies in the multiplications and summations. H. J. Nussbaumer showed that the method of polynomial transforms substantially reduces these redundancies and, therefore, the arithmetic to compute the DFT [4, 30]. For example, suppose we are required to compute an $N \times N$ 2-D DFT. The normal row–column rule requires N DFTs to transform the rows and N more to transform the columns, for a total of $2N$ DFTs. If N is a prime number, the polynomial transform method computes the $N \times N$ DFT with $N + 1$ N-point DFTs, thus cutting the computation in half for $N \gg 1$. The N-point DFTs are computed in the most efficient manner possible.

Developing the polynomial transforms would take us somewhat away from the approach we have followed in this chapter. We therefore refer the reader to several other publications [2, 4, 30, 45] for details. However, in the next section we give some results for DFT computation using polynomial transforms plus nesting, so we will illustrate this method for the case of transforming an $N \times N$ array $(x(n, m))$, $N = N_1 N_2$, and $\gcd(N_1, N_2) = 1$. Let $\mathbf{D}_1$ and $\mathbf{D}_2$ be N_1- and N_2-point DFTs, and let $\mathbf{D} = \mathbf{D}_2 \otimes \mathbf{D}_1$. Then the 2-D DFT is

$$(X(k, l)) = \mathbf{D}(x(m, n))\mathbf{D}^{\text{T}} = \mathbf{D}_2 \otimes \mathbf{D}_1(x(m, n))(\mathbf{D}_2 \otimes \mathbf{D}_1)^{\text{T}} \tag{7.120}$$

Let k and l be represented by the CRT, and m and n by the RC. Then the 2-D arrays become 4-D arrays, $(X(k,l)) = (X(k_2,k_1,l_2,l_1))_{CRT}$ and $x(m,n)) = (x(m_2,m_1,n_2,n_1)_{RC})$, that may be transformed by applying $\mathbf{D}_2$ to first the k_2 index and then the l_2 index, followed by applying $\mathbf{D}_1$ to the k_1 and l_1 indices, written symbolically as

$$(X(k_2,k_1,l_2,l_1)_{CRT}) = [\mathbf{D}_1[\mathbf{D}_1[\mathbf{D}_2[\mathbf{D}_2(x(m_2,n_2,m_1,n_1)_{RC})]^T]^T]^T]^T \quad (7.121)$$

The computations in Eq. (7.121) can be performed by nesting $N_2 \times N_2$ DFTs inside of $N_1 \times N_1$ DFTs, and these DFTs can be computed efficiently by polynomial transforms. Thus, the 2-D DFT $(X(k,l))$ is obtained from polynomial transforms plus nesting.

XIII   COMPARISON OF ALGORITHMS

Data giving arithmetic computational requirements were obtained from a number of sources [15, 17, 24, 29–34]. The data is in Table VIII and is plotted in Fig. 7.18. Note that approximately a 3:1 reduction in multiplications results from using the WFTA or a polynomial transform algorithm instead of a radix-2 FFT. Note also that for the data in Fig. 7.18, the SRFFT minimizes additions and offers a compromise multiplication count. Since the SRFFT has a butterfly structure that implies in-place computation, no reordering of the data is required, and this leads to efficient program execution. Multidimensional DFT computation is compared in Table IX, which shows that there is often a sizable reduction in multiplications using polynomial transforms plus nesting.

Figure 7.19 compares the ratio of theoretically computed computational times using the nonorthogonal coordinate system with the basis $(1, W_3)$ described in Section V.A and (a) a standard radix-3 algorithm, (b) a radix-2 algorithm, and (c) a radix-4 algorithm. The comparison is for large values of N. The cost of a multiplication is r times that of an addition, and the time comparison does not include time for data transfers or computational overhead. Four real multiplications and three real additions were assumed for implementing multiplications using the basis $(1, W_3)$, and four and two, respectively, were assumed in the complex plane. The costs are relative, since a radix-2 or radix-4 algorithm and a radix-3 algorithm cannot both exist for the same N. Note that the radix-3 algorithm, which is described in Section V.C and uses nonorthogonal coordinates, is more efficient than a radix-2 or a standard radix-3 algorithm but is less efficient than the radix-4 algorithm, discussed in Section VI, based on a multiplication–addition comparison.

Similar to Fig. 7.19, Fig. 7.20 shows the ratio of computational times using a radix-6 FFT implemented using the nonorthogonal coordinate system with the basis $(1, W_3)$ (see Section V.D) and several other FFTs, one of which is a 6-point FFT using Good's algorithm (see Section X). Note that the radix-6 FFT is more

TABLE VIII

Number of Real Multiplications and Real Additions to Compute 1-D FFT Algorithms with Complex Input Data

N	Factors	WFTA Multiplications	WFTA Additions	Good algorithm Multiplications	Good algorithm Additions	Polynomial transform Multiplications	Polynomial transform Additions	Radix-2 FFT Multiplications	Radix-2 FFT Additions	FFT Multiplications	FFT Additions
30	5, 3, 2	68	384	68	384						
32	2^5							102	422	68	388
48	16, 3	108	636								
60	5, 4, 3	144	888								
63	7, 9					172	1,424				
80	5, 16					188	1,340				
120	5, 8, 3	288	2,076	512	2,920						
126	9, 7, 2	424	3,312								
128	2^7							774	2,566	516	2,308
168	7, 8, 3	432	3,492								
240	5, 16, 3	648	5,016			596	4,980				
252	9, 7, 4	848	7,128	1,024	6,344						
256	2^8							1,926	6,022	1,284	5,380
315	9, 5, 7	1,292	11,286	1,784	8,812						
360	9, 5, 8	1,152	9,492	1,396	8,708						
504	9, 7, 8	1,704	15,516	2,300	13,948						
512	2^9					1,380	14,668	4,614	13,830		
840	5, 7, 8, 3	2,592	24,804	4,244	23,172	2,580	24,804				
1,008	9, 7, 16	4,212	35,244			3,116	34,956				
1,024	2^{10}							10,758	31,238		
1,260	9, 5, 7, 4	5,168	50,184	7,136	40,288						
2,048	2^{11}							24,582	69,638	16,388	61,444
2,520	9, 5, 7, 8	10,344	106,667	15,532	86,876	8,340	95,532				

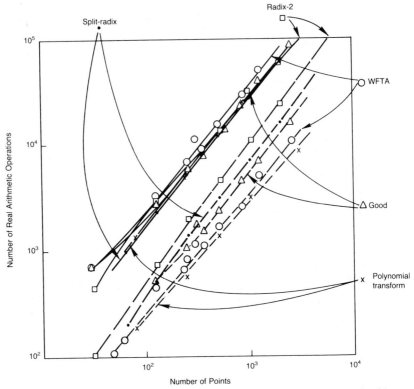

Fig. 7.18. Comparison of real arithmetic operations to compute 1-D FFT algorithms with complex input data: solid line, additions; dashed line, multiplications.

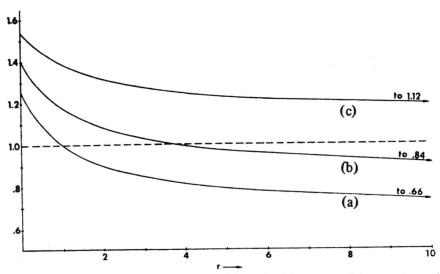

Fig. 7.19. Ratio of computational times of radix-3 algorithm computed in nonorthogonal coordinates and (a) standard radix-3, (b) radix-2, (c) radix-4 algorithms [20] © 1978 IEEE.

TABLE IX

Number of Real Multiplications and Additions per Output Point for Multidimensional DFTs with Complex Input Data (Trivial Multiplications by ± 1, $\pm j$ Are Not Counted)[a]

DFT size	Polynomial transform method plus nesting		WFTA		Good	
	Multiplications per point	Additions per point	Multiplications per point	Additions per point	Multiplications per point	Additions per point
24×24	1.86	20.75	1.87	21.00	3.67	21.00
30×30	2.47	29.68	2.87	26.96	6.67	25.60
36×36	2.57	27.38	2.96	29.73	4.44	27.56
40×40	2.43	30.43	2.83	27.96	5.00	26.60
48×48	2.30	25.69	2.48	27.66	5.17	26.50
56×56	2.63	38.67	3.28	36.51	5.57	33.57
63×63	3.44	51.63	4.94	56.85	9.02	40.13
72×72	2.58	32.14	2.97	34.73	5.44	32.56
80×80	2.93	38.68	3.62	38.59	6.50	32.10
112×112	3.14	48.47	4.17	49.41	7.07	39.07
120×120	2.47	38.43	2.87	35.96	7.67	34.60
144×144	3.07	40.70	3.78	47.16	6.94	38.06
240×240	2.94	46.68	3.64	46.59	9.17	40.10
504×504	3.44	64.38	4.94	69.85	10.02	53.13
1008×1008	4.08	79.00	6.25	91.61	11.52	58.63
$120 \times 120 \times 120$	2.50	57.85	3.46	56.25	11.50	51.90
$240 \times 240 \times 240$	3.04	50.74	4.92	78.61	13.75	60.15

[a] From [30]. ©1979 IEEE.

583

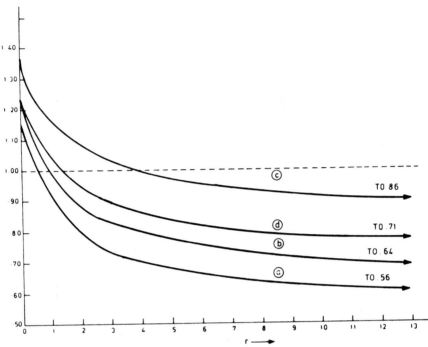

Fig. 7.20. Ratio of computation time of radix-6 algorithm computed in nonorthogonal coordinates and (a) standard radix-6, (b) radix-2, (c) radix-4, (d) standard radix-6 implemented with Good's FFT [21] © 1981 IEEE.

efficient than the radix-4 FFT for $r > 4$. The comparison is for large values of N and neglects data transfer times.

Algorithms have been found for radix-3, -6, and -12 FFTs that are computed in the $(1, j)$ plane rather than by using the basis $(1, \mu)$ [35]. These algorithms are the most efficient of known FFTs for these radices, do not require input-output coordinate transformations, and are simpler to implement and use than the algorithms described in Figs. 7.19 and 7.20.

Although a particular algorithm reduces multiplications, it may require numerous data transfers so that computer run time may be longer than for another algorithm with more multiplications and fewer data transfers. For example, Morris compared WFTA and radix-4 algorithms on several computers that compile a relatively time-efficient program for execution [36]. He found that data transfers, an increase in the number of additions, and data reordering resulted in execution times 40–60% longer for the WFTA than those for radix-4 FFTs for a comparable number of data points.

Table X is an evaluation of five FFT algorithms on seven different computers [37]. Each execution time is an average value obtained by repeated execution of the algorithm. Comparing 1008- and 1024-point FFTs, note that an ordering of the algorithms based on execution time is different for each computer.

TABLE X
FFT Execution Time in Milliseconds[†]

Computer	Length	Radix-2	Mixed radix	WFTA	Good's	Radix-4
Cray-1	504		5.75	2.73	3.71	
	512	4.25				
	630		7.50	4.72	5.84	
	1008		10.55	6.77	7.77	
	1024	8.98				
	1260		15.31	8.60	11.41	
	2048	18.97				
	2520		32.20	17.25	23.03	
Cyber 750	504		28	15	13	
	512	10				
	630		36	21	20	
	1008		52	35	29	
	1024	24				35
	1260		76	41	43	
	2048	50				
	2520		160	92	88	
IBM 370	504		237	134	103	
	512	194				
	630		307	203	147	
	1008		441	314	226	
	1024	404				
	1260		657	408	314	
	2048	920				
	2520		1423	873	682	
VAX 11/780	504		192	133	85	
	512	183				
	630		240	207	152	
	1008		344	317	213	
	1024	360				300
	1260		521	423	308	
	2048	779				
	2520		1127	917	610	
PDP 11/60	504		295	250	183	
	512	266				
	630		411	367	261	
	1008		566	[a]	384	
	1024	566				390
	1260	[a]	849	[a]	511	
	2048	1211				
	2520		1800	[a]	[a]	
PDP 11/50	504		793	551	411	
	512		678			
PDP 11/50	630		1054	835	602	
	1008		1543	1291	952	
	1024	1452				783
	1260		2250	[a]	1240	
	2048	3128				
	2520		4780	[a]	2651	

[†] From [37]. © 1985 IEEE.

[a] Unable to execute due to insufficient memory.

(continued)

TABLE X (*Continued*)

Computer	Length	Radix-2	Mixed radix	WFTA	Good's	Radix-4
Cromemco	504		21000	a	8000	
	512	18000				
	630		29000	a	12000	
	1008		43000	a	15000	
	1024	40000				
	1260		62000	a	23000	
	2048	97000				
	2520		135000	a	a	

Mehalic, Rustan, and Route [37] explain why certain algorithms perform better on certain computers in terms of the computer architecture, hardware, and software. They relate the execution times to four different instructions: (1) floating-point additions and subtractions, (2) floating-point multiplications and divisions, (3) integer operations, and (4) data transfers. The correlation coefficients between the instruction categories and run times are shown in Table XI. In all cases the number of data transfers is highly correlated with the execution time. For processors whose architecture favors floating-point operations, it was found that FFTs minimizing data transfers did best and the radix-2 FFT was fastest. Architectures especially suited to data transfers favor FFTs minimizing multiplications, so the WFTA and Good's algorithm run fastest. Computers designed for vector operations (i.e., array processing) execute the WFTA fastest.

Table XII lists the instruction counts obtained by analyzing assembly language listings of the FORTRAN source codes. Typically, over 99.5% of the floating-point multiplications and divisions were multiplications, and over 90% of the

TABLE XI

Correlation Coefficients between Execution Time and Instruction Type[a]

| | Data | Floating point | | Integer |
| | transfers | Mult. & Div. | Add. & Subt. | operations |
Computer				
Cray-1	0.95	0.88	0.93	0.97
Cyber 750	1.00	0.73	0.92	0.96
IBM 370/155	0.95	0.87	0.95	0.78
VAX 11/780	0.97	0.66	0.95	0.92
PDP 11/60	1.00	0.97	0.98	0.98
PDP 11/50	1.00	0.92	0.96	0.98
Cromemco Z-2D	0.99	1.00	0.97	1.00

[a] From [37]. © 1985 IEEE.

TABLE XII

Instruction Count for 1008- or 1024-Point FFT[a]

| Computer | Algorithm | Floating point | | Integer | Data transfers |
		Add. & Subt.	Mult. & Div.		
Cray-1	Radix-2	29,702	25,615	40,921	242,663
	MFFT	33,671	23,205	62,183	178,997
	WFTA	34,290	3,654	61,385	200,282
	Good's	29,548	5,810	36,909	140,144
Cyber 750	Radix-2	32,766	24,592	13,805	68,680
	MFFT	34,655	22,877	32,772	144,005
	WFTA	34,353	3,584	1,463	114,530
	Good's	29,100	5,807	10,740	81,582
	Radix-4	28,336	7,856	6,430	83,984
IBM 370/155	Radix-2	32,776	24,582	15,357	103,064
	MFFT	33,660	23,096	20,711	150,560
	WFTA	34,353	3,564	22,652	167,125
	Good's	29,100	5,804	5,649	68,325
VAX 11/780	Radix-2	32,766	24,592	13,299	59,335
	MFFT	33,653	23,110	20,807	68,083
	WFTA	34,353	3,564	17,921	77,917
	Good's	29,100	5,804	5,781	37,360
PDP 11/60 and PDP 11/50	Radix-2	32,766	24,582	37,812	136,086
	MFFT	32,099	22,852	47,368	162,467
	WFTA	34,353	3,564	44,279	163,910
	Good's	29,100	5,804	21,745	93,280
	Radix-4	28,336	7,856	6,714	78,034
Cromemco Z-2D	Radix-2	32,766	24,582	122,143	444,363
	MFFT	33,641	22,601	129,872	447,076
	WFTA	34,290	3,564	130,224	368,802
	Good's	29,244	5,804	56,424	267,127
	Radix-4	28,336	7,856	55,098	201,782

[a] From [37]. © 1985 IEEE.

integer operations were additions or subtractions. The number of floating-point operations depends on the FFT algorithm and is approximately equal to the number predicted in theory, whereas the number of integer operations and data transfers depends on the compiler and the computer architecture and is different for each computer [37].

FFT WORD LENGTHS   XIV

A sufficient number of bits must be allocated to number representation in an FFT mechanization if the FFT is to be used to its full potential. In this section we show how to determine word lengths for a radix-2 FFT and state results that show the Good FFT and WFTA require up to $\frac{1}{2}$ and 2 extra bits, respectively, for the same (approximately) length FFT. We shall investigate word lengths using dynamic range analysis, which is an analytical technique that investigates whether a system has sufficient digital word lengths in the digital filters, FFT, and other processor components. We shall illustrate FFT word-length allocation in a spectral analysis system (see Chapters 8 and 9). Chapter 14 further discusses FFT implementation, including microprogramming the FFT butterfly (Section VI.A) and distributed arithmetic (Section VIII).

a. Dynamic Range Analysis.   Dynamic range for a spectral analysis system is stated in terms of the maximum difference that can be detected in the power level of high- and low-amplitude pure-tone signals (i.e., single-frequency sinusoids). The high-amplitude signal drives a fixed-point system near to saturation. The low-amplitude signal is detectable after processing, even though it is indiscernible in the noise before processing. We shall illustrate dynamic range analysis using a fixed-point, sign-and-magnitude representation of numbers and shall briefly discuss other representations.

Word lengths in a fixed-point spectral analysis system must be sufficient to accomplish the following objectives:

1. They must allow signals with a low signal-to-noise ratio (SNR) to be filtered so that noise is reduced to a level at which the signal can be detected. This requires that noise due to quantizing the outputs of arithmetic operations contribute negligible noise power compared to a reference input. In a fixed-point system this implies that the least significant bit (lsb) represents a small enough magnitude so that the FFT roundoff noise does not become a dominant noise source compared to the reference.

2. They must prevent high-amplitude signals from overflowing in fixed-point mechanizations. This requires that the processed words contain a sufficient number of bits to prevent high-level signals from clipping while keeping low-level signals from being lost in roundoff noise.

3. They must accomplish an accurate spectra analysis. This requires that multiplier coefficients W^{kn} in the FFT be represented by a sufficient number of bits to maintain the accuracy of the sinusoidal correlation function.

b. Spectral Analysis System with AGC.   Figure 7.21 shows the block diagram of a fixed-point spectral analysis system. The analog filter is an antialiasing filter prior to the ADC. The width of the signal transition band (see Chapter 2, Section III) is appreciably reduced by the digital filter so that the sampling frequency can be reduced, permitting the FFT to run at a lower rate. The magnitude or magnitude-squared digital filter outputs are averaged in a digital lowpass (LPF), and filter automatic gain control (AGC) action is accomplished by comparing the difference of average and desired LPF outputs. The integrated difference adjusts the gain of the amplifier so that the difference goes to zero. The magnitude or magnitude squared of the properly ordered transform sequence from the FFT is displayed completing the spectral analysis system functions in Fig. 7.21.

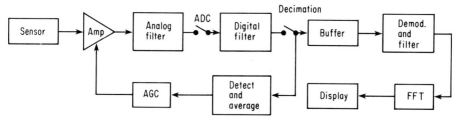

Fig. 7.21. Special analysis system using fixed-point arithmetic.

The AGC adjusts the power level to keep high-amplitude signals from overflowing (objective 2). Thus the real signal at the digital filter output has a power level of typically -12 dB, as shown in Figure 7.22. In general, the AGC is controlled by a mixture of signals and noise. Suppose, for illustration purposes, that the only signal in the system is pure tone with a period P s and a phase angle θ. If the signal is oscillating from $+1$ to -1, its average power is

$$\frac{1}{P}\int_{-P/2}^{P/2}\cos^2\left(\frac{2\pi t}{P}+\theta\right)dt = \frac{1}{2} \qquad \text{(equivalent to } -3 \text{ dB)} \qquad (7.122)$$

A bit, which represents a magnitude change of 2 or a power change of 4, is equivalent to 6 dB, so bits convert to decibels in the ratio of 6 dB/bit. Bit number, bit magnitude, and power level in decibels are shown in Fig. 7.22. The power level corresponds to a signal whose rms value is given by the bit magnitude. We assume that the fixed-point word out of the ADC is a real sign-magnitude number with the form $s \cdot a_1 a_2 a_3 \cdots a_k \cdots a_b$, where $a_k = 0$ or 1, a_b is the lsb, $k = 1, 2, \ldots,$ b is the bit number, s is the sign bit,

$$s = \begin{cases} 0 & \text{if } \dfrac{x}{|x|} = 1 \\[2mm] 1 & \text{if } \dfrac{x}{|x|} = -1 \end{cases} \qquad (7.123)$$

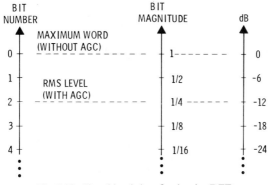

Fig. 7.22. Signal levels in a fixed-point DFT.

where $x = s + \sum_{k=1}^{b} a_k 2^{-k}$, and the maximum magnitude of x is

$$0.111 \cdots 1 = \frac{1}{2} + \frac{1}{4} + \frac{1}{8} + \cdots + \frac{1}{2^b} \approx 1$$

See Section II in Chapter 5 and Section IV in Chapter 14 for further discussion of number representations.

c. Impact of Scaling within a Fixed-Point FFT.   We mentioned in Chapter 1, Section VII.D, that the factor of $1/N$ is often incorporated in fixed-point FFTs to prevent overflowing. In a radix-2 FFT with $N = 2^L$ this is usually accomplished by dividing the inputs to a butterfly by 2 or scaling by $\frac{1}{2}$ in each of the L butterfly stages. To illustrate the need for the scaling in a fixed-point FFT. consider a complex sinusoid $x(n) = e^{j2\pi kn/N}$ at the FFT input. At the FFT output the sinusoid, which is centered in frequency bin k, yields an output

$$X(k) = \frac{1}{N} \sum_{n=0}^{N-1} W^{kn} e^{j2\pi kn/N} = 1 \tag{7.124}$$

since $W = e^{-j2\pi/N}$. This is a *coherent summation*; the signal phase is the negative of the phase of the kernel of the summation so that the FFT output is maximized at 1. Without the $1/N$ scaling, we would have $X(k) = N$, which might cause overflow in the spectral analysis system, depending on the scaling. Tracing the complex sinusoid, for example, the sinusoid for a normalized frequency of k/N Hz in Fig. 7.9, through the FFT on its path to the kth bin output shows that it doubles at the output of each stage without scaling; with a scaling of $\frac{1}{2}$ at each stage it remains unity. Thus, the scaling strategy is to scale by a factor of $\frac{1}{2}$ at each stage.

To further illustrate the consequences of scaling, consider zero mean, independently distributed noise at the FFT input, that is,

$$E[x(n)] = 0, \quad E[x(n)x(m)] = 0, \quad n \neq m, \tag{7.125}$$

$$E[x(n)x^*(n)] = \sigma_x^2 = \text{FFT input noise power}$$

The output power for the kth DFT coefficient after scaling the DFT by $1/N$ is

$$E[X(k)X^*(k)] = E\left[\frac{1}{N^2} \sum_{n=0}^{N-1} x(n)W^{kn} \sum_{m=0}^{N-1} x^*(m)W^{-km}\right]$$

$$= \frac{1}{N^2} \sum_{n=0}^{N-1} W^{kn} \sum_{m=0}^{N-1} W^{-km} E[x(n)x^*(m)] = \frac{\sigma_x^2}{N} \tag{7.126}$$

$$= \frac{1}{N} \text{FFT input noise power}$$

If the $1/N$ factor results from doubling the noise power at each summing junction and then attenuating it by a factor of 4 by using a scaling of $\frac{1}{2}$, the net attenuation is $\frac{1}{2}$ at each of the L stages. Since the signal power remained unity, the SNR increases by 2 per stage and the rms SNR increases by $\sqrt{2}$ per stage.

We have considered noise at the FFT input and its attenuation going through the FFT due to the scaling of $\frac{1}{2}$ per stage. In addition, quantization noise is generated internally in the FFT, and this noise must be accounted for; we consider this topic next.

d. Quantization Noise. Reducing digital word lengths by truncation or rounding introduces *quantization noise*. We shall assume rounding is used in the spectral analysis system. Quantization noise due to rounding in the FFT results from scaling by $\frac{1}{2}$ and from rounding the output of multiplications.

Consider first division by 2. If there is uncorrelated noise at the FFT input, it is equally probable that the lsb of a given word is 0 or 1, and furthermore it is equally probable that the 1 represents 2^{-b} or -2^{-b}. Thus, the probabilities that the lsb is zero, -2^{-b}, and 2^b are $\frac{1}{2}, \frac{1}{4}$, and $\frac{1}{4}$, respectively. For real data the mean error m_s after scaling by $\frac{1}{2}$ is zero and the variance σ_s^2 is 2^{-2b-1}, as shown in Fig. 7.23. For complex data $\sigma_s^2 = 2^{-2b}$, since the real and imaginary components each contribute a variance (noise power) of 2^{-2b-1}.

Consider next multiplication roundoff noise. Let the inputs to the multiplier, x and y, satisfy $|x| < 1$ and $|y| < 1$ so that overflow will not occur. Let x and y be sign-magnitude numbers of b bits plus sign each. Let the $2b$-bit output be rounded to b bits. Then assuming that $b \gg 1$, we can approximate the rounding error as uniformly distributed as shown in Fig. 7.24 so that the mean error is zero and the variance σ_m due the rounding the multiplication is $2^{-2b}/12$. For a complex input with $x = a + jb$ and $y = c + jd$, $xy = ac - bd + j(ad + bc)$, so the variance is increased by 4, yielding $\sigma_m^2 = 4(2^{-b}/12)$, as shown in Fig. 7.25.

e. Roundoff Noise in an FFT. Roundoff noise is a function of the hardware utilized and the algorithm. As an example of the effect of the hardware, a microprocessor may have a recoverable overflow bit so that scaling by $\frac{1}{2}$ can be accomplished after addition of two numbers rather than before, but this overflow bit recovery also entails a loss of speed due to additional logic. An example of the effect of the algorithm, the FFT quantization noise power output is slightly different for a DIF than a DIT FFT [38]. We shall make reasonable assumptions and give indicative results using the DIT FFT.

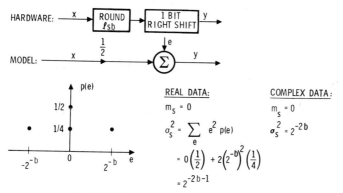

Fig. 7.23. Noise introduced by division by 2.

- LET THE NUMBER OF BITS, b , BE LARGE, I.E., $b \gg 1$
- THEN, THE ERROR IS UNIFORMLY DISTRIBUTED BETWEEN $-\dfrac{1}{2^{b+1}}$ AND $\dfrac{1}{2^{b+1}}$

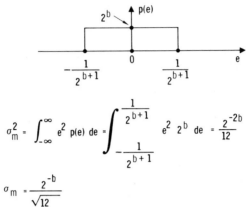

$$\sigma_m^2 = \int_{-\infty}^{\infty} e^2 \, p(e) \, de = \int_{-\frac{1}{2^{b+1}}}^{\frac{1}{2^{b+1}}} e^2 \, 2^b \, de = \frac{2^{-2b}}{12}$$

$$\sigma_m = \frac{2^{-b}}{\sqrt{12}}$$

Fig. 7.24. Mean-squared error due to rounding the product of the two b-bit numbers to b bits.

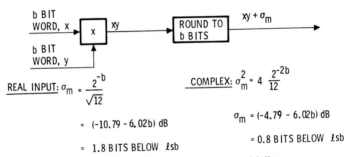

REAL INPUT: $\sigma_m = \dfrac{2^{-b}}{\sqrt{12}}$

$= (-10.79 - 6.02b)$ dB

$= 1.8$ BITS BELOW ℓsb

COMPLEX: $\sigma_m^2 = 4\,\dfrac{2^{-2b}}{12}$

$\sigma_m = (-4.79 - 6.02b)$ dB

$= 0.8$ BITS BELOW ℓsb

Fig. 7.25. Quantization noise from a multiplier.

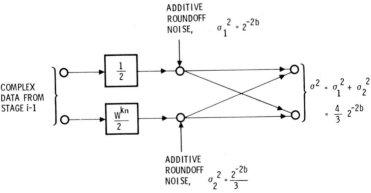

Fig. 7.26. Example of quantization noise at the output of stage i in a DIT FFT.

Figure 7.26 is an example of one stage in a butterfly computation for a DIT FFT showing that output roundoff noise at each node of the stage is $\sigma^2 = 4(2^{-2b})/3$. The first two stages and half the butterflies in subsequent stages have no multiplications, and for these butterflies the noise is due only to scaling by $\frac{1}{2}$, which yields $\sigma^2 = 2(2^{-2b})$. Thus, the output at stage i due to noise power at stages i and $i - 1$ is bounded by

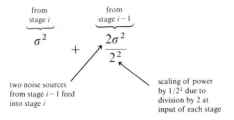

At the final stage, stage L, the output roundoff noise power at any node is the sum of powers from stages $L, L - 1, \ldots, 1$. This roundoff noise power is bounded by σ^2 from stage L, $2\sigma^2/2^2$ from stage $L - 1, \ldots, 2^m\sigma^2/2^{2m}$ from stage $L - m$. Adding these powers gives

$$\sigma^2_{output} < \sigma^2\left[1 + \frac{1}{2} + \cdots + \frac{1}{2^{L-1}}\right] = 2\sigma^2(1 - 2^{-L}) \approx 2\sigma^2 \qquad (7.128)$$

as a bound on the DIT FFT roundoff noise power.

f. Graphical Approach to FFT Word-Length Specification. We shall present a simple graphical approach to FFT word-length specification [2] to meet a requirement for a dynamic range of 38 dB. Figure 7.27 applies to an 8-stage FFT using a word length of 12 bits (i.e., 11 + sign). The vertical axis is the bit level, where

$$\text{bit level} = -\log_2(\text{rms level}) \qquad (7.129)$$

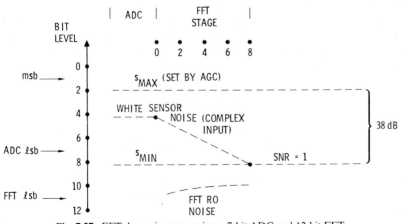

Fig. 7.27. FFT dynamic range using a 7-bit ADC and 12-bit FFT.

The curves in Fig. 7.27 show the signal and rms noise levels at the ADC output and at FFT stages 0 (input) through 8 (output). The signals and noise include

1. A pure tone that is centered in a DFT frequency bin and has a power level of $s_{MAX} = -12$ dB set by AGC.

2. White sensor noise with an rms level $4\frac{1}{3}$ bits (26 dB) below the 0 bit level. This noise loses $\frac{1}{2}$ bit per stage relative to s_{MAX} due to the scaling of $\frac{1}{2}$ per stage. After L stages the white noise is attenuated to $8\frac{1}{3}$ bits (50 dB) below the 0 bit level.

3. A pure tone that is centered in a different DFT bin than the pure tone in (1) and has a power level of $s_{MIN} = -50$ dB. The power levels of this tone and the white noise in (2) are equal at the DFT output. Assume that a SNR = 1 is sufficient for detection at the DFT output. (Noncoherent integration, i.e., periodogram averaging, may be used to further increase this SNR, thereby enhancing detection.) The difference between pure tones (1) and (3) is -12 dB $-$ (-50 dB) = 38 dB, and this is the dynamic range of the system (neglecting FFT roundoff noise).

4. FFT roundoff noise with a power bounded by $2(2^{-2b})$ at a stage 1 output and by $2^2(2^{-2b})$ at the DFT output. Figure 7.27 is for a 12- (11 + sign) bit data word, so the roundoff noise is bounded by the tenth bit below the 0 bit level. The roundoff noise added at each stage leading up to the output of pure tone (3) is assumed to be independently distributed. That is, the pure tones (1) and (3) are assumed not to generate correlated noise in the butterflies leading up to the DFT bin in which pure tone (3) is centered. Under these assumptions, the ratio of FFT roundoff noise power to white sensor noise power increases as $[2^2/2^{-2b}]/[(2^{-13/3})^2/2^{\mathscr{S}}] \propto 2^{\mathscr{S}}$, where $\mathscr{S}$ is the stage number going through the FFT [39]. The FFT roundoff noise at the output of the FFT is approximately 2 bits below the sensor white noise, and, even though it is approximately 16 times lower in power, it represents a loss in the FFT processor that slightly degrades the dynamic range. We next describe how to account for this loss.

g. Treating Quantization Noise as a Loss. Good FFT design keeps all roundoff noise negligible with respect to some reference input noise, for example, ADC quantization noise. As additional roundoff noise is introduced, it can be treated as a loss. The loss is an SNR degradation due to the additional roundoff noise and is given by

$$\text{loss} = 10 \log \left[\frac{P_R + P_Q}{P_R} \right] \tag{7.130}$$

where P_R is the noise power due to the reference noise and P_Q is the additive quantization noise power. Losses are correction terms subtracted from total processor gain. The output of every arithmetic operation must be considered as a source of roundoff noise in the loss calculations. Keeping losses to an insignificant level relative to ADC roundoff noise ensures that word lengths are sufficient.

h. Impact of Rounding Multiplier Coefficients. One other source of error in the FFT is rounding the multiplier coefficients W^{kn}. The FFT spectral analysis becomes more and more inaccurate as fewer and fewer bits are used for the cosine and sine terms of W^{kn}. Assessment of the number of bits to mechanize W^{kn} has shown that if the cosine and sine terms are rounded to the word length of the FFT computations, then negligible error is introduced into the DFT output by this quantization [40, 41].

i. Impact of Other Number Representations. The results we have given apply when rounding is used to quantize fixed-point numbers including 1's- and 2's-complement as well as sign-and-magnitude representations. The FFT roundoff noise results also are applicable to truncation after doubling the error magnitudes and noting that truncation of 2's complement numbers leads to an undesirable bias error. In floating-point arithmetic the quantization noise depends on the magnitude of the numbers in the FFT, but in general the noise effects are significantly less [5, 42]. For example, the quantization noise to input white noise (e.g., sensor noise, ADC roundoff) ratio increases as L for floating-point arithmetic compared to $2^L = N$ for fixed-point arithmetic in a radix-2 FFT.

j. Impact of Other FFT Algorithms. The dynamic range analysis illustrated with Fig. 7.27 generally applies to other FFT algorithms. The main variation is in the accumulation of FFT quantization noise. Due to noise accumulation characteristics, the WFTA requires 1 or 2 more bits for number representation to give an error comparable to the radix-2 FFT, and the Good FFT requires up to $\frac{1}{2}$ bit more [43].

SUMMARY XV

This chapter has exploited the correspondence of computing 1-D and 2-D DFTs to develop a number of 1-D FFTs. The radix-4, and -6 algorithms are examples of 1-D DFTs that can be computed in 2-D space using DFT computations along each axis with twiddle factors between the DFTs. The twiddle factors are eliminated by using the CRT and/or the RC to represent integers in an N-point DFT. The CRT and RC impose the constraint that N must factor into the product of relatively prime integers. Several FFTs result from using only the CRT or only the RC. Good's FFT and the WFTA result from using the CRT and RC to represent the transform and data sequence indices k and n, respectively (or vice versa). Polynomial transforms minimize the arithmetic computations in 2-D DFT computations and can be combined with other approaches. Computational comparisons were given for the arithmetic required to compute various FFTs, and computational word lengths were derived to ensure that the FFT has sufficient dynamic range.

APPENDIX A   Small-N DFT Algorithms

This appendix summarizes the small-N DFT algorithms, i.e., the Winogard short fast Fourier transforms [2, 3, 14, 15, 24, 29, 31–34]. The following statements describe the algorithms.

1. The algorithms are structured to compute $X(k) = \sum_{n=0}^{N-1} x(n) W^{kn}$.
2. Input data to the small-N algorithm are $x(0), x(1), \ldots, x(N-1)$ in NO. This input data may be a complex sequence.
3. Output data are $X(0), X(1), \ldots, X(N-1)$ in NO.
4. $m_0, m_1, \ldots, m_{M-1}$ are the results of the M multiplications.
5. $t_1, t_2, \ldots$ are temporary storage areas for input data.
6. $s_1, s_2, \ldots$ are temporary storage areas for output data.
7. The lists of input and output additions are sequenced and must be executed in the specified order. When there are several equations to a line, read left to right before proceeding to the next line.
8. Multiplications stated for each factor include multiplications by ± 1 or $\pm j$. These trivial multiplications are stated in parentheses. Shifts due to factors of $\frac{1}{2}$ are counted as a multiplication.

The inverse DFT (IDFT) can be computed from the preceding algorithms by one of the following methods:

1. Substitute $-u$ for u (if u is defined).
2. Use any of the methods that compute the IDFT with a DFT (see Table VI in Chapter 1).

Summary of Small-N Algorithms

$N = 2$:

$$m_0 = 1 \times [x(0) + x(1)], \qquad m_1 = 1 \times [x(0) - x(1)]$$
$$X(0) = m_0, \qquad X(1) = m_1$$

2 multiplications (2), 2 additions.

$N = 3$: $u = \frac{2}{3}\pi$.

$$t_1 = x(1) + x(2)$$
$$m_0 = 1 \times [x(0) + t_1], \qquad m_1 = (\cos u - 1) \times t_1, \qquad m_2 = (j \sin u) \times [x(2) - x(1)]$$
$$s_1 = m_0 + m_1$$
$$X(0) = m_0, \qquad X(1) = s_1 + m_2, \qquad X(2) = s_1 - m_2$$

3 multiplications (1), 6 additions.

$N = 4$:

$$t_1 = x(0) + x(2), \qquad t_2 = x(1) + x(3)$$
$$m_0 = 1 \times (t_1 + t_2), \qquad m_1 = 1 \times (t_1 - t_2)$$
$$m_2 = 1 \times [x(0) - x(2)], \qquad m_3 = j \times [x(3) - x(1)]$$
$$X(0) = m_0, \qquad X(1) = m_2 + m_3, \qquad X(2) = m_1, \qquad X(3) = m_2 + m_3$$

4 multiplications (4), 8 additions.

(continued)

Summary of Small-N Algorithms (*Continued*)

$N = 5$: $u = \frac{2}{5}\pi$.

$$t_1 = x(1) + x(4), \qquad t_2 = x(2) + x(3), \qquad t_3 = x(1) - x(4),$$
$$t_4 = x(3) - x(2) \qquad t_5 = t_1 + t_2$$
$$m_0 = 1 \times [x(0) + t_5], \qquad m_1 = [\tfrac{1}{2}(\cos u + \cos 2u) - 1] \times t_5$$
$$m_2 = \tfrac{1}{2}(\cos u - \cos 2u) \times (t_1 - t_2), \qquad m_3 = -j(\sin u) \times (t_3 + t_4)$$
$$m_4 = -j(\sin u + \sin 2u) \times t_4, \qquad m_5 = j(\sin u - \sin 2u) \times t_3$$
$$s_1 = m_0 + m_1, \qquad s_2 = s_1 + m_2, \qquad s_3 = m_3 - m_4$$
$$s_4 = s_1 - m_2, \qquad s_5 = m_3 + m_5$$
$$X(0) = m_0, \qquad X(1) = s_2 + s_3, \qquad X(2) = s_4 + s_5$$
$$X(3) = s_4 - s_5, \qquad X(4) = s_2 - s_3$$

6 multiplications (1), 17 additions.

$N = 7$: $u = \frac{2}{7}\pi$.

$$t_1 = x(1) + x(6), \qquad t_2 = x(2) + x(5), \qquad t_3 = x(3) + x(4)$$
$$t_4 = t_1 + t_2 + t_3, \qquad t_5 = x(1) - x(6), \qquad t_6 = x(2) - x(5)$$
$$t_7 = x(4) - x(3)$$
$$m_0 = 1 \times [x(0) + t_4]$$
$$m_1 = \tfrac{1}{3}[(\cos u + \cos 2u + \cos 3u) - 1] \times t_4$$
$$m_2 = \tfrac{1}{3}(2\cos u - \cos 2u - \cos 3u) \times (t_1 - t_3)$$
$$m_3 = \tfrac{1}{3}(\cos u - 2\cos 2u + \cos 3u) \times (t_3 - t_2)$$
$$m_4 = \tfrac{1}{3}(\cos u + \cos 2u - 2\cos 3u) \times (t_2 - t_1)$$
$$m_5 = -j\tfrac{1}{3}(\sin u + \sin 2u - \sin 3u) \times (t_5 + t_6 + t_7)$$
$$m_6 = j\tfrac{1}{3}(2\sin u - \sin 2u + \sin 3u) \times (t_7 - t_5)$$
$$m_7 = j\tfrac{1}{3}(\sin u - 2\sin 2u - \sin 3u) \times (t_6 - t_7)$$
$$m_8 = j\tfrac{1}{3}(\sin u + \sin 2u + 2\sin 3u) \times (t_5 - t_6)$$
$$s_1 = m_0 + m_1, \qquad s_2 = s_1 + m_2 + m_3, \qquad s_3 = s_1 - m_2 - m_4, \qquad s_4 = s_1 - m_3 + m_4$$
$$s_5 = m_5 + m_6 + m_7, \qquad s_6 = m_5 - m_6 - m_8, \qquad s_7 = m_5 - m_7 + m_8$$
$$X(0) = m_0, \qquad X(1) = s_2 + s_5, \qquad X(2) = s_3 + s_6, \qquad X(3) = s_4 - s_7$$
$$X(4) = s_4 + s_7, \qquad X(5) = s_3 - s_6, \qquad X(6) = s_2 - s_5$$

9 multiplications (1), 36 additions.

$N = 8$: $u = \frac{2}{8}\pi$.

$$t_1 = x(0) + x(4), \qquad t_2 = x(2) + x(6), \qquad t_3 = x(1) + x(5), \qquad t_4 = x(1) - x(5)$$
$$t_5 = x(3) + x(7), \qquad t_6 = x(3) - x(7), \qquad t_7 = t_1 + t_2, \qquad t_8 = t_3 + t_5$$
$$m_0 = 1 \times (t_7 + t_8), \qquad m_1 = 1 \times (t_7 - t_8), \qquad m_2 = 1 \times (t_1 - t_2), \qquad m_3 = 1 \times [x(0) - x(4)]$$
$$m_4 = (\cos u) \times (t_4 - t_6), \qquad m_5 = j \times (t_5 - t_3), \qquad m_6 = j \times [x(6) - x(2)], \qquad m_7 = (-j\sin u) \times (t_4 + t_6)$$
$$s_1 = m_3 + m_4, \qquad s_2 = m_3 - m_4, \qquad s_3 = m_6 + m_7, \qquad s_4 = m_6 - m_7$$
$$X(0) = m_0, \qquad X(1) = s_1 + s_3, \qquad X(2) = m_2 + m_5, \qquad X(3) = s_2 - s_4$$
$$X(4) = m_1, \qquad X(5) = s_2 + s_4, \qquad X(6) = m_2 - m_5, \qquad X(7) = s_1 - s_3$$

8 multiplications (6), 26 additions.

(*continued*)

Summary of Small-N Algorithms (*Continued*)

$N = 9$: $u = \frac{2}{9}\pi$.

$$t_1 = x(1) + x(8), \qquad t_2 = x(2) + x(7), \qquad t_3 = x(3) + x(6)$$
$$t_4 = x(4) + x(5), \qquad t_5 = t_1 + t_2 + t_4, \qquad t_6 = x(1) - x(8)$$
$$t_7 = x(7) - x(2), \qquad t_8 = x(3) - x(6), \qquad t_9 = x(4) - x(5)$$
$$t_{10} = t_6 + t_7 + t_9$$
$$m_0 = 1 \times [x(0) + t_3 + t_5], \qquad m_1 = \tfrac{3}{2} \times t_3, \qquad m_2 = -\tfrac{1}{2} \times t_5$$
$$m_3 = \tfrac{1}{3}(2\cos u - \cos 2u - \cos 4u) \times (t_1 - t_2)$$
$$m_4 = \tfrac{1}{3}(\cos u + \cos 2u - 2\cos 4u) \times (t_2 - t_4)$$
$$m_5 = \tfrac{1}{3}(\cos u - 2\cos 2u + \cos 4u) \times (t_4 - t_1)$$
$$m_6 = (-j\sin 3u) \times t_{10}, \qquad m_7 = (-j\sin 3u) \times t_8, \qquad m_8 = (j\sin u) \times (t_7 - t_6)$$
$$m_9 = (j\sin 4u) \times (t_7 - t_9), \qquad m_{10} = (j\sin 2u) \times (t_6 - t_9)$$
$$s_1 = m_0 + m_2 + m_2, \qquad s_2 = s_1 - m_1, \qquad s_3 = s_1 + m_2$$
$$s_4 = m_3 + m_4 + s_2, \qquad s_5 = -m_4 + m_5 + s_2, \qquad s_6 = -m_3 - m_5 + s_2$$
$$s_7 = m_8 + m_9 + m_7, \qquad s_8 = -m_9 + m_{10} + m_7, \qquad s_9 = -m_8 - m_{10} + m_7$$
$$X(0) = m_0, \qquad X(1) = s_4 + s_7, \qquad X(2) = s_5 - s_8$$
$$X(3) = s_3 + m_6, \qquad X(4) = s_6 + s_9, \qquad X(5) = s_6 - s_9$$
$$X(6) = s_3 - m_6, \qquad X(7) = s_5 + s_8, \qquad X(8) = s_4 - s_7$$

11 multiplications (1), 44 additions.

$N = 11$:

$$t_1 = x(1) + x(10), \qquad t_2 = x(2) + x(9), \qquad t_3 = x(3) + x(8)$$
$$t_4 = x(4) + x(7), \qquad t_5 = x(5) + x(6), \qquad t_6 = x(1) - x(10),$$
$$t_7 = x(2) - x(9), \qquad t_8 = x(3) - x(8), \qquad t_9 = x(4) - x(7)$$
$$t_{10} = x(5) - x(6), \qquad t_{11} = t_1 + t_2, \qquad t_{12} = t_3 + t_5,$$
$$t_{13} = t_4 + t_{11} + t_{12}, \qquad t_{14} = t_7 - t_8 \qquad t_{15} = t_6 + t_{10}$$
$$m_0 = x(0) + t_{13}, \qquad m_1 = 1.10 t_{13}, \qquad m_2 = 0.33166250(t_{14} - t_{15} - t_9)$$
$$m_3 = 0.51541500(t_2 - t_4), \qquad m_4 = 0.941253500(t_1 - t_4), \qquad m_5 = 1.41435370(t_2 - t_1)$$
$$m_6 = 0.185949300(t_5 - t_4), \qquad m_7 = 0.04231480(t_3 - t_4), \qquad m_8 = 0.38639280(t_5 - t_3)$$
$$m_9 = 0.51254590(t_2 - t_5), \qquad m_{10} = 1.07027569(t_1 - t_3), \qquad m_{11} = 0.55486070(t_{12} - t_{11})$$
$$m_{12} = 1.24129440(t_7 + t_9), \qquad m_{13} = 0.20897830(t_6 - t_9), \qquad m_{14} = 0.37415717(t_6 - t_7)$$
$$m_{15} = 0.04992992(t_9 - t_{10}), \qquad m_{16} = 0.65815896(t_8 - t_9), \qquad m_{17} = 0.63306543(t_8 - t_{10})$$
$$m_{18} = 1.08224607(t_7 + t_{10}), \qquad m_{19} = 0.81720738(t_8 - t_8), \qquad m_{20} = 0.42408709(t_{14} + t_{15})$$
$$s_0 = m_0 - m_1, \qquad s_1 = m_3 + m_4, \qquad s_2 = m_4 + m_5, \qquad s_3 = m_3 - m_5$$
$$s_4 = m_6 + m_7, \qquad s_5 = m_7 + m_8, \qquad s_6 = m_6 - m_8, \qquad s_7 = m_{10} + m_{11}$$
$$s_8 = m_9 + m_{11}, \qquad s_9 = m_{13} + m_{14}, \qquad s_{10} = m_{12} - m_{14}, \qquad s_{11} = m_{16} + m_{17}$$
$$s_{12} = m_{15} - m_{17}, \qquad s_{13} = m_{19} + m_{20}, \qquad s_{14} = m_{18} - m_{20}, \qquad s_{15} = s_5 + s_7 + s_0$$
$$s_{16} = s_0 - s_2 - s_7, \qquad s_{17} = s_0 + s_6 + s_8, \qquad s_{18} = s_0 - s_3 - s_8,$$
$$s_{19} = s_0 + s_1 - s_4, \qquad s_{20} = m_2 + s_{11} + s_{13}, \qquad s_{21} = s_{13} - s_9 - m_2$$
$$s_{22} = m_2 + s_{14} + s_{12}, \qquad s_{23} = s_{12} - s_{10} - m_2, \qquad s_{24} = s_{20} - s_{21} + s_{22} - s_{23}$$

(*continued*)

Summary of Small-N Algorithms (*Continued*)

$$X(0) = m_0$$

$$X(1) = s_1 + js_{24}, \qquad X(2) = s_{15} + js_{20}, \qquad X(3) = s_{16} + js_{21}, \qquad X(4) = s_{17} - js_{22}$$

$$X(5) = s_{18} + js_{23}, \qquad X(6) = s_{18} - js_{23}, \qquad X(7) = s_{17} + js_{22}, \qquad X(8) = s_{16} - js_{21}$$

$$X(9) = s_{15} - js_{20}, \qquad X(10) = s_{19} - js_{24}$$

multiplications, 83 additions

$N = 13$

$$t_1 = x(1) + x(12), \qquad t_2 = x(2) + x(11), \qquad t_3 = x(3) + x(10), \qquad t_4 = x(4) + x(9)$$

$$t_5 = x(5) + x(8), \qquad t_6 = x(6) + x(7), \qquad t_7 = x(1) - x(12), \qquad t_8 = x(2) - x(11)$$

$$t_9 = x(3) - x(10), \qquad t_{10} = x(4) - x(9), \qquad t_{11} = x(5) - x(8), \qquad t_{12} = x(6) - x(7)$$

$$t_{13} = t_2 + t_5 + t_6, \qquad t_{14} = t_1 + t_3 + t_4, \qquad t_{15} = t_{13} + t_{14}, \qquad t_{16} = t_8 + t_{11} + t_{12}$$

$$t_{17} = t_7 + t_9 - t_{10}, \qquad t_{18} = t_2 - t_6, \qquad t_{19} = t_3 - t_4, \qquad t_{20} = t_1 - t_4$$

$$t_{21} = t_5 - t_6, \qquad t_{22} = t_{18} - t_{19}, \qquad t_{23} = t_{20} - t_{21}, \qquad t_{24} = t_{18} + t_{19}$$

$$t_{25} = t_{20} + t_{21}, \qquad t_{26} = t_8 - t_{12}, \qquad t_{27} = t_7 - t_9, \qquad t_{28} = t_8 - t_{11}$$

$$t_{29} = t_9 + t_{10}, \qquad t_{30} = t_{11} - t_{12}, \qquad t_{31} = -t_9 - t_{10}$$

$$m_0 = X(0) + t_{15}, \qquad m_1 = 1.08333333t_{15}, \qquad m_2 = 0.30046261(t_{14} - t_{13})$$

$$m_3 = 0.74927933t_{16}, \qquad m_4 = 0.40113213t_{17}, \qquad m_5 = 0.57514073(t_{16} + t_{17})$$

$$m_6 = 0.52422664t_{22}, \qquad m_7 = 0.51642078t_{23}, \qquad m_8 = 0.00770586(t_{22} + t_{23})$$

$$m_9 = 0.42763400t_{24}, \qquad m_{10} = 0.15180600t_{25}, \qquad m_{11} = 0.57944000(t_{24} + t_{25})$$

$$m_{12} = 1.15439500t_{26}, \qquad m_{13} = 0.9065220t_{27}, \qquad m_{14} = 0.81857030(t_{26} + t_{27})$$

$$m_{15} = 1.19713680t_{28}, \qquad m_{16} = 0.86131170t_{29}, \qquad m_{17} = 1.10915485(t_{28} + t_{29})$$

$$m_{18} = 0.04274140t_{30}, \qquad m_{19} = 0.04524049t_{31}, \qquad m_{20} = 0.29058500(t_{30} + t_{31})$$

$$s_0 = m_0 - m_1, \qquad s_1 = m_7 + m_6 - m_2, \qquad s_2 = m_7 + m_8 + m_2, \qquad s_3 = m_8 - m_6 - m_2$$

$$s_4 = s_0 - m_9 + m_{10}, \qquad s_5 = s_0 - m_{10} - m_{11}, \qquad s_6 = s_0 - m_9 + m_{11}, \qquad s_7 = m_{12} - m_{14}$$

$$s_8 = m_{13} - m_{14}, \qquad s_9 = m_{15} - m_{17}, \qquad s_{10} = m_{16} - m_{17}, \qquad s_{11} = m_{18} - m_{20}$$

$$s_{12} = m_{19} + m_{20}, \qquad s_{13} = m_3 - m_5, \qquad s_{14} = m_4 - m_5, \qquad s_{15} = s_1 + s_4$$

$$s_{16} = s_2 + s_5, \qquad s_{17} = s_5 - s_2, \qquad s_{18} = s_3 + s_6, \qquad s_{19} = s_4 - s_1$$

$$s_{20} = s_6 - s_3, \qquad s_{21} = s_4 + j(s_7 - s_7), \qquad s_{22} = s_{12} - s_{13} - s_{10}, \qquad s_{23} = s_7 + s_{11} + s_{14}$$

$$s_{24} = s_9 + s_{11} - s_{14}, \qquad s_{25} = s_8 - s_{12} - s_{13}, \qquad s_{26} = s_3 + j(s_8 - s_{10})$$

$$X(0) = m_0$$

$$X(1) = s_{15} + s_{21}, \qquad X(2) = s_{15} + js_{22}, \qquad X(3) = s_{17} + js_{23}, \qquad X(4) = s_{18} - js_{24}$$

$$X(5) = s_{19} + js_{25}, \qquad X(6) = s_{20} - s_{26}, \qquad X(7) = s_{20} + s_{26}, \qquad X(8) = s_{19} - js_{25}$$

$$X(9) = s_{18} + js_{24}, \qquad X(10) = s_{17} + js_{23}, \qquad X(11) = s_{16} - js_{22}, \qquad X(12) = s_{15} - s_{21}$$

20 multiplications, 94 additions

$N = 16$: $\quad u = \frac{2}{16}\pi$.

$$t_1 = x(0) + x(8), \qquad t_2 = x(4) + x(2), \qquad t_3 = x(2) + x(10)$$

$$t_4 = x(2) - x(10), \qquad t_5 = x(6) + x(14), \qquad t_6 = x(6) - x(14)$$

$$t_7 = x(1) + x(9), \qquad t_8 = x(1) - x(9), \qquad t_9 = x(3) + x(11)$$

$$t_{10} = x(3) - x(11), \qquad t_{11} = x(5) + x(13), \qquad t_{12} = x(5) - x(13)$$

(continued)

Summary of Small-N Algorithms (*Continued*)

$$t_{13} = x(7) + x(15), \qquad t_{14} = x(7) - x(15), \qquad t_{15} = t_1 + t_2$$

$$t_{16} = t_3 + t_5, \qquad t_{17} = t_{15} + t_{16}, \qquad t_{18} = t_7 + t_{11}$$

$$t_{19} = t_7 - t_{11}, \qquad t_{20} = t_9 + t_{13}, \qquad t_{21} = t_9 - t_{13}$$

$$t_{22} = t_{18} + t_{20}, \qquad t_{23} = t_8 + t_{14}, \qquad t_{24} = t_8 - t_{14}$$

$$t_{25} = t_{10} + t_{12}, \qquad t_{26} = t_{12} - t_{10}$$

$$m_0 = 1 \times (t_{17} + t_{22}), \qquad m_1 = 1 \times (t_{17} - t_{22})$$

$$m_2 = 1 \times (t_{15} - t_{16}), \qquad m_3 = 1 \times (t_1 - t_2)$$

$$m_4 = 1 \times [x(0) - x(8)], \qquad m_5 = (\cos 2u) \times (t_{19} - t_{21})$$

$$m_6 = (\cos 2u) \times (t_4 - t_6), \qquad m_7 = (\cos 3u) \times (t_{24} + t_{26})$$

$$m_8 = (\cos u + \cos 3u) \times t_{24}, \qquad m_9 = (\cos 3u - \cos u) \times t_{26}$$

$$m_{10} = j \times (t_{20} - t_{18}), \qquad m_{11} = j \times (t_5 - t_3)$$

$$m_{12} = j \times (x(12) - x(4)), \qquad m_{13} = (-j \sin 2u) \times (t_{19} + t_{21})$$

$$m_{14} = (-j \sin 2u) \times (t_4 + t_6), \qquad m_{15} = (-j \sin 3u) \times (t_{23} + t_{25})$$

$$m_{16} = j(\sin 3u - \sin u) \times t_{23}, \qquad m_{17} = -j(\sin u + \sin 3u) \times t_{25}$$

$$s_1 = m_3 + m_5, \qquad s_2 = m_3 - m_5, \qquad s_3 = m_{11} + m_{13}, \qquad s_4 = m_{13} - m_{11}$$

$$s_5 = m_4 + m_6, \qquad s_6 = m_4 - m_6, \qquad s_7 = m_8 - m_7, \qquad s_8 = m_9 - m_7$$

$$s_9 = s_5 + s_7, \qquad s_{10} = s_5 - s_7, \qquad s_{11} = s_6 + s_8, \qquad s_{12} = s_6 - s_8$$

$$s_{13} = m_{12} + m_{14}, \qquad s_{14} = m_{12} - m_{14}, \qquad s_{15} = m_{15} + m_{16}, \qquad s_{16} = m_{15} - m_{17}$$

$$s_{17} = s_{13} + s_{15}, \qquad s_{18} = s_{13} - s_{15}, \qquad s_{19} = s_{14} + s_{16}, \qquad s_{20} = s_{14} - s_{16}$$

$$X(0) = m_0, \qquad X(1) = s_9 + s_{17}, \qquad X(2) = s_1 + s_3, \qquad X(3) = s_{12} - s_{20}$$

$$X(4) = m_2 + m_{10}, \qquad X(5) = s_{11} + s_{19}, \qquad X(6) = s_2 + s_4, \qquad X(7) = s_{10} - s_{18}$$

$$X(8) = m_1, \qquad X(9) = s_{10} + s_{18}, \qquad X(10) = s_2 - s_4, \qquad X(11) = s_{11} - s_{19}$$

$$X(12) = m_2 - m_{10}, \qquad X(13) = s_{12} + s_{20}, \qquad X(14) = s_1 - s_3, \qquad X(15) = s_9 - s_{17}$$

18 multiplications (8), 74 additions.

APPENDIX B.   FFT COMPUTER PROGRAMS

This appendix summarizes some FFTs available in the literature. The literature includes computer codes that in some cases are available on magnetic tape. The algorithms are discussed according to type.

Radix-2.   See Appendix C for code.

Radix-2 SRFFT.   See [18, Appendix] for DIF and DIT SRFFT code. According to [18+], "An analysis of the arithmetic complexity showed that the SRFFT is a significant improvement over the Cooley–Tukey FFT and is probably optimal in the sense of minimum floating point arithmetic. It has an efficiency exceeding a radix-8 FFT, a size comparable to a radix-4 FFT, and the flexibility of a radix-2 FFT."

Radix-2 RCFA See [22 Appendixes I and II] for code for transforming complex- and real-valued sequences, respectively. The RCFA is the same as the SRFFT for sequences of length 2^L. It offers a slight advantage in computation time, at least on the VAX-11/750 computer and uses a smaller program to implement the calculation as compared to Good's FFT and the WFTA.

Radix-2,-4, and *-8*. See [44] for code. Tape available from IEEE. These subroutines, by G. D. Bergland and M. T. Dolan, are written to produce very fast programs at the expense of instruction memory and program complexity.

Time-Efficient Radix-4. See [44] for code. Tape available. This time-efficient radix-4 fast Fourier transform by L. R. Morris is an example of trading off memory for timewise efficiency when many DFTs of sequences with the same length N are to be performed.

Mixed Radix. See [44] for code. Tape available. This mixed-radix FFT by R. C. Singleton permits one to use values of N containing factors other than 2. In general, the larger the prime factors of N, the less efficient will be the calculation in terms of numbers of operations per output point.

Ruritanian Correspondence. See [28] for code designated PFA2 to compute an N-point DFT, where $N = N_1 N_2 \cdots N_L$ and the N_i are mutually relatively prime, $i = 1, 2, \ldots, L$ The computation involves N_i-point DFTs and since indexing in the N_i-point DFT involves the value of N/N_i, this program by Burrus and Eschenbacher was written to be recompiled for the particular value of N. This algorithm has the in-order, in-place feature.

Good's Algorithm (Also called the Good–Thomas PFA or simply the PFA). Appendixes D and E present two programs for efficient implementation of the PFA. Each has been tested and debugged on IBM ATs and XTs. The first (Appendix D) is in Microsoft FORTRAN and runs a 504-point transform in 2 s. The second (Appendix E) is an assembly language listing written to make optimal use of an 8087 coprocessor in performing a 1008-point PFA and runs in 1.43 s.

See also [28] for code designated PFA1. The code for this program by Burrus and Eschenbacher uses the RC and CRT for the input and output maps, respectively.

Winograd Fourier Transform Algorithm. See [44] for code and [3] for discussion. Tape available from IEEE. This program by J. H. McClellan and H. Nawab offers an improvement in run time, but the required subroutines take a lot of instruction storage compared with FFT programs using butterfly or butterfly-like computational structures.

APPENDIX C.   RADIX-2 FFT PROGRAM

```
C                      FORTRAN program "TRANS"
C Program author: fred harris
C                      Electrical & Computer Engineering Department
C                      San Diego State University
C                      San Diego, CA 92182
C Interactive driver program for performing forward or inverse
C radix-2 fast Fourier transform of real or complex data array.
C Input array, transform length N (N=2**p), and forward or inverse
C direction are selected by prompt. Program zero extends data to
C the selected transform length. Output is selected as transform
C index (0 -> N-1) and complex array or as normalized frequency
C (-0.5 -> +0.5) and log magnitude (with 0.0 dB = max level).

             DIMENSION X(2048),Y(2048), FMAG(2048)
             CHARACTER*60 FILEIN,FILEOUT,QANS

C PROMPT ASKING FOR INPUT FILE NAME
      2      WRITE(*,'(A\)')')' ENTER DATA FILE TO BE TRANSFORMED         -> '
             READ(*,'(A)') FILEIN
             OPEN(10,FILE=FILEIN,ERR=5,STATUS='OLD')
             GO TO 8
             WRITE(*,*)' '
      5      WRITE(*,*)' THIS FILE DOES NOT EXIST'
             WRITE(*,*)' '
             GO TO 2
      8      write(*,*)' '
             WRITE(*,'(A\)')')' FILE? [i,X(i)] (0) OR [i,X(i),Y(i)] (1)   -> '
             READ(*,*) IANS
C READING INPUT FILE
             II=0
             IF(IANS.EQ.1) GO TO 25
             DO 20, I=1,2048
             READ(10,*,END=30) NUMBR,X(I)
             II=II+1
      20     CONTINUE
             GO TO 30

      25     DO 28, I=1,2048
             READ(10,*,END=30) NUMBR,X(I),Y(I)
             II=II+1
      28     CONTINUE

      30     CLOSE(10)

C PROMPT ASKING FOR DESIRED TRANSFORM LENGTH, II.LE.2**P.LE.2048
      44     write(*,45)ii
      45     format(' THERE WERE ',I4,' POINTS')
             WRITE(*,'(A\)')')' ENTER EXPONENT OF TRANSFORM SIZE 2**P     -> '
             READ(*,47) aP
      47     FORMAT(f3.0)
             NN=2**ifix(aP)
             IF(NN.GT.2048) GO TO 44
             IF(NN.LE.1) GO TO 44
             write(*,48)nn
      48     format(' YOU HAVE SELECTED A ',i4,'-POINT TRANSFORM')

             DO 49, I=II+1,NN
             X(I)=0.0
             Y(I)=0.0
      49     CONTINUE

             WRITE(*,'(A\)')')' FORWARD (0) OR INVERSE (1) TRANSFORM?     -> '
             READ(*,*) IANS
             WRITE(*,'(A\)')')' REAL & IMAGINARY (0) OR LOG MAGNITUDE (1) -> '
             READ(*,*) IOPT
```

```
         IF(IOPT.EQ.0) GO TO 55
         SGN=+1.

         DO 50, I=1,II
         X(I)=SGN*X(I)
         Y(I)=SGN*Y(I)
         SGN=-SGN
  50     CONTINUE

C CALL TO FFT
  55     INDX=1
         IF(IANS.EQ.1) INDX=-1
         CALL FFT2(X,Y,NN,INDX)
         WRITE(*,'(A\)')' DISPLAY TRANSFORM? (Y,N)              -> Y '
         READ(*,'(A)') QANS
         IF(IOPT.EQ.1) GO TO 65
         IF(QANS.EQ.'N'.OR.QANS.EQ.'n') GO TO 80
         WRITE(*,*)' '

         DO 64 I=1,NN
         WRITE(*,63)I-1,X(I),Y(I)
  63     FORMAT(' A(',I4,') = ',F8.4,',',F8.4)
  64     CONTINUE
         GOTO 80

C CONVERSION TO LOG MAGNITUDE AND SCALING MAXIMUM AMPLITUDE TO 0 DB
  65     FMAX=0.0
         DO 70, I=1,NN
         FMAG(I)=X(I)*X(I)+Y(I)*Y(I)
         IF(FMAG(I).GT.FMAX) FMAX=FMAG(I)
  70     CONTINUE

         DO 75,I=1,NN
         FMAG(I)=FMAG(I)/FMAX
         IF(FMAG(I).LE.0.000000001) FMAG(I)=0.000000001
         FMAG(I)=10.0*ALOG10(FMAG(I))
  75     CONTINUE

         IF (QANS.EQ.'N'.OR.QANS.EQ.'n') GO TO 80
         WRITE(*,*)' '
         DO 79, I=1,NN
         WRITE(*,78) I-1,FMAG(I)
  78     FORMAT(' A(',I3,') = ',F8.4)
  79     CONTINUE

C OUTPUTTING DATA
  80     WRITE(*,*)' '
         WRITE(*,'(A\)')' ENTER NAME OF OUTPUT FILE                -> '
         READ(*,'(A)') FILEOUT
         OPEN(11,FILE=FILEOUT,STATUS='NEW')
         IF(IOPT.EQ.0) GO TO 90
         DEL=1./FLOAT(NN)
         CRCL=-0.5

         DO 85,I=1,NN
         WRITE(11,82) CRCL,FMAG(I)
  82     FORMAT(F8.4,5X,F8.4)
         CRCL=CRCL+DEL
  85     CONTINUE
         GO TO 100

  90     DO 95 I=1,NN
         WRITE(11,92) I-1,X(I),Y(I)
  92     FORMAT(I4,2(5X,F9.4))
  95     CONTINUE

 100     CLOSE(11)
         WRITE(*,*)' '
         WRITE(*,'(A)') ' GOODBY'
         END
```

```
        subroutine FFT2(X,Y,N,INDX)
        DIMENSION X(N),Y(N)
        REAL PI
        M=NINT(ALOG(FLOAT(N))/ALOG(2.))

        NV2=N/2
        NM1=N-1

        J=1
        DO 40 I=1,NM1
          IF(I.GE.J) GO TO 10
          TX=X(J)
          TY=Y(J)
          X(J)=X(I)
          Y(J)=Y(I)
          X(I)=TX
          Y(I)=TY
10        K=NV2
20        IF(K.GE.J) GO TO 30
          J=J-K
          K=K/2
          GO TO 20
30        J=J+K
40      CONTINUE
        PI=4.*ATAN(1.0)
        SIGN=1.0
        IF(INDX.EQ.-1) SIGN=-1.0
        DO 70 L=1,M
          LE=2**L
          FLE=FLOAT(LE)
          LE1=LE/2
          FLE1=FLE/2.
          UR=1.0
          UI=0.0
          WR=COS(PI/FLE1)
          WI=-SIGN*SIN(PI/FLE1)
          DO 60 J=1,LE1
            DO 50 I=J,N,LE
              IP=I+LE1
              TX=X(IP)*UR-Y(IP)*UI
              TY=Y(IP)*UR+X(IP)*UI
              X(IP)=X(I)-TX
              Y(IP)=Y(I)-TY
              X(I)=X(I)+TX
              Y(I)=Y(I)+TY
50            CONTINUE
            TR=UR
            TI=UI
            UR=TR*WR-TI*WI
            UI=TI*WR+TR*WI
60        CONTINUE
70      CONTINUE

        IF(INDX.EQ.1) GO TO 90
        SCALE=1.0/FLOAT(N)
        DO 80 I=1,N
        X(I)=X(I)*SCALE
        Y(I)=Y(I)*SCALE
80      CONTINUE

90      RETURN
        END
```

APPENDIX D.   PRIME FACTOR ALGORITHM
(PFA) PROGRAM LISTINGS FOR PRIME FACTOR TRANSFORM

Appendixes D and E present two program listings for efficient implementation of the discrete Fourier transform prime factor algorithm (PFA). Both programs were written as part of a master's thesis at San Diego State University under the guidance of Professor Fred Harris. Each has been tested and debugged and is running on IBM ATs and XTs at SDSU's College of Engineering.

The first program, written by Eric Johnson, is listed in Appendix D, is in Microsoft FORTRAN, and is extremely portable. This algorithm performs a forward or inverse prime factor transform on a complex input array. The algorithm is performed in place and in natural order, so there is no need for a second array to perform address rearrangement. The inverse transform is scaled by the transform length N. The choice of prime factors for the transform is limited to the integers $1, 2, 3, 4, 5, 7, 8, 9, 16$.

Timing tests were conducted on this algorithm running on an IBM XT with an 8087 coprocessor operating at the standard $4.77 = $ MHz clock. The 504-$(7 \times 8 \times 9)$ point transform is performed in 2.0 s.

The second program, written by Mike Orchard, is listed in Appendix E and is an assembly language listing intended to be used with Microsoft FORTRAN. This program was written to make optimal use of the 8087 coprocessor. The algorithm performs the forward prime factor transform on a complex input array of length 1008 $(7 \times 9 \times 16)$. The algorithm is performed in-place and in natural order. This algorithm is a section of a general-purpose prime factor transform for factors $2, 3, 4, 5, 7, 8, 9, 16$. Three factors (7, 9, and 16) are present in this version. The code is quite compact, and the required memory space is significantly less than a radix-2 Cooley–Tukey algorithm if we account for the space allocated to the SIN-COS array.

Timing tests were performed on this algorithm on an IBM XT with an 8087 coprocessor operating at the standard 4.77 MHz clock. The 1008-point transform of nonzero data is performed in 1.43 s. The transform is slightly faster if the input array has a significant number of zero-valued data points.

```
C               Fortran version of the prime factor (Winograd) FFT.
C
C       Program author:     Eric S. Johnson
C                           Graduate student, SDSU
C                           April, 1986
C       Program extracted from Master's thesis.
C
C       Thesis advisor:     fred harris
C
C       Inquiries concerning this program are directed to:
C
C                       fred harris
C                       Electrical & Computer Engineering Department
C                       San Diego State University
C                       San Diego, CA 92182
C
C           This program computes the forward and inverse discrete
C       Fourier transform using the prime factor algorithm and the
C       Winograd short fast Fourier transform algorithms.
C           This program prompts the user to enter four relatively
C       prime factors. If the application requires less than four
C       factors, than enter the number 1 until the limit of four
C       factors is reached. The factors may be entered in any order.
C       The choice of factors is limited to 1,2,3,4,5,7,8,9,16.
C           The program is structured as follows:
C
C       1. Input data
C       2. If an inverse transform is specified, then a second set
C          of coefficients is used, where all values associated
C          with the operator j are of opposite polarity.
C       3. Map the data into subdata sections of factor lengths
C          by applying the Good-Thomas prime factor algorithm.
C          This is accomplished by an in-place addressing scheme.
C       4. Transform the subdata sections by applying the Winograd
C          short fast Fourier transform. These transforms have been
C          reduced as much as possible to a sequence of subroutine
C          calls.  These subroutines are shared by the different
C          Winograd short transforms, the result being a smaller,
C          more organized program.
C
C               Program variables
C
C       N         Transform length
C       NI( )     Factor lengths
C       X( ,1)    Real data
C       X( ,2)    Imaginary data
C       Z( ,1)    Forward coefficients
C       Z( ,2)    Inverse coefficients
C       I( )      Input address vectors
C       IP( )     Scrambled output address vectors
C       A( , )    Intermediate data
C
C/////////////////////////////////////////////////////////////////////////
C
        PROGRAM FFTPFAS
C
        REAL X
        INTEGER N,NI
        DIMENSION X(512,2),NI(4)
        COMMON /A/ X /D/ NI
C
                CALL INPUT (N)
                CALL PFA (N)
                CALL OUTPUT (N)
```

```
                STOP
            END
C
C-------------------------------------------------------
C
            SUBROUTINE INPUT (N)
C
            REAL X
            COMMON /A/X /D/NI
            CHARACTER*20 FILENAME
            DIMENSION X(512,2),NI(4)
            INTEGER N,NI
C
            WRITE (*,*) 'Enter length of transform'
            READ (*,*) N
            WRITE (*,*) 'Enter the factor lengths (N1,N2,N3,N4)'
            READ (*,*) NI(1),NI(2),NI(3),NI(4)
C
            WRITE(*,*)'Enter the input data file name'
            READ(*,'(A)') FILENAME
            OPEN(10,FILE=FILENAME,STATUS='OLD')
C
C           Prepare for zero extension.
C
            DO 16, I=1,N
                    X(I,1) = 0
                    X(I,2) = 0
   16       CONTINUE
C
            DO 26, I=1,N
                    READ(10,*,END=27) X(I,1), X(I,2)
   26       CONTINUE
   27       CONTINUE
            CLOSE(10)
C
            RETURN
            END
C
C
C-------------------------------------------------------
C
            SUBROUTINE OUTPUT (N)
C
            COMMON /A/X
            CHARACTER*20 OUTFILE
            INTEGER N
            REAL X
            DIMENSION X(512,2)
C
            WRITE(*,*)'Enter the output file name'
            READ(*,'(A)')OUTFILE
            OPEN(10,FILE=OUTFILE,STATUS='NEW')
C
            DO 49, I=1,N
                    RMAG=(X(I,1)**2+X(I,2)**2)**0.5
                    ARG=1
                    IF (X(I,1).EQ.0) THEN
                            ARG=90
                            IF (X(I,2).EQ.0)  ARG=0
                    END IF
                    IF (ARG.NE.1) GOTO 48
                    ARG=ATAN(X(I,2)/X(I,1))
                    ARG=ARG*57.29577951
   48               K1=I-1
C
C       Output format:  Real  Imag  Mag  Phase  Position
```

```
C
                    WRITE(10,51)X(I,1),X(I,2),RMAG,ARG,K1
   49       CONTINUE
   51       FORMAT(4(E12.4,','),I4)
            CLOSE(10)
            RETURN
            END
C
C-----------------------------------------------------------
C
            SUBROUTINE PFA (N)
            INTEGER NI,I,IP,LP,E,INV
            COMMON /A/ X /B/ A /C/I,IP,E
            COMMON /D/ NI /E/ Z,INV
            REAL X,A,Z,T,R
            DIMENSION X(512,2),A(16,2),Z(29,2),T(29),R(72)
            DIMENSION NI(4),I(16),IP(16),E(72),LP(16)
C
            WRITE(*,*) 'FFT or inverse FFT? (1,2)'
            READ (*,*) INV
C
C           Look up table for in-place scrambled outputs.
C
            DATA    R(1),R(2),R(3),R(4)        / 1,2,2,3 /
            DATA    R(5),R(6),R(7),R(8)        / 2,3,1,3 /
            DATA    R(9),R(10),R(11),R(12)     / 2,4,2,5 /
            DATA    R(13),R(14),R(15),R(16)    / 4,3,2,5 /
            DATA    R(17),R(18),R(19),R(20)    / 4,3,2,7 /
            DATA    R(21),R(22),R(23),R(24)    / 5,4,3,6 /
            DATA    R(25),R(26),R(27),R(28)    / 2,7,3,6 /
            DATA    R(29),R(30),R(31),R(32)    / 5,4,1,5 /
            DATA    R(33),R(34),R(35),R(36)    / 3,7,2,4 /
            DATA    R(37),R(38),R(39),R(40)    / 6,8,4,7 /
            DATA    R(41),R(42),R(43),R(44)    / 8,3,2,9 /
            DATA    R(45),R(46),R(47),R(48)    / 5,6,4,7 /
            DATA    R(49),R(50),R(51),R(52)    / 2,9,5,6 /
            DATA    R(53),R(54),R(55),R(56)    / 8,3,1,9 /
            DATA    R(57),R(58),R(59),R(60)    / 5,13,3,7 /
            DATA    R(61),R(62),R(63),R(64)    / 11,15,12,6 /
            DATA    R(65),R(66),R(67),R(68)    / 4,14,2,16 /
            DATA    R(69),R(70)                / 8,10 /
C
            DO 2    K=1,70
                    E(K)=R(K)
    2       CONTINUE
C
C                   Coefficients
C
            DATA    T(1),T(2)     / -1.5,         -0.86602540 /
            DATA    T(3),T(4)     / -1.25,        -1.53884180 /
            DATA    T(5),T(6)     /  0.55901699,   0.36327126 /
            DATA    T(7),T(8)     /  0.58778525,  -1.16666667 /
            DATA    T(9),T(10)    / -0.44095855,   0.73430220 /
            DATA    T(11),T(12)   / -0.79015647,   0.34087293 /
            DATA    T(13),T(14)   / -0.87484229,   0.05585427 /
            DATA    T(15),T(16)   /  0.53396936,   0.70710678 /
            DATA    T(17),T(18)   /  0.5,          0.76604444 /
            DATA    T(19),T(20)   / -0.17364818,   0.93969262 /
            DATA    T(21),T(22)   / -0.64278761,  -0.98480775 /
            DATA    T(23),T(24)   /  0.34202014,   0.54119610 /
            DATA    T(25),T(26)   / -0.54119610,   1.30656296 /
            DATA    T(27),T(28)   / -0.92387953,  -0.38268343 /
            DATA    T(29)         / -0.70710678 /
C
            DO 3    K=1,29
                    Z(K,1) = T(K)
```

```
                       Z(K,2) = -T(K)
      3       CONTINUE
C
C------------------NESTED LOOPS-------------------
C
C       Map to multidimensions through selective addressing.
C
        DO 10 K=1,4
                N1=NI(K)
                N2=N/N1
C
                L=1
                N3=N2-N1*(N2/N1)
                DO 15 J=2,N1
                        L=L+N3
                        IF (L.GT.N1) L=L-N1
                        LP(J)=L
     15         CONTINUE
C
                DO 5 J=1,N,N1
                        IT=J
                        I(1)=J
                        IP(1)=J
                        DO 30 L=2,N1
                                IT=IT+N2
                                IF (IT.GT.N) IT=IT-N
                                I(L)=IT
                                IP(LP(L))=IT
     30                 CONTINUE
        GOTO(5,102,103,104,105,5,107,108,109,5,5,5,5,5,5,116),N1
C
C-------------- WFTA Length=2 ---------------------------
C
    102 CALL BFLY1 (1,1,2,0,0)
        X(IP(1),1) = A(1,1)
        X(IP(2),1) = A(2,1)
        X(IP(1),2) = A(1,2)
        X(IP(2),2) = A(2,2)
        GOTO 5
C
C-------------- WFTA Length=3 ---------------------------
C
    103 CALL BFLY1 (1,2,3,0,2)
        A(1,1) = X(I(1),1)
        A(1,2) = X(I(1),2)
        CALL KERMIT (1,2,1)
        S3 = -Z(2,INV)*A(3,2)
        A(3,2) = Z(2,INV)*A(3,1)
        A(3,1) = S3
        CALL BFLY3 (1,2,3,4)
        X(IP(1),1) = A(1,1)
        X(IP(1),2) = A(1,2)
        GOTO 5
C
C-------------- WFTA Length=4 ---------------------------
C
    104 CALL BFLY1 (2,1,3,1,0)
C
        E1 = A(4,2)
        A(4,2) = -A(4,1)
        A(4,1) = E1
        IF (INV.EQ.2) THEN
                A(4,1) = -A(4,1)
                A(4,2) = -A(4,2)
        END IF
C
```

```
        CALL BFLY3 (1,1,2,6)
        CALL BFLY3 (1,3,4,8)
        GOTO 5
C
C-------------- WFTA Length=5 -----------------------------
C
  105   A(1,1) = X(I(1),1)
        A(1,2) = X(I(1),2)
        CALL BFLY1 (1,2,3,0,10)
        CALL BFLY1 (1,4,5,0,12)
        CALL BFLY2 (1,2,4)
        CALL KERMIT (1,2,3)
        CALL ERNIE (3,5,4,7,6,0)
        A(4,1) = Z(5,1)*A(4,1)
        A(4,2) = Z(5,1)*A(4,2)
        X(IP(1),1) = A(1,1)
        X(IP(1),2) = A(1,2)
        CALL BFLY2 (1,2,4)
        CALL BFLY3 (1,2,3,14)
        CALL BFLY3 (1,4,5,16)
        GOTO 5
C
C-------------- WFTA Length=7 -----------------------------
C
  107   A(1,1) = X(I(1),1)
        A(1,2) = X(I(1),2)
        CALL BFLY1 (1,2,3,0,18)
        CALL BFLY1 (1,4,5,0,20)
        CALL BFLY1 (1,6,7,0,22)
        CALL GROVER (2,4,6)
        CALL GROVER (3,5,7)
        CALL ERNIE (4,6,11,10,14,1)
        CALL ERNIE (5,7,12,13,15,0)
        CALL KERMIT (1,2,8)
        E1     = -A(3,2)*Z(9,INV)
        A(3,2) = A(3,1)*Z(9,INV)
        A(3,1) = E1
        CALL BIGBIRD (3,5,7)
        CALL BIGBIRD (2,4,6)
        CALL BFLY3 (1,2,3,24)
        CALL BFLY3 (1,4,5,26)
        CALL BFLY3 (1,6,7,28)
        X(IP(1),1) = A(1,1)
        X(IP(1),2) = A(1,2)
        GOTO 5
C
C-------------- WFTA Length=8 -----------------------------
C
  108   CALL BFLY1 (4,1,5,1,0)
        CALL BFLY2 (2,1,3)
        CALL BFLY2 (1,6,8)
C
        E1     = A(4,2)
        A(4,2) = -A(4,1)
        A(4,1) = E1
        IF (INV.EQ.2) THEN
                A(4,1) = -A(4,1)
                A(4,2) = -A(4,2)
        END IF
C
        E1     = -Z(29,INV)*A(6,2)
        A(6,2) = Z(29,INV)*A(6,1)
        A(6,1) = E1
C
        E1 = A(7,2)
        A(7,2) = -A(7,1)
```

```
              A(7,1) = E1
              IF (INV.EQ.2) THEN
                       A(7,1) = -A(7,1)
                       A(7,2) = -A(7,2)
              END IF
C
              A(8,1) = Z(16,1)*A(8,1)
              A(8,2) = Z(16,1)*A(8,2)
C
              CALL BFLY3 (1,1,2,30)
              CALL BFLY3 (1,3,4,32)
              CALL BFLY2 (1,5,6)
              CALL BFLY2 (1,7,8)
              CALL BFLY3 (2,5,7,34)
              GOTO 5
C
C
C-------------- WFTA Length=9 ----------------------------
C
  109    A(1,1) = X(I(1),1)
         A(1,2) = X(I(1),2)
         CALL BFLY1 (1,2,3,0,38)
         CALL BFLY1 (3,5,8,0,40)
C
         CALL KERMIT (1,2,1)
         CALL COOKMON (5,6,7,4,18,19,20,17,1)
         CALL COOKMON (8,9,10,11,21,22,23,2,0)
         E1     = -Z(2,INV)*A(3,2)
         A(3,2) = Z(2,INV)*A(3,1)
         A(3,1) = E1
C
         X(IP(1),1) = A(1,1) + A(4,1) + A(4,1)
         X(IP(1),2) = A(1,2) + A(4,2) + A(4,2)
         A(4,1) = A(1,1) - A(4,1)
         A(4,2) = A(1,2) - A(4,2)
C
         CALL MSPIGGY (5,6,7,2)
         CALL MSPIGGY (8,9,10,3)
         CALL BFLY3 (1,4,11,46)
         CALL BFLY3 (3,5,8,48)
C
         GOTO 5
C
C-------------- WFTA Length=16 --------------------------
C
  116    CALL BFLY1 (8,1,9,1,0)
         CALL BFLY2 (4,1,5)
         CALL BFLY2 (1,10,16)
         CALL BFLY2 (1,11,15)
         CALL BFLY2 (1,12,14)
         A(14,1) = -A(14,1)
         A(14,2) = -A(14,2)
         CALL BFLY2 (2,1,3)
         CALL BFLY2 (1,6,8)
C
         CALL ERNIE (10,12,24,27,26,0)
         CALL ERNIE (14,16,25,28,26,1)
C
         E1     = A(4,2)
         A(4,2) = -A(4,1)
         A(4,1) = E1
         IF (INV.EQ.2) THEN
                  A(4,1) = -A(4,1)
                  A(4,2) = -A(4,2)
         END IF
C
```

```
          E1    = -Z(29,INV)*A(6,2)
          A(6,2) = Z(29,INV)*A(6,1)
          A(6,1) = E1
C
          E1    = A(7,2)
          A(7,2) = -A(7,1)
          A(7,1) = E1
          IF (INV.EQ.2) THEN
                  A(7,1) = -A(7,1)
                  A(7,2) = -A(7,2)
          END IF
C
          A(8,1) = Z(16,1)*A(8,1)
          A(8,2) = Z(16,1)*A(8,2)
C
          E1    = -Z(29,INV)*A(11,2)
          A(11,2)= Z(29,INV)*A(11,1)
          A(11,1)= E1
C
          E1    = A(13,2)
          A(13,2)=-A(13,1)
          A(13,1) = E1
          IF (INV.EQ.2) THEN
                  A(13,1) = -A(13,1)
                  A(13,2) = -A(13,2)
          END IF
C
          A(15,1) = Z(16,1)*A(15,1)
          A(15,2) = Z(16,1)*A(15,2)
C
          CALL BFLY3 (1,1,2,54)
          CALL BFLY3 (1,3,4,56)
C
          CALL BFLY2 (1,5,6)
          CALL BFLY2 (1,7,8)
          CALL BFLY3 (2,5,7,58)
C
          CALL BFLY2 (1,9,15)
          CALL BFLY2 (1,11,13)
          A(14,1) = -A(14,1)
          A(14,2) = -A(14,2)
C
          CALL BFLY2 (1,10,11)
          CALL BFLY2 (1,13,12)
          CALL BFLY2 (1,15,14)
          CALL BFLY2 (1,9,16)
C
          CALL BFLY3 (2,14,12,62)
C
          CALL BFLY3 (1,9,10,66)
          CALL BFLY3 (1,16,11,68)
C
          GOTO 5
C----------------------------------------------------------
   5              CONTINUE
  10      CONTINUE
C
C
C         Divide data by length if doing inverse transform.
C
          IF (INV.EQ.2) THEN
                  DO 11 K=1,N
                          X(K,1) = X(K,1)/N
                          X(K,2) = X(K,2)/N
  11              CONTINUE
          END IF
```

```
C
            RETURN
            END
C
C/////////////////////////////////////////////////////////
C
C
C           These subroutines are easily understood when
C           accompanied by the corresponding flowgraphs.
C
C----------------------------------------------------------
            SUBROUTINE BFLY1 (M,C1,C2,J,H)
C
C                   X  TO  A
C
            REAL X,A
            INTEGER C1,C2,K1,K2,I,M,E,H,R1,R2
            COMMON /A/X /B/A /C/I,IP,E
            DIMENSION X(512,2),A(16,2),I(16),E(72),IP(16)
C
            K1 = 0
            K2 = 0
     5      IF (J.EQ.1) THEN
                    R1 = C1+K1
                    R2 = C2+K1
            ELSE
                    R1 = E(K2+H+1)
                    R2 = E(K2+H+2)
            END IF
C
            DO 6 N=1,2
                    A(C1+K1,N) = X(I(R1),N) + X(I(R2),N)
                    A(C2+K1,N) = X(I(R1),N) - X(I(R2),N)
     6      CONTINUE
C
            K1 = K1 + 1
            K2 = K1 + K1
            IF (K1.NE.M) GOTO 5
C
            RETURN
            END
C
C----------------------------------------------------------
            SUBROUTINE BFLY2 (M,C1,C2)
C
C           A  TO  A
C
            REAL A
            INTEGER C1,C2,M,K1
            COMMON /B/ A
            DIMENSION A(16,2)
C
            K1 = 0
     7      DO 8 N=1,2
                    E1 = A(C1+K1,N) + A(C2+K1,N)
                    A(C2+K1,N) = A(C1+K1,N) - A(C2+K1,N)
                    A(C1+K1,N) = E1
     8      CONTINUE
C
            K1 = K1 + 1
            IF (K1.NE.M) GOTO 7
C
            RETURN
            END
C
C----------------------------------------------------------
            SUBROUTINE BFLY3 (M,C1,C2,H)
```

```
C
C        A  TO  X
C
         REAL X,A
         INTEGER C1,C2,M,K1,K2,IP,E,H
         COMMON /A/X /B/A /C/ I,IP,E
         DIMENSION X(512,2),A(16,2),IP(16),E(72),I(16)
C
         K1 = 0
         K2 = 0
   9     DO 10 N=1,2
                 X(IP(E(K2+H+1)),N) = A(C1+K1,N) + A(C2+K1,N)
                 X(IP(E(K2+H+2)),N) = A(C1+K1,N) - A(C2+K1,N)
   10    CONTINUE
C
         K1 = K1 + 1
         K2 = K1 + K1
         IF (K1.NE.M) GOTO 9
C
         RETURN
         END
C
C-----------------------------------------------------------
         SUBROUTINE KERMIT (C1,C2,T1)
C
         REAL A,Z
         COMMON /B/ A /E/ Z,INV
         INTEGER C1,C2,T1
         DIMENSION Z(29,2),A(16,2)
C
         DO 11 N=1,2
                 A(C1,N) = A(C1,N) + A(C2,N)
                 A(C2,N) = A(C1,N) + Z(T1,1)*A(C2,N)
   11    CONTINUE
C
         RETURN
         END
C
C-----------------------------------------------------------
         SUBROUTINE ERNIE (C1,C2,T1,T2,T3,W1)
C
         COMMON /B/ A /E/ Z,INV
         DIMENSION Z(29,2),A(16,2)
         INTEGER C1,C2,T1,T2,T3,W1
C
         U1 = A(C1,1) + A(C2,1)
         V1 = A(C1,2) + A(C2,2)
C
         IF (W1.EQ.1) THEN
                 U2 = Z(T2,1)*U1
                 V2 = Z(T2,1)*V1
C
                 E1     = A(C1,1)*Z(T1,1) + U2
                 A(C1,2)= A(C1,2)*Z(T1,1) + V2
                 A(C1,1)= E1
C
                 E1     = A(C2,1)*Z(T3,1) + U2
                 A(C2,2)= A(C2,2)*Z(T3,1) + V2
                 A(C2,1)= E1
         ELSE
                 U2 = -Z(T2,INV)*V1
                 V2 = Z(T2,INV)*U1
C
                 E1     = -A(C1,2)*Z(T1,INV) + U2
                 A(C1,2) = A(C1,1)*Z(T1,INV) + V2
```

```
C                      A(C1,1) = E1

                       E1      = -A(C2,2)*Z(T3,INV) + U2
                       A(C2,2) = A(C2,1)*Z(T3,INV) + V2
                       A(C2,1) = E1
              END IF
C
              RETURN
              END
C
C-----------------------------------------------------------
              SUBROUTINE GROVER (C1,C2,C3)
C
              REAL A
              COMMON /B/ A
              DIMENSION A(16,2)
              INTEGER C1,C2,C3
C
              DO 12 N=1,2
                       E1      = A(C1,N) + A(C2,N) + A(C3,N)
                       E2      = A(C1,N) - A(C2,N)
                       A(C3,N) = A(C2,N) - A(C3,N)
                       A(C2,N) = E2
                       A(C1,N) = E1
     12       CONTINUE
C
              RETURN
              END
C
C-----------------------------------------------------------
              SUBROUTINE BIGBIRD (C1,C2,C3)
C
              REAL A
              COMMON /B/ A
              DIMENSION A(16,2)
              INTEGER C1,C2,C3
C
              DO 13 N=1,2
                       E1      = A(C1,N) - A(C2,N) + A(C3,N)
                       E2      = A(C1,N) + A(C2,N)
                       A(C3,N) = A(C1,N) - A(C3,N)
                       A(C2,N) = E2
                       A(C1,N) = E1
     13       CONTINUE
C
              RETURN
              END
C
C-----------------------------------------------------------
              SUBROUTINE COOKMON (C1,C2,C3,C4,T1,T2,T3,T4,J)
C
              INTEGER C1,C2,C3,C4,T1,T2,T3,T4
              REAL A,Z,G
              COMMON /B/ A /E/ Z,INV
              DIMENSION A(16,2),Z(29,2),G(4,2)
C
              DO 14 N=1,2
                  IF (J.EQ.1) THEN
                  G(1,N) = Z(T1,1)*(A(C2,N) - A(C1,N))
                  G(2,N) = Z(T2,1)*(A(C3,N) - A(C2,N))
                  G(3,N) = Z(T3,1)*(A(C1,N) - A(C3,N))
                  G(4,N) = Z(T4,1)*(A(C1,N) + A(C2,N) + A(C3,N))
                  ELSE
                  G(1,N) = Z(T1,INV)*(A(C2,N) - A(C1,N))
                  G(2,N) = Z(T2,INV)*(A(C3,N) - A(C2,N))
                  G(3,N) = Z(T3,INV)*(A(C1,N) - A(C3,N))
```

```
                G(4,N) = Z(T4,INV)*(A(C1,N) + A(C2,N) + A(C3,N))
                END IF
 14      CONTINUE
C
         IF (J.EQ.1) THEN
                DO 15 N=1,2
                        A(C1,N) = G(1,N)
                        A(C2,N) = G(2,N)
                        A(C3,N) = G(3,N)
                        A(C4,N) = G(4,N)
 15             CONTINUE
         ELSE
                A(C1,1) = -G(1,2)
                A(C2,1) = -G(2,2)
                A(C3,1) = -G(3,2)
                A(C4,1) = -G(4,2)
                A(C1,2) = G(1,1)
                A(C2,2) = G(2,1)
                A(C3,2) = G(3,1)
                A(C4,2) = G(4,1)
         END IF
C
         RETURN
         END
C
C-----------------------------------------------------------
         SUBROUTINE MSPIGGY (C1,C2,C3,C4)
C
         INTEGER C1,C2,C3,C4
         REAL A
         COMMON /B/ A
         DIMENSION A(16,2)
C
         DO 16 N=1,2
                E1 = A(C1,N) + A(C3,N) + A(C4,N)
                E2 = A(C4,N) - A(C2,N) - A(C1,N)
                A(C3,N) = A(C4,N) - A(C3,N) + A(C2,N)
                A(C2,N) = E2
                A(C1,N) = E1
 16      CONTINUE
C
         RETURN
         END
```

Subroutines used in the FORTRAN version of the Winograd short FFTs follow.

BFLY1

For almost all the algorithms, the input consisted of a number of stacked 2-point convolutions (butterflies). To let us take advantage of this, subroutine BFLY1 allows any number of consecutive loops, with the addresses being incremented every time.

Another consideration was that the ordering of the inputs was often not sequential. Thus, this subroutine had to allow for the specification of each input address. The variable X represents an input or output address, whereas the variable A represents the intermediate in-place variable. The back slashes indicate a multiplication by -1. The direction of flow is left (input) to right (output).

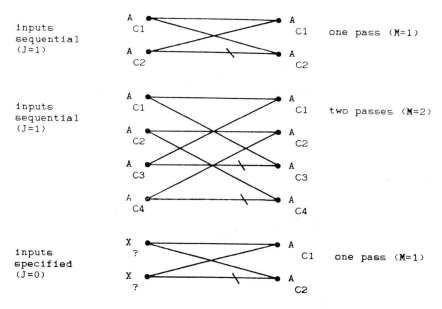

BFLY2

Same as BFLY1, except that inputs and outputs are strictly sequential (in-place).

BFLY3

Same as BFLY1, except that outputs have the option of being specified.

KERMIT

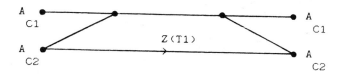

Strictly an in-place algorithm. The passed variable T1 determines which coefficient value to use.

ERNIE

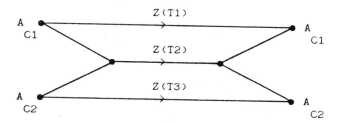

GROVER

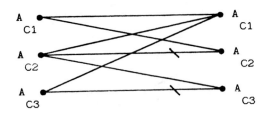

BIGBIRD

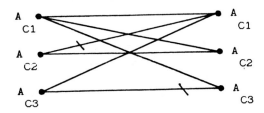

COOKMON

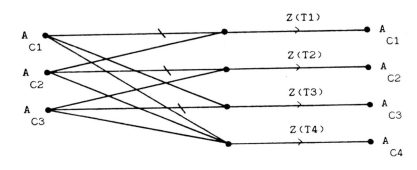

MSPIGGY

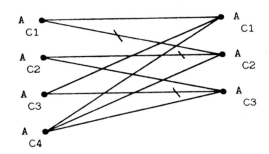

Winograd Short FFT Algorithms

Flow diagrams for Winograd's short FFTs, that is, for the Winograd small-N DFTs, follow.

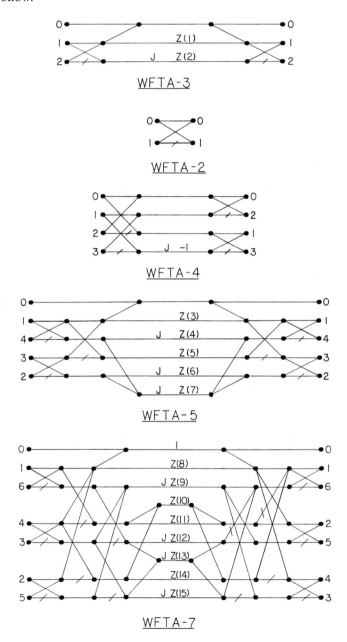

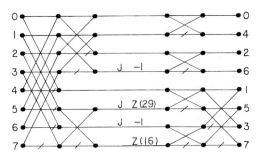

WFTA-8

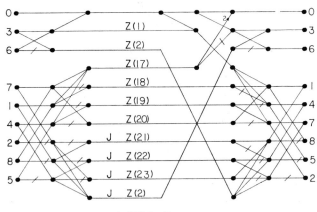

WFTA-9

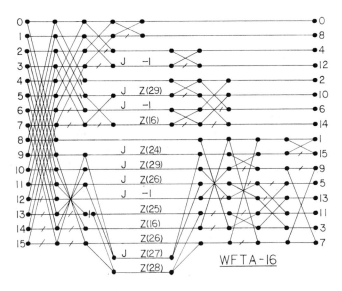

WFTA-16

APPENDIX E. HIGHLY EFFICIENT PFA ASSEMBLY LANGUAGE COMPUTER PROGRAM

```
;                    FORTRAN subroutine "ONEK()".
;
;        Program author:   Mike Orchard
;                          Graduate student, SDSU
;                          April, 1986
;        Program extracted from Master's thesis.
;
;        Thesis advisor:   fred harris
;
;        Inquires concerning this program are directed to:
;
;                    Mike Orchard
;                    Princeton University
;                    Princeton, NJ
;                         or
;                    fred harris
;                    Electrical & Computer Engineering Department
;                    San Diego State University
;                    San Diego, CA 92182
;
;        This program listing is a highly efficient assembly language
;        implementation of a 1008-point prime factor transform. This
;        program is described in the introduction to appendix D.
;        ONEK() has been optimized for use with the 8087 coprocessor.
;        ONEK() is intended to be used with the Microsoft FORTRAN compliler
;        for the IBM PC. Special attention should be paid to the passing
;        of arguments when interfacing to other compilers.
;
;        Description:
;            ONEK() performs a 1008-point DFT on an array of complex
;            data passed to it from the FORTRAN calling program.
;        Calling format:
;            COMPLEX*16  TEST(1008)
;            CALL ONEK(TEST)
;        Hardware requirements:
;            IBM PC with 8087 coproccessor (or emulating library).
;        Memory Requirements:
;            ONEK() adds 1172 bytes of code to the program CODE segment
;            and 266 bytes of data to the program DATA segment.
;        Timing:
;            ONEK() completes a typical 1008-point DFT in 1.43 seconds.
;            *Note: this typical timing was measured on an IBM-PC, using
;            a 4.77 MHz clock, on an array of non-zero data. This time
;            decreases when operating on data sequences with a substantial
;            number of zeros.
;        Theory of Operation:
;            ONEK() implements the Good-Thomas prime factor algorithm (PFA)
;            using factors of 7, 9, and 16 to obtain the 1008-point DFT.
;            The following techniques are used to minimize code and
;            maximize speed:
;
;        1.      Unscrambling: Direct implementation of the PFA produces
;        an output array in scrambled order.  An unscrambling stage
;        can be avoided by proper permutation of the output of the
;        individual factor algorithms, but this approach adds code and
;        time required to manipulate separate input and output index
;        pointers into the array.  This program uses a technique
;        suggested by Burrus (IEEE ASSP Proc. Feb. 1985), which achieves
;        correct output array ordering by permuting the multiplier
;        coefficients used by each algorithm.
;
;        2.      Winograd Small FFT: The development of efficient 7-, 9-,
;        and 16-point DFT algorithms involves recognizing that much of
;        the computation required can be organized as cyclic convolu-
;        tions. A cyclic convolution can be modeled as a polynomial
```

```
;        product modulo a third polynomial. If we reduce the polynomial
;        product modulo each of the factors of the third polynomial,
;        perform each of these residue products independently, and
;        reconstruct the original product using the Chinese remainder
;        theorem, we obtain savings in required computation. (Refer to
;        texts on fast algorithms for more detailed treatment.) The
;        structure of algorithms developed in this way is determined
;        by the size of the cyclic convolutions identified in each DFT
;        and the particular factors used in the reduction and recon-
;        struction of polynomial products.
;            This program recognizes that the 7-, 9-, and 16 point
;        algorithms share some convolution sizes and polynomial factors.
;        The resulting similarities in structure are exploited to minimize
;        code. For example, the 7- and 9-point algorithms both include a
;        6-point cyclic convolution. The structure of this convolution is
;        implemented in the subroutines INTO and OUTOF and the 7- and
;        9-point programs, SV and NN, call these subroutines. Similar
;        code sharing is achieved in the 16-point algorithm.
;
;   3.       Indexing: Accessing data from the array to be processed
;        by each of the small DFT algorithms can be time consuming and
;        can require overhead code.  This program greatly reduces this
;        effort by accessing all data in-place (never moved from the
;        original large array) addressed by index registers.  The
;        standard indexing calculations usually required to determine
;        the order of data to be sent to the small DFTs is eliminated
;        by incrementing the index registers in a way that reflects
;        the desired order in which data should be sent to each small
;        DFT algorithm.  For example:  When performing the 7-point
;        DFTs, all indexes are incremented by (9 * 16) mod 1008.
;        Starting indexes are initialized in the storage locations
;        SVPOS, NNPOS, and HXPOS.
;
; *NOTE:   This program has been extracted from the larger program NPFA(),
;          which is a general purpose PFA algorithm for factors 2, 3, 4,
;          5, 7, 8, 9, and 16.
;

PAGE 60,120
DATA    SEGMENT PUBLIC 'DATA'
SEVCF   DQ      -1.166666666666667      ;D(1)
        DQ       -.4409585518440984     ;D(5)
        DQ       -.7901564685254002     ;D(3)
        DQ        .7343022012357524     ;D(2)
        DQ        .05585426728964767    ;D(4)
        DQ        .3408729306239314     ;D(7)
        DQ       -.8748422909616567     ;D(6)
        DQ        .5339693603377252     ;D(8)
NINCF   DQ       -.5000000000000000     ;D(2)
        DQ      -1.5000000000000000     ;D(1)
        DQ       -.8660254037844387     ;D(6),D(7)
        DQ       -.1736481776669304     ;D(3)
        DQ        .9396926207859083     ;D(5)
        DQ       -.7660444431189780     ;D(4)
        DQ       -.9848077530122080     ;D(8)
        DQ        .3420201433256689     ;D(10)
        DQ        .6427876096865393     ;D(9)
OCTCF   DQ        .7071067810000000     ;D(7)
        DQ        .7071067810000000     ;D(4)
HXCF    DQ       -.3826834323650898     ;D(14)
        DQ       -.5411961001461969     ;D(13)
        DQ       1.3065629648763770     ;D(12)
        DQ       -.9238795325112867     ;D(17)
        DQ        .5411961001461969     ;D(16)
        DQ       1.3065629648763770     ;D(15)
TWSTAT  DB      0
```

```
CNT       DB      ?
SVPOS     DW      0CA00H,0F700H,0D300H,0EE00H,0DC00H,0E500H,0C100H
THPOS     DW      0D600H,0EB00H,0C800H,0F900H,0DD00H,0E400H,0CF00H,0F200H,0C100H
TWPOS     DW      0C8E0H,0F820H,0D8A0H,0E860H,0F040H,0D0C0H,0C100H,0E080H
          DW      0C4F0H,0FC10H,0DC90H,0E470H,0CCD0H,0F430H,0D4B0H,0EC50H
DATA      ENDS

DGROUP    GROUP   DATA
CODE      SEGMENT 'CODE'
          ASSUME  CS:CODE,DS:DGROUP,SS:DGROUP;
PUBLIC    SV,NN,SUB1,SUB2,INTO,OUTOF,SVSCL,NNSCL,DUMP,EIGHT,HX,SUB5,SUB6,ONEK
ONEK      PROC    FAR
          PUSH    BP
          MOV     BP,SP
          LES     BX,[BP+6]
          ADD     BX,16128
          MOV     DX,16128
          CALL    HX
          CALL    NN
          CALL    SV
          POP     BP
          RET     4
ONEK      ENDP
;
HX        PROC    NEAR
          PUSH    BP
          MOV     BP,SP
          SUB     SP,260
HXBG:     LEA     DI,TWPOS
          CALL    SUB4
          CALL    SUB5
          CALL    EIGHT
          MOV     CX,6
HXLP1:    SUB     BP,10
          FSTP    TBYTE PTR [BP]
          LOOP    HXLP1
          ADD     BP,140
          MOV     CX,6
HXLP2:    SUB     BP,10
          FLD     TBYTE PTR [BP]
          LOOP    HXLP2
          LEA     DI,HXCF
          CALL    OUTOF
          ADD     BP,60
          CALL    SUB6
          MOV     CX,4
HXLP3:    SUB     BP,10
          FSTP    TBYTE PTR [BP]
          LOOP    HXLP3
          FLD     TBYTE PTR [BP-30]
          FLD     TBYTE PTR [BP-40]
          CALL    SUB6
          MOV     CX,4
HXLP4:    SUB     BP,10
          FSTP    TBYTE PTR [BP]
          LOOP    HXLP4
          ADD     BX,8
          LEA     DI,TWPOS
          CALL    SUB4
          SUB     BP,60
          CALL    SUB5
          CALL    EIGHT
          ADD     BP,120
          MOV     CNT,3
          MOV     CX,256
          LEA     DI,TWPOS+8
```

```
                CALL    DUMP
                ADD     BP,20
                MOV     CX,6
HXLP5:          SUB     BP,10
                FLD     TBYTE PTR [BP]
                LOOP    HXLP5
                LEA     DI,HXCF
                CALL    OUTOF
                ADD     BP,180
                MOV     CNT,2
                CALL    SUB6
                MOV     CX,256
                LEA     DI,TWPOS+28
                CALL    DUMP
                SUB     BP,160
                FLD     TBYTE PTR [BP+10]
                FLD     TBYTE PTR [BP]
                CALL    SUB6
                MOV     CNT,2
                ADD     BP,160
                CALL    DUMP
                SUB     BX,8
                LEA     DI,TWPOS+14
                ADD     [DI],CX
                JL      HXLP6
                SUB     [DI],DX
HXLP6:          ADD     [DI-2],CX
                JGE     HXFIN
                ADD     BP,100
                JMP     HXBG
HXFIN:          SUB     [DI-2],DX
                ADD     SP,260
                POP     BP
                RET
                HX      ENDP
;
NN              PROC    NEAR
                PUSH    BP
                MOV     BP,SP
                SUB     SP,100
NNBG:           LEA     DI,THPOS
                MOV     CX,1
                CALL    SUB1
                SUB     BP,20
                FSTP    TBYTE PTR [BP+10]
                FSTP    TBYTE PTR [BP]
                CALL    INTO
                CALL    NNSCL
                CALL    OUTOF
                ADD     BX,8
                LEA     DI,THPOS
                CALL    SUB2
                MOV     CX,6
NLP1:           SUB     BP,10
                FSTP    TBYTE PTR [BP]
                LOOP    NLP1
                MOV     CX,1
                CALL    SUB1
                SUB     BP,20
                FSTP    TBYTE PTR [BP+10]
                FSTP    TBYTE PTR [BP]
                CALL    INTO
                CALL    NNSCL
                CALL    OUTOF
                ADD     BP,60
                MOV     CNT,3
```

```
            MOV       CX,144
            CALL      SUB2
            LEA       DI,THPOS+12
            CALL      DUMP
            FLD       TBYTE PTR [BP]
            FLD       TBYTE PTR [BP+10]
            ADD       BP,80
            MOV       CNT,1
            CALL      DUMP
            SUB       BX,8
            LEA       DI,THPOS+16
            ADD       [DI],CX
            JGE       NNFIN
            ADD       BP,40
            JMP       NNBG
NNFIN:      SUB       [DI],DX
            ADD       SP,100
            POP       BP
            RET
            NN        ENDP
;
SV          PROC      NEAR
            PUSH      BP
            MOV       BP,SP
            SUB       SP,60
SVBG:       LEA       DI,SVPOS
            CALL      INTO
            CALL      SVSCL
            CALL      OUTOF
            ADD       BX,8
            LEA       DI,SVPOS
            CALL      SUB2
            MOV       CX,6
LP1:        SUB       BP,10
            FSTP      TBYTE PTR [BP]
            LOOP      LP1
            CALL      INTO
            CALL      SVSCL
            CALL      OUTOF
            ADD       BP,40
            MOV       CNT,3
            MOV       CX,112
            CALL      SUB2
            LEA       DI,SVPOS+8
            CALL      DUMP
            SUB       BX,8
            LEA       DI,SVPOS+12
            ADD       [DI],CX
            JGE       SVFIN
            ADD       BP,80
            JMP       SVBG
SVFIN:      SUB       [DI],DX
            ADD       SP,60
            POP       BP
            RET
            SV        ENDP
;
FVDC        PROC      NEAR
            MOV       SI,[DI]
            FLD       ST(0)
            FADD      QWORD PTR [BX+SI]
            XCHG      AX,DI
            FST       QWORD PTR [BX+SI]
            FXCH      ST(1)
            FMUL      QWORD PTR [DI]
            FADDP     ST(1),ST
```

```
          RET
          FVDC      ENDP
;
EIGHT     PROC      NEAR
          FLD       ST(1)
          FXCH      ST(1)
          FADD      ST(1),ST
          FSUBRP    ST(2),ST
          FLD       ST(2)
          FXCH      ST(5)
          FADD      ST(5),ST
          FSUBRP    ST(3),ST
          FLD       ST(3)
          FXCH      ST(6)
          FADD      ST(4),ST
          FSUBP     ST(6),ST
          FLD       ST(4)
          FXCH      ST(1)
          FADD      ST(1),ST
          ADD       BP,10
          FSUBRP    ST(5),ST
          MOV       SI,[DI-4]
          FSTP      QWORD PTR ES:[BX+SI]
          MOV       SI,[DI-2]
          FXCH      ST(3)
          FSTP      QWORD PTR ES:[BX+SI]
          LEA       DI,OCTCF
          FLD       TBYTE PTR [BP]
          FLD       ST(0)
          FXCH      ST(3)
          FMUL      QWORD PTR [DI]
          FADD      ST(3),ST
          ADD       DI,8
          SUB       BP,10
          FSUBRP    ST(1),ST
          FXCH      ST(4)
          FLD       TBYTE PTR [BP]
          FLD       ST(0)
          FXCH      ST(3)
          FMUL      QWORD PTR [DI]
          FADD      ST(1),ST
          FSUBP     ST(3),ST
          ADD       BP,20
          FXCH      ST(4)
          RET
          EIGHT     ENDP
;
NNSCL     PROC      NEAR          ;BX: BASE OF ARRAY
                                  ;DI: (IN) ADDRESS OF OFFSET INDICES
                                  ;    (OUT) ADDRESS OF COEFFICIENTS
                                  ;SI: USED - (NOT PRESERVED)
                                  ;BP: ADDRESS OF t5 ON STACK
                                  ;    (t1 AND t5 ARE REPLACED ON THE STACK
                                  ;     BY T4 AND m7 WITH BP POINTING TO m7)
          ADD       BP,10
          MOV       SI,[DI]
          FLD       TBYTE PTR [BP]
          FLD       ST(0)
          FADD      QWORD PTR ES:[BX+SI]
          FADD      ST,ST(2)
          LEA       DI,NINCF
          FST       QWORD PTR ES:[BX+SI]
          FXCH      ST(2)
          FMUL      QWORD PTR [DI]
          FADD      ST(2),ST
          ADD       DI,8
```

```
              FADD        ST(2),ST
              FADD        ST,ST(2)
              FSTP        TBYTE PTR [BP]
              FMUL        QWORD PTR [DI]
              FADDP       ST(1),ST
              ADD         DI,16
              SUB         BP,10
              FLD         TBYTE PTR [BP]
              FMUL        QWORD PTR [DI-8]
              FXCH        ST(2)
              FMUL        QWORD PTR [DI-8]
              FSTP        TBYTE PTR [BP]
              RET
     NNSCL    ENDP
;
SVSCL         PROC        NEAR              ;BX: BASE OF ARRAY
                                           ;DI: (IN) ADDRESS OF OFFSET INDICES
                                           ;    (OUT) ADDRESS OF COEFFICIENTS
                                           ;SI: USED - (NOT PRESERVED)

              LEA         AX,SEVCF
              CALL        FVDC
              ADD         DI,16
              FXCH        ST(1)
              FMUL        QWORD PTR [DI-8]
              FXCH        ST(1)
              RET
     SVSCL    ENDP
;
DUMP          PROC        NEAR
LP2:          FLD         TBYTE PTR [BP]
              FLD         ST(0)
              FADD        ST,ST(2)                    ;IM(N)
              MOV         SI,[DI]
              ADD         [DI],CX
              JL          L1
              SUB         [DI],DX
L1:           FSTP        QWORD PTR ES:[BX+SI]
              FSUBP       ST(1),ST                    ;IM(N*)
              ADD         BP,10
              ADD         DI,2
              MOV         AX,SI
              MOV         SI,[DI]
              FSTP        QWORD PTR ES:[BX+SI]
              FLD         TBYTE PTR [BP]
              FLD         ST(0)
              FSUB        ST,ST(2)                    ;RL(N)
              SUB         BP,30
              SUB         BX,8
              XCHG        AX,SI
              FSTP        QWORD PTR ES:[BX+SI]
              FADDP       ST(1),ST                    ;RL(N*)
              XCHG        AX,SI
              ADD         [DI],CX
              JL          L2
              SUB         [DI],DX
L2:           SUB         DI,6
              FSTP        QWORD PTR ES:[BX+SI]
              ADD         BX,8
              DEC         CNT
              JG          LP2
              RET
     DUMP     ENDP
;
INTO          PROC        NEAR              ;DI: ADDRESS OF OFFSET INDICES
                                           ;BX: BASE OF ARRAY
              MOV         CX,3
```

```
            CALL    SUB1
            CALL    SUB2
            RET
            INTO    ENDP
;
OUTOF       PROC    NEAR
            FLD     ST(3)
            FSUBR   ST,ST(6)
            FLD     ST(3)
            FSUBR   ST,ST(6)
            MOV     CX,2
OUTLP:      FMUL    QWORD PTR [DI]
            ADD     DI,8
            FXCH    ST(4)
            FMUL    QWORD PTR [DI]
            FSUB    ST,ST(4)
            ADD     DI,8
            FXCH    ST(4)
            FXCH    ST(6)
            FMUL    QWORD PTR [DI]
            ADD     DI,8
            FADDP   ST(6),ST
            LOOP    OUTLP
            RET
            OUTOF   ENDP
;
SUB1        PROC    NEAR                ;DI: ADDRESS OF OFFSET INDEXES
                                        ;BX: BASE OF ARRAY
                                        ;SI: USED - (NOT PRESERVED)
                                        ;CX: COUNT - (NOT PRESERVED)
LONE:       MOV     SI,[DI]
            FLD     QWORD PTR ES:[BX+SI]
            ADD     DI,2
            MOV     SI,[DI]
            FLD     ST(0)
            FLD     QWORD PTR ES:[BX+SI]
            FADD    ST(1),ST
            ADD     DI,2
            FSUBP   ST(2),ST
            LOOP    LONE
            RET
            SUB1    ENDP
;
SUB2        PROC    NEAR
            FLD     ST(5)
            FADD    ST,ST(4)
            FLD     ST(5)
            FADD    ST,ST(4)
            FXCH    ST(2)
            FADD    ST(2),ST
            FSUBR   ST(4),ST
            FSUBRP  ST(6),ST
            FXCH    ST(2)
            FSUB    ST(2),ST
            FADD    ST(4),ST
            FADDP   ST(6),ST
            RET
            SUB2    ENDP
;
SUB4        PROC    NEAR
            MOV     CX,2
            CALL    SUB1
            FLD     ST(2)
            FXCH    ST(1)
            FADD    ST(3),ST
            FSUBP   ST(1),ST
```

```
          FLD     ST(3)
          FXCH    ST(2)
          FADD    ST(2),ST
          FSUBP   ST(4),ST
          RET
          SUB4    ENDP
;
SUB5      PROC    NEAR
          INC     CX
          CALL    SUB1
          LEA     SI,OCTCF
          FLD     ST(1)
          FXCH    ST(4)
          FMUL    QWORD PTR [SI]
          FADD    ST(2),ST
          INC     CX
          FSUBRP  ST(4),ST
          FXCH    ST(3)
          FSTP    TBYTE PTR [BP-70]
          FSTP    TBYTE PTR [BP-50]
          CALL    SUB1
          LEA     SI,OCTCF+8
          FLD     ST(1)
          FXCH    ST(3)
          FMUL    QWORD PTR [SI]
          FADD    ST(3),ST
          FSUBP   ST(2),ST
          FXCH    ST(2)
          FSTP    TBYTE PTR [BP-80]
          FSTP    TBYTE PTR [BP-60]
          FLD     ST(0)
          FXCH    ST(2)
          FADD    ST(1),ST
          FSUBP   ST(2),ST
          SUB     BP,80
          MOV     CX,4
          TEST    TWSTAT,1
          FXCH    ST(3)
          JZ      S5LP
          FCHS
S5LP:     SUB     BP,10
          FSTP    TBYTE PTR [BP]
          LOOP    S5LP
          CALL    SUB4
          ADD     BP,20
          FSTP    TBYTE PTR [BP+80]
          FSTP    TBYTE PTR [BP+90]
          CALL    SUB4
          SUB     DI,16
          FSTP    TBYTE PTR [BP+60]
          FSTP    TBYTE PTR [BP+70]
          FLD     TBYTE PTR [BP-10]
          FLD     TBYTE PTR [BP-20]
          RET
          SUB5    ENDP
;
SUB6      PROC    NEAR
          FLD     ST(0)
          FXCH    ST(3)
          FADD    ST(3),ST
          FSUBP   ST(1),ST
          FLD     ST(3)
          FXCH    ST(2)
          FADD    ST(4),ST
          FSUBP   ST(2),ST
          RET

          SUB6    ENDP
;
          CODE    ENDS
END
```

REFERENCES

1. E. O. Brigham, *The Fast Fourier Transform*. Prentice-Hall, Englewood Cliffs, N.J., 1974.
2. D. F. Elliott and K. R. Rao, *Fast Transforms—Algorithms, Analyses and Applications*. Academic Press, New York, 1982.
3. J. H. McClellan and C. M. Rader, *Number Theory in Digital Signal Processing*, Prentice-Hall, Englewood Cliffs, N.J., 1979.
4. H. J. Nussbaumer, *Fast Fourier Transform and Convolution Algorithms*, Springer-Verlag, Berlin and New York, 1981.
5. A. V. Oppenheim and R. W. Schafer, *Digital Signal Processing*, Prentice-Hall, Englewood Cliffs, N.J., 1975.
6. M. T. Heideman, D. H. Johnson, and C. S. Burrus, Gauss and the history of the fast Fourier transform, *IEEE ASSP Mag.* **1**, 14–21 (1984).
7. J. W. Cooley and J. W. Tukey, An algorithm for the machine calculation of complex Fourier series, *Math. Comput.* **19**, 297–301 (1965).
8. I. J. Good, The interaction algorithm and practical Fourier series, *J. R. Statist. Soc. Sect. B.* **20**, 361–372 (1958); **22**, 372–375 (1960).
9. I. J. Good, The relationship between two fast Fourier transforms, *IEEE Trans. Comput.* **C-20**, 310–317 (1971).
10. S. Winograd, On computing the discrete Fourier transform, *Math. Comput.* **32**, 175–199 (1978).
11. R. C. Singleton, An algorithm for computing the mixed radix fast Fourier Transform, *IEEE Trans. Audio Electroacoust.* **AU-17**, 93–103 (1969).
12. G. Brunn, Z-transform DFT filters and FFT's, *IEEE Trans. Acoust. Speech Signal Process.* **ASSP-26**, 56–63 (1978).
13. H. W. Johnson and C. S. Burrus, An in-order, in-place radix-2 FFT, *Proc. IEEE Int. Conf. on Acoust. Speech Signal Process.* pp. 28A.2.1–28A.2.4, 1984.
14. D. F. Elliott, In-place, in-order mixed-radix FFTs, *Proc. Nineteenth Asilomar Conf. Circuits, Systems, Computers*, 688-692, 1985.
15. D. P. Kolba and I. W. Parks, A prime factor FFT algorithm using high-speed convolution, *IEEE Trans. Acoust. Speech Signal Process.* **ASSP-25**, 281–294 (1977).
16. R. Duhamel and H. Hollmann, Split-radix FFT algorithm, *Electron. Letters* **20**, 14–16 (1984).
17. P. Duhamel, Implementation of "split-radix" FFT algorithms for complex, real, and real symmetric-data, *IEEE Trans. Acoust. Speech Signal Process.* **ASSP-34**, 285–295 (1986).
18. H. V. Sorensen, M. T. Heideman, and C. S. Burrus, On computing the split-radix FFT, *IEEE Trans. Acoust. Speech Signal Process.* **ASSP-34**, 152–156 (1986).
19. M. T. Heideman and C. S. Burrus, On the number of multiplications necessary to compute a length-2^n DFT, *IEEE Trans. Acoust. Speech Signal Process.* **ASSP-34**, 91–95 (1986).
20. E. Dubois and A. N. Venetsanopoulos, A new algorithm for the radix-3 FFT, *IEEE Trans. Acoust. Speech Signal Process.* **ASSP-26**, 222–225 (1978).
21. S. Prakash and V. V. Rao, A new radix-6 FFT algorithm, *IEEE Trans. Acoust. Speech Signal Process.*, **ASSP-29**, 939–941 (1981).
22. J. B. Martens, Recursive cyclotomic factorization—A new algorithm for calculating the discrete Fourier transform, *IEEE Trans. Acoust. Speech Signal Process.* **ASSP-32**, 750–761 (1984).
23. S. S. Narayan, M. J. Narasimha, and A. M. Peterson, DFT algorithms—Analaysis and Implementation, Technical Report No. 3606–12, Stanford Electronic Laboratories, Department of Electrical Engineering, Stanford University, Stanford, Calif., May 1978.
24. R. C. Agarwal and J. C. Cooley, New algorithms for digital convolution, *IEEE Trans. Acoust. Speech Signal Process.* **ASSP-25**, 392–410 (1977).
25. R. E. Blahut, *Fast Algorithms for Digital Signal Processing*, Addison-Wesley, Reading, Mass., 1985.
26. D. M. Burton, *Elementary Number Theory*, Allyn and Bacon, Boston, 1976.
27. C. S. Burrus, Index mappings for multidimensional formulation of the DFT and convolution, *IEEE Trans. Acoust. Speech Signal Process.* **ASSP-25**, 239–242 (1977).

28. C. S. Burrus and P. W. Eschenbacher, An in-place, in-order prime factor FFT algorithm, *IEEE Trans. Acoust. Speech Signal Process.* **ASSP-29,** 806–817 (1981).

29. H. F. Silverman, An introduction to programming the Winograd Fourier transform algorithm (WFTA), *IEEE Trans. Acoust. Speech Signal Process.* **ASSP-25,** 152–165 (1977).

30. H. J. Nussbaumer and P. Quandalle, Fast computation of discrete Fourier transforms using polynomial transforms, *IEEE Trans. Acoust. Speech Signal Process.* **ASSP-27,** 169–181 (1979).

31. R. C. Agarwal, Comments on "A prime factor algorithm using high speed convolution," *IEEE Trans. Acoust. Speech Signal Process.* **ASSD-26,** 254 (1978).

32. H. F. Silverman, Corrections and an addendum to "An introduction to programming the Winograd Fourier transform algorithm (WFTA)," *IEEE Trans. Acoust. Speech Signal Process.* **ASSP-26,** 268 (1978).

33. H. F. Silverman, Further corrections to "An introduction to programming the Winograd Fourier transform algorithm (WFTA)," *IEEE Trans. Acoust. Speech Signal Process.* **ASSP-26,** 482 (1978).

34. B. D. Tseng and W. C. Miller, Comments on "An introduction to programming the Winograd Fourier transform algorithm (WFTA)," *IEEE Trans. Acoust. Speech Signal Process.* **ASSP-26,** 268–269 (1978).

35. Y. Suzuki, T. Sone, and K. Kido, A new FFT algorithm of radix 3, 6, and 12, *IEEE Trans. Acoust. Speech Signal Process.* **ASSP-34,** 300–383 (1986).

36. L. R. Morris, A comparative study of time efficient FFT and WFTA programs for general purpose computers, *IEEE Trans. Acoust. Speech Signal Process* **ASSP-26,** 141–150 (1978).

37. M. A. Mehalic, P. L. Rustan, and G. P. Route, Effects of Architecture Implementation on DFT Algorithm Performance, *IEEE Trans. Acoust. Speech Signal Process.* **ASSP-33,** 684–693 (1985).

38. Tran-Thong and B. Liu, Fixed-point fast Fourier transform error analysis, *IEEE Trans. Acoust. Speech Signal Process.* **ASSP-24,** 563–573 (1976).

39. P. P. Welch, A fixed point fast Fourier transform error analysis, *IEEE Trans. Audio Electroacoust.* **AU-17,** 151–157 (1969).

40. A. V. Oppenheim and C. J. Weinstein, Effects of finite register length in digital filtering and the fast Fourier transform, *Proc. IEEE 60.* 957–976 (1972).

41. C. J. Weinstein, Roundoff noise in floating point fast Fourier transform computation, *IEEE Trans. Audio Electroacoust.* **AU-17,** 209–215 (1969).

42. Tran-Thong and B. Liu, Accumulation of roundoff errors in floating point FFT, *IEEE Trans. Circuits Syst.* **CAS-24,** 132–143 (1974).

43. R. W. Patterson and J. H. McClellan, Fixed-point error analysis of Winograd Fourier transform algorithms, *IEEE Trans. Acoust. Speech Signal Process.* **ASSP-26,** 447–455 (1978).

44. C. J. Weinstein *et. al., Programs for Digital Signal Processing, IEEE Press* New York, 1979.

45. H. Chung, A new 2-D FFT algorithm requiring only one data pass, *Proc. Twentieth Asilomar Conf. Signals, Systems, Computers,* 25–29, (1986).

Chapter **8**

Time Domain Signal Processing with the DFT

FREDERIC J. HARRIS
Department of Electrical and Computer Engineering
San Diego State University
San Diego, California 92182-0190

INTRODUCTION I

The discrete Fourier transform (DFT), implemented by one of the computationally efficient fast Fourier transform (FFT) algorithms, has become the core of many digital signal processing systems. These systems can perform general time domain signal processing as well as classical frequency domain processing. We can partition these FFT-based processors into three broad categories, which are shown in Table I. This partitioning is based upon the domains of the input and output of the processing, the domains being time and frequency (or distance and wave number for spatial processing).

In the first category, spectral analysis, the input data is in the time domain (or frequency domain), and the output data is in the frequency domain (or time domain). The DFT performs the transformation between the two domains. This form of processing is the easiest to visualize because it is a simple extension of classical continuous spectral analysis.

TABLE I

Categories of DFT-Based Processing

1. Spectrum analysis and estimation
2. Fast convolution and correlation
3. Multiband channelizers

HANDBOOK OF DIGITAL SIGNAL PROCESSING

The second category, fast convolution, has the input and the output in the same domain (such as time). Here the DFT is used to transform the input time, signal to the frequency domain, where each frequency component is multiplied by the corresponding spectral component of a second signal. The inverse transform returns, the resultant signal to the time domain. The value of the FFT for this processing is that it efficiently transforms the convolution operation in one domain to a product in the second domain. This too is a simple extension of the use of the Fourier transform to convert a convolution operator to a product operator.

The third category, multiband channelizers, like the second category, has both the input data and the output data in one domain. Unlike the second category, the signal does not pass through the frequency domain between the input and the output. Here, as in the first category, the transform is applied only once per output set.

A   Systems that Use the DFT for Time Domain Processing

We describe some signal processing applications that use the DFT to perform specific time domain filtering tasks [1–4]. Two basic filtering tasks can be performed with DFT: (1) convolution (or correlation) between two arbitrary arrays and (2) narrowband channelization. The DFT gives us access to the computational efficiency of the FFT. Some very clever perspectives have evolved that allow classical filtering operations to be implemented by the FFT. We will develop these perspectives shortly.

1   Channelized Digital In-Phase Quadrature (I-Q) Receivers

In this example we offer an intuitive description of how a DFT is used to synthesize a bank of narrowband filters. In conventional DFT processing a block of time data $f(n)$ (of length N) is weighted; that is, a time domain window is applied to the data, and the data is presented to a transform algorithm. The output of the transform is N points of what is classically interpreted as the weighted data spectrum, denoted $F(k)$. We can imagine that blocks of overlapped time data are sequentially delivered to the transform for spectral processing.

From the classical viewpoint, a time domain window (i.e., a weighting function) is applied to the overlapped data blocks to reduce the levels of spectral leakage at the output of the transform by controlling the severity of discontinuities at the boundaries of the observation interval. From another viewpoint, the time domain window shapes the spectral width and controls the spectral sidelobes of equivalent narrowband filters of the spectral decomposition. The outputs of these equivalent filters can be sampled at a rate consistent with the filter bandwidth to obtain samples of the narrowband complex envelope. The sample rate is controlled by selecting the overlap of consecutive time intervals processed by the transform.

An output data point is obtained from a single transform bin for each time block processed by the transform. We can emphasize the time dependence of the output data by stacking the succession of transform outputs in a two-dimensional array; one array dimension is the spectral sample number of the transform, and the other is a time index identifying the center position of the processed time interval. This two-dimensional array is of the form $F(k, m)$ and is indicated in Fig. 8.1. Suppose we select a particular frequency, say the rth bin i.e.,-rth DFT filter output), and view how that spectral output evolves with time. We

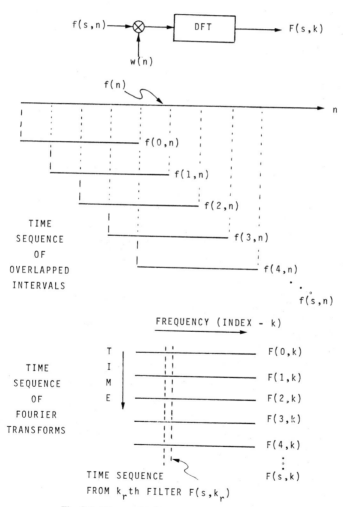

Fig. 8.1. Time series from sequential transforms.

do this by running down the time axis in the two-dimensional frequency–time array. What we encounter is a time series! The first index, the frequency variable, is now interpreted as the index identifying the center frequency of that particular narrowband (filtered) time series.

Note that blocks of time data are delivered to the transform, and that the output block computed by the transform is now seen as a collection of time samples from a bank of contiguous narrowband filters. The center frequencies of the bank are the bin centers of the classic spectral analysis performed by a single transform. Their bandwidth is controlled and shaped by the time domain window applied to the input time blocks. The output sample rate of the narrowband filter(s) is controlled by overlap of the blocks processed by the transform. Note again that for each block of time data a single time sample from each filter in the set is obtained from the operation of time-domain-window overlapped data and transform. In this light the DFT is now a collection of narrowband time domain processors. We will expand upon this example in Section II and show how to maintain independent control of bandwidth, center frequency, and sample rate of the equivalent filter set. The process just described directly convert a frequency-division-multiplexed signal to a time-division-multiplexed signal and is known as *transmultiplexing*.

2   *High-Resolution Interpolator*

The DFT can be used to synthesize the output of an interpolating filter. In Chapter 3 we demonstrated how a polyphase interpolating filter could be formed by lowpass filtering a zero-packed data set. The zero-packing was the process of multiplexing the input data with a set of zero-valued data samples. The purpose of the zero-packing was to increase the input sample rate to the lowpass filter. The effect of the zero-packing was to replicate the signal spectrum at intervals equal to the input sample rate and to fill the spectral width covered by the output sample rate. The filter then eliminated the spectral replicates so that the input spectra became periodic at the (higher) output rate. We can achieve the same set of effects with DFT processing.

We shall demonstrate the technique by a specific example, say that of $4:1$ interpolation. The process starts by selection of an input data block of length N. We do not zero-pack the block but simply transform it. The resultant N spectral points cover a bandwidth equal to the input sample rate with a resolution equal to the sample rate divided by the transform size (f_s/N). Had we zero-packed the data by $4:1$ and then performed a $4N$-point transform, we could find four identical replicates of the original length-N transform in the $4N$ output bins. Remember that the zero-packing replicates the transform by redefining the sample rate. We really have no need for the replicates. (If we really had need for a replicated transform, we would replicated the copy of the spectrum we already have without requiring the use of the extended length transform.) The function of the time domain (polyphase) lowpass filter was to remove (or attenuate) the spectral content in the regions in which the spectral replicates are located. The composite effect of the zero-packing and lowpass filtering in the time domain was to increase the spectral distance between the baseband spectra and its first replicate (i.e., increase the sample rate for a given bandwidth).

We can accomplish the same result indirectly in the frequency domain by simply zero-extending the N points of spectral data to $4N$ points. We do this by splitting the array at address $N/2$ and inserting $3N$ zeros between the two halves, thus extending the transform array to a total length of $4N$. The data point at address $N/2$ (assuming N is even) is split between two addresses; half is placed in address $+N/2$, and half in address $-N/2$ (actually, $4N - N/2$). We then perform an inverse DFT (IDFT) to obtain the interpolated time series. This example, modified for $2:1$ interpolation, is demonstrated in Fig. 8.2.

In Chapter 3 we derived the workload to perform this interpolation by polyphase filtering and showed it to be eight multiplications and eight additions per output point. The workload for the transform-based processing is approximately $\log(4N)$ multiplications and $\log(4N)$ additions per output point, so the transform is computationally more efficient for output blocks smaller than 64 points. Significant computational savings occur when many such processing tasks are performed simultaneously.

A second example of using the DFT as an interpolator is spectral shifts and frequency domain multiplexing, which can also be imbedded in the transform-based processing. We can carry this example to its logical end by viewing it as the inverse of the first example. We can consider the first example to be applied analysis and this one to be applied synthesis. The transmultiplexing process of interpolation, bandshifting, and summation of narrowband signals to form a frequency-division-multiplexed signal from a set of baseband time domain signals can also be performed efficiently by using the DFT.

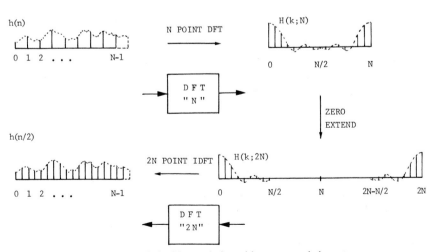

Fig. 8.2. Bandlimited interpolation with zero-extended spectra.

3   Arbitrary Matched Filter

The DFT can be used to synthesize an arbitrary finite impulse response (FIR) filter. Applications for such a filter include the matched filter, which maximizes signal-to-noise ratio (SNR) in communication applications, pulse compressors for high-resolution (large time-bandwidth) ranging signals in sonar and radar, and phase-coded sequences used for spread spectrum communication systems. These applications are examples of the classic problem of detecting known signals with unknown time of arrival in the presence of (white) noise. The filtering task is one of searching through the arriving signal for a good match to a copy (or template) of the known signal of interest. The searching task is performed by sequentially projecting the signal upon the (set of) template(s). This is often called a correlation receiver. The search mode requires repeated application of the inner product processing task. The workload for an N-tap filter is about N multiplications and N–additions per output sample. Thus a search over $2N$ samples would require N-squared operations. For large N (such as 1000 points) this is a formidable processing task.

The linear correlation required for the matched filtering task can be performed with a circular convolution. It is reasonable to ask just why we want to do this. We are willing to imbed the linear correlation in a circular convolution because the latter can be performed with a sequence of DFTs, which in turn can be implemented with FFT algoroithms. (The convolution can perform correlation by simply reversing one of the data (time) series prior to the convolution, and this reversal can be accomplished in the transform domain as a simple conjugate.)

The DFT is a block process, and the linear correlation is a continuous process. A technique known as overlap and discard (or overlap and add) is used to synthesize the continuous process with the block processor. The input data is partitioned into double-length ($2N$) blocks that overlap the previous interval by length N. In the overlap-and-discard technique, $2N$ points are circularly convolved via the DFT with the N-point matched filter. The first N points of the output correspond to time-aliased (or circularly wrapped) data and are discarded. The second N points are alias free and correspond precisely to the output of a linear convolver; this segment is saved and is appended to successively processed blocks. This example is demonstrated in Fig. 8.3 where $d(s, n)$ is the overlapped data sequence, $G(k)$ is the filter's transform sequence, and $r(s, k)$ is the convolution output.

4   Overview of Chapter

In the remaining part of this chapter we examine various tasks in which time domain processing is accomplished with a DFT. We show how a judicious choice of window, overlap, block size, and circular indexing, coupled with simple pre- and postprocessing tasks, leads to use of the DFT to perform general time

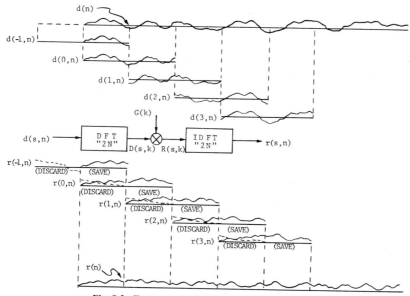

Fig. 8.3. Fast convolution by overlap and discard.

domain processing. We site the computational advantages gained by performing specific time domain tasks with an FFT. These gains are quite impressive when multichannel processing is synthesized with the FFT. In particular, we examine how simple pre- and postprocessing tasks significantly enhance the degrees of freedom available to the designer of multichannel processors. We pay particular attention to how processing parameters are coupled and to how a choice of processing parameters impacts important system considerations, such as total computational burden, and classical fidelity measures, such as channel crosstalk and noise levels.

THE DFT AS A BANK OF NARROWBAND FILTERS II

The time series obtained from the output of a uniform sampler can be described as a broadband series formed by the summation of numerous narrowband signals distributed over contiguous frequency bands within the analysis bandwidth. Our desired processing goal is the decomposition of this broadband series into narrowband series by banks of narrowband filters. The sampling rate for each narrowband time series is reduced (relative to the input rate) in proportion to the bandwidth reduction. Filters that operate at different input and output sample rates are called multirate filters (see Chapter 3).

The narrowband channelization of the input time series can be computation-ally intensive. The desire to control this processing burden has motivated searches for channelization schemes with reduced computation load, such as those centered around the FFT [5–9]. When all of the channel filters have the same bandwidth and hence the same output sample rate, they can be realized efficiently (and simultaneously) by windowed and overlapped FFTs. If the channels have different bandwidths, the filtering task can be performed in a two-stage multirate process, which is somewhat akin to a dual-conversion communi-cation receiver. In the initial stage, standard overlapped FFT processing is used to form a series with a reduced bandwidth at a reduced sample rate. The second stage performs additional coherent processing either to further reduce the bandwidth by additional filtering or to increase the bandwidth by merging the outputs of adjacent filters. Both forms of second-stage processing can be performed by any suitable signal processing technique, including additional DFT processing.

The DFT is a block process, and we must take care to control the artifacts that may arise from partitioning the data into convenient block sizes. The transform parameters through which we exercise this control are the transform length N, the data sequence window shape $h(n)$, the window length L, and the transform overlap $1 - p/N$ (or transform shift p). These parameters are interrelated in various ways. Understanding how they are related is made easier if we first examines the relationships in an equivalent process. In particular, the process is the bank of generic narrowband filters we are forming with the DFT. The correspondence between the parameters of the two processes are listed in Table II. Note that the transform size and the window length are distinct parameters. The window can be shorter than the transform, and the difference in lengths is easily accommodated by zero-extending. We will also show that the window length can exceed the transform length and that the excess length is cyclically wrapped (or folded) to the transform size.

TABLE II

Corresponding Parameters of Generic Filter Bank and DFT-Based Filter Bank

Generic filter bank	DFT-based filter bank	Parameter
Number of filters spanning input bandwidth	Transform size	N
Prototype (or baseband) impulse response	Data sequence window	$W(n)$
Filter length (or bandwidth)	Window length (or resolution)	L
Ratio of input to output sample rates	Data shift	P

We first demonstrate a simple relationship between the DFT and the convolution operator, using the initial steps in the derivation of the Goertzel algorithm. Recall that the definition of the DFT is

$$F(k) = \sum_{m=0}^{N-1} W^{mk} f(m), \qquad k = 0, 1, 2, \ldots, N-1 \tag{8.1}$$

where $W = e^{-j2\pi/N}$

We note that W, the kernel of the transform, is periodic in N. Thus Eq. (8.1) can be written as

$$F(k) = \sum_{m=0}^{N-1} W^{-(N-m)k} f(m) \tag{8.2}$$

Modifying Eq. (8.2) by replacing the constant N with a variable index n gives Eqs. (8.3a)–(8.c).

$$F(k) = F_k(n) \bigg|_{n=N} = F_k(N) \tag{8.3a}$$

where $F_k(n)$ is defined by the *Goertzel algorithm*

$$F_k(n) = \sum_{m=0}^{N-1} W^{-(n-m)k} f(m) \tag{8.3b}$$

or

$$F_k(n) = f(n) * W^{-nk} \tag{8.3c}$$

We recognize Eq. (8.3b) as a convolution of the data $f(n)$ with the complex exponential $\exp(-j2\pi k/N)$. Here the superscript k emphasizes that the frequency index now denotes the center frequency of a time sequence. The Goertzel algorithm demonstrates that the DFT can be implemented as a convolution. Our interest in this demonstration is found "on the other side of the coin;" namely the DFT output is equivalent to a time sample vector from a bank of narrow-band filters.

The Block diagram of a generic bank of filters that can dechannelize a broadband input signal is shown in Fig. 8.4. Also indicated is the spectral coverage of the separate channel filters. We note that the filtering process is equivalent to convolving the input series with a matrix (i.e., a set of impulse responses, one for each center frequency). Note that the number of filters and the length of each filter's are impulse response not constrained in any way. Thus the

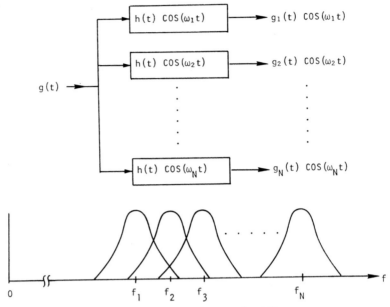

Fig. 8.4. Bank of generic narrowband filters.

equivalent matrix of filter coefficients is not constrained to be square. We call attention to this because when we imbed the filter bank in the DFT (which is described as a square matrix), we have to handle the unequal dimension of the equivalent filter bank. We shall demonstrate that in DFT-based processing, the synthesized filter banks have lengths that are two to four times the number of filters formed.

C FIR Digital Filter

The basic digital filtering process of the filter bank is described by the finite weighted summation

$$r(k, n) = \sum_{m=0}^{N-1} g(k, m)d(n - m), \qquad n = 0, 1, 2, \dots; k = 0, 1, 2, \dots, K - 1 \quad (8.4)$$

where $d(n)$ is the data sequence and

$$g(k, n) = h(n)e^{jn\theta(k)}$$

Figure 8.5 suggests one possible structure of this filter. Note that the filter impulse response coefficients $g(k, n)$ are formed as the product of a prototype lowpass filter $h(n)$ and a complex exponential $\exp[jn\theta(k)]$ that translates the lowpass spectral characteristics to the arbitrary center frequency of $\theta(k)$ radians per

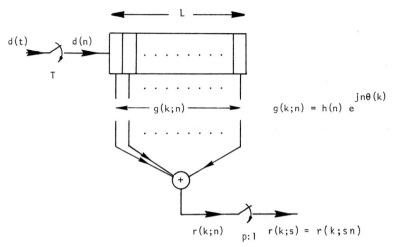

Fig. 8.5. Finite impulse response digital filter.

sample. If we explicitly show this form of the filter in Eq. (8.4), we obtain

$$r(k, n) = \sum_{m=0}^{N-1} d(n - m)h(m)e^{+jm\theta(k)} \qquad (8.5a)$$

$$= e^{+jn\theta(k)} \sum_{m=0}^{N-1} h(m)d(n - m)e^{-j(n-m)\theta(k)} \qquad (8.5b)$$

The form of the filter suggested by Eq. (8.5b) is shown in Fig. 8.6. In this form, the

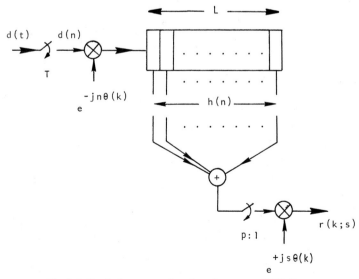

Fig. 8.6. Equivalent narrowband carrier-centered FIR filter.

desired center frequency is heterodyned down to baseband, rather than having the spectral characteristics of the baseband filter moved up to the center frequency of the desired channel. The spectrally shifted data is filtered and then heterodyned back to the original center frequency. The two forms of the process are indistinguishable! We see, in this form of the filter, that the heterodyne process and the convolution process occur as distinct operations. From this we conclude that the center frequency of the filter (established with the heterodyne) and the bandwidth (established with the convolution) are independent parameters. This independence can be preserved when the filter bank is realized as a DFT.

D   Filter Length, Bandwidth, and Desampling Ratio

From the equivalence demonstrated in the last section, we see that the spectral structure of each filter in a bank of bandpass filters is the same as the spectral structure of a heterodyned lowpass prototype. Let us examine this prototype to review the relationship between filter length, bandwidth, and desampling ratio.

The narrowest spectral bandwidth, called a resolution cell, that can be realized with an M-point FIR filter (or an M-point DFT) is $1/M$. This minimum bandwidth filter is the periodic extension of the cardinal $(\sin \pi f M)/\pi f$ function (called the *Dirichlet* kernel) and is shown in Chapter 1 Section VII.E, to have a $\sin(\pi f M)/\sin(\pi f)$ response. The frequency response of this filter, shown in Fig. 8.7, is the equivalent filter set obtained when the DFT is used for spectral analysis with uniform (or rectangular) weighting. In the spectral analysis task the high sidelobes of the Dirichlet kernel lead to an additive bias term known as *spectral leakage*. This term reflects the characteristic that the high sidelobes allow a filter at one spectral location to respond to signals at remote locations, particularly those outside the mainlobe response interval. Control of this bias term requires an alternative weighting function, one exhibiting reduced sidelobes. For weighting terms of fixed lengths, sidelobe reduction is always achieved at the expense of an increase in mainlobe width. The trade of mainlobe width for sidelobe level is well understood, and a concise statement of this relationship is presented in Table III. In this table, as in the rest of this chapter, it is convenient to borrow the terminology of spectral analysis, in which the minimum width of $1/M$ is defined as a resolution bin (or quantization cell). This permits arbitrary bandwidths to be described with respect to this cell dimension in terms of number of bin widths (not necessarily an integer).

The primary message to be found in Table III is that mainlobe width must be increased to obtain reduced sidelobe levels (for a given rate of sidelobe decay). For desampling operations a sidelobe decay rate between -6 and -12 dB/ octave is desired to minimize the total sum of the sidelobe terms that fold

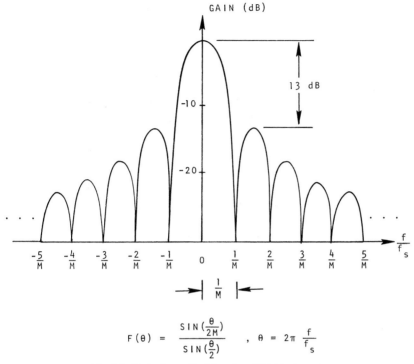

$$F(\theta) = \frac{SIN(\frac{\theta}{2M})}{SIN(\frac{\theta}{2})} \quad , \quad \theta = 2\pi \frac{f}{f_s}$$

Fig. 8.7. Periodic cardinal function, Dirichlet kernel.

TABLE III

Highest Sidelobe Level as Function of Mainlobe Width

Mainlobe width	Sidelobe assymptotic rate of falloffing dB			
	0 dB/oct	−6 dB/oct	−12 dB/oct	−18 dB/oct
2/M	−48	−46	−42	−38
3/M	−75	−72	−66	−62
4/M	−102	−98	−96	−91

back into the mainlobe under desampling. Thus we see that to obtain narrowband filters with −70-dB peak sidelobes and good decay characteristics, the mainlobe width of the filter must be equal to or greater than three resolution cells. An example of such a filter response is given in Fig. 8.8. We shall soon show that the processing overlap is controlled directly by the mainlobe width and, hence, indirectly by the sidelobe levels of the window (or filter).

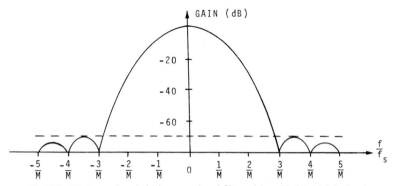

Fig. 8.8. Minimum bandwidth narrowband filter with -70-dB sidelobe level.

E   Output Sample Rate or Processing Overlap

We now address the sample rate required to satisfy the Nyquist criterion for the time series at the filter output. The spectral characteristics of the input data, of the FIR filter, and of the filter output data are periodic in the input sample frequency. The function of the filtering process is to reduce the bandwidth of the output series. Without loss of information, we are permitted to reduce the output sample rate (relative to the input rate) in the same ratio as that of the output to input bandwidths.

We can assume that the input signal to the filter exhibits a white spectrum so that the filter's response has the same power spectral shape as the filter. In reducing the output sample rate, we reduce the separation between the filter response spectral replicates. As this separation is reduced, the filter mainlobe response starts overlapping the filter sidelobe response. We anticipate this overlap by specifying the acceptable levels of sidelobes permitted to fold into the mainlobe interval. Upon further reduction of output sample rate, the filter mainlobe response starts to overlap its first replicate. This overlap is called *spectral aliasing*. We control the amount of aliasing by choosing an output sample rate sufficiently high to prevent the spectral folding (or overlap) into the mainlobe bandwidth of interest.

Figure 8.9 shows sketches of the prototype output spectra with possible spectral replicates formed by selecting different output sample rates. The resampling operation entails the computation of one output point for every P input points, which is an input-to-output sample rate ratio of $1/P$. This ratio can be normalized to the filter length of M points as indicated by

$$\frac{1}{P} = \frac{l}{M} \tag{8.6}$$

We note that l, the new sampling frequency in multiples of filter resolution

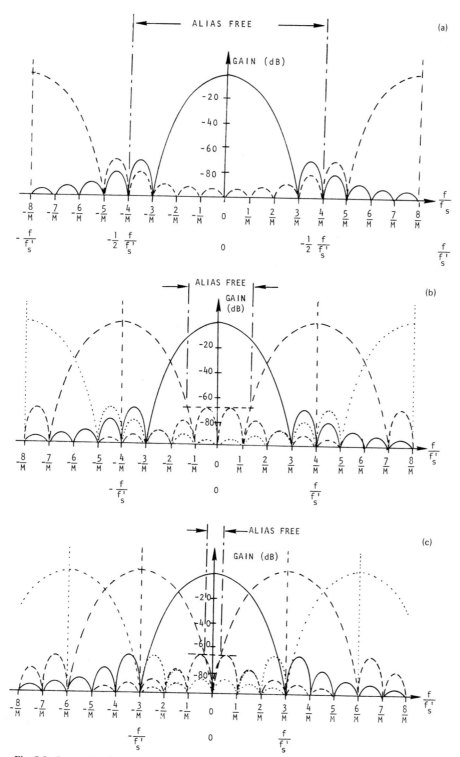

Fig. 8.9. Spectral replicates of desampled lowpass filter sample rate reductions of (a) $M/8$, (b) $M/4$, and (c) $M/3$.

widths, is not constrained to be an integer. For instance, $1:10$ resampling $(P = 10)$ with a 128-point filter $(M = 128)$ results in the spectral replicate being located at 12.8 spectral bins. Keep in mind that although the sketches of Fig. 8.9 show the spectral replicates at integer multiples of $1/M$, this is an arbitrary assignment to demonstrate a set of relationships.

In the normalized spectral coordinates of Fig. 8.9, the resampling operation of computing l output filter points for each M input data points shifts the spectral replicates from unity to the new output rate l/M. We are concerned with the relationships between this output sample rate and the useful alias-free band within the mainlobe response. For the specific example presented, the sidelobes are chosen to be down by $-70\ \text{dB}$ and this requires that the mainlobe width be $3/M$. A choice of other sidelobe levels would alter the required mainlobe width and would change the specific numbers but not the form of the relationships we are discussing. From Fig. 8.9(a) we see that when the sample rate exceeds the two-sided spectral width of the filter, the entire spectrum is alias free. On the other hand, when the sample rate is less than the one-sided spectral width of the filter, there is no alias-free bandwidth. Thus, for this example, an alias-free bandwidth is available if the output sample rate is lower bounded by $3/M$. This means that the processing overlap must exceed $3:1$. Also there is no alias-related advantage to having the processing overlap exceed $6:1$, which would have the output sample rate exceed an upper bound $6/M$. Finally, to realize an alias-free region of one resolution cell, we would need an output sample rate exceeding $3.5/M$, and to realize an alias-free region of two resolution cells, we require an output sample rate of $4/M$.

Although the higher output sample rates extend the alias-free bandwidth, the increased attenuation at the limits of the extended bandwidth (called *scalloping loss*) restricts the useful bandwidth to approximately two resolution cells. Thus it appears that an output sample rate corresponding to one output point for each $M/4$ input points (a $4:1$ processing overlap) is the natural sample rate to minimize output rate (hence processing load) while maximizing useful output bandwidth.

F DFT Implementation of a Channelized Filter Bank

The complete channelization and basebanding of the input signal is conceptually performed with a bank of digital FIR filters. The form of such a system is shown in Fig. 8.10. The computational burden to perform the filtering task was presented in Eq. (8.5b) and is repeated here:

$$r(k, n) = e^{-jn\theta(k)} \sum_{m=0}^{M-1} d(n - m)h(m)e^{+jm\theta(k)} \tag{8.7a}$$

$$k = 0, 1, 2, \ldots, K - 1, n = 0, 1, 2, 3, \ldots$$

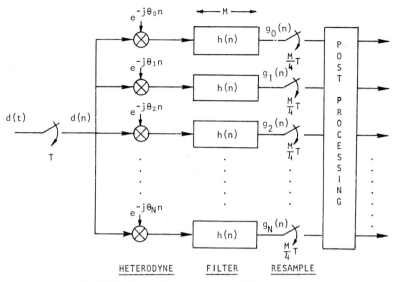

Fig. 8.10. Channelized system with FIR digital filters.

If we now account for the resampling operation by computing the output at indices $n = s(M/4)$, we have

$$r(k, s) = r(k, n)\Big|_{n = (M/4)s}$$

$$= e^{-j(M/4)s\theta(k)} \sum_{m=0}^{M-1} d\left(\frac{M}{4}s - m\right) h(m) e^{+jm\theta(k)} \qquad (8.7b)$$

We will next describe how to implement the collection of channeling filters in a single DFT (performed as an FFT) and to realize significant computational advantage over the direct implementation of the individual filters. If a data sequence window (weighting) $w(n)$ is multiplied point by point with a data sequence $f(n)$, the DFT computes

$$F(k) = \sum_{n=0}^{N-1} w(n) f(n) e^{-j(2\pi/N)nk}, \qquad k = 0, 1, 2, \ldots, N - 1 \qquad (8.8)$$

The transform performs an inner product of the sequence $w(n)f(n)$ with the complex exponential sequence. The bank of narrowband filters, cast as FIR filters, also performs a set of inner products with complex exponential sequences. In this light we can use the block processing of the DFT to accomplish processing equivalent to the desampled FIR filters by applying the transform to overlapped intervals of the input time series. This block processing generally requires that each interval be processed l times; we will refer to this as $l:1$ overlap processing. Figure 8.11 illustrates a 4:1 overlap.

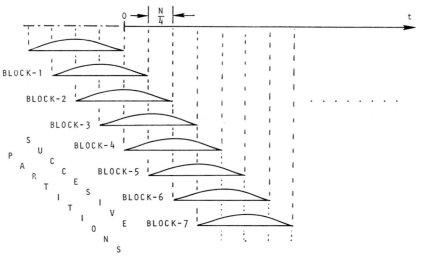

Fig. 8.11. Block partitions of data stream for 4:1 overlap processing.

We can denote the shifting block partitions with a shift index s, given by

$$F(k, s) = \sum_{n=0}^{N-1} w(n) f\left[\frac{N}{4}s - (N-1) + n\right] e^{-j(2\pi/N)nk} \tag{8.9a}$$

$$k = 0, 1, 2, \ldots, N-1; \; s = 0, 1, 2, 3, \ldots$$

Changing the variable of summation to n', where

$$n' = (N - 1 - n) \qquad \text{or} \qquad n = (N - 1 - n')$$

yields

$$F(k, s) = \sum_{n'=0}^{N-1} w(N - 1 - n') f\left(\frac{N}{4}s - n'\right) e^{+j(2\pi/N)(n'+1)k} \tag{8.9b}$$

We now define $w(N - 1 - n)$ as $h(n)$, a flipped and translated version of the desired prototype lowpass filter impulse response. In doing so we see that the window used in transform-based channelizing is an arbitrary lowpass filter that can be designed by one of the techniques presented in Chapters 2 and 3. Substituting for $w(N - 1 - n)$ and redefining the index of summation in Eq. (8.9b), we obtain

$$F(k, s) = e^{+j(2\pi/N)k} \sum_{n=0}^{N-1} f\left(\frac{N}{4}s - n\right) h(n) e^{+j(2\pi/N)nk} \tag{8.9c}$$

Comparing Eq. (8.9c) to Eq. (8.7b), we see that the two summations that represent the filtering and resampling operations are of identical forms. Denoting the pair of summations by $p(k, s)$ and $q(k, s)$, respectively, we compare the two expressions as follows:

$$r(k, s) = e^{-j(N/4)s\theta(k)}p(k, s) \qquad (8.10a)$$

$$F(k, s) = e^{+j(2\pi/N)k}q(k, s) \qquad (8.10b)$$

We note that the primary difference in the expressions is that the transform-based operation does not include the complex heterodyne. Thus the narrowband output is not basebanded, and the transform-based filter responses exhibit a residual phase rotation term that must be removed (or at least accounted for) by pre- or post-transform processing. Setting $d(n) = f(n)$ and $\theta(k)$ in Eq. (8.10a) equal to the specific $\theta(k)$ in Eq. (8.10b) makes the two summations in Eq. (8.7c) and (8.9c) identical. Then the two expressions in Eq. (8.10) become

$$r'(k, s) = e^{-j(2\pi/4)ks}q(k, s) \qquad (8.11a)$$

$$F(k, s) = e^{+j(2\pi/N)k}q(k, s) \qquad (8.11b)$$

The prime on the variable $r(k, s)$ distinguishes between the arbitrary center frequencies and the specific center frequencies implied by integer values of s. After this section, the prime will be dropped. Furthermore, postprocessing is required to make the output of the transform-based processing match that of the direct FIR-filter-based processing. This postprocessing is a phase rotation, so the phase-corrected (or heterodyned) transform output matches the output of the filter; in other words,

$$r'(k, s) = e^{-j(2\pi/4)ks}e^{-j(2\pi/N)k}F(k, s) \qquad (8.12)$$

The second phase term in Eq. (8.12) is independent of the output time index s; hence it represents a constant phase angle in the carrier-centered signal. Since the phase term is arbitrary, it can be ignored. Alternatively, we can remove it by imbedding it as the initial phase offset of the first phase term in Eq. (8.12), or we can avoid it entirely by performing a single cyclic shift of the input windowed data before performing the DFT.

Note that for 4:1 overlap, the apparent shift (in radians per sample) required to phase correct the kth filter is $(\pi/2)k$. Since the phase progression is periodic in 2π, we can rewrite the apparent frequency as

$$2\pi\left[\frac{sk}{N} \bmod N\right] \qquad (8.13a)$$

For the specific case of 4:1 overlap (i.e., with $s = lN/4$) the apparent shift is

$$2\pi\left[\frac{kl}{4} \bmod 4\right] \qquad (8.13b)$$

Thus, depending on the value of $(kl/4) \bmod 4$, the phase rotation (per output time sample) will be one of four possible values, as shown in Table IV. Note that (for the processing overlap of $N/4$ chosen for this example) the phase-correction

TABLE IV

Residual Phase Rotation of FFT Bins for 4:1
Overlap Processing

Bin [(kl/4) mod (4)]	Frequency (rad/sample)
0	0
1	$\pi/2$
2	π
3	$-\pi/2$

terms are trivial and can be performed with simple indexing. For arbitrary overlap the phase correction is not quite as trivial. In a later section we will discuss the phase correction required for arbitrary overlap. At that time we will also present processing options to account for or eliminate the computations required to apply the phase rotation terms.

As a final note to this section, we observe that the center frequencies of the channel bank that were identified as $\theta(k)$ in Eq. (8.7) have now been constrained by transform-based processing to be the equally spaced frequencies $(2\pi/N)k$— that is, integer multiples of $1/N$ of the sampling frequency. At this point it appears that the filter length and the filter spacing are defined by default by the same integer N, the transform length. This conclusion is not valid, as we shall soon show.

G   Data Folding; Independent Control of Filter Spacing and Filter Bandwidth

To this point the DFT-based channelizer has led to a bank of filters whose spectral separation is $1/N$ and whose spectral bandwidths are b/N. Here b is the bandwidth broadening factor which resulted from control of the filter bandwidth and the sidelobe levels. We are assuming a normalized sampling frequency 1 and a transform length N. The spectral characteristics of such a filter bank are shown in Fig. 8.12. Whereas Fig. 8.8 shows the spectral response of a single filter, Fig. 8.12 presents the spectral response of a bank of contiguous filters. Each filter in this bank is periodic in the sampling frequency, but the span of frequencies presented is too small to see the periodicity.

Note that for the filter responses selected in this example (a filter with a first sidelobe peak of -70 dB and with a -9-dB/octave falloff of sidelobe peaks) adjacent DFT filter bins cross at their -1.0-dB points, alternate filters cross at their -4.0-dB points, and filters separated by three bins cross at their -20.0-dB points. Thus adjacent filters are considerably wider than their separation, and therefore adjacent filters span overlapping bands of frequencies. As a result, the time series obtained from adjacent filters are highly correlated. We can reduce this high degree of correlation by forming filters with narrower bandwidths (at

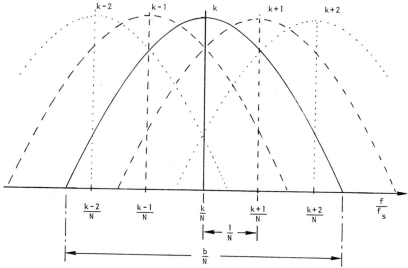

Fig. 8.12. Resolution (spectral width) and spectral spacing of an FFT-based bank of narrow-band filters.

the same center-frequency locations) and/or by using fewer filters and increasing the separation of center-frequency locations [10, 11].

Recall that the transform length N is chosen to establish the spacing between channel center frequencies. Classically, by default, we accept the bandwidth obtained for a window (or filter) of the same length as the transform. We do not have to accept that constraint. If we examine the structure of the generic FIR filter channelizer (Fig. 8.4), we note that the center frequency of the filter is selected by the heterodyne and the bandwidth is selected by the lowpass prototype weights. Thus there is no fundamental restriction that the number of filters and the number of data points being processed be the same value. From the perspective of classical Fourier transform analysis, we know that the unweighted complex vectors of the DFT form an orthogonal basis set that spans the N-dimensional vector space (in which the data resides). In that case the number of filters matches the dimension of the space (the number of data points). However, if the channelization is being performed with filter sets that span the spectrum but, due to mainlobe spectral overlap, are highly correlated, then we have two options by which we can reduce the mainlobe spectral overlap and thereby reduce the correlation (or crosstalk) between adjacent channels. First, we can keep the filter lengths (hence bandwidths) fixed and increase the separation between filters. This involves computing fewer filter outputs without reducing the filter length. Second, we can keep the separation between filter centers constant but decrease the filter spectral width by increasing the length of the filter. Again, this involves computing outputs from fewer filters than there are data points. We shall show that the two options are the same.

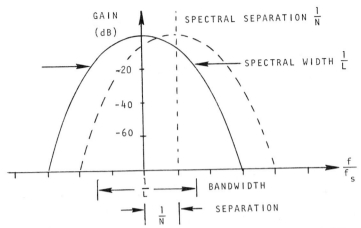

Fig. 8.13. Filter specification showing how to reduce spectral width (by control of filter length L) for a given set of spectral centers (defined by transform size N).

We choose the initial perspective that the filter spacing is $1/N$, the spacing of an N-point transform, and that the filter length L is greater than N, so the bandwidth b/L is comparable to the spacing $1/N$. The form of the filter bank in terms of the filter length L and number of filters N, where $L < N$, is given by

$$q(k, s) = \sum_{n=0}^{N-1} d\left(\frac{L}{4}s - n\right)h(n)e^{+j(2\pi/N)kn} \tag{8.14}$$

For our needs, $L > N$. When $L < N$, the frequencies dictated by the transform length are computed by zero-extending the filter length to match the length of the transform. Zero-extended data is the most common example of the bandwidth being determined by the data length L while the spectral spacing is determined by the transform length N. Figure 8.13 shows how the filter center frequencies are related to the fixed transform length N and how the filter widths can be altered by changing the filter length L (relative to N). The processing required to form the filter bank $g(k, s)$ with spectral spacing $1/N$ and with filter length L, where $L > N$, is

$$p(k, s) = \sum_{n=0}^{L-1} d\left(\frac{L}{4}s - n\right)h(n)e^{+j(2\pi/N)kn} \tag{8.15}$$

Knowing that the complex exponential in Eq. (8.15) is periodic in N, we can replace the index of summation n by a mixed-radix integer representation (see Section III.A) of the form

$$n = n_1 + Nn_2, \qquad n_1 = 0, 1, 2, \ldots, N - 1; n_2 = 0, 1, 2, \ldots, c - 1 \tag{8.16a}$$

where c satisfies

$$(c - 1)N < L \leq cN,$$

and obtain

$$p(k, s) = \sum_{n_1 = 0}^{N-1} \sum_{n_2 = 0}^{c-1} d\left[\frac{L}{4} s - (n_1 + n_2 N)\right] h(n_1 + n_2 N) e^{+j(2\pi/N)n,k} \quad (8.16b)$$

We know from the sampling theorem that, to avoid aliasing, a function must be sampled at a spacing that is less than the reciprocal width of its two-sided spectrum. Violating this constraint results in aliasing of the transform. Likewise, if the spectra of a signal is undersampled, the time signal will exhibit circular wrap-around or time folding. Conversely, circular wrap-around of a time function is always an indication of spectral undersampling. In this light the inner summation of Eq. (8.16b) represents the intentional time domain aliasing of the input signal to support the undersampling of the signal's spectrum by the N-point DFT.

A reasonable selection criterion for choosing the filter length L is that the adjacent filters have nearly uncorrelated outputs. As mentioned in Chapter 1, uncorrelated signals with a zero mean are orthogonal. We will assume zero-mean white noise inputs to the filters and derive conditions under which the filter outputs are orthogonal. We can achieve precise orthogonality by placing a subset of the filter's spectral zeros at the center frequencies of the other filters. The class of filters with equally spaced zeros was presented in Chapter 3 as having impulse responses that are Nyquist pulses. Standard filters that match this spectral characteristic are Blackman–Harris windows and Taylor windows. For instance, a three-term Blackman–Harris window can achieve complete orthogonality with a triple-length window (which requires 3:1 data folding). Complete orthogonality requires very narrow filters and results in excessive scalloping loss (i.e., the reduction in gain for a signal located between bin centers). A reasonable compromise for the filter length (in terms of scalloping loss and folding length) is twice the transform length. For a window of length $2N$ with -70-dB sidelobes, the spectral responses of adjacent filters cross at their -4.3-dB points, have a gain of -19.1 dB at adjacent centers, and have zero gain (i.e., infinite rejection) at the center of all other filters. By comparison, the Dirichlet kernel filters with -13-dB sidelobes cross at their -3.9-dB points and have zero gain at the center of all other filters.

The processing corresponding to the length-$2N$ filter with center frequencies at $1/N$ can be visualized with the aid of Fig. 8.14. The data sequence is $d(n) = 1$ for representational purposes; it is windowed and folded. This latter operation adds the first half of the windowed data to the second half. The data folding simulates the time domain overlap of adjacent time intervals due to undersampling the spectral data.

An alternative visualization explains the folding process that occurs when an N-point transform is applied to $2N$ data points. First we envision a $2N$-point transform applied in the usual manner to $2N$ data points as

$$F(k) = \sum_{n=0}^{2N-1} f(n) e^{+j(2\pi/2N)nk} \quad (8.17a)$$

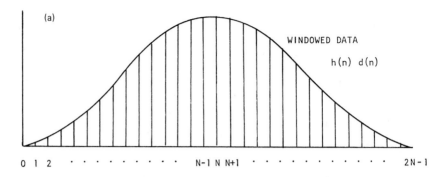

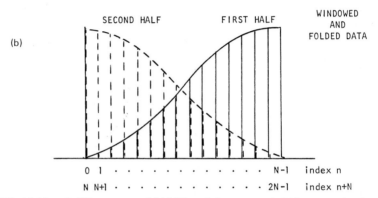

Fig. 8.14. (a) A length-$2N$ sequence and (b) folding of the sequence in (a) in preparation for an N-point FFT.

We now examine the even-indexed frequency bins of this transform as shown in

$$F(2k) = \sum_{n=0}^{2N-1} f(n)e^{+j(2\pi/2N)2nk} = \sum_{n=0}^{2N-1} f(n)e^{+j(2\pi/N)nk} \tag{8.17b}$$

$$F(2k) = \sum_{n=0}^{N-1} [f(n) + f(n+N)]e^{+j(2\pi/N)nk} \tag{8.17c}$$

We note that Eq. (8.17c) is simply the transform of 2:1 folded data. Thus an alternative perspective of the 2:1 folding operation is that we are computing alternate spectral points of a length-$2N$-point transform. Note again there is no loss of spectral or time information in the folded DFT processing provided that the window has broadened the filter bandwidth to include the alternate (and not computed) spectral cells. From this perspective, the folded DFT filter bank has formed reduced-bandwidth filters to realize a closer match between the filter spacing and the filter width.

A complete DFT-based channelizer has the form in Fig. 8.15(a). Here we have a 2:1 data folding and 4:1 overlap of the windowed time intervals. The overlap establishes the time sample rate to satisfy the Nyquist criterion for the filter

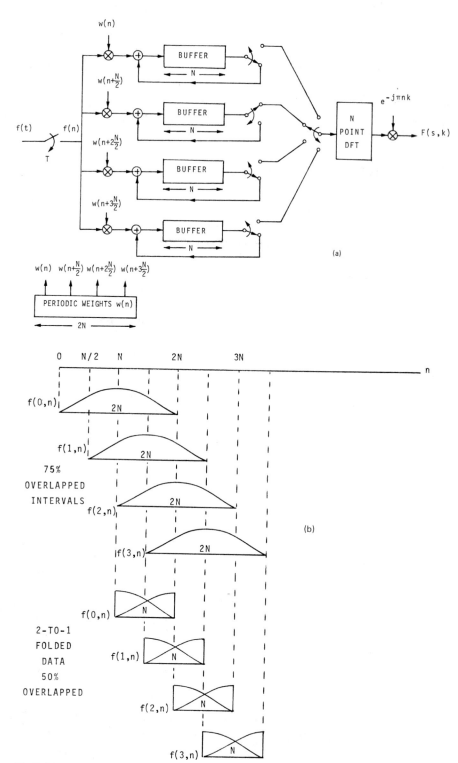

Fig. 8.15. (a) Overlapped, windowed, and folded DFT bank of filters. (b) Overlapped intervals, before and after folding.

bank, and the folding reduces the filter bandwidth to compensate for the filter broadening due to the windowing operation. We emphasize that the 4:1 overlap of the filter impulse response is required independent of the folding; but due to the folding, the transforms are performed with 2:1 overlap (as opposed to 4:1). This relationship is presented in Fig. 8.15(b).

H   Residual Phase Rotation Term of DFT Channelizer

In Section II.F and particularly in Eq. (8.10) we cited the residual phase rotation in the time series obtained from the DFT channelizer. We noted that the amount of phase rotation was bin dependent and the phase angle for any given bin was time dependent. The residual phase term for the arbitrary transform length N, filter length L, and filter overlap L/p is given by

$$e^{+j\theta(k,s)} = e^{+j(2\pi L/Np)ks} \tag{8.18}$$

When $L = N$, with $p = 4$, the phase term for the kth bin increments by $(\pi/2)k$ radians per sample, which agrees with Eq. (8.10). When $L = 2N$, with $p = 4$, the phase term increments by πk radians per sample, which is the phase-correction term indicated in Fig. 8.15. These phase-angle terms are trivially corrected or removed from the output data by simple sign reversals and data steering (i.e., reversal of real and imaginary components of the output). For the arbitrary case, the phase correction is not a trivial operation. For instance, if the transform length N is 32, filter length L is 96, and overlap L/p is 6 (i.e., $p = 16$, or 1 output point for each 16 input points), then the phase term for the kth filter increments by $\frac{3}{8}\pi k$ radians per sample. Figure 8.16 presents the filtering process implemented with these parameters.

We have previously identified the output of the DFT channelizer as the output of a desampled narrowband filter bank. The phase-incrementing terms in the DFT output series are the residual phase terms caused by desampling the carrier-centered narrowband time series. We are, in effect, using spectral replicates (normally called aliased spectra) to produce an output heterodyne. For some bins (those for which $(L/p)k$ mod N is zero) the equivalent heterodyning results in a basebanding to zero frequency. For other bins the equivalent heterodyning results in a residual carrier. This carrier term can be removed by a postprocessing heterodyne as indicated in Fig. 8.16.

An alternative to the postprocessing heterodyne correction is a preprocessing technique that avoids the residual phase rotation by synthesizing the zero-frequency basebanding for each output channel. Keep in mind that the phase rotation is related to the overlap processing, not to the data folding. We first present a graphical description that explains the cause of the residual phase rotation. The graphical description leads to an intuitive understanding of the technique that avoids the residual phase. We will then cast the solution in equation form.

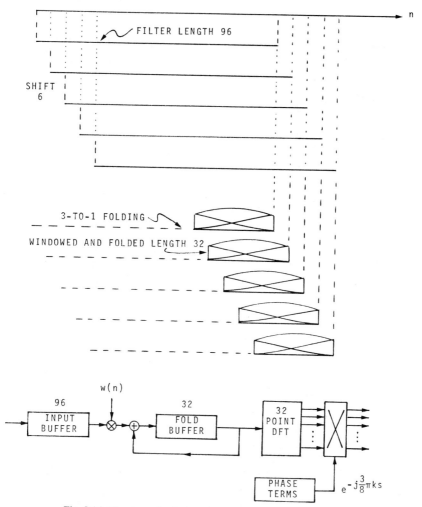

Fig. 8.16. Overlapped, windowed, and folded DFT channelizer.

Figure 8.17(a) indicates the overlapped partitions of the input data and one component of a filter vector (i.e., filter impulse response). For illustrative purposes we set $d(n)$ equal to a constant. Each successive data block is projected onto the filter vector to obtain the output time samples for that filter. Note that each successive position of the filter vector (caused by the shifting) overlaps the same portion of a time-delayed sinusoid. The time delay is equivalent to a phase shift in the sinusoid. This phase shift is the cause of the residual phase term removed by the heterodyne at the output of each successive transform. If the overlapped data blocks were projected onto successive filter vectors that were phase continuous, the residual phase term would not appear.

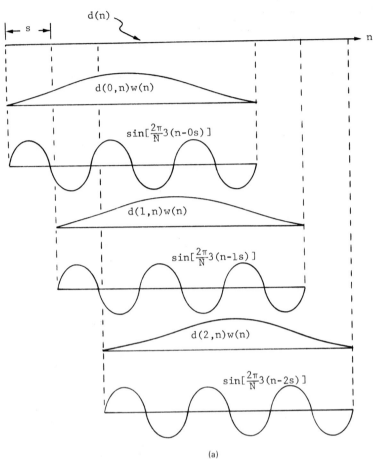

(a)

Fig. 8.17(a). Relationship between overlapped and windowed intervals to basis filter of DFT.

We can visualize a set of modified filter vectors of the form indicated in Fig. 8.17(b). Since the filter vectors exhibit an integer number of cycles in the data interval, this modified set could be obtained as an end-around shift of the original filter vector. The problem is that the new vector set does not correspond to the set defined by the DFT, which always starts at an initial phase angle of zero. However, this difficulty may be overcome because the transform not only considers the basis set to be periodic, but it also considers the data set to be periodic. Thus, rather than perform a cyclic shift of the basis set, we can achieve the same effect by applying the desired end-around shift (in the opposite direction) to the data block. This end-around shift of the windowed (and folded) data results in a linear phase-shift (with frequency index) that just cancels the residual phase we have been discussing. To preserve phase continuity for

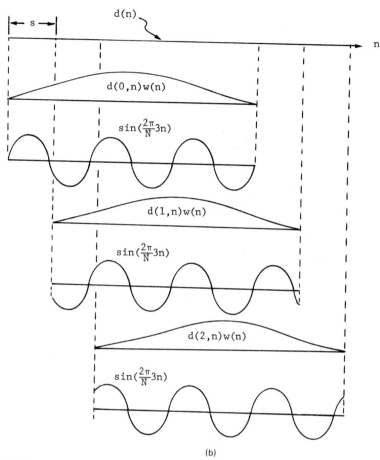

(b)

Fig. 8.17(b). Relationship between overlapped and windowed intervals to phase-shifted basis filters.

successive applications of the filter sets, we must have the end-around shift applied to each successive data block equal to the total amount of shift between that block and an arbitrary origin. Since the shift is cyclic, the actual shift is $sp \bmod N$, where s is the output time index, p is the shift distance between adjacent partitions, and N is the size of the transform. The cyclic shift of the windowed data prior to the transform is actually performed during the transfer operation that loads the input memory of the DFT. Thus by simple precessed indexing of the input memory during the data transfer, the output of the DFT is converted from a bank of narrowband filters to a bank of basebanded filters. Incidently, the constant phase-shift term that appeared in Eq. (8.10b) can also be removed in this manner by a nonprecessing (i.e., fixed) cyclic shift of a single data point during the data transfer.

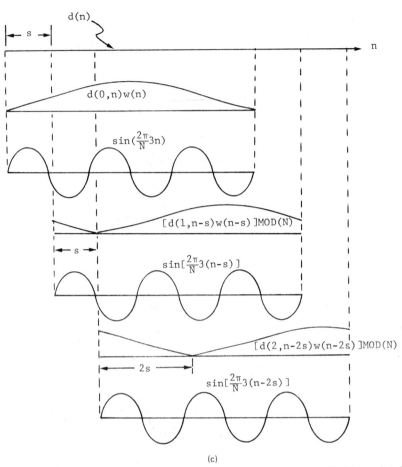

(c)

Fig. 8.17(c). Relationship between overlapped, windowed, and circularly-shifted intervals to DFT basis filter.

The general form of the desired filter output including the filter length L, resampling shift L/p, and transform length N is given by

$$r'(k,s) = e^{-j(2\pi L/Np)ks} \sum_{n=0}^{L-1} d\left(\frac{L}{p}s - n\right)h(n)e^{+j(2\pi/N)kn} \tag{8.19a}$$

$$= \sum_{n=0}^{L-1} h(n)d\left(\frac{L}{p}s - n\right)e^{-j(2\pi/N)(Ls/p - n)k} \tag{8.19b}$$

$$= \sum_{n=0}^{L-1} g(s,n)e^{-j(2\pi/N)(Ls/p - n)k} \tag{8.19c}$$

where $g(s,n) = h(n)d(Ls/p - n)$ is the sth windowed data block. Define the sth windowed and folded data block as

$$f(s, n') = \sum_{n''=0}^{c-1} g(s, n' + n''N)$$

Then

$$r'(k, s) = \sum_{n'=0}^{N-1} f(s, n')e^{-j(2\pi/N)(Ls/p - n')k} \tag{8.19d}$$

Letting $n_1 = (L/p)s - n'$ yields

$$r'(k, s) = \sum_{n_1=(L/p)s}^{(L/p)s-(N-1)} g(s, n_1)e^{-j(2\pi/N)n_1 k} \tag{8.19e}$$

Since the summation is periodic in N, circularly, shifting the index on $g(s, n')$ yields

$$r'(k, s) = \sum_{n_1=0}^{N-1} g[s, (n_1 \bmod N)]e^{-j(2\pi/N)n_1 k} \tag{8.19f}$$

Thus the desired set of basebanded, filtered, and resampled time sequences is obtained by taking DFTs overlapped, windowed, folded, and circularly shifted blocks of data. The kth sequence is equivalent to the demodulated and filtered output in Fig. 8.6 for $\theta(k) = (2\pi L/Np)s$.

Sample Design of DFT-Based Channelizer I

In this section we present a sample design for a DFT-based channelizer. We start with a set of channel specifications and show the sequence of design steps required to formulate the final design. The example we choose is the task of demultiplexing a standard single-sideband frequency-division-multiplexed (SSB-FDM) collection of 12 voice-grade telephone channels. In the telephone community, such a bank of 12 channels is called a channel group. Each channel is 4.0 kHz wide, and the FDM group is located between 60 kHz and 108 kHz. The task is to demultiplex this FDM group to a set of 12 single real baseband channels each sampled at an 8.0-kHz data rate. Each channel should exceed the specifications of a C4-channel-conditioned line. The specifications listed in Table V

TABLE V

FDM Channel Demultiplexer Specifications
(300–3000 Hz)

Phase slope deviation	$< 300\ \mu s$
Amplitude deviation	< -0.5 dB
Crosstalk levels	< -55 dB
Quantization noise	< -55 dB

more than satisfy C4 specifications and represent a simple set of specifications for our example.

The spectrum of the channel group is presented in Fig. 8.18(a). In this design we will frequency shift the analog channel-group signal to baseband with a complex heterodyne. We will also analog filter the heterodyned signal before sampling to minimize the sample rate. Let the analog lowpass filter require one octave to achieve -50-dB attenuation level. The basebanded channel spectrum and the spectrum of a reasonable analog lowpass filter are shown in Fig. 8.18(b). We see from the figure that the minimum sampling frequency required to prevent aliasing into the analysis band is (twice the foldover frequency of 39 kHz) 78 kHz.

We require the sampling frequency to be an integer multiple of the channel spacing, because the DFT channel centers are spaced at f_s/N, where N is the transform size. The minimum sampling frequency to preclude aliasing, 78 kHz, is not divisible by the 4-kHz channel centers, so the sample rate is changed to 80 kHz, the next highest multiple of 4 kHz. The channelization can be performed with an $80/4 = 20$-point DFT implemented as a (5×4)-point mixed-radix FFT. An alternative is to select a larger transform with a convenient size and a smaller computational load. For instance, a 24-point DFT [implemented as a (3×8)-point mixed-radix FFT] will demultiplex the desired 12 channels if the input data is sampled at $24 \times 4 = 96$ kHz. The slightly higher sampling frequency also relaxes the transition bandwidth requirements for the analog antialiasing filters. Choosing the second option, we now must select the filter length. The filter specification to allow resampling to the 8-kHz output rate from the 96-kHz input rate is computed from the spectral description in Fig. 8.19. From the design criterion in Chapter 3 we determine that the filter length is

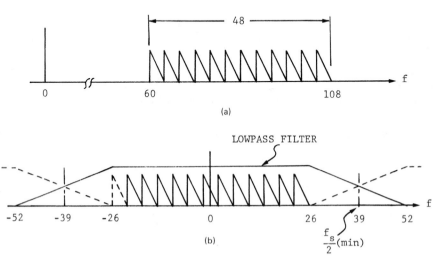

Fig. 8.18. (a) Spectrum of channel group and (b) heterodyned channel group with minimum bandwidth lowpass filter.

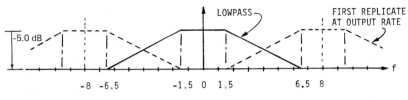

Fig. 8.19. Spectral description of lowpass prototype filter used to resample DFT-based channelizer.

48 points:

$$L = K(A)\frac{f_s}{f^d} = 2.5\frac{96.0}{6.5 - 1.5} = 2.5\frac{96.0}{5.0} = 48 \qquad (8.20)$$

Thus the filter is specified to be 48 points with a passband between 0.0 and 1.5/96.0 and with a stopband between 6.5/96.0, based on a normalized sampling frequency of 1 Hz. The Remez algorithm design (using a 1:40 passband-to-stopband relative penalty weighting) exhibited -0.43-dB deviation in the passband and -58.0-dB attenuation in the stopband which easily satisfy the specifications of Table V. Further, to achieve the -55-dB quantization noise level (relative to full-scale signal), we would require 10-bit ADC. Finally, the resampling from 96 to 8 kHz (a 12:1 ratio) requires that a new transform be performed for every 12 new input points. Thus the processing is performed with a 48-point filter folded 2:1 to fit the 24-point transform. The transform is performed for every 12 new points, which means a 4:1 overlap of the filter but a 2:1 overlap of the transform processing. Thus the 24-point transform must finish processing in the time it takes to bring in 12 new data points. At the 96-kHz rate this time is 125 μs, which by no coincidence is the design output rate of the filter bank.

Note that the transform is of length 24, but the number of required filters is 12. Hence, only half the output points have to be computed. By forming the FFT as three transforms of length 8, we can eliminated unused computations (*prune*) to avoid the unnecessary computations in the radix-3 "small-N" DFT.

The 24-point DFT implemented as a pruned prime factor transform (see Section X of Chapter 7) requires only 28 multiplications. Coupling this workload with the 96 multiplications of the 48-point filter, we find that the 12 filters can be implemented with less than 11 multiplications per filter. For the same performance using separate FIR filters and input data sampled at 78 kHz, the required filter length is only 39 points. Using the symmetry of the impulse response and the complex input data, the workload per FIR filter is 39 multiplications per output point. Thus, for this sample problem the multiplication rate for the FFT demultiplexer is less than one-third that of the direct FIR filter implementation. Note that we chose the complex output rate of the DFT channelizer to match the final desired 8-kHz output rate. In doing so we have arranged for the complex-to-real conversion to be trivial. The details of that conversion are presented in

Chapter 3. Also note that by selecting the complex output rate to be unnecessarily high, we have increased the rate at which the data windowing and transforming must be performed. A larger system would call for finer tuning, which would reduce the input workload at the expense of increasing the output workload by requiring nontrivial operations in the complex-to-real conversion. The details of conversion from a 6.0-kHz complex sample rate to an 8.0-kHz real sample rate are in Section V.D of Chapter 3.

III FAST CONVOLUTION AND CORRELATION

A primary signal processing operation is the decomposition of a signal into two or more subclasses. The subclasses may be as simple as signal and noise, or they may be as complex as a 600-channel FDM communication system. The signal subclasses are separated by a set of distinct parameters, such as center frequency, bandwidth, and modulation structure. These parameters are usually imbedded in a minimal set of template signals with which the input signal is to be compared. The comparison entails the projection of the input signal upon the template signals. In digital signal processing the input signal is represented by N data points and can be interpreted as an N-dimensional vector. From this perspective the projection is performed by a classic inner product—that is, by a weighted summation of the input signal samples. This projection process is known as cross-correlation or as matched filtering (i.e., convolution).

When the input signal is characterized to within a set of unknown parameters, the signal is projected on a collection of template signals that span the expected range of these unknown parameters. Examples include signals with unknown Doppler frequencies or unknown times of arrival (see Chapter 10). Then the matching process is not a single projection but a collection of such projections. For instance, a bank of narrowband filters (such as those of a windowed DFT) resolves the Doppler uncertainty of a signal, whereas a single filter shifted through successive time increments resolves the unknown time of arrival. The computational workload required for each inner product (or filter output) is N multiplications and additions. Thus the workload to compute the output from a bank of M matched filters is about $N \times M$. In the previous section the matched filtering required to separate signals of known (and reduced) bandwidth but distinct center frequencies, was imbedded in a DFT process. This imbedding offered significant computational advantages. Rather than requiring $N \times M$ operations, we have demonstrated that the (2:1) folding would require about $(N/4)\log(M)$ operations.

In the next section we demonstrate how the DFT can reduce the computational load for an arbitrary matched filter operating over successive time intervals. We describe the fast convolution (or fast correlation) technique, which is applicable to any filtering task. Furthermore, we demonstrate how resampling can be imbedded in the DFT process.

Discrete Linear Convolution and Correlation   **A**

The expression for computing the linear convolution of the sequence $h(n)$ of length L, denoted $[h(n):L]$, and the sequence $x(n)$ of arbitrary length greater than L is given by

$$y(n) = \sum_{m=0}^{L-1} x(n - m)h(m) \qquad (8.21a)$$

$$y(n) = x(n) * h(n) \qquad (8.21b)$$

$$Y(Z) = X(Z) \circ H(Z) \qquad (8.21c)$$

Equation (8.21b) indicates the conventional symbolic notation used to denote linear convolution. Noting the one-to-one correspondence between finite sequences and polynomials with the same coefficients as the sequence (equivalent to the finite z-transform), we also indicate, in Eq. (8.21c), the polynomial representation of finite convolution.

The corresponding expression for computing the linear correlation of two real sequences is

$$y(n) = \sum_{m=0}^{L-1} x(n + m)h(m), \qquad (8.22a)$$

$$y(n) = x(n) * h(-n), \qquad (8.22b)$$

$$y(n) = x(n) \,\,\text{☆}\,\, h(n), \qquad (8.22c)$$

$$Y(Z) = X(Z) \circ H(Z^{-1}). \qquad (8.22d)$$

Equations (8.22b) and (8.22c) indicate the conventional symbolic notation used to denote linear correlation, and Eq. (8.22d) is the polynomial representation. The summations indicated in Eqs. (8.22) and (8.23) represent running weighted sums. The difference in their indexing is best illustrated in Fig. 8.20, in which the indices of the summations have been indicated on a pair of parallel ribbons.

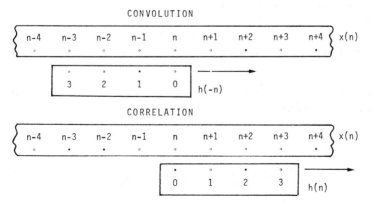

Fig. 8.20. Relationship between the indices for convolution and for correlation.

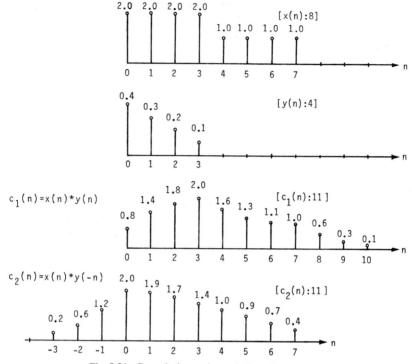

Fig. 8.21. Convolution and correlation of sequences.

To demonstrate an important consideration, Fig. 8.21 presents an example of linear convolution and linear correlation of two sequences. Note in particular that for both operations the number of resultant terms is one less than the sum of the number of original terms. That is, the linear convolution (or correlation) of two sequences of lengths P and Q, respectively, will produce a third sequence of length $P + Q - 1$. Also note the location of the zero index for the two operations of convolution and correlation.

B   The DFT and Circular Sequences

As stated in Section VII of Chapter 1, the DFT relationship between two sequences $h(n)$ and $H(k)$ is

$$H(k) = \sum_{n=0}^{N-1} h(n)e^{-j(2\pi/N)nk}, \qquad k = 0, 1, 2, \dots, N-1 \qquad (8.23a)$$

$$h(n) = \frac{1}{N}\sum_{k=0}^{N-1} H(k)e^{+j(2\pi/N)NK}, \qquad n = 0, 1, 2, \dots, N-1 \qquad (8.23b)$$

Note, via the Euclidean division algorithm, that for all k' and n' there are integer values of k, r, n, and s that satisfy

$$k' = k + rN \tag{8.24a}$$

$$n' = n + sN \tag{8.24b}$$

Substituting Eq. (8.24) into Eqs. (8.21) and (8.22) yields

$$H(k') = H(k + rN), \tag{8.25a}$$

$$H(k') = \sum_{n=0}^{N-1} h(n)e^{-j(2\pi/N)(k+rN)n} \tag{8.25b}$$

$$H(k') = \sum_{n=0}^{N-1} h(n)e^{-j(2\pi/N)kn} \tag{8.25c}$$

or

$$H(k') = H(k + rN) = H(k) \tag{8.25d}$$

$$h(n') = h(n + sN) \tag{8.25e}$$

$$h(n') = \frac{1}{N}\sum_{k=0}^{N-1} H(k)e^{+j(2\pi/N)(n+sN)k} \tag{8.25f}$$

$$h(n') = \frac{1}{N}\sum_{k=0}^{N-1} H(k)e^{+j(2\pi/N)nk} \tag{8.25g}$$

or

$$h(n') = h(n + sN) = h(n) \tag{8.25h}$$

Equations (8.25) show that sequences $H(k)$ and $h(n)$ are periodic in N, the size of the transform. Even if the original data $h(n)$ is not periodic, use of the transform implies a periodic extension of the data set. It is often convenient to envision the two sequences as circular sequences—that is, sequences defined on the perimeter of a circle.

Circular Convolution and Circular Correlation   C

The convolution (or correlation) of two continuous functions can be implemented indirectly through the product of their respective Fourier transforms and an inverse Fourier transform [12, 13]. This well-known equivalency is indicated in Fig. 8.22 for right-sided functions.

Analogously, the convolution (or correlation) of two discrete sequences can be implemented indirectly by the DFT, as discussed briefly in Section VII.E of Chapter 1. For computational efficiency the DFT is implemented by an FFT algorithm, which is why the transform-based convolution schemes are referred to as fast convolution. We must keep in mind, however, that the DFT describes a

DIRECT CONVOLUTION

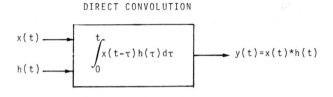

INDIRECT CONVOLUTION

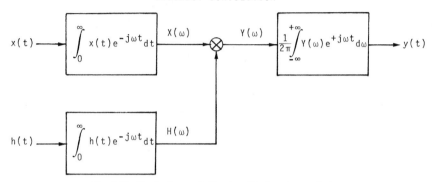

Fig. 8.22. Equivalency of direct and indirect convolution.

circular sequence (obtained by periodically extending the sequence) so that discrete convolution realized by a DFT is circular convolution. The expressions for the circular convolution of two sequences $h(n)$ and $x(n)$, now both of length L, are

$$y(n) = \sum_{m=0}^{L-1} x[(n - m) \mod(L)]h(m) \tag{8.26a}$$

$$y(n) = x(n) \circledast_L h(n) \tag{8.26b}$$

$$Y(Z) = X(Z) \cdot H(Z) \mod(Z^L - 1) \tag{8.26c}$$

Equation (8.26b) indicates the conventional notation used to denote circular convolution, and Eq. (8.26c) indicates how the polynomial representation denotes circular convolution. The L in Eq. (8.26b) is often omitted if the modulo is understood in context. For notational convenience, after this section, the circle (about the convolution operator, i.e., the asterisk) will also be omitted. The reader will understand that circular convolution is implied by the method used to implement the convolution. The corresponding expressions for computing the circular correlation of the same two sequences are

$$y(n) = \sum_{m=0}^{L-1} x[(n + m) \mod(L)]h(m) \tag{8.27a}$$

$$y(n) = x(n) \circledast_L h(-n) \tag{8.27b}$$

$$Y(Z) = X(Z) \cdot H(Z^{-1}) \mod(Z^L - 1) \tag{8.27c}$$

Equations (8.27b) and (8.27c) indicate the standard notational convention for circular correlation.

Figure 8.23 emphasizes the circular relationship between the indices of Eqs. (8.26) and (8.27) by assigning the indices to equally spaced intervals on a pair of concentric rings.

The indexing required for circular convolution requires that the two sequences be the same length. If a given pair of sequences is not (of the same length), we make them so by zero-extending the shorter one to match the longer. In many cases we choose to zero-extend both sequences to match a third convenient length (for instance, the length of a convenient circular convolver). Alternatively, we zero-extend data so that we can perform linear convolution with a circular convolver.

CIRCULAR CONVOLUTION

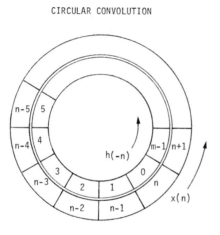

CIRCULAR CORRELATION

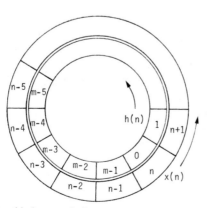

Fig. 8.23. Relationship between indices for circular convolution and correlation.

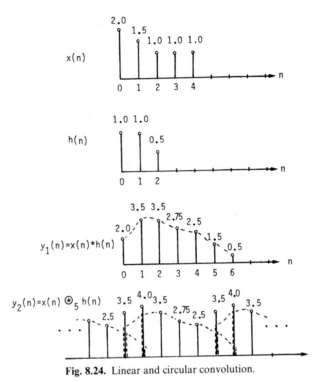

Fig. 8.24. Linear and circular convolution.

We note in Fig. 8.24 that circular convolution is related to linear convolution by the summation of end-around shifted data points. This is stated concisely in Eqs. (8.26c) and (8.27c). These end-around shifted and added points are equivalent to time domain aliasing described mathematically by

$$y_1(n) = x(n) * h(n) \tag{8.28a}$$

$$y_2(n) = x(n) \circledast_L h(n) \tag{8.28b}$$

$$y_2(n) = \sum_r y_1(n + rL), \qquad n = 0, 1, 2, \ldots, L - 1 \tag{8.28c}$$

We denote the zero-extended versions of $[x(n):p]$ and $[h(n):Q]$ by $[\tilde{x}(n):L]$ and $[\tilde{h}(n):L]$, respectively, and examine the relationships defined by

$$[y_1(n):P + Q - 1] = [x(n):P] * [y(n):Q] \tag{8.29a}$$

$$[y_2(n):L] = [x'(n):L] \circledast_L [y'(n):L] \tag{8.29b}$$

if

$$L \geq P + Q - 1, \qquad y_1(n) = y_2(n), \quad n = 0, 1, 2, \ldots, L - 1. \tag{8.29c}$$

As noted in Eq. (8.29c), if the zero-extended length L of a circular convolution

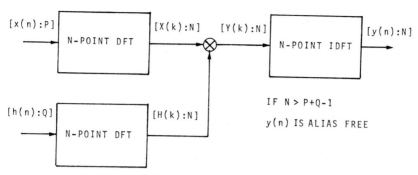

Fig. 8.25. DFT-based fast convolution.

exceeds the sum (less 1) of the preextended lengths, the circular convolution is identical to the linear convolution of the two sequences. Thus the DFT can be used to perform the linear convolution of two sequences by zero-extending the length of each to the next conveniently sized algorithm, say of length L, that satisfies Eq. (8.29c). This processing is indicated in Fig. 8.25 (see also Fig. 1.8).

Computational Workload for an N-Point FFT   **D**

A simple upper bound to the computational workload for implementing an N-point complex FFT is indicated in (7.60a) and (7.60b). The assumptions made in deriving (7.60) are that the FFT is a Cooley–Tukey radix-2 algorithm with a complex multiplication required in all butterflies except those in the first two passes and that each butterfly requires a pair of complex additions. The arithmetic operations in (7.60a) and (7.60b) are repeated as

$$\frac{N}{2}\log_2\left(\frac{N}{2}\right) \quad \text{complex multiplications} \tag{8.30a}$$

$$N\log_2(N) \quad \text{complex additions} \tag{8.30b}$$

These equations are equivalent to

$$N[2\log_2(N) - 4] \quad \text{real multiplications} \tag{8.30c}$$

$$N[3\log_2(N) - 2] \quad \text{real additions} \tag{8.30d}$$

If we assume real data sequences, we have the option of reducing the average computational workload by using the transform to process two arrays of data simultaneously. One array goes in the real component of the FFT input and one goes in the imaginary component (see Table VI in Chapter 1 entry for the DFT of two real N-point sequences by means of one N-point DFT). The workload per array in dual N-point transforms, accounting for the extra additions required for the odd–even separation, is

$$N[\log_2(N) - 2] \qquad \text{real multiplications} \qquad (8.31a)$$

$$N[1.5\log_2(N) + 1] \qquad \text{real additions} \qquad (8.31b)$$

E   Computational Workload for Fast Correlation

The computational burden required to perform a fast convolution consists of two forward transforms, one point-by-point complex product of the transform output vectors, and an inverse transform (see Fig. 8.25). The workload to perform this sequence of tasks might be reduced if we have access to a priori information about the two sequences. As one example, autocorrelation requires one, not two, forward transforms for the fast correlation method. As another example, if the sequences have even or odd symmetry, the spectral products become real products. These examples represent special cases that we will no longer consider. Hence, we will interpret the following results as tight upper bounds to the computational workload for the arbitrary signal sets.

Let the two real sequences to be correlated have the same length M, and let $2M$ be shorter than the size of an available FFT. The computational workload for direct computation of the full $2M - 1$ points of a cross-correlation is

$$M^2 \qquad \text{(real multiplications)} \qquad (8.32a)$$

$$(M - 1)^2 \qquad \text{(real additions)} \qquad (8.32b)$$

This workload will result in $2M - 1$ output points. The average computational workload per output point is

$$\frac{M^2}{2M - 1} \simeq \frac{M}{2} \qquad \text{(real multiplications)} \qquad (8.33a)$$

$$\frac{(M - 1)^2}{2M - 1} \simeq \frac{M}{2} \qquad \text{(real additions)} \qquad (8.33b)$$

For fast correlation the data length M is zero-extended to N, the next power of 2 greater (or equal) to $2M - 1$. The integers M and N satisfy

$$\frac{N}{2} < 2M \leq N, \qquad N = 2^p \qquad (8.34)$$

where we assume that a radix-2 FFT will be used. The pair of zero-extended data sequences is then transformed, conjugate multiplied, and inverse transformed. The computational workload for each step in this process, for two real sequences, is indicated in Table VI. Here we have assumed that dual forward transforms are performed simultaneously [see Eq. (8.31)] and then separated by the even and odd parts of the real and imaginary output (see Table VI in Chapter 1). The

TABLE VI

Multiplications and Additions for Fast Correlation

Task	Real multiplications	Real additions
Forward FFT	$N[2\log(N) - 4]$	$N[3\log(N) - 2]$
Odd–even separation	—	$2N$
Forward FFT	$N[2\log(N) - 4]$	$N[3\log(N) - 2]$
Odd–even separation	—	$2N$
Spectral products	$4N$	$2N$
Odd–even merging	—	$2N$
Inverse FFT	$N[2\log(N) - 4]$	$N[3\log(N) - 2]$
Total	$N[6\log(N) - 4]$	$N[9\log(N) + 2]$
Total/array	$N[3\log(N) - 2]$	$N[4.5\log(N) + 1]$

spectral products are formed over half of the frequencies of each transform and then merged again by the odd and even symmetries of the real and imaginary components for a dual inverse (real) transform. The computational workload indicated in Table VI will result in $2M - 1$ output points. Equations (8.35) indicate the computational workload per output point. The bounds indicated in Eq. (8.35) result from substituting the bounds of Eq. (8.34).

Number of real multiplications:

$$[2\log_2(2M) - 2] < \frac{N[3\log_2(N) - 2]}{2M - 1} < [6\log_2(4M) - 4] \quad (8.35a)$$

Number of real additions:

$$[4.5\log_2(2M) + 1] < \frac{N[4.5\log_2(N) + 1]}{2M - 1} < [9\log_2(4M) + 2] \quad (8.35b)$$

Figure 8.26 is a graph of Eqs. (8.33) and (8.35) for a wide range of sequence lengths M and the associated transform lengths N. Also shown in the figure are graphs of Eq. (8.36) that present estimates for the number of calls to data memory per output data point (per array) for direct and fast correlation. We have assumed 10 calls to memory per full butterfly and 8 calls to memory for the odd–even separation or merging operation (which is equivalent to a butterfly without any multiplications).

Number of calls to data memory:

$$\frac{2M^2}{2M - 1} \simeq M \quad \text{(direct)} \quad (8.36a)$$

$$\frac{N[7.5\log_2(N) - 1]}{2M - 1} \simeq 3.75\frac{N}{M}\log_2(N) \quad \text{(fast)} \quad (8.36b)$$

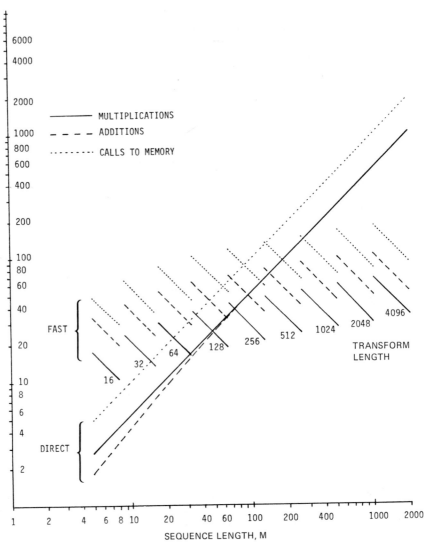

Fig. 8.26. Number of multiplications, additions, and calls to memory for direct and for fast correlations of length M.

The significant results from Fig. 8.26 are the crossover points at which fast correlation becomes computationally more efficient than direct correlation. These points are tabulated in Table VII. We note from Table VII, depending on the particular measure, that fast correlation is computationally more efficient if the two sequences are longer than 75 to 150 points. If a correlation is to be performed only once, it probably doesn't matter how it is implemented. On the other hand, if the correlation is performed regularly as a production task, it may well be worth optimizing the implementation.

TABLE VII

Range of Length M for Which Fast Correlation Is More Efficient than Direct Correlation

Real multiplications	$M > 75$
Real additions	$M > 150$
Calls to memory	$M > 130$

Fast Convolution with the FFT   F

A recurring task in digital signal processing is the filtering of an essentially unending stream of input data. If the filtering is performed as a direct convolution with a FIR filter of length M, having a symmetric impulse response, the computational load is approximately $M/2$ multiplications and M additions per output point. By performing the convolution with an FFT, we can significantly reduce the workload per data point. In the previous section we performed a correlation by using a transform long enough to avoid circular convolution. Here we make the assumption that the data length exceeds the length of any practical DFT algorithm. We still perform the convolution with the DFT, but we arrange to partition (or block) the problem into a set of smaller problems that fit into DFT algorithms of computationally practical length.

In performing convolution (which is a continuous process) by the DFT (which is a block process) we must be careful to avoid artifacts related to the artifically induced block boundaries. Two block processing techniques totally avoid boundary-related processing artifacts. The first is known as *overlap and add*, and the second is called *overlap and discard* (often called overlap and save). In both methods data blocks are processed by an N-point FFT algorithm. Each successive block overlaps the previous block by M-1 data points, where M is the length of the FIR filter impulse response.

If the two sequences, of lengths N and M, respectively, are linearly convolved, the resultant sequence has length $N + M - 1$. If the same two sequences (including a required zero-extension of one sequence to length N) are circularly convolved, the resultant sequence also has length N and exhibits, relative to the linearly convolved sequence, a circular wrap-around of $M - 1$ points. Figure 8.27 demonstrates the relationship between the linearly and circularly convolved sequences. We see that the first $M - 1$ points are circulary wrapped; consequently, $N - (M - 1)$ points are alias free. Thus each successive block processed by the N-point DFT gives $N + 1 - M$ good data points. Accordingly, blocks of new input data should be separated by $N + M - 1$ points, the alias-free distance of the output blocks. The boundaries for each new input block are found by sliding the previous boundary forward $N + 1 - M$ points to include these new $N + 1 - M$ input data points. The two options (discard or add) differ in how they handle the remaining $M - 1$ data positions of the length-N input array for the transform.

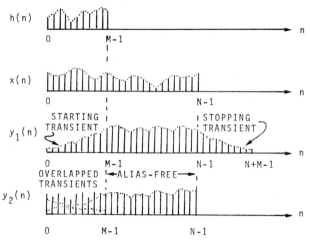

Fig. 8.27. Alias-free interval for circular convolver performing linear convolution.

In overlap and add processing, we avoid circular wrap-around by using the remaining $M - 1$ positions as zero-extending points. Then the resultant circular convolution exactly matches the equivalent linear convolution [see Eq. (8.29)]. The resultant convolution exhibits two transients; the starting transient, which corresponds to the data block entering the filter, and the stopping transient, which corresponds to the data block leaving the filter. Since the transients are responses to artificial block boundaries, they can be eliminated by adding the stopping transient from a given block to the starting transient of the next block. Merging successively processed blocks by adding transient responses in the overlapped intervals is demonstrated in Fig. 8.28. Note that the name "overlap and add" describes the processing performed to avoid the artifacts related to processing the data in blocks.

In overlap and discard processing, the circular wrap-around is not avoided in the output of the intermediate block processing, but is prevented from contributing to the final merged output by our recognizing and discarding the locations at which the aliasing does occur. In this technique the free $M - 1$ positions are relegated to the left side of the input array, where they overlap the previous interval by the $M - 1$ positions. The circular convolution of the length-N array with the length-M array produces $M - 1$ points of circularly wrapped output data. The locations of these wrapped points in the output array coincide with the overlapped interval of the input array. Since the end of each processing block is alias free, the output points associated with the aliased interval in the current processing block are available from the processing of the previous block. Hence, the data in the aliased interval is simply discarded, and the merging of successive blocks is performed by simple juxtaposition of the alias-free intervals. This is simpler (and less work than) adding the responses in the overlapped intervals as required by the overlap-and-add technique. This processing technique is also demonstrated in Fig. 8.28. The name "overlap and discard" describes

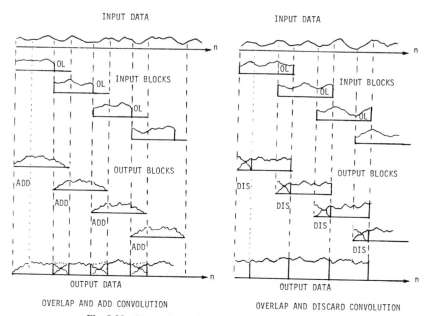

Fig. 8.28. Comparison of overlap convolution techniques.

the processing performed to account for the artificially induced boundaries in the input data.

The signal-flow diagram for the overlapped fast convolution processing is shown in Fig. 8.29. If the input data is real, we can more efficiently use the DFT by having it perform two simultaneous tasks. One such option is to perform the block process on two successive blocks of data from the same sequence by treating the blocks from two time intervals as the real and imaginary parts of a complex input series (see the Table VI entry in Chapter 1 for the DFT of two real N-point sequences by means of one N-point DFT). If performed as a real-time process, this option requires additional input buffering to hold the two input blocks. Waiting for the last data point in the second block before initiating the

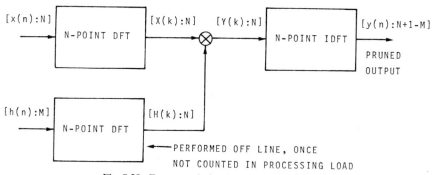

Fig. 8.29. Fast convolution by overlap and discard.

Frederic J. Harris

processing means there will be additional latency between the arrival of the first input data point and the delivery of the first output data point. The second option is to use the same FFT to perform the forward transform for a given interval while simultaneously performing the inverse transform for the previous interval. In the first option there is no extra overhead to separate the two arrays being simultaneously processed, whereas in the second option there is a minor overhead involved to perform an odd–even decomposition of the two arrays. The signal-flow diagrams for the two options are shown in Fig. 8.30. The square box with the plus symbol is not an arithmetic operation but an association of two real data sets as a complex data set. The same box with the bar over the plus symbol is the equivalent disassociation that separates a complex data set into a pair of real data sets.

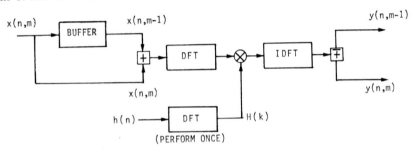

PROCESSING DUAL REAL ARRAYS SIMULTANEOUSLY

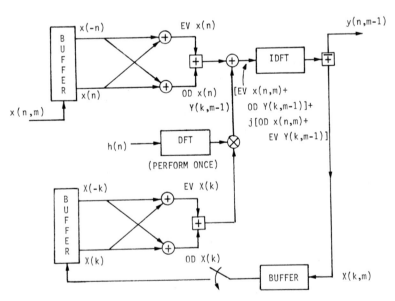

PROCESSING FORWARD AND INVERSE TRANSFORMS SIMULTANEOUSLY

Fig. 8.30. Processing two transforms simultaneously.

TABLE VIII

TABLE VIII

Real Multiplications and Additions for Fast Convolution Using Dual Simultaneous Real Input Arrays

Task	Real multiplications	Real additions
Forward FFT	$N[2\log(N) - 4]$	$N[3\log(N) - 2]$
Spectral products	$4N$	$2N$
Inverse FFT	$N[2\log(N) - 4]$	$N[3\log(N) - 2]$
Total	$N[4\log(N) - 4]$	$N[6\log(N) - 2]$
Total/array	$N[2\log(N) - 2]$	$N[3\log(N) - 1]$

Table VIII lists the processing tasks and the computational burden required at each step to perform the fast convolution using the option of dual simultaneous input arrays. Table IX lists the equivalent tasks and burdens for fast convolution using the option of simultaneous forward and inverse transforms.

The computational workload indicated in Tables VIII and IX gives $N - (M - 1)$ useful output points. The computational workload per output point for the option of dual simultaneous real array processing is

$$\text{Number of real multiplications} = \frac{N[2\log_2(N)]}{N + 1 - M} \qquad (8.37a)$$

$$\text{Number of real additions} = \frac{N[3\log_2(N) - 1]}{N + 1 - M} \qquad (8.37b)$$

Figure 8.31 is a graph of Eq. (8.37) for a wide range of filter lengths M and associated transform lengths N [14]. Also shown are graphs of Eq. (8.38), which presents estimates for the number of calls to memory per output data point (per array) for direct and fast convolutions. We have assumed that odd–even

TABLE IX

Multiplications and Additions for Fast Convolution Using Simultaneous Forward and Inverse Transforms

Task	Real multiplications	Real additions
Odd–even separation (input array)	—	$2N$
Odd–even separation (output array)	—	$2N$
Spectral product	$4N$	$2N$
Summing arrays	—	$2N$
Forward FFT	$N[2\log(N) - 4]$	$N[3\log(N) - 2]$
Total	$N[2\log(N)]$	$N[3\log(N) + 6]$

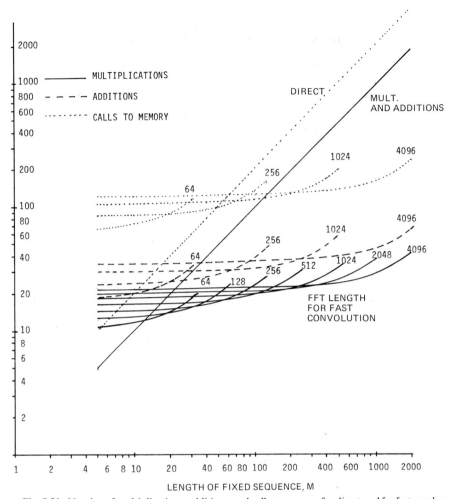

Fig. 8.31. Number of multiplications, additions, and calls to memory for direct and for fast overlap and discard convolution.

separation is equivalent to a butterfly without multiplication that requires eight calls to memory and that a butterfly with multiplication requires 10 calls.

Calls to memory:

$$2M \qquad \text{(direct)} \tag{8.38a}$$

$$\frac{N[10\log_2(N) + 2]}{N + 1 - M} \qquad \text{(fast)} \tag{8.38b}$$

Figure 8.31 has some interesting results. First we note that the transform technique is relatively insensitive to filter length M till the length approaches half the transform length, where the workload climbs rapidly. Also note that the

TABLE X

Range of Filter Length M for Which
Fast Convolution Is More Efficient
than Direct Convolution

Real multiplications	$M > 25$
Real additions	$M > 32$
Calls to memory	$M > 60$

largest transform is not always the best transform for a given length convolution. For example, for a filter of length 80, a 512-point FFT gives the fewest operations per output point. The other significant result from Fig. 8.31 is the crossover points at which fast convolution becomes computationally more efficient than direct convolution. These points are tabulated in Table X for a 4096-point DFT.

We may be tempted to compare the results in Table X to those in Table VII. Remember, the tables correspond to different conditions. Here the parameter M is the filter length, and the transform size N is larger than the filter to allow for an alias-free data interval. In Table VII M is the data length and N is limited to twice the data size.

THE DFT AS AN INTERPOLATOR AND SIGNAL GENERATOR   IV

The DFT can be used to increase the sample rate of an input time series. Interpolation with the DFT is a common signal processing task. Usually the interpolation is performed in the frequency domain as part of a spectral analysis or beamforming task. We will review why and how the spectral interpolation is performed and then apply the technique to time domain interpolation. An interesting aspect of the DFT-based time domain interpolator is the option of performing a spectral shift during the interpolation. The attraction of this option is the ability to simultaneously interpolate and heterodyne a set of input signals. We will then have an efficient way to convert a time-domain-multiplexed (TDM) signal to a frequency-domain-multiplexed (FDM) signal. This task is the inverse of the one we examined in Section II. An extension of this technique is the formulation of a technique to efficiently generate signals with arbitrary time-varying spectral parameters.

Interpolation by Zero-Extended DFTs   A

Let us return for a moment to the perspective of the DFT as a bank of narrowband filters. The adjacent filters of the bank exhibit a variation in gain as a function of frequency (see, e.g., Fig. 8.4). This variation is called the *picket-fence effect* because the computed amplitude of a single sinusoid with a slowly varying frequency that causes it slide through adjacent filters will vary similar to the peaks of a picket fence. The reduced amplitude of a sinusoid located between two filters (or DFT bins) relative to the amplitude exhibited by the sinusoid located at the filter (or bin) center is known as the *scalloping loss*. Figure 8.32 demonstrates that the peak scalloping loss is for a sinusoid located at the bin crossover points of a DFT. The scalloping loss reduces detection performance when the DFT is used to detect sinusoids of unknown frequency and amplitude in the presence of additive noise. This performance loss is minimized by forming additional filters positioned at the crossover points of the original set of DFT filters, as indicated by the dotted lines in Fig. 8.32. The increased overlap of adjacent filters (in the enhanced filter bank) increases the correlation between the outputs from adjacent filters. Computing the outputs of the additional filters in the set is equivalent to interpolating between the spectral samples of the original DFT. We actually form the additional filter outputs by simply zero-extending the input data set with an equal number of zeros and applying a double-length DFT to the zero-extended set.

By interchanging the domains in which we perform the zero-extension, we move the interpolation to the time domain. Thus we can take the DFT of a block of time data, zero-extend its transform, and then take the inverse DFT to obtain the bandlimited (circular) interpolation of the original block. This procedure is very similar to the fast convolution technique described in Section III. The difference is that the spectral modification, which is equivalent to the time domain convolution, is not multiplicative but a simple redefinition of the sample rate (i.e., the spectral span) by zero-extension.

This technique can also be described in the vocabulary of the FIR interpolator we presented in Section V in Chapter 3. Assume that the original data is

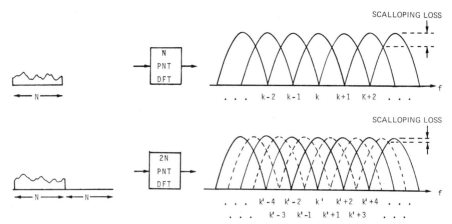

Fig. 8.32. Scalloping loss of adjacent filters in DFT.

transformed and then zero-extended by a factor of M. We now demonstrate that this is the same as performing a two-step operation simultaneously, and we can gain insight by separating the two steps. We can visualize the first step as replicating the original transform M times. This is equivalent to zero-packing the original data using an $M:1$ multiplexer (see Fig. 3.32) and then transforming the zero-packed data. We eliminate the replicates using the techniques of fast convolution, which involves multiplying the spectrum with the spectrum of the interpolating lowpass filter. Since the multiplication is by zero, we couple the two operations by simply loading zeros in the extended spectral locations. Later we may choose to actually perform the spectral products, because we may want to reduce the signal bandwidth (i.e., perform a filtering task) along with the interpolation.

We now know that the zero-extension in the frequency domain is equivalent to raising the sampling rate of the input data by zero-packing and filtering. The increase in sampling rate is the same as the ratio of the output transform size to the input transform size. For instance, if the input transform size is 256 and the inverse transform of the zero-extended spectrum is 768, the output time series will have three times as many data points in the same time span as the original input data will. Often the interpolation ratio is chosen to be a power of 2 so that the transform is simply a larger radix-2 FFT. This restriction is arbitrary and not inherent in the technique. We can interpolate by any ratio of integers by judiciously choosing transform sizes. For example, we can interpolate by $\frac{3}{2}$ by using an input transform of length 512 and an output transform of length 768.

Note that once the transform of the input data has been zero-extended, we are free to circularly shift the spectrum to an arbitrary position in the longer array. We know that rotation of the spectrum is equivalent to a complex heterodyne in the time domain. This manipulation and its equivalent time domain process are indicated in Fig. 8.33. Since the spectral data has been zero-extended, there is no spectral wrapping past the half sampling frequency, and the spectral rotation is equivalent to a spectral shift. This subtlety is equivalent to the zero-extension in the time domain to perform linear convolution with a circular convolver. If we require the output time series to be real, we must perform the spectral shift over equal positive and negative increments. This shifting operation is identical to heterodyning the original signal with a cosine carrier. If the spectral shift operation is combined with a $\pm 90°$ phase shift, the resultant heterodyned signal is on a sine carrier.

The heterodyne is accomplished by address manipulations rather than multiplications. To complete this preliminary discussion, we recognize that we can perform this operation on signals with the same bandwidth and initial sample rate. If there were M input signals, we could perform an $M:1$ increase in sample rate and arrange for the spectrum of each signal to occupy nonoverlapping spectral positions. We then inverse transform each spectral array and add the resultant interpolated and bandshifted time signals to obtain a FDM output signal. But wait; we can obtain the FDM spectrum directly by forming a single

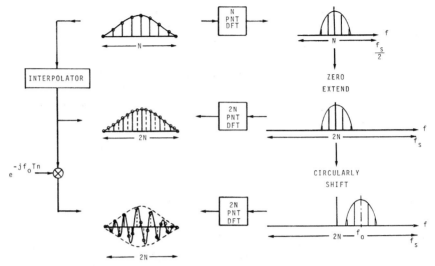

Fig. 8.33. Interpolation and spectral shift in time domain and with DFT.

spectrum containing the sum of the separate nonoverlapping spectra. Then a single inverse transform will construct the FDM time series. This equivalency is indicated in Fig. 8.34. Note that we perform the heterodynes and (since they are nonoverlapped) the spectral summations by simple memory addressing. We still have to address the problem that the FDM process we are synthesizing is an

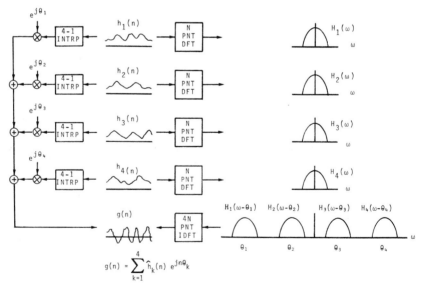

Fig. 8.34. Interpolation and frequency-division multiplexing in time domain and with discrete Fourier transform.

operation on a continuous stream of input data, but the transform-based process is a block process. As we did for the fast convolution routines, we have to devise a method to handle the edge effects generated by the data blocking.

Merging Overlapped and Interpolated Data Blocks   B

The time domain interpolation using a zero-extended DFT, described in the previous section, performs a time domain circular convolution of the zero-packed data sequence (by a factor of M) with the bandlimited and periodic $\sin(\pi n)/\sin(\pi n/N)$ interpolation function described in Section VII.E of Chapter 1, where the DFT length is MN. This is the default function realized by the inverse transform of the (implied) sampled spectral rectangle that was used in the fast convolution spectral product. Thus the resultant interpolation exhibits circular aliasing, which may not be the desired result. We have access to techniques with which we can avoid the circular wrapping.

Since we have identified the interpolator as a variant of fast convolution, we might first examine the solution we derived to avoid circular aliasing with fast convolution in Section III. There circular convolution was avoided by simple overlap-and-discard processing. Figure 8.35 presents sketches of the time and frequency responses for the DFT convolver along with the equivalent time domain processor whose spectrum would replicate the output of the DFT. We see that the output of the DFT is the same as that obtained by circularly

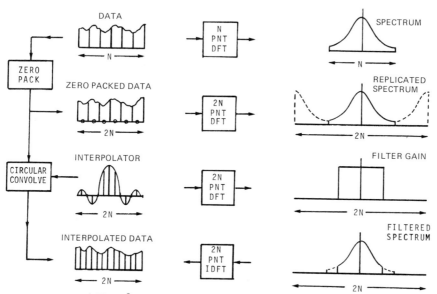

Fig. 8.35. Time domain and DFT-based interpolator.

convolving a $\sin(\pi f)/\sin(\pi f/N)$ filter, which has the same length as the zero-packed input data, with the DFT spectrum. The zero-packing by the factor M raises the number of input points N to the number of output points NM from the circular convolver.

At first glance it would seem we have our solution. To avoid the circular aliasing, we would zero-extend the filter impulse response by one length, and the processing would then proceed as normal 50% overlap-and-discard fast convolution. A surprise awaits us, however, when we return to the frequency domain and examine the transform of the equivalent rectangular filter. Before the zero-extension, the $\sin(\pi n)/\sin(\pi n/N)$ impulse response of the filter used in the fast convolver had the very convenient values of unity at just one sample and zero at all other samples. The spectral description of the double-length version of the filter is more complicated. The most striking feature of what we now have is spectral mainlobe broadening and nonzero sidelobe peaks from the $\sin(\pi n)/\sin(\pi n/N)$, which is attributable to the time limiting of the original filter response. As seen in Fig. 8.36, the sidelobes of this filter do not completely reject the spectral replicates, hence this is not the appropriate filter to perform the interpolation.

The form of the proper filter required for the interpolation is shown in Figure 8.36(b). We could design the impulse response of the filter by using any of the FIR filter design techniques. Then a DFT of the response supplies the spectral description needed for the fast convolver. A particularly attractive option for time domain design is to convolve on M-point rectangular interpolator with the mainlobe samples of a good weighting function (i.e., time domain) window, such as the Kaiser–Bessel or Blackman–Harris. The resultant interpolator spectrum has unity or zero values at all DFT samples except at the transition region of the filter. Thus the spectral samples in the transition bands are scaled when forming the filtered spectrum while all remaining DFT data points are zeroed or are passed with no attenuation. We now have access to a modification of the fast convolution technique that can simultaneously interpolate, heterodyne, and form an FDM signal from a set of input signals.

C   Merging Data Blocks by Inverse Synthesis

Figure 8.32 shows that there is a marked increase in computational workload for fast convolution when the length of the filter impulse response approaches half the size of transform (i.e., there is a 50% overlap in the convolver output data). This is the processing required for the interpolation technique described in the last section for 2:1 zero-packing. We can improve the efficiency of the process by seeking an alternative form of the interpolating filter process. The alternative technique imbeds the spectral product of the fast convolution in the windowing operation that precedes the original forward transform. In addition to forming an

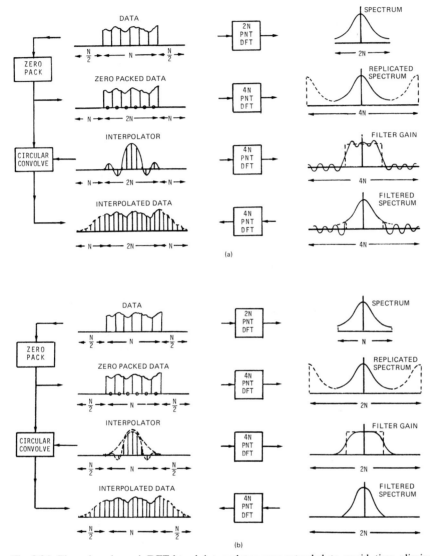

Fig. 8.36. Time domain and DFT-based interpolator zero-extended to avoid time aliasing. (a) Filter with appreciable sidelobes; (b) filter shaping to minimize spectral sidelobes.

alternative interpolator and FDM synthesizer, this technique is the core of an efficient arbitrary function generator [15–19].

We first demonstrate the alternative technique of simultaneous interpolation and spectral shifting for a single channel. Let us assume we want to increase the sample rate for a time series by a factor of 32 and heterodyne the signal to a new frequency at $\frac{3}{32}$ of the new sampling frequency. Figure 8.37 presents an initial naive attempt to interpolate and heterodyne. Here we simply replace each sample

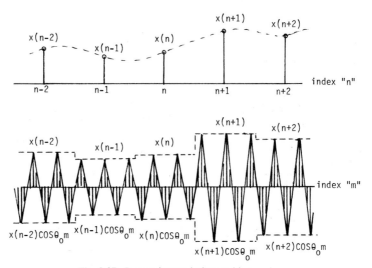

Fig. 8.37. Boxcar interpolation and heterodyne.

value of the input series with a tone burst of the proper length (32 sample) and of the proper frequency scaled by that sample. This is equivalent to replicating each sample 32 times (performing coarse interpolation) and then applying the desired heterodyne.

The amplitude discontinuities every M data points in Fig. 8.37 suggest the presence of higher frequencies that must be eliminated. These higher frequencies can be visualized as the result of a two-step process. In the first step we zero-pack the input data by M, the desired increase in sampling frequency. This redefines the sample rate, and the spectrum of the zero-packed data will exhibit M replicates in the band of frequencies defined by this rate (see Fig. 8.38). To eliminate these replicates, we can pass the zero-extended data through an averager, which for this initial example has the impulse response of an M-point rectangle. The MN-point DFT frequency-response magnitude of the M-point averager is $\sin(\pi f N)/\sin(\pi f)$. The zeros of this response coincide with the positions of the spectral replicates, so the spectral product significantly reduces their amplitude. The residual amplitudes are the high-frequency terms that account for the time domain envelope discontinuities. We can eliminate these terms by convolving the DFT of the zero-packed data with a smoother window, say a four-term Blackman–Harris window. If the duration (or width) of the smooth data sequence window is confined to the zero-packing interval (of M points), the corresponding increased mainlobe spectral width will extend beyond the first spectral replicate. Thus those spectral replicates outside the mainlobe will be eliminated, but those within the widened mainlobe will still be present. For the four-term Blackman–Harris window three replicates on either side of the primary spectrum will be present. We wish to keep the primary copy and remove

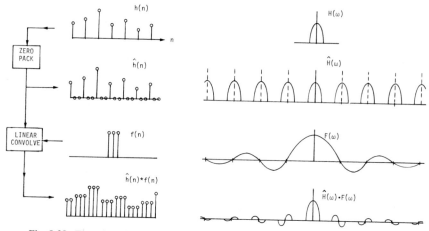

Fig. 8.38. Time domain and equivalent spectral description of boxcar interpolation.

the three pairs of (attenuated) duplicates. To eliminate the replicas inside the mainlobe, we must reduce the width at the mainlobe response. We accomplish this by increasing the duration of the time domain weighting to be four zero-packed intervals wide. Then the frequency domain width precisely matches the separation of the spectral replicates. The spectral product between the zero-padded data spectrum and the lengthened filter effectively eliminates the spectral replicates within a reasonable fidelity criteria (such as greater than 80-dB attenuation). This is shown in Fig. 8.39.

The equivalent DFT-based operation to perform this same task is to load the spectral points for a given channel into the address of a quadruple-length IDFT

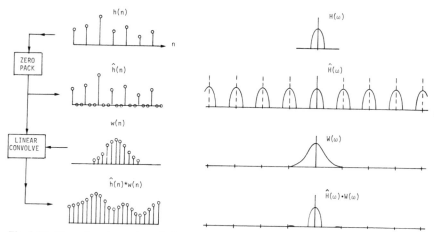

Fig. 8.39. Time domain and equivalent spectral description of 4:1 overlapped window (or arbitrary filter) interpolator.

corresponding to the desired output frequency, perform the inverse transform, and weight the data. For our specific example the transform length is 128 and the output bin is bin 12, corresponding to $\frac{3}{32}$ of the new sampling rate. This is repeated for each input data point. The sequence of 128-point windowed time series is displaced by 32 points and merged by simple addition with a bin-dependent phase-correction term of the form of Eq. (8.11a). For the 4:1 processing overlap the phase corrections are combinations of sign reversals and data exchanges between the real and imaginary components of the data.

This sequence of operations is the reversal of the transmultiplexer example we examined in Section II.F. There successive blocks of time samples were processed by a 4:1 overlapped and weighted input to the DFT to obtain successive time samples from each filter to a bank of narrowband filters. We obtain a single output point per filter per input data block. Counter to conventional DFT processing, this operation is characterized by time in and time out. Reversing this, we sequentially input single time samples into each desired center-frequency bin of an inverse DFT and obtain a sequence of data blocks associated with 4:1 overlapped intervals. The data from each overlapped interval is weighted (to control edge effects) and then merged into the desired output series by simple addition.

The weighting operation applied multiplicatively at the output of the IDFT can also be applied as a convolution at the input to the transform. This is a desirable option if the composite bandwidth of the output signal is only a small fraction of the output sample rate. In that case a spectral convolution with the few nonzero spectral terms of the window may require fewer multiplications.

D Function Generator with Arbitrary Spectra

In the previous section we described a technique to form a composite output time series from the spectral components of an input time series. In this section we describe a related method to synthesize a composite output series with specified but arbitrary power spectrum [20]. The specified spectrum can be stationary or slowly time varying, and it can be described with any mix of deterministic and stochastic attributes. Conceptually, generating stochastic signals with a specified power spectra (or correlation function) is accomplished by filtering a white noise time series with a filter exhibiting the desired power spectrum. The filtering can be implemented with a conventional fast convolution algorithm as indicated in Fig. 8.40. This approach is characterized by simplicity but suffers from implementation problems.

The first problem is the task of obtaining the broadband random series to be filtered. One common solution is to generate the samples with a pseudo-random-noise (P-N) algorithm. Algorithms exist to generate P-N sequences with a uniform distribution on (0, 1), which in turn can be converted to an arbitrary

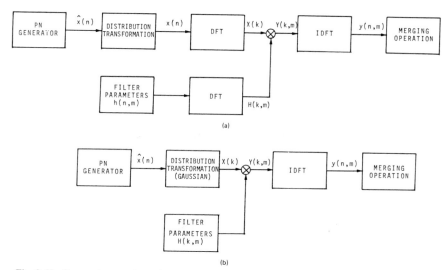

Fig. 8.40. Generating random signals with specified power spectra given specifications in the (a) time domain and (b) frequency domain.

distribution, such as Gaussian. This method is indicated in Fig. 8.40. Random-number generators based on modulo arithmetic operations are periodic in a fixed (possibly large) number of calls. As such, a high data rate from the random-number generator may inadvertently permit the time series to become periodic in the observation interval. This happens, for instance, when the *central limit theorem* is invoked to effect the transformation of a uniformly distributed random variable to a Gaussian distributed random-variable distribution. In this method samples of a Gaussian process are approximated by summing many independent identically distributed (i.i.d) input samples. The same problem, in a slightly different form, occurs when the output process exhibits a high ratio of sample rate to bandwidth, such as for a narrowband process. For this case the input data to the filtering process is generated at the input (and output) sample rate rather than at the reduced rate consistent with the reduced bandwidth. Shortly we will examine a technique in which the DFT performs indirect time domain interpolation. This will permit calls to the random-number generator to proceed at the reduced bandwidth rate while outputting time samples at the higher output rate.

The second weakness of this method for generating random signals with an arbitrary power spectral is the filtering process. The computational burden for the filtering process can be very large, particularly when the time series being generated has high sample-to-sample correlation, such as in a narrowband process. We minimize this burden by using a fast convolution algorithm to perform the filtering.

We can lengthen the period of the output series and reduce the overall generation and filtering work load by recognizing that we have a complete statistical description for the DFT of a white noise series. Hence there is no need to perform the DFT of the input series as part of the fast convolution. We first assume that the input series is a sequence of i.i.d. samples of a Gaussian random variable with zero mean and known (say unit) variance. Since the N-point DFT is a linear process, we know the output must also be a sequence of complex Gaussian random variables with zero mean and variance N. (The phases of the complex sequence are independently distributed on $(0, 2\pi)$. (We can also invoke the central limit theorem to argue that the output of the N-point DFT is such a sequence as long as the input is any set of i.i.d. random variables.) Thus rather than load samples of noise into a DFT and then perform the DFT to obtain the white noise spectral input to the fast convolution, we simply treat the white Gaussian noise samples as the spectral samples.

We can now describe the structure of the random-function generator with arbitrary power spectrum. We compute a spectral set of zero-mean unit-variance Gaussian random variables to cover the span of the nonzero bandwidth for the desired output series, and scale these samples by the desired spectral envelope. This scaling corresponds to the spectral product of a fast convolution routine (or of the synthesis by an analysis algorithm). The phase of the scaled spectral lines is then randomized with uniformly distributed phase angles obtained by calls to the uniform random-number generator. Alternatively, two sets of zero-mean unit-variance Gaussian data samples can be generated and treated as real and imaginary components of the complex samples to be scaled by the spectral envelope. The latter approach avoids the need to randomize the phase of the shaped spectrum. By either technique we have formed the input spectral data required by the IDFT in the synthesis section of the fast convolver. By this technique we are generating the spectral data at the Nyquist rate rather than at the high sample rate as described earlier, and we are using the IDFT as an interpolator as we did in the previous section. The resultant synthesized series from the IDFT is then windowed and merged with other similarly generated offset intervals, as was also done in the previous section. Again we note that when the input bandwidth is small compared to the sample rate, the window is more efficiently applied as a convolution in the frequency domain than as a product in the time domain.

We also note that the bandwidth and/or center frequency of the spectral weighting applied to the spectral noise samples can be slowly varying functions of time. This allows us to generate nonstationary signals with arbitrary spectral descriptions. For example, we can generate samples of a narrowband time series with a slowly shifting center frequency by translating the spectral window by an appropriate interval on successive IDFT inputs. The sample points of the spectrum in the translating window are fixed at the positions of the DFT coefficients $X(k)$. The translation of the window is synthesized by positioning the center of the mainlobe at the desired spectral position and scaling the $X(k)$ in the window according to the window amplitude at point k. Figure 8.41 demonstrates the shift and resample operation required to move a narrowband process.

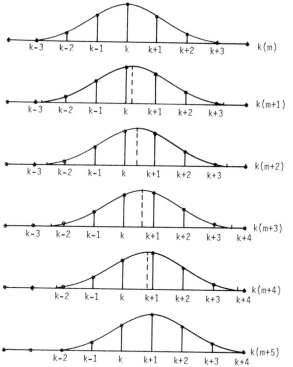

Fig. 8.41. Samples of a sliding spectral window at times $m, m + 1, \ldots, m + 5$.

Bear in mind that the amount of spectral shift per transform must be less than the effective width of the spectral window. For the 4:1 overlapped (low sidelobe level) merging windows of total width 4 bins, the effective width (ENBW) is approximately one bin or f_s/N. The time interval between inverse transforms for 4:1 overlap is $N/4$. Thus the maximum rate of spectral shift is bounded by

$$\frac{\Delta f_{max}}{\text{sample}} = \frac{f_s/N}{N/4} = \frac{4f_s}{N^2} \tag{8.39}$$

The parameter to adjust to obtain higher rates of spectral shift for a given sample rate is the transform length N. For instance, at a sample rate of 500 Hz a transform length of 512 would allow synthesis of a slow frequency shift of 7.6 mHz/s, and 256-point and 128-point transforms would allow frequency shifts of 30.5 and 122 mHz/s, respectively.

Special Function Generators 1

In the previous section we described how to form random signals with specified (possibly time-varying) spectra. We also can use the same technique to construct deterministic signals with specific spectral or time domain attributes. One such signal is a slowly varying sinusoid. The technique described at the end of the previous section is directly applied to this task. The only modification results from the need to eliminate the random amplitude and phase due to the Gaussian random variables that are scaled by the shifting spectral window. To eliminate the random amplitude, we directly use the amplitude of the window values with a single arbitrary phase (such as zero phase). A time-evolving (and bin-number-dependent) phase shift is also applied to the spectral bins to reflect the time shift of the overlapped time intervals. This evolving phase term must also reflect the frequency shift of a sliding tone. The spectral description of a sliding tone is given by

$$F(k, m) = \sum_{n=0}^{N-1} W(n) f\left[n + m\left(\frac{N}{4}\right) \right] e^{-j(2\pi/N)nk} \qquad (8.40a)$$

where

$$f\left[n + m\left(\frac{N}{4}\right) \right] = e^{j(2\pi/N)[n + m(N/4)][k + \Delta km(N/4)]} \qquad (8.40b)$$

Therefore,

$$F(k, m) = \sum_{n=0}^{N-1} W(n) e^{j(2\pi/N)[n + m(N/4)][k + \Delta km(N/4)]} e^{-j(2\pi/N)nk} \qquad (8.40c)$$

$$F(k, m) = e^{j(\pi/2)mk} e^{j(\pi/2)\Delta km^2(N/4)} \sum_{n=0}^{N-1} W(n) e^{-j(2\pi/N)m\Delta k(N/4)} \qquad (8.40d)$$

where we assume the tone is shifting Δk bins per $N/4$ input points, so it appears to be stationary over each block interval. The overlapped merging operation, which follows the block generation, modifies the spectra so that they are nonstationary per sample (as opposed to per block). The first phase term in Eq. (8.40d) is the bin-dependent phase rotation applied to each bin to reflect the shifting time origin for successive time intervals. This was described in Section II.F, particularly in Table IV. The second phase term is a constant phase angle (i.e., independent of frequency index k but quadratic with block index m) applied to each spectral bin to reflect the shifting offset of the spectral peak. The summation is the DFT of the offset window, from which we obtain the offset samples shown in Fig. 8.41. Note that the quadratic phase term that evolves with the block index m is the phase coupling (or correlation) between successive output blocks to reflect the slowly shifting sinusoid.

We have seen two examples of signal generation for which spectral phase control is required (e.g., randomized or correlated) to form a desired time series. We now observe that by using various combinations of random or correlated phase between adjacent spectral bins as well as between successive spectral realizations, we can form significantly different time domain envelopes for a given power spectrum. As one example, we can generate a broadband time series that looks like random noise but has an absolutely flat power spectrum. This signal is called *synchronous noise*. The magnitudes of its nonzero spectral components are identical (note that this is much stronger than saying that the expected value of the magnitudes are identical). To generate this signal, we load a constant (say N) into an array corresponding to the nonzero spectral bins of an IDFT. The IDFT of this spectrum is the Dirichlet kernel, which has a high *crest factor* (ratio of peak to rms value). To reduce the crest factor, we uniformly randomize the phase of the spectral terms. This entails calls to a scaled random-number generator yielding uniformly distributed outputs on $(0, 1)$ (scaling factor is 2π) followed by cosine and sine functions to effect a complex spectral component. The resultant time series generated by an IDFT has an approximately Gaussian density function and a crest factor very close to 3.0. This signal is useful as a test signal (to probe filters, for instance) because it has the structure of a white noise sequence but does not require the ensemble averaging we usually associate with white noise testing of systems to obtain low-variance (high-degree-of-freedom) spectral estimates.

As another example, rather than randomize the phase of adjacent spectral bins to control the time domain crest factor, we can correlate the phase and actually achieve tighter control of the crest factor. We can apply a quadratic phase term to successive spectral bins to synthesize a linear FM sweep over the data interval. The quadratic phase for the kth spectral bin for a flat power spectrum is

$$\theta(k) = \theta(0) + \left(\frac{\pi}{N}\right)k^2, \qquad k = -\frac{N}{2} + 1, \ldots, 1, 0, +1, \ldots, +\frac{N}{2} \quad (8.41a)$$

where $\theta(0)$ is an arbitrary phase factor. If the power spectrum is not flat, the phase terms for each bin must reflect the relative power in that bin, as indicated in Eq. (8.41b).

$$\theta(k) = \theta(0) + \frac{2\pi}{P}\sum_{n=0}^{k-1}(k-n)p(k) \qquad (8.41b)$$

$$P = \sum_{k=0}^{N-1}p(k).$$

If the bin-dependent power $p(k)$ in Eq. (8.41b) is a constant, then Eq. (8.41b) simplifies (within a linear phase-term) to Eq. (8.41a). The resultant FM signal has a peak-to-rms ratio of $\sqrt{2}$, which is the crest factor of a sinusoid. The crest factor of the time function can be varied by replacing the scale factor π in Eq. (8.41) with a smaller (or larger) angle. Smaller angles move the time series toward the Dirichlet kernel, and larger angles move the time series toward noiselike sequences. Control over crest factor for a given power spectrum is useful for generating the drive signals of random shaker control systems. In this application large crest factors are avoided to prevent transducer clipping for high input power levels.

V SUMMARY

In this chapter we have reviewed ways to use the DFT for time domain signal processing and signal generation. We have shown how to synthesize the output of a desampled bank of narrowband filters with the DFT. This processing is equivalent to converting a frequency-division-multiplexed signal to a time-division-multiplexed signal; hence it is called transmultiplexing. We took care to describe those design considerations needed to control crosstalk between channels, dynamic range of the channels, and aliasing under the resampling operation.

We then reviewed the process of fast convolution via the DFT and showed how linear convolution is performed with the circular convolver through overlap block processing. A slight modification of the fast convolution technique led us to fast interpolators. As indicated in Chapter 3, the interpolation process is useful for increasing the sample rate of a data set.

One additional modification of the interpolator and fast convolution method led us to use the DFT as a versatile and efficient signal generator. Signals with specified but arbitrary power spectra can be generated by this method. This includes any mix of stationary, nonstationary, stochastic, or deterministic attributes in the signal. Further, we showed how certain constraints on the envelope of the time series could be accommodated by controlling the phase of the spectrum being processed.

REFERENCES

1. J. B. Allen and L. R. Rabiner, A unified approach to short-time Fourier analysis and synthesis, *Proc. IEEE* **65**, 1558–1564 (November 1977).
2. V. K. Jain and R. E. Crochiere, A novel approach to the design of analysis/Synthesis filter banks, *Proc. 1983, IEEE Int. Conf. Acoust. Speech Signal Process.*, April 1983.
3. E. Paulus, A fast convolution procedure for discrete short-time spectral analysis with frequency dependent resolution, *IEEE Trans. Speech Signal Process.* **ASSP-32**, 1100–1104 (October 1984).
4. E. A. Ferrara, Frequency-Domain Implementation of Periodically Time Varying Filters, *IEEE Trans. Acoust. Speech Signal Process.* **ASSP-33**, 883–892 (August 1985).
5. M. Bellanger and J. L. Daguet, TDM–FDM transmultiplexer; Digital polyphase and FFT, *IEEE Trans. Commun.* **COM-22**, 1199–1205 (September 1974).
6. IEEE, Special issue on TDM–FDM conversion, *IEEE Trans. Commun.* **COM-26**, No. 5 (May 1978).
7. M. J. Narasimha and A. Peterson, Design of a 24-channel transmultiplexer, *IEEE Trans. Speech Signal Process.* **ASSP-27**, 752–761 (December 1979).
8. H. Scheuermann and H. Gockler, A comprehensive survey of digital transmultiplexing methods, *Proc. IEEE* **69**, 1419–1450 (November 1981).
9. IEEE, Special issue on transmultiplexers, *IEEE Trans. Commun.* **COM-30**, No. 7 (July 1982).
10. F. J. Harris, The discrete Fourier transform applied to time domain signal processing, *IEEE Comm. Mag.* 13–22 (May 1982).
11. D. F. Elliott and K. R. Rao, *Fast Transforms: Algorithms, Analyses, and Applications*, Academic Press, New York, 1982.

12. A. V. Oppenheim and R. W. Schafer, *Digital Signal Processing*, Prentice-Hall, Englewood Cliffs, N.J., 1975.
13. L. R. Rabiner and R. W. Schafer, *Digital Processing of Speech Signals*, Prentice-Hall, Englewood Cliffs, N.J., 1978.
14. F. J. Harris, Convolution, correlation, and narrowband filtering with the fast Fourier transform, *IEEE–ESIME Conf., Semana de la Ingenieria en Comunicaciones Electricas*, Mexico City, (July 1980).
15. R. W. Schafer and L. R. Rabiner, Design and simulation of a speech analysis-synthesis system based on short-time Fourier analysis, *IEEE Trans. Audio Electroacoust.* **AU-21,** 165–174 (June 1973).
16. M. R. Portnoff, Implementation of the digital phase vocoder using the fast Fourier transform, *IEEE Trans. Speech Signal Process.* **ASSP-24,** 243–247 (June 1976).
17. J. B. Allen, Short Term Spectral Analysis, Synthesis, and Modification by discrete Fourier transform, *IEEE Trans. Speech Signal Process.* **ASSP-25,** 235–238 (June 1977).
18. M. R. Portnoff, time–frequency representation of digital signals and systems based on short-time Fourier analysis, *IEEE Trans. Acoust. Speech Signal Process.* **ASSP-28,** 55–69 (February 1980).
19. R. E. Crochiere, A weighted overlap-add method of Fourier analysis/synthesis, *IEEE Trans. Acoust. Speech Signal Process.* **ASSP-28,** 99–102 (February 1980).
20. F. J. Harris, On the use of merged overlapped, and windowed FFT's to generate synthetic time series data with a specified power spectrum, *Sixteenth Annual Asilomar Conf. Circuits, Systems, and Computers,* 8–10 (November 1982).

Chapter **9**
Spectral Analysis

JAMES A. CADZOW
Department of Electrical and Computer Engineering
Arizona State University
Tempe, Arizona 85287

INTRODUCTION   **I**

In such varied applications as radar Doppler processing adaptive filtering, speech processing, underwater acoustics, seismology, econometrics, spectral estimation, and array processing, we want to estimate the statistical characteristics of a wide-sense stationary (WSS) time series. More often than not, this required characterization is embodied in the WSS time series' underlying *autocorrelation lag sequence* as specified by [see (1.117)]

$$r_{xx}(n) = E\{x(m)x^*(n-m)\} = E\{x(n+m)x^*(m)\} \qquad (9.1)$$

in which the symbols E and $*$ denote the operations of expectation and complex conjugation, respectively. From this definition the complex conjugate symmetric property possessed by the autocorrelation sequence [i.e., $r_{xx}^*(-n) = r_{xx}(n)$] is readily established (see Section IX.B in Chapter 1). We will automatically invoke this property whenever negative-lag autocorrelation elements (or their estimates) are required.

The second-order statistical characterization as represented by the autocorrelation sequence may be given an equivalent frequency domain interpretation. Namely, upon taking the discrete time Fourier transform (DTFT) of the autocorrelation sequence, that is,

$$S_{xx}(e^{j\omega}) = \sum_{n=-\infty}^{\infty} r_{xx}(n)e^{-jn\omega} \qquad (9.2)$$

we obtain the associated *power spectral density function* (PSD) $S_{xx}(e^{j\omega})$ where the normalized frequency variable is denoted by ω. The spectral density function possesses the salient properties of being a positive semidefinite, even (if the time

701

HANDBOOK OF DIGITAL SIGNAL PROCESSING

series is real valued), periodic function of ω (Table VII in Chapter 1). This function has a Fourier series interpretation in which the autocorrelation lags play the role of the Fourier coefficients. It therefore follows that these coefficients may be determined from the spectral density function through the Fourier series coefficient integral expression

$$r_{xx}(n) = \frac{1}{2\pi} \int_{-\pi}^{\pi} S_{xx}(e^{j\omega}) e^{j\omega} \, d\omega \tag{9.3}$$

Relationships (9.2) and (9.3) form a Fourier transform pair, so knowledge of the autocorrelation sequence is equivalent to knowledge of the spectral density function, and vice versa. We belabor this point to establish the viewpoint that spectral estimation and autocorrelation lag estimation are conceptually equivalent concepts. In this chapter we briefly explore issues that are central to estimating spectral density functions from time series observations.

II RATIONAL SPECTRAL MODELS

In the classical spectral estimation problem we want to estimate the underlying PSD function, with this estimate based on a finite set of time series observations. Typically, these observations are composed of a set of contiguous data measurements taken at equispaced time intervals T, as represented by

$$x(0), x(1), \ldots, x(N-1) \tag{9.4}$$

where N is called the data length, in which the sampling period T argument has been suppressed. Unless some constraints are imposed on the basic nature of the PSD function, there exists a fundamental incompatibility in seeking an estimate of the infinite-parameter spectral function [Eq. (9.2)] (i.e., the infinite set of autocorrelation lag parameters) based on the finite set of observations [Eq. (9.4)]. Investigators have often resolved this dilemma by postulating a finite-parameter model for the spectral density function. The time series observations [Eq. (9.4)] are then used to fix the parameters of this parametric model by an appropriate estimation procedure.

Without doubt, the most widely used the studied of finite parametric models are the so-called rational models. When employing a rational model, we are seeking to approximate the generally infinite series expansion [Eq. (9.2)] by a magnitude-squared ratio of polynomials in the variable $e^{-j\omega}$, that is,

$$S(e^{j\omega}) = \left| \frac{b_0 + b_1 e^{-j\omega} + \cdots + b_q e^{-jq\omega}}{1 + a_1 e^{-j\omega} + \cdots + a_p e^{-jp\omega}} \right|^2 . \tag{9.5}$$

The finite number of a_k and b_k parameters in this model then provides the mechanism for circumventing the aforementioned parameter mismatch dilemma. Namely, if the data length parameter N adequately exceeds this rational function's number of parameters (i.e., $N \gg p + q + 1$), then it is feasible to utilize the given time series observations [Eq. (9.4)] to estimate values for these parameters. A few words are now appropriate concerning the adequacy of rational models in representing power spectral density functions. It is known that if a spectral density function is a continuous function of ω, then it may be approximated arbitrarily closely by a rational function of form Eq. (9.5) if the order parameters p and q are selected suitably large [1]. Comforted by this knowledge, engineers have made rational functions a standard tool in spectral estimation.

W now consider three classes of rational spectral density functions and give a brief historical perspective of their usage in spectral estimation theory. The first two classes are commonly referred to as the moving average (MA) and the autoregressive (AR) spectral models. An MA model is defined to be a rational function (9.5) in which all the a_k parameters are zero (i.e., it has only numerator dynamics); an AR model is one for which all the b_k parameters are zero except for b_0 (i.e., it has only denominator dynamics). By and large, these two classes of rational functions have formed the basic modeling tools in contemporary spectral estimation theory. The more general ARMA model Eq. (9.5), however, is receiving an increasing amount of attention. A schematic representation of the types of spectral estimation procedures to be developed is shown in Fig. 9.1.

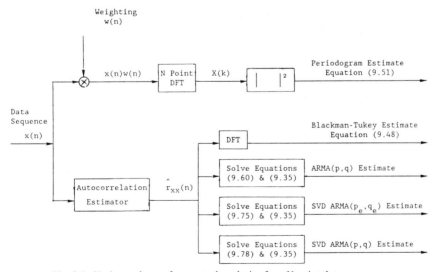

Fig. 9.1. Various schemes for spectral analysis of an N-point data sequence.

A MA Model

A spectral model is said to be an MA *model of order q* [i.e., MA(q)] if it may be put into the form

$$S_{MA}(e^{j\omega}) = |b_0 + b_1 e^{-j\omega} + \cdots + b_q e^{-j\omega}|^2 = |B_q(e^{j\omega})|^2. \qquad (9.6)$$

The $q + 1$ parameters $b_0, b_1, \ldots, b_q$ that identify this MA(q) model are seen to form a qth-order polynomial $B_q(e^{j\omega})$ in the variable $e^{-j\omega}$. An MA model is then a special case of the more general rational model Eq. (9.5), in which the denominator has been set equal to unity.

If the polynomial constituting the MA model [Eq. (9.6)] is factored, it is possible to provide additional insight into an MA model's properties. This factorization leads to the equivalent representation

$$S_{MA}(e^{j\omega}) = |b_0|^2 \prod_{k=1}^{q} (1 - z_k e^{-j\omega})(1 - \bar{z}_k e^{j\omega}) \qquad (9.7)$$

in which z_k are the roots of the polynomial $B_q(z)$. The zeros of an MA spectral model occur in reciprocal pairs. Due to the basic nature of this factorization, MA models are also commonly referred to as *all-zero* models. If any of the roots z_k are close to the unit circle (i.e., $z_k \approx e^{j\omega_k}$), it is clear that $S_{MA}(e^{j\omega})$ will then contain sharply defined notches at frequencies in a neighborhood associated with these roots (i.e., at $\omega = \omega_k$). Thus MA models are particularly effective when approximating spectra that contain sharply defined notches (zerolike behavior) but not sharply defined peaks. Whenever a spectrum contains sharply defined peaks, it is possible to simulate their effect at the cost of many additional zeros (i.e., a high MA order) for an adequate representation. With this is mind, MA models should normally be avoided whenever a peaky-type behavior in the underlying spectrum is suspected (i.e., narrowband sources).

Fourier analysis has played a primary role in much of the earlier, as well as more recent, efforts at spectrally characterizing experimentally collected data. For example, Schuster developed the periodogram method for detecting hidden periodicities in sunspot activity data at the turn of the century [2]. In a more recent classical work, Blackman and Tukey presented a generalized procedure for effecting spectral estimates [3]. This involved the two-step procedure of (i) determining autocorrelation lag estimates $\hat{r}_{xx}(n)$ using the provided data and (ii) taking the Fourier transform of these estimates.[‡] The PSD estimate which this approach yields takes the form

$$\hat{S}_{xx}(e^{j\omega}) = \sum_{n=-q}^{q} w(n)\hat{r}_{xx}(n)e^{-j\omega n} \qquad (9.8)$$

[‡] We shall hereafter use the caret symbol (ˆ) to denote a statistical estimate.

where $w(n)$ is a symmetric *data sequence window* chosen to achieve various desirable effects such as sidelobe reduction. This window is often selected to be rectangular, in which case $w(n) = 1$, although other choices may be more suitable for the application. Descriptions of some popular choices for the data window can be found in signal processing texts (e.g., see [4–6]).

In the Blackman–Tukey estimate, (9.8), only a finite number of summand terms (i.e., $2q + 1$) are involved in the spectral estimate, because only a finite set of autocorrelation lag estimates are obtainable from the observed data set [Eq. (9.4)] if standard lag-estimation methods are employed. Due to this finite sum structure we now show that the Blackman–Tukey estimation method is a special case of the more general rational MA spectral model [Eq. (9.6)].

To establish the fact that the Blackman–Tukey approach to spectral estimation is of an MA structure, we can give yet another equivalent representation to the MA(q) expression [Eq. (9.6)]. This will entail explicitly carrying out the indicated polynomial product $B_q(e^{j\omega}) \bar{B}_q(e^{j\omega})$, thereby giving

$$S_{\text{MA}}(e^{j\omega}) = \sum_{n=-q}^{q} c_n e^{-j\omega n} \tag{9.9}$$

in which the complex-conjugate symmetric c_n parameters are related to the original b_n parameters according to

$$c_n = \sum_{k=0}^{q} b_k \bar{b}_{k-n}, \qquad -q \leq n \leq q \tag{9.10}$$

where b_k is taken to be zero outside the set $k \in [0, q]$. Setting the c_n equal to $w(n)\hat{r}_x(n)$ shows that the Blackman–Tukey estimate [Eq. (9.8)] is a special-form MA(q) model. This fact is usually overlooked by investigators who have considered the Blackman–Tukey method as well as the periodogram method as nonparametric spectral estimators. When viewed from our approach here, however, we can recognize each of these procedures as a realization of an MA parametric model.

AR Model   B

When we compare the MA(q) spectral model expression [Eq. (9.9)] with the theoretical PSD function [Eq. (9.2)] being estimated, we see that a serious modeling mismatch can occur whenever the underlying autocorrelation lags are such that the $r_x(n)$ are not approximately equal to zero for $n > q$. In recognition of this potential shortcoming of MA models, investigators have examined alternative rational spectral models that do not invoke the unnecessarily harsh requirement of a truncated autocorrelation lag behavior. Undoubtedly, the most widely used of such models is the AR model. A spectral model is an AR model of order p [i.e., $AR(p)$] if it may be put into the form

$$S_{AR}(e^{j\omega}) = \left| \frac{b_0}{1 + a_1 e^{-j\omega} + a_2 e^{-j2\omega} + \cdots + a_p e^{-jp\omega}} \right|^2$$

$$= \frac{|b_0|^2}{|A_p(e^{j\omega})|^2} \tag{9.11}$$

This $AR(p)$ model has a functional behavior completely characterized by its $p + 1$ parameters $b_0, a_1, a_2, \ldots, a_p$. The characteristic pth-order polynomial $A_p(e^{j\omega})$ influences the frequency behavior of the estimate, and b_0 controls the level.

As in the MA model, we gain valuable insight into the capabilities of AR modeling by factoring the polynomial $A_p(e^{j\omega})$. We get the equivalent representation.

$$S_{AR}(e^{j\omega}) = \frac{|b_0|^2}{\displaystyle\prod_{k=1}^{p} (1 - p_k e^{-j\omega})(1 - \bar{p}_k e^{j\omega})} \tag{9.12}$$

where p_k are the roots of $A_p(z)$. The poles of this AR spectral model occur in reciprocal pairs. The $AR(p)$ spectral model is also commonly called an all-pole model. As such, it is particularly appropriate for modeling spectra with sharply defined peaks (polelike behavior) but not sharply defined notches. If a spectrum does possess notches, however, it is possible to simulate their effect at the cost of many additional poles (i.e., a high-AR order). In terms of parameter parsimony it is therefore prudent to avoid AR models whenever notches in the underlying spectrum are suspected.

AR models first were used by Yule [7] and Walker [8] to forecast trends of economically based time series. These models were employed by Burg [9] in 1967 and Parzen [10] in 1968 to achieve spectral estimates that did not possess the aforementioned deficiencies of the MA model. The Burg method is of particular interest, since it offered new insight into spectral modeling and introduced concepts that are now standard tools of spectral estimation. This included an efficient lattice-structured implementation of the Burg method, which has since been examined and advanced by many investigators (e.g., see [11]). It is not an exaggeration to say that Burg's method gave rise to a literal explosion in research activity directed toward evolving improved rational modeling methods.

C   ARMA Models

In many applications the underlying spectral density function contains both notchlike and peaklike behavior. As such, neither the MA nor the AR model is an appropriate model representation from a parameter parsimony viewpoint. The more general rational model [Eq. (9.5)], however, is capable of efficiently representing such behavior. This most general rational model is commonly referred to as an ARMA *model* of order (p, q) [i.e., ARMA(p, q)] and its frequency characterization is

$$S_{\text{ARMA}}(e^{j\omega}) = \left|\frac{b_0 + b_1 e^{-j\omega} + \cdots + b_q e^{-jq\omega}}{1 + a_1 e^{-j\omega} + \cdots + a_p e^{-jp\omega}}\right|^2 = \left|\frac{B_q(e^{j\omega})}{A_p(e^{j\omega})}\right|^2 \tag{9.13}$$

An ARMA model has a frequency characterization that is the composite of an MA model and an AR model. To further reinforce this interpretation, we have the following equivalent representation after factoring the polynomials $A_p(e^{j\omega})$ and $B_q(e^{j\omega})$ which characterize its frequency behavior:

$$S_{\text{ARMA}}(e^{j\omega}) = |b_0|^2 \frac{\displaystyle\prod_{k=1}^{q} (1 - z_k e^{-j\omega})(1 - \bar{z}_k e^{j\omega})}{\displaystyle\prod_{k=1}^{p} (1 - p_k e^{-j\omega})(1 - \bar{p}_k e^{j\omega})} \tag{9.14}$$

An ARMA model has q zeros and p poles; therefore it is generally a much more effective model than are its more specialized MA (all-zero) and AR (all-pole) model counterparts. These poles and zeros occur in reciprocal pairs. Although ARMA models are the preferred choice for various applications, many practitioners use the more specialized MA or AR models. There is an increasing awareness, however, of the general usefulness of ARMA modeling.

RATIONAL MODELING: EXACT AUTOCORRELATION KNOWLEDGE   III

In this section the theoretical autocorrelation characteristics of MA, AR, and ARMA random processes are examined separately. This characterization, in turn, enables us to intelligently select the most appropriate rational model that best represents a given set of exact autocorrelation lags

$$r_{xx}(0), r_{xx}(1), \ldots, r_{xx}(s) \tag{9.15}$$

Moreover, we develop a systematic procedure for identifying the selected model's parameters from these given autocorrelation lag values. Although our assumption of exact autocorrelation information is highly idealistic and almost never met in applications, the insight provided is helpful when we consider the more practical problem of generating rational model estimates from raw time series observations.

To begin this analysis, we hereafter assume that the time series under examination is generated (or can be adequately modeled) as the response associated with a linear operator

$$x(n) = \sum_{k=1}^{p} a_k x(n - k) = \sum_{k=0}^{q} b_k \epsilon(n - k) \tag{9.16}$$

in which the unobserved excitation time series $\{\epsilon(n)\}$ is taken to be a sequence of zero-mean, unit-variance, uncorrelated random variables (i.e., normalized white noise). This excitation–response behavior is depicted in Fig. 9.2. Taking the z-transform of Eq. (9.16), setting $z = e^{j\omega}$, and using the fact that the PSD of white noise is unity shows that the PSD function associated with the response time series is given by the ARMA(p,q) rational form

$$S_{xx}(e^{j\omega}) = \left| \frac{b_0 + b_1 e^{-j\omega} + \cdots + b_q e^{-jq\omega}}{1 + a_1 e^{-j\omega} + \cdots + a_p e^{-jp\omega}} \right|^2$$

Thus there is an equivalency between an assumed ARMA(p,q) spectral model and the response of the recursive linear operator [Eq. (9.16)] to white noise. In this section we use the required rational modeling to develop the time series description [Eq. (9.16)] and its associated autocorrelation characterization. Most available rational spectral estimation techniques are based on such a time domain characterization.

The mechanism for effecting the required rational modeling is the *Yule–Walker equations*, which govern linear relationship [Eq. (9.16)]: multiplying both sides of Eq. (9.16) by $\bar{x}(n - m)$ and taking expected values gives the Yule–Walker equations

$$\sum_{k=0}^{p} a_k r_{xx}(n - k) = \sum_{i=0}^{q} b_i \bar{h}(i - n) \tag{9.17}$$

where $a_0 = 1$. The entity $h(n)$ appearing in this expression corresponds to the unit-impulse (i.e., Kronecker delta) response of the linear system operator corresponding to the system given by (9.16). This unit-impulse response may also be interpreted as the inverse Fourier transform of the linear operator's frequency response $B_q(e^{j\omega})/A_p(e^{j\omega})$. In the following we assume that this linear operator is *causal*, which implies that $h(n) = 0$ for n negative. Although this assumption is not essential in the analysis, we impose it because most applications are inherently involved with causal operations. Adaption to the case where noncausal operations are more appropriate is straightforward and is not given. We now investigate the behavior of the Yule–Walker equations for the special case MA and AR models.

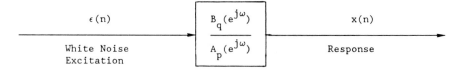

Fig. 9.2. Model of WSS rational time series.

The time series $\{x(n)\}$ is an MA random process if it is generated according to the linear nonrecursive relationship

$$x(n) = \sum_{k=0}^{q} b_k \epsilon(n - k) \tag{9.18}$$

where $\{\epsilon(n)\}$ is the aforementioned normalized white noise excitation process. According to the general Yule–Walker Eq. (9.17), the response's autocorrelation sequence is therefore specified by

$$r_{xx}(n) = \begin{cases} \sum_{k=0}^{q} b_k \bar{b}_{k-n}, & -q \le n \le q \\ 0, & \text{otherwise} \end{cases} \tag{9.19}$$

where we used the facts that $a_k = 0$ for $1 \le k \le p$ and $h(n) = b_n$ for $0 \le n \le q$. Thus the autocorrelation sequence associated with an MA process has finite length (i.e., $2q + 1$), with the length identifying the order of the MA(q) process.

We now consider the problem of identifying the MA parameters b_k that correspond to a given length-$(2q + 1)$ autocorrelation sequence $r_{xx}(n)$ for $-q \le n \le q$. We do this by examining the spectral density function associated with this truncated autocorrelation sequence. After taking the z-transform of the given length-$(2q + 1)$ autocorrelation sequence given by Eq. (9.19), we have

$$S_{xx}(z) = \sum_{n=-q}^{q} r_{xx}(n) z^{-n} = \sum_{n=-q}^{q} \sum_{k=0}^{q} b_k \bar{b}_{k-n} z^{-n} = \sum_{k=0}^{q} b_k z^{-k} \sum_{m=0}^{q} \bar{b}_m z^{m} \tag{9.20}$$

Since the spectral density function $S_{xy}(z)$ has complex-conjugate symmetrical coefficients [i.e., $r_{xx}(-n) = \bar{r}_{xx}(n)$], it follows that the zeros of this function must occur in reciprocal pairs. Therefore we can always factor the spectral density function as

$$S_{xx}(z) = \alpha^2 \prod_{k=1}^{q} (1 - z_k z^{-1})(1 - \bar{z}_k z) \tag{9.21}$$

where α is a real-valued scalar. Comparing Eqs. (9.20) and (9.21), we see that

$$B_q(z) = \sum_{k=0}^{q} b_k z^{-k} = \alpha \prod_{k=1}^{q} (1 - z_k z^{-1}) \tag{9.22}$$

Thus we obtain the required b_k parameter identification by carrying out the multiplications on the right side of Eq. (9.22) and equating coefficients of equal powers of z^{-k}. The most critical step of this identification procedure is the factorization of the known power series $S_{xx}(z)$ as given in Eq. (9.21).

We caution that, although the factorization of $S_{xx}(z)$ into its $2q$ first-order product terms is unique, the decomposition Eq. (9.22) is certainly not, because the roots of $S_x(z)$ occur in reciprocal pairs. Thus $1 - z_1 z^{-1}$ may be replaced by $1 - z_1^{-1} z^{-1}$ in Eq. (9.21) without destroying the required structure [Eq. (9.20)]. This replacement, however, generally leads to a different set of b_k parameters. Since there are typically q different first-order reciprocal pairs in Eq. (9.21), it then follows that there are 2^q different b_n parameter sets compatible with the autocorrelation identity [Eq. (9.19)]. The one normally chosen corresponds to the *minimum-phase* selection in which the z_k roots used in Eq. (9.22) are selected so that they all have magnitudes less than 1.

B   AR Modeling

The time series $\{x(n)\}$ is an AR process of order p if it is generated according to the recursive relationship

$$x(n) + \sum_{k=1}^{p} a_k x(n-k) = b_0 \epsilon(n)$$

where $\{\epsilon(n)\}$ is a normalized white noise process. The Yule–Walker Eq. (9.17) as they apply to this special model indicate that the AR(p) autocorrelation elements are related by

$$r_{xx}(n) + \sum_{k=1}^{p} a_k r_{xx}(n-k) = \begin{cases} |b_0|^2, & n = 0 \\ 0, & n \geq 1 \end{cases} \tag{9.23}$$

where we used the facts that $h(0) = b_0$ and $h(n) = 0$ for $n < 0$.

To derive a direct procedure for identifying the AR(p) model's $p + 1$ parameters $a_1, a_2, \ldots, a_p, b_0$ that best represent the set of autocorrelation lag values [Eq. (9.15)], we may evaluate the first $p + 1$ of these governing Yule–Walker equations. In matrix format this evaluation takes the form

$$\begin{bmatrix} r_{xx}(0) & r_{xx}(-1) & \cdots & r_{xx}(-p) \\ r_{xx}(1) & r_{xx}(0) & \cdots & r_{xx}(-p+1) \\ & & \cdots & \\ \vdots & \vdots & \vdots & \vdots \\ r_{xx}(p) & r_{xx}(p-1) & \cdots & r_{xx}(0) \end{bmatrix} \begin{bmatrix} 1 \\ a_1 \\ a_2 \\ \vdots \\ a_p \end{bmatrix} = \begin{bmatrix} |b_0|^2 \\ 0 \\ 0 \\ \vdots \\ 0 \end{bmatrix} \tag{9.24}$$

$$\mathbf{R}_x \mathbf{a} = |b_0|^2 \mathbf{e}_1 \tag{9.25}$$

In Eq. (9.25) $\mathbf{R}_x$ is the $(p + 1) \times (p + 1)$ AR *correlation matrix* with elements

$$R_x(i, j) = r_{xx}(i - j) \qquad \text{for } 1 \leq i, j \leq p + 1 \tag{9.26}$$

and $\mathbf{a}$ is the $(p + 1) \times 1$ augmented *AR parameter vector* with first component equal to 1 (i.e., it is augmented by a leading 1); that is,

$$\mathbf{a} = [1, a_1, a_2, \ldots, a_p]^T \tag{9.27}$$

where e_1 is the $(p + 1) \times 1$ standard basis vector whose elements are all zero except for its first, which is 1, and the superscript T denotes transposition. We obtain the required parameter identification by solving this sytem of $p + 1$ linear equations in $p + 1$ unknowns.[‡] Conceptually, we obtain this solution by solving

$$\mathbf{a} = |b_0|^2 \mathbf{R}_x^{-1} \mathbf{e}_1 \tag{9.28}$$

in which the normalizing coefficient b_0 is selected so that the first component of $\mathbf{a}$ is 1, as required in Eq. (9.27). In this solution procedure we are tacitly assuming the invertibility of the correlation matrix. If the matrix $\mathbf{R}_x$ is singular, however, this invariably implies that the underlying time series is an AR process of order less than p. In this case it is necessary to decrease the order parameter p until $\mathbf{R}_x$ first becomes invertible.

From Eq. (9.24), the resultant $AR(p)$ model parameters are seen to be dependent totally on the first $p + 1$ given autocorrelation lags $r_{xx}(0), r_{xx}(1), \ldots, r_{xx}(p)$. Although the associated AR model has an autocorrelation behavior that perfectly matches these first $p + 1$ lags, it may provide a very poor representation for the remaining given autocorrelation lags $r_{xx}(p + 1)$, $r_{xx}(p + 2), \ldots, r_{xx}(s)$ (which were not used in the parameter identification). To provide a representation for these higher lags by the procedure taken here, we may have to increase the AR model order to s (i.e., $p = s$). In many applications, however, the underlying goal will be that of providing an AR model of relatively low order (i.e., $p \ll s$) that adequately represents the entire set of autocorrelation lags. We shall address this issue shortly.

The system of equations (9.25) also occurs when one solves the optimum one-step predictor problem or uses the maximum entropy principle [4] and [13]. In the one-step predictor problem we went to select the pth-order linear predictor filter parameters a_k so that the prediction

$$\hat{x}(n) = -\sum_{k=1}^{p} a_k x(n - k) \tag{9.29}$$

best approximates $x(n)$ in the sense of minimizing the mean-squared prediction error $E\{|x(n) - \hat{x}(n)|^2\}$. We find the optimum prediction parameters by solving Eq. (9.25) and letting $|b_0|^2$ play the role of the minimum mean-square prediction error. On the other hand, when applying the maximum entropy principle, we tacitly assume that the time series $\{x(n)\}$ is a zero-mean Gaussian process. The objective is to then find a spectral density function $S_{xx}(e^{j\omega})$ that will maximize the entropy measure

$$\int_{-\pi}^{\pi} \log[S_{xx}(e^{j\omega})] \, d\omega \tag{9.30}$$

[‡] As will be discussed in Section IV of Chapter 10, the Levinson–Durbin algorithm provides an elegant procedure for sequentially solving these equations as the order parameter p is incrementally increased [12].

subject to the constraint that this function be consistent with the given set of $p + 1$ autocorrelation lags $r_{xx}(0), r_{xx}(1), \ldots, r_{xx}(p)$ through the Fourier transform relationship (9.3). Maximizing Eq. (9.30) yields an AR process of order p whose parameters are given by Eq. (9.25).

C ARMA Modeling

The time series $\{x(n)\}$ is an ARMA process of order (p, q) if it is generated (or can be modeled) according to the recursive relationship

$$x(n) + \sum_{k=1}^{p} a_k x(n - k) = \sum_{k=0}^{q} b_k \epsilon(n - k) \tag{9.31}$$

in which the excitation sequence $\{\epsilon(n)\}$ is a normalized white noise process. Our task is then to determine values for the a_k and b_k parameters of this model that are most compatible with the given autocorrelation lags [Eq. (9.15)]. We initially assume that these autocorrelation lags are perfectly compatible with an ARMA(p, q) model. The mechanism for identifying the required model parameters is the Yule–Walker Eqs. (9.17), which characterize the above ARMA model. This mechanism yields ARMA parameters that appear in a nonlinear fashion through the system unit-impulse response $h(n)$. If we want a best least squares model, then to generate the optimal a_k, b_k parameters we must solve the highly nonlinear Yule–Walker equations. This usually involves computationally burdensome nonlinear programming algorithms, difficult initial parameter value selection, and the possibilities of convergence, or even nonconvergence, to a local extremum.

If we evaluate the a_k and b_k parameters separately, however, we have far less work. This approach provides a linear solution procedure for the a_k parameters. Although suboptimal in nature, it often provides a near-optimal modeling. The mechanism for this separate parameter evaluation is obtained from the Yule–Walker equations [Eq. (9.17)], which characterize the ARMA model [Eq. (9.31)]. If this model is taken to be causal, it follows that the Yule–Walker equations assume a particularly simple form for indices $n > q$; that is,

$$r_{xx}(n) + \sum_{k=1}^{p} a_k r_{xx}(n - k) = 0 \qquad \text{for } n \geq q + 1 \tag{9.32}$$

We shall refer to this particular subset of the Yule–Walker equations as the *higher-order Yule–Walker* equations. The obvious attractiveness of these equations lies in that they are linear in the a_k parameters.

To determine the a_k AR parameters that are most compatible with the given set of autocorrelation lags [Eq. (9.15)], we first adopt the approach that characterized most recent AR and ARMA modeling methods. In particular, this entails evaluating the first p higher-order Yule–Walker equations (i.e., $q + 1 \leq n \leq$

$q + p$); that is,

$$
\begin{bmatrix}
r_{xx}(q) & r_{xx}(q-1) & \cdots & r_{xx}(q+1-p) \\
r_{xx}(q+1) & r_{xx}(q) & \cdots & r_{xx}(q+2-p) \\
\vdots & \vdots & & \vdots \\
r_{xx}(q+p-1) & r_{xx}(q+p-2) & \cdots & r_{xx}(q)
\end{bmatrix}
\begin{bmatrix}
a_1 \\ a_2 \\ \vdots \\ a_p
\end{bmatrix}
= -
\begin{bmatrix}
r_{xx}(q+1) \\ r_{xx}(q+2) \\ \vdots \\ r_{xx}(q+p)
\end{bmatrix}
$$

$$(9.33)$$

We next solve this linear system of equations for the required a_k AR parameters. There is a simple test for determining the appropriateness of this ARMA(p, q) model selection method: the higher-order Yule–Walker Eqs. (9.32) using the a_k parameters obtained from solving expression (9.33) must be also satisfied over the additional indices $q + p + 1 \leq n \leq s$. If they are not all satisfied, then an ARMA(p, q) model is incompatible with the given autocorrelation lags. One might seek a higher-order ARMA model to rectify this incompatibility.

Once we have determined the AR parameters by solving Eq. (9.33), we then find the MA coefficients. Let the time series $\{x(n)\}$ be conceptually applied to a pth-order nonrecursive filter with transfer function

$$
A_p(z) = 1 + a_1 z^{-1} + \cdots + a_p z^{-p}
$$

whose a_k coefficients correspond to the solution of Eq. (9.33). This filtering produces the *residual time series* $\{s(n)\}$, as depicted in Fig. 9.3, and causes it to be an MA process of order q with a PSD function of $|B_q(e^{j\omega})|^2$, which is evident from Fig. 9.3. This presumes that $\{x(n)\}$ is an ARMA(p, q) process. Computing the length-$(2q + 1)$ autocorrelation sequence of this residual time series yields

$$
r_{ss}(n) =
\begin{cases}
\displaystyle\sum_{k=0}^{p} \sum_{m=0}^{p} a_k \bar{a}_m r_{xx}(n + m - k), & -q \leq n \leq q \\
0, & \text{otherwise}
\end{cases}
\qquad (9.34)
$$

With these computed MA(q) autocorrelation lags, it follows from Eq. (9.19) that the unknown b_k parameters must be such that

$$
r_{ss}(n) = \sum_{k=0}^{p} b_k \bar{b}_{k-n}, \qquad -q \leq n \leq q
\qquad (9.35)
$$

A spectral factorization along the lines mentioned in this section's MA time series subsection then yields the desired b_k parameters, which completes the ARMA model.

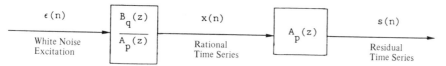

Fig. 9.3. Residual time series generation.

IV OVERDETERMINED EQUATION MODELING APPROACH

In determining the AR parameters (i.e., the a_k) that govern AR and ARMA models, we evaluated the higher-order Yule–Walker equations at the fewest indices n compatible with the model under consideration. To obtain AR parameters that better represent the entire set of given autocorrelation lags [Eq. (9.15)], we find it is generally more effective to use more than the fewest evaluations [14]. To illustrate this approach, let us evaluate the higher-order Yule–Walker Eqs. (9.32) over the enlarged indexed set $q + 1 \le n \le q + t$ where $t \ge p$ in which the s in Eq. (9.15) is set equal to $t + q$. We get the following overdetermined system of t linear equations in the AR parameter unknowns.[‡]

$$\begin{bmatrix} r_{xx}(q+1) & r_{xx}(q) & \cdots & r_{xx}(q-p+1) \\ r_{xx}(q+2) & r_{xx}(q+1) & \cdots & r_{xx}(q-p+2) \\ \cdot & \cdot & \cdots & \cdot \\ \cdot & \cdot & \cdots & \cdot \\ \cdot & \cdot & \cdots & \cdot \\ r_{xx}(q+t) & r_{xx}(q+t-1) & \cdots & r_{xx}(q-p+t) \end{bmatrix} \begin{bmatrix} 1 \\ a_1 \\ a_2 \\ \vdots \\ a_p \end{bmatrix} = \begin{bmatrix} 0 \\ 0 \\ \vdots \\ 0 \end{bmatrix}$$

or

$$\mathbf{R}_1 \mathbf{a} = \mathbf{0} \tag{9.36}$$

where 0 denotes the $t \times 1$ zero vector, $\mathbf{R}_1$ is the $t \times (p + 1)$ ARMA autocorrelation matrix with Toeplitz-type structure having elements

$$R_1(i,j) = r_{xx}(q + 1 + i - j), \qquad 1 \le i \le t, 1 \le j \le p + 1 \tag{9.37}$$

and $\mathbf{a}$ is the $(p + 1) \times 1$ augmented AR parameter vector in which a 1 has been inserted in it first component position: that is,

$$\mathbf{a} = [1, a_1, a_2, \ldots, a_p]^{\mathrm{T}} \tag{9.38}$$

Examination of Eq. (9.36) reveals that the ARMA model's a_k parameters are obtained upon solving a system of t overdetermined (assuming $t > p$) linear equations. Due to the overdetermined nature of these equations, the fundamental question of whether a solution exists naturally arises. The following theorem provides an answer to this question and is a direct result of the higher-order Yule–Walker equations that govern ARMA processes.

Theorem 9.1. If the autocorrelation lag entries used in the $t \times (p + 1)$ correlation matrix $\mathbf{R}_1$ in Eq. (9.36) correspond to those of an ARMA(p_1, q_1) process, then the rank of $\mathbf{R}_1$ is p_1, if that $p \ge p_1, q \ge q_1$, and $t \ge p$.

[‡] In certain applications it may be desirable to use evaluations other than a contiguous set of extended Yule–Walker evaluations.

Hence the existence of a solution to Eq. (9.36) depends on the rank of $\mathbf{R}_1$. We shall now consider separately the cases in which $\mathbf{R}_1$ has less than full rank $(\text{Rank}[\mathbf{R}_1] \leq p)$ and full rank $(\text{Rank}[\mathbf{R}_1] = p + 1)$.

For $\text{Rank}[\mathbf{R}_1] \leq p$ an augmented AR parametric vector solution $\mathbf{a}$ is ensured. We can obtain an interesting algebraic characterization of this solution by premultiplying both sides of Eq. (9.36) by the complex conjugate transpose of R_1 $(\mathbf{R}_1^\dagger)$:

$$\mathbf{R}_1^\dagger \mathbf{R}_1 \mathbf{a} = \mathbf{0} \tag{9.39}$$

Equation (9.39) shows that the required augmented AR parameter vector may be also identified with any properly normalized eigenvector (i.e., its first component is 1) associated with a zero eigenvalue of the $(p + 1) \times (p + 1)$ matrix $\mathbf{R}_1^\dagger \mathbf{R}_1$. As such, we may then use standard eigenvector–eigenvalue routines when finding the required ARMA model AR parameters.

The matrix $\mathbf{R}_1$ has full rank whenever the autocorrelation lag entries used are associated with either a nonrational random time series, an MA process, or a higher-order ARMA rational process. Since $\mathbf{R}_1$ has full rank, there is no nontrivial solution to Eq. (9.36). Nonetheless, we still want an ARMA model that "best fits" these overdetermined extended Yule–Walker equations. Namely, we seek an augmented AR parameter vector $\mathbf{a}$ so that $\mathbf{R}_1 \mathbf{a}$ most closely equals the required ideal zero vector as specified in Eq. (9.36). Although a variety of procedures may be used for accomplishing this selection, the following two approaches typify many spectral estimation algorithms.

1. In the first selection procedure we want to find an augmented AR parameter vector lying on the unit hypersphere that will minimize the Euclidean norm of $\mathbf{R}_1 \mathbf{a}$. We must therefore solve the constrained optimization problem

$$\min_{\mathbf{a}^\dagger \mathbf{a} = 1} \mathbf{a}^\dagger \mathbf{R}_1^\dagger \mathbf{R}_1 \mathbf{a}$$

By standard Lagrange multiplier concepts, we easily solve this problem by selecting an eigenvector of the positive definite Hermitian matrix $\mathbf{R}_1^\dagger \mathbf{R}_1$ associated with its minimum eigenvalue. If $\mathbf{x}_1$ corresponds to such an eigenvector, then the required augmented AR parameter vector with first component 1 is obtained by the normalization

$$\mathbf{a}^0 = [x_1(1)]^{-1} \mathbf{x}_1 \tag{9.40}$$

where $x_1(1)$ denotes the first component of $\mathbf{x}_1$. This AR augmented parameter vector selection procedure characterizes many spectral algorithms that are variants of the Pisarenko method [15].

2. In the second selection procedure we wish to minimize the Euclidean norm of $\mathbf{R}_1 \mathbf{a}$ over all $(p + 1) \times 1$ vectors $\mathbf{a}$ with first components of 1:

$$\min_{a(1) = 1} \mathbf{a}^\dagger \mathbf{R}_1^\dagger \mathbf{R}_1 \mathbf{a}$$

Again appealing to the Lagrange multiplier approach, we solve this problem by solving the linear system

$$\mathbf{R}_1^\dagger \mathbf{R}_1 \mathbf{a}^0 = \alpha \mathbf{e}_1 \qquad (9.41)$$

where the normalized constant α is selected so that the first component of $\mathbf{a}^0$ is 1 and $\mathbf{e}_1$ is the standard basis vector.

In using either procedure, we want to best satisfy Eq. (9.36) in the least squares sense subject to appropriate constraints.[‡] The application dictates which AR parameter vector selection procedure provides the best performance. It has been the author's experience that Eq. (9.40) has often provided reasonable modeling [4]. In terms of computational efficiency and general effectiveness, however, the linear selection Eq. (9.41) is clearly superior due to the availability of efficient adaptive algorithms for its computation. Therefore we shall mainly focus our attention in Section VIII on Eq. (9.41). These ARMA results are also applicable to the special AR modeling problem, in which case we simply enter $q = 0$ when forming the ARMA autocorrelation matrix $\mathbf{R}_1$.

V   DETECTION OF MULTIPLE SINUSOIDS IN WHITE NOISE

The procedures developed in the preceding section are applicable to the task of generating rational models for the general class of WSS time series. To demonstrate the relative effectiveness of MA, AR, and ARMA modeling, we now consider the classical problem of the detection and frequency identification of the sinusoids in white noise time series. Although this does represent a restricted application of rational spectral estimation, it provides a meaningful basis for measuring the relative performance capabilities of MA, AR, and ARMA models. In particular, the time series now being examined is taken to be the sum of m real sinusoids in additive noise, as specified by

$$x(n) = \sum_{k=1}^{m} A_k \sin[2\pi f_k n + \theta_k] + w(n) \qquad (9.42)$$

in which the θ_k are independent, uniformly distributed random variables on the interval $[-\pi, \pi)$, and $w(n)$ is a zero-mean variance σ^2 white noise process. Recall that the problem of detecting sinusoids in noise originally gave rise to spectral estimation theory. The periodogram method was developed for this very purpose by Schuster in 1898 [2].

The task at hand is to generate MA, AR, and ARMA models from the autocorrelation lags associated with this time series using the procedures

---

[‡] It is possible to generalize the constraints to be a quadratic surface (giving rise to a generalized eigenvector solution) or a hyperplane, respectively [16].

outlined in the previous section. The autocorrelation sequence characterizing time series [Eq. (9.42)] is

$$r_{xx}(n) = \sum_{k=1}^{m} 0.5 A_k^2 \cos[2\pi f_k n] + \sigma^2 \delta(n) \tag{9.43}$$

in which $\delta(n)$ denotes the unit-impulse (Kronecker delta) sequence. The spectral density function associated with this process is composed of $2m$ Dirac delta impulses of amplitudes $0.5 A_k^2$ located at frequencies $\pm f_k$ riding on top of a constant value σ^2. As such, this *discontinuous* spectral density function may not be associated with a finite-order MA, AR, or ARMA process. Nonetheless, we may still use such models to achieve estimates for this spectral behavior.

Numerical Example A

To illustrate the effectiveness of rational models for sinusoids embedded in white noise, we now consider the specific time series

$$x(n) = \sin(0.4\pi n + \theta_1) + \cos(0.43\pi n + \theta_2) + w(n) \tag{9.44}$$

The white noise series $\{w(n)\}$ is taken to have a variance of 0.5, thereby creating a 0-dB SNR (signal-to-noise ratio) environment. According to Eq. (9.43), the autocorrelation sequence associated with this time series is

$$r_{xx}(n) = 0.5 \cos(0.4\pi n) + 0.5 \cos(0.43\pi n) + 0.5 \delta(n) \tag{9.45}$$

We shall now use these autocorrelation lags along with the concepts developed in the previous two sections to generate appropriate MA, AR, and ARMA models. We briefly discuss the resultant modeling performances in this idealistic situation.

MA Models 1

When using the classical spectral modeling expression

$$S_{xx}(e^{j\omega}) = \sum_{n=-q}^{q} r_{xx}(n) e^{-j\omega n} \tag{9.46}$$

we are, in effect, invoking an MA(q) model. Plots of this expression with entries [Eq. (9.45)] for model order selections of $q = 32$ and $q = 64$ are shown in Fig. 9.4 over the range normalized frequencies $0 \leq f \leq 0.5$. These results show that a resolution of the two equal-amplitude sinusoids was not achieved for a thirty-second-order MA model but was achieved for a sixty-fourth-order MA model. Thus an artificially high-order MA model was required to resolve the two sinusoids even when exact autocorrelation lags were used. This example nicely demonstrates the difficulties that can occur when we invoke an MA model if the underlying assumption that $r_{xx}(n) = 0$ for $n > q$ thereby implied is not satisfied

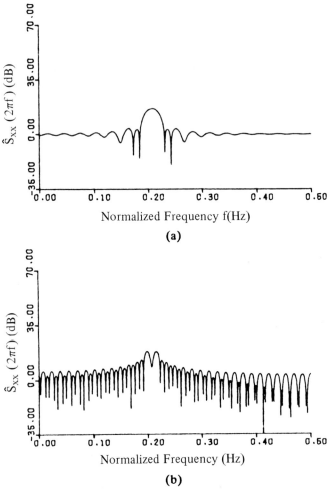

Fig. 9.4. MA spectral models using Eq. (9.46) with exact autocorrelation lags: (a) MA(32) with $q = 32$; (b) MA(64) with $q = 64$.

(or approximately satisfied). Clearly, the nondamped nature of the autocorrelation sequence [Eq. (9.45)] indicates that the MA modeling of a time series composed of sinusoids in white noise can be inappropriate unless a sufficiently large selection of the MA model order q is made.

2   AR Models

We next used the same autocorrelation lag information [Eq. (9.45)] to generate AR models of order $p = 20$ and $p = 24$ after solving the system of AR Eqs. (9.25). The resultant spectral estimates $1/|A_p(e^{j\omega})|^2$ are shown in Fig. 9.5(a),(b) for these

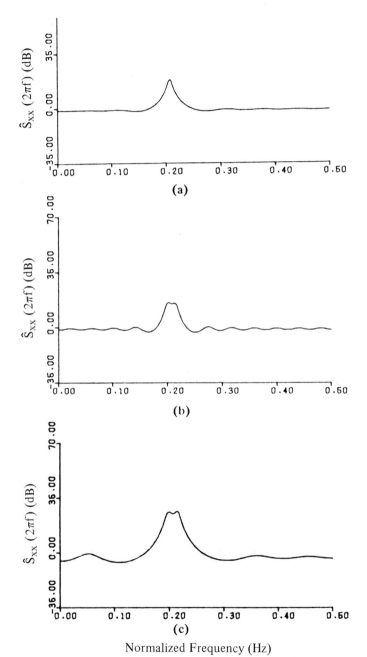

Fig. 9.5. AR spectral models using Eq. (9.25) with exact autocorrelation lags: (a) AR(20) with $p = t = 20$; (b) AR(24) with $p = t = 24$; (c) AR(10) with $p = 10, t = 100$.

two AR models. The twentieth-order model was unable to resolve the two
sinusoids, and the twenty-fourth was just able to achieve a resolution. Since the
specific autocorrelation lags $r_{xx}(n)$ for $0 \leq n \leq p$ were required for generating an
AR(p) model, fewer autocorrelation lags were needed to resolve the two sinusoids
when using an AR(24) model compared to the MA(64) model. This simply gives
credence to the previously made suggestion that AR models provide a more
effective instrument for representing peaklike spectra than do MA models.

To illustrate the effect of using more than the minimal number of higher-order
Yule–Walker equations (i.e., $t > p$) when generating an AR model, we next used
the overdetermined AR modeling Eqs. (9.36) with parameters $p = 10$, $q = 0$, and
$t = 100$. The AR(10) model that we got after solving Eq. (9.41) for this choice of
order parameters has a spectral behavior as depicted in Fig. 9.5(c). This AR(10)
spectral estimate is significantly better than that achieved by the higher-order
AR(24) estimate. Clearly, the process of using 100 (i.e., $t = 100$) higher-order
Yule–Walker equation evaluations instead of the minimal number 10 produced
this improvement.

3   ARMA Models

We next used the given autocorrelation lag information [Eq. (9.45)] to
generate an ARMA(4, 4) model by solving Eq. (9.41) with $p = q = t = 4$. The
resultant ARMA-based spectral estimate $1/|A_4(e^{j\omega})|^2$ without the MA compo-
nent is plotted in Fig. 9.6. The two sinusoids are nicely resolved, and when we
factored the fourth-order polynomial $A_4(e^{j\omega})$, its four roots were located on the
unit circle at $e^{\pm j 2\pi f_k}$ for $k = 1, 2$ in which $f_1 = 0.2$ and $f_2 = 0.215$. This should not
be surprising, since it is well known that an ARMA-type model is perfectly

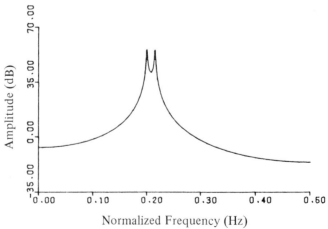

Fig. 9.6. ARMA spectral modeling using Eq. (9.41) with exact autocorrelation lags and $p = t = 4$.

compatible with a sinusoid in white noise time series [14] (MA and AR models are not compatible). Only the autocorrelation lags $r_{xx}(n)$ for $1 \leq n \leq 8$ were required to generate the spectral model shown in Fig. 9.6.

MA MODELING: TIME SERIES OBSERVATIONS   VI

From a practical viewpoint the situation in which exact autocorrelation lag values are given to produce a spectral estimate almost never occurs. More typically, the required spectral estimate is to be generated from a finite set of contiguous time series observations as represented by

$$x(0), x(1), \ldots, x(N-1) \tag{9.47}$$

In this section we are concerned with achieving MA spectral estimates from this observation set. The methods to be presented for this purpose are largely influenced by the theoretical developments in Section III.

Two popular primary MA spectral estimation procedures *indirect methods* based on first generating autocorrelation estimates from the given data, as proposed by Blackman and Tukey [3], and *direct methods* based on Fourier transforming the given data. Direct methods are represented by the periodogram (or the method of averaged periodograms due to Welch [17]). As we will shortly see, the periodogram is a special case of the Blackman–Tukey approach.

Blackman–Tukey Approach   A

In the Blackman–Tukey method one first obtains autocorrelation estimates $\hat{r}_{xx}(n)$ from the given observation set [Eq. (9.47)]. These estimates are then inserted into Eq. (9.8) to give the required spectral estimate. For a variety of reasons it is often beneficial to introduce a data sequence window $w(n)$ to achieve the windowed MA spectral estimate of order q:

$$\hat{S}(e^{j\omega}) = \sum_{n=-q}^{q} w(n)\hat{r}_{xx}(n)e^{-j\omega n} \tag{9.48}$$

Considerations to be made in selecting the window sequence are well documented, and the reader is referred to Chapters 3 and 8 as well as to [4–6]. Two of the more popular selections are the rectangular window (i.e., $w(n) = 1$) and the Bartlett triangle window [i.e., $w(n) = (1 - |n|)/(q + 1)$]. The standard unbiased and biased autocorrelation estimates are among the most popular candidates to be used in the spectral estimate [Eq. (9.48)] (e.g., see [18] for a detailed development).

B Periodogram Approach

The periodogram is defined by

$$\hat{S}_{xx}(e^{j\omega}) = \frac{1}{N}|X_N(e^{j\omega})|^2 \tag{9.49}$$

where $X_N(e^{j\omega})$ is the DTFT of the time series observations (see Chapter 1, Section III); that is,

$$X_N(e^{j\omega}) = \sum_{n=0}^{N-1} x(n)e^{-jn\omega} \tag{9.50}$$

The subscript N explicitly denotes the dependency of $X_N(e^{j\omega})$ on the observation length parameter. The periodogram is identical to the Blackman–Tukey approach when the standard biased autocorrelation estimates are used in Eq. (9.48) with $q = N - 1$ and $w(n) = 1$.

The primary advantage of the periodogram approach is computational in nature. Specifically, the values of the periodogram at the N discrete set of uniformly spaced radian frequencies $\omega_k = 2\pi k/N$ for $0 \le k \le N - 1$ involve evaluating

$$X_N(e^{j(2\pi k/N)}) = \sum_{n=0}^{N-1} x(n)e^{-j(2\pi kn/N)}, \qquad 0 \le k \le N - 1 \tag{9.51}$$

We easily carry out these evaluations by the N-point fast Fourier transform (FFT) algorithm (see Chapter 7). With the FFT algorithm the N sampled quantities [Eq. (9.51)] may be computed, in which the required number of complex additions and multiplications is of the order $N \log_2 N$. The computational saving is considerable when compared to the direct evaluation of Eq. (9.51), which needs N^2 complex additions and multiplications. Hence spectral estimates of long data sequences became feasible with the FFT's development.

Although the FFT algorithm offers a computationally efficient means for numerically evaluating the periodogram [Eq. (9.49)], it possesses a potentially serious drawback. The FFT implementation provides a sampled version of the periodogram in which the frequency samples are separated by $2\pi/N$ radians. For many applications this sampling may be too coarse in that the detailed continuous-frequency behavior of the periodogram may be somewhat obscured through the sampling proce ss. To alleviate this potential difficulty, we may apply the concept of *zero*-padding whereby we simply append L zeros to the given set of time series observations:

$$x(0), x(1), \ldots, x(N - 1), 0, 0, \ldots, 0 \tag{9.52}$$

where L is a yet unspecified positive integer. If we were to take the Fourier transform of this padded time series, we would obtain the same transform [Eq. (9.50)] and therefore the same periodogram function [Eq. (9.49)]. On the other hand, if we were to take an $(N + L)$-point FFT of this padded time series, the following more finely spaced samples of the Fourier transform would be generated:

$$X_N(e^{j(2\pi k/(N+L))}) = \sum_{n=0}^{N-1} x(n)e^{-j(2\pi kn/(N+L))}, \qquad 0 \le k < N + L \qquad (9.53)$$

If these sampled values were then substituted into Eq. (9.49), we would obtain sampled values of the periodogram at the more finely spaced frequencies $\omega_k = 2\pi/(N + L)$ for $\le k < N + L$. The L zero-padding reduces the frequency sampling interval from $2\pi/N$ to $2\pi/(N + L)$. By selecting L suitably large, we can reduce this sampling interval to any degree desirable.

AR MODELING TIME SERIES OBSERVATIONS   VII

The task of generating AR spectral models from a set of time series observations has been of primary concern to many investigators over the last several years. Undoubtedly, the most widely used AR modeling procedure is the Burg algorithm, as first proposed in 1967 [9]. This algorithm not only provided a spectral resolution capability that was theretofore lacking, it also inspired an intense search for improved rational spectral estimation procedures. Much of contemporary spectral estimation theory has been directly influenced by the philosophy of the Burg approach. Many of the more recent rational estimation procedures were developed to oversome some of the deficiencies observed in the Burg spectral estimates, as typified by line splitting and biased frequency estimates. Nonetheless, the Burg algorithm still occupies an important position among contemporary AR modeling methods. Since its operational behavior is so well documented, we refer the interest reader to the relevant literature (e.g., see [13, 19]).

Many of the popularly used AR methods (which include the Burg algorithm) may be interpreted as providing statistical estimates of the fundamental Yule–Walker Eqs. (9.25) that govern AR processes. These estimates are to be obtained from the set of contiguous time series observations

$$x(0), x(1), \ldots, x(N - 1) \qquad (9.54)$$

which are made available through some measurement mechanism. More specifically, it is well known that various contemporary methods either explicitly or implicitly use these observations to generate estimates of the $(p + 1) \times (p + 1)$ autocorrelation matrix $\mathbf{R}_x$ that appears in the fundamental relationship [Eq. (9.25)]. Clearly, the elements of the matrix estimate $\hat{\mathbf{R}}_x$ must be such that

$$\hat{\mathbf{R}}_x(i, j) \text{ is an estimate of } r_{xx}(i - j) \qquad \text{for } 1 \le i, j \le p + 1 \qquad (9.55)$$

Once these estimates have been computed from the given time series observations, the resultant augmented AR parameter vector estimate is, in accordance with Eq. (9.25), given by solving the system of equations

$$\hat{\mathbf{R}}_x \mathbf{a} = |b_0|^2 \mathbf{e}_1 \tag{9.56}$$

in which the normalizing parameter b_0 is selected so that the first component of $\mathbf{a}$ is 1.

The quality of the AR modeling approach as embodied in Eq. (9.56) is critically dependent on the choice of the autocorrelation lag-estimation procedure used. For many applications the standard unbiased autocorrelation estimates typically provide the best selection in terms of spectral estimation performance. The correlation matrix formed from this particular set of estimates is Toeplitz and complex-conjugate symmetric; properties shared by the actual correlation matrix being approximated. Moreover, this estimate is *consistent* in the sense that as N approaches infinity, we have $\hat{\mathbf{R}}_x \to \mathbf{R}_x$ under the second-order ergodic assumption on the underlying time series. In view of all of these favorable qualities it is not surprising that the standard unbiased estimator generally provides excellent AR modeling performance. Since AR models are a special case of the more general ARMA model, we now direct our efforts toward ARMA model estimation.

VIII ARMA MODELING: TIME SERIES OBSERVATIONS

The methods for generating ARMA models based upon time series observations fall into basically two categories: the a_k and b_k parameters are evaluated (i) simultaneously or (ii) separately. In the first category, maximum-likelihood-based techniques are prominent. They include exact maximum-likelihood approaches (e.g., [19]) and least squares methods that approximate the exact likelihood function (e.g., [20, 21]). Although promising optimum modeling, these maximum-likelihood methods involve nonlinear programming solution procedures. As such, these solution procedures are computationally inefficient and suffer the obvious drawbacks associated with nonlinear programming methods. Other techniques in category (i) have been proposed (e.g. [22]). These alternative methods also use nonlinear programming solution procedures.

Because of the obvious shortcomings of nonlinear-programming-based techniques, methods have been proposed that employ a separate evaluation of the AR and MA parameters. With this approach it is generally possible to obtain satisfactory modeling without the drawbacks inherent with nonlinear programming. These techniques usually use the first p higher-order Yule–Walker equations to obtain the a_k estimates in a linear fashion as demonstrated in Eq. (9.33). Unfortunately, the use of the minimal number of higher-order Yule–Walker equations (i.e., p) can cause an undesirable parameter hypersensitivity. Therefore procedures have been proposed for using an overdetermined set of Yule–Walker equation evaluations to decrease this hypersensitivity (e.g., see [14]). We now give a detailed development of the overdetermined equation approach to estimating the a_k parameters of an ARMA model. These estimates are based on the finite set of time series observations

$$x(0), x(1), \ldots, x(N-1) \tag{9.57}$$

In this parameter estimation we seek to incorporate the philosophy embodied in the higher-order Yule–Walker ARMA model Eq. (9.36) for estimating the model's a_k parameters.

The modeling approach uses the given time series observations to generate an estimate of the $t \times (p+1)$ autocorrelation matrix $\mathbf{R}_1$ in Eq. (9.36). Using one of several available procedures, we first compute the autocorrelation lag estimates

$$\hat{R}_1(i, j) = \text{an estimate of } r_{xx}(q+1+i-j), \qquad 1 \le i \le t, 1 \le j \le p+1 \tag{9.58}$$

Regardless of the procedure used, the net result of this first step produces the $t \times (p+1)$ correlation matrix estimate $\hat{\mathbf{R}}_1$. Due to errors inherent in the autocorrelation estimation process, however, this matrix estimate generally has full rank [i.e. $\min(p+1, t)$] instead of the theoretical rank p possessed by the matrix $\mathbf{R}_1$ being estimated [even if the time series is an ARMA(p, q) process]. Therefore it is not generally possible to find an augmented AR parameter vector with first component equal to 1 that satisfies the theoretical relationship $\mathbf{R}_1\mathbf{a} = \mathbf{0}$ as given in Eq. (9.36). As such, the $t \times 1$ higher-order Yule–Walker equation error vector

$$\mathbf{e} = \hat{\mathbf{R}}_1\mathbf{a} \tag{9.59}$$

is generated. In accordance with the theoretical results of Section IV, a logical choice for the augmented AR parameter vector $\mathbf{a}$ is obtained by solving the constrained quadratic model error problem

$$\min_{a(1)=1} \mathbf{a}^\dagger\hat{\mathbf{R}}^\dagger\mathbf{W}\hat{\mathbf{R}}\mathbf{a}$$

in which $\mathbf{W}$ is a $t \times t$ positive semidefinite weighting matrix that is normally chosen to be the identity matrix. Using standard Lagrange multiplier techniques, we obtain the solution to this constrained minimization problem by solving the system of $(p+1) \times (p+1)$ linear equations

$$\hat{\mathbf{R}}_1^\dagger\mathbf{W}\hat{\mathbf{R}}_1\mathbf{a}^0 = \alpha\mathbf{e}_1 \tag{9.60}$$

where α is a normalizing constant selected so that the first component of a^0 is 1, as required. Equation (9.60) constitutes the so-called overdetermined AR parameter vector selection [4, 14]. In effect, we have selected a to best satisfy the theoretical ARMA relationship given by $\mathbf{R}_1\mathbf{a} = \mathbf{0}$. The real advantage of the overdetermined equation model approach is achieved when the integer t is selected to be larger than p. In this case more than the minimal number of extended Yule–Walker equation evaluations (i.e., t instead of p) are being used in fixing the model's p AR coefficients. So it is not surprising that *parameter hypersensitivity* decreases when $t > p$. See the example in Section V. A similar advantage occurs for ARMA models estimated from raw time series observations. In the situation here the integer parameter t is typically selected to lie within the range

$$p \leq t \leq N - q - 1 \tag{9.61}$$

Generally, larger values than the minimum p are preferred for modeling fidelity and parameter desensitization.

To complete the ARMA modeling, we need to compute an estimate for the MA component $|B_q(e^{j\omega})|^2$. A logical procedure is to use correlation lag estimates in the method outlined in Section III as represented by Eqs. (9.34) and (9.35). However, regardless of the procedure used, this MA component estimate is almost always significantly lower in quality than the associated AR component estimate $|\tilde{A}_p(e^{j\omega})|^2$.

IX   ARMA MODELING: A SINGULAR VALUE DECOMPOSITION APPROACH

The important issue of ARMA model order determination has yet to be addressed: in particular, whether we have exact autocorrelation lags or time series observations for effecting the modeling, how should we choose appropriate values for the order parameters p and q? This model order information is implicitly contained in the autocorrelation matrices that characterize ARMA models [4]. In this section we give a procedure for extracting the prerequisite model order values that uses a singular value decomposition of an extended correlation matrix. An important by-product of this procedure is an adaption of the ARMA modeling procedure of the previous section, which significantly improves spectral estimation.

A   Theoretical Considerations

When the ARMA model order parameters are not known a priori, it is judicious to select the initial model order to be much larger than the anticipated order. In particular, let us consider the extended order ARMA (p_e, q_e) model for which p_e is selected to be larger (usually much larger) than the eventual model order. Although we typically do not know p a priori, it is generally possible to make an educated guess of p to ensure that

$$p_e > p \tag{9.62}$$

From Eq. (9.36) it then follows that the $t \times (p_e + 1)$ extended-order autocorrelation matrix associated with this ARMA(p_e, q_e) model may be expressed as

$$\mathbf{R}_e = \begin{bmatrix} r_x(q_e + 1) & r_x(q_e) & \cdots & r_x(q_e - p_e + 1) \\ r_x(q_e + 2) & r_x(q_e + 1) & \cdots & r_x(q_e - p_e + 2) \\ \vdots & \vdots & \vdots & \vdots \\ r_x(q_e + t) & r_x(q_e + t - 1) & \cdots & r_x(q_e - p_e + t) \end{bmatrix} \qquad (9.63)$$

If the autocorrelation lag entries in Eq. (9.63) correspond to an ARMA(p, q) process for which $q_e - p_e \geq q - p$, it then follows from the results of Section IV that the rank of the $t \times (p_e + 1)$ matrix $\mathbf{R}_e$ is p. In arriving at this result, we assume that t is selected to at least equal p. To determine the required order parameter p, we then simply set p equal to the rank of $\mathbf{R}_e$ for the ideal case in which exact autocorrelation lag information is available.

To obtain the ARMA model's $(p + 1) \times 1$ augmented AR parameter vector $\mathbf{a}$ from this extended-order autocorrelation matrix, we can appeal to the theoretical developments of Sections III and IV. In particular, let us consider the set of submatrices of $\mathbf{R}_e$ formed from any of its $p + 1$ contiguous columns. This set of $t \times (p + 1)$ matrices is specified by

$$\mathbf{R}_k = [\text{submatrix of } \mathbf{R}_e \text{ composed of its } k\text{th through}$$
$$p + k\text{th column vectors inclusively}] \qquad \text{for } 1 \leq k \leq p_e - p + 1 \quad (9.64)$$

In accordance with the ARMA model's higher-order Yule–Walker equations, it is readily established that the required unique augmented AR parameter vector $\mathbf{a}$ satisfies the set of homogeneous relationships

$$\mathbf{R}_k \mathbf{a} = \mathbf{0} \qquad \text{for } 1 \leq k \leq p_e - p + 1 \qquad (9.65)$$

where the first component of $\mathbf{a}$ is constrained to be 1. Equation (9.65) provides a matrix representation for the t higher-order Yule–Walker Eqs. (9.32) defined on the specific indices $q_e + 2 - k \leq n \leq q_e + t + 1 - k$. Note that this conclusion is valid only if the correlation lag entries used in forming $\mathbf{R}_e$ correspond to an ARMA(p, q) process, and the order parameters are such that $p_e \geq p$ and $q_e - p_e \geq q - p$. How we use Eq. (9.65) to generate an ARMA(p, q) model is made clear shortly.

We shall now apply this rank characterization of $\mathbf{R}_e$ to the practical problem in which the ARMA modeling is to be based only on the time series observations

$$x(0), x(1), \ldots, x(N - 1) \qquad (9.66)$$

and not an exact autocorrelation lag information. In this case we must first compute autocorrelation lag estimates from these observations. We then substitute these estimates into the matrix format Eq. (9.63) to generate the extended-order correlation matrix estimate $\hat{\mathbf{R}}_e$. Since the autocorrelation lag-estimate entires will be invariably in error, it follows that $\hat{\mathbf{R}}_e$ normally has full rank [i.e., $\min(p_e + 1, t)$] even when the time series under study corresponds to an ARMA(p, q) process. Nonetheless, the *effective rank* of $\hat{\mathbf{R}}_e$ still tends to be p. To better quantify the vague term "effective rank," we introduce the concept of *singular value decomposition* (SVD).

B   Singular Value Decomposition

In a variety of applications the primary objective is to solve a linear system of equations. The matrix associated with this system of equations not only characterizes the desired solution, but it often conveys useful additional information. Hence, it behooves us to examine the salient properties of this characterizing matrix. The singular value decomposition of a matrix, as outlined in the following theorem, serves this role particularly well (e.g., [23]).

Theorem 9.2   Let $\mathbf{A}$ be an $m \times n$ matrix of generally complex-valued elements. This matrix may be equivalently represented as the weighted sum of outer products given by[‡]

$$\mathbf{A} = \sum_{k=1}^{r} \sigma_k \mathbf{u}_k \mathbf{v}_k^{\dagger} \tag{9.67}$$

in which $r = \text{Rank}[\mathbf{A}]$ and the positive scalars σ_k satisfy the eigenrelationships

$$\mathbf{A}\mathbf{A}^{\dagger}\mathbf{u}_k = \sigma_k^2 \mathbf{u}_k, \quad \mathbf{A}^{\dagger}\mathbf{A}\mathbf{v}_k = \sigma_k^2 \mathbf{v}_k, \quad 1 \leq k \leq r$$

where $\mathbf{u}_k$ and $\mathbf{v}_k$ are the $m \times 1$ and $n \times 1$ associated orthonormal eigenvectors [i.e., $\mathbf{u}_k^{\dagger}\mathbf{u}_m = \mathbf{v}_k^{\dagger}\mathbf{v}_m = \delta(k - m)$].

The scalar elements σ_k are commonly referred to as the *singular values* of the matrix $\mathbf{A}$ and are ordered as $\sigma_1 \geq \sigma_2 \geq \cdots \geq \sigma_r > 0$. They convey valuable information about the rank characterization of $\mathbf{A}$, as the following theorem shows.

Theorem 9.3.   The unique $m \times n$ matrix of rank $k \leq \text{Rank}[A]$ that best approximates the $m \times n$ matrix $\mathbf{A}$ in the least squares difference (i.e., Frobenius norm) sense is given by

$$\mathbf{A}^{(k)} = \sum_{i=1}^{k} \sigma_i \mathbf{u}_i \mathbf{v}_i^{\dagger} \tag{9.68}$$

The quality of this optimum approximation [Eq. (9.68)] is given by

$$\|\mathbf{A} - \mathbf{A}^{(k)}\|^2 = \sum_{i=1}^{m} \sum_{j=1}^{n} |a_{ij} - \hat{a}_{ij}|^2$$

$$\sum_{j=k+1}^{r} \sigma_j^2, \quad 0 \leq k \leq n \tag{9.69}$$

where $\mathbf{A}^{(k)} = (\hat{a}_{ij})$.

[‡] The $m \times n$ rank 1 matrix $\mathbf{u}_k \mathbf{v}_k^{\dagger}$ formed from the $m \times 1$ and $n \times 1$ vectors $\mathbf{u}_k$ and $\mathbf{v}_k$, respectively, is called an *outer product*.

The degree to which $\mathbf{A}^{(k)}$ approximates $\mathbf{A}$ depends on the sum of the $r - k$ *smallest singular values squared*. As k approaches r, this sum becomes progressively smaller and eventually goes to zero at $k = r$. To provide a convenient measure for this behavior independent of the size of $\mathbf{A}$, let us consider the *normalized matrix approximation ratio*

$$v(k) = \frac{\|\mathbf{A}^{(k)}\|}{\|\mathbf{A}\|} = \left[\frac{\sigma_1^2 + \sigma_2^2 + \cdots + \sigma_k^2}{\sigma_1^2 + \sigma_2^2 + \cdots + \sigma_r^2}\right]^{1/2}, \qquad 1 \leq k \leq r \qquad (9.70)$$

Clearly, this normalized ratio approaches its maximum value of 1 as k approaches r. For matrices of low effective rank, $v(k)$ is close to 1 for values of k significantly smaller than r. On the other hand, matrices for which m must take on high values (i.e., $k \approx r$) to achieve a $v(k)$ near 1 are said to be of high effective rank.

Application of SVD to ARMA Modeling   C

To determine the required order for an ARMA model, we shall now make an SVD of the $tx(p_e + 1)$ extended-order correlation matrix estimate of form Eq. (9.63), that is,

$$\mathbf{R}_e = \sum_{k=1}^{r} \hat{\sigma}_k \hat{\mathbf{u}}_k \hat{\mathbf{v}}_k^\dagger \qquad (9.71)$$

To obtain the required order p, we examine the normalized ratio $\hat{v}(k)$. We set the underlying order p equal to the smallest value of k for which $\hat{v}(k)$ is deemed adequately close to 1. The terminology "adequately close to 1" is subjective and depends on the particular application under consideration as well as user experience gained through empirical experimentation. In any case the net result of this step yields a rank p approximation of the $t \times (p_e + 1)$ extended-order correlation matrix estimation; that is,

$$\hat{\mathbf{R}}_e^{(p)} = \sum_{k=1}^{r} \hat{\sigma}_k \hat{\mathbf{u}}_k \hat{\mathbf{v}}_k^\dagger \qquad (9.72)$$

We now give two procedures for using this rank p approximation to obtain AR parameter estimates.

Method I: ARMA(p_e, q_e) Model   1

In this approach the rank p approximation [Eq. (9.72)] is interpreted as an improved estimate of the underlying extended correlation matrix. It is convenient to decompose Eq. (9.72) as follows:

$$\hat{\mathbf{R}}_e^{(p)} = [\hat{\mathbf{r}}_1^{(p)} \vdots \hat{\mathbf{R}}^{(p)}] \qquad (9.73)$$

where $\hat{\mathbf{r}}_1^{(p)}$ is the leftmost $t \times 1$ column vector of $\hat{\mathbf{R}}_e^{(p)}$ and $\hat{\mathbf{R}}^{(p)}$ is a $t \times p_e$ matrix composed of the p_e rightmost $t \times 1$ column vectors of $\hat{\mathbf{R}}_e^{(p)}$. We now seek a

$(p_e + 1) \times 1$ augmented AR parameter vector $\mathbf{a}$ (i.e., its first component equals 1) that satisfies the theoretical relationship

$$\mathbf{R}_e^{(p)}\tilde{\mathbf{a}} = \mathbf{0} \tag{9.74}$$

Since the rank of $\hat{\mathbf{R}}_e^{(p)}$ is less than full if $p \leq p_e$, there exists an infinite number of solutions to this problem. From decomposition Eq. (9.73) each solution must satisfy $\hat{\mathbf{R}}^{(p)}\mathbf{a} = -\mathbf{r}_1^{(p)}$. We here select the minimum-norm solution, which is specified by [14]

$$\begin{bmatrix} a_1^0 \\ a_2^0 \\ \vdots \\ a_{pe}^0 \end{bmatrix} = -[\hat{\mathbf{R}}^{(p)}]^{\#}\hat{\mathbf{r}}_1^{(p)} \tag{9.75}$$

where $[\hat{\mathbf{R}}^{(p)}]^{\#}$ denotes the pseudo inverse of matrix $\hat{\mathbf{R}}^{(p)}$.

2 Method II: Lower-Order ARMA(p, q) Model

The best rank p approximation matrix [Eq. (9.72)] contains within its column structure the characteristics required to estimate AR parameters of a lower-order ARMA(p, q) model [4, 14]. In particular, the submatrices of $\hat{\mathbf{R}}_e^{(p)}$ composed of its columns k through $p + k$ inclusively yield rank p approximations of the $t \times (p+1)$ correlation matrices $\mathbf{R}_k$ for $1 \leq k \leq p_e - p + 1$ as specified by Eq. (9.64). We shall denote these rank p approximations by $\hat{\mathbf{R}}_k^{(p)}$. Due to the SVD operation and errors inherent in generating $\hat{\mathbf{R}}_e$, there generally does not exist a unique augmented AR parameter vector that satisfies all of the $p_e - p + 1$ homogeneous relationships [Eq. (9.65)]. Nonetheless, it is still desirable to find an AR parameter vector for which each of these relationships is almost satisfied. A functional that measures the degree to which this is accomplished is

$$f(\tilde{\mathbf{a}}) = \mathbf{a}^{\dagger}\mathbf{S}^{(p)}\mathbf{a} \tag{9.76}$$

where

$$\mathbf{S}^{(p)} = \sum_{k=1}^{p_e - p + 1} \hat{\mathbf{R}}_k^{(p)\dagger}\hat{\mathbf{R}}_k^{(p)} \tag{9.77}$$

The $(p + 1) \times (p + 1)$ matrix $\mathbf{S}^{(p)}$ is nonnegative definite Hermitian.

Upon generating the $(p + 1) \times (p + 1)$ matrix $\mathbf{S}^{(p)}$, we next wish to select that augmented AR parameter vector $\mathbf{a}$ to minimize quadratic functional Eq. (9.76). This constrained minimization results in the best least squares approximation of the theoretical relationships [Eq. (9.65)]. Using standard procedures, we find the required optimum augmented AR parameter vector by solving the linear system[‡]

$$\mathbf{S}^{(p)}\mathbf{a}^0 = \alpha\mathbf{e}_1 \tag{9.78}$$

[‡] In those rare cases where $\mathbf{S}^{(p)}$ is singular, the required augmented AR parameter vector is set equal to any appropriately normalized eigenvector associated with a zero eigenvalue of $\mathbf{S}^{(p)}$.

in which the normalizing constant α is selected so that the first component of **a** is 1, as required. We show in the next section that these SVD versions of ARMA modeling procedures can significantly improve modeling performance.

NUMERICAL EXAMPLES X

In this section we investigate the comparative spectral estimation performance of the ARMA modeling procedures as developed in Sections VIII and IX with those of popularly used alternatives. The first example treats the problem of obtaining a rational spectral estimate from a set of observations of an ARMA(4, 4) process. In the second and third examples we examine the modeling performance for the special case of sinusoids in white noise.

Example 1. We examine the time series as characterized by (see [24])

$$x(n) = x_1(n) + x_2(n) + 0.5\epsilon(n) \tag{9.79a}$$

which is composed of the two AR(2) time series generated according to

$$x_1(n) = 0.4x_1(n-1) - 093x_1(n-2) + \epsilon_1(n) \tag{9.79b}$$

$$x_2(n) = -0.5x_2(n-1) - 0.93x_2(n-2) + \epsilon_2(n) \tag{9.79c}$$

where $\epsilon(n)$, $\epsilon_1(n)$, and $\epsilon_2(n)$ are pairwise uncorrelated Gaussian zero-mean white noise processes with variance 1. A simple analysis indicates that the PSD function associated with time series [Eq. (9.79)] is

$$S_x(\omega) = |1 - 0.4e^{-j\omega} + 0.93e^{-j2\omega}|^{-2}$$

$$+ |1 + 0.5e^{-j\omega} + 0.93e^{-j2\omega}|^{-2} + 0.25 \tag{9.80}$$

and is plotted in Fig. 9.7(c).

Using the time series description [Eq. (9.79a)], we generated 20 statistically independent realizations each of length 125. These realizations were used to compare the modeling effectiveness of the overdetermined ARMA method herein described with the Box–Jenkin maximum-likelihood method [21]. The 20 (one for each realization) superimposed ARMA (4, 4) spectral estimates obtained using the Box-Jenkin iterative method are shown in Fig. 9.7(b). The number of iterations required to achieve these estimates ranged from 10 to 700, with 50 being a typical requirement. Next, we used the ARMA modeling method represented by Eq. (9.60) with unbiased autocorrelation lag estimates and $W = 1$ to obtain the ARMA(4.4) AR parameter estimates. We used a direct adaptation of Eqs. (9.34) and (9.35) to form the MA component of the spectral estimates. The 20 superimposed ARMA(4.4) spectral estimates obtained are shown in Fig. 9.6(c)–(e) for various choices of t. These plots show that progressively imporved estimates are achieved when t is increased from its minimal value 4 to 8 and then to 20. Moreover, these spectral estimates were of higher quality

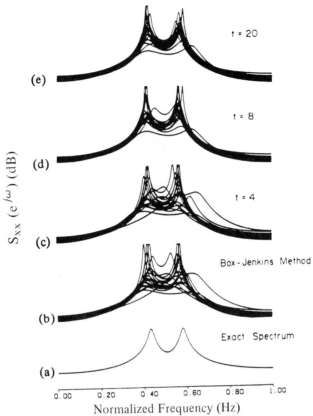

Fig. 9.7. ARMA (4.4) spectral estimates: (a) Exact; (b) Box–Jenkins maximum-likelihood method; (c) Eq. (9.60) with $t = 4$; (d) Eq. (9.60) with $t = 8$; (e) Eq. (9.60) with $t = 20$.

than those obtained with the maximum-likelihood Box–Jenkins method, which exhibited a larger variance in estimate.

Example 2. We investigated the comparative spectral estimation performances of various widely used methods on the classical sinusoids in additive white noise problem. The particular time series considered is

$$x(n) = \sin(2\pi f_1 n) + \sin(2\pi f_2 n) + w(n), \qquad 0 \le n \le N - 1 \qquad (9.81)$$

where $f_1 = 0.2, f_2 = 0.215$, and $w(n)$ is a Gaussian white noise process of variance $\sigma_w^2 = 0.5$. This time series was previously examined in Section V, where different rational models were generated from exact autocorrelation lag information. This time series is particularly appropriate for testing the resolution capabilities of spectral estimators, because of the closeness of the sinusoidal frequencies (i.e., $f_2 - f_1 = 0.015$) and the prevailing low SNR of 0 dB (individual sinusoid power to total noise power).

To gain a reasonably good statistical basis for comparison, we generated 10 statistically independent realizations of the time series [Eq. (9.81)] with each realization being of length 128 (i.e., $N = 128$). From these 10 different sets of time series observations, we made 10 spectral estimates for each rational spectral estimator being tested. These estimates were then plotted in Figs. 9.8 to 9.11 in a superimposed fashion (except for the periodogram) to depict consistency of estimate. The ideal estimate would be two sharply defined peaks at frequencies 0.2 and 0.215. We now briefly describe the different estimators and their performance on these test samples.

MA Estimates   A

The periodogram as implemented by the FFT was first used to generate spectral estimates for each of the 10 different 128 data length realizations. Specifically, the FFT [Eq. (9.51)] with $N = 128$ was incorporated into the MA spectral estimator [Eq. (9.49)] to generate the sample periodogram estimate

$$\hat{S}_{xx}(e^{j(2\pi k/N)}) = \frac{1}{N}\left|\sum_{n=0}^{N-1} x(n+1)e^{-j(2\pi k/N)}\right|^2, \qquad 0 \le k \le N-1 \qquad (9.82)$$

Each of the 10 periodograms produced remarkably similar results. A typical 128-point FFT periodogram estimate arising from one of these trials is shown in Fig. 9.8(a). From this plot (and the nine others not shown) it was not possible

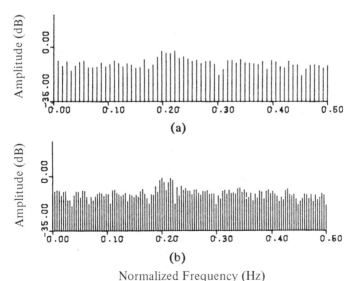

(a)

(b)

Normalized Frequency (Hz)

Fig. 9.8. MA spectral estimate using the FFT algorithm implementation of the periodogram: (a) $N = 128$ with no zero-padding; (b) $N = 256$ with 128 zero-padding.

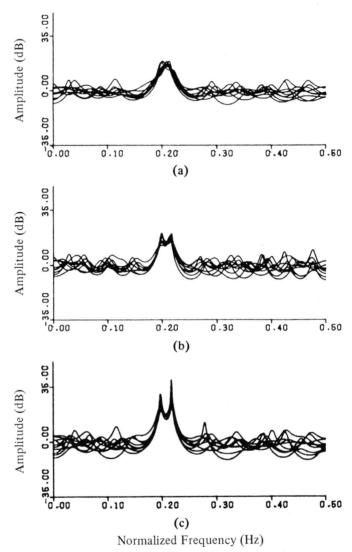

Fig. 9.9. AR spectral estimates from 128 time series observations: (a) AR(20) with $p = 20$, Burg estimate; (b) AR(24) with $p = 24$, Burg estimate; (c) AR(20) with $p = 20$, $q = 0$ using Eq. (9.60).

to unambiguously detect the presence of two spectral peaks at frequencies 0.2 and 0.215.

To ease the potential ambiguity created by the finite-frequency sampling of the periodogram (i.e., $\Delta\omega = 2\pi/N$), we used the concept of padding (Section VI). The original time series observation of length 128 was appended with 128 zeros. The resultant 256-point padded FFT periodogram is shown in Fig. 9.8(b). In this padded case we are able to unambiguously detect the presence of the two spectral peaks at 0.2 and 0.215.

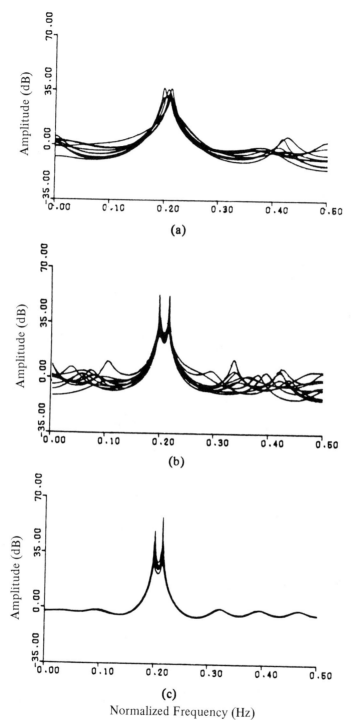

Fig. 9.10. ARMA estimate using 128 times series observations: (a) ARMA(8,8) model, using Eq. (9.60) with $p = q = 8, t = 70$; (b) ARMA(12,12) estimate using Eq. (9.60) with $p = q = 12, t = 70$; (c) ARMA(4.4) SVD estimate using Eq. (9.60) with $p = q = 14, p = 4, t = 50$.

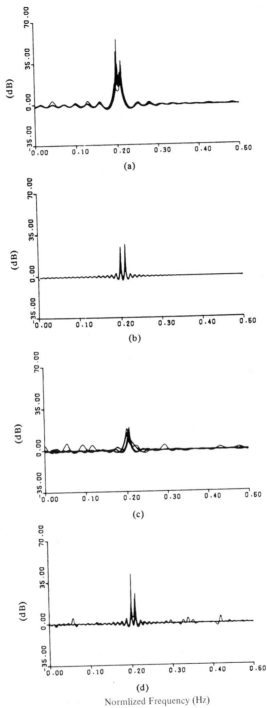

Normlized Frequency (Hz)

Fig. 9.11. AR spectral models: (a) Eq. (9.75) with $p = 35$; (b) Eq. (9.75) with $p = 96$; (c) Kumaresan–Tufts method, $p = 35$; (d) Kumaresan–Tufts method—optimum order $p = 96$.

AR Estimates   B

In AR modeling, one of the most widely used procedure is the Burg algorithm. We used it to generate spectral estimates for each of the aforementioned 10 observation sets of length 128. The 10 superimposed Burg AR(20) estimates that resulted are depicted in Fig. 9.9(a). Although a detection of spectral energy in the region about $f = 0.2$ is evident, the appearance of two spectral peaks is absent. The ordering selection $p = 20$ was evidently not sufficient for the required resolution. When the AR order was increased to $p = 24$, however, the Burg AR(24) estimates produced two reasonably well-defined peaks about $f = 0.2$ and $f = 0.215$ in 9 out of the 10 estimates. These estimates are plotted in superimposed fashion in Fig. 9.9(b). It was further determined that even more sharply defined peaks are achieved in all 10 estimates when the order was increased to 40. The Burg algorithm provides satisfactory resolution performance for the time series under study when the AR order is larger than 24.

To demonstrate the effect of using more than the minimal number of extended Yule–Walker equations in arriving at an AR model (the Burg algorithm uses the minimal number), we used the overdetermined equation modeling technique as embodied in Eq. (9.60) with $W = I$ and unbiased autocorrelation lag estimates with $p = 20$, $q = 0$, and $t = 50$. The 10 AR(20) spectral estimates obtained are shown in Fig. 9.9(c). A resolution of the two sinusoids was achieved in all 10 estimates. The lower-order AR(20) spectral estimates generated with the overdetermined equation approach provided more sharply defined peaks than did the high-order Burg AR(24) spectral estimates. This occurred primarily because 50 higher-order Yule–Walker equations were used to specify the 20 AR parameters. The degree of smoothing achieved in applying this approach is evident from this numerical example.

ARMA Estimates   C

We next used the overdetermined equation ARMA modeling procedure as represented by Eq. (9.60) with $W = I$ and unbiased autocorrelation lag-estimate entries to generate estimates of the AR coefficients of an ARMA(p, p) model for $p = 8$ and $p = 12$. Using the remarks in Section V, we plotted $|A_p(e^{j\omega})|^{-2}$ to reveal the required spectral information for the sinusoids in white noise case (i.e., the zeros are not used). In Fig. 9.10(a) the 10 AR(8, 8) spectral estimates that arose for a choice of $t = 70$ are shown superimposed. Although spectral energy in the neighborhood of $f = 0.2$ is detected, the presence of the required two spectral peaks is not. Clearly, the order selection $p = 8$ was not sufficient to achieve the desired resolution. When we increased the order to ARMA(12, 12), retaining $t = 70$, the resultant 10 spectral estimates in Fig. 9.10(b) each achieved the desired spectral resolution with two sharply defined peaks about $f = 0.2$ and $f =$

0.215. These spectral estimates were obtained with only 12 AR parameters and are superior to the Burg AR(24) estimates, which required 24 AR parameters, and the overdetermined AR(20) estimate. In terms of spectral estimation fidelity and parameter parsimony (i.e., effective use of parameters), the overdetermined equation ARMA modeling method was clearly superior to the other methods.

Spectral estimation performance is significantly improved when we adopt the SVD approaches to ARMA modeling as outlined in Section IX. After setting $p_e = q_e = 14$ and $t = 50$ we found that the effective rank of the extended-order autocorrelation matrix estimate $\hat{R}_e$ was 4. Next, for $p = 4$ in Eq. (9.78) the 10 SVD derived lower-order ARMA(4,4) spectral estimates that arose are shown superimposed in Fig. 9.10(c). In all 10 estimates the two sinusoids were detected, and the spectrum was approximately at the theoretical 0-dB noise level for most other frequencies. These spectral estimates are not only of uniformly high quality, but they represent the lowest-order rational model compatible with the two sinusoids in white noise.

To demonstrate the worthiness of singular values in model order determination when using the SVD approach, we give the 15 singular values that characterized the extended-order autocorrelation matrix estimate $\hat{R}_e$ for one of the 10 observation sets: $\hat{\sigma}_1 = 18.3$, $\hat{\sigma}_2 = 18.2$, $\hat{\sigma}_3 = 5.30$, $\hat{\sigma}_4 = 4.69$, $\hat{\sigma}_5 = 0.85$, $\hat{\sigma}_6 = 0.78, \ldots, \hat{\sigma}_{15} = 0.21$. The first four singular values are dominant (i.e., $\hat{v}(4) = 0.99$), which indicates that the effective rank of $\hat{R}_e$ is 4. Thus we correctly choose ARMA order $p = q = 4$ after examining the behavior of the singular values.

Example 3. We next consider a time series of form Eq. (9.81) in which the relevant parameters are $f_1 = 0.2$, $f_2 = 0.21$, $\sigma_W^2 = 1.778$. This particular parameter choice provides a more challenging test of resolution capability because the frequency spacing $f_2 - f_1 = 0.01$ is smaller and the SNR of -5 dB is lower than that of the time series in Example 2. Again, 10 statistically sample runs each of length 128 were used for testing four AR-type models. In the first, we used the overdetermined equation AR model [Eq. (9.36)] with $q_e = -1$, $p_e = 35$, $t = 90$ (giving 90 Yule–Walker equation approximations). We then used unbiased autocorrelation estimates to form the 90×36 autocorrelation matrix estimate $\hat{R}_e$. Finally, we used Eq. (9.75) to generate the optimum AR parameter estimates. The resultant 10 AR(35) spectral estimates are shown in superimposed plots in Fig. 9.11(a), where resolution was achieved in each of the 10 runs. Next, we tested the overdetermined equation AR model [Eq. (9.36)] with $q_e = -1$, $p_e = 96$, $t = 96$, and unbiased autocorrelation lags. We need Eq. (9.75) with $p = 4$ to generate the a_k estimates of the AR(96) model. A plot of the resultant spectra is shown in Fig. 9.11(b), where resolution was achieved for each of the 10 runs.

The pseudo-maximum-likelihood Kumaresan–Tufts (KT) method, which provides a near maximum-likelihood performance, was next tested on these same 10 sample runs [25]. The resultant AR-type thirty-fifth and ninety-sixth (the optimum KT order choice) order spectra are plotted in Fig. 9.11(c) and 9.11(d), respectively. The thirty-fifth-order model was unable to resolve the sinusoids in any of the 10 runs but the ninety-sixth-order model achieved a resolution in each case. For this example the overdetermined equation modeling approach outperformed the pseudo-maximum-likelihood approach.

CONCLUSIONS XI

A philosophy directed toward the rational modeling of WSS time series has been presented. The method is explicitly based on the Yule–Walker equations, which characterize the autocorrelation sequence associated with the rational time series being modeled. In particular, the key concepts were (1) using an overdetermined set of Yule–Walker equation evaluations and (2) employing a mode overordering for estimating the parameters of a postulated rational model. This approach reduced the data-induced hypersensitivity of the parameter estimates in comparison to many of the more popular parametric approaches that invoke a minimum set of evaluations for obtaining the parameter estimates. These latter methods include the Burg algorithm and many LMS methods. Comparative examples illustrating this reduced hypersensitivity have been given in which the modeling is based on both exact autocorrelation lag information and raw time series observations.

The SVD method was next introduced and used to obtain an effective rational model order determination procedure and provide a novel rational modeling procedure whose performance has been empirically found usually to exceed that of more traditional techniques.

REFERENCES

1. L. M. Koopmans, *The Spectral Aanalysis of Time Series*, Academic Press, New York, 1974.
2. A. Schuster, On the investigation of hidden periodicities with application to a supposed 26 days period of meteorological phenomena, *Terrestrial Magnetism* **3**, 13–41 (March 1898).
3. R. B. Blackman and J. W. Tukey, *The Measurement of Power Spectra*, Dover, New York, 1959.
4. J. A. Cadzow, *Foundations of Digital Signal Processing and Time Series Analysis*, MacMillan Press, New York, 1987.
5. A. V. Oppenheim and R. W. Schafer, *Digital Signal Processing*, Prentice-Hall, Englewood Cliffs, 1975.
6. M. B. Priestly, *Spectral Analysis and Time Series*, Vols. 1, 2, Academic Press, London, 1981.
7. G. U. Yule, On a method of investigating periodicities in disturbed series with special reference to Wolder's sunspot numbers, *Philosoph. Trans. Roy. Soc. London, Ser. A.* **226**, 276–298 (July 1927).
8. G. Walker, On periodicity in series of related terms, *Proc. Roy. Soc. London, Ser. A.* **131**, 518–531 (1931).
9. J. P. Burg, Maximum entropy spectral analysis, *Proc. 37th Meet. Society of Exploration Geophysicists* (Oklahoma City, OK), October 31, 1967.
10. E. Parzen, Statistical spectral analysis (single channel case) in 1968, Dept. Statistics, Stanford Univ., Stanford, Calif., Tech. Report 11, June 1968.

11. J. Makhoul, Stable and efficient lattice methods for linear prediction, *IEEE Trans. Acoust. Speech Signal Process.* **ASSP-25**, 423–428 (October 1977).

12. N. Levinson, The Wiener (root mean square) error criterion in filter design and prediction, *J. Math. Phys.* **25**, 261–278 (1947).

13. S. S. Haykin, Editors *Nonlinear Methods of Spectral Analysis*, Springer, New York, 1979.

14. J. A. Cadzow, Spectral estimation: An overdetermined rational model equation approach, *IEEE Proc.* **70**, 907–939 (September 1982).

15. V. F. Pisarenko, The retrieval of harmonics from a covariance function, *Geophys. J. Royal Astron. Soc.* **33**, 347–366 (1973).

16. T. P. Bronez and J. A. Cadzow, An algebraic approach to super-resolution array processing, *IEEE Trans. Aero. Elect. Syst.* **AES-19**, 123–133 (January 1983).

17. P. D. Welch, The use of fast Fourier transform for the estimation of power spectra, *IEEE Trans. Audio Electroacoust.* **AU-15**, 70–73 (June 1970).

18. G. M. Jenkins and D. G. Watts, *Spectral Analysis and its Applications*, Holden Day, San Francisco 1968.

19. F. G. Childers, Editor, *Modern Spectral Analysis*, IEEE Press, New York, 1978.

20. H. Akaike, Maximum likelihood identification of Gaussian autoregressive moving-average models, *Biometrica* **60**, 255–265 (August 1973).

21. G. E. P. Box and G. M. Jenkins, *Jenkins, Time Series Analysis: Forecasting and Control*, rev. ed., Holden Day, San Francisco, 1976.

22. S. A. Tretter and K. Steiglitz, Power spectrum identifications in terms of rational models, *IEEE Trans, Automat. Contr.* **AC-12**, 185–188 (April 1967).

23. G. Golub and W. Kahan, Calculating the singular values and pseudo-inverse of a matrix, *J. SIAM Numer. Anal. (Ser. B)* **2**, 205–224 (1965).

24. S. Bruzzone and M. Kaveh, On some suboptimum ARMA spectral estimators, *IEEE trans. Acoust. Speech Signal Process.* **ASSP-28**, 753–754 (December 1980).

25. D. W. Tufts and R. Kumaresan, Estimation of frequencies of multiple sinusoids: Making linear prediction perform like maximum likehood, *IEEE Proceedings* **70**, 975–989 (September 1982).

Chapter **10**

Deconvolution

MANUEL T. SILVIA
Allied Signal Aerospace Company
Bendix Oceanics Division
Sylmar, California 91342

INTRODUCTION **I**

Many physical phenomena can be described by the methods of linear time-invariant (LTI) systems theory. When the LTI theory is applicable, the underlying physical process is usually described as the response of an LTI system to some physical source excitation. The corresponding mathematical model is composed of an input (the source excitation), an impulse response (the LTI system function), and an output (the physical process). The process of *convolution* transforms the input to the output by the LTI impulse response. For example, let us consider the physical process of speech. When air pressure is forced from the glottis to the lips by means of the vocal tract, human sounds (i.e., speech) are produced [1]. Here, the input or source excitation is the air pressure in the glottis, the LTI impulse response is derived from the physical properties of the vocal tract (see [1]), and the output of the LTI system is the physical process of speech. Figure 10.1 gives a physical description of speech generation. Figure 10.2 gives an LTI systems theory description of speech. For continuous-time speech processes the convolution integral

$$y(t) = \int_{-\infty}^{\infty} h(\tau)x(t - \tau)\,d\tau = h(t) * x(t) \tag{10.1}$$

transforms the glottis source $x(t)$ into the speech output $y(t)$ by means of the vocal tract's impulse response $h(t)$. Thus, speech can be modeled as the convolution of $h(t)$ and $x(t)$.

Given a particular vocal tract or $h(t)$ and a glottis source $x(t)$, convolution generates the speech waveform $y(t)$. We say that *convolution describes the forward problem*. Let us now consider the problem of trying to evaluate $h(t)$ from knowledge of $y(t)$ and $x(t)$. That is, given the speech output and knowledge of the

741

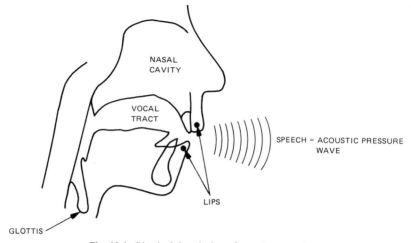

Fig. 10.1. Physical description of speech generation.

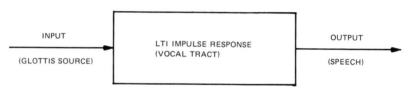

Fig. 10.2. LTI systems theory description of speech.

glottis input, what is the vocal tract's impulse response? This question defines the inverse problem. From Eq. (10.1) we see that the convolution of $y(t)$ and some function $q(t)$, that is,

$$y(t) * q(t) = h(t) * x(t) * q(t) \qquad (10.2)$$

would equal $h(t)$ if

$$x(t) * q(t) = \delta(t) \qquad (10.3)$$

Here, $\delta(t)$ is the familiar Dirac delta function (Chapter 1). If Eq. (10.3) exists, then the convolution Eq. (10.2) gives $h(t)$, and the inverse problem has a solution. The quantity $q(t)$ is called a *deconvolution filter*, since it "deconvolves" the input $x(t)$ from the speech waveform $y(t)$. Thus, we say that *deconvolution describes the inverse problem*. The problem of deconvolution is concerned with the development of fast and stable algorithms that produce accurate deconvolution filters. Once the deconvolution filter $q(t)$ is known, the impulse response $h(t)$ follows from Eqs. (10.2) and (10.3).

Let us now consider another physical process involving the inverse problem of deconvolution. In the exploration for oil and natural gas, seismic sources or

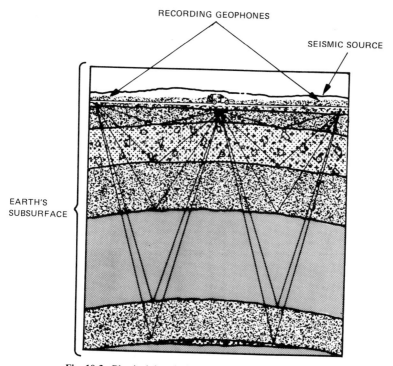

Fig. 10.3. Physical description of recorded seismic waves.

vibrators (located at or near the earth's surface) excite the earth and produce seismic waves [2]. Geophysicists record these waves with geophones (for land exploration) or hydrophones (for offshore exploration). For this discussion let us consider the case where the geophones or hydrophones are located at or near the earth's surface. Again, we can use LTI systems theory to describe this physical process. This time the input or source excitation is the seismic vibrator, the LTI impulse response is derived from the physical properties of the earth's subsurface (see [2]), and the output of the LTI system is the recorded seismic waves. Figure 10.3 gives a physical description of the recorded seismic waves that occur in the exploration for oil and natural gas. Figure 10.4 gives the corresponding LTI system description. For convenience let us assume that the recorded seismic

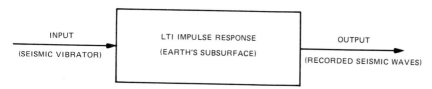

Fig. 10.4. LTI systems theory description of recorded seismic waves.

waves represent one-dimensional continuous-time phenomena. Therefore, after analog-to-digital conversion (ADC) the convolution integral Eq. (10.1) becomes the convolution sum

$$y(n) = \sum_{m=-\infty}^{\infty} h(m)x(n-m) = h(n) * x(n) \tag{10.4}$$

In words, the recorded seismic wave samples $y(n)$ are generated by the convolution of the earth's discrete-time impulse response $h(n)$ and the source samples $x(n)$. Thus, given $h(n)$ and $x(n)$, we solve the forward problem for $y(n)$ by convolving $h(n)$ with $x(n)$. Now given $y(n)$ and $x(n)$, we solve the inverse problem for $h(n)$ by deconvolving $x(n)$ from $y(n)$. That is,

$$y(n) * q(n) = h(n) * x(n) * q(n) \tag{10.5}$$

would equal $h(n)$ if

$$x(n) * q(n) = \delta(n) \tag{10.6}$$

Here, $\delta(n)$ is the discrete-time impulse function (Chapter 1). The discrete-time deconvolution filter $q(n)$ is obtained from Eq. (10.6), provided it exists. Once $q(n)$ is known, the deconvolution problem is solved, and $h(n)$ is obtained from Eqs. (10.5) and (10.6). The seismic deconvolution problem plays an important role in the exploration for oil and natural gas, since knowledge of the earth's impulse response is tantamount to knowledge about oil and gas reservoirs [2].

The deconvolution problem also appears in the sonar signal processing area. For example, in passive sonar operations a target radiates an acoustic signal into

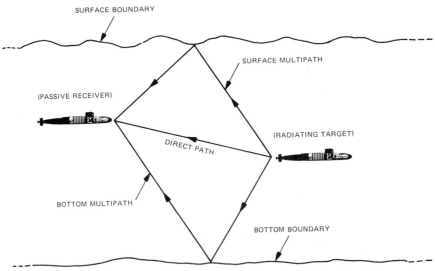

Fig. 10.5. Passive sonar receives distorted version of radiated signal.

an acoustic medium with surface and bottom boundaries. Generally, the boundaries of this medium produce multipath interference [3]. Consequently, a passive sensor/receiver could receive a distorted version of the radiated signal (see Fig. 10.5). Now if we let the input $x(t)$ be the radiated signal, the output or received signal $y(t)$ can be modeled by (Fig. 10.5)

$$y(t) = x(t) + A_s x(t - \tau_s) + A_b x(t - \tau_b)$$
$$= \int_{-\infty}^{\infty} h(\lambda) x(t - \lambda) \, d\lambda = h(t) * x(t) \tag{10.7}$$

where the multipath impulse response $h(t)$ can be expressed as

$$h(t) = \delta(t) + A_s \delta(t - \tau_s) + A_b \delta(t - \tau_b) \tag{10.8}$$

Here, A_s and A_b represent surface and bottom signal amplitude parameters, and τ_s and τ_b represent the signal time delays due to the surface and bottom multipaths, respectively. Hence, the multipath interference or distortion can be described by the convolution of the source $x(t)$ and the LTI impulse response $h(t)$, which depends on the physical characteristics of the ocean medium.

Normally, a passive sonar receiver is interested in the radiated signal $x(t)$. As we have just seen, when multipath distortion is present, $y(t)$ is a distorted version of $x(t)$. Thus, to obtain $x(t)$, we must deconvolve $h(t)$ from $y(t)$. Mathematically,

$$y(t) * q(t) = h(t) * x(t) * q(t) = x(t) * h(t) * q(t) \tag{10.9}$$

equals $x(t)$ if

$$h(t) * q(t) = \delta(t) \tag{10.10}$$

As before, we obtain the deconvolution filter $q(t)$ by solving Eq. (10.10) for $q(t)$. Notice that the continuous-time Fourier transform of Eq. (10.10) gives

$$H(F)Q(F) = 1 \tag{10.11a}$$

or

$$Q(F) = \frac{1}{H(F)} \tag{10.11b}$$

which shows that deconvolution is equivalent to division in the frequency domain. Although the mathematical solution for $Q(F)$ seems straightforward, numerical divison on a digital computer must be done with caution. Further, some Fourier transforms might contain zeros. For these situations exact deconvolution filters do not exist. As we will soon see, deconvolution algorithms must be carefully designed in order to handle noisy signals, finite-length 16-bit integer arithmetic problems, and signals with zeros in their Fourier transforms.

Deconvolution plays an important role in the identification of physical systems. As we have just seen, the deconvolution of a speech signal $y(t)$ can provide useful information about the vocal tract [i.e., $h(t)$]. In seismic signal processing, the deconvolution of a seismic waveform $y(t)$ can be used to identify the earth's impulse response $h(t)$. In passive sonar signal processing, the deconvolution of a received signal $y(t)$ can be used to estimate the target's radiated signal $x(t)$. In the literature, deconvolution is sometimes called *systems identification* [4–6].

The subject of deconvolution is rich in theory and computational algorithms. The main purpose of this chapter is to briefly review the essential components of deconvolution theory and a few computational algorithms. In Section II we consider the deconvolution of LTI systems with no measurement noise. In Section III we consider the more difficult problem of the deconvolution of LTI systems that contain measurement noise. In Section IV we discuss the Levinson or Toeplitz recursion and its relationship to deconvolution. In Section V we discuss the deconvolution or inverse problem as it appears in speech and seismic signal processing. The appendixes provide some references where computational FORTRAN IV algorithms can be obtained, and some useful program source codes.

II DECONVOLUTION AND LTI SYSTEMS WITH NO MEASUREMENT NOISE

A Discrete-Time Linear Time-Invariant (DTLTI) Systems

Deconvolution applies to both continuous-time and DTLTI systems. From now on we will consider only DTLTI systems. This is done for convenience, since most deconvolution algorithms are performed on a digital computer.

A DTLTI system can be described by its impulse response $h(n)$. The corresponding z-transform $H(z)$ is the system transfer function. In general, $H(z)$ is a two-sided z-transform (i.e., the sequence $h(n)$ is nonzero for positive and negative indices n). For our discussion we consider only right-sided or causal sequences $h(n)$, so $h(n) = 0$ for $n < 0$. Further, we assume that $H(z)$ can be described by a rational function:

$$H(z) = \frac{b_M(0) + b_M(1)z^{-1} + b_M(2)z^{-2} + \cdots + b_M(M)z^{-M}}{1 + a_N(1)z^{-1} + a_N(2)z^{-2} + \cdots + a_N(N)z^{-N}}, \qquad M < N \qquad (10.12)$$

Thus, the coefficients $a_N(m)$ $(m = 1, 2, \ldots, N)$ and $b_M(l)$ $(l = 0, 1, 2, \ldots, M)$ characterize the DTLTI system.

We further assume that all the poles of Eq. (10.12) are inside the unit circle in the complex z-plane, so $h(n)$ is a stable sequence. For a right-sided input sequence $x(n)$ and a right-sided output sequence $y(n)$, Eq. (10.12) gives rise to the linear constant-coefficient difference equation

$$y(n) + a_N(1)y(n-1) + a_N(2)y(n-2) + \cdots + a_N(N)y(n-N)$$
$$= b_M(0)x(n) + b_M(1)x(n-1) + b_M(2)x(n-2)$$
$$+ \cdots + b_M(M)x(n-M), \quad n \geq 0 \tag{10.13}$$

Thus, a right-sided, stable DTLTI system can be described by its impulse $h(n)$, its system transfer function [Eq. (10.12)], or its difference equation [Eq. (10.13)]. Here, we have assumed that both the input and output sequences $x(n)$ and $y(n)$, respectively, are right-sided, stable sequences.

Given the coefficients $a_N(m)$ $(m = 1, 2, \ldots, N)$, $b_M(l)$ $(l = 0, 1, 2, \ldots, M)$, and $x(n)$, we can find the output $y(n)$ from Eq. (10.13). Given $h(n)$ and $x(n)$, we can find the output $y(n)$ from the convolution sum

$$y(n) = \sum_{m=0}^{n} h(m)x(n-m) = h(n) * x(n), \quad n \geq 0 \tag{10.14}$$

If we define the finite-length sequences

$$a_N(n) \equiv (a_N(0) = 1, a_N(1), a_N(2), \ldots, a_N(N))$$
$$b_M(n) \equiv (b_M(0), b_M(1), b_M(2), \ldots, b_M(M)) \tag{10.15}$$

with right-sided z-transforms

$$A_N(z) = \sum_{n=0}^{N} a_N(n)z^{-n} = 1 + a_N(1)z^{-1} + a_N(2)z^{-2} + \cdots + a_N(N)z^{-N}$$

$$B_M(z) = \sum_{n=0}^{M} b_M(n)z^{-n} = b_M(0) + b_M(1)z^{-1} + b_M(2)z^{-2} + \cdots + b_M(M)z^{-M}$$
$$\tag{10.16}$$

then Eq. (10.12) becomes

$$H(z) = \frac{B_M(z)}{A_N(z)} \tag{10.17}$$

and Eq. (10.13) can be written in convolution form as

$$y(n) * a_N(n) = x(n) * b_M(n) \tag{10.18}$$

Equations (10.12)–(10.18) are useful for convolution and deconvolution operations.

Minimum Phase, Minimum Delay, and Deconvolution   B

An important concept often encountered in the study of deconvolution is minimum phase or minimum delay [2, 7]. The concept of minimum phase and its relationship to feedback control systems were introduced by Bode, who worked in the domain of continuous-time, linear, time-invariant systems. Working with the Laplace complex frequency variable $s = \sigma + j\Omega$ associated with continuous time, Bode originally stated that a transfer function, derived from a linear differential equation with constant coefficients, is minimum phase if it contains no zeros or poles in the right-half s-plane. Systems having poles and/or zeros in the right-half s-plane are called non-minimum-phase systems. Based on Bode's original work, we now give the following definitions for right-sided sequences and DTLTI systems:

Definition of Stability.   A right-sided sequence is *stable* if its one-sided z-transform has no poles outside or on the unit circle in the complex z-plane. A right-sided DTLTI system of the forms (10.12) and (10.17) is *stable* if the polynomial $A_N(z)$ has no zeros outside or on the unit circle in the complex z-plane.

Definition of Minimum Phase.   A right-sided stable sequence is called *minimum phase* if its one-sided z-transform has no zeros outside or on the unit circle in the complex z-plane. A right-sided DTLTI system of the forms (10.12) and (10.17) is called minimum phase if the polynomial $B_M(z)$ has no zeros outside or on the unit circle in the complex z-plane

Any right-sided stable sequence or DTLTI system that is not minimum phase is called *non-minimum phase.*

The spectrum or frequency content of a right-sided stable sequence $s(n)$ is given by the discrete-time Fourier transform (DTFT) (Chapter 1)

$$S(\omega) = |S(\omega)|e^{j\theta_s(\omega)} \tag{10.19}$$

where $|S(\omega)|$ is termed the magnitude spectrum or gain and $\theta_s(\omega)$ is the phase spectrum. One important consequence of a minimum-phase sequence is that if the gain is specified for $-\pi \le \omega \le \pi$, then the corresponding phase spectrum is uniquely specified for $-\pi \le \omega \le \pi$. Conversely, if the phase spectrum is specified for $-\pi \le \omega \le \pi$, then the gain is uniquely specified for $-\pi \le \omega \le \pi$. Thus, the magnitude and phase spectra of a minimum-phase sequence are uniquely related: they form a Hilbert transform pair. If we assume that Eq. (10.19) represents a minimum-phase sequence, then we have the Hilbert transform pair

$$\log|S(\omega)| = \tilde{s}(0) - \frac{1}{2\pi}(P)\int_{-\pi}^{\pi}\theta_s(\lambda)\cot\left(\frac{\lambda - \omega}{2}\right)d\lambda$$

$$\theta_s(\omega) = \frac{1}{2\pi}(P)\int_{-\pi}^{\pi}\log|S(\omega)|\cot\left(\frac{\lambda - \omega}{2}\right)d\lambda \tag{10.20}$$

where

$$\tilde{S}(z) = \log S(z) = \sum_{n=0}^{\infty}\tilde{s}(n)z^{-n} \tag{10.21}$$

and (P) denotes the Cauchy principal value of the integral [8].

Example 1.   Consider the right-sided stable DTLTI system in Fig. 10.6. Let us assume that the input sequence $\underline{x}(n)$ is a zero mean wide-sense stationary (WSS) random process with autocorrelation sequence (refer to Section IX in Chapter (1),

$$r_{xx}(m) = E[\underline{x}(n)\underline{x}^*(n-m)] \tag{10.22}$$

Thus, the input power spectral density (PSD) is, for $-\pi \le \omega \le \pi$,

$$S_{xx}(\omega) = \sum_{m=-\infty}^{\infty} r_{xx}(m)e^{-jm\omega} \tag{10.23}$$

It follows that the output sequence $y(n)$ is also a zero-mean WSS random process. The corresponding output PSD is

$$S_{yy}(\omega) = |H(\omega)|^2 S_{xx}(\omega) \tag{10.24}$$

for $-\pi \le \omega \le \pi$. Here, $H(\omega)$ is the DTFT of $h(n)$ or the frequency response of the DTLTI system.

Let us now consider the following deconvolution problem. Given the random WSS input [with PSD $S_{xx}(\omega)$ and autocorrelation sequence $r_{xx}(m)$] and the random WSS output [with PSD $S_{yy}(\omega)$ and autocorrelation sequence $r_{yy}(m)$] associated with the DTLTI system in Fig. 10.6, determine the impulse response $h(n)$. To solve this problem, we proceed as follows. The fundamental idea is to deconvolve $\underline{x}(n)$ from $y(n)$, as explained by Eqs. (10.4) and (10.5). However, since we are attempting to determine a nonrandom sequence $h(n)$ from two random sequences $\underline{x}(n)$ and $y(n)$, it makes more sense to deal with the corresponding PSDs or autocorrelation functions. Thus, let us first proceed to obtain the magnitude of $H(\omega)$ from Eq. (10.24); that is,

$$|H(\omega)| = \left[\frac{S_{yy}(\omega)}{S_{xx}(\omega)}\right]^{1/2} \tag{10.25}$$

provided that $S_{xx}(\omega) > 0$ for $-\pi \le \omega \le \pi$. (In general, $S_{xx}(\omega)$ is nonnegative for $-\pi \le \omega \le \pi$ [9]. The requirement that $S_{xx}(\omega)$ be positive is not stringent, for it includes many physical WSS random processes such as white noise.) The next step is to obtain the phase spectrum $\theta_H(\omega)$ associated with $H(\omega)$. If we assume that $H(\omega)$ represents a minimum-phase system, then we know that $\log|H(\omega)|$ and $\theta_H(\omega)$ form a Hilbert transform pair [Eq. (10.20)]. Thus, $H(\omega)$ is totally specified from just the magnitude information, since the phase is uniquely reconstructed by Eq. (10.20). At this point we have determined the total frequency response $H(\omega)$.

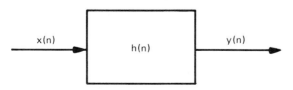

Fig. 10.6. Right-sided stable DTLTI system.

The impulse response $h(n)$ follows from the inverse DTFT (IDTFT) (Chapter 1) of $H(\omega)$. This completes the solution to the deconvolution problem.

A key assumption in our solution was that $H(\omega)$ represented a minimum-phase system. When $H(\omega)$ is not minimum phase, the phase reconstruction is not unique [2, 7]. Consequently, we cannot obtain a unique answer to the deconvolution problem. Therefore, we make the important observation that the concept of minimum phase and the concept of a unique deconvolution go hand in hand.

Let us now discuss the concept of minimum delay [10]. Any right-sided stable sequence or system can be described by its magnitude spectrum (gain) or its phase spectrum (a measure of delay). The delay of a system is a measure of the time delay from input to output. It is possible to have many different right-sided systems with the same gain but each with a different delay. It is always possible to have right-sided systems with very large delays, because there is no theoretical limit to the largeness of a delay that can be incorporated into a right-sided system. On the other hand, there is a limit to the smallness of a delay that can be incorporated into a right-sided system. The reason is that it always takes some finite amount of time for a right-sided system to respond significantly to an input. Thus, the minimum-delay sequence or system is the one with the smallest possible delay for its gain. It turns out that the mathematical properties of minimum phase and minimum delay are identical [2]. For a more detailed discussion of minimum delay see [2, 9].

Example 2.   Let us once again consider the right-sided stable DTLTI system in Fig. 10.6. Let us assume that the input sequence $x(n)$ is a nonrandom right-sided stable sequence. It follows that the output sequence $y(n)$ is also a nonrandom right-sided stable sequence that can be derived from the convolution sum [Eq. (10.3)]. We now wish to solve the following deconvolution problem. Given the right-sided stable impulse response $h(n)$ and the right-sided stable output sequence $y(n)$, determine the right-sided stable input sequence $x(n)$. Let us now proceed to solve this problem.

The basic idea is to deconvolve $h(n)$ from the output $y(n)$. In mathematical terms there exists a deconvolution filter $q(n)$ such that

$$y(n) * q(n) = h(n) * x(n) * q(n) = x(n) * h(n) * q(n) \tag{10.26}$$

equals $x(n)$ if

$$h(n) * q(n) = \delta(n) \tag{10.27}$$

The one-sided z-transform of Eq. (10.27) gives

$$H(z)Q(z) = 1 \tag{10.28}$$

or

$$Q(z) = \frac{1}{H(z)} \tag{10.29}$$

which is the one-sided z-transform of the deconvolution filter $q(n)$. This filter must be right-sided and stable; otherwise, $x(n) = y(n) * q(n)$ will not be right-sided and stable. Thus, in order for Eq. (10.29) to yield a right-sided stable deconvolution filter, $Q(z)$ must have no poles outside or on the unit circle in the complex z-plane. In other words, $H(z)$ must be minimum phase or minimum delay. If $H(z)$ is not minimum phase, we cannot recover $x(n)$ from $y(n)$; that is, we cannot deconvolve $h(n)$ from $y(n)$.

In summary, the above deconvolution problem has solution $x(n) = y(n) * q(n)$ if and only if $h(n)$ is minimum phase or minimum delay. Under this condition $q(n)$ follows from Eq. (10.27) or Eq. (10.29). As we saw in Example 1, the concepts of minimum phase and deconvolution are intimately related.

We now close this section with the following key points. Let S denote the set of right-sided, stable sequences. If we assume that $x(n)$, $h(n)$, and $y(n)$ are all contained in S and $y(n) = h(n) * x(n)$, then

1. In order to deconvolve $x(n)$ from $y(n)$, $x(n)$ must be minimum phase or minimum delay.

2. In order to deconvolve $h(n)$ from $y(n)$, $h(n)$ must be minimum phase or minimum delay.

3. All deconvolution filters $q(n)$ that are contained in S must be minimum phase or minimum delay.

4. A minimum-phase sequence can be uniquely reconstructed from only partial knowledge of its Fourier transform (e.g., from its magnitude or phase spectrums; see the Hilbert transform pair (10.20) and (10.21).

Deconvolution and the Identification of DTLTI Systems with No Measurement Noise   C

DTLTI Systems with Nonrandom Inputs   1

In this section we assume that $x(n)$, $h(n)$, and $y(n)$ all belong to the set S of all right-sided stable sequences. Further, we assume that our DTLTI system transfer function $H(z)$ has the rational form [Eq. (10.12)], so this DTLTI system can also be described by the difference equation [Eq. (10.13)]. Thus, the coefficients $a_N(m)$ $(m = 1, 2, \ldots, N)$, $b_M(l)$ $(l = 0, 1, 2, \ldots, M)$ in Eqs. (10.12) and (10.13) completely define or identify the impulse response $h(n)$. Given the input $x(n)$ and the noise-free output $y(n)$ for $n \geq 0$, we will now show how to determine the $a_N(m)$ and $b_M(l)$ coefficients. That is, we will perform a DTLTI systems identification [4–6].

The first step is to obtain the impulse response $h(n)$ by deconvolving the input or source $x(n)$ from the noise-free output $y(n)$. If we assume that $x(n)$ is a minimum-phase sequence, then the deconvolution is proper; that is, we can uniquely reconstruct $h(n)$ (see Section II.B). Now to perform this deconvolution in the frequency domain, we first take the DTFT of $x(n)$ to get $X(\omega)$. We then take the DTFT of $y(n)$ to get $Y(\omega)$. Next, we perform the spectral division or frequency domain deconvolution

$$H(\omega) = \frac{Y(\omega)}{X(\omega)} \qquad (10.30)$$

for $-\pi \leq \omega \leq \pi$. The IDTFT of Eq. (10.30) gives a stable $h(n)$ for $n \geq 0$ (provided that $x(n)$ is minimum phase). This completes the deconvolution of the minimum-phase source $x(n)$.

For $n \geq 0$ we note that $h(n)$ satisfies the difference equation

$$h(n) + a_N(1)h(n-1) + a_N(2)h(n-2) + \cdots + a_N(N)h(n-N)$$
$$= b_M(0)\delta(n) + b_M(1)\delta(n-1) + b_M(2)\delta(n-2)$$
$$+ \cdots + b_M(M)\delta(n-M), \qquad n \geq 0 \qquad (10.31)$$

For $n > M$ we have the difference equation

$$h(n) + a_N(1)h(n-1) + a_N(2)h(n-2) + \cdots + a_N(N)h(n-N) = 0, \qquad n > M \qquad (10.32)$$

Since Eq. (10.32) does not contain any of the $b_M(l)$ coefficients, it provides a useful vehicle for obtaining the $a_N(m)$ coefficients. That is, for $n = M+1, M+2, \ldots, M+N$ we can use Eq. (10.32) to generate N simultaneous equations in the N unknowns $a_N(1), a_N(2), \ldots, a_N(N)$. Doing so, we get the matrix equation

$$
\begin{bmatrix}
h(M) & h(M-1) & \cdots & h(M+1-N) \\
h(M+1) & h(M) & \cdots & h(M+2-N) \\
& & \vdots & \\
h(M+N-1) & h(M+N-2) & \cdots & h(M)
\end{bmatrix}
\begin{bmatrix}
a_N(1) \\
a_N(2) \\
\vdots \\
a_N(N)
\end{bmatrix}
= -
\begin{bmatrix}
h(M+1) \\
h(M+2) \\
\vdots \\
h(M+N)
\end{bmatrix}
$$
$$(10.33)$$

which can be solved for the $a_N(m)$ coefficients. Once the $a_N(m)$ coefficients are known, we can then use Eq. (10.31) to obtain the $b_M(l)$ coefficients. Specifically, Eq. (10.31) can be written in the convolution form

$$b_M(l) = \sum_{m=0}^{l} a_N(m)h(l-m), \qquad a_N(0) \equiv 1, l = 0, 1, 2, \ldots, M \qquad (10.34)$$

At this point we have solved the systems identification problem; that is, we have identified the $a_N(m)$ and $b_M(l)$ coefficients that define the DTLTI system described by Eqs. (10.12) and (10.13).

Rational DTLTI systems of the form (10.12), (10.13), or (10.17) are commonly referred to as autoregressive–moving average [ARMA(M, N)] systems [11, 12]. An ARMA(M, N) system, with M zeros and N poles, can always be expressed as the cascade of an autoregressive [AR(N)] or all-pole system and a moving average [MA(M)] or all-zero system. [In the digital filtering literature ARMA is usually replaced by infinite impulse response (IIR) and MA is usually replaced by

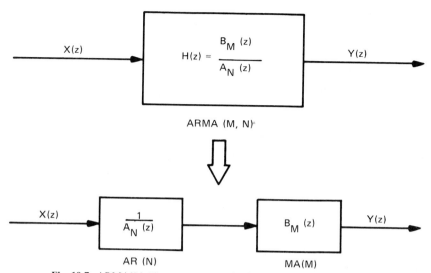

Fig. 10.7. ARMA(M, N) system as cascade of AR(N) and MA(M) systems.

finite impulse response (FIR).] See Fig. 10.7. Thus, if we let $p(n)$ denote the impulse response of the AR(N) system and $b_M(n)$ denote the impulse response of the MA(M) system, then the output $y(n)$ can be explained in terms of two convolutions. Mathematically,

$$y(n) = x(n) * p(n) * b_M(n) \tag{10.35}$$

Therefore, we can think of our ARMA(M, N) systems identification as a double deconvolution. That is, first we perform a source deconvolution on $y(n)$ to remove the effect of $x(n)$ and obtain $h(n)$. The corresponding deconvolution filter $q_1(n)$ satisfies the relation

$$q_1(n) * x(n) = \delta(n) \tag{10.36}$$

Second, we perform an AR(N) deconvolution on $h(n)$ to remove the effect of $p(n)$ and obtain $b_M(n)$. The corresponding deconvolution filter $q_2(n)$ satisfies the relation

$$q_2(n) * p(n) = \delta(n) \tag{10.37}$$

It turns out that $q_2(n) = a_N(n)$ (with $a_N(0) = 1$) is also the sequence of desired AR(N) coefficients. Table I summarizes the double deconvolution algorithm required for our ARMA(M, N) systems identification.

Note that the double deconvolution algorithm made only one restrictive assumption—namely, the source $x(n)$ had to be a minimum-phase sequence. Otherwise, the algorithm is capable of identifying both minimum-phase and non-minimum-phase ARMA(M, N) systems. A block diagram description of the double deconvolution algorithm is in Fig. 10.8.

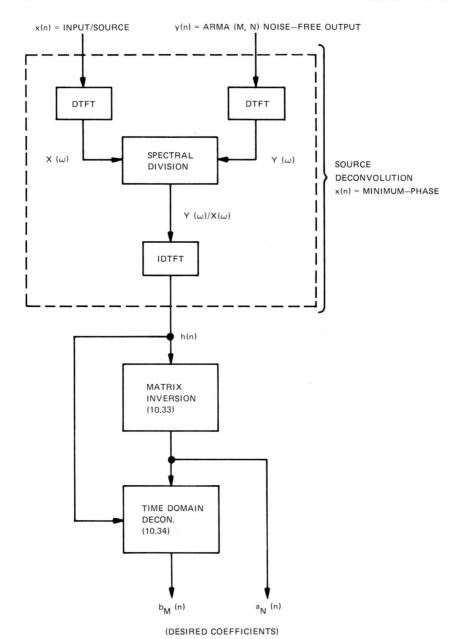

Fig. 10.8. Block diagram of the double deconvolution algorithm used in the ARMA (M, N) system identification.

TABLE I

Double Deconvolution Algorithm for ARMA(M, N) Systems Identification

Step 1. Take the DTFT of the noise-free output $y(n)$ and the input $x(n)$. We assume that $x(n)$ is a minimum-phase sequence.

Step 2. Perform the first deconvolution in the frequency domain. That is, perform the spectral division

$$H(\omega) = Q_1(\omega)Y(\omega) = \frac{Y(\omega)}{X(\omega)}$$

Then take the IDFT of this spectral division to yield $h(n)$.

Step 3. Solve the matrix equation (10.33) to obtain the second deconvolution filter $q_2(n) = a_N(n)$ (with $a_N(0) = 1$). This step yields the desired AR(N) coefficients $a_N(1), a_N(2), \ldots, a_N(N)$.

Step 4. Solve the convolution equation (10.34) to obtain the desired MA(M) coefficients $b_M(0)$, $b_M(1), b_M(2), \ldots, b_M(M)$. Equation (10.34) is actually the second deconvolution; that is, it is the deconvolution $q_2(n) * h(n)$ that removes the effect of $p(n)$ on $h(n)$.

DTLTI Systems with WSS Random Inputs 2

a. A Power Spectrum Approach.   Once again, we assume that $h(n)$ is a right-sided, stable impulse response with system transfer function [Eq. (10.12)]. This time we assume that the input $x(n)$ is a real zero-mean WSS random process with autocorrelation sequence $r_{xx}(m)$ and PSD $S_{xx}(\omega)$. Thus, the output $y(n)$ is also a real zero-mean WSS random process with autocorrelation sequence $r_{yy}(m)$ and PSD $S_{yy}(\omega)$. Given the input $x(n)$ and output $y(n)$, we will now show how to identify the system Eq. (10.12). That is, we will discuss an algorithm for determining the $a_N(m)$ and $b_M(l)$ coefficients in Eq. (10.12).

Our first approach is to assume that both the input and output PSDs are known for $-\pi \le \omega \le \pi$. For this case $|H(\omega)|$ is obtained from Eq. (10.25), and the corresponding phase spectrum $\theta_H(\omega)$ follows from the Hilbert transform relation between $\log|H(\omega)|$ and $\theta_H(\omega)$ (refer to Example 1). Thus, the impulse response $h(n)$, which must be minimum phase (Example 1), follows from the IDTFT of

$$H(\omega) = |H(\omega)|e^{j\theta_H(\omega)} \qquad (10.38)$$

Given $h(n)$ for $n \ge 0$, we can use steps 2 and 3 of the double deconvolution algorithm to complete the systems identification. Note that the systems identification algorithm proposed in this section can only identify minimum-phase systems.

b. An Autocorrelation–Cross-Correlation Approach.   In the previous section we assumed that only PSD information was available. In this section we assume that only the autocorrelation and cross-correlation information are available. That is, we assume that $r_{xx}(m)$, $r_{yy}(m)$, and $r_{yx}(m)$ are known for all lags m. Given this "time domain" information, let us now discuss some system identification algorithms.

Example 3. Let us assume that $B_M(z) = 1$, so $H(z)$ is the minimum-phase all-pole model $H(z) = 1/A_N(z)$. Under this condition we get the difference equation

$$y(n) + a_N(1)\underline{y}(n-1) + a_N(2)\underline{y}(n-2) + \cdots + a_N(N)\underline{y}(n-N) = \underline{x}(n) \quad (10.39)$$

for $-\infty < n < \infty$. Further, if we assume that $\underline{x}(n)$ is a zero-mean white noise WSS process, then the autocorrelation function $r_{xx}(m)$ becomes

$$r_{xx}(m) = \sigma_x^2 \delta(m) \quad (10.40)$$

Equations (10.39) and (10.40) describe an AR(N) process of order N. The output $y(n)$ represents an AR process [12]. By multiplying both sides of Eq. (10.39) by $\underline{y}(n-m)$ and taking expected values, we can show that the real AR(N) process Eq. (10.39) has the autocorrelation model

$$r_{yy}(m) + a_N(1)r_{yy}(m-1) + a_N(2)r_{yy}(m-2) + \cdots + a_N(N)r_{yy}(m-N) = 0 \quad (10.41)$$

for $m > 0$. The model [Eq. (10.41)] provides a useful vehicle for obtaining the AR coefficients $a_N(1)$, $a_N(2), \ldots$, $a_N(N)$. That is, for $m = 1, 2, \ldots, N$ we can use Eq. (10.41) to generate N simultaneous equations in the N unknowns—that is, the AR coefficients. Doing so, we get the matrix equation

$$\begin{bmatrix} r_{yy}(0) & r_{yy}(1) & \cdots & r_{yy}(N-1) \\ r_{yy}(1) & r_{yy}(0) & \cdots & r_{yy}(N-2) \\ & & \vdots & \\ r_{yy}(N-1) & r_{yy}(N-2) & \cdots & r_{yy}(0) \end{bmatrix} \begin{bmatrix} a_N(1) \\ a_N(2) \\ \vdots \\ a_N(N) \end{bmatrix} = - \begin{bmatrix} r_{yy}(1) \\ r_{yy}(2) \\ \vdots \\ r_{yy}(N) \end{bmatrix} \quad (10.42)$$

where we have used the fact that $r_{yy}(m) = r_{yy}(-m)$ for real WSS processes $y(n)$. The set of equations (10.42) is commonly referred to as the *Yule–Walker* equations. These equations were previously discussed in Chapter 9 (Section III) in conjunction with spectral analysis. In Section IV we shall discuss a fast matrix inversion algorithm for solving the Yule–Walker equations.

The identification of an AR(N) process has an interesting interpretation in terms of *linear prediction* [2, 13]. For example, if $y(n)$ is the "true value" at time n and

$$\hat{\underline{y}}(n) = - \sum_{m=1}^{N} a_N(m)\underline{y}(n-m) \quad (10.43)$$

represents the "linear prediction" of $y(n)$ based on the past N samples $\underline{y}(n-1)$, $\underline{y}(n-2), \ldots, \underline{y}(n-N)$, then the corresponding "prediction error" is

$$\underline{e}(n) = \underline{y}(n) - \hat{\underline{y}}(n) \quad (10.44)$$

Notice that Eq. (10.44) resembles the AR(N) difference equation [Eq. (10.39)]. The set of $a_N(m)$ coefficients that minimize the mean-squared prediction error, namely,

$$E[\underline{e}^2(n)] = E[\underline{y}(n) - \hat{\underline{y}}(n)]^2 \quad (10.45)$$

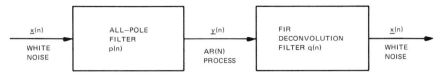

Fig. 10.9. Convolution and deconvolution operations associated with an AR(N) process.

satisfies the set of equations (10.42). In the context of mean-squared error (MSE) linear prediction, the $a_N(m)$ coefficients represent a prediction filter and Eq. (10.42) is referred to as the normal equations. In the context of AR(N) systems identification, the $a_N(m)$ coefficients represent the AR coefficients and Eq. (10.42) are referred to as the Yule–Walker equations. In any event, there is a one-to-one correspondence between AR(N) systems identification and linear prediction.

The coefficients $q(n) = (1, a_N(1), a_N(2), \ldots, a_N(N))$ represent an FIR minimum-phase deconvolution filter. That is, if $y(n)$ is generated by the convolution

$$\underline{y}(n) = p(n) * \underline{x}(n) \tag{10.46}$$

then $\underline{x}(n)$ is generated by the deconvolution

$$q(n) * \underline{y}(n) = \underline{x}(n) \tag{10.47}$$

Notice that the deconvolution Eq. (10.47) resembles the AR(N) difference equation [Eq. (10.39)]. The deconvolution filter $q(n)$ is sometimes called a *whitening filter*, since colored noise $\underline{y}(n)$ gets convolved with $q(n)$ to produce white noise $\underline{x}(n)$. See Fig. 10.9.

Example 4. Here we assume that $A_N(z) = 1$, so $H(z)$ is the all-zero or FIR model $H(z) = B_M(z)$. For this case we get the difference equation

$$\underline{y}(n) = b_M(0)\underline{x}(n) + b_M(1)\underline{x}(n-1) + b_M(2)\underline{x}(n-2) + \cdots + b_M(M)\underline{x}(n-M) \tag{10.48}$$

for $-\infty < n < \infty$. If $\underline{x}(n)$ is a white noise source with autocorrelation function [Eq. (10.40)], then Eq. (10.48) represents an MA(M) process of order M. We say that the output $\underline{y}(n)$ represents an MA process.

By multiplying both sides of Eq. (10.48) by $\underline{x}(n-m)$ and taking expected values, we obtain

$$b_M(l) = \frac{r_{yx}(l)}{\sigma_x^2}, \qquad l = 0, 1, 2, \ldots, M \tag{10.49}$$

That is, the MA coefficients are completely specified from the first M lags of the cross-correlation sequence $r_{yx}(m)$ and σ_x^2 [i.e., the variance of $\underline{x}(n)$]. Thus, the identification of an FIR filter driven by white noise with variance σ_x^2 is accomplished by Eq. (10.49). In Section IV we discuss fast algorithms that perform an FIR filter systems identification.

The above FIR systems identification algorithm can handle minimum-phase and non-minimum-phase systems. From the results in Section II.C.2.a we see that when the input and output information is in the form of power spectra (or autocorrelation sequences), the systems identification algorithms are limited to minimum-phase systems. In this example we assumed that we were given the cross-correlation sequence $r_{yx}(m)$ and input autocorrelation sequence $r_{xx}(m)$. Under these conditions the phase spectrum of $H(\omega) = B_M(\omega)$ is preserved, so in addition to minimum-phase systems we were also able to identify non-minimum-phase systems.

Example 5.   Let us now assume that $H(z)$ represents a pole–zero model; that is, $H(z) = B_M(z)/A_N(z)$. For this case we get the difference equation

$$\underline{y}(n) + a_N(1)\underline{y}(n-1) + a_M(2)\underline{y}(n-2) + \cdots + a_N(N)\underline{y}(n-N)$$

$$= b_M(0)\underline{x}(n) + b_M(1)\underline{x}(n-1) + b_M(2)\underline{x}(n-2) + \cdots + b_M(M)\underline{x}(n-M)$$

$$\text{(10.50)}$$

for $-\infty < n < \infty$. If $\underline{x}(n)$ is the WSS white noise process [Eq. (10.40)], then Eqs. (10.50) and (10.40) describe an ARMA(M, N) process of order (M, N). The output $y(n)$ represents an ARMA process [12].

The $\bar{\text{A}}$RMA(M, N) process can also be generated by the convolution

$$\underline{y}(n) = \sum_{k=0}^{\infty} h(k)\underline{x}(n-k) \tag{10.51}$$

Multiplying both sides of Eq. (10.51) by $\underline{x}(n-m)$ and taking expected values yields

$$r_{yx}(m) = \begin{cases} \sigma_x^2 h(m) & \text{for } m \geq 0 \\ 0 & \text{for } m < 0 \end{cases} \tag{10.52}$$

Equation (10.52) implies that the right-sided stable impulse response $h(n)$ can be completely recovered from knowledge of the cross-correlation sequence $r_{yx}(m)$ and white noise variance σ_x^2. That is,

$$h(n) = \frac{r_{yx}(n)}{\sigma_x^2}, \qquad n \geq 0 \tag{10.53}$$

Thus, to identify the $a_N(m)$ and $b_M(l)$ coefficients in Eq. (10.50), we can first use Eq. (10.53) to generate $h(n)$. Then we can use steps 3 and 4 in the double deconvolution algorithm to complete the ARMA(M, N) systems identification. This procedure will identify both minimum-phase and non-minimum-phase systems.

Let us now discuss another algorithm for identifying the ARMA(M, N) process. Multiplying both sides of Eq. (10.50) by $\underline{y}(n-m)$ and taking expected values yields

$$r_{yy}(m) + a_N(1)r_{yy}(m-1) + a_N(2)r_{yy}(m-2) + \cdots + a_N(N)r_{yy}(m-N)$$
$$= b_m(0)r_{yx}(-m) + b_M(1)r_{yx}(1-m) + b_M(2)r_{yx}(2-m)$$
$$+ \cdots + b_M(M)r_{yx}(M-m) \tag{10.54}$$

for $-\infty < m < \infty$. Here we used the fact that $r_{xy}(m) = r_{yx}(-m)$. Now for $m = M+1, M+2, \ldots, M+N$ we can use Eq. (10.54) to generate the matrix equation

$$\begin{bmatrix} r_{yy}(M) & r_{yy}(M-1) & \cdots & r_{yy}(M+1-N) \\ r_{yy}(M+1) & r_{yy}(M) & \cdots & r_{yy}(M+2-N) \\ & & \vdots & \\ r_{yy}(M+N-1) & r_{yy}(M+N-2) & \cdots & r_{yy}(M) \end{bmatrix} \begin{bmatrix} a_N(1) \\ a_N(2) \\ \vdots \\ a_N(N) \end{bmatrix} = - \begin{bmatrix} r_{yy}(M+1) \\ r_{yy}(M+2) \\ \vdots \\ r_{yy}(M+N) \end{bmatrix} \tag{10.55}$$

which can be solved for the AR coefficients. The set of equations (10.55) is commonly referred to as the *extended, modified,* or *high-order Yule–Walker equations* [14–16] which also appear in Chapter 9, Section III.C, in conjunction with spectral analysis. In Section IV we discuss a fast matrix inversion algorithm for solving these equations.

At this point we have identified the N AR parameters or coefficients from knowledge of the first $M+N$ lags of the autocorrelation sequence $r_{yy}(m)$. If we now consider Eq. (10.54) for $m = 0, 1, 2, \ldots, M$, we get the matrix equation

$$\begin{bmatrix} r_{yx}(0) & r_{yx}(1) & r_{yx}(2) & \cdots & r_{yx}(M) \\ 0 & r_{yx}(0) & r_{yx}(1) & \cdots & r_{yx}(M-1) \\ 0 & 0 & r_{yx}(0) & \cdots & r_{yx}(M-2) \\ & & & \vdots & \\ 0 & 0 & 0 & \cdots & r_{yx}(0) \end{bmatrix} \begin{bmatrix} b_M(0) \\ b_M(1) \\ b_M(2) \\ \vdots \\ b_M(M) \end{bmatrix} = \begin{bmatrix} R_{yy}(0) \\ R_{yy}(1) \\ R_{yy}(2) \\ \vdots \\ R_{yy}(M) \end{bmatrix} \tag{10.56}$$

where

$$R_{yy}(m) = r_{yy}(m) + \sum_{k=1}^{N} a_N(k)r_{yy}(m-k), \qquad m = 0, 1, 2, \ldots, M \tag{10.57}$$

The inversion of the upper triangular matrix in Eq. (10.56) yields the $M+1$ MA parameters or coefficients. Equations (10.55)–(10.57) provide the necessary information for a complete systems identification. This identification procedure can handle both minimum-phase and non-minimum-phase systems.

We close this section with the following key remarks:

1. The identification of a non-minimum-phase system driven by white noise requires (i) knowledge of the cross-correlation sequence $r_{yx}(m)$ for all lags m [refer

to (10.53)], or (ii) knowledge of the first $M + N$ lags of $r_{yy}(m)$ and the first M lags of $r_{yx}(m)$ [refer to Eqs. (10.55)–(10.57)]. Non-minimum-phase systems cannot be identified from knowledge of only $r_{yy}(m)$ and $r_{xx}(m)$.

2. Minimum-phase ARMA(M, N) systems driven by white noise can be identified from knowledge of only the input and output autocorrelation sequence (or the input and output PSDs). Refer to Section II.C.1.

3. The Yule–Walker equations (10.42) and the high-order Yule–Walker equations (10.55) can be solved by fast inversion algorithms. Refer to Section IV.

III   DECONVOLUTION AND THE IDENTIFICATION OF DTLTI SYSTEMS WITH MEASUREMENT NOISE

A   DTLTI Systems with Nonrandom Inputs

1   *Statement of the Deconvolution Problem for Noisy Outputs*

As in Section II.C.1 we assume that $x(n)$, $h(n)$, and $y(n)$ all belong to the set of right-sided stable sequences. This time, we assume that the output $y(n)$ is corrupted by an additive zero-mean WSS random noise process $\underline{v}(n)$, $\underline{n} = 0, 1, 2, \ldots$. With these assumptions let us now state the deconvolution problem for noisy outputs. Given the DTLTI system in Fig. 10.10,

$$y(n) = \sum_{k=0}^{n} h(k)x(n - k), \qquad n = 0, 1, 2, \ldots$$

$$\underline{z}(n) = y(n) + \underline{v}(n), \qquad n = 0, 1, 2, \ldots$$

$$(10.58)$$

the noisy deconvolution problem is to estimate the sequence $h(n)$ from knowledge of $\underline{z}(n)$ and $x(n)$.

In general, $h(n)$ and $x(n)$ are infinite-length sequences, so $y(n)$ and $\underline{z}(n)$ are infinite-length sequences. To make the problem amenable to the digital computer, we assume that $x(n)$ ($n = 0, 1, 2, \ldots, L_x - 1$) is a finite-length sequence of length L_x and that $h(n)$ ($n = 0, 1, 2, \ldots, L_h - 1$) is a finite-length sequence

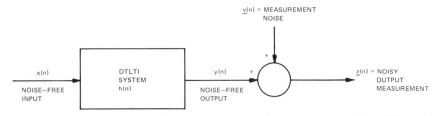

Fig. 10.10. Block diagram showing the output of a convolution model corrupted by additive noise.

of length L_h, so $h(n) * x(n)$ is the finite-length sequence $y(n)$ $(n = 0, 1,\ldots, L_x + L_h - 2)$ of length $L_y = L_x + L_h - 1$. Further, we assume that $\underline{z}(n)$ $(n = 0, 1, 2,\ldots, L_x + L_h - 2)$ is a sequence of length $L_z = L_x + L_h - 1$. With these finite-length assumptions, Eq. (10.58) has the matrix representation

$$\underbrace{\begin{bmatrix} z(0) \\ \underline{z}(1) \\ \underline{z}(2) \\ \vdots \\ \underline{z}(L_z - 1) \end{bmatrix}}_{L_z \times 1} = \underbrace{\begin{bmatrix} x(0) & 0 & 0 & \cdots & 0 \\ x(1) & x(0) & 0 & \cdots & 0 \\ x(2) & x(1) & x(0) & \cdots & 0 \\ & & & \vdots & \\ x(L_z - 1) & x(L_z - 2) & x(L_z - 3) & \cdots & x(L_x - 1) \end{bmatrix}}_{L_z \times L_h} \underbrace{\begin{bmatrix} h(0) \\ h(1) \\ h(2) \\ \vdots \\ h(L_h - 1) \end{bmatrix}}_{L_h \times 1} + \underbrace{\begin{bmatrix} \underline{v}(0) \\ \underline{v}(1) \\ \underline{v}(2) \\ \vdots \\ \underline{v}(L_z - 1) \end{bmatrix}}_{L_z \times 1}$$

(10.59)

which can be written in matrix–vector notation as

$$\underline{z} = \mathbf{A}\mathbf{h} + \underline{v} \tag{10.60}$$

Here, $\underline{z}$ is the $L_z \times 1$ column vector of noisy measurements, $\mathbf{A}$ is the $L_z \times L_h$ sparse matrix of input data, $\mathbf{h}$ is the $L_h \times 1$ column vector of unknown coefficients, and $\underline{v}$ is the $L_z \times 1$ column vector of noise samples. Thus, in the context of the matrix equation [Eq. (10.60)] the noisy deconvolution problem is to estimate the vector $\mathbf{h}$ given the known vector $\underline{z}$ and matrix $\mathbf{A}$. As we shall soon see, the noisy deconvolution problem is equivalent to the linear multiple regression problem [12].

Deconvolution and Linear Multiple Regression   2

In the previous section we saw that the noisy deconvolution problem came about because $\underline{z}(n)$ was a noisy observation of $\mathbf{y}(n)$. It turns out that in the matrix form [Eq. (10.60)], the deconvolution problem can be viewed as a linear multiple regression problem, with the unknown impulse response vector $\mathbf{h}$ playing the role of the multiple regression coefficients [12]. The linear multiple regression solution of Eq. (10.60) for $\mathbf{h}$ is that vector $\mathbf{h}_{LS}$ that minimizes the (MSE)

$$\text{MSE} = \sum_{n=0}^{L_z - 1} |\underline{v}(n)|^2 = \underline{v}^T\underline{v} = (\underline{z} - \mathbf{A}\mathbf{h})^T(\underline{z} - \mathbf{A}\mathbf{h}) \tag{10.61}$$

where the superscript T denotes the matrix transpose. The vector $\mathbf{h}_{LS}$ that minimizes Eq. (10.61) is obtained from the least squares normal equations

$$\mathbf{A}^T\mathbf{A}\mathbf{h}_{LS} = \mathbf{A}^T\underline{z} \tag{10.62}$$

We assume that $\mathbf{A}^T\mathbf{A}$ is nonsingular. Thus, the solution to Eq. (10.62),

$$\mathbf{h}_{LS} = (\mathbf{A}^T\mathbf{A})^{-1}\mathbf{A}^T\underline{z} \tag{10.63}$$

is unique. Further, if $\underline{v}(n)$ is a zero-mean WSS white noise process with variance

σ_v^2, then Eq. (10.63) is an unbiased efficient estimator of $\mathbf{h}$ [17]. The corresponding error covariance matrix is

$$\mathbf{P} = E[(\mathbf{h}_{LS} - \mathbf{h})(\mathbf{h}_{LS} - \mathbf{h})^T] = \sigma_v^2(\mathbf{A}^T\mathbf{A})^{-1} \tag{10.64}$$

As we have just seen, Eq. (10.63) provides a least squares solution to the noisy deconvolution problem. Our success in performing a noisy deconvolution should depend on the number of impulse response values L_h, the properties of the input sequence (or $\mathbf{A}^T\mathbf{A}$), and the signal-to-noise ratio (SNR). As a quantitative measure of our success, let us consider the ratio

$$R \equiv \frac{\mathrm{Tr}(\mathbf{P})}{\|\mathbf{h}\|^2} \tag{10.65}$$

where $\mathrm{Tr}(\mathbf{P})$ denotes the trace of the error covariance matrix [Eq. (10.64)] and

$$\|\mathbf{h}\|^2 \equiv h^2(0) + h^2(1) + h^2(2) \cdots + h^2(L_h - 1) \tag{10.66}$$

The smaller the value of R, the greater our success in performing an accurate noisy deconvolution. If

$$\mathrm{SNR} \equiv \frac{\|\mathbf{y}\|}{\sigma_v\sqrt{L_z}} \tag{10.67}$$

then [18] gives the upper and lower bounds for R:

$$\frac{1}{c\rho(\mathrm{SNR})^2} \leq R \leq \frac{c}{\rho(\mathrm{SNR})^2} \tag{10.68}$$

where $c = \lambda_{max}/\lambda_{min}$ and $\rho = L_z/L_h$. Here, λ_{max} and λ_{min} are the maximum and minimum eigenvalues of $\mathbf{A}^T\mathbf{A}$, respectively. The ratio c is often referred to as the condition number of $\mathbf{A}^T\mathbf{A}$. If c is small and ρ and SNR are large, our noisy deconvolution will be successful (i.e., accurate). We note that a minimum-phase source tends to have a small value of c; many data points and few regression parameters will yield a large value of ρ or "good" least squares fit, and a high SNR tends to give good results. The quantitive performance bounds [Eq. (10.68)] not only give us a good measure of deconvolution performance, but they also quantify our intuitive notions.

If the input $x(n)$ is a bandlimited or non-minimum-phase sequence, $\mathbf{A}^T\mathbf{A}$ will sometimes be singular (i.e., $\lambda_{min} = 0$). Then we cannot perform an exact and unique deconvolution. However, we can perform an "approximate" deconvolution by considering the modified normal equations

$$(\mathbf{A}^T\mathbf{A} + \sigma^2\mathbf{I})h_{MLS} = \mathbf{A}^T\mathbf{z} \tag{10.69}$$

where σ^2 is a judiciously chosen parameter that forces $\mathbf{A}^T\mathbf{A}$ to be nonsingular; that is, σ^2 is chosen so that λ_{min} is nonzero. Here, $\mathbf{I}$ is the $L_h \times L_h$ identity matrix. In the statistical literature the process of selecting an "optimal" value of σ^2 is called *ridge regression* [19]. Another rationale for selecting σ^2 is called *total least squares* [20]. In either case the fundamental idea is to load the diagonal elements of $\mathbf{A}^\mathrm{T}\mathbf{A}$ so that $\lambda_{\min}$ is nonzero. Since the collection of all the eigenvalues of $\mathbf{A}^\mathrm{T}\mathbf{A}$ is called the spectrum of $\mathbf{A}^\mathrm{T}\mathbf{A}$, the idea of selecting an optimal value of σ^2 is also referred to as *spectral balancing*.

The numerical solution of the normal equations (10.62) and the modified normal equations (10.69) is a fundamental problem in linear estimation theory. Chapter 13 discusses the batch and recursive solutions of Eq. (10.62), and [20] discusses a singular value decomposition (SVD) algorithm for the solution of Eq. (10.69). (For a brief discussion of the SVD technique, refer to Chapter 9.) In any event, we have shown that the noisy deconvolution problem can be formulated as a linear multiple regression or linear least squares problem. In this form many numerical algorithms are available for its solution. More will be said about numerical deconvolution algorithms in Section IV.

If $h(n)$ represents the impulse response of an FIR filter, then the noisy deconvolution algorithms discussed in this section are appropriate. However, if $h(n)$ represents the impulse response of an arbitrary IIR filter, then, based on our discussions in this section, we can only estimate the first L_h values of $h(n)$. However, if $H(z)$ has the rational form [Eq. (10.12)] and we wish to identify the sequences $a_N(m)$ and $b_M(l)$, then we can still use h_LS to estimate the sequences, provided that $L_h \geq M + N$ [see Eq. (10.33)]. That is, we can estimate the first $L_h = M + N$ values of $h(n)$ from Eq. (10.62) (when $x(n)$ is minimum phase); then we can use the vector $\mathbf{h}_\mathrm{LS}$ in steps 3 and 4 of the double deconvolution algorithm (discussed in Section II.C.1) to obtain estimates for the coefficients $a_N(m)$, $m = 1, 2, \ldots, N$, and $b_M(l)$, $l = 0, 1, \ldots, M$. We must be careful when attempting to invert the matrix in Eq. (10.33), since the elements of this matrix come from the vector of random variables $\mathbf{h}_\mathrm{LS}$. The inversion of noisy matrices is discussed in [20, 21].

When $x(n)$ is a non-minimum-phase input sequence, we can use Eq. (10.69) to get a least squares approximation to $h(n)$. Then we can use the vector $\mathbf{h}_\mathrm{MLS}$ in steps 3 and 4 of the double deconvolution algorithm to obtain approximate $a_N(m)$ and $b_M(l)$ sequences. Again, we must be careful when attempting to invert the matrix in Eq. (10.33).

DTLTI Systems with Random Inputs   B

Statement of the Deconvolution Problem for Noisy Outputs   1

As in Section II.C.2, we assume that $h(n)$ is right-sided and stable and that $\underline{x}(n)$ and $\underline{y}(n)$ belong to the set of zero-mean WSS random processes. We now make the additional assumption that $\underline{y}(n)$ is corrupted by an additive zero-mean, WSS random-noise process $\underline{v}(n)$, so we have the noisy WSS measurement $\underline{z}(n) = \underline{y}(n) + \underline{v}(n)$ for all integers n (see Fig. 10.11). With these assumptions let us now

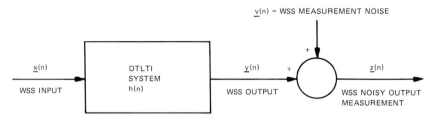

Fig. 10.11. A DTLTI system with a noisy WSS output corrupted by WSS additive noise.

state the noisy deconvolution problem for randon inputs. That is, given $x(n)$ and $z(n)$, the deconvolution problem is to estimate $h(n)$.

Example 6. Let us now extend the results of Example 3 to the noisy deconvolution problem. Recall that the AR(N) noise-free output $y(n)$ satisfied the difference equation [Eq. (10.39)] and $x(n)$ was the WSS white noise process [Eq. (10.40)]. We now assume that we have the noisy output $z(n) = y(n) + v(n)$, so $y(n)$ is corrupted by the additive WSS white noise process $v(n)$, where

$$r_{vv}(m) = \sigma_v^2 \delta(m) \tag{10.70}$$

We further assume that $x(n)$ and $v(n)$ are uncorrelated and that $y(n)$ and $v(n)$ are uncorrelated. If we now replace $y(n)$ in Eq. (10.39) by $z(n) - v(n)$ and multiply both sides of this new Eq. (10.39) by $z(n - m)$, we get the autocorrelation model

$$r_{zz}(m) - \sigma_v^2 \delta(m) + a_N(1)[r_{zz}(m - 1) - \sigma_v^2 \delta(m - 1)]$$
$$+ a_N(2)[r_{zz}(m - 2) - \sigma_v^2 \delta(m - 2)] + \cdots$$
$$+ a_N(N)[r_{zz}(m - N) - \sigma_v^2 \delta(m - N)] = 0 \tag{10.71}$$

for $m > 0$. The "new" Yule–Walker equations are

$$\begin{bmatrix} (r_{zz}(0) - \sigma_v^2) & r_{zz}(1) & \cdots & r_{zz}(N-1) \\ r_{zz}(1) & (r_{zz}(0) - \sigma_v^2) & \cdots & r_{zz}(N-2) \\ & & \vdots & \\ r_{zz}(N-1) & r_{zz}(N-2) & \cdots & (r_{zz}(0) - \sigma_v^2) \end{bmatrix} \begin{bmatrix} a_N(1) \\ a_N(2) \\ \vdots \\ a_N(N) \end{bmatrix} = - \begin{bmatrix} r_{zz}(1) \\ r_{zz}(2) \\ \vdots \\ r_{zz}(N) \end{bmatrix} \tag{10.72}$$

Comparing Eqs. (10.42) and (10.72), we see that for the noisy deconvolution problem, $r_{yy}(m)$ gets replaced by $r_{zz}(m)$ and the diagonals of the autocorrelation matrix get incremented by $-\sigma_v^2$. Thus, the noisy deconvolution of an AR(N) process uses the output autocorrelations $r_{zz}(m)$ ($m = 0, 1, 2, \ldots, N$) and a diagonal loading factor $-\sigma_v^2$, which compensates for the effects of the additive noise $v(n)$. In Section IV we discuss a fast matrix inversion algorithm for solving Eq. (10.72).

Example 7. In this example we extend the results of Example 4 to the noisy deconvolution problem. When the MA(M) process $y(n)$ is corrupted by the additive noise process [Eq. (10.70)], the noisy MA($\overline{M}$) measurement model becomes

$$\underline{z}(n) = \underline{y}(n) + \underline{v}(n) = \sum_{l=0}^{M-1} b_M(l)\underline{x}(n-l) + \underline{v}(n) \qquad (10.73)$$

for all integers n. As before, we assume that $\underline{y}(n)$ and $\underline{v}(n)$ are uncorrelated and that $\underline{x}(n)$ and $\underline{v}(n)$ are uncorrelated. Multiplying both sides of Eqs. (10.73) by $\underline{x}(n-m)$ and taking expected values gives

$$r_{zx}(m) = \sum_{l=0}^{M-1} b_M(l)r_{xx}(m-l) \qquad (10.74)$$

for all integers m. Here, we used the fact that $r_{vx}(m) = 0$. When $\underline{x}(n)$ is the white noise process [Eq. (10.40)], Eq. (10.74) yields

$$b_M(l) = \frac{r_{zx}(l)}{\sigma_x^2}, \qquad l = 0, 1, 2, \dots, M \qquad (10.75)$$

which extends Eq. (10.49) to the noisy deconvolution problem.

An alternative approach for identifying the MA(M) parameters $b_M(l)$ is to minimize the MSE

$$\text{MSE} = E\left[\left(\underline{z}(n) - \sum_{l=0}^{M-1} b_M(l)\underline{x}(n-l) \right)^2 \right] \qquad (10.76)$$

Doing so, we get Eq. (10.74). In the context of linear least squares estimation, Eq. (10.74) is called the *discrete-time Wiener–Hopf equation* [22]. The orthogonality condition $r_{vx}(m) = 0$ and the minimization of Eq. (10.76) go hand in hand (refer to Chapter 13). In Section VI we discuss a fast algorithm for solving the discrete-time Wiener–Hopf equation [Eq. (10.74)].

Example 8. In this example we assume that we have a noisy measurement $\underline{z}(n) = \underline{y}(n) + \underline{v}(n)$ (for all integers n) of the ARMA(M, N) process $\underline{y}(n)$ discussed in Example 5. Here, $\underline{v}(n)$ is the measurement noise discussed in Examples 6 and 7. Given the noisy measurement $\underline{z}(n)$, we now wish to identify the AR and MA coefficients.

Since we have assumed the $\underline{v}(n)$ and $\underline{y}(n)$ are uncorrelated and $\underline{v}(n)$ and $\underline{x}(n)$ are uncorrelated, it follows that

$$r_{zz}(m) = r_{yy}(m) + \sigma_v^2 \delta(m), \qquad r_{zx}(m) = r_{yx}(m). \qquad (10.77)$$

Thus, the first $M + N$ values of $h(n)$ can be found from Eq. (10.53) with $r_{yx}(m)$ replaced by $r_{zx}(m)$. Then we can use steps 3 and 4 of the double deconvolution algorithm to obtain the N AR and M MA parameters. Alternatively, we can find the AR coefficients by solving a "new" set of high-order Yule–Walker equations, namely, Eq. (10.55) with $r_{yy}(m)$ replaced by $r_{zz}(m)$. Then we find the MA coefficients by solving Eq. (10.56) with $r_{yy}(0)$ replaced by $r_{zz}(0) - \sigma_v^2$, $r_{yy}(m)$ ($m = 1, 2, \dots, M$) replaced by $r_{zz}(m)$, and $r_{yx}(m)$ replaced by $r_{zx}(m)$. This extends the results in Example 5 to the noisy deconvolution or systems identification problem. In Section IV we discuss fast algorithms for the solution of deconvolution problems.

IV FAST ALGORITHMS FOR DECONVOLUTION PROBLEMS

A The Levinson or Toeplitz Recursion: Direct Form

1 A Fast Algorithm for Identifying an AR(N) Process with Known Statistics

An uncorrupted AR(N) process $y(n)$ satisfies the difference equation [Eq. (10.39)], which can be schematically described by the direct-form diagram in Fig. 10.12. From Section II.C.2.b, Example 3, we know that an uncorrupted AR(N) process $y(n)$ can be completely defined from the first N lags of its autocorrelation function $r_{yy}(m)$. For known AR(N) statistics (i.e., known autocorrelation values) we must solve the Yule–Walker equations (10.42), which are compatible with the direct-form diagram in Fig. 10.12, to obtain the N AR(N) parameters. We now discuss a fast algorithm for solving the Yule–Walker equations.

Example 9. Let us consider the simplest of all AR(N) processes, the AR(1) process. The Yule–Walker equations become the single equation

$$r_{yy}(0)a_1(1) = -r_{yy}(1) \tag{10.78}$$

The algorithm for solving Eq. (10.78) is trivial, since it involves only the division

$$a_1(1) = -\frac{r_{yy}(1)}{r_{yy}(0)} \tag{10.79}$$

Notice that $|a_1(1)| < 1$.

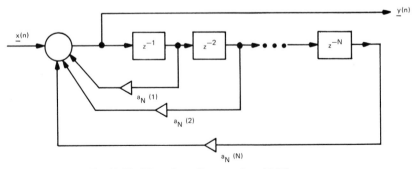

Fig. 10.12. Direct-form diagram of an AR(N) process.

Let us now consider the AR(2) process. The Yule–Walker equations are now

$$r_{yy}(0)a_2(1) + r_{yy}(1)a_2(2) = -r_{yy}(1)$$
$$r_{yy}(1)a_2(1) + r_{yy}(0)a_2(2) = -r_{yy}(2)$$
(10.80)

To solve Eq. (10.80) for $a_2(1)$ and $a_2(2)$, we will proceed according to the Gaussian elimination algorithm [23]. That is, we first define $k_1 \equiv -r_{yy}(1)/r_{yy}(0)$; notice that $|k_1| < 1$. Next, we multiply both sides of the first equation in (10.80) by k_1, and add the resulting equation to the second equation. This eliminates the variable $a_2(1)$ and allows us to solve for $a_2(2)$. Thus

$$a_2(2) = -\frac{r_{yy}(2) + k_1 r_{yy}(1)}{r_{yy}(0) + k_1 r_{yy}(1)}$$
(10.81)

which can be rewritten as

$$a_2(2) = -\frac{r_{yy}(2) + k_1 r_{yy}(1)}{r_{yy}(0)(1 - k_1^2)}$$
(10.82)

A little algebra will show that $|a_2(2)| < 1$. The last step in the Gaussian elimination algorithm is the back substitution. That is, given $a_2(2)$, we use the first equation in Eq. (10.80) to solve for $a_2(1)$. Thus

$$a_2(1) = k_1 + k_1 a_2(2)$$
(10.83)

We now can use the algorithm in Table II to solve the Yule–Walker equations (10.80).

Let us now consider the AR(3) process. The Yule–Walker equations are

$$r_{yy}(0)a_3(1) + r_{yy}(1)a_3(2) + r_{yy}(2)a_3(3) = -r_{yy}(1)$$
$$r_{yy}(1)a_3(1) + r_{yy}(0)a_3(2) + r_{yy}(1)a_3(3) = -r_{yy}(2)$$
$$r_{yy}(2)a_3(1) + r_{yy}(1)a_3(2) + r_{yy}(0)a_3(3) = -r_{yy}(3)$$
(10.84)

Using the Gaussian elimination algorithm to eliminate $a_3(1)$ and $a_3(2)$, we solve for $a_3(3)$:

$$a_3(3) = -\frac{r_{yy}(3) + \alpha_2(1)r_{yy}(2) + \alpha_2(2)r_{yy}(1)}{r_{yy}(0)(1 - k_1^2)(1 - k_2^2)}$$
(10.85)

TABLE II

Algorithm for Solving Yule–Walker Equations Given by Eq. (10.80)

Step 1. Define $k_1 \equiv -r_{yy}(1)/r_{yy}(0)$. Notice that $|k_1| < 1$.

Step 2. Given k_1 and the known autocorrelation values $r_{yy}(0)$, $r_{yy}(1)$, and $r_{yy}(2)$, solve (10.82) for the last AR(2) parameter, $a_2(2)$. Notice that $|a_2(2)| < 1$.

Step 3. Given k_1 and $a_2(2)$, solve (10.83) for the first AR(2) parameter, $a_2(1)$. At this point we have solved the Yule–Walker equations (10.80) for the AR(2) parameters $a_2(1)$ and $a_2(2)$.

where

$$k_1 \equiv \alpha_1(1) \equiv -\frac{r_{yy}(1)}{r_{yy}(0)} \tag{10.86}$$

$$k_2 \equiv \alpha_2(2) \equiv -\frac{r_{yy}(2) + \alpha_1(1)r_{yy}(1)}{r_{yy}(0)(1 - k_1^2)} \tag{10.87}$$

$$\alpha_2(1) = \alpha_1(1) + \alpha_1(1)\alpha_2(2) \tag{10.88}$$

The back substitution part of the Gaussian elimination algorithm gives $a_3(2)$ and $a_3(1)$:

$$a_3(2) = \alpha_2(2) + \alpha_2(1)a_3(3) \tag{10.89}$$

$$a_3(1) = \alpha_2(1) + \alpha_2(2)a_3(3) \tag{10.90}$$

Based on the above simplification of a Gaussian elimination algorithm to solve Eq. (10.84), we now propose the algorithm in Table III as a fast efficient method for solving the matrix equation

$$\begin{bmatrix} r_{yy}(0) & r_{yy}(1) & r_{yy}(2) \\ r_{yy}(1) & r_{yy}(0) & r_{yy}(1) \\ r_{yy}(2) & r_{yy}(1) & r_{yy}(0) \end{bmatrix} \begin{bmatrix} a_3(1) \\ a_3(2) \\ a_3(3) \end{bmatrix} = - \begin{bmatrix} r_{yy}(1) \\ r_{yy}(2) \\ r_{yy}(3) \end{bmatrix} \tag{10.91}$$

Recall that we started to solve Eq. (10.91) by the Gaussian elimination algorithm. However, we used a lot of algebra and simplification to reduce the general

TABLE III

Efficient Algorithm for Solving the Yule–Walker Equations (10.84)

Step 1. Initialization. Set $P_1 \equiv r_{yy}(0)$ and compute $k_1 \equiv \alpha_1(1)$.

Step 2. Compute $P_2 = P_1(1 - k_1^2)$. Then compute k_2 from [see (10.87)]

$$k_2 = \alpha_2(2) = -\frac{r_{yy}(2) + \alpha_1(1)r_{yy}(1)}{P_2}$$

Compute $\alpha_2(1)$ from (10.88). At this point we have defined $\alpha_2(1)$ and $\alpha_2(2)$ from knowledge of $r_{yy}(0)$, $r_{yy}(1)$, and $r_{yy}(2)$.

Step 3. Compute $P_3 = P_2(1 - k_2^2)$. Then compute k_3 from

$$k_3 = \alpha_3(3) = -\frac{r_{yy}(3) + \alpha_2(1)r_{yy}(2) + \alpha_2(2)r_{yy}(1)}{P_3}$$

Compute $\alpha_3(1)$ and $\alpha_2(2)$ from the relations

$$\alpha_3(1) = \alpha_2(1) + \alpha_2(2)k_3$$

$$\alpha_3(2) = \alpha_2(2) + \alpha_2(1)k_3$$

At this point we have defined $\alpha_3(1)$, $\alpha_3(2)$, and $\alpha_3(3)$ from knowledge of $r_{yy}(0)$, $r_{yy}(1)$, $r_{yy}(2)$, and $r_{yy}(3)$.

Step 4. Set $a_3(1) = \alpha_3(1)$, $a_3(2) = \alpha_3(2)$, and $a_3 = k_3 = \alpha_3(3)$. At this point we have solved (10.84) for the AR(3) parameters $a_3(1)$, $a_3(2)$, and $a_3(3)$.

---

approach of the Gaussian algorithm to the fast efficient algorithm in Table III.
Let us now explain why this simplification was possible.

Without thinking, we could have solved Eq. (10.91) or inverted the matrix

$$\begin{bmatrix} r_{yy}(0) & r_{yy}(1) & r_{yy}(2) \\ r_{yy}(1) & r_{yy}(0) & r_{yy}(1) \\ r_{yy}(2) & r_{yy}(1) & r_{yy}(0) \end{bmatrix} \qquad (10.92)$$

by a direct application of the Gaussian elimination algorithm. However, a little
thought reveals the following important point. Gaussian elimination does not
care about the structure or symmetry properties of the matrix [Eq. (10.92)]. The
only consideration is that the matrix be nonsingular. Thus, an $N \times N$ matrix
generally has N^2 independent elements, and the Gaussian elimination algorithm
would require N^2 storage locations and $O(N^3)$ operations in order to invert an
$N \times N$ nonsingular matrix. However, the Yule–Walker matrix [Eq. (10.92)]
has only three independent elements, not nine. Further, the elements of this matrix have symmetry; that is, they are the same along any northwest–southeast
diagonal. In mathematics a square matrix with this symmetry property is called a
Toeplitz matrix [2]. The mathematical properties of a Toeplitz matrix allowed us
to simplify the Gaussian elimination solution of Eq. (10.84) to a fast efficient
algorithm.

Since the Yule–Walker equations (10.42) have a Toeplitz structure, it follows
that the fast algorithm in Table III for solving Eq. (10.84) [or Eq. (10.91)] can be
generalized to solve the Yule–Walker equations (10.42). Levinson exploited the
Toeplitz structure of Eq. (10.42) and published the efficient approach to its
solution [24, 25] stated in Table IV. Since Eq. (10.94) in Table IV yields $|k_m| < 1$
for $m = 1, 2, \ldots, N$ (see Example 9), the Levinson or Toeplitz recursion is
numerically stable.

It turns out that the Toeplitz exploitation of the Levinson algorithm reduces
the Gaussian elimination algorithm from N^2 storage locations and $O(N^3)$
operations to N storage locations and $O(N^2)$ operations. The Levinson or
Toeplitz recursion is not only more efficient than the conventional Gaussian
elimination algorithm, but it also has an interesting interpretation. For example,
notice that $\alpha_1(1)$ could be thought of as the AR parameter of some AR(1) process.
The coefficients $\alpha_2(1)$ and $\alpha_2(2)$ could also be thought of as AR parameters of
some AR(2) process. Similarly, $\alpha_3(1), \alpha_3(2)$, and $\alpha_3(3)$ could belong to some AR(3)
process, and so on. The Levinson or Toeplitz recursion uses $\alpha_1(1)$ to generate
$\alpha_2(1), \alpha_2(2)$; then it uses $\alpha_2(1), \alpha_2(2)$ to generate $\alpha_3(1), \alpha_3(2), \alpha_3(3)$, etc. Thus, the
Levinson algorithm recursively generates AR parameters of increasing order
from the parameter of some AR(1) process to the desired parameters of the
AR(N) process. In this sense the fast efficient Levinson algorithm is correctly
named a recursion. It is one of the most important recursive algorithms in digital
signal processing. Although we have explained the Levinson recursion in terms of
the AR(N) systems identification problem, it is also used to solve the linear
prediction and whitening filter problems (see Section II.C.2.b, Example 3). An
IBM PC-compatible BASIC computer program is given in Appendix B.

TABLE IV

The Levinson or Toeplitz Recursion: Direct Form[a]

Given the autocorrelation values $r_{yy}(0), r_{yy}(1), r_{yy}(2), \ldots, r_{yy}(N)$ associated with an AR(N) process of order N, the Levinson recursion provides a fast efficient algorithm for solving the Yule–Walker equations (10.42). The algorithm gives the N AR parameters $a_N(1), a_N(2), \ldots, a_N(N)$.

Step 1. Initialization. Set $m = 1$.

$$P_1 = r_{yy}(0), \qquad k_1 = \alpha_1(1) \equiv -\frac{r_{yy}(1)}{r_{yy}(0)} \tag{10.93}$$

Step 2. Basic recursion ($m = 2, 3, \ldots, N$)

$$P_m = P_{m-1}[1 - k_{m-1}^2]$$

$$k_m = \alpha_m(m) = -\frac{r_{yy}(m) + \sum_{n=1}^{m-1} \alpha_{m-1}(n) r_{yy}(m-n)}{P_m} \tag{10.94}$$

$$\alpha_m(n) = \alpha_{m-1}(n) + [\alpha_{m-1}(m-n)]k_m, \qquad n = 1, 2, \ldots, m-1$$

Step 3. $a_N(n) = \alpha_N(n), \qquad n = 1, 2, \ldots, N$ $\qquad\qquad\qquad\qquad$ (10.95)

[a] Provides a fast efficient algorithm for solving the Yule–Walker equations (10.42).

2 Identifying an AR(N) Process with Unknown Statistics

In practice, one seldom knows the exact autocorrelation values. Instead, we usually observe a finite number of data samples, say $\underline{y}(1), \underline{y}(2), \ldots, \underline{y}(L_y)$. Given these L_y data samples, we now propose a fast algorithm for estimating the AR(N) parameters.

The basic idea is to first estimate the autocorrelation values by using the asymptotically unbiased estimate

$$\hat{r}_{yy}(m) = \frac{1}{L_y} \sum_{n=1}^{L_y - |m|} \underline{y}(n)\underline{y}(n-m), \qquad |m| \ll L_y, \ m = 0, 1, 2, \ldots, N \tag{10.96}$$

and replacing $r_{yy}(m)$ by $\hat{r}_{yy}(m)$ in the fast Levinson recursion. To do this successfully, we must have $N \ll L_y$. This will ensure that the variance of Eq. (10.96) will be small for large lags, so Eq. (10.96) will be a good estimate of $r_{yy}(m)$ for lags near $m = N$ [2].

B The Levinson or Toeplitz Recursion: Lattice Form

1 The Lattice Structure

Let us consider an arbitrary sequence $y(n)$; that is, this sequence could be either random or nonrandom, finite length or infinite length. Let us also consider the idea of passing this sequence through a two-point FIR minimum-phase filter

Fig. 10.13. Input-output relationship of linear minimum phase filter.

with transfer function

$$\text{Min}(z) = 1 + kz^{-1} \tag{10.97}$$

where $|k| < 1$. Thus, the input $y(n)$ and output $f(n)$ of this FIR minimum-phase filter are described by the difference equation

$$y(n) + ky(n-1) = f(n) \tag{10.98}$$

for all integers n (see Fig. 10.13).

In Section II.B we discussed the concept of minimum phase or minimum delay. It turns out that for every minimum-phase filter, we have a corresponding maximum-phase filter [11]. The coefficients of this maximum-phase filter are obtained by reversing the order of the minimum-phase filter coefficients. For example, the minimum-phase filter [Eq. (10.97)] has the maximum-phase counterpart

$$\text{Max}(z) = k + z^{-1} \tag{10.99}$$

Note that Eqs. (10.97) and (10.99) have the same magnitude spectrum.

Let us now consider the idea of passing the arbitrary sequence $y(n)$ through the two-point FIR maximum-phase filter that corresponds to Eq. (10.97), namely, Eq. (10.99). The input $y(n)$ and output $\beta(n)$ of this FIR maximum-phase filter are described by the difference equation

$$ky(n) + y(n-1) = \beta(n) \tag{10.100}$$

for all integers n (Fig. 10.14).

We now come to the fundamental idea behind the lattice structure. That is, if we combine the minimum-phase system [Eq. (10.98)] and the corresponding maximum-phase system [Eq. (10.100)], we obtain an overall block diagram that resembles a lattice configuration (Fig. 10.15).

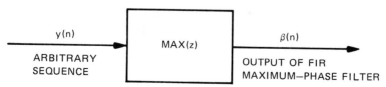

Fig. 10.14. Input-output relationship of linear maximum-phase filter.

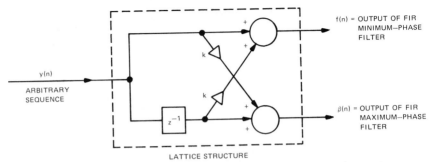

LATTICE STRUCTURE

Fig. 10.15. Combination of minimum-phase system and maximum-phase system.

2 The Lattice Structure and Its Relationship to the Levinson Recursion

As we saw in Section IV.A.1, the Levinson algorithm recursively generates AR parameters at each stage of the recursion. For example, at the first stage ($m = 1$) we get the parameter $\alpha_1(1)$. At the second stage ($m = 2$) we get $\alpha_2(1)$, $\alpha_2(2)$. At the final stage ($m = N$) we get the desired AR(N) parameters $a_N(1)$, $a_N(2)$, ..., $a_N(N)$ associated with the underlying AR(N) process. Note that the intermediate parameters $\alpha_m(n)$ ($m = 1, 2, \ldots, N - 1$; $n = 1, 2, \ldots, m$) are simply useful by-products of the Levinson recursion. Let us elaborate. At stage m of the Levinson recursion ($m = 1, 2, \ldots, N$), we generate $\alpha_m(1)$, $\alpha_m(2), \ldots, \alpha_m(m) = k_m$. These parameters can be used to form the FIR minimum-phase filter

$$A_m(z) = 1 + \alpha_m(1)z^{-1} + \alpha_m(2)z^{-2} + \cdots + k_m z^{-m} \qquad (10.101)$$

We obtain the corresponding FIR maximum-phase filter by reversing the order of the coefficients in the minimum-phase filter [Eq. (10.101)]: Thus

$$R_m(z) = k_m + \alpha_m(m - 1)z^{-1} + \alpha_m(m - 2)z^{-2} + \cdots + z^{-m} \qquad (10.102)$$

Now let $y(n)$ denote the WSS AR(N) process. If we pass $y(n)$ through the minimum-phase filter [Eq. (10.101)], we get the output $\underline{f}_m(n)$. The input $\underline{y}(n)$ and output $\underline{f}_m(n)$ are related by the difference equation

$$\underline{y}(n) + \sum_{k=1}^{m} \alpha_m(k)\underline{y}(n - k) = \underline{f}_m(n) \qquad (10.103)$$

for $-\infty < n < \infty$. The output $\underline{f}_m(n)$ is not necessarily white noise, since the $\alpha_m(k)$ parameters are not the AR(N) parameters. Thus, only at the final stage ($m = N$) does $a_N(k) = \alpha_N(k)$ and $\underline{f}_N(n) = \underline{x}(n)$ = white noise.

Similarly, if we pass $\underline{y}(n)$ through the maximum-phase filter [Eq. (10.102)], we get the output $\underline{\beta}_m(n)$. The input $\underline{y}(n)$ and output $\underline{\beta}_m(n)$ are related by the difference equation

$$\underline{y}(n - m) + \sum_{k=1}^{m} \alpha_m(m - k + 1)\underline{y}(n - k + 1) = \underline{\beta}_m(n) \qquad (10.104)$$

for $-\infty < n < \infty$. Recall that the minimum-phase and maximum-phase filters (10.101) and (10.102), respectively, have the same magnitude spectrum. Thus, it follows that $\underline{f}_m(n)$ and $\beta_m(n)$ have the same power spectrum.

Let us now show how Eqs. (10.103) and (10.104) can be combined to form a lattice structure. From our knowledge of the Levinson or Toeplitz recursion [see step 2, (10.94) in Table 10.4], we know that the α parameters at stage m and stage $m - 1$ are related by

$$\alpha_m(k) = \alpha_{m-1}(k) + [\alpha_{m-1}(m - k)]k_m, \qquad m = 2, 3, \ldots, N; k = 1, 2, \ldots, m - 1$$

$$(10.105)$$

If we now substitute Eq. (10.105) into Eq. (10.103) and rearrange terms based on the forms of Eqs. (10.103) and (10.104), we obtain

$$\underline{f}_m(n) = \underline{f}_{m-1}(n) + k_m\beta_{m-1}(n - 1) \qquad (10.106)$$

for $m = 2, 3, \ldots, N$ and $-\infty < n < \infty$. Similarly, if we substitute Eq. (10.105) into Eq. (10.104) and rearrange terms based on the forms of Eqs. (10.103) and (10.104), we obtain

$$\beta_m(n) = \underline{\beta}_{m-1}(n - 1) + k_m\underline{f}_{m-1}(n) \qquad (10.107)$$

for $m = 2, 3, \ldots, N$ and $-\infty < n < \infty$. Equations (10.106) and (10.107) represent a set of coupled difference equations that relate the minimum-phase and maximum-phase filter outputs at the mth stage ($m = 2, 3, \ldots, N$). A schematic diagram of the combination of these two equations at stage m gives the lattice structure in Fig. 10.16. This lattice structure contains only the parameter $k_m \equiv \alpha_m(m)$. Recall that $|k_m| < 1$ for $m = 1, 2, \ldots, N$.

The first stage ($m = 1$) of the Levinson algorithm was the initialization of the

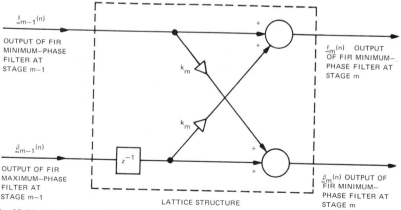

$\underline{f}_{m-1}(n)$

OUTPUT OF FIR
MINIMUM–PHASE
FILTER AT
STAGE m–1

$\underline{\beta}_{m-1}(n)$

OUTPUT OF FIR
MAXIMUM–PHASE
FILTER AT
STAGE m–1

k_m

k_m

z^{-1}

LATTICE STRUCTURE

$\underline{f}_m(n)$ OUTPUT
OF FIR MINIMUM–
PHASE FILTER AT
STAGE m

$\beta_m(n)$ OUTPUT OF
FIR MINIMUM–
PHASE FILTER AT
STAGE m

Fig. 10.16. At each stage of the Levinson recursion ($m = 2, 3, \ldots, N$), a lattice structure relates the minimum-phase and maximum-phase filter outputs at stage $m - 1$ to the minimum-phase and maximum-phase filter outputs at stage m.

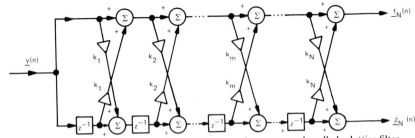

Fig. 10.17. Schematic diagram of the lattice recursion, commonly called a lattice filter.

recursion [see step 1, (10.93) in Table IV. For $m = 1$ Eq. (10.103) reduces to

$$\underline{f}(n) = \underline{y}(n) + k_1 \underline{y}(n - 1) \tag{10.108}$$

and Eq. (10.104) reduces to

$$\underline{\beta}(n) = \underline{y}(n - 1) + k_1 \underline{y}(n) \tag{10.109}$$

Comparing Eq. (10.108) with Eq. (10.106) and Eq. (10.109) with Eq. (10.107), we can say that

$$\underline{\beta}_0(n) \equiv \underline{y}(n), \qquad \underline{f}_0(n) \equiv \underline{y}(n) \tag{10.110}$$

Thus we have the lattice recursion in Table V. Figure 10.17 gives a schematic diagram description of the lattice recursion. The input to this lattice is the AR(N) process $y(n)$, and one of the outputs is the white noise process $f_N(n) = \underline{x}(n)$. Thus, this lattice structure acts as a "whitening filter." In the digital signal processing literature the lattice recursion and its schematic representation in Fig. 10.17 are referred to as the *lattice filter* [26], which is also discussed in Section V of Chapter 12.

We close this section with two key points:

1. The Levinson recursion depends on the numbers $k_1, k_2, \ldots, k_m, \ldots, k_N$,

TABLE V

Lattice Recursion

Step 1.   Initialization. Set $m = 0$, $-\infty < n < \infty$.

$$\underline{f}_0(n) = \underline{y}(n), \qquad \underline{\beta}_0(n) = \underline{y}(n) \tag{10.111}$$

Step 2.   Lattice recursion ($m = 1, 2, \ldots, N$), $-\infty < n < \infty$.

$$\underline{f}_m(n) = \underline{f}_{m-1}(n) + k_m \underline{\beta}_{m-1}(n - 1)$$
$$\underline{\beta}_m(n) = \underline{\beta}_{m-1}(n - 1) + k_m \underline{f}_{m-1}(n) \tag{10.112}$$

Step 3.   Final stage ($m = N$), $-\infty < n < \infty$.

$$\underline{f}_N(n) = \underline{x}(n) = \text{white noise}$$
$$\underline{\beta}_N(n) = \text{white noise} \tag{10.113}$$

---

where $|k_m| < 1$. Because of this property, these numbers are commonly referred to as *reflection coefficients* (see Section V).

2. We have shown that the Levinson recursion has a corresponding lattice recursion that depends only on the k_m's. The lattice recursion, or lattice filter, is a multistage whitening filter.

In the next section we show how the lattice recursion can be used to identify an AR(N) process with unknown statistics.

A Fast Lattice Algorithm for Identifying an AR(N) Process with Unknown Statistics   3

We assume that we have only L_y samples of an AR(N) process, namely, $y(1), y(2), \ldots, y(L_y)$. We further assume that $N \ll L_y$. We now show how to identify the N AR parameters by means of a lattice algorithm.

The quantity $f_m(n)$ in Eq. (10.103) was shown to be the output of an FIR minimum-phase filter. In the context of linear prediction we can interpret $f_m(n)$ as a *forward* prediction error. Similarly, $\beta_m(n)$ in Eq. (10.104) was shown to be the output of an FIR maximum-phase filter. In the context of linear prediction we can interpret $\beta_m(n)$ as a *backward* prediction error. The terms "forward" and "backward" refer to the problem of predicting $y(n)$ on the basis of m past samples (forward prediction) and predicting $y(n - m)$ on the basis of m future samples (backward prediction). In this context we can define the forward-prediction-error sample variance by

$$E_f \equiv \frac{1}{L_y - m} \sum_{n=m+1}^{L_y} f_m^2(n) \tag{10.114}$$

and the backward-prediction-error sample variance by

$$E_\beta \equiv \frac{1}{L_y - m} \sum_{n=m+1}^{L_y} \beta_m^2(n) \tag{10.115}$$

We chose the summation indices $n = m + 1$ to $n = L_y$ to avoid going outside the data window $n = 1$ to $n = L_y$. In this way we make no assumption about the data outside the data window. Now since $y(n)$ was assumed to be a WSS process, the theoretical forward-prediction- and backward-prediction-error variances are equal. Thus, we may combine the sample variances [Eqs. (10.114) and (10.115)] by the standard statistical technique of forming their arithmetic mean. Thus

$$E \equiv \tfrac{1}{2}(E_f + E_\beta) \tag{10.116}$$

or

$$E = \frac{1}{2(L_y - m)} \sum_{n=m+1}^{L_y} [f_m^2(n) + \beta_m^2(n)] \tag{10.117}$$

Substituting Eq. (10.112) into Eq. (10.117) gives

$$E = \frac{1}{2(L_y - m)} \sum_{n=m+1}^{L_y} \{[\underline{f}_{m-1}(n) + k_m \underline{\beta}_{m-1}(n-1)]^2$$

$$+ [\underline{\beta}_{m-1}(n-1) + k_m \underline{f}_{m-1}(n)]^2\} \quad (10.118)$$

for $n = 1, 2, \ldots, N$. Differenting E in Eq. (10.118) with respect to k_m and setting the result equal to zero gives the coefficient $\underline{k}_m$ that minimizes E:

$$\underline{k}_m = \underline{\hat{a}}_m(m) = \frac{-2\sum_{n=m+1}^{L_y} \underline{f}_{m-1}(n)\underline{\beta}_{m-1}(n-1)}{\sum_{n=m+1}^{L_y} [\underline{f}_{m-1}^2(n) + \underline{\beta}_{m-1}^2(n-1)]} \quad (10.119)$$

for $m = 1, 2, \ldots, N$.

We are now in a position to give a lattice-filter-type algorithm for identifying the N AR(N) parameters. The algorithm in Table VI is basically the lattice form of the Levinson or Toeplitz recursion and is due to J. P. Burg [11]. In Appendix C we give an IBM PC-compatible BASIC computer program for implementing the Burg algorithm.

We note that the direct form of the Levinson algorithm discussed in Section IV.A.2 and the lattice form of the Levinson algorithm given here are very similar, since they are derived from the same mathematical assumptions. However, the direct form explicitly estimates the autocorrelation values $r_{yy}(m)$, whereas the lattice form implicitly estimates $r_{yy}(m)$. In either case they both handle the case of unknown statistics.

TABLE VI

Lattice Form of the Levinson Recursion: The Burg Algorithm

Step 1. Initialization. Set $m = 0, 1 \le n \le L_y$

$$\underline{f}_0(n) = \underline{y}(n), \qquad \underline{\beta}_0(n) = \underline{y}(n)$$

Step 2. Recursion for $m = 1, 2, \ldots, N$.

  (i) Compute $\underline{k}_m$ from (10.119), $1 \le m \le N$.

  (ii) $\underline{\hat{a}}_m = \underline{k}_m$, $1 \le m \le N$

  $\underline{\hat{a}}_m(k) = \underline{\hat{a}}_{m-1}(k) + \underline{k}_m \underline{\hat{a}}_{m-1}(m-k)$, $2 \le m \le N; 1 \le k \le m - 1$

  (iii) $\underline{f}_m = \underline{f}_{m-1}(n) + \underline{k}_{y_m} \underline{\beta}_{m-1}(n-1)$

  $\underline{\beta}_m = \underline{\beta}_{m-1}(n-1) + \underline{k}_{y_m} \underline{f}_{m-1}(n)$, $m + 1 \le n \le L_y$

Step 3. After cycling through step 2 for $m = 1, 2, \ldots, N$, we come to the final stage $m = N$. At this point we have

$$\hat{a}_N(m) = \underline{\hat{a}}_N(m), \qquad m = 1, 2, \ldots, N$$

The quantities $\hat{a}_N(m)$ are estimates of the true AR(N) parameters $a_N(m)$.

There are many variations of the lattice filter. In this section we have presented only one. However, once you master the material in this section, you will appreciate the numerous results in [26].

Extended Levinson Algorithms   C

As we have seen, the mathematics of Toeplitz matrices allows for fast efficient direct-form or lattice-type algorithms. However, situations do arise (e.g., in linear predictive least squares analysis [27]) when the matrices are not Toeplitz. To handle this situation, we use the concept of displacement rank, which is a measure of how far a matrix is from being Toeplitz [28]. References [28] and [29] provide a good discussion on fast algrithms for inverting matrices that are not too far from being Toeplitz.

Linear Least Squares Estimation and   D
Kalman Filtering Algorithms

Many deconvolution problems can be cast into linear regression problems (see Section III.A.2) or Kalman filtering state-space filtering problems. For these situations we can use the well-known Kalman filtering or least squares algorithms, which are discussed in Chapter 13.

SOME PRACTICAL APPLICATIONS OF DECONVOLUTION   V

Deconvolution and Speech Signal Processing   A

In our introductory remarks we noted that deconvolution defines the inverse problem. In speech the forward problem is to produce the speech waveform from knowledge of the glottis excitation waveform and the vocal tract shape (Figs. 10.1 and 10.2). The inverse problem for speech is to define the vocal tract shape from knowledge of the speech waveform and glottis excitation waveform. Let us now show how the theory of deconvolution is related to the inverse problem for speech.

To perform deconvolution on a physical process such as speech, we need a model. That is, to solve the inverse problem for speech, we need a model of the vocal tract shape. It must be a simple, tractable model of the physical vocal tract shape, which is pictorially described in Fig. 10.1. A very useful one is the *acoustic tube model* [1], based on the important assumption that the physical vocal tract shape can be approximated by an interconnected–cascaded network of cylindrical sections as illustrated in Fig. 10.18. It is also assumed that each cylindrical section has the same length *l* and is of uniform cross-sectional area.

From a purely physical argument we know that when the glottis creates an acoustic excitation, speech or sound is produced. Further, as the speech is being uttered, the cross-sectional area of each cylindrical section is changing as a function of time. Hence, if we knew the glottis excitation waveform as a function of time and the cross-sectional areas $A_1, A_2, \ldots, A_N$ of the N sections as functions of time (Fig. 10.18), then, in principle, we could produce speech. This idea forms the basis of speech analysis and synthesis [1].

For any given sound, let the cross-sectional area of the mth cylindrical section be denoted by A_m, where m runs from 1 to N. Let section 1 be closest to the lips, and let section N be closest to the glottis. For descriptive purposes we speak of the glottis as being at the left and the lips as being at the right.

Under the preceding assumptions and some additional assumptions involving one-dimensional plane-wave propagation in a homogeneous acoustic tube, the acoustic velocity wave in each homogeneous cylindrical section satisfies the one-dimensional acoustic wave equation

$$\frac{\partial^2 U_m(x,t)}{\partial t^2} = c^2 \frac{\partial^2 U_m(x,t)}{\partial x^2} \tag{10.120}$$

where $U_m(x, t)$ is the acoustic velocity wave in the mth cylindrical section, c is the speed of sound in the vocal tract, x is the spatial variable ($x > 0$ is to the right), and t is time. Since the solution to Eq. (10.120) is of the form

$$U_m(x,t) = C_1 U_m\left(\frac{t-x}{c}\right) + C_2 U_m^-\left(\frac{t+x}{c}\right) \tag{10.121}$$

we see that in each cylindrical section of the acoustic tube model we have two traveling waves. One traveling wave, $U_m^+(t - x/c)$, moves to the right; the other

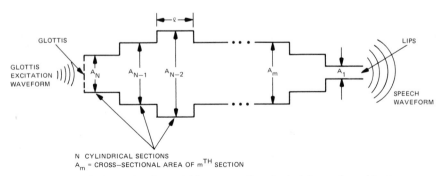

Fig. 10.18. Acoustic tube model for representing physical shape of vocal tract.

traveling wave, $U_m^-(t + x/c)$, moves to the left. At the interface between sections $m - 1$ and m, there is a discontinuity in cross-sectional area; that is, section $m - 1$ has cross-sectional area A_{m-1}, and section m has cross-sectional area A_m. Thus, because of this discontinuity in cross-sectional area at each interface between two adjacent sections, a traveling wave will be partially reflected and partially transmitted at each interface. The division of acoustic energy between the reflected and transmitted parts of the traveling wave is governed by the *reflection coefficient* associated with a particular interface. For example, if A_{m-1} is the cross-sectional area of section $m - 1$ and A_m is the cross-sectional area of section m, then, from continuity of pressure and velocity and physical considerations, it can be shown that the reflection coefficient at the interface between sections $m - 1$ and m is given by [1]

$$k_m = \frac{A_{m-1} - A_m}{A_{m-1} + A_m} \qquad (10.122)$$

After taking into account the boundary conditions at each interface and performing several mathematical transformations on the dependent and independent variables, we obtain [1]

$$y_m^+(t) \equiv c_m U_m^+(t + \tau - t_m), \qquad y_m^-(t) \equiv -c_m U_m^-(t - \tau - t_m) \quad (10.123)$$

where

$$c_m \equiv \prod_{j=1}^{m} (1 + k_j), \quad m = 1, 2, \ldots, N, \qquad c_0 \equiv 1 \qquad (10.124)$$

$t_m = 2(m + 1)\tau$, and $\tau = l/2c$. Performing some additional mathematical transformations on Eq. (10.123), we obtain the coupled equations

$$y_m^+(t) = y_{m-1}^+(t) + k_m y_{m-1}^-(t)$$
$$y_m^-(t) = y_{m-1}^-(t - T) + k_m y_{m-1}^+(t - T) \qquad (10.125)$$

for $m = 1, 2, \ldots, N$. Here, $T = 4\tau = 2l/c$ is twice the time needed for a wave to propagate through a single cylindrical section. If we let $t = nT$, then we can convert the continuous-time relations [Eq. (10.125)] to discrete time. Doing so gives

$$y_m^+(n) = y_{m-1}^+(n) + k_m y_{m-1}^-(n)$$
$$y_m^-(n) = y_{m-1}^-(n - 1) + k_m y_{m-1}^+(n - 1) \qquad (10.126)$$

for $m = 1, 2, \ldots, N$ and all integers n.

The coupled equations in (10.126) relate the right- and left-going waves in section $m - 1$ to the right- and left-going waves in section m. It turns out that this traveling wave relationship is described by the lattice structure in Fig. 10.19. Further, notice that $y_0^+(n)$ is proportional to the sampled speech waveform and $y_N^-(n)$ is proportional to the sampled glottis excitation waveform. If we let $x(n) = y_N^-(n)$ and $y(n) = y_0^+(n)$, then we can show that $y(n)$ and $x(n)$ are related by

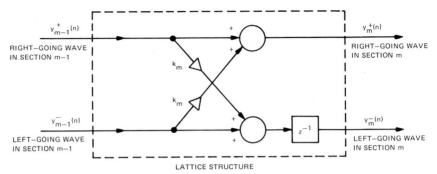

LATTICE STRUCTURE

Fig. 10.19. The lattice structure relates the right-going and left-going waves in section $m - 1$ to the corresponding waves in section m.

the all-pole or AR model [1]

$$y(n) + a_N(1)y(n-1) + a_N(2)y(n-2) + \cdots + a_N(N)y(n-N) = x(n) \quad (10.127)$$

For certain speech sounds $y(n)$ can be approximated by a WSS AR(N) process, which implies that $x(n)$ is white noise. Under these conditions we can use the direct form of the Levinson recursion to estimate the N AR(N) parameters $a_N(1), a_N(2), \ldots, a_N(N)$. However, the lattice form of the Levinson recursion is more desirable, since the lattice parameters $k_1, k_2, \ldots, k_N$ are proportional to the physical reflection coefficients of the acoustic tube model [1]. Once the reflection coefficients are known, then the vocal tract shape follows from Eq. (10.122).

In summary, we solve the deconvolution or inverse problem for speech by using the lattice filter algorithms discussed in Section IV.B. The lattice parameters $k_1, k_2, \ldots, k_N$ turn out to be the physical reflection coefficients associated with the acoustic tube model of the vocal tract shape. The relationship between lattice filters and right- and left-going waves in the acoustic tube model is important, for it shows how deconvolution algorithms are related to the physics of the problem.

B Deconvolution and Seismic Signal Processing

In the introduction we discussed the real-world nature of the seismic deconvolution or inverse problem (see Figs. 10.3 and 10.4). Recall that the speech inverse problem needed a model of the vocal tract shape. Similarly, the seismic inverse problem needs a model of the earth's subsurface. However, the mathematical model for the real-world seismic deconvolution or inverse problem involves a three-dimensional elastic wave equation with spatially variant coefficients [30]. This three-dimensional subsurface model is quite difficult to analyze; it is still in the research stages. As a result, we will consider a one-dimensional (1-D) subsurface model—that is, a 1-D elastic wave equation, which is mathematically easier to analyze.

Let us first review the seismic experiment. We will consider the 1-D seismic system in Fig. 10.20, where $z < 0$ defines a homogeneous half-space (e.g., air) and $z \geq 0$ defines an inhomogeneous half-space (e.g., the earth's subsurface). A seismic source located at $z = 0$ excites the 1-D model in Fig. 10.20 with the waveform $x(t)$ at $t = 0$. Thus, $x(t)$ is a right-sided or causal waveform. The response to this excitation is the seismic signal $y(t) = u(z = 0, t)$, where $u(z, t)$ is the seismic wave field for all z and t, and $u(z = 0, t)$ is the seismic wave field measured at $z = 0$. Hence, the source and receiver are located at the same point, $z = 0$. This differs from the speech problem, where the source was located at the glottis and the measurement was performed at the lips. We now state the 1-D seismic inverse problem. Given knowledge of the source $x(t)$ and the response $y(t) = u(z = 0, t)$ for $t \geq 0$ and the 1-D elastic model

$$\rho(z)\frac{\partial^2 u(z, t)}{\partial t^2} - \frac{\partial}{\partial z}\left[E(z)\frac{\partial u(z, t)}{\partial z}\right] = -\delta(z)x(t) \tag{10.128}$$

find the parameters $\rho(z)$ and $E(z)$ for $z > 0$. Here, $\rho(z)$ is the density, and $E(z)$ is an elastic parameter; both are known constants for $z < 0$.

A little thought reveals that there is not enough information to solve the 1-D inverse problem. In other words, how can we estimate two independent functions, $\rho(z)$ and $E(z)$, from only one measurement or time series, $u(z = 0, t)$? To obtain a 1-D solution, we can do one of three things: (i) obtain another independent measurement of the wave field or measure the gradient of the wave field; (ii) obtain a priori information on $\rho(z)$ or $E(z)$ that is, assume that one of these functions is known; or (iii) solve for the ratio or product of $\rho(z)$ and $E(z)$. It turns out that the seismic impedance is the square root of $\rho(z)E(z)$. Since this quantity is physically meaningful, let us now discuss the digital signal processing functions required to convert the sampled wave field $y(n)$ into an estimate of the seismic impedance for $z > 0$. Doing so, we will have solved the 1-D seismic deconvolution or inverse problem.

According to [31], it is often observed that the graph of $\rho(z)$ and $E(z)$ as a function of depth can well be approximated by piecewise constant values on the spatial scales of physical interest. Given that this observation is correct, the 1-D

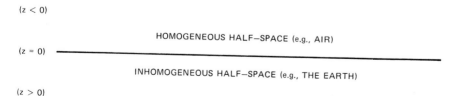

($z < 0$)

HOMOGENEOUS HALF−SPACE (e.g., AIR)

($z = 0$)

INHOMOGENEOUS HALF−SPACE (e.g., THE EARTH)

($z > 0$)

Fig. 10.20. Pictorial representation of a 1-D seismic medium.

seismic model [Eq. (10.128)] can be analyzed in terms of a *layered medium model* [2, 32]. This means that the inhomogeneous half-space in Fig. 10.20 for $z \geq 0$ can be replaced by an interconnected–cascaded network of homogeneous sections or layers, as shown in Fig. 10.21. Therefore each layer has its own constant-coefficient wave equation, and there are up-going and down-going traveling waves in each layer. For the nth layer we have the wave equation

$$\rho_n \frac{\partial^2 u_n(z,t)}{\partial t^2} = E_n \frac{\partial^2 u_n(z,t)}{\partial z^2} \tag{10.129}$$

where ρ_n and E_n are constants. Also, $c_n = [E_n/\rho_n]^{1/2}$ is the constant wave propagation speed for layer n, and $Z_n = \rho_n c_n = [\rho_n E_n]^{1/2}$ is the constant seismic impedance for layer n. In solving the seismic inverse problem, we define, for convenience, the travel time variable

$$\tau(z) = \begin{cases} \dfrac{z}{c_0} & \text{for } z \leq 0 \\[2ex] \displaystyle\int_0^z \dfrac{dx}{c(x)} & \text{for } z \geq 0 \end{cases} \tag{10.130}$$

For a layered medium the up-going and down-going waves in each layer take a finite amount of time to travel from one interface to the other. In general, the waves experience different travel times between interfaces, since each layer has a different wave propagation speed. References [2] and [32] solved the seismic inverse problem for layered media with the assumption of layers of equal travel time and minimum-phase sources. Under these conditions a lattice-filter-type algorithm relates the sampled wave field $y(n)$ to a set of numbers k_n called

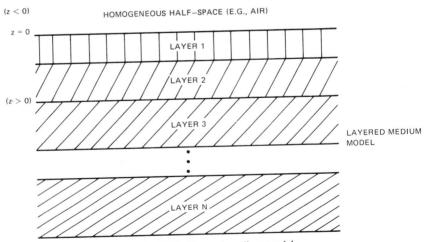

Fig. 10.21. Layered medium model.

TABLE VII

Fast Seismic Deconvolution Algorithm for Layers of Unequal Travel Time

---

Fundamental Assumptions

(a) The impedance of the 1-D elastic medium varies continuously with travel time or depth.

(b) The sampling frequency is high enough so that the sample spacing Δ is very small.

(c) The source excitation is minimum phase.

(d) The measured backscattered wave field is noise free.

Step 1. Excite the layered medium with a minimum-phase source $x(t)$ at time $t = 0$ and at depth $z = 0$. Record the wave field $u(z, t)$ for $t > 0$ at depth $z = 0$. Let $y(t) = u(z = 0, t)$. Convert $y(t)$ to discrete time; that is, let $t = n\Delta$ for $n = 0, 1, \ldots, N - 1$. Choose Δ to be "small" and N to be "large." At this point we have the sampled wave field $y(n)$ for $0 \le n \le N - 1$.

Step 2. Deconvolve the minimum-phase source from $y(n)$ to obtain the impulse response of the medium at $z = 0$. That is, first convert $x(t)$ to discrete time to obtain $x(n)$ for $0 \le n \le N - 1$. Next, compute the DFTs of $x(n)$ and $y(n)$ to obtain $X(k)$ and $Y(k)$, respectively, for $k = 0, 1, \ldots, N - 1$. (Refer to Chapter 1, Section VII.B). Since $y(t) = x(t) * g(t)$, where $g(t)$ is the impulse response of the layered medium at $z = 0$, it follows that

$$G(k) = \frac{Y(k)}{X(k)}, \quad k = 0, \ldots, N - 1$$

and $g(n) = \text{IDFT}[G(k)], n = 0, 1, \ldots, N - 1$. At this point we have the discrete-time impulse response $g(n)$ for $0 \le n \le N - 1$.

Step 3. Perform the initialization for the lattice algorithm. Set $n = 0$, $k_0 = \Delta g(1)$, $f_0(0) = 1$, $\beta_0(0) = k_0$, and $Q_0 = 1 - k_0^2$.

Step 4. Perform the first stage ($n = 1$) of the lattice algorithm. Compute the auxiliary quantities:

$$P_n = \sum_{i=0}^{n-1} f_i(n - 1)\Delta g(n + 1 - i) \tag{10.133}$$

$$k_n = \frac{P_n}{Q_{n-1}} \tag{10.134}$$

$$Q_n = Q_{n-1}(1 - k_n^2) \tag{10.135}$$

Use the lattice equations

$$f_i(n) = f_i(n - 1) + k_n \beta_{i-1}(n - 1)$$
$$\beta_i(n) = \beta_{i-1}(n - 1) + k_n f_i(n - 1) \tag{10.136}$$

for $i = 0, 1, \ldots, n$. Here, $f_0(n) = 1$, $\beta_0(n) = k_n$ for $n = 0, 1, \ldots, N - 1$ and $f_n(n - 1) = 0$ for $n = 1, 2, \ldots, N - 1$.

Step 5. Proceed to the next stage and repeat step 4 for $n = 2$. Continue this recursion for $n = 3, 4, \ldots, N - 1$.

Step 6. At this point we have the N reflection coefficients $k_0, k_1, \ldots, k_{N-1}$. Since $Z_0 = [\rho_0 E_0]^{1/2}$ is assumed to be known, the impedance Z_n as a function of discrete travel time follows from (10.132).

---

reflection coefficients. The impedance Z_n follows from

$$Z_{n+1} = Z_0 \prod_{i=0}^{n} \frac{1 - k_i}{1 + k_i} \tag{10.131}$$

For this solution the sampling interval Δ is equivalent to the two-way travel time in a layer, which is a constant for all layers.

The more general problem of layers of unequal travel time is solved in [31]. Under the assumptions that Δ is small, the medium impedance varies continuously, and the sources are minimum phase, [31] shows that a lattice-filter-type algorithm relates the sampled wave field $y(n)$ to a set of numbers k_n called reflection coefficients. Given k_n, the impedance follows from

$$Z_{n+1} = \frac{Z_0}{1 - k_n} \prod_{i=0}^{n} \frac{1 - k_i}{1 + k_i} \tag{10.132}$$

The impedances in Eqs. (10.131) and (10.132) are functions of discrete travel time, not discrete depth. To convert Eq. (10.131) or Eq. (10.132) to a function of discrete depth, we need to know the wave propagation speed c as a function of travel time—that is, $c(\tau)$, where τ is the travel time independent variable defined in Eq. (10.130). Given $c(\tau)$, we can use Eq. (10.130) to find $\tau(z)$. Thus, once the relationship between travel time τ and depth z is known, then Eq. (10.131) or Eq. (10.132) can be modified to become impedance as a function of depth z. However, since we have only one measurement, $c(\tau)$ cannot be found. Hence, with this restriction, we can only obtain impedance as a function of discrete travel time.

We close this section with Table VII, which states a fast seismic deconvolution algorithm that can handle layered media with layers of unequal travel time [31]. Note that the algorithm assumes noise-free measurements. The seismic deconvolution problem when the measurements are noisy is considered in [21, 33].

VI SUMMARY

This chapter provided the reader with the necessary tools to understand the basic theory, physics, and computational algorithms associated with deconvolution. Although deconvolution is a general term, it does have some specific applications. This chapter showed that it is the core element in speech and seismic signal processing.

Deconvolution is an inverse problem. Like most inverse problems, it requires a good understanding of physics as well as signal processing. We hope that the material in this chapter will give the reader the incentive to probe further into the study of inverse problems.

The deconvolution of parametric models, such as the AR, MA, and ARMA models, involves algorithms that appear in many other areas of digital signal processing. For example, the deconvolution algorithm for an AR process, namely, the Burg algorithm, is used in maximum entropy spectral analysis as described in Chapter 9. Deconvolution is a rich subject full of computational challenges.

APPENDIX A.   REFERENCES FOR OBTAINING
COMPUTATIONAL ALGORITHMS

The Levinson or Toeplitz Recursion: Direct Form   *A.1*

FORTRAN IV programs for solving the Yule–Walker equations (10.42) are listed in [2, 32]. Both references also give FORTRAN IV computer programs for solving the discrete-time Wiener–Hopf equation (10.74). Appendix B is a program written in IBM PC-compatible BASIC to solve the Yule–Walker equations.

The Levinson or Toeplitz Recursion: Lattice Form   *A.2*

Reference [2] gives a FORTRAN IV program for computing the Burg algorithm, and [1] gives FORTRAN IV programs that perform speech analysis and synthesis. Although [26] does not provide computer programs, it gives a detailed treatment of lattice filters. Appendix C is a program written in IBM PC-compatible BASIC to solve the Burg algorithm.

Extended Levinson Algorithms and Least Squares Analysis   *A.3*

A FORTRAN IV program for performing FIR systems identification by least squares analysis is in [27]. A key point is that this computer program gives a fast algorithm for systems that are not Toeplitz.

APPENDIX B.   IMPLEMENTING THE LEVINSON OR
TOEPLITZ RECURSION

In this appendix we give an IBM PC-compatible BASIC computer program for implementing the Levinson or Toeplitz recursion (refer to Table IV). This program solves the Yule–Walker equations. We assume that the autocorrelation values have already been computed; they are an input to the following BASIC computer program.

```
100 REM ...   LEVINSON OR TOEPLITZ RECURSION : DIRECT FORM
110 REM ...            ( REFER TO TABLE IV )
120 REM ...   THIS PROGRAM WAS WRITTEN BY DR. JACK-KANG CHAN
130 REM ...            OF NORDEN SYSTEMS
140 REM ...   INPUT   :  AUTOCORRELATION VALUES  R(1),R(2), ... ,R(N+1)
150 REM ...   OUTPUTS :  AR(N) FILTER COEFFICIENTS  A(1),A(2), ... ,A(N)
160 REM ...            REFLECTION COEFFICIENTS  K(1),K(2), ... ,K(N)
170 REM ...            MEAN-SQUARED ERRORS  P(1),P(2), ... ,P(N+1)
180 REM ...
190 REM ...
200 DIM A(N),AO(N),K(N),P(N+1)
210 REM ...   INITIALIZE ARRAYS
220 FOR I=1 TO N
230 A(I)=0
240 K(I)=0
250 P(I+1)=0
260 NEXT I
270 REM ...    BEGIN LEVINSON RECURSION
280 P(1)=R(1)
290 FOR J=1 TO N
300 FOR I=1 TO N
310 AO(I)=A(I)
320 NEXT I
330 KO=R(J+1)
340 FOR I=1 TO J-1
350 KO=KO+AO(I)*R(J+1-I)
360 NEXT I
370 KO=-KO/P(J)
380 K(J)=KO
390 A(J)=KO
400 P(J+1)=P(J)*(1-KO*KO)
410 IF J<2 THEN 450
420 FOR I=1 TO J-1
430 A(I)=AO(I)+KO*AO(J-I)
440 NEXT I
450 NEXT J
460 RETURN
```

APPENDIX C. IMPLEMENTING THE LATTICE FORM
OF THE LEVINSON RECURSION

In this appendix we give an IBM PC-compatible BASIC computer program for implementing the lattice form of the Levinson recursion. In the literature, this program is referred to as the Burg algorithm (see Table VI). We assume that L_y time series values are available; they are an input to the following BASIC computer program.

```
100 REM ...   LATTICE FORM OF THE LEVINSON RECURSION   : BURG ALGORITHM
110 REM ...           ( REFER TO TABLE VI )
120 REM ...   THIS PROGRAM WAS WRITTEN BY DR. JACK-KANG CHAN
130 REM ...           OF NORDEN SYSTEMS
140 REM ...   INPUT  : TIME SERIES VALUES  Y(1),Y(2), ... ,Y(LY)
150 REM ...   OUTPUT : REFLECTION COEFFICIENTS  K(1),K(2), ... ,K(N)
160 REM ...
170 REM ...
180 DIM F(LY),B(LY),K(LY)
190 REM ...   INITIALIZE ARRAYS
200 FOR I=1 TO LY
210 F(I)=Y(I)
220 B(I)=F(I)
230 NEXT I
240 REM ...   BEGIN BURG ALGORITHM
250 FOR J=1 TO N
260 F1=0
270 F2=0
280 FOR I=J+1 TO LY
290 F1=F1+B(I-1)*F(I)
300 F2=F2+F(I)*F(I)+B(I-1)*B(I-1)
310 NEXT I
320 K0=-2*F1/F2
330 K(J)=K0
340 FOR I=J+1 TO LY
350 F0=F(I)+K0*B(I-1)
360 B0=K0*F(I)+B(I-1)
370 B(I-1)=F1
380 F(I)=F0
390 F1=B0
400 NEXT I
410 NEXT J
420 RETURN
```

REFERENCES

1. J. D. Markel and A. H. Gray, *Linear Prediction of Speech*, Springer-Verlag, New York, 1976, pp. 1–16.
2. M. T. Silvia and E. A. Robinson, *Deconvolution of Geophysical Time Series in the Exploration for Oil and Natural Gas*, Elsevier, New York, 1979, pp. 1–14.
3. G. Rand, New solutions appear to solve old sonar problems, *Defense Electronics Mag.* **12**, 17–20 (October 1980).
4. S. Lawrence Marple, Fast algorithms for linear prediction and system identification filters with linear phase, *IEEE Trans. Acoust. Speech Signal Process.* **ASSP-30**, 942–953 (December 1982).
5. P. Eykhoff, *System Identification*, Wiley, New York, 1974.
6. D. Graupe, *Identification of Systems*, Van Nostrand Reinhold, New York, 1972.
7. A. V. Oppenheim and R. W. Schafer, *Digital Signal Processing*, Prentice-Hall, Englewood Cliffs, N.J., 1975, pp. 345–353.

8. F. B. Hildebrand, *Advanced Calculus for Applications*, Prentice-Hall, Englewood Cliffs, N.J., 1962.

9. E. A. Robinson, *Statistical Communication and Detection*, Hafner Press, New York, 1967, 206–213.

10. E. A. Robinson, *Random Wavelets and Cybernetic Systems*, Charles Griffin, London, 1962.

11. E. A. Robinson and M. T. Silvia, *Digital Signal Processing. and Time Series Analysis*, Holden Day, San Francisco, 1978.

12. E. A. Robinson and M. T. Silvia, *Digital Foundations of Time Series Analysis: Vol. I. The Box–Jenkins Approach*, Holden Day, San Francisco, 1979.

13. J. Makhoul, Linear prediction: A tutorial review, *Proc. IEEE* **63**, 561–580 (1975).

14. R. L. Moses and J. A. Cadzow, A recursive procedure for ARMA modeling, *IEEE Trans. Acoust. Speech, Signal Process.* **ASSP-33**, 1188–1196 (October 1985).

15. P. Stoica, T. Söderström, and B. Friedlander, Optimal instrumental variable estimates of the AR parameters of an ARMA process, *IEEE Trans. Automat. Contr.* **AC-30**, 1066–1074 (November 1985).

16. D. F. Gingras, Asymptotic properties of high-order Yule—Walker estimates of the AR parameters of an ARMA time series, *IEEE Trans. Acoust. Speech Signal Process.* **ASSP-33**, 1095–1101 (October 1985).

17. R. Deutsch, *Estimation Theory*, Prentice-Hall, Englewood Cliffs, N.J., 1965.

18. D. Commenges, The deconvolution problem: Fast Algorithms including the preconditioned conjugate-gradient to compute a MAP estimator, *IEEE Trans. Automat. Contr.* **AC-29**, 229–243 (March 1984).

19. S. D. Hodgers and P. C. Moore, Data uncertainties and least squares regression, *Applied Statistics* **12**, 185–195 (1972).

20. G. H. Golub and C. F. Van Loan, An analysis of the total least squares problem, *SIAM J. Numer. Anal.* **17**, 883–893 (December 1980).

21. M. T. Silvia and E. C. Tacker, Regularization of Marchenko's integral equation by total least squares, *J. Acoust. Soc. Am.* **72**, 1202–1207 (1982).

22. T. Kailath, A view of three decades of linear filtering theory, *IEEE Trans. Information Theory*, **IT-20**, 146–181 (March 1974).

23. B. Noble and J. W. Daniel, *Applied Linear Algebra*, Prentice-Hall, Englewood Cliffs, N.J., 1977, pp. 179–198.

24. N. Levinson, The Weiner rms (root mean square) error criterion in filter design and prediction, *J. Math. Phys.* **25**, 261–278 (1947).

25. N. Weiner, *The Extrapolation, Interpolation, and Smoothing of Stationary Time Series with Engineering Applications*, Wiley, New York, 1949, App. C.

26. B. Friedlander, Lattice filters for adaptive processing, *Proc. IEEE* **70**, 829–867 (August 1982).

27. S. L. Marple, Efficient least squares FIR system identification, *IEEE Trans Acoust. Speech Signal Process.* **ASSP-29**, 62–73 (February 1981).

28. B. Friedlander, T. Kailath, M. Morf, and L. Ljung, Extended Levinson and Chandrasekhar equations for general discrete-time linear estimation problems, *IEEE Trans. Automat. Contr.* **AC-23**, 653–659 (August 1978).

29. M. Morf, G. S. Sidhu, and T. Kailath, Some new algorithms for recursive estimation in constant linear discrete-time systems, *IEEE Trans. Automat. Contr.* **AC-19**, 315–323 (August 1974).

30. M. T. Silvia and A. B. Weglein, Method for obtaining a nearfield inverse scattering solution to the acoustic wave equation, *J. Acoust. Soc. Am.* **69**, 478–482 (1981).

31. J. G. Berryman and R. R. Greene, Discrete inverse methods for elastic waves in layered media, *Geophysics* **45**, 213–233 (February 1980).

32. E. A. Robinson, *Multichannel Time Series Analysis with Digital Computer Programs*, Holden Day, San Francisco, 1967, pp. 117–148.

33. J. M. Mendel, *Optimal Seismic Deconvolution: An Estimation-Based Approach*, Academic Press, New York, 1983.

Chapter **11**

Time Delay Estimation

MANUEL T. SILVIA
Allied Signal Aerospace Company
Bendix Oceanics Division
Sylmar, California 91342

INTRODUCTION   I

The estimation of time delay (or time difference) has become an important problem in digital signal processing. For example, an ideal active radar or sonar, which employs a single omnidirectional sensor to transmit and receive signals, can measure the time difference between the time a signal was transmitted and the time a backscattered signal was received to estimate the range of a radar or sonar target. If these active systems employ an array of omnidirectional sensors, then, in addition to estimating range, the time delays between these sensors can also be used (i) to focus the transmitted energy in a specified direction and (ii) to estimate the direction of a radar or sonar target [see Fig. 11.1(a)]. On the other hand, an ideal passive sonar or radar generally employs an array of omnidirectional sensors (at least two) for the sole purpose of receiving acoustic or electromagnetic radiation from distant targets. When the radiation is received at the passive array, time delay estimation methods are used to estimate the travel time of an acoustic or electromagnetic wavefront between the sensors. Wavefront travel time gives the range and direction of a radiating target [see Fig. 11.1(b)]. In either case the estimation of these time delays is often corrupted by ambient and receiver-generated noise, and multipath and finite-length observation intervals [1].

In seismology an underground disturbance creates seismic waves. Seismic detectors, located on the earth's surface, record these waves at different times. By estimating the time delays associated with the propagation of these seismic waves to the various detectors, a seismologist can decide whether an underground disturbance was natural or created (e.g., disturbances that are localized deep within the earth are more likely to be natural, whereas shallow disturbances are more likely to be created [2]). In the speech and hearing area time delay estimation has been explored to measure the travel time of sound waves from the

789

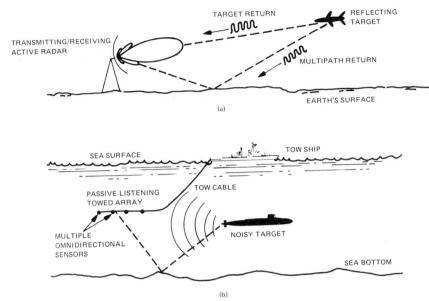

Fig. 11.1. (a) Active radar system. (b) Passive sonar system.

external ear to the eardrum and other parts of the internal ear. Analyzing these time delays helps researchers understand the hearing mechanisms of man and other species [3]. In biomedicine the electroencephalogram (EEG) represents the spontaneous electrical activity of the brain as measured from electrodes placed on a patient's scalp. When the patient is subjected to a sensory stimulus, electrical signals in the EEG are observed. By studying the time delays in these electrical signals, biomedical researchers can help doctors improve their neurological assessment of patients [4].

Hyperbolic location systems, commonly referred to as time difference of arrival systems, locate an active source or transmitter by processing signal arrival-time measurements at three or more passive stations [5]. The measurements at these passive stations are sent to another station, designated the master station, that does the time delay processing. The basic idea behind hyperbolic location systems is as follows. The arrival-time measurements at two stations are combined to produce a relative arrival time that, in the absence of noise and other interference, restricts the possible transmitter location to a hyperboloid with the two stations as foci. The transmitter location is then estimated from the intersection of three or more independently generated hyperboloids determined from at least four stations. If the transmitter and the passive stations lie in the same plane, then the transmitter location is estimated from the intersections of two or more hyperbolas determined from three or more stations. Figure 11.2 illustrates two hyperbolas, each of which has two branches, derived from the measurements at three stations. Notice that the two hyperbolas have two points

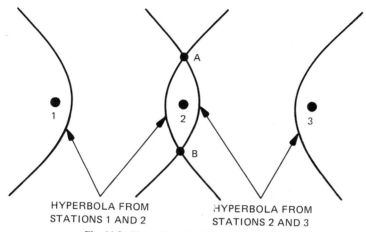

HYPERBOLA FROM   HYPERBOLA FROM
STATIONS 1 AND 2   STATIONS 2 AND 3

Fig. 11.2. Planar hyperbolic location system.

of intersection. We can resolve the resulting ambiguity in transmitter location by using a priori information about the location or a fourth station to generate an additional hyperbola.

If we now consider the three or more passive stations to be active sources and the one transmitter to be a passive station or receiver, then the single passive receiver can determine its own position by processing the signal arrival-time measurements from the three or more active sources. Similar to the previous hyperbolic location system, the position of the passive receiver will be determined by the intersection of three or more hyperbolas. This simple idea describes the fundamental principle behind a military and commercial navigation system called LORAN C [6]. Today, nearly every yachtsman has a commercial LORAN C receiver that estimates the signal arrival-time differences or time delays and converts these measurements into latitude and longitude coordinates, which are useful for navigational purposes (refer to Fig. 11.3). Thus, time delay estimation forms the basis of nearly all hyperbolic location and/or navigation systems.

As we have just seen, the time delay estimation problem spans the fields of radar, sonar, seismology, speech and hearing, biomedical research, and hyperbolic localization, just to name a few. The main purpose of this chapter is to provide a summary of the basic principles behind time delay estimation. In Section II we consider the time delay problem for active sensors (e.g., active radars or sonars). In Section III we discuss the time delay problem for passive sensors (e.g., passive sonars or radars). In Section IV we concern ourselves with the statistical theory of correlation and its relationship to the time delay estimation problem. In Section V we consider the implementation of some time delay estimation algorithms using the fast Fourier transform (FFT). Section VI, provides a table of various algorithms and some numerical results.

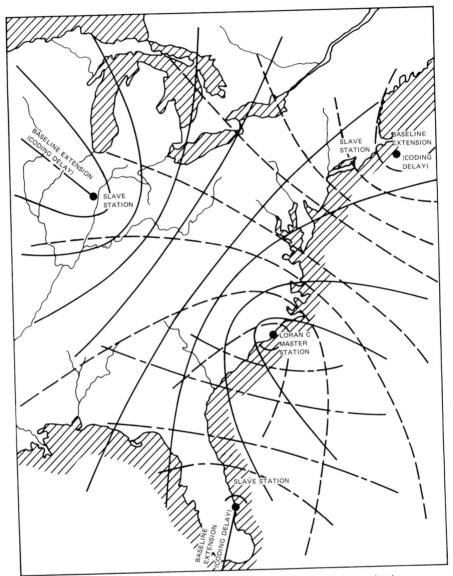

Fig. 11.3. LORAN C chart showing hyperbolas used for time delay navigation.

TIME DELAY ESTIMATION FOR ACTIVE SENSORS   II

The Time Delay Estimation Problem for a   A
Single Omnidirectional Active Sensor

In general, an active radar or sonar system contains an array of omni-directional sensors, a transmitter, and a receiver. The sole purpose of the transmitter is to excite the sensors with electrical signals. In radar the sensors convert these electrical signals into electromagnetic energy and radiate electromagnetic waves. In sonar the sensors convert these electrical signals into acoustic energy and radiate acoustic waves. In both cases the radiated waves eventually strike a target. However, only some of the transmitted energy returns to the radar or sonar sensors. Since the sensors are assumed to be reciprocal devices, they convert the returned waves back to electrical signals. The sole purpose of the receiver is to filter or prepare these electrical signals for further signal processing.

If the active system employs only one omnidirectional reciprocal sensor, then it radiates the same amount of energy in all directions and it receives energy in the same way for every direction. See Fig. 11.4 for a graphical illustration.

In the theory of analog and digital filters the most trival of all linear time-invariant filters is the one whose frequency response treats all the frequencies of an input signal in the same way. That is, its frequency response has a constant gain of unity and a constant phase shift of zero. This filter is sometimes referred to as the trival all-pass filter. Its frequency response is shown in Fig. 11.5. Thus, we can think of the single omnidirectional reciprocal sensor as a trival all-pass *spatial filter*. That is, this sensor has a spatial response that treats all the angles ϕ associated with an input signal in the same way. Analogously, its radiation and receive spatial response has a constant gain of unity and a constant phase shift of zero. The radiation and receive spatial response of a single omnidirectional reciprocal sensor is shown in Fig. 11.6. Although the spatial gain function $G(\phi)$ can be plotted in either Cartesian or polar coordinates [Fig. 11.6(a), (c), respectively], a commonly used graphical representation of the spatial gain function is the *beam pattern*, as defined in Fig. 11.6(d).

As we have just seen, a single omnidirectional active sensor cannot focus its transmitted energy in a specified direction. Since we have assumed that the sensor is a reciprocal device, it cannot tell which direction the returned or backscattered energy came from. Thus, any radar or sonar that uses a single omnidirectional reciprocal sensor to transmit and receive cannot estimate the direction of a reflecting target. However, by estimating the time delay or time difference between the time a signal was transmitted and the time a signal was received, a "single-sensor" active radar or sonar can estimate the reflecting target's range. Hence, the time delay estimation problem for a single omnidirectional active sensor is equivalent to the range estimation problem. Let us elaborate.

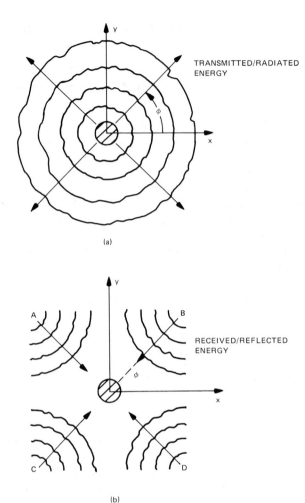

Fig. 11.4. Graphical illustration. (a) A single omnidirectional active sensor radiates the same amount of energy in all directions ϕ. (b) A single omnidirectional active sensor, which is assumed to be a reciprocal device, receives reflected energy in the same way for every direction ϕ. That is, this sensor would receive the same reflected energy regardless of where the target is located (e.g., at points A, B, C, or D). Thus, it has no spatial discrimination.

Suppose the transmitter creates an electrical signal, say $s_T(t)$, which excites a single omnidirectional sensor. The resulting electromagnetic or acoustic waves radiate outward [Fig. 11.4(a)] toward a reflecting target. When the waves strike the target, a complicated backscattering process generates a reflected or backscattered wave that returns to the sensor. The sensor then converts this returned wave to an electrical signal, say $s_R(t)$. If the ambient noise of the medium and the noise generated in the receiver can be combined into an additive process,

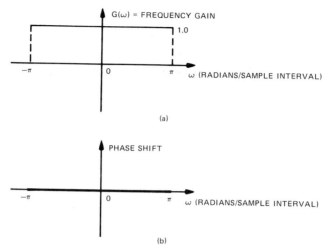

Fig. 11.5. Frequency response of a trivial all-pass digital filter: (a) frequency gain function; (b) frequency phase shift function.

then the electrical signal, as seen by the receiver, is

$$\underline{z}(t) = s_R(t) + \underline{v}(t)$$

where $\underline{v}(t)$ is the electrical signal that represents the combined additive noise process. In general, we note that $s_R(t)$ depends on the physical properties and shape of the reflecting target, $s_T(t)$, and the spatial response of the sensor. For example, it could happen that the direction in which the active sensor decides to focus its transmitted energy may not coincide with the target's direction, which would cause a reduction in the amplitude of $s_R(t)$ (refer to Fig. 11.7). However, since we are considering a single omnidirectional reciprocal sensor, the amplitude of $s_R(t)$ will not be affected by the spatial response of the sensor.

We are now ready to state the time delay estimation problem for the case of a single omnidirectional active sensor. That is, given $\underline{z}(t)$ for $t_p \leq t \leq t_p + t_0$, where t_0 is the length of the observation interval, the problem is to estimate the time delay between the time $s_T(t)$ was transmitted, say $t = 0$, and the time $s_R(t)$ was received, say $t = \tau$. See Fig. 11.8.

In the absence of additive noise [e.g., $\underline{v}(t) = 0$], estimating the time delay τ is not difficult, because the onset or leading edge of $s_R(t)$ is easily detected when no interference or noise is present, provided the amplitude of $s_R(t)$ is not too small. For the noise-free case this onset detection problem seems to be independent of the shape and amplitude of $s_R(t)$. However, when noise is present, then detecting the leading edge of $s_R(t)$ becomes more difficult. By examining Fig. 11.8(b), we can intuitively argue that the level of difficulty increases as the signal-to-noise ratio (SNR) decreases. That is, the onset of $s_R(t)$ becomes more difficult to detect when the noise amplitudes approach the signal amplitudes. Moreover, this onset

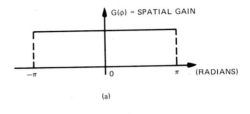

(a)

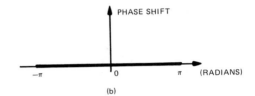

(b)

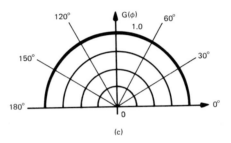

(c)

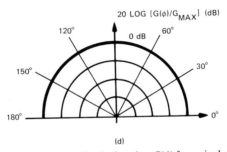

(d)

Fig. 11.6. Spatial response. (a) spatial gain function $G(\phi)$ for a single omnidirectional reciprocal sensor. Graph is in Cartesian coordinates; (b) spatial phase-shift function for a single omnidirectional reciprocal sensor; (c) spatial gain function plotted in polar coordinates. Graph is for $0 \leq \phi \leq \pi$; (d) the function $20 \text{ Log } [G(\phi)/G_{\text{max}}]$, plotted in polar coordinates, is commonly called the beam pattern. Graph is for $0 \leq \phi \leq \pi$.

detection problem could be made less difficult if, for example, $s_R(t)$ had a large amplitude and a fast rise time or a sharp leading edge. This implies that our success in detecting $s_R(t)$'s leading edge, in the presence of noise, depends on the shape and amplitude of $s_R(t)$. In any event, we can intuitively argue [see Fig. 11.8(b)] that the accuracy of our time delay estimate will be greater if the

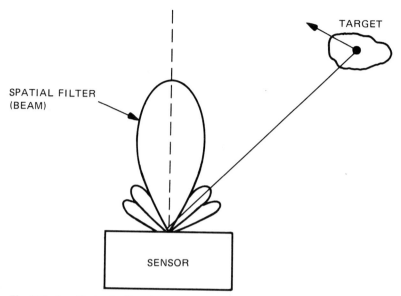

Fig. 11.7. Amplitude of reflected signal (echo) is affected by spatial response of sensor.

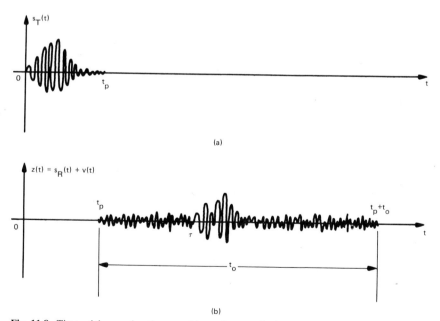

(a)

(b)

Fig. 11.8. Time delay estimation problem for a single omnidirectional active sensor: (a) transmitted signal; (b) backscattered signal as seen by the receiver.

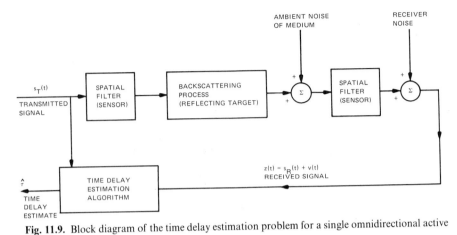

Fig. 11.9. Block diagram of the time delay estimation problem for a single omnidirectional active sensor.

rise time of $s_R(t)$ is small and the SNR is high. In the following sections we will quantify these intuitive notions.

We close this section with Fig. 11.9, a block diagram of the time delay estimation problem for a single omnidirectional active sensor.

B The Time Delay Estimation Problem for an Array of Omnidirectional Active Sensors

In the previous section we considered the most trivial of all active systems—that is, the one with a single omnidirectional reciprocal sensor. This system had no spatial discrimination capability. In this section we consider a more practical active system, one that employs an array of omnidirectional reciprocal sensors. As we will soon see, active systems that use more than one omnidirectional reciprocal sensor have the ability to perform spatial discrimination or spatial filtering.

1 Two-Sensor Array

Let us begin by considering the simplest of all arrays—the linear array containing only two omnidirectional reciprocal sensors separated by a distance l. Figure 11.10 gives a pictorial description of this array.

To explain how the two-sensor array can provide spatial discrimination, let us consider the following experiment. We assume that the radar or sonar transmitter is capable of generating the waveform or pulse

$$s_T(t) = \begin{cases} a(t)\cos[2\pi F_0 t + \theta(t)], & 0 \le t \le t_p \\ 0 & \text{otherwise} \end{cases} \tag{11.1}$$

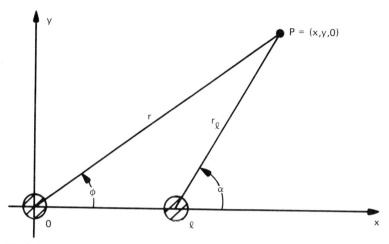

Fig. 10. A simple array with two omnidirectional reciprocal sensors a distance l apart. The z-axis is pointing out of the page.

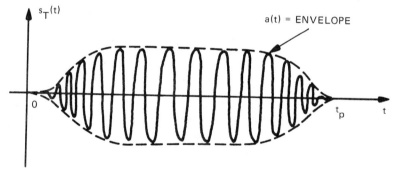

Fig. 11.11. Description of a radar or sonar pulse whose amplitude and phase are both slowly varying with respect to the sine-wave fluctuations.

where $a(t)$ is the envelope, F_0 is the carrier frequency in hertz, $\theta(t)$ is the phase modulation, and t_p is the pulse duration. Figure 11.11 is a graphical description of Eq. (11.1). At $t = 0$ the omnidirectional sensor located at $x = 0$ is excited by $s_T(t)$. After a time delay δ the omnidirectional sensor located at $x = l$ is also excited by $s_T(t)$. If the two sensors radiate waves into a homogeneous, isotropic, and lossless medium, then the resulting waveform at point P in Fig. 11.10 has the approximate form [7]

$$s_P(t) \simeq \frac{1}{r} s_T\left(t - \frac{r}{c}\right) + \frac{1}{r} s_T\left(t - \frac{r}{c} + \Delta - \delta\right) \qquad (11.2)$$

where c is the wave propagation speed in the medium of interest and

$$\Delta = \frac{r}{c} - \frac{r_l}{c} \simeq \frac{l}{c} \cos\phi \qquad (11.3)$$

represents the *travel time difference*. Equations (11.2) and (11.3) assume that $l \ll r$, the lines r and r_l are approximately parallel (e.g., $\alpha \simeq \phi$), and point P is "very far" from the array, so $s_P(t)$ is essentially a plane wave.

Notice that Δ depends on the sensor spacing l and the array angle ϕ. For fixed l, Δ is controlled by ϕ. Now if the $x = 0$ sensor is always excited at $t = 0$, then at what later time should we excite the $x = l$ sensor? That is, how should we select the excitation or *intersensor time delay* δ? Let us proceed to answer this question.

Suppose that the radar or sonar wishes to transmit most of its energy in a specific direction, say $\phi = \phi_0$. It turns out that $s_P(t)$ [refer to Eq. (11.2)] experiences "constructive interference" along a specific direction ϕ_0 when the time delay δ satisfies the condition

$$\delta = \Delta_0 = \frac{l}{c} \cos \phi_0 \tag{11.4}$$

In other words, the radiated energy will be a maximum along the line $\phi = \phi_0$ when δ satisfies Eq. (11.4). To see this let us consider the angular distribution of radiated energy under Eq. (11.4). Mathematically, the radiated energy at a "distant" point P for all angles ϕ is

$$E_P \equiv \int |s_P(t)|^2 \, dt = \int |S_P(F)|^2 \, dF$$

$$\equiv \int |S_T(F)|^2 |A(F, \phi)|^2 \, dF \tag{11.5}$$

which follows from the Fourier transform of Eq. (11.2). Here, the quantity

$$A(F, \phi) \equiv \sum_{n=0}^{1} a(n) e^{j2\pi n F \Delta} \tag{11.6}$$

describes a *spatial filter*, where

$$a(0) \equiv 1, \qquad a(1) \equiv e^{-j2\pi F\delta} \tag{11.7}$$

Δ is given by Eq. (11.3), and δ is given by Eq. (11.4). Since most radars and sonars transmit narrowband waveforms, most of the energy associated with $s_T(t)$ is concentrated around the carrier frequency F_0. Thus, we can say

$$E_P \propto |A(F_0, \phi)|^2 \tag{11.8}$$

From Eqs. (11.3), (11.4), (11.6), and (11.7) we conclude that the radiated energy E_P is a maximum along the line $\phi = \phi_0$ when $\delta = \Delta_0$. When $\delta = \Delta_0$, the line $\phi = \phi_0$ is generally referred to as the *main response axis* (MRA) of the array.

The *beam pattern*, defined by

$$B(\phi) \equiv 20 \log \left[\frac{G(\phi)}{G_{max}} \right] \tag{11.9}$$

where

$$G(\phi) \equiv |A(F_0, \phi)| = \text{spatial gain}$$

describes the angular distribution of radiated energy for a given spacing l, analog carrier frequency F_0, and intersensor time delay δ. $B(\phi)$ is an important quantity in the design of radar and sonar arrays.

Example 1. We wish to design a two-sensor linear sonar array that will transmit most of its energy in the direction $\phi = \phi_0 = 90°$. If $F_0 = 5000$ Hz $= 5$ kHz and $c = 5000$ ft/s, how do we select the intersensor time delay δ and the sensor spacing l?

From Eq. (11.4) we see that $\phi = \phi_0 = 90°$ gives $\delta = \Delta_0 = 0$ s for any array length l. However, $\phi_0 = 270°$ also gives $\delta = 0$ s for any spacing l. This means that for $\delta = 0$ s this array will provide maximum radiated energy along *two* directions ($\phi_0 = 90°$ and $\phi_0 = 270°$), so it has two MRAs. Hence, we cannot focus this array in only *one* direction. Nevertheless, our design would select $\delta = 0$ s, so we should excite both sensors at the same time, say $t = 0$, with the same narrowband waveform, say $s_T(t)$. Let us now consider the selection of l.

If we let $l = 0.5$ ft, the resulting beam pattern for $0° \le \phi \le 180°$ is shown in Fig. 11.12(a). [The beam pattern for $180° \le \phi \le 360°$ is the mirror image of Fig. 11.12(a).] The angular sector defined by the -3-dB point to the left of the MRA (e.g., consider the MRA at $\phi_0 = 90°$) and the -3-dB point to the right of the MRA is called the 3-dB or *half-power beamwidth*. For $l = 0.5$ ft the beamwidth is $60°$. Thus, this array can focus energy in two main beams or mainlobes; one $60°$ wide beam is aimed in the intended direction $\phi_0 = 90°$, and the other $60°$ wide beam is aimed in the direction $\phi_0 = 270°$. Although these main beams are very wide, this two-sensor array still provides more spatial discrimination or spatial filtering than the single omnidirectional sensor does [compare Figs. 11.6(d) and 11.12(a)].

Suppose we increase the sensor spacing to $l = 2$ ft. The resulting beam pattern for $0° \le \phi \le 180°$ is shown in Fig. 11.12(b). [The beam pattern for $180° \le \phi \le 360°$ is the mirror image of Fig. 11.12(b).] For this case we still have two main beams or mainlobes at the MRAs $\phi_0 = 90°$ and $\phi_0 = 270°$. Notice that the beamwidth is $14.4°$, which is considerably narrower than when $l = 0.5$ ft. The $l = 2$-ft pattern did produce a narrower beamwidth than the $l = 0.5$-ft pattern, but it introduced *grating lobes*. Here, a grating lobe is defined as a radiation beam or lobe in any direction, other than the intended MRA directions, that produces the same maximum radiation levels as the MRAs. Thus, the $l = 2$-ft array has grating lobes at $\phi = 0°, 60°, 120°, 180°, 240°,$ and $300°$ [Fig. 11.12(b)]. Clearly, these grating lobes are undesirable.

From the above analysis we see that for a fixed wavelength λ the beamwidth of the mainlobe got smaller as the sensor spacing l got larger. For $l = \lambda/2 = 0.5$ ft we had a $60°$ wide main beam but no grating lobes. For $l = 2\lambda = 2$ ft we had a $14.4°$ wide main beam but several grating lobes. It turns out that the sensor spacing l

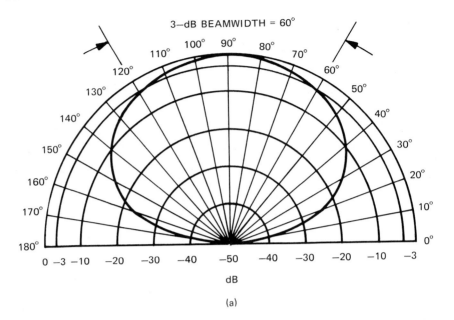

(a)

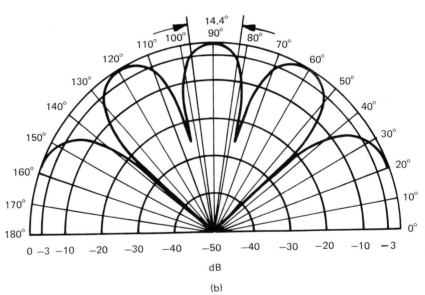

(b)

Fig. 11.12. Beam patterns. (a) Plot is for $0° \leq \phi \leq 180°$; for $180° \leq \phi \leq 360°$, we get the mirror image. Note: $l = \lambda/2 = 0.5$ ft, no grating lobes. (b) $l = 2\lambda = 2$ ft, grating lobes at $\phi = 0°$, $60°$, $120°$, $180°$, $240°$, and $300°$.

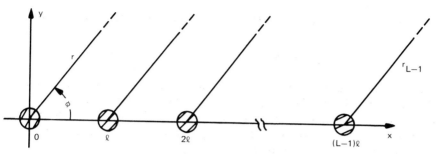

Fig. 11.13. A linear array with L equally spaced omnidirectional reciprocal sensors: l = sensor spacing; $r \simeq (L-1)l\cos\phi + r_{L-1}$.

should be chosen so that $l \le \lambda/2$. For this choice of l the grating lobes will be eliminated. Thus, this two-sensor linear sonar array should be designed for $\delta = 0$ s and $l \le \lambda/2$ ft. The narrowest beamwidth with no grating lobes occurs when $l = \lambda/2 = 0.5$ ft. In summary:

1. The intersensor time delay $\delta = 0$ s gives maximum radiated energy along *two* directions, $\phi_0 = 90°$ and $\phi_0 = 270°$. This linear array cannot focus its energy in *one* direction, say $\phi_0 = 90°$.

2. The sensor spacing $l = \lambda/2$ gives the narrowest 3-dB beamwidth with no grating lobes. This beamwidth is $60°$.

Multisensor Arrays 2

In practice a two-sensor linear array with $l = \lambda/2$ does not provide enough spatial filtering. Thus, if the sensor spacing is constrained by $l = \lambda/2$, how can we achieve narrower beamwidths? One way is to simply add more sensors to the array. Let us elaborate.

Let us now consider an equally spaced linear array with L omnidirectional reciprocal sensors (Fig. 11.13). As before, we assume that the $x = 0$ sensor is the time reference sensor. That is, we assume that at $t = 0$ the omnidirectional sensor located at $x = 0$ is excited by $s_T(t)$. After a time delay δ_1 the omnidirectional sensor located at $x = l$ is excited by $s_T(t)$. After a time delay δ_2 the omnidirectional sensor located at $x = 2l$ is excited by $s_T(t)$, and so on. Finally, the sensor located at $x = (L-1)l$ is excited by $s_T(t)\delta_{L-1}$ s later. Here, $0 < \delta_1 < \delta_2 < \cdots < \delta_{L-1}$, and all the intersensor time delays δ_n $(n = 1, 2,\ldots, L-1)$ are referenced to $t = 0$. If all of these sensors radiate waves into a homogeneous and isotropic medium, then the resultant waveform at a distant point P can be approximated by

$$s_P(t) \simeq \frac{1}{r}s_T\left(t - \frac{r}{c}\right) + \frac{1}{r}s_T\left(t - \frac{r}{c} + \Delta - \delta_1\right)$$

$$+ \cdots + \frac{1}{r}s_T\left(t - \frac{r}{c} + (L-1)\Delta - \delta_{L-1}\right) \qquad (11.10)$$

which is a generalization of Eq. (11.2). If the time delays δ_n satisfy the condition

$$\delta_n = n\left(\frac{l}{c}\cos\phi_0\right) = n\Delta_0 \qquad (n = 0, 1, 2,\dots, L-1) \tag{11.11}$$

then $s_P(t)$ experiences constructive interference at a "distant" point along the line $\phi = \phi_0$. Hence, Eq. (11.11), which is a generalization of Eq. (11.4), represents the condition for maximum radiated energy in the direction ϕ_0. The angular distribution of energy is still given by Eqs. (11.5) and (11.8). However, for the L-sensor array we have the corresponding spatial filter

$$A(F,\phi) \equiv \sum_{n=0}^{L-1} a(n)e^{j2\pi nF\Delta} \tag{11.12}$$

where

$$a(n) \equiv e^{-j2\pi F\delta_n} \qquad (n = 0, 1, 2,\dots, L-1) \tag{11.13}$$

Δ is given by Eq. (11.3), and δ_n is given by Eq. (11.11). Equations (11.12) and (11.13) are generalizations of Eqs. (11.6) and (11.7), respectively.

Example 2. Let us consider the linear sonar array in Example 1. If l/λ is constrained to be 0.5, then the element spacing is $l = 0.5$ ft, since $F_0 = 5$ kHz and $c = F_0\lambda = 5000$ ft/s. Thus, for $L = 20$ omnidirectional equally spaced sensors, the array length is $(L-1)l = 9.5$ ft. For $\phi_0 = 90°$ the timing sequence is $\delta_n = 0$ s for $n = 1, 2,\dots, L-1$, so all the sensors are excited at $t = 0$. Figure 11.14(a) shows the beam pattern (for $0° \le \phi \le 180°$) that results when $\phi_0 = 90°$, $l/\lambda = 0.5$, and $L = 20$ sensors. [The beam pattern for $180° \le \phi \le 360°$ is the mirror image of Fig 11.14(a).]

We can easily see the effect of using $L = 20$ sensors instead of $L = 2$ sensors, all other factors being the same, by comparing Figs. 11.14(a) and 11.12(a), respectively. For the $L = 20$ case the beamwidth is $5°$, whereas for the $L = 2$ case the beamwidth is $60°$. Although the $L = 20$ sensor array generates a desirable $5°$ beamwidth, it also generates *sidelobes*. Here, a sidelobe is defined as a radiation beam or lobe in any direction other than the desired or intended direction $\phi = \phi_0$. The largest sidelobe occurs at about $\phi = 82°$. It is about 13.3 dB down from the mainlobe, which occurs at $\phi = \phi_0 = 90°$. Although sidelobes are not desirable, they are not as bad as the grating lobes encountered in Example 1.

Let us now show how we can "steer" this ($L = 20$) array in a specific direction by controlling the time delay sequence δ_n ($n = 1, 2,\dots, 19$). Specifically, suppose we wish to steer the array or form a beam in the direction $\phi = \phi_0 = 53°$. For this case

$$\delta_n = n\left(\frac{l}{c}\cos\phi_0\right) = n60 \times 10^{-6} \text{ s} = n60 \ \mu\text{s}$$

for $n = 1, 2,\dots, 19$. That is, at $t = 0$ we excite the $x = 0$ sensor with $s_T(t)$. At $t = 60$ μs we excite the $x = l$ sensor with $s_T(t)$. At $t = 120$ μs we excite the $x = 2l$ sensor with $s_T(t)$. Finally, at $t = 1140$ μs we excite the $x = (L-1)l$ sensor with $s_T(t)$. The resulting radiation beam pattern for $0° \leq \phi \leq 180°$ is shown in Fig. 11.14(b). [The beam pattern for $180° \leq \phi \leq 360°$ is the mirror image of Fig. 11.14(b).] Comparing Fig. 11.14(a) (b), we see how steering the array or forming beams effects the linear array's beam pattern (e.g., beamwidth and sidelobe structure).

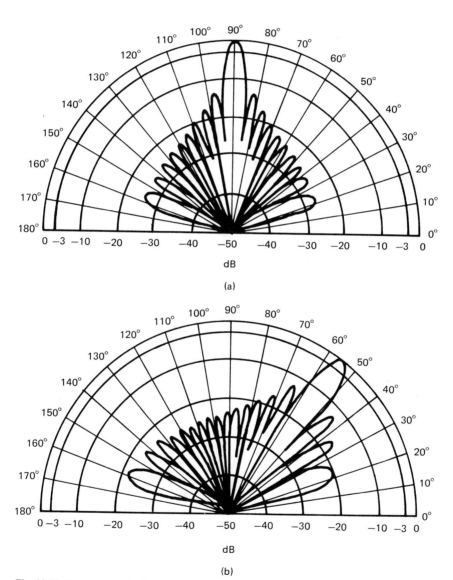

Fig. 11.14. Beam pattern for linear sonar array. (a) Plot is for $0° \leq \phi \leq 180°$; for $180° \leq \phi \leq 360°$, we get the mirror image. Note $l/\lambda = 0.5$, $\phi_0 = 90°(270°) =$ broadside, 3-dB beamwidth = 5°. (b) $l/\lambda = 0.5$, $\phi_0 = 53°(307°)$, 3-dB beamwidth 5°.

In the terminology of radar or sonar we can "form a beam" in a specific direction, say $\phi = \phi_0$, by exciting the sensors according to Eq. (11.11). As we have just seen, the intersensor or excitation time delays δ_n can be used to form beams in any direction. The ability to form beams in different directions by controlling the time delay sequence δ_n is called *beamforming*.

In sonar applications l/c is on the order of microseconds, whereas in radar applications l/c is on the order of nanoseconds, sometimes even fractions of nanoseconds. Therefore, the accurate control of δ_n in radar can be a problem. Because $s_T(t)$ is a narrowband waveform (refer to Eq. (11.1) and Fig. 11.11), we can change the phase of $s_T(t)$ rather than the time delay. Mathematically,

$$s_T(t - \delta) = a(t - \delta)\cos[2\pi F_0(t - \delta) + \theta(t - \delta)]$$

$$\simeq a(t)\cos[2\pi F_0 t + \theta(t) - 2\pi F_0 \delta] \tag{11.14}$$

since $a(t)$ and $\theta(t)$ are assumed to be slowly varying waveforms. Hence, in radar, the steering or beamforming can be accomplished by *phase shifters*, which vary the phase, $-2\pi F_0 \delta$, in Eq. (11.14). By electronically phasing $s_T(t)$ at each sensor, we can effectively control the timing sequence δ_n and therefore steer or scan the beam. This idea forms the basis of *phased-array radar* [8].

In summary:

1. Adding more elements to the linear array produces a narrower beamwidth but generates *sidelobes*.
2. A linear array with $L = 20$ omnidirectional reciprocal sensors and $l/\lambda = 0.5$ can generate a $5°$ beam in two directions. It provides good spatial filtering in two directions but cannot provide spatial filtering in just a single direction.
3. In sonar the beamforming is generally done with time delay controls, whereas in radar the beamforming is done with electronic phase shift controls.

Example 3. In the design of radar or sonar arrays one usually specifies the analog carrier frequency F_0 (or wavelength λ) and a desired 3-dB beamwidth. These quantities will generally control the physical size of the array. The ratio l/λ for a linear array is generally set at 0.5, because $l = \lambda/2$ is the maximum sensor spacing allowed by the spatial version of Nyquist's sampling theorem. Moreover, the choice $l = \lambda/2$ also prevents grating lobes. Thus, the physical extent of a linear array will be $(L - 1)\lambda/2$, where L is determined by the design specifications F_0 and the 3-dB beamwidth.

Hence an important quantity in the design of linear arrays is the spatial filter $A(F, \phi)$ in Eq. (11.12). For a fixed analog frequency F_0 and $l = \lambda/2$, Eq. (11.12) can be rewritten as

$$A(\omega) = \sum_{n=0}^{L-1} a(n)e^{jn\omega} \tag{11.15}$$

where $\omega = \pi \cos \phi$,

$$a(n) = e^{-jn\omega_0} \qquad (n = 0, 1, 2, \ldots, L - 1) \tag{11.16}$$

and $\omega_0 = \pi \cos \phi_0$. So far we have assumed that

$$|a(n)| = \begin{cases} 1 & \text{for } 0 \leq n \leq L - 1 \\ 0 & \text{otherwise} \end{cases} \qquad (11.17)$$

and

$$\angle a(n) = \begin{cases} -n\omega_0 & \text{for } 0 \leq n \leq L \\ 0 & \text{otherwise} \end{cases} \qquad (11.18)$$

That is, the magnitude of $a(n)$ is unity, and the phase angle of $a(n)$ is linear in n. To properly form beams for a linear array, we want the phase angle of $a(n)$ to satisfy Eq. (11.18) and the phase spectrum of $A(\omega)$ to be linear in ω. This implies that the magnitude of $a(n)$ can be any positive sequence that is symmetric over $0 \leq n \leq L - 1$. Hence, $|a(n)|$ need not be limited to the positive uniform sequence Eq. (11.16). It turns out that we can judiciously select the positive symmetric sequence $|a(n)|$ to obtain reduced sidelobe levels at the expense of a modest increase in beamwidth. The values of $|a(n)|$ that accomplish this are called the *sensor shading factors*.

Except for a difference in the sign of ω, the spatial filter $A(\omega)$ can be viewed as the discrete-time Fourier transform (DTFT) of the complex sequence $a(n)$, where ω is the corresponding radian frequency. Refer to Eq. (11.15) and Chapters 1 and 2. Thus, we can use the theory of finite impulse response (FIR) linear-phase digital filters to select $|a(n)|$ or, equivalently, to shape $|A(\omega)|$. Also, the shading factors $|a(n)|$ produce the same mathematical effects as the "window functions" used in spectral analysis. Hence, the theory of window functions, as used in spectral analysis, can be useful in the design of linear arrays.

In summary:

1. The physical size of a radar or sonar array is controlled by F_0 (or λ) and the 3-dB beamwidth.

2. The sensor spacing of a linear array is generally set at $l = \lambda/2$ to comply with the spatial version of Nyquist's sampling theorem. This choice of l also eliminates grating lobes.

3. The complex sequence $a(n)$ completely defines the linear array. The magnitude of $a(n)$ must be symmetric over $0 \leq n \leq L - 1$; we can judiciously select the shading factors $|a(n)|$ to reduce the sidelobe levels at a modest increase in beamwidth. The phase angle of $a(n)$ must be linear in n; the intersensor time delays appear in $\angle a(n)$ and are used to steer the array.

4. The spatial filter (11.12) can be viewed as the DTFT of $a(n)$. Thus, the mathematics of linear-phase FIR digital filters and window functions, as used in spectral analysis, can be useful in the design of linear arrays.

5. In practice, radar and sonar arrays can be different geometrical shapes (e.g., planar, spherical, cylindrical, and linear). Thus, the intersensor time delays will depend on the shape of the array. For a more detailed treatment of array theory see [9].

The linear array (and other types of arrays) can focus its transmitted energy in a specific direction ϕ_0. The *transmit beamformer* is responsible for steering the array to ϕ_0; it does so by exciting the sensors according to Eq. (11.11). The waves radiated outward along ϕ_0 eventually strike a target and return to the array. The *receive beamformer* is responsible for delaying (or phase shifting) the back-scattered waveforms received at each sensor by an amount that would maximize the received energy along ϕ_0. It turns out that the receive beamformer uses the same intersensor time delays (or phase shifts) as the transmit beamformer, namely, Eq. (11.11). Further, since all the sensors are assumed to be reciprocal, the receive beam patterns are exactly the same as the transmit beam patterns. The following example summarizes the basic function of the receiver beamformer.

Example 4. For simplicity let us assume that a stationary point target is located at some distant range $r = R$ and at some angle $\phi = \phi_0$ defined by the point $P = (r, \phi, z = 0)$. See Fig. 11.13. If the transmit beamformer of a linear array forms a beam in the direction $\phi = \phi_0$, then the waveform at P (just before it strikes the target) can be expressed as

$$s_P(t) \simeq \frac{G(\phi_0)}{R} s_T\left(t - \frac{R}{c}\right) \tag{11.19}$$

where

$$G(\phi_0) = \sum_{n=0}^{L-1} |a(n)| \tag{11.20}$$

represents the spatial gain of the linear array. The simplicity of Eq. (11.19) is due to the "constructive interference" pattern set up by the transmit beamformer. Now after $s_P(t)$ in Eq. (11.19) strikes the stationary point target, the backscattered waveform returns to the array. The approximate waveform, as seen by each sensor in the array, is [10] as follows:

Sensor Location	Backscattered Waveform (relative to $t = 0$)	
$x = 0$	$\dfrac{AG(\phi_0)}{R^2} s_T\left(t - \dfrac{2R}{c}\right)$	
$x = l$	$\dfrac{AG(\phi_0)}{R^2} s_T\left(t - \dfrac{2R}{c} + \Delta_0\right)$	
$x = 2l$	$\dfrac{AG(\phi_0)}{R^2} s_T\left(t - \dfrac{2R}{c} + 2\Delta_0\right)$	(11.21)
$\vdots$	$\vdots$	
$x = (L-1)l$	$\dfrac{AG(\phi_0)}{R^2} s_T\left(t - \dfrac{2R}{c} + (L-1)\Delta_0\right)$	

Here, A is a backscattering amplitude factor and $\Delta_0 = (l/c)\cos\phi_0$.

Due to the assumed reciprocity of the array, the *receive beamformer* acts the same way as the transmit beamformer. That is, the backscattered waveform received at $x = 0$ gets zero delay (or phase shift). The backscattered waveform received at $x = l$ gets delayed (or phase shifted) by $\delta_1 = \Delta_0$. The waveform received at $x = 2l$ gets a delay of $\delta_2 = 2\Delta_0$. Finally, the waveform received at $x = (L - 1)l$ gets delayed by $\delta_{L-1} = (L - 1)\Delta_0$. Thus, after $s_P(t)$ strikes the stationary point target and returns to the array, the output of the receive beamformer can be expressed as

$$
s_R(t) \simeq \frac{AG(\phi_0)}{R^2}|a(0)|s_T\left(t - \frac{2R}{c}\right) + \frac{AG(\phi_0)}{R^2}|a(1)|s_T\left(t - \frac{2R}{c} + \Delta_0 - \delta_1\right)
$$

$$
+ \cdots + \frac{AG(\phi_0)}{R^2}|a(L - 1)|s_T\left(t - \frac{2R}{c} + (L - 1)\Delta_0 - \delta_{L-1}\right)
$$

$$
\simeq \frac{AG(\phi_0)}{R^2}s_T\left(t - \frac{2R}{c}\right)[|a(0)| + |a(1)| + \cdots + |a(L - 1)|] \qquad (11.22)
$$

or

$$
s_R(t) \simeq \frac{AG^2(\phi_0)}{R^2}s_T(t - \tau) \qquad (11.23)
$$

Here

$$
\tau \equiv \frac{2R}{c} \qquad (11.24)
$$

is the time delay we must estimate in order to obtain an estimate of the target's range R. Once again, the simplicity of Eq. (11.23) is due to the "constructive interference" pattern set up by the receive beamformer.

In the preceding discussion we made a very important assumption. That is, we assumed that the transmit beamformer pointed the MRA of the beam directly at the target. Thus the dominant backscattering is contained in the beam's mainlobe, the electrical signal out of the receive beamformer has the simple form [Eq. (11.23)], $G(\phi_0)$ is a maximum, and the energy in $s_R(t)$ is a maximum. If the transmit beamformer had pointed the MRA in any other direction, the dominant backscattering would have probably been contained in the beam's sidelobes, $s_R(t)$ would experience "destructive interference," and the energy in $s_R(t)$ would be less. Thus, the spatial filter $A(F, \phi)$ is "matched" when the beam's MRA is pointed directly at the target. Under this matched condition the receive beamformer signal $s_R(t)$ has maximum energy.

Using the notion of a *matched spatial filter*, we can derive a simple algorithm for obtaining a coarse estimate of the target's direction. We make the following assumptions:

1. We consider a stationary point target located in a homogeneous, isotropic, lossless medium.

2. We assume that the target is known to exist in the sector $0° \leq \phi \leq 180°$.
3. We assume no background or receiver noise.

For a linear array we propose the following algorithm:

Algorithm for Obtaining a Coarse Estimate of the Target's Direction

Step 1. Given a 3-dB beamwidth of $\Delta\phi°$, form $180°/\Delta\phi°$ beams. In each beam transmit, receive, and record the detected energy.

Step 2. The beam that has the largest detected energy is the beam that probably contains the target. The MRA angle associated with this beam gives a coarse estimate of the target's direction. Here, a coarse estimate means that the target is somewhere in the $\Delta\phi°$ beam.

This algorithm is a "common sense" type. That is, it steers the beam in steps of the 3-dB beamwidth until the MRA is matched to the target's direction. When this matching occurs, $s_R(t)$ has maximum energy, and we can assume that the matched beam is the beam that probably contains the target. In practice, many phased-array search radars use this simple concept to obtain a coarse estimate of the target's direction. Once a coarse estimate is obtained, these phased-array radars refine this estimate by using monopulse techniques [11]. Figure 11.15 gives a pictorial description of the algorithm. The "common sense" can be rigorously justified by the theory of maximum likelihood estimation [12].

We are now ready to state the time delay estimation problem for the case of any array containing numerous omnidirectional active sensors. We make the following assumptions:

1. The target is a stationary point target located in a homogeneous, isotropic, lossless medium.

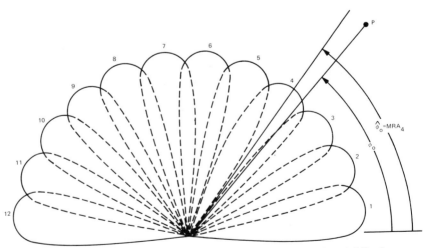

Fig. 11.5. Coarse estimate of target direction by means of matched spatial filtering.

2. The target's range R is well within the active system's detection range (e.g., the SNR is relatively large—greater than 15 dB).

3. The active system has an array of omnidirectional reciprocal sensors, so it can perform both transmit and receive beamforming; that is, it can perform spatial filtering. It transmits $s_T(t)$ in Eq. (11.1).

Let the above active system form numerous densely packed beams that fill a hemisphere. For beam j the receive beamformer output has the form

$$z_j(t) = s_{Rj}(t) + v_j(t) \tag{11.25}$$

where $t_p \le t \le t_p + t_0$ and t_0 is the length of the observation interval (Fig. 11.8). Here, $v_j(t)$ represents the additive noise process associated with beam j, and $s_{Rj}(t)$ represents the receive beamformer output of beam j when no noise is present. For some beam $j = M$ the MRA will match (approximately) the target's direction. Under this condition

$$z_M(t) \simeq \frac{AG^2}{R^2} s_T(t - \tau) + v_M(t) \tag{11.26}$$

where A is a backscattering factor, G is the spatial gain of the array, R is the target range, and τ is the desired time delay (e.g., two-way travel time) given by Eq. (11.24). The problem is to estimate the target direction $\mathbf{R}/R$ and target range R by forming many beams that fill the hemisphere containing the target, where $\mathbf{R}$ denotes the target range vector. As we have seen, the beam with the maximum received energy (say $j = M$) gives an estimate of $\mathbf{R}/R$. In the next section we will show how Eq. (11.26) can be processed to obtain an estimate of τ. The target range R can then be obtained from Eq. (11.24).

We close this section with Figs. 11.16 and 11.17, which summarize the process of beamforming and the time delay estimation problem for an array of omni-directional active sensors, respectively.

A Time Delay Estimation Algorithm for Active Sensors   C

Stationary Point Target Backscattering Model   1

Before we discuss the details of a time delay estimation algorithm, let us examine the stationary point target backscattering model used earlier. Recall that when the beam's MRA is pointed directly at a stationary point target, the output of the receive beamformer, $s_R(t)$, has the form of Eq. (11.23). In words, $s_R(t)$ is simply a scaled, time-delayed replica of $s_T(t)$. However, in practice, this assumption is not always true, because the scattering of electromagnetic or acoustic waves off targets of different shapes is generally a more complicated process. For example, Fig. 11.18 shows what happens when a continuous wave (CW) acoustic pulse is incident on a stationary aluminum sphere embedded in water. Depending on the size parameter $ka = 2\pi(a/\lambda)$, where λ is the wavelength

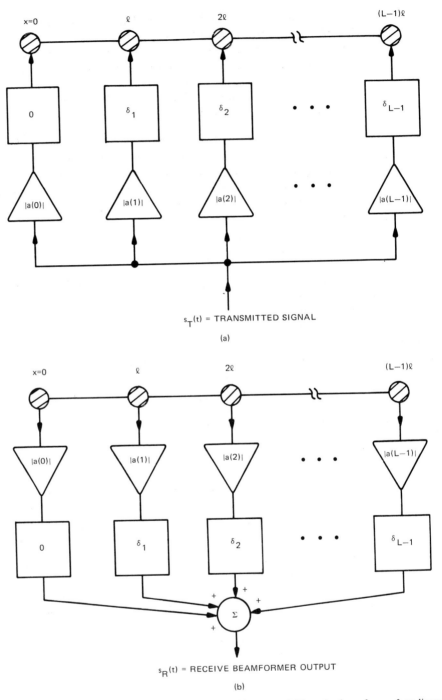

Fig. 11.16. Block diagram of the (a) transmit beamformer and (b) receive beamformer for a linear arrary.

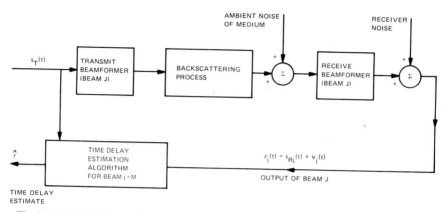

Fig. 11.17. Block diagram of the time delay estimation problem for an array of omnidirectional active sensors.

of the incident wave and a is the radius of the sphere, different backscattering occurs [13]. Figure 11.18(b), (c) shows that $s_R(t)$ is not a scaled, time-delayed version of $s_T(t)$.

To properly describe the backscattering that results from probing these differently shaped targets, we would have to solve the partial differential equations that describe the backscattering. This requires detailed knowledge of the target's size and orientation, which are generally not known. However, suppose that the backscattering process, described in the block diagrams of Figs. 11.9 and 11.17, could be described by a linear time-invariant filter, say $h(t)$. Then the noisy beamformer output $\underline{z}(t)$ could be written as

$$\underline{z}(t) = s_R(t) + \underline{v}(t) = \int h(\sigma)s_T(t - \sigma)\,d\sigma + \underline{v}(t) \qquad (11.27)$$

for $t_p \le t \le t_p + t_0$. Thus, given $\underline{z}(t)$ for t_0 s, we could estimate $h(t)$. Once $h(t)$ is known, the backscattering process is known, and we could estimate the time delay τ. Equation (11.27) is a *convolution* process. The process of estimating $h(t)$ from Eq. (11.27) is called *deconvolution* [14].

Since deconvolution usually involves the estimation of a complete time function, algorithms that perform deconvolution can be computationally involved, depending on the nature of $h(t)$. The deconvolution problem is considered further in Chapter 10.

One attractive feature of the stationary point target backscattering model is that the time delay τ appears in $s_R(t)$ as a simple parameter. Since most of the research on time delay estimation for active systems has focused on the parameter estimation approach, we will consider that approach here.

Thus, although the stationary point target model is a gross simplification of the real received echo, it is commonly used to keep the mathematical model of the receive beamformer output as simple as possible. From a time delay estimation point of view, this makes the time delay problem mathematically tractable.

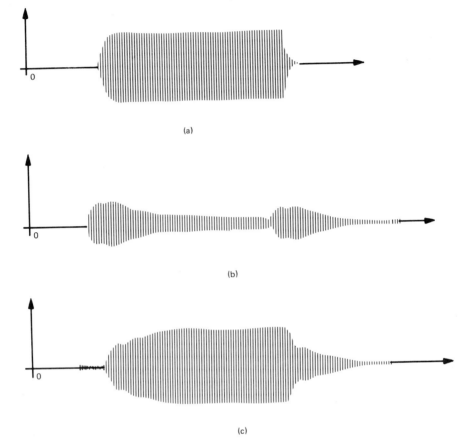

(a)

(b)

(c)

Fig. 11.18. Aluminum sphere, incident-backscattered pulse. (a) A 500 microsecond-long transmitted acoustic CW pulse, incident on a stationary aluminum sphere embedded in water. (b) The
pulse reflected by an aluminum sphere when the pulse in (a) is incident for $ka = 20.78$, where $ka = 2\pi(a/\lambda)$ is the wavelength of the incident wave, and a is the radius of the sphere. (c) The backscattered
pulse for $ka = 21.21$.

2 A Least Squares Approach to Time Delay Estimation

We assume that an active system has gone through the beamforming process
and has obtained a coarse estimate of the target's direction. That is, the target is
definitely located in some beam. The corresponding noisy beamformer output
has the form

$$\underline{z}(t) = \frac{AG^2}{R^2} s_T(t - \tau) + \underline{v}(t) \tag{11.28}$$

for $t_p \leq t \leq t_p + t_0$. For example, see Fig. 11.8. We now wish to estimate the time
delay τ.

We assume that τ is the true but unknown time delay. We further assume that τ can be treated as a time-independent parameter. To estimate τ, we form the quantity

$$J(\tilde{\tau}) = \int_{t_p}^{t_p + t_0} \left[\underline{z}(t) - \frac{AG^2}{R^2} s_T(t - \tilde{\tau}) \right]^2 dt \tag{11.29}$$

which is a function of the parameter $\tilde{\tau}$. We then vary $\tilde{\tau}$ until $J(\tilde{\tau})$ is a minimum. The value of $\tilde{\tau}$ that produces the smallest J is labeled $\hat{\underline{\tau}}$ and is called the *least squares estimate* of τ. Let us now derive a least squares algorithm for estimating τ.

Differentiating Eq. (11.29) with respect to $\tilde{\tau}$ gives

$$\frac{\partial J}{\partial \tilde{\tau}} = \int_{t_p}^{t_p + t_0} 2 \left[\underline{z}(t) - \frac{AG^2}{R^2} s_T(t - \tilde{\tau}) \right] \left[-\frac{AG^2}{R^2} \frac{\partial s_T(t - \tilde{\tau})}{\partial \tilde{\tau}} \right] dt \tag{11.30}$$

Now we can obtain the minimum of Eq. (11.29) by setting Eq. (11.30) equal to zero. Thus

$$\int_{t_p}^{t_p + t_0} \underline{z}(t) \frac{\partial s_T(t - \tilde{\tau})}{\partial \tilde{\tau}} dt = \frac{AG^2}{R^2} \int_{t_p}^{t_p + t_0} s_T(t - \tilde{\tau}) \frac{\partial s_T(t - \tilde{\tau})}{\partial \tilde{\tau}} dt$$

$$= \frac{AG^2}{R^2} \int_{t_p}^{t_p + t_0} \frac{\partial}{\partial \tilde{\tau}} [\tfrac{1}{2} s_T^2(t - \tilde{\tau})] dt \tag{11.31}$$

In practice, $t_0 \gg t_p$. That is, the observation interval t_0 is much longer than the transmitted pulse width t_p. So if we assume that $t_p \leq \tilde{\tau} \leq t_0$, then the right side of Eq. (11.31) is approximately zero:

$$\int_{t_p}^{t_p + t_0} \frac{\partial}{\partial \tilde{\tau}} [\tfrac{1}{2} s_T^2(t - \tilde{\tau})] dt \simeq \frac{\partial}{\partial \tilde{\tau}} \int_{t_p}^{t_p + t_0} \tfrac{1}{2} s_T^2(t - \tilde{\tau}) dt$$

$$\simeq \frac{1}{2} \frac{\partial}{\partial \tilde{\tau}} (E_T) = 0 \tag{11.32}$$

where

$$E_T = \int_{t_p}^{t_p + t_0} s_T^2(t - \tilde{\tau}) dt = \int_0^{t_p} s_T^2(t) dt = \text{constant} \tag{11.33}$$

is the energy contained in the transmitted signal $s_T(t)$. Thus, it follows that Eq. (11.31) can be rewritten as

$$\int_{t_p}^{t_0 + t_p} \underline{z}(t) \frac{\partial s_T(t - \tilde{\tau})}{\partial \tau} \simeq 0 \tag{11.34}$$

or

$$\frac{\partial}{\partial \tilde{\tau}} [\underline{y}(\tilde{\tau})] \simeq 0 \tag{11.35}$$

where

$$y(\tilde{\tau}) \equiv \int_{t_p}^{t_p + t_0} \underline{z}(t) s_T(t - \tilde{\tau})\, dt \qquad (11.36)$$

In summary, the value of $\tilde{\tau}$, say $\tilde{\tau} = \hat{\tau}$, that produces a unique global maximum in Eq. (11.36) also satisfies Eq. (11.35) and therefore minimizes Eq. (11.29). The value $\hat{\tau}$ is called the *least squares estimate* of τ.

Equation (11.36) is a key equation in the study of time delay estimation algorithms for active sensors. Mathematically $y(\tilde{\tau})$ in Eq. (11.36) can be viewed as a cross-correlation function with independent variable $\tilde{\tau}$. That is, under the ergodic hypothesis an estimate of $y(\tilde{\tau})$ can be interpreted as the correlation between the noise-free transmitted signal $s_{\hat{\tau}}(t)$ and the noisy beamformer output $\underline{z}(t)$. Thus, we can vary the *lag* $\tilde{\tau}$ for all $\tilde{\tau}$ in the interval $t_p \leq \tilde{\tau} \leq t_0$. At some lag $\tilde{\tau} = \hat{\tau}$ the cross-correlation function $y(\tilde{\tau})$ achieves a maximum. This maximum occurs at the least squares estimate of τ. Figure 11.19 is a block diagram of a time delay estimation algorithm that implements Eq. (11.36) as a bank of cross-correlators.

Let us now consider another way to interpret Eq. (11.36). Specifically, let us assume that $\underline{z}(t)$ is passed through a linear time-invariant filter with impulse response $s_T(-t)$. If we sample the output of this filter, say $y(t)$, at $t = \tilde{\tau}$, we obtain the same mathematical result as in Eq. (11.36). The maximum output of this filter occurs at $t = \hat{\tau}$.

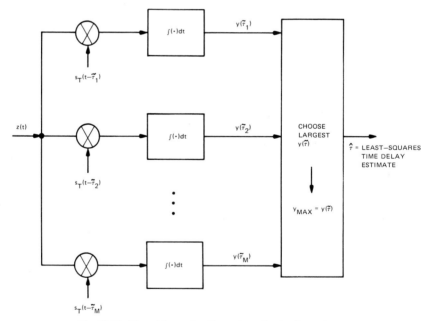

Fig. 11.19. Time delay estimation using a bank of correlators.

The preceding interpretation is possible because of the mathematical similarity of correlation and convolution. The impulse response $s_T(-t)$ not only reproduces (11.36), but it is also the only linear time-invariant filter that produces the maximum SNR at $t = \hat{\tau}$. For $\underline{v}(t)$ a white noise process with autocorrelation function

$$E[\underline{v}(t)\underline{v}(t + \beta)] = \tfrac{1}{2}N_0\delta(\beta) \tag{11.37}$$

the maximum SNR at $t = \hat{\tau}$ is $2E_T/N_0$, where E_T is given by (11.33). Here, $\delta(\beta)$ is

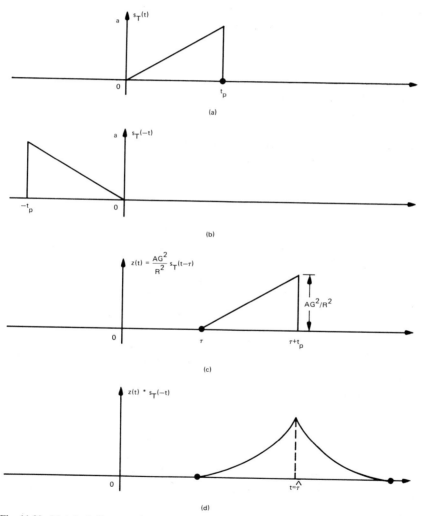

Fig. 11.20. Matched filter produces maximum SNR at $t = \hat{\tau}$. (a) Transmitted signal $s_T(t)$; (b) matched filter; (c) receive beamformer output when no noise is present (e.g., $\underline{v}(t) = 0$); (d) output of the matched filter; (c) convolved with (b).

the familiar Dirac delta function. The filter $s_T(-t)$, which corresponds to $s_T(t)$, is called the *matched filter* for $s_T(t)$ [15] (Fig. 11.20). The matched filter not only produces the maximum SNR at $t = \hat{t}$, but it can also be implemented as a correlator. Matched filters or correlators also play an important role in the signal detection problem [16].

When the noise process $\underline{v}(t)$ is Gaussian, Eq. (11.36) can be derived from the theory of maximum-likelihood estimation. In any event, Eq. (11.36) is a key equation. In Section V we will consider a practical implementation of Eq. (11.36) or Fig. 11.19.

In closing this section we refer the reader to Figs. 11.15–11.17 and 11.19, which summarize the important concepts involved in beamforming and time delay estimation for active systems.

III   Time Delay Estimation for Passive Sensors

A   The Time Delay Estimation Problem for a Passive Array with Two Omnidirectional Reciprocal Sensors

In general, a passive sonar or radar contains an array of omnidirectional sensors and a receiver. The purpose of the passive array is to sense the acoustic or electromagnetic waves that are radiated by a target (refer to Fig. 11.1). The passive receiver converts these waves into electrical signals and decides if a target was really present. Further signal processing can ultimately localize the target (i.e., estimate the target's range and direction).

Let us begin our discussion of passive arrays by considering the simplest of all passive arrays, the one with only two sensors. See Fig. 11.10. We assume that a target, located at point P, radiates the signal $s(t)$. Now if the target radiates $s(t)$ at $t = 0$, the signal received at the $x = l$ sensor has the form $s(t - r_l/c)/r_l$, and the signal received at the $x = 0$ sensor has the form $s(t - r/c)/r$. Here, we have assumed that the medium is noise free, homogeneous, isotropic, and lossless; c is the corresponding wave propagation speed. If the sensor outputs are now combined according to the rule

$$s_R(t) = \frac{|a(0)|}{r}s\left(t - \frac{r}{c}\right) + \frac{|a(1)|}{r_l}s\left(t - \frac{r_l}{c} - D\right) \tag{11.38}$$

then we have performed *receive beamforming* on the sensor outputs [refer to Fig. 11.16(b)]. Recall that $|a(0)|$ and $|a(1)|$ are the shading factors and D is a time delay parameter. When D is equal to the *intersensor time delay*

$$\Delta = \frac{r}{c} - \frac{r_l}{c} \tag{11.39}$$

Eq. (11.38) reduces to

$$s_R(t)\Big|_{D=\Delta} = s\left(t - \frac{r}{c}\right)\left[\frac{|a(0)|}{r} + \frac{|a(1)|}{r_l}\right] \tag{11.40}$$

That is, for $D = \Delta$ we experience a "constructive interference" effect, and Eq. (11.38) achieves its maximum, Eq. (11.40). Thus, we can vary D until $s_R(t)$ achieves a maximum. The values of D that maximizes the receive beamformer output $s_R(t)$ is the intersensor time delay Δ. Given an estimate of Δ, can we localize a radiating target with a two-sensor, linear, passive array? Let us proceed to answer this question.

From Fig. 11.10 we see that

$$r_l^2 = r^2 + l^2 - 2rl\cos\phi \tag{11.41}$$

where r is the target range and ϕ is the target bearing or direction. Examination of Eqs. (11.39) and (11.41) reveals that we have two equations but three unknowns, r, r_l, and ϕ. Hence, given Δ, we cannot obtain r and ϕ for all ranges and bearings. However, if the radiating target is "very far" from the passive array, such that $\phi \simeq \alpha$, then r and r_l are approximately parallel. It follows that

$$r \simeq r_l + l\cos\phi \tag{11.42}$$

and

$$\Delta \simeq \frac{l}{c}\cos\phi \tag{11.43}$$

Under this special condition (i.e., $r \to \infty$) we can use Δ to get an approximate estimate of ϕ by means of Eq. (11.43). Hence, the two-sensor, linear, passive array cannot localize a radiating target. However, when the target is very far from the array, we can estimate the target's bearing.

The two-sensor, linear, passive-array, time delay estimation problem is equivalent to the bearing estimation problem for distant targets. The basic idea is to estimate the intersensor time delay Δ and use Eq. (11.43) to estimate the bearing ϕ.

The Time Delay Estimation Problem for a Passive Array **B** with Three Omnidirectional Reciprocal Sensors

In the previous section we saw that the two-sensor problem produced one intersensor time delay (11.39), two equations [(11.39) and (11.41)], and three unknowns. The end result was that a radiating target could not be localized by a two-sensor, linear, passive array. Let us now see what happens to the passive localization problem when we add one more sensor to the two-sensor array in Fig. 11.10. For example, Fig. 11.21 shows a three-sensor, linear, passive array and a target located at a range r and bearing ϕ. If this target radiates the waveform $s(t)$

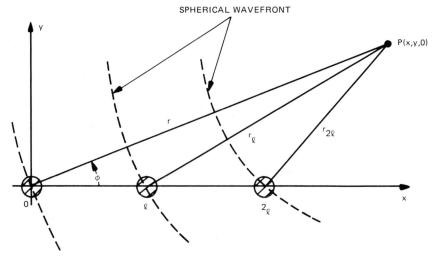

Fig. 11.21. Three-sensor linear passive array.

at $t = 0$, the waveform received at the $x = 2l$ sensor has the form $s(t - r_{2l}/c)/r_{2l}$, the waveform received at the $x = l$ sensor has the form $s(t - r_l/c)/r_l$, and the waveform received at the $x = 0$ sensor has the form $s(t - r/c)/r$. Now

$$\Delta_{01} = \frac{r}{c} - \frac{r_l}{c} \tag{11.44}$$

is the intersensor time delay between the $x = 0$ and $x = l$ sensors and

$$\Delta_{02} = \frac{r}{c} - \frac{r_{2l}}{c} \tag{11.45}$$

is the intersensor time delay between the $x = 0$ and $x = 2l$ sensors. Since the intersensor time delay between the $x = l$ and $x = 2l$ sensors can be expressed as

$$\Delta_{12} = \frac{r_l}{c} - \frac{r_{2l}}{c} = \Delta_{02} - \Delta_{01} \tag{11.46}$$

we see that the three-sensor, linear, passive array has only two independent intersensor delays. Moreover, due to the spherical nature of the wavefronts in Fig. 11.21, Δ_{02} is not, in general, an integer multiple of Δ_{01}; only when $r \to \infty$ is this approximately true. Therefore, if we attempt to perform beamforming according to the assumption that $\Delta_{02} \simeq 2\Delta_{01}$ [see Fig. 11.16(b)], we are not likely to obtain the correct result. Hence, we should consider a beamformer that combines the three sensor outputs according to the rule

$$s_R(t) = \frac{|a(0)|}{r} s\left(t - \frac{r}{c}\right) + \frac{|a(1)|}{r_l} s\left(t - \frac{r_l}{c} - D_{01}\right) + \frac{|a(2)|}{r_{2l}} s\left(t - \frac{r_{2l}}{c} - D_{02}\right) \tag{11.47}$$

where D_{01} and D_{02} are two independent time delay parameters. The beamformer output Eq. (11.47) achieves a global maximum when $D_{01} = \Delta_{01}$ and $D_{02} = \Delta_{02}$. Thus, we now have the following "intuitive" algorithm for estimating Δ_{01} and Δ_{02} under noise-free conditions:

1. Perform the beamforming operation (11.47) on the three sensor outputs.
2. Vary D_{01} and D_{02} in a two-dimensional fashion until $s_R(t)$ in (11.47) achieves a global maximum. The location of this maximum should occur at the intersensor time delays Δ_{01} and Δ_{02}.

Finally, given Δ_{01} and Δ_{02}, can the three-sensor, linear, passive array solve the passive localization problem? Let us proceed to answer this question.

From Fig. 11.21 we see that

$$r_l^2 = l^2 + r^2 - 2rl\cos\phi \tag{11.48}$$

and

$$r_{2l}^2 = (2l)^2 + r^2 - 2r(2l)\cos\phi \tag{11.49}$$

Given that Δ_{01} and Δ_{02} are known (or can be estimated), we now have four independent equations [(11.44), (11.45), (11.48), (11.49)] and four unknowns (r, ϕ, r_l, r_{2l}). Thus, the three-sensor, linear, passive array shows that a solution to the passive localization problem exists. Doing some algebra we obtain the target's range

$$r = \frac{l^2 + (c\Delta_{01})^2 - \frac{1}{2}(c\Delta_{02})^2}{2c\Delta_{01} - c\Delta_{02}} \tag{11.50}$$

and the target's bearing

$$\phi = \cos^{-1}\left[\frac{l^2 - (c\Delta_{01})^2 + 2rc\Delta_{01}}{2rl}\right] \tag{11.51}$$

However, although a solution exists, it is not unique. For example, a target located at the point $(r, -\phi, z = 0)$ (e.g., below the x-axis in Fig. 11.21) would give the same time delays (and therefore the same localization solution) as a target located at the point $(r, \phi, z = 0)$. Hence, we have an ambiguity in target bearing. Recall that this ambiguity also existed for the array with active sensors. It turns out that this bearing ambiguity is directly related to the fact that each sensor has an omnidirectional spatial characteristic instead of a directional one. Thus, to resolve the bearing ambiguity, (i) we must have a priori knowledge that the target exists in the sector $0° \leq \phi \leq 180°$ (or $180° \leq \phi \leq 360°$), or (ii) we must use directional or baffled sensors.

In summary, the three-sensor, linear, passive array provides a solution to the passive localization problem. In the next section we consider various signal processing strategies for estimating the two independent time delays Δ_{01} and Δ_{02}.

C   A Time Delay Estimation Algorithm for Passive Sensors

1   *An Alogrithm for the Two-Sensor Linear Array*

Although we cannot solve the passive localization problem with a two-sensor, linear, passive array, we can obtain the bearing of a distant target by estimating the intersensor time delay Δ_{01}. Let us elaborate.

Assume that the point P in Fig. 11.10 represents a distant, stationary target that radiates a real, zero-mean, wide-sense stationary (WSS), random process $\underline{s}(t)$. Further, we assume that the passive receiving array is stationary and that the position of the sensors is exactly known. Hence, the signal received at the $x = 0$ sensor has the form

$$\underline{z}_0(t) = \frac{1}{r}\underline{s}\left(t - \frac{r}{c}\right) + \underline{v}_0(t) \tag{11.52}$$

and the signal received at the $x = l$ sensor has the form

$$\underline{z}_1(t) = \frac{1}{r_l}\underline{s}\left(t - \frac{r_l}{c}\right) + \underline{v}_1(t) \tag{11.53}$$

Here, $\underline{v}_0(t)$ and $\underline{v}_1(t)$ are assumed to be real, uncorrelated, WSS noise processes. If we now perform receive beamforming on these two sensor, the beamformer output has the form

$$\underline{z}(t) = |a(0)|\underline{z}_0(t) + |a(1)|\underline{z}_1(t - D_{01}) \tag{11.54}$$

where $|a(0)|$ and $|a(1)|$ are the shading factors and D_{01} is a time delay parameter. Since $\underline{s}(t)$, $\underline{v}_0(t)$, and $\underline{v}_1(t)$ are assumed to be real, zero-mean, WSS, random processes, it follows that $\underline{z}(t)$ is also a real, zero-mean, WSS random process.

Based on our discussions in Section III.A, we could vary D_{01} until $\underline{z}(t)$ achieves a maximum. However, since $\underline{z}(t)$ is a random process, this procedure does not make sense. Rather than maximizing the beamformer output [Eq. (11.54)], let us consider maximizing the mean-squared value of the beamformer output, namely,

$$J(D_{01}) = E[\underline{z}(t)]^2 = E[|a(0)|\underline{z}_0(t) + |a(1)|\underline{z}_1(t - D_{01})]^2 \tag{11.55}$$

The value of D_{01} that maximizes Eq. (11.55) will be our estimate of the intersensor time delay Δ_{01}. Now Eq. (11.55) can be rewritten as

$$J(D_{01}) = |a(0)|^2 E[\underline{z}_0(t)]^2 + 2|a(0)||a(1)|R_{01}(D_{01}) + |a(1)|^2 E[\underline{z}_1(t - D_{01})]^2 \tag{11.56}$$

where

$$R_{01}(D_{01}) \equiv E[\underline{z}_0(t)\underline{z}_1(t - D_{01})] \tag{11.57}$$

is the statistical cross-correlation function between the real processes $\underline{z}_0(t)$ and $\underline{z}_1(t)$. Here, D_{01} is the correlation or lag parameter. Since $\underline{z}_0(t)$ and $\underline{z}_1(t)$ were assumed to be zero-mean, WSS random processes, it follows that

$$E[\underline{z}_0(t)]^2 = \text{var}[\underline{z}_0(t)] = \text{constant}$$

$$E[\underline{z}_1(t - D_{01})]^2 = E[\underline{z}_1(t)]^2 = \text{var}[\underline{z}_1(t)] = \text{constant} \quad (11.58)$$

Consequently, from Eq. (11.55) through Eq. (11.58) we conclude that maximizing Eq. (11.55) is equivalent to maximizing the cross-correlation function Eq. (11.57). Hence, locating the peak of the cross-correlation function is equivalent to estimating the intersensor time delay Δ_{01}.

Notice that $R_{01}(D_{01})$, as defined in Eq. (11.57), requires ensemble averaging. However, if the zero-mean, WSS processes $\underline{z}_0(t)$ and $\underline{z}_1(t)$ are ergodic (see Chapter 1) and are observed for $t_p \le t \le t_p + t_0$, then Eq. (11.57) can be approximated by

$$\hat{R}_{01}(D_{01}) = \int_{t_p}^{t_p + t_0} \underline{z}_0(t)\underline{z}_1(t - D_{01})\, dt \quad (11.59)$$

provided that the observation interval t_0 is very long. Here, $\hat{R}_{01}(D_{01})$ denotes an estimate of $R_{01}(D_{01})$. Figure 11.22 summarizes a cross-correlation time delay estimation algorithm for the two-sensor, linear, passive array. Once Δ_{01} is known, the target's bearing follows from Eq. (11.43).

We can also implement the cross-correlation algorithm of Fig. 11.22 in the frequency domain. For example, the cross-spectral density associated with Eq. (11.57) is defined by the Fourier transform

$$G_{01}(F) \equiv \int_{-\infty}^{\infty} R_{01}(D_{01})e^{-j2\pi FD_{01}}\, dD_{01} \quad (11.60)$$

Substituting Eq. (11.59) into Eq. (11.60) gives the estimate

$$\hat{G}_{01}(F) = \underline{Z}_0(F)\underline{Z}_1^*(F) \quad (11.61)$$

provided that t_0 is very long. Here, $\underline{Z}_0(F)$ and $\underline{Z}_1(F)$ are the Fourier transforms of $\underline{z}_0(t)$ and $\underline{z}_1(t)$, respectively, and $\hat{G}_{01}(F)$ denotes an estimate of $G_{01}(F)$. Figure 11.23 shows the frequency domain implementation of Fig. 11.22. Notice that the sensor outputs are not prefiltered. That is, the received waveforms at $x = 0$ and $x = l$ go directly into a Fourier transform.

Let us now consider prefiltering $\underline{z}_0(t)$ with a linear time-invariant filter $h_0(t)$ and prefiltering $\underline{z}_1(t)$ with a linear time-invariant filter $h_1(t)$. Since the time delays show up in the phase spectra, let us assume that both prefilters have the same phase spectrum. This will prevent any distortion due to prefiltering. Hence, this idea generalizes the cross-correlation algorithms in Figs. 11.22 and 11.23. Figure 11.24 shows a time domain implementation of a generalized cross-correlation (GCC) algorithm, whereas Fig. 11.25 shows a frequency domain implementation of a GCC algorithm. In either case $\hat{R}_{01}^h(D_{01})$ is commonly called the *generalized cross-correlation function*.

We have introduced the ideas of prefiltering and GCC (see Figs. 11.24 and 11.25) as natural, intuitive extensions of Figs. 11.22 and 11.23. A more rigorous justification of the GCC method is given in [17]. Further, there has been a great

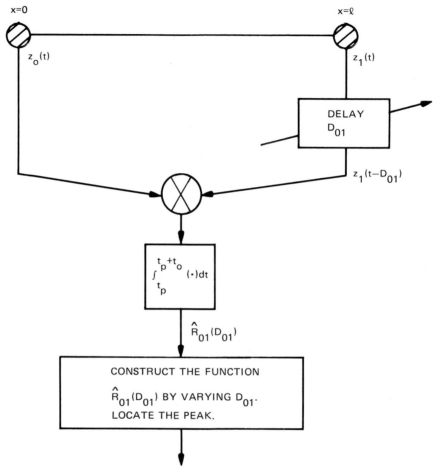

Fig. 11.22. Estimating Δ_{01} by a cross-correlation algorithm.

deal of research conducted on the selection of an "optimal" frequency weighting function $W(F) = |H_0(F)| \cdot |H_1(F)|$ for use in the frequency domain implementation of the GCC method [17]. (See Fig. 11.25.) For example, when the underlying spectral densities of $\underline{z}_0(t)$ and $\underline{z}_1(t)$ are known, when $\underline{s}(t)$, $\underline{v}_0(t)$, and $\underline{v}_1(t)$ are Gaussian and mutually uncorrelated, and when $\hat{G}_{01}(F)$ is obtained by averaging periodogram-type estimates of the cross-spectral density according to [18], then we can choose $W(F)$ to minimize the variance of the time delay estimate $\hat{\Delta}_{01}$. The resulting frequency weighting function is

$$W(F) = \frac{1}{G_{ss}(F)} \left[\frac{|\gamma_{01}(F)|^2}{1 - |\gamma_{01}(F)|^2} \right] \qquad (11.62)$$

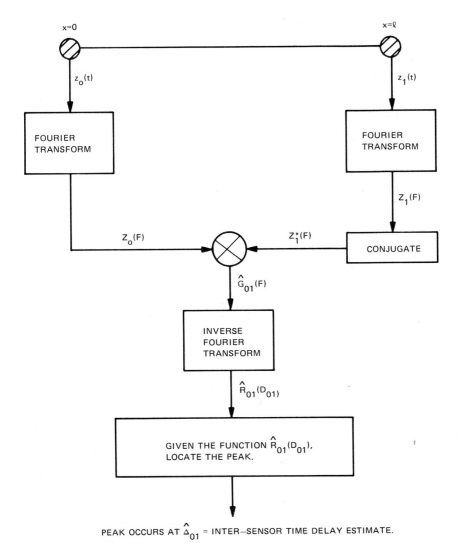

Fig. 11.23. Frequency domain implementation of the cross-correlation algorithm in Fig. 11.22. The sensor outputs $\underline{z}_0(t)$ and $\underline{z}_1(t)$ are not prefiltered—they go directly into a Fourier transform.

where

$$\gamma_{01}(F) = \frac{G_{01}(F)}{\sqrt{G_{00}(F)G_{11}(F)}} \tag{11.63}$$

Here, $G_{ss}(F)$ is the spectral density of $\underline{s}(t)$, $G_{00}(F)$ is the spectral density of $\underline{z}_0(t)$, $G_{11}(F)$ is the spectral density of $\underline{z}_1(t)$, and $G_{01}(F)$ is the cross-spectral density between $\underline{z}_0(t)$ and $\underline{z}_1(t)$. The quantity $\gamma_{01}(F)$ is called the *coherence function* between $\underline{z}_0(t)$ and $\underline{z}_1(t)$. Under the above assumptions and the assumption that t_0

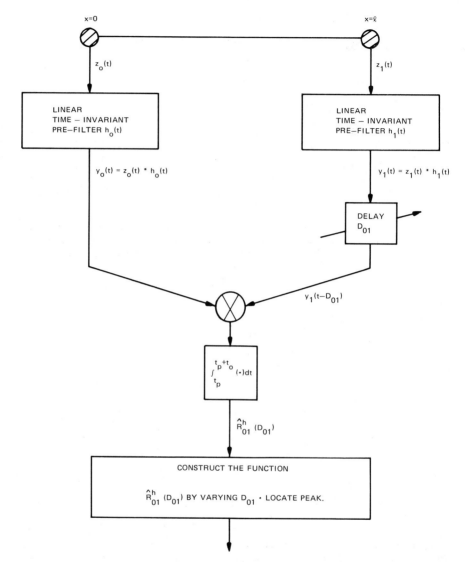

PEAK OCCURS AT $\hat{\Delta}_{01}$ = INTER–SENSOR TIME DELAY ESTIMATE.

Fig. 11.24. Generalized Cross Correlation (GCC) method.

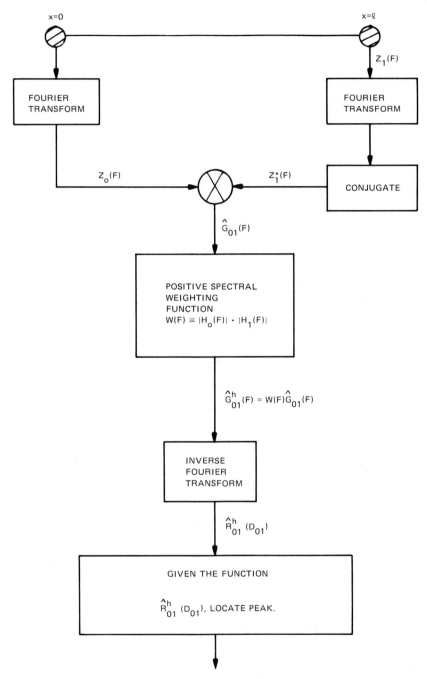

PEAK OCCURS AT $\hat{\Delta}_{01}$ = INTER–SENSOR TIME DELAY ESTIMATE.

Fig. 11.25. Frequency domain implementation of the GCC method.

is a very long observation time, we can show that the GCC algorithm (Fig. 11.25) that uses Eqs. (11.62) and (11.63) is the *maximum-likelihood estimate* of Δ_{01} [17, 19].

There are other reasons for choosing $W(F)$. For example, the weighting function

$$W(F) = \frac{1}{\sqrt{G_{00}(F)G_{11}(F)}} \qquad (11.64)$$

can be used to desensitize the GCC method to the bandwidth properties of $\underline{s}(t)$ [20]. That is, Eq. (11.64) has a prewhitening effect on $\hat{G}_{01}(F)$. Reference [21] provides a good discussion on several commonly used weighting functions and the reasons for their selection.

2 An Algorithm for the Three-Sensor Linear Array

As we saw in Section III.B, the three-sensor, linear, passive array solves the passive localization problem; that is, we can obtain the target's range r and bearing ϕ. However, we do have an ambiguity in target bearing that can be resolved by using (i) a priori knowledge or (ii) directional, rather than omnidirectional, sensors. Nevertheless, we are now faced with the problem of estimating the two independent time delays Δ_{01} and Δ_{02}. The third time delay, Δ_{12}, can be obtained from Eq. (11.46).

Let us assume that the radiating target and receiving passive array are both stationary. Further, we assume that the sensor positions are exactly known. We will also assume that the signal $\underline{s}(t)$ and the three noise processes $\underline{v}_0(t)$, $\underline{v}_1(t)$, and $\underline{v}_2(t)$ are all real, zero-mean, Gaussian, mutually uncorrelated, WSS random processes. Now the waveform received at the $x = 0$ and $x = l$ sensors are given by Eqs. (11.52) and (11.53), respectively, and the waveform received at the $x = 2l$ sensor is given by

$$\underline{z}_2(t) = \frac{1}{r_{2l}} s\left(t - \frac{r_{2l}}{c}\right) + \underline{v}_2(t) \qquad (11.65)$$

As we discussed in Section III.B, to obtain the target's range, we cannot assume that $\Delta_{02} \simeq 2\Delta_{01}$, which is equivalent to assuming that $r \to \infty$. In other words, we cannot perform the receive beamforming according to Fig. 11.16(b). Thus, we should perform the beamforming according to the rule

$$\underline{z}(t) = |a(0)|\underline{z}_0(t) + |a(1)|\underline{z}_1(t - D_{01}) + |a(2)|\underline{z}_2(t - D_{02}) \qquad (11.66)$$

where $|a(0)|$, $|a(1)|$, and $|a(2)|$ are the shading factors and D_{01} and D_{02} are the two independent time delay parameters. The values $\hat{D}_{01} = \hat{\Delta}_{01}$ and $\hat{D}_{02} = \hat{\Delta}_{02}$ that maximize the mean-squared value of the beamformer output [Eq. (11.66)] will be taken as our estimates of Δ_{01} and Δ_{02}, respectively.

Now the mean-squared value of Eq. (11.66) is

$$J(D_{01}, D_{02}) = E[\underline{z}(t)]^2$$

$$= E[|a(0)|\underline{z}_0(t) + |a(1)|\underline{z}_1(t - D_{01}) + |a(2)|\underline{z}_2(t - D_{02})]^2 \quad (11.67)$$

which represents a surface or two-dimensional function. Expanding Eq. (11.67), we get

$$J(D_{01}, D_{02}) = |a(0)|^2 E[\underline{z}_0(t)]^2 + |a(1)|^2 E[\underline{z}_1(t)]^2$$

$$+ |a(2)|^2 E[\underline{z}_2(t)]^2 + 2|a(0)||a(1)|R_{01}(D_{01})$$

$$+ 2|a(0)||a(2)|R_{02}(D_{02}) + 2|a(1)||a(2)|R_{12}(D_{02} - D_{01}) \quad (11.68)$$

which follows from the WSS assumption on $\underline{z}_0(t)$, $\underline{z}_1(t)$, and $\underline{z}_2(t)$. The statistical cross-correlation function $R_{01}(D_{01})$ is defined in Eq. (11.57). The other two cross-correlation functions are defined by

$$R_{02}(D_{02}) = E[\underline{z}_0(t)\underline{z}_2(t - D_{02})] \quad (11.69)$$

and

$$R_{12}(D_{02} - D_{01}) = E[\underline{z}_1(t - D_{01})\underline{z}_2(t - D_{02})] \quad (11.70)$$

where $\underline{z}_0(t)$, $\underline{z}_1(t)$, and $\underline{z}_2(t)$ are real processes. If these processes are ergodic and observed over a very long observation interval of length t_0, then the ensemble averages in Eqs. (11.57), (11.69), and (11.70) can be approximated by the time averages Eq. (11.59),

$$\hat{\underline{R}}_{02}(D_{02}) = \int_{t_p}^{t_p + t_0} \underline{z}_0(t)\underline{z}_2(t - D_{02})\, dt \quad (11.71)$$

and

$$\hat{\underline{R}}_{12}(D_{02} - D_{01}) = \int_{t_p}^{t_p + t_0} \underline{z}_1(t - D_{01})\underline{z}_2(t - D_{02})\, dt \quad (11.72)$$

respectively. Here, $\hat{R}_{01}(D_{01})$, $\hat{R}_{02}(D_{02})$, and $\hat{R}_{12}(D_{02} - D_{01})$ are estimates of $R_{01}(D_{01})$, $R_{02}(D_{02})$, and $R_{12}(D_{02} - D_{01})$, respectively,

The first three terms in Eq. (11.68) are constants. Thus, instead of maximizing Eq. (11.68) we could maximize the two-dimensional function

$$M(D_{01}, D_{02}) = 2|a(0)||a(1)|R_{01}(D_{01}) + 2|a(0)||a(2)|R_{02}(D_{02})$$

$$+ 2|a(1)||a(2)|R_{12}(D_{02} - D_{01}) \quad (11.73)$$

which is really the last three terms of Eq. (11.68). To locate the peak of Eq. (11.73), which is equivalent to maximizing the mean-squared value of the beamformer output, we could use the following algorithm:

Step 1. Select a point (D_{01}, D_{02}) from the set of all points in the $D_{01}D_{02}$ plane.
Step 2. Compute the three cross-correlation estimates (11.59), (11.71), and (11.72).

Step 3. Compute (11.73) for a given set of shading factors.

Step 4. Repeat steps 1–3 until (11.73) becomes a surface.

Step 5. Locate the peak of this surface. Say the peak occurs at the point $(\hat{\underline{\Delta}}_{01}, \hat{\underline{\Delta}}_{02})$. Take $(\hat{\underline{\Delta}}_{01}, \hat{\underline{\Delta}}_{02})$ as the estimate of $(\Delta_{01}, \Delta_{02})$.

Step 6. Use (11.50) and (11.51) to convert $(\hat{\underline{\Delta}}_{01}, \hat{\underline{\Delta}}_{02})$ into range and bearing estimates.

In Fig. 11.26 we show how to implement steps 1–6 by using three cross-correlators. We use the output of these correlators to construct the surface Eq. (11.73), and after locating the peak of this surface we label it $(\hat{\underline{\Delta}}_{01}, \hat{\underline{\Delta}}_{02})$. Given that $(\hat{\underline{\Delta}}_{01}, \hat{\underline{\Delta}}_{02})$ is an estimate of the intersensor time delays $(\Delta_{01}, \Delta_{02})$, we can find the target's range and bearing by evaluating Eqs. (11.50) and (11.51), respectively, at $(\hat{\underline{\Delta}}_{01}, \hat{\underline{\Delta}}_{02})$.

The algorithm described in Fig. 11.26 searches, in an unconstrained fashion, through all possible time delay values (D_{01}, D_{02}) before selecting the optimum pair $(\hat{\underline{\Delta}}_{01}, \hat{\underline{\Delta}}_{02})$. With $(\hat{\underline{\Delta}}_{01}, \hat{\underline{\Delta}}_{02})$, it then transforms these time delay estimates into range and bearing estimates by Eqs. (11.50) and (11.51), respectively. An alternative approach to range-bearing estimation would be to constrain the time-delay values (D_{01}, D_{02}) in Fig. 11.26 to follow the range-bearing Eqs. (11.50) (11.51). That is, we would first pick a range-bearing pair (r, ϕ), use Eqs. (11.50) and (11.51) to convert this pair to (D_{01}, D_{02}), and then use Fig. 11.26 to maximize the mean-squared value of the beamformer output [Eq. (11.68)]. Thus, the time delay pair that maximized Eq. (11.68) would immediately imply a range-bearing estimate; that is, we would not have to use Eqs. (11.50) and (11.51) after performing the time delay estimation algorithm is Fig. 11.26. In the literature this latter approach is known as the *focused beamformer*, because it constrains the time delay parameters (D_{01}, D_{02}) to "focus" on a specific (r, ϕ) pair [22]. The focused beamformer and Fig. 11.26 provide theoretically equivalent approaches to range-bearing estimation. However, for practical applications, it is sometimes more convenient to perform an unconstrained search (e.g., Fig. 11.26), rather than a constrained search (e.g., the focused beamformer), in the time delay parameters [23].

The time delay estimation algorithm in Fig. 11.26 requires a two-dimensional (2-D) peak detector. Although this represents an optimum algorithm, it would be convenient for practical reasons to reduce the algorithm to several one-dimensional (1-D) peak detectors. For example, reference [24] considers a time delay estimation procedure that processes each sensor pair (e.g., three pairs in Fig. 11.26) by a GCC algorithm. See Figs. 11.24 and 11.25. The time delay estimates from each GCC pair are then judiciously combined to produce the overall time delay estimate $(\hat{\underline{\Delta}}_{01}, \hat{\underline{\Delta}}_{02})$ [24]. Thus, this procedure replaces the 2-D peak detection algorithm of Fig. 11.26 by several (e.g., three) judiciously combined GCC algorithms (i.e., 1-D peak detectors).

Let us now discuss a conventional time delay estimation algorithm used for estimating range and bearing with a passive sonar array. As we saw in Section III.B, the three-sensor, linear, passive array solves the range and bearing

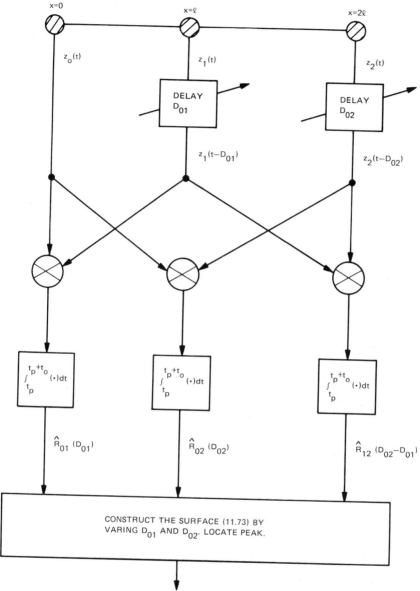

Fig. 11.26. Optimum 2-D algorithm for estimating intersensor time delays.

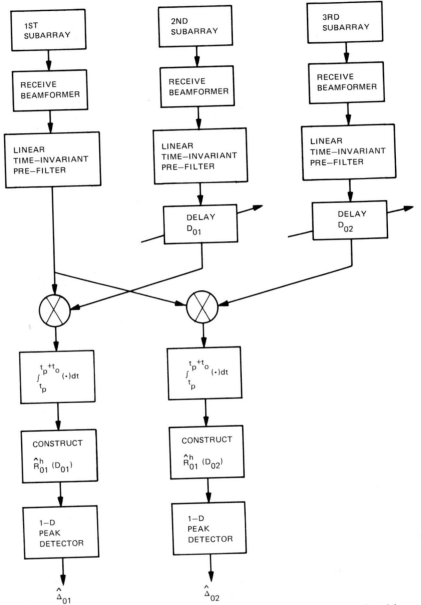

Fig. 11.27. Conventional suboptimum realization for estimating intersensor time delays.

estimation problem. Now instead of using three omnidirectional sensors, let us consider the idea of using three *subarrarys*. (Here, a subarray generally contains several omnidirectional sensors.) First, we will perform receive beamforming on each subarray. Next, we will perform a GCC algorithm on the beamformer outputs associated with the first and second subarrays. The resulting time delay estimate is approximately $\hat{\Delta}_{01}$. Then we will perform a GCC algorithm on the beamformer outputs associated with the first and third subarrays. The resulting time delay estimate is approximately $\hat{\Delta}_{02}$. Given $(\hat{\Delta}_{01}, \hat{\Delta}_{02})$, we use Eqs. (11.50) and (11.51) to obtain the range and bearing estimates, respectively. This conventional time delay estimation algorithm is shown in Fig. 11.27.

Although the conventional algorithm of Fig. 11.27 is not the theoretically optimum algorithm (e.g., the GCC version of Fig. 11.26 and the focused beamformer), it is very practical and easy to implement. That is, it can be implemented at a lower cost than the optimum algorithm and performs almost as well [1].

Recall that there are only two independent time delays (e.g., Δ_{01} and Δ_{02}). The remaining time delay, Δ_{12}, can be obtained from Eq. (11.46). Thus, we need not perform a GCC algorithm on the second and third subarrays in Fig. 11.27. However, in practice, this is done for redundancy; that is, it can be used to verify that the algorithm is working properly.

As we have seen, cross-correlation and time delay estimation go hand in hand. In the next section we will discuss the theory of cross-correlation and its relationship to the time delay estimation problem.

CROSS-CORRELATION AND ITS RELATIONSHIP TO THE   IV
TIME DELAY ESTIMATION PROBLEM

Cross-Correlation: A Measure of Similarity   A

Two geometrical vectors, say $\mathbf{x}$ and $\mathbf{y}$, two continuous-time waveforms, say $x(t)$ and $y(t)$, and two discrete-time sequences, say $x(n)$ and $y(n)$, are commonly classified as similar or dissimilar. For example, if two geometrical vectors have the same magnitude and direction, they are similar; specifically, they are equivalent. Sometimes, two vectors could have the same magnitude but different directions. Then the vectors are similar but not equivalent. To quantify the term "similar" for two geometrical vectors, we frequently use the inner product, scalar product, or dot product. For two geometrical vectors $\mathbf{x}$ and $\mathbf{y}$ the *dot product* is defined by

$$\mathbf{x} \cdot \mathbf{y} = |\mathbf{x}||\mathbf{y}| \cos \theta \qquad (11.74)$$

where θ is the angle between the vectors. When two geometrical vectors have the same magnitude and are pointed in the same direction, we have $\mathbf{x} \cdot \mathbf{y} = |\mathbf{x}|^2$. For this case the dot product is a maximum, and the two vectors are identical. When two geometrical vectors have the same magnitude but are perpendicular (i.e., $\theta = 90°$), we have $\mathbf{x} \cdot \mathbf{y} = 0$. For this case the dot product is zero, and the two vectors are dissimilar. In any case the *dot product* quantifies the terms *similar* and *dissimilar* for two *geometrical vectors*.

Let us now consider the two real, continuous-time waveforms $x(t)$ and $y(t)$. If the two waveforms have the same amplitude and time distributions, they are *equivalent*. In the time delay estimation problem the two waveforms generally have the same amplitude distributions but different time distributions; that is, the two waveforms can be expressed as $x(t)$ and $y(t) = x(t - \tau)$. To quantify the term "similar" for two continuous-time waveforms $x(t)$ and $y(t)$, we define the inner product

$$\langle x(t), y(t) \rangle = \int_a^b x(t)y(t)\,dt \tag{11.75}$$

where $a \le t \le b$ defines the time interval of interest. If $y(t) = x(t - \tau)$, then

$$\langle x(t), y(t) \rangle = \int_a^b x(t)x(t - \tau)\,dt \tag{11.76}$$

When $\tau = 0$ the waveforms $x(t)$ and $x(t - \tau)$ are aligned. For this case the inner product [Eq. (11.76)] is a maximum, and the two waveforms are similar; specifically, they are identical. When either the waveform $x(t)$ or $x(t - \tau)$ does not partially occupy the time interval $[a, b]$ (i.e., they are disjoint in time), then Eq. (11.76) is zero. For this case the waveforms are dissimilar. The inner product Eq. (11.76), plotted as a function of τ, is the autocorrelation function of $x(t)$. Thus, a measure of *similarity* for two continuous-time waveforms is the *inner product* Eq. (11.75).

For discrete-time sequences we define the inner product

$$\langle x(n), y(n) \rangle = \sum_{n=0}^{N-1} x(n)y(n) \tag{11.77}$$

where $0 \le n \le N - 1$ is the interval of interest. Again, for time delay problems we have $y(n) = x(n - m)$. For this case Eq. (11.77) can be written as the discrete-time autocorrelation function of $x(n)$. Hence, a measure a *similarity* for two discrete-time sequences is the *inner product* Eq. (11.77).

The cross-correlation function between ergodic sequences $x(n)$ and $y(n)$ is defined by

$$r_{xy}(m) = \sum_{n=\infty}^{\infty} x(n)y^*(n - m) \tag{11.78}$$

where $x(n)$ and $y(n)$ are usually complex sequences. Here, the independent variable m is called the lag variable. Notice that Eq. (11.78) is really the inner product $\langle x(n), y(n - m) \rangle$, which is a function of the lag m. Thus, the cross-correlation function, like the other inner products, provide a general measure of similarity between two waveforms.

Figure 11.28 shows two different waveforms and the corresponding cross-correlation function. Notice that the cross-correlation function is, in general, not symmetrical and not unimodal. Figure 11.29 shows the cross-correlation function between a waveform $x(n)$ and a delayed version of this waveform, $x(n - D)$. Here, D is an integer value of time delay. For this case the cross-correlation function is always symmetrical and always unimodal, provided the SNR is large. Thus, the time delay estimation problem allows $r_{xy}(m)$ to be unimodal. Hence time delay estimation algorithms that locate the peak of $r_{xy}(m)$ will always select one maximum or peak, which occurs at the time delay D.

In summary, the cross-correlation function is an inner-product-type function that provides a measure of similarity between two waveforms. For time delay estimation problems the cross-correlation function is equivalent to the

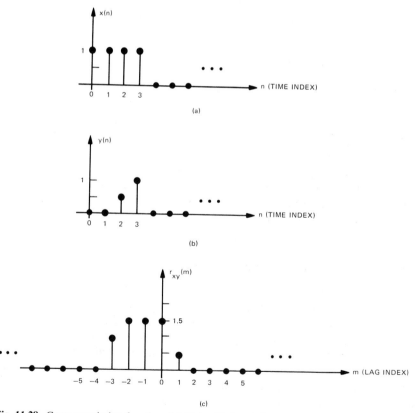

Fig. 11.28. Cross-correlation function. (a) Right-sided waveform $x(n)$; (b) right-sided waveform $y(n)$; (c) $R_{xy}(m)$ = cross correlation function between $x(n)$ and $y(n)$.

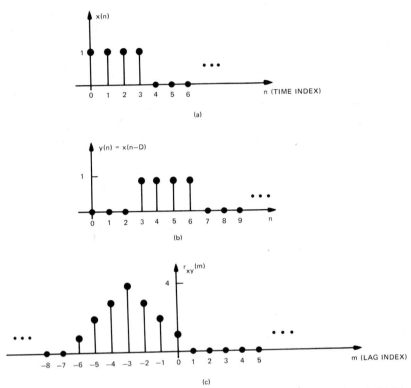

Fig. 11.29. Cross-correlation function. (a) Right-sided waveform $x(n)$; (b) waveform in (a) delayed by $D = 3$ units; (c) cross correlation function $r_{xy}(m) =$ autocorrelation function $r_{xx}(m + 3)$.

autocorrelation function centered at the true time delay. Hence time delay estimation algorithms that locate the peak of $r_{xy}(m)$ will always obtain a unique global peak (provided the SNR is large) due to the unimodal, symmetrical nature of the autocorrelation function.

B Cross-Correlation and Mean-Squared Criteria

The cross-correlation function arises quite naturally when one attempts to minimize or maximize mean-squared objective functions. For example, in the active sensor problem we assumed that the optimal time delay estimate was the one that minimized Eq. (11.29). Equation (11.29) represents the mean-squared (i.e., average-squared) error between the observation $z(t)$ and the model $(AG^2/R^2)s_T(t - \tau)$. The end result was the cross-correlation function Eq. (11.36); the location of the peak of Eq. (11.36) is the active time delay estimate.

For the passive sensor problem we assumed that the optimal intersensor time delay estimates were the ones that maximized the mean-squared value of the beamformer output. Refer to Eqs. (11.55) and (11.67). The end result was the cross-correlation functions between the sensor outputs (or subarray beamformer outputs); the peaks of these cross-correlation functions were related to the intersensor time delay estimates.

In general, if one has a mean-squared objective function of the form

$$J(D) = E[x(n) + ay(n - D)]^2$$

$$= E[x^2(n) + 2ax(n)y(n - D) + a^2y^2(n - D)] \quad (11.79)$$

if $x(n)$ and $y(n)$ are zero mean WSS processes, if a is a constant, and if D is a time delay parameter, then

$$J(D) \propto r_{xy}(D) \quad (11.80)$$

That is, the cross term in the mean-squared objective function [Eq. (11.79)] gives rise to a cross-correlation function. Hence, locating the peak of a cross-correlation function is equivalent to maximizing Eq. (11.79).

In summary, mean-squared objective functions and cross-correlation functions go hand in hand. However, if one chooses to select an objective function that is not of the mean-squared type, then there is no obvious reason why cross-correlation functions should appear in the resulting time delay estimation algorithms. Nevertheless, the mean-squared value of the beamformer output makes physical sense, so maximizing this quantity is not only reasonable but wise in terms of the ease of implementation. For the mathematical properties of cross-correlation functions, see Chapter 1.

THE IMPLEMENTATION OF SOME TIME DELAY ESTIMATION V ALGORITHMS USING THE FAST FOURIER TRANSFORM (FFT)

From Theory to Implementation A

In previous sections we covered the basic theory and functional flow diagrams for both the active and passive time delay estimation algorithms. We now discuss some practical implementation issues.

With the advent of high-speed digital electronics, there has been a steady transition from analog signal processing to digital signal processing. Today, many radar and sonar systems are moving toward computer-controlled, automated software-based systems. Both radar and sonar signal processing have been heavily influenced by the commerical availability of gate arrays, CMOS devices, high-speed digital signal processing chips, microprocessors, microcomputers, and FFT algorithms. The implementation of many time delay estimation algorithms rely quite heavily on the FTT. Thus, we will discuss the role of the FFT in both the active and passive problems.

B Implementation Issues for the Active Case

The front end of an active radar or sonar receiver generally contains a receive beamformer, analog filters, amplifiers, and dynamic range controllers [e.g., automatic gain control (AGC)]. These devices prepare the radar or sonar analog signal for digital signal processing. For a stationary point target located in a homogeneous, isotropic, lossless medium, the analog signal, after front-end processing, has the form

$$\underline{z}(t) = M s_T(t - \tau) + \underline{v}(t) \tag{11.81}$$

for $t_p \le t \le t_p + t_0$. Here, t_p is the duration of the transmitted pulse, t_0 is the length of the observation interval, $s_T(t)$ is the transmitted waveform [refer to Eq. (11.1)], M is a constant, $\underline{v}(t)$ is a zero-mean, white Gaussian noise process, and τ is the desired time delay.

Equation (11.81) is an analog signal with a corresponding analog spectrum $\underline{Z}(F)$. In active radar and sonar $\underline{z}(t)$ generally has a narrowband spectrum. That is, $\underline{Z}(F)$ is centered about some carrier frequency F_0 (Hz) and has a bandwidth W (Hz) that is much smaller than F_0 [25]. For example, Figure 11.30 shows a typical magnitude spectrum of a narrowband process $\underline{z}(t)$. Let us now discuss the analog-to-digital conversion (ADC) of this narrowband process.

Suppose $\underline{z}(t)$ was associated with an X-band radar whose carrier frequency was $F_0 = 9 \times 10^9$ Hz $= 9$ GHz and whose bandwidth was $W = 1 \times 10^6$ Hz $= 1$ MHz. Naively, we could sample this process at the Nyquist rate of $2(F_0 + W/2)$ Hz or 18 GHz. However, the current ADC technology cannot support this sampling requirement. Further, if the observation interval was $t_0 = 0.75 \times 10^{-3}$ s, then sampling $\underline{z}(t)$ at 18 GHz would result in 13.5×10^6 digital samples, an enormous amount of data.

To circumvent these problems and make the ADC practical, we first translate the narrowband process $\underline{z}(t)$ down to baseband (i.e., a lowpass spectrum centered

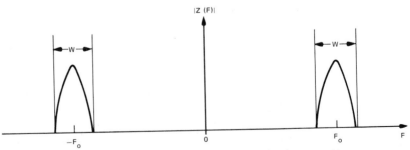

Fig. 11.30. Magnitude spectrum of a narrowband process $\underline{z}(t)$.

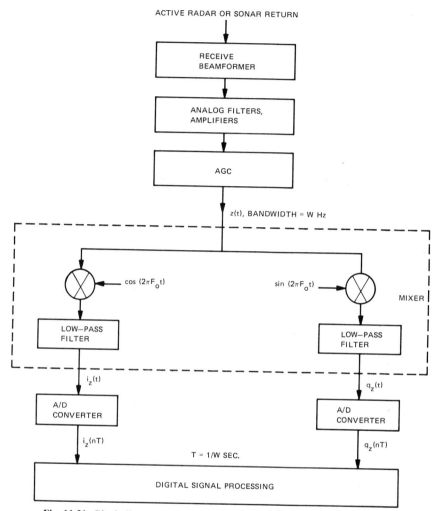

Fig. 11.31. Block diagram of the narrowband-to-baseband translation process.

at $F = 0$), then sampled at a much lower rate. The narrowband-to-baseband translation, common practice in active radar and sonar, is generally done with analog multipliers and filters. Figure 11.31 is a block diagram description of this.

Figure 11.31 shows that the narrowband-to-baseband translation, commonly referred to as *mixing*, decomposes $\underline{z}(t)$ into an *in-phase* (I) component $i_z(t)$ and a *quadrature* (Q) component $q_z(t)$. Mathematically, the mixing process generates a lowpass *complex analog signal*

$$\tilde{\underline{z}}(t) = \underline{i}_z(t) + j\underline{q}_z(t) \tag{11.82}$$

for $t_p \le t \le t_p + t_0$. The magnitude of $\underline{\tilde{z}}(t)$ is

$$|\underline{\tilde{z}}(t)| = \{[\underline{i}_z(t)]^2 + [\underline{q}_z(t)]^2\}^{1/2} \tag{11.83}$$

and the phase angle associated with $\underline{\tilde{z}}(t)$ is

$$\arg[\underline{\tilde{z}}(t)] = \tan^{-1}\left\{\frac{\underline{q}_z(t)}{\underline{i}_z(t)}\right\} \tag{11.84}$$

Since each analog component of $\underline{\tilde{z}}(t)$ has a lowpass spectrum with cutoff frequency $W/2$ Hz, this means that $\underline{i}_z(t)$ and $\underline{q}_z(t)$ can be sampled at W Hz. Thus, the above X-band radar would require 10 MHz ADCs in the I and Q paths. The current ADC technology can easily support this sampling requirement. Further, for $t_0 = 0.75$ ms, the 10-MHz sampling rate generates 7500 I samples and 7500 Q samples instead of the 13.5×10^6 z-samples generated by the 18-GHz sampling rate. This represents a data compression ratio of approximately 1000 to 1.

At this point the active radar or sonar return has been front-end filtered, mixed, and converted to discrete-time form. We assume that the time origin has been shifted so that $0 \le t \le t_0$. Hence, if $t_0 = (N - 1)T$, then we have the N complex samples $\underline{\tilde{z}}(nT)$ $(n = 0, 1, \ldots, N - 1)$. Equivalently, we now have the N in-phase samples $\underline{i}_z(nT)$ $(n = 0, 1, \ldots, N - 1)$ and the N quadrature samples $\underline{q}_z(nT)$ $(n = 0, 1, \ldots, N - 1)$. The radar or sonar return is now ready for digital signal processing (Fig. 11.31).

Recall the discussion in Section II.C.2. For real data $z(t)$ and a stationary point target in an ideal medium, we showed that the least squares solution to the active time delay estimation problem was to locate the peak of the correlator output. Refer to Eq. (11.36) and Fig. 11.19. For complex data $\underline{\tilde{z}}(t)$ [refer to Eq. (11.82) and Fig. 11.31], Eq. (11.36) becomes

$$\underline{\tilde{y}}(\tilde{\tau}) = \underline{i}_y(\tilde{\tau}) + j\underline{q}_y(\tilde{\tau}) = \int_{t_p}^{t_p+t_0} \underline{\tilde{z}}(t)\tilde{s}_T^*(t - \tilde{\tau})\, dt \tag{11.85}$$

Here, $\underline{\tilde{z}}(t)$ and

$$\tilde{s}_T(t) = s_{Ti}(t) + js_{Tq}(t) \tag{11.86}$$

are obtained by mixing $\underline{z}(t)$ and $s_T(t)$, respectively. See Fig. 11.31. The quantities $\underline{i}_y(\tilde{\tau})$ and $\underline{q}_y(\tilde{\tau})$ are the real and imaginary components, respectively, of the complex correlator output [Eq. (11.85)]. If we implement Eq. (11.85) on a digital computer than $\underline{\tilde{y}}(\tilde{\tau})$ can be approximated by

$$\underline{\tilde{y}}(mT) = \sum_{n=0}^{N-1} \underline{\tilde{z}}(nT)\tilde{s}_T^*(nT - mT) \tag{11.87}$$

where $\tilde{\tau} = mT$ $(m = 0, \pm 1, \ldots, \pm M \mp 1)$, $t = nT$ $(n = 0, 1, \ldots, N - 1)$, and T is the uniform sampling increment. Generally, the length of $\tilde{s}_T(nT)$, say S, is shorter than N, so $M > N > S$.

Many active radars and sonars compute Eq. (11.87) by the FFT. Specifically, if

$$\tilde{\underline{Z}}(k) = \sum_{n=0}^{NL-1} \tilde{\underline{z}}(n)e^{-j2\pi nk/NL} \qquad (k = 0, 1, \ldots, NL-1) \qquad (11.88)$$

represents the discrete Fourier transform (DFT) of $\tilde{\underline{z}}(n) = \tilde{\underline{z}}(nT)$ and

$$\tilde{S}_T(k) = \sum_{n=0}^{NL-1} \tilde{s}_T(n)e^{-j2\pi nk/NL} \qquad (k = 0, 1, \ldots, NL-1) \qquad (11.89)$$

represents the DFT of $\tilde{s}_T(n) = \tilde{s}_T(nT)$, then

$$\tilde{\underline{Y}}(k) = \tilde{\underline{Z}}(k)S_T^*(k) \qquad (k = 0, 1, \ldots, NL-1) \qquad (11.90)$$

represents the discrete cross-spectrum between $\tilde{\underline{z}}(n)$ and $\tilde{s}_T(n)$, provided that t_0 is "large." The DFT

$$\tilde{\underline{y}}(m) = \frac{1}{NL} \sum_{k=0}^{NL-1} \tilde{\underline{Y}}(k)e^{j2\pi nk/NL} \qquad (m = 0, 1, \ldots, NL-1) \qquad (11.91)$$

gives the correlator output Eq. (11.87). We note that the size of the DFTs, namely NL, is usually much larger than N because $\tilde{\underline{z}}(n)$ and $\tilde{s}_T(n)$ are appended with $NL - N$ and $NL - S$ zeros, respectively. This zero-padding is necessary to avoid the circular convolution effects that one encounters when using DFTs to perform convolution or correlation. Refer to Chapter 1, Section VII.D. Now once the zero-padding and DFT size NL have been established, the FFT algorithm (see Chap. 7) is used to implement the DFTs (11.88) and (11.89). Next, the cross-spectrum Eq. (11.90) is computed; then the inverse FFT algorithm is used to implement the DFT Eq. (11.91). At this point the complex correlator output $\tilde{\underline{y}}(m)$ is available for further processing.

The time delay τ appears in both the magnitude and phase of $\tilde{\underline{y}}(m)$. However, for active radar and sonar the phase of $\tilde{\underline{y}}(m)$ is a very sensitive function of τ; that is, the smallest change in τ produces large phase fluctuations. Therefore the phase of $\tilde{\underline{y}}(m)$ is generally not stable, so it is not used for time delay estimation. On the other hand, the magnitude of $\tilde{\underline{y}}(m)$ is less sensitive to small changes in τ. Consequently, the magnitude of $\tilde{\underline{y}}(m)$ is generally used for time delay estimation. Thus, the FFT processing gives $\tilde{\underline{y}}(m)$, and the peak location of

$$|\tilde{\underline{y}}(m)| = |\underline{i}_y(m) + j\underline{q}_y(m)| = \left| \sum_{n=0}^{N-1} \tilde{\underline{z}}(n)\tilde{s}_T^*(n-m) \right| \qquad (11.92)$$

gives the final active time delay estimate. Figure 11.32 summarizes the above discussion.

When no noise is present [e.g., $v(t) = 0$], the magnitude of $\tilde{\underline{y}}(\tilde{\tau})$ can be written as

$$|\tilde{\underline{y}}(\tilde{\tau})| = \left| \int_{-\infty}^{\infty} M\tilde{s}_T(t-\tau)\tilde{s}_T^*(t-\tilde{\tau})\,dt \right| \qquad (11.93)$$

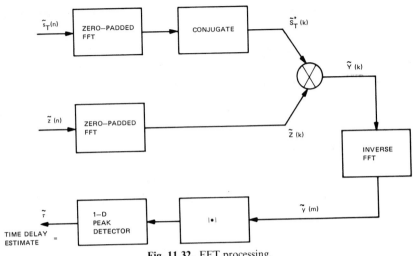

Fig. 11.32. FFT processing.

Under the no-noise assumption, Eq. (11.93) is entirely dependent on the properties of the transmitted waveform $s_T(t)$. Further, $\tilde{y}(\tilde{\tau})$ achieves its maximum value when $\tilde{\tau} = \tau$ (i.e., when $\tilde{\tau}$ equals the true time delay τ). Notice that this maximum value is proportional to the energy E_T in $s_T(t)$.

Up to now we have assumed that the active radar or sonar operated against a stationary point target. For constant-velocity point targets (see [26]), Eq. (11.93) can be generalized to

$$|\tilde{y}(\tilde{\tau}, \tilde{F}_d)| = \left| \int_{-\infty}^{\infty} M \tilde{s}_T(t - \tau) \tilde{s}^*(t - \tilde{\tau}) e^{-j2\pi(F_d - \tilde{F}_d)t}\, dt \right| \tag{11.94}$$

where F_d is the *Doppler shift*. If Eq. (11.94) is normalized such that

$$A(\tilde{\tau} = \tau, \tilde{F}_d = F_d) = \frac{|\tilde{y}(\tau, F_d)|}{|M| E_T = 1} \tag{11.95}$$

we obtain

$$A(\tilde{\tau}, \tilde{F}_d) = \left| \int_{-\infty}^{\infty} \tilde{s}_T(t - \tau) \tilde{s}_T^*(t - \tilde{\tau}) e^{-j2\pi(F_d - \tilde{F}_d)t}\, dt \right| \tag{11.96}$$

The square of Eq. (11.96) is commonly referred to as the *ambiguity function*, which was originally introduced by Ville [27]. The ambiguity function represents the magnitude squared of the complex correlator output or matched filter output under the constant-velocity point target and no-noise assumptions. Notice that $A(\tilde{\tau}, \tilde{F}_d)$ is a 2-D surface with a global maximum at the point (τ, F_d). Thus, we can perform time delay and Doppler estimations simultaneously by locating the global peak of Eq. (11.96). Further, since $s_T(t)$ controls the shape of the ambiguity function, one can judiciously select an "optimal" transmitted waveform by means of Eq. (11.96). In any event, the ambiguity function plays a major role in radar and sonar signal processing. References [25] and [28] provide good discussions on the ambiguity function as well as numerous 3-D pictures.

Implementation Issues for the Passive Case   C

The front end of a passive radar or sonar receiver generally contains a receive beamformer, analog filters, amplifiers, and AGC circuitry. Just like the active case these devices prepare the analog signals for digital signal processing.

As we saw in Section III.C, the GCC algorithm plays an important role in the passive time delay estimation problem. Figure 11.25 is a block diagram for implementing the GCC algorithm in the frequency domain. Since we are interested in an FFT implementation, our discussion will be centered around Fig. 11.25.

The analog signals $\underline{z}_0(t)$ and $\underline{z}_1(t)$ that experience that front-end processing are generally *broadband*. That is, the spectra $Z_0(F)$ and $Z_1(F)$ are generally spread out over a fairly wide bandwidth. Although these bandwidths are wide, they are usually compatible with practical ADCs. Thus, the samples $z_0(nT)$ ($n = 0, 1,..., N - 1$) and $z_1(nT)$ ($n = 0, 1,..., N - 1$) are usually obtained by direct analog-to-digital conversion of $\underline{z}_0(t)$ and $\underline{z}_1(t)$, respectively. For example, a passive sonar receiver with a 0–10 kHz bandwidth would require at least a 20-kHz ADC. For an observation interval of $t_0 = 25.6$ msc, this means that the length of $\underline{z}_0(nT)$ and $\underline{z}_1(nT)$ is $N = 512$ points. Here, $T = \frac{1}{20}$ kHz $= 50 \ \mu s$ is the uniform sampling increment.

Given that

$$Z_0(k) = \sum_{n=0}^{NL-1} z_0(n)e^{-j2\pi nk/NL} \qquad (k = 0, 1,..., NL - 1) \qquad (11.97)$$

is the DFT of $\underline{z}_0(n) = \underline{z}_0(nT)$ and

$$Z_1(k) = \sum_{n=0}^{NL-1} z_1(n)e^{-j2\pi nk/NL} \qquad (k = 0, 1,..., NL - 1) \qquad (11.98)$$

is the DFT of $\underline{z}_1(n) = \underline{z}_1(nT)$, then the cross-spectrum between $\underline{z}_0(n)$ and $\underline{z}_1(n)$ is

$$\hat{G}_{01}(k) = Z_0(k)Z_1^*(k) \qquad (k = 0, 1,..., NL - 1) \qquad (11.99)$$

For a given spectral weighting function $W(k)$ ($k = 0, 1,..., NL - 1$), the GCC algorithm modifies the cross-spectrum according to the multiplicative rule

$$\hat{G}_{01}^h(k) = W(k)\hat{G}_{01}(k) \qquad (k = 0, 1,..., NL - 1) \qquad (11.100)$$

Finally, the IDFT

$$\hat{R}_{01}^h(n) = \frac{1}{NL} \sum_{k=0}^{NL-1} \hat{G}_{01}^h(k)e^{j2\pi nk/NL} \qquad (n = 0, 1,..., NL - 1) \quad (11.101)$$

gives the GCC function. The location of the peak of Eq. (11.101) gives the "optimal" time delay estimate.

For an FFT implementation of Fig. 11.25, the DFTs Eqs. (11.97) and (11.98) can be implemented by an FFT algorithm. Similarly, Eq. (11.101) can be implemented by an IFFT algorithm.

As we saw, Fig. 11.27 can be used to solve the passive localization problem. The practical aspect of Fig. 11.27 is that it involves two independent GCC algorithms. Since we have just shown how a GCC algorithm can be implemented by FFTs, it follows that Fig. 11.27 has an FFT implementation.

In summary, we can use the FFT algorithm to solve the active and passive time delay estimation problems. When applying the FFT to correlation or convolution problems, be careful to avoid the effects of circular convolution. This is why the FFT input sequences are zero-padded. That is, the FFT size NL is composed of N data points and a sufficient number of zeros.

VI ALGORITHM PERFORMANCE

A Performance for the Active Case

In Section II we discussed the time delay estimation problem for active sensors. Recall that we considered a simple backscattering model (i.e., a stationary point target model) and an additive white noise model. Although these models represent a gross simplification of a real-world target echo, they keep the mathematics tractable, so we can obtain a feel for the problem.

Let us now make the following assumptions:

1. The transmitted signal $s_T(t)$ has the form (11.1).
2. The backscattering process is described by a single stationary point target located in a homogeneous, isotropic, lossless medium. Thus, the noise-free target echo is simply a scaled time-delayed version of (11.1), there are no other scatterers, and no multipath.
3. The additive noise model is a zero-mean, WSS, Gaussian white noise process with autocorrelation function (11.37).
4. The transmitted pulse width t_p is much smaller than the observation interval t_0.
5. The MRA of the transmit beam is pointed directly at the target, so the target's direction is exactly known.
6. The time delay estimate $\hat{\tau}$ is obtained by locating the peak of the magnitude of the cross-correlation function. The phase of the cross-correlation function is not used.

Based on these assumptions and the additional assumption of a large SNR (e.g., greater than 15 dB), the variance of the time delay estimate $\hat{\tau}$ is [16, 26]

$$\operatorname{var}(\hat{\tau}) = \frac{1}{d^2 \beta^2} \tag{11.102}$$

where

$$d^2 \equiv \frac{2E_T}{N_0} = \frac{E_T}{N_0/2} \tag{11.103}$$

$$E_T = \int_0^{t_p} s_T^2(t)\,dt = \int_{-\infty}^{\infty} |S_T(F)|^2\,dF \tag{11.104}$$

and

$$\beta^2 = \frac{\displaystyle\int_{-\infty}^{\infty} (2\pi F)^2 |S_T(F)|^2\,dF}{\displaystyle\int_{-\infty}^{\infty} |S_T(F)|^2\,dF} \tag{11.105}$$

Here, E_T is the energy of the transmitted signal, $N_0/2$ is the magnitude of the white noise power spectral density (PSD), and $S_T(F)$ is the Fourier (analog) spectrum of $s_T(t)$. It is common practice to interpret d^2 as a measure of SNR and β^2 as a mean-squared measure of transmitted signal bandwidth [16]. Thus, if the square root of $\operatorname{var}(\hat{\tau})$ represents the time delay estimation accuracy, then large SNRs (e.g., greater than 15 dB) and large bandwidths produce accurate time delay estimates.

Such results are intuitively pleasing. For example, Fig. 11.8(b) shows a stationary point target echo in additive white noise. We see that when the signal amplitude is large compared to the noise amplitudes and when the rise time of the pulse is small (which translates into a large signal bandwidth), we can intuitively argue that the time delay estimate $\hat{\tau}$ will be more accurate. Equation (11.102) [or the square root of Eq. (11.102)] quantifies these intuitive notions.

Performance for the Passive Case   B

In Section III we discussed the time delay estimation problem for passive sensors. Recall that to perform target localization by a passive array, we must be able to accurately estimate the intersensor time delays Δ_{01} and Δ_{02} [see Eqs. (11.44), (11.45) and Fig. 11.21].

Let us now make the following assumptions:

1. The passive array receives a radiated signal $s(t)$ from a stationary target. When appropriate, the radiated signal $s(t)$ belongs to a zero mean, WSS Gaussian process with power spectral density $G_{ss}(F)$.

2. The passive array is stationary, and the elements or sensors are all collinear.

3. The additive noise $\underline{v}(t)$ in the received signal model is a zero-mean, WSS Gaussian white noise process with autocorrelation function (11.37) and power spectral density $G_{vv}(F)$.

4. The radiating target and linear passive array are located in a homogeneous, isotropic, and lossless medium. Further, there is no multipath corruption of the received signal.

5. The radiated signal and additive noise process are uncorrelated.

Based on these assumptions, the variance of the time delay estimate $\hat{\underline{\tau}}$ between two sensors is [17]

$$\text{var}(\hat{\underline{\tau}}) = \left\{ 2t_0 \int_0^\infty (2\pi F)^2 \left[\frac{|\gamma(F)|^2}{1 - |\gamma(F)|^2} \right] dF \right\}^{-1} \tag{11.106}$$

where

$$|\gamma(F)|^2 = \frac{G_{ss}^2(F)}{[G_{ss}(F) + G_{vv}(F)]^2} \tag{11.107}$$

and t_0 is the length of the observation interval.

For the active case, $\text{var}(\hat{\underline{\tau}})$, given by Eq. (11.102), was self-explanatory. That is, given a transmitted signal $s_T(t)$, d^2 and β^2 clearly defined the notions of SNR and bandwidth. However, for the passive case it is not clear how Eq. (11.106) relates to SNR and bandwidth. Thus, to make things clear, we will consider a simple example.

Example 5.   Let us assume that both the signal and noise PSDs are constant over a finite-length frequency band and zero otherwise. Refer to Fig. 11.33. Under this condition Eq. (11.106) reduces to

$$\text{var}(\hat{\underline{\tau}}) = \frac{3}{8\pi^2 t_0} \frac{1 + 2(S_0/N_0)}{(S_0/N_0)^2 (F_2^3 - F_1^3)} \tag{11.108}$$

Since the signal power S is

$$S = \int_{-\infty}^{\infty} G_{ss}(F) \, dF = S_0(F_2 - F_1) \tag{11.109}$$

and the noise power N is

$$N = \int_{-\infty}^{\infty} G_{vv}(F) \, dF = N_0(F_2 - F_1) \tag{11.110}$$

Eq. (11.108) can be rewritten in terms of signal-power-to-noise-power ratios; that is,

$$\text{var}(\hat{\underline{\tau}}) = \frac{3}{8\pi^2 t_0} \frac{1 + 2(S/N)}{(S/N)^2 (F_2^3 - F_1^3)} \tag{11.111}$$

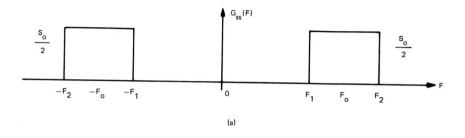

(a)

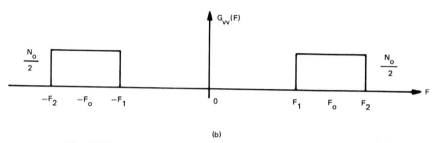

(b)

Fig. 11.33. Assumed PSDs for (a) the signal $s(t)$ and (b) the noise $\underline{v}(t)$.

For low SNRs (i.e., SNR $\ll 1$) we have

$$\text{var}(\hat{\underline{\tau}}) \simeq \frac{3}{8\pi^2 t_0} \frac{1}{(S/N)^2(F_2^3 - F_1^3)} \qquad (11.112)$$

whereas for high SNRs (i.e., SNR $\gg 1$) we have

$$\text{var}(\hat{\underline{\tau}}) \simeq \frac{3}{8\pi^2 t_0} \frac{2}{(S/N)(F_2^3 - F_1^3)} \qquad (11.113)$$

In summary:

1. Like the active case, large SNRs and large bandwidths produce accurate time delay estimates.

2. For the low SNR case the accuracy of $\hat{\underline{\tau}}$ [or the square root of (11.112)] is inversely proportional to SNR.

3. For the high SNR case the accuracy of $\hat{\underline{\tau}}$ [or the square root of (11.113)] is inversely proportional to $\sqrt{\text{SNR}}$.

Note that Eq. (11.102) for the active case and Eq. (11.106) for the passive case represent a lower bound on the variance of the time delay estimate $\hat{\underline{\tau}}$. That is, under the given assumptions, Eqs. (11.102) and (11.106) represent the best we can do. In the theory of maximum-likelihood estimation this lower bound is commonly referred to as the *Cramèr–Rao lower bound*. The derivation of the Cramèr–Rao lower bound can be found in [12, 16, 29].

In terms of the passive localization problem, $\text{var}(\hat{\underline{\Delta}}_{01}) = \text{var}(\hat{\underline{\Delta}}_{02}) = \text{var}(\hat{\tau})$ [Eq. (11.106)]. Recall that $\hat{\underline{\Delta}}_{01}$ was the time delay estimate between sensors 0 and 1, and $\hat{\underline{\Delta}}_{02}$ was the time delay estimate between sensors 0 and 2. The variance of the range r [Eq. (11.50)] and of the bearing ϕ [Eq. (11.51)] can be found in [1]. It turns out that an accurate range estimate requires very accurate time delay estimates, whereas an accurate bearing estimate is less sensitive to time delay accuracy.

The performance of time delay estimation algorithms has been the subject of many research papers. For a good overview of the active and passive cases, see [30] and the references there.

C   A Numerical Example

For the active case we showed that Fig. 11.32 was an FFT implementation of Fig. 11.19. Let us now show how to compute the necessary quantities shown in Fig. 11.32 and the time delay estimate $\hat{\tau}$.

First, we compute the complex signal

$$\tilde{s}_T(n) = s_{Ti}(n) + js_{Tq}(n) \tag{11.114}$$

which is the complex demodulated version of the transmitted waveform $s_T(t)$. Figure 11.34(a) shows a ficticious transmitted pulse [i.e., $s_T(t)$] of duration $t_p = 678.9$ μs and rise time 234.5 μs. The narrowband spectrum of $s_T(t)$ is shown in Fig. 11.34(b). Figure 11.34(c) shows the complex signal $\tilde{s}_T(n)$ [see Eq. (11.114)]. The narrowband-to-baseband translation of $s_T(t)$ [i.e., the complex demoduation of $s_T(t)$] was done digitally, with the FIR linear-phase lowpass filter shown in Fig. 11.35 (see Chapters 2 and 3). The sampling frequency was 512 kHz.

Next, bandlimited Gaussian white noise was added to the waveform in Fig. 11.34(a) to produce the received noisy echo $\underline{z}(t)$. Refer to Fig. 11.36(a). The duration of this noisy echo, or the length of the observation interval t_0, was $t_0 = 1000$ μs, or 1 ms. Figure 11.36(b) shows the narrowband spectrum of $\underline{z}(t)$, and Fig. 11.36(c) shows the complex demodulated signal

$$\tilde{\underline{z}}(n) = z_i(n) + j\underline{z}_q(n) \tag{11.115}$$

Again, the narrowband-to-baseband translation of $z(t)$ was done digitally, with the FIR filter in Fig. 11.35; the sampling frequency was 512 kHz.

To form the cross-spectrum,

$$\tilde{\underline{Y}}(k) = \tilde{S}_T^*(k)\tilde{\underline{Z}}(k) \tag{11.116}$$

we must compute the FFT of the complex sequence $\tilde{s}_T(n)$ and the FFT of the complex sequence $\tilde{\underline{z}}(n)$. These FFTs must be zero-padded in order to avoid the effects of circular convolution, as explained in Section V.B. Thus, 1 ms of data gives 512 data points, so a zero-pad of 512 zeros requires a 1024-point FFT.

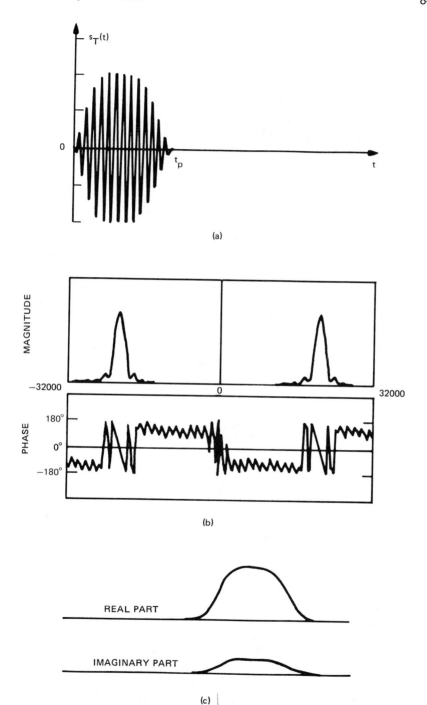

Fig. 11.34. (a) Transmitted pulse. (b) Magnitude and phase spectra. (c) Complex demodulation.

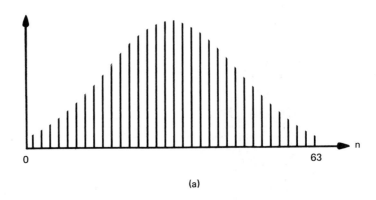

(a)

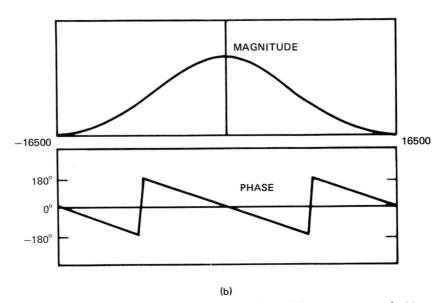

(b)

Fig. 11.35. (a) A 64 tap, linear-phase FIR lowpass digital filter. (b) Frequency response for (a).

Figure 11.37(a) shows a 1024-point FFT of $\tilde{s}_T(n)$, and Fig. 11.37(b) shows a 1024-point FFT of $\tilde{z}(n)$. The cross-spectrum $\tilde{Y}(k)$ is shown in Fig. 11.37(c).

Now that the FFTs have been properly zero-padded, the IFFT of $\underline{Y}(k)$ [Fig. 11.37(c)] gives the complex cross-correlation $\tilde{y}(m)$ [Refer to Eq. (11.91)]. The magnitude and phase of $\tilde{y}(m)$ are shown in Fig. 11.38. The peak of $|\tilde{y}(m)|$ is located at $\hat{\tau} = 248.047\ \mu s$, which is the time delay estimate of τ.

The SNR for this numerical example was 15 dB. The error in our estimate was $-1.247\ \mu s$. When the SNR increases, the error decreases.

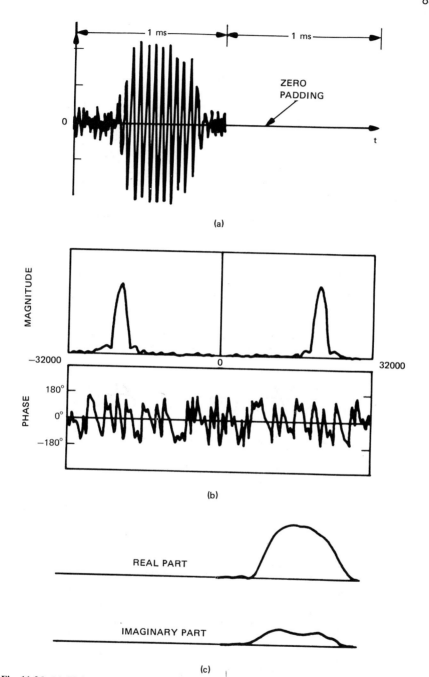

Fig. 11.36. (a) Noisy echo; zero-padding for FFT. (b) Magnitude and phase spectra for $\underline{z}(t)$. Baseband translation of $\underline{z}(t)$.

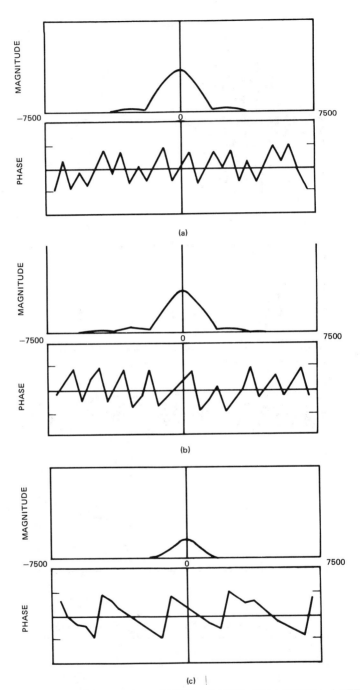

Fig. 11.37. Spectrum and cross-spectrum. (a) 1024-point FFT of $\tilde{\underline{s}}_T(n)$; (b) 1024-point FFT of $\tilde{\underline{z}}(n)$; (c) cross spectrum $\tilde{Y}(k)$ 0.

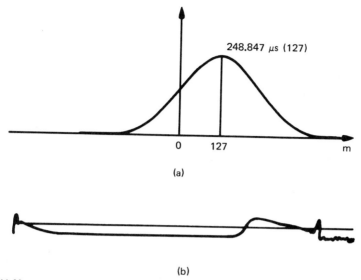

248.847 μs (127)

0   127   m

(a)

(b)

Fig. 11.38. (a) The magnitude and (b) phase angle of the complex cross-correlation function.

SUMMARY   VII

In this chapter we presented an overview of the time delay estimation problem. We discussed the active and passive radar and sonar problems, beamforming, and active and passive localization. We then discussed the theory and algorithms involved in estimating the intersensor time delays.

In real-world applications we do not have stationary point target models and simple backscattering; in addition, there are multipath, finite-length observations, and nonstationary, non-Gaussian noise. However, this chapter will give the reader a good understanding of the basic principles; then the more difficult problems will be easier to analyze. For example, a good reading of this chapter will allow the reader to understand some current real-world problems, namely, the fundamental limitations of the passive theory when narrowband energy is present and the problem of tracking a time-variant time delay [31, 32].

REFERENCES

1. G. C. Carter, Time Delay Estimation for passive sonar signal processing, *IEEE Trans. Acoust. Speech Signal Process.* **ASSP-29**, 463–470 (June 1981).
2. B. P. Bogert, M. J. R. Healy, and J. W. Tukey, The quefrency analysis of time series for echoes, *Proc. Symp. on Time Series Analysis*, edited by M. Rosenblatt, Wiley, New York, 1963, pp. 209–243.
3. M. M. Gibson, Delay estimation of disturbances on the basilar membrane, *IEEE Trans. Acoust. Speech Signal Process.* **ASSP-29**, 621–623 (June 1981).

4. M. A. Rodriguez, R. H. Williams, and T. J. Carlow, Signal delay and waveform estimation using unwrapped phase averaging, *IEEE Trans. Acoust. Speech Signal Process.* **ASSP-29,** 508–513 (June 1981).

5. D. J. Torrieri, Statistical theory of passive location systems, *IEEE Trans. Aerospace Electronic Systems* **AES-20,** 183–198 (March 1984).

6. J. P. Van Etten, LORAN C system product and development, *ITT Electrical Communication* **45,** 100–115 (1970).

7. P. M. Morse and H. Feshback, *Methods of Theoretical Physics*, Part I, McGraw-Hill, New York, 1953, pp. 838–841.

8. M. I. Skolnik, *Introduction to Radar Systems*, 2nd ed., McGraw-Hill, New York, 1980, pp. 278–337.

9. W. L. Stutzman and G. A. Thiele, *Antenna Theory and Design*, Wiley, New York, 1981, pp. 537–550.

10. M. T. Silvia and A. B. Weglein, Method for obtaining a near-field inverse scattering solution to the acoustic wave equation, *J. Acoust. Soc. Am.* **69,** 478–482 (February 1981).

11. S. M. Sherman, *Monopulse Principles and Techniques*, Artech House, Dedham, Mass., 1984, pp. 1–21.

12. H. L. Van Trees, *Detection, Estimation, and Modulation Theory*, Part III, Wiley, New York, 1971, pp. 167–187.

13. W. G. Neubauer, R. H. Vogt, and L. R. Dragonette, Acoustic reflection from elastic spheres. I: Steady-state signals, *J. Acoust. Soc. Am.* **55,** 1123–1129 (1974).

14. M. T. Silvia and E. A. Robinson, *Deconvolution of Geophysical Time Series in the Exploration for Oil and Natural Gas*, Elsevier, New York, 1979, pp. 1–45.

15. G. L. Turin, An introduction to matched filters, *IRE Trans. Information Theory* **IT-6,** 311–329 (June 1960).

16. C. W. Helstrom, *Statistical Theory of Signal Detection*, Pergamon Press, New York, 1968, pp. 112–115.

17. C. H. Knapp and G. C. Carter, The generalized correlation method for estimation of time delay, *IEEE Trans. Acoust. Speech Signal Process.* **ASSP-24,** 320–327 (August 1976).

18. G. M. Jenkins and D. G. Watts, *Spectral Analysis and Its Applications*, Holden Day, San Francisco, 1968, pp. 363–421.

19. E. J. Hannan and P. J. Thomson, Estimating group delay, *Biometrika* **60,** 241–253 (1973).

20. G. C. Carter, A. H. Nuttall, and P. G. Cable, The smoothed coherence transform, *Proc. IEEE* **61,** 1497–1498 (1973).

21. J. C. Hassab and R. E. Boucher, Optimum estimation of time delay by a generalized correlator, *IEEE Trans. Acoust. Speech Signal Process.* **ASSP-27,** 373–380 (August 1979).

22. G. C. Carter, Variance bounds for passively locating an acoustic source with a symmetric line array, *J. Acoust. Soc. Amer.* **62,** 922–926 (1977).

23. C. Lawrence Ng and Y. Bar-Shalom, "Optimum multisensor, multitarget time delay estimation," *NUSC Technical Report* 65757, Naval Underwater Systems Center, New London, Conn. April 20, 1983, pp. 57–75.

24. W. R. Hahn, Optimum signal processing for passive ssonar range and bearing estimation, *J. Acoust. Soc. Amer.* 201–207 (1975).

25. T. H. Glisson, C. I. Black, and A. P. Sage, On sonar signal analysis, *IEEE Trans. Aerospace Electronic Systems* **AES-6,** 37–49 (January 1970).

26. J. V. DiFranco and W. L. Rubin, *Radar Detection*, Prentice-Hall, Englewood Cliffs, N.J., 1968, pp. 623–625.

27. J. Ville, Theorie et application de la notion de signal analytique, *Cables et Transmission* **2,** 61–74 (1948).

28. C. E. Cook and M. Bernfeld, *Radar Signals: An Introduction to Theory and Applications*, Academic Press, New York, 1967.

29. A. D. Whalen, *Detection of Signal in Noise*, Academic Press, New York, 1971, pp. 321–362.

30. A. H. Quazi, An overview on the time delay estimate in active and passive systems for target localization, *IEEE Trans. Acoust. Speech Signal Process.* **ASSP-29,** 527–533 (June 1981).
31. E. Weinstein and A. J. Weiss, Fundamental limitations in passive time delay estimation. Part II: Wide-band systems, *IEEE Trans. Acoust. Speech Signal Process.* **ASSP-32,** 1064–1078 (October 1984).
32. J. O. Smith and B. Friedlander, Adaptive interpolated time delay estimation, *IEEE Trans Aerospace Electronic Systems* **AES-21,** 180–199 (March 1985).

Chapter 12
Adaptive Filtering

NASIR AHMED
Department of Electrical and Computer Engineering
University of New Mexico
Albuquerque, New Mexico 87131

INTRODUCTION   I

By "filtering" we mean a linear process designed to alter the spectral content of an input signal (or data sequence) in a specified manner. Filtering is done by filters whose magnitude and/or phase responses satisfy certain specifications in the frequency domain. Examples of two magnitude responses are given in Fig. 12.1. The term "adaptive filtering" implies that filter parameters such as bandwidth and notch frequency change with time. As such, the coefficients (weights) of adaptive filters vary with time. In contrast, the coefficients of fixed filters are time invariant.

Fixed and adaptive filters are usually represented as block diagrams (see Fig. 12.2). The arrow in Fig. 12.2(b) implies that the filter weights are changing with time. We will restrict our attention to digital filters, which means that the input, output, and filter weights are quantized and coded in binary form.

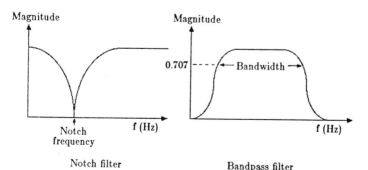

Notch filter   Bandpass filter
Fig. 12.1. Examples of magnitude responses.

857

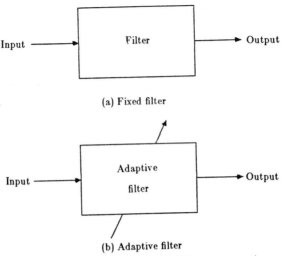

(a) Fixed filter

(b) Adaptive filter

Fig. 12.2. (a) Fixed and (b) adaptive filter representation.

The input-output equation of an adaptive digital filter is

$$y(n) = \sum_{i=0}^{N} a_i(n) x(n - i) - \sum_{j=1}^{M} b_j(n) y(n - j), \qquad n \geq 0$$

where $x(n)$ and $y(n)$ are the input and output samples (values) at time n, $a_i(n)$ and $b_j(n)$ are the ith and jth filter weights at time n, and $N + M + 1$ is the total number of weights. Thus, if a_i and b_j are used in place of $a_i(n)$ and $b_j(n)$, respectively, then the equation represents the input-output equation of a fixed filter.

If $b_j(n) = 0$, $1 \leq j \leq M$, in the adaptive digital filter input-output equation, then the resulting class of filters is called FIR (finite impulse response) adaptive. We shall restrict this chapter to a subset of FIR adaptive filters whose weights are changed by a technique called steepest descent. This subset of adaptive filters is widely used and is described in terms of tapped-delay-line (transversal filter) and lattice models. Our objective is to provide an introduction and working knowledge of such adaptive digital filters.

II SOME MATRIX OPERATIONS

This section introduces some matrix operations that we will use to derive a class of optimal least squares filters in Section II.

Let

$$x^T = [x_1 \quad x_2 \quad \cdots \quad x_d]$$

and

$$A = \begin{bmatrix} a_{11} & a_{12} & \cdots & a_{1d} \\ a_{21} & a_{22} & \cdots & a_{2d} \\ \vdots & \vdots & \vdots & \vdots \\ a_{d1} & a_{d2} & \cdots & a_{dd} \end{bmatrix} \qquad (12.1)$$

denote a vector and matrix, respectively, where the superscript T implies the matrix transpose operation. Taking the matrix–vector product $\mathbf{Ax}$, forming the scalar $q = \mathbf{x}^T\mathbf{A}^T\mathbf{Ax}$, and taking the appropriate partial derivatives yield

$$\nabla_{\mathbf{A}}(\mathbf{x}^T\mathbf{A}^T A\mathbf{x}) = 2\, A(\mathbf{xx}^T) \qquad (12.2)$$

where ∇ is the gradient (derivative) operator, and $\nabla_{\mathbf{A}}$ denotes the gradient of the quantity enclosed in parentheses with respect to $\mathbf{A}$. To illustrate, let $d = 2$. Then

$$q = (a_{11}x_1 + a_{12}x_2)^2 + (a_{21}x_1 + a_{22}x_2)^2 \qquad (12.3)$$

By definition

$$\nabla_{\mathbf{A}}(q) = \begin{bmatrix} \dfrac{\partial q}{\partial a_{11}} & \dfrac{\partial q}{\partial a_{12}} \\ \dfrac{\partial q}{\partial a_{21}} & \dfrac{\partial q}{\partial a_{22}} \end{bmatrix} \qquad (12.4)$$

From Eqs. (12.3) and (12.4) it follows that

$$\nabla_{\mathbf{A}}(q) = 2\begin{bmatrix} a_{11} & a_{12} \\ a_{21} & a_{22} \end{bmatrix}\begin{bmatrix} x_1^2 & x_1x_2 \\ x_1x_2 & x_2^2 \end{bmatrix} = 2\mathbf{Axx}^T$$

since

$$\begin{bmatrix} x_1^2 & x_1x_2 \\ x_1x_2 & x_2^2 \end{bmatrix} = \begin{bmatrix} x_1 \\ x_2 \end{bmatrix}[x_1 \quad x_2] \qquad (12.5)$$

The right side of Eq. (12.5) is known as the *outer product* of the vector $\mathbf{x}$. Similarly, if $\mathbf{v}^T = [v_1 \quad v_2 \quad \cdots \quad v_d]$, then

$$\nabla_{\mathbf{A}}(\mathbf{x}^T\mathbf{A}^T\mathbf{v}) = \mathbf{vx}^T \qquad (12.6a)$$

and

$$\nabla_{\mathbf{x}}(\mathbf{x}^T\mathbf{v}) = \nabla_{\mathbf{x}}(\mathbf{v}^T\mathbf{x}) = \mathbf{v} \qquad (12.6b)$$

The identities in Eqs. (12.2) and (12.6) are summarized as follows:

1. $\nabla_{\mathbf{A}}(\mathbf{x}^T\mathbf{A}^T\mathbf{Ax}) = 2\mathbf{A}(\mathbf{xx}^T)$.
2. $\nabla_{\mathbf{A}}(\mathbf{x}^T\mathbf{A}^T\mathbf{v}) = \mathbf{vx}^T$.
3. $\nabla_{\mathbf{x}}(\mathbf{x}^T\mathbf{v}) = \nabla_{\mathbf{x}}(\mathbf{v}^T\mathbf{x}) = \mathbf{v}$.

III   A CLASS OF OPTIMAL FILTERS

This class of filters is optimum with respect to the mean square error (MSE) criterion. The filters are causal in that their impulse responses are zero for negative values of time. One may refer to this class of filters as Wiener filters, in the sense that they are a subset of the general class of filters considered by Wiener.

We shall introduce three configurations. The motivation for doing so is that adaptive versions of the same will be considered in Sections IV and V.

A   Predictor Configuration

A predictor configuration is shown in Fig. 12.3, where the input $x(n)$ is assumed to be a stationary random process, and $\mathbf{w}$ represents the weights $\{w_i\}$ of a digital filter in vector form; that is,

$$\mathbf{w}^{\mathsf{T}} = [w_1 \quad w_2 \quad \cdots \quad w_M] \tag{12.7}$$

where M is the number of filter weights. The filter output at time n is

$$\underline{g}(n) = \mathbf{w}^{\mathsf{T}} \underline{\mathbf{x}}_n = \underline{\mathbf{x}}_n^{\mathsf{T}} \mathbf{w} \tag{12.8}$$

where

$$\underline{\mathbf{x}}_n^{\mathsf{T}} = [x(n - \Delta) \quad x(n - \Delta - 1) \quad \cdots \quad x(n - \Delta - [M - 1])]$$

is the input vector at time n and $\Delta \geq 1$ is an integer. We seek a weight vector $\mathbf{w}$ such that the output $\underline{g}(n)$ is a least squares approximation to the current (present) sample $\underline{x}(n)$, using M of its past values. The special case $\Delta = 1$ is referred to as a one-step predictor.

In Fig. 12.3 the error at time n is

$$\underline{e}(n) = \underline{x}(n) - \mathbf{w}^{\mathsf{T}} \underline{\mathbf{x}}_n \tag{12.9a}$$

or

$$\underline{e}(n) = \underline{x}(n) - \underline{\mathbf{x}}_n^{\mathsf{T}} \mathbf{w} \tag{12.9b}$$

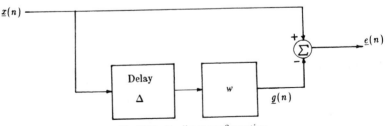

Fig. 12.3. Predictor configuration.

Defining the MSE

$$\epsilon = E\{\underline{e}^2(n)\} \tag{12.10}$$

where E denotes statistical expectation,[‡] and using Eq. (12.9) shows that ϵ is a quadratic ("bowl-shaped") surface in a space whose coordinates are w_1, $w_2, \ldots, w_M$. Thus we obtain the optimal (unique) value of $\mathbf{w}$ by solving the matrix equation

$$\nabla_\mathbf{w}\epsilon = \mathbf{0} \tag{12.11}$$

where $\mathbf{0}$ is a null vector. Equations (12.9)–(12.11) yield

$$E\{e(n)\underline{\mathbf{x}}_n\} = \mathbf{0} \tag{12.12}$$

known as the *orthogonality principle*, which states that the process of minimizing the MSE $E\{\underline{e}^2(n)\}$ is equivalent to making the error $\underline{e}(n)$ orthogonal to each of the inputs $x(n - \Delta - j)$, $0 \le j \le (M - 1)$. Substituting Eq. (12.9b) into Eq. (12.12) leads to

$$\mathbf{w}^* = \mathbf{S}_{xx}^{-1}\mathbf{p}_{xx} \tag{12.13}$$

where $\mathbf{w}^{*\mathrm{T}} = [w_1^* \quad w_2^* \quad \cdots \quad w_M^*]$ is the desired optimal solution for $\mathbf{w}$,

$$\mathbf{S}_{xx} = E\{\underline{\mathbf{x}}_n\underline{\mathbf{x}}_n^\mathrm{T}\} \text{ is the } M \times M \text{ input autocorrelation matrix}$$

and

$$\mathbf{p}_{xx} = E\{\underline{x}(n)\underline{\mathbf{x}}_n\} \text{ is the } M \times 1 \text{ input correlation vector}$$

In practice, $\mathbf{S}_{xx}$ is almost always positive definite; that is, all of its eigenvalues are positive. This condition ensures that $\mathbf{S}_{xx}$ is nonsingular, so $\mathbf{S}_{xx}^{-1}$ exists.

To illustrate the matrix form of Eq. (12.13), consider a two-weight, one-step predictor (i.e., $M = 2$ and $\Delta = 1$). Then we can obtain $\mathbf{w}^*$ by evaluating the matrix product

$$\mathbf{w}^* = \mathbf{S}_{xx}^{-1}\mathbf{p}_{xx} \tag{12.14}$$

where

$$\mathbf{S}_{xx} = \begin{bmatrix} E\{\underline{x}^2(n - 1) & E\{\underline{x}(n - 1)\underline{x}(n - 2)\} \\ E\{\underline{x}(n - 2)\underline{x}(n - 1)\} & E\{\underline{x}^2(n - 2)\} \end{bmatrix}$$

and

$$\mathbf{p}_{xx} = \begin{bmatrix} E\{\underline{x}(n)\underline{x}(n - 1)\} \\ E\{\underline{x}(n)\underline{x}(n - 2)\} \end{bmatrix}$$

[‡] When the input is not random, E is replaced by a time-averaging operation.

1 Minimum MSE

Substituting Eq. (12.9a) in Eq. (12.10), we get

$$\epsilon_{\min} = E\{\underline{e}(n)\underline{x}(n)\} - \mathbf{w}^{T} E\{\underline{e}(n)\underline{\mathbf{x}}_{n}\}$$

the second term of which is $\mathbf{0}$ because of the orthogonality principle in Eq. (12.12). Thus

$$\epsilon_{\min} = E\{\underline{e}(n)\underline{x}(n)\}$$

which yields the desired result

$$\epsilon_{\min} = E\{\underline{x}^{2}(n)\} - \mathbf{w}^{*T}\mathbf{p}_{xx} \tag{12.15}$$

since $\underline{e}(n) = \underline{x}(n) - \mathbf{w}^{*T}\underline{\mathbf{x}}_{n}$; see Eq. (12.9a). In Eq. (12.15) $E\{\underline{x}^{2}(n)\}$ represents the total power in the input $\underline{x}(n)$.

An important property of the predictor configuration is that it strives to remove correlated (linearly dependent) components in the input $\underline{x}(n)$. As such, the output error $\underline{e}(n)$ tends to be uncorrelated. In fact, as the number of weights tends to infinity, the output error sequence is completely uncorrelated. This de-correlation property enables one to achieve data compression. Related schemes are called *linear predictive coding* (LPC) and *differential pulse code podulation* (DPCM), respectively; see [1] and [2], for example.

Example 1.   Consider the sinusoidal input

$$\underline{x}(n) = \sqrt{2}\,\sin(n\omega_{0}T + \underline{\theta}), \qquad n \geq 0 \tag{12.16}$$

where $\underline{\theta}$ is a uniformly distributed random variable in the interval $(0, 2\pi)$; ω_{0} is the radian frequency, and T is the sampling interval. Find $\mathbf{w}^{*}$ for a two-weight, one-step predictor, and evaluate the corresponding value of $\epsilon_{\min}$.

Solution   It can be shown that $\underline{x}(n)$ in Eq. (12.16) is an ergodic process in that its first- and second-order ensemble and time averages are equivalent. Its autocorrelation sequence $r_{xx}(m)$ is

$$r_{xx}(m) = E\{\underline{x}(n)\underline{x}(n - m)\} = \cos(m\omega_{0}T), \qquad |m| < \infty$$

where m is the shift index. Thus

$$r_{xx}(0) = E\{\underline{x}^{2}(n)\} = E\{\underline{x}^{2}(n - 1)\} = 1$$
$$r_{xx}(1) = E\{\underline{x}(n)\underline{x}(n - 1)\} = \cos(\omega_{0}T)$$

and

$$r_{xx}(2) = E\{\underline{x}(n)\underline{x}(n - 2)\} = \cos(2\omega_{0}T) \tag{12.17}$$

Substituting Eq. (12.17) into Eq. (12.14) leads to

$$\mathbf{w}^{*T} = [w_{1}^{*} \quad w_{2}^{*}] \tag{12.18}$$

where $w_{1}^{*} = 2\cos(\omega_{0}T)$ and $w_{2}^{*} = -1$, which is the desired solution.

Next, from Eqs. (12.14), (12.15), (12.17), and (12.18) it follows that

$$\epsilon \equiv 0 \qquad (12.19)$$

which means that we can predict $\underline{x}(n)$ exactly in Eq. (12.16), using a two-weight predictor with $\Delta = 1$. This is also true for $\Delta > 1$.

The main results of the above discussion are summarized in Fig. 12.4 where a tapped-delay-line (or transversal filter) model for the predictor configuration is also included. In the general case the predictor weights w_i are time varying and are updated from the input and error information.

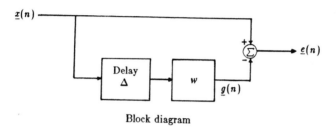

Block diagram

Notation: $\mathbf{w}^T = [w_1 w_2 \cdots w_M]$

$\mathbf{x}_n^T = [\underline{x}(n - \Delta)\underline{x}(n - \Delta - 1) \cdots \underline{x}(n - \Delta - [M - 1])]$

$\underline{g}(n) = \mathbf{x}_n^T \mathbf{w}$

$\mathbf{S}_{xx} = E\{\underline{\mathbf{x}}_n \underline{\mathbf{x}}_n^T\}; \; \mathbf{P}_{xx} = E\{\underline{x}(n)\underline{\mathbf{x}}_n\}$

Orthogonality principle: $E\{\underline{e}(n)\underline{\mathbf{x}}_n\} = \underline{0}$

Optimum solution: $\mathbf{w}^* = \mathbf{S}_{xx}^{-1} \mathbf{P}_{xx}$

Minimum mse: $\epsilon_{\min} = E\{\underline{x}^2(n)\} - \mathbf{w}^{*T} \mathbf{P}_{xx}$

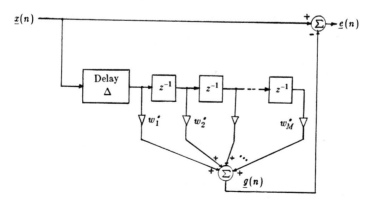

Tapped-delay-line model

Fig. 12.4. Predictor configuration summary.

B Filter Configuration

Figure 12.5 shows this configuration where $\underline{x}(n)$ is the input to a digital filter whose weights are represented by the weight vector

$$\mathbf{w}^{\mathsf{T}} = [w_0 \quad w_1 \quad \cdots \quad w_M] \tag{12.20}$$

The sequence $\underline{y}(n)$ is generally called the desired output of the filter. The object is to find $\mathbf{w}$ so that the actual output $\underline{g}(n)$ is a least squares approximation to $\underline{y}(n)$. Thus we define the error sequence

$$\underline{e}(n) = \underline{y}(n) - \underline{g}(n) \tag{12.21}$$

where $\underline{g}(n) = \mathbf{w}^{\mathsf{T}}\underline{x}_n$ and $\underline{x}_n = [\underline{x}(n) \quad \underline{x}(n-1) \quad \cdots \quad \underline{x}(n-M)]$ is the input vector.

Next, we minimize the MSE $\epsilon = E\{\underline{e}^2(n)\}$ with respect to $\mathbf{w}$. The procedure is similar to that for the predictor configuration. The final results are summarized in Fig. 12.6.

For example, consider a two-weight filter and suppose $\underline{x}(n)$ and $\underline{y}(n)$ are such that

$$E\{\underline{x}(n)\underline{x}(n-m)\} = \alpha^m \quad \text{and} \quad E\{\underline{y}(n)\underline{x}(n-l)\} = \beta_l$$

where $|\alpha| < 1$ and $|\beta_l| < 1$, and m and l are shift indices. Then evaluating $\mathbf{S}_{xx}$ and $\mathbf{p}_{yx}$ and substituting them in Eq. (12.23) gives the optimal weights

$$w_1^* = \frac{\beta_0 - \alpha\beta_1}{1 - \alpha^2}, \qquad w_2^* = \frac{\beta_1 - \alpha\beta_0}{1 - \alpha^2}$$

C Noise-Canceler Configuration

The two inputs to the noise-canceler configuration are denoted by ① and ② in Fig. 12.7. Input ① consists of the sum of the signal sequence $\underline{x}(n)$ and the noise sequence $\underline{v}_1(n)$, and is usually called the *primary input*. Input ② is usually called the *reference input*, the consists of the noise sequence $\underline{v}_2(n)$.

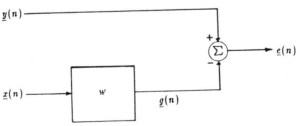

Fig. 12.5. Filter configuration.

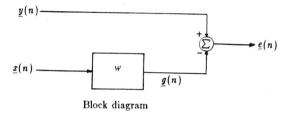

Block diagram

Notation: $\mathbf{w}^T = [w_0 w_1 \cdots w_M]$

$\underline{\mathbf{x}}_n^T = [\underline{x}(n)\underline{x}(n-1)\cdots\underline{x}(n-M)]$

$\underline{g}(n) = \underline{\mathbf{x}}_n^T \mathbf{w}$

$\mathbf{S}_{xx} = E\{\underline{\mathbf{x}}_n \underline{\mathbf{x}}_n^T\}; \ \mathbf{p}_{yx} = E\{\underline{y}(n)\underline{\mathbf{x}}_n\}$

Orthogonality Principle: $E\{\underline{e}(n)\underline{\mathbf{x}}_n\} = \underline{0}$ (12.22)

Optimum Solution: $\mathbf{w}^* = \mathbf{S}_{xx}^{-1}\mathbf{p}_{yx}$ (12.23)

Minimum mse: $\epsilon_{min} = E\{\underline{y}^2(n)\} - \mathbf{w}^{*T}\mathbf{p}_{yx}$ (12.24)

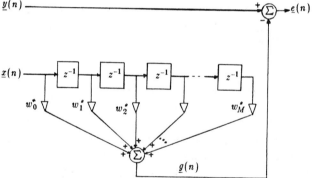

Tapped-delay-line model

Fig. 12.6. Filter configuration summary.

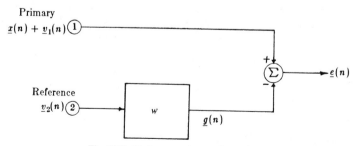

Fig. 12.7. Noise-canceler configuration.

The output $g(n)$ in Fig. 12.7 is

$$g(n) = \mathbf{w}^T \underline{\mathbf{v}}_{2,n} = \underline{\mathbf{v}}_{2,n}^T \mathbf{w} \qquad (12.25)$$

where

$$\mathbf{w}^T = \begin{bmatrix} w_0 & w_1 & \cdots & w_M \end{bmatrix} \quad \text{and} \quad \mathbf{v}_{2,n}^T = \begin{bmatrix} v_2(n) & v_2(n) & \cdots & v_2(n-M) \end{bmatrix}$$

Thus the error at time n is

$$\underline{e}(n) = \underline{x}(n) + \underline{v}_1(n) - \underline{g}(n) \qquad (12.26)$$

We now make the following assumptions, which are valid in many applications.

1. $\underline{v}_1(n)$ and $\underline{v}_2(n)$ are correlated (linearly dependent), zero-mean noise sequences; that is, $E\{\underline{v}_1(n)\underline{v}_2(n)\} \neq 0$, and $E\{\underline{v}_i(n)\} = 0$ for $i = 1, 2$.
2. The signal $\underline{x}(n)$ is uncorrelated (linearly independent) with respect to $\underline{v}_1(n)$ and $\underline{v}_2(n)$; that is, $E\{\underline{v}_i(n)\underline{x}(n)\} = E\{\underline{v}_i(n)\}E\{\underline{x}(n)\}$ for $i = 1, 2$.

The problem is to choose $\mathbf{w}$ so that $g(n)$ is a least squares approximation of $\underline{v}_1(n)$. As such, the canceler output $\underline{e}(n)$ in Eq. (12.26) will be $\underline{e}(n) \simeq \underline{x}(n)$ when noise cancellation has occurred. We achieve the optimal $\mathbf{w}$ by minimizing the MSE $E\{\underline{e}^2(n)\}$ with respect to $\mathbf{w}$. Again, the steps involved for doing so parallel those for the predictor configuration. The final results are summarized in Fig. 12.8.

IV LEAST-MEAN-SQUARES (LMS) ALGORITHM

The optimal solutions derived in the previous section all involve autocorrelation matrices and cross-correlation vectors that are assumed to be known. In many applications this is not the case. They may be difficult to estimate, or the data statistics may be changing with time; that is, the data sequences may be nonstationary. In such cases adaptive filtering techniques are employed. A very useful algorithm in this regard is the LMS algorithm, and is attributed to Widrow [3–5]. It is sometimes referred to as the Widrow–Hoff algorithm [6].

The notion of steepest descent plays a key role in arriving at the LMS algorithm. The steepest-descent technique is ideally suited to deriving adaptive versions of the fixed filter configurations discussed in Section III, since the related error surfaces are guaranteed to be quadratic ("bowl-shaped") with respect to the filter weights w_i. This property of the error surface is illustrated in Fig. 12.9 for two weights w_0 and w_1.

Let $\epsilon(0)$ represent the value of the sequence $\underline{e}^2(n)$ with an arbitrary choice of the weight vector $\mathbf{w}_0$. Then the boundary of the corresponding cross section of the bowl-shaped surface in Fig. 12.9 is an ellipse. The steepest-descent technique enables us to descend to the bottom of the bowl to $\mathbf{w}^*$ in a systematic manner. The idea is to leave an ellipse in a direction that is orthogonal

Primary
$\underline{z}(n)+\underline{v}_1(n)$ ①

Reference
$\underline{v}_2(n)$ ② w $g(n)$

$\to \underline{e}(n)$

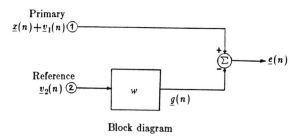

Block diagram

Notation: $\mathbf{w}^T = [w_0 w_1 \cdots w_M]$

$\quad \underline{\mathbf{v}}_{2,n}^T = [\underline{v}_2(n)\underline{v}_2(n-1)\cdots \underline{v}_2(n-M)]$

$\quad \underline{g}(n) = \underline{\mathbf{v}}_{2,n}^T \mathbf{w}$

$\quad \mathbf{S}_{v_2v_2} = E\{\underline{\mathbf{v}}_{2,n}\underline{\mathbf{v}}_{2,n}^T\}; \; \mathbf{p}_{v_1v_2} = \{\underline{v}_1(n)\underline{\mathbf{v}}_{2,n}\}$

Orthogonality Principle: $E\{\underline{e}(n)\underline{\mathbf{v}}_{2,n}\} = \underline{0}$ (12.27)

Optimum Solution: $\mathbf{w}^* = \mathbf{S}_{v_2v_2}^{-1}\mathbf{p}_{v_1v_2}$ (12.28)

Minimum mse: $\epsilon_{\min} = E\{\underline{x}^2(n)\} + E\{\underline{v}_1^2(n)\} - \mathbf{w}^{*T}\mathbf{p}_{v_1v_2}$ (12.29)

Primary
$\underline{z}(n)+\underline{v}_1(n)$ ① $\to \underline{e}(n)$

Reference
$\underline{v}_2(n)$ ②

$w_0^{\bullet} \quad w_1^{\bullet} \quad w_2^{\bullet} \qquad\qquad w_M^{\bullet}$

$g(n)$

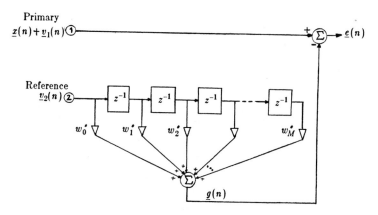

Tapped-delay-line model
Fig. 12.8. Noise-canceler configuration summary.

to the tangent at that point. We do this by the recursive relation [7]

$$\underline{\mathbf{w}}_{n+1} = \underline{\mathbf{w}}_n + \tilde{v}[-\mathbf{g}]$$ (12.30)

where $\tilde{v}$ is a convergence constant that governs the rate of descent to the bottom of the bowl; the larger $\tilde{v}$ is, the faster is the rate of descent. The term $[-\mathbf{g}]$ denotes the negative gradient of the error $E\{\underline{e}^2(n)\}$ with respect to $\underline{w}$. In practice, we usually must estimate $\mathbf{g}$. Widrow's estimate for $\mathbf{g}$ is given by $\hat{\mathbf{g}}$, where

$$\hat{\underline{\mathbf{g}}} = \nabla_{\mathbf{w}_n}\{\underline{e}^2(n)\} = 2\underline{e}(n)\nabla_{\mathbf{w}_n}\{\underline{e}(n)\}$$ (12.31)

In other words, the true gradient $\mathbf{g}$ is approximated by the instantaneous gradient $\hat{\underline{\mathbf{g}}}$ in Eq. (12.31). Hence the steepest-descent relation in Eq. (12.31)

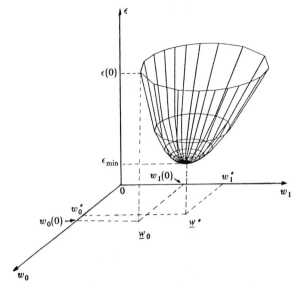

Fig. 12.9. An illustration of the method of steepest descent.

becomes

$$\underline{w}_{n+1} = \underline{w}_n - 2\tilde{v}\underline{e}(n)\nabla_{\mathbf{w}_n}\{\underline{e}(n)\} \tag{12.32}$$

Equation (12.32) was originally called the "noisy" LMS algorithm to indicate that $\hat{\underline{g}} = \nabla_{\mathbf{w}_n}\{\underline{e}^2(n)\}$ is a noisy gradient. However, it is convenient to simply refer to Eq. (12.32) as the LMS algorithm.

To illustrate, we consider the filter configuration in Fig. 12.5. Then [see Eq. (12.21)]

$$\underline{e}(n) = \underline{y}(n) - \mathbf{w}_n^T \underline{\mathbf{x}}_n$$

where

$$\underline{\mathbf{x}}_n^T = [\underline{x}(n) \quad \underline{x}(n-1) \quad \cdots \quad \underline{x}(n-M)]$$

Thus

$$\nabla_{\mathbf{w}_n}\{\underline{e}(n)\} = -\mathbf{x}_n \tag{12.33}$$

From Eqs. (12.32) and (12.33) we obtain

$$\underline{w}_{n+1} = \underline{w}_n + v\underline{e}(n)\underline{\mathbf{x}}_n \tag{12.34}$$

where $v = 2\tilde{v}$ is a convergence parameter.

Equation (12.34) is the LMS algorithm for the filter configuration. With stationary inputs, if we assume that $\underline{\mathbf{x}}_n$ is uncorrelated over time (i.e, that $E\{\underline{\mathbf{x}}_n\underline{\mathbf{x}}_{n+j}^T\} = 0, \forall j \neq 0$), then the expected value of the gradient estimate equals the true gradient. As such, the expected value of $\underline{w}_n$ converges to $\underline{w}^* = \mathbf{S}_{xx}^{-1}\mathbf{p}_{yx}$ in

Eq. (12.23) under these conditions, as long as v lies in the range

$$0 < v < \frac{2}{\lambda_{max}} \qquad (12.35)$$

where λ_{max} is the largest eigenvalue of $\mathbf{S}_{xx}$. See [4, 8] for details.

We may also write the LMS algorithm in Eq. (12.34) in scalar form to obtain

$$\underline{w}_i(n + 1) = \underline{w}_i(n) + v\underline{e}(n)\underline{x}(n - i), \qquad 0 \le i \le M \qquad (12.36)$$

where $\underline{e}(n) = \underline{y}(n) - \underline{g}(n)$.

The above results are summarized in Fig. 12.10. A tapped-delay-line model is also included. This is the adaptive counterpart of the model in Fig. 12.6.

Example 2. Suppose $y(n)$ is a 25-Hz sinusoid with peak value 1 and phase 18° (arbitrary). Let $x(n)$ be the sum of two sinusoids: (1) the first has frequency 25 Hz, peak value 0.5, and phase 75° (arbitrary); (2) the second has frequency 10 Hz, peak

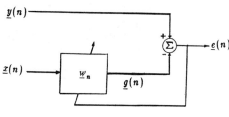

Block diagram

Notation: $\underline{\mathbf{w}}_n^T = [\underline{w}_0(n)\underline{w}_1(n)\cdots\underline{w}_M(n)]$

$\underline{\mathbf{x}}_n^T = [x(n)x(n - 1)\cdots x(n - M)]$

LMS Algorithm: $\underline{w}_i(n + 1) = \underline{w}_i(n) + v\underline{e}(n)\underline{x}(n - i), 0 \le i \le M$

where $\underline{e}(n) = \underline{y}(n) - \underline{g}(n) = \underline{y}(n) - \mathbf{w}_n^T\mathbf{x}_n$.

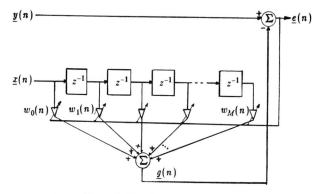

Tapped-delay-line model

Fig. 12.10. Adaptive filter configuration summary.

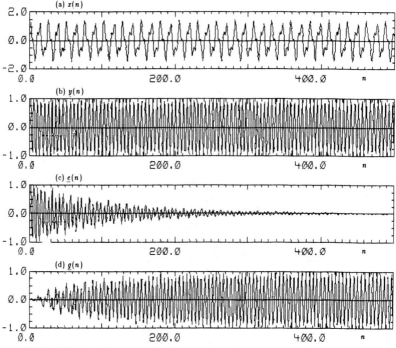

Fig. 12.11. LMS algorithm example; filter configuration: (a) $x(n)$; (b) $y(n)$; (c) $e(n)$; (d) $g(n)$.

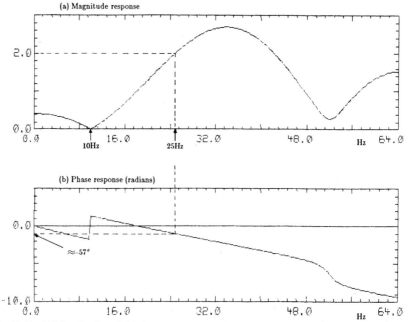

Fig. 12.12. (a) Magnitude and (b) phase responses implemented by adaptive filter in Example 12.1.

value 1, and phase 63° (arbitrary). With a sampling frequency of 128 samples/s (sps), the resulting $x(n)$ and $y(n)$ are plotted in Fig. 12.11(a),(b), respectively.

The error $\underline{e}(n)$ and output $\underline{g}(n)$ that result with the LMS algorithm in Eq. (12.36) with $M = 6$ and $v = 0.05$ are plotted in Fig. 12.11(c),(d), respectively. We observe that $\underline{e}(n)$ decays exponentially, whereas $\underline{g}(n)$ builds up toward the desired output $\underline{y}(n)$.

The magnitude and phase responses implemented by the weights $w_i(n)$ at $n = 1000$ are displayed in Fig. 12.12. We observe that the magnitude response is 0 and 2 at 10 and 25 Hz, respectively. Thus the 10-Hz component in $x(n)$ does not appear in the output $\underline{g}(n)$. Also, the phase is adjusted appropriately so that $\underline{g}(n)$ is gradually brought in phase with $\underline{y}(n)$, thus causing $\underline{e}(n)$ to decay to 0.

Adaptive Predictor Configuration   A

Here $\underline{e}(n)$ is given by Eq. (12.9a) as

$$\underline{e}(n) = \underline{x}(n) - \underline{\mathbf{w}}_n^T \underline{\mathbf{x}}_n$$

where

$$\underline{\mathbf{w}}_n^T = [\underline{w}_1(n) \quad \underline{w}_2(n) \quad \cdots \quad w_M(n)]$$

and

$$\underline{\mathbf{x}}_n^T = [\underline{x}(n - \Delta) \quad \underline{x}(n - \Delta - 1) \quad \cdots \quad \underline{x}(n - \Delta - [M - 1])]$$

Thus

$$\nabla_{\underline{\mathbf{w}}_n}\{\underline{e}(n)\} = -\underline{\mathbf{x}}_n \tag{12.37}$$

Substituting Eq. (12.37) into Eq. (12.32) leads to

$$\underline{\mathbf{w}}_{n+1} = \underline{\mathbf{w}}_n + v\underline{e}(n)\underline{\mathbf{x}}_n \tag{12.38}$$

where $v = 2\tilde{v}$ is a convergence parameter. Equation (12.38) is the LMS algorithm for the predictor configuration. In scalar form this algorithm is equivalent to

$$\underline{w}_i(n + 1) = \underline{w}_i(n) + v\underline{e}(n)\underline{x}(n - \Delta + 1 - i) \tag{12.39}$$

for $1 \leq i \leq M$.

If the input $\underline{x}(n)$ is stationary and $\underline{\mathbf{x}}_n$ is assumed to be uncorrelated over time, then [4, 8] the expected value of $\underline{\mathbf{w}}_n$ in Eq. (12.38) converges to $\underline{\mathbf{w}}^* = \mathbf{S}_{xx}^{-1}\mathbf{p}_{xx}$ in Eq. (12.13), provided v is chosen to lie in the range specified by Eq. (12.35).

Example 3. Let

$$x(n) = \sqrt{2} \sin\left[\frac{(2\pi)(25)}{128} + 30°\right] \tag{12.40}$$

which is a special case of $x(n)$ in Eq. (12.16). Equation (12.40) simply represents a

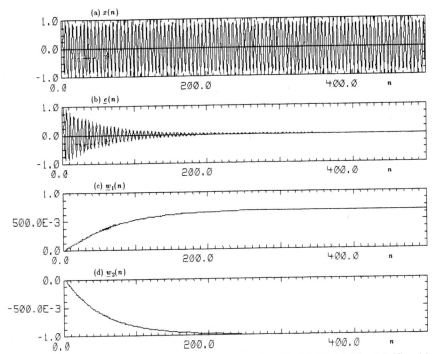

Fig. 12.13. LMS algorithm example; predictor configuration: (a) $x(n)$; (b) $e(n)$; (c) $w_1(n)$; (d) $w_2(n)$.

25-Hz sinusoid with peak value $\sqrt{2}$, phase $30°$, that is sampled at 128 sps. Its plot is shown in Fig. 12.13(a). The corresponding error output of a two-weight one-step predictor using the LMS algorithm in Eq. (12.39) with $M = 2$, $\Delta = 1$, and $v = 0.05$ is plotted in Fig. 12.13(b). The initial values $w_1(0)$ and $w_2(0)$ were set equal to zero.

From Fig. 12.13(b) it is apparent that the steady-state prediction error is close to 0, which agrees with the result in Eq. (12.19). The values of the weights $w_1(n)$ and $w_2(n)$ are plotted in Figs. 12.13(c),(d), respectively. These weights settle down at the values $w_1 = 0.673$ and $w_2 = -1$, which agree with the optimal weights w_1^* and w_2^* given by (12.18), with $w_0 T = (2\pi)(25)/128$.

The adaptive predictor results are summarized in Fig. 12.14.

B   Adaptive Noise-Canceler Configuration

Since $\underline{g}(n) = \mathbf{\underline{w}}_n^T \mathbf{\underline{v}}_{2,n}$, Eq. (12.26) yields the error sequence

$$\underline{e}(n) = \underline{x}(n) + \underline{v}_1(n) - \mathbf{\underline{w}}_n^T \mathbf{\underline{v}}_{2,n}$$

where

$$\mathbf{\underline{w}}_n^T = [\underline{w}_0(n) \quad \underline{w}_1(n) \quad \cdots \quad \underline{w}_M(n)]$$

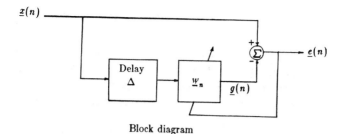

Block diagram

Notation: $\underline{w}_n^T = [\underline{w}_1(n)\underline{w}_2(n)\cdots\underline{w}_M(n)]$

$\underline{x}_n^T = [\underline{x}(n-\Delta)\underline{x}(n-\Delta-1)\cdots\underline{x}(n-\Delta[M-1])]$

LMS Algorithm: $\underline{w}_i(n+1) = \underline{w}_i(n) + v\underline{e}(n)\underline{x}(n-\Delta+1-i), 1 \le i \le M$

where $\underline{e}(n) = \underline{x}(n) - \underline{g}(n) = \underline{x}(n) - \underline{w}_n^T\underline{x}_n$.

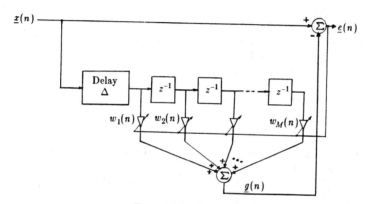

Tapped-delay-line model

Fig. 12.14. Adaptive predictor configuration summary.

and

$$\underline{v}_{2,n}^T = [\underline{v}_2(n) \quad \underline{v}_2(n-1) \quad \cdots \quad \underline{v}_2(n-M)]$$

Hence

$$\nabla_{\underline{w}_n}\{\underline{e}(n)\} = -\underline{v}_{2,n}$$

which on substitution in Eq. (12.32) yields the following LMS algorithm for the noise-canceler configuration.

$$\underline{\mathbf{W}}_{n+1} = \underline{\mathbf{W}}_n + v\underline{e}(n)\underline{\mathbf{v}}_{2,n} \tag{12.41}$$

The scalar form of Eq. (12.41) is

$$\underline{w}_i(n+1) = \underline{w}_i(n) + v\underline{e}(n)\underline{v}_2(n-i) \tag{12.42}$$

for $0 \le i \le M$.

If the inputs are stationary, and if we assume that $\underline{v}_{2,n}$ is uncorrelated over time, then [4, 8] the expected value of $\underline{w}_n$ in Eq. (12.41) converges to $\mathbf{w}^* = \mathbf{S}_{v_2v_2}^{-1}\mathbf{P}_{v_1v_2}$

in Eq. (12.28), provided $0 < v < 2/\lambda_{max}$, where λ_{max} is the maximum eigenvalue of $S_{v_2 v_2}$.

Example 4. Let $x(n)$ be a 25-Hz sinusoid with peak value 1 and phase $18°$ (arbitrary), which is sampled at 128 sps; let $\underline{v}_1(n)$ be bandpassed noise and $\underline{v}_2(n)$ a shifted and scaled version of $\underline{v}_1(n)$. Plots of $x(n)$, the primary input $x(n) + \underline{v}_1(n)$, and the reference input $\underline{v}_2(n)$ for $n = 800$ to 1000 are displayed in Fig. 12.15(a)–(c), respectively.

The variance of $\underline{v}_1(n)$ is 0.5. It was obtained by passing white noise through an eighth-order Butterworth bandpassed filter with lower and upper cutoff frequencies of 10 Hz and 15 Hz, respectively [9]. The reference $\underline{v}_2(n)$ has a variance of 0.084. We obtained it by multiplying $\underline{v}_1(n)$ by 0.41 and delaying it by four samples.

The error output obtained via the LMS algorithm in Eq. (12.42) with $M = 16$ and $v = 0.1$ is plotted in Fig. 12.15(d). Comparing Fig. 12.15(a),(b),(d), we see that a substantial reduction in additive bandpass noise is achieved. We can also come to this conclusion by examining the power density spectra of the primary input and error output shown in Fig. 12.15(e),(f), respectively.

Figure 12.16 summarizes the adaptive noise-canceler results.

C On Choosing v

Consider the adaptive filter case whose convergence condition, given by Eq. (12.35), is $0 < v < 2/\lambda_{max}$, where λ_{max} is the largest eigenvalue of the input autocorrelation matrix $\mathbf{S}_{xx}$. In practice it is very difficult to estimate $\mathbf{S}_{xx}$. Hence an alternative condition for convergence is

$$0 < v < 2 \bigg/ \sum_i \lambda_i \qquad (12.43)$$

In Eq. (12.43) we note that $\sum_i \lambda_i$ represents the total power in the input signal. Thus, in practice v is made inversely proportional to the input power. One useful way of doing so is to modify the LMS algorithm in Eq. (12.36) to obtain [10]

$$\underline{w}_i(n + 1) = \underline{w}_i(n) + \frac{\alpha}{\sigma_x^2(n)} \underline{e}(n)\underline{x}(n - i), \qquad 0 \le i \le M \qquad (12.44)$$

where $0 < \alpha < 1$ is a convergence parameter, and $\underline{\sigma}_x^2(n)$ is an estimate of the input average power at time n.

Equation (12.44) is referred to as the modified LMS (MLMS) algorithm for the filter configuration. A very effective way of estimating $\underline{\sigma}_x^2(n)$ is given by [10]

$$\underline{\sigma}_x^2(n) = \beta\underline{\sigma}_x^2(n - 1) + (1 - \beta)\underline{x}^2(n) \qquad (12.45)$$

where $0 < \beta < 1$ is a smoothing parameter. It follows that

$$\underline{\sigma}_x^2(n) = (1 - \beta)[\underline{x}^2(n) + \beta\underline{x}^2(n - 1) + \beta^2\underline{x}^2(n - 2) + \cdots]$$

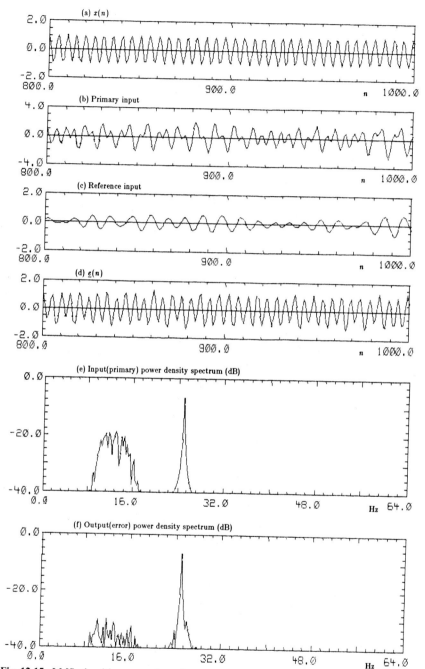

Fig. 12.15. LMS algorithm example; noise-canceler configuration: (a) $x(n)$; (b) primary input; (c) reference input; (d) $\underline{e}(n)$; (e) input primary power density spectrum dB; (f) output (error) power density spectrum (dB).

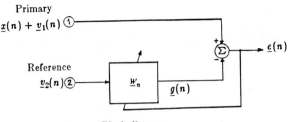

Block diagram

Notation: $\mathbf{w}_n^T = [\underline{w}_0(n)\underline{w}_1(n)\cdots\underline{w}_M(n)]$

$\mathbf{v}_{2,n}^T = [\underline{v}_2(n)\underline{v}_2(n-1)\cdots\underline{v}_2(n-M)]$

LMS Algorithm: $\underline{w}_i(n+1) = \underline{w}_i(n) + v\underline{e}(n)\underline{v}_2(n-i), 0 \le i \le M$

where $\underline{e}(n) = \underline{x}(n) + \underline{v}_1(n) - \underline{g}(n) = \underline{x}(n) + \underline{v}_1(n) - \mathbf{w}_n^T\mathbf{v}_{2,n}.$

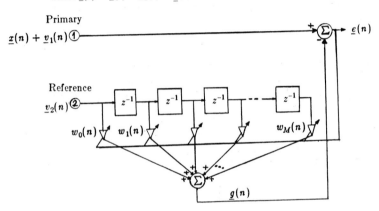

Tapped-delay-line model

Fig. 12.16. Adaptive noise-canceler configuration summary.

which means that (12.45) yields an exponentially weighted average of the squared input samples. The number of samples (say N), for which $\beta^N = 1/e$ may be defined as the *time constant* of the recursion in Eq. (12.45). From $\beta^N = 1/e$ it follows that

$$N \simeq \frac{1}{1-\beta} \tag{12.45a}$$

Thus if α is set equal to $1 - \beta$, then the above MLMS algorithm becomes

$$\underline{w}_i(n+1) = \underline{w}_i(n) + \frac{1-\beta}{\underline{\sigma}_x^2(n)}\underline{e}(n)\underline{x}(n-i), \qquad 0 \le i \le M \tag{12.46}$$

where $\underline{\sigma}_x^2(n)$ is continuously estimated using (12.45).

These MLMS algorithms are very effective for a variety of applications and are summarized in Table I.

TABLE I

MLMS Algorithm Summary

Adaptive filter configuration (see Fig. 12.10):

$$\underline{w}_i(n+1) = \underline{w}_i(n) + \frac{1-\beta}{\sigma_x^2(n)}\underline{e}(n)\underline{x}(n-i), \qquad 0 \le i \le M$$

where $\underline{e}(n) = \underline{y}(n) - \underline{g}(n)$, and

$$\sigma_x^2(n) = \beta\sigma_x^2(n-1) + (1-\beta)\underline{x}^2(n), \qquad 0 < \beta < 1$$

Adaptive predictor configuration (see Fig. 12.14):

$$\underline{w}_i(n+1) = \underline{w}_i(n) + \frac{1-\beta}{\sigma_x^2(n)}\underline{e}(n)\underline{x}(n-\Delta+1-i), \qquad 1 \le i \le M; \Delta = 1, 2, \ldots, K, K < \infty$$

where $\underline{e}(n) = \underline{x}(n) - \underline{g}(n)$, and

$$\sigma_x^2(n) = \beta\sigma_x^2(n-1) + (1-\beta)\underline{x}^2(n), \qquad 0 < \beta < 1$$

Adaptive noise-canceler configuration (see Fig. 12.16):

$$\underline{w}_i(n+1) = \underline{w}_i(n) + \frac{1-\beta}{\sigma_{v_2}^2(n)}\underline{e}(n)\underline{v}_2(n-i), \qquad 0 \le i \le M$$

where $\underline{e}(n) = \underline{x}(n) + v_1(n) - \underline{g}(n)$, and

$$\sigma_{v_2}^2(n) = \beta\underline{\sigma}_{v_2}^2(n-1) + (1-\beta)v_2^2(n), \qquad 0 < \beta < 1$$

Example 5. Consider the problem of improving the signal-to-noise ratio (SNR) of a sinusoid buried in broadband noise. If the frequency of the sinusoid is known, then we can use a fixed bandpass filter to improve the SNR. We consider the case in which the sinusoidal frequency is unknown. Hence an adaptive approach is used, as depicted in Fig. 12.17. It is apparent that this is simply a predictor configuration (see block diagram in Fig. 12.14).

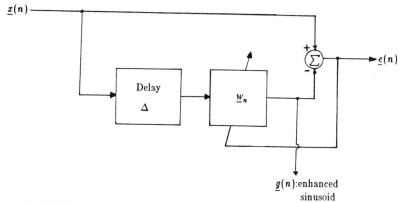

Fig. 12.17. Adaptive configuration for enhancing a sinusoid in broadband noise.

The basic idea in Fig. 12.17 is to choose the delay Δ to be sufficiently large so that the noise component in $\underline{x}(n - \Delta)$ is decorrelated with respect to the noise component in the input $\underline{x}(n)$. Then the only correlated component in $\underline{x}(n)$ and $\underline{x}(n - \Delta)$ is the sinusoid. As such, the filter weights adapt to the sinusoidal component and implement a bandpass characteristic about the frequency of the sinusoidal component. The resulting output $\underline{g}(n)$ is an enhanced sinusoid.

Figure 12.18(a) shows the input $\underline{x}(n)$, which consists of a 30-Hz sinusoid with peak value 1 and white noise with variance 1. This yields an SNR of -3 dB. The sampling frequency is 256 sps. Two thousand samples of $\underline{x}(n)$ were processed using the MLMS predictor algorithm in Table I with $M = 32$, $\Delta = 32$, and $\beta = 0.999$. To illustrate, we plot $\underline{x}(n)$ and $\underline{g}(n)$ in Fig. 12.18(b),(c), respectively, for sample numbers 1800 to 2000, and an improvement in SNR is apparent. One can also come to this conclusion by examining the input and output power density spectra displayed in Fig. 12.19(a),(b), respectively. This SNR improvement occurs because the 32-weight adaptive filter gradually implements a bandpass magnitude response around 30 Hz, the frequency of the sinusoid. The bandpass response implemented by the filter at $n = 2000$ is displayed in Fig. 12.19(c).

It has been shown that the optimal value a^* of the magnitude response at the

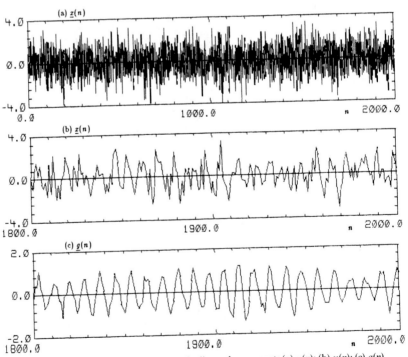

Fig. 12.18. MLMS algorithm example; line enhancement: (a) $\underline{x}(n)$; (b) $\underline{x}(n)$; (c) $\underline{g}(n)$.

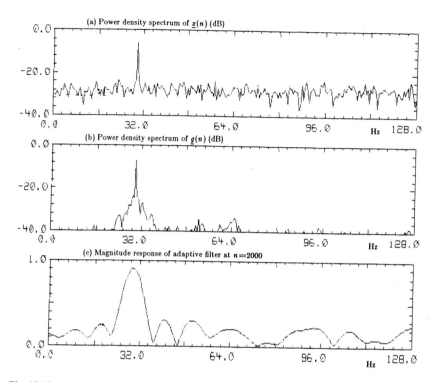

Fig. 12.19. Input-output power density spectra of (a) $\underline{x}(n)$ and (b) $\underline{g}(n)$ in dB and (c) related magnitude response at $n = 2000$.

frequency of the input sinusoid is [3]

$$a^* = \frac{(\text{SNR})(M/2)}{1 + (\text{SNR})(M/2)} \tag{12.47}$$

where M is the number of adaptive weights. Equation (12.47) shows that at high SNRs, $a^* \simeq 1$. At low SNRs $a^* < 1$. The desired condition $a^* \simeq 1$ may be attained at low SNRs if M is increased. However, this may cause the weights to be "noisy," which could produce a degradation in the overall bandpass response. If the noise components of the weights are assumed to have the same variance and to be mutually uncorrelated, then [3] the variance of the noise in each weight is $v\epsilon_{min}$, where ϵ_{min} is given by Eq. (12.15). Therefore, if M is increased to make $a^* \simeq 1$ at low SNRs, the adaptation rate should be reduced; that is, v should be made smaller for the LMS algorithm, and β should be made larger for the MLMS algorithm.

Although one sinusoid was considered in the foregoing example, the approach can be used to enhance several sinusoids in the input $\underline{x}(n)$. Since sinusoids have line spectra, the process of enhancing them is called line enhancement, and the configuration in Fig. 12.17 is called an *adaptive line enhancer* (ALE).

D   Miscellaneous Considerations

1 A detailed discussion pertaining to the properties of the LMS algorithm is available in the literature; see [3–5].

2. During adaptation the squared error $\underline{e}^2(n)$ is nonstationary as the weight vector $\mathbf{w}_n$ adapts toward $\mathbf{w}^*$. The corresponding MSE can thus be defined only on the basis of ensemble averages. A plot of the MSE versus n may be referred to as the *learning curve* for a given adaptive algorithm.

3. Excess MSE is caused by random noise in the weight vector. If the vector is noise free and the condition in Eq. (12.35) is satisfied, then $\mathbf{w}_n$ converges to $\mathbf{w}^*$ and the MSE would be ϵ_{min}. However, this usually does not occur in practice since the weight vector is, on the average, "misadjusted" from its optimal setting. The misadjustment is due to gradient noise, which is attributed to the gradient estimate $\hat{\mathbf{g}}$ in Eq. (12.31). This misadjustment (say m_ϵ) is defined as [5]

$$m_\epsilon = \frac{\text{average excess MSE}}{\epsilon_{min}}$$

It can be shown that m_ϵ is related to the speed of adaptation via the relation

$$m_\epsilon = v\lambda_{av}M$$

where λ_{av} is the average of the eigenvalues of the pertinent input autocorrelation matrix, v is the convergence constant for the LMS algorithm, and M is the number of weights. From the above relation for m_e it follows that if m_e is to be kept at a specified value, then v will have to be decreased if M is increased, and vice versa. That is, one has to seek a compromise between rate of adaptation and the number of weights while using the LMS algorithm. This is also the case with the MLMS algorithm.

4. In certain applications the LMS or MLMS algorithm for the predictor configuration may result in the so-called no-pass phenomenon [11] that was observed during long-term field tests of a perimeter intrusion-detection algorithm. Here transient signals (due to human intruders) buried in correlated noise were enhanced prior to using a threshold-detection scheme. In the absence of intruder signals the predictor served to reduce the level of background noise, thereby reducing the number of nuisance alarms. In essence, the no-pass phenomenon implies that over a period of time, an adaptive predictor with a *surplus* number of weights not only removes correlated noise but removes intruder transient signals as well. A detailed discussion and related analysis of this undesired effect is given in [11], which shows that a simple modification of the LMS or MLMS algorithm avoids the no-pass phenomenon. The modification involves the introduction of a parameter u, $0 < u < 1$, that multiplies the term $w_i(n)$ in the LMS or MLMS algorithm. Thus, for example the LMS algorithm in Fig. 12.14 becomes

$$\underline{w}_i(n+1) = u\underline{w}_i(n) + v\underline{e}(n)\underline{x}(n - \Delta + 1 - i), \qquad 1 \le i \le M$$

where $0 < u < 1$ and $\underline{e}(n) = \underline{x}(n) - \underline{g}(n)$. In practice, u is set very close to 1 [e.g., 0.999878 ($\simeq 1 - 2^{-13}$)].

5. The time taken for the LMS algorithm to produce a steady-state output component that corresponds to the ith input component (mode) is called a *time constant*. It has been shown that the time constant τ_i associated with the ith component is given by [3–5],

$$\tau_i \simeq \frac{1}{v\lambda_i} \tag{12.48}$$

where v is the convergence constant, and λ_i is the ith eigenvalue of the input autocorrelation matrix $\mathbf{S}_{xx}$.

Equation (12.48) shows that for a specified v the components that correspond to smaller eigenvalues of $\mathbf{S}_{xx}$ take much longer to reach their steady-state values when compared to components that correspond to larger eigenvalues. Hence the overall convergence rate of the LMS algorithm depends on the eigenvalue distribution of $\mathbf{S}_{xx}$.

To illustrate, suppose the input to an adaptive predictor consists of two sinusoids whose frequencies are 5 and 30 Hz, respectively. Let the respective peak values of the sinusoids be 1 and 10, and the sampling be 128 sps. A plot of this input for $n = 1$ to 1000 is shown in Fig. 12.20(a). Using the MLMS algorithm in

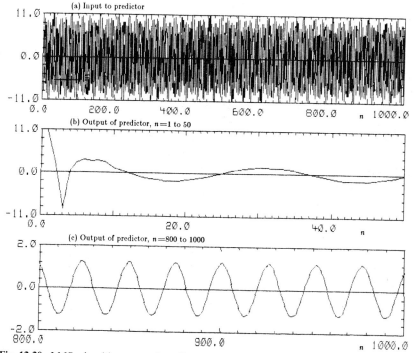

Fig. 12.20. LMS algorithm example; effect of eigenvalue distribution on convergence rate: (a) input to predictor; (b) output of predictor ($n = 1$–50); (c) output of predictor ($n = 800$–1000).

Fig. 12.14 with $\Delta = 1$, $M = 6$, and $\beta = 0.999$, we obtain the error output $\underline{e}(n)$ in Figs. 12.20(b),(c) for $n = 1$ to 50 and $n = 800$ to 1000, respectively. We observe that the input component with peak value 10 is immediately canceled output, but the component with peak value 1 remains through the 1000 input samples. Eventually, it will also be removed. The reason that it takes much longer is that the effective convergence parameter $(1 - \beta)/\underline{\sigma}_x^2(n)$ in the MLMS algorithm is small as far as the component with peak value 1 is concerned, since $\underline{\sigma}_x^2(n)$ is dominated by the component with peak value 10.

In the next section we consider a very effective LMS type algorithm whose convergence rate does not depend on the eigenvalue distribution of $\mathbf{S}_{xx}$.

V LMS LATTICE ALGORITHMS

The previous section shows that the LMS and MLMS algorithms are implemented with the tapped-delay-line model. We now implement these algorithms using lattice models. We consider two models: the one-step predictor model and the filter model.

A One-Step Predictor Model

The lattice model for the one-step predictor is given in Fig. 12.21, where $\underline{e}_i(n)$ and $\underline{w}_i(n)$ refer to the forward and backward prediction errors, respectively; k_i denotes the ith lattice weight and is occasionally referred to as a "reflection coefficient." The input to the N-stage lattice is $\underline{x}(n)$, and $\underline{e}_N(n)$ is the final error output; each z^{-1} represents a unit delay.

The notions of forward and backward predictions are keys to obtaining the lattice structure in Fig. 12.21. If $\hat{\underline{x}}(n)$ is an estimate for predicting $\underline{x}(n)$ using the past samples $\underline{x}(n - 1)$, $\underline{x}(n - 2), \ldots, \underline{x}(n - N)$, then

$$\underline{e}_N(n) = \underline{x}(n) - \hat{\underline{x}}(n) \tag{12.49}$$

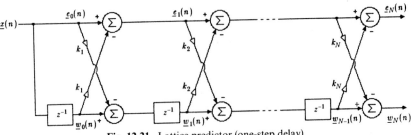

Fig. 12.21. Lattice predictor (one-step delay).

is called the forward prediction error. Again, if we wish to "predict" $\underline{x}(n - N - 1)$, given $\underline{x}(n - 1), \underline{x}(n - 2), \ldots, \underline{x}(n - N)$, then

$$\underline{w}_N(n) = \underline{x}(n - N - 1) - \hat{\underline{x}}(n - N - 1) \tag{12.50}$$

is called the backward prediction error, where $\hat{\underline{x}}(n - N - 1)$ denotes an estimate of $\underline{x}(n - N - 1)$. The $\underline{e}_i(n)$, $1 \leq i \leq N$, and $\underline{w}_j(n)$, $0 \leq j < N$, are the intermediate forward and backward prediction errors, respectively.

Details for deriving the lattice model are available elsewhere [12, 13]. If the input $\underline{x}(n)$ is stationary, then the respective steady-state values of $\underline{e}^2(n)$ and $\underline{e}_N^2(n)$ for the tapped-delay line (Fig. 12.14 with $\Delta = 1$) and lattice models are the same. See references [12, 14] for a discussion of some interesting properties of the lattice model.

Adaptive Considerations   1

If the input to the lattice predictor in Fig. 12.21 is nonstationary, then the lattice weights are time varying. Several strategies for updating the weights are discussed in [14]. We consider the approach in [15] that employs the method of steepest descent, introduced in the last section. As such, we update the lattice weights using the relation [see Eq. (12.30)]

$$\underline{k}_l(n + 1) = \underline{k}_l(n) - \tilde{u}\left[\frac{\partial \underline{r}_l^2(n)}{\partial \underline{k}_l(n)}\right], \qquad 1 \leq l \leq N \tag{12.51}$$

where $\underline{r}_l^2(n) = \underline{e}_l^2(n) + \underline{w}_l^2(n)$ is the total prediction error at stage l and time $n, \underline{k}_l(n)$ denotes the value of $\underline{k}_l$ at time n, and $\tilde{u}$ is a convergence parameter.

The recursive equations that describe the lattice model in Fig. 12.21 are

$$\underline{x}(n) = \underline{e}_0(n); \qquad \underline{w}_0(n) = \underline{x}(n - 1)$$

$$\underline{e}_l(n) = \underline{e}_{l-1}(n) - \underline{k}_l(n)\underline{w}_{l-1}(n) \tag{12.52}$$

$$\underline{w}_l(n) = \underline{w}_{l-1}(n - 1) - \underline{k}_l(n)\underline{e}_{l-1}(n - 1), \qquad 1 \leq l \leq N$$

Using Eq. (12.52) in Eq. (12.51) yields

$$\underline{k}_l(n + 1) = \underline{k}_l(n) + 2\tilde{u}[\underline{e}_l(n)\underline{w}_{l-1}(n) + \underline{w}_l(n)\underline{e}_{l-1}(n - 1)] \tag{12.53}$$

for $1 \leq l \leq N$.

It can be shown that the power in the forward and backward error sequences decreases as the number of stages in the lattice is increased. Therefore, a normalized convergence parameter has to be used in Eq. (12.53) in place of $2\tilde{u}$, and Eq. (12.53) is modified to obtain [15]

$$\underline{k}_l(n + 1) = \underline{k}_l(n) + \frac{\alpha}{\underline{\sigma}_l^2(n)}[\underline{e}_l(n)\underline{w}_{l-1}(n) + \underline{w}_l(n)\underline{e}_{l-1}(n - 1)] \tag{12.54}$$

where $0 < \alpha < 1$ and $\underline{\sigma}_l^2(n)$ is the input power estimate at the lth stage. It can be computed recursively as [see Eq. (12.45)]

$$\underline{\sigma}_l^2(n) = \beta\underline{\sigma}_l^2(n-1) + (1-\beta)[\underline{e}_{l-1}^2(n) + \underline{w}_{l-1}^2(n)] \qquad (12.55)$$

where $0 < \beta < 1$ is a smoothing parameter. As with the MLMS algorithm, a convenient choice in Eq. (12.54) is $\alpha = 1 - \beta$. Then we have the update equation

$$\underline{k}_l(n+1) = \underline{k}_l(n) + \frac{1-\beta}{\underline{\sigma}_l^2(n)}[\underline{e}_l(n)\underline{w}_{l-1}(n) + \underline{w}_l(n)\underline{e}_{l-1}(n-1)] \qquad (12.56)$$

for $1 \leq l \leq N$, which we refer to as the LMS lattice equation for a one-step predictor, where $\underline{\sigma}_l^2(n)$ is updated via Eq. (12.55).

Example 6. An important property of the LMS lattice algorithm in Eq. (12.56) is that its convergence rate is independent of the eigenvalue distribution of the input autocorrelation matrix $\mathbf{S}_{xx}$. To illustrate, we repeat the experiment related to Fig. 12.20. The input to a six-stage one-step LMS lattice predictor is the same as that plotted in Fig. 12.20(a); that is, the sum of 5- and 30-Hz sinusoids of peak values 1 and 10, respectively, sampled at 128 sps. With $\beta = 0.999$ and $N = 6$ in the LMS lattice algorithm in (12.56), the output that results is shown

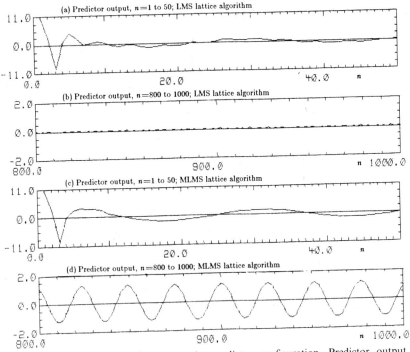

Fig. 12.22. LMS lattice algorithm example; predictor configuration. Predictor output for (a) $n = 1$–50, LMS lattice algorithm; (b) $n = 800$–1000, LMS lattice algorithm; (c) $n = 1$–50, MLMS algorithm; (d) $n = 800$–1000, MLMS algorithm.

in Fig. 12.22(a),(b) for $n = 1$ to 50 and (c) for $n = 800$ to 1000, respectively. From this output it is apparent that both sinusoidal components in the input $x(n)$ are removed. In contrast, the larger component was removed quickly by the MLMS algorithm, but the smaller component was not; see Fig. 12.20(b),(c), which is repeated for convenience as Fig. 12.22(c),(d), respectively.

Filter Model   B

Figure 12.23 shows the lattice model for the filter configuration whose equivalent tapped-delay-line model is given in Fig. 12.6. See [13] for a detailed derivation of this lattice model. If the inputs $x(n)$ and $y(n)$ are stationary, then the respective steady-state values of $\underline{e}^2(n)$ and $\underline{s}_N^2(n)$ for the tapped-delay-line and lattice models are the same.

The filter model in Fig. 12.23 consists of N stages. Its upper half (solid lines) is simply the predictor model considered earlier; see Fig. 12.21. The lower portion (dashed lines) consists of N additional weights k_l', $1 \leq l \leq N$. The basic idea involved in obtaining an adaptive algorithm is to continuously adjust the lattice weights $\underline{k}_l(n)$ and $\underline{k}_l'(n)$. The $\underline{k}_l(n)$ are adjusted to minimize the instantaneous error $\underline{e}_l^2(n) + \underline{w}_l^2(n)$ by the one-step predictor LMS algorithm in Eq. (12.56). Next, the $\underline{k}_l'(n)$ are adjusted to minimize the filter error $\underline{s}_l^2(n)$ by the steepest-descent technique [15], where $\underline{s}_l(n) = \underline{y}(n) - \hat{y}_N(n)$, and $\hat{y}_N(n)$ is an estimate of $y(n)$ using an N-stage lattice. Thus we have

$$\underline{k}_l'(n + 1) = \underline{k}_l'(n) - \tilde{u}\left[\frac{\partial \underline{s}_l^2(n)}{\partial \underline{k}_l'(n)}\right], \qquad 1 \leq l \leq N, \tag{12.57}$$

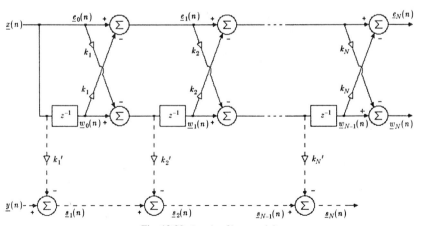

Fig. 12.23. Lattice filter model.

where $\tilde{u}$ is a convergence parameter. Again from Fig. 12.23 it follows that

$$\underline{s}_l(n) = \underline{s}_{l-1}(n) - \underline{k}'_l(n)\underline{w}_{l-1}(n+1) \tag{12.58}$$

with $\underline{s}_0(n) = \underline{y}(n)$. Substituting Eq. (12.58) into Eq. (12.57) gives

$$\underline{k}'_l(n+1) = \underline{k}'_l(n) + 2\tilde{u}\underline{s}_l(n)\underline{w}_{l-1}(n+1) \tag{12.59}$$

for $1 \le l \le N$. As in the predictor case, the constant convergence term $2\tilde{u}$ is replaced by a normalized convergence parameter [15]. The final result is

$$\underline{k}'_l(n+1) = \underline{k}'_l(n) + \frac{1-\tilde{\beta}}{\underline{\tilde{\sigma}}_l^2(n)}[\underline{s}_l(n)\underline{w}_{l-1}(n+1)] \tag{12.60}$$

where

$$\underline{\tilde{\sigma}}_l^2(n) = \tilde{\beta}\underline{\tilde{\sigma}}_l^2(n-1) + (1-\tilde{\beta})\underline{s}_l^2(n)$$

where $\tilde{\beta}, 0 < \tilde{\beta} < 1$, is a smoothing parameter and $1 \le l \le N$.

The LMS lattice algorithm for the filter configuration is given by Eqs. (12.56) and (12.60). This algorithm can also be used for prediction with $\Delta > 1$ and noise

TABLE II
LMS Lattice Algorithm Summary

One-step adaptive lattice predictor model (see Fig. 12.21)

$$\underline{k}_l(n+1) = \underline{k}_l(n) + \frac{1-\beta}{\sigma_l^2(n)}[\underline{e}_l(n)\underline{w}_{l-1}(n) + \underline{w}_l(n)e_{l-1}(n-1)]$$

where

$$\underline{\sigma}_l^2(n) = \beta\underline{\sigma}_l^2(n-1) + (1-\beta)[\underline{e}_{l-1}^2(n) + \underline{w}_{l-1}^2(n)], \qquad 0 < \beta < 1,$$

$$\text{for } 1 \le l \le N; \underline{e}_0(n) = \underline{x}(n) \text{ and } \underline{w}_0(n) = \underline{x}(n-1)$$

Note: $\underline{e}_l(n)$ and $\underline{w}_l(n)$, $1 \le l \le N$, are defined in Eq. (12.52).
Adaptive lattice filter configuration (see Fig. 12.23)
    The above predictor algorithm and the following:

$$\underline{k}'_l(n+1) = \underline{k}'_l(n) + \frac{1-\beta}{\underline{\tilde{\sigma}}_l^2(n)}[\underline{s}_l(n)\underline{w}_{l-1}(n+1)]$$

where

$$\underline{\tilde{\sigma}}_l^2(n) = \tilde{\beta}\underline{\tilde{\sigma}}_l^2(n-1) + (1-\tilde{\beta})\underline{s}_l^2(n), \qquad 0 < \tilde{\beta} < 1,$$

$$\text{for } 1 \le l \le N; \underline{w}_0(n+1) = \underline{x}(n)$$

Note: $\underline{s}_l(n)$, $1 \le l \le N$, is defined in Eq. (12.58).
Prediction with $\Delta > 1$.
    Replace $\underline{x}(n)$ by $\underline{x}(n-\Delta)$ and $\underline{y}(n)$ by $\underline{x}(n)$ in Fig. 12.23
Noise cancellation
    In Fig. 12.23 replace $\underline{y}(n)$ by the primary input $\underline{x}(n) + \underline{v}_1(n)$, and $\underline{x}(n)$ by the reference input $\underline{v}_2(n)$.

cancellation as follows:

Prediction with $\Delta > 1$:   Replace $\underline{x}(n)$ by $\underline{x}(n - \Delta)$ and $\underline{y}(n)$ by $\underline{x}(n)$.

Noise cancellation: Replace $x(n)$ by the reference input $\underline{v}_2(n)$ and $y(n)$ by the primary input $\underline{x}(n) + \underline{v}_1(n)$. We assume that $\underline{v}_1(n)$ and $\underline{v}_2(n)$ are correlated zero-mean noise sequences and that the signal $\underline{x}(n)$ is uncorrelated with respect to $\underline{v}_1(n)$ and $\underline{v}_2(n)$.

The above lattice algorithms are summarized in Table II.

Example 7.   We repeat the noise-cancellation experiment of Example 4. For convenience, Fig. 12.15(a)–(c) is repeated as Fig. 12.24(a)–(c).

A 16-stage lattice was used. The resulting output $\underline{s}_{16}(n)$ is plotted in Fig. 12.24(d) for $n = 800$ to 1000. We obtained this output using the LMS lattice algorithm in Table II with $N = 16$ and $\beta = \tilde{\beta} = 0.99$. Clearly, the output in Fig. 12.24(d) provides a good approximation to the original 25-Hz sinusoid in Fig. 12.24(a), indicating a significant improvement in SNR. This SNR improvement is also evident from the corresponding input and output power density spectra shown in Fig. 12.25.

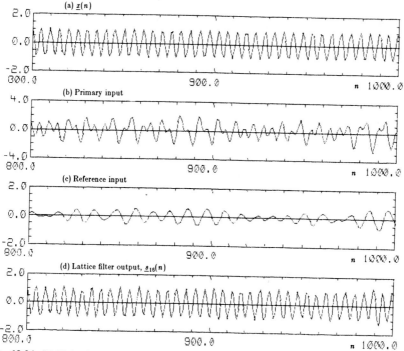

Fig. 12.24. LMS lattice algorithm example; noise-cancellation: (a) $x(n)$; (b) primary input; (c) reference input; (d) lattice filter output, $\underline{s}_{16}(n)$.

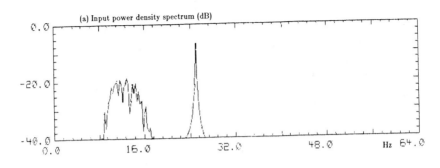

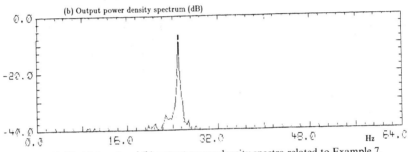

Fig. 12.25. (a) Input and (b) output power density spectra related to Example 7.

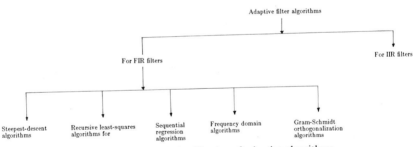

Fig. 12.26. A broad classification of adaptive algorithms.

VI CONCLUDING REMARKS

We have studied a class of steepest-descent algorithms that are relevant to tapped-delay-line and lattice models of FIR filters. These algorithms are widely used since they are efficient and easy to implement in hardware. This class of algorithms is one of several that are available in the literature. The available algorithms may be broadly classified as indicated in Fig. 12.26.

Recursive least squares (RLS) algorithms for lattice as well as transversal filter models have been developed [16–18]. RLS algorithms converge very rapidly compared to steepest-descent algorithms and are especially suited to applications where rapid convergence is required, such as fast start-up channel equalization [19, 20]. Faster convergence is achieved at a relatively modest increase in computational requirements compared to corresponding steepest-descent algorithms; see [18, Table I].

Sequential regression (SER) algorithms [21–23] also have superior convergence properties compared to the steepest-descent algorithms. However, they are computationally inefficient.

Several frequency domain adaptive algorithms for FIR filters have been presented in the literature [24, 25]. The main objective of this class of algorithms is to exploit the computational advantages of performing convolutions via the fast Fourier transform (FFT). In addition, the steepest-descent approach is used to update weights in the frequency domain. In this regard, the LMS algorithm for complex data sequences [26, 27] is used.

Additional adaptive configurations that are intriguing from a theoretical point of view have also been studied. These configurations [28, 29] are pertinent to the Gram–Schmidt orthogonalization method.

More recently there has been a growing interest in the development of adaptive algorithms for IIR filters. The main difficulty in this area is that the related MSE error surfaces are not guaranteed to be quadratic (bowl-shaped) with respect to the filter weights. Therefore, the related analysis is much more difficult than that for FIR adaptive filters. See [30–34] for details of the approaches that have been undertaken.

APPENDIX: FOUR FORTRAN-77 PROGRAMS

Listings of four FORTRAN-77 programs are presented in this appendix. Program 1 implements the LMS and MLMS algorithms for the predictor, filter, and noise-cancellation configurations. Program 2 implements the LMS lattice algorithms for the predictor and filter configurations.

Programs 1 and 2 are interactive. Either program enables us to store the adaptive filter weights at any desired sample point (iteration).

Input and output data files are read and written via subroutines LREAD and LWRITE, available as Program 3 and Program 4, respectively.

Solutions for several of the examples in this chapter were obtained from these programs.

Program 1

```
c************************************************************************
c
c
c        purpose
c                   This program implements the LMS and MLMS algorithms for
c                   the predictor, filter, and noise-canceler configurations.
c
c        description of i/o files
c
c                input:   * predictor configuration:
c                             input x(n) file
c
c                         * filter configuration:
c                             desired output y(n) file
c                             input    x(n)  file
c
c                         * noise-canceler configuration:
c                             primary input file
c                             reference input file
c
c                output:    error  e(n) file
c                           output q(n) file
c                           weights     file
c
c************************************************************************
c
        parameter ( mem=20000, eps=0.0000001 )
        real pri(mem),ref(-255:mem),err(mem),est(mem),coef(256)
        character*1 icon
c
c        ** read in parameters **
c
        write(*,*) 'do you want predictor  mode [1]'
        write(*,*) '               filter     mode [2]'
        write(*,*) '                    noise-canceler [3]'
        write(*,110)
        read(*,*) iqp
110     format(2x,'enter  the  mode number [1,2,3]  = ',$)
        write(*,111)
        read(*,*) beta
111     format(2x,'the value of smoothing parameter = ',$)
        write(*,112)
        read(*,*) icon
112     format(2x,'Do you want MLMS [y] or LMS [n]  = ',$)
        if (iqp.eq.1) then
                write(*,113)
113             format(2x,'enter the predictor delay(0-128) = ',$)
                read(*,*) id
                        else
                id=0
        endif
        write(*,114)
        read(*,*) nco
114     format(2x,'number of filter weights (1-256) = ',$)
        write(*,115)
        read(*,*) idata
115     format(2x,'enter the number of  iterations  = ',$)
        var=1.0
```

Program 1, cont.

```
         if (icon.eq.'y'.or.icon.eq.'Y') var=0.0
         write(*,116)
         read(*,*) idump
116      format(2x,'iteration # to dump out weights  = ',$)
c
c        ** initialization **
c
         do 15 ii=1,256
           ref(ii)=0.0
           ref(1-ii)=0.0
           coef(ii)=0.0
15       continue
c
c        ** read input files **
c
         if (iqp.eq.1) then
                 call lread(' predictor input file name  = ',pri,is1)
                 do 20 ii=1,idata
                     ref(id+ii)=pri(ii)
20               continue
         endif
         if (iqp.eq.2) then
                 call lread(' desired output y(n) file name  = ',pri,is1)
                 call lread(' input    x(n)        file name  = ',ref(1),is2)
         endif
         if (iqp.eq.3) then
                 call lread(' primary   input file name  = ',pri,is1)
                 call lread(' reference input file name  = ',ref(1),is2)
         endif
         do 1000 i=1,idata
           est(i)=0.0
           do 50 ii=1,nco
             est(i)=est(i)+coef(ii)*ref(i-ii+1)
50         continue
           err(i)=pri(i)-est(i)
           if (icon.eq.'y'.or.icon.eq.'Y') then
                 var=beta*var+(1.-beta)*ref(i)*ref(i)
           endif
           if(var.le.eps) goto 70
           do 51 ii=1,nco
             coef(ii)=coef(ii)+(1.-beta)*err(i)*ref(i-ii+1)/var
51         continue
70         if (i.ne.idump) goto 1000
           write(*,117) idump
117        format(1x,/,2x,'The values of weight at',i5,' iteration',/)
           do 52 ii=1,nco
             write(*,*) '      weight(',ii,')=',coef(ii)
52         continue
           write(*,*)
           call lwrite(' weights output file name = ',coef,nco)
1000     continue
         call lwrite(' error  e(n) file name = ',err,idata)
         call lwrite(' output g(n) file name = ',est,idata)
         end
```

Program 2

```
C************************************************************************
c
c
c          purpose
c                    This program implements the lattice algorithm for
c                    one-step predictor and filter configurations, as
c                    given in Reference [10].
c
c          description of i/o files
c
c                    [1] one-step predictor configuration
c
c                              input:  input x(n) file
c                              output: forward prediction error e(n) file
c
c                    [2] filter mode
c
c                              input:  input x(n) file
c                                      input y(n) file
c                              output: forward prediction error e(n) file
c                                      filter  error v(n) file
c
C************************************************************************
          paraneter (nem=50000,eps=0.0000001)
          real pri(mem),ref(mem),f(256),b(256),bb(256),del(256)
          real kk(256),err(0:256),g(256),gam(256),for(mem),fil(mem)
          character*1 ip,iqv
c
c          ** read in parameter **
c
          write(*,111)
          read(*,*) ip
111       format(2x,'predictor[y],filter[n] routine = ',$)
          write(*,112)
          read(*,*) lstage
112       format(2x,'the  number  of  stage (1-256) = ',$)
          write(*,113)
          read(*,*) beta
113       format(2x,'smoothing    parameter   beta  = ',$)
          write(*,114)
          read(*,*) iqv
114       format(2x,'time varying[y], fixed[n] var. = ',$)
          write(*,115)
          read(*,*) idata
115       format(2x,'the number of iteration[def:0] = ',$)
c
c          ** read in input files **
c
          if(ip.eq.'y'.or.ip.eq.'Y') then
                  call lread(' input x(n) file name = ',ref,is)
                      else
                  call lread(' input x(n) file name = ',pri,is)
                  call lread(' input y(n) file name = ',ref,isl)
                  if(isl.lt.is) is=isl
          endif
          if(idata.le.0.or.idata.gt.is) idata=is
```

```
c          ** memory initialization **
c
           alpha=1.-beta
           do 21 i=1,256
              bb(i)=0.
              g(i)=0.
              kk(i)=0.
              if(iqv.eq.'y'.or.iqv.eq.'Y') then
                  del(i)=0.
                  gam(i)=0.
                     else
                  del(i)=1.
                  gam(i)=1.
              endif
21         continue
c
c          ** compute one-step predictor **
c
           do 100 j=1,idata
             f(1)=ref(j)
             b(1)=ref(j)
             do 34 i=1,lstage
               f(i+1)=f(i)-kk(i)*bb(i)
               b(i+1)=bb(i)-kk(i)*f(i)
               if (iqv.eq.'y'.or.iqv.eq.'Y') then
                  del(i)=del(i)*beta+(1.-beta)*(bb(i)*bb(i)+f(i)*f(i))
                  if (del(i).lt.eps) del(i)=eps
               endif
               kk(i)=kk(i)+alpha*(f(i+1)*bb(i)+b(i+1)*f(i))/del(i)
34           continue
             do 35 i=1,lstage+1
               bb(i)=b(i)
35           continue
             for(j)=f(lstage+1)
c
c            ** compute filter output **
c
             if(ip.eq.'n'.or.ip.eq.'N') then
                  err(0)=pri(j)
                  do 54 i=1,lstage+1
                    err(i)=err(i-1)-g(i)*b(i)
                    if(iqv.eq.'y'.or.iqv.eq.'Y') then
                         gam(i)=gam(i)*beta+(1.-beta)*b(i)*b(i)
                         if (gam(i).lt.eps) gam(i)=eps
                    endif
                    g(i)=g(i)+alpha*err(i)*b(i)/gam(i)
54                continue
                  fil(j)=err(lstage+1)
             endif
100        continue
           if(ip.eq.'y'.or.ip.eq.'Y') then
           call lwrite('  prediction error e(n) file = ',for,idata)
                     else
           call lwrite('  prediction error e(n) file = ',for,idata)
           call lwrite('  filter     error v(n) file = ',fil,idata)
           endif
           end
```

Program 3

****

    subroutine lread(prompt,array,datlen)

This subroutine reads a floating-point data file into an array.
The file to be read contains real values in a form corresponding
to FORTRAN direct-access unformatted mode.

Definitions:

prompt   CHARACTER   Prompt for filename.
datlen   INTEGER   Data length (number of values read)
                          At present, max data length is 20,000 values.
                          datlen is returned to the calling program.
array   REAL   The name of the array into which the values
                          will be read. The array name must be
                          dimensioned in the calling program.

Operation:

    Subroutine lread accepts a prompt and an array name, prompts for
    a data file name, opens the file, reads each 4-byte floating-
    point value into the array, closes the file, and returns the
    number of values read in the variable datlen.

****

```
      subroutine lread(prompt,array,datlen)
      integer datlen
      real array(1)
      character*80 fname
      character*(*) prompt
      write(6,10) prompt
10    format(' ',a,$)
      read(5,12)fname
12    format(a)
      open(unit=3,file=fname,access='direct',status='old',
     &  form='unformatted',iostat=ierro,recl=4)
      rewind (unit=3)
      do 100 i=1,20000
              read(3,rec=i,end=200) array(i)
100   continue
200   datlen = i -1
      close(unit=3)
      return
      end
```

Program 4

```
*****************************************************************************
*
*          subroutine lwrite(prompt,array,datlen)
*
*     This subroutine writes  a floating-point data file from an array.
*     The file will contain real values in a form corresponding
*     to FORTRAN direct access unformatted mode.
*     Definitions:
*     prompt   CHARACTER        Prompt for filename.
*     datlen   INTEGER          Data length (number of values to be written)
*                               datlen is received from the calling program.
*     array    REAL             The name of the array from which the values will
*                               be read.  The array name must be furnished and
*                               dimensioned by the calling program.
*     Operation:
*          Subroutine lwrite accepts a prompt and an array name, prompts
*          for a data file name, opens the file, writes 4-byte floating-
*          point values from the array to the file, and closes the file.
*          The number of values to be written is specified by the variable
*          datlen.
*****************************************************************************
          subroutine lwrite(prompt,array,datlen)
          character*80 fname
          character*1 answer
          character*(*) prompt
          integer datlen, length
          real array(1:datlen)
    8     write(6,10) prompt
   10     format(' ',a,$)
          read(5,12) fname
   12     format(a)
          length = datlen*4
          open(unit=3,file=fname,access='direct',status='new',
     &    form='unformatted',recl=length,iostat=ierrw)
          if(ierrw.eq.117) then
                  write(6,14)
   14             format(' ','FILE EXISTS ',/
     &            1x,'DO YOU WISH TO OVERWRITE?',$)
                  read(5,12) answer
                  if(answer.eq.'n'.or.answer.eq.'N') then
                          write(6,16)
   16                     format(' ','PICK ANOTHER FILENAME')
                          go to 8
                  else
                          open(unit=3,file=fname,access='direct',
     &                    status='old',form='unformatted',
     &                    recl=length,iostat=ierrw2)
                          close(unit=3, status = 'delete')
                          open(unit=3,file=fname,access='direct',
     &                    status='new',form='unformatted',
     &                    recl=length,iostat=ierrw2)
                  endif
          else
          endif
          write(3,rec=1) array
          return
          end
```

ACKNOWLEDGMENT

The author is grateful to Mr. Sangil Park of the Electrical and Computer Engineering Department at the University of New Mexico for his assistance in preparing this chapter.

REFERENCES

1. J. D. Markel and A. H. Gray, *Linear Prediction of Speech*, Springer-Verlag, Berlin and New York, 1976.
2. A. Habibi, Comparision of *n*-th order DPCM encoder with linear transformations and block quantization techniques, *IEEE Trans. Commun.* **COM-19**, 948–956 (1971).
3. B. Widrow *et al.*, Adaptive noise cancelling: Principles and applications, *Proc. IEEE* **63**, 1692–1716 (1975).
4. B. Widrow, Adaptive filters in *Aspects of Network and System Theory*, edited by R. Kalman and N. De Claris, Holt, Reinhart and Winston, New York, 1971 pp. 563–587.
5. B. Widrow *et al.*, Stationary and nonstationary learning characteristics of the LMS adaptive filters, *Proc. IEEE* **64**, 1151–1162 (1976).
6. B. Widrow and M. Hoff, Jr., Adaptive switching circuits, *IRE WESCON Conv. Rec.* **4**, 96–104 (1960).
7. D. K. Faddeev and V. N. Faddeeva, *Computational Methods of Linear Algebra*, W. H. Freeman, San Francisco, 1963.
8. B. Widrow *et al.*, Adaptive antenna systems, *Proc. IEEE* **55**, 2143–2159 (1967).
9. N. Ahmed and T. Natarajan, *Discrete-Time Signals and Systems*, Appendix 6.2 Rseton, Reston, Va., 1983.
10. L. J. Griffiths, Adaptive lattice structure for noise-cancelling applications, *Proc. Int. Conf. Acoust. Speech Signal Process.*, pp. 87–90, 1978.
11. K. J. Hass, D. H. Lenhert, and N. Ahmed, On a microcomputer implementation of an intrusion-detection algorithm, *IEEE Trans. Acoust. Speech Signal Process.* **ASSP-27**, 782–789 (1979).
12. S. A. Tretter, *Introduction to Discrete-Time Signal Processing*, Wiley, New York, 1976, pp. 182–191.
13. N. Ahmed and R. J. Fogler, A matrix bordering approach for deriving lattice models, *IEEE Trans. Aerosp. Electron. Syst.* **AES-20**, 835–838 (1985).
14. J. Makhoul, Stable and efficient lattice model for linear prediction, *IEEE Trans. Acoust. Speech Signal Process.* **ASSP-25**, 423–428 (1977).
15. L. J. Griffiths, A continuously-adaptive filter implementated as a lattice structure, *Proc. Int. Conf. Acoust. Speech Signal Process.* pp.683–686, 1977.
16. M. Morf and D. Lee, Recursive least-squares ladder forms for fast parameter tracking, *Proc. IEEE Int. Conf. Decision and Control*, pp. 1352–1367, 1979.
17. D. Lee, M. Morf, and B. Friedlander, Recursive least-squares ladder estimation algorithms, *IEEE Trans. Acoust. Speech Signal Process.* **ASSP-29**, 627–641 (1981).
18. J. M. Cioffi and T. Kailath, Fast, recursive-least-squares transversal filters for adaptive filtering, *IEEE Trans. Acoust. Speech Signal Process.* **ASSP-32**, 304–337 (1984).
19. E. Satorius and S. T. Alexander, Channel equalization using adaptive lattice algorithms, *IEEE Trans. Commun.* **COM-29**, 899–905 (1979).
20. E. Satorius and J. Pack, Application of least-squares lattice algorithms to adaptive equalization, *IEEE Trans. Commun.* **COM-29**, 136–142 (1981).
21. R. D. Gitlin and F. R. McGee, Self-orthogonalizing adaptive equalization algorithm, *IEEE Trans. Commun.* **COM-25**, 666–672 (1972).
22. N. Ahmed *et al.*, Sequential regression considerations of adaptive filtering, *Electronics Letters* **13**, 446–448 (1977).
23. N. Ahmed *et al.*, A short-term sequential regression algorithm, *IEEE Trans. Acoust. Speech Signal Process.* **ASSP-27**, 453–457 (1979).

24. S. Shankar Narayan, A. M. Peterson, and M. J. Narsimha, Transformation domain LMS algorithm, *IEEE Trans. Acoust. Speech Signal Process.* **ASSP-31,** 609–615 (1983).
25. G. A. Clark, S. R. Parker, and S. K. Mitra, A unified approach to time- and frequency-domain realization of FIR adaptive digital filters, *IEEE Trans. Acoust. Speech Signal Process.* **ASSP-31,** 1073–1083 (1983).
26. B. Widrow, J. McCooll and M. Ball, The complex LMS algorithm, *Proc. IEEE* **63,** 719–720 (1975).
27. B. Fisher and N. J. Bershad, The complex LMS adaptive algorithm—transient weight mean and covariance with applications to the ALE, *IEEE Trans. Acoust. Speech Signal Process.* **ASSP-31,** 34–44 (1983).
28. L. J. Griffiths, Adaptive structures for multiple-input noise cancelling applications, *Proc. Int. Conf. Acoust. Speech Signal Process.,* pp. 925–928, 1979.
29. N. Ahmed and D. H. Youn, On a realization and related algorithm for adaptive prediction, *IEEE Trans. Acoust. Speech Signal Process.* **ASSP-28,** 493–497 (1980).
30. P. L. Feintuch, An adaptive recursive LMS filter, *Proc. IEEE* **64,** 1622–1624 (1976).
31. S. A. White, An adaptive recursive filter, *Proc. Asilomar Conf. Circuits Systems Comput.,* pp. 21–25, 1975.
32. J. R. Treichler, M. G. Larimore, and C. R. Johnson, Simple adaptive IIR filtering, *Proc. Int. Conf. Acoust. Speech Signal Process.,* pp. 118–122, 1978.
33. D. Parikh and N. Ahmed, On an adaptive algorithm for IIR filters, *Proc. IEEE* **66,** 585–588 (1978).
34. D. V. Bhaskar Rao and S. Kung, Adaptive notch filtering for the retrieval of sinusoids in noise, *IEEE Trans. Acoust. Speech Signal Process.* **ASSP-32,** 791–802 (1984).

Chapter **13**

Recursive Estimation

GENE H. HOSTETTER
Electrical Engineering Department
University of California, Irvine
Irvine, California 92717

INTRODUCTION I

In 1795 Karl Friedrich Gauss (1777–1855) invented the method of least squares estimation in the course of calculating planetary and comet orbits from telescopic measurement data [1]. Six precise measurements would suffice to determine the six parameters characterizing each orbit, but individual measurements were likely to be quite inaccurate. More measurements than the minimum number were used, and the "best fit" to an orbit was found, in the sense of minimizing the sum of squares of the corresponding parameter measurement errors. Gauss's approach was to develop the method, then argue eloquently that it yielded the "most accurate" estimate. Adrien Marie Legendre (1707–1783) independently developed least squares estimation and published the results first, in 1806.

Through the years least squares methods have become increasingly important in many applications, including communications, control systems, navigation, and signal and image processing [2, 3]. The next section develops the fundamental ideas of least squares estimation. The solution involves a linear transformation of the measurements to obtain the optimal estimate. Then a recursive formulation [4, 5] of the least squares solution is derived in which the measurements are processed sequentially. The digital processing for recursive least squares constitutes filtering of incoming discrete-time measurement signals to produce discrete-time outputs representing estimates of the measured system parameters. Several illustrative examples are given. The section concludes with discussion of probabilistic interpretations of least squares and an indication of how recursive least squares methods can be generalized.

In 1960, building on the work of others, Rudolph E. Kalman published his first paper [6] on linear minimum mean square (MMS) estimation. The approach was

899

a fundamental departure from that of Gauss in that it began with a stochastic formulation rather than giving stochastic interpretation to an already developed procedure. The result, now known as the Kalman filter [7–10], is an elegant generalization of recursive least squares that nicely unifies and extends many earlier results. It is especially convenient for digital computer implementation.

With the ideas of recursive least squares established, we formulate the basic linear MMS estimation problem in Section III and derive the recursive Kalman filter equations. Measurements to be processed are represented by a state-variable noise-driven model that has additive measurement noise. As each measurement is incorporated, the Kalman filter produces an optimal estimate of the model state based on all previous measurements through the latest one. With each filter iteration the estimate is updated and improved by the incorporation of new data. If the noises involved have Gaussian probability distributions, the filter produces minimum mean-square error (MSE) estimates. Otherwise, it produces estimates with the smallest MSE obtainable with a linear filter; nonlinear filters could be superior.

Section IV begins with a summary of the matrix Kalman filtering equations and a block diagram of the filter, which includes a replica of the state-variable model for the measurements. A BASIC language computer program for demonstrating first-order Kalman filters is given, and important considerations in the programming of multivariable filters are discussed. The next section introduces extensions of the Kalman filter to situations involving noise coupling matrices, deterministic inputs to the model, nonzero mean values, known initial conditions, correlated noises, and bias estimation.

Section VI is concerned with some of the computational aspects of Kalman filtering [11–14]. Insufficient care in modeling can lead to unrealistic confidence in the estimation accuracy, to the point where additional measurements are effectively ignored by the filter—a situation called *divergence*. The effects of computational inaccuracies can be reduced by using alternative arrangements of the computations, such as square-root filtering. Examples [15–22] are given to illustrate key concepts.

The final section is a short bibliography that includes references to other material on optimal smoothing [23–28], to filtering for continuous-time systems [26–28], and to several papers describing applications of Kalman filtering.

II LEAST SQUARES ESTIMATION

A Direct Least Squares

The basic least squares problem [29, 30] involves estimating an n-vector quantity $\mathbf{x}$ from an m-vector [31–33] of linearly related known measurements

$$\underline{z} = \mathbf{Hx} + \underline{v} \tag{13.1}$$

where the matrix $\mathbf{H}$ has the dimensions $m \times n$ with $m \geq n$, and where $\mathbf{v}$ is an m-vector of unknown measurement errors. Every estimate of $\mathbf{x}$, denoted by $\hat{\mathbf{x}}$, corresponds to some error (or noise) vector $\hat{\mathbf{v}}$ in

$$\mathbf{z} = \mathbf{H}\hat{\mathbf{x}} + \hat{\mathbf{v}} \tag{13.2}$$

We want to find, using the measurements $\mathbf{z}$, the estimate $\hat{\mathbf{x}}$ that minimizes the performance measure, which is the sum of squares of errors

$$J = \hat{\mathbf{v}}^{\mathsf{T}}\hat{\mathbf{v}} = \hat{v}_1^2 + \hat{v}_2^2 + \cdots + \hat{v}_m^2 \tag{13.3}$$

The solution is found by expressing $\hat{\mathbf{v}}$ in terms of $\hat{\mathbf{x}}$ then setting the derivatives of J with respect to each component of $\underline{x}$ to zero:

$$\hat{\mathbf{v}}^{\mathsf{T}}\hat{\mathbf{v}} = (\mathbf{z} - \mathbf{H}\hat{\mathbf{x}})^{\mathsf{T}}(\mathbf{z} - \mathbf{H}\hat{\mathbf{x}}) \tag{13.4}$$

$$\left(\frac{\partial J}{\partial \hat{\mathbf{x}}}\right) = \begin{bmatrix} \dfrac{\partial J}{\partial x_1} \\[6pt] \dfrac{\partial J}{\partial x_2} \\[6pt] \vdots \\[6pt] \dfrac{\partial J}{\partial x_n} \end{bmatrix} = -\mathbf{H}^{\mathsf{T}}(\mathbf{z} - \mathbf{H}\hat{\mathbf{x}}) = \mathbf{0} \tag{13.5}$$

$$\mathbf{H}^{\mathsf{T}}\mathbf{H}\hat{\mathbf{x}} = \mathbf{H}^{\mathsf{T}}\mathbf{z} \tag{13.6}$$

$$\hat{\mathbf{x}} = (\mathbf{H}^{\mathsf{T}}\mathbf{H})^{-1}\mathbf{H}^{\mathsf{T}}\mathbf{z} \tag{13.7}$$

It turns out that the matrix of second derivatives of J,

$$\frac{\partial^2 J}{\partial \hat{\mathbf{x}}^2} = \mathbf{H}^{\mathsf{T}}\mathbf{z} \tag{13.8}$$

is positive definite if $\mathbf{H}$ has full rank, so the solution is unique and is a minimum. Since $\mathbf{H}^{\mathsf{T}}\mathbf{H}$ is positive definite, $(\mathbf{H}^{\mathsf{T}}\mathbf{H})^{-1}$ exists. Equation (13.7) shows that the least squares estimate $\hat{\mathbf{x}}$ is linearly related to the measurements $\mathbf{z}$. This is not surprising, since derivatives of quadratic functions are linear functions.

Scalar Least Squares Example. Suppose that a scalar quantity x to be estimated and three measurements $\mathbf{z}$ are related by

$$\begin{aligned} \underline{z}_1 &= 3 = 2x + \underline{v}_1, \\ \underline{z}_2 &= 0 = -x + \underline{v}_2, \\ \underline{z}_3 &= -2 = -2x + \underline{v}_3 \end{aligned} \tag{13.9}$$

or

$$\mathbf{z} = \begin{bmatrix} 3 \\ 0 \\ -2 \end{bmatrix} = \begin{bmatrix} 2 \\ -1 \\ -2 \end{bmatrix} x + \begin{bmatrix} v_1 \\ v_2 \\ v_3 \end{bmatrix} = \mathbf{h}x + \mathbf{v} \tag{13.10}$$

The least squares estimate of x is

$$\hat{x} = (h^Th)^{-1}h^Tz$$

$$= \left([2 \quad -1 \quad -2]\begin{bmatrix} 2 \\ -1 \\ -2 \end{bmatrix}\right)^{-1}[2 \quad -1 \quad -2]\begin{bmatrix} 3 \\ 0 \\ -2 \end{bmatrix} = \frac{10}{9} \qquad (13.11)$$

Vector Least Squares Example. Suppose we want to estimate the vector quantity

$$\mathbf{x} = \begin{bmatrix} x_1 \\ x_2 \end{bmatrix} \qquad (13.12)$$

from the measurements

$$
\begin{aligned}
\underline{z}_1 &= & 3 &= & -x_1 + & x_2 + \underline{v}_1 \\
\underline{z}_2 &= -5 &= & 2x_1 - & x_2 + \underline{v}_2 \\
\underline{z}_3 &= & 2 &= & x_1 + & x_2 + \underline{v}_3 \\
\underline{z}_4 &= & 6 &= & -2x_1 + 2x_2 + \underline{v}_4
\end{aligned}
\qquad (13.13)
$$

or

$$\underline{z} = \begin{bmatrix} 3 \\ -5 \\ 2 \\ 6 \end{bmatrix} = \begin{bmatrix} -1 & 1 \\ 2 & -1 \\ 1 & 1 \\ -2 & 2 \end{bmatrix}\begin{bmatrix} x_1 \\ x_2 \end{bmatrix} + \begin{bmatrix} \underline{v}_1 \\ \underline{v}_2 \\ \underline{v}_3 \\ \underline{v}_4 \end{bmatrix} = \mathbf{H}\mathbf{x} + \underline{v} \qquad (13.14)$$

The least squares estimate of $\mathbf{x}$ is

$$\hat{\underline{x}} = (\mathbf{H}^T\mathbf{H})^{-1}\mathbf{H}^T\underline{z}$$

$$= \left(\begin{bmatrix} -1 & 2 & 1 & -2 \\ 1 & -1 & 1 & 2 \end{bmatrix}\begin{bmatrix} -1 & 1 \\ 2 & -1 \\ 1 & 1 \\ -2 & 2 \end{bmatrix}\right)^{-1}\begin{bmatrix} -1 & 2 & 1 & -2 \\ 1 & -1 & 1 & 2 \end{bmatrix}\begin{bmatrix} 3 \\ -5 \\ 2 \\ 6 \end{bmatrix}$$

$$= \begin{bmatrix} 10 & -6 \\ -6 & 7 \end{bmatrix}^{-1}\begin{bmatrix} -23 \\ 22 \end{bmatrix} = \frac{1}{34}\begin{bmatrix} 7 & 6 \\ 6 & 10 \end{bmatrix}\begin{bmatrix} -23 \\ 22 \end{bmatrix} = \begin{bmatrix} -0.853 \\ 2.41 \end{bmatrix} \qquad (13.15)$$

B Recursive Least Squares

Computationally, Eq. (13.7) is difficult to implement when m, which is the dimension of $\underline{z}$ and one of the dimensions of $\mathbf{H}$, is large. If new measurements are accumulated so that a sequence of least squares solutions $\hat{\mathbf{x}}$ each based upon additional measurements is desired, each solution of Eq. (13.7) involves a progressively higher dimension m. In the recursive least squares solution [4, 5], the solution $\hat{\mathbf{x}}$ is a linear transformation of the measurements $\underline{\mathbf{z}}$, so a solution based on the first $k + 1$ measurements may be expressed as a linear transformation of the solution based on k measurements plus a correction term based on the $(k + 1)$st measurement alone.

Denote the number of measurements used by arguments of the various quantities; then the least squares solution based on k measurements is

$$\hat{\underline{\mathbf{x}}}(k) = [\mathbf{H}^{\mathrm{T}}(k)\mathbf{H}(k)]^{-1}\mathbf{H}^{\mathrm{T}}(k)\underline{\mathbf{z}}(k) \tag{13.16}$$

Then

$$\hat{\underline{\mathbf{x}}}(k + 1) = [\mathbf{H}^{\mathrm{T}}(k + 1)\mathbf{H}(k + 1)]^{-1}\mathbf{H}^{\mathrm{T}}(k + 1)\underline{\mathbf{z}}(k + 1) \tag{13.17}$$

where $\mathbf{H}(k + 1)$ is $\mathbf{H}(k)$ with an additional row, $\mathbf{h}^{\mathrm{T}}(k + 1)$:

$$\mathbf{H}(k + 1) = \left[\begin{array}{c} \mathbf{H}(k) \\ \hline \mathbf{h}^{\mathrm{T}}(k + 1) \end{array}\right] \tag{13.18}$$

Let the vector of measurements $\underline{\mathbf{z}}(k + 1)$ be the measurement vector $\underline{\mathbf{z}}(k)$ with one additional scalar measurement, z_{k+1}:

$$\underline{\mathbf{z}}(k + 1) = \left[\begin{array}{c} \underline{\mathbf{z}}(k) \\ \hline z_{k+1} \end{array}\right] \tag{13.19}$$

Now

$$\mathbf{H}^{\mathrm{T}}(k + 1)\mathbf{H}(k + 1) = \left[\begin{array}{c|c} \mathbf{H}^{\mathrm{T}}(k) & \mathbf{h}(k + 1) \end{array}\right]\left[\begin{array}{c} \mathbf{H}(k) \\ \hline \mathbf{h}^{\mathrm{T}}(k + 1) \end{array}\right]$$

$$= \mathbf{H}^{\mathrm{T}}(k)\mathbf{H}(k) + \mathbf{h}(k + 1)\mathbf{h}^{\mathrm{T}}(k + 1) \tag{13.20}$$

Defining

$$\mathbf{P}(k) = [\mathbf{H}^{\mathrm{T}}(k)\mathbf{H}(k)]^{-1} \tag{13.21}$$

$$\mathbf{P}(k + 1) = [\mathbf{H}^{\mathrm{T}}(k + 1)\mathbf{H}(k + 1)]^{-1}$$

$$= [\mathbf{H}(k)^{\mathrm{T}}\mathbf{H}(k) + \mathbf{h}(k + 1)\mathbf{h}^{\mathrm{T}}(k + 1)]^{-1}$$

$$= [\mathbf{P}^{-1}(k) + \mathbf{h}(k + 1)\mathbf{h}^{\mathrm{T}}(k + 1)]^{-1} \tag{13.22}$$

and applying the matrix inversion lemma [5, pp. 56–57]

$$(\mathbf{\Gamma} + \mathbf{u}\mathbf{v}^{\mathrm{T}})^{-1} = \mathbf{\Gamma}^{-1} - \frac{\mathbf{\Gamma}^{-1}\mathbf{u}\mathbf{v}^{\mathrm{T}}\mathbf{\Gamma}^{-1}}{1 + \mathbf{v}^{\mathrm{T}}\mathbf{\Gamma}^{-1}\mathbf{u}} \tag{13.23}$$

gives an update equation for $\mathbf{P}(k + 1)$ in terms of $\mathbf{P}(k)$ and the next measurement equation coefficients $\mathbf{h}(k + 1)$:

$$\mathbf{P}(k + 1) = \mathbf{P}(k) - \mathbf{P}(k)\mathbf{h}(k + 1)[\mathbf{h}^{\mathrm{T}}(k + 1)\mathbf{P}(k)\mathbf{h}(k + 1) + 1]^{-1}\mathbf{h}^{\mathrm{T}}(k + 1)\mathbf{P}(k)$$

$$= \mathbf{P}(k) - \mathbf{P}(k)\mathbf{h}(k + 1)c(k + 1)\mathbf{h}^{\mathrm{T}}(k + 1)\mathbf{P}(k) \tag{13.24}$$

where

$$c(k + 1) = [\mathbf{h}^T(k + 1)\mathbf{P}(k)\mathbf{h}(k + 1) + 1]^{-1} \tag{13.25}$$

is a scalar. The inversion involved is then simply a division.

The least squares estimate at step $k + 1$ is

$$\hat{\underline{x}}(k + 1) = \mathbf{P}(k + 1)\mathbf{H}^T(k + 1)\underline{z}(k + 1) = \mathbf{P}(k + 1)[\mathbf{H}^T(k) \mid \mathbf{h}(k + 1)] \begin{bmatrix} \underline{z}(k) \\ \hline \underline{z}_{k+1} \end{bmatrix}$$

$$= \mathbf{P}(k + 1)[\mathbf{H}^T(k)\underline{z}(k) + \mathbf{h}(k + 1)\underline{z}_{k+1}]$$

$$= [\mathbf{P}(k) - \mathbf{P}(k)\mathbf{h}(k + 1)c(k + 1)\mathbf{h}^T(k + 1)\mathbf{P}(k)][\mathbf{H}^T(k)\underline{z}(k)$$

$$\qquad + \mathbf{h}(k + 1)\underline{z}_{k+1}]$$

$$= \mathbf{P}(k)\mathbf{H}^T(k)\underline{z}(k) + \mathbf{P}(k)\mathbf{h}(k + 1)\underline{z}_{k+1}$$

$$\qquad - \mathbf{P}(k)\mathbf{h}(k + 1)c(k + 1)\mathbf{h}^T(k + 1)\mathbf{P}(k)\mathbf{H}^T(k)\underline{z}(k)$$

$$\qquad - \mathbf{P}(k)\mathbf{h}(k + 1)c(k + 1)\mathbf{h}^T(k + 1)\mathbf{P}(k)\mathbf{h}(k + 1)\underline{z}_{k+1}$$

$$= \hat{\underline{x}}(k) + \mathbf{P}(k)\mathbf{h}(k + 1)c(k + 1)[\underline{z}_{k+1} - \mathbf{h}^T(k + 1)\hat{\underline{x}}(k)] \tag{13.26}$$

This remarkable result is that the least squares based on $k + 1$ measurements is the previous estimate, based on k measurements, plus a gain

$$\mathbf{K}(k + 1) = \mathbf{P}(k)\mathbf{h}(k + 1)c(k + 1) \tag{13.27}$$

times the difference between the new measurement $\underline{z}_{k+1}$ and the predicted measurement $\mathbf{h}^T(k + 1)\hat{\underline{x}}(k)$ based on the previous estimate.

The equations for recursive least squares calculation are collected in Table I. To apply them for the estimation of the n-vector $\underline{x}$, we first obtain an initial estimate based on the first n measurements:

$$\hat{\underline{x}}(n) = [\mathbf{H}^T(n)\mathbf{H}(n)]^{-1}\mathbf{H}^T(n)\underline{z}(n) \tag{13.28}$$

TABLE I
Collected Recursive Least Squares Equations

Measurement model (for scalar measurements)

$$\underline{z}_{k+1} = \mathbf{h}^T(k + 1)\mathbf{x}(k + 1) + \underline{v}_{k+1}$$

Predictor–corrector

$$\hat{\underline{x}}(k + 1) = \hat{\underline{x}}(k) + \mathbf{K}(k + 1)[\underline{z}_{k+1} - \mathbf{h}^T(k + 1)\hat{\underline{x}}(k)]$$

Corrector gain

$$\mathbf{K}(k + 1) = \mathbf{P}(k)\mathbf{h}(k + 1)c(k + 1)$$

Gain quantities

$$c(k + 1) = [\mathbf{h}^T(k + 1)\mathbf{P}(k)\mathbf{h}(k + 1) + 1]^{-1}$$

$$\mathbf{P}(k + 1) = \mathbf{P}(k) - \mathbf{P}(k)\mathbf{h}(k + 1)c(k + 1)\mathbf{h}^T(k + 1)\mathbf{P}(k)$$

$$= [\mathbf{I} - \mathbf{K}(k + 1)\mathbf{h}^T(k + 1)]\mathbf{P}(k)$$

At the same time the initial $\mathbf{P}$ matrix

$$\mathbf{P}(n) = [\mathbf{H}^T(n)\mathbf{H}(n)]^{-1} \qquad (13.29)$$

is obtained. Thereafter, the least squares estimate is updated with each new scalar measurement.

Figure 13.1 is a block diagram of the recursive least squares estimator. The filter processes one scalar measurement at a time and generates the least squares estimate based on that and all preceding measurements.

Scalar Recursive Least Squares Example. For the equations and measurements (13.9) considered previously, a recursive solution is

initialization

$$P(1) = [h^T(1)h(1)]^{-1} = \tfrac{1}{4}$$
$$\hat{\underline{x}}(1) = P(1)h^T(1)z_1 = (\tfrac{1}{4})(2)(\underline{3}) = \tfrac{3}{2} \qquad (13.30)$$

update with measurement 2

$$c(2) = [h^T(2)P(1)h(2) + 1]^{-1} = [(-1)(\tfrac{1}{4})(-1) + 1]^{-1} = \tfrac{4}{5}$$
$$K(2) = P(1)h(2)c(2) = (\tfrac{1}{4})(-1)(\tfrac{4}{5}) = -\tfrac{1}{5}$$
$$P(2) = [1 - K(2)h^T(2)]P(1) = [1 - (-\tfrac{1}{5})(-1)](\tfrac{1}{4}) = \tfrac{1}{5} \qquad (13.31)$$
$$\hat{\underline{x}}(2) = \hat{\underline{x}}(1) + K(2)[z_2 - h(2)\hat{\underline{x}}(1)]$$
$$= \tfrac{3}{2} + (-\tfrac{1}{5})[\underline{0} - (-1)(\tfrac{3}{2})] = \tfrac{6}{5}$$

update with measurement 3

$$c(3) = [h^T(3)P(2)h(3) + 1]^{-1} = [(-2)(\tfrac{1}{5})(-2) + 1]^{-1} = \tfrac{5}{9}$$
$$K(3) = P(2)h(3)c(3) = (\tfrac{1}{5})(-2)(\tfrac{5}{9}) = -\tfrac{2}{9}$$
$$P(3) = [1 - K(3)h^T(3)]P(2) = [1 - (-\tfrac{2}{9})(-2)](\tfrac{1}{5}) = \tfrac{1}{9} \qquad (13.32)$$
$$\hat{\underline{x}}(3) = \hat{\underline{x}}(2) + K(3)[z_3 - h(3)\hat{\underline{x}}(2)]$$
$$= \tfrac{6}{5} + (-\tfrac{2}{9})[-2 - (-2)(\tfrac{6}{5})] = \tfrac{10}{9}$$

The process could be continued if there were more measurements.

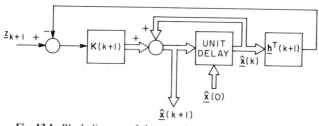

Fig. 13.1. Block diagram of the recursive least squares estimator.

Vector Recursive Least Squares Example.   A recursive solution of the vector estimation problem [Eq. (13.13)] considered previously is

initialization

$$P(2) = [H^T(2)H(2)]^{-1} = \left(\begin{bmatrix} -1 & 2 \\ 1 & -1 \end{bmatrix} \begin{bmatrix} -1 & 1 \\ 2 & -1 \end{bmatrix} \right)^{-1}$$

$$= \begin{bmatrix} 5 & -3 \\ -3 & 2 \end{bmatrix}^{-1} = \begin{bmatrix} 2 & 3 \\ 3 & 5 \end{bmatrix} \tag{13.33}$$

$$\hat{\underline{x}}(2) = P(2)H^T(2)\underline{z}_2 = \begin{bmatrix} 2 & 3 \\ 3 & 5 \end{bmatrix} \begin{bmatrix} -1 & 2 \\ 1 & -1 \end{bmatrix} \begin{bmatrix} 3 \\ -5 \end{bmatrix} = \begin{bmatrix} -2 \\ 1 \end{bmatrix}$$

update with measurement 3

$$c(3) = [h^T(3)P(2)h(3) + 1]^{-1} = \left(\begin{bmatrix} 1 & 1 \end{bmatrix} \begin{bmatrix} 2 & 3 \\ 3 & 5 \end{bmatrix} \begin{bmatrix} 1 \\ 1 \end{bmatrix} + 1 \right)^{-1}$$

$$= \tfrac{1}{14} = 0.071$$

$$K(3) = P(2)h(3)c(3) = \begin{bmatrix} 2 & 3 \\ 3 & 5 \end{bmatrix} \begin{bmatrix} 1 \\ 1 \end{bmatrix} \left(\frac{1}{14} \right) = \begin{bmatrix} 0.357 \\ 0.571 \end{bmatrix}$$

$$P(3) = [I - K(3)h^T(3)](P2)$$

$$= \left(\begin{bmatrix} 1 & 0 \\ 0 & 1 \end{bmatrix} - \begin{bmatrix} 0.357 \\ 0.571 \end{bmatrix} \begin{bmatrix} 1 & 1 \end{bmatrix} \right) \begin{bmatrix} 2 & 3 \\ 3 & 5 \end{bmatrix} \tag{13.34}$$

$$= \begin{bmatrix} 0.215 & 0.145 \\ 0.145 & 0.432 \end{bmatrix}$$

$$\hat{\underline{x}}(3) = \hat{\underline{x}}(2) + K(3)[z_3 - h^T(3)\hat{\underline{x}}(2)]$$

$$= \begin{bmatrix} -2 \\ 1 \end{bmatrix} + \begin{bmatrix} 0.357 \\ 0.571 \end{bmatrix} \left(2 - \begin{bmatrix} 1 & 1 \end{bmatrix} \begin{bmatrix} -2 \\ 1 \end{bmatrix} \right)$$

$$= \begin{bmatrix} -0.929 \\ 2.714 \end{bmatrix}$$

update with measurement 4

$$c(4) = [h^1(4)P(3)h(4) + 1]^{-1}$$

$$= \left(\begin{bmatrix} -2 & 2 \end{bmatrix} \begin{bmatrix} 0.215 & 0.145 \\ 0.145 & 0.432 \end{bmatrix} \begin{bmatrix} -2 \\ 2 \end{bmatrix} + 1 \right)^{-1} = 0.412$$

$$K(4) = P(3)h(4)c(4) = \begin{bmatrix} 0.215 & 0.145 \\ 0.145 & 0.432 \end{bmatrix} \begin{bmatrix} -2 \\ 2 \end{bmatrix} (0.412) \tag{13.35}$$

$$= \begin{bmatrix} -0.0577 \\ 0.236 \end{bmatrix}$$

$$P(4) = [I - K(4)h^T(4)]P(3)$$

$$= \left(\begin{bmatrix} 1 & 0 \\ 0 & 1 \end{bmatrix} - \begin{bmatrix} -0.0577 \\ 0.236 \end{bmatrix} [-2 \quad 2] \right) \begin{bmatrix} 0.215 & 0.145 \\ 0.145 & 0.432 \end{bmatrix}$$

$$= \begin{bmatrix} 0.206 & 0.178 \\ 0.178 & 0.296 \end{bmatrix}$$

$$\hat{\underline{x}}(4) = \hat{\underline{x}}(3) + K(4)[z_4 - h^T(4)\hat{\underline{x}}(3)] \tag{13.35}$$

$$= \begin{bmatrix} -0.929 \\ 2.714 \end{bmatrix} + \begin{bmatrix} -0.0577 \\ 0.236 \end{bmatrix} \left(\underline{6} - [-2 \quad 2] \begin{bmatrix} -0.929 \\ 2.714 \end{bmatrix} \right)$$

$$= \begin{bmatrix} -0.853 \\ 2.41 \end{bmatrix}$$

as we found earlier. If there were additional measurements, they could be incorporated into the estimate in a similar way.

Probabilistic Interpretation of Least Squares   C

If the least squares estimate is interpreted as yielding the "best" or "most likely" value of the estimated quantity, probabilistic assumptions are being made about the measurement errors $\underline{v}_1, \underline{v}_2, \ldots$, as was known to and discussed by Gauss. For the basic least squares problem considered so far, equal weightings of the squares of the measurement errors in the performance measure J to be minimized imply that each measurement has equal likelihood of error and that the errors are independent of one another.

A more general least squares problem minimizes

$$J = \underline{v}^T W \underline{v} \tag{13.36}$$

where W is a symmetric, positive definite, weighting matrix. Then J is a quadratic form in the measurement errors. When we have more confidence in the accuracy of some measurements than of others, we can choose the elements of W to weigh them more heavily than others. In this case the solution for the least squares estimate is

$$\hat{\underline{x}} = (H^T W H)^{-1} H^T W \underline{z} \tag{13.37}$$

This, too, can be expressed recursively.

If the errors $\underline{v}$ are zero mean,

$$E[\underline{v}] = 0 \tag{13.38}$$

with known covariance R,

$$E[\underline{v}\underline{v}^T] = R \tag{13.39}$$

it is natural to choose

$$\mathbf{W} = \mathbf{R}^{-1} \tag{13.40}$$

Indeed, for a constant vector $\mathbf{x}$ to be estimated, this gives the same estimate $\hat{\mathbf{x}}$ as the more general results to follow.

Recursive least square methods can also be designed to incorporate vector, rather than scalar, measurements at each step and to estimate a quantity $\mathbf{x}(n)$ that itself changes with the step number n in a known way.

III LINEAR MINIMUM MEAN SQUARE ESTIMATION

A Kalman Filtering

Rather than adopting a least squares criterion and arguing that the resulting estimate is most probable, Kalman began with a stochastic formulation, including a probabilistic performance index to be minimized. As did Fisher, Kolmogorov, Wiener, and others before him, Kalman sought estimates that were linearly related to the measurements such that the expected sum of squares of the errors between the actual and estimated states,

$$J = E[(\mathbf{x} - \hat{\underline{\mathbf{x}}})^{\mathsf{T}}(\mathbf{x} - \hat{\underline{\mathbf{x}}})] \tag{13.41}$$

was minimized. The state to be estimated could vary in a known way with the step, the state as well as the measurements could be influenced by noise, and the initial state could be described stochastically. The result is now called a *Kalman filter* [6–10].

In general, an estimate linearly related to the measurements may not minimize J; a nonlinear relation might be superior. Kalman found the linear estimator that minimizes (13.41) for any (reasonable) noise statistics. If the noises involved have *Gaussian* probability distributions, it can be shown that the linear estimator is optimum; it is the *best* that can be done.

The problem of linear MMS estimation is straightforward to solve but involves a good deal of detail. Consequently, we will first develop the solution to the basic problem, then indicate how to generalize those results to more complicated situations.

B Stochastic System Model

A sequence of vector measurements $\underline{\mathbf{z}}(1), \underline{\mathbf{z}}(2), \dots$ is modeled as the output of a discrete-time stochastic system [34–38] of the form

$$\underline{\mathbf{x}}(k + 1) = \mathbf{F}(k)\underline{\mathbf{x}}(k) + \underline{\mathbf{w}}(k)$$

$$\underline{\mathbf{z}}(k + 1) = \mathbf{H}(k + 1)\underline{\mathbf{x}}(k + 1) + \underline{\mathbf{v}}(k + 1) \tag{13.42}$$

The state equations of the model are

$$\begin{bmatrix} \underline{x}_1(k+1) \\ \underline{x}_2(k+1) \\ \vdots \\ \underline{x}_n(k+1) \end{bmatrix} = \begin{bmatrix} f_{11}(k) & f_{12}(k) & \cdots & f_{1n}(k) \\ f_{21}(k) & f_{22}(k) & \cdots & f_{2n}(k) \\ \vdots & \vdots & \vdots & \vdots \\ f_{n1}(k) & f_{n2}(k) & \cdots & f_{nn}(k) \end{bmatrix} \begin{bmatrix} \underline{x}_1(k) \\ \underline{x}_2(k) \\ \vdots \\ \underline{x}_n(k) \end{bmatrix} + \begin{bmatrix} \underline{w}_1(k) \\ \underline{w}_2(k) \\ \vdots \\ \underline{w}_n(k) \end{bmatrix} \qquad (13.43)$$

where $\underline{w}(k)$ is a white noise sequence with zero mean and known step-by-step covariance matrix. That the sequence $\underline{w}(k)$ is zero mean is expressed by

$$E[\underline{w}(k)] = 0 \qquad (13.44)$$

where E denotes the expected value. Whiteness of the sequence means that

$$E[\underline{w}(j)\underline{w}^T(k)] = 0 \qquad (13.45)$$

unless $j = k$. That is, $\underline{w}(k)$ is uncorrelated with itself at any other step. At the same step

$$E[\underline{w}(k)\underline{w}^T(k)] = \mathbf{Q}(k) \qquad (13.46)$$

where $\mathbf{Q}(k)$ is a symmetric, positive semidefinite, covariance matrix.

The effects of known inputs can be computed separately, so they are omitted from the model. The measurement equations are

$$\begin{bmatrix} \underline{z}_1(k+1) \\ \underline{z}_2(k+1) \\ \vdots \\ \underline{z}_m(k+1) \end{bmatrix} = \begin{bmatrix} h_{11}(k+1) & h_{12}(k+1) & \cdots & h_{1n}(k+1) \\ h_{21}(k+1) & h_{22}(k+1) & \cdots & h_{2n}(k+1) \\ \vdots & \vdots & \vdots & \vdots \\ h_{m1}(k+1) & h_{m2}(k+1) & \cdots & h_{mn}(k+1) \end{bmatrix} \begin{bmatrix} \underline{x}_1(kH) \\ \underline{x}_2(kH) \\ \vdots \\ \underline{x}_n(k+1) \end{bmatrix} + \begin{bmatrix} \underline{v}_1(k+1) \\ \underline{v}_2(k+1) \\ \vdots \\ \underline{v}_m(k+1) \end{bmatrix}$$

$$(13\text{-}47)$$

where $\underline{v}(k)$ is a white noise sequence with zero mean, known covariance matrix, and is uncorrelated with $\underline{w}(k)$:

$$E[\underline{v}(k)] = 0, \quad E[\underline{v}(j)\underline{v}^T(k)] = 0, \qquad j \neq k$$
$$E[\underline{v}(k)\underline{v}^T(k)] = \mathbf{R}(k), \qquad E[\underline{v}(j)\underline{w}^T(k)] = 0 \qquad (13.48)$$

where $\mathbf{R}(k)$ is symmetric and positive semidefinite.

The initial system state $\underline{x}(0)$ is probabilistic, with zero mean, known positive semidefinite covariance matrix, uncorrelated with $\underline{w}(k)$ and $\underline{v}(k)$:

$$E[\underline{x}(0)] = 0, \qquad E[\underline{x}(0)\underline{x}^T(0)] = \mathbf{P}_0$$
$$E[\underline{x}(0)\underline{w}^T(k)] = 0, \qquad E[\underline{x}(0)\underline{v}^T(k)] = 0 \qquad (13.49)$$

The relationships between the signals in the stochastic model are shown in Fig. 13.2.

Example of Stochastic System Response. For a probabilistic initial condition $x(0)$, a typical response of the first-order stochastic discrete-time system

$$\underline{x}(k+1) = 0.9\underline{x}(k) + \underline{w}(k), \qquad \underline{z}(k) = \underline{x}(k) + \underline{v}(k) \qquad (13.50)$$

is plotted in Fig. 13.3 for the white noise sequences $\underline{w}(k)$ and $\underline{v}(k)$ shown.

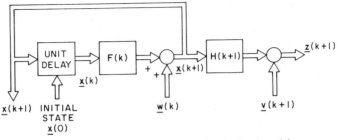

Fig. 13.2. Block diagram of the stochastic signal model.

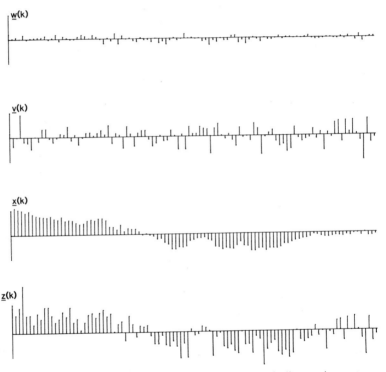

Fig. 13.3. Noise inputs and response of an example stochastic discrete-time system.

C Problem Statement and Notation

As measurements are received in time sequence, we want to estimate the state $\underline{x}$ of the stochastic system model, using all measurements presently available. At each time step the system state $\underline{x}$ changes, and a new measurement $\underline{z}$ becomes available.

For the stochastic system model described by Eqs. (13.42)–(13.49) involving zero-mean uncorrelated white noise sequences driving the state and corrupting the measurements, we want to find, at each step k, the linear MMS estimate of $\underline{x}(k)$ based on the measurements from step 1 through the present step k.

The notation used here, which is common, is that the estimate of a quantity such as $\underline{x}$ is denoted by a "hat" over the symbol for the quantity (i.e., $\hat{\underline{x}}$). The arguments for estimates are written in the form (i/j), where the first index i is the step of the quantity estimated, and the second index j is the number of measurements used in making the estimate. Some examples follow:

$\hat{\underline{x}}(k + 1 \mid k)$ is the linear MMS estimate of $\underline{x}(k + 1)$ based on
$\underline{z}(1), \underline{z}(2), \ldots, \underline{z}(k)$.
$\hat{\underline{x}}(k + 1 \mid k + 1)$ is the linear MMS estimate of $\underline{x}(k + 1)$ based on
$\underline{z}(1), \underline{z}(2), \ldots, \underline{z}(k + 1)$.
$\hat{\underline{z}}(k + 1 \mid k)$ is the linear MMS estimate of $\underline{z}(k + 1)$ based on
$\underline{z}(1), \underline{z}(2), \ldots, \underline{z}(k)$.

Similar definitions are made for estimates $\hat{\underline{w}}(k \mid k)$, $\hat{\underline{v}}(k + 1 \mid k)$, etc. Some other useful definitions are the following:

$\underline{\Delta x}(k \mid k) = \underline{x}(k) - \hat{\underline{x}}(k \mid k)$ is the state estimation error.
$\underline{\Delta x}(k + 1 \mid k) = \underline{x}(k + 1) - \hat{\underline{x}}(k + 1 \mid k)$ is the state prediction error.
$\underline{\Delta z}(k + 1 \mid k) = \underline{z}(k + 1) - \hat{\underline{z}}(k + 1 \mid k)$ is the measurement prediction error.

Linear MMS Estimation Properties   D

Four results for linear MMS estimation are keys to the development to follow:

Solution in Terms of Expected Values. If $\underline{x}$ and $\underline{z}$ are zero-mean random vectors, the linear MMS estimate of $\underline{x}$ based on $\underline{z}$ is

$$\hat{\underline{x}} = E[\underline{x}\underline{z}^{\mathrm{T}}]\{E[\underline{z}\underline{z}^{\mathrm{T}}]\}^{-1}\underline{z} \tag{13.51}$$

Orthogonality of Estimate Error and Data. This result, known as the *orthogonality principle*, is that if $\underline{x}$, $\underline{z}$, and $\hat{\underline{x}}$ are as above, then

$$E[\underline{z}(\underline{x} - \hat{\underline{x}})^{\mathrm{T}}] = \mathbf{0} \tag{13.52}$$

The collection of measurements $\underline{z}$ and the estimate error $\underline{x} - \hat{\underline{x}}$ are orthogonal.

Estimate of a Linear Composition. If

$$\underline{x} - A\underline{y} + B\underline{w} \tag{13.53}$$

the linear MMS estimate of $\underline{x}$ based on $\underline{z}$ is

$$\hat{\underline{x}} = A\hat{\underline{y}} + B\hat{\underline{w}} \tag{13.54}$$

where $\hat{\underline{y}}$ is the estimate of $\underline{y}$ and $\hat{\underline{w}}$ is the estimate of $\underline{w}$.

Incorporation of Orthogonal Data.   If $\underline{x}$, $\underline{z}_1$, and $\underline{z}_2$ are zero-mean random vectors, with $\underline{z}_1$ and $\underline{z}_2$ orthogonal,

$$E[\underline{z}_1\underline{z}_2^T] = 0 \tag{13.55}$$

the linear MMS estimate of $\underline{x}$ based on $\underline{z}_1$ and $\underline{z}_2$ is

$$\hat{\underline{x}} = \hat{\underline{x}}_1 + \hat{\underline{x}}_2 \tag{13.56}$$

where $\hat{\underline{x}}_1$ is the estimate of $\underline{x}$ based on $\underline{z}_1$ and $\hat{\underline{x}}_2$ is the estimate of $\underline{x}$ based on $\underline{z}_2$.

E   Prediction and Correction

The derivation of the Kalman filter is now outlined, and key results are highlighted with asterisks by the equation numbers. Using the linear composition result [Eq. (13.54)], we obtain the optimal estimate of $\underline{x}(k + 1)$ given data through the kth step:

$$\hat{\underline{x}}(k + 1\,|\,k) = \mathbf{F}(k)\hat{\underline{x}}(k\,|\,k) + \hat{\underline{w}}(k\,|\,k) \tag{13.57}$$

Since $\underline{w}(k)$ and $\underline{z}(j)$, $j = 1, 2, \ldots, k$, are uncorrelated,

$$\hat{\underline{w}}(k\,|\,k) = 0 \tag{13.58}$$

and

$$\hat{\underline{x}}(k + 1\,|\,k) = \mathbf{F}(k)\hat{\underline{x}}(k\,|\,k), \qquad \hat{\underline{x}}(0\,|\,0) = 0 \tag{13.59}*$$

The best prediction of the state at the next step is to pass the previous step's estimate through the system state coupling matrix $\mathbf{F}$.

Similarly, applying the linear composition result (13.54) to the stochastic system output equation

$$\underline{z}(k + 1) = \mathbf{H}(k + 1)\underline{x}(k + 1) + \underline{v}(k + 1) \tag{13.60}$$

gives

$$\hat{\underline{z}}(k + 1\,|\,k) = \mathbf{H}(k + 1)\hat{\underline{x}}(k + 1\,|\,k) + \hat{\underline{v}}(k + 1\,|\,k) \tag{13.61}$$

Since $\underline{v}(k)$ and $\underline{z}(j)$ are uncorrelated for $k \neq j$,

$$\hat{\underline{v}}(k + 1\,|\,k) = 0 \tag{13.62}$$

so

$$\hat{\underline{z}}(k + 1\,|\,k) = \mathbf{H}(k + 1)\hat{\underline{x}}(k + 1\,|\,k) \tag{13.63}*$$

The best prediction of the next measurement is to pass the predicted state through the measurement coupling matrix $\mathbf{H}$.

The measurement prediction errors

$$\underline{\Delta z}(k + 1\,|\,k) = \underline{z}(k + 1) - \hat{\underline{z}}(k + 1\,|\,k) \tag{13.64}*$$

are also termed the *measurement residuals*. Rather than using the original measurements $\underline{z}(1), \underline{z}(2), \ldots, \underline{z}(k), \ldots$, it is expedient for us to use the measurement residuals $\underline{\Delta z}(1\,|\,0), \underline{\Delta z}(2\,|\,1), \ldots, \underline{\Delta z}(k\,|\,k-1), \ldots$ as the measurements. The two are equivalent, since either may be found deterministically from the other. Collecting the residuals through step k into a single vector of measurements,

$$
\underline{\Delta z}_k = \begin{bmatrix} \underline{\Delta z}(1\,|\,0) \\ \hline \underline{\Delta z}(2\,|\,1) \\ \hline \vdots \\ \hline \underline{\Delta z}(k\,|\,k-1) \end{bmatrix} \tag{13.65}
$$

we have that the quantity $\hat{\underline{x}}(k+1\,|\,k)$ denotes the linear MMS estimate of $\underline{x}(k+1)$ based on $\underline{\Delta z}_k$. Using the orthogonality principle [Eq. (13.53)], we see that the measurement and the estimate error are orthogonal:

$$
E\{\underline{\Delta z}_k[\underline{x}(k+1) - \hat{\underline{x}}(k+1\,|\,k)]^T\} = \mathbf{0} \tag{13.66}
$$

Postmultiplying by $\mathbf{H}^T(k+1)$, we get

$$
E\{\underline{\Delta z}_k[\underline{x}(k+1) - \hat{\underline{x}}(k+1\,|\,k)]^T\mathbf{H}^T(k+1)\} = E\{\underline{\Delta z}_k[\underline{z}(k+1) - \hat{\underline{z}}(k+1\,|\,k)]^T\}
$$
$$
= E[\underline{\Delta z}_k\underline{\Delta z}^T(k+1\,|\,k)] \tag{13.67}
$$

Since the collection of measurements through step k, $\underline{\Delta z}_k$, and the step $k+1$ measurements, $\underline{\Delta z}(k+1\,|\,k)$, are orthogonal, any linear MMS estimates based on $\underline{\Delta z}_k$ and $\underline{\Delta z}(k+1\,|\,k)$ are, according to Eq. (13.57), the sum of the two individual estimates:

$$
\hat{\underline{x}}(k+1\,|\,k+1) = \hat{\underline{x}}(k+1\,|\,k)
$$
$$
+ \text{[linear MMS estimate of } \underline{x}(k+1) \text{ based on } \underline{\Delta z}(k+1\,|\,k)] \tag{13.68}
$$

Incorporation of new data in the form of the residuals only involves making additive corrections to the previous predictions, not complete recalculation. Applying Eq. (13.55) and defining the *Kalman gain* $\mathbf{K}(k+1)$ as

$$
\mathbf{K}(k+1) = E[\underline{x}(k+1)\underline{\Delta z}^T(k+1\,|\,k)]\{E[\underline{\Delta z}(k+1\,|\,k)\underline{\Delta z}^T(k+1\,|\,k)]\}^{-1}
$$
$$
\tag{13.69}
$$

yields the result

$$
\hat{\underline{x}}(k+1\,|\,k+1) = \hat{\underline{x}}(k+1\,|\,k) + \mathbf{K}(k+1)\underline{\Delta z}(k+1\,|\,k) \tag{13.70}*
$$

Kalman Gain and Error Covariances   F

   The most involved part of Kalman filtering is the calculation of the sequence of Kalman gains $\mathbf{K}(1), \mathbf{K}(2), \mathbf{K}(3), \ldots$. We now derive formulas for recursive calculation of the gain sequence. The result is a set of three coupled matrix equations, from which the Kalman gains can be computed. Using

$$\underline{\Delta z}(k + 1 \mid k) = \underline{z}(k + 1) - \hat{\underline{z}}(k + 1 \mid k)$$

$$= \mathbf{H}(k + 1)\underline{x}(k + 1) + \underline{v}(k + 1) - \mathbf{H}(k + 1)\hat{\underline{x}}(k + 1 \mid k) \quad (13.71)$$

and the fact that $\underline{v}(k + 1)$ and $\underline{\Delta x}(k + 1 \mid k)$ are uncorrelated,

$$E[\underline{\Delta x}(k + 1 \mid k)\underline{v}^{\mathrm{T}}(k + 1)] = E[\underline{v}(k + 1)\underline{\Delta x}^{\mathrm{T}}(k + 1 \mid k)] = \mathbf{0} \quad (13.72)$$

yields the result that

$$E[\underline{\Delta z}(k + 1 \mid k)\underline{\Delta z}^{\mathrm{T}}(k + 1 \mid k)] = \mathbf{H}(k + 1)\mathbf{P}(k + 1 \mid k)\mathbf{H}^{\mathrm{T}}(k + 1) + \mathbf{R}(k + 1)$$

$$(13.73)$$

where

$$\mathbf{P}(k + 1 \mid k) = E[\underline{\Delta x}(k + 1 \mid k)\underline{\Delta x}^{\mathrm{T}}(k + 1 \mid k)] \quad (13.74)$$

is the *state prediction error covariance.*

Similarly, since $\underline{v}(k + 1)$ and $\underline{\Delta x}(k + 1 \mid k)$ are uncorrelated,

$$E[\underline{\Delta x}(k + 1 \mid k)\underline{v}^{\mathrm{T}}(k + 1)] = \mathbf{0} \quad (13.75)$$

it follows that

$$E[\underline{x}(k + 1)\underline{\Delta z}^{\mathrm{T}}(k + 1 \mid k)] = \mathbf{P}(k + 1 \mid k)\mathbf{H}^{\mathrm{T}}(k + 1) \quad (13.76)$$

so the Kalman gain [Eq. (13.69)] is

$$\mathbf{K}(k + 1) = \mathbf{P}(k + 1 \mid k)\mathbf{H}^{\mathrm{T}}(k + 1)[\mathbf{H}(k + 1)\mathbf{P}(k + 1 \mid k)\mathbf{H}^{\mathrm{T}}(k + 1) + \mathbf{R}(k + 1)]^{-1}$$

$$(13.77)^*$$

We can also express the state prediction error covariance in terms of the *state estimation error covariance,*

$$\mathbf{P}(k \mid k) = E[\underline{\Delta x}(k \mid k)\underline{\Delta x}^{\mathrm{T}}(k \mid k)] \quad (13.78)$$

using the fact that $\underline{\Delta x}(k \mid k)$ and $\underline{w}(k)$ are uncorrelated:

$$E[\underline{\Delta x}(k \mid k)\underline{w}^{\mathrm{T}}(k)] = E[\underline{w}(k)\underline{\Delta x}^{\mathrm{T}}(k)] = \mathbf{0} \quad (13.79)$$

The result is

$$\mathbf{P}(k + 1 \mid k) = \mathbf{F}(k)\mathbf{P}(k \mid k)\mathbf{F}^{\mathrm{T}}(k) + \mathbf{Q}(k), \qquad \mathbf{P}(0 \mid 0) = \mathbf{P}_0 \quad (13.80)^*$$

Since $\underline{\Delta x}(k + 1 \mid k)$ and $\underline{v}(k + 1)$ are uncorrelated,

$$E[\underline{v}(k + 1)\underline{\Delta x}^{\mathrm{T}}(k + 1 \mid k)] = E[\underline{\Delta x}(k + 1 \mid k)\underline{v}^{\mathrm{T}}(k + 1)] = 0 \quad (13.81)$$

the state estimate error covariance is expressible as

$$\mathbf{P}(k + 1 \mid k + 1) = [\mathbf{I} - \mathbf{K}(k + 1)\mathbf{H}(k + 1)]\mathbf{P}(k + 1 \mid k)[\mathbf{I} - \mathbf{K}(k + 1)\mathbf{H}(k + 1)]^{\mathrm{T}}$$

$$+ \mathbf{K}(k + 1)\mathbf{R}(k + 1)\mathbf{K}^{\mathrm{T}}(k + 1) \quad (13.82)$$

which, using Eq. (13.77), simplifies to

$$\mathbf{P}(k + 1 \mid k + 1) = [\mathbf{I} - \mathbf{K}(k + 1)\mathbf{H}(k + 1)]\mathbf{P}(k + 1 \mid k) \quad (13.83)^*$$

DISCRETE KALMAN FILTERING EXAMPLES   IV

The Basic Filter   A

The equations connected with Kalman filtering are collected in Table II. The Kalman filter for an nth-order linear discrete-time stochastic system is another nth-order linear discrete-time system. The filter input is the system measurement, and the filter output is the optimally estimated system state, as indicated in Fig. 13.4.

Figure 13.5 is a block diagram showing the relationships between the signals in the Kalman filter. The filter consists of a model of the system with zero noise inputs replacing the actual (unknown) system noise inputs and initial conditions determined by the measurement residuals through the Kalman gain **K**.

Fig. 13.4. Kalman filtering a system output to optimally estimate the system state.

TABLE II
Kalman Filter Equations

System model

$$\underline{x}(k + 1) = F(k)\underline{x}(k) + \underline{w}(k)$$

$$\underline{z}(k + 1) = H(k + 1)\underline{x}(k + 1) + \underline{v}(k + 1)$$

Predictor

$$\hat{\underline{x}}(k + 1 \,|\, k) = F(k)\hat{\underline{x}}(k \,|\, k), \qquad \hat{\underline{x}}(0 \,|\, 0) = \mathbf{0}$$

$$\hat{\underline{z}}(k + 1 \,|\, k) = H(k + 1)\hat{\underline{x}}(k + 1 \,|\, k)$$

Corrector

$$\hat{\underline{x}}(k + 1 \,|\, k + 1) = \hat{\underline{x}}(k + 1 \,|\, k) + K(k + 1)\underline{\Delta z}(k + 1 \,|\, k)$$

$$\underline{\Delta z}(k + 1 \,|\, k) = \underline{z}(k + 1) - \underline{z}(k + 1 \,|\, k)$$

Kalman filter gain

$$K(k + 1) = P(k + 1 \,|\, k)H^{T}(k + 1)[H(k + 1)P(k + 1 \,|\, k)H^{T}(k + 1) + R(k + 1)]^{-1}$$

Covariances

$$P(k + 1 \,|\, k) = F(k)P(k \,|\, k)F^{T}(k) + Q(k), \qquad P(0 \,|\, 0) = P_0$$

$$P(k + 1 \,|\, k + 1) = [I - K(k + 1)H(k + 1)]P(k + 1 \,|\, k)$$

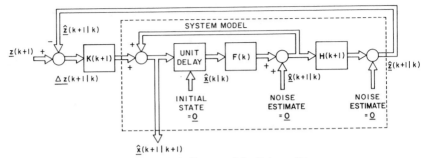

Fig. 13.5. Block diagram of the Kalman filter.

Some of the advantages of the recursive solution are

1. The filtering is readily performed by a digital computer.
2. A fixed amount of computer memory is required.
3. The required matrix inversions are of fixed order.
4. The algorithm is in a feedback configuration.
5. The **P** matrix computations constitute a built-in error analysis.
6. Kalman filtering is a cornerstone to a general estimation and control design philosophy.

B First-Order System Example

Consider the first-order stochastic system model

$$x(k + 1) = 0.5\underline{x}(k) + \underline{w}(k), \qquad \underline{z}(k + 1) = 3\underline{x}(k + 1) + \underline{v}(k + 1) \quad (13.84)$$

with

$$E\{\underline{x}^2(0)\} = P_0 = 10$$

$$E\{\underline{w}^2(k)\} = Q = 4 \qquad \text{for each step } k \qquad (13.85)$$

$$E\{\underline{v}^2(k)\} = R = 5 \qquad \text{for each step } k$$

A block diagram of the system is given in Fig. 13.6(a). The Kalman filter predictor equations for the system are

$$\hat{\underline{x}}(k + 1 \,|\, k) = \tfrac{1}{2}\hat{\underline{x}}(k \,|\, k), \qquad \hat{\underline{x}}(0 \,|\, 0) = 0$$

$$\hat{\underline{z}}(k + 1 \,|\, k) = 3\hat{\underline{x}}(k + 1 \,|\, k) \qquad (13.86)$$

The corrector equations are

$$\hat{\underline{x}}(k + 1 \,|\, k + 1) = \hat{\underline{x}}(k + 1 \,|\, k) + K(k + 1)\underline{\Delta z}(k + 1)$$

$$\underline{\Delta z}(k + 1) = \underline{z}(k + 1) - \hat{\underline{z}}(k + 1 \,|\, k) \qquad (13.87)$$

A block diagram of the filter is given in Fig. 13.6(b).

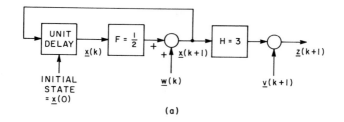

(a)

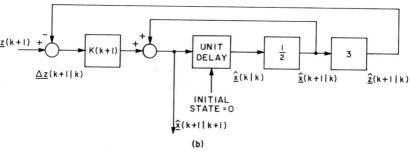

(b)

Fig. 13.6. Block diagrams for an example first-order stochastic system and the corresponding Kalman filter: (a) stochastic system model; (b) Kalman filter for the system.

In the general case, calculation of the sequence of Kalman gains, $\mathbf{K}(0), \mathbf{K}(1), \ldots$, which may be computed and stored in advance, involves repetitive cycles of three computations:

1. estimate error covariance $\mathbf{P}(k \mid k)$, beginning with $\mathbf{P}(0 \mid 0) = \mathbf{P}_0$
2. prediction error covariance $\mathbf{P}(k + 1 \mid k)$
3. Kalman gain $\mathbf{K}(k + 1)$

For the scalar example,

$$
\begin{aligned}
\text{first} \quad & \begin{cases} P(0 \mid 0) = 10 \\ P(1 \mid 0) = \tfrac{1}{4} P(0 \mid 0) + 4 = 6.5 \\ K(1) = \dfrac{3P(1 \mid 0)}{9P(1 \mid 0) + 5} = 0.307 \end{cases} \\[2ex]
\text{second} \quad & \begin{cases} P(1 \mid 1) = \{1 - 3K(1)\} P(1 \mid 0) = 0.512 \\ P(2 \mid 1) = \tfrac{1}{4} P(1 \mid 1) + 4 = 4.13 \\ K(2) = \dfrac{3P(2 \mid 1)}{9P(2 \mid 1) + 4} = 0.294 \end{cases} \qquad (13.88) \\[2ex]
\text{third} \quad & \begin{cases} P(2 \mid 2) = \{1 - 3K(2)\} P(2 \mid 1) = 0.49 \\ \vdots \end{cases}
\end{aligned}
$$

Computer-generated calculations of these quantities are given in Table III.

TABLE III

Computer-Generated Covariances and Kalman Gain for the Example System

Step k	$P(k\,|\,k)$	$P(k+1\,|\,k)$	$K(k+1)$
0	10	6.5	0.307086614
2	0.511811024	4.127952756	0.293793490
3	0.489655817	4.122413954	0.293746674
4	0.489577790	4.122394448	0.293746509
5	0.489577515	4.122394379	0.293746508
6	0.489577514	4.122394379	0.293746508
7 ⎫ ⋮ ⎬		No change from the line above	

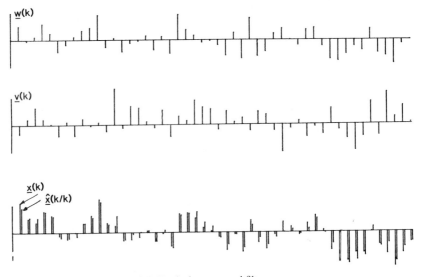

Fig. 13.7. Typical system and filter responses.

Typical white noise sequences $w(k)$ and $v(k)$, the corresponding actual system state $x(k)$, and the Kalman filter estimates of the system state $\hat{x}(k\,|\,k)$, from the noise-corrupted measurements, are plotted in Fig. 13.7.

C Scalar Kalman Filters in BASIC

Table IV gives the listing for a digital computer program, written in BASIC, for generating first-order stochastic system states and measurements, then Kalman filtering the measurements to estimate the states. Data for the example of the previous section was obtained with this program.

TABLE IV

BASIC Program to Compute First-Order Stochastic Model States and Measurements and Kalman Filter Estimates of the Model States from the Measurements

```
100        PRINT "FIRST ORDER KALMAN FILTER"
110        REM SET SYSTEM PARAMETERS
120        F = 0.5
130        H = 3
140        P = 10
150        Q = 4
160        R = 5
170        REM XE IS STATE ESTIMATE X(K/K)
180        K = 0
190        XE = 0

200        REM SET INITIAL STATE X OF MODEL
210        C = 0
220        FOR I = 1 TO 12
230        C = C + RND
240        NEXT I
250        X = P * P * (C-6)

260        REM PRINT TABLE HEADING
270        PRINT "STEP K", "STATE X", "NOISE W", "NOISE V", "MEAS Z",
           "P(K/K)", "P(K + 1/K)", "K(K + 1)", "EST XE"

300        REM COMPUTE MODEL STATE X
310        C = 0
320        FOR I = 1 TO 12
330        C = C + RND
340        NEXT I
350        W = Q * Q * (C-6)
360        X = F * X + W

400        REM COMPUTE MEASUREMENT Z
410        C = 0
420        FOR I = 1 TO 12
430        C = C + RND
440        NEXT I
450        V = R * R * (C-6)
460        Z = H * X + V

500        REM COMPUTE PREDICTION COVARIANCE P1
510        P1 = F * P * F + Q
520        REM COMPUTE KALMAN GAIN A
530        A = (P1 * H)/(H * P1 * H + R)

550        REM COMPUTE STATE PREDICTION X1
560        X1 = F * XE
570        REM COMPUTE MEASUREMENT PREDICTION Z1
580        Z1 = H * X1

600        REM COMPUTE STATE ESTIMATE XE
610        XE = A * (Z - Z1) + X1
```

(continued)

TABLE IV (*Continued*)

650	REM PRINT RESULTS
660	PRINT K, W, V, X, Z, P, P1, A, XE
700	REM UPDATE ESTIMATE COVARIANCE
710	P = (1 − A ∗ H) ∗ P1
750	REM INCREMENT STEP K AND LOOP
760	K = K + 1
770	GO TO 300
800	STOP
810	END

The program uses the RND function, which supplies random numbers in the range (0, 1). Some BASIC compilers instead recognize RND1 or RND(1) as this function. Twelve such random numbers are added, and their mean of 6 subtracted to give a nearly Gaussian probability distribution with unit covariance.[‡] A typical sequence of program steps ending with X being zero-mean Gaussian random with covariance P are 200–250 in the table.

D Multivariable Kalman Filter Programs

Programming a second-order Kalman filter in a language such as BASIC or FORTRAN is probably easiest if we code the individual scalar equations. For Kalman filters of third and higher order it is expedient to organize the computations in matrix form. Below is an outline of the program steps that may be used to perform Kalman filtering according to the equations summarized at the beginning of this section:

1. Set the step index $k = 0$.
2. Initialize the state estimate vector $\hat{\mathbf{x}}(0|0) = \mathbf{0}$.
3. Initialize the state estimate error covariance matrix $\mathbf{P}(0|0) = \mathbf{P}_0$.
4. Compute the next state prediction error covariance $\mathbf{P}(k + 1|k) = \mathbf{F}(k)\mathbf{P}(k|k)\mathbf{F}^T(k) + \mathbf{Q}(k)$.
5. Compute the matrix $\mathbf{S} = \mathbf{H}(k + 1)\mathbf{P}(k + 1)|k)\mathbf{H}^T(k + 1) + \mathbf{R}(k + 1)$.
6. Compute the matrix inverse $\mathbf{S}^{-1}$.
7. Compute the next Kalman gain $\mathbf{K}(k + 1) = \mathbf{P}(k + 1|k)\mathbf{H}^T(k + 1)\mathbf{S}^{-1}$.
8. Compute the next state estimate error covariance $\mathbf{P}(k + 1|k + 1) = [\mathbf{I} − \mathbf{K}(k + 1)\mathbf{H}(k + 1)]\mathbf{P}(k + 1|k)$.
9. Compute the next predicted state $\hat{\mathbf{x}}(k + 1|k) = \mathbf{F}(k)\hat{\mathbf{x}}(k|k)$.
10. Read the next measurement $\mathbf{z}(k + 1)$.

[‡] R. W. Hamming, *Introduction to Applied Numerical Analysis*, McGraw-Hill, New York, 1971, Chap. 14.

11. Compute the measurement residual

$$\underline{\Delta z}(k + 1 \mid k) = \underline{z}(k + 1) - \mathbf{H}(k + 1)\hat{\underline{x}}(k + 1).$$

12. Compute the state estimate

$$\hat{\underline{x}}(k + 1 \mid k + 1) = \hat{\underline{x}}(k + 1 \mid k) + \mathbf{K}(k + 1)\underline{\Delta z}(k + 1 \mid k).$$

13. Increment k by 1.
14. Output the state estimate.
15. Return to step 4.

The complexity of the operations in these steps is relatively high if matrix operation commands are not available to the programmer. Each matrix multiplication, for example, if programmed in terms of scalar elements, involves three nested program loops or the equivalent number of individual scalar assignments.

Some measure of the computational requirement is given below, where each of the above steps is implemented in a straightforward way, as one might do in hand calculation. Some savings are possible through clever combination of some of the operations and through exploiting the symmetries of $\mathbf{Q}(k)$, $\mathbf{R}(k)$, $\mathbf{P}(k + 1 \mid k)$, and $\mathbf{P}(k \mid k)$. However, it is evident that the computations are not trivial. Clearly, a careful and systematic approach is needed.

In the following analysis of the arithmetic operations to accomplish Kalman filtering, n is the order of the stochastic system model (and of the Kalman filter) and m is the dimension of the system measurement vector:

1. Assignment of zero to scalar
2. Assignment of zero to an n-vector
3. Assignment of zero to an $n \times n$ matrix
4. Two $n \times n$ matrix multiplications and one $n \times n$ matrix addition
5. Multiplication of an $n \times n$ matrix by an $n \times m$ matrix, multiplication of an $m \times n$ matrix by an $n \times m$ matrix, and addition of two $m \times m$ matrices
6. Inversion of an $m \times m$ matrix.
7. Multiplication of an $n \times m$ matrix by an $m \times m$ matrix, and multiplication of an $n \times n$ matrix by an $n \times m$ matrix
8. Multiplication of an $n \times m$ matrix by an $m \times n$ matrix, subtraction of two $n \times n$ matrices, and multiplication of two $n \times n$ matrices
9. Multiplication of an $n \times n$ matrix by an n-vector
10. Acquisition of an m-vector of measurements
11. Multiplication of an $m \times n$ matrix by an n-vector, and subtraction of two m-vectors
12. Multiplication of an $n \times m$ matrix by an m-vector, and subtraction of two n-vectors
13. Addition of unity to a scalar
14. Transfer of an n-vector
15. Performance of a program jump

The matrix inversion needed in step 6 is $m \times m$, where m is the dimension of the measurement vector. It is common to deal with systems of order n up to perhaps 18, but with the measurement dimension m only up to about 6. If the number of model outputs m is 1, then the matrix inversion needed is simply division by a scalar. If m is 2, the inverse of the resulting 2×2 matrix is

$$\begin{bmatrix} s_{11} & s_{12} \\ s_{12} & s_{22} \end{bmatrix}^{-1} = \frac{1}{s_{11}s_{22} - s_{12}s_{21}} \begin{bmatrix} s_{22} & -s_{12} \\ -s_{21} & s_{11} \end{bmatrix} \qquad (13.89)$$

For m larger than 2 a numerical matrix inversion routine, such as Gauss–Jordan pivoting,[‡] is used. The existence of the inverse is guaranteed if $\mathbf{R}(k + 1)$ is positive definite (i.e., if some measurement noise is modeled).

If the model system is step-varying so that $\mathbf{F}(k)$ and $\mathbf{H}(k + 1)$ are not constant, or if its statistics $\mathbf{Q}(k)$ and $\mathbf{R}(k)$ vary with step, then these quantities must be stored in advance or calculated at each step from formulas.

V EXTENSIONS

A Noise Coupling Matrices

If the system model has a matrix $\mathbf{L}(k)$ coupling the noise $\underline{\mathbf{w}}(k)$ to the state equations

$$\underline{\mathbf{x}}(k + 1) = \mathbf{F}(k)\underline{\mathbf{x}}(k) + \mathbf{L}(k)\underline{\mathbf{w}}(k) = \mathbf{F}(k)\underline{\mathbf{x}}(k) + \underline{\mathbf{w}}'(k) \qquad (13.90)$$

the previous Kalman filter equations apply, but the state noise covariance $\mathbf{Q}(k)$ is replaced by

$$\mathbf{Q}'(k) = E[\underline{\mathbf{w}}'(k)\underline{\mathbf{w}}'^{\mathrm{T}}(k)] = E[\mathbf{L}(k)\underline{\mathbf{w}}(k)\underline{\mathbf{w}}^{\mathrm{T}}(k)\mathbf{L}^{\mathrm{T}}(k)]$$

$$= \mathbf{L}(k)E[\underline{\mathbf{w}}(k)\underline{\mathbf{w}}^{\mathrm{T}}(k)]\mathbf{L}^{\mathrm{T}}(k) = \mathbf{L}(k)\mathbf{Q}(k)\mathbf{L}^{\mathrm{T}}(k) \qquad (13.91)$$

Similarly, if the system model has a matrix coupling of the noise $\underline{\mathbf{v}}(k)$ to the measurements,

$$\underline{\mathbf{z}}(k) = \mathbf{H}(k)\underline{\mathbf{x}}(k) + \mathbf{M}(k)\underline{\mathbf{v}}(k) = \mathbf{H}(k)\underline{\mathbf{x}}(k) + \underline{\mathbf{v}}'(k) \qquad (13.92)$$

The measurement noise covariance $\mathbf{R}(k)$ is simply replaced in the filter equations by

$$\mathbf{R}'(k) = E[\underline{\mathbf{v}}'(k)\underline{\mathbf{v}}'^{\mathrm{T}}(k)] = E[\mathbf{M}(k)\underline{\mathbf{v}}(k)\underline{\mathbf{v}}^{\mathrm{T}}(k)\mathbf{M}^{\mathrm{T}}(k)]$$

$$= \mathbf{M}(k)\mathbf{R}(k)\mathbf{M}^{\mathrm{T}}(k) \qquad (13.93)$$

[‡] M. L. James, G. M. Smith, and J. C. Wolford, *Applied Numerical Methods for Digital Computations*, 2nd ed. Harper and Row, New York, 1977, chap. 3.

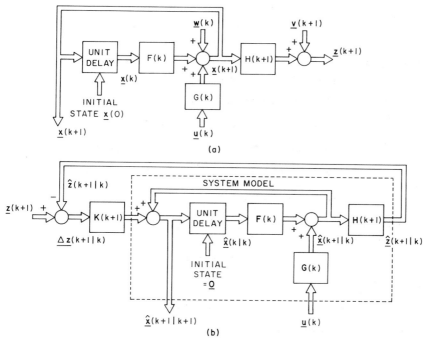

Fig. 13.8. Incorporating deterministic inputs into the Kalman filter: (a) stochastic system model; (b) Kalman filter.

Deterministic Inputs   B

If the system model has deterministic inputs $\mathbf{u}(k)$,

$$\underline{\mathbf{x}}(k + 1) = \mathbf{F}(k)\underline{\mathbf{x}}(k) + \underline{\mathbf{w}}(k) + \mathbf{G}(k)\mathbf{u}(k) \tag{13.94}$$

they are incorporated into the system model portion of the Kalman filter, as shown in Fig. 13.8. In essence, the filter is adding the known effects of the inputs to the estimates while removing them from the measurement residuals. Only the Kalman filter predictor equation is changed; the term involving the input $\mathbf{u}(k)$ is added as follows:

$$\hat{\underline{\mathbf{x}}}(k + 1 \,|\, k) = \mathbf{F}(k)\hat{\underline{\mathbf{x}}}(k \,|\, k) + \mathbf{G}(k)\mathbf{u}(k) \tag{13.95}$$

Nonzero Noise and Initial Condition Means   C

If a noise source, say $\underline{\mathbf{w}}(k)$, has known nonzero mean,

$$E[\underline{\mathbf{w}}(k)] = \mathbf{b}(k) \tag{13.96}$$

a new zero-mean noise signal

$$\underline{w}'(k) = \underline{w}(k) - b(k) \qquad (13.97)$$

is defined, and the system is considered to have zero-mean noise input $\underline{w}'(k)$ plus the deterministic input $b(k)$. The covariance of $\underline{w}'(k)$ is

$$\begin{aligned}
Q'(k) &= E\{[\underline{w}(k) - b(k)][\underline{w}(k) - b(k)]^T\} \\
&= E[\underline{w}(k)\underline{w}^T(k) - b(k)\underline{w}^T(k) - \underline{w}(k)b^T(k) + b(k)b^T(k)] \\
&= Q(k) - b(k)E[\underline{w}^T(k)] - E[\underline{w}(k)]b^T + b(k)b^T(k) \\
&= Q(k) - b(k)b^T(k) - b(k)b^T(k) + b(k)b^T(k) \\
&= Q(k) - b(k)b^T(k) \qquad (13.98)
\end{aligned}$$

This quantity should replace $Q(k)$ in the Kalman filtering equations.

For a known nonzero measurement noise mean,

$$E[\underline{v}(k)] = a(k) \qquad (13.99)$$

define

$$\underline{v}'(k) = \underline{v}(k) - a(k) \qquad (13.100)$$

with $a(k)$ a deterministic input to the measurements. Then let

$$R'(k) = R(k) - a(k)a^T(k) \qquad (13.101)$$

replace $R(k)$ in the Kalman filtering equations.

If the initial system state has nonzero mean,

$$E[\underline{x}(0)] = c \qquad (13.102)$$

the Kalman filter is simply begun with the initial state

$$\hat{\underline{x}}(0\,|\,0) = c \qquad (13.103)$$

rather than with a zero initial condition.

Incorporation of known means into the Kalman filter is shown in Fig. 13.9.

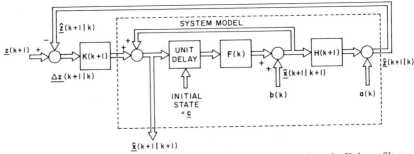

Fig. 13.9. Incorporating known noise and initial condition means into the Kalman filter.

The system model is described by

$$\underline{x}(k + 1) = \mathbf{F}(k)\underline{x}(k) + \underline{w}(k), \qquad \underline{z}(k) = \mathbf{H}(k)\underline{x}(k) + \underline{v}(k), \qquad (13.104)$$

where

$$E[\underline{w}(k)] = \mathbf{b}(k), \qquad E[\underline{v}(k)] = \mathbf{a}(k), \qquad E[\underline{x}(0)] = \mathbf{c} \qquad (13.105)$$

and

$$E\{[\underline{w}(j) - \mathbf{b}(j)][\underline{w}(k) - \mathbf{b}(k)]^{\mathsf{T}}\} = \mathbf{0}, \qquad j \neq k$$
$$E\{[\underline{w}(k) - \mathbf{b}(k)][\underline{w}(k) - \mathbf{b}(k)]^{\mathsf{T}}\} = \mathbf{R}'(k)$$
$$E\{[\underline{v}(j) - \mathbf{a}(j)][\underline{v}(k) - \mathbf{a}(k)]^{\mathsf{T}}\} = \mathbf{0}, \qquad j \neq k$$
$$E\{[\underline{v}(k) - \mathbf{a}(k)][\underline{v}(k) - \mathbf{a}(k)]^{\mathsf{T}}\} = \mathbf{Q}'(k)$$
$$E\{[\underline{w}(j) - \mathbf{b}(j)][\underline{v}(k) - \mathbf{a}(k)]^{\mathsf{T}}\} = \mathbf{0} \qquad \text{for all } j, k$$
$$E\{[\underline{x}(0) - \mathbf{c}][\underline{x}(0) - \mathbf{c}]^{\mathsf{T}}\} = \mathbf{P}'_0$$
$$E\{[\underline{x}(0)] - \mathbf{c}][\underline{w}(k) - \mathbf{b}(k)]^{\mathsf{T}}\} = \mathbf{0} \qquad \text{for all } k$$
$$E\{[\underline{x}(0) - \mathbf{c}][\underline{v}(k) - \mathbf{a}(k)]^{\mathsf{T}}\} = \mathbf{0} \qquad \text{for all } k \qquad (13.106)$$

The Kalman filter predictor equations are then

$$\hat{\underline{x}}(k + 1 \,|\, k) = \mathbf{F}(k)\hat{\underline{x}}(k \,|\, k) + \mathbf{b}(k), \qquad \hat{\underline{x}}(0 \,|\, 0) = \mathbf{c}$$
$$\hat{\underline{z}}(k + 1 \,|\, k) = \mathbf{H}(k + 1)\hat{\underline{x}}(k + 1 \,|\, k) + \mathbf{a}(k) \qquad (13.107)$$

The corrector equations are unchanged. The prediction error covariances, estimation error covariances and Kalman gains are calculated as in the basic problem, with $\mathbf{Q}'(k)$ replacing $\mathbf{Q}(k)$ and $\mathbf{R}'(k)$ replacing $\mathbf{R}(k)$.

Known Initial Conditions D

If the initial conditions of the stochastic model system are known,

$$\mathbf{x}(0) = \mathbf{c} \qquad (13.108)$$

then

$$E[\mathbf{x}(0)] = \mathbf{c} \qquad (13.109)$$

and

$$E\{[\mathbf{x}(0) - \mathbf{c}][\mathbf{x}(0) - \mathbf{c}]^{\mathsf{T}}\} = \mathbf{P}'_0 = \mathbf{0} \qquad (13.110)$$

The Kalman filter is begun with the known mean

$$\hat{\mathbf{x}}(0 \,|\, 0) = \mathbf{c} \qquad (13.111)$$

initially. The initial variance from the mean is zero, so the Kalman gain calculations begin with

$$\mathbf{P}(0\,|\,0) = \mathbf{P}_0 = \mathbf{0} \qquad (13.112)$$

E   Correlated Noises

It may happen that the noise sequences $\underline{w}(k)$ and $\underline{v}(k)$ are not white and are possibly correlated with one another. That is, one or more of the following may hold for some or all j and k:

$$E[\underline{w}(j)\underline{w}^\mathsf{T}(k)] \neq \mathbf{0}, \quad E[\underline{v}(j)\underline{v}^\mathsf{T}(k)] \neq \mathbf{0}, \quad E[\underline{w}(j)\underline{v}^\mathsf{T}(j)] \neq \mathbf{0} \quad (13.113)$$

In this event the basic results for uncorrelated white noise sequences can be applied, provided that a filter can be found that turns uncorrelated white noise sequences $\underline{w}'(k)$ and $\underline{v}'(k)$ into sequences that accurately model the correlations of $\underline{w}(k)$ and $\underline{v}(k)$:

$$\underline{\xi}(k + 1) = \mathbf{A}(k)\underline{\xi}(k) + \mathbf{B}(k)\underline{w}'(k)$$

$$\underline{w}(k) = \mathbf{C}(k)\underline{\xi}(k)$$

$$\underline{v}(k) = \mathbf{D}(k)\underline{\xi}(k) + \underline{v}'(k) \qquad (13.114)$$

Figure 13.10 is a block diagram of such a *shaping filter*.

The system consisting of the original nth-order stochastic model plus an rth order shaping filter is then described by the $(n + r)$th-order model

$$\begin{bmatrix} \underline{x}(k + 1) \\ \hline \underline{\xi}(k + 1) \end{bmatrix} = \begin{bmatrix} \mathbf{F}(k) & \mathbf{C}(k) \\ \hline \mathbf{0} & \mathbf{A}(k) \end{bmatrix} \begin{bmatrix} \underline{x}(k) \\ \hline \underline{\xi}(k) \end{bmatrix} + \begin{bmatrix} \mathbf{0} \\ \hline \mathbf{B}(k) \end{bmatrix} \underline{w}'(k)$$

$$= \mathbf{F}'(k)\underline{\psi}(k) + \mathbf{D}'(k)\underline{w}'(k)$$

$$\underline{z}(k) = [\mathbf{H}(k) \,|\, \mathbf{D}(k)] \begin{bmatrix} \underline{x}(k) \\ \hline \underline{\xi}(k) \end{bmatrix} + \underline{v}'(k) = \mathbf{H}'(k)\underline{\psi}(k) + \underline{v}'(k) \quad (13.115)$$

This combination system is of the type for which the basic Kalman filter applies (with input noise coupling matrix $\mathbf{D}'$) and for which the $(n + r)$th-order Kalman filter will generate optimal estimates of $\underline{\psi}(k)$, that is, of both $\underline{x}(k)$ and $\underline{\xi}(k)$. The fundamental problem here is the determination of a shaping filter that will model the actual correlations sufficiently accurately.

Example of Correlated State Noise.   When scalar, zero-mean, Gaussian white noise $\underline{w}'(k)$ with constant covariance R is passed through the first-order filter

$$\underline{\xi}(k + 1) = 0.8\underline{\xi}(k) + \underline{w}'(k), \qquad \underline{w}(k + 1) = \underline{\xi}(k + 1) \qquad (13.116)$$

the resulting filtered noise $\underline{w}(k)$ is Gaussian, since Gaussian noise passed through a linear, step-invariant filter remains Gaussian. It is no longer white, however, since $\underline{\xi}(k) = \underline{w}(k)$ depends on all past values of the filter input $\underline{w}'$. Suppose that the

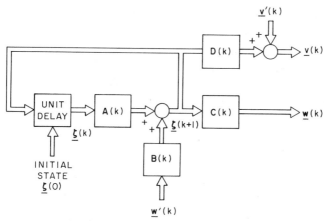

Fig. 13.10. Block diagram of a shaping filter.

shaping filter's initial condition is also zero mean with covariance Γ, uncorrelated with $\underline{w}'(k)$.

The shaping filter output at step k is

$$\underline{w}(k) = \underline{\xi}(k) = (0.8)^k \underline{\xi}(0) + (0.8)^{k-1} \underline{w}'(0) + (0.8)^{k-2} \underline{w}'(1)$$
$$+ \cdots + 0.8 \underline{w}'(k-2) + \underline{w}'(k-1) \qquad (13.117)$$

Making use of the fact that $\underline{\xi}(0)$ and $\underline{w}'(j)$ are uncorrelated for all steps j and that

$$E[\underline{w}'(i)\underline{w}'(j)] = 0, \qquad i \neq j \qquad (13.118)$$

give

$$E[\underline{w}(j)\underline{w}(k)] = (0.8)^{k+j} E[\underline{\xi}^2(0)] + (0.8)^{k+j-2} E[\underline{w}'^2(0)]$$
$$+ (0.8)^{k+j-4} E[\underline{w}'^2(1)] + \cdots$$
$$= (0.8)^{k+j}\Gamma + [(0.8)^{k+j-2} + (0.8)^{k+j-4} + \cdots]R \qquad (13.119)$$

Suppose that the covariance structure of this filtered white noise accurately models that of the correlated state noise $\underline{w}(k)$ in the scalar stochastic system model

$$x(k+1) = 0.5x(k) + \underline{w}(k), \qquad z(k+1) = 3x(k+1) + v(k+1) \qquad (13.120)$$

Combining the shaping filter and original system model into a second-order model with white noise inputs yields

$$\begin{bmatrix} x(k+1) \\ \xi(k+1) \end{bmatrix} = \begin{bmatrix} 0.5 & 1 \\ 0 & 0.8 \end{bmatrix} \begin{bmatrix} x(k) \\ \xi(k) \end{bmatrix} + \begin{bmatrix} 0 \\ 1 \end{bmatrix} \underline{w}'(k)$$

$$z(k) = \begin{bmatrix} 3 & 0 \end{bmatrix} \begin{bmatrix} x(k) \\ \xi(k) \end{bmatrix} + v(k) \qquad (13.121)$$

which fits the basic Kalman filter form with a noise input coupling matrix.

F   Bias Estimation

In practice, it often happens that we wish to estimate unknown constant signals, termed *biases*, in a system. In navigation systems, for example, there are constant or slowly varying component alignment errors that must be modeled. A constant signal is modeled by a scalar difference equation of the form

$$x_i(k + 1) = x_i(k) \tag{13.122}$$

An equation of this form is used for each bias.

Care must be taken when simultaneously modeling several system biases, because biases on top of biases may result in an unobservable system. For example, if a system's outputs depend only on the sum of two cumulative unknown constants (say two different additive alignment errors from different sources), it is not possible to estimate the two unknowns separately; only their sum is observable.

Example of Bias Augmentation.   A stochastic system is described by

$$\begin{bmatrix} x_1(k+1) \\ x_2(k+1) \end{bmatrix} = \begin{bmatrix} 0.5 & 1 \\ 0.25 & 0 \end{bmatrix} \begin{bmatrix} x_1(k) \\ x_2(k) \end{bmatrix} + \begin{bmatrix} w_1(k) \\ w_2(k) \end{bmatrix}$$

$$z(k+1) = [1 \quad 0] \begin{bmatrix} x_1(k+1) \\ x_2(k+1) \end{bmatrix} + b + v(k+1) \tag{13.123}$$

where b is an unknown constant bias of the measurements. Modeling b as

$$b = x_3(k+1) = x_3(k) + w_3(k) \tag{13.124}$$

we collect the three state equations and form a resulting model of the standard form:

$$\begin{bmatrix} x_1(k+1) \\ x_2(k+1) \\ x_3(k+1) \end{bmatrix} = \begin{bmatrix} 0.5 & 1 & 0 \\ 0.25 & 0 & 0 \\ 0 & 0 & 0 \end{bmatrix} \begin{bmatrix} x_1(k) \\ x_2(k) \\ x_3(k) \end{bmatrix} + \begin{bmatrix} w_1(k) \\ w_2(k) \\ w_3(k) \end{bmatrix}$$

$$z(k+1) = [1 \quad 0 \quad 1] \begin{bmatrix} x_1(k+1) \\ x_2(k+1) \\ x_3(k+1) \end{bmatrix} + v(k+1) \tag{13.125}$$

The previous methods for constructing a Kalman filter then apply, with the measurement bias becoming an additional state variable to be estimated.

G   Extended Kalman Filtering

Many of the most successful applications of Kalman filtering have been in areas such as navigation and trajectory determination, where the system model is nonlinear and typically of the form

$$\underline{x}(k + 1) = \underline{f}[k, \underline{x}(k)] + \underline{w}(k), \qquad \underline{z}(k + 1) = \underline{h}[k, \underline{x}(k)] + \underline{v}(k) \quad (13.126)$$

where $\underline{f}$ and $\underline{h}$ are known deterministic functions depending on the present state of the system, $\underline{x}(k)$. Possibly, the noise covariances of $\underline{w}(k)$ and of $\underline{v}(k)$ also depend on $\underline{x}(k)$. In this situation the system state is not known exactly; it is the quantity being estimated. In the *extended Kalman filter* [39–41] the *estimated* state $\hat{\underline{x}}(k \mid k)$ is used to obtain an *approximate* linearized discrete-time system model of the form

$$\underline{x}(k + 1) = F[k, \hat{\underline{x}}(k \mid k)]\underline{x}(k) + \underline{w}(k)$$
$$\underline{z}(k + 1) = H[k, \hat{\underline{x}}(k \mid k)]\underline{x}(k) + \underline{v}(k) \tag{13.127}$$

that is used in place of Eq. (13.126) in the Kalman filter. For a discrete-time model of a continuous-time system this amounts to linearizing the inherently nonlinear equations about the current estimated state trajectory.

In the extended Kalman filter the system model for the next step is not determined until the state estimate at the present step has been computed, so the Kalman gain depends on the estimated state at each prior step. It is therefore usually necessary to compute the Kalman gain sequence on-line as the measurement data and state estimates are processed. The approximation involved in using Eq. (13.127) in place of Eq. (13.126), if too crude because of large state changes between measurements, can cause poor, even unstable, filter behavior.

SOME COMPUTATIONAL CONSIDERATIONS   VI

Steady-State Solutions   A

If the stochastic system model is step invariant and completely observable, the solutions for the prediction error covariance, estimation error covariance, and Kalman gain will converge to unique steady-state values after a sufficiently large number, k, of steps. If $P(k + 1 \mid k)$, $P(k \mid k)$, and $K(k + 1)$ reach limiting values for large k,

$$\lim_{k \to \infty} P(k + 1 \mid k) = P_1$$

$$\lim_{k \to \infty} P(k \mid k) = P \tag{13.128}$$

$$\lim_{k \to \infty} K(k + 1) = K$$

then the gain and covariance equations become, for large k and constant system matrices,

$$P = [I - KH]P_1$$
$$P_1 = FPF^T + Q \qquad (13.129)$$
$$K = P_1 H^T [HP_1 H^T + R]^{-1}$$

Example of Steady-State Covariances and Kalman Gain. For the previous scalar system, with

$$\underline{x}(k + 1) = 0.5\underline{x}(k) + \underline{w}(k), \qquad \underline{z}(k + 1) = 3\underline{x}(k + 1) + \underline{v}(k + 1)$$
$$Q = 4 \qquad R = 5 \qquad (13.130)$$

the steady-state solution is

$$P = (1 - 3K)P_1, \qquad P_1 = 0.25P + 4, \qquad K = \frac{3P_1}{9P_1 + 5} \qquad (13.131)$$

Substituting gives

$$P = \left[1 - \frac{9P_1}{9P_1 + 5}\right]P_1 = \frac{5P_1}{9P_1 + 5} = \frac{5(0.25P + 4)}{9(0.25P + 4) + 5} = \frac{5P + 80}{9P + 164}$$
$$9P^2 + 159P - 80 = 0 \qquad (13.132)$$
$$P = \frac{-159 \pm \sqrt{(159)^2 - (36)(80)}}{18} = 0.4896, \; -18.16$$

The positive solution is the value previously found by iteration (see Table III). The limiting values of P_1 and K are

$$P_1 = 0.25P + 4 = 4.122, \qquad K = \frac{3P_1}{9P_1 + 5} = 0.2937 \qquad (13.133)$$

Example of Steady-State with Zero Measurement Noise. For the same system, but with $Q = 4, R = 0$, the steady-state solution is

$$P = (1 - 3K)P_1, \qquad P_1 = 0.25P + 4, \qquad K = \frac{3P_1}{9P_1} = \frac{1}{3} \qquad (13.134)$$

Substituting then gives

$$P = [1 - (\tfrac{1}{3})(3)]P_1 = 0, \qquad P_1 = 0.25(0) + 4 = 4 \qquad (13.135)$$

Each prediction has an error covariance equal to $Q = 4$. Once the measurement is received, the estimate is perfect, however, since $P = 0$. The Kalman gain simply undoes the output gain $H = 3$ to obtain the system state.

Example of Steady-State with Zero-State Noise. For the same system, but with $Q = 0, R = 5$, the steady-state solution is

$$P = (1 - 3K)P_1, \qquad P_1 = 0.25P, \qquad K = \frac{3P_1}{9P_1 + 5}$$

Substituting gives

$$P = \left[1 - \frac{5P_1}{9P_1 + 5}\right] = \frac{5P_1}{9P_1 + 5} = \frac{5(0.25P)}{9(0.25P) + 5} = \frac{5P}{9P + 20} \qquad (13.136)$$

$$9P^2 + 15P = 0; \qquad \text{so} \quad P = 0, -\tfrac{15}{9} \qquad (13.137)$$

The physical solution is $P = 0$. Then $P_1 = 0$ and $K = 0$.

If this filter should reach its limiting behavior, for all practical purposes the Kalman gain is zero and all future measurements will have no further effect upon the estimate. Were the system to undergo an unexpected disturbance, the filter would not respond to it. If there are slight modeling errors of the system (especially if it is unstable), huge errors can occur as the Kalman gain goes to zero.

In practical filters, even when there is negligible state noise, $\mathbf{Q}$ is taken to be nonzero so that the Kalman gain will not go to zero. Alternatively, the Kalman gain may not be allowed to drop below a threshold value.

Divergence   B

Insufficient care in modeling the system can lead to the following unacceptable result: after an extended period of filter operation, the estimate errors have values entirely out of proportion to those predicted by the filter covariance [42–44]. The calculated covariance matrix becomes unrealistically small so that undue confidence is placed in the estimates, and subsequent measurements are effectively ignored.

Causes may be classified as follows:

1. System model errors
2. Noise model errors
3. Biases
4. Numerical errors

The errors due to numerical roundoff or truncation may be modeled as noise, and their effects may be incorporated into the filter.

Example of System Model Error.   For the system

$$x(k + 1) = 0.9\underline{x}(k) + \underline{w}(k), \qquad \underline{z}(k + 1) = \underline{x}(k + 1) + \underline{v}(k + 1) \qquad (13.138)$$

with

$$P_0 = 10, \qquad Q = 0.01, \quad R = 5 \qquad (13.139)$$

the steady-state error covariances and Kalman gain are

$$P = (1 - K)P_1, \qquad P_1 = 0.81P + 0.01, \qquad K = \frac{P_1}{P_1 + 5} \qquad (13.140)$$

Substituting, we get

$$P = \left(1 - \frac{P_1}{P_1 + 5}\right)P_1 = \frac{5P_1}{P_1 + 5} = \frac{5(0.81P + 0.01)}{0.81P + 0.01 + 5}$$

$$0.81P^2 + 0.96P - 0.05 = 0, \qquad P = 0.0494 \qquad (13.141)$$

taking the positive solution. Then

$$P_1 = 0.05, \qquad K = 0.0099 \qquad (13.142)$$

If the *true* system is, instead,

$$x(k + 1) = 1.02\underline{x}(k) + \underline{w}(k), \qquad \underline{z}(k + 1) = \underline{x}(k + 1) + \underline{v}(k + 1) \quad (13.143)$$

typical noise sequences give states and estimates as in Fig. 13.11.

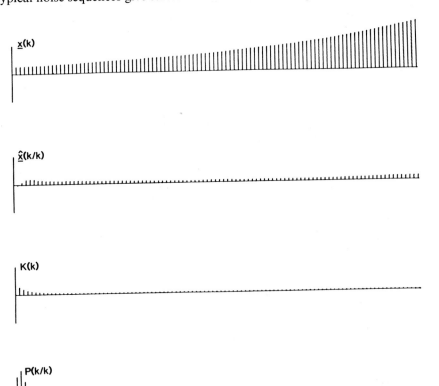

Fig. 13.11. Divergence due to system model error.

Example of Noise Model Error.   For the system

$$x(k + 1) = 0.9x(k) + w(k), \qquad z(k + 1) = x(k + 1) + v(k + 1) \quad (13.144)$$

with

$$P_0 = 10, \qquad Q = 0.01, \qquad R = 5 \qquad\qquad (13.145)$$

the steady-state error covariances and Kalman gains were found in the previous example to be

$$P = 0.0494, \qquad P_1 = 0.05, \qquad K = 0.0099 \qquad (13.146)$$

If the *true* covariance of $w(k)$ is $Q = 4$, typical noise sequences give system states and estimates as in Fig. 13.12. Actual steady-steady error covariance is far larger than P above. Hence P can be very misleading if the noise statistics are not accurate.

Example of Bias Error.   For the previous system and noise models suppose the *true* system involves a bias on the measurements (e.g., v is biased):

$$z(k + 1) = x(k + 1) + v(k + 1) + 1 \qquad\qquad (13.147)$$

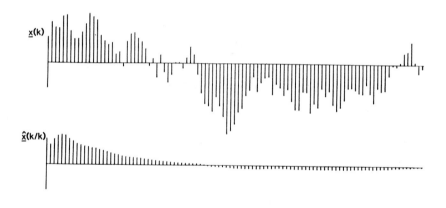

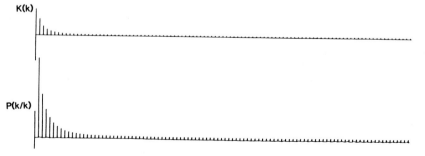

Fig. 13.12. Divergence due to noise model error.

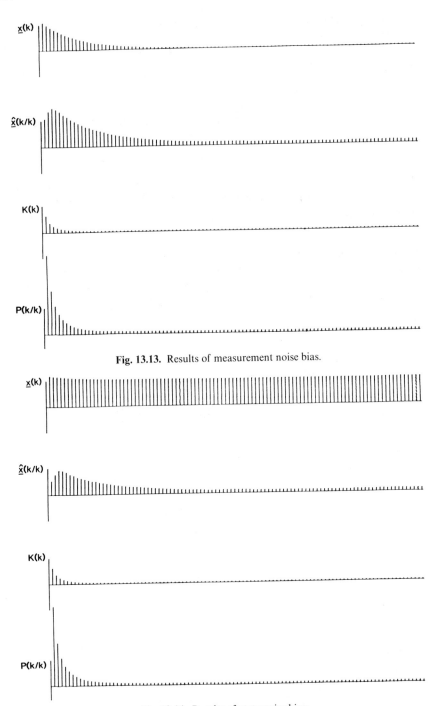

Fig. 13.13. Results of measurement noise bias.

Fig. 13.14. Results of state noise bias.

Typical noise sequences give system states and estimates as in Fig. 13.13. Actual steady-state error covariance is far larger than that assumed, namely, $P = 0.0494$.
If, instead, the state equation is biased (e.g., w is biased),

$$\underline{x}(k + 1) = 0.9\underline{x}(k) + \underline{w}(k) + 1 \tag{13.148}$$

the results in Fig. 13.14 are obtained.

Suboptimal Filters   C

If the noise statistics $\mathbf{Q}(k)$ and $\mathbf{R}(k)$ are accurately known, the filter error covariance will accurately assess filter performance. However, if $\mathbf{Q}(k)$ and $\mathbf{R}(k)$ are inaccurate, the error covariance may not be correct.

The error covariance is determined by the previous equations for the *optimal* Kalman gain $\mathbf{K}(k + 1)$. If either purposely or because of numerical error $\mathbf{K}$ is *not* optimum, then the state estimate error covariance is still given by Eq. (13.82), which holds for any gain $\mathbf{K}$ and which is repeated here as

$$\mathbf{P}(k + 1 \,|\, k + 1) = [\mathbf{I} - \mathbf{K}(k + 1)\mathbf{H}(k + 1)]\mathbf{P}(k + 1 \,|\, k)[\mathbf{I} - \mathbf{K}(k + 1)\mathbf{H}(k + 1)]^{\mathrm{T}}$$
$$+ \mathbf{K}(k + 1)\mathbf{R}(k + 1)\mathbf{K}^{\mathrm{T}}(k + 1) \tag{13.149}$$

This relation is particularly useful when the steady-state Kalman gain is used for a (suboptimal) filter.

Square-Root Filtering Using Covariance   D

Use of the usual Kalman filter equations for calculation of the error covariance can produce a matrix that fails to be positive semidefinite due to numerical errors, particularly for small $\|\mathbf{Q}\|$ (i.e., relatively accurate measurements). If $\mathbf{P}$ is positive semidefinite and symmetric, it may always be represented as [38, pp. 307–308]

$$\mathbf{P} = \mathbf{M}\mathbf{M}^{\mathrm{T}} \tag{13.150}$$

where $\mathbf{M}$ is square but not necessarily positive semidefinite and symmetric. $\mathbf{M}$ is generally not unique, but $\mathbf{M}\mathbf{M}^{\mathrm{T}}$ is always positive semidefinite and symmetric. Matrices $\mathbf{M}$ are termed square roots of $\mathbf{P}$.

Forming the error covariance equations in terms of $\mathbf{M}$ has the following advantages:

1. Since $\mathbf{M}\mathbf{M}^{\mathrm{T}}$ is always positive semidefinite and symmetric, $\mathbf{P} = \mathbf{M}\mathbf{M}^{\mathrm{T}}$ will not give a matrix that fails to have these properties as a result of numerical errors.

2. Numerical errors in $\mathbf{M}$ are generally of much less consequence than in the direct calculation of $\mathbf{P}$. Only half as many significant digits of $\mathbf{M}$ need to be accurate, compared to $\mathbf{P}$, to give freedom from numerical difficulty.

If the Kalman filtering equations are expressed and implemented in terms of square roots M instead of P, the result is termed a square-root filter. Generally, square-root filters require more computations than the ordinary type do. Square-root filters give improved performance with a fixed number of digits in the computations, but they by no means give the "double precision" improvement that would be possible if the number of computations was the same for the two types.

Since the square root of a symmetric matrix is generally nonunique, there are many different possibilities for these filters. Most popular are methods involving upper triangular square roots, M.

Example of Scalar Square-Root Filter. For a first-order stochastic system model (see Fig. 13.5) with $Q = 0$, the Kalman filter covariance and gain equations are

$$P(k + 1 \mid k) = F^2 P(k \mid k), \qquad P(0 \mid 0) = P_0$$

$$K(k + 1) = \frac{P(k + 1 \mid k)H}{H^2 P(k + 1 \mid k) + R}$$

$$P(k + 1 \mid k + 1) = [I - K(k + 1)H]P(k + 1 \mid k) \qquad (13.151)$$

Letting

$$M(k + 1 \mid k) = \sqrt{P(k + 1 \mid k)}, \qquad M(k \mid k) = \sqrt{P(k \mid k)}, \qquad (13.152)$$

We can rewrite these relations as

$$M(k + 1 \mid k) = FM(k \mid k), \qquad M(0 \mid 0) = \sqrt{P_0}$$

$$K(k + 1) = \frac{M^2(k + 1 \mid k)H}{H^2 M^2(k + 1 \mid k) + R}$$

$$M(k + 1 \mid k + 1) = \sqrt{1 - K(k + 1)H} \, M(k + 1 \mid k) \qquad (13.153)$$

E   Information Matrix Filters

The information matrices for a Kalman filter are defined to be the matrix inverses of the corresponding state estimate error covariances:

$$\Omega(k + 1 \mid k) = P^{-1}(k + 1 \mid k), \qquad \Omega(k \mid k) = P^{-1}(k \mid k) \qquad (13.154)$$

These matrices exist for positive definite P. When the Kalman filter equations are expressed and implemented in terms of the information matrices, the filter is termed an information filter. The advantage of using the information filter formulation is that, as $\|P\|$ nears zero, $\|\Omega\|$ becomes large. It is the nature of finite word-length digital computation that the information contained in matrices with small nonzero norms is more accurately conveyed through computation by the inverse matrix.

Example of Scalar Information Filter. For a first order Kalman filter with $Q = 0$, the filter covariance equations are (13.51). Letting

$$\Omega(k + 1 \mid k) = P^{-1}(k + 1 \mid k) = \frac{1}{P(k + 1 \mid k)}$$

$$\Omega(k \mid k) = P^{-1}(k \mid k) = \frac{1}{P(k \mid k)} \qquad (13.155)$$

these equations become

$$\Omega(k + 1 \mid k) = (1 \mid F^2)\Omega(k \mid k)$$

$$K(k + 1) = \frac{H}{\Omega(k + 1 \mid k)[(H^2 + R\Omega(k + 1 \mid k))/\Omega(k + 1 \mid k)]}$$

$$\Omega(k + 1 \mid k + 1) = \frac{1}{1 - K(k + 1)H}\Omega(k + 1 \mid k) \qquad (13.156)$$

Square-Root Information Matrix Filters   F

The inverse of a symmetric positive definite matrix is also symmetric and positive definite, so positive definite covariance matrices have corresponding symmetric, positive definite information matrices. Using square roots of the information matrices will, as with the covariances, maintain positive definiteness in the face of numerical error and, for a fixed computer word length, offer improvements in accuracy:

$$\mathbf{\Omega}(k + 1 \mid k) = \mathbf{P}^{-1}(k + 1 \mid k) = \mathbf{N}(k + 1 \mid k)\mathbf{N}^{\mathsf{T}}(k + 1 \mid k)$$
$$\mathbf{\Omega}(k \mid k) = \mathbf{P}^{-1}(k \mid k) = \mathbf{N}(k \mid k)\mathbf{N}^{\mathsf{T}}(k \mid k) \qquad (13.157)$$

Example of Scalar Square-Root Information Filter. For the first-order Kalman filter with $Q = 0$, the corresponding square-root information filter equations are

$$N(k + 1 \mid k) = (1 \mid F)N(k \mid k)$$

$$K(k + 1) = \frac{H}{H^2 + RN^2(k + 1 \mid k)}$$

$$N(k + 1 \mid k + 1) = \frac{1}{1 - K(k + 1)H}N(k + 1 \mid k + 1) \qquad (13.158)$$

VII SUMMARY

An introduction to recursive estimation was presented in this chapter. We began with a derivation and examples of least squares estimation. We then derived and demonstrated recursive least squares methods in which new data is used to sequentially update previous least squares estimates. Generalizations of the basic least squares problem and probabilistic interpretations of the results were discussed.

The basic linear MMS estimation problem, which can be viewed as a generalization of least squares, was then formulated. The recursive Kalman filter equations were derived, and computer programming considerations were discussed. Several extensions to the basic Kalman filter were developed. The chapter concluded with a discussion of some of the computational aspects of Kalman filtering, including alternative algorithms, such as square-root filtering, that can improve computational accuracy.

REFERENCES

Below are listed, by topic, references that the author feels will be especially helpful to engineers and scientists who wish to study these ideas further. No attempt has been made to be comprehensive or to assess credit for various developments. The references listed here are selected on the basis of their suitability as extensions of this discussion to greater depth and to related topics.

Historical Perspective

1. K. F. Gauss, *Theory of Motion of the Heavenly Bodies about the Sun in Conic Section*, Dover, New York, 1963.
2. H. W. Sorenson, Least-squares estimation: from Gauss to Kalman, *IEEE Spectrum*, 63–68 (July 1970).
3. T. Kailath, A view of three decades of linear filtering theory, *IEEE Trans. Information Theory* **IT-20**, 146–181 (March 1974).

Recursive Least Squares

4. R. C. K. Lee, *Optimal Estimation, Identification and Control*, MIT Press, Cambridge, 1964.
5. H. W. Sorenson, *Parameter Estimation*, Dekker, New York, 1980.

The Kalman Filter

6. R. E. Kalman, A new approach to linear filtering and prediction problems, *Trans. ASME J. Basic Engr.* **82D**, 35–45 (March 1960).
7. H. W. Sorenson, Kalman filtering techniques, in *Advances in Control Systems*, edited by C. T. Leondes, Academic Press, New York, 1966.
8. J. S. Meditch, *Stochastic Optimal Linear Estimation and Control*, McGraw-Hill, New York, 1967.
9. B. D. O. Anderson and J. B. Moore, *Optimal Filtering*, Prentice-Hall, Englewood Cliffs, N.J., 1979.
10. G. F. Franklin and J. D. Powell, *Digital Control of Dynamic Systems*, Addison-Wesley, Reading, Mass., 1980.

Computation

11. I. A. Gura and G. J. Bierman, On computational efficiency of linear filtering algorithms, *Automatica* **7**, 299–314 (1971).
12. R. A. Singer and R. G. Sea, Increasing the computational efficiency of discrete Kalman filters, *IEEE Trans. Automatic Control* **AC-16**, 254–257 (June 1971).
13. J. M. Mendel, Computational requirements for a discrete Kalman filter, *IEEE Trans. Automatic Control* **AC-16**, 748–758 (December 1971).
14. G. J. Bierman, *Factorization Methods for Discrete Sequential Estimation*, Academic Press, New York, 1979.

Application Examples

15. R. W. Larson *et al.*, State estimation in power systems I, II: Theory of feasibility, *IEEE Trans. Power Applications and Systems* **PAS-89**, 345–353 (March 1970).
16. B. D. Tapley, Orbit determination in the presence of unmodeled accelerations, *IEEE Trans. Automatic Control* **AC-18**, 369–373 (August 1973).
17. J. B. Pearson, Kalman filter applications in airborne radar tracking, *IEEE Trans. Aerospace Electronic Systems* **AES-10**, 319–329 (May 1974).
18. D. Goddard, Channel equalization using a Kalman filter for fast data transmissions, *IBM J. Research Development* **18**, 267–273 (May 1974).
19. H. J. Parlis and B. Okumseinde, Multiple Kalman filters in a distributed steam monitoring system, *Proc. Fifteenth Joint Automatic Control Conf.* Austin, Texas, pp. 615–623, 1974.
20. Y. Sawaragi *et al.*, The prediction of air pollution levels by nonphysical models based on Kalman filtering method, *J. Dynamic Systems, Measurement and Control* **98**, 375–386 (December 1976).
21. P. K. Tam and J. B. Moore, Improved demodulation of sampled-FM signals in high noise, *IEEE Trans. Communications* **COM-25**, 1052–1053 (September 1977).
22. C. R. Szelag, A short-term forecasting algorithm for trunk demand servicing, *Bell System Tech. J.* **61**, 67–96 (January 1982).

Optimal Smoothing

23. J. S. Meditch, *Stochastic Optimal Linear Estimation and Control*, McGraw-Hill, New York, 1969.
24. J. S. Meditch, A survey of data smoothing for linear and nonlinear dynamic systems, *Automatica* **9**, 151–162 (March 1973).
25. A. Gelb, Editor, *Applied Optimal Estimation*, MIT Press, Cambridge, Mass., 1974.

Filtering for Continuous-Time Systems

26. N. Wiener, *The Extrapolation, Interpolation, and Smoothing of Stationary Time Series*, Wiley, New York, 1949.
27. R. E. Kalman and R. S. Bucy, New results in linear filtering and prediction theory, *Trans. ASME J. Basic Engr.* **83**, 95–108 (1961).
28. T. P. McGarty, *Stochastic Systems and State Estimation*, Wiley, New York, 1974.

Least Squares Estimation

29. J. M. Mendel, *Discrete Techniques of Parameter Estimation*, Dekker, New York, 1973.
30. C. L. Lawson and R. J. Hanson, *Solving Least Squares Problems*, Prentice-Hall, Englewood Cliffs, N.J., 1974.

State Variable Models

31. R. Bellman, *Introduction to Matrix Analysis*, McGraw-Hill, New York, 1960.

32. R. E. Kalman, Mathematical description of linear dynamical systems, *J. SIAM* **1**, 152–192 (1963).
33. P. M. DeRusso, R. J. Roy, and D. M. Close, *State Variables for Engineers*, Wiley, New York, 1965.

Stochastic Systems

34. A. Papoulis, *Probability, Random Variables, and Stochastic Processes*, McGraw-Hill, New York, 1965.
35. G. R. Cooper and C. D. McGillem, *Probabilistic Methods of Signal and System Analysis*, Holt, Rinehart, and Winston, New York, 1971.
36. J. L. Melsa and A. P. Sage, *An Introduction to Probability and Stochastic Processes*, Prentice-Hall, Englewood Cliffs, N.J., 1973.
37. F. C. Schweppe, *Uncertain Dynamic Systems*, Prentice-Hall, Englewood Cliffs, N.J., 1973.
38. R. G. Brown, *Introduction to Random Signal Analysis and Kalman Filtering*, Wiley, New York, 1983.

Extended Kalman Filter

39. H. W. Sorenson, Kalman filtering techniques, in *Advances in Control Systems*, Vol. 3, edited by C. T. Leondes, Academic Press, New York, 1966.
40. H. W. Sorenson, *Parameter Estimation*, Dekker, New York, 1980.
41. R. G. Brown, *Introduction to Random Signal Analysis and Kalman Filtering*, Wiley, New York, 1983.

Divergence

42. F. H. Schlee, C. J. Standish, and N. F. Toda, Divergence in the Kalman filter, *AIAA J.* **5**, 1114–1120 (June 1967).
43. C. F. Price, An analysis of the divergence problem in the Kalman filter, *IEEE Trans. Automatic Control* **AC-13**, 699–702 (December 1968).
44. R. J. Fitzgerald, Divergence of the Kalman filter, *IEEE Trans. Automatic Control* **AC-16**, 736–747 (December 1971).

Chapter **14**

Mechanization of Digital Signal Processors

LESTER MINTZER
Rockwell International Corporation
Anaheim, California 92803

INTRODUCTION   I

The field of digital signal processing is too young to talk of conventional mechanizations and too dynamic to expect them to emerge at some point in the future. Nonetheless, this chapter shall present a body of basic knowledge that will enable the reader to recognize and assess the various digital signal processing resources at his or her disposal and to fashion by selection, design, or adaptation the appropirate digital signal processing mechanization for a specific application.

Digital signal processors (DSPs) are basically digital machines that differ from the more pervasive digital data processors in the following ways.

1. DSPs are primarily involved in computationally intensive ("number crunching") operations where the same arithmetic operations are applied to large data streams. The processors are vector-like and are for the most part data independent.

2. DSPs often operate under real-time requirements; that is, they are data driven.

3. The processes are arithmetic intensive, and the algorithms are limited. Thus convolution, filtering, and FFT (fast Fourier transform) algorithms account for a large part of the digital signal processes.

4. Speed–cost considerations have favored fixed-point data representation. However, applications requiring a large dynamic range as well as very-large-scale-integration (VLSI) economies in memory and arithmetic elements have fostered the use of the floating-point and/or large-word (double-precision) data format.

HANDBOOK OF DIGITAL SIGNAL PROCESSING

This chapter will present the fundamentals underlying all digital machines [1] and then show how the sum of products [see, for example, (7.1)] that is basic to many important signal processing algorithms is mechanized. Machine behavior at fundamental levels is important for efficient mechanization and microprogramming which can offer both flexibility and efficiency is illustrated. The translation of signal processing requirements into efficient hardware mechanizations requires the ability to partition and size the algorithms (i.e., turn them into data flow and computation loads and then select the appropriate architectural and hardware realization [2–4]). Designers are largely on their own, for there are really no cookbook solutions available.

VLSI developments are shaping the digital signal processing design process by offering more powerful processing elements, of which the single chip DSP and the systolic array are outstanding examples [5–10], and are encouraging new algorithmic approaches.

II DIGITAL MACHINE FUNDAMENTALS

A The Digital Machine

A digital machine of arbitrary size and complexity may be distilled to a basic digital machine whose essence is shown in Fig. 14.1. This basic machine, sometimes referred to as a sequential network, consists of two elements: a

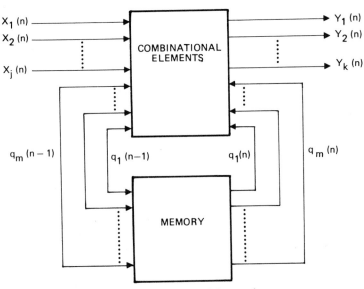

Fig. 14.1. The sequential network.

combinatorial or combinational network of gates, and a set of memory elements [1]. Ideally, the gates (or switching circuits) perform functions that can be fully described by Boolean equations. Zero time delay is implied. The memory elements provide a historical record of past conditions or states of the machine. Since memory size in a real machine is finite, these machines are sometimes referred to as finite state machines. The behavior of such a machine is described by the expression

$$y_i(n) = F\,[x_1(n), x_2(n), \ldots, x_j(n), q_1(n-1), \ldots, q_m(n-1)], \qquad i = 0, 1, 2, \ldots, k$$

where x, y, and q are two-state Boolean variables representing input, output, and internal states, respectively. Each output, $y_i(n)$, is a function of all present and previous inputs, $x_1(n), \ldots, x_j(n)$, which are reflected in the current state of the machine, $q_1(n-1), \ldots, q_m(n-1)$.

Switching Circuits B

Switching circuits or gates are circuits that perform well-defined logic or arithmetic operations on binary variables. Binary variables are two-valued variables expressed as 1's or 0's in algebraic form, or true or false in syllogistic forms, or as high or low voltage, positive or negative remanence (magnetic flux), etc., in circuit forms. The logic behavior of a gate network is fully characterized by Boolean equations. The resulting gate response is ideal in the sense that propagation time through the gates is not included, nor are variations in circuit behavior (e.g., change of thresholds) covered. Arithmetic and control functions are developed from the basic switching circuits that are described next.

Basic Switching Circuits C

The logic functions performed by a switching circuit are fully described by Boolean equations. Boolean algebra is a branch of mathematics that is a well-defined discipline with a set of basic postulates and theorems that serve as the foundation and justification for all Boolean relations (equations). The two fundamental logic or Boolean processes that link two binary variables are the AND and OR operations. The AND gate will provide a true output when both input (binary) variables are true. When either or both outputs are false, the AND gate will provide a false output. In Boolean form we write

$$C = A \cdot B \tag{14.1a}$$

where A and B are Boolean input variables and C is the Boolean output variable. Very often the dot linking the two input variables is not included, and the expression, which will be used in this chapter, becomes

$$C = AB \tag{14.1b}$$

The OR gate provides a true output when either or both inputs are true. The plus symbol denotes this relationship, as

$$C = A + B \qquad (14.2\text{a})$$

Boolean expressions (14.1) and (14.2) look like ordinary algebraic equations describing multiplication and addition operations. Where the notation can cause confusion, it is possible to fall back on an archaic notation used by logicians:

$$A + B = A \vee B \qquad (14.2\text{b})$$

$$AB = A \wedge B \qquad (14.1\text{c})$$

These two operations are expressed in tabular or truth table forms as shown in Table I. The table describes the AND and OR operations for all possible combinations of the input variables. This exhaustive description is sometimes referred to as perfect induction. The Boolean equation is a more succinct way of expressing the same relation.

These two operations are not sufficient to describe all relations between two variables. It is obvious that more functional relations are possible. Trivial examples are an output that is 0 (or 1) for all combinations of the input variables. A more significant relationship is the exclusive-OR (EXOR), $\oplus$, which generates a true (1) response when either input is true (1) but not when both are true.

An additional operation, the complement, completes the set of operations to realize any Boolean relationship. The complement is an operation on a single variable that negates its value. Thus for a true variable, the complement gate would produce a false output, and vice versa. The EXOR gate can now be expressed as

$$A \oplus B = AB' + A'B \qquad (14.3)$$

where the prime denotes complement.

TABLE I

**Truth Tables for Boolean Equations with Variables
Expressed as either True and False or 1 or 0**

A	B	$C = AB$	$C = A + B$
F	F	F	F
F	T	F	T
T	F	F	T
T	T	T	T
A	B	$C = AB$	$C = A + B$
0	0	0	0
0	1	0	1
1	0	0	1
1	1	1	1

Other functional relationships involving two variables are possible. There are 16 relationships (Table II), among which are the AND, OR, EXOR, null (0), and unit (1). As the number of variables grows, the number of relationships increases exponentially—that is, 2^{2^n} where n is the number of variables. Nonetheless, the important relationships among two variables are extendable to more. This is illustrated by the multivariable expression

$$F = ABCD + AB'C + BCD'E' \tag{14.4}$$

Among the important two-variable relationships are the NAND and NOR functions. They are important because they are universal logic elements; that is, they can be configured to realize any arbitrary Boolean equation and, fortunately, are most easily realized in circuit form. Also, NAND and NOR functions are duals of one another; one function is transformed into the other by complementing the input and output variables or simply by interpreting 1 as 0, and vice versa. Thus, a physical NAND gate can become a NOR gate by reversing the interpretation of high- and low-level signals. With this understanding we can focus our attention initially on the NAND gate without really neglecting the NOR.

The NAND gate is represented in logic schematic form in Fig. 14.2. The

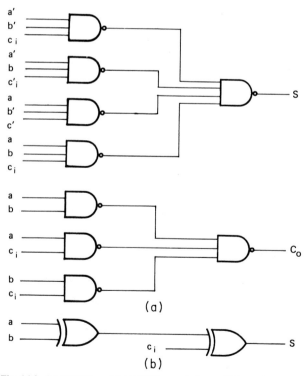

Fig. 14.2. (a) NAND and (b) EXOR gate designs of binary full adder.

TABLE II

Boolean Functions of Two Variables

x y	F_0	F_1	F_2	F_3	F_4	F_5	F_6	F_7	F_8	F_9	F_{10}	F_{11}	F_{12}	F_{13}	F_{14}	F_{15}
0 0	0	0	0	0	0	0	0	0	1	1	1	1	1	1	1	1
0 1	0	0	0	0	1	1	1	1	0	0	0	0	1	1	1	1
1 0	0	0	1	1	0	0	1	1	0	0	1	1	0	0	1	1
1 1	0	1	0	1	0	1	0	1	0	1	0	1	0	1	0	1

	F_0	F_1	F_2	F_3	F_4	F_5	F_6	F_7	F_8	F_9	F_{10}	F_{11}	F_{12}	F_{13}	F_{14}	F_{15}
Symbol		$\wedge$ $\cdot$					$\veebar$ $\oplus$	$\vee$ $+$	$\rightarrow$	$\odot$ $\oplus$	$'$	$\cup$	$'$	$\cap$	$\uparrow$ $\mid$	
Name	Null	AND	Inhibition	Transfer	Inhibition	Transfer	EX-OR	OR	NOR	Match	Complement	Implication	Complement	Implication	NAND	Identity
Boolean Equation	$F_0 = 0$	$F_1 = xy$	$F_2 = xy'$	$F_3 = x$	$F_4 = x'y$	$F_5 = y$	$F_6 = x'y + xy'$	$F_7 = x + y$	$F_8 = (x+y)'$	$F_9 = x'y' + xy$	$F_{10} = y'$	$F_{11} = x + y'$	$F_{12} = x'$	$F_{13} = x' + y$	$F_{14} = (xy)'$	$F_{15} = 1$
Function Description	Constant 0	x and y	x but not y	x	y but not x	y	x or y but not both	x or y	Not OR	x equals y	not y	If y then x	not x	If x then y	Not AND	Constant 1

Boolean expressions for the NAND are

$$C = (AB)' \quad \text{or} \quad C = A' + B' \tag{14.5}$$

The equivalence of these expressions can be established by applying DeMorgan's theorem, which states that

$$(x + y)' = x'y', \qquad (xy)' = x' + y' \tag{14.6}$$

where x and y are Boolean variables.

THE ESSENCE OF DIGITAL SIGNAL PROCESSING   III

Just as there are fundamental equations that speak for an entire body of knowledge—for example, $F = ma$ and $E = mc^2$—so too there is a fundamental equation that covers many important signal processes. The difference equation describing the filter response $y(nT)$ plays this role [see Eq. (4.6)]:

$$y(nT) = a_0 x(nT) + a_1 x[(n - 1)T] + a_2 x[(n - 2)T]$$
$$+ \cdots + b_1 y[(n - 1)T] + b_2 y[(n - 2)T] + \cdots \tag{14.7}$$

Here the filter response at time nT, where T is the sample period and n is a running index, is the sum of product terms of past responses, $y[(n - 1)T]$, etc., and past and present inputs, $x(nT)$ and $x[(n - 1)T]$, etc., respectively. With fixed coefficients the equation describes a linear, time-invariant system. With all the a and b coefficients beyond a_2 and b_2 set to zero, the equation describes a second-order recursive filter with the a and b coefficients defining the zeros and the poles, respectively [see Eq. (4.10)].

With all b's set to zero and with $a_i = e^{-j2\pi ki/N}$, the equation expresses the discrete Fourier transform (DFT) for the kth spectral element. This sum of products equation has many extensions in digital signal processing.

The dependence on present and past values is reminiscent of the state equation describing the sequential network. Memory elements are involved. However, we are dealing here with the algebraic sum of product terms that require further resolution into their Boolean representations. The very high-speed computation of sums of product terms is commonly referred to as number crunching. Therefore, it is appropriate to discuss numbers and their representation in Boolean variables.

NUMBER REPRESENTATIONS   IV

Numbers are a systematic representation of the counting process. Large numbers are efficiently represented by a weighted number system wherein a few symbols are used repeatedly with different weights. Thus, in our well-known decimal system there are the 10 symbols 0 through 9, forming a radix-number system. The digits in a number have weightings of one, ten, hundred, thousand, etc., in each decimal (radix) position. The advent of computers has made us aware of other number systems with radices different from 10 (see Section III.A of Chapter 7). Historically, other radices have been known to the Egyptians (binary), Babylonians (radix 60), Mayans (radices 18 and 20), etc.

The radix-2 or binary number system fits nicely with circuits that handle logic using two levels (expressed by the symbols 0 and 1). Any integer can be represented in binary notation as

$$k = \sum_{i=0}^{M} a_i 2^i, \tag{14.8}$$

where the coefficients a_i assume the binary values 0, 1, and the ith power of 2 denotes the weight at the ith position. Conversion from decimal to binary representation proceeds from this expression by dividing the decimal number by the radix 2 and observing the remainder:

$$\frac{k}{2} = \frac{a_0}{2} + \sum_{i=1}^{M} a_i 2^{i-1} \tag{14.9}$$

The fractional component (if one exists) of the result has numerator $a_0 = 1$. The integer component is the second term of the expression. The process is repeated in the integer until only a fraction term is left.

Example. Convert 579 to a binary number.

$$\frac{579}{2} = \frac{1}{2} + 289; \quad \text{therefore} \quad a_0 = 1, \quad 2^0 = 1$$

$$\frac{289}{2} = \frac{1}{2} + 144; \quad \text{therefore} \quad a_1 = 1, \quad 2^1 = 2$$

$$\frac{144}{2} = \frac{0}{2} + 72; \quad \text{therefore} \quad a_2 = 0$$

Likewise, $a_3 = a_4 = a_5 = a_7 = a_8 = 0$. However, $a_6 = 1$ and $a_9 = 1$; $2^6 = 64$ and $2^9 = 512$.

$$\begin{array}{ccccccccccc} & 9 & 8 & 7 & 6 & 5 & 4 & 3 & 2 & 1 & 0 \leftarrow \text{powers of 2} \end{array}$$

therefore $(579)_{10} = 1 \quad 0 \quad 0 \quad 1 \quad 0 \quad 0 \quad 0 \quad 0 \quad 1 \quad 1$

A Fractional 2's Complement Representation

Number values are unbounded; computer representation of them is not. Conventionally, computer word size grows in increments of 8-bit bytes. The 16-bit word has been the computer standard for two decades. Extensions beyond this require economic justification since hardware cost in both logic and memory is proportional to word size. Today, with decreasing circuit costs due to advancements in LSI technology, 32-bit word machines are becoming prevalent. Nonetheless, arithmetic operations do increase the word size, and it becomes necessary to maintain constancy of word size by restricting the outcome of all arithmetic operations. A fractional number representation scheme serves this purpose.

The 2's complement fractional number representation is the form found in most computers. As discussed in Section II of Chapters 5, 2's complement numbers must be scaled to be representable by the expression

$$k = -s + \sum_{i=1}^{b} a_i 2^{-i} \tag{14.10}$$

where s is the sign bit and is 1 for negative numbers. This is followed by the binary point and then a positive component made up of a decreasing order of b binary weighted fractions. Two important features of this form are (a) the number 0 is represented unambiguously with all coefficients (a_i) equal to 0; and (b) subtraction is easily realized by complementing the subtrahend bit by bit, doing a binary addition of the two operands, and then adding 1×2^{-b}, to the results, i.e. 1 in the lsb (least significant bit) position. The latter may be done by a single addition step with an input carry. The range of values represented by the 2's complement is indicated in Fig. 14.3. Note that the range is not symmetric about the origin. This has important implications; for example, the offset that occurs when full-scale limiting is effected can cause undesirable artifacts in the output signal. Clamping to symmetrical end points $1 - 2^{-M}$ and $-1 + 2^{-M}$ eliminates this problem.

The Significance of a Bit in Digital Signal Processing   B

Signals are subject to losses and gains in the path from source to destination. The operations affecting signal level are expressed in logarithmic form (specifically, decibels) so that cascaded gain changes may be added rather than multiplied when converted to decibels (dB). The change in signal level Δs in one stage of the data path may be expressed as

$$\Delta s = 20 \log\left(\frac{S_o}{S_i}\right) \quad \text{dB} \tag{14.11}$$

where S_o is the output signal and S_i is the input signal. Now consider expressing these signals as binary numbers. If the input signal range requires M bits for representation and if the signal level is scaled up by a factor of 2 at the output of the stage, then $M + 1$ bits are required to represent the output signal. The signal

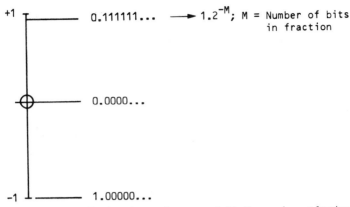

Fig. 14.3. Range of values that can be represented in 2's complement fractions.

change in conventional terms is

$$20 \log(\tfrac{2}{1}) = 20 \log 2 = 6.02 \quad \text{dB}$$

Thus, each bit added to a binary word extends the signal representation range by approximately 6 dB. An 8-bit word has a 48-dB signal range, and a 16-bit word has a 96-dB signal range. For most applications a 6-dB-per-bit rule of thumb applies.

V HARDWARE COMPONENTS

The first consideration in the mechanization of digital processors is available components. In this section we discuss adders, multipliers, registers and memory, and serial-to-parallel forms.

A The Binary Full-Adder

The general digital computation contains only two arithmetic operations: multiplication and summation. The latter, the simpler of the two, will be discussed here. A single stage of a binary full-adder requires three operands: an addend bit a, an augend bit b, and a carry-in bit c_i. The results are a sum bit s and a carry-out bit c_o.

The behavior of a single stage of the full-adder is described by the truth table in Table III. The table lists all possible combinations of the three operands and the corresponding responses for the addition algorithm. The sum is true whenever an odd number of operands is present, and the carry is true whenever two or more operands are present.

TABLE III

Single-Stage Binary Full Adder

a	b	c_i	Sum s	c_0
0	0	0	0	0
0	0	1	1	0
0	1	0	1	0
0	1	1	0	1
1	0	0	1	0
1	0	1	0	1
1	1	0	0	1
1	1	1	1	1

Implementation with NAND gates [Fig. 14.3(a)] requires the conversion of Table III to Boolean equations as follows:

$$s = a'b'c_i + a'bc_i' + ab'c_i' + abc_i \qquad (14.12a)$$

$$c_0 = a'bc_i + ab'c_i + abc_i' + abc_i = ab + ac_i + bc_i \qquad (14.12b)$$

The sum expression may be transformed into simple EXOR operations, which may be implemented with EXOR gates as shown in Fig. 14.3(b).

$$s = a'b'c_i + a'bc_i' + ab'c_i' + abc_i$$

$$= (a'b' + ab)c_i + (a'b + ab')c_i'$$

$$= (a \oplus b)'c_i + (a \oplus b)c_i'$$

$$= (a \oplus b) \oplus c_i \qquad (14.13)$$

Parallel addition is achieved by replicating the adder stage M times for an M-bit word length. The carry-out of one stage serves as the carry-in to the next higher stage. The long propagation path involved in generating the outputs of the final stages can be reduced by using additional gates that generate fast carries that span several stages.

Subtraction is performed as addition with the bits of the subtrahend complemented, and for 2's complement numbers the carry-in to the least significant stage is set to a 1. Where the same circuit is used for both addition and subtraction, the complementing is done with EXOR gates preceding the adder. An add/subtract control line is the second input to the EXOR gates and is set true for subtraction.

Array Multiplication   B

Multiplication is familiar to most as the generation of partial products—that is, multiplying the multiplicand with each of the product digits, and then scaling (shifting) and adding the partial products to obtain the full product. The same process holds for binary arithmetic; there are, however, a number of different algorithms for achieving the final product. The algorithms extend from a serial shift-and-add technique to a fully parallel approach. The former is circuit efficient but takes longer; the latter is circuit intensive but offers very high-speed results. The very regular structure of the multiplier array, like that of a storage array, lends itself to VLSl implementation. Single-chip multipliers producing 16×16 bit products within 200 ns are common. The application of array multipliers predominates, and by focusing on this algorithm we are covering the most important multiplication technique and also providing insight to other approaches.

Array multiplication will be described by an 8×8 array example. Assume 2's complement fractional numbers X and Y.

$$X = -x_0 + \sum_{i=1}^{7} x_i 2^{-i}, \qquad Y = -y_0 + \sum_{i=1}^{7} y_i 2^{-i} \qquad (14.14)$$

The multiplier array with its partial products is shown in Fig. 14.4. The pattern of partial products is similar to that encountered in the standard multiplication process. Here we are working with binary elements and simple logic, and binary arithmetic operations produce the partial products and the final sum. The logic expressions for the partial products are

$$a_0 = x_0 y_7, \qquad a_1 = x_1 y_7 \qquad a_2 = x_2 y_7, \ldots, \qquad a_7 = x_7 y_7$$

$$b_0 = x_0 y_6, \qquad b_1 = x_1 y_6 \qquad b_2 = x_2 y_6, \ldots, \qquad b_7 = x_7 y_6$$

$$c_0 = x_0 y_5, \qquad c_1 = x_1 y_5, \qquad c_2 = x_2 y_5, \ldots, \qquad c_7 = x_7 y_5 \qquad (14.15)$$

$$\vdots$$

$$h_0 = x_0 y_0, \qquad h_1 = x_1 y_0, \qquad h_2 = x_2 y_0, \ldots, \qquad h_7 = x_7 y_0$$

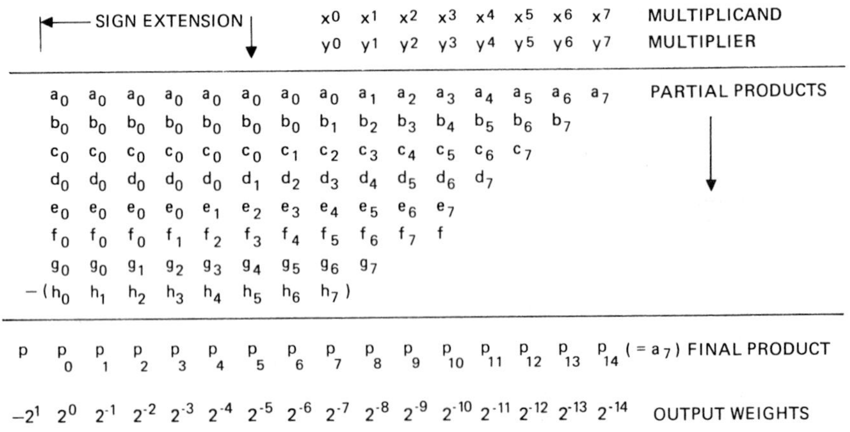

Fig. 14.4. 8×8 multiplier array.

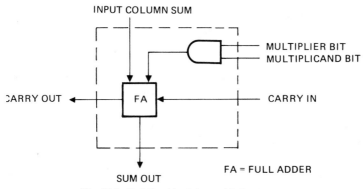

Fig. 14.5. Building block for multiplier array.

Each partial product term is the output of a two-input AND gate; however, in the last partial product the multiplicand bits are complemented if the multiplier sign bit is negative. The resulting bit values are summed within each column with binary carries passed to the next higher (left) column. With the binary full-adder discussed earlier, this involves adding the resulting partial product bit to the result of previous additions of the bits above it in the same column. A building block consisting of a full-adder, with one addend the output of a two-input AND gate (Fig. 14.5), can be replicated in an array pattern (Fig. 14.6) to implement the summing of partial products to obtain the final product. Although this building block can be used exclusively in the array, two additional circuits—a two-input AND and a half-adder—serve to reduce the component count. Nevertheless, a

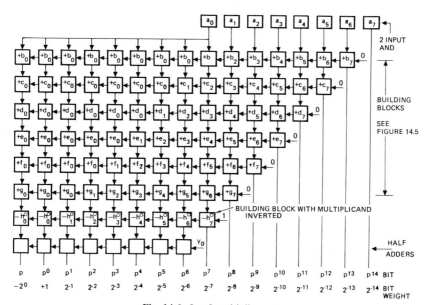

Fig. 14.6. 8×8 multiplier array.

very regular configuration suitable for VLSl implementation remains. Variations of this simple multiplier array are discussed in [11–13]. Even with earlier VLSl technology a 24×24 single-chip array multiplier was commercially available.

The array in Fig. 14.6 handles 2's complement number formats. Each partial product is expressed in fractional 2's complement form with the binary point set at the final product position. This requires all partial products to include sign extension to the output sign bit (i.e., one position left of the binary point). The additional sign extension bits account for the departure from the rhomboid array for magnitude-only multiplication. In addition, a final product value of $+1$ is possible (-1×-1). Since it is beyond the fractional 2's complement range, the final product is augmented by an additional bit to the left of the binary point. The bit weights are indicated at the bottom of Fig. 14.6.

The final multiplier bit is the sign bit y_0. If true, the last partial product must be complemented before the adder. Furthermore, a 1 must be added at the lsb portion to restore the 2's complement format. An additional stage of half-adders provides this function. The final product is a 16-bit number ranging from -2 to $+2 - 2^{-14}$. If the input condition (-1×-1) is precluded, then the 2's complement final product may be obtained by discarding P2 and interpreting P1 as the sign bit, -1.

If the product is accumulated in the same VLSl chip, the input restriction is removed, since accumulation produces several bits above the binary point. The TRW 8×8 multiplier–accumulator (MAC) chip (TDC 1008) provides a 5-bit extension above the binary point (i.e., 3 bits above P1). If the accumulated result serves as an operand in subsequent computations in 2's complement, it must be scaled down or clamped to fit within the 2's complement range.

C   Registers and Memory

A practical array multiplier requires more than the combinational elements shown in Fig. 14.6. The two factors must be held constant while their values ripple through the array; the final results must again be held constant for the combinational circuits that may follow. Flip-flop memory elements will capture input data values and present them as constant output values until they are triggered to respond to new input conditions. The flip-flop memory elements are basically two NAND gates connected in tandem.

The NAND gate pair in Fig. 14.7 constitutes the primitive SR (set/reset) flip-flop. With no input signal (i.e., both S' and R' are false) the output Q remains in either a true or false state, which was determined by an earlier input. The coupling between the two NAND gates ensures a stable response with Q true and Q' false, or vice versa. The flip-flop functions as a single-bit memory that indicates what the previous excitation had been.

Linear groupings of flip-flop stages serve as registers and counters, and large two-dimensional arrays serve as random access memories (RAMs). Variations in

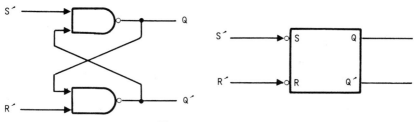

Fig. 14.7. *SR* flip-flop.

response are available in different flip-flop types. Two important types are the *D* flip-flop, which captures the state of a single input line, and the JK flip-flop, with two inputs for set, reset, or toggle. In register configurations the *D* flip-flops serve as data buffers and shift registers, and the *JK* flip-flops serve as counters.

The flip-flops change state in response to the input only after the triggering edge of a clock has occurred. The behavior of these flip-flop types is indicated in Table IV, which indicates the response $Q+$ after the clock trigger due to input conditions preceding the clock. Note that the response depends not only on the input but also on the present stage Q of the flip-flop.

Flip-flops in linear arrays controlled by a common clock are called registers or synchronous counters. The two-dimensional register array in Fig. 14.8 is the basis of a random-access memory (RAM). The flip-flops or cells are linked by common address lines (horizontal) and bit lines (vertical). One of $2n$ address lines is selected for either reading (observing the cell output) or writing (setting the cell). Selection for reading or writing requires two AND gates with the address lines as input to both. A third input on the input AND gate is the write control. The write control is distributed to all cells of the array.

The selection of address lines is made in an address decoder that includes 2^n AND gates, each with n coded address inputs. These gates represent a considerable amount of hardware and control lines. By factoring the selection logic into two levels of gating, we obtain significant reductions. This tends to

TABLE IV

Flip-Flop Truth Tables

(a) SR				(b) D			(c) JK			
S	R	Q	Q^+	D	Q	Q^+	J	K	Q	Q^+
0	0	0	0	0	0	0	0	0	0	0
0	0	1	1	0	1	0	0	0	1	1
0	1	0	0	1	0	1	0	1	0	0
0	1	1	0	1	1	1	0	1	1	0
1	0	0	1				1	0	0	1
1	0	1	1				1	0	1	1
1	1	0	Undefined				1	1	0	1
1	1	1	Undefined				1	1	1	0

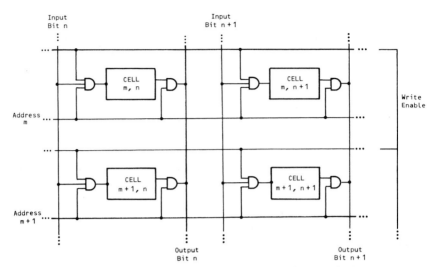

Fig. 14.8. Two-dimensional register array used as the basis of RAM.

increase the propagation delay through the address decoder and thus extends the time needed to write into and read from these arrays. As word size increases so does the delay or memory read or write cycle time.

D   Serial-to-Parallel Multipliers

It is possible to trade off speed for economy in multipler design. The opportunity for processing bit serially (slow and economical) versus bit parallel (fast but requires more components) occurs often in digital designs. The multiplier array described in Section V.B represents an all-parallel approach where the operands are captured in two 8-bit registers and are then applied to the array building blocks. The data propagate through all the combinational circuits, and when the final product bit paths have settled they may be captured in an output product register. The total propagation delay is the sum of the switching time of the operand registers, the delay through the longest path of the array, and the setup time of the final product register. This effectively defines the multiplication time. Parallel 8×8 multipliers in bipolar technology offer multiply times of 60 ns.

We may derive a serial-to-parallel multiplier by observing how the partial products are linked in the multiplier array. If a row of 16 building blocks (Fig. 14.6) is arranged so that the sum outputs are loaded into register stages whose contents serve as augends to the next lower stage (to the right), and if the registers are clocked as each multiplier bit is advanced (lsb first), the final sum would reside in this register after the eighth clock. The 8×8 version of the

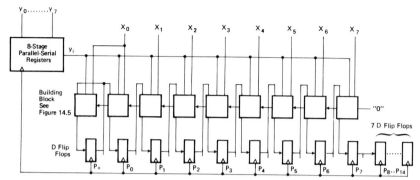

Fig. 14.9. 8 × 8 serial/parallel multiplier.

serial-to-parallel multipler in Fig. 14.9 uses nine building blocks of the array multiplier. There are also 16 D-type flip-flops to hold the running sum as the partial products are added. The offset of the partial products to the left is accounted for by the data flow to the right. The sign extension only requires one stage beyond the sign bit. The multiplier is loaded bit parallel into a register and then applied bit serially to generate the partial products.

There are at least five additional design solutions for the serial-to-parallel multipler [14]. Indeed, the number of design approaches, particularly for the more complex algorithms, should challenge rather than frustrate the new designer. Let us consider another serial-to-parallel multipler design (Fig. 14.10) and show a systematic way of describing how the partial products and final sum are developed. This technique serves as an analysis tool and as a design tool for the microprogram development discussed in the next section.

The functional blocks of Fig. 14.9 have already been defined. The register transfer nature of the processes is apparent. Signals flow from sources to destination register with, in some instances, combinational circuits sandwiched in between. Each register through which data flow is being traced is labeled as well as the sum output port of the full-adder circuit. A single phase clock (not shown) causes all flip-flops to switch to the state present at the input. The process flow is

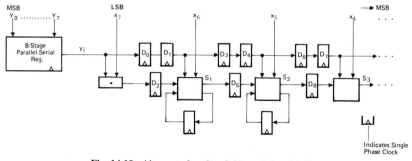

Fig. 14.10. Alternate 8 × 8 serial/parallel multiplier.

TABLE V
Tabular Description of Stages of Serial/Parallel Multiplier

Clock	D1	D2	S1	D5	D4	S2	D8	D7	S3
1	0	0	0	0	0	0	0	0	0
2	$x_7 \cdot y_7 = a_7$	0	a_7	0	0	0	0	0	0
3	$x_7 \cdot y_6 = b_7$	y_7	$b_7 + (x_6 y_7 = a_6)$	a_7	0	a_7	0	0	0
4	$x_7 \cdot y_5 = c_7$	y_6	$c_7 + (x_6 y_6 = b_6)$	$b_7 + a_6$	0	$b_7 + a_6$	a_7	0	a_7
5	$x_7 \cdot y_4 = d_7$	y_5	$d_7 + (x_6 y_5 = c_6)$	$c_7 + b_6$	y_7	$c_7 + b_6 + (x_5 \cdot y_7 = a_5)$	$b_7 + a_6$	0	$b_7 + a_6$
6	$x_7 \cdot y_3 = e_7$	y_4	$e_7 + (x_6 y_4 = d_6)$	$d_7 + c_6$	y_6	$d_7 + c_6 + (x_5 \cdot y_6 = b_5)$	$c_7 + b_6 + a_5$	0	$c_7 + b_6 + a_5$
7		y_3		$e_7 + d_6$	y_5	$e_7 + d_6 + (x_5 \cdot y_5 = c_5)$	$d_7 + c_6 + b_5$	y_7	$d_7 + c_6 + b_5 + (x_4 \cdot y_7 = a_4)$
8							$e_7 + d_6 + c_5$	y_6	$e_7 + d_6 + c_5 + (x_4 \cdot y_6 = b_4)$

described in Table V. The tabulation starts with all flip-flops reset and the least significant multiplier bit, y_7, being shifted out of the eight-stage parallel-to-serial (PSR) register. The table entries denote the computation results that would be observed at the indicated points once the clock trigger has been applied and the flip-flops switched to their new states. For the columns of the output sum the result takes into account the switching of the source flip-flops and the propagation delay through the adder.

There are three additional flip-flops per stage in Fig. 14.10. However, the carry propagates through only one stage before it is reclocked, whereas in Fig. 14.9 the carry propagates through all eight multiplicand stages. If the same circuits are used in both designs, it is apparent that considerably greater speed is obtained at the cost of three additional flip-flops per stage—an example of the speed–cost tradeoffs possible in digital design. The speedup is achieved by essentially reclocking the data after passage through combinational paths embracing a few functions. Although the reclocking causes the data to be delayed (causing latency), the data flow rate (i.e., multiplication rate) is increased.

The breakup of long combinational delay paths into short sections with intermediate reclocking registers is commonly referred to as pipelining, which is often used in digital design. An $M \times M$ multiplier with pipelined stages patterned after Fig. 14.10 will offer a speed improvement factor of M over a design based on Fig. 14.9, but the product appears only after $2M$ clock intervals. The final product is generated after eight clocks. However, a higher clock frequency than that for the array may be used.

MICROPROGRAMMING VI

A revision of the sequential network organization of Fig. 14.1 offers another perspective of the digital machine. If the memory is split into source and destination memories, as in Fig. 14.11, a basic data path can be defined as a register transfer process from source to destination registers via combinational elements. Register transfer descriptions, notations, and even languages have been used to describe this aspect of machine behavior. Again, all data paths can be articulated in this form. For example, a simple binary counter can be described as a single register that serves as both source and destination register with combinational elements that provide the binary counting logic.

A more significant example is the array multiplier discussed earlier. Two registers holding the multiplier and multiplicand are the source of data for the combinational elements of the multiplier array. Some time after the source registers have been loaded, the final product value can be captured in a destination register.

The data transfer process, in general, involves the selection of source register(s), enabling the desired switching functions to achieve arithmetic or logic opera-

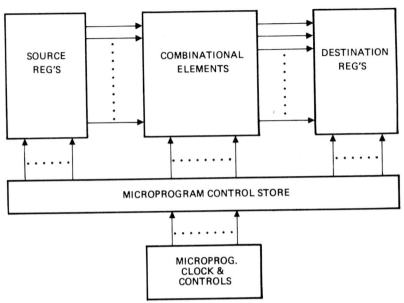

Fig. 14.11. Basic register transfer network with microprogram control.

tions, and destination register(s). The transfer takes place within one clock period, wherein all controls are held fixed for the duration of the period. If the source of all control signals is a control store or memory, as shown in Fig. 14.11, in effect, a microprogram control is realized. The microprogram approach [15, 16] to controls is used extensively in signal processing applications, since it provides control of processes at the lowest functional level. This is necessary to ensure that processing resources (i.e., adders and multipliers) are being used most efficiently.

A Microprogramming the FFT Butterfly

The microprogram process is illustrated by a radix-2 FFT butterfly. (See Section IV in Chapter 7 for a discussion of radix-2 FFTs and Section XIV of Chapter 7 for FFT word length and dynamic range considerations.) The data path resources are given in Fig. 14.12. A RAM holds a block of complex data for a storage-in-place FFT computation. The data from the real and imaginary blocks are multiplexed before loading the X input register of the MAC chip. The second operand is obtained from a sin/cos programmable read-only memory (PROM) and loaded into the Y input register of the MAC. The single-precision most significant half accumulation of final products is captured in the most significant product (MSP) register. Any auxiliary register buffers the MSP from the data bus that loads the RAM.

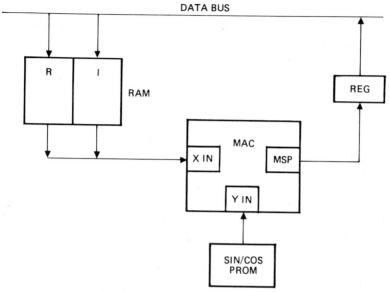

Fig. 14.12. Data paths for FFT butterfly.

The computations for the radix-2 butterfly shown in Fig. 14.13 are

$$A_i = \tfrac{1}{2}\{\overbrace{X_{Ri} + X_{Rj}\cos\theta_k + X_{Ij}\sin\theta_k}^{\alpha}$$
$$\underbrace{+ j[X_{Ii} + X_{Ij}\cos\theta_k - X_{Rj}\sin\theta_k]\}}_{\beta} \qquad (14.16a)$$

$$A_j = \tfrac{1}{2}\{X_{Ri} - (X_{Rj}\cos\theta_k + X_{Ij}\sin\theta_k)$$
$$+ j[X_{Ii} - (X_{Ij}\cos\theta_k - X_{Rj}\sin\theta_k)]\} \qquad (14.16b)$$

A computation strategy is necessary to ensure efficient microprogramming. From the butterfly equations we observe that four real products are computed and that two pairs of products are added together and two are subtracted.

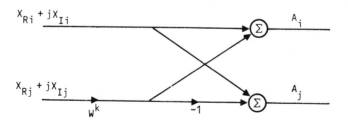

$$w^k = \cos\theta_k - j\sin\theta_k$$

Fig. 14.13. Radix-2 butterfly.

Although the product pairs are used in both equations, the addition and subtraction need be done only once. Further, there are two additions and two subtractions of the real and imaginary terms; finally, to prevent overflow in the next stage of this 2's complement fractional representation, all terms are scaled by $\frac{1}{2}$ before they are stored back in memory. (See discussions in Section XIV of Chapter 7.)

The MAC is the single arithmetic resource and must handle all the operations indicated above. The scaling must therefore be done as a full multiplication. The subtrahend in subtraction resides in the MAC. With these constraints the microprogram steps are listed in Table VI. Note that the contents of the PROM are already scaled by $\frac{1}{2}$.

The listings in the RAM column indicate the data variables being accessed. The addressing of the RAM and the PROM will be discussed later. One clock period is allowed for simultaneous access of both RAM and PROM; the operands X_{Rj} and $\frac{1}{2}\cos\theta_k$ are loaded into the X_{in} and Y_{in} registers of the MAC. Although these registers are not accessible, their contents are shown in the X_{in} and Y_{in} columns. One clock period later the accumulated products appear in the output MSP register. The accumulator has initially been cleared so the first accumulated product is $X_{Rj}(\frac{1}{2}\cos\theta_k)$. The next operands are accessed from the two memories and loaded into the MAC input register. One clock later the sum α of the two products appears in the output register.

The real component A_{Ri} of the first output term is next computed by adding another product, $\frac{1}{2}X_{Ri}$, to the accumulator α. The result A_{Ri} is passed on to the buffer register. To restore the accumulator to α for the next subtraction, the

TABLE VI
Process Steps for Microprogramming the Radix-2 Butterfly

Clock	RAM	PROM	X_{in}	Y_{in}	MAC MSP Reg.	Reg.
1	X_{Rj}	$\frac{1}{2}\cos\theta_k$			0	
2	X_{Ij}	$\frac{1}{2}\sin\theta_k$	X_{Rj}	$\frac{1}{2}\cos\theta_k$	0	
3	X_{Ri}	$\frac{1}{2}*$	X_{Ij}	$\frac{1}{2}\sin\theta_k$	$\frac{1}{2}X_{Rj}\cos\theta_k$	
4			X_{Ri}	$\frac{1}{2}$	$\frac{1}{2}X_{Rj}\cos\theta_k + \frac{1}{2}X_{Ij}\sin\theta_k = \alpha$	
5			X_{Ri}	$\frac{1}{2}$	$\alpha + \frac{1}{2}X_{Ri} = A_{Ri}$	
6	W A_{Ri}		X_{Ri}	$\frac{1}{2}$	$-A_{Ri} + \frac{1}{2}X_{Ri} = -\alpha$	A_{Ri}
7	X_{Rj}	$\frac{1}{2}\sin\theta_k$			$-\alpha + \frac{1}{2}X_{Ri} = A_{Rj}$	
8	X_{Ij}	$\frac{1}{2}\cos\theta_k$	X_{Rj}	$\frac{1}{2}\sin\theta_k$		A_{Rj}
9	X_{Ii}	$\frac{1}{2}*$	X_{Ij}	$\frac{1}{2}\cos\theta_k$	$\frac{1}{2}X_{Rj}\sin\theta_k$	
10	W A_{Rj}		X_{Ii}	$\frac{1}{2}$	$-\frac{1}{2}X_{Rj}\sin\theta_k + \frac{1}{2}\cos\theta_k = \beta$	
11			X_{Ii}	$\frac{1}{2}$	$\beta + \frac{1}{2}X_{Ii} = A_{Ii}$	
12	W A_{Ii}		X_{Ii}	$\frac{1}{2}$	$-A_{Ii} + \frac{1}{2}X_{Ii} = -\beta$	A_{Ii}
13					$-\beta + \frac{1}{2}X_{Ii} = A_{Ij}$	
14	W A_{Ij}					A_{Ij}

$* \frac{1}{2}\cos 0° = \frac{1}{2}$
W = Ram write

accumulated value A_{Ri} is subtracted from the input product, still $\frac{1}{2}X_{Ri}$. The result is $-\alpha$, which is then added to the same product from A_{Rj}, the real component of the second butterfly output. The computation of the imaginary components is similar and may be observed in the table.

The accessing of RAM data to keep the MAC utilized has the highest priority. Any time data are not being read, the RAM may be written into. The buffer register provides flexibility in choosing the write period. Once data are loaded into this register, and with no real access, the data may be written into the RAM as indicated in lines 6, 10, 12, and 14.

The microprogram controls for this data flow involve the following:

1. Addressing the RAM for reading and writing and also for generating the write pulse
2. Addressing the PROM
3. Generating the clocks to load X_{in} and Y_{in}
4. Setting the multiply–accumulate for one of the following modes:

    a. Multiply only
    b. Multiply and add
    c. Multiply and subtract

5. Clocking the data into the output, MSP, register

Table VI has been set up based solely on data flow requirements. A 14-clock cycle is indicated. The MAC is actively engaged for 10 cycles; that is, it operates with a duty factor of 71%. This is reasonably good use of the computing resources; indeed, duty factors of 50% are common. In any microprogram design the raw power of the processor (multiply–accumulates peer second) must be derated in assessing performance.

Performance is further reduced by the architectural constraints that necessitated a nonoptimal butterfly algorithm. Except in dedicated processors one cannot expect to find an optimal match of hardware and algorithm.

KEEPING THINGS IN PERSPECTIVE   VII

Designers have characterized the performance of an FFT circuit by the speed of its multiplier, because until the advent of LSl technologies it was the pacing element. Now, multipliers and adders are of comparable speed, and attention has shifted to the six additions required in the butterfly. However, for these six additions there are four accesses of complex data (eight memory cycles) and two accesses of table (ROM) data. Indeed, the memory access times may now be the limiting factor.

In addition to the arithmetic operations and memory accessing, there are the procedures to generate the memory addresses and FFT pass controls and other system interfaces. A review of the FFT flow diagram indicates that addressing is more than simply sequential. Separate address generation circuits operating in parallel with the FFT butterfly computation are often provided to restore balanced processing wherein the speed potential of the arithmetic number crunching circuits can be approached.

VIII   DISTRIBUTED ARITHMETIC

An implementation known variously as distributed arithmetic (DA), inner product, or Peled–Liu multiplier [17, 18, 19, 20] offers an interesting alternative to the dedicated hardware multiplier. The DA is a direct implementation of the sum of products (see Section III) that describes many input and signal processing algorithms. One essential restriction is that data are represented in fixed point formats. Consider the general sum of products expression.

$$Y = \sum_{i=0}^{N} A_i X_i, \tag{14.17}$$

where A_i is a constant term and X_i is an input variable. Let X_i be a fractional 2's complement number.

$$X_i = -x_{i0} + \sum_{j=i}^{b} x_{ij} 2^{-j} \tag{14.18}$$

Substituting Eq. (14.18) into Eq. (14.17) yields

$$Y = \sum_{i=0}^{N} A_i \left(-x_{i0} + \sum_{j=1}^{b} x_{ij} 2^{-j} \right) \tag{14.19a}$$

$$Y = -\sum_{i=0}^{N} x_{i0} A_i + \sum_{i=0}^{N} \sum_{j=1}^{b} x_{ij} A_i 2^{-j} \tag{14.19b}$$

and writing out the product terms within each summation yields

$$\begin{aligned}
Y = & -(x_{00} A_0 + x_{10} A_1 + x_{20} A_2 + \cdots + x_{N0} A_N) \\
& + 2^{-1}(x_{01} A_0 + x_{11} A_1 + x_{21} A_2 + \cdots + x_{N1} A_N) \\
& + 2^{-2}(x_{02} A_0 + x_{12} A_1 + x_{22} A_2 + \cdots + x_{N2} A_N) \\
& + \cdots + 2^{-b}(x_{0b} A_0 + x_{1b} A_1 + x_{2b} A_2 + \cdots + x_{Nb} A_N)
\end{aligned} \tag{14.19c}$$

Whereas Eq. (14.17) accomplishes a sum of the products of coefficients and data, Eq. (14.19c) distributes the arithmetic to products of coefficients and single bits of data; hence the name distributed arithmetic (DA). That is, the terms within each group of parentheses are the sums of all the coefficients or constants weighted by the binary (bit) values, that is, the jth bit of all the input variables. There are

TABLE VII

The Coefficient of 2^{-j} in Eq. (14.19c) as Determined
by X_{ij}, $i = 0, 1, \ldots, b$

Bit pattern				Parenthesis value
x_{bj} $\cdots$	x_{2j}	x_{1j}	x_{0j}	
0 $\cdots$	0	0	0	0
0 $\cdots$	0	0	1	A_0
0 $\cdots$	0	1	0	A_1
0 $\cdots$	0	1	1	$A_1 + A_0$
0 $\cdots$	1	0	0	A_2
0 $\cdots$	1	0	1	$A_2 + A_0$
0 $\cdots$	1	1	0	$A_2 + A_1$
0 $\cdots$	1	1	1	$A_2 + A_1 + A_0$
$\vdots$				$\vdots$
1 $\cdots$	1	1	1	$A_N + A_{N-1} + \cdots + A_2 + A_1 + A_0$

$2M + 1$ combinations of jth-bit patterns that translate into a corresponding number of different values within the parentheses; these are tabulated in Table VII. The table can be represented as a RAM or PROM that is addressed by the bits and with the address contents in memory indicated by the table. The contents within each set of parentheses of Eq. (14.19c) can be represented by the same table. In the final summation each parentheses is simply binary scaled in the manner indicated and the results are added. The summation of the partial products is effectively a distribution of the arithmetic process as opposed to a summation of all partial product terms. We have converted the multiply and accumulate process in Eq. (14.17) to a table look-up, shift accumulate process. The table look-up is possible because the coefficient values in Eq. (14.17) are fixed.

The implementation in Fig. 14.14 calls for a PSR to convert each input variable to bit serial data for addressing the memory (either PROM or RAM). The address

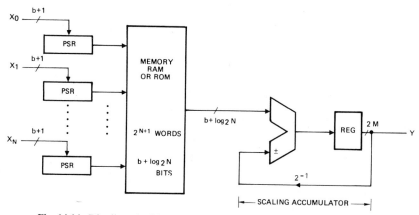

Fig. 14.14. Distributed arithmetic processor (PSR = parallel to serial register).

bits are sequenced with the lsb first. The memory output is scaled down by $\frac{1}{2}$ and stored in an accumulator register. The next lsb then addresses the memory whose contents are added to the accumulator with the sum, which is again scaled by $\frac{1}{2}$ and stored in the accumulator. The process repeats until the sign bit addresses the memory. Now the memory contents are subtracted from the accumulator, and the difference is the complete sum of products, which is now passed on to the next processing stage.

The bit-serial nature of the process tends to preclude high-speed processing. However, this is partially compensated by processing all inputs in parallel. The regularity of the memory array and the simplicity of the surrounding circuits (registers and adders) make the DA algorithm an attractive candate for VLSI implementation.

Unlike conventional hardware multipliers and MACs, the DA allows for different word sizes for input variables and stored constants. The input word (variable) length sets the speed of operation; the number of shift periods (clocks) matches the number of bits in the input word. To the hardware to accomplish this, we must add a few clocks for pipeline effects. By using two or more bits per word at a time to address memory, the number of shifts is reduced and the speed is thereby increased. However, this comes at the expense of increased memory size.

The number of words of memory is set by the number of input variables and the number of bits per word. The latter is set by the desired coefficient accuracy, which does not have to match the dynamic range of the input variables. The size of the parallel adder must match the memory word size. The accumulation of sums of partial products yields a double-precision result that may be rounded or truncated to the desired bit length of the output result.

A   FIR Filters in Distributed Arithmetic

The finite impulse response (FIR) filter is a simple realization of the sum of products (see Section III) and is easily configured in distributed arithmetic. An N-tap FIR filter is shown in Fig. 14.15 in both functional flow form and as it would be designed in DA form. Input samples are loaded in bit-parallel format into a PSR and thereafter sequenced serially through $N - 1$ serial shift registers. With the loading of each input word, the data are shifted by the b bits that represent the input word length. The precomputed combination of coefficient sums (see Table VII) are stored in a 2^{N+1} word PROM.

The PROM size becomes a limiting factor for FIR DA designs. For example, a 20-tap FIR filter (not extraordinarily large) requires $2^{20}(b + 1)$ or over $10^6 b$ words of PROM. Fortunately, very significant reductions in PROM size can be achieved for symmetrical FIR filters. If the outputs of symmetrical tap pairs are added bit-serial before addressing the PROM, the number of address lines is

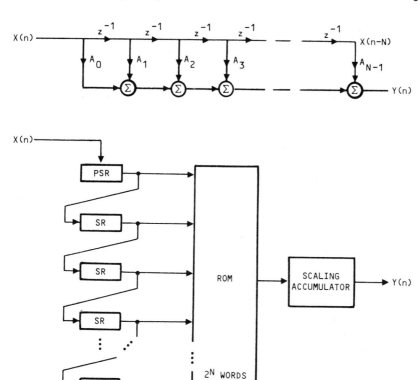

Fig. 14.15. An N-top FIR filter using distributed arithmetic.

halved. Thus in the example above, there are effectively 10 coefficients so that the PROM shrinks to $2^{10}(b + 1)$, or a little over $10^3 b$ words, which can be satisfied by standard PROM chips. A DA memory size of 1K words by 16 bits requires only two 1K × 8 PROM chips.

IIR Filters in Distributed Arithmetic   B

The infinite impulse response (IIR) filter difference equation can be written as a pair of sums of products expression:

$$y(n) = \sum_{i=0}^{M} X(n-i)A_i + \sum_{j=1}^{N} y(n-j)B_j \qquad (14.20)$$

There are several ways of implementing Eq. (14.20). If the two summing nodes are processed separately, then two separate DA circuits are employed and their outputs are added. The two summations may be incorporated into a single summing node with a single DA circuit. A single DA two-pole, two-zero IIR filter

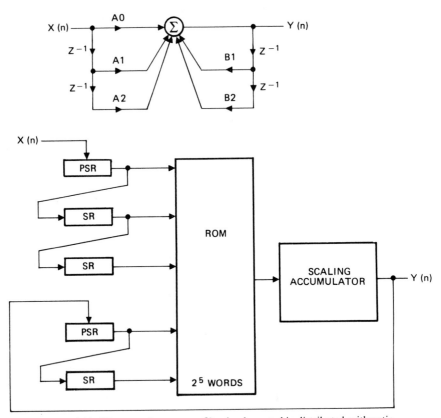

Fig. 14.16. IIR two-pole, two-zero filter implemented in distributed arithmetic.

is shown in Fig. 14.16. The input samples are loaded bit-parallel into a PSR just as in the FIR filter. The samples are then sequenced through a pair of serial shift registers. The output samples are similarly loaded bit-parallel and sequenced through one serial shift register. With a 20-MHz shift clock, an input sample rate of 1 million samples per second is possible.

Only five data lines address the PROM and, therefore, only 2^5 $(b + 1)$-bit words are prestored. The additional memory capacity available in standard PROM chips may be used to hold several different filter coefficient sets (i.e., filters with different transfer characteristics).

C The Radix-2 Butterfly in Distributed Arithmetic

The computations of the radix-2 butterfly [see Eq. (14.16)] can be partially implemented in DA. The pair of terms denoted by α in Eq. (14.16a) is a sum of products. The prestored coefficients are $\cos \theta_k$ and $\sin \theta_k$, and these will extend over $N/2$ values (see, e.g., Figs. 7.9 and 7.10), where N is the FFT size. The PROM address lines are now $2 + \log_2 N/2$ lines where the two lines are for the radix-2 butterfly data inputs. Thus, for a 4096-point FFT the number of address lines is 13; an 8K word PROM is required. As each radix-2 butterfly is computed, the index k, $0 \leq k \leq \log_2 N/2$, is incremented in accordance with the FFT pass number.

The same PROM may serve for the computation of β of Eq. (14.16). The data input lines are swapped, and the line addressing the $\sin \theta_k$ port is complemented. The implementation may be realized by time sharing a single PROM and scaling accumulator over two cycles or by using a pair of PROMs and scaling accumulators over a single cycle.

Halving the DA Memory D

An ingenious scheme offers the possibility of halving the DA memory at the cost of additional controls in the address lines [18, 19]. The scheme is predicated on a 2's complement number representation and follows a development similar to our earlier expressions (14.17)–(14.19). We start with an almost trivial identity

$$X_i = \tfrac{1}{2}[X_i - (-X_i)] \tag{14.21}$$

In 2's complement notation a negative value is obtained by complementing bit by bit and then adding an lsb. Substituting the 2's complement number of Eq. (14.18) into Eq. (14.21), we obtain

$$X_i = \frac{1}{2}\left[-x_{i0} + \sum_{j=1}^{b} x_{ij}2^{-j} - \left(-x'_{i0} + \sum_{j=1}^{b} x'_{ij}2^{-j} + 2^{-b}\right)\right] \tag{14.21a}$$

$$= \frac{1}{2}\left[-(x_{i0} - x'_{i0}) + \sum_{j=1}^{b} (x_{ij} - x'_{ij})2^{-j} - 2^{-b}\right] \tag{14.21b}$$

where prime means complement (see Table II). Substituting Eq. (14.21b) in the product terms of Eq. (14.19c) yields

$$Y = -2^{-1}[(x_{00} - x'_{00})A_0 + (x_{10} - x'_{10})A_1 + \cdots + (x_{N0} - x'_{N0})A_N]$$
$$+ 2^{-2}[(x_{01} - x'_{01})A_0 + (x_{11} - x'_{11})A_1 + \cdots + (x_{N1} - x'_{N1})A_N]$$
$$\vdots$$
$$+ 2^{-b-1}[(x_{0b} - x'_{0b})A_0 + (x_{1b} - x'_{1b})A_1 + \cdots + (x_{Nb} - x'_{Nb})A_N]$$
$$- 2^{-b-1}[(N + 1)(A_0 + A_1 + \cdots + A_N)] \tag{14.21c}$$

Note that $x_{ij} - x'_{ij}$ is either $+1$ or -1 for all i, j values. Thus, a coefficient table similar to Table VIII will contain all possible ways in which the coefficients may be added or subtracted, as shown in Table VIII for $N = 2$. A single-cycle

TABLE VIII

Coefficients of 2^{-j} for $N = 2$

Bit (address) pattern			Memory content		
x_2	x_1	x_0			
0	0	0	$-A_2$	$-A_1$	$-A_0$
0	0	1	$-A_2$	$-A_1$	$+A_0$
0	1	0	$-A_2$	$+A_1$	$-A_0$
0	1	1	$-A_2$	$+A_1$	$+A_0$
1	0	0	$+A_2$	$-A_1$	$+A_0$
1	0	1	$+A_2$	$-A_1$	$+A_0$
1	1	0	$+A_2$	$+A_1$	$-A_0$
1	1	1	$+A_2$	$+A_1$	$+A_0$

implementation of the radix-2 butterfly of Fig. 14.13 is shown in Fig. 14.17. Since this is a block process, the computations can be pipelined to include serial addition to obtain the complete butterfly result.

Note that only half the memory contains independent values; the other half may be obtained by a sign change of the contents. A simple algorithm for

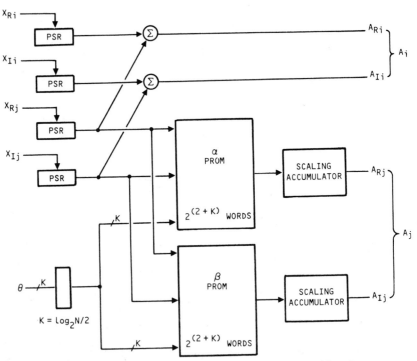

Fig. 14.17. Radix-2 butterfly implemented in distributed arithmetic.

TABLE IX

Address Translation and Add/Subtract Control

Original address			Modified address			
x_2	x_1	x_0	$x\hat{x}_2$	$x\hat{x}_1$	$x\hat{x}_0$	A/S
0	0	0	0	0	0	A
0	0	1	0	0	1	A
0	1	0	0	1	0	A
0	1	1	0	1	1	A
1	0	0	0	1	1	S
1	0	1	0	1	0	S
1	1	0	0	0	1	S
1	1	1	0	0	0	S

realizing this involves an address modification and slightly more elaborate control of the add/subtract functions of the scaling accumulator. The address modification and add/subtract control are illustrated in Table IX for $N = 2$. The table may be summarized by the Boolean relations

$$\hat{x}_0 = x_2 \oplus x_0, \qquad \hat{x}_1 = x_2 \oplus x_1 \qquad (14.22)$$

Here x_2 serves as a control bit; this is an arbitrary assignment, and any variable may serve this purpose. Note that one less bit is required to address the memory; that is, half the original memory is used. The add/subtract control must not only conform to the table but must also provide the subtract function when the sign bits are accumulated at T_s:

$$A = x_2 \oplus T_s, \qquad S = A'$$

The modified DA functional block diagram is shown in Fig. 14.18. Note that the accumulator register is initially set to the initial condition $-(N + 1)(A_0 + A_1 + \cdots + A_N)$. This method may be extended by separating the input words

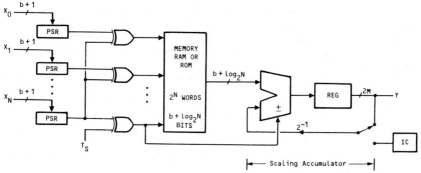

Fig. 14.18. Distributed arithmetic processor that halves the DA memory (PSR = parallel to serial register).

into equal-length segments (e.g., bytes) and applying each segment to replicated circuitry [20]. This increases multiplier speed at the expense of increased DA hardware. DA offers a wide range of configurations to satisfy many system requirements.

IX SUMMARY

The rapid pace of hardware development in DSP tends to render any material obsolete before the printer's ink dries. We have thus attempted to present hardware concepts that are fundamental and invariant under any future changes. Boolean algebra, switching circuits, and memory elements provide the basis for all digital mechanizations, whether be dedicated processors, programmable processors, or networks of processors. An input design principle is the desirability to maintain appropriate balance among arithmetic speed, data movement, and system control.

The expression that characterizes many of the important signal processing algorithms is the sum of products. Multiplication is the pervading arithmetic operation and is covered by a discussion of both parallel (array) and serial multiplier circuits. Microprogramming, whether user accessible or embedded in the hardware, provides efficient control of the arithmetic functions.

An alternative to the hardware multiplier is the memory-based distributed arithmetic direct realization of the sum of products. The simplicity and regularity of this structure makes it attractive for VLSI implementation.

REFERENCES

1. M. Mano, *Digital Logic and Computer Design*, Prentice-Hall, Englewood Cliffs, N.J., 1979.
2. J. Allen, Computer architecture for digital signal Processing, *Proc. IEEE* **73**, 832–873 (May 1985).
3. S. L. Freeny, Special purpose hardware for digital Filtering, *Proc. IEEE* **63**, 633–648 (April 1975).
4. H. T. Kung and C. E. Leiserson, Systolic arrays for VLSI, in *Introduction to VLSI Systems*, edited by C. A. Mead and L. A. Conway, Addison-Wesley, Reading, Mass., 1980, Sec. 8.3.
5. S. Y. Kung, On supercomputing with systolic/wavefront array processors, *Proc. IEEE* **72**, 862–884 (July 1984).
6. J. Roesgen and S. Tung, DSP chip with external memory, *Electronic Design*, 131–144 (February 1985).
7. M. Schwartz *et al.*, Multiple Bus DSP, *Electronic Design*, 147–153 (February 1985).
8. B. Eichen *et al.*, 32-bit DSP, *Electronic Design*, 159–165 (February 1985).
9. T. V. Kampen and P. Anders, DSP chip with parallel architecture, 1377 *Electronic Design*, 169–174 (February 1985).
10. K. Marin, Six DSP processors tackle high-end signal processing applications, *Computer Design*, 21–25 (March 1986).
11. C. S. Wallace, A suggestion for a fast multiplier, *IEEE Trans. Electronic Comput.* **EC-13**, 14–17 (February 1984).

12. W. J. Stenzel *et al.*, A compact high speed parallel multiplication scheme, *IEEE Trans. Computers.* **C-26,** 948–957 (October 1977).
13. E. E. Swartzlander and B. K. Gilbert, Arithmetic for ultra-high-speed tomography, *IEEE Trans. Computers* **C-29,** 341–353 (May 1980).
14. P. E. Danielsson, Serial/parallel convolvers, *IEEE Trans. Computers* **C-33,** 652–667 (July 1984).
15. D. A. Patterson, Microprogramming, *Scientific American,* 50–57 (March 1983).
16. A. Agrawala and T. Rauscher, *Foundations of Microprogramming,* Academic Press, New York, 1984.
17. A. Peled and B. Liu, A new hardware realization of digital filters, *IEEE Trans. Acoust. Speech Signal Process.* **ASSP-22,** 456–462 (1974).
18. M. Buttner and H. W. Schuessler, On structures for the implementation of the distributed arithmetic, *NTZ Communication J.* **Z29,** 472–477, **6,** (1976).
19. S. A. White, A simple FFT butterfly arithmetic unit, *IEEE Trans., Circuits Systems* **CAS-28,** 352–355 (April 1981).
20. C. S. Burrus, Digital filter realization by distributed arithmetic, *Proc. Int. Sym. on Circuits and Systems, Munich,* 106–109, (April 1976).

Addendum to Chapter **3**
Window Generation Computer Program

```
C
C     Program author:    Fred Harris
C
C     Inquiries concerning this program are directed to:
C
C          Fred Harris
C          Electrical & Computer Engineering Department
C          San Diego State University
C          San Diego, CA 92182
C
C     This program generates classic data windows, of arbitrary length,
C     to be applied multiplicatively in the time domain. The program is
C     menu driven and controlled by prompts. In addition to the window,
C     the program computes and presents standard figures of merit (see
C     F. Harris, "On the use of Windows for Harmonic Analysis with the
C     Discrete Fourier Transform", Proc. of IEEE, Vol. 66, No. 1, Jan.
C     1978, pp. 51-83) for the particular window.
C
C     A TYPICAL PROMPTED INTERACTION HAS THE FOLLOWING FORM
C
C               ***** SELECT WINDOW TYPE FROM MENU *****
C                1. TRIANGLE                (-27 DB SIDELOBE)
C                2. HANN                     (-32 DB SIDELOBE)
C                3. HAMMING                  (-43 DB SIDELOBE)
C                4. GAUSSIAN            (SELECTABLE SIDELOBE)
C                5. DOLPH-TCHEBYSHEV    (SELECTABLE SIDELOBE)
C                6. KAISER-BESSEL       (SELECTABLE SIDELOBE)
C                7. TAYLOR              (SELECTABLE SIDELOBE)
C                8. EXACT BLACKMAN           (-68 DB SIDELOBE)
C                9. MIN  3-TERM BH           (-71 DB SIDELOBE)
C               10. GOOD 4-TERM BH           (-80 DB SIDELOBE)
C               11. MIN  4-TERM BH           (-98 DB SIDELOBE)
C               12. RECTANGLE                (-13 DB SIDELOBE)
C               13. HARRIS FLAT TOP          (-80 DB SIDELOBE)
C
C               ENTER CHOICE (1-13)                    -> 2
C
C               SELECT WINDOW SIZE (1 < N < 2049)      -> 20
C
C                    COHERENT GAIN   =    .5000
C                            ENBW    =   1.5000 (BINS)
C                                    =   1.7609 dB
C               MAX SCALLOP LOSS     =  -1.4235 dB
C          CORRELATION  \  C(75%)   =    .6592
C          COEFFICIENTS /  C(50%)   =    .1667
C                       3 dB WIDTH   =   1.4398 (BINS)
C                       6 dB WIDTH   =   2.0000 (BINS)
C
C               WRITE A WINDOW FILE? (Y,N)          ->Y   N
C               DO YOU WANT ANOTHER WINDOW? (Y,N)  ->Y   N
C
C
```

```
        PROGRAM WINDOW

        DIMENSION WW(2048),alist(10)
        DIMENSION T2(2),T3(2),T7(20),T8(3)
        DIMENSION T9(3),T10(4),T11(4),T13(4)
        CHARACTER*10 FNAME,QANS
        DATA T2/0.5,-0.5/
        DATA T3/0.54,-0.46/
        DATA T8/0.42659071,-0.49656062,0.07684867/
        DATA T9/0.4243801,-0.4973406,0.0782793/
        DATA T10/0.3780294,-0.4940071,0.1221416,-0.0058219/
        DATA T11/0.3635819,-0.4891775,0.1365995,-0.0106411/
        DATA T13/0.3066923,-0.4748398,0.1924696,-0.0259983/

1       WRITE(*,*)' '
        WRITE(*,*)' ****** SELECT WINDOW TYPE FROM MENU ******'
        WRITE(*,*)'  1. TRIANGLE                  (-27 DB SIDELOBE)'
        WRITE(*,*)'  2. HANN                       (-32 DB SIDELOBE)'
        WRITE(*,*)'  3. HAMMING                    (-43 DB SIDELOBE)'
        WRITE(*,*)'  4. GAUSSIAN            (SELECTABLE SIDELOBE)'
        WRITE(*,*)'  5. DOLPH-TCHEBYSHEV (SELECTABLE SIDELOBE)'
        WRITE(*,*)'  6. KAISER-BESSEL       (SELECTABLE SIDELOBE)'
        WRITE(*,*)'  7. TAYLOR              (SELECTABLE SIDELOBE)'
        WRITE(*,*)'  8. EXACT BLACKMAN         (-68 DB SIDELOBE)'
        WRITE(*,*)'  9. MIN   3-TERM BH        (-71 DB SIDELOBE)'
        WRITE(*,*)' 10. GOOD 4-TERM BH         (-80 DB SIDELOBE)'
        WRITE(*,*)' 11. MIN   4-TERM BH        (-98 DB SIDELOBE)'
        WRITE(*,*)' 12. RECTANGLE              (-13 DB SIDELOBE)'
        WRITE(*,*)' 13. HARRIS FLAT TOP        (-80 DB SIDELOBE)'
        WRITE(*,*)' '
5       WRITE(*,'(A\)')' ENTER CHOICE (1-13)                      -> '
        READ(*,*) ISLCT
        IF(ISLCT.LE.0.OR.ISLCT.GE.14) GO TO 5
        WRITE(*,*)' '
8       WRITE(*,'(A\)')' SELECT WINDOW SIZE (1 < N < 2049)        -> '
        READ(*,*) NWNDO
        IF(NWNDO.LE.0.OR.NWNDO.GE.2049) GO TO 8

        GO TO (10,20,30,40,50,60,70,80,90,100,110,120,130), ISLCT

C  CALL TO TRIANGLE WINDOW
 10     CALL TRNGL(NWNDO,WW)
        GO TO 200

C  CALL TO TRIG WINDOW WITH HANN COEFFICIENTS
 20     CALL TRIG(NWNDO,WW,T2,2)
        GO TO 200

C  CALL TO TRIG WINDOW WITH HAMMING COEFFICIENTS
 30     CALL TRIG(NWNDO,WW,T3,2)
        GO TO 200

C CALL TO GAUSSIAN WINDOW
 40     WRITE(*,'(A\)')' SELECT DESIRED SIDELOBE LEVELS      -> '
        READ(*,*) SLL
        SLL=ABS(SLL)
        CALL GAUSS(NWNDO,SLL,WW,ALPHA)
        WRITE(*,45) ALPHA
 45     FORMAT(' GAUSSIAN PARAMETER ALPHA = ',F6.4)
        GO TO 200

C  CALL TO DOLPH-TCHEBYSCHEV WINDOW
```

```
  50       WRITE(*,'(A\)')' SELECT DESIRED SIDELOBE LEVELS    -> '
           READ(*,*) SLL
           SLL=ABS(SLL)
           CALL TCHEBY(NWNDO,SLL,WW)
           GO TO 200

C CALL TO KAISER-BESSEL WINDOW
  60       WRITE(*,'(A\)')' SELECT DESIRED SIDELOBE LEVELS    -> '
           READ(*,*) SLL
           SLL=ABS(SLL)
           CALL KAISER(NWNDO,SLL,WW,ALPHA)
           WRITE(*,65) ALPHA
  65       FORMAT(' KAISER-BESSEL PARAMETER ALPHA = ',F10.4)
           GO TO 200

C CALL TO TAYLOR WINDOW
  70       WRITE(*,'(A\)')' SELECT DESIRED SIDELOBE LEVELS    -> '
           READ(*,*) SLL
           SLL=ABS(SLL)
           NBAR=1
           CALL TAYLOR(NWNDO,SLL,T7,NBAR)
           CALL TRIG(NWNDO,WW,T7,NBAR)
           GO TO 200

C CALL TO BLACKMAN WINDOW
  80       CALL TRIG(NWNDO,WW,T8,3)
           GO TO 200

C CALL TO MINIMUM 3-TERM BLACKMAN-HARRIS WINDOW
  90       CALL TRIG(NWNDO,WW,T9,3)
           GO TO 200

C CALL TO 4-TERM 80 DB BLACKMAN-HARRIS WINDOW
 100       CALL TRIG(NWNDO,WW,T10,4)
           GO TO 200

C CALL TO MINIMUM 4-TERM BLACKMAN-HARRIS WINDOW
 110       CALL TRIG(NWNDO,WW,T11,4)
           GO TO 200

C CALL TO RECTANGLE
 120       CALL RECT(NWNDO,WW)
           GO TO 200

C CALL TO HARRIS FLATOP
 130       CALL TRIG(NWNDO,WW,T13,4)
           GO TO 200

C WINDOW TEST PARAMETERS
 200       CONTINUE
           CALL TEST(nwndo,ww,alist)
           write(*,220) alist(1)
 220       format(/,10x,'  COHERENT GAIN = ',f7.4)
           write(*,221) alist(2),alist(3),alist(6)
 221       format( 10x,'           ENBW = ',f7.4,' (BINS)',/,25x,
     c     ' = ',f7.4,' dB',/,9x,'MAX SCALLOP LOSS = ',f7.4,' dB')
           write(*,222) alist(4),alist(5)
 222       format('   CORRELATION  \  C(75%) = ',f7.4,/,
     c     '   COEFFICIENTS /  C(50%) = ',f7.4)
           CALL DBTEST(nwndo,ww)
           WRITE(*,*)' '
           WRITE(*,'(A\)')' WRITE A WINDOW FILE? (Y,N)       ->Y '
           READ(*,'(A)') QANS
```

```
         IF(QANS.EQ.'N'.OR.QANS.EQ.'n') GO TO 320
         WRITE(*,'(A\)')' NAME OF OUTPUT FILE ?                  -> '
         READ(*,309)FNAME
  309    FORMAT(A)
         OPEN(20,FILE=FNAME,status='NEW')

         DO 310 I=1,NWNDO
         WRITE(20,*) I,WW(I)
  310    CONTINUE
         CLOSE(UNIT=20)
         WRITE(*,*)' '
         WRITE(*,*)'       THE WINDOW COEFFICIENTS HAVE BEEN WRITTEN.'
         WRITE(*,*)' '
  320    WRITE(*,'(A\)')' DO YOU WANT ANOTHER WINDOW? (Y,N)      ->Y '
         READ(*,'(A)') QANS
         IF(QANS.NE.'N'.AND.QANS.NE.'n') GO TO 1
         WRITE(*,*)' '
         WRITE(*,*)'          BY'
         END

CCC
C SUBROUTINE TRNGL FORMS TRIANGLE WINDOW

         SUBROUTINE TRNGL(NWNDO,WW)
         REAL WW(1)
         integer nwndo

         NN=(NWNDO+1)/2
         STEP=0.0
         DSTEP=1.0/FLOAT(NN)

         WW(NWNDO/2+1)=1.0

         DO 10 I=1,NN
         WW(I)=STEP
         WW(NWNDO+2-I)=WW(I)
         STEP=STEP+DSTEP
  10     continue

         RETURN
         END

CCC
C SUBROUTINE TRIG FORMS WINDOW FROM SHORT COSINE SERIES

         SUBROUTINE TRIG(NWNDO,WW,COEF,NTRMS)
         DIMENSION W(20)
         REAL WW(1),COEF(1)
         integer nwndo,ntrms

         DO 10 I=1,NTRMS
C        W(I)=COEF(I)/SUM
         W(I)=COEF(I)
  10     continue

         TWOPI=8.0*ATAN(1.0)
         THETA=0.0
         DDTHETA=TWOPI/FLOAT(NWNDO)
         NN=(NWNDO/2)+1

         DTHETA = DDTHETA
         DO 15 J=1,NN
```

```
         WW(J)=W(1)
15       continue

C        WW(NWNDO/2+1)=1.0

         DTHETA=DDTHETA
         DO 25 I=2,NTRMS
         THETA=0.0
         DO 20 J=1,NN
         WW(J)=WW(J)+W(I)*COS(THETA)
         THETA=THETA+DTHETA
20       continue
         DTHETA=DTHETA+DDTHETA
25       continue

         DO 30 J=1,NN
         WW(NWNDO+2-J)=WW(J)
30       continue

         RETURN
         END

CCC
C SUBROUTINE GAUSS  FORMS GAUSSIAN WINDOW

         SUBROUTINE GAUSS(NWNDO,SLL,WW,ALPHA)
         REAL SLL,WW(1),ALPHA
         integer nwndo

         ETA=-(SLL-19.0)/20.0
         ETA=10.0**ETA
         ALPHA=-2.0*ALOG(ETA)
         ALPHA=SQRT(ALPHA)

         FN=FLOAT(NWNDO)
         NN=(NWNDO/2)+1
         FNN=FN/2.

         WW(NWNDO/2+1)=1.0

         ALPHA=ALPHA/FNN
         DO 10 K=1,NN
         FK=FNN-FLOAT(K-1)

         ARG=ALPHA*FK
         ARG=-0.5*ARG*ARG

         WW(K)=EXP(ARG)
         WW(NWNDO-K+2)=WW(K)
10       continue

         RETURN
         END

CCC
C SUBROUTINE TCHEBY FORMS DOLPH-TCHEBYSHEV WINDOW

         SUBROUTINE TCHEBY(NWNDO,SLL,WW)
         REAL SLL,WW(1)
         integer nwndo
         DOUBLE PRECISION A,B,C,D,FK,FI,FJ,FN,SCL
```

```
          FN=FLOAT(NWNDO)+1.
          NN=(NWNDO+2)/2

          S=10.0**(SLL/20.0)
          AA=ALOG(S+SQRT(S*S-1.0))/(FN-1.0)
          BB=EXP(AA)
          BBI=1.0/BB
          A=(BB - BBI)/(BB + BBI)
          A=A*A

          DO 35 K=2,NN
          FK=FLOAT(K)
          KK=K-1
          B=0.0

          DO 30 J=1,KK
          FJ=FLOAT(J)
          JJ=J-1
          C=1.0
          D=1.0
          IF(J-1) 1,3,1

1         DO 25 I=1,JJ
          FI=FLOAT(I)
          C=C*(FK-1.0-FI)/FI
25        continue

3         DO 20 I=1,J
          FI=FLOAT(I)
          D=D*(FN-FK+1.0-FI)/FI
20        continue
          B=B+C*D*(A**FJ)
30        continue
          SCL=(FN-1.)/(FN-FK)
          WW(K)=B*SCL
35        continue

          WW(1)=1.0
          WW(NWNDO)=1.0
          SCL=WW(NN)
          DO 15 K=1,NN
          WW(K)=WW(K)/SCL
          WW(NWNDO+2-K)=WW(K)
15        continue

          RETURN
          END

CCC
C SUBROUTINE KAISER FORMS KAISER-BESSEL WINDOW

          SUBROUTINE KAISER(NWNDO,SLL,WW,ETA)
          REAL SLL, WW(1),ETA
          integer nwndo
          DOUBLE PRECISION X,EXPX,EXPX1,Y,YDOT,DX

          PI=4.0*ATAN(1.0)
          SCL=0.75*PI
          ETA=10.0**(SLL/20.0)
          X=1.14*ALOG(ETA)

10        EXPX=EXP(X)
```

```
          EXPXI=1.0/EXPX
          Y=SCL*((EXPX-EXPXI)/X)-ETA
          YDOT=SCL*((EXPX+EXPXI)-((EXPX-EXPXI)/X))/X
          DX=Y/YDOT
          IF(ABS(DX).LT.0.000001.OR.ABS(Y).LT.0.001) GO TO 20
          X=X-DX
          GO TO 10

20        ETA=X
          FN=FLOAT(NWNDO)+1.0
          NN=(NWNDO+2)/2
          FNN=FLOAT(NN-1)

          DO 101 K=1,NN
          FK=FLOAT(NN-K)
          B=1.0
          ADD=1.0

          ARG=0.5*ETA*SQRT(1.0 -(FK/FNN)**2.0)
          ARG=ARG*ARG
          FJ=1.0
30        ADD=ADD+ARG/(FJ*FJ)
          B=B+ADD
          FJ=FJ+1.0
          IF(ADD.LE.0.000001.OR.FJ.GE.40.0) GO TO 40
          GO TO 30

40        WW(K)=B
101       continue

          SCL=WW(NN)
          DO 15 K=1,NN
          WW(K)=WW(K)/SCL
          WW(NWNDO+2-K)=WW(K)
15        continue

          RETURN
          END

CCC
C SUBROUTINE TAYLOR FORMS TAYLOR WINDOW

          SUBROUTINE TAYLOR(NWNDO,SLL,T7,NBAR)
          REAL SLL,T7(1)
          integer nwndo,NBAR

          PI=4.0*ATAN(1.0)

          ETA=10.0**(SLL/20.0)
          ASQ=ALOG(ETA+SQRT(ETA*ETA-1.0))/PI
          ASQ=ASQ*ASQ
          ENBAR=1.0
          SGMA1=0.0

10        CONTINUE
          SGMA2=(ENBAR*ENBAR)/(ASQ+(ENBAR-0.5)*(ENBAR-0.5))
          IF(SGMA2.LT.SGMA1) GO TO 20
          ENBAR=ENBAR+1.0
          SGMA1=SGMA2
          GO TO 10

20        ENBAR=ENBAR-1.0
          NBAR=IFIX(ENBAR)
```

```
        DO 101 M=1,NBAR-1
        FM=FLOAT(M)
        RMM=FM*FM
        PROD1=1.0
        PROD2=1.0

        DO 15 N=1,NBAR-1
        IF(N.EQ.M) GO TO 50
        FN=FLOAT(N)
        RNN=FN*FN
        PROD1=PROD1*(1.0-RMM/RNN)
50      CONTINUE
15      continue

        Q=0.5/PROD1
        DO 201 N=1,NBAR-1
        FN=FLOAT(N)
        ZNSQ=SGMA1*(ASQ+(FN-0.5)*(FN-0.5))
        PROD2=PROD2*(1.0-RMM/ZNSQ)
201     continue

        SM=PROD2*(-1.0)**(M+1)
        T7(M+1)=2.0*Q*SM
101     continue

        T7(1)=1.0
        SUM=0.0
        DO 25 I=1,NBAR
        SUM=SUM+T7(I)
25      continue

        SIGN=+1.0
        DO 30 I=1,NBAR
        T7(I)=SIGN*T7(I)/SUM
        SIGN=-SIGN
30      continue

        return
        end

C SUBROUTINE RECT
        SUBROUTINE RECT(NWNDO,WW)
        REAL WW(1)
        INTEGER NWNDO

        DO 10 I=1,NWNDO
        WW(I)=1.0
10      continue
        RETURN
        END

CCC
C SUBROUTINE TO COMPUTE PARAMETERS OF WINDOW

        subroutine test(nwndo,ww,alist)
        real ww(1),alist(1)
        dimension trns(2049)
        integer nwndo

        fn=float(nwndo)
        sum1=0.0
        sum2=0.0
```

```
          do 10 i=1,nwndo
          sum1=sum1+ww(i)
          sum2=sum2+ww(i)*ww(i)
10        continue

          alist(1)=sum1/fn

C         COMPUTE SCALLOP LOSS
          call xform(nwndo,ww,.5,alist(6))
          alist(6)=alist(6)/sum1
          alist(6)=20*alog10(alist(6))
          alist(2)=fn*sum2/(sum1*sum1)
          alist(3)=10.0*alog10(alist(2))
          SMSQ=SUM2

c 75% O.L. correlation
          sum1=0.0
          sum2=0.0
          n1=NWNDO/4

          do 15 i=1,nwndo-n1
          sum1=sum1+ww(i)*ww(i+n1)
15        continue
          sum1=sum1/SMSQ

          do 20 i=1,nwndo-n1-1
          sum2=sum2+ww(i)*ww(i+n1+1)
20        continue
          sum2=sum2/SMSQ

          c75=sum1 -(sum1-sum2)*(float(nwndo-4*(nwndo/4)))/4.0

c 50% O.L. correlation
          sum1=0.0
          sum2=0.0
          n2=nwndo/2

          do 25 i=1,nwndo-n2
          sum1=sum1+ww(i)*ww(i+n2)
25        continue
          sum1=sum1/SMSQ

          do 30 i=1,nwndo-n2-1
          sum2=sum2+ww(i)*ww(i+n2+1)
30        continue
          sum2=sum2/SMSQ

          c50=sum1 -(sum1-sum2)*(float(nwndo-2*(nwndo/2)))/2.0
          alist(4)=c75
          alist(5)=c50

          RETURN
          END

CCC
C         SUBROUTINE DBTEST FINDS THE THREE DB AND SIX DB POINTS OF THE
C         WINDOW.

          SUBROUTINE DBTEST(nwndo,ww)
          REAL WW(1),x(2)
          integer nwndo,j
          real dc,half,lx,hx,flx,fhx
```

```
        real error,bound
        real dx,dy,deltax,deltay

c       find dc value
        call xform(nwndo,ww,0,dc)

c       find half power point
c       x(2) is 6 db point
c       x(1) is 3 db point
        x(2)=dc/2.0
        x(1)=dc*(sqrt(2.0)/2.0)

        do 100 j=1,2
          half=x(j)
c       box the 6db region with lx and hx
        hx=1.0
        flx=dc
        lx=0
10      continue
        call xform(nwndo,ww,hx,fhx)
        if(fhx.lt.half)goto 15
        lx=hx
        hx=hx+1.0
        flx=fhx
        goto 10
15      bound=10e-3

c       find slope
60      deltax=hx-lx
        deltay=flx-fhx
        dy=flx-half
        dx=dy*(deltax/deltay)
        lx=lx+dx
        call xform(nwndo,ww,lx,flx)
        error=flx-half
        if(error.le.bound)goto 55
        goto 60

55      if(j.eq.2)write(*,99)lx*2
        if(j.eq.1)write(*,98)lx*2
98      format(10x,'      3 DB WIDTH = ',f7.4,' (BINS)')
99      format(10x,'      6 DB WIDTH = ',f7.4,' (BINS)')
100     continue
        return
        end


        subroutine xform(nwndo,ww,k,fk)
        integer nwndo,i
        real ww(1),twopi,k,fk,fnwndo,c1,c2,w0,w1,w2
        real phi,dphi,re,im

        twopi=8*atan(1.0)
        fnwndo=float(nwndo)

c       take DFT at specific points

        phi=(twopi/fnwndo)*k

        c1=-2.0*cos(phi)
        c2=1.0
        w0=0.0
        w1=0.0
```

```
        w2=0.0

        do 10 i=1,nwndo
          w0=ww(i)-c1*w1-c2*w2
          w2=w1
          w1=w0
10        continue
        w0=-c1*w1-c2*w2
        re=w0-w1*(c1/(-2.0))
        im=-w1*sin(phi)
        fk=sqrt(re*re+im*im)

        return
        end
```

Index

A

Acoustic tube model, 778
  for deconvolution, 778
  reflection coefficients, 779
Acoustic wave equation, 778
  model for speech signal processing, 778
Active linear two-sensor array, 798, 799
Active radar and sonar, 837
Adaptive filtering, 857
  See also adaptive filters
  frequency domain, 889
  channel equalizer, 889
  finite impulse response, 858
  forward prediction, 882
  infinite impulse response, 889
  lattice structure, 882
  learning curve, 880
  least-squares configuration, 864
  line enhancer, 879
  misadjustment of weighting vector in, 880
  modified algorithm for, 874
  noise canceler configuration, 864, 872
  predictor configuration, 871, 882
  noisy gradient's impact on design of, 868
  no-pass phenomena, 880
  signal-to-noise ratio, 878
  steepest-descent design technique, 866
  time constant, 876
Aliasing
  See spectral aliasing
All-pass filters
  basics, 453
  gray and marked structure, 454
  structures for, 454
  structures based on, 444
  trivial all-pass filter, 793, 795
Alternation theorem, 73
Ambiguity function, 842

Amplitude-change function, 110
And gate
  See gates
Angle estimation, 810
  by means of matched spatial filter, 810
  algorithm for, 810
Arithmetic operations
  See complex bandshifting, fast Fourier
    transforms, and operations per output
    point
Array multiplication, 951
Assembly language prime factor algorithm,
    621
Attenuation, 60, 305
Autocorrelation, 45, 702, 749, 770
  See also correlation
  unbiased estimate of, 770
Autoregressive (AR) system
  See also spectral analysis
  deconvolution, 766
  fast algorithm for, 766
  lattice filters for, 774
  identification
    with known statistics, 766
    with unknown statistics, 770
  models, 766, 780
  speech signal processing, for, 780
  process, 766
    direct form block diagram, 766
    linear prediction, and, 756
Autoregressive-moving average (ARMA)
    systems, 752
  See also discrete-time linear time-invariant
    systems and spectral analysis
    process, 758
  deconvolution, 753
  double deconvolution algorithm, 754
  identification, 758
  relationships to AR(N) and MA(M)
    systems, 752

B

Backscattered signal, 797
Backscattering model, 811
  sphere, for a, 814
  stationary point target for, 811
Backward prediction, 775, 882
  relationship to linear prediction and lattice
    filter, 775
BASIC programs, 785–787
  Levinson or Toeplitz recursion, direct form,
    786
  Burg algorithm, lattice filter, 787
Beamforming, 806, 818
Beam pattern, 793, 796, 797, 800
  for two-sensor array, 802
  for 20-sensor array, 805
Bessel filters
  See infinite impulse response filters
Bias estimation using Kalman filters, 928
Bilinear z-transformations, 337
  warping effect, 339
Binary adder, 950
Binary Fourier transform (BIFORE), 503
Binary numbers, 361, 589, 948
  fixed-point, 362
  floating-point, 362
  negative number representation of, 363
  one's complement, 365
  quantization of, 366, 591
    magnitude-truncation, 368
    rounding, 368
    truncation, 367
  two's complement, 364, 948
Bit-reversed order, 553
  for an eight-point DIT FFT, 556
Blackman-Tukey spectral analysis method,
    705, 721
Boolean
  algebra, 943
  functions of two variables, 946
Box-Jenkins, spectral analysis method, 731
Brick-wall filter characteristics, 301
Broadband signals, 843
Bessel filters
  See infinite impulse response filters
Burg algorithm, 706, 776
  lattice form of Levinson or Toeplitz
    recursion, 776
  computer program, 787
Butterworth filters
  See infinite impulse response filters

C

C matrix transform, 500
Cardinal function
  dirichlet kernel, 644
  in signal reconstruction, 235
Carrier frequency, 799
Cascade realization of IIR filters, 299
Cauchy
  integral theorem, 18
  residue theorem, 19
Channel equalization, 889
Chebyshev filters
  See infinite impulse response filters
Chebyshev polynomials
  FIR filters applied to, 101, 130
Chinese remainder theorem (CRT) integer
    respresentation, 571
Circular convolution
  See convolution
Complex analytic signal, 839
  in mixing, 839
Complex bandshifting, complex
    demodulation, complex hetrodyning
  See frequency shifting
Complex-to-real data conversion, 177, 241
Computer programs
  See BASIC programs and FORTRAN
    programs
Condition number, 762
Congruence
  See modulo
Constant-Q spectrum analysis, 175, 228
Convolution
  aperiodic, 32
  circular, 32, 638, 655, 668, 670, 672, 678,
    688
  discrete-time sequences, of, 10, 290, 744
  fast, 638, 666, 677, 687
    arithmetic operations for, 674, 675, 681,
      682
  forward problem describing, 741, 744
  frequency domain, 14, 23
  integral, 741
  linear, 667, 672, 678
  model for DTLTI system corrupted by
    additive noise, 760
  relationship to backscattering powers, 813
  z-plane, 22
Correlation
  See also autocorrelation, cross-correlation,
    674
  arithmetic operations, for, 674, 681

matrix used in AR modeling, 710
properties, 47
vectors, 861
Coupled form structures, 417
conventional, 418
modified, 415
Covariance sequence
autocovariance, 46
cross-covariance, 46
properties, 47–49
Covariance matrix, 485, 512
Cramèr-Rao lower bound, 847
relationship to time delay estimation
performance, 847
Cross-correlation, 46, 513, 822, 833
approximation of, 823
Fourier transform of, 823
locating peak of, 823
mean-square criteria relation to, 836
measure of similarity, 833
relationship to time delay estimation
problem, 833
time delay estimation algorithm
time domain implementation, 824
frequency domain implementation, 825
Cross-spectral density, 823
Fourier transform of cross-correlation
function, 823
Cuttoff frequency, 302
Butterworth filter, 309
Chebyshev filter, 317

D

Decimation of a data sequence
DTFT relationships before and after, 13
z-transform relationships before and after,
21
Deconvolution, 741, 751, 757, 762, 813
approximated by modified normal
equations, 762
ridge regression, 762
spectral balancing, 763
total least squares, 762
AR(N) process, of, 757
double, 754
filter, 742
discrete-time, 744
frequency domain, performed in, 751, 752
inverse problem, 742, 744
measure of effectives R, 762
minimum phase sources, of, 752

minimum phase and minimum delay,
relationship to, 751
rational DTLTI systems, of, 751, 752
relationship to backscattering process, 813
seismic, 744
Deconvolution and LTI systems with no
measurement noise, 746
Deconvolution and identification of DTLTI
systems
with measurement noise, 760
with no measurement noise, 451
Deconvolution and linear multiple regression,
761
least-square normal equations, 761
Delta function
See Dirac delta function, discrete-time
impulse, Kronecker delta function
Demodulation
See frequency shifting
Desampling, 173, 205
See also multirate filters
arithmetic operations for, 214
sampling rate reduction using cascaded FIR
filters, 215
Differentiators
See finite impulse response filters
Digit-reversed order (DRO), 535
Digital filter
See also finite impulse response and infinite
impulse response digital filters,
adaptive filters, Kalman filters,
recursive filters
design specifications, 59, 181, 300
frequency response, 57, 290
infinite impulse response filter building
blocks, 295
magnitude response specifications
ideal, 59, 301
practical, 57, 303
phase response, 57
Dirac delta function
acting as a sampling function, 8
convolution yielding, 742
Direct form structures
See also infinite impulse response filter
realizations
quantization effects in FIR filter, 460
signal-to-noise ratio in second order IIR
filter, 383
Discrete cosine transform (DCT), 486
even, 517
inverse, 499

Discrete cosine transform (DCT) (*cont.*)
  N-point DCT by a N-point IDFT, 500
  N-point DCT by a 2N-point FFT. 518
Discrete Fourier transform (DFT)
  See also fast Fourier transform
  channelization of signals using, 634, 639,
      644, 648, 651, 658
  channelizer residual phase rotation, 658
  computing a 1-D DFT with 2-D operations,
      537, 538, 551
    with multidimensional processing, 549
  discrete cosine transform developed from
      DFT, 519
  Goertzel algorithm relationship with, 641
  inverse 1-D, 30
  matrix representation of, 529, 541
  multidimensional, 41
  one-dimensional, 31
  properties, 32–40
  systems use of for time domain processing,
      634
  time delay estimation using, 841
  two-dimensional, 532
  Winograd's small-N, 565, 596, 616
  zoom transform for linear spectral analysis,
      174
  2-point, 539
  3-point, 543
  4-point, 547, 551
  6-point, 539, 545
  8-point, 553
  15-point, 577
Discrete sine transforms, 493, 494
  inverse DSTs, 499
Discrete-time Fourier transform (DTFT)
  definition of 1-D, 9
  inverse 1-D, 9
  properties, 10–14
  relationship to linear arrays, 806, 807
  spectral analysis with, 701
  two-dimensional, 15
Discrete-time impulse, 18
  deconvolution using, 744
  discrete-time Fourier transform of, 11
Discrete-time linear time-invariant (DTLTI)
      systems, 746
  with nonrandom inputs, 751, 760
    deconvolution problem for noisy
        outputs, 760
  with random inputs, 763
    deconvolution problem for noisy
        outputs, 763
  with WSS random inputs, 755
    output autocorrelation and cross-
        correlation, 755
    output power spectrum, 755
Discrete-time random sequence (DTRS), 41
  jointly distributed sequences, 44
  stationary, 44
  wide-sense stationary, 45
Discrete-time spectra
  See power spectral density
Discrete W-transform, 486
Discrimination factor, 309
Distributed arithmetic (DA), 964
  halving the DA memory, 969
Divergence of Kalman filters, 931
Dolph-Chebyshev polynomials
  See Chebyshev polynomials
Doppler
  processing, 701
  shift, 842
Dot product, 833
  relationship to cross-correlation, 833
Double deconvolution algorithm, 754
Doubly-terminated LC structures, 420
Dynamic range
  analysis, 588
  constraints in filters, 373

                              E

Eigenvalue
  distribution in adaptive lattice filter design,
      881
  maximum and minimum, 762
Elastic wave model, 781
  for seismic signal processing, 781
  for seismic deconvolution, 781
Elliptic filters
  See infinite impulse response
      filters
Energy packing efficiency (EPE), 511
Equiripple filters
  See finite and infinite impulse response filters
Equivalent noise bandwidth (ENBN), 256, 695
Ergodic
  process, 862
  sequences, 47
Error covariance matrix, 762
  trace of, 762
Error spectrum shaping (ESS), 387, 399
  Agarwal-Burrus approach, 394

compromise between single and double
    precision, 393
  in cascade forms, 400
  in first order sections, 388
  in second order sections, 391
Euler's approximations, 333
Expectation (expected value), 44, 45
Extended Kalman filtering, 928

                    F

Fast convolution
  See convolution
Fast algorithms for deconvolution problems,
    766
  Levinson or Toeplitz, 770
  Burg or lattice recursion, 776
Fast Fourier transform (FFT)
  See also discrete Fourier transform
  arithmetic operations
    comparison of algorithms, 580
      for a radix-2 FFT, 527, 556
      for a six-point FFT, 543
  butterfly, 540, 555, 960, 969
  butterfly-like structures, 558
    efficient microprogramming of, 961
    in distributed arithmetic, 968
  by means of matrix transpose, 548
  Chinese remainder theorem algorithm, 572
  computed in nonorthogonal coordinates
    six-point, 561
    3^L-point, 561
    6^L-point, 564
  computer programs available, 600
  decimation-in-frequency (DIF) algorithm
    eight-point, 557
    four-point, 547
    reason for nomenclature, 540
    six-point, 539, 545
    2^L-point, 557
  decimation-in-time (DIT) algorithm
    eight-point, 554
    four-point, 547
    reason for nomenclature, 540
    six-point, 539, 545
    2^L-point, 556
  fast convolution use of, 677
  frequency domain adaptive algorithms use
    of, 889
  Good's algorithm, 573
  in-order computation, 549

  of a four-point FFT, 552
  of a twelve-point FFT, 550
  that is also in-place, 552
  in-place computation, 549
  matrix factorization, 530
    for a four-point FFT, 531, 548
    for a six-point DIT FFT, 541
    for a six-point DIF FFT, 542, 545
    for an eight-point DIT FFT, 555
  mixed-radix integer representation (MIR)
    algorithms, 532, 664
  nested operations, 577
  polynomial transform algorithm, 579
  prime factor algorithm (PFA), 573, 605
    computer programs, 605
      in FORTRAN, 606
      in assembly language, 621
  quantization noise, 591
    radix-2, 553, 602
    computer program, 602
    radix-3, 558
    radix-4, 564
    radix-6, 558
  recursive cyclotomic factorization
    algorithm, 564
  ruritanian correspondence (RC) algorithm,
    567
  six-point, 570
  split-radix algorithm, 558
  time delay estimation use of, 842
  Winograd's algorithm, 576
  word length requirements, 587
Filter configuration
  in a least squares approximation, 864
Finite impulse response (FIR) digital filter
  architectural models for, 245
  bandwidth reduction using, 180
  bounded real structures, 465
  building-block extractions, 134
  coefficient quantization effects, 460
    accuracy estimate, 462
    low sensitivity using passivity, 465
      complex-to-real data conversion, for,
        177
  cutoff frequency, 60
  deconvolution, used for, 753, 757, 771
  desampling using, 215
  design specifications, 59
  desired response, 61
  differentiators, 83
  design charts, 147–148
  distributed arithmetic mechanization, 966

Finite impulse response (FIR) digital filter (*cont.*)
  equiripple approximations, 71
  extraripple solution, 76
  four basic types, 71
  flat-passband equiripple stopband filters, 132
  frequency transformations in, 100
  halfband filters, 141
  Hilbert transformers, 85, 233
    design charts, 149
  interpolated FIR (IFIR) design approach, 119
  interpolating, 173, 234, 241
    beamforming, for, 179
  length, 68, 76, 77, 183, 210
  linear programming approach to design, 95
  linear-phase, 57
  low noise, low sensitivity, 359
  magnitude response, 57
  maximally flat response design, 91
    implementation, 94
  McClellan-Parks (MP) algorithm, 79, 180, 183, 210
    FORTRAN program, 152
  minimum phase, 136, 748
  multirate for interpolating and desampling, 173
  narrowband filter bank, 642
  numerical gain, 202
  optimal
    equiripple, 71
    maximally flat, 90
  order estimate for
    window design, 68
    quiripple design, 76, 77
  phase response, 57
  prefilter-equalizer design approach, 125
  recursive running sum (RRS), 123
  response sharpening, 108
  roundoff noise
    in direct form structures, 460
    in cascade form structures, 561
    impact of section ordering, 462
  scaling, 191
  sidelobes, 183, 644
  transmission zero placement, 88
  two-dimensional, 112
    design with McClellan's transformation, 113
  weighted error, 71
  weighted error function, 78
  window design, 61
    limitations of, 71

Finite word length
  See quantization
Flip-flop memory elements, 954
Focused beamformer, 830
  for time delay estimation, 830
  for passive localization, 830
FORTRAN programs
  See also specific topic
  McClellan-Parks FIR filter design, 152
  prime factor algorithm FFT, 605
  radix-2 FFT, 602
  window generation, 975
Forward prediction error, 775
  relationship to linear prediction and lattice filters, 775
Fourier series
  one-dimensional, 2
  representation of periodic spectra, 7
  two-dimensional, 5
  used by Gauss, 528
Fractional octave spectrum analyses, 175, 210
Frequency
  normalized variables f and ω and analog variables F and Ω, 9
Frequency division multiplexing (FDM), 636, 663, 683, 685, 689
Frequency response, 57, 290, 749
Frequency shifting, 10, 174, 223, 229
  See also interpolating filters
  active radar and sonar using, 839
  arithmetic operations for, 225
  DFT, accomplished with, 686
  in-phase component, 839
  relationship to complex analytic signal, 839
Frequency transformation
  See spectral transformations
Frequency weighting functions, 824, 828
  for time delay estimation, 824
Frobenius norm, 728
Function generator, 683, 692, 695

G

Gates, 943
Gauss, Carl Friedrich
  algorithm for Fourier series, 527
  development of least squares estimation, 899, 907
Gaussian
  density and distribution function, 43
  elimination related to Levinson or Toeplitz recursion, 676
  function, 43

process, 382
Generalized cross-correlation (GCC)
    algorithms
    time domain implementation, 826
    frequency domain implementation, 827
    function, 832
Geometric series
    summation formula, 17
Gibbs phenomenon explaining
    overshoot in a square wave Fourier series
        representation, 4
    ripple in a filter response, 62
Goertzel algorithm, 641
Good's algorithm
    See fast Fourier transform
Gradient operator, 859
Gram-Schmidt orthogonalization, 889
Grating lobes, 801
Gray and Markel structures
    See all-pass filters
Group delay, 302

H

Haar
    function, 505
    matrices, 505
    rationalized, 506
    transform, 504
Hadamard or natural ordered transform, 502
Half-band filters
    See finite impulse response filters
Half-power beamwidth, 801
Hermann's method, 74
Hetrodyning
    See frequency shifting
Hilbert transform pair, 748
    transformers
        See finite impulse response filters
Hybrid transform, 508
Hyperbolic location systems, 790
    time difference of arrival systems, 790, 791
    Loran C navigation, 792

I

Identification of FIR filters, 757
    moving average MA(M) processes, 757
Impulse function
    See Dirac delta function, discrete-time
        impulse, Kronecker delta function
Impulse-invariant transformation, 334
Infinite impulse response (IIR) digital filter, 289

See also digital filter, low sensitivity filters
Bessel design, 330
Butterworth design
    cutoff frequency, 309
    factored polynomials, 308
    magnitude response, 307
    pole location, 307
    transfer function, 308
Chebyshev design
    Chebyshev polynomials, 312
    magnitude response, 314
    order, 317
    pole location, 315
    tables of characteristic polynomials, 319
comparison with FIR filters, 289, 290
elliptic design
    magnitude response, 326
    transfer function, 327
    pole-zero calculation, 327
    equiripple magnitude response
        both in passband and stopband, 324
        passband, in, 311
        stopband, in, 323
internal signal appearance, 388
inverse Chebyshev design
    transfer function, 323
    poles location, 324
    zeros location, 324
limit cycles, 469
low-noise low-sensitivity design, 359
maximally flat design
    magnitude response, 306
mechanized using distributed arithmetic, 967
order
    Butterworth, 309
    Chebyshev, 316
    elliptic, 327
    Inverse Chebyshev, 323
realizations, 295
    cascade, 299
    direct-form 1, 296
    direct-form 2, 297
    direct-form 2, canonic, 298, 360
    parallel, 298
signal-to-noise ratio in, 378
transformations converting analog filters to
    digital
    bilinear, 337
    impulse-invariant, 334
    matched z-transform, 335
Information Kalman filters, 936
In-order and in-place
    See FFT

Inner product, 834
  See also DOT product
  continuous time waveform for, 834
  discrete time waveform for, 834
Integer representations
  See also binary numbers
  Chinese remainder theorem, 571
  mixed-radix integer representation, 534
  Ruritanian correspondence, 567
Interpolating filters, 234
  changing sample rate by a rational
      fraction, 241
  increasing the data rate by a given factor,
      234
Interpolation, 173
  See also desampling and interpolating
      filters
  complex-to-real data conversion, for, 177
  DFT, using the, 636, 683
  merging overlapped data blocks after, 687
      by inverse synthesis, 691
  time domain beamforming, for, 178
  upsampling, 173
      increasing data rate by an integer factor,
          234
      by a rational fraction, 241
Intersensor time delay, 800, 818
  for two-sensor array, 818
Inverse problems in
  See also deconvolution
  speech, 777
  seismic signal processing, 780

J

Jury's
  array, 293
  stability test, 293

K

Kaiser window, 68
Kalman filtering, 908
  advantages of, 916
  bias estimation using, 928
  computer programs for, 918
  divergence of, 931
  examples of, 916
  extended, 928
  extensions of, 922
  filter equations table, 915
  information formulation, 936

linear estimation properties, 911
  prediction and correction, 912
  relationship to deconvolution, 777
  shaping filters for modeling colored noise,
      926
  square root formulation, 935
  steady state, 929
  stochastic model, 908
  suboptimal, 935
Karhunen-Loeve transform, 483
  advantages, 484
  disadvantages, 484
Kronecker
  delta function, 2
  product, 503, 575
Kumaresan-Tufts method for spectral
      analysis, 738

L

Lagrange multipliers, 725
Laplace transform
  definition, 24
  pairs, 28, 29
  properties, 26
  representation of IIR filters, 307, 313, 323,
      327, 330, 332
Lattice recursion, 774
  algorithms for AR(N) decimation, 774
Lattice structures, 455, 770
  adaptive filtering, 882
  related to
      Levinson or Toeplitz recursion, 772
      minimum and maximum phase filters,
          773
  tapped cascaded to implement arbitrary
      transfer functions, 457
Layered media
  model for 1-D seismic deconvolution, 782
Leapfrog structure, 345
Least-mean-square (LMS)
  algorithm, 866
  filter model, 885
  lattice algorithm, 882
  modified algorithm, 874
  predictor model, 882
Least-squares estimation, 814, 900
  approach to time-delay estimation, 814
  direct, 900
  examples of, 901, 905
  probabilistic interpretation of, 907
  recursive, 902
  time delay of, 814

weighted, 907
Least-squares normal equations, 761
  relationship to deconvolution, 761
Legendre, Adrein Marie, 899
Levinson algorithms, extended, 777
  non-Toeplitz system, 777
  displacement rank, 777
Levinson or Toeplitz recursion, 766
  direct form, 766
  relationship to AR(N) process, 766–770
  fast algorithm for Yule-Walker equation, 770
  lattice form, 770
Limit cycles, 469
  granular or roundoff type, 469
  overflow type, 470
    limit cycle-free structure, 472
    closed form for, 475
  Linear array
    design of, 804
    beam pattern, 805
  prediction in AR(N) processes, 756
  system output in response to a DTRS input, 48
Linear time-invariant system, 741
  impulse response, 741, 742
Loran C navigation, 792
  hyperbolic location system, 792
Lossless bounded real (LBR) filter design, 434
  reduced-order remainder, 438
  two-pair, 438
Lossless discrete integrator (LDI), 346
Low noise filters, 359
  cascade form, 396
  error spectrum shaping, 387, 399
  state-space optimized designs, 402
Low sensitivity filters, 359
  allpass-based structures, 444
  FIR filters, 465
  FIRBR filters, 465
  lossless bounded real (LBR) design approach, 434
  orthogonal filters, 458
  second order sections, 416
  structural losslessness, 443
  wave digital filters, 419

M

Main response axis (MRA), 800
Markov-1 model, 510
Matched

filter, 816, 817
  for course angle estimation, 809, 810
  z-transform, 335
Maximally flat filter response
  See finite and infinite impulse response filters
Maximum entropy, 711, 712
Maximum likelihood theory, 810
  for angle estimation, 810
Maximum phase filter, 771
McClellan's transformation to convert 1-D filters to 2-D, 113
McClellan-Parks' algorithm, 76
  FORTRAN program, 152
Mean-squared
  criteria, 836
    relationship to cross-correlation, 836
  error, 513, 756, 761, 765, 860
  value of beamformer output, 822, 828
Measurement residuals, 913
Memory in a digital system, 954
Microprogramming, 959
Minimum-norm structures, 473
Minimum
  delay, 750
  phase, 748
    filter, 136, 748
Misadjustment of adaptive filter weighting vector, 880
Mixed-radix integer representation (MIR), 534
Mixing
  See frequency shifting
Modified LMS algorithm, 874
Modified normal equations
  See deconvolution
Modulo
  congruence modulo an integer, 27
  representation of an integer mod N, 27
Moving average (MA) systems
  See also finite impulse response filters and spectral analysis
  MA(M) process, 757
Multirate filters, 173
  See also desampling, interpolating filters, and interpolation
Multisensor linear array, 803
Multipath impulse response, 745

N

Narrowband signals, 838
Narrowband-to-baseband translation, 839
  relationship to

Narrowband-to-baseband translation (*cont.*)
  complex analytic signal, 839
  mixing, 839
Natural order (NO), 535
Nested operations
  See fast Fourier transform
Noise
  due to quantizing digital words, 591
  transfer function, 371, 407
Noise-canceler adaptive filter configuration,
  864
Noisy gradient in adaptive filter design, 868
Nonminimum phase systems, 748, 763
Non-orthogonal coordinates, 560
No-pass phenomenon in adaptive filters, 880
Norm
  L_2, 375
  L_p, 375
  of a matrix, 473
Normal form digital filters, 473
Normalized frequency, 9, 60
Normalized structures, 378, 455
Number representations, 361, 947
  See also binary numbers, integer
    representations
Nyquist theorem/rate, 209

                                O

Omnidirectional sensor, 794
  for active case, 794
Operations per output point, 214, 225, 239,
  673, 681
Or gate
  See gates
Orthogonal
  Complex exponential functions, 2
  discrete-time random functions, 48
  filters, 458
Orthogonality principle, 861, 911, 913
Outer product, 859
Overdetermined equation modeling, 714
Overflow, 374, 382
Overlap processing, 214, 638, 646, 651, 665,
  677, 679, 687

                                P

Parallel realization of an IIR filter, 298
Partial sum filters, 179, 250
Parseval's theorem
  DFT, 37

DTFT, 13, 21
Passband, 59
  attenuation, 305
  edge frequency, 302
Picket fence
  See scallop/loss
Passive localization, 819
  with three-sensor array, 819
Passive sonar, 744, 790
Periodogram, 722, 733, 734
Pole stabilization, 294
Pole-crowding, 413
Poles of a function, 17
Polynomial transforms
  See fast Fourier transform
Polyphase filter, 180, 217, 250
Power spectral density (PSD), 50, 701, 749
  convergence conditions, 50
  cross-power spectral density, 50
  properties, 52
Phase modulation, 799
Phased-array radar, 806
Predictor
  approximation, 348
  configuration for adaptive filtering, 860
Prime factor algorithm
  See fast Fourier transform

                                Q

Quadratic sections, 299, 300
Quadratic component, 839
  relationship to complex analytic signal, 839
Quadratic mirror filters, 73, 228, 233, 244
Quantization
  of binary numbers, 366, 591
    magnitude-truncation, 368
    rounding, 368
    truncation, 367
  of filter coefficients, 202, 359
  of internal signals, 359

                                R

Radar system, 790, 837
Radii of convergence
  See z-transform
Rapid transform, 507
Random variables
  binomial distributed, 42
  definition, 41
  Gaussian distributed, 42

Rate distortion and maximum reducible bits, 514
Rate distribution function, 515
Rational spectral models, 702
Receive beamformer, 808
  linear array, 812
Recursive cyclotomic factorization algorithm (RCFA)
  See fast Fourier transform
Recursive least squares (RLS) algorithm, 889, 899
  See also Kalman filtering and least squares estimation
Reflection coefficients, 775
  relationship to lattice filters, 775
  acoustic tube model, 779
  seismic model, 782
Region of convergence
  See z-transform
Remez exchange procedure, 79
Residual
  correlation, 512
  time series, 713
Ridge regression, 762
Ripple factor, 302
Ruritanian correspondence (RC) integer representation, 567

S

Sample variance, 775
  prediction error
    backward, 775
    forward, 775
Sampling frequency, 6
  See also desampling, interpolation
  changed by a rational fraction, 173
  increased by an integer factor, 13, 21, 37, 173
  reduced by an integer factor, 13, 121, 173
Scallop loss, 257, 648, 684
Scaling, 373
  conservative scaling, 376
  L_2, 375, 407
  L_p, 375
  state space structures, 408
  transfer function, 374, 407
  types of policies for, 376
Seismic
  deconvolution algorithm, 783
    for layers of unequal traveltime, 783
  detectors, 789
  model, 781

one-dimensional, 781
  layered-medium, 782
signal processing, 780
  relationship to deconvolution, 780
waves, 743
Selectivity parameter, 309
Sensitivity measures for filter design, 414
Sensor shading factors, 807
Sequential regression (SER) algorithms, 889
Serial-to-parallel multipliers, 956
Shaping filters for modeling colored noise in Kalman filtering, 926
Sidelobes of sensor arrays, 804, 806
Signal-to-noise ratio (SNR)
  adaptive filter, in an, 878
  deconvolution, impact on, 762
  digital filter structures, in, 395
  FFTs, in, 588
    due to roundoff errors, 591
  filter output, at, 372
  matched filter, relationship to, 817
  roundoff noise in an IIR filter, due to, 378
  time delay estimation, impact on, 795, 844
  Wiener filter design, in, 514
Simultaneous transforms, 675, 680
Sinusoidal detection, 588, 716
Singular value decomposition in ARMA modeling, 726–731
Slant transform, 506
Sparse matrices, 530
Spatial filter, 793, 794, 797, 800, 804
  beam pattern, 793, 796, 797, 800
Spectral analysis, 701
  autoregressive (AR) model, 703, 705, 710, 718, 723, 737
    overdetermined equation modeling, 714
    parameter vector, 710, 714
  autoregressive moving average (ARMA) model, 703, 706, 712, 720, 724, 737
  Blackman-Tukey method, 705, 721
  Box-Jenkins maximum-likelihood ARMA method, 731
  Burg autoregressive model, 706
  DFT and FFT, use of, 701, 722
  fractional octave, 175, 210
    system with AGC, 588
  moving average (MA) models, 702, 709, 717, 721, 733
  periodogram approach, 722, 733
Spectral aliasing
  cause of, 6
  description of, 211

Spectral aliasing (*cont.*)
elimination using complex narrowband
filtering, 223
resampling after single and two-stage, due
to, 216
Spectral
balancing, 763
leakage, 39, 644
transformations
lowpass to bandpass, 343
lowpass to bandstop, 344
lowpass to highpass, 343
lowpass to lowpass, 343
transformations (in situ)
lowpass to highpass, 349
lowpass to bandpass, 349
Speech
generation, 742
glottis, 741
vocal tract, 741
signal processing relationship to
deconvolution, 777
Square root Kalman filters, 935
Stability, 291, 748
converting poles outside the unit circle to
inside, by, 294
tests, 292
State space structures for low-noise filters, 402
analysis, 404
complexity of, 405
impulse response, 404
K and W matrices, 407
minimum noise, 409
roundoff noise, 406
similarity transforms, 405
Stationary sequences
See discrete-time random sequence
Steady state Kalman filter, 929
Steepest-descent adaptive filter design
technique, 866
Stopband, 60, 302
attenuation, 60, 305
edge frequency, 60, 302
Structural boundedness, 435, 443
losslessness and passivity, 443, 448
Subband coding, 143
Switching circuits, 943
Synchronous noise, 697
System
identification, 746
AR(N), 756
ARMA(M,N), 758
MA(M), 757
transfer function, 746

impulse response, 746
rational function, 746

T

Tempered scale, 176
Three-sensor array, 831
time delay estimation algorithm
optimal, 831
suboptimal, 832
Three-sensor linear array, 819
Time delay estimation, 789
active sensors, for, 793, 811
algorithm performance, of, 844
omnidirectional array of, 813
omnidirectional single, 793, 795, 798
omnidirectional, two, 798
algorithms, 824, 831, 837, 844
FFT implementation, 837
numerical example, 848
performance of active sensor, 844
performance of passive sensor, 845
three-sensor array, 831
two-sensor array, 822, 824
correlators, using, 816
least squares, 814–816
linear time-invariant filter, 823, 826
passive sensor for, 818
two-sensor array, 818
three-sensor array, 819
Toeplitz matrix, 510
Total least squares, 762
Transfer function, 24, 56, 290, 291
Transform pair
discrete-time Fourier transform, 8
Transition bandwidth, 59, 181, 182, 209
Transmit beamformer, 808
linear array, for, 812
Transmitted pulse, 797
narrowband signal, 800
Transmultiplex, 636
Travel time difference, 799, 800
Truth table, 944
Twiddle factor, 537, 544
in nonorthogonal coordinates, 560
Two-dimensional FIR filters, 112
Two pairs, 437
constrained, 436
Two-sensor linear array, 798, 799, 818
bearing estimation, 819
design of active array, 801
passive time delay estimation, 818

U

Unit circle, 16
Upsampling
  See interpolation

W

Walsh-Hadamard function, 501
Walsh-Hadamard transform
  cal-sal ordered, 500
  Hadamard or natural ordered, 502
  Paley or dyadic ordered, 503
Warping phenomena using bilinear
  z-transform, 338
Wave digital filters, 419
Weighted DFT input, 39, 40
Whitening filters, 757
  and AR(N) deconvolution, 757
  lattice filters, 774
  computer program, 787
Wide-sense stationary
  See also discrete-time random sequence
  definition, 45
  error sequences in filters, 371
  sequences in spectral estimation, 701
Widrow-Hoff algorithm, 866
Wiener filtering, 513, 860
Wiener transfer function, 513
Wiener-Hopf equation, 765
Windowed DFT output, 40
Windows, 39, 61, 203, 253, 704
  Blackman, 66
  Blackman-Harris, 264, 286, 655, 688, 690
  Dolph-Chebyshev, 278, 286, 975
  Hamming, 66, 262
  Hann, 66, 259

Kaiser, 68
Kaiser-Bessel, 264, 280, 286, 688
  rectangular, 61, 66
  Taylor, 279, 286, 655
  triangular, 63
Window folding, 652, 655, 658
Winograd Fourier transform algorithm
  (WFTA), 576
Winograd small-N DFTs
  See discrete Fourier transform

Y

Yuke-Walker equations, 708, 714, 756
  extended, high-order, or modified, 759

Z

Zero extending data sequences, 637, 684
Zero packing data sequences, 237, 636, 687,
  689
Zero-padding, 841
  for cross-correlation by means of FFT, 841
Zoom transform, 174
z-transform
  definition of 1-D, 16
  inverse 1-D, 18
  properties, 20, 21
  radii of convergence, 16
  region of convergence, 16
  right- and left-sided sequence pairs, 20
  right-sided sequence pairs, 28, 29
  two-dimensional, 23
Zeros of a function, 17